A SOCIAL HISTORY OF THE WELSH LANGUAGE

'Let's do our best for the ancient tongue'

*The Welsh Language in the
Twentieth Century*

Editors

GERAINT H. JENKINS and MARI A. WILLIAMS

UNIVERSITY OF WALES PRESS

www.uwp.co.uk

British Library Cataloguing-in-Publication Data

A catalogue record for this book is available from the British Library.

ISBN   978-1-78316-178-2

Printed by CPI Antony Rowe, Chippenham, Wiltshire

Let's do our best for the ancient tongue,
Its music's so delightful,
We clearly love to hear it sung,
But speak it? Oh, how frightful

'The art of the possible', Harri Webb

Contents

Maps and Figures

Preface

As a result of sweeping demographic and socio-economic changes, during the course of the twentieth century the Welsh language lost its position as the predominant spoken tongue within the communities of Wales. Wider exposure to the English tongue and to Anglo-American culture has meant that the linguistic profile of Wales is much more diverse and fractured than it was a hundred years ago, and it remains to be seen whether the enhanced public status now enjoyed by the native language and its marked resurgence in urban communities, especially in south-east Wales, can adequately compensate for the loss of the age-old communal and territorial base in the heartlands. The reaction to these changes has been mixed and, long before Saunders Lewis broadcast his gloomy forebodings in 1962, the fate of the language had been a source of morbid fascination among the Welsh. Indeed, over the past century the Welsh language has revealed a curious capacity to generate, among Welsh speakers and non-Welsh speakers alike, indifference, scepticism, hostility, noble gestures and self-sacrifice. The aim of this volume, written from the convenient vantage point of the late 1990s, is to set the major linguistic changes which occurred in a variety of key domains within a broad social and historical perspective. We seek neither to sentimentalize nor weep over the world we have lost.

This collaborative research project has been one of the most challenging and rewarding enterprises with which I have been associated. On many occasions I have marvelled at the enthusiasm and good humour of the young research fellows who have formed the core of the project and whose findings have enriched both this and other volumes in the series. Their stimulating ideas and constant support have sustained my occasional flagging spirits and made the venture a happy and fulfilling experience. The team effort at the University of Wales Centre for Advanced Welsh and Celtic Studies has received admirably robust support from a wide range of scholars from within the constituent institutions of the University of Wales and beyond, each of whom has been encouraged to offer complementary or different views according to his or her own particular expertise and perspective. All of them, and especially those who have contributed to this volume, are eager to join with me in thanking my fellow editor, Dr Mari A. Williams, for leading this project with unfailing courtesy and efficiency. It is gratifying for everyone associated with this series that each publication has been warmly received and has also generated vigorous debate. Not least among those who made Welsh and its literature a subject of scrutiny and debate were Dr W. Gareth Evans and Mr R. Gerallt Jones, two contributors to this volume whose recent untimely demise greatly saddened their wide circle of friends.

It gives me great pleasure to acknowledge the guidance and kindness of members of the Advisory Committee of this project, namely Professor Emeritus Harold Carter, Professor Emeritus Ieuan Gwynedd Jones, Dr Brynley F. Roberts and Professor Emeritus J. Beverley Smith. In a variety of ways the staff of the National Library of Wales and the University of Wales Dictionary of the Welsh Language have given generous assistance and ready access to their holdings. A sincere debt of gratitude is owed to Mr Andrew Hawke whose computer skills are a thing of wonder, and to Mr Ian Gulley and Mr Antony Smith whose splendid cartographic work at the Institute of Geography and Earth Sciences, University of Wales Aberystwyth, has rendered this volume all the more pleasant and attractive. I gratefully acknowledge the wise counsel and expertise of Mrs Dot Jones (former leader of the project), Mr Dewi Morris Jones, Mrs Meinir McDonald and Dr Huw Walters. Mr Elgan Davies of the Welsh Books Council deserves high praise for designing the entire series. For the editorial skills of Mrs Glenys Howells, mere thanks seem utterly inadequate. Unstinting administrative assistance was provided by Mrs Aeres Bowen Davies, Ms Siân Lynn Evans and Ms Elin Humphreys, and Mr William H. Howells completed the index with characteristically brisk efficiency. I am also glad to recognize the support of the staff of the University of Wales Press, especially Ruth Dennis-Jones.

Soothsaying and history make uncomfortable bedfellows and no one can predict what the march of events in the twenty-first century will hold for what Emyr Humphreys has affectionately (and correctly) called our 'senior language'. Although it is a commonplace that the future prospects of all lesser-used languages, including Welsh, remain uncertain and perhaps even parlous, it would be absurd for a Welsh-speaking editor of a multi-volume series like this to end this preface on a negative note. Historians, too, have a duty to 'keep house amidst a cloud of witnesses' and it is sufficient to say that this book and the series of which it is part are not meant to be a poignant epitaph. The story we have told is unfinished.

June 2000   *Geraint H. Jenkins*

Preface to the Reprinted Edition

Whatever the imperfections of decennial censuses, they remain a rich statistical source and a key benchmark for analyses of socio-linguistic trends in Wales. Since the first publication of this book in 2000, two enumerations – in 2001 and 2011 – have been held, each of which throws light on many of the challenges which confronted the Welsh language in the second half of the twentieth century. The results of the 2001 census were joyously greeted by promoters of the native tongue. For the first time since the early twentieth century the percentage of Welsh-speakers had increased; in this case by 2% since the previous enumeration in 1991. Buoyed by this seemingly remarkable turnaround, the Welsh Assembly Government set itself the aim of creating 'a truly bilingual' Wales. More cautious commentators, so used to experiencing post-enumeration angst, were unconvinced by such a surprising result and their doubts were confirmed when the 2011 census revealed a decrease in the number of Welsh-speakers over the age of three from 20.8% to 19%.

As was made very clear in our volume, while the public status of Welsh is assured, its long-term future as a spoken language remains uncertain. Many of the complex challenges and problems, prefigured earlier, have if anything intensified. Population mobility is a key factor, notably in the rural heartlands. The in-migration of affluent retirees, second-home owners and unemployed people has seriously undermined the age-old status of Welsh as a living community language. As one anonymous blogger pithily exclaimed: 'Johnny Englishman has the money, Penuwch couple don't. English trumps Welsh: survival of the fittest.' Just as troubling is the out-flow from Wales of young, gifted Welsh-speakers whose employment and housing opportunities are shamefully few. While the appreciable increase in the number of Welsh-speakers aged between 3 and 15 is heartening, especially in urban areas, the problem remains of ensuring that the post-15 cohort are afforded opportunities to speak Welsh outside the school environment. In an increasingly globalized society, it is harder than ever for young Welsh-speakers to resist the invasive powers of the English tongue. It remains to be seen whether the Welsh Assembly Government has the political will to address these issues and provide the resources required to deal with them. Maintaining a lesser-used language calls for the strongest possible commitment and unfailing vigilance. If Welsh is to prosper, our leaders need to do a good deal more and to do it a good deal better.

I am grateful to my fellow editor for her support and it is a pleasure to acknowledge the valuable advice received from Llion Wigley at the University of Wales Press.

Geraint H. Jenkins   June 2014

Abbreviations

AC	*Archaeologia Cambrensis*
BBCS	*Bulletin of the Board of Celtic Studies*
CW	*Contemporary Wales*
FHSJ	*Flintshire Historical Society Journal*
NLW	Manuscript at National Library of Wales
NLWJ	*National Library of Wales Journal*
PH	*Pembrokeshire Historian*
TCHS	*Transactions of the Caernarvonshire Historical Society*
THSC	*Transactions of the Honourable Society of Cymmrodorion*
TIBG	*Transactions of the Institute of British Geographers*
UWBL	University of Wales Bangor Library
WHR	*Welsh History Review*

The Fortunes of the Welsh Language 1900–2000: Introduction

GERAINT H. JENKINS and MARI A. WILLIAMS

BY ANY STANDARDS, the twentieth century was a tumultuous period in the history of the world. In many significant ways, people's lives were markedly different from anything which their forebears had either experienced or imagined. The pace of change was unprecedented throughout the world and the horrors of total war, the rise and fall of totalitarian regimes, anti-semitism, genocide, stepping on the moon, the threat of nuclear annihilation and ecological catastrophe, and the emergence of new technology all left a deep imprint on the minds of those who lived through the best part of the century. For the social historian and sociolinguist interested in the fate of Celtic languages and lesser-used languages in western Europe, the rise of the English language to a position of genuine world status was just as momentous.[1] During the course of the century English became the principal medium of linguistic exchange and the dominant language of business, academia, advertising, diplomacy, electronic retrieval systems, leisure, sport and much else. As the use of the English language swept through the world, other languages disappeared at an unprecedented rate. Indeed, the overwhelming majority of human languages spoken on the planet are likely to perish before the end of the twenty-first century.[2] Paradoxically, however, the seemingly un-stoppable advent of the English language to the status of a truly global tongue has served to focus attention on the importance of lesser-used languages together with their cultural identity. Among these beleaguered tongues is Welsh, the oldest spoken language in Britain and one of the oldest literary languages in Europe. Having been a vibrant, living medium of communication for the majority of Welsh people at the dawn of the twentieth century, as the decades rolled by the

---

[1] See David Crystal, *The Cambridge Encyclopedia of the English Language* (Cambridge, 1995); idem, *English as a Global Language* (Cambridge, 1997).

[2] Steven Pinker, *The Language Instinct: The New Science of Language and Mind* (London, 1994), pp. 259–61.

future well-being of the Welsh language was placed in considerable jeopardy.[3] Francis Fukuyama has reminded us that the twentieth century has turned us into 'historical pessimists'[4] and, as a result of the complex and cumulative effects of modernization, urbanization, total war, depopulation, in-migration, market forces and globalization, Welsh now finds itself in what might prove to be irretrievable decline. Of all the memorable phrases coined in the twentieth century none has had greater resonance for the Welsh speaker than 'Tynged yr Iaith' (The Fate of the Language),[5] the title and theme of the path-breaking BBC Annual Lecture, delivered by Saunders Lewis in 1962, which still haunts or inspires champions of the native tongue on the cusp of the new millennium.

The history of the Welsh language in the twentieth century is both the story of numerical decline and of the struggle for official recognition. At the turn of the nineteenth century Welsh appeared to command a secure place in the cultural profile of the nation and, notwithstanding the gloomy predictions of a small number of *fin de siècle* commentators, there was no reason to suspect that its future was in jeopardy. Indeed, the 1901 census bore witness to its robust position: it was spoken by 929,824 people (49.9 per cent of the population), of whom 280,905 (30.2 per cent) were monoglot Welsh. Most of the Welsh monoglots were clustered in the Welsh-speaking heartland ('Y Fro Gymraeg'), where over 90 per cent of the population spoke Welsh and where it was perfectly possible for individuals and families to live their lives almost entirely through the medium of Welsh. The native tongue was still numerically strong in the South Wales Coalfield and throughout most of the country it was robust in the domains of home, neighbourhood, religion, popular culture, literature and even politics. All this had changed by the time of the 1991 census. Welsh monoglottism was a thing of the past, 'Y Fro Gymraeg' was a pale shadow of its former self, and four-fifths

---

[3] Previous studies include the following: Harold Carter, 'Dirywiad yr Iaith Gymraeg yn yr Ugeinfed Ganrif' in Geraint H. Jenkins (ed.), *Cof Cenedl V: Ysgrifau ar Hanes Cymru* (Llandysul, 1990), pp. 147–76; Janet Davies, *The Welsh Language* (Cardiff, 1993); eadem, 'The Welsh Language' in Trevor Herbert and Gareth Elwyn Jones (eds.), *Post-War Wales* (Cardiff, 1995), pp. 55–77; John Davies, *A History of Wales* (London, 1993), chapters 9 and 10; Bedwyr Lewis Jones, 'Welsh: Linguistic Conservatism and Shifting Bilingualism' in Einer Haugen, J. Derrick McClure and Derick Thomson (eds.), *Minority Languages Today* (Edinburgh, 1990), pp. 40–52; R. Merfyn Jones, *Cymru 2000: Hanes Cymru yn yr Ugeinfed Ganrif* (Caerdydd, 1999), chapter 11; Robert Owen Jones, *'Hir Oes i'r Iaith': Agweddau ar Hanes y Gymraeg a'r Gymdeithas* (Llandysul, 1997), pp. 327–436; idem, 'The Sociolinguistics of Welsh' in Martin J. Ball (with James Fife) (eds.), *The Celtic Languages* (London, 1993), pp. 536–605; Marion Löffler, *Englisch und Kymrisch in Wales: Geschichte der Sprachsituation und Sprachpolitik* (Hamburg, 1997), pp. 110–88; Meic Stephens (ed.), *The Welsh Language Today* (Llandysul, 1973); Colin H. Williams, 'Language Contact and Language Change in Wales, 1901–71: A Study in Historical Geolinguistics', *WHR*, 10, no. 2 (1980), 207–38; idem, 'The Anglicisation of Wales' in Nikolas Coupland (ed.), *English in Wales: Diversity, Conflict and Change* (Cleveland, 1990), pp. 19–47.

[4] Francis Fukuyama, *The End of History and the Last Man* (London, 1992), p. 3.

[5] Saunders Lewis, *Tynged yr Iaith* (London, [1962]). For an English translation, see Gruffydd Aled Williams, 'The Fate of the Language (1962)' in Alun R. Jones and Gwyn Thomas (eds.), *Presenting Saunders Lewis* (Cardiff, 1973), pp. 127–41.

of the population had no grasp of the language. By 1991 only 508,098 (18.6 per cent) spoke Welsh, and 56 per cent of them lived in Gwynedd and Dyfed. Such startling figures speak for themselves.[6] Yet, paradoxically, the numerical and territorial decline of Welsh was accompanied by the latter decades of the century by enhanced legal status and considerably greater political and economic clout.[7]

As previous volumes in this series have revealed,[8] even by the late Victorian period Welsh was increasingly at risk from the influential tongue of its nearest neighbour. Although the 1911 census recorded the highest number of Welsh speakers (977,366) ever known, in proportional terms Welsh speakers had become a minority (43.5 per cent) in their own land for the first time in history. Bilingualism was more prevalent than ever before and the influx of English-speaking workers and their families to the industrial counties of Glamorgan and Monmouth was so considerable that their assimilation into the Welsh-speaking society was impossible. By the eve of the First World War the trend was unmistakably pointing in favour of the English language as the language of prosperity, modernity and fashion.

The Great War inevitably took its toll on native Welsh speakers, and memorials in Welsh towns and villages bear mute witness to grievous losses. Of c.280,000 men who enlisted in the armed forces, around 35,000 were killed, an appreciable number of whom presumably spoke Welsh.[9] The poet R. Williams Parry spoke for the nation when he referred to 'the wrench of losing the lads' ('y rhwyg o golli'r hogiau')[10] and the poignant occasion when Ellis Humphrey Evans (Hedd Wyn) of Trawsfynydd was posthumously awarded the Chair at the National Eisteddfod at Birkenhead in 1917 was a symbolic expression not only of the futility of total war but also of the vulnerability of a precious tongue. On joining the armed forces, Welsh speakers swiftly realized that theirs was a second-class language. Although the authorities went to considerable pains to produce and disseminate Welsh posters and recruiting forms, and to summon the names of ancient Welsh princes in a bid to excite popular interest and support, Welsh speakers were discriminated against in active duty and, until the latter stages of the war, their language was proscribed.[11] According to Lewis Valentine, 'officers tended to look upon us the

[6] See Chapter 1.
[7] See Chapter 5; Gwilym Prys Davies, 'Yr Iaith Gymraeg a Deddfwriaeth / The Welsh Language and Legislation' in Rhian Huws Williams, Hywel Williams and Elaine Davies (eds.), *Gwaith Cymdeithasol a'r Iaith Gymraeg / Social Work and the Welsh Language* (Caerdydd, 1994), pp. 41–73; idem, 'Statws Cyfreithiol yr Iaith Gymraeg yn yr Ugeinfed Ganrif', *Y Traethodydd*, CLIII (1998), 76–95.
[8] Geraint H. Jenkins (ed.), *Language and Community in the Nineteenth Century* (Cardiff, 1998); Gwenfair Parry and Mari A. Williams, *The Welsh Language and the 1891 Census* (Cardiff, 1999); Geraint H. Jenkins (ed.), *The Welsh Language and its Social Domains 1801–1911* (Cardiff, 2000).
[9] Angela Gaffney, *Aftermath: Remembering the Great War in Wales* (Cardiff, 1998), pp. 150–1.
[10] Alan Llwyd (ed.), *Cerddi R. Williams Parry: Y Casgliad Cyflawn 1905–1950* (Dinbych, 1998), p. 66.
[11] Aled Eurig, 'Agweddau ar y Gwrthwynebiad i'r Rhyfel Byd Cyntaf yng Nghymru', *Llafur*, 4, no. 4 (1987), 60; Gervase Phillips, 'Dai Bach y Soldiwr: Welsh Soldiers in the British Army 1914–1918', ibid., 6, no. 2 (1993), 101.

Welsh as barely civilized, wild men from the hills' ('tuedd y swyddogion oedd edrych arnom ni'r Cymry fel dynion gwyllt o'r mynydd ac yn hanner gwâr') and many poked fun at 'the very Welsh Welshmen . . . who had an imperfect command of English'.[12] Welsh speakers who could not reconcile shedding blood on the Western Front with their Christian principles were forced to endure public scorn and private beatings,[13] and in the post-war years the 'conshi' (conscientious objector) was reminded of his lack of fibre by countless war memorials bearing the inscription 'Gwell Angau na Chywilydd' (Better Death than Dishonour). It was hard, too, for the common soldier to feel any loyalty to a system which prevented him from communicating the horrors of trench warfare by letter in his native language. Although soldiers were encouraged to sing 'Hen Wlad fy Nhadau' (Land of my Fathers) and Welsh hymns as they climbed over the parapet, many of them complained that every Welsh letter sent to their loved ones was returned 'as if it were a bad penny' ('fel pe bai'n geiniog ddrwg').[14] Nothing caused more bitter resentment among the next-of-kin in monoglot Welsh-speaking communities than to receive from the War Office notification in English of the death of relatives.[15] It was also a measure of the lack of status accorded to Welsh that, in the aftermath of war, the inclusion on war memorials of an inscription in Welsh, alongside English and Latin, was usually an afterthought and that the unveiling ceremonies were invariably conducted in English.

It is a commonplace that the Great War marked a critical break with the past. In terms of collective destruction and suffering, its like had never been witnessed before. In the context of language and culture, too, it had profound implications. The movement of people and the dissemination of propaganda meant that contact with the English language increased. Between 1911 and 1921 the percentage of Welsh monoglots fell from 8.5 per cent to 6.3 per cent, and around 10 per cent of bilingual speakers aged 15–25 in 1911 had become monoglot English speakers by 1921.[16] Having experienced unimaginable trauma in the trenches, many soldiers who returned to a land supposedly fit for heroes renounced the Christian faith. Chapel-based religion was thrown on the defensive and its public image was further tarnished when Caradoc Evans's *My People* (1915) 'came in like a bad smell through the window'.[17] Yet, in a curious way, the terror of war and its

---

[12] Lewis Valentine, *Dyddiadur Milwr a Gweithiau Eraill*, ed. John Emyr (Llandysul, 1988), p. 11; Gerwyn Wiliams, *Tir Neb: Rhyddiaith Gymraeg a'r Rhyfel Byd Cyntaf* (Caerdydd, 1996), p. 13.

[13] See Ithel Davies, *Bwrlwm Byw* (Llandysul, 1984), pp. 62–79.

[14] Alan Llwyd and Elwyn Edwards, *Y Bardd a Gollwyd: Cofiant David Ellis* (Cyhoeddiadau Barddas, 1992), pp. 59, 93.

[15] For a superb evocation of a quarrying family losing its menfolk in the Great War, see Kate Roberts, *Traed mewn Cyffion* (Aberystwyth, 1936). An English translation, *Feet in Chains*, was published in 1977.

[16] Glyn Lewis, 'Migration and the Decline of the Welsh Language' in Joshua A. Fishman (ed.), *Advances in the Study of Societal Multilingualism* (The Hague, 1978), pp. 295–6.

[17] Sam Adams and Gwilym Rees Hughes (eds.), *Triskel One: Essays on Welsh and Anglo-Welsh Literature* (Llandybïe, 1971), p. 79. Gwyn Jones coined the phrase.

dramatic effects on patterns of behaviour also worked in favour of the Welsh language. In the case of Lewis Valentine and Saunders Lewis, for instance, both of whom experienced the gruesome brutality of war, it led to the rejection of British rhetoric and the espousal of a new sense of Welsh identity based on the native language and culture. At Miraumont on St David's day 1917, Valentine wrote in his diary: 'I know today in the marrow of my bones that henceforth I must become embroiled in the cause of Wales' ('Gwn heddiw ym mêr fy esgyrn fod yn rhaid i mi fod byth mwy ynghlwm wrth achos Cymru').[18] Sentiments such as these would shortly become both a powerful stimulant and an irritant in the cultural life of Wales.

The inter-war years witnessed sweeping demographic and socio-economic changes which deeply affected the fortunes of the Welsh language.[19] Structural weaknesses within the economy were laid bare and mass unemployment, poor health and adverse living conditions scarred the lives of thousands of people. Farming was in poor shape and it is hard to convey the bleak misery of life in the industrial valleys. Between 1921 and 1936, 241 mines were closed in the South Wales Coalfield and nearly half the male workforce of 270,000 were laid off. Agrarian depression and the slump in the coalfields led to an exodus of biblical proportions. Whereas the nineteenth-century Welsh had colonized their own land, their descendants took part in a massive out-migration, and where migration had once signified dynamism and virility, it was now viewed as a haemorrhage. Improved communications by road and rail made it much easier for people to seek work elsewhere and, as a result of voluntary, assisted or enforced migration, between 1920 and 1939 Wales lost 442,000 people to the new industrial conurbations of the Midlands and south-east England. Around 66 per cent of the out-migrants from south Wales were under thirty and 87 per cent were under forty-five.[20] The linguistic implications were far-reaching. Young and active out-migrants left behind them middle-aged or elderly people whose command of Welsh was not transmitted to the new generation. Moreover, the industrialized counties of south Wales were beginning to reap the cultural consequences of heavy in-migration of monoglot English speakers during the early decades of the century.[21] In his recollections the poet Harri Webb emphasized not only the adverse consequences of the Welsh diaspora but also the shifting linguistic balance:

---

[18] Valentine, *Dyddiadur Milwr*, p. 43.

[19] Mari A. Williams, '"In the Wars": Wales 1914–1945' in Gareth Elwyn Jones and Dai Smith (eds.), *The People of Wales* (Llandysul, 1999), pp. 179–206.

[20] Andrew J. Chandler, 'The Re-making of a Working Class: Migration from the South Wales Coalfield to the New Industry Areas of the Midlands *c*.1920–1940' (unpubl. University of Wales PhD thesis, 1988), pp. 3–4, 14.

[21] See Chapter 3.

until about that time [1914] Wales was still fifty per cent Welsh-speaking, and the other fifty per cent were culturally inert – unassimilated immigrants or denaturalised natives. A generation later, assimilation was under way, and there was in existence a large population, Welsh in feeling, but English in language, something totally new in our history.[22]

Large parts of the rural heartland of north and west Wales, of course, remained robustly Welsh-speaking, but the striking fall in the number of Welsh speakers in some of the traditional urban strongholds of Glamorgan boded ill: between 1921 and 1951 the total Welsh-speaking population of Merthyr Tydfil County Borough and the Rhondda Urban District plummeted from 30,948 to 14,538 and from 68,519 to 31,215 respectively.[23] W. J. Gruffydd, *soi-disant* 'chief devil of the Welsh' ('prif gythraul y Cymry'), did not mince his words in *Y Llenor*:

y ffaith anhyfryd [yw] (1) bod y Gymraeg yn marw yn gyflym ym mhob rhan o Forgannwg i'r dwyrain o afon Nedd; (2) bod rhannau helaeth ohoni'n barod wedi mynd mor Seisnig â Sir Faesyfed neu Sir Fynwy; (3) mai hoelen arall yn arch y Gymraeg yw pob ymgais i guddio'r ffeithiau, ac i gymryd arnom fod popeth o'r gorau.[24]

(the unlovely fact [is] (1) that Welsh is dying swiftly in every part of Glamorgan to the east of the Neath river; (2) that substantial parts of it are already as Anglicized as Radnorshire or Monmouthshire; (3) that every effort to conceal the facts, and to pretend that all is well, is another nail in the Welsh coffin.)

Demographic and linguistic shifts were also linking with dramatic changes in mobility and technology which had the potential to undermine the native tongue even in its most cherished heartlands. Improvements in the means of communication and the wider availability of cars, buses and trains enabled people to cover distances more quickly and to reach the most popular tourist and recreational destinations. By 1938 there were 55,000 licensed cars in south Wales and 21,000 in the north.[25] The arrival of the telegraph, the telephone and especially the wireless enabled the English language to cross national boundaries and penetrate the homes of people who seldom spoke English. No longer were

---

[22] Letter from Harri Webb to Meic Stephens, 7 October 1966, published in *Poetry Wales*, II, no. 3 (1966), 37.

[23] John Williams, *Digest of Welsh Historical Statistics* (2 vols., Cardiff, 1985), I, p. 83.

[24] 'Nodiadau'r Golygydd', *Y Llenor*, X, no. 2 (1931), 66. For similar comments, see Gwynfor Evans, '"Eu Hiaith a Gadwant" –?', *Y Ddraig Goch*, XI, no. 7 (1937), 8, as quoted in D. Hywel Davies, *The Welsh Nationalist Party 1925–1945: A Call to Nationhood* (Cardiff, 1983), p. 78: 'The cancer has driven deeply into the valleys of the Rhondda, Ogmore, Rhymney, Aberdare and Merthyr Tydfil; where fifty years ago there was almost only Welsh, English is now the language of the majority . . .' See also Ceri W. Lewis, 'The Welsh Language: Its Origin and Later History in the Rhondda' in K. S. Hopkins (ed.), *Rhondda Past and Future* (Rhondda Borough Council, n.d.), pp. 210–11.

[25] Deian Hopkin, 'Social Reactions to Economic Change' in Trevor Herbert and Gareth Elwyn Jones (eds.), *Wales between the Wars* (Cardiff, 1988), p. 57.

even the rugged mountain peaks of Wales a barrier to the progress of Anglo-American culture. The wireless was an invention of enormous cultural significance since it spelled the end of domestic isolation.[26] As well as providing fireside information, it influenced the minds, mores and behaviour of listeners. During the inter-war years the BBC used its monopolistic control to realize John Reith's dream of 'making the nation one man'.[27] Reith did not believe in making any concessions to vulgar minority interests and some of his views on the Celtic peoples and their languages were unprintable. As a result, sound radio, which broadcast through the only proven medium of the English language, became a vehicle for a 'British' view of things expressed in royal broadcasts, anniversary programmes and all manner of celebrations, festivities and rituals. This cultural hegemony was also reinforced by the concentration of newspapers into a smaller number of controlling agencies.[28] Welsh-language newspapers could not hope to compete with the powerful Berry newspaper empire and it was a sign of the times when *Y Darian* (formerly *Tarian y Gweithiwr*) folded in 1934 and *Y Genedl Gymreig*, which had aspired to the status of a national Welsh newspaper, was absorbed into the Herald company in 1932. Even the National Eisteddfod appeared to have entirely succumbed to Anglicizing forces. By 1931, when English was dominant on the eisteddfod stage, in adjudications and the ceremonies of the Gorsedd of the Bards, W. J. Gruffydd dubbed it 'our old cannon . . . fallen into the hands of the enemy' ('ein hen fagnel ni ydyw wedi mynd i ddwylo'r gelyn').[29]

Another disturbing factor which generated a sense of insecurity among Welsh speakers was the declining influence of Christianity.[30] The fervour generated by the last great spiritual revival of 1904–5 had swiftly dissipated and, as we have seen, the horrors of total war prompted many people to repudiate their religious upbringing. Ministers bemoaned the loss of worshippers as many of the young, who despised hell-fire sermons and gloomy hymns, voted with their feet. In the

---

[26] See Chapter 8.

[27] David Cardiff and Paddy Scannell, 'Broadcasting and National Unity' in James Curran, Anthony Smith and Pauline Wingate (eds.), *Impacts and Influences: Essays on Media Power in the Twentieth Century* (London, 1987), p. 157. See also Asa Briggs, *The BBC: The First Fifty Years* (Oxford, 1985), p. 55.

[28] Aled Gruffydd Jones, *Press, Politics and Society: A History of Journalism in Wales* (Cardiff, 1993), pp. 200, 202, 209; idem, 'The Newspaper Press in Wales 1804–1945' in Philip Henry Jones and Eiluned Rees (eds.), *A Nation and its Books: A History of the Book in Wales* (Aberystwyth, 1998), pp. 209–20.

[29] 'Nodiadau'r Golygydd', *Y Llenor*, X, no. 4 (1931), 193.

[30] See 'The English Language and the Welsh Churches', *The Welsh Outlook*, 1 (1914), 247; M. H. Jones, 'The Sunday School in Wales', ibid., VII (1920), 68–70; John Jenkins (Gwili), 'Y Gymraeg yn ei Pherthynas ag Addysg ac â Chrefydd Heddyw', *Y Geninen*, XXXVIII, no. 3 (1920), 141–4; D. Tecwyn Evans, 'Yr Iaith Gymraeg a Chrefydd Cymru', ibid., XLII, no. 1 (1924), 17–23; W. R. Watkins, 'Y Bedyddwyr a'r Comisiwn ar y Gymraeg', *Seren Gomer*, XVIII, no. 6 (1926), 225–37; Annie E. Jones and Gwladys Thomas, 'Yr Iaith Gymraeg a Chrefydd Cymru', *Yr Efrydydd*, IX, no. 8 (1933), 197–9.

urban communities of south Wales, growing numbers of the young generation were unfamiliar with the Welsh language[31] and in 1927 it was reported that 'in many churches the Gospel is preached to the old and middle-aged *in the presence of* the young whose faces only light up when the preacher lapses into an English quotation'.[32] The emergence of the labour movement, as well as new scientific and philosophical ideas, challenged the cultural dominance of Nonconformity by associating the Welsh language with discredited Liberal politics and blinkered rural lifestyles.[33] Especially in industrialized and urban communities in south Wales, chapel-based religion, which attached so much importance to thrift, self-help, sobriety and respectability, held little appeal to people who queued outside the soup kitchens or were subjected to the Means Test. As a result, different and more attractive competitors were the beneficiaries. By the mid-1930s, a period which witnessed what David Berry refers to as the 'Talkies and the Picture Palace Boom',[34] there were more cinemas per head of the population in south Wales than anywhere else in Britain. 'Thank God for the pictures', cried working-class people as they strove to cope with their economic misery.[35] The glitter of Hollywood and its Americanisms offered cheap and exciting entertainment against which staid Welsh-language activities like the *seiat* and *ysgol gân* could never compete. Cinema stars and sporting heroes became irresistible icons in working-class communities. Yet, we should not exaggerate the decline of organized religion in Welsh-speaking Wales. Chapels continued to retain a significant hold on people's lives until at least the 1960s, especially in rural areas, and the influence of the Sunday schools, prayer meetings, eisteddfodau, Bands of Hope, drama groups and temperance societies helped to counter Anglicizing influences.

One of the most striking features of the period was the demand for English-medium schooling in the most densely populated areas where there were compelling incentives to acquire and use English at the expense of Welsh.[36] Mothers might urge their sons and daughters to raise their children to speak Welsh ('Cofiwch eu bod nhw'n wilia Cwmbreg'), but there was unmistakable evidence that children who had formerly been bilingual had adopted English monoglottism in adulthood and rejected Welsh as being inadequate for modern

---

[31] See Chapter 10.

[32] Departmental Committee on Welsh in the Educational System of Wales, *Welsh in Education and Life* (London, 1927), p. 150.

[33] D. Miall Edwards, 'The Present Religious Situation', *The Welsh Outlook*, VII (1920), 141–3; Robert Pope, *Building Jerusalem: Nonconformity, Labour and the Social Question in Wales, 1906–1939* (Cardiff, 1998); idem, *Seeking God's Kingdom: The Nonconformist Social Gospel in Wales, 1906–1939* (Cardiff, 1999).

[34] David Berry, *Wales and the Cinema: The First Hundred Years* (Cardiff, 1994), pp. 113–95.

[35] Stephen Ridgwell, 'South Wales and the Cinema in the 1930s', *WHR*, 17, no. 4 (1995), 595. See also Peter Miskell, 'Imagining the Nation: The Changing Face of Wales in the Cinema 1935–1955' (unpubl. University of Wales MA thesis, 1996).

[36] See Chapter 9.

needs.[37] Language vitality depends on the socio-economic prestige value of the language, and the truth is that powerful psychological pressures were brought to bear on parents to discriminate against Welsh without ever pausing to reflect on the heritage being lost. It was dinned into their heads that learning or sustaining Welsh was futile. English was the language of 'getting on' and the old language was viewed as a source of shame. 'What do they want to speak [Welsh] for?', 'Welsh doesn't pay' and 'No good fiddling about with Welsh' were commonly used phrases as English rapidly became the lingua franca in both school and playground in the industrial south.[38] Of course, linguistic practices varied from place to place and in the solidly Welsh-speaking quarters of Wales Anglicizing education policies had less serious linguistic consequences. But for a new generation the 'old tongue' was simply part of 'the old, abandoned ways'.[39] Although they were intensely aware of their Welshness they were not greatly troubled by the declining fortunes of Welsh.

One of the consequences of this substantial linguistic shift was the emergence of eloquent new voices who spoke to Wales in the English tongue.[40] Not all Anglo-Welsh writers were hostile to the native tongue. For instance, although Idris Davies sensed that English was likely 'to conquer the world' he believed that this was 'no reason why the "Anglo-Welsh" should neglect their first language. I shall cling to it as long as I live'.[41] But there were certainly writers among them who viewed Welsh with open disdain and who were determined to realize the creative potential of Welsh writing in English. Stung by the jibes of the Welsh-speaking intelligentsia ('Is there an Anglo-Welsh Literature?' asked Saunders Lewis sardonically),[42] an unusually gifted group of writers, which included Jack Jones, Glyn Jones, Margiad Evans, Alun Lewis, Dylan Thomas, Gwyn Thomas and Vernon Watkins, sought to raise the profile of Wales by encouraging their fellow countrymen to compose in the majority tongue. In Keidrych Rhys's provocative *Wales* and Gwyn Jones's innovative *Welsh Review*, new talent emerged and won international fame which Welsh speakers greatly envied.[43] Of late, sensible calls

---

[37] D. Hywel Davies, 'South Wales History which almost Excludes the Welsh', *New Welsh Review*, 26 (1994), 11; Hywel Francis, 'Language, Culture and Learning: The Experience of a Valley Community', *Llafur*, 6, no. 3 (1994), 85–96.

[38] Glyn Jones, *The Dragon Has Two Tongues: Essays on Anglo-Welsh Writers and Writing* (London, 1968), pp. 9, 21, 24; Fiona Bowie and Oliver Davies (eds.), *Discovering Welshness* (Llandysul, 1992), p. 119; Dafydd Johnston, 'Idris Davies a'r Gymraeg' in M. Wynn Thomas (ed.), *DiFfinio Dwy Lenyddiaeth Cymru* (Caerdydd, 1995), p. 108.

[39] John Stuart Williams and Meic Stephens (eds.), *The Lilting House: An Anthology of Anglo-Welsh Poetry 1917–67* (Llandybïe, 1969), p. 184. The phrase 'the old abandoned ways' is taken from Herbert Williams's poem 'The Old Tongue'.

[40] See Jones, *The Dragon Has Two Tongues*; Raymond Garlick, *An Introduction to Anglo-Welsh Literature* (Cardiff, 1970); Roland Mathias, *Anglo-Welsh Literature: An Illustrated History* (Bridgend, 1986).

[41] NLW MS 10812D, p. [87], 26 December 1939.

[42] Saunders Lewis, *Is there an Anglo-Welsh Literature?* (Caerdydd, 1939).

[43] See Chapter 13.

have been made for a greater appreciation of the degree to which writers in the two languages were the product of a common cultural source and shared social experiences,[44] but the fact remains that at that time champions of the Welsh language strongly believed that the emergence of a prickly school of Anglo-Welsh writers was a further symptom of the unwelcome Anglicization of inter-war Wales. The most that can be said is that during this period the two cultures co-existed in a spirit of mutual suspicion.

In the light of all these trends, it would have been remarkable had the articulate, educated Welsh-speaking lobby failed to rally opinion in favour of the beleaguered native tongue. Since the bulk of the common people did not grasp the full extent and implications of large-scale linguistic shifts and more subtle patterns of attitudinal change, it was left to the middle-class intelligentsia to seek ways and means of countering the widely-held belief that Welsh was redundant and its decline inevitable. As each census portrayed a language in retreat, new initiatives were launched to revive confidence in Welsh and its capacity to cope with the needs and demands of modern life.[45] The initial groundwork was carried out by Undeb Cenedlaethol y Cymdeithasau Cymraeg (the National Union of Welsh Societies), whose branches throughout Wales helped to carry the torch of Welsh-language maintenance in difficult times.[46] Distancing itself from nationalist politics *per se*, the Union closely monitored the effects of English-medium education and broadcasting on the young and achieved modest, unsung victories as a result of assiduous lobbying. More successful and long-lasting, however, was the Welsh-language youth movement, Urdd Gobaith Cymru (the Welsh League of Youth), founded by Ifan ab Owen Edwards in 1922 with the avowed aim of cherishing the literature, traditions, religion and language of Wales. Its efforts to promote the language among the young were endorsed by *Welsh in Education and Life*, a Board of Education report, published in 1927, which bore the unmistakable imprint of W. J. Gruffydd's views and which pricked consciences regarding the limited or non-use of Welsh in education and broadcasting. The influence of academics within the University of Wales began to make itself felt, notably within the hard-hitting columns of *Y Llenor* in which the iconoclasm and social realism of poets like R. Williams Parry, T. H. Parry-Williams and D. Gwenallt Jones (Gwenallt) were vented.[47] Although many believed that by making English the language of education and administration within its ivory towers, the University of Wales had failed to repay its debt to the *gwerin* who had founded it, the University Broadcasting Committee played a decisive role in the campaign to

---

[44] M. Wynn Thomas, *Corresponding Cultures: The Two Literatures of Wales* (Cardiff, 1999), p. 73.

[45] See Chapter 4.

[46] Marion Löffler, '"Eu Hiaith a Gadwant": The Work of the National Union of Welsh Societies, 1914–1941', *THSC*, new series, 4 (1998), 124–52.

[47] See Chapter 11.

establish the Welsh Region of the BBC in 1937.[48] Even though Welsh-language programmes remained few in number, the initiatives launched by Sam Jones at Bangor helped to dispel the image of the BBC as a 'Big Bumptious Concern'.[49] Indeed, such was his influence on broadcasting in north Wales that the catchphrase 'Babi Sam yw'r BiBiSi' (The BBC is Sam's Baby) entered the broadcasting vocabulary.[50]

By this stage, however, it had become clear that the problems associated with the loss of prestige and respect for the language were not likely to be resolved by the Labour Party, whose dominance at the polls ensured its political ascendancy, especially in the industrial constituencies. Labour was little concerned with the declining fortunes of the native tongue, and the only political party to make extensive use of Welsh, to advocate its wider usage, and to campaign for enhanced status was Plaid Genedlaethol Cymru (the Welsh Nationalist Party) which, from 1925 onwards, derived most of its support from middle-class intellectuals.[51] Its initial aim was to establish a 'Welsh Wales', but its lamentable performance at the polls robbed it of credibility as a political force. Its policies heavily bore the imprint of Saunders Lewis, a founder member of the Party and its president from 1926 to 1939. By any standards, Lewis was a towering figure and the reader will discover his name in most chapters in this volume. This urbane, élitist, right-wing scholar and literary critic was beyond question the most able Welsh writer of his day. Fired by the conviction that cultural well-being and social cohesion sprang from the moral and spiritual integrity of the individual, Lewis sacrificed his personal career as a writer in order to champion the political cause of the Welsh language. His provocative ideas and ideologies attracted admiration and revulsion in equal measures. He urged his fellow writers and campaigners to boycott Anglicizing influences in favour of native and European aesthetics, and, like Leavis, he believed that industrialization had corrupted society and grievously weakened its culture. Lewis despised socialism as much as capitalism and although his 'back to the land' programme was not necessarily a regressive notion[52] it outraged Labour activists and alienated non-Welsh speakers. Hardly any of his arguments, however, left any impression on the bulk of the populace and, with the wisdom of hindsight, we can see that his interpretation of the history of Wales was massively flawed. Yet, at two critical junctures – in 1936 and 1962 – he intervened decisively in the political arena in order to defend the interests of the Welsh language. Both interventions had a far-reaching influence on people's minds.

---

[48] John Davies, *Broadcasting and the BBC in Wales* (Cardiff, 1994), p. 79; J. Gwynn Williams, *The University of Wales 1893–1939* (Cardiff, 1997), pp. 385–6.

[49] R. Alun Evans, *Stand By! Bywyd a Gwaith Sam Jones* (Llandysul, 1998), p. 60.

[50] Dyfnallt Morgan (ed.), *Babi Sam yn Dathlu Hanner Can Mlynedd o Ddarlledu o Fangor, 1935–1985* (Bangor and Caernarfon, 1985), p. 15.

[51] See Chapter 6.

[52] See Chapter 2; Pyrs Gruffudd, 'Tradition, Modernity and the Countryside: The Imaginary Geography of Rural Wales', *CW*, 6 (1994), 45.

The first intervention – the symbolic burning of the bombing school at Penyberth in September 1936 – was important not only because it exposed the political bankruptcy of the Welsh lobby in Parliament but also because it underlined the subordinate status of the Welsh language. The fact that the case was transferred to the Old Bailey and that the three defendants refused to speak English strengthened public sympathy for Welsh. At the National Eisteddfod in Cardiff in 1938 a non-political, non-sectarian national petition, organized by the barrister Dafydd Jenkins (who optimistically predicted that a million signatures was his goal), was launched.[53] In the event, over 360,000 signatures came to hand in support of the repeal of the so-called 'language clause' of the Act of Union of 1536. War had intervened by the time the Welsh Language Petition was presented to the House of Commons in 1941 and the culmination of the campaign – the Welsh Courts Act 1942 – was greeted with cries of betrayal. Although this was the first piece of legislation to grant a degree of recognition to Welsh, it fell considerably short of the aim of enabling a party or witness to use freely the Welsh language in court. Small wonder that Welsh-language campaigners felt themselves cut off from the central institutions of government.

In many ways, however, the legal standing of Welsh was less important than the deteriorating situation of the language at grass roots level. Had a census been held in 1941 it would certainly have shown that Welsh was running into serious trouble. Although the effect of war-demands on Anglicizing trends is a subject which deserves further scrutiny, all the signs are that its impact was hardly conducive to the well-being of Welsh. The bulk of the Welsh public naturally pledged their full support to the war effort and complied with every attempt by the wartime government to present a united British front. The exigencies of war, however, meant that fewer resources were made available for Welsh-language broadcasting and over the six long years of hostilities nearly half a million licence-holders in Wales became familiar with propaganda on behalf of the 'British nation' and a daily diet of English-language programmes. The influx of thousands of evacuees who were removed from vulnerable urban communities in England to safer havens in rural Wales also generated a deep sense of insecurity. According to local reports, the young incomers brought bugs and body lice to their billets as well as Scouse, Brummie and Cockney accents. The Education Officer of Anglesey County Council gloomily observed that the evacuees 'spoke a different language and had generally formed different habits from the native children'.[54] In the short-term, evacuees adversely affected the speech patterns of young Welsh

[53] J. Graham Jones, 'The National Petition on the Legal Status of the Welsh Language, 1938–1942', *WHR*, 18, no. 1 (1996), 92–124.

[54] Gillian Wallis, 'North Wales Receives – An Account of the First Government Evacuation Scheme, 1939–40', *FHSJ*, 32 (1989), 128. See also eadem, 'North Wales: A Case Study of a Reception Area under the Government Evacuation Scheme, 1939–1945' (unpubl. University of Wales MA thesis, 1979).

speakers, but over time they adjusted smoothly to rural life and at least some of those who settled permanently became fluent in Welsh.

Those who strenuously sought to safeguard Welsh culture were also outraged by the confiscation of land by the wartime government. In 1940 fifty-four households on the Epynt Mountain in Breconshire were impounded by the government for military purposes and 219 people were ejected from their homes without adequate explanation or compensation.[55] Pwyllgor Diogelu Diwylliant Cymru (the Committee for the Defence of the Culture of Wales), hastily convened in December 1939 to forestall such developments, was powerless to prevent the appropriation of land which had been farmed by Welsh-speaking families for generations. Public protests by Saunders Lewis and Iorwerth C. Peate fell on deaf ears, and even when the Committee allied with the National Union of Welsh Societies to form Undeb Cymru Fydd (the New Wales Union) in 1941, the government continued to ride roughshod over what the Welsh-speaking lobby considered to be legitimate grievances. In the 'people's war', undermining Hitler's regime was the chief priority, and since the humiliating ejections which accompanied the appropriation of 40,000 acres of land on Epynt Mountain were undertaken in wartime the episode never acquired the symbolic significance of Penyberth or Tryweryn in folk memory.

The Second World War, therefore, accelerated long-term trends which had become apparent by the late 1930s. The breakdown of isolation, greater and swifter mobility, and the incursions of the mass media all meant that English was sweeping remorselessly even into remote areas. By 1951 the number of Welsh speakers had plummeted to 714,686 (28.9 per cent of the total population over the age of three). Considerable inroads had been made into the Welsh-speaking heartland along the swiftly-Anglicizing coastline as well as along the traditional east–west routes into Wales. Adult Welsh monoglots were becoming as rare as gold sovereigns and in the predominantly English-speaking towns of industrial Wales the native language was viewed as a badge of ignorance. The long-term trend seemed to point to greater exposure to the English language, decreasing competence in spoken (and certainly written) Welsh, and a lack of confidence about using a language which was clearly in an advanced stage of decay. The public status of Welsh was well-nigh invisible. There were no public signs or notices in Welsh, and all official forms distributed by central and local government were entirely in English. Bold acts of civil disobedience – those by Eileen and Trefor Beasley of Llangennech are the most oft-quoted examples – were openly derided, and the plight of Welsh appeared to be so pitiable that in his science-fiction novel, *Wythnos yng Nghymru Fydd* (A Week in the Wales of the Future),

---

[55] Ronald Davies, *Epynt without People . . . and Much More* (Talybont, 1971); Herbert Hughes, *An Uprooted Community: A History of Epynt* (Llandysul, 1998); Ann Gruffydd Rhys, 'Colli Epynt', *Barn*, 366–7 (1993), 30–4.

published in 1957, Islwyn Ffowc Elis dispatched his principal character on two separate journeys into the future. The first visit was immensely reassuring, for he encountered an independent, bilingual Wales at ease with itself. The second visit, however, was profoundly unnerving: he found himself in a Wales which had become a province of western England and in which no Welsh was spoken. On a tour of this unhappy land, he met a deranged old lady in Bala whom he invited to recite with him in Welsh the familiar words of the twenty-third Psalm. She joined him and completed the Psalm before lapsing irrevocably into English: 'I had seen with my own eyes the death of the Welsh language' ('Yr oeddwn wedi gweld â'm llygaid fy hun farwolaeth yr iaith Gymraeg').[56] For the Welsh-language campaigner the 1950s was a deeply dispiriting decade and it was becoming increasingly clear that only a determined challenge involving a considerable degree of organization and perhaps self-sacrifice would awaken the public conscience to the plight of the native tongue.

That defining moment in the history of the Welsh language occurred in February 1962 when Saunders Lewis, who had spent the post-war years in relative seclusion, returned to the glare of publicity by delivering his historic radio lecture *Tynged yr Iaith*, in which he declared that as long as the linguistic status quo prevailed there was a strong likelihood that the demise of Welsh would occur early in the twenty-first century.[57] As in 1936, he threw down the gauntlet in order to shame his countrymen, especially members of Plaid Cymru, into developing a coherent and effective strategy to revive the fortunes of the language he cherished above all others. Lewis reiterated his long-held belief that the survival of the language was more important than self-government and, although we do not know how many actually heard the lecture, its content reverberated around Welsh-speaking Wales for many years afterwards. Indeed, it is hard not to reflect on how radically different things might have been had he not fashioned such a scintillating and timely polemic. It brought the plight of Welsh into the public, and especially the political, domain as never before. Lewis's message was clear: the situation could only be rectified by revolutionary means. Ironically, therefore, although the 1960s witnessed a catastrophic decline of 17.3 per cent in the number of Welsh speakers, *Tynged yr Iaith* ushered in a new sense of commitment to the recovery of Welsh. In particular, it heralded the entry of the young into the political arena.

In many parts of Europe and America, the 1960s was a decade of student activism notable for its idealism, bravery and daring. Non-violent civil disobedience became a central feature of what Martin Luther King liked to call

---

[56] Islwyn Ffowc Elis, *Wythnos yng Nghymru Fydd* (Caerdydd, 1957), p. 214.
[57] Lewis, *Tynged yr Iaith*, p. 5.

'creative extremism'[58] and in Wales the civil rights movement focused on the native language. The fact that for every one Welsh speaker there were three non-Welsh speakers in Wales concentrated the minds of the young, relatively affluent, middle-class student activists who joined Cymdeithas yr Iaith Gymraeg (the Welsh Language Society) from 1962 onwards and who embarked on a programme of public protest designed to redress the inequitable treatment of the Welsh language in public life.[59] Although the total number of fully-fledged members seldom exceeded 2,000 at any stage, they exercised an influence far beyond their numbers.[60] The constitutional methods and polite decency of their predecessors were replaced by militant non-violent direct action deliberately calculated to invite police intervention, prosecution, fines and imprisonment. A variety of unconventional, foolhardy and heroic stratagems were devised to attract publicity, most of it unfavourable, and to compel the authorities to take the language issue seriously. Over a period of time, the Society also published sophisticated manifestos which went beyond symbolic battles and which provided cogent ways and means of reviving the fortunes of Welsh. The 'madcap campaign'[61] (in the words of George Thomas, Secretary of State for Wales) of the Welsh Language Society can only be understood in the context of the realization that to lose a language is to lose a cultural identity which, in turn, leads to the impoverishment of mankind. The Society's actions were underpinned and legitimized by what the philosopher J. R. Jones movingly described as 'the experience of knowing, not that you are leaving your country, but that your country is leaving you, is ceasing to exist under your very feet, being sucked away from you, as it were by a rapacious swallowing wind, into the hands and possession of another country and civilization' ('[y] profiad o wybod, nid eich bod chwi yn gadael eich gwlad, ond fod eich gwlad yn eich gadael chwi, yn darfod allan o fod o dan eich traed chwi, yn cael ei sugno i ffwrdd oddiwrthych, megis gan lyncwynt gwancus, i ddwylo ac i feddiant gwlad a gwareiddiad arall').[62]

Having traditionally been baulked at every turn by the inertia and indifference of Whitehall officialdom, the language movement discovered its ability to jolt people into action. Grudging concessions were achieved on issues such as bilingual road signs, car tax discs and official documentation, and the pace of

---

[58] Arthur Marwick, *The Sixties: Cultural Revolution in Britain, France, Italy, and the United States, c.1958–c.1974* (Oxford, 1998), p. 288. See also Norman F. Cantor, *The Age of Protest* (London, 1970).

[59] See Chapter 16.

[60] Dylan Phillips, *Trwy Ddulliau Chwyldro . . .? Hanes Cymdeithas yr Iaith Gymraeg, 1962–1992* (Llandysul, 1998), p. 62. See also idem, '"Crea Anniddigrwydd drwy Gyrrau'r Byd": Oes y Brotest a Brwydr yr Iaith yng Nghymru' in Geraint H. Jenkins (ed.), *Cof Cenedl XIII: Ysgrifau ar Hanes Cymru* (Llandysul, 1998), pp. 165–95.

[61] Phillips, *Trwy Ddulliau Chwyldro . . . ?*, pp. 253–4; Colin H. Williams, 'Non-Violence and the Development of the Welsh Language Society, 1962–c.1974', *WHR*, 8, no. 4 (1977), 426–55.

[62] J. R. Jones, *Gwaedd yng Nghymru* (Cyhoeddiadau Modern Cymreig, 1970), pp. 81–2.

change quickened in legislation. However, the Welsh Language Act of 1967, which extolled the merits of equal validity, was a bitter disappointment to language campaigners since it failed to place an obligation on public bodies to use the Welsh language or to enable users to insist upon a Welsh service. Even before the ink had dried on this piece of legislation, clamorous cries were being heard calling for greater recognition for Welsh in public life and a positive response to the impact of socio-economic change on the cultural heritage.

The failure of the broadcasting authorities to match up to the expectations of language campaigners became an immediate priority. From the 1970s onwards sound and television broadcasting became a highly contentious and divisive domain. Late in the day, it had dawned on language activists that the television screen was a powerful Anglicizing agent and that a separate service for Welsh-language programmes was not only feasible but imperative. Indeed, in the eyes of the Welsh Language Society, it was 'Yr Unig Ateb' (The Only Answer) likely to satisfy both Welsh and English speakers. Television became a symbol of the fate of the Welsh language, especially when Gwynfor Evans, an iconic figure in nationalist circles, declared his intention to fast unto death unless the Conservative government honoured its pledge to establish a fourth channel devoted to Welsh-medium broadcasting. In November 1982 a major watershed in the cultural history of Wales was reached when Sianel Pedwar Cymru (S4C) began broadcasting twenty-two hours of Welsh-language programmes a week. In the considered view of Geraint Stanley Jones, the fact that around half a million people were able to sustain a complex radio[63] and television service 'in their historically buffeted language is a creative, political and economic achievement of some magnitude'.[64]

Over a longer period of time language campaigners over a broad spectrum of society had also been flexing their muscles on behalf of Welsh-language education. For much of the period after 1945 local education authorities were permitted to launch schemes for the teaching of Welsh according to the needs and aspirations of local communities. This led not only to maldistribution of provision but also considerable disaffection. By 1961 less than a fifth of Welsh children between the ages of five and fifteen were able to speak or understand Welsh.[65] It swiftly became clear that, in part, the salvation of the language lay in extending the provision of bilingual or Welsh-medium education so that it would reach not only families in robustly Welsh-speaking communities but also parents in industrial and urban areas who had either failed to transfer the mother tongue to

---

[63] Radio Cymru, the Welsh-language radio service, began broadcasting in 1977 and was relaunched in 1979 on VHF.

[64] Geraint Stanley Jones, 'A Sense of Place' in Patrick Hannan (ed.), *Wales in Vision: The People and Politics of Television* (BBC Cymru Wales, 1990), p. 157; Hugh Mackay and Anthony Powell, 'Wales and its Media: Production, Consumption and Regulation', *CW*, 9 (1996), 8–39.

[65] Gareth Elwyn Jones, *Modern Wales: A Concise History c.1485–1979* (Cambridge, 1984), p. 291.

their children or had resented its very presence in public life. Belatedly it was recognized that pre-school children needed to be immersed in Welsh and this led to the formation of Mudiad Ysgolion Meithrin (the Welsh-medium Nursery Schools Movement) in 1971. It proved spectacularly successful and by 1998–9 there were around a thousand Welsh-medium playgroups, parent and toddler groups, and nurseries offering a full range of pre-school activities.[66] Its influence as a pre-condition of successful bilingual education cannot be overemphasized. The establishment of Welsh-medium schools, at primary and secondary level, helped to dispel the notion that English was the only worthwhile and effective medium of education, and among appreciable numbers of non-Welsh-speaking parents the old language, which had formerly been a source of shame, came to be highly cherished as a source of identity and self-esteem. As bilingual education grew by leaps and bounds, Welsh shed its negative overtones and, by the Education Reform Act of 1988, it became compulsory, either as a first or second language, within the curriculum of primary schools and early classes within secondary schools. Conversely, the University of Wales, one of the finest achievements of late Victorian society, proved less than equal to the task of retaining its talented sons and daughters and providing them with a satisfying fare of Welsh-medium courses. Until the 1960s Welsh-medium teaching within Welsh universities was confined to Departments of Welsh, Welsh History and Biblical Studies but, although a wide range of subjects in the humanities were subsequently taught in Welsh, calls for a Welsh-medium College were rejected out of hand and the piecemeal provision appeared to confirm Saunders Lewis's verdict of 'a cata-strophic lack of moral courage and decision'.[67] Ironically, therefore, even though Welsh dons were chiefly responsible for the post-war flowering of creative literary and historical writing, their students were denied adequate scope to develop their talents through the Welsh language. Overall, however, the development of bilingual education during the second half of the century provided a solid base for linguistic regeneration.[68]

In the domain of religion, formerly a fortress for the Welsh language, the story was very different. Although spiritual matters had historically been interlinked with education, in the post-1945 period the Welsh were not disposed to shore up their spiritual heritage. Indeed, they abandoned it in droves. No longer was it the case that to be a Christian was an integral part of being Welsh. Church membership in Wales declined from 808,161 in 1905 to 523,100 in 1982, a fall of

---

[66] Mudiad Ysgolion Meithrin, *Adroddiad Blynyddol / Annual Report 1998–99*. For a full account, see Catrin Stevens, *Meithrin: Hanes Mudiad Ysgolion Meithrin 1971–1996* (Llandysul, 1996).

[67] Lewis, *Is there an Anglo-Welsh Literature?*, p. 13. See also Dafydd Glyn Jones, 'Problem Prifysgol', *Y Traethodydd*, CLIII (1998), 71–5.

[68] See the stimulating work of Colin Baker, especially *Aspects of Bilingualism in Wales* (Clevedon, 1985), *Key Issues in Bilingualism and Bilingual Education* (Clevedon, 1988), *Attitudes and Language* (Clevedon, 1992) and (with Sylvia Prys Jones), *Encyclopedia of Bilingualism and Bilingual Education* (Clevedon, 1998).

36 per cent.[69] The tide had turned emphatically against Christian worship and practice. The rise of secularism, the association of Nonconformity with out-dated practices and an ageing population, and the emergence of more attractive alternatives meant that many thousands were not only deeply disillusioned with organized religion but had also lost their faith. Post-modern Wales had little patience with, or room for, the pieties of the past and, despite the commendable efforts of conservationists, chapels which had once been the pride and joy of congregations were allowed to crumble into ruins, to become a prey for vandals, or to be converted into cinemas, pubs, bingo halls, factories and garages.[70] 'The fire now burns on Cambria's altars', wrote Glanmor Williams in 1991, 'only with a smoky and fitful flame.'[71] Such disenchantment had cultural implications. From the Reformation onwards, especially following the publication of the Welsh Bible in 1588, Welsh had been the language of religion in Wales. This conferred dignity on the language and ensured that Welsh remained the predominant medium of worship in churches and chapels for the best part of four centuries. But when religion became of marginal importance to community life in Wales during the second half of the twentieth century, the loss of exposure to Welsh in church and chapel services, Sunday schools and literary gatherings deprived the native tongue of one of its most powerful and respected domains. It should also be emphasized that those Welsh speakers who repudiated Christianity also turned their back on a rich cultural legacy which included the prose of William Morgan, Charles Edwards and Ellis Wynne, the pulpit rhetoric of John Elias and Christmas Evans, and the hymns of Williams Pantycelyn and Ann Griffiths. In a land formerly known as 'the country of the Book', William Owen Pughe's aphorism about Welsh as the 'language of heaven' carried a hollow ring, and it is hard to imagine that it will ever again draw strength from the domain of religion.

As the influence of religion began to wane in the post-war years, it became increasingly evident that the book culture which had sustained Welsh culture since the days of the Renaissance scholars was also likely to crumble unless considerable subventions were made available by the state. In 1952 the Ready Report flagged up the paramount importance of securing state assistance for Welsh publishing:

> A bookless people is a rootless people . . . if Welsh goes, a bastardised vernacular will take its place, lacking both pride of ancestry and hope of posterity.[72]

---

[69] Glanmor Williams, *The Welsh and their Religion* (Cardiff, 1991), p. 72. See also Chris Harris, 'Religion' in Richard Jenkins and Arwel Edwards (eds.), *One Step Forward? South and West Wales Towards the Year 2000* (Swansea, 1990), pp. 49–59; Christopher Harris and Richard Startup, *The Church in Wales: The Sociology of a Traditional Institution* (Cardiff, 1999), pp. 37–9; D. Densil Morgan, *The Span of the Cross: Christian Religion and Society in Wales 1914–2000* (Cardiff, 1999).

[70] Anthony L. Jones, *Welsh Chapels* (revised ed., Stroud, 1996), pp. 118–20.

[71] Williams, *The Welsh and their Religion*, p. 72.

[72] Gwilym Huws, 'Welsh-Language Publishing 1919 to 1995' in Jones and Rees (eds.), *A Nation and its Books*, p. 343.

The dearth of an attractive range of Welsh-language books, magazines and newspapers made it all the more difficult to cope with what Gwynfor Evans called the 'daily onslaught'[73] of English words, idioms and phrases which poured into Wales and strongly affected patterns of speech and regional dialects.[74] The mass media became extraordinarily powerful cultural agents, and a coherent strategy was required to foster book-reading and literacy in Welsh. As Colin Baker has emphasized, 'Welsh oracy without literacy is like a body devoid of limbs.'[75] Thanks to highly resourceful entrepreneurial work carried out by Alun R. Edwards, at the time Chief Librarian of Cardiganshire Joint Library, the Welsh Books Council (Cyngor Llyfrau Cymraeg and subsequently Cyngor Llyfrau Cymru) was established in 1961. In tandem with the Welsh Joint Education Committee (established in 1948) and the Welsh Arts Council (subsequently the Arts Council of Wales), established in 1967, the Welsh Books Council rejuvenated Welsh-language book culture by increasing the number of published Welsh books from 109 in 1963 to 573 in 1998–9 and by encouraging the proliferation of Welsh bookshops throughout the land. Within the context of lesser-used languages in western Europe, this was an extraordinary achievement.[76] Although the bulk of this material was designed for the benefit of children and schools, the more general literary culture continued to find vigorous expression through print. Kate Roberts, queen of Welsh fiction writers, continued to publish novels and short stories until the 1980s, while in the 1950s Islwyn Ffowc Elis (who was voted the most popular Welsh-language writer of all time in a poll conducted by the *Western Mail* in 1999) began publishing a series of highly readable novels which not only gave the genre a new lease of life but also reached a wider range of readers. The more recent post-modernist era produced experimentalist fiction by remarkably self-confident young writers like Robin Llywelyn, Mihangel Morgan and Wiliam Owen Roberts.[77] Nor were historians unaffected by the rise of national sentiment and the flowering of Welsh-language writing. From 1986 *Cof Cenedl*, a successful annual publication of Welsh historical essays, sought to re-establish the notion that a healthy nation writes its history in its own tongue, a sentiment amply borne out by the publication of the magisterial *Hanes Cymru* (1990) by John Davies, the first Welsh-language study of the whole span of the history of Wales. It is worth noting, too, that Welsh-language writers and those who used to be called Anglo-Welsh writers buried the hatchet and, by the 1990s, were better able to focus on that which bound rather than divided the

---

[73] Gwynfor Evans, *Byw neu Farw? Y Frwydr dros yr Iaith a'r Sianel Deledu Gymraeg / Life or Death? The Struggle for the Language and a Welsh T.V. Channel* (n.d.), p. [10].

[74] See Chapter 12.

[75] Baker, *Aspects of Bilingualism*, p. 21.

[76] See Chapter 20 and Glanville Price (ed.), *Encyclopedia of the Languages of Europe* (Oxford, 1998).

[77] For the background to these developments, see Dafydd Johnston (ed.), *A Guide to Welsh Literature c.1900–1996* (Cardiff, 1998).

two cultures.[78] Some of the most prominent literary figures in the English-speaking world – R. S. Thomas, Emyr Humphreys and Gillian Clarke – were Welsh speakers deeply committed to the ancient language, and the publication of *Cydymaith i Lenyddiaeth Cymru* and its English equivalent *The Oxford Companion to the Literature of Wales* in 1986 was a celebrated milestone in this marriage of interests.

Even as the literary culture began to prosper, the Welsh-language newspaper press became increasingly enfeebled. A sharp reduction occurred in the number and diversity of Welsh titles as newspapers suffered from the competition of radio, television, cinema and mass entertainment in general. The dream of establishing a Welsh-language daily appeared to be all the more impractical when *Sulyn*, the first Welsh-language Sunday newspaper, perished after only fourteen issues in 1983. The loss of the longstanding *Y Faner* in acrimonious circumstances in 1992 was a grievous blow, and the relatively small circulation of weeklies like *Golwg* and *Y Cymro* was a symptom of the decay of the reading habit on the hearth. A more reassuring success story was the proliferation of *papurau bro*, community newspapers whose titles – *Y Cardi Bach*, *Eco'r Wyddfa*, *Y Gloran* and *Llanw Llŷn* – reflected their local nature. Between 1973 and 1988 fifty-two *papurau bro* were established, with a total monthly circulation of around 70,000 and a readership of *c.*280,000. By 1990 this community venture commanded a higher proportion of readers than the combined readership of the *Daily Post* and *Western Mail*.[79] On the other hand, on a daily basis Wales was and continues to be a net importer of English-language tabloid newspapers which speak from outside the Welsh culture and exercise a powerful influence on speech patterns and language skills as well as the ideology and thought processes of the colonizer. The torrent of printed words in English newspapers thus swelled the tide of Anglicization in all parts of Wales.

The experience of the National Eisteddfod of Wales was rather different in the second half of the century. Since the days of Hugh Owen its attitude towards Welsh had been at best ambivalent, and even its most enthusiastic sponsors believed that it was more important for Wales's national festival to project itself to the English-speaking world than to cherish and promote Welsh as a living language. However, when the all-Welsh rule was instituted at the Caerffili Eisteddfod in 1950, this annual event became a standard-bearer of Welsh language and culture.[80] For all its shortcomings – uneven literary standards, erratic adjudications and apolitical judgements – the Eisteddfod exercised a catalytic effect on Welsh learners and on the diffusion of literary, musical and dramatic skills.[81] It also

---

[78] See Thomas, *Corresponding Cultures* and idem (ed.), *DiFfinio Dwy Lenyddiaeth Cymru*, and the series *Welsh Writing in English: A Yearbook of Critical Essays* (1995–).

[79] See Chapter 7; Emyr W. Williams, *Y Papurau Bro – Y Presennol a'r Dyfodol* (n.d.); Gwilym Huws, 'Papurau Bro', *Planet*, 83 (1990), 55–61.

[80] Hywel Teifi Edwards, 'Eisteddfod Genedlaethol Caerffili, 7–12 Awst 1950' in idem (ed.), *Ebwy, Rhymni a Sirhywi* (Llandysul, 1999), pp. 190–218.

[81] Idem, *The Eisteddfod* (Cardiff, 1990), p. 43.

played a vital role in fostering the healthy poetic culture which flourished after the Second World War and which was reflected in the success of *Barddas*, the monthly magazine of Cymdeithas Cerdd Dafod (lit. the Society of Poetic Art), and the poetic jousts of 'Talwrn y Beirdd'. The revival of poetry, exemplified in the renewed interest in *cynghanedd* and also in the emergence of female poets, was significant because those who mastered the bardic craft became remembrancers of the language. Welsh *prifeirdd* (chief poets) became a more reassuring presence than ever before.

Despite this (admittedly mixed) evidence of cultural gains, the censuses of 1971, 1981 and 1991 appeared to supply incontestable evidence that Welsh was a dying language. In absolute terms the number of Welsh speakers fell from 542,425 in 1971 to 508,207 in 1981 and to 508,098 in 1991. This decline was inextricably bound up with socio-economic problems, including in-migration, depopulation, deindustrialization, poverty and the environment, all of which seemed to point to the fact that language legislation and schooling provision were not foolproof life-support machines for the native tongue. The traditional Welsh-speaking core had been eroded and fragmented so alarmingly that by the 1990s it was no longer possible or sensible to refer to Inner and Outer Wales, to Heartland and Hinterland, and to Core, Domain and Periphery.[82] The overall picture was much more subtle and complex. Even the popular (if vague) phrase 'Y Fro Gymraeg' (Welsh Wales), so beloved of geographers and social historians in the 1960s and 1970s, had lost its currency and relevance. A broad cluster of interconnected changes were clearly at work. The rise of new technology and the decline of smallholdings, which had always been sustained by ties of family and kinship, aggravated the age-old problem of depopulation. As a result of the 'crisis of poverty' which afflicted large parts of the rural countryside, young people who were the mainstay of Welsh-language culture drifted away from the land.[83] This coincided with a twin-phased inward movement of non-Welsh-speaking urban dwellers from England. In 1989 Graham Day graphically entitled an article 'A Million on the Move?' to illustrate the scale of outward and inward migration in rural Wales.[84] The first phase was an influx of second-home owners (including retired persons, commuters, tourists and even some hippies), together with their families, in search of property in the most desirable and picturesque parts of rural

---

[82] Of central importance here is John Aitchison and Harold Carter, *The Welsh Language 1961–1981: An Interpretative Atlas* (Cardiff, 1985); Harold Carter, *Mewnfudo a'r Iaith Gymraeg / Immigration and the Welsh Language* (Llys yr Eisteddfod Genedlaethol, 1988); idem, 'Patterns of Language and Culture: Wales 1961–1990', *THSC* (1990), 261–80; John Aitchison and Harold Carter, 'Cultural Empowerment and Language Shift in Wales', *Tijdschrift voor Economische en Sociale Geografie*, 90, no. 2 (1999), 168–83; idem, *Language, Economy and Society: The Changing Fortunes of the Welsh Language in the Twentieth Century* (Cardiff, 2000).

[83] See Chapter 17.

[84] Graham Day, '"A Million on the Move"? Population Change and Rural Wales', *CW*, 3 (1989), 137–59.

and coastal Wales.[85] The second involved the beneficiaries of the Thatcherite boom in the 1980s: celebrating their financial gains, these in-migrants were sufficiently affluent to purchase (sometimes with hard cash) Welsh properties as permanent dwellings. The influx occurred so swiftly that it had calamitous cultural effects on rural communities which had hitherto been relatively resistant to Anglicization. A survey conducted in four rural communities in the early 1990s evoked comments such as 'English immigrants are swamping the village and changing the character' and 'There's so many strangers in the village now'.[86] It is true that some incomers mastered Welsh and brought up their children bi-lingually, but the overwhelming majority, blissfully unaware of the otherness of Wales and its native language, remained steadfastly English-speaking. In-migra-tion adversely affected teaching methods, the size of congregations in chapels, the medium of communication in community councils, post offices and village shops, and ushered in massive problems for local authorities who desperately sought to protect their delicately balanced linguistic and cultural profiles.

The result of this extraordinary geographic mobility, industrial decline and agricultural depression were critical language shifts which necessitated political action in the form of comprehensive language policies. It is one of the bitter ironies of Welsh history that Conservative governments, whose monetary policies enormously increased the socio-economic and cultural dislocation experienced in Wales in the period 1979–97, were able to defuse popular discontent and appease the Welsh-speaking lobby with a series of important concessions. Whereas the Labour Party took refuge in masterly inactivity on language issues, the Conservatives provided the essential political dynamic which led to the setting up of the advisory body Bwrdd yr Iaith Gymraeg (the Welsh Language Board) in 1988 in order to formulate language planning policies and prepare the way for a new Welsh Language Act to replace the discredited 1967 Act. Five years later the Welsh Language Act of 1993, which fell a good deal short of the expectations of the majority of language campaigners, established a statutory Welsh Language Board whose strategy, published in 1996, focused on increasing the number of Welsh speakers, providing opportunities to use the language, encouraging people to avail themselves of those opportunities, and strengthening the position of Welsh as a community language.[87] In the light of the rapid pace of social and technological change, we suspect that the first and last of these objectives will prove the most difficult to attain.

---

[85] See Chapter 14.

[86] Paul Cloke, Mark Goodwin and Paul Milbourne, ' "There's So Many Strangers in the Village Now": Marginalization and Change in 1990s Welsh Rural Life-Styles', *CW*, 8 (1995), 47–74. See also Llinos Dafis (ed.), *The Lesser-Used Languages – Assimilating Newcomers: Proceedings of the Conference held at Carmarthen, 1991* (Carmarthen, 1992).

[87] Colin H. Williams and Jeremy Evas, *The Community Research Project: A Report Prepared for the Welsh Language Board* (Cardiff, 1997).

As the curtain falls on the twentieth century, we may pause briefly to reflect on the current position of the language and to consider tentatively its future prospects. It is evident that several crucial and sometimes antithetical processes are at work. Paradoxically, a war of attrition and a regenerative drive seem to co-exist and it is not easy to digest and interpret evidence which is sometimes ambiguous, subjective and self-contradictory. Nevertheless, it is possible to offer the following broad generalizations.

In several important ways, Welsh is much stronger in 2000 than it was in 1900. Institutionally it is more robust and, although the Welsh Language Act of 1993 failed to confer upon it equality of status with English, its public status is high, its use in daily life – on official forms, public notices, place-names – is extensive, and it figures prominently in education, the media, law and local government. Its own people no longer regard it as a stumbling block or an incubus, and only a minority of egregious outsiders continue to disparage or patronize it. Conversely, the numbers who speak Welsh are a shrinking minority. During the course of the century the absolute number of resident Welsh speakers nearly halved and the proportion of the total population fell from around 50 per cent in 1901 to 18.6 per cent in 1991. The numerical decline was matched by territorial decline and significant language shift. Welsh is no longer principally associated with farming, slate quarries, coal mines, chapels and eisteddfodau. Following the erosion and fragmentation of Welsh Wales or 'Y Fro Gymraeg', the growth points of the language are linked with the bilingual, articulate, upwardly mobile middle-class élite who are rapidly colonizing a wide range of commercial, service and media occupations in the formerly Anglicized towns and cities of south-east Wales where Welsh carries greater socio-economic prestige than ever before.[88]

Parallel to this is the decline of Welsh as a community language. The diminishing role of agriculture in the Welsh economy, the collapse of the smokestack industries, the effects of out-migration and in-migration, and the impact of tourism have all precipitated or intensified language loss in Welsh-speaking communities. The spatial continuum which characterized the dominance of Welsh in 1900 has vanished and the prevalence and distribution of Welsh speakers are patchy and fragile. The linguistic profile of Wales is therefore much more diverse and fractured than it was a hundred years ago, and it remains to be seen whether the increase in the number of bilingual speakers in urban areas (the percentage of those aged 3–15 able to speak Welsh increased from 18 per cent in 1981 to 24.9 per cent in 1991) will compensate for the decline of the language among native Welsh speakers in the traditional heartlands. The auguries are not promising and only gloomy conclusions can be drawn from David Greene's comment: 'a

---

[88] John Aitchison and Harold Carter, 'Language and Class in Wales: New Data from the 1991 Census', *Planet*, 105 (1994), 11–16; David Blackaby and Stephen Drinkwater, 'Welsh-Speakers and the Labour Market', *CW*, 9 (1996), 158–70.

network is no substitute for a community'.[89] A large percentage of the population is elderly, divorce rates are high and lone-parent families proliferate.[90] All these factors have critical significance for language transmission. An alarmingly high proportion of Welsh speakers are linguistically isolated within their households. Fifty-one per cent of households have only one Welsh speaker and 70 per cent have no Welsh-speaking children within them.[91] The percentage of Welsh speakers who claim Welsh as their first language was as low as 56 per cent in 1992, and the number of households where all the adults and children speak Welsh accounted for only 2.5 per cent of the population.[92] Despite the proliferation of adult learners' classes, the number of in-migrants in rural and urban areas who either speak or have learnt Welsh is distressingly low. Language networks are so tenuous that Welsh, despite its enhanced status, rarely impinges on the lives of four of every five persons living in Wales. It is legitimate, therefore, to pose the question: is it possible for a language bereft of a core of adult monoglot speakers and which is no longer robustly community-based to survive?[93]

Since families and communities are no longer reproducing Welsh speakers in sufficiently large numbers and since a third of Welsh children acquire the native tongue outside their homes, the role of education has assumed critical importance. The significant advances which occurred in this domain in the period following the Second World War reversed the trend of more than a century. None of this could have been achieved without enlightened planning and tireless effort.[94] However, the results have not matched the rhetoric, since only a fifth of the children of Wales are fluent in Welsh by the age of eleven. Further deterioration occurs at secondary level and by the stage of GCSE and Advanced level examinations only 5.7 per cent and 5.2 per cent respectively of all examination entries are through the medium of Welsh. Four of every ten students from Wales attend universities in England and the percentage of higher education students (1.6 per cent) pursuing Welsh-medium courses in Welsh universities is lamentable.[95] It has recently been argued that current teaching practices in adult

---

[89] Haugen, McClure and Thomson (eds.), *Minority Languages Today*, p. 8.

[90] Jane Aaron, Teresa Rees, Sandra Betts and Moira Vincentelli (eds.), *Our Sisters' Land: The Changing Identities of Women in Wales* (Cardiff, 1994), pp. 20–1, 30.

[91] John Aitchison and Harold Carter, 'Household Structures and the Welsh Language', *Planet*, 113 (1995), 31–2.

[92] Idem, 'The Welsh Language Today' in David Dunkerley and Andrew Thompson (eds.), *Wales Today* (Cardiff, 1999), p. 98.

[93] Robyn Parri, 'Facing Reality', *Planet*, 136 (1999), 40–6. For a more optimistic view, see Robert Owen Jones, 'The Welsh Language: Does it Have a Future?' in Ronald Black, William Gillies and Roibeard Ó Maolalaigh (eds.), *Celtic Connections: Proceedings of the 10th International Congress of Celtic Studies. Volume One. Language, Literature, History, Culture* (East Linton, 1999), pp. 425–56. See also John Aitchison and Harold Carter, 'The Regeneration of the Welsh Language: An Analysis', *CW*, 11 (1998), 167–85.

[94] The most enlightened bilingual policy was implemented in Gwynedd. See Chapter 18.

[95] Colin Baker and Meirion Prys Jones, *Dilyniant mewn Addysg Gymraeg / Continuity in Welsh Language Education* (Bwrdd yr Iaith Gymraeg / The Welsh Language Board, 1999).

learners' classes are based on false and discredited methodologies, and the high drop-out rate in such classes is deeply unsettling.[96] It is abundantly clear, therefore, that even if education were adequately resourced and implemented by thousands of imaginative, energetic and well-paid teachers, it cannot, of itself, guarantee the survival of the Welsh language.

Language maintenance is also dependent on cultural networks, be they sustained by the state or by voluntary means. Here it is difficult to predict what the future holds, but a reasonable interim report would clearly show that Welsh-language publishing is too heavily dependent on state support, that sales and circulation figures are disappointingly low (even the most successful biography or novel is unlikely to sell more than 5,000 copies) and that the yawning gap between Welsh oracy and literacy bodes ill for the culture.[97] We still await a national daily Welsh-language newspaper. It is evident, too, that the cultural mission of Welsh broadcasting has been profoundly affected by cable and satellite television, and since digital television will offer hundreds of channels to the viewer (most of them in English) the ability of the BBC, HTV and S4C (the most heavily subsidized television channel in the world) to influence Welsh-language maintenance will be severely curtailed. Indeed, there are already signs that both Radio Cymru and S4C are prepared to deCymricize their programme content and encourage language degeneration in order to improve their ratings. What began life as highly acclaimed Welsh-medium services are in danger of becoming a vehicle for bilingualism, a shift which has incensed traditional listeners and viewers. As we have seen, too, Welsh-language literature, heavily buttressed by state support, is seeking new modes of expression, and it is reassuring to learn that 'no period can compare with the twentieth century in terms of quantity or quality of literature'.[98] Moreover, despite the slovenliness of a great deal of spoken Welsh,[99] institutions like the National Eisteddfod, Urdd Gobaith Cymru, Merched y Wawr (lit. Daughters of the Dawn) and the Young Farmers' Clubs ensure that the Welsh cultural tradition remains unbroken at grass roots level.

Recent constitutional changes may well release creative energies in the language domain. The coming of the Welsh Assembly has certainly made this an exhilarating time to be Welsh. However, ringing declarations of support for the

[96] Jeremy Evas, 'Rhwystrau ar Lwybr Dwyieithrwydd' (unpubl. University of Wales PhD thesis, 1999), chapter 5. For a robust defence of adult learners' classes, see Bobi Jones, *Language Regained* (Llandysul, 1993).

[97] D. Roy Thomas, 'Welsh-Language Publications: Is Public Support Effective?', *CW*, 9 (1996), 40–55.

[98] Johnston (ed.), *A Guide to Welsh Literature*, p. vii. See, for instance, Geraint Bowen (ed.), *Y Traddodiad Rhyddiaith yn yr Ugeinfed Ganrif* (Llandysul, 1976) and John Rowlands (ed.), *Sglefrio ar Eiriau* (Llandysul, 1992).

[99] See Chapter 15; Dafydd Glyn Jones, *John Morris-Jones a'r 'Cymro Dirodres'* (Undeb y Gymraeg, 1997); Dafydd Jenkins, 'Cyfarthion Corieithgi', *Taliesin*, 102 (1998), 66–77; Heini Gruffudd, 'Young People's Use of Welsh: The Influence of Home and Community', *CW*, 10 (1998), 200–18.

native language are no substitute for regular deployment of the language in the public proceedings of the Assembly. In its first year, contributions from the floor in Welsh constituted only 10 to 12 per cent of the total proceedings and the Irish example should forewarn us of the ability of politicians to allow a language to die by stealth.[100] The acquisition of political institutions can serve to marginalize the language as a political issue and it is entirely possible that the Assembly will not perceive Welsh as the most important badge of the national identity within a land in which four of every five do not speak it. It is also possible to argue that the growth of political institutions in Wales from 1964 onwards will lead to a culture based on common citizenship rather than linguistic considerations. The other possibility is that the growing desire to share a wider European identity might prompt the Welsh to root their Europeanization in their native tongue. In the words of Ned Thomas: 'To be a linguistic minority . . . is to share a very' widespread European experience, to be normal in one's abnormality, and to have a common aim at the European level – the normalization of one's status so that we become just one more part of an extensive linguistic and cultural mosaic.'[101]

One final, and perennial, problem remains: the growing power of the English language, the world's first truly global language. It is a commonplace that English is currently more widely spoken and written than any other language, and its dominance implies the slow death of cultures which are embodied in other, different languages. The odds are heavily stacked against half a million Welsh speakers living in the shadow of 56 million English speakers in Britain and 221 million speakers of English in America.[102] How will Welsh succeed in fulfilling its needs and aspirations in a world increasingly dominated by computers, cellular telephones, fax, cable and satellite television, multimedia and, above all, the World Wide Web? The new information and communication technologies which have reduced the world to a 'Global Village' are underpinned by the English language.[103] Cyberspace is synonymous with English and the implications for linguistic diversity and the fate of marginal languages are obvious. The challenge for Wales is to maintain its linguistic and cultural identity and to share, and participate in, the benefits of the new information age. As *Geiriadur Prifysgol Cymru* (The University of Wales Dictionary) has revealed, the Welsh language is an extremely adaptable tongue, well able to lend itself to a wide range of modern requirements. Within the amorphous globalism of the World Wide Web lie

---

[100] See *Y Cymro*, 29 December 1999; Dylan Phillips, *Pa Ddiben Protestio Bellach?* (Talybont, 1998), pp. 11–12.

[101] Ned Thomas, 'Cymry Cymraeg fel Lleiafrif yn y Gymuned Ewropeaidd / Welsh Speakers as a Territorial Linguistic Minority in the European Community' in Williams, Williams and Davies (eds.), *Gwaith Cymdeithasol a'r Iaith Gymraeg / Social Work and the Welsh Language*, p. 157. See also Chapters 19 and 21.

[102] Price (ed.), *Encyclopedia of the Languages of Europe*, p. 148.

[103] See John Naughton, *A Brief History of the Future: The Origins of the Internet* (London, 1999) and *The Encarta World English Dictionary* (London, 1999).

special niches for sites in minority languages which offer opportunities for Welsh-language versions of front-end interfaces, website home pages and entry points. Just as Welsh speakers appropriated the printing press in Tudor times, so must they now promote a progressive image of themselves by penetrating the fastest-growing communications phenomenon in history.

Despite the levelling out revealed in the 1991 census figures, the current trend points towards what sociolinguists morbidly refer to as language death. Only wise and far-seeing language planning can reverse this trend by ensuring that Welsh becomes a normal medium of communication in a wide range of domains, including leisure, recreation and entertainment. The experience of Mentrau Iaith (Language Initiatives) in Mold, Llanelli, the Aman, Gwendraeth, Tawe and Teifi Valleys has shown that massive financial resources will be required to regenerate Welsh as a community language and enable it to prosper within the prevailing youth culture.[104] Without the means to undertake a creative role as a language planning body, the Welsh Language Board will simply become a complacent exercise in public relations. As Saunders Lewis never tired of emphasizing, benign inertia and passive goodwill are the principal enemies of Welsh, and his foreword to the second edition of *Tynged yr Iaith*, published in 1972, reminds us that the battle goes on:

> Y mae'n iawn ymdrechu tra galler dros gynnal yr iaith Gymraeg yn iaith lafar ac yn iaith lên oblegid mai felly'n unig yn y darn daear hwn y gellir parchu'r ddynoliaeth a fagwyd arno ac y sydd eto'n ei arddel. Dirmygu dyn yw bodloni i iaith a fu'n etifeddiaeth i'n tadau ni fil a hanner o flynyddoedd farw. Gwae'r gymdeithas a ddirmygo ddyn.[105]

> (It is right to struggle as long as possible to preserve Welsh as a spoken and literary tongue because only thus on this portion of the earth can one respect the men bred there who still lay claim to it. To acquiesce in the death of a language which was the heritage of our forefathers for one thousand five hundred years, is to despise man. Woe betide the society that despises man.)

---

[104] See Chapter 21; Colin H. Williams, *Welsh Language Planning: Opportunities and Constraints* (Cardiff, n.d.); idem, 'Governance and the Language', *CW*, 12 (1999), 130–54. The most recent study of planning and Welsh language use is Delyth Morris and Glyn Williams, *Language Planning and Language Use* (Cardiff, 2000).

[105] Lewis, *Tynged yr Iaith* (2nd ed., Cymdeithas yr Iaith Gymraeg, 1972), pp. 5–6.

1

The Welsh Language 1921–1991:
A Geolinguistic Perspective

JOHN W. AITCHISON and HAROLD CARTER

Introduction: Conceptual Framework

THIS CHAPTER analyses the changes which have characterized the spatial distribution of the Welsh language in the period 1921–91. As such, it is essentially an essay in geolinguistics. While geolinguistics emphasizes regional variations and trends, as an analytic framework it offers a good deal more than the simple carto-graphical representation of language data.[1] As Figures 1a and 1b demonstrate,[2] an evaluation of the patterns and processes which have shaped the geography of the Welsh language during the major part of the twentieth century requires reference to a wide variety of variables, operating at many differing scales – a nexus of closely related socio-economic, demographic and political influences. Figure 1a identifies a set of structural variables which could be regarded as having significantly influenced the vitality of the Welsh language during the twentieth century. Here three main determining factors are specified: the changing status of the language, its demographic context and the emergence of various forms of institutional support.

Status is divided into social status – the degree of esteem a linguistic group affords itself – and economic status – the degree of control a language group has gained over the economic life of its nation, region or community. To these are added socio-historic status or the symbolic value of the language, and the evalu-ation of the language both from within and from without. The second set of variables are 'demographic', of which there are two main components. The first is

---

[1] See Colin H. Williams, 'Language Contact and Language Change in Wales, 1901–1971: A Study in Historical Geolinguistics', *WHR*, 10, no. 2 (1980), 207–38; idem, 'An Introduction to Geolinguistics' and William F. Mackey, 'Geolinguistics: Its Scope and Principles' in Colin H. Williams (ed.), *Language in Geographic Context* (Clevedon, 1988), pp. 1–19, 20–46. For further discussion on this theme, see *Geolinguistics: The Journal of the American Society of Geolinguistics* and Colin H. Williams (ed.), *Discussion Papers in Geolinguistics* (Department of Geography and Recreation Studies, Staffordshire Polytechnic, 1981–).

[2] H. Giles, R. Y. Bourhis and D. M. Taylor, 'Towards a Theory of Language in Ethnic Group Relations' in H. Giles (ed.), *Language, Ethnicity and Intergroup Relations* (London, 1977), pp. 307–48.

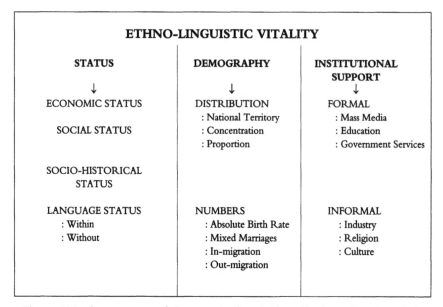

Figure 1(a). A taxonomy of the structural variables affecting ethno-linguistic vitality (after Giles, Bourhis and Taylor)

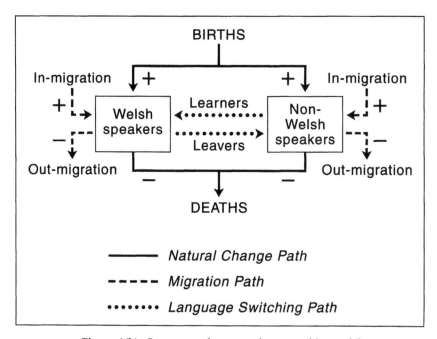

Figure 1(b). Language change: a demographic model

the relation of language to territory and the numbers and proportions of speakers within that territory. Closely related to these features are the standard demographic processes of population change, including increase or decrease by natural causes (the excess of births over deaths, or vice versa), and by in-migration or out-migration. The only unusual element in this scheme is that of mixed marriages, which have an obvious impact on language shift. Figure 1b seeks to summarize these demographic movements and their possible consequences for the numbers of Welsh speakers in a simple model. In addition to the population variables identified, it also takes into account second-language learning and language loss (that is, the subsequent rejection of the language either by native speakers or by learners). To varying degrees, each of these movements can significantly affect the numbers of speakers within particular localities. The third set of variables relates to the issue of institutional support; it emphasizes the whole gamut of formal and informal sources of language maintenance and reproduction. These include the role of government, the media, education and religion, together with a host of others.

While these three broad areas of discourse serve to capture the diversity of factors operating within the language domain, there is a further matter which needs to be taken into account. This relates to the fact that the mapping of language is a means of expressing in tangible form the intangible notion of culture, of which language is one of the most significant diagnostic criteria. Immediately language is regarded as an aspect of culture, a new series of relationships warrant consideration – for instance, the relationship between language, ethnic identity and nationhood. Although clearly important, such matters are not broached in this particular study.[3] The principal aim of this chapter is to chart the changing fortunes of the Welsh language, largely from 1921 to the present, as manifested in the regional distribution of various language indices.

Statistical and Technical Issues

In seeking to describe and explain patterns of language change in Wales during the twentieth century the prime information source must be census data. This poses certain problems with regard to the interpretation of language patterns and trends.[4] The first is that the study must chiefly draw upon aggregate statistics, i.e. data for geographical areas (e.g. parishes/communities) derived from summations of enumerations for individuals within households. The difficulty here is that conclusions drawn from such data are necessarily constrained by the scale at which

---

[3] A discussion of this issue may be found in John Aitchison and Harold Carter, *A Geography of the Welsh Language 1961–1991* (Cardiff, 1994), pp. 1–13. See also R. Y. Bourhis and H. Giles, 'Language as a Determinant of Welsh Identity', *European Journal of Social Psychology*, 3 (1973), 447–60.

[4] See W. T. R. Pryce and Colin H. Williams, 'Sources and Methods in the Study of Language Areas: A Case Study of Wales' in Williams (ed.), *Language in Geographic Context*, pp. 167–237.

they are set. They are certainly at one remove from the processes of language change which take place on the ground (e.g. within households). For example, the actual process of language change or shift can be seen to start with an initial move to code mixing, where words or phrases of a majority language will be introduced into the speech patterns of those using a minority language. There ensues code switching, where communication on specific occasions, or in special contexts, will switch to the majority language. The final consummation is the more frequent use of the majority language and the slow eradication of the minority tongue. A multitude of influences act upon that process which need to be identified and measured. However, none of this can be achieved through analyses of aggregate data where nothing can be directly established regarding the motivation and the behaviour of individuals. The last phrase is the key; only behavioural studies at an individual level, and set within particular social contexts, can reveal these crucial aspects of language change. None can be revealed from aggregate analysis, although inferences can be tentatively drawn.

That said, such difficulties in no way affect the validity of aggregate study. This approach allows general patterns to be identified, many of which can be accounted for by their spatial or regional settings (e.g. accessibility considerations, urban/rural contrasts). Maps can be used both to test and generate hypotheses regarding language change, and they can certainly serve to capture the changing vitality of language over space and time.

Before considering more substantive matters, it is necessary to draw attention to other technical issues concerning the census data on which this chapter is largely based. Firstly, it should be noted that decennial population censuses since 1891 have included a question on the Welsh language in Wales, but not in the rest of the United Kingdom. Secondly, the questions asked have varied in form and range. Thus, the phrasing adopted for the 1991 census – 'Does the person speak Welsh?' – differs from that used in previous censuses. Whatever the precise phrasing of this question in the census returns, it is evident that attitudes to such questions have changed over the years and with them the nature of the responses, in particular the willingness of the respondent to claim or deny the ability to speak Welsh. This last point can be illustrated by reference to the 1951 census when a decision was made by the Registrar General to interpret all those who claimed to be monoglot Welsh, but who completed and returned the census form in English, as being able to speak English. The implication is that the 'facts' on the forms of such respondents reflected an attitude rather than an actual condition. Moreover, the question regarding ability to read and write Welsh was not included until 1971, and in 1991 part of the question which had previously been asked about the ability to speak English was deleted.

A third technical issue is that census data can be processed and mapped in a variety of ways, and to suit different purposes. Needless to say, the choices made significantly determine the ensuing interpretations. With regard to the Welsh-speaking population, for instance, maps can be compiled of absolute numbers or of percentages of speakers. The two yield different patterns, and when used to trace the magnitude and directions of change can result in contradictory tendencies. Thus, the absolute number of speakers in a particular locality might increase, but the percentage of the population able to speak Welsh might decline. The reverse could also apply.

Finally, reference should be made to the differing statistical bases of various censuses. A critical issue, and one which can seriously affect calibrations of the intensity of change, concerns the way in which data have been collected and published. Until 1971, for example, the census was based on the location of the individual respondent on census night. This created problems, especially in relation to visitors who were counted as resident. It gave rise to a particular difficulty in 1921 when the census was held in June, yielding results which were notably out of line with the preceding and succeeding censuses taken at the usual time in the spring. Even the spring date can create problems for interpretation since whether or not universities and colleges are in session or on vacation can produce substantial anomalies in small towns. In 1981, because of these anomalies, the base was changed to the more logical 'usual place of residence', but at the cost of an awkward discontinuity in series data. Also in 1981 'wholly absent' households were omitted; confusingly in 1991 they were either included by means of an additional census form or were 'imputed'. Thus a further discontinuity was introduced. Indeed, it created misunderstanding. The 1981 figure for the total of Welsh speakers was 503,549 and that published for 1991, on the new 1991 base, was 508,098. This apparent increase was heralded as being of major consequence, suggesting a historic reversal in the numbers of speakers after decades of persistent decline. But calculated on the same 1981 base, the total for 1991 was actually 496,530, thus depicting a continuing, if small, decline in the number of Welsh speakers.

Related to these matters, and yielding further complications, are changes in the areal units for which data are available. During the period under review, administrative reorganization and boundary changes have made it increasingly difficult, even impossible, to produce maps for different dates which are directly comparable. In Wales the change from civil parishes to communities, with extensive modification in the process, is a particular difficulty. This is not crucial in the general comparison of maps at different dates, but it totally undermines the mapping of change at the local level, where constant boundaries are obviously essential. For the period from 1961 to 1981 the problem has been overcome by the complex and tedious process of reassembling enumeration districts on the 1961 basis, and by using the location of residents on census night as the criterion. But the extent of change, even in enumeration districts, has made this impossible for 1991.

With these technical and statistical caveats duly recorded, it is possible to proceed to an empirical consideration of the changes which have characterized the geography of the Welsh language in the period 1921–91.

The Inter-War Years

Table 1. The percentage of the population who spoke Welsh and the percentage of the Welsh-speaking population who were monoglots, 1901, 1921 and 1931

County	1901		1921		1931	
	Welsh speakers	Monoglot Welsh	Welsh speakers	Monoglot Welsh	Welsh speakers	Monoglot Welsh
Anglesey	91.7	52.3	84.9	36.5	87.4	27.4
Brecon	45.9	20.2	37.2	12.2	37.3	5.4
Caernarfon	89.6	53.1	75.0	34.9	79.2	27.1
Cardigan	93.0	54.2	82.1	32.5	87.0	22.9
Carmarthen	90.4	39.3	82.4	20.0	82.3	11.1
Denbigh	61.9	29.6	48.4	17.5	48.5	11.1
Flint	49.1	15.3	32.7	7.1	31.7	3.0
Glamorgan	43.5	15.2	31.6	6.9	30.5	2.6
Merioneth	93.7	54.0	82.1	36.1	86.1	25.6
Monmouth	13.0	5.6	6.4	3.6	6.0	2.0
Montgomery	47.5	32.8	42.3	21.0	40.7	16.7
Pembroke	34.4	34.6	30.3	19.2	30.6	13.1
Radnor	6.2	3.7	6.3	7.4	4.7	0.7
Wales	49.9	30.2	37.1	16.9	36.8	10.7

Table 1 summarizes the numerical status of the Welsh language during the inter-war period. For comparative purposes, the data for 1901 have also been included as an indication of the situation at the beginning of the century. The number of Welsh speakers in 1921 was 922,092, as compared with 929,824 in 1901. In interpreting these figures it should be recalled that the 1921 census was held during the summer period. It is probably for this reason, as well as the form in which the question was posed, that for nearly 87,000 returns the language section was not completed; this compares with an equivalent figure of just 2,751 in 1901. The proportion speaking Welsh in 1901 had been 49.9 per cent, virtually half of the population over 3 years of age. By 1921 this had fallen to 37.1 per cent; it was marginally lower in 1931 at 36.8 per cent. Over the period a decline in the number and proportion of Welsh speakers was manifest, but perhaps not quite as great as might have been envisaged given the loss of isolation brought about by the vastly improved communications of the latter part of the nineteenth century and the upheavals of the First World War.[5] Indeed, if the Welsh-speaking population alone is examined, a loss of only 7,732 (0.8 per cent) occurred between 1901 and 1921, with a further fall of 12,831 (1.4 per cent) between 1921 and 1931. Although the pace of decline was apparently quickening, the figures testify to the immense resilience of the language, especially at a time when a perceived low social status and an Anglicized education system worked so strongly against it.

It must be said, however, that other census statistics point to less positive trends. At the beginning of the century the percentage of the Welsh-speaking population who were monoglots was over 50 per cent in four counties (Table 1); it was 30.2 per cent for the whole of Wales. By 1921 the percentage for Wales had fallen sharply to 16.9 per cent, and to just 10.7 per cent in 1931. In absolute numbers the Welsh monoglot population had declined from 280,905 in 1901 to 155,989 in 1921 (44.5 per cent), with a further reduction of 58,057 (37.2 per cent) in the decade 1921–31. It is tempting to ascribe this to the impact of the First World War, but between 1911 and 1931 there was an even greater loss (49.5 per cent) among females than among males (47.6 per cent). Even so, Lord Kitchener certainly ordered that Welsh should not be spoken on the parade ground and even in billets; presumably this must have had some impact, at least on the monoglot recruit. Yet Gervase Phillips has maintained that 'the widely held view that Welshmen were prevented from speaking Welsh, while serving in the First World War seems to be incorrect . . . and, by 1918 at least, the Army seems to have provided for, rather than discriminated against, Welsh speakers in France'.[6] Nevertheless, even if the native language had been permitted, a more extensive knowledge of English was also undoubtedly acquired.

Despite these general trends, at the beginning of the century in the counties which would later be called 'Y Fro Gymraeg' over 90 per cent of the population were able to speak Welsh, over 50 per cent of whom were monoglot (Table 1). This confirms that in certain regions there was still extant a culture and a way of life which was wholly Welsh. During the inter-war period, however, the situation changed dramatically. In all parts monolingual communities were rapidly transformed into bilingual communities. This trend was significant, for bilingualism can be seen as a stage in the process of language loss; it can be viewed as an aggregate equivalent of code mixing.

The data presented in Table 1 suggest that five groups of counties (including two single counties) can be differentiated in terms of basic language characteristics. The first includes the counties of Merioneth, Cardigan, Anglesey, Caernarfon and Carmarthen. Throughout the period they were overwhelmingly Welsh-speaking,

---

[5] See Dot Jones, 'The Coming of the Railways and Language Change in North Wales 1850–1900' in Geraint H. Jenkins (ed.), *The Welsh Language and its Social Domains 1801–1911* (Cardiff, 2000), pp. 131–49; Angela Gaffney, *Aftermath: Remembering the Great War in Wales* (Cardiff, 1998).

[6] Gervase Phillips, 'Dai Bach y Soldiwr: Welsh Soldiers in the British Army 1914–1918, *Llafur*, 6, no. 2 (1993), 101.

with proportions at both the 1921 and 1931 censuses of over 80 per cent. It should be noted that the anomalously lower proportion for Caernarfonshire in 1921 was a reflection of the June date of the census – a factor of some significance in a county with an emerging tourist industry, most notably in the Creuddyn peninsula. The monoglot speakers were only a third of the Welsh-speaking population in 1921, and even lower in 1931, but even so the five counties unmistakably constituted Welsh Wales.

The second group of counties comprised Denbigh, Montgomery, Brecon and Pembroke. These are all counties of the Welsh March with their eastern parts – southern in the case of Pembrokeshire – predominantly Anglicized. They occur as a group simply because the divide between Welsh Wales and Anglo-Wales runs through them. The divide varied in sharpness, depending partly on the physical terrain, where unpopulated uplands often marked the break, and partly on history. It was at its sharpest in Pembrokeshire, where the *Landsker* recognized a long-standing and well-defined boundary line.

Denis Balsom has proposed a three-model Wales which differentiates the industrial south since it does not easily fit into a simple Welsh/Anglo-Welsh divide.[7] To a degree this is supported by the data in Table 1, where the more rapid decline of both Welsh speakers and monoglot Welsh speakers suggests a somewhat different condition. However, industrial Flintshire is very similar to Glamorgan and would constitute an equivalent northern area of contrast.

Radnorshire can be regarded as unique, given that it was almost totally Anglicized at an early date. By 1931, when only 4.7 per cent were able to speak Welsh and when a mere 0.7 per cent of these were monoglot, Radnorshire represented Anglo-Wales. Monmouthshire, too, stands out on its own, but only because Blaenau Gwent matched Glamorgan and the Vale of Gwent matched Radnorshire.

Although there were complexities which modified the simplest division of Wales into two, the contrast between Welsh Wales of the north and west and Anglo-Wales of the south and east remains the most appropriate framework. It is fully confirmed by the analysis of the 1931 returns based on the much finer parish scale.[8] At that time, a convincing 80 per cent Welsh-speaking isopleth defined Welsh Wales (Figure 2); furthermore, as it was crossed, it was marked by a steep gradient of decline over most of its length. There were even places where the highest value of 80 per cent abutted the lowest of under 20 per cent.

But even if a twofold division dominated the distribution of the Welsh language during the inter-war years, there was also evidence of the first signs of

---

[7] Denis Balsom, 'The Three-Wales Model' in John Osmond (ed.), *The National Question Again: Welsh Political Identity in the 1980s* (Llandysul, 1983), pp. 1–17.

[8] D. Trevor Williams, 'A Linguistic Map of Wales according to the 1931 Census, with some Observations on its Historical and Geographical Setting', *The Geographical Journal*, LXXXIX, no. 2 (1937), 146–51.

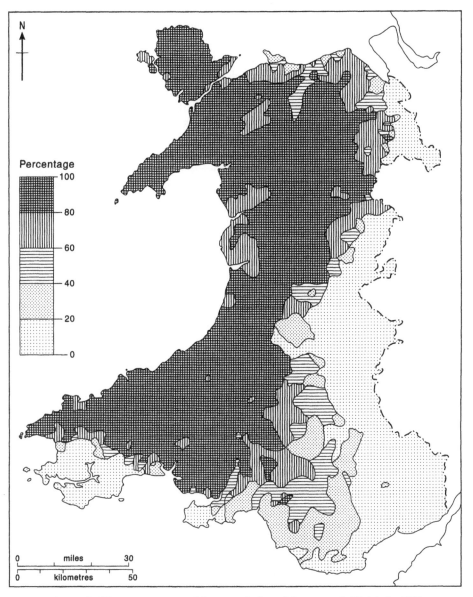

**Figure 2. The percentage of the population able to speak Welsh in 1931
(after D. T. Williams)**

inroads being made into the heartland of Welsh speech. The first of these appeared in the middle Conwy valley and along its tributaries, the Llugwy and Nantgwryd, a section of the old cantref of Arllechwedd or the Geirionnydd Rural District, as it was in 1931. The lower proportions formed an area extending from Betws-y-coed to Capel Curig. The relevant data are set out in Table 2, where the northern part of the Geirionnydd Rural District, with its quasi-urban character, contrasts with the southern section. Here, remarkably, in 1931 the parish of Eidda recorded 100 per cent Welsh speakers, with 65.9 per cent returned as monoglot Welsh speakers.

Table 2. The percentage of the population who spoke Welsh and the percentage of the Welsh-speaking population who were monoglots, Geirionnydd Rural District, 1931

Parish	Welsh speakers	Monoglot Welsh
Betws-y-coed	69.8	12.2
Capel Curig	77.3	21.0
Llanrhychwyn	77.0	25.7
Trefriw	81.0	10.9
Dolwyddelan	91.6	31.4
Maenan	93.0	19.5
Penmachno	96.1	47.7
Eidda	100.0	65.9

The reason for this discontinuity within the area, where over 80 per cent spoke Welsh, is evident. These were locations involved in the early development of mass tourism. Betws-y-coed was already a holiday town visited by charabancs, while Capel Curig had become a major centre for hillwalking and mountain climbing. These activities attracted visitors and entrepreneurs who spoke no Welsh. The low monoglot proportions in Betws-y-coed and Trefriw are especially significant, for they are indicative of the switch to English as the standard means of communication in areas where tourism was growing. The contrast with Eidda, only a few miles away, could not have been sharper.

The second area of decline within the heartland demonstrates the same process. The growth of tourism along the north Wales coast, from Prestatyn and Rhyl in the east to Llandudno and beyond in the west, was accompanied by a progressive decline in the proportions speaking Welsh. Llandudno was typical with only 32.5 per cent Welsh speakers, of whom only 1.4 per cent were monoglots in 1931. It is also indicative of the town's function that of the 4,306 Welsh speakers 1,933 were male, but 2,373 female. That function is again apparent in the much lower proportion of Welsh speakers (23.1 per cent) recorded at the June census of 1921. Even by 1931, therefore, the ribbon of Anglicization along the north coast was well established. Indeed, there was only a small extension of the 80 per cent area to the coast before Bangor was reached. There was also a parallel extension along the south-east coast of Anglesey from Menai Bridge to Beaumaris.

A third area of decline, more akin to the Conwy valley since it lay within the heartland itself, was the coast of Merioneth between the estuaries of the Dyfi and the Mawddach. However, as might be expected, given the westerly location, the proportions were a little higher than those along the north coast. Barmouth returned 64.4 per cent able to speak Welsh, of whom only 3 per cent were monoglots; the respective figures for Tywyn were 74.3 per cent and 9.9 per cent. Here, too, the cause was tourism, especially seaside holidays. Perhaps the most important aspect of the language situation along the Merioneth coast is that it revealed an incipient frontier of retreat along the western coastal margin, a feature which would develop in later decades.

Two other features of Figure 2 require comment. The first is the markedly lower proportions of Welsh speakers in the towns, one of the long-standing traits examined by Stephen W. Williams.[9] This urban concentration of non-Welsh speakers was partly a consequence of the past, for the towns of Wales were largely Anglo-Norman creations and centres of English influence.[10] It was also partly a consequence of the role of towns as central places where the mixing of populations was at its greatest and where English was most likely to become the lingua franca.

The other feature is the clear departure in the coalfields from the notion of a sharp gradient across the language border. Although apparent in the north-east, it is even more strongly marked in the south where the sharp divide is replaced by broad bands at each of the percentage values mapped. Moreover, the isopleths which define the bands turn westward as they approach the Glamorgan coast, producing the well-known pattern of Welsh-language use increasing from the east to west, and from south to north, across the coalfield. Conventionally in the 1930s the Vale of Neath marked a break in the economic and cultural geography of the coalfield, for it delimited the boundary between the bituminous coal of the east and the anthracite coal of the west. Different dates and patterns of industrial exploitation were reflected in language patterns. But the Vale of Neath was no longer a clear language divide, for Anglicization had advanced further to the west.

The crucial significance of these characteristics of the 1931 distribution is that each represented the beginnings of patterns of erosion which were to become

[9] Stephen W. Williams, 'The Urban Hierarchy, Diffusion and the Welsh Language: A Preliminary Analysis 1901–71', *Cambria*, 8, no. 1 (1981), 35–50.

[10] Harold Carter, 'Whose City? A View from the Periphery', *TIBG*, 14, no. 1 (1989), 4–23.

dominant in subsequent decades. Moreover, in addition to these specific spatial features there was a much more general process of decline which stemmed from the wider socio-economic and demographic conditions of the inter-war years. Industrial depression and agricultural reorganization produced a period of extensive out-migration. Given the problems of the 1921 census and the absence of a census in 1941 because of the war, it is necessary to illustrate the situation by considering changes between 1931 and 1951. Figure 3 depicts the demographic situation. Most of Welsh-speaking Wales showed population decrease by migration loss. There is no evidence that migration was language specific, i.e. that Welsh speakers were more likely to migrate than monoglot English speakers, but the direct loss of numbers undermined the strength of the language. Furthermore, the majority of emigrants were young people, so that an increasingly ageing population remained. In consequence, natural increase fell to a level below that of deaths and populations declined also by natural loss. The extensive areas in Category A in Figure 3 mark these areas of both migratory and natural loss; their relationship to Welsh-speaking Wales is clear. As an example, the population of the Machynlleth Rural District fell by 10.5 per cent between 1931 and 1951; emigration accounted for 9 per cent of the decline. The Welsh-speaking population over the same period fell by 11.3 per cent.

Table 3 sets out the proportions in selected age groups of the total population (3 years and over), and of the Welsh-speaking population, between 1901 and 1931. The total population shows a transfer to the older groups, but it is significant that this shift is exacerbated among the Welsh speakers. In 1901, 24.8 per cent of Welsh speakers were in the youngest group, but this proportion had fallen to 17.2 per cent by 1931. For the two older groups, i.e. those over 45 and generally beyond child-bearing age, the proportions had risen from 24.7 per cent to 35.8 per cent. Against the background of specifically located losses, therefore, there was a general demographic malaise which sapped linguistic strength. It is also worth noting that virtually all the areas of demographic vitality, with both migratory and natural gains, were in Anglo-Wales. Ironically, the only such areas in Welsh Wales were the consequence of wartime military establishments at Tonfannau in Merioneth and Valley in Anglesey, both of which introduced an Anglicizing influence.

In the inter-war years there were also responses to these indications of decline which prefigured the much greater reaction of the post-war years. It was manifest that one of the greatest threats to the language lay in the educational system which, since the Report of the Commissioners on the State of Education in Wales of 1847 and the Welsh Intermediate Education Act of 1889, had equated progress in all its interpretation with English-medium education. At a meeting of the governors of the newly-opened Aberystwyth Intermediate School in December 1896, Mary Vaughan Davies, wife of the Liberal MP for Cardiganshire, even expressed the view that Welsh should not be taught at all: 'It was not used outside

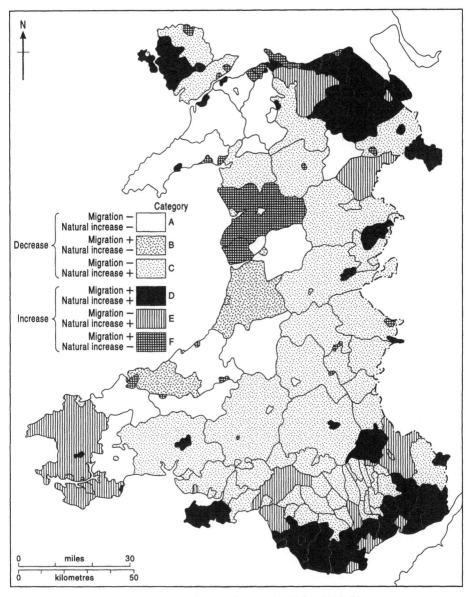

Figure 3. Population changes in Wales 1931–51

Table 3. The percentage of the total population and the percentage of Welsh speakers by age group (3 years and over), 1901, 1921 and 1931

Age group	1901 Total population	Welsh speakers	1921 Total population	Welsh speakers	1931 Total population	Welsh speakers
3–14	28.7	24.8	25.7	21.0	23.0	17.2
15–24	20.7	19.8	19.2	17.8	17.7	16.1
25–44	30.0	30.6	30.5	30.4	30.4	30.9
45–64	15.6	18.3	19.0	23.0	21.8	26.2
65+	5.1	6.4	5.6	7.8	7.1	9.6

Cardiganshire. French or German were of greater commercial value.'[11] The equating of Welsh with two foreign languages was particularly revealing. Welsh in education is discussed elsewhere in this volume, but it can be noted here that, following the establishment of the Welsh Department of the Board of Education in 1907, a departmental committee published a widely cited Report, *Welsh in Education and Life*, in 1927.[12] This report was an important landmark in the reclamation of the domain of education for the language. In many ways the fight back of the Welsh language would constitute the successive reoccupation of lost domains, and given the data in Table 3 it is clear that education was of vital importance.

In the domain of law and administration some progress was also made. In 1942 the Welsh Courts Act was passed, allowing the use of Welsh in court proceedings.[13] In what can somewhat unsatisfactorily be called the voluntary sector, the concern for the language and its evident decline was best expressed by the growth of Undeb Cenedlaethol y Cymdeithasau Cymraeg (the National Union of Welsh Societies) and, in response to wartime pressures, the eventual coming together of a range of Welsh cultural organizations and the establishment of Undeb Cymru Fydd (the New Wales Union) in 1941.[14] However, the most influential of the inter-war developments was the founding of Urdd Gobaith

---

[11] *Cambrian News*, 25 December 1896. See also W. Gareth Evans, 'The Aberdare Report and Cardiganshire: An Assessment of Educational Conditions and Attitudes in 1881', *Ceredigion*, IX, no. 3 (1982), 221.

[12] Departmental Committee on Welsh in the Educational System of Wales, *Welsh in Education and Life* (London, 1927).

[13] Robyn Lewis, 'The Welsh Language and the Law' in Meic Stephens (ed.), *The Welsh Language Today* (Llandysul, 1973), pp. 196–7; J. A. Andrews and L. G. Henshaw, *The Welsh Language in the Courts* (Aberystwyth, 1984), pp. 12–17.

[14] See Marion Löffler, '*Iaith Nas Arferir, Iaith i Farw Yw*': *Ymgyrchu dros yr Iaith Gymraeg rhwng y Ddau Ryfel Byd* (Aberystwyth, 1995); eadem, '"Eu Hiaith a Gadwant": The Work of the National Union of Welsh Societies, 1913–1941', *THSC*, new series, 4 (1998), 124–52; R. Gerallt Jones, *A Bid for Unity: The Story of Undeb Cymru Fydd 1941–1966* (Aberystwyth, 1971).

Cymru (the Welsh League of Youth) by Ifan ab Owen Edwards in 1922.[15] Writing in 1973, Dafydd Glyn Jones observed: 'All in all, *Yr Urdd*'s . . . history constitutes an impressive feat in combining idealism, enthusiasm and ambition with careful planning and skilled manipulation of resources. Of all the different branches of the Welsh language movement today, it must be accounted the one most immediately successful.'[16]

Direct action, too, had its pre-war representation. In September 1936 Saunders Lewis, Lewis Valentine and D. J. Williams symbolically lit a fire at the bombing school which had been founded at Penyberth near Penrhos in Llŷn. In his address to the jury at his first trial at Caernarfon, Saunders Lewis declared:

It is the plain historical fact that, from the fifth century on, Lleyn has been Welsh of the Welsh, and that so long as Lleyn remained unanglicised, Welsh life and culture were secure. If once the forces of anglicisation are securely established behind as well as in front of the mountains of Snowdonia, the day when Welsh language and culture will be crushed between the iron jaws of these pincers cannot be long delayed. For Wales, the preservation of the Lleyn Peninsula from this anglicisation is a matter of life and death.[17]

This was a voice which was to become louder and more strident after the war as the continued decline in the numbers of Welsh speakers proceeded apace. It is also significant, given the terms in which this chapter has been written, that a literary figure should have couched his argument in geolinguistic terms.

By the end of the war, therefore, perhaps the major change had been not so much the decline of the language, however manifest that was, but the near elimination of Welsh monoglottism. This can be regarded as the first and the most severe manifestation of the undermining of language integrity. In addition, the broad geographical patterns of decline had been set and they would become more acute. But the main lines of reaction had also been established. In the following decades both decline and reaction would become more evident and a phase of conflict would ensue.

Post-War Depression and Crisis: 1951–71

There is little doubt that the period after the Second World War marked a nadir in the fortunes of the Welsh language. In 1931, 909,261 people declared that they could speak Welsh, representing 36.8 per cent of the population (3 years and over). By 1951 the number had shrunk to 714,686, representing 28.9 per cent of

---

[15] See R. E. Griffith, *Urdd Gobaith Cymru: Cyfrol I. 1922–1945* (Aberystwyth, 1971).

[16] Dafydd Glyn Jones, 'The Welsh Language Movement' in Stephens (ed.), *The Welsh Language Today*, p. 288.

[17] Dafydd Jenkins, *A Nation on Trial: Penyberth 1936* (Cardiff, 1998), p. 78.

Table 4a. The percentage of Welsh speakers among the enumerated population by county, 1931–71

County	1931	1951	1961	1971
Anglesey	87.4	79.8	75.5	65.7
Brecon	37.3	30.3	28.1	22.9
Caernarfon	79.2	71.7	68.3	62.0
Cardigan	87.0	79.5	74.8	67.6
Carmarthen	82.3	77.3	75.1	66.5
Denbigh	48.5	38.5	34.8	28.1
Flint	31.7	21.1	19.0	14.7
Glamorgan	30.5	20.3	17.2	11.8
Merioneth	86.1	75.4	75.9	73.5
Monmouth	6.0	3.5	3.4	2.1
Montgomery	40.7	35.1	32.3	28.1
Pembroke	30.6	26.9	24.4	20.7
Radnor	4.7	4.5	4.5	3.7
Wales	36.8	28.9	26.0	20.8

Table 4b. The percentage loss in numbers of Welsh speakers by county, 1931–71[1]

County	1931–51	1951–61	1961–71
Anglesey	−6.3	−3.5	−0.03
Brecon	−20.5	−9.5	−21.2
Caernarfon	−1.9	−6.1	−8.5
Cardigan	−12.2	−5.2	−7.1
Carmarthen	−9.8	−5.5	−14.2
Denbigh	−14.5	−7.3	−14.5
Flint	−14.5	−6.6	−10.2
Glamorgan	−34.8	−13.2	−15.0
Merioneth	−15.7	−7.3	−10.4
Monmouth	−43.4	+2.3	−35.9
Montgomery	−18.6	−11.3	−14.8
Pembroke	−8.8	−6.0	−10.7
Radnor	−12.0	−7.8	−17.1
Wales	−21.4	−8.2	−17.3

[1] Because no census was held in 1941 the data in the first column (1931–51) covers a period of twenty years. These figures refer to the Welsh-speaking population only.

the population. By 1961 there had been a further decline to 656,002 or 26 per cent. The losses by county are shown in Tables 4a and 4b.

The situation revealed in Tables 4a and 4b is one of 'inexorable decay', a phrase used by J. Gareth Thomas to conclude his study of the language at the 1951 census.[18] Apart from one anomalous gain in Monmouthshire, where numbers were very small and erratic, there was a universal pattern of substantial decline. Even by 1971 there was no sign of improvement; indeed, the decade 1961–71 recorded the highest loss of Welsh speakers in any census. In general terms, moreover, there had been an increase in the status of the English language. In his study of Tregaron in 1947, at a time when it was a wholly Welsh community, Emrys Jones recorded, 'in spite of the children's ability in spoken Welsh and even their preference for it in conversation, they prefer to express themselves in English in writing'; young girls especially used English as a symbol of sophistication and urbanity. Jones concluded that 'the stress on English is a result of the belief that it is the language of success'.[19] If such forces were at work in Tregaron it needs little imagination to realize how much more powerful they were in localities where the two languages were directly in contact. By this period, too, the geographical pattern of decline which was to continue throughout the second half of the century had become evident. It is epitomized in the patterns which emerge from the superimposition of D. Trevor Williams's 1931 map and that of J. Gareth Thomas for 1951 (Figure 4).

The first element in that pattern was the shift westward of the long-standing divide between Welsh Wales and Anglo-Wales. That frontier, evident from much earlier times, had been relatively stable. Indeed, Jones and Griffiths in their analysis of the 1961 census were to write of 'a predominantly Welsh Wales, fairly sharply divided from a highly anglicized area, and yielding territorially only reluctantly to the small peripheral advances of the latter'.[20] In fact, these peripheral advances, identifiable in Figure 4, were to become a clear manifestation of the retreat of Welsh. That can best be demonstrated by taking two transects across the divide, one in the north and one in the south. They are set out in Tables 5a and 5b. There is, of course, the reservation that it is difficult to select parishes which give a neat transect. In the north the seven parishes form a general line which straddles the eastern edge of Mynydd Hiraethog, to the south and west of Denbigh. It is apparent that the proportion of Welsh speakers was sustained remarkably well between 1931 and 1951. In 1931, of all the parishes with percentages of 80 and over, only one, Efenechdyd, the most easterly, had fallen below that proportion

---

[18] J. Gareth Thomas, 'The Geographical Distribution of the Welsh Language', *The Geographical Journal*, 122, part 1 (1956), 71–9.

[19] Emrys Jones, 'Tregaron: The Sociology of a Market Town in Central Cardiganshire' in Elwyn Davies and Alwyn D. Rees (eds.), *Welsh Rural Communities* (Cardiff, 1960), pp. 101–2.

[20] Emrys Jones and Ieuan L. Griffiths, 'A Linguistic Map of Wales: 1961', *The Geographical Journal*, 129, part 2 (1963), 195.

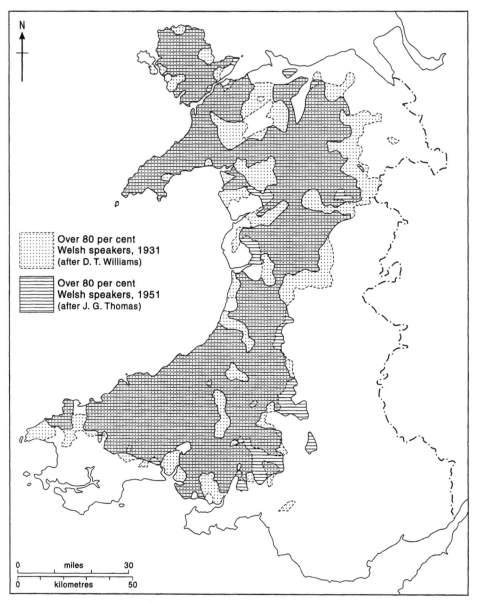

Figure 4. Areas where over 80 per cent spoke Welsh in 1931 and 1951

Table 5a. The percentage of the population able to speak Welsh, Eastern Mynydd Hiraethog, 1931–71

Parish	1931	1951	1961	1971
Cerrigydrudion	94.5	89.3	90.8	89.6
Nantglyn	90.8	85.9	82.8	77.1
Llanrhaeadr-yng-Nghinmeirch	88.5	84.2	87.6	80.1
Y Gyffylliog	97.6	86.2	86.6	75.0
Clocaenog	91.0	89.1	88.9	75.0
Llanynys	84.9	80.7	79.4	72.8
Efenechdyd	82.9	71.0	74.4	69.8

Table 5b. The percentage of the population able to speak Welsh, Brecon Beacons – Fforest Fawr – Black Mountain, 1931–71

Parish	1931	1951	1961	1971
Llanddeusant	96.3	91.4	85.1	81.8
Traean-glas	85.7	76.5	67.1	54.2
Crai	80.8	78.0	77.8	60.8
Senni	81.8	81.1	71.6	57.7
Glyn	36.9	35.9	25.7	15.6
Modrydd	32.5	22.0	16.7	12.5

by 1951. By 1971, however, only two of the seven returned over 80 per cent and one of these, Llanrhaeadr-yng-Nghinmeirch, did so only marginally. If a line at a value of 80 per cent were to be taken as defining the border, then clearly it had shifted well to the west during the period under review.

The second set of parishes in the south are arranged west to east in Table 5b and follow a line of hills running from Brecon westwards through Fforest Fawr to the Black Mountain south of Llandeilo. There the sharpness of the divide is more in evidence, with a major fall between Senni and Glyn. If the Welsh/Anglo-Welsh divide is taken as 70 per cent, then in 1931 it lay between those two parishes. But by 1971 it had retreated well to the west and lay between Llanddeusant and Traean-glas. One reason for this retreat was the acquisition of land in Breconshire for military purposes, particularly the firing range on the Epynt Mountain, and the consequent enforced eviction of the indigenous Welsh-speaking population.[21] The effect which this had on the Welsh language is evident in the relative data set out in Table 5c.

The two cross-sections set out in Tables 5a and 5b demonstrate the retreat of the frontier, the shrinking of what came to be called 'Y Fro Gymraeg'. Even more

[21] See Herbert Hughes, *An Uprooted Community: A History of Epynt* (Llandysul, 1998), pp. 85–112.

Table 5c. The percentage of the population able to speak Welsh, Llangynidr Mountain and Epynt Mountain, 1931–71

Parish	1931	1951	1961	1971
Llangatwg	13.7	5.8	6.4	5.3
Llangynidr	24.4	16.0	8.7	8.0
Merthyr Cynog	49.9	36.2	31.9	23.4
Llanfihangel Nant Brân	72.6	63.6	46.0	48.0

Table 6. The percentage of the population able to speak Welsh in the *Landsker* zone of Pembrokeshire, 1931–71

Parish	1931	1951	1961	1971
Band 1				
Brawdy	71.5	61.4	22.3	36.3
Hayscastle	84.7	69.7	68.1	53.7
Treffgarne	55.8	50.5	37.5	40.0
St Dogwells	94.2	85.9	65.7	55.6
Ambleston	79.1	68.8	69.5	57.4
Walton East	64.1	48.2	46.2	39.1
Llys-y-frân	79.1	83.5	74.2	76.9
New Moat	89.9	78.2	68.5	61.5
Bletherston	84.6	82.0	68.3	50.0
Llawhaden	45.0	36.5	37.5	32.9
Llanddewi Velfrey	88.5	74.4	68.7	58.2
Band 2				
Llandeloy	90.6	78.2	77.2	74.2
St Lawrence	85.3	66.4	85.1	63.2
Letterston	87.3	78.1	71.0	59.6
Little Newcastle	97.1	83.4	86.2	83.3
Puncheston	95.9	87.4	96.3	88.2
Castleblythe	97.5	87.6	92.0	75.0
Henry's Moat	96.7	89.1	88.8	80.8
Llan-y-cefn	94.1	96.3	82.2	78.8
Llandysilio West	91.3	94.3	88.2	78.5

Table 7. The total population (aged 3 and over), the total Welsh-speaking population and the percentage of Welsh speakers, in selected administrative areas of the South Wales Coalfield, 1951–71

	Total population	Welsh-speaking population	Percentage of Welsh speakers
1951			
Mynyddislwyn	13544	747	5.5
Rhondda	106098	31215	29.4
Neath	36962	17563	44.2
Pontardawe	31179	24699	79.2
Cwmaman	4400	4007	91.1
Ebbw Vale	27779	1054	3.8
Merthyr Tydfil	58058	14538	25.0
1961			
Mynyddislwyn	14718	724	4.9
Rhondda	95846	23233	24.2
Neath	39089	14710	37.6
Pontardawe	29491	22483	76.2
Cwmaman	4107	3755	91.4
Ebbw Vale	27218	1049	3.9
Merthyr Tydfil	56244	11169	19.9
1971			
Mynyddislwyn	14635	390	2.7
Rhondda	85140	11295	13.3
Neath	38980	10035	25.7
Pontardawe	28245	18565	65.7
Cwmaman	3810	3395	89.1
Ebbw Vale	24730	410	1.7
Merthyr Tydfil	52725	5945	11.3

significant was a parallel retreat in that area where the divide had traditionally been regarded as being at its sharpest, and where it was most stable. This was the *Landsker* in Pembrokeshire. In 1971 Brian S. John claimed that 'the present day divide is a cultural feature of surprising tenacity; it is quite as discernible, and only a little less strong, than the divide of four centuries ago. In the Landsker we have a unique cultural heritage'.[22]

Table 6 sets out a series of parishes which lie east-west along the *Landsker*. Band 1 is close to the traditional border, while Band 2 is to the north of Band 1 and follows the southern flanks of the Preselau mountains. All the evidence in Table 6 indicates

[22] Brian S. John, 'The Linguistic Significance of the Pembrokeshire Landsker', *PH*, no. 4 (1972), 27.

a substantial fall in the proportions speaking Welsh. In the crucial band along the *Landsker* (Band 1), eight of the parishes recorded percentages in excess of 60 in 1951; by 1961 the number had fallen to seven out of eleven, and by 1971 to only two.

There are two further areas at the periphery of Welsh-speaking Wales which are greatly significant and require comment. The first is the South Wales Coalfield. The nature of the losses of Welsh speech are captured in Table 7 and in Figure 5. Underlying language loss in the region was the basic out-migration which dominated the demography of south Wales both before and after the Second World War. This was caused by de-industrialization. Thus, Table 7 shows the extent of the loss for areas which straddle the coalfield from east to west. Two of the former iron and steel towns, Merthyr Tydfil and Ebbw Vale, have also been included. All figures relate to the population aged 3 and over. The population of the Rhondda fell from 134,603 in 1931 to 106,098 in 1951, and to 95,846 in 1961. Obviously, a proportion of these was Welsh-speaking, so that an element of language decline was simply a facet of people emigrating to destinations which were largely outside Wales. There is the well-known story by the writer Gwyn Thomas of his climbing to the cemetery above Trealaw in the Rhondda to find a tombstone engraved 'Not dead but gone to Slough'. To that must be added the loss of language caused by the failure of parents to pass on the ability to speak Welsh to their children. This was a time when the language was believed to have no value in the struggle for a livelihood; indeed, it was often regarded as a hindrance. A much more prudent investment was to acquire both English and an English accent if the future lay in England. Thus, Table 7 reveals that the decline in the numbers of Welsh speakers was always in excess of a balanced share of the total. Between 1951 and 1961 the population of the Rhondda fell by 9.66 per cent, but that of the Welsh-speaking population by 25.57 per cent. Neath Rural District lost only 1.52 per cent of its population between the same dates, but the Welsh-speaking section fell by 16.24 per cent. The arrangement of the areas in Table 7 again demonstrates the east–west retreat of the language, but it also shows that the western anthracite coalfield was much more resistant to change, and that to the west of the Vale of Neath the language held on with some tenacity. The population of Pontardawe Rural District fell by 5.4 per cent between 1951 and 1961, while the proportion of Welsh speakers declined by 8.97 per cent. The percentage difference between the two was considerably less than in the eastern coalfield. The old irontowns of the northern outcrop of the coalfield showed drastic losses. The population of Merthyr Tydfil fell by only 3.17 per cent in the decade 1951–61, but the Welsh-speaking section fell by 23.27 per cent. Figure 5, for the succeeding decade, amply demonstrates the same process of disastrous decline in the coalfield and the pushing westwards of anything that could be considered part of Welsh-speaking Wales.

The second area at the periphery of 'Y Fro Gymraeg' is the north Wales coast, which has already been highlighted as a special part of the process of retreat. The

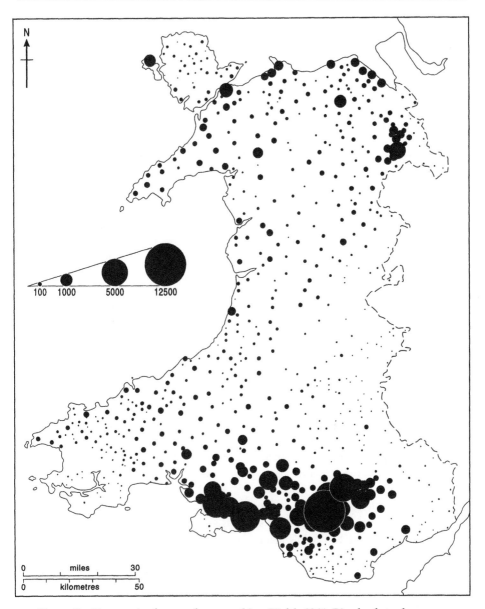

Figure 5. Changes in the numbers speaking Welsh 1961–71: absolute decreases

Table 8. Percentage of the population able to speak Welsh, the north Wales coast: Conwy to Bangor, 1931–71

Parish	1931	1951	1961	1971
Bangor	76.1	69.8	65.6	53.4
Llandygái	93.0	88.9	82.3	73.5
Llanllechid	95.4	91.1	87.0	77.1
Aber	86.1	82.2	77.5	69.8
Llanfairfechan	74.0	65.1	65.7	56.5
Penmaen-mawr	72.3	62.8	58.1	46.5
Conwy	57.2	47.9	42.1	34.7

relevant data are set out in Table 8. The diminution east to west is again apparent, with the exception of Bangor which demonstrates the impact of urbanization. But also quite clear is the way in which the arrowhead of Anglicization had progressed. In 1931, six out of the seven parishes returned Welsh-speaking proportions of over 70 per cent; by 1971 there were only two.

While the extension of Anglicization along the long-standing frontier of contact, indeed along the whole periphery of the March, showed clear signs of increase, even more apparent during the post-war period was the further development of already extant points of Anglicization within the heartland of the language itself, and the development of new ones. The pressure on the language in the middle valley of the Conwy and its tributaries between Capel Curig and Betws-y-coed was evident in 1931 (Table 2). By 1951 it had greatly extended and by 1961 (Figure 6) it had become part of a developing line of Anglicization which cut through Snowdonia from Conwy south-west to Porthmadog. By 1971 (Figure 7) it had further widened and deepened. The proportions speaking Welsh recorded in Table 2 had been greatly reduced. At Capel Curig the 1931 percentage of 77.3 had fallen to 45.5. Another feature, incipient in 1931, had been considerably enlarged and extended, namely the Anglicization of the west coast. The proportions of Welsh speakers in many communities from Harlech in the north to the St David's peninsula in the south had fallen considerably, and continued to do so.

In central Wales a line of Anglicization had traditionally advanced along the Severn valley and also the upper reaches of the Wye. As a result, whereas the low proportions of Welsh speakers in the towns of Welshpool and Newtown had remained unchanged at about 10 per cent, those further into the heartland had fallen. Llandinam registered only 18.7 per cent in 1931 and had declined to 15.8 per cent by 1961; Llanidloes had fallen from 33.4 per cent to 21.2 per cent over the same period, and Llangurig, well into the mountain country of mid-Wales, had fallen from 64.5 per cent in 1931 to 45.9 per cent in 1961. The effect of these declining proportions was to drive a wedge of Anglicization through the centre of Wales.

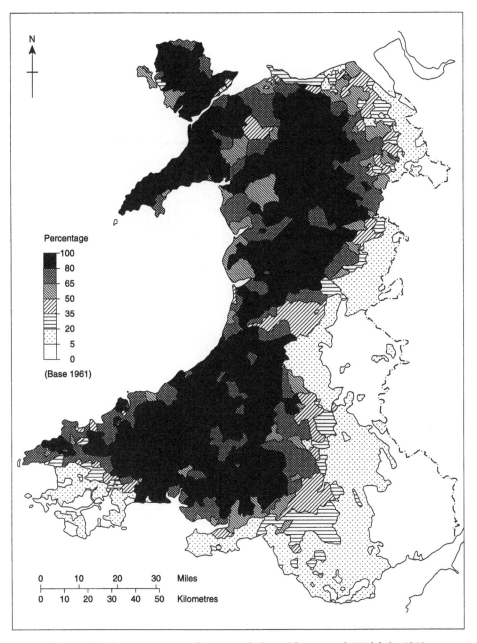

Figure 6. The percentage of the population able to speak Welsh in 1961

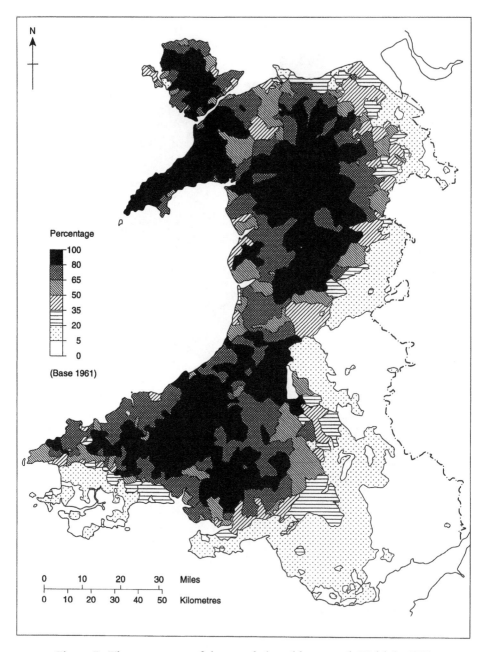

Figure 7. The percentage of the population able to speak Welsh in 1971

One further area of decline needs to be noted. A fall occurred in the proportions of Welsh speakers along a line running north-east from Carmarthen Bay, largely along the Tywi valley. This feature also created a wedge of Anglicization which pushed between the high Welsh-speaking area of the anthracite coalfield and the equally high Welsh-speaking parts of south Cardiganshire and north Carmarthenshire.

The crucial effect of these areas of change within the heartland led to a process of its own internal fractionization, which became clearly apparent by 1961 (Figure 6) and had further exacerbated by 1971 (Figure 7). The push along the north coast, along with falls on the south coast of Anglesey, created a linguistic break to parallel the physical break of the Menai Straits. The line across Snowdonia separated the Welsh core of Llŷn and Arfon, or Dwyfor as the District was to be called, from the other significant core in Merioneth with its heart in Penllyn. The Severn/Wye wedge isolated the Merioneth core from that of rural Dyfed, while the line of Anglicization along the fringe of rural Dyfed separated that core from the only Welsh-speaking industrial core area in east Dyfed and west Glamorgan. In essence, the once continuous heartland of Welsh speech was breaking into a series of separate and smaller cores. The fragmentation of the heartland at this time could be likened to the drying up of a lake, where the main body of water gave way to a series of isolated pools, with the implication that these, too, would in turn disappear. There seemed to be a clear geographical pattern which identified the decline and fall of the Welsh language.

Thus far, the discussion of the post-war period has emphasized the proportions speaking Welsh. If to that is added a review of the changes in absolute numbers the situation of the language is seen to be even more parlous. The losses in numbers between 1961 and 1971 are shown in Figure 5. The massive fall from 656,002 to 542,425 in the decade 1961–71 has already been noted. As Figure 5 so vividly demonstrates, losses were greatest in the industrial valley regions of south Wales. By 1971 Rhondda had 11,938 fewer Welsh speakers, Merthyr Tydfil 5,224 and Aberdare 5,039. Further west the Welsh-speaking population of Swansea declined by 6,517 and that of Llanelli by 5,035. The basic industrial reasons have already been indicated. The same was true of the north where, between the same dates, the community of Rhosllannerchrugog lost 1,778 Welsh speakers. Communities bordering the Dee estuary recorded similar, if less dramatic, decreases, as did other settlements along the north Wales coast. The industrial regions of south and north-east Wales, as well as the retirement areas along the northern coast, contained high proportions of elderly people, a factor which also contributed to the fall in numbers. But the main feature which emerges from a consideration of numbers is that they did not necessarily occur where the fall in proportions were worst, but served to reduce the vitality of the language in those areas where it seemed to be strongest. The loss of vitality was a regrettable addition to the proportional decline in the geographical context.

Table 9. The percentage of the population able to speak Welsh
and percentage change, by number of communities, 1961–71

Classes	1961	1971	Percentage change
Under 5 per cent	194	224	15.5
5–20 per cent	239	243	2.1
21–35 per cent	59	51	−13.6
36–50 per cent	47	60	27.7
51–65 per cent	61	76	24.6
66–80 per cent	114	148	29.8
Over 80 per cent	279	191	−31.5

All the evidence which has been presented to this point would suggest that the 1960s must be classified as a period of substantial decline in the fortunes of the Welsh language, at least as revealed in the census figures. Table 4b, which includes the percentage losses in the decade 1961–71, indicates that the decade was the most disastrous of the century. Every county showed a loss of Welsh speakers, most of them quite considerable, while Wales as a whole showed a loss of 17.3 per cent. As Table 9 reveals, the decline in the numbers of communities with 80 per cent and more of the population able to speak Welsh was particularly marked.

The map of the proportions speaking Welsh in 1971 (Figure 7) shows that the areas where significant decline had been observed since the inter-war period, and which had been enlarged by each successive census, had been further extended and deepened to such an extent that the former heartland had effectively been broken into pieces. It is true that the heartland could still be identified, but only by lowering the defining proportion of Welsh speakers to 65 per cent. It is difficult to identify a minimum percentage of speakers below which it can be said that a language is not in daily use in a spread of domains, but certainly 65 per cent would be below most suggestions for such a minimum. Moreover, even with that lowered defining percentage of the heartland the fragmentation which has been identified as the crucial feature of decline was still apparent. If absolute numbers are examined (Figure 5), the evidence of decline becomes even more pronounced. The whole of the country showed widely distributed losses, but they were particularly severe in those areas where the numbers of Welsh speakers were greatest, namely both the eastern and western sections of the South Wales Coalfield, the area around Wrexham in the north, and the Dee estuary. There were some communities which showed increases, but they were very limited and were largely the result of suburbanization.

The 1971 census was the first to ask respondents whether or not they could read and write Welsh as well as speak it; it is only at this point that a measure of literacy becomes available. It is not easy to identify the significance of the

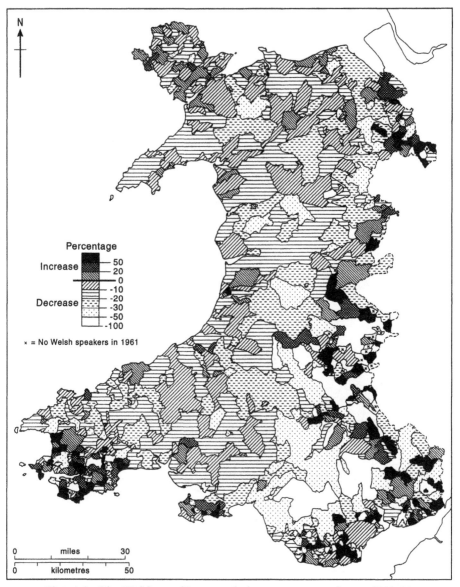

Figure 8. The Welsh-speaking population: percentage change 1961–71

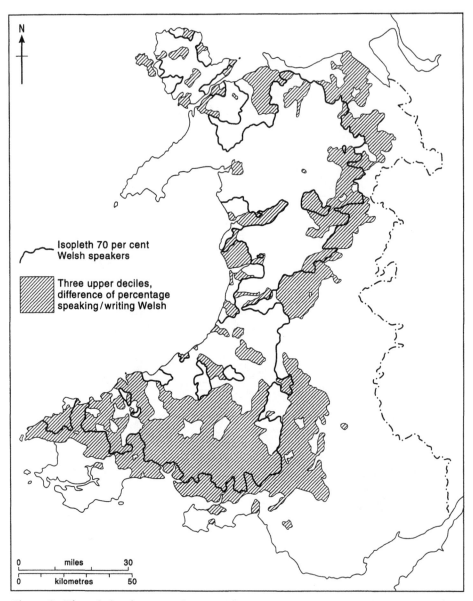

Figure 9. The relation between the area where 70 per cent spoke Welsh and the three upper deciles of the difference of percentage speaking/writing Welsh in 1971

difference between speaking and reading and writing. It can be argued that where the ability to write a language has been lost or not acquired, the language survives in limited domains only and that limitation is an indicator of potential total loss. Figure 9 shows the relationship between the area where over 70 per cent spoke Welsh in 1971, and the three upper deciles of the difference of percentage speaking/writing the language by community. Two features stand out. The first is the close coincidence between the boundary and the identified parishes, which suggests that loss of language takes place by a process in which literacy is lost first; again this can be taken as an aggregate reflection of code switching. The second feature is the large area of low literacy in the south-west, especially in the industrial parts of east Carmarthenshire and west Glamorgan. This conforms with the substantial loss of numbers already noted and underlines the parlous state of the language in an area where the numbers of speakers was the largest in Wales. All this is confirmed by a consideration of the map of the percentage losses of Welsh speakers between 1961 and 1971 (Figure 8). Certainly there are complexities. Decreases dominate and sections of greater decrease correspond to the critical areas which have been identified. Thus the Porthmadog–Conwy axis can be identified as a line of higher decrease. But there are also increases, some of which are attributable to suburban extension. Significantly, the greatest increases were in the most Anglicized areas; there was a virtual correspondence with the old Marcher lands. These indicated that there were changes in progress which suggested a very different direction for the language in the succeeding years.

To comprehend these changes it is necessary to return to the beginning of the 1960s. The forerunners of the language movement in the inter-war period have already been noted. But it was after the war, when the extent of what was believed to be a threat of extinction was apparent, that the mobilization of forces in support of the language occurred. Undoubtedly the key event in that process was the radio lecture *Tynged yr Iaith* (The Fate of the Language) broadcast in 1962. Written and delivered by Saunders Lewis, one of the three men imprisoned for their action against the military installation in Llŷn in 1936, the lecture was in effect a renewed call for decisive action if the language was to survive. 'I shall presuppose', he declared, 'that the figures which will shortly be published [the 1961 census] will shock and disappoint those of us who consider that Wales without the Welsh language will not be Wales. I shall also presuppose that Welsh will end as a living language, should the present trend continue, about the beginning of the twenty-first century.'[23] Lewis's polemic was not directed at forces external to Wales, but rather at the neglect of, and even worse, the disdain for the language which the Welsh people themselves had shown. He believed that hostility and resistance to the furtherance of the language, 'the opposition – harsh,

[23] Saunders Lewis, *Tynged yr Iaith* (London, [1962]), p. 5. Translated into English by Gruffydd Aled Williams, 'The Fate of the Language (1962)' in Alun R. Jones and Gwyn Thomas (eds.), *Presenting Saunders Lewis* (Cardiff, 1973), p. 127.

vindictive and violent – would come from Wales'.[24] Furthermore, he claimed that 'if any kind of self-government for Wales were obtained before the Welsh language was acknowledged and used as an official language in local authority and state administration in the Welsh-speaking parts of our country, then the language would never achieve official status at all, and its demise would be quicker than it will be under English rule'.[25] Lewis set out no coherent policy for the promotion of the language in his broadcast other than to demand the use of Welsh in public life. But his radio lecture led to the formation in the same year of Cymdeithas yr Iaith Gymraeg (the Welsh Language Society), which ushered in a new era in the struggle to maintain and advance the language in a much more vibrant and determined manner.[26]

There also developed a range of organizations and activities whose main aim was to promote the language. Among the most notable, and perhaps the most influential, were developments in the field of education. As early as 1953 the Central Advisory Council for Education (Wales), under the Welsh Department of the Ministry of Education, had published a report entitled *The Place of Welsh and English in the Schools of Wales*. It stressed the relationship between language and culture, arguing that 'the culture of Wales is so bound up with its linguistic expression that separated from the latter it has very little meaning or worth', and recommended that children throughout Wales and Monmouthshire 'should be taught Welsh and English according to their ability to profit from such instruction'.[27] The first local authority Welsh-medium school was opened in Llanelli in 1947, and from that initiative there grew what was to become an effective and elaborate system of Welsh-medium and bilingual education from nursery to postgraduate stages. Perhaps most significant of all was the growth of nursery education from its initial location at Maesteg in 1949 to the founding of Mudiad Ysgolion Meithrin (the Welsh-medium Nursery Schools Movement) at the 1971 National Eisteddfod at Bangor.[28]

Against the background of the growing agitation for support of the language, a committee chaired by Sir David Hughes Parry was set up in 1963[29] whose recommendations led to the Welsh Language Act of 1967 which effectively gave the right to unrestricted use of the language in the courts, although practice was to

[24] Williams, 'The Fate of the Language', p. 137.

[25] Ibid., p. 141.

[26] See Cynog Dafis, 'Cymdeithas yr Iaith Gymraeg' in Stephens (ed.), *The Welsh Language Today*, pp. 248–63; Janet Davies, *The Welsh Language* (Cardiff, 1993), pp. 94–7; Gwilym Tudur, *Wyt Ti'n Cofio? Chwarter Canrif o Frwydr yr Iaith* (Talybont, 1989); Dylan Phillips, *Trwy Ddulliau Chwyldro . . .? Hanes Cymdeithas yr Iaith Gymraeg, 1962–1992* (Llandysul, 1998).

[27] Ministry of Education, Central Advisory Council for Education (Wales), *The Place of Welsh and English in the Schools of Wales* (London, 1953), pp. 52, 55.

[28] Catrin Stevens, *Meithrin: Hanes Mudiad Ysgolion Meithrin 1971–1996* (Llandysul, 1996).

[29] The Welsh Office, *Legal Status of the Welsh Language: Report of the Committee under the Chairmanship of Sir David Hughes Parry, 1963–1965* (London, 1965) (PP 1964–5 (Cmd. 2785) XXIII).

prove rather different.[30] There was a general conviction that little in fact had been accomplished by the 1967 Act and that feeling led to the establishment of the Council for the Welsh Language and the preparation of yet another report. In that document – *A Future for the Welsh Language* (1978) – it was stated categorically that: 'We find the concept of "equal validity" totally inadequate to the needs of the Welsh language today. Nor do we share the Hughes-Parry concept of bilingualism. To us, bilingualism means that throughout Wales every individual should be enabled and encouraged to achieve sufficient facility in both Welsh and English to *choose* which of the two languages to use on all occasions and for all purposes in Wales.'[31] Not all of the report's recommendations were acted upon, but it is evident how much the general attitude to the language had changed by the very nature of the proposals.

This very brief and limited review of developments in the fields of language movements, education and legal status, dealt with elsewhere in this volume, have been included here in order to give a clear indication of the rapidly changing attitude to the language. Whereas in 1947 the children of Tregaron might have felt that Welsh was a symbol of rural naivety and of things past, by the 1970s the language was being regarded as a symbol of cultural identity and of a new and different future. Nowhere was the change more apparent than in the realm of the media. The Anglicizing impact of television had become a major concern.[32] The demand for a Welsh-medium channel grew throughout the 1970s and the report, *A Future for the Welsh Language*, highlighted the urgent need for such a provision. In the seventh recommendation it stated that 'in the case of Welsh, the most powerful external influence affecting the home at present is broadcasting . . . We also recommend that the Government, in the very near future, should make funds available to enable the fourth television channel in Wales to be established and maintained'.[33] In 1982, following decisive intervention by some influential Welshmen, Sianel Pedwar Cymru (S4C) was established. To this aspect of the media must be added the drive towards publishing in Welsh and especially the founding of the Welsh Books Council in 1961.

In summary, the 1960s and the early 1970s represent a phase of distinct contrasts. All the hard evidence, epitomized by the 1971 census returns, indicated continued, even devastating, decline, fully in keeping with Saunders Lewis's prophecy that the language would virtually be dying by the next century. On the other hand, there occurred the beginning and rapid development of measures to restore the fortunes of the language. None of this took place against an inert

---

[30] Lewis, 'The Welsh Language and the Law' in Stephens (ed.), *The Welsh Language Today*, pp. 199–210; Andrews and Henshaw, *The Welsh Language in the Courts*, pp. 27–8.

[31] The Council for the Welsh Language, *A Future for the Welsh Language* (Cardiff, 1978), p. 49.

[32] Alwyn D. Rees, 'The Welsh Language in Broadcasting' in Stephens (ed.), *The Welsh Language Today*, pp. 174–94.

[33] The Council for the Welsh Language, *A Future for the Welsh Language*, pp. 63–4.

background. Great changes were beginning to occur in the Welsh economy. Agriculture was subject to radical restructuring and rural depopulation continued. Furthermore, industry was about to embark on the process of complete transformation which was to characterize the 1980s. It is to that crucial period and the evidence of the 1981 census that attention must now be directed.

New Challenges and Responses: 1971–81

At first glance the 1981 census gave some hope that a severe period of language decline had been survived. The most obvious element of encouragement was the fact that the total Welsh-speaking population (1971 base) had declined by only 6.34 per cent to a total of 508,207 (Table 10), as compared with the figure of 17.31 per cent for the previous decade. Yet, an examination of the relevant maps points to an exacerbation of the trends which had become established over the preceding decades; in addition, it pinpoints new and threatening tendencies. In 1971 there were 191 communities where over 80 per cent of the population spoke Welsh (Table 9); by 1981 there were only 66 such communities. Even so, Table 10 shows some counties registering gains and emphasizes that the most significant losses occurred in the main industrial counties.

Table 10. The percentage changes in the numbers able to speak Welsh in pre-1974 counties, 1961–71 and 1971–81

County (pre-1974)	Change 1961–71	Change 1971–81
Anglesey	−0.03	5.98
Brecon	−21.18	−10.30
Caernarfon	−8.49	−2.28
Cardigan	−7.10	−1.79
Carmarthen	−14.15	−10.27
Denbigh	−14.45	−6.99
Flint	−10.22	−4.48
Glamorgan	−14.96	−29.79
Merioneth	−10.37	−4.77
Monmouth	−35.85	27.78
Montgomery	−14.80	−3.74
Pembroke	−10.74	−2.98
Radnor	−17.09	58.17
Wales	−17.31	−6.34

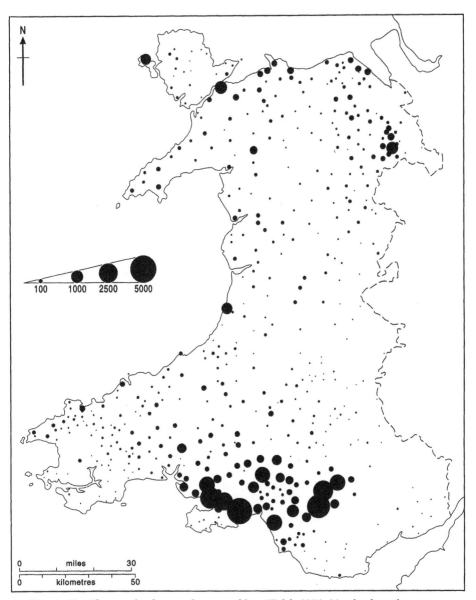

Figure 10. Changes in the numbers speaking Welsh 1971–81: absolute decreases

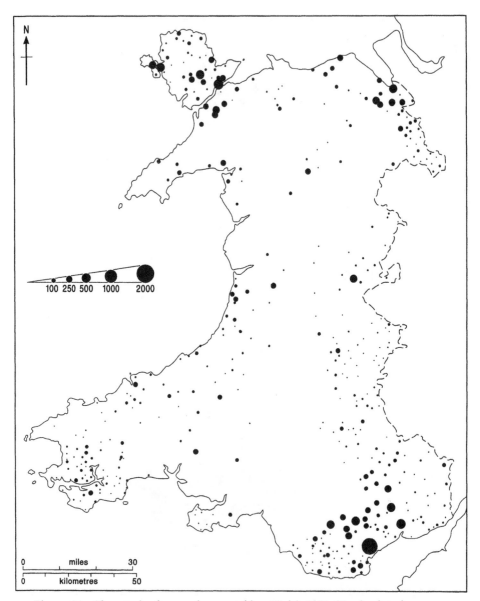

Figure 11. Changes in the numbers speaking Welsh 1971–81: absolute increases

Figure 10, which records absolute decreases in the numbers of Welsh speakers between 1971 and 1981, clearly demonstrates that the industrial heartlands of south and north-east Wales suffered the bulk of the losses, although the actual numbers are smaller than for the preceding decade. Perhaps more disturbing was the apparent swing of losses westward in south Wales, which suggested that numbers had already fallen to such a level in the Glamorgan coalfield that there was simply no possibility of large losses there. Throughout rural Wales the reductions were noticeably smaller. The university towns of Aberystwyth and Bangor showed relatively high losses, 775 and 951 respectively, possibly due to the absence of students from the returns, but also reflecting a decline of urban populations as suburbanization accelerated. Thus, the communities immediately surrounding the towns showed increases. Figure 11 identifies those increases. Apart from the suburbs of towns, the predominant feature is the marked growth in the numbers of Welsh speakers in south-east and north-east Wales. There was also a scattering of small increases along the Marcher lands.

The distribution of the proportion speaking Welsh emphasizes the negative impact of the period. This is most clearly seen if reference is made to the areas where over 80 per cent of the population spoke Welsh. It has been noted that in 1951 those areas constituted a continuous extent which, in spite of reservations, could justifiably be called 'Y Fro Gymraeg'. Such a position was still maintained in 1961. At that date it was still possible to traverse Wales from Llanfair-yng-Nghornwy at the north-western extremity of Anglesey to Cydweli on the Carmarthenshire coast of south Wales without having to leave a community (parish at that time) in which over 80 per cent of the population spoke Welsh. Perhaps, more suprisingly, it would have been possible to do the same from west to east, from the tip of Llŷn to very near the English border at the south-eastern edge of the parish of Llanrhaeadr-ym-Mochnant in the county of Montgomery. By 1971, however, this was no longer feasible because the once continuous 80 per cent core had been broken into a series of separated sub-cores and the defining percentage of a reasonable continuous core had been reduced to 65 per cent Welsh-speaking. In 1981 all that was left of the 80 per cent area was a series of isolated fragments (Figure 12), and even these are exaggerated by the nature of the map which is reproduced. In an equivalent map in the *National Atlas of Wales*,[34] unpopulated areas are left blank (i.e. without shading), so the extensive mountain tracts are uncoloured. The result is to reduce the actual extent of Welsh-speaking areas quite considerably, especially the largest single area of Meirionnydd Nant Conwy. Moreover, to give any semblance of conviction to a continuous Welsh-speaking Wales, the defining criterion would have to be reduced to 60 per cent.

---

[34] John W. Aitchison and Harold Carter, 'The Welsh Language, 1981: Percentage Speaking Welsh' in Harold Carter (ed.), *National Atlas of Wales* (Cardiff, 1989), Map 3.4b.

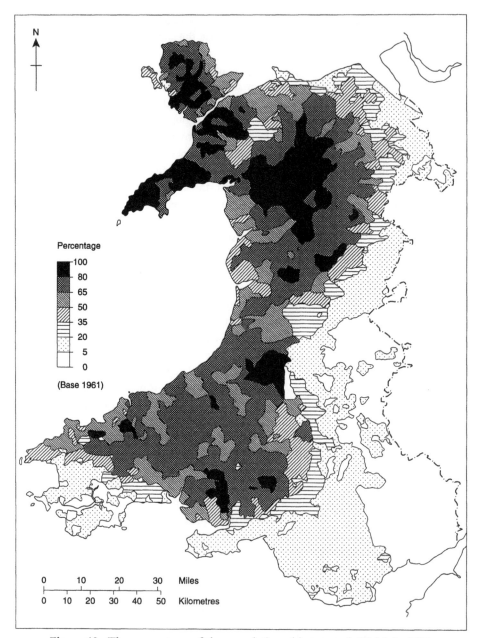

Figure 12. The percentage of the population able to speak Welsh in 1981

Table 11. The number of Welsh speakers: change categories,[1]
1961–71 and 1971–81

Categories	Number of communities	Mean percentage 1961–71	Mean percentage 1971–81
1	143	–15.6	–28.1
2	277	–24.1	–12.6
3	87	58.2	–34.5
4	260	–24.1	40.1
5	80	100.5	24.3
6	82	19.5	55.4

[1] See Figure 15 for the definition of the six categories.

The enlargement of the main lines of decline along the north Wales coast, the Conwy–Porthmadog axis, the Severn valley to the west coast at Aberystwyth, and the separator line between rural and industrial Dyfed, are too obvious to require comment. But there were other complexities which are much more evident, if not new. These were most clearly apparent in Ceredigion. On the one hand, there were manifest areas of decrease, some of them quite disastrous. The wholly Welsh community of Llangeitho with 92 per cent speaking Welsh in 1961 and 83 per cent in 1971 had, by 1981, seen the proportion fall to 54.5 per cent. The key lay in the proportion born in Wales, which in 1981 was only 54.2 per cent. Crucially there had been a considerable migration of non-Welsh speakers into the heartland of Welsh speech. On the other hand, in communities not far removed from Llangeitho there was evidence of an increase in Welsh speakers. At Llanybydder the total of 937 speakers in 1961 had fallen to 920 in 1971, but by 1981 had risen to 1,059. Similarly, numbers at Llangynnwr increased from 845 in 1961 to 1,140 in 1971, and by 1981 had increased to 1,321. Figure 13, which shows change in the decade 1971–81, demonstrates both the areas of decrease and the great complexity which had been introduced by these widely varying trends. It also shows considerable increases in those urban and Marcher areas to which attention has already been drawn.

Figure 14 provides a classification of communities according to patterns of change in the numbers of Welsh speakers for two intercensal periods, while Table 11 lists the associated number of communities, together with the mean rate of change for the decades concerned. Category 1 is made up of those communities in which the number of Welsh speakers declined continuously over the two decades and where the pace of decline actually increased between 1971 and 1981. Although they are scattered throughout Wales, close examination reveals that they approximate to those parts of the country which, throughout the twentieth

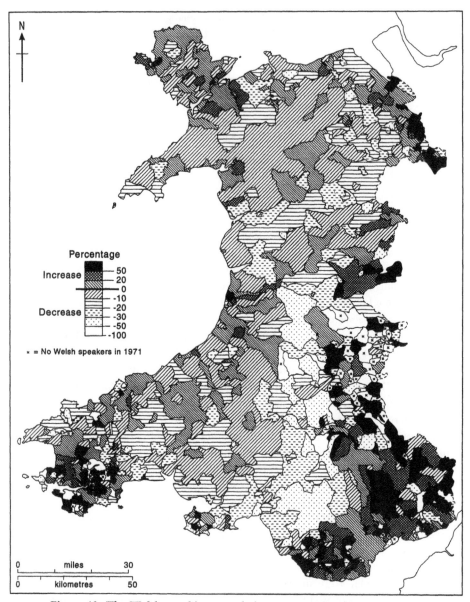

Figure 13. The Welsh-speaking population: percentage change 1971–81

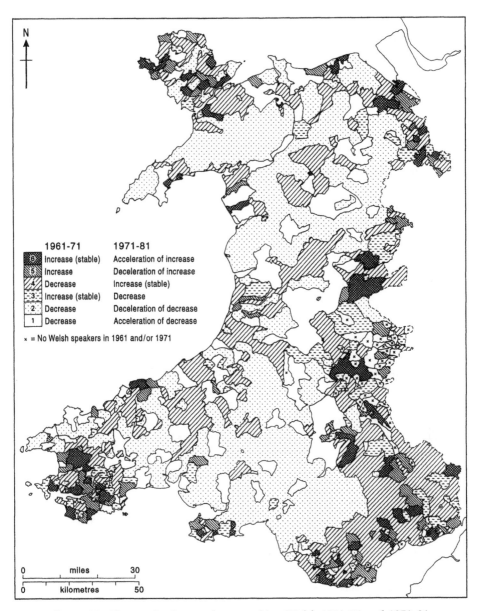

Figure 14. Changes in the numbers speaking Welsh 1961–71 and 1971–81

century, had been most vulnerable. An arc follows the line from Porthmadog to Conwy, and at the Conwy end expands along the north Wales coast. Also in the northern half of the country, a parallel arc can be identified along the line of the retreating language frontier. There is also a suggestion of a similar relation of this category in the Severn–west coast line of decline and again with the eastern language frontier, although in the south it is less coherent. Within the heartland itself the feature of a scattering of areas of significant decline amid areas of increment is also apparent.

Category 2, which shows decreases which became smaller over the decade, contains the greatest number of communities and can be identified as the 'background' category for Welsh Wales, although both in the north and the south it extended eastward. The pattern of slowing decrease provides evidence that the measures and activities which were considered for the previous period were at last beginning to have some impact and that the decline which had so dominated the very heartland of the language was at last being offset.

Category 3 constitutes those communities which experienced an increase in the number of Welsh speakers during the period 1961–71, but where there was a subsequent decrease. There were only 87 such communities, all located in the Welsh border. In view of the small numbers concerned, it is difficult to provide any general explanation for this unusual reversal of trends.

In contrast, Category 4 is a highly significant one, comprising those communities which replaced a loss in the decade 1961–71 with a gain in the period 1971–81. The most consistent grouping appears in the east along the border, especially in south Glamorgan. It confirmed the general pattern of increase which characterized areas once firmly Anglicized. A parallel representation along the western coast reflected the complex of increases and decreases already identified. A similar heterogeneity characterized the north, but one common factor was a feature previously noted, namely the tendency for suburbanization to produce areas of increment around the towns. Category 5 has a distribution which accords with Category 4, and the two can effectively be linked together. Finally, Category 6 includes communities which experienced accelerating increase. Evidence of this increase was also to be found in scatters in the Marcher lands of Wales, testifying to the growth of Welsh speech there. The one clear exception was the island of Anglesey, where there were communities with growing numbers of Welsh speakers alongside others which revealed accelerated decline.

Three fundamental influences have critically conditioned the positive and negative changes which have been outlined. The first, while apparently local in derivation, was nevertheless a reflection of more general European trends. The other two were explicitly of a broader western provenance.

All the local influences coalesce around what was the most crucial of the changes, namely the enhanced social status of the Welsh language (Figure 1a).

Throughout the twentieth century the economic advantages and the social evaluation of the language were both rated so lowly that little effort was made to maintain the language. However, the continuing efforts of pressure groups and the response of government led to a creeping revolution in attitude. It took off from the active movements of the 1960s and gathered strength in the succeeding decades. The response of government, already noted, continued into the 1980s. Formally, the most noteworthy was the creation in 1988 by the Secretary of State for Wales of yet another body with a special commitment to the needs of the language, namely Bwrdd yr Iaith Gymraeg (the Welsh Language Board). Its remit was to advise on language matters in general and to promote the wider use of Welsh in both public and private spheres. The Board outlined a strategy for the period 1989–94 which recognized the need to 'improve the infrastructure for bilingualism' and 'to ensure that both languages and the two linguistic communities can live together and thrive'.[35] Although the Board placed emphasis on bilingualism, it accepted that it was unrealistic to expect everything to be available bilingually throughout the country, including those areas where political and social constraints would have a strong influence. Even so, the concept of 'normalization' was stressed. Normalization is a term widely used in the European arena of lesser-used languages and was construed by the Welsh Language Board to mean that 'it is possible, convenient and normal for everyone, in every situation where a public service is provided, to choose which language he or she wishes to use'.[36] Although this refers to a date somewhat after the period which has been reviewed, it is a clear indication of attitudes which had been formulated during the preceding decade or even earlier.

A wide-ranging summary of these initiatives is available in the report *Language Strategy 1991–2001* published by the National Language Forum,[37] and they are treated in detail in other chapters in this volume. Even so, two aspects need to be briefly discussed because of their overriding significance.

The first is education. Considerable advances were made on this particular front. Mudiad Ysgolion Meithrin continued to expand. Indeed, by 1990 there were 553 nursery groups and 345 'mother and toddler' groups which together catered for some 13,000 children. There was also a steady expansion of Welsh-medium primary schools and secondary education. The impact of this was to be clearly seen in the growth in the proportion of young people speaking Welsh. In 1971, 14.95 per cent of children aged between 3 and 14 spoke Welsh; by 1981 this proportion had increased to 17.75. The second area which demands comment is the media. The establishment of Radio Cymru in 1977 contributed significantly to the promotion of the language, but it was the establishment of S4C in 1982 which was of pivotal importance. To a large extent the growth of

---

[35] The Welsh Language Board, *The Welsh Language: A Strategy for the Future* (Cardiff, 1989), p. 5.
[36] Ibid.
[37] National Language Forum, *Language Strategy 1991–2001* (Caernarfon, 1991).

television created a new problem for the language. The impact of English upon Welsh had in the past been limited to those areas of direct contact. Hence the retreat of the eastern frontier and the clear losses wherever tourism brought non-Welsh speakers into the heartland. But with television, even more so than radio, English speech was brought into the home, one domain where the language had been relatively secure. In a sense, the geographic element was outflanked and Welsh subjected to great pressures regardless of location. It was for this reason that the Welsh television channel was so crucial. Moreover, it was to provide a new and influential source of employment for many young Welsh-speaking people.

It would seem from the discussion above that during this period there was a major change of attitude and action within Wales itself. This was certainly the case, but it is important to stress that these shifts were a local reflection of much wider movements. If universal movements of modern times have been generally threatening to the language, the nature of the post-modern world can be considered very different.[38] Post-modernism can be described as the ultimate in eclecticism, and if that is inadequate as a definition it at least gives some indication of what has characterized recent decades. The western world has been marked by the decline of large-scale certainties, and by a breakdown into ideas and movements which are far more ragged and less dominated by overriding notions. The development of the European Community has, by its questioning of the pre-eminence of the nation state, revivified the claims and rights of 'regions'; the very existence of the European Bureau for Lesser Used Languages is symptomatic of this trend. Moreover, the rise of what has been called the single-issue fanatic, one who devotes total effort to a single issue which is not necessarily related to any standard or coherent philosophy – animal rights, anti-smoking, green matters are examples – is an associated phenomenon. All this has implications for language. The Welsh Language Society, it could be argued, was one of the earliest of the single-issue organizations. As the old universalist philosophies of the right and the left, of both Thatcherite conservatism and pure socialism, declined into variant forms of pragmatism, so the Welsh Language Society was able to exert more influence. Together with other movements, it succeeded in placing the language firmly at the centre of the political agenda in a way it could not have hoped to do when monolithic parties and their philosophies dominated the political scene.

The concomitant attitude to the nation state has been of central relevance. Many contemporary states came into being during the early modern period through the agglomeration of territories, either by conquest or marriage. Currently the constituent parts are asserting their own rights to separate or devolved government and emphasizing their cultural differences and identities. As a result, the confrontation of the great powers has been replaced by regional conflicts. The present is not witnessing 'the end of history', but a different post-

---

[38] See Harold Carter, *Yr Iaith Gymraeg mewn Oes Ôl-Fodern* (Caerdydd, 1992).

modern history. Internal colonization as a concept is now less fashionable, but it is possible to argue that the post-war decolonization of the external pieces of empire is now being followed by internal decolonization, a recognition of the culturally different pieces out of which modern states had been created. If Wales is considered in relation to all these trends then, superficially at least, there would seem to be considerable advantage to the language. A clear continent-wide trend to devolution must be of benefit. No longer are large-scale movements inimical to minority languages: the new values and ideologies favour the 'regions'. It is for these reasons that the success of the language movement in Wales needs to be seen not in isolation, but as part of a complex of transformations in the western world.

The second influence upon the language was the incoming of non-Welsh speakers from England. This was part of the movement widespread throughout the western world and which is usually termed counterurbanization or rural retreating.[39] That the first term is of American origin, and the second the common Australian usage, indicates the international character of the phenomenon. It was a reaction against urbanism as a way of life which was perceived as increasingly materialistic. Moreover, the urban environment was increasingly polluted and characterized by crime and violence. Ironically, suburbanization at an earlier date had been an attempt to escape the problems of the city centre, but now suburbia itself was being engulfed. One solution was to escape to the countryside. The result was an astonishing counter-revolution, with people leaving the metropoles and large cities for a reformed way of life in a country town, a village or the remote countryside. Movements of this sort were made easier by enhanced mobility. With the widespread ownership of the motor car, no location was too remote. In local terms it meant that the way in which Welsh had survived by virtue of simple distance from the forces of Anglicization was no longer operative. With television directly beamed into the home and the countryside open to mobile newcomers, the traditional defences of the language were being breached. It meant that language change was no longer necessarily limited to location where the languages were in propinquity; thus, a potentially devastating new process of change was under way.

The impact upon Wales took place in two stages. The first is sometimes called 'seasonal suburbanization', namely the buying of second or holiday homes by people not resident in an area. The Gwynedd County Council Planning Department produced a series of Census Information Sheets and Research Bulletins on, and following, the 1981 census which revealed that there were several communities in the county with abnormal proportions of second homes. Table 12 sets out the relevant statistics for the communities with the highest percentages of second homes in Gwynedd. Although there is some variation in these percentages, the

---

[39] Anthony G. Champion, *Counterurbanization: The Pace and Nature of Population Decentralization* (London, 1989).

Table 12. The percentage of second homes in 1981, and the percentage of Welsh speakers in selected communities in Gwynedd, 1961–81

Community	Percentage of second homes 1981	Welsh speakers 1961	Welsh speakers 1971	Welsh speakers 1981
Penmachno	37	86.8	84.4	69.5
Beddgelert	30	55.2	51.5	46.7
Llanbedrog	33	59.9	58.3	60.2
Llanengan	34	78.3	74.8	67.0
Llangelynnin	34	58.6	56.0	45.0
Llangywer	30	85.3	90.9	73.8
Tal-y-llyn	30	92.0	80.0	66.0

detrimental effect upon the degree of Welsh speech retention was manifest, for these were communities at the very heart of the traditional language strength.

The second phase was the direct in-migration of population into rural Wales. Figure 15 shows both inward movements in Gwynedd for two periods between 1976 and 1984 by age groups. Such data are obtained from the NHS Family Practitioner Committees. The in-migration figures indicate what is perhaps a surprising dominance of people in their late teens and early twenties, as opposed to the assumed retired group movement – although the expected upward swing between 55 and 65 is apparent. The out-migration, however, shows a complete dominance of young people and young adults. This is the critical aspect of the demographic context, for it shows that there was still a substantial rural depopulation in operation. Whereas for some people rural Wales provided much in the way of isolation from the stresses and disadvantages of the city, on the other hand it provided little for local youth in the provision of attractive employment opportunities.

In the late 1970s, in a study entitled 'Consciousness and Lifestyle: Alternative Developments in the Culture and Economy of Rural Dyfed',[40] Nicholas J. Ford interviewed a hundred migrants into the county. Twenty-three came from London, twenty-six from the area called Roseland (the remainder of south-east England), and only seven from other parts of Wales. He concluded that in nearly all cases people were seeking a new way of life or a further extension of certain aspects of an old one. Many of the householders saw themselves as embarking on something new – a new skill, for instance in gardening, farming, craftwork or art; more abstractly, many were seeking to 're-create' or 'refine' themselves. For those endeavouring to develop a 'more meaningful' lifestyle, the move to rural Wales

---

[40] Nicholas J. Ford, 'Consciousness and Lifestyle: Alternative Developments in the Culture and Economy of Rural Dyfed' (unpubl. University of Wales PhD thesis, 1982).

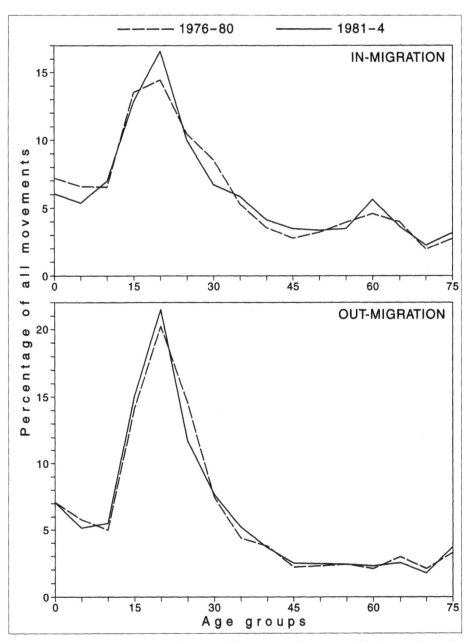

Figure 15. Migration patterns in Gwynedd 1976–84 (after Gwynedd County Council Planning Department)

Table 13. Migration patterns in Dyfed, 1984–8

Year	In-migrants	Out-migrants	Net balance
1984–5	10091	8511	+1580
1985–6	11584	9120	+2464
1986–7	13122	9599	+3523
1987–8	15324	10354	+4970

Table 14. Population characteristics, Dyfed, 1971–87

District	Natural change		Net migration	
	1971–81	1981–7	1971–81	1981–7
Carmarthen	−1300	−900	+2100	+3500
Ceredigion	−2000	−900	+9200	+5100
Dinefwr	−1600	−800	+1700	+1800
Llanelli	−2200	−900	−	−1300
Preseli Pembs	+600	+600	+3500	+1000
South Pembs	+200	+200	+2000	+2500
Dyfed	−6300	−2800	+18500	+12600

involved leaving behind the inessentials and trappings of a consumer society. It was this situation and its impact which led Dyfed County Council Planning Department to produce a special report on migration.[41] The migration patterns in Table 13 show exactly the same pattern as those for Gwynedd, with an out-migration pattern more than balanced by that of in-migration. Table 14 (Pembrokeshire excepted) demonstrates the substantial inward movement of population against a general pattern of natural loss. The impact of these population changes upon the Welsh language were immediate and clear, and they help to explain the patterns of losses which have already been traced in the maps of distribution.

The third element which greatly affected the language and which was also worldwide in its province was the complex process of de-industrialization and the growth of the transactional city. Thus the old smokestack industries which once dominated the Welsh economy have almost disappeared. Where there has been growth, it has occurred in new 'high-tech' electronic industries in new locations and in occupations based on the handling and processing of information. A

---

[41] Dyfed County Council Planning Department, *Migration in Dyfed* (Technical Paper No. 3, Carmarthen, 1989).

significant part of this is the service industries which underpin a substantial bureaucracy. Blackaby and others write in a recent survey of the Welsh economy:

> As for the distribution of total employment within Wales, the largest employing sector is the service sector, where roughly seven out of every ten employees are employed. Of its constituent industries it is Education, Health and Other Services and Wholesale, Distribution, Hotels, Catering and Repairs which make up the main-stay of employment . . . Meanwhile, manufacturing employment accounts for approximately one quarter of all employees, with electrical engineering and electronic manufacture being an important component of this. The overall picture, though, is one of a service-sector based economy . . . traditional heavy industry playing a small role in industrial employment.[42]

Although the date advances the discussion into the 1990s (to be discussed below), the numbers employed in agriculture in Wales fell by 5.26 per cent between 1992 and 1995, and by a massive 27.27 per cent in energy and water supply. In contrast, in banking and finance it rose by 19.72 per cent.[43] The areas which benefited most in Wales were those along the M4, the continuation of the English M4 corridor, and those in proximity to the reconstructed A55 in north-east Wales.

The impact of these changes on the language was twofold. The collapse of coal mining and heavy industry was in part responsible for the large falls in the number of Welsh speakers in the valleys of south Wales. The decline in agricultural employment underlined the outflow of Welsh speakers from the rural heartland. But the growth of financial and other services in the south-east and the north-east created a new middle class closely related to two great growth areas in occupations, the administrative bureaucracy and the media, especially the Welsh-language media. In many of these jobs the ability to speak Welsh, if not essential, was a great advantage. In response to the demand by language activists for normal-ization, employment opportunities for those with a command of the language were considerably enhanced. The result was a highly visible increase in the number and proportions of Welsh speakers in the transactional centres of Wales, above all in Cardiff. The increases which have been identified were no more than a reflection of major developments in economy and society throughout the western world. Elsewhere in Europe intellectual groups were active in the pro-motion of regional identity. The intellectual, often a product of the University of Wales, had replaced the industrialist as a prime mover in national development. For confirmation, it is revealing to examine the percentages speaking Welsh in some of the former county towns (Table 15).

At first sight these figures do not appear to lend support to the argument advanced above. But in each case, with the notable exception of Swansea, the

---

[42] D. Blackaby, P. Murphy, N. O'Leary and E. Thomas, 'Wales: An Economic Survey', *CW*, 8 (1995), 236.
[43] Ibid., 237 (Table 11.12).

**Table 15. The percentage of the population able to speak Welsh in the
county towns of Wales, 1961–81**

Town	1961	1971	1981
Caernarfon	87.9	86.5	86.5
Cardiff	5.0	4.9	5.7
Carmarthen	57.2	51.8	50.0
Llandrindod	8.6	6.8	8.9
Newport	2.2	1.7	2.3
Mold	18.9	16.7	18.4
Swansea	17.5	12.9	10.4
Llandrindod Rural	4.1	4.1	8.9

proportion of Welsh speakers had either been maintained or had increased, in
defiance of the general trend. Moreover, many of the increases occurred in the
suburban and commuter belts of these places. One example only has been
included in Table 15, that of Llandrindod Rural. Traditionally a highly Anglicized
district, the percentages highlight the emergence of a Welsh-speaking bourgeoisie
which was slowly taking control of the levers of power.

Having considered linguistic change in the broadest sense, it is now appropriate
to illustrate the intricacy of the changes which were taking place through three
case examples. The emerging significance of a newly empowered Welsh-speaking
middle class during the latter part of the 1970s manifested itself most clearly in the
capital city of Cardiff and its region.[44] The data presented below have been
derived from the Small Area Statistics of the 1981 census. The basic areal unit is
the enumeration district (ED) of which there were 575 in the area (excluding 20
institutional EDs), but reference is also made to the 25 wards of the city (Figure
16).

Figure 17 charts the proportion of the population (3 years and over) able to
speak Welsh in EDs of the city at the 1981 census. The resultant pattern is largely
sectoral in structure, with three dominant zones of above average percentages,
generally in excess of 9 per cent, extending out from the city centre, and
ultimately coalescing in the suburban and rural periphery. The first and the most
evident of these sectors or wedges runs westward through Llandaff to Radyr and
St Fagans (for locations, see Figure 16). The two other sectors worthy of note are
more fragmented in form and have a common focus in the south-east of the city
at Roath. From there one band of EDs reaches north-westwards to Llanishen and
Rhiwbeina, while the other strikes due north through Pen-y-lan – the ward
containing the greatest number of Welsh speakers (2,244) to Lisvane. The sectors

---

[44] J. W. Aitchison and Harold Carter, 'The Welsh Language in Cardiff: A Quiet Revolution',
TIBG, 12, no. 4 (1987), 482–92.

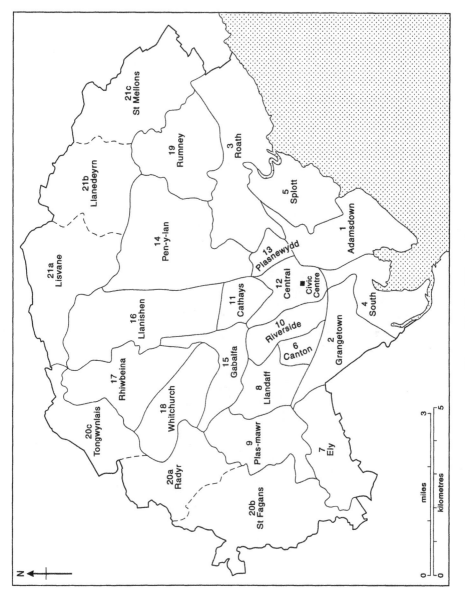

Figure 16. Cardiff: wards

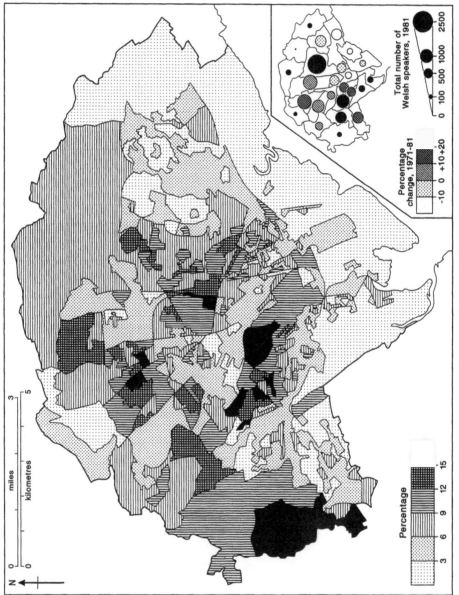

Figure 17. The percentage of the population able to speak Welsh in Cardiff in 1981

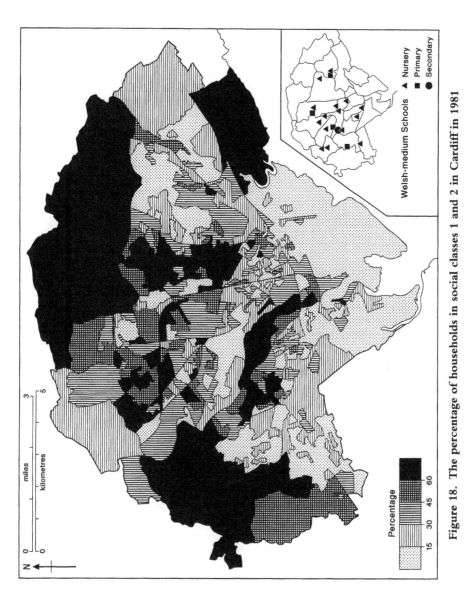

Figure 18. The percentage of households in social classes 1 and 2 in Cardiff in 1981

merge into a peripheral zone of relatively high proportions, but with sharp breaks in the old industrial region of Tongwynlais in the north-west, at Ely in the south-west, and at St Mellons to the east of the city.

Because of boundary changes it is not possible to calculate rates of change in numbers of Welsh speakers over the decade 1971–81 at the ED level, but from the ward level data in Figure 17 (inset) it is evident that increases were generally greatest in the sectors identified above. In eight wards, all in these sectors, growth rates between 1971 and 1981 actually exceeded 25 per cent. In the light of the analysis in the last section, it is appropriate to relate this pattern to social class and age structure within the city.

In Figure 18 the EDs of Cardiff are classified according to the proportion of households in social classes 1 and 2 defined in the census. Included in these are households whose heads are engaged in professional and what are termed 'intermediate' forms of employment. It must be emphasized that the data are derived from a 10 per cent sample and include all households, not simply Welsh-speaking households, since it is impossible to disaggregate the 1981 data according to language spoken. Whatever the difficulties, however, the two distributions – Figures 17 and 18 – reveal a high degree of concordance. The sectoral and peripheral areas identified above are again apparent, as are the breaks in the outer ring at Ely, Tongwynlais and St Mellons. Within the sectors many EDs have over half of their households in social classes 1 and 2. Percentages of less than 15 characterize those areas with very low proportions of Welsh speakers, such as Grangetown, South, Splott and parts of Ely. A seeming anomaly is Roath, but it is a large ED which takes in a small dairy-farming community on the Wentloog Levels. Despite the inadequacies of the data, these patterns would suggest that the linkage between Welsh-speaking areas and areas of high social class is strongly evident. This situation is truly a revolutionary departure from previous patterns.

However, in order to underline the fact that such social contexts can vary spatially, it is instructive to compare this case study with another carried out in north Wales by Glyn Williams.[45] Table 16 is selected from his work. Williams refers to the much-debated 'internal colonialism' hypothesis of Hechter[46] whereby a cultural division of labour emerges, with the incoming colonists occupying positions of influence and of power. Williams maintains that:

> the argument focusing on the cultural division of labour can be substantiated by looking, for example, at an area such as the county of Gwynedd where there have been profound developments of branch plant and new manufacturing industries. The most obvious feature of such development is that . . . most of the higher-level managerial or

[45] Glyn Williams, 'Recent Trends in the Sociology of Wales' in I. Hume and W. T. R. Pryce (eds.), *The Welsh and their Country* (Llandysul, 1986), pp. 176–92.

[46] Michael Hechter, *Internal Colonialism: The Celtic Fringe in British National Development, 1536–1966* (London, 1975).

Table 16. Over- and under-representation[1] of Welsh speakers and the population born outside Wales in socio-economic groups, Gwynedd, 1981

Socio-economic groups	Welsh speakers	Extent of over/under representation	Population born outside Wales
Employer/managers large establishments	–	10.8	+
Employers/managers small establishments	–	21.6	+
Professional workers: self-employed	–	12.6	+
Professional workers: employers	–	29.2	+
Skilled manual	+	9.3	–
Semi-skilled	+	4.7	–
Unskilled	+	12.2	–

[1] The negative sign indicates under-representation and the positive sign over-representation of the relevant statistics.

professional posts will be held by in-migrants. On the other hand, the proletarian labour will be local. There are, therefore, two different labour markets for different class locations.[47]

Williams was able to demonstrate the linguistic implications of this process through the use of unpublished census data for the region (Table 16). These indicate that there is 'a heavy over-representation of non-Welsh born and an under-representation of Welsh-speakers at the top four official socio-economic groups used in the census tabulations'.[48] Williams was prepared, however, to recognize the distinct advance in the status of the language as a consequence of its significance to a new bourgeoisie.

The conclusions presented by Williams were reinforced by a study carried out by Delyth Morris in Ynys Môn in 1987.[49] She writes: 'Following the intervention of the state in the local economy, branches of manufacturing firms started to come into the area, bringing with them their managerial staff whilst employing their labour locally (usually part-time, low-waged, and often female labour).'[50] She refers to the major capital works on the island and notes that the contracts for construction were awarded to outside firms which brought both a skilled and labouring force with them. Moreover, the tourist industry was being developed largely by English-speaking incomers, while most of the derived profits leaked out

[47] Williams, 'Recent Trends in the Sociology of Wales', p. 187.
[48] Ibid.
[49] Delyth Morris, 'A Study of Language Contact and Social Networks in Ynys Môn', *CW*, 3 (1989), 99–117.
[50] Ibid., 115.

of the area. The situation was aggravated by the purchase of holiday homes and by an influx of people retiring: 'It was apparent that a split economy was developing in Ynys Môn: a relatively prosperous enclave, together with an associated marginalised sector.' It follows from the earlier review of employment that, whereas the prosperous enclave was closely related to the non-Welsh-speaking incomers, marginalization was associated with the Welsh.[51] Morris's study is one of social networks where the close linkages of the Welsh are in contrast to the less coherent relationships of the incomers. From this a general Welsh resentment of the in-migrant English was derived which cut across class barriers. There was widespread support for the ability to speak Welsh to be made a requirement for professional and managerial level jobs under Gwynedd County Council even from among those who did not possess the qualifications to compete for them. Thus, although the situation seems directly opposite to that identified in Cardiff, the kind of reaction which created the Cardiff condition is apparent.

It would seem from the analysis of the distribution maps of the 1981 census and the consideration of the more detailed studies that a series of contradictory tendencies were in operation during the 1970s and the early 1980s. The first of these relates to the class location of the language. It has been shown that fundamental changes in the nature of the Welsh economy had generated a social transformation and had brought to the fore an educated, articulate Welsh-speaking middle class which exercised considerable influence, especially within the media. New support and a new status had been brought to the language. On the other hand, if the work of Williams and Morris is accepted, in the world of business and industry the old cultural division of labour still existed and the dichotomy of an English-speaking managerial sector and a Welsh labour force still appertained. The corollary of this situation was that, whatever the evidence was for a cultural division of labour, the language had achieved enhanced status. No longer was it widely regarded as having low esteem: attitudes had changed to support rather than antipathy. The establishment of the European Bureau for Lesser Used Languages undoubtedly played a part in this development. Welsh was seen not as an isolated case but rather as one of a large range of languages seeking equal recognition and standing. Even so, there was still a well-publicized counter-movement among some intellectuals, mainly but not wholly non-Welsh speaking, who saw the language as subject to inevitable decay and as a hindrance to economic, and in some cases, political progress.

The second of these contradictory characteristics relates to the rural areas of 'Y Fro Gymraeg'. It was paradoxical that the forces most inimical to the language had developed in the heartland of Welsh speech. Here, the long-established rural depopulation continued and, given the very nature of job opportunity, it seemed evident that it would continue. On the other hand, counterurbanization had

<hr>

[51] Ibid., 116.

generated a steady stream of non-Welsh-speaking in-migrants. It is true that not all these newcomers rejected the Welsh language. Many saw its acquisition as part of their changed lifestyle and encouraged their children to learn it. Even so, a conflict situation had arisen which focused on the language. The third anomaly is the longest standing. This is the argument first developed in full by Brinley Thomas.[52] He maintained that the growing towns and industrial villages had retained in nineteenth-century Wales a Welsh-speaking population which would otherwise have had to migrate overseas. Unlike the case in Ireland, the language did not decline into one spoken by a few in an isolated western Gaeltacht:

> During the course of the twentieth century Welsh children could not have stayed on the farm; they would have had to emigrate to England and overseas, as the Irish did. The likelihood is that the Welsh nation would be an aged society surviving in a small rural bunker, a *casa geriatrica*, instead of a large youthful urban society which can afford cultural institutions to express and strengthen the national identity.[53]

At the same time, however, the mixing of population which was the inevitable concomitant of urban growth led to eventual decline. This has remained an anomaly. In terms of numbers Welsh is an urban language, yet its traditions are essentially of the rural heartland. The greatest threat in regional terms lies in the continuing decline in the western parts of what was west Glamorgan and east Dyfed. Again, it is paradoxical that many of the movements most supportive of the language in recent times have come from the industrial areas; Mudiad Ysgolion Meithrin is an example. Fourthly, and as a consequence of educational change, the final anomaly is that in the nineteenth century and the first part of the twentieth century children spoke Welsh at home and English in school; nowadays, at least in some cases, they speak Welsh in school and English at home.

All the above conditions had a significant impact upon language, and continue to do so. This is evident from an analysis of data generated by the 1991 census.

The 1991 Census

The 1991 census recorded a total Welsh-speaking population of 508,098, 18.6 per cent of the total resident population (aged 3 and over). Table 17 shows the distribution of Welsh speakers at county level. The counties of Dyfed and Gwynedd remained the main strongholds of the language, accounting for over half of all Welsh speakers (283,411 or 55.7 per cent). At the other extreme were

---

[52] Brinley Thomas, 'A Cauldron of Rebirth: Population and the Welsh Language in the Nineteenth Century' in Jenkins (ed.), *The Welsh Language and its Social Domains 1801–1911*, pp. 81–99.
[53] Ibid., p. 97.

Table 17. Total resident population, total Welsh-speaking population and the percentage of the population able to speak Welsh 1991

County	Resident population (3 years and over)	Population able to speak Welsh	Percentage able to speak Welsh
Clwyd	392812	71405	18.2
Dyfed	331528	144998	43.7
Gwent	423794	10339	2.4
Gwynedd	226862	138413	61.0
Mid Glamorgan	511656	43263	8.4
Powys	113335	22871	20.2
South Glamorgan	375857	24541	6.5
West Glamorgan	347779	52268	15.0
Wales	2723623	508098	18.6

the counties of Gwent, Powys and South Glamorgan, where resident Welsh-speaking populations were in each case less than 25,000. This regional pattern of absolute figures is repeated in the proportions able to speak the language: in Gwynedd and Dyfed the percentages were 61 and 43.7 respectively, while in Gwent and South Glamorgan they were 2.4 and 6.5 respectively. In spite of its lower absolute numbers, Powys returned 20.2 per cent, while Mid Glamorgan, with 43,263 speakers, reached only 8.4 per cent.

Figure 19 depicts the absolute distribution of Welsh speakers in 1991 on a ward basis. It confirms the dominance of two areas. The first, and the prime concentration, covers the urban and industrial parts of what can still be called the western coalfield of south Wales. Wards such as Tumble (2,770), Morriston (2,755), Gors-las (2,602), Gwauncaegurwen (2,204), Ystalyfera (2,110) and Pontardawe (2,093) all returned over 2,000 Welsh speakers. Manifestly the size of the ward influenced the numbers, but there was a marked falling off within and to the east of the Vale of Neath. None of the wards in the Vale of Neath recorded more than a thousand Welsh speakers, and only two – Glynneath with 893 and Seven Sisters (Blaendulais) with 621 – returned over 500, marking the retreat of the language within the coalfield. To the east of the Vale of Neath, a dense swarm of wards returned relatively small numbers. In Mid Glamorgan only Aberdare West (1,098) and Treorci (1,048) recorded over 1,000. A much stronger cluster existed in the neighbourhood of Cardiff. All this was in line with the trends already noted.

The second main zone of concentration lay along the north coast from Prestatyn to Caernarfon, with a somewhat slighter extension along the Dee estuary to Wrexham and Ruabon. Two coagulations lay within the zone. The first was along the Menai Straits formed by the suburban wards of Caernarfon and

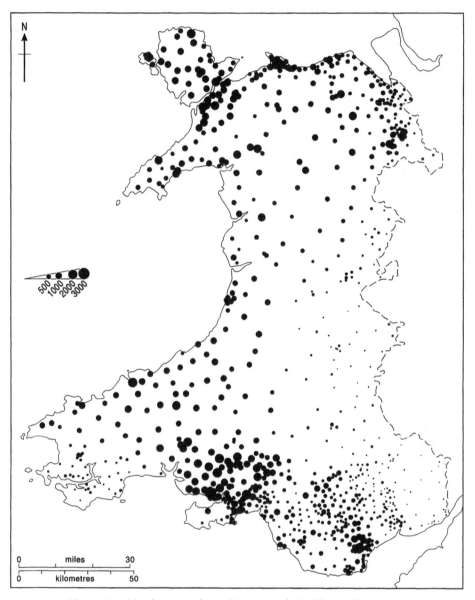

Figure 19. Absolute numbers able to speak Welsh in 1991

Bangor, while the second was associated with the Creuddyn peninsula and the towns of Conwy and Llandudno. In addition to these two major groupings, other concentrations emerged along the west coast in the towns of Holyhead, Pwllheli, Porthmadog, Blaenau Ffestiniog, Dolgellau, Aberystwyth and Cardigan, a line which could be extended to Fishguard and Carmarthen. Elsewhere, the market towns stood out: Llandeilo in the Tywi valley, Denbigh and Ruthin in the Vale of Clwyd, Llanrwst in the Conwy valley, Bala in Penllyn and possibly Newtown in the Severn valley. There were clearly appreciable numbers of Welsh speakers in the rural heartlands of Gwynedd and Dyfed, but they were widely dispersed in distribution. Indeed, the establishment of larger wards in the rural areas exaggerated the concentration in these parts. Thus a major feature of the language, which has already been noted, was emphasized by these figures: Welsh was now predominantly an urban language.

At this point it is necessary to turn to consider the distribution of the proportions or percentages speaking Welsh in 1991. At the expense of some repetition, it is worth setting out the process by which the core area of Welsh speech in the north and west had been successively reduced during the twentieth century. For the various censuses, the following briefly summarizes the changing situation:

1901   A clear and dominant core could be identified where over 90 per cent of the population spoke Welsh. There were indications of some parts within the core where decrease was perceptible.

1931   The situation was in general as it had been at the beginning of the century, but the qualifying proportion for a continuous core was reduced to 80 per cent.

1951   The core area could still be identified with some confidence, but the qualifying proportion was nearer 75 per cent. Internal fracture lines had by this date become apparent.

1961   In order to propose a core area the qualifying proportion was reduced to 65 per cent, a level at which daily use in all domains would be unlikely. Four fracture lines had become apparent:
- the Menai Straits
- the Conwy–Porthmadog line extending across the heart of Snowdonia
- the Severn–Dyfi break across mid-Wales
- the break between rural and industrial Dyfed, roughly following the Tywi river

1971   The fracture lines had become very clear and the retention of a 65 per

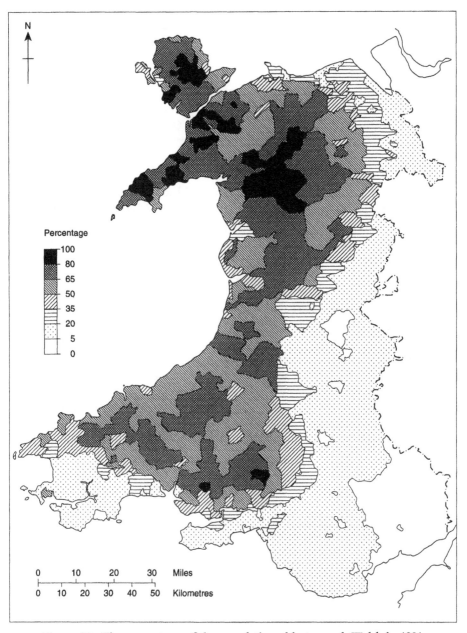

Figure 20. The percentage of the population able to speak Welsh in 1991

cent qualifying figure meant that a continuous core could not be maintained and a series of separated sub-cores had to be identified, namely:

- Ynys Môn
- Llŷn and Arfon
- Meirionnydd Nant Conwy
- rural Dyfed, north of the *Landsker* and west of the Tywi river
- industrial eastern Dyfed and West Glamorgan, west of the Vale of Neath

1981   The process which had been evident since the end of the First World War had continued apace and the heartland had been substantially reduced in terms of its defining proportions speaking Welsh. The figure now was nearer 60 per cent, and the parts where over 80 per cent spoke the language had been reduced to a series of isolated fragments, mainly in Dwyfor and Meirionnydd. No areas of this character remained in rural Dyfed.

The distribution for 1991 (Figure 20) shows a further development of the same tendencies.[54] To identify a continuous core area in the west and north it is necessary to lower the defining percentage to 50. The parts where over 80 per cent speak the language have been further diminished. They can no longer be legitimately referred to as sub-cores, for they are merely remnant fragments. To identify the strongholds of Welsh, one no longer seeks wards where more than 80 per cent speak Welsh, but rather those where proportions exceed 65 per cent. It is also pertinent that the largest continuous area with over 65 per cent speaking Welsh was Meirionnydd Nant Conwy, where a great part of the terrain was unpopulated mountain and high plateau, so that the reality is a great deal less than the appearance on the map.

Changes in the population base for the 1991 census and modifications to community boundaries make it impossible to record detailed shifts in numbers and percentages of Welsh speakers. Reference, however, can be made to statistics for the constituent counties. Table 18 reveals that the overall decline in the number of speakers was but 1.4 per cent, compared with the 6.3 per cent for the previous decade. Changes in the counties varied greatly, however, but conformed to the trends which have been identified already. South Glamorgan showed a high increase of 14 per cent, in line with the socio-economic processes which characterized that part of the country. In contrast, West Glamorgan returned a massive loss of 11.2 per cent, again identifying it as one of the key areas for the

---

[54] See John Aitchison and Harold Carter, 'The Welsh Language in 1991 – A Broken Heartland and a New Beginning?', *Planet*, 97 (1993), 3–10; idem, 'The Language Patterns of Wales' in Merfyn Griffiths (ed.), *The Welsh Language in Education* (Cardiff, 1997), pp. 21–5.

Table 18. Numbers of Welsh speakers and percentage change, 1981–91 (1981 base)

County	1981	1991	Percentage change
Clwyd	69578	69945	0.5
Dyfed	146213	142209	−2.7
Gwent	10550	9936	−5.8
Gwynedd	135067	135366	0.2
Mid Glamorgan	42691	42150	−1.3
Powys	21358	22355	4.7
South Glamorgan	20684	23393	14.0
West Glamorgan	57408	50976	−11.2
Wales	503549	496530	−1.4

Table 19. The percentage of the population able to speak Welsh according to age, 1921–91

Age group	1921	1931	1951	1961	1971	1981	1991
3–4	26.7	22.1	14.5	13.1	11.3	13.3	16.1
5–9	29.4	26.6	20.1	16.8	14.5	17.8	24.7
10–14	32.2	30.4	22.2	19.5	17.0	18.5	26.9
15–24	34.5	33.4	22.8	20.8	15.9	14.9	17.1
25–44	36.9	37.4	27.4	23.2	18.3	15.5	14.5
45–64	44.9	44.1	35.4	32.6	24.8	20.7	17.3
65+	51.9	49.9	40.7	37.2	31.0	27.4	22.6

Table 20. The percentage of the population aged 3–15 able to speak Welsh and percentage change, 1981–91 (1981 base)

County	Percentage of speakers 1981	Percentage of speakers 1991	Number of speakers 1981	Number of speakers 1991	Percentage change 1981–91
Clwyd	18.6	27.9	13796	18617	31.7
Dyfed	40.3	47.7	23163	25811	11.4
Gwent	2.3	4.8	1921	3490	81.1
Gwynedd	69.3	77.6	28785	27889	−3.1
Mid Glamorgan	8.6	16.1	8906	14604	64.0
Powys	16.7	30.0	3284	5436	66.4
South Glamorgan	7.4	11.9	5152	7690	49.3
West Glamorgan	9.3	15.0	6064	8719	43.8

**Table 21. Numbers and percentage of Welsh speakers aged
under 15 and over 65, 1991**

County	Under 15		Over 65	
	Number	Percentage	Number	Percentage
Clwyd	18335	25.7	15187	21.3
Dyfed	26086	18.0	33820	23.3
Gwent	3558	34.4	1456	14.1
Gwynedd	28256	20.4	25974	18.7
Mid Glamorgan	14786	34.2	9801	22.7
Powys	5517	24.1	5100	22.3
South Glamorgan	7888	32.1	3028	12.3
West Glamorgan	8810	16.9	16527	31.6

future of the language. Elsewhere, the impact of in-migration appeared in the decline of 2.7 per cent recorded for the county of Dyfed.

Of crucial significance to an interpretation of these and future trends are the age profiles of Welsh speakers. Three tabulations serve to highlight the main features. Table 19 shows the age structure of the Welsh-speaking population for the whole of Wales from 1921 to 1991; Table 20 shows the changes in the numbers and percentage of Welsh speakers between 3 and 15 between 1981 and 1991; and Table 21 records the age profiles of Welsh speakers at the 1991 census.

Table 19 demonstrates the significant changes which had occurred in the age structure of the Welsh-speaking population. Whereas until 1971 every decade had revealed a progressive decrease in the proportion speaking Welsh in every age group, after that date the situation changed dramatically. All the youngest age groups showed an increase in the proportion speaking Welsh, and by 1991 the increase had advanced to the 15–24 group. All the older age groups showed the expected continuing decline. These data serve as indicators of a substantial language shift as the teaching of Welsh in the schools of Wales began to bear fruit. Moreover, contrary to some suggestions, the extension of increase to the 15–24 cohort would appear to indicate that the speaking of the language was being sustained after school-leaving age.

Table 20 reveals that the proportion of those aged 3–15 speaking Welsh increased in every county, although in Gwynedd the actual *numbers* fell. Although based on rather small numbers, the increases in some counties were spectacular. Of the eight counties, three recorded increases of over 60 per cent, and two of over 40 per cent between 1981 and 1991.

Table 21 depicts the age profiles of Welsh speakers on a county basis, contrasting the proportions of those under 15 with those over 65. The patterns which have already been identified were reaffirmed. Gwent and South Glamorgan revealed the expected contrast between the high percentages in the

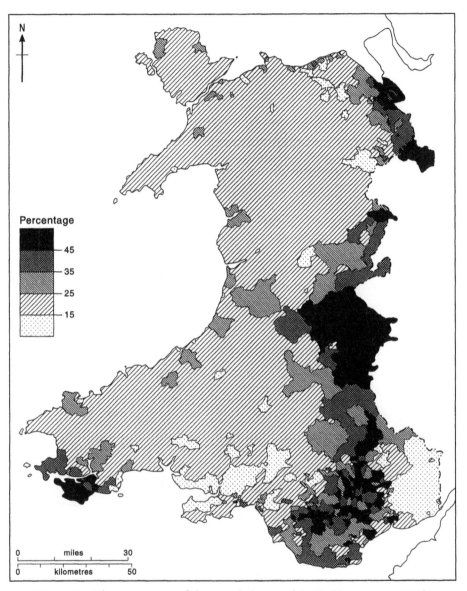

Figure 21. The percentage of the population aged 3–15 able to speak Welsh in 1991

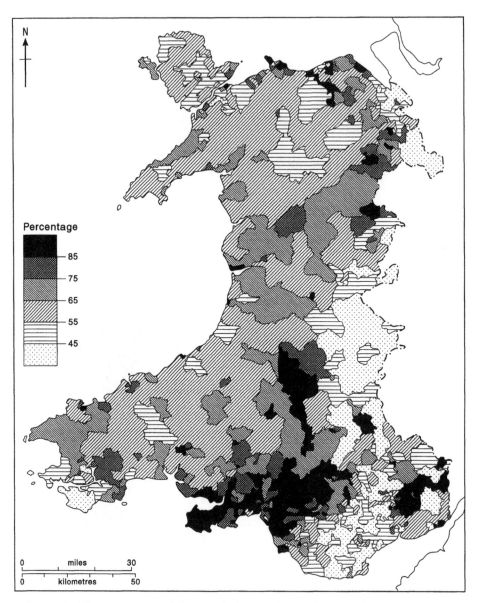

Figure 22. The percentage of the population aged 65 and over able to speak Welsh in 1991

younger group and the lower percentages in the over 65s. But the problem area of West Glamorgan also stood out, neatly reversing the situation in the other two counties.

The indications from these data are that there has been a marked revival of Welsh among the young and that future censuses will reveal a rise in the number of Welsh speakers by the beginning of the twenty-first century.[55] However, such predictions need to be treated with some circumspection. It could be argued that a language primarily learnt and spoken in school will soon be forgotten in the world of work, and that there is certainly a tendency for parents answering census forms on behalf of their children to exaggerate fluency.

Figures 21 and 22 map the distribution of Welsh speakers in 1991 by age on a ward basis. Figure 21, which shows the distribution of those over 3 but under 15, is dominated by an extensive zone where young Welsh speakers account for between 15 and 25 per cent of the Welsh-speaking population. In the main this zone occupies the western and northern Welsh-speaking areas of rural Wales. It is surrounded by an irregular but clearly demarcated fringe where the proportions are higher. Although the absolute numbers are small, these are the areas where a significant impact had been made by Welsh-language teaching initiatives. The percentage frequently exceeded 35 per cent and in many wards over 45 per cent of young people claimed to speak Welsh. In contrast, the map of the over 65s speaking Welsh (Figure 22) is much more fragmented. It is noteworthy that the greatest concentration was to be found in West Glamorgan and the western parts of Mid Glamorgan, including the Ogmore and Garw valleys. A very sharp and telling gradient divided this region from areas in South Glamorgan where young Welsh speakers dominated. Again, given the crudity of the categories, much of rural Wales shows a uniform pattern.

The 1991 census presented a much greater range of detail relating to language skills than any previous census. A total of 546,551 persons were returned as able to speak or read or write Welsh, a significantly higher total than speakers alone. Presumably, if the question as to ability to understand Welsh had been added the total would have been even greater. Figure 23 charts by ward the proportion of Welsh speakers who were also able to read and write the language. This presented an interesting distribution since it encapsulated many of the features which have already been identified. The western and northern heartland is clearly discernible, but the sub cores which were suggested can also be seen as having high proportions of literate Welsh speakers. The major contrast lay in the western part of the former coalfield. A wedge of low literacy runs north-eastward from Gower and along the Vale of Neath. It corresponds with the wedge of elderly speakers which can be seen in Figure 22. Here again, the tenuous nature of the language in

---

[55] John Aitchison and Harold Carter, 'Rural Wales and the Welsh Language', *Rural History*, 2, no. 1 (1991), 61–79.

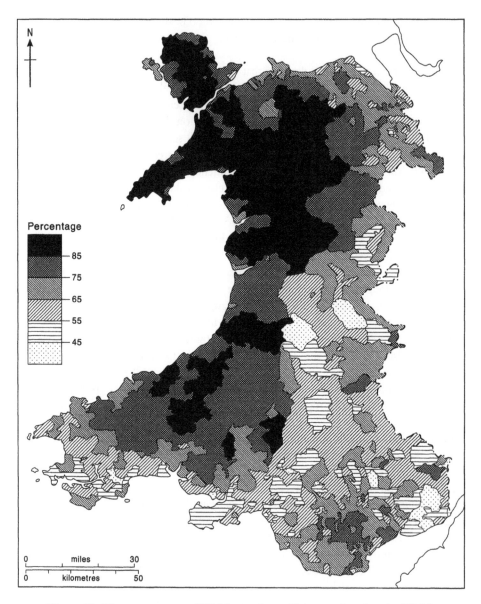

Figure 23. The percentage of Welsh speakers able to read and write Welsh in 1991

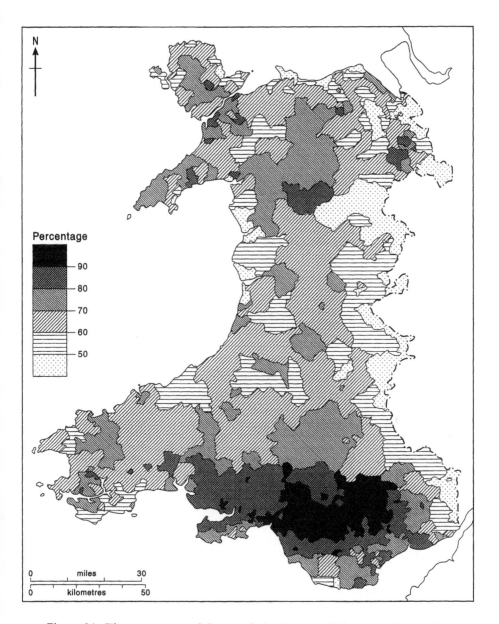

Figure 24. The percentage of the population born in Wales according to the 1991 census

this crucial area is demonstrated, for if loss of literacy is regarded as a phase of decline, then here is further evidence of the threat to the language in an area where numbers are highest. It will also be recalled (Table 18) that West Glamorgan stood out as the county with the largest decrease in speakers in the period 1981–91. In contrast, the areas with a preponderance of young speakers and the areas which showed the greatest increase between 1981 and 1991 also returned high percentages of literacy, not of the order of the heartland, but considerably in excess of the immediate fringes of that core. To a degree, therefore, the distribution of literacy is a summary of the variety of influences which have affected the language in the recent past.

Finally, there is one further piece of evidence which is relevant to the understanding of the pattern of Welsh speakers. The census provides data regarding the birthplace of the population. In 1991, of the total resident population in Wales, some 77 per cent had been born in Wales. Figure 24 shows the distribution, on a ward basis, of those born in Wales. One area dominates the map, namely the old industrial and coal-mining region of south Wales. There, percentages generally exceed 80, with a large cluster of wards actually returning over 90 per cent. Elsewhere, there is only a random scattering of wards with such high values and over most of rural Wales values tend to range between 60 and 70 per cent. The borderlands with England show an expected low percentage, but so also do those parts strongly affected by in-migration. The coast of north Wales stands out, as does the west coast and especially the interior parts of Ceredigion. It is part of the series of paradoxes which have already been sketched that many of those areas which are regarded as quintessentially Welsh show the higher proportion of those born in England. It is also of interest that of the total population able to speak Welsh (508,098), nearly 10 per cent (48,919) were born outside Wales. It is impossible to identify who these were; whether, for example, they were brought up in Welsh-speaking families and came to Wales speaking Welsh, or whether they were incomers who had learned Welsh. It does suggest, however, the degree to which in-migrants have committed themselves to learning the language.

The published data for the 1991 census for the first time included a tabulation of in-migrants and their language abilities. Its value is somewhat limited since it was based on change of address in the year before the census, so that the bulk of the movement recorded is within-county change of address. Even so, the evidence of continued in-migration to rural Welsh-speaking Wales is clear. Dyfed recorded 29,833 movements, but of these 19,682 were relocations within the county. Of the remaining 10,151, some 6,486 were from outside Wales. However, of that number 732 or 11.3 per cent spoke Welsh. Assuming it is unlikely that many learnt Welsh within the year, this would suggest that there was some element of return movement. Even so, the figure of 11.3 per cent is well below the figure for Dyfed (43.1 per cent). Thus, the overall influence was one of Anglicization, a trend noted in the preceding decade. Gwynedd saw 5,060 inward movements during the year,

Table 22. Occupation profiles of Welsh speakers, 1991

Occupation	Percentage of Welsh speakers	Relation to total percentage[1]
Corporate managers and administrators	12.99	−
Managers/proprietors in agricultural services	25.30	+
Science and engineering professionals	11.16	−
Health professionals	19.24	o
Teaching professionals	33.28	+
Other professionals	20.36	o
Science and engineering associate professionals	14.28	−
Health associate professionals	21.66	+
Other associate professionals	18.70	o
Clerical occupations	15.72	o
Secretarial occupations	14.29	−
Skilled construction trades	18.60	o
Skilled engineering trades	13.05	−
Other skilled trades	14.40	−
Protective services	15.35	o
Personal services	17.27	o
Buyers, brokers and sales representatives	13.88	−
Other sales occupations	13.84	−
Industrial plant and machine operators/assemblers	11.49	−
Drivers and mobile machinery operators	16.70	o
Other occupations in agriculture/forestry/fishing	41.86	+
Other elementary occupations	14.22	−
Unemployed	11.61	−
Students (economically inactive)	23.94	+
Permanently sick, retired and other inactive	18.60	o

[1]   In the column 'Relation to total percentage', the relation of the percentage of each group to that for the national percentage speaking Welsh (17.49) is shown. Where the deviation is more than 3 per cent above the national figure, the symbol + is inserted; where it is more than 3 per cent below the national figure, the symbol − is inserted. Where the proportion is within a 3 per cent range of the national figure, the symbol o is inserted. The data are based on a 10 per cent sample.

with 16.6 per cent able to speak Welsh compared with the county figure of 58.8 per cent. It is also noteworthy that South Glamorgan recorded 3,475 in-migrants from the rest of Wales, of whom 557 or 16 per cent spoke Welsh, in that case considerably in excess of the county proportion of 6.5 per cent. Unfortunately, these are flawed data which are only published on a county basis. Nevertheless, they confirm the general conclusions which have been presented earlier regarding migration processes and their impact on language.

Unlike earlier censuses, that of 1991 provided a much greater range of data not only in relation to population movements but also in relation to such key variables as occupation, social class and family structure. The statistical information presented in Table 22 appears to support many of the general statements already made concerning the relationship between language and occupation. Thus, in business management there is a clear under-representation of Welsh speakers, which confirms the notion of a cultural division of labour. But it is also note-worthy that Welsh speakers are also under-represented in both the 'elementary occupations' and 'unemployed' categories, which suggests the opposite. More clearly there is a substantial under-representation among science and engineering professionals and associate professionals in those occupations, indicating the limited commitment to the Welsh language in such areas, and perhaps the cultural division of labour in industry. Over-representation is most apparent in the agricultural and associated areas, reflecting the rural base of the language in spite of its predominant urban location. The other notable area is education, in which both teaching professionals and students are heavily in excess of the general proportion.

The somewhat limited conclusions which can be derived from the published data can be extended by resource to sample sets of data made available by the Office of Population Censuses and Surveys and which are described as Samples of Anonymized Records or SARs.[56] The sample is 2 per cent for individuals and one per cent for families, so that the files contain information on 11,152 Welsh speakers and 44,574 non-Welsh speakers. The main advantage of these data is that cross-tabulations with other variables can be derived from them. The notion of class, as opposed to occupational groups, is difficult to define, but Table 23 uses the standard six class category of OPCS.[57] At first sight it would seem that these data are at odds with those in Table 22, but the anomaly presumably depends on the high proportion of agricultural employers who are Welsh-speaking and are placed in the managerial class. Taken at face value, however, the figures imply that there is now no social disadvantage implicit in speaking Welsh.

The question as to whether incomers have gained control of the most prominent class locations can be examined further in Table 24. Here a division has been made based on place of birth, so that non-Welsh speakers born in Wales (Anglo-Welsh) can be set alongside non-Welsh speakers born outside Wales. From the table it is evident that, as a group, non-Welsh-speaking in-migrants have a much stronger representation among the higher social classes than both Welsh speakers and indigenous non-Welsh speakers. The statistics could clearly be used to support the notion of the cultural division of labour. Yet, the data also

---

[56] The SARs have been made available for academic use by ESRC/JISC/DENI and CMU. They are Crown Copyright.

[57] See also John Aitchison and Harold Carter, 'Language and Social Class in Wales', *Planet*, 105 (1994), 11–16.

Table 23. The percentage of Welsh speakers and non–Welsh speakers employed in each social class, 1991

Social class	Percentage employed	
	Welsh speakers	Non–Welsh speakers
Professional	3.5	3.4
Managerial/professional	31.6	23.9
Skilled: non–manual	21.2	22.0
Skilled: manual	20.1	23.1
Part–skilled	16.9	19.4
Unskilled	6.7	8.1

Table 24. Social class by ethno–linguistic groups, 1991

Social class	Percentage employed in ethno–linguistic groups		
	Welsh speakers	Anglo–Welsh	Non–Welsh-speaking in-migrants
Professional	3.5	2.2	6.2
Managerial/technical	31.6	20.1	32.6
Skilled: non–manual	21.2	22.1	21.7
Part–skilled	16.9	21.1	15.7
Unskilled	6.7	9.3	5.5

show that the most disadvantaged section of Welsh society was not so much the Welsh-speaking community, as is frequently argued, but the Anglo-Welsh. The Anglo-Welsh were doubly disadvantaged. On the one hand, they were unable to compete for high level positions where an ability to speak Welsh was a necessity or an advantage; on the other, they were obliged to face strong competition both from incomers and indigenous Welsh speakers. These data go some way to explaining the anomalies derived from the analysis of the 1981 census figures. The apparent success of both Welsh speakers *and* non-Welsh-speaking incomers had been obtained at the expense of the Welsh-born non-Welsh speakers who constituted the disadvantaged.[58]

Further insight into the situation can be gained by considering the regional variation within the above data. In Table 25 the group proportions have been recorded in each of three categories of social class where the 'upper' category includes professional and managerial/technical employees; the 'middle' category refers to skilled manual and non-manual workers, while the 'lower' category includes the part-skilled and unskilled. In four counties – Gwent, South Glamorgan, Mid Glamorgan and Clwyd – there was a stronger relative

---

[58] John Giggs and Charles Pattie, 'Wales as a Plural Society', *CW*, 5 (1992), 25–63.

Table 25. Social class and ethno-linguistic groups by county, 1991

| County | Percentage employed in ethno-linguistic group | | | | | | | | |
| | Upper | | | Middle | | | Lower | | |
	A	AW	NW	W	AW	NW	A	AW	NW
Clwyd	35	20	34	43	48	43	21	32	23
Dyfed	34	25	41	41	45	37	25	30	22
Gwent	54	22	41	34	46	41	12	33	18
Gwynedd	29	22	41	42	50	38	29	28	22
Mid Glamorgan	40	20	35	41	48	42	19	32	24
Powys	38	33	39	36	41	38	26	26	23
South Glamorgan	53	27	44	37	50	38	10	24	18
West Glamorgan	36	20	39	42	48	38	23	32	23

W = Welsh speakers; AW = Anglo-Welsh; NW = non-Welsh-speaking in-migrants

representation of upper class locations within the Welsh-speaking population than in each of the two other categories. This would appear to underline the importance of the growth in job opportunities for bilinguals in the more economically dynamic regions of Wales. As has been noted, it is ironic that the language was now gaining ground in these long Anglicized areas – a development clearly related to the expansion of employment in national, local and other public services. The associated establishment of Welsh-medium educational facilities in borderland and urban environments which was noted earlier was a further manifestation of the prevailing social trends.

In contrast, Table 25 also demonstrates that in the main heartland regions of the Welsh language, non-Welsh-speaking incomers retained the highest representation in upper class locations. In Dyfed, Gwynedd and West Glamorgan nearly 40 per cent of the group were in professional or managerial positions. Equivalent figures for Welsh-speaking sectors of the population ranged from 29 per cent in Gwynedd to 34 per cent in Dyfed. This reinforces the conclusions of Williams and Morris considered earlier. It is in these fragile rural areas and the declining industrial county of West Glamorgan, more than anywhere else, that Hechter's concept of the cultural division of labour applies. Finally, it can be noted that it was the Anglo-Welsh who had the lowest proportions in the upper class category, ranging from 20 to 25 per cent.

Further census tabulations provide evidence of language in relation to household composition. Table 26 is derived from Table 5 of the published report on the Welsh language for the 1991 census.[59] It provides data on the language by

[59] 1991 Census / Cyfrifiad 1991, *Welsh Language* / *Cymraeg: Wales* / *Cymru* (London, 1994), pp. 70–1 (Table 5).

Table 26. Household composition and language spoken, 1991

Total households	1111689	
		Percentage
Households with no dependent children	762898	
No adults speak Welsh	589278	77.24
Some adults speak Welsh	56786	7.44
All adults speak Welsh	116834	15.31
Households with dependent children		
No adults speak Welsh		
Children under the age of 3	38201	
No children speak Welsh	208544	86.62
Some children speak Welsh	8663	3.60
All children speak Welsh	23549	9.78
Households with dependent children		
Some adults speak Welsh		
Children under the age of 3	4469	
No children speak Welsh	13002	42.43
Some children speak Welsh	2483	8.10
All children speak Welsh	15139	49.41
Households with dependent children		
All adults speak Welsh		
Children under the age of 3	4114	
No children speak Welsh	2215	7.23
Some children speak Welsh	899	2.94
All children speak Welsh	27513	89.83

household and the data confirm conclusions which were drawn earlier.[60] Welsh was spoken by at least one individual in some 21.9 per cent of households. However, totally Welsh households, where all adults and dependent children (aged 3 and over) spoke Welsh, accounted for only 13.5 per cent of the total. In contrast, of the households where no adults spoke Welsh, 3.6 per cent returned some children as able to speak the language and there were 9.78 per cent where all the children spoke Welsh. In households where some adults spoke Welsh the proportions increased to 8.1 and 49.4 per cent respectively; where all adults spoke Welsh, the percentages were 2.94 and 89.83. It was impressive that non-Welsh-

---

[60] See also John Aitchison and Harold Carter, 'Household Structures and the Welsh Language', *Planet*, 113 (1995), 25–32; idem, 'Language Reproduction: Reflections on the Welsh Example', *Area*, 29, no. 4 (1997), 357–66.

Table 27. Language attributes and household types, 1991

Household types	Percentage households within each type
Type 1. All households	100
(i) Households without Welsh speakers	73.6
(ii) Households with Welsh speakers	26.4
Type 2. Households with Welsh speakers	100
(i) Households wholly Welsh-speaking	53.6
(ii) Households partly Welsh-speaking	46.4
Type 3. Household composition and Welsh speech	100
a. Households wholly Welsh-speaking	53.6
(i) With children	10.9
(ii) Without children	42.7
b. Households partly Welsh-speaking	46.4
(i) With Welsh-speaking children	18.9
(ii) With non-Welsh-speaking children	5.8
(iii) With no children	21.7
Type 4. Household size, composition and Welsh speech	100
a. Households wholly Welsh-speaking	53.6
(i) With children	10.9
(ii) Single person households: Welsh-speaking	21.3
(iii) Without children: more than one Welsh speaker	21.5
b. Households partly Welsh-speaking	46.4
(i) Households with Welsh-speaking children: single speaker	6.2
(ii) Households with Welsh-speaking children: more than one Welsh speaker	12.7
c. Households partly Welsh-speaking but without Welsh-speaking children	
(i) Single Welsh speaker	4.9
(ii) More than one Welsh speaker	0.9
d. Households partly Welsh-speaking but without children	
(i) Single Welsh speaker	18.6
(ii) More than one Welsh speaker	3.1

speaking households should have returned such high figures, and this was clearly a reflection of the success of Welsh-medium teaching, but there was an element of concern in the fact that in 7.23 per cent of households where all the adults spoke Welsh, the children could not speak the language.

If the households in West Glamorgan where all adults spoke Welsh are examined, those where none of the children spoke Welsh accounted for 17.9 per cent of the total, those where some children spoke the language accounted for a further 3.3 per cent, but no more than 78.7 per cent were homes where all the children were Welsh-speaking. These can be simplified as ratios of 18:3:79 and compare with the national ratio of 7:3:90. Clearly the language was not being transmitted down the generations. The equivalent ratio for South Glamorgan was 12:4:84 and indicated the contrasting attitudes to the language between new areas of revival and those in the older industrial areas. The ratio for the county of Gwynedd was 2:2:96, which indicated that, in spite of in-migration, the transmission of the language remained secure in the heartland.

It is also possible to use the 1991 SARs to examine the relationship between family structure and language more closely, and a classification is presented in Table 27. The first division into households with at least one Welsh speaker, referred to henceforth as 'Welsh-speaking' households, and those without any Welsh speaker break in the ratio of 26.4 to 73.6 per cent. This compares with the 24.8 to 75.2 per cent of the total data in the census volume. But further analysis of the SARs data shows that over half the Welsh-speaking households (51 per cent) had just one Welsh speaker within them. This significantly high ratio implied that members were able to communicate through the medium of Welsh in fewer than half the Welsh-speaking households. The linguistic influence of the home, which had always been one of the crucial domains for the Welsh language, was apparently strongly circumscribed. It must be added that households with but a single Welsh speaker accounted for 28 per cent of the Welsh-speaking population, and of these nearly 37 per cent were over 65 years of age.

It is possible now to move on to examine Welsh-speaking households on the basis of whether they are wholly or partly Welsh-speaking (Table 27: Types 2i and 2ii). The data indicated that only 14 per cent of households in Wales were wholly Welsh-speaking and that a further 12 per cent were linguistically mixed. Of the households with only one Welsh speaker, 42 per cent were single-occupation households. The group of households which were wholly Welsh-speaking can be further subdivided into those with and without children (aged 3–17) (Table 27: Types 3ai and 3aii). The picture which emerged here was also disconcerting for the language, for only 3 per cent of all households in Wales were entirely Welsh-speaking and had children. Moreover, the vast majority of wholly Welsh-speaking households, some 89 per cent, were without children. A similar pattern was displayed by the households which were partly Welsh-speaking. Of these, nearly two thirds (64 per cent) had only a single Welsh speaker, the majority of whom dwelt in households which had no children. It is also worth adding that a high proportion of Welsh-speaking households (30 per cent) had heads who were able to speak Welsh but where there were no recorded spouses or cohabitees. This high ratio serves to confirm that there existed a strong preponderance of single-person, and mainly elderly, households among the Welsh-speaking population.

One dominant conclusion emerges from this analysis. An extremely high proportion of Welsh speakers were linguistically isolated within their home environments. Some 28 per cent of speakers either lived alone or were the only member of the household who spoke Welsh. Significantly, 70 per cent of the Welsh-speaking households had no Welsh-speaking children within them, and the role of the home as the critical domain wherein Welsh was preserved was in severe jeopardy. However, this was essentially the end-product of a long period of decline and represented the past, perhaps, rather than the future. The high proportions of Welsh speakers among the young may indicate that the condition reported here might well change considerably in forthcoming decades if the age cohorts retain the language as they move up the age groups and ensure that their children are Welsh speakers.

Conclusion

This chapter has sought to trace the principal changes which characterized the geography of the Welsh language following the 1921 census. Inevitably, the progressive diminution in the area of preponderant Welsh speech has been emphasized. By 1991 two elements stood out. Either a low percentage of speakers, as low as 50 per cent, must be adopted to justify and identify a continuous area of Welsh speech in the north and west, or it must be accepted that fragmentation has already occurred and that only vestigial remnants of a once continuous Welsh Wales can be found. The clear division between Inner and Outer Wales is no longer apparent as a result of the in-migration of non-Welsh speakers into rural Wales and the language revival led by the middle-class bourgeoisie of the towns and cities.

At the heart of these changes are a number of paradoxes. The anomalies relating to the older cultural division of labour, the new social clout of the Welsh bourgeoisie, the impact of counterurbanization in rural Wales, the urban nature of the language, and the role of education in language revival, have all created a new Wales. Part of that transformation has been the evident diminution of the two great domains in which Welsh survived during centuries of neglect and oppression, namely the chapel and the home. Secularization has long undermined the significance of the chapel, and especially the Sunday school, and a materialistic and laodicean society has abandoned its former values. These changes are difficult to demonstrate, but analyses of the several referenda on the Sunday opening of licensed premises in Wales have shown how the westward advance of such a cultural icon can be closely correlated with the westward shift of the language frontier.[61] If

---

[61] Harold Carter and J. G. Thomas, 'The Referendum on the Sunday Opening of Licensed Premises in Wales as a Criterion of a Culture Region', *Regional Studies*, 3, no. 1 (1969), 61–71; Harold Carter, 'Y Fro Gymraeg and the 1975 Referendum on Sunday Closing of Public Houses in Wales', *Cambria*, 3, no. 2 (1976), 89–101.

nothing more, it symbolizes the declining influence of Nonconformist chapel culture. Likewise, in considering family structures, it has been demonstrated how tenuous the domain of home and hearth has become. This, of course, is partly a consequence of age structure, but it is also a reflection of new patterns of living and new lifestyles. The tightly-knit nuclear family wherein the language was nurtured and cherished is no longer predominant.

All these characteristics of late twentieth-century society might imply a hastening language decline. In fact, the opposite has occurred. For if the old domains have been attenuated, some key ones have been successfully reclaimed. In this context nothing is more important than education. Thus, if the Sunday school has lost its role as the keeper of the language, then the 'ysgol feithrin' and the Welsh-medium primary school have come to replace it; the same is true of adult language-learning, for the Sunday school was by no means limited to children. Education at all levels has developed to provide a vigorous basis for language transmission not only for indigenous families but also for children of monoglot English newcomers who choose to learn and speak Welsh.

This introduces the concept of status. There is little doubt that there has been a revolution in the status of the language within Wales. Whereas at the beginning of the period under review there was no social cachet in the ability to speak Welsh, that ability now seems to carry social and economic advantages. Much more importantly, it is perceived to do so. This, too, is partly related to the reclaiming of lost domains and is epitomized by the Welsh Language Act 1993. The Act established 'a body corporate to be known as Bwrdd yr Iaith Gymraeg or the Welsh Language Board' with 'the function of promoting and facilitating the use of the Welsh language'. The Act declared that every public body which 'provides services to the public in Wales, or exercises statutory functions in relation to the provision by other public bodies of services to the public in Wales, shall prepare a scheme specifying the measures which it proposes to take . . . as to the use of the Welsh language'.[62] It ensured the right to use Welsh in the law courts, as long as due notice was given, and dictated that all official forms and circulars should be issued in Welsh. Here is evidence of the reclaiming of language domains which were lost when Wales was assimilated into England.

The crucial point is that there have been radical changes in the nature of western society from which Wales has not been isolated. Secularization, materialism, the break-up of the nuclear family as the standard social unit, have all had an impact and cannot be reversed. The Welsh language faces a different and challenging future. If the monoglot, isolated rural Wales of the past has disappeared, never to be restored, the future of a bilingual Wales remains to be achieved.

---

[62] *Welsh Language Act 1993* (c. 38) (London, 1993), pp. 2–3.

2

The Welsh Language and the Geographical Imagination 1918–1950

PYRS GRUFFUDD

Introduction

SEVERAL RECENT studies[1] have suggested that the nation can no longer be considered a material reality; it is, rather, a form of discourse in which imaginative processes inevitably assume a central role. Benedict Anderson argues that the nation is an 'imagined community', whose members bond through cultural and psychological, as much as explicitly political, networks.[2] Forms of communication such as 'national' languages or 'national' media therefore assume greater significance. Similarly, the ideological programme of nationalism has both material and cultural aspects – aimed at capturing structures of power as well as the mindset of the citizenry. Thus the concept of 'national *identity*' has assumed almost as much significance in academic debates as the more material aspects of nationhood. There is a geographical significance to these processes of imagination and reconstruction because, according to Colin Williams and Anthony D. Smith, 'Whatever else it may be, nationalism is always a struggle for control of land; whatever else the nation may be, it is nothing if not a mode of constructing and interpreting social space.'[3]

Notions of geography, territory and national space are crucial in understanding the development of nationalist politics. Nevertheless, as a number of geographers have pointed out, territory is frequently reified, particularly in studies of the original state nationalisms where the imposition of cultural homogeneity on a newly unified space casts attention on bureaucratic processes.[4] Studies of the national construction of social space must examine the relationship between politics, territory and identity because, as James Anderson has argued, nations are

---

[1] See, for instance, Homi K. Bhabha (ed.), *Nation and Narration* (London, 1990); Andrew Parker, Mary Russo, Doris Sommer and Patricia Yaeger (eds.), *Nationalisms and Sexualities* (London, 1992); Raphael Samuel (ed.), *Patriotism: The Making and Unmaking of British National Identity* (3 vols., London, 1989); Geoffrey Cubitt (ed.), *Imagining Nations* (Manchester, 1998).

[2] Benedict Anderson, *Imagined Communities* (London, 1991).

[3] Colin Williams and Anthony D. Smith, 'The National Construction of Social Space', *Progress in Human Geography*, 7, no. 4 (1983), 502.

[4] See, for instance, R. J. Johnston, David B. Knight and Eleonore Kofman (eds.), *Nationalism, Self-determination and Political Geography* (London, 1988).

not simply located in geographical space, 'rather they explicitly claim particular territories and derive distinctiveness from them. Indeed nationalists typically over-emphasise the particular uniqueness of their own territory and history'.[5] In understanding the role of territory in nationalism, therefore, we must be sensitive to geographical, historical and cultural context. Williams and Smith identify eight major dimensions of national territory which figure in nationalist ideologies.[6] Notions of 'habitat' and 'folk culture', for instance, embody the romantic nationalism which opposes urban corruption with rural purity, and the concept of 'homeland' shifts the understanding of territory from a material to a symbolic role: 'History has nationalized a strip of land, and endowed its most ordinary features with mythical content and hallowed sentiments.'[7] The interplay between land and language is a crucial aspect of this mythologizing and nationalizing. There is now a growing appreciation of the symbolic attributes of land and landscape, and their role in the construction and mobilization of national identity. The invention of national traditions often draws heavily on geographical imagery and myth, and Anthony D. Smith notes how 'legends and landscapes' or, equally, 'maps and moralities' furnish people with a geographical understanding of their nation.[8] In the field of cultural geography, landscape imagery has long been viewed as an integral component of national identity, with visual or textual images of landscape read as a series of iconographic discourses embedded in broader cultural and political debates.[9] Particular landscapes have emblematic roles in the articulation of national identity and debates about their preservation can thus assume wider symbolic significance. In this way apparently 'neutral' state processes like physical planning become highly charged and politically contentious.

This chapter examines the negotiation of a particular version of Welsh national identity through land and landscape. It assesses how a territorially-rooted sense of national identity was created in academic circles, and especially in geography, and how that was mirrored in nationalist political discourse and action in Wales in the first half of the twentieth century. This identity was fundamentally geographical in that it located Welshness within a particular rural environment and a version of a rural 'moral economy'. It also exhibited a profound territorial sense in its defence of 'national space', an issue examined here in the context of military land

---

[5] James Anderson, 'Nationalist Ideology and Territory' in ibid., p. 18.

[6] Williams and Smith, 'The National Construction of Social Space', 502–18.

[7] Ibid., 509.

[8] Anthony D. Smith, *The Ethnic Origins of Nations* (Oxford, 1986); idem, *National Identity* (Harmondsworth, 1991). See also Eric Hobsbawm and Terence Ranger (eds.), *The Invention of Tradition* (Cambridge, 1983).

[9] See *Landscape Research*, 16 (1991), theme issue on 'Landscape and National Identity'; Denis Cosgrove and Stephen Daniels (eds.), *The Iconography of Landscape* (Cambridge, 1988); Stephen Daniels, *Fields of Vision: Landscape Imagery and National Identity in England and the United States* (Cambridge, 1993).

requisitioning in Wales. And, finally, the nationalist understanding of territory led to an ideology of nation-building incorporating both symbolic and material acts. Central to any understanding of these processes, however, is the question of the Welsh language and its political significance. The language occupied a central role in the nationalist geographical imagination – as a symbol of cultural continuity, as a marker for monitoring the incursions of Anglicization, as that which must be defended against those incursions, and as that which must be mobilized for nation-building. Ultimately, language emerged as the vital core of the nationalist geographical imagination.

Defining the Nation

Lacking full political recognition since the Acts of Union, Wales is, in many senses, an 'imagined nation' and the cultural imagination has always played a role in Welsh political discourses.[10] Prys Morgan's study of the creation of 'an invented Wales, a Wales of the imagination' in the eighteenth century suggests that historiography and the cultural imagination were essential ingredients of a radical political agenda.[11] What is pertinent here is the role of geography in this imagination and its relationship to other markers of identity such as language. Gwyn A. Williams suggests that there are two intersecting discourses of Welshness – the rural *gwerin* and the industrial working class – each with its own geographical imagination.[12] The former will be examined here. From the Romantic period onwards, Welsh patriots viewed the rural areas and the *gwerin* as the bastions of national strength and morality. Welsh-speaking, devout and in some kind of sustainable relationship with their land, they were the very epitome of that broader European romantic nationalization of the *völk*. Although debates have centred on the extent to which the rural identity can be considered to be the more 'authentically Welsh', it is clear that speculations on the national character and environment run through the history of Welsh national identity, and that the rural element has played a significant role.[13]

The concept of the *gwerin*, arguably, survived undisturbed until the inter-war period when a whole series of cultural and economic changes – most of them bringing profoundly geographical effects in their wake – altered the imaginary processes surrounding rural Wales. This reading of a threatened rural Wales was

---

[10] See Tony Curtis (ed.), *Wales: The Imagined Nation. Essays in Cultural and National Identity* (Bridgend, 1986).

[11] Prys Morgan, 'Keeping the Legends Alive' in ibid., p. 29.

[12] Gwyn A. Williams, *When was Wales? A History of the Welsh* (London, 1985), pp. 237–40.

[13] For instance, Kenneth O. Morgan claims that the 'cradle of the Welsh national revival' was 'not in the agrarian hinterland, so beloved of many apostles of "peasant culture", but amid the blast furnaces and winding-shafts of the working-class metropolis of Merthyr Tydfil'. Kenneth O. Morgan, 'Welsh Nationalism: The Historical Background', *Journal of Contemporary History*, 6, no. 1 (1971), 156.

influenced by academic studies in the inter-war period and their location of a version of Welsh identity in the remote countryside of the Celtic west. For H. J. Fleure, Professor of Geography and Anthropology at the University College of Wales, Aberystwyth from 1917, rural Wales was a spiritual resource, 'a refuge of old ways and old types', as revealed by anthropological and archaeological evidence.[14] Although Fleure believed that physical type was the major factor – he had trained as a zoologist and was concerned with the evolutionary relationship between organism and environment – the Welsh language was also crucial. His research examined local variations in dialect as a reflection of difference in physical type, and folk tales as records of historical changes like culture contacts.[15] Perhaps more significant, however, was the role of the language as a symbol of cultural continuity and of the imagined geography of rural Wales:

> The hill countries of Europe keep alive inheritances from the remote past, though in most cases the languages of the plains have spread up the valleys and have ousted ancient forms of speech save for a few words used in the farmyard or the kitchen. There are, however, a few old tongues surviving here and there, Basque on the Franco-Spanish frontier in the west, Romansch, Ladin and Frioul in the Eastern Alps. In none of the cases just mentioned does the ancient language gather around it powerful emotional associations affecting large numbers of people, but this is the case in Wales. We may say that in many ways Wales is the refuge and repository of ancient heritages England once possessed, but we must also say that associations gathering in comparatively recent times around the Celtic language, still widely spoken and possessing a growing literature, have helped to keep up and even in some ways to accentuate distinctions that are rooted in a long and involved history.[16]

According to Fleure, geography was the key to this cultural vitality. The westerly position and the upland terrain of Wales, with its rivers running east to west from the barrier of the Cambrian mountains, had prevented the nation from developing a centre of political expression, a capital city, but it had promoted cultural continuity and the survival of the Welsh language. In Fleure's words:

> the Celtic fringe is in a sense the ultimate refuge in the far west, wherein persist, among valleys that look towards the sunset, old thoughts and visions that else had been lost to the world . . . The physical features of the country, the framework of mountain-moorland that separates the Wye and Severn region from the valleys that radiate out to

---

[14] H. J. Fleure, 'Problems of Welsh Archaeology', *AC*, LXXVIII (1923), 233. On Fleure and his fieldwork, see Pyrs Gruffudd, 'Back to the Land: Historiography, Rurality and the Nation in Inter-war Wales', *TIBG*, 19, no.1 (1994), 61–77.

[15] See, for instance, H. J. Fleure and T. C. James, 'Geographical Distribution of Anthropological Types in Wales', *Journal of the Royal Anthropological Institute*, XLVI (1916), 35–153; H. J. Fleure, 'The Place of Folklore in a Regional Survey', *Folklore*, XLII, no. 1 (1931), 51–4.

[16] Idem, 'Wales' in Alan G. Ogilvie (ed.), *Great Britain: Essays in Regional Geography* (Cambridge, 1928), p. 230.

sea, have broken the force of many waves of change ere they have reached the quiet western cwms.[17]

This theorization of rural Wales, and of the persistence of the language as a marker of continuity, was mirrored elsewhere. In *The Personality of Britain* (1932), the archaeologist Cyril Fox divided Britain into a lowland zone in flux and a highland zone of continuity.[18] The 'Celtic language' was one of his indicators of a resilient western culture, along with the persistence of old racial stocks and the importance of tribal custom and the clan.[19] More influential was the work of Iorwerth C. Peate, one of Fleure's first students. He pursued doctoral research on the links between physical type and Welsh language dialect in the Dyfi basin, uncovering both heartlands of continuity and an advancing frontier of Englishness (a theme which is considered below).[20] His later work on the craft industries and the organic communities supporting them argued that the language was central to any understanding of rural social continuity: 'Tradition and language in Wales are as weft and warp; without either the final pattern of our society is ruined.'[21] For Peate, too, Wales – especially the west – was a refuge from the waves of new cultures that had washed over the east. It was a storehouse of cultural continuity and linguistic resilience. The key to that continuity was the very geography of Wales and its capacity to resist cultural change: 'We see in the language, as we see in other aspects of Welsh society, the same reliance on geography. We certainly cannot separate language from locality' ('Fe welir yn yr iaith megis ag a welir mewn agweddau eraill o'r gymdeithas Gymreig yr un ymddibyniaeth ar ddaearyddiaeth. Ni ellir yn sicr wahanu iaith oddi wrth ei bro').[22]

Mapping Culture

However, these imagined geographies of rural Wales were becoming unstable during the inter-war period. The Celtic west was threatened and, according to Fleure, the cultural barrier provided by the geography of Wales was 'likely to count for less and less in these days of powerful charabancs, listening-in, and universal education'.[23] Tourism, broadcasting, and the school curriculum were all

---

[17] H. J. Fleure, *Wales and her People* (Wrexham, 1926), p. 1.

[18] Cyril Fox, *The Personality of Britain: Its Influence on Inhabitant and Invader in Prehistoric and Early Historic Times* (Cardiff, 1932).

[19] Ibid., p. 32.

[20] Iorwerth C. Peate, 'The Dyfi Basin: A Study in Physical Anthropology and Dialect Distribution', *Journal of the Royal Anthropological Institute*, LV (1925), 58–72.

[21] Idem, 'The Crafts and a National Language' in Edgar L. Chappell (ed.), *Welsh Housing and Development Year Book 1933* (Cardiff, 1933), p. 77; see also idem, 'The Social Organization of Rural Industries' in Chappell (ed.), *Welsh Housing and Development Year Book 1928* (Cardiff, 1928), pp. 103–5.

[22] Iorwerth C. Peate, *Cymru a'i Phobl* (Caerdydd, 1931), p. 84.

[23] Fleure, *Wales and her People*, p. 2.

making rural Wales more accessible and, in the process, transforming its moral geography. Peate, too, was profoundly aware of the manifold ways in which Anglicized culture was transcending the old geographical barriers:

> Daeth cerbyd modur a bws yn gyffredin i ddwyn gwlad a thref yn nes nag erioed; esgorodd hynny ar ffyrdd newyddion a dorrai trwy ardaloedd a fu gynt yn anhygyrch. Tyfodd olion digamsyniol y fasnach foduron fel dolurion cochion ar eu hyd. Datblygodd y radio trwy'r gwledydd megis ar amrantiad gan wneud y byd yn llai fyth a dwyn iaith pob gwlad i geginau Cymru. Ond yn arbennig yr iaith Saesneg a'r holl ddiwylliant a oedd ynghlwm â'r iaith honno ac a welid eisoes megis haenen amryliw o olew tros wyneb dyfroedd llonydd yr hen ddiwylliant.[24]

> (The motor car and bus became commonplace and drew country and town closer than ever before; that process generated new roads that cut through areas that were once remote. The unmistakable marks of the motor trade grew like red bruises along them. Radio developed through the countries in an instant making the world smaller still and bringing the language of every nation to the kitchens of Wales. But especially the English language and the whole culture associated with that language which had already been seen like a multicoloured film of oil over the still waters of the old civilization.)

While debates elsewhere on the relationship between tradition and modernity revolved around certain key icons, like the roadside detritus mentioned by Peate,[25] the most significant element threatened here was the Welsh language.

Census returns in the early part of the twentieth century offered conclusive evidence for the first time that the number of Welsh speakers had begun to decline. This linguistic and social process soon acquired geographical resonances which challenged the stable readings of rurality outlined above. In the first geographical study of the Welsh language based on census statistics, Trevor Lewis traced the decline of the language from the Edwardian Conquest (Figure 1).[26] His analysis was based in part on the socio-biological characteristics of sectors of the Welsh population (based on Fleure's physical surveys), on the dynamics of rural depopulation, and on historical factors such as the rise of Nonconformity. But one central theme was the interplay between topography and cultural continuity. In essence, the decline was manifested in the gradual retreat of the Welsh-speaking areas from the south and east to the upland western heartlands of the north and

---

[24] Iorwerth C. Peate, *Diwylliant Gwerin Cymru* (Lerpwl, 1942), pp. 124–5.

[25] For an example of this perceived relationship between aesthetic and social order, see Pyrs Gruffudd, '"Propaganda for Seemliness": Clough Williams-Ellis and Portmeirion, 1918–1950', *Ecumene*, 2, no. 4 (1995), 399–422.

[26] Trevor Lewis, 'Sur la distribution du parler gallois dans le Pays de Galles d'après le recensement de 1921', *Annales de Géographie*, XXXV, no. 197 (1926), 413–18. Due to the poor quality of the original map, it was impossible to distinguish between areas where 50–80 per cent and 80–100 per cent of the population spoke Welsh, and both areas have been reproduced here as one group (50–100 per cent).

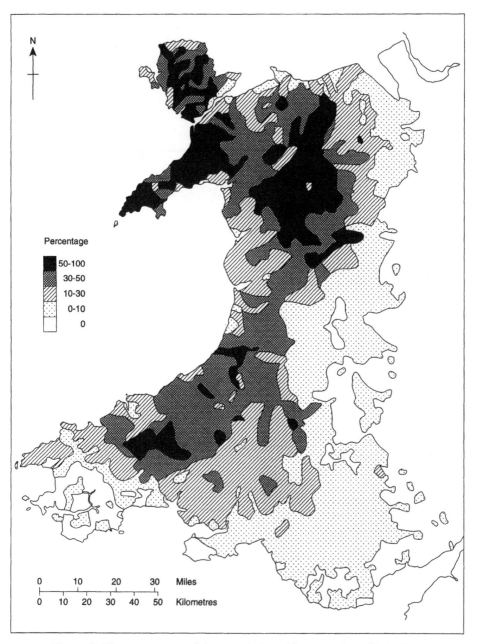

Figure 1. The percentage of the population able to speak Welsh in 1921
(after Trevor Lewis)

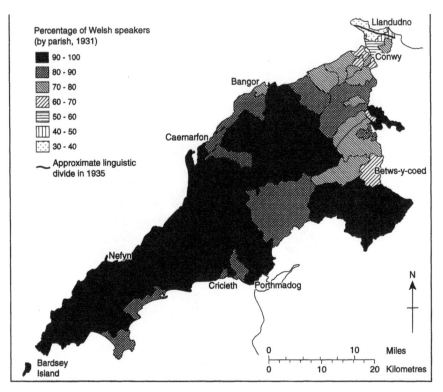

Figure 2. Linguistic divides in Caernarfonshire in 1935 (after D. T. Williams)

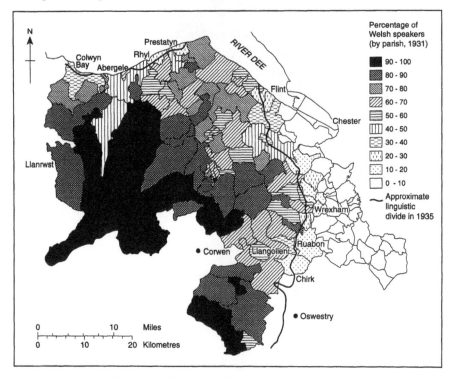

Figure 3. Linguistic divides in Flintshire and Denbighshire in 1935
(after D. T. Williams)

west, sheltering behind the protective wall of the Cambrian mountains: 'ancient Gwynedd, the north west corner of Wales, remains the fortress of the old language'.[27] But, in addition to this gradual incursion, Anglicization was penetrating the heartland more rapidly along communication corridors like the London–Holyhead railway, and through the tourist trade of the coastal strips which catered for the working classes of the Potteries.

D. Trevor Williams's later studies attempted to bring greater sophistication to the analysis of language. He criticized some of the inaccuracies of census mapping – including the map produced by Lewis which, Williams claimed, under-represented the Welsh-speaking population – and summarized some of the pitfalls facing the researcher:

> The County Borough of Swansea for example extends 3–4 miles inland from the coast over an area in which the Welsh language is dominant, and yet the entire district is represented as one in which there are between 60–80 per cent English monoglots. South, from Abergele, on the north coast of Wales, a long, narrow belt of anglicization is shown extending into the uplands, but the parish so represented, Llanfair Talhaiarn, has a population of only thirty-one individuals, aged three years and over, of whom seventeen are English monoglots. The writer has attempted elsewhere to overcome this limitation by personal investigation and survey in such areas.[28]

While Williams's analysis of the 1931 census figures tended to reinforce the earlier conclusions of Trevor Lewis, his particular contribution was the concept of the linguistic divide – a border based on parish level figures and complemented by fieldwork in the apparent border zone between Welsh and English. The divide was a more detailed demarcation of the cultural frontier, and although it barely impinged on heartlands such as Caernarfonshire (Figure 2), it reflected an intensity of concern about the state of the language elsewhere: 'From the neigh-bourhood of Chirk the boundary is drawn through Cefnmawr . . . thence within a mile west of Ruabon and through Johnstown, Rhostyllen, one and a half miles west of Wrexham, and Moss to the environs of Caergwrle. From Caergwrle the language frontier follows closely the main road in the Vale of Alyn to Mold' (Figure 3).[29] But, in addition, the linguistic divide was believed to be a concept relevant to the lived experience of Welshness: 'It defines the limits of anglicisation, the area in which Welsh is no longer the medium of cultural

---

[27] Ibid., 417–18.

[28] D. Trevor Williams, 'A Linguistic Map of Wales according to the 1931 Census, with some Observations on its Historical and Geographical Setting', *The Geographical Journal*, LXXXIX, no. 2 (1937), 146.

[29] Idem, 'Linguistic Divides in North Wales: A Study in Historical Geography', *AC*, XCI, part 2 (1936), 198.

interpretation or of ordinary conversation to the majority of the population.'[30] Hence, 'At Pentyrch, only seven miles from Cardiff, the parish meetings are still held entirely in Welsh and the minutes recorded in that language. However, this hamlet is becoming a residential suburb of Cardiff, and the language change is shown by the necessity to give, at the annual parish meeting, the minutes in English as well as in Welsh.'[31]

The linguistic divide also introduced a dynamic and strategic sense of the patterns and processes of language which, when related to the advance of English, was imaginatively powerful. Thus, the Townhill and Mayhill housing estates were represented as cresting the highland ridges to the north of Swansea and displacing the Welsh-speaking settled agricultural life, while the tourist towns of the west coast came alive as nuclei of Englishness.[32] In Breconshire the English language was represented almost as an active agent, albeit facilitated by human impacts on the landscape:

> The English tongue has spread across the river into Breconshire and is customarily spoken by all, except the very old, along the entire valley from Rhayader to Newbridge and Builth. It has also spread westwards for some miles along the Irfon Valley from Builth towards Llangammarch. Communication by road and rail and the construction of many bridges have aided the linguistic change during the last fifty years . . . The anglicising influence of the town of Builth is seen spreading westwards in a semi-circle of gradually increasing radius.[33]

This strategic and dynamic understanding of language was echoed in the work of Iorwerth C. Peate. He had been influenced by the concept of the 'frontier' – a concept which held considerable currency in the discipline of geography at that time – which asserted that a culture's most creative energies were exhibited at its margins. This, he suggested, accounted for the geographical development of Welsh Nonconformity.[34] However, between Wales's frontier and that of England (manifested in Shropshire's poetic and literary vitality, for instance), Peate identified a 'no man's land' – an Anglicized zone of 'half things' which had lost touch with tradition by losing the language. This was demonstrated, for instance, in east Montgomeryshire's neglect of traditional Welsh crafts.[35] Furthermore, the frontier of Welshness had been penetrated and the heartland was, accordingly, in

---

[30] Idem, 'Linguistic Divides in South Wales: A Historico-geographical Study', ibid., XC, part 2 (1935), 240.

[31] Ibid., 260.

[32] Idem, 'Gower: A Study in Linguistic Movements and Historical Geography', ibid., LXXXIX, part 2 (1934), 302–27.

[33] Idem, 'Linguistic Divides in South Wales', 246.

[34] Iorwerth C. Peate, 'Lle'r Ffiniau yn Natblygiad Annibyniaeth yng Nghymru', Y Cofiadur, no. 7 (1929), 3–21.

[35] Idem, 'The Crafts and a National Language', pp. 75–6.

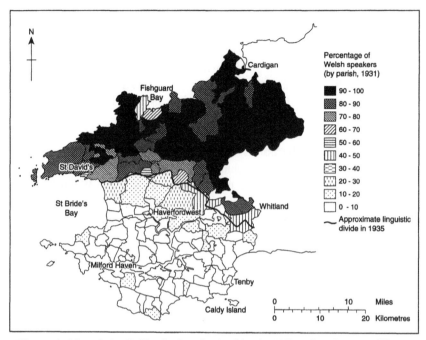

Figure 4. Linguistic divides in Pembrokeshire in 1935 (after D. T. Williams)

retreat. Peate identified 'tongues' of lowland – the north Wales coastal strip and the valleys of rivers like the Severn and Wye – pushing into the Cambrian mountains from the Anglicized east: 'These lowland tongues are the gateways of the east, easy routes from the English plains to the heart of the mountains of the west. And along them came wave after wave of new habits, new people, a new language and a new culture' ('Pyrth y dwyrain yw'r tafodau tir isel hyn, llwybrau hawdd o iseldir Lloegr i galon mynydd-dir y gorllewin. Ac ar eu hyd daeth yn eu tro don ar ôl ton o arferion newydd, pobl newydd, iaith newydd a diwylliant newydd').[36] Significantly, the cultural division between Welshness and Englishness was also a geographical division – the watershed between the Dyfi and Severn, which Peate referred to as the 'Talerddig divide'.[37] Peate did not, however, share Cyril Fox's faith in an overwhelming highland resilience: 'And as the people and their habits,

---

[36] Idem, *Cymru a'i Phobl*, p. 9.

[37] The 'Talerddig divide' was 'the watershed between Dyfi and Severn, the boundary between things Welsh and things English, the great barrier to invasion from the Saxon east'. Peate, 'The Dyfi Basin', 59. It was also in proximity to Peate's home village of Llanbryn-mair – a 'frontier' village, therefore – to which he gave a position of some significance in modern Welsh history. H. J. Fleure, too, commented on the significance of the 'Talerddig divide' as experienced when travelling by train from England to rural Wales when, typically, 'the talk in a railway compartment changes from betting to chapels, or from horse-racing to the eisteddfod. It is this simple peasant heritage that is even now struggling to escape destruction'. Fleure, 'The Celtic West', *Journal of the Royal Society of Arts*, LXXXVIII, no. 4571 (1940), 883.

their language and culture succeed in transforming the mountain-lands around the gateways, so is their influence extended over the native life of the country, and so is the continuation of the culture of the mountain-land threatened unless a transformation in government can be achieved' ('Ac fel y llwydda'r bobl a'u harferion, yr iaith a'i diwylliant i drawsnewid y mynydd-dir o gwmpas y pyrth, lledaenir eu dylanwad tros fywyd cysefin y wlad ac ansicr fydd parhad diwylliant y mynydd-dir oni cheir rhyw gyfnewidiad rheolaeth').[38]

The explanation offered by Williams and Peate for these shifts in language patterns was rooted in the history – early and modern – of Welsh political, demographic and economic relationships with England and with other European nations. For Williams, however, the more recent history of the Welsh language was also shot through with a profound awareness of the transcending of geographical barriers: 'Modern expansion, new cultural influences made possible by rapid transport, the cinema, the wireless, and the powerful influence of the teachers in the elementary schools since 1870 all enter into the linguistic changes that are taking place in . . . Wales to-day.'[39] Transportation had brought with it the Anglicized, but perhaps moral, economy of the coalfields and of quarrying. More recently, however, road and rail had facilitated the leisure traveller and parts of north Wales had become 'the seasonal playgrounds of visitors from [the] populated manufacturing districts and, to some extent, the dormitory "villages" of more wealthy industrialists'.[40] The organic advance of the frontier had, as it were, been transgressed by modernity. In Pembrokeshire, the historically-rooted *Landsker* divide was counterposed with the more recent transport-related growth (Figure 4) and in Cardiganshire the 35 per cent monoglot English population in Aberystwyth was understood as 'a possible reflection of its urban character, its tourist industry, its University College, and its railway terminus'.[41] Williams's moral ambivalence about the transient age of tourism and leisure was widely reflected,[42] but, as Fleure and Peate had suggested, the barrier of the Cambrian mountains was losing its effectiveness in the light of modernization and modernity and this posed a grave threat to cultural continuity.

A Geographical Politics

It was in response to the perceived loss of Welsh identity caused by the processes of modernization and of geographical upheaval that Plaid Genedlaethol Cymru

---

[38]　Peate, *Cymru a'i Phobl*, p. 9.

[39]　Williams, 'Gower', 325.

[40]　Idem, 'Linguistic Divides in North Wales', 204.

[41]　Idem, 'Linguistic Divides in South Wales', 263.

[42]　For instance, H. J. Fleure suggested that rural populations which came to rely entirely on the city tourist might become socially degenerate, and he advocated co-operative schemes of economic development to combat this dependence. See Gruffudd, 'Back to the Land', 61–77.

(the Welsh Nationalist Party) was formed in 1925. It has been argued that during its first twenty years Plaid Genedlaethol Cymru was less a political party than a cultural and educational movement which sought to re-establish a traditional, organic and rural form of Welsh identity: 'The formation of the Welsh Nationalist Party was an explicit challenge to the growing idea of British nationality, and an attempt to resist and reverse all those trends that were assimilating Wales into England.'[43]

The profound influence of its president, Saunders Lewis, was based not on economic or political grievances as much as on threats to Welsh cultural identity. According to Colin H. Williams, Lewis was committed to a form of 'organic' rather than 'state' nationalism which had at its core cultural continuity rather than what he called nationalist materialism.[44] Eliciting a sense of a common ethnic identity, primarily through the defence and promotion of the Welsh language, was the strategy of the Welsh Nationalist Party and the link between language, culture and territory was a fundamental part of its philosophy. The unveiling of the Party's symbol, the *Triban* (a stylized representation of the mountains), in 1933 testified to the importance of the geographical imagination in nationalist discourse. J. E. Jones, the Party's secretary, welcomed the symbol thus: 'The mountains! The perpetual witnesses of our history, and the unchanging background of our language: we can express it in symbolic form – therefore our sign – the TRIBAN' ('Y mynyddoedd! Tystion tragwyddol ein hanes, a chefndir digyfnewid ein hiaith: gallwn ei fynegi mewn ffurf symbolig – gan hynny ein harwydd – arwydd y Blaid – y TRIBAN').[45] In *Y Ddraig Goch*, the Party's paper, Iorwerth C. Peate extended this geographical historiography by arguing that, due to its physical character, Wales could be seen as 'an immortal *nucleus* containing . . . the finest heart of the western world's traditions. There has grown in Wales a society which possessed an inheritance of incomparable tradition, and . . . a culture almost as old as the world itself' ('*nucleus* anfarwol yn cynnwys . . . r[h]uddin goreu traddodiadau'r byd gorllewin. Ac felly fe dyfodd i fyny yng Nghymru gymdeithas a feddai etifeddiaeth o draddodiadau digymar, ac a feddai ddiwylliant mor hen bron a'r byd ei hunan').[46] Having been born into such a perfect society, the Welsh had a duty to civilization to ensure the perpetuation of their nation. This meant resisting English cultural encroachments.

The geographical dimension to the Welsh Nationalist Party's politics was also represented by a moralized notion of the *gwerin* and of the countryside as a civiliz-ing storehouse of the Welsh language and identity. It was argued that the Party

[43] D. Hywel Davies, *The Welsh Nationalist Party 1925–1945: A Call to Nationhood* (Cardiff, 1983), p. vii.
[44] Colin H. Williams, 'Separatism and the Mobilization of Welsh National Identity' in idem (ed.), *National Separatism* (Cardiff, 1982), pp. 145–201; idem, 'Minority Nationalist Historiography' in Johnston et al. (eds.), *Nationalism, Self-determination and Political Geography*, pp. 203–21.
[45] J. E. Jones, *Tros Gymru: J. E. a'r Blaid* (Abertawe, 1970), p. 92.
[46] Iorwerth C. Peate, 'Y Genedl ac Awdurdod', *Y Ddraig Goch*, 1, no. 2 (1926), 4.

had emerged from Welsh rural life and many of its members contributed, particularly as writers and poets, to the location of the Welsh character in the countryside. This idealization of the rural was common elsewhere in Europe, among both the Left and the Right. In Ireland, for instance, the Gaeltacht served as the main locus of Irish cultural aspiration, its linguistic strength and rural cultural continuity read as a condition of virtue.[47] In Wales, this alliance between geography, language and identity found expression, for instance, in campaigns against the urbanizing tendency of modern education. Writers such as W. Ambrose Bebb mourned a lost age of rural prosperity and vitality in the pages of *Y Ddraig Goch*, and blamed an Anglicized educational system for alienating the *gwerin* from their cultural and geographical roots.[48] More radically, Saunders Lewis argued that agriculture should be Wales's primary industry 'and the foundation of its civilization'.[49] One central Party policy was a move 'back to the land', realigning the dispossessed of the Anglicized industrial areas with their 'true' cultural heritage. Saunders Lewis argued for the resettlement of former industrial workers in farming colonies and Moses Gruffydd, the Party's agricultural spokesman, argued that the policy was 'essential if the Welsh Nation is to live. The Welsh Nation is a nation with its roots in the country and the soil'.[50] But the policy also integrated economic with cultural logic. A cartoon which appeared in *Y Ddraig Goch* in 1936 was clearly idealistic in its representation of the awkward ugliness of the capitalist and the nobility of the peasant farmer, but, with the capitalist begging 'For the free market's sake, don't become self-sufficient!', the cartoon referred to notions of Welsh economic independence.[51] To reject industrial capitalism was to resist English influence and to attain the conditions of nationhood.

Defending the Nation

This theoretical understanding of the cultural role of geography in Welsh nationalist politics was translated into campaigns in which the defence and control

---

[47] See, for instance, Nuala C. Johnson, 'Building a Nation: an Examination of the Irish Gaeltacht Commission Report of 1926', *Journal of Historical Geography*, 19, no. 2 (1993), 157–68; Catherine Nash, '"Embodying the Nation": The West of Ireland Landscape and Irish Identity' in Barbara O'Connor and Michael Cronin (eds.), *Tourism in Ireland: A Critical Analysis* (Cork, 1993), pp. 86–112.

[48] W. Ambrose Bebb, 'Bywyd Gwledig Cymru Heddiw', *Y Ddraig Goch*, 1, no. 12 (1927), 4.

[49] Saunders Lewis, 'Deg Pwynt Polisi' in idem, *Canlyn Arthur: Ysgrifau Gwleidyddol* (Aberystwyth, 1938), p. 12.

[50] Cited in Davies, *The Welsh Nationalist Party*, p. 92. Gruffydd worked closely with the agricultural scientist R. George Stapledon, who expressed influential ideas on the socio-cultural importance of rural civilization, at the University of Wales's experimental farm near Aberystwyth. See R. George Stapledon, *The Land Now and Tomorrow* (London, 1935) and Anna Bramwell, *Ecology in the Twentieth Century: A History* (London, 1989).

[51] *Y Ddraig Goch*, 10, no. 8 (1936), 7.

of Welsh territory assumed both a material and symbolic role. These campaigns revealed a profound awareness of the geography of language and the dynamics of Anglicization as exposed by academic research in the 1930s. Gradually there emerged a strategic awareness of threats to the geographical integrity of Welshness, particularly in the rural areas, and of the potential redefinition of Wales as part of British space. These themes were demonstrated dramatically in the late 1930s by large-scale land requisitioning by the military authorities for munitions works and training areas. The location of training areas was particularly controversial since they posed immediate threats both to the organic rural communities which served as the nationalists' definition of the nation, and to their ideal of national territorial control. One proposed requisitioning provided a defining moment in Welsh nationalist history. In May 1935 plans were announced for the establishment of an aerodrome at Porth Neigwl (known in English as Hell's Mouth) in the Llŷn peninsula, an area identified as a cultural heartland by the mappers of Welshness. The Welsh Nationalist Party immediately opposed 'another nation's seizure of our lands for *any* purpose, and especially its seizure for filthy work' ('Gwrthdystia'r Blaid Genedlaethol yn erbyn i genedl arall feddiannu ein tiroedd ni i *unrhyw* bwrpas, ac yn arbennig yn erbyn ei feddiannu ar gyfer ei budrwaith').[52] Notably, the Party's 'geographical imagination' of Wales – an amalgam of territorial, linguistic and moral stances – served to define this response and its opposition to the numerous claims made on Welsh territory before, during, and after the Second World War. The following section examines the mobilization of that geographical imagination and especially an interpretation of the organic unity between the *gwerin* and the land. It then considers the ways in which these targeted areas came to be understood as strategically important for the Welsh nation, in relation to the geography of the language.

One of the key definers of the contribution of the *gwerin* to Welshness in the inter-war years was Iorwerth C. Peate. In response to the aerodrome proposal, Peate claimed that the population of the Llŷn peninsula was 'an excellent example of . . . an unsophisticated peasant community. It seems to me to be a heinous sin to introduce any kind of camp into that area'.[53] Opposition to the scheme was immediately defined in terms of threats by an 'alien civilization' to the cultural and geographical integrity of the Welsh nation. Peate claimed that the peninsula was wholly untouched by nineteenth- and twentieth-century industrialism and thus, was 'virgin ground almost completely unaffected by modern building and

---

[52] Ibid., 9, no. 7 (1935), 1.

[53] NLW, CPRW Papers 9/19, letter from Iorwerth C. Peate to Clough Williams-Ellis, 31 May 1935. Peate's campaigning involved the preservationist group, the Council for the Preservation of Rural Wales (CPRW). The CPRW's refusal to protest saw them labelled an Anglicized body with little understanding of indigenous interpretations of rural life and landscapes. This itself was part of a broader debate on the 'meaning' of Wales's landscapes between the wars. See Pyrs Gruffudd, 'Landscape and Nationhood: Tradition and Modernity in Rural Wales, 1900–1950' (unpubl. University of Loughborough PhD thesis, 1989).

the effects of tourist and English influences'.[54] This continuity was, in part, caused by remoteness and by the under-development of transport networks; the railway stopped at Pwllheli and most of the roads were narrow and unimproved. Geography had, therefore, provided the foundation for cultural continuity in Llŷn and the peninsula had consequently become, like other western European peninsulas, a storehouse of the Celtic tradition. An essentially modern folk-life offered vital knowledge to sociologists and ethnographers. Peate referred to Trevor Lewis's research in *Annales de Géographie* and suggested that 'Llŷn is monoglot Welsh to a degree unknown in any other part of the country'. He continued by arguing that:

> The purity of the linguistic tradition, with its comprehensive agricultural and craft vocabularies unadulterated by any mass-borrowing from English, is a fact of the greatest importance to the linguistic scholar. To introduce any extraneous element into this homogeneous society, by developing the peninsula or any part of it on modern lines or by any other form of exotic settlement would therefore be most unfortunate. It would destroy evidence in all the directions indicated which would be a loss to international scholarship and culture.[55]

In short, it was 'imperative that the peninsula should maintain the unsophisticated purity of its native tradition'.[56] Thus the main themes of Wales's inter-war cultural geography were represented here. There was considerable emphasis on cultural and linguistic continuity, on folk wisdom, and on the existence of an organic community. In this way, the case came to symbolize for the Welsh Nationalist Party the struggle to define and defend its preferred version of Welsh national identity. Proposed exactly four hundred years after the first Act of Union, Saunders Lewis argued in *The Listener* that the Porth Neigwl aerodrome would be:

> an English garrison set up in an area where the Welsh language has ever since the fifth century been established and undisturbed, where Welsh speech has moulded a countryside rich in intelligence, noble in the purity of its idiom, and with its native culture harmoniously developed through fifteen centuries of unbroken tradition . . . In the Lleyn Peninsula the English Air Ministry threatens . . . one of the few remaining homes of Welsh national culture and pure idiom.[57]

---

[54] NLW, CPRW Papers 9/19, Iorwerth C. Peate, *The Llŷn Peninsula: Some Cultural Considerations.* Sent to CPRW, 27 July 1935.

[55] Ibid. This theme was identified in the contributions of others to the debate. Iorwerth Jones of Swansea, in a letter published in the *Western Mail* on 30 June 1936, used the contemporary jargon of conservationist debates to suggest that 'Lleyn to Wales is a linguistic national park, to be guarded jealously while the language and Welsh life remain separate from the cosmopolitan tide of modern life. And England should have enough sense and consideration to realise this fact . . .'

[56] NLW, CPRW Papers 9/19, Peate, *The Llŷn Peninsula.*

[57] Saunders Lewis, 'The Case for Welsh Nationalism', *The Listener*, XV, no. 383, 13 May 1936, 915.

Elsewhere, the foundations of Welsh rural culture were similarly threatened. In 1940 Iorwerth C. Peate described the shattering of cultural continuity on the Epynt Mountain in mid-Wales, where 40,000 acres were requisitioned for military training. Here, too, there existed what was interpreted as an organic, Welsh-speaking *gwerin*. Peate witnessed the death of a Welsh community:

Canys er imi deithio tua phedwar can milltir yn ôl ac ymlaen, ar hyd ac ar draws y fro, ni chlywais odid ddim Saesneg. Rhyw ddau neu dri a gyfarfûm na ddeallent Gymraeg. Trwy wasgaru gwerin Mynydd Epynt, drylliwyd un o'r darnau cadarn olaf – o unrhyw faint – o'r diwylliant Cymraeg ym Mrycheiniog. Ac er y gellir o bosibl ail-boblogi'r fro pan ddêl dynion atynt eu hunain o'r gwallgofrwydd presennol, nid gwerin Mynydd Epynt fydd yno, nid gwŷr a gwragedd a'u gwreiddiau ers canrifoedd yn y fro, a'r iaith gynhenid ar eu gwefusau ond yn hytrach 'ddynion dwad'. Ac fe gymer ganrifoedd eto i'r rheini wreiddio yn y tir fel y gwreiddiasai'r gymdeithas a lofruddiwyd yn 1940. Nid oes ond gobeithio – a gofalu – mai'r Gymraeg fydd eu hiaith hwythau.[58]

(Because although I travelled around four hundred miles to and fro, the length and breadth of the locality, I heard virtually no English. I only met two or three who did not understand Welsh. By dispersing the *gwerin* of Epynt, one of the last secure pieces of the Welsh tradition in Breconshire – of meaningful size – has been destroyed. And although it may be possible to re-populate the area when men come to their senses after the present madness, it will not be the *gwerin* of Epynt that will be there, not men and women with their roots in the locality for centuries, and the native language on their lips, but rather incomers. And it will take centuries again for them to root in the soil as had the community that was murdered in 1940. We can only hope – and ensure – that their language will be Welsh.)

The *gwerin* of the Preselau mountains in north Pembrokeshire, where the War Office proposed to retain 16,000 acres after the war, was similarly represented as part of the cultural wealth of the nation. As late as 1930 it was claimed that 80 per cent of the inhabitants of the village of Mynachlog-ddu attended chapel and that 99 per cent were Welsh-speaking.[59] Campaigners argued that the area had produced theologians, preachers and scholars, and the clerical leadership of the campaign also stressed the spiritual and religious qualities of the remaining *gwerin*. They juxtaposed the wisdom of those born and bred on the hills with the materialistic folk of the plains: 'To us, the mountain is the bread of life, and is a holy sacrament. Our lives are woven into its essence. If we lose the mountains nothing will remain but "snobbery" and "chip" shops' ('I ni, y mae'r mynydd yn fara'r bywyd, ac yn sagrafen gysegredig. Mae ein bywyd ni wedi ei wau i'w hanfod. Os collwn y mynyddoedd ni bydd dim yn aros ond "snobbery" a siop "chips" ').[60]

---

[58] Iorwerth C. Peate, 'Mynydd Epynt', *Y Llenor*, XX, no. 4 (1941), 185.
[59] Janet Davies, 'The Fight for Preseli, 1946', *Planet*, 58 (1986), 3–9.
[60] *Baner ac Amserau Cymru*, 5 February 1947.

Descriptions of the cultural integrity of the threatened areas aligned them with definitions of the nation, but also located them on another central part of the geographical imagination in Wales, namely the national cultural map. Fundamental claims on Welsh land were expressly made – 'Wales free, every inch of her – that is the policy of Plaid Cymru' ('Cymru'n rhydd, bob modfedd ohoni – dyna bolisi Plaid Cymru')[61] – but there was also a strategic understanding of the implications of the schemes. In the same way as studies of the Welsh language had highlighted linguistic 'fortresses', 'divides' and 'frontiers', so politicians adopted geopolitical discourse to represent the struggle between English and Welsh culture over the western and upland strongholds. For Saunders Lewis, the Porth Neigwl aerodrome threatened a cultural heartland of national importance. It was one place where 'we could until very recently assume that the purity of the Welsh language could be maintained despite all alien educational regimes. Whilst Llŷn was Welsh we did not need fear for the Welsh nation' ('Yno o leiaf, gellid tybio hyd yn ddiweddar iawn, fe gedwid purdeb yr iaith Gymraeg er gwaethaf pob cyfundrefn addysg estron. Tra byddai Llŷn yn Gymraeg ni ddarfyddai am genedl y Cymry').[62] But Saunders Lewis also maintained that 'this threat by the Air Force aims straight and true at the heart and life of our language and literature and culture and existence as a nation' ('y mae'r bygythiad hwn gan y Fyddin Awyr yn anelu'n union ac yn ddiffael at galon ac at einioes ein hiaith a'n llenyddiaeth a'n diwylliant a'n bodolaeth fel cenedl').[63] Welshness was understood in profoundly geographical terms, as illustrated in a remarkable letter to the press by a group of prominent nationalists, pacifists and theologians:

> The advance of Anglicising influences along the northern seaboard, powerful and disturbing though they were, could still be regarded with a certain qualified equanimity, so long as the mountains of Snowdonia offered a barrier behind which, in the profoundly Welsh peninsula of Lleyn, the forces of defence, and ultimately of counter-attack could safely rally. The value of Lleyn, Welsh of the Welsh as it is, is absolutely irreplaceable in our national life, and any blow to the security of Welsh culture here is a mortal blow. The establishment of the bombing school here will do for modern Welsh culture what the occupation of Anglesey by Edward I in the thirteenth century did for Welsh political independence – destroy it by cutting its communications and vital supplies.[64]

[61] *Y Ddraig Goch*, 21, no. 5 (1947), 2.
[62] Saunders Lewis, 'Paham y Gwrthwynebwn yr Ysgol Fomio?', *Y Ddraig Goch*, 10, no. 3 (1936), 6–7.
[63] Ibid.
[64] The signatories were George M. Ll. Davies, the Revd Peter Hughes-Griffiths, Professor W. J. Gruffydd, the Revd W. Harris Hughes, the Revd J. J. Williams and Professor J. E. Daniel. The letter appeared in the *Western Mail*, 24 March 1936, as part of an article entitled 'Hellsmouth Bombing School – Opposition Falsely Based – Pilgrims' Way Untouched' which expressed apparent support for the air base in north Wales and astonishment at attacks on the proposal. The letter was given the sub-headings 'Bones of Saints' and 'Welsh Culture'.

The geopolitical imagery and rhetoric in this letter clearly illustrates the power of the geographical imagination in the cultural and political discourse of inter-war Wales. In this one scheme the process of diffusion by which Wales had been steadily Anglicized for centuries was replaced by a form of internal colonialism, and the mountains, the traditional protectors of Wales, were defeated:

> If the plan is persevered with the future holds for Welsh life and culture a black outlook indeed. Taken in front and rear by the forces of Anglicisation, its total destruction can only be a matter of years. If the Government had deliberately set out to deal them as deadly a wound as it possibly could, it could hardly have made a more diabolically effective choice.[65]

Similar geopolitical arguments were developed elsewhere, before, during and after the war. At one stage Epynt was referred to as the Alsace of Wales.[66] As noted above, Iorwerth C. Peate believed that the range would destroy one of the last linguistic strongholds in Breconshire but, viewed alongside other proposals in the post-war period, it was clear that the plan also threatened to divide Wales into north and south, denying the Anglicized and urbanized south its tentative links with a linguistically 'pure' and rural Welshness: 'Linguistically, it [the Epynt range] has driven the border of Welsh-speaking Wales back ten miles towards Llanwrtyd, where the position is more than precarious, and whence another huge training area reaches out towards the Cardigan coast. When the War Office went to Epynt a part of Wales died.'[67] This threatened to undermine the geographical and cultural integrity of the Welsh nation itself. Pembrokeshire was historically divided into Welsh north and Anglicized south by the *Landsker* line, but the Preselau tank range now threatened to Anglicize the north, thus achieving (according to one local paper) what the Saxons, Normans and Flemings had failed to do.[68] According to the Revd R. Parri Roberts, this would crystallize Wales's role as merely a western base for the English military, facilitated by Welsh roads running from east to west (from England to Wales) rather than from north to south.[69] Plaid Cymru summarized their case in a similarly profound manner. The mountains and uplands had been:

> . . . for centuries the inner fortress of Wales, the source of her spiritual and political strength. To this wild hinterland her people withdrew when attacked, until they were strong enough to recover their lost territory. What is now threatened is geographically

---

[65] Ibid.

[66] *Y Ddraig Goch*, 14, no. 6 (1940), 1.

[67] Welsh Nationalist Party, *Havoc in Wales: The War Office Demands* (Cardiff, 1947), p. 12.

[68] *Western Telegraph*, 28 November 1946.

[69] 'Cymru – Gwersyll Milwrol Lloegr', *Baner ac Amserau Cymru*, 25 December 1946.

the very heart of Wales, and to do violence to it endangers not her welfare only, but her very existence.[70]

These campaigns of resistance and appeals to the cultural and geographical politics of the Welsh enjoyed varying success. The protests against and the subsequent attack upon the Penyberth base are a celebrated part of nationalist history that does not require repeating here.[71] Protests at the end of the Second World War, however, were equally impassioned, with half a million acres (almost 10 per cent) of Welsh land still held by the military. Campaigners appealed to the spirit of the *gwerin*: 'the yeomen of Wales still have the power to defeat the militarists who would desecrate and destroy their homes. Though they have none of the mechanism of slaughter with which to defend their birthright, they have justice on their side. Their right is their might'.[72] Welshness was inextricably aligned with the land, with each individual threat read as a challenge to the territorial integrity of the nation. After a war fought ostensibly for the rights of small nations, it was ironic to see a post-war socialist government now threaten the life of Wales. Using the campaign's spirit of resistance, Plaid Cymru hoped to 'sweep away the last vestiges of alien misrule from Wales, and to found a new Welsh civilisation with a sound re-organisation of our economic, social and cultural life'.[73]

Rebuilding the Nation

As the above quotation implies, the definition of Welsh identity as being rooted in the soil and the subsequent defence of that soil was only one characteristic of the nationalist programme. According to Williams and Smith, the concept of the 'homeland' can also inspire 'a project of self-renewal, achieved by externalizing the struggle for collective identity in acts of environmental manipulation and by attaining mastery over a recalcitrant nature'.[74] Notions of the land, territory and language also played central roles in the proposed reorganization of Welsh life – the process of nation-building. Alongside the defence of Welsh cultural integrity, therefore, was a corresponding drive to integrate linguistic politics into all aspects of the 'nationalization' and management of Welsh territory, and to create a culturally integrated 'nation' out of a disparate and fluctuating mosaic of regions.

In the opinion of Plaid Cymru, the British state treated Wales as a peripheral region of Britain, resisting calls for greater autonomy. This was reflected in several ways, for instance, in the official treatment of the language. But planning and the

---

[70] Welsh Nationalist Party, *Havoc in Wales*, pp. 3–4.
[71] See, for example, Dafydd Jenkins, *A Nation on Trial: Penyberth 1936* (Cardiff, 1998).
[72] *The Welsh Nationalist*, XVI, no. 7 (1947), 1.
[73] Ibid., XVII, no. 4 (1948), 4.
[74] Williams and Smith, 'The National Construction of Social Space', 511.

management of territory had also kept Wales firmly in a broader British space and had implications for linguistic geographies. The decline of the Liberal hegemony had left Wales dominated by a Labour bloc largely suspicious of the issue of Welsh nationality. Thus Welsh Labour MPs had no wish to deviate from traditional socialist centralism which provided the basic framework for any integrated economic planning for Britain as a whole.[75] For Plaid Cymru and other 'nationalists', these concerns were heightened by the government's reconstruction proposals of the 1940s, which were themselves part of a discourse of *British* nation-building. Iorwerth C. Peate criticized the Scott Report on *Land Utilisation in Rural Areas*, published in 1942, which conceived of the countryside as an 'amenity' area dependent upon the towns.[76] It established a division which Peate claimed was alien to Wales, a country where rural and industrial activities were historically integrated. The 'national character' had emerged in part, he argued, from the co-operative patterns of rural industries, which he sought to revive on the basis of new technologies like electrification. By denying an evolving role for the countryside, the Scott Report appeared to attack the vital role of the rural in Welsh national identity. A future of depopulation, economic stagnation and a superficial form of 'heritage tourism' beckoned. Plaid Cymru also criticized the assumptions of this and other reports that, on the basis of existing links, Wales and England should form one unit for the purposes of planning. Wales was a nation with its own geographic and economic logic and 'at no time should geographical and economic links between areas of Wales and areas of England be allowed to endanger the wholeness, unity and personality of that Welsh society. That would be a sin against civilization' ('ac ni ddylid un amser ganiatáu i gysylltiadau daearyddol ac economaidd rhwng ardaloedd yng Nghymru ac ardaloedd yn Lloegr beryglu cyfanrwydd ac undod a phersonoliaeth y gymdeithas Gymreig honno. Byddai hynny'n bechod yn erbyn gwareiddiad').[77]

Plaid Cymru argued that Wales required a national plan calculated to revive the depopulated rural areas and to give a territorial basis to Welsh national aspirations: 'planning or lack of it', one representative argued, 'is very closely linked with the political and cultural survival of our nation.'[78] The existing planning system, however, was politically and culturally defective in failing to address the damaging role of industrialism in Welsh life. Sustaining their location of Welshness in the Welsh-speaking countryside, Plaid Cymru argued that the industrial revolution had shattered the Welsh national community which had once been knit together by language, culture and tradition, and had replaced it with a denationalized proletariat. Thus 'if it is part of the planner's job to replace the dark satanic mills

---

[75] Kenneth O. Morgan, *Rebirth of a Nation: Wales 1880–1980* (Oxford, 1981), pp. 297–8.

[76] Iorwerth C. Peate, 'Yr Ardaloedd Gwledig a'u Dyfodol', *Y Llenor*, XXII, nos. 1 and 2 (1943), 10–18.

[77] *Y Ddraig Goch*, 16, no. 9 (1942), 1.

[78] Roy A. Lewis, 'This is not what we want', *The Welsh Nationalist*, XVIII, no. 8 (1949), 1.

of last century by industrial towns fit to live in, it is in Wales also his task to counteract, as far as it lies in his field, the tide of anglicisation and the shattering of community life which resulted from the chaotic industrial exploitation of the past.'[79] Many nationalists looked to the Tennessee Valley Authority for inspiration. Its comprehensive revival of rural life was seen as an attractive model of state-sponsored self-determination. In a debate prompted by large-scale hydroelectric developments in Wales, a number of nationalists detected potential parallels between Wales and Tennessee and saw electricity as a revitalizing force that could resurrect the old rural social order on a new foundation.[80]

The Way to Unite Wales

Electrification was to be one element in the work of an integrated, democratic planning authority that 'would find a potent ally in the national spirit, and it would realize that its plans were meant not for a region, but for a nation'.[81] However, another frequently advocated policy was even more radical in its aim of shifting Wales's geographical orientation away from England and of physically reuniting the nation. It was also explicitly understood in terms of the rural geographical imagination and its linguistic dimensions, as outlined above. Roads in Wales largely radiated to the east and west, in practice linking Wales to England, and as early as 1917 it had been argued that a road from north to south Wales would do more to bring the nation 'into common accord than generations of patriotic meetings'.[82] The Welsh Nationalist Party had discussed such a plan in the early 1930s, and in 1936 an article in *Y Ddraig Goch* revived the idea.[83] The scheme had many economic virtues, according to the Party, including the revival of quarrying and lead mining in north and mid-Wales and a new impetus for agriculture and associated industries. New tracts of agricultural land could be made available to resettle Welsh families from the industrial areas as part of the Party's 'back to the land' policy. Thus, while retaining a romantic bent, the Party addressed itself to all aspects of the nation's economy. The *Western Mail* also offered a number of variations on the scheme in a series of articles extolling its economic virtues.[84] But for the Welsh Nationalist Party the road also offered

---

[79] Ibid., 8.

[80] On electricity, see Pyrs Gruffudd, '"Uncivil Engineering": Nature, Nationalism and Hydro-Electrics in North Wales' in Denis Cosgrove and Geoff Petts (eds.), *Water, Engineering and Landscape: Water Control and Landscape Transformation in the Modern Period* (London, 1990), pp. 159–73.

[81] Welsh Nationalist Party, *TVA for Wales* (Caernarfon, 1945), p. 15.

[82] J. H. Davies, 'The Development of Transport in Rural Wales' in Chappell (ed.), *Welsh Housing and Development Year Book 1917* (Cardiff, 1917), p. 57.

[83] Oswald Rowlands, 'Asgwrn Cefn Newydd i Gymru', *Y Ddraig Goch*, 10, no. 12 (1936), 7, 9.

[84] See the report of a speech by Robert Webber, the director of the *Western Mail*, in *The Times*, 20 August 1937.

political and cultural opportunities. Popular mobilization for road-building might make the proletariat aware of its place in the Welsh nation. Work camps would 'become centres of Welsh culture and social life as well as of economic activity, and a means of revivifying the district where they were situated; the workers would be conscious that they were engaged for the first time on work for their own nation'.[85]

The road would also integrate language, culture and territory in two ways. Firstly, it would promote a 'hardening' of Welsh space by shifting the focus of national life away from the accessible and Anglicized coastal and border areas. It would follow a bold route across the uplands of central Wales, thus linking north and south. In its very geography the road would symbolize a new Wales and sponsor a national, rather than regional or local, regeneration. As the prominent nationalist, R. O. F. Wynne claimed: 'A scheme such as this would require the patriotic support of the whole nation, and would achieve that vital object – the unification of Wales.'[86] Secondly, by passing through the uplands of mid-Wales – 'the source and sanctuary of Welsh life' ('tarddle a noddfa'r bywyd Cymreig')[87] – the road would tap the cultural heartland of the nation. Travelling through this area would bring the urban population into contact with their lost cultural and environmental heritage, thus reintegrating them into nationhood. In a material as well as symbolic sense, therefore, this road would, according to its advocates, dismantle cultural, linguistic and economic differences between north and south and would safeguard Welsh rural culture.

Voices raised against the road scheme, however, expressed a significantly different geographical conception of the Welsh nation. Supporters of the scheme represented the modernizing tendency which suggested that national conscious-ness could be manufactured. They highlighted the reciprocal relationship that would be created between north and south, rural and industrial. Opposition came, most notably, from Iorwerth C. Peate and his more organic conception of Welshness rooted in geographical and cultural continuity.[88] According to Peate and Fleure, among others, the geography of Wales had protected Welsh culture, and to transcend that geography was to threaten that continuity. Peate was not anti-modern; in many respects he was the nationalist cause's most ardent modern-izer, welcoming new technology and its potential for reviving the pattern of Welsh rural life. But unless Welsh sovereignty were first achieved, the transcend-ing of Wales's geography would expose rural society to Anglicization:

[85] D. J. Davies and Nöelle Davies, *Can Wales Afford Self-Government?* (Caernarfon, 1939), p. 60. For a comparison on this, and other aspects of the road-building programme, see James D. Shand, 'The Reichsautobahn: Symbol for the Third Reich', *Journal of Contemporary History*, 19 (1984), 189–200.

[86] R. O. F. Wynne, 'A Trunk Road for Wales', *The Welsh Nationalist*, VI, no. 9 (1937), 9.

[87] Rowlands, 'Asgwrn Cefn Newydd i Gymru', 9.

[88] Iorwerth C. Peate, 'Ffordd i "Uno Cymru"', *Heddiw*, 3, no. 4 (1937), 126–9.

Petai Cymru'n wladwriaeth, petai'n rheoli ei hun, petai'n trefnu ei bywyd a'i thrafnidiaeth ar 'dir hollol genedlaethol' gyda grym gwladwriaeth Gymreig y tu ôl iddi; petai ganddi allu gwladwriaethol i osod yr iaith Gymraeg ar sylfaen sicr ym mhob ysgol trwy Gymru; petai addysg Cymru yn fagwriaeth i'r traddodiad cenedlaethol, yna'n sicr ni cheid dim hyfrytach na'r ffordd hon o draethau Hafren hyd at lannau Menai i greu gytgord a chymdogaeth dda a masnach rhwng holl siroedd Cymru.[89]

(Were Wales a state, ruling itself, planning its life and transport along 'national lines' with the power of the Welsh state behind it; had it a statutory ability to place the Welsh language on a strong foundation in every school throughout Wales; were Welsh education a breeding ground for the national tradition, then certainly there would be nothing finer than this road from the beaches of the Severn to the shores of the Menai Straits to create union, good neighbourliness and trade between all the counties of Wales.)

However, as Peate argued, Welshness was gravely threatened, and the uplands of the north and west were the final barriers against the Anglicizing forces of the outside world. In the uplands the language and the way of life that depended upon it was a daily reality. But, Peate insisted, were the 'road to unite Wales' built before self-determination was achieved, then 'the influences which drowned Welshness in the Vale of Glamorgan, the Severn valley and Colwyn Bay will flow like the red floods of August over the plains of Pumlumon, and to the feet of the Aran' ('Daw'r dylanwadau a foddodd gymreictod bro Morgannwg a dyffryn Hafren a Cholwyn Bay fel llifogydd coch Awst tros wastadeddau Pumlumon, ac at draed yr Aran').[90] A road would be a natural product of unity and a symbol of it, but it could not, Peate compellingly argued, be its generating force. To suggest that the nation might literally be built was a sign of the weakness of Welshness. Invoking his geographical and anthropological understanding of Welshness, Peate concluded: 'Only in the remotest places do we today find Wales in her glory of language and tradition. Are we ready to kill her in her last sanctuary?' ('Yn y lleoedd anhygyrch yn unig heddiw y ceir Cymru, yn ei hiaith a'i thraddodiadau, yn ei gogoniant. A ydym yn barod i'w lladd yn ei noddfa olaf?').[91]

Conclusion

According to Gwyn A. Williams:

Wales . . . is a process, a process of continuous and dialectical historical development, in which human mind and human will interact with objective reality. Wales is an artefact

---

[89] Ibid., 128.
[90] Ibid.
[91] Ibid., 129.

which the Welsh produce; the Welsh make and remake Wales day by day and year after year. If they want to.[92]

This chapter has argued that the geographical imagination was a central feature of this remaking, and that part of the process of mobilizing for nationalist ends is the politicization of the cultural heritage through the cultivation of a nation's 'poetic spaces'. But Wales was remade, with its 'poetic spaces' at the core of the process, in both an exclusive and an integrative way. On the one hand, Wales was understood as an expression of an ethnic and linguistic identity and Welshness came to be defined in exclusive terms as 'the rural'. Rural areas located far from the Anglicizing influences of the accessible lowlands harboured both the 'national language' and the 'national character', and so nationalist politics centred on monitoring and defending that cultural integrity. The ultimate aim of this identity-based politics was the realignment of the dispossessed with their cultural heritage through a shift 'back to the land'. Therefore, there existed an integrative form of nationalism based on the assumption of sovereignty over territory. The sense of national unity inevitably led to demands for the control and manipulation of national space. For Plaid Cymru, this meant achieving an economic and, perhaps more importantly, a cultural and psychological unity between the industrial, Anglicized south and the rural, Welsh-speaking north. Clearly, the north–south road had immense potential both in a material and a symbolic sense. Yet, intellectuals like Peate – who had been central in identifying the cultural repository of rural Wales and the dynamics of threats to it – questioned the very project of nation-building and national modernization as the route to cultural unity. For Peate, sovereignty was the key to linguistic and cultural expression.

This debate on cultural integrity, national space and planning was continued in the post-war period. The most notable theoretical expression of it was J. R. Jones's volume *Prydeindod* (1966), in which he focused on the *cydymdreiddiad* (interpenetration) of land and language.[93] According to Jones, when a people feel themselves to be an organic part of its land, this is manifested through language, such as the naming of mountains and vales, rivers and villages – the endowing of land with nationality, history and mythology: 'the people take hold of their land, as it were, and assimilate it into the texture of their lives through the medium of their language. It is as if they see and handle and love their land through the mirror of their language' ('fe welir Pobl megis yn gafaelyd yn eu tir a'i gymhathu i mewn i wead eu bywyd yng nghyfryngwriaeth eu hiaith. Byddant, fel petai, yn gweld a thrafod a charu eu daear yn nrych eu hiaith').[94] In parts of contemporary Wales the interpenetration of land and language remained as a reminder of how

---

[92] Gwyn A. Williams, *The Welsh in their History* (London, 1982), p. 200.
[93] J. R. Jones, *Prydeindod* (Llandybïe, 1966).
[94] Ibid., p. 14.

the Welsh *might still* be a distinct people, but elsewhere Wales was evidently characterized by retreating Welshness and advancing Britishness. All that remained
were the relics of place names. Parts of Wales – Tryweryn and the Gwendraeth
valley – had already been lost, and these were not merely parcels of land but parts
of the very being of the Welsh people. The people were annihilated by having
their foothold on earth sucked into a wider space as part of another nation. Jones
quoted Tillich: 'Being means having space . . . This is the reason for the
tremendous importance of geographical space and the fight for its possession by
power groups. The struggle is not simply the attempt to remove another group
from a given space. The real purpose is to draw this space into a larger power
field, to deprive it of a centre of its own.'[95] The Welsh people – as the drowning
of Tryweryn and the proposals to establish a new town in mid-Wales as a West
Midlands 'overspill' proved – did not have a centre of power to resist the
English/British nation.

David Harvey has suggested that 'appeals to mythologies of place, person and
tradition, to the aesthetic sense, have played a vital role in geopolitical history.'[96]
This is certainly true of the geographical politics which emerged in Wales in the
inter-war period. Given the role of territory in nationalist ideology, it is clear that
a historical and geographical reading of the nation offers an insight into the
dynamism of nationalist movements and into the construction of their political
discourses. There are dangers, however, of generating closed, essentialist readings
of identity. J. R. Jones suggests that 'a People's identity emerges from the
interpenetration of their one *native* land and their one *native* language; that is, their
two-fold *distinctness* is that which makes them that People with a particular name
and history' ('Daw hunaniaeth Pobl, meddaf, o gydymdreiddiad un *priod* dir ag un
briod iaith; hynny yw, eu *gwahanrwydd* deuglwm a bair mai'r Bobl arbennig hynny
ydynt ag iddynt eu henw a'u hanes arbennig').[97] He concedes that there are
positions between possession of a *whole* identity and a total *absence* of identity –
that non-Welsh speakers are *partly* Welsh – but Welsh identity is still seen in a
relatively closed, singular and linguistically-defined way. In an era of increasing
globalization, we need to move towards what Doreen Massey calls a 'progressive
sense of place'.[98] This challenges the idea of places as being composed of, or
reflecting, single, stable, essential identities. It involves, instead, looking at the
multiple identities which are articulated in any one locality, and seeing places as
processes in motion. In addition, places are seen as being characterized by flows
and networks which make the construction of boundaries around them

---

[95] Ibid., p. 15.
[96] David Harvey, 'Between Space and Time: Reflections on the Geographical Imagination', *Annals of the Association of American Geographers*, 80, no. 3 (1990), 430.
[97] Jones, *Prydeindod*, pp. 15–16.
[98] Doreen Massey, 'Power-Geometry and a Progressive Sense of Place' in J. Bird, B. Curtis, T. Putnam, G. Robertson and L. Tickner (eds.), *Mapping the Futures: Local Cultures, Global Change* (London, 1993), pp. 59–69.

superfluous. None of this, however, denies the uniqueness and importance of place, but 'what gives a place its specificity is not some long internalized history but the fact that it is constructed out of a particular constellation of relations, articulated together at a particular locus'.[99] This approach would help us to see the nation in general and Welshness more specifically as fluid, contested and, ultimately, imagined.

---

[99] Ibid., p. 66.

3

Women and the Welsh Language in the Industrial Valleys of South Wales 1914–1945

MARI A. WILLIAMS

In 1927 the Welsh-language column of one of Glamorgan's weekly newspapers published an article by the Revd W. R. Jones (Gwenith Gwyn) on a subject which had already been discussed at length in the Welsh press that year.[1] Following the publication of the Departmental Committee of the Board of Education's weighty report, *Welsh in Education and Life*, one might have assumed that Gwenith Gwyn would wish to contribute to the lively debate which that publication had generated by drawing on his experiences as a Baptist minister in Glamorgan since 1894.[2] His concern, however, focused on only one aspect of the difficult 'language problem', namely the failure of so many Welsh mothers and daughters to support their native language and culture. Since members of the fair sex were, in his opinion, the lifeblood of the Welsh language ('colofn a sylfaen, bywyd a bwyd iaith'), it was extremely distressing for him to see so many of them forsaking their priceless heritage. For Gwenith Gwyn and others like him, the responsibility for maintaining the language in the home, transmitting it to children, and securing its place among future generations, lay squarely with the Welsh female population.

Placing such an enormous responsibility on the shoulders of half the population was clearly totally unrealistic. During the period under consideration Welsh communities in the industrial valleys faced unprecedented social changes that were not easy to withstand. Traditional cultural patterns and customs were transformed by the powerful effects of two world wars and communal stability was destroyed by acute economic depression. Welsh-language aspects of life in the valleys suffered immensely as a result of this dislocation and the English language reigned supreme in the world of education, politics and commerce. Several historians have wrestled with the complex relationship between language and society in industrial south

---

[1] *Barry and District News*, 28 October 1927.
[2] Departmental Committee on Welsh in the Educational System of Wales, *Welsh in Education and Life* (London, 1927).

Wales in an attempt to explain the attitudes of those who turned their back on the Welsh language,[3] but much further research is required on many aspects of the social history of the Welsh language in the region.[4] In view of Gwenith Gwyn's sweeping observations regarding the linguistic role of Welsh women, gaining further insight into their special relationship with the Welsh language during this period is essential. In examining the linguistic and cultural experiences of women, due attention must be given to the use made of the Welsh language in the informal domains of the coalfield society and to the special significance of social affiliations created by women through their oral networks with family and friends.

On the eve of the First World War the English language had already secured a firm grip on both the formal and public domains of daily life in the eastern valleys of Glamorgan. English was the official language of local government and admin-istration, the language associated with business, commerce and economic advancement, and the primary language of the new political force, socialism. The census of 1911 revealed that the vast majority of people living in the urban districts of the Rhondda, Aberdare, Ogmore and Garw were proficient in the English language, and over half the men and women in the lower age groups, particularly in the Ogmore, Garw and Rhondda valleys, were monoglot English speakers. However, the 1911 census also revealed that over half the population of the Rhondda (55 per cent) and Aberdare (64 per cent) could speak Welsh and it must be recognized that the language retained an important role in the daily lives of its speakers.[5] As the opportunities for using the Welsh language became increasingly restricted to informal social domains, the linguistic and cultural role played by the home was heightened. Since only 14.4 per cent of women in the Rhondda were classed as being in full-time employment in 1911, and 76 per cent of women aged between 20 and 40 were married, it is not surprising that the

---

[3] Ieuan Gwynedd Jones, 'Language and Community in Nineteenth Century Wales' in David Smith (ed.), *A People and a Proletariat: Essays in the History of Wales 1780–1980* (London, 1980), pp. 47–71; David Smith, 'The Future of Coalfield History in South Wales', *Morgannwg*, XIX (1975), 57–70; Dai Smith, *Wales! Wales?* (London, 1984), pp. 98–106, 161–2; Sian Rhiannon Williams, 'Iaith y Nefoedd mewn Cymdeithas Ddiwydiannol: Y Gymraeg a Chrefydd yng Ngorllewin Sir Fynwy yn y Bedwaredd Ganrif ar Bymtheg' in Geraint H. Jenkins and J. Beverley Smith (eds.), *Politics and Society in Wales 1840–1922: Essays in Honour of Ieuan Gwynedd Jones* (Cardiff, 1988), pp. 47–60; eadem, *Oes y Byd i'r Iaith Gymraeg: Y Gymraeg yn Ardal Ddiwydiannol Sir Fynwy yn y Bedwaredd Ganrif ar Bymtheg* (Caerdydd, 1992); T. I. Williams, 'Patriots and Citizens. Language, Identity and Education in a Liberal State: The Anglicisation of Pontypridd 1818–1920' (unpubl. University of Wales PhD thesis, 1989); idem, 'Language, Religion and Culture' in Trevor Herbert and Gareth Elwyn Jones (eds.), *Wales, 1880–1914* (Cardiff, 1988), pp. 73–105.

[4] Dyfnallt Morgan, *Y Wlad Sydd Well* (Llanbedr Pont Steffan, 1984); Colin Morgan, review of *Oes y Byd i'r Iaith Gymraeg* by Sian Rhiannon Williams, *WHR*, 17, no. 1 (1994), 130–2; D. Hywel Davies, 'South Wales History which almost Excludes the Welsh', *New Welsh Review*, 26 (1994), 8–13.

[5] Census of England and Wales, 1911, *Vol. XII, Language Spoken in Wales and Monmouthshire* (London, 1913), pp. 27, 31.

responsibility of shouldering the linguistic burden in the home was placed firmly on women.[6]

The importance of the linguistic experiences of women in the industrial valleys, therefore, should not be underestimated, for it was in the home that decisions were made either to foster or abandon the Welsh language. While recognizing that the experience of every family differed greatly, the home had a crucial role to play in the shaping of linguistic attitudes. As the historian Ieuan Gwynedd Jones (b. 1920) has argued:

> my own experience as a child in a heavily anglicized part of Glamorgan in the 1920s – convinces us that this is true . . . at a time when education, even at its best, was for the vast majority of persons but fragmentary and brief in its duration and of doubtful quality, the family was of paramount importance in the education and socialization of the young.[7]

The linguistic experience of every home was evidently determined by many complex factors, including the linguistic and geographical background of its members, the linguistic profile of the community, and the strength of the family's affiliations with Welsh-language networks or institutions. It should be borne in mind that the relatively young valley communities were home to a mixed population and that families of differing cultural backgrounds could be found living next to one another. The scale and nature of the migration into the counties of Glamorgan and Monmouth during the first decade of the twentieth century undoubtedly had a considerable influence on the native language and culture of those industrial communities, particularly since 63 per cent of the migrants who came to Glamorgan between 1901 and 1911 were from England.[8] Many in-migrants came from further afield and over 2,000 foreigners resided in the Rhondda alone in 1911.[9] The multilingual nature of this industrial community was brought to life in B. L. Coombes's account of a miners' gathering in the Neath valley:

> What a mixture of languages and dialects were there sometimes! Yorkshire and Durham men, Londoners, men from the Forest of Dean, North Welshmen – whose language is much deeper and more pure than the others from South Wales – two Australians, four Frenchmen, and several coloured gentlemen.[10]

---

[6] Dot Jones, 'Serfdom and Slavery: Women's Work in Wales, 1890–1930' in Deian R. Hopkin and Gregory S. Kealey (eds.), *Class, Community and the Labour Movement: Wales and Canada, 1850–1930* (Llafur/CCLH, 1989), pp. 86–100.

[7] Ieuan Gwynedd Jones, *Towards a Social History of the Welsh Language* (Aberystwyth, 1994), p. 6.

[8] John Davies, *A History of Wales* (London, 1993), p. 490.

[9] Census of England and Wales, 1911, *Vol. IX, Birthplaces of Persons Enumerated in Administrative Counties, County Boroughs, &tc., and Ages and Occupations of Foreigners* (London, 1913), pp. 258–9, 276–7.

[10] B. L. Coombes, *These Poor Hands: The Autobiography of a Miner Working in South Wales* (London, 1939), p. 88.

Although the majority of in-migrants were males, their families and partners often accompanied them to their places of settlement. In 1911, 12.9 per cent of the female population of the Rhondda were of English extraction, while 34.5 per cent were from other parts of Wales (mostly Cardiganshire and Carmarthenshire). Over half, however, had been born in the Rhondda, a greater proportion than the number of men who were natives of the valley. To the north-east at Aberdare, an area which had experienced earlier industrial development, the stability of the female population was even more pronounced. Only 9.2 per cent of Aberdare's females hailed from England, while 60.9 per cent had been born in the district.[11] This pattern of migration ensured that a greater number of females than males were Welsh speakers. Indeed, in Aberdare 73 per cent of women over the age of 25 were Welsh-speaking in 1911, while 66.3 per cent were returned as Welsh speakers in the Rhondda.[12]

It cannot be denied, however, that the flood of in-migrants during the first decade of the twentieth century had totally transformed the linguistic character of the industrial settlements. Such was the impact upon some communities that the likes of H. Parry Jones, who wrote in 1914, feared for the future of the native tongue and culture:

Yn y rhuthr i'r pyllau glo a'r gweithfeydd, daeth Morgannwg a Mynwy yn grochan y cenhedloedd. Cleddir y wythïen Gymreig o'r golwg ymron o dan haenau tewion o Saeson, Gwyddelod, Ysbaenwyr, Eidalwyr, Negroaid, ac agos bob cenedl dan haul, fel y mae'n anodd ofnadwy i'r Gymraeg gadw'i phen yn y siroedd hynny.[13]

(In the rush to the coal pits and works, Glamorgan and Monmouthshire have become a melting-pot of nationalities. The Welsh seam is buried almost out of sight under thick layers of English, Irish, Spanish, Italians, Negroes and almost every nation under the sun, so that it is very difficult for the Welsh language to keep its head above ground in those counties.)

Reflecting upon his childhood in Dowlais in the 1920s, the writer Dyfnallt Morgan believed that the linguistic and cultural dilution which followed this period of in-migration was inevitable. In his opinion, such a mixture of Welsh speakers, non-Welsh speakers, Irish, English, Jews, Spaniards and others could never possess a common memory nor maintain any kind of tradition ('Pa obaith oedd gan gymysgfa o Gymry Cymraeg, Cymry di-Gymraeg, Gwyddelod, Saeson, Iddewon, Sbaenwyr ac eraill feddu ar gof cyffredinol iddynt oll a thrwy hynny gynnal unrhyw fath ar draddodiad?').[14] Perhaps the descriptions of Rhondda's

---

[11] Census of England and Wales, 1911, *Vol. IX*, pp. 258–9, 276–7.

[12] Ibid., *Vol. XII*, pp. 27, 31.

[13] H. Parry Jones, 'Y Gymraeg a'r Ugeinfed Ganrif', *Y Beirniad*, IV, no. 3 (1914), 166–7.

[14] Morgan, *Y Wlad Sydd Well*, p. 11.

environs in the 1920s as 'hotch-potch' communities, where 'foreigners' lived almost every second door from the native 'Brython', were not far removed from the truth.[15] It would not be an exaggeration to claim that by the mid-1920s the Welsh language was under siege in the eastern valleys of Glamorgan as social, economic and political forces increasingly favoured the English language. It soon became apparent that the Welsh language needed to strengthen its hold on existing social networks and institutions, and it was on their homes that many Welsh speakers in the valleys focused their attention.

Many communities in these industrial districts were relatively young settlements and the majority of their Welsh-speaking residents were descendants of the first wave of in-migrants from rural Wales. However, as one Welsh-language columnist made clear in 1916, irrespective of their dominantly Welsh-speaking backgrounds, the task of maintaining the Welshness of the home in this urban and industrial society was immensely difficult for many families:

Ond wele chwi yn ceisio codi plant yng Nghwm y Rhondda, lle y mae amgylchedd eich teulu mor wahanol ag y gallai fod i amgylchedd eich plentyndod, ac mewn oes sydd mor wahanol i'r oes o'r blaen ag y bu unrhyw oes i'w blaenorydd. Yr ydych yn byw ymhlith pobl o bob math, wedi ymdyrru at eu gilydd o bob rhan o'r byd. Yn yr un ystryd a chwi triga rhai o ddynion goreu a gwaethaf Cymru a Lloegr, a rhai o wehilion yr Ysbaen a'r Eidal. Y mae papurau Northcliffe a Bottomley yn gwthio eu hunain i'r aelwydydd, ac yn bygwth gyrru allan y Beibl a chylchgronau Cymru. Ymladda cyfarfodydd yr eglwys, yr eisteddfod a'r gyngherdd am eu bodolaeth gyda'r chwaraedy, y rhedegfeydd ceffylau a'r sinema.[16]

(Here you are trying to raise your children in the Rhondda Valley, where your family's environment is as different as could be from your childhood environment, and in an age which is as different from the previous age as any age could be from its predecessor. You live among people of all sorts, thrown together from every part of the world. In the same street as you live some of the best and worst men from England and Wales, and some of the dregs of Spain and Italy. Northcliffe and Bottomley's newspapers force themselves into the homes and threaten to drive out the Bible and Welsh journals. Church meetings, the eisteddfod and the concert fight for their existence against the playhouse, horse-races and the cinema.)

Many families succeeded in maintaining their Welsh-language affiliations by regularly visiting their relations in the predominantly Welsh-speaking rural areas. For many children living in the valleys, such connections proved an important link which gave them a transfusion of Welshness and enhanced their attachment

---

[15] D. J. Saer, F. Smith and J. Hughes, *The Bilingual Problem: A Study Based Upon Experiments and Observations in Wales* (Wrexham, 1924), p. 90; 'Bedford', 'Iaith a Chenedlaetholdeb', *Y Geninen*, XLIII, no. 3 (1925), 155.

[16] 'Yr Atwebyd', 'At fy Nghydwladwyr: Llythyr II', *Y Darian*, 15 June 1916.

to the Welsh language and culture. Dyfnallt Morgan was indebted to his regular visits to Llanddewibrefi in Cardiganshire for the opportunity to practise and 'strengthen' his knowledge of the Welsh language.[17] Communication through the medium of Welsh was essential in order to socialize with cousins who were not always fluent in English, while in the presence of older members of the family this was even more necessary. Indeed, those who ventured to greet their elderly relatives in English were often scolded for their insolent behaviour.[18] For the writer Glyn Jones (1905–95), who was brought up amid the vibrant 'ethnic mix' of Merthyr Tydfil, the close family connection with a Welsh-speaking aunt proved of great importance and 'it was she who was perhaps the strongest link between me and the Welsh language when I was a boy'.[19]

In homes where Welsh-language networks were comparatively strong and where there were opportunities to hear and speak the language on a daily basis, there was some hope that Welsh could be kept alive among children. But linguistic continuity could not be guaranteed in a multicultural society where individuals of many different backgrounds came into daily contact with one another. It would appear that 'mixed marriages' between Welsh speakers and non-Welsh speakers were becoming increasingly common in the industrial communities of south Wales and it was inevitable that if the English language came to be used daily by parents it would establish itself as the main language of the home and the children. Since no detailed information is available in censuses, however, it is extremely difficult to know exactly how many marriages of this kind occurred, let alone ascertain which language was spoken in their homes. The marriage registers of three Welsh Nonconformist causes in the Rhondda reveal that marriages between chapel members and people from outside the Rhondda area were extremely rare, and although it is not known what language was spoken in the homes of couples who married in local Welsh chapels it may be inferred that linguistically-mixed marriages were not common, at least among members of Welsh chapels.[20] The evidence of many contemporary commentators, however, suggests that the 'mixed marriage' was one of the greatest scourges in Welsh society, since it was the Welsh language which lost its place, almost without exception, in the homes of such couples.[21] It was alleged that 'mongrel' marriages

---

[17] Dyfnallt Morgan, ' ". . . Deigryn am a fu": Atgofion am Ddowlais 1917–1935', *Taliesin*, 71 (1990), 41–8.

[18] Museum of Welsh Life [MWL], tape 7537, evidence of female from Ogmore Vale (b. 1921); South Wales Miners' Library [SWML], tape 115, evidence of male from Bedlinog (b. 1915).

[19] Glyn Jones, 'The Making of a Poet – Part I', *Planet*, 112 (1995), 72.

[20] NLW, CM Archives O25/1–2. Marriage Registers of Jerusalem, Tonpentre, 1913–32, 1935–45; O27/1 Marriage Register of Bethesda, Blaenrhondda, 1912–47; O29/1 Marriage Register of Horeb, Treherbert, 1908–48.

[21] L. F. Taylor, 'Welsh *v.* English: The Position in Industrial South Wales as Revealed by the Census of 1911', *Wales*, V, no. 3 (1914), 161–3; Departmental Committee on Welsh in the Educational System of Wales, *Welsh in Education and Life*, p. 301.

were 'weakening Wales' because the non-Welsh-speaking partner, 'whether man or wife, father or mother, possessed little love or affection for Welsh ideals' ('Gwyddom . . . trwy brofiad fod priodasau cymysg yn andwyol i wladgarwch a datblygiad cenedlaethol Cymru, gan nad oes gan yr estron, bydded ŵr neu wraig, tad neu fam, nemawr o honynt serch ac atdyniad at ddelfrydau Cymreig').[22] It cannot be conclusively proven, however, that such marriages were any more detrimental to the Welsh language than marriages between Welsh speakers who were apathetic towards the language. Even so, one contemporary commentator, who gave vent to his frustrations in 1932, clearly believed that the 'mixed marriage' was responsible for polluting the native tongue in the industrial valleys. The bastardized tongue which he heard spoken by children along the length of the two Rhondda valleys reduced him to tears.[23]

In discussing the failings of the 'mixed marriage', commentators agreed that there was some glimmer of hope that the Welsh language could be transmitted to the children if their mother was a Welsh speaker. Ultimately, it was believed that the mother's linguistic ability would have the greatest bearing upon the language of her children.[24] Since married women in the industrial districts were denied access and opportunities to undertake full-time employment and therefore spent a great part of their day occupied with domestic chores, it is likely that there was an element of truth in this claim. Evidence presented to the Board of Education's departmental inquiry in 1927 confirms this view:

> The key to the whole situation lies with the *mothers* of Wales. As one of our witnesses wrote:- 'The trouble and its cure lie with the *mothers* of Wales, for be the fathers as patriotic as they may, it is the mothers who are always at home with the children, and who have the most influence over them during the most plastic years of their lives.'[25]

The writer, Robert Morgan, who was brought up at Penrhiw-ceibr in the 1920s, noted that since his mother could not speak Welsh the only language heard on the hearth was English: 'At home my father spoke in English, for my mother was not Welsh speaking, consequently my sisters and I grew up with only a smattering of the language.'[26] The mother's role was clearly crucial in the early education of her

---

[22] *Y Darian*, 21 June 1923, 31 December 1931.

[23] Ibid., 7 January 1932.

[24] NLW MS 9356E. Memorandum no. 82, evidence presented by the Presbyterian Church of Wales before the Departmental Committee of the Board of Education; William Jones, 'Dylanwad ac Addysg Mam', *Y Drysorfa*, LXXX, no. 959 (1910), 412–14; D. Miall Edwards, *Iaith a Diwylliant Cenedl* (Dolgellau, 1927), p. 67.

[25] Departmental Committee on Welsh in the Educational System of Wales, *Welsh in Education and Life*, p. 305. See also NLW MS 9354E. Memorandum no. 35, evidence presented by Mrs J. E. Evans, Swansea (a teacher at Palmerston Road Infants' School, Barry), before the Departmental Committee of the Board of Education, 10 October 1925.

[26] Robert Morgan, *My Lamp Still Burns* (Llandysul, 1981), p. 20.

child and doubtless there was considerable truth in the claim that she was the child's 'most important teacher' and the one who 'determined his language'.[27] There was a deeper significance, therefore, to the teasing poem by Thomas Jacob Thomas (Sarnicol), 'Iaith fy Mam' (My Mother's Tongue), published in 1935:

> 'Cymraeg yw'ch iaith chwi, ond, Dadi, pam
> 'Rych chwi yn ei galw yn Iaith fy Mam?'
> 'Am fod dy fam, mae'n debyg, Johnny,
> Yn siarad llawer mwy ohoni.'[28]

('Your language is Welsh, Daddy, but why / Do you call it my Mother Tongue?'/ 'Probably, Johnny, because your mother / Speaks a great deal more of it.')

In some instances, the efforts of the Welsh-speaking mother to transmit her native tongue to the children against the will of her partner could lead to conflict. A woman from Clydach Vale found herself in the local police court in 1917 appealing for a maintenance order against her estranged Irish Catholic husband. He had deserted her some years previously, claiming that she had broken their marriage contract by insisting on speaking Welsh to their son, giving him Welsh books to read, and raising him in a Welsh Nonconformist chapel.[29] This was evidently an extraordinary and exceptional case, and it is difficult to believe that many women would be willing to sacrifice their marriage for the sake of the Welsh language. However, some of the staunchest supporters of the language believed that women should make a stand to ensure the place of Welsh in their homes. Placing such emphasis upon the woman's role in the complex process of language transmission fuelled the argument for protecting the sacred role of women in the home as mothers and wives. In their spirited campaigns to win over the linguistic allegiance of Welsh mothers, Welsh societies and writers in Welsh-language newspaper columns drew particular attention to this point. 'Eluned', who wrote in the Aberdare-based *Tarian y Gweithiwr* in 1914, deplored the fact that Welsh women seemed to be more concerned about winning the vote than winning their children's support for the Welsh language. She hoped to see a company of Welsh suffragettes join together, 'not to win the vote and the right to go to Parliament to talk nonsense, but to demand that every Welsh woman brought her children up to speak Welsh' ('Gresyn na chodai cwmni o "suffragettes" yng Nghymru [*sic*], nid i hawlio'r "vote" a chael myned i St Stephan i siarad ynfydrwydd, ond i hawlio fod pob Cymraes i siarad Cymraeg a'i

---

[27] Remarks made by the Revd R. J. Jones at the St David's day dinner of the Aberdare Cymrodorion Society, *Tarian y Gweithiwr*, 12 March 1914; and the columnist, 'Yr Atwebyd', *Y Darian*, 30 November 1916.

[28] Thomas Jacob Thomas (Sarnicol), 'Iaith fy Mam', *Blodau Drain Duon* (Llandysul, 1935), p. 35.

[29] *Rhondda Leader*, 17 February 1917.

phlentyn').[30] Such demands came from a certain section of society, and were voiced mainly in the Welsh-language columns of local newspapers and in the pages of Welsh denominational and literary journals. It was no accident, therefore, that during the early 1930s several editors of these Welsh columns published a poem by the late R. J. Derfel (1824–1905), 'Magwch Blant i Gymru' (Raise Children for Wales), doubtless in the hope that its message would prick the conscience of its readers.[31] The 'appeal to mothers' was a recurring theme in the literature of the inter-war period, as the rallying cry in the poem of the collier, Walter Morgan (Murmurydd), of Gelli, Rhondda, made clear:

> Famau Cymru, ymwrolwch
> Dewch ymaflwch yn y llyw
> Dewch o ddifrif ymegnïwch
> Os am gadw'r iaith yn fyw;
> Famau, rhowch yng ngenau'r plentyn
> Y Gymraeg – iaith ore'r byd,
> Dewch lledaenwch ein hiaith ddillyn
> O! parablwch hi o hyd.[32]

(Mothers of Wales, strive / Come, take charge at the helm / Come, make an earnest effort / To keep the language alive / Mothers, in your child's mouth / Place the Welsh language – the finest in the world / Come popularize our precious tongue / Oh! converse in Welsh at all times.)

It was the mothers, therefore, who were held responsible for the decline of the Welsh language in the homes of the industrial valleys. The Revd T. Eli Evans of Aberdare declared emphatically during a St David's day dinner, organized by the local Cymrodorion Society, that the Anglicized nature of the town could be attributed to the mothers and not the fathers of Aberdare.[33] In 1927 another Nonconformist minister went so far as to claim that if the Welsh language died, members of the female population would be held directly responsible for its demise ('os marw a wna'r Gymraeg bydd ei gwaed ar ben y rhywdeg').[34] Such notions had also been advocated in earlier decades by Welsh language supporters who had blamed women for the linguistic failings of their children. It was claimed that women not only surrendered too readily to the English language in the home but also had the audacity to make deliberate attempts to teach English to their

---

[30] *Tarian y Gweithiwr*, 21 May 1914.
[31] See *Glamorgan Free Press and Rhondda Leader*, 26 August 1933; *Aberdare Leader*, 26 August 1933.
[32] *Y Darian*, 24 February 1927.
[33] *Tarian y Gweithiwr*, 12 March 1914.
[34] NLW, Gwenith Gwyn Papers A/4.

children.[35] Writing in 1932, one commentator decried the efforts of Welsh-speaking mothers who inflicted their poor English on their children ('Ac onid yw yn drueni clywed mamau Cymru yn gwastraffu eu Saesneg gwael ac yn Cymreigyddio eu Saesneg am na allant wneuthur yn well').[36] As the columnist 'Yr Atwebyd' noted in his provocative column to his 'Fellow Countrymen': 'those who speak the poorest English are the children who are taught clumsy English by mothers who could teach them to speak good Welsh . . . and – gracious – what English' ('y plant sydd yn siarad y Saesneg waethaf yw'r plant a ddysgant Saesneg carbwl oddiwrth famau allent ddysgu Cymraeg da iddynt . . . ac – o'r arswyd – y fath Saesneg').[37] Delegates who assembled at a district meeting of the Baptists held at Bridgend in 1928 were treated to the following example of the corrupt English spoken by many mothers in their homes: 'I know it's my umbrella by its leg.'[38]

It is hard to exaggerate the effect of socio-economic pressures on the linguistic choices of Welsh mothers. It is fairly certain that many mothers spoke English to their children because they believed that it was the language which would be of greatest benefit to them in the future. This was certainly the opinion of Lewis Morgan of Cymer, who believed that many Welsh families in the Rhondda were neglecting their mother tongue because English was respectable and the key to high society ('Esgeulusir yr iaith hefyd mewn cartrefi eraill o dan y dybiaeth mai Saesneg sy'n rispectabl ac yn allwedd i gymdeithas y bobl fawr').[39] The secretary of a Welsh chapel in Pontypridd noted in 1925 that many parents who attended the chapel believed that they were degrading themselves by speaking the Welsh language ('Gwreiddyn y mater yn ddiddadl yw balchder y rhieni yn barod i gredu eu bod yn iselhau eu hunain wrth siarad yr Iaith Gymraeg').[40] Although working-class mothers were generally pilloried for such 'treasonable' acts, members of the Welsh establishment themselves were criticized for their hypocrisy in this context. It was alleged that the 'professional patriots' who publicly denounced apathetic Welsh speakers were among the worst for disregarding the language in the privacy of their own homes.[41] In 1921 the editor of the *Rhondda Leader* urged Welsh societies to 'purge' their organizations of such 'undesirable elements' as:

[35] Williams, *Oes y Byd i'r Iaith Gymraeg*, p. 17; Dan Isaac Davies, *1785, 1885, 1985, neu Tair Miliwn o Gymry Dwy-ieithawg mewn Can Mlynedd* (Dinbych, 1886), p. 22; Owen Morgan (Morien), *History of Pontypridd and Rhondda Valleys* (Pontypridd, 1903), p. 9.

[36] E. J. Jones, *Eneideg Cenedl a Phwnc yr Iaith Gymraeg* (Caerdydd, 1932), p. 9.

[37] 'Yr Atwebyd', 'At Fy Nghydwladwyr', *Y Darian*, 30 November 1916.

[38] A remark made by S. Griffiths, Bridgend, before a meeting of the Bridgend and District Baptists, *Y Darian*, 8 March 1928.

[39] Taken from Lewis Morgan's address entitled 'Adfer y Gymraeg' (Reviving the Welsh Language), delivered before the Porth and District Welsh Society in 1926, *Y Darian*, 23 May 1929.

[40] NLW, CM Archives C2/23. Questionnaire returns concerning the use of the Welsh language in the chapels of the Presbytery of East Glamorgan, evidence of T. J. Perrott, Secretary of Soar, Hopkinstown, 15 October 1925.

[41] *Y Darian*, 4 August 1921.

the schoolmaster who bans Welsh in his own school, the minister who has neglected to bring up his own children in the knowledge of the mother tongue, the tradesman who persists in conducting his business in English, and the snobs of the Welsh churches who speak the alien tongue as soon as they are out of the chapel.[42]

Writing in 1913, the Welsh-language columnist of the *Rhondda Socialist* noted that it was not surprising that the language was rapidly losing ground and respect in the district in view of the fact that a significant number of those individuals who publicly lamented the loss of the native tongue spoke English to their children at home ('Cwynir fod y Gymraeg yn colli tir yn y Rhondda, a llawer o'r bobl hyny a wylant ddagrau hidl am golli'r famiaith yn siarad Saesneg efo'u plant ar yr aelwyd').[43]

In view of the changing nature of Welsh family and social life, it was inevitable that social attitudes formed by new experiences outside the home would greatly influence linguistic attitudes on the hearth. Powerful social and cultural changes were already afoot before the outbreak of the First World War and several preachers voiced their concern over the possible effects upon the traditional role of the home.[44] In 1920 D. Miall Edwards, Professor of Theology at the Memorial College in Brecon, declared that the traditional role of the home as a combination of school, eisteddfod, senate and church had been completely undermined by recent social developments. In his opinion, if the traditional culture of the hearth was to be revived, it was of critical importance that the social status of the home be reaffirmed.[45] It was extremely difficult, however, to withstand the socio-linguistic impact of improved transport and communications. Patterns of mobility were transformed by the revolution in public transport and the emergence of local bus companies and the motor car. Furthermore, it was no longer necessary to leave the comfort of one's home to experience new and foreign sounds and environments since the world of broadcasting and publishing penetrated deeply into Welsh homes. To women who spent a great deal of their time in their homes, the arrival of the radio-set or wireless in 1922 was a highly significant development.[46] Indeed, in his advertising campaign in 1923, a radio salesman from Pontypridd was quick to point out that this new device was 'the greatest boon to all housewives'.[47] Many Welsh language protagonists were clearly

---

[42] *Rhondda Leader*, 13 January 1921.

[43] *Rhondda Socialist*, 15 March 1913.

[44] See, for example, R. G. R. [R. Gwylfa Roberts], 'Cerrig Llam: Yr Aelwyd Gymreig', *Y Dysgedydd*, 93 (1914), 127–33; D. Price, 'Lle'r Cartref ym Mywyd y Genedl', *Seren Gomer*, VI, no. 3 (1914), 113–21; T. Mason, 'Dylanwad yr Aelwyd', *Glamorgan Free Press*, 11 January 1917.

[45] D. Miall Edwards, 'Y Rhagolwg Newydd yng Nghymru', *Y Beirniad*, VIII, no. 4 (1920), 236.

[46] NLW, Jack Jones MSS 146. 'Report on a Survey of the Social Effects of the Coming of Broadcasting in South Wales for the BBC, 1938.'

[47] *Rhondda Gazette*, 13 October 1923.

dismayed to discover that so many Welsh speakers were buying wireless sets, thereby transforming the Welsh character and atmosphere of their homes. Commenting upon such changes, one observer noted that many homes, where previously only Welsh was heard, now resounded to the sound of jazz music.[48] By 1937 Eluned Bebb, writing in the Welsh-language monthly *Yr Efrydydd*, believed that the situation in many Welsh households had degenerated beyond belief and betokened a bleak future for the Welsh language and culture. She maintained that the cultural life of the majority of Welsh households was simply a pale replica of an alien tradition, and that 'true' Welsh homes where not a word of English was heard had become a rare feature ('Un o wendidau mwyaf Cymru heddiw yw'r bywyd yn ei chartrefi. Nid ydyw namyn drych egwan o fywyd estron. Mor brin yw'r aelwydydd gwirioneddol Gymreig, lle na chlywir gair o Saesneg').[49]

Many other social factors were also responsible for weakening the cultural influence of the Welsh home. Murmurydd believed that poor housing conditions in the Rhondda had a direct bearing upon the future of the traditional Welsh home, forcing its inhabitants to 'pollute' their minds in vacuous playhouses and in the unhealthy atmosphere of the cinemas.[50] Certainly, poor living conditions drove many women and young girls to seek comfort and entertainment elsewhere.[51] It was not surprising, therefore, that females were deemed to be the staunchest supporters of the cinema during the years of the depression.[52] For miners' wives like Meri Williams, a character in a short story by D. Jacob Davies, one of the greatest pleasures in life was her weekly trip to the cinema, where she could relax, immerse herself in the film and blot out the harsh realities of daily life.[53] Powerful American images portrayed on Welsh cinema screens clearly held a great attraction for audiences. Writing in 1924, Dorothy Roberts maintained that the cinema had undermined the *seiat* as an influential social force, an opinion echoed by Walter Haydn Davies in 1933.[54]

It would appear, therefore, that there were grounds for concern regarding the effects of new entertainment centres upon the native Welsh culture. It was no

---

[48] T. Davies, 'Dylanwad Estronol ym Mywyd y Cymro Heddiw', *Y Tyst*, 28 May 1931. Note also the comments of 'Welsh people in Glamorgan (Cardiff especially)' in 1930, regarding the effects of English-language broadcasting: 'Our children hear enough in the streets, and in the schools, but they never heard anything but Welsh on the hearth; now with the wireless English has invaded our very Hearth.' NLW, Thomas Jones Papers, Class H, vol. 18, no. 25, 18 February 1930.

[49] Eluned Bebb, 'Ni Ellir Cenedl Heb y Cartrefi', *Yr Efrydydd*, II, no. 3 (1937), 38.

[50] *Glamorgan Free Press*, 17 April 1919.

[51] *Rhondda Leader*, 2 September 1920; Madeline Rooff, *Youth and Leisure: A Survey of Girls' Organisations in England and Wales* (Edinburgh, 1935), p. 85.

[52] *Y Darian*, 18 February 1932.

[53] D. Jacob Davies, 'Ar Goll', *Y Dyddiau Main: Cyfrol o Storïau* (Llandybïe, 1967), pp. 16–28.

[54] Dorothy E. Roberts, *Oriau Hamdden ac Adloniant* (Wrecsam, 1924), p. 2; Walter Haydn Davies, 'The Influence of Recent Changes in the Social Environment on the Outlook and Habits of Individuals, with Special Reference to Mining Communities in South Wales' (unpubl. University of Wales MA thesis, 1933), p. 67.

easy task, however, to persuade the vast majority of the population of the long-term linguistic implications of their new social and cultural affiliations. In the Rhondda in 1918 the Nonconformist establishment called upon mothers to use their influence in the home to quash what it regarded as new and undesirable social habits.[55] However, as 'Llais Llafur', a correspondent who supported the campaign to open licensed halls on Sundays, pointed out, those critics who enjoyed a life of plenty could never truly appreciate the misery experienced by many working-class families in the Rhondda, nor fully realize the irrelevance of their appeal to the mothers of the district.[56] The editorial of the *Rhondda Leader* in 1920 also stressed that unless 'wholesome clubs' were provided to cater for the needs of its female population as well as its males, Rhondda women could not be blamed for seeking entertainment in picture houses and dance halls: 'It is useless to expect the churches to provide wholesome amusement, where young people can meet each other without being bored to viciousness by goody-goody methods.'[57]

For many ordinary mothers, making ends meet was a heavy enough burden without the added responsibility of fretting about 'declining' social and cultural standards. Because of lack of money, many already shared their homes with others, either by offering rooms to lodgers or by sub-letting part of their house to other families. Since they shared the same home, it was inevitable that the language and customs of other residents would affect the daily lives of others in the house, and under such circumstances it was extremely difficult to escape the influence of non-Welsh-speaking lodgers.[58] As Rhobet Esmor, a character in Rhydwen Williams's autobiographical novel, *Y Siôl Wen*, discovered, the presence of English-speaking lodgers in his home undermined its distinctive Welsh character. Indeed, he was not sure whether his mother had invited 'an alien into the home to pollute its Welsh-speaking environment and threaten the position of the language' ('nid oedd yn rhy siŵr . . . ai ryw fath o elyn estronol a gyraeddasai i wenwyno awyrgylch yr aelwyd a sarhau iaith yr aelwyd a pheryglu bywyd yr aelwyd').[59] Ironically, Rhobet Esmor himself, through his friendship with the lodger, Will Kingston, eventually forsook his 'foolish Welsh' and insisted on conversing in English with his mother.[60]

Indeed, the pressure to change the language of the home invariably came from the children as they attempted to 'simplify and unify their mental lives by insisting

---

[55] See the address given by H. H. Evans, Cilfynydd, President of the East Glamorgan Baptists' Union before the Union's Annual Conference at Pontypridd, *Glamorgan Free Press*, 11 July 1918. Similarly, the Revd Rowland Hughes, Congregational minister at Tylorstown, suggested that local mothers should be consulted before any decision was made regarding the Sunday opening of licensed halls. *Y Darian*, 11 May 1916.

[56] *Y Darian*, 11 May 1916.

[57] *Rhondda Leader*, 2 September 1920.

[58] NLW MS 9356E. Memorandum no. 82, p. 19.

[59] Rhydwen Williams, *Y Siôl Wen* (Llandybïe, 1970), p. 132.

[60] Ibid., p. 139.

at all times on using one language only'.[61] In a period when children spent the best part of their day outside the confines of the home, often in the company of friends from non-Welsh-speaking backgrounds, there was a great danger, as a study in 1924 confirmed, that the English language would 'invade the Welsh-speaking home'.[62] During the same year, Rhys Elias, Director of Education for Merthyr Tydfil, declared that the influence of the home on the language of the child 'frequently falls short of becoming the determining influence on account of the language of play'.[63] A witness who gave evidence before the Departmental Committee of the Board of Education during the same period maintained that 'to the child . . . his playmate can be a more important linguistic factor than his parents, his minister and his schoolmaster combined'.[64] Among children, in particular, the desire to conform was strong and the fear of being considered different prompted some of them to deny knowledge of Welsh.[65] The headmaster of Blaenrhondda school noted in 1919 how 'the pupils of Fernhill – when on their own "pitch" on the hillside – invariably spoke Welsh', but spoke English in the precincts of the school when they mixed with other pupils.[66] Under such circumstances, parents could do very little to resist the linguistic shift, for even their own children insisted upon answering them in English. A native of Blaen-llechau, who was born in 1928, believed that the conflict between the language of the home and that of school and play had eventually led his parents to abandon the use of Welsh in the home.[67] The situation led to discord within many Welsh homes as children refused to respond to their parents' Welsh commands.[68] In such divided households it was inevitable that parents and their children would become linguistically 'estranged' from one another, and that the mother tongue would become no more than a language in which parents shared secrets.[69]

---

[61] Departmental Committee on Welsh in the Educational System of Wales, *Welsh in Education and Life*, p. 301.

[62] Saer, Smith and Hughes, *The Bilingual Problem*, p. 44.

[63] Merthyr Tydfil Education Committee, *Director's Report on the Teaching of Welsh* (Merthyr Tydfil, 1924), p. 3.

[64] Departmental Committee on Welsh in the Educational System of Wales, *Welsh in Education and Life*, p. 301.

[65] MWL, tape 7019, evidence of a female from Llwynypia (b. 1904).

[66] NLW MS 9354E. Memorandum no. 36, report by O. Jones Owen, headmaster of Blaenrhondda School, before the Departmental Committee of the Board of Education, 16 October 1925.

[67] Evidence of Elfed Evans (b. 1928) in Dei Treanor et al. (eds.), *Green, Black and Back: The Story of Blaenllechau* (Treorchy, 1994), p. 57.

[68] SWML, tape 83, evidence of a female from Maerdy, and tape 148, evidence of a female from Seven Sisters (b. 1921); evidence of Gwyneth Fricker in Mark Davies (ed.), *The Valleys' Autobiography: A People's History of the Garw, Llynfi and Ogmore Valleys* (Bridgend, 1992), p. 59; Morgan, *My Lamp Still Burns*, pp. 20–1.

[69] See Jones, 'Y Gymraeg a'r Ugeinfed Ganrif', and the report of an address delivered by Megfam before the Annual Conference of the East Glamorgan and Monmouthshire Section of the National Union of Welsh Societies at Porth, 30 April 1921. *Y Darian*, 5 May 1921.

There was no doubt in the minds of many commentators that the education system was culpable in this process and that the Anglicized schools of the valleys were chiefly responsible for polluting the children's language. The schools of the Rhondda were severely criticized in 1915 in an address delivered before the Porth Welsh Society, during which it was claimed that they had opened a 'flood-gate' of Englishness which threatened to drown the beneficial influences of the home.[70] This accusation was seconded by a columnist in *Y Darian*, who believed that the child's first day in school was a fateful one, since it was at that point that the anxieties of the mother for her Welsh-speaking child began.[71] In a letter to the Director of Education of Merthyr Tydfil in 1924 the Revd Fred Jones, Treorci, claimed that local Welsh-speaking parents were heartbroken within six weeks of sending their eldest child to school.[72] The chapels, too, voiced concern about the detrimental influence of schools on the linguistic ability of their younger members. In 1925 the secretary of the Welsh Calvinistic Methodist chapel at Tonyrefail pointed out that many of its members experienced great difficulty in keeping their children Welsh-speaking once they had begun their education at local schools.[73] It would appear, however, that chapel officials and language supporters were only too aware of the fact that the main problem lay within the home itself, for it was the apathy of parents more than anything else which occasioned the language shift which occurred in so many Welsh homes in the valleys.

The many surveys conducted by local education authorities within schools showed clearly that, in spite of the parents' ability to speak Welsh, a steady decline in the number of Welsh-speaking pupils was under way. A survey carried out by the Pontypridd Education Committee in 1911 found that only 5 per cent of children in the schools of the authority spoke Welsh at home with their parents, while a panel of schools' inspectors from Mountain Ash noted in 1914 that Welsh was already a 'foreign language' among a very large proportion of the children in attendance at local schools.[74] A report prepared in 1915 by the East Glamorgan Baptists' Council noted that ignorance of the Welsh language among the younger generation was also creating problems in many of its Welsh chapels. It was revealed that 86 per cent of its chapels in the Rhondda, 82 per cent in Pontypridd, 73 per cent in Rhymney and 70 per cent in the Merthyr Tydfil district were experiencing difficulties because of their members' ignorance of the Welsh language.[75] Constant requests by chapel officials for greater support from the

---

[70] *Y Darian*, 9 December 1915.
[71] Ibid., 9 March 1916.
[72] Ibid., 10 April 1924.
[73] NLW, CM Archives C2/23. Evidence of David Adam, secretary of Capel y Ton, Tonyrefail, 31 August 1925.
[74] *Pontypridd Observer*, 20 June 1914; *Aberdare Leader*, 21 February 1914.
[75] Cymanfa Ddwyreiniol Bedyddwyr Morgannwg, *Cwestiwn yr Iaith Gymraeg, sef Ymchwil yn Egluro Dwys Gyfyngder y Cyfnod parthed Anwybodaeth y Plant a'n Hieuenctid o'r Iaith Gymraeg, yn bennaf yn eu Perthynas a'r Gwasanaeth Crefyddol* (Aberdâr, 1915), p. 14.

parents fell on deaf ears. Although many parents continued to send their children to the Welsh chapel services and Sunday schools, the inability of the younger members to comprehend the proceedings boded ill for the future.[76] It was claimed in 1921 that preachers in Glamorgan's Welsh chapels and churches were forced to deliver sermons 'in hotch-potch, half Welsh, half English – neither fish, flesh nor fowl – but a wretched mixture of both languages'.[77] Indeed, the poet and theologian John Jenkins (Gwili) was informed that a Welsh service was like a sermon in Greek to hundreds of youngsters living in the Rhondda in the early 1920s.[78] The parents of such children were chastized by members of the Welsh societies and D. Arthen Evans, secretary of Undeb Cenedlaethol y Cymdeithasau Cymraeg (the National Union of Welsh Societies), poured scorn on those who raised their children as 'foreigners in their own homes' and expected the chapels to compensate for their own linguistic deficiencies.[79]

It is extremely difficult to explain why the Welsh language was abandoned in so many homes. Evidently, many parents felt they could no longer struggle against the powerful forces of an Anglicizing society. The belief that the 'complete cleavage' between the languages of the home and school could lead to 'deleterious "interferences" in the young mind' was strong.[80] A columnist in the Welsh Nationalist Party's monthly, *Y Ddraig Goch*, admitted in 1929 that the desire to maintain continuity between the life of the hearth and of the wider community persuaded many Welsh parents to use English in their homes.[81] Small wonder that so many local councils and education authorities believed that expanding Welsh-language teaching provision in their schools was futile when many parents showed so little support for the language in their own homes.[82] An Aberdare headmistress, who had been criticized for her 'scornful' attitude towards the Welsh language in 1922, was quick to lay the blame on mothers at home.[83] Although individuals such as O. Jones Owen, headmaster of Blaenrhondda school, endeavoured to

---

[76] See *Y Tyst*, 27 October 1915; NLW, CM Archives C2/23. Evidence of D. R. Morgan, Secretary of Bethania, Llwynypia, 15 September 1925; *Adroddiad Capel y Bedyddwyr, Tabernacl, Pontypridd am y flwyddyn 1925* (Pontypridd, 1926), p. 4; *Adroddiad Capel y Tabernacl MC, Abercynon am y flwyddyn 1927* (Abercynon, 1928), p. 2.

[77] *Rhondda Leader*, 20 October 1921.

[78] John Jenkins (Gwili), 'Y Gymraeg yn ei Pherthynas ag Addysg ac â Chrefydd Heddyw', *Y Geninen*, XXXVIII, no. 3 (1920), 143.

[79] D. Arthen Evans, 'Cymry Heddyw', ibid., XLI, no. 5 (1923), 268. See also Caleb Rees, 'Dysgu'r Gymraeg yn yr Ysgolion', *Y Beirniad*, I, no. 4 (1911), 225–40; D. Tecwyn Evans, 'Yr Iaith Gymraeg a Chrefydd Cymru', *Y Geninen*, XLII, no. 1 (1924), 17–23.

[80] NLW MS 9356E. Memorandum no. 105, evidence presented by D. T. Davies, His Majesty's Assistant Inspector of Schools, before the Departmental Committee of the Board of Education.

[81] Daisy Harker, 'Ymuno â'r Blaid Genedlaethol – Sut yr Edrych Merch ar y Mater', *Y Ddraig Goch*, 3, no. 9 (1929), 7.

[82] *Glamorgan Free Press*, 20 April 1916; NLW MSS 9353E and 9355E. Memoranda nos. 12 and 62, evidence presented by the National Union of Teachers and Aberdare Education Authority before the Departmental Committee of the Board of Education.

[83] *Y Darian*, 30 March 1922.

convince parents of the potential value of the Welsh language for their children's future, it was clear that changing the attitude of the majority was practically impossible.[84] Indeed, some parents who had already abandoned the language in their homes were resentful of the fact that many education authorities in the valleys had developed schemes to increase the provision of Welsh-medium education.[85] According to J. Vyrnwy Morgan, many parents believed they could give their children adequate instruction through the medium of Welsh in the home and that the main duty of the school was to provide instruction through the medium of the commercial, competitive and truly useful language of English.[86] This was a commonly held view among parents bent on giving their children every opportunity to secure employment or pursue a career.[87] In the opinion of Herbert Morgan, a minister and lecturer raised in the Rhondda, a combination of social and economic forces lay at the heart of the linguistic priorities of parents in the Rhondda: 'a certain servile and snobbish attitude which regarded the English language as the cachet of a superior education, and . . . the well intentioned but utilitarian desire of parents to provide their children with better opportunities for self-advancement'.[88]

Many found the battle against Anglicizing influences too great a burden to bear.[89] In a letter to W. J. Gruffydd in the mid-1920s, George Davies of Treorci noted that the many obstacles which faced ordinary families in the Rhondda had led to cultural apathy and indifference.[90] This trend was encapsulated in the novel *Ffynnonloyw* (1939), written by Elizabeth Mary Jones (Moelona), which depicted thoroughly Welsh families who succumbed to the English tongue in their homes.[91] As many of those who were raised in Welsh homes during this period have testified, sustaining the Welsh language required considerable effort and perseverance on the part of their parents.[92] In a bid to encourage Welsh mothers

---

[84] O. Jones Owen, *The Value of the Welsh Language for English Youth in Wales* (Tonpentre, 1917); idem, *Welsh for the English: English for the Welsh* (Wrexham, 1925).

[85] For evidence of some local parents' objection to the proposed introduction of compulsory Welsh-language education, see *Glamorgan Free Press and Rhondda Leader*, 16 October 1925; ibid., 13 November 1925; *Rhondda Gazette*, 14 November 1925.

[86] J. Vyrnwy Morgan, *The Welsh Mind in Evolution* (London, 1925), p. 136.

[87] See J. Parry Lewis, 'The Anglicisation of Glamorgan', *Morgannwg*, IV (1960), 28–49; Colin H. Williams, 'The Anglicisation of Wales' in Nikolas Coupland (ed.), *English in Wales: Diversity, Conflict and Change* (Clevedon, 1990), pp. 19–47.

[88] NLW MS 9356E. Memorandum no. 90, evidence presented by Herbert Morgan before the Departmental Committee of the Board of Education.

[89] See NLW BBC (Wales) Archives: Scripts, Radio Talk by Emily Stanley Davies, 'Y Broblem o fagu plentyn Cymraeg mewn tre' Saesneg a cheisio cymodi'r ddau fywyd yn ei brofiad' (The Problem of raising a Welsh child in an English town and how to reconcile the two languages in his life-experience), broadcast 27 April 1938.

[90] NLW, W. J. Gruffydd Papers II, 207, letter from George Davies, Treorci, to Gruffydd [n.d.].

[91] Elizabeth Mary Jones (Moelona), *Ffynnonloyw* (Llandysul, 1939), p. 69.

[92] MWL, tape 7019; SWML, tape 103, evidence of a male from Bedlinog (b. 1899); Morgan, '". . . Deigryn am a fu"'.

to act accordingly, Catherine John (Megfam) contributed a series of articles to *Y Darian* in 1917 giving advice and instruction on 'How to Raise a Welsh Child' ('Sut i Fagu'r Baban yn Gymro').[93] On the basis of her own experiences as a mother in Senghennydd, she was acutely aware of the difficulties involved in withstanding the unfavourable influences of the industrial community, but she strongly believed that every responsible mother should make a determined effort to ensure that her child was brought up through the medium of Welsh. Indeed, in December 1928, at a conference held under the auspices of the National Union of Welsh Societies, Megfam called on mothers to be 'callous' in their insistence on a Welsh-medium upbringing.[94] The columnist 'Yr Atwebyd', who also wrote in *Y Darian*, preached a similar message, urging mothers to turn a deaf ear to any English spoken by their children and to steep them in the sounds of Welsh legends, nursery rhymes and folk songs.[95]

It was evident, however, that many Welsh mothers had already succumbed to the English language in their homes. 'Meiriona', a regular contributor to the Welsh press on such matters, feared that the majority of Welsh women had no sympathy with the 'best ideals' of the nation ('Nid yw mwyafrif merched Cymru mewn cydymdeimlad a dyheuadau goreu ein cenedl').[96] The gradual linguistic shift occurring in many Welsh homes was reflected in the differing linguistic ability of children from the same family. In 1922 Megfam was forced to acknowledge that the number of mothers willing to defend the Welsh language against a flood of Anglicizing influences was rapidly diminishing; consequently, the younger children in many families now spoke English only.[97] This was a common phenomenon in many homes in the industrial valleys: parents had succeeded in raising their older children as Welsh speakers, but had failed to maintain the language among their younger children.[98] Indeed, while discussing with Saunders Lewis themes for her proposed novel in 1932, a novel which would portray the experiences of an ordinary Welsh mining family, Kate Roberts resolved to depict the linguistic shift which was taking place within many Welsh-speaking families all around her in the Rhondda.[99] The experience of the writer Gwyn Thomas, born in Cymer in 1913, provides a shining example of this process of language slippage, for knowledge of the Welsh language in his home was confined to the six older children. As Thomas himself commented in 1979:

[93] *Y Darian*, 1 and 8 February 1917, 1 March 1917, 10 May 1917, 21 and 28 June 1917.
[94] *Western Mail*, 3 December 1928.
[95] *Y Darian*, 30 November 1916.
[96] Meiriona, 'Ein Hiaith – Ei Choledd a'i Chadw', *Cymru*, LX, no. 358 (1921), 209.
[97] *Y Darian*, 6 July 1922.
[98] SWML, tape 148; Mary Wiliam, *Blas ar Iaith Blaenau'r Cymoedd* (Llanrwst, 1990), p. 6; evidence of Vernon Evans in Davies (ed.), *The Valleys' Autobiography*, p. 59.
[99] Dafydd Ifans (ed.), *Annwyl Kate, Annwyl Saunders: Gohebiaeth 1923–1983* (Aberystwyth, 1992), p. 89.

'The death of Welsh ran through our family of twelve children like a geological fault.'[100]

By analysing census statistics and reports compiled by individual schools, the scale of linguistic change within the homes of the industrial communities becomes immediately apparent. In the Rhondda the number of children (aged between 3 and 9) brought up through the medium of Welsh fell from 43.9 per cent in 1911 to 27.7 per cent in 1931, while in Merthyr Tydfil the decline from 37.4 per cent to 17.3 per cent was even more pronounced.[101] Surveys conducted by local education authorities furnished further evidence of the seriousness of the situation. A report by the headteachers of selected schools in the Rhondda and Aberdare districts in 1927 revealed that only 8.8 per cent and 15.7 per cent of children in the two respective areas spoke Welsh at home, despite the fact that over half the parents of those children were Welsh speakers.[102] In 1928 only 2.3 per cent of the 9,529 children who attended schools at Pontypridd were recorded as Welsh speakers, and in the same year an inquiry by the Mountain Ash Education Committee revealed that English was spoken in the homes of 78.7 per cent of the 8,897 pupils under its care, even though nearly 40 per cent of the parents spoke Welsh.[103]

Despite such serious losses among the younger population, the Welsh language continued to play an important part in the social life of a large proportion of the older generation. Women in industrial communities were highly dependent on informal oral networks and, as Beth Thomas noted in her study of the language patterns of female residents in Pont-rhyd-y-fen, the close-knit and self-contained nature of their social contacts strengthened their allegiance towards the Welsh language.[104] It is difficult to estimate precisely how much use was made of the Welsh language in their daily discourse, but since more than 60 per cent of women (aged over 45) in the Rhondda and Merthyr Tydfil, and nearly 70 per cent in Aberdare, were Welsh speakers in 1931, it can be assumed that many conversations were conducted through the medium of Welsh.[105] Although bilingualism had become the norm, the Welsh language still had an important role to play in the lives of many local women, particularly when discussing confidential matters in select company or keeping secrets from children.[106]

[100] Gwyn Thomas, *The Subsidence Factor* (Cardiff, 1979), p. 13.

[101] Census of England and Wales, 1911, *Vol. XII*, pp. 30–1; Census of England and Wales, 1931, *County of Glamorgan (Part I)* (London, 1932), pp. 36–7.

[102] NLW MS 9353E. Memorandum no. 14, evidence presented by the Welsh Federation of Headteachers before the Departmental Committee of the Board of Education.

[103] *Glamorgan Free Press and Rhondda Leader*, 28 July 1928; *Aberdare Leader*, 7 July 1928.

[104] Beth Thomas, 'Differences of Sex and Sects: Linguistic Variation and Social Networks in a Welsh Mining Village' in Jennifer Coates and Deborah Cameron (eds.), *Women in their Speech Communities: New Perspectives on Language and Sex* (New York, 1988), pp. 51–60.

[105] Census of England and Wales, 1931, *County of Glamorgan (Part I)*, pp. 36–7.

[106] See the evidence of the author Alun Richards (b. 1929, Pontypridd) in Meic Stephens (ed.), *Artists in Wales* (Llandysul, 1971), p. 57; Eileen Baker, *Yan Boogie: The Autobiography of a Swansea Valley Girl* (Johannesburg, 1992), p. 49.

In their studies of working-class communities, many historians have drawn attention to the existence of what has been called 'a female culture', a self-sufficient, independent culture which fulfilled an important function in the daily lives of the female population.[107] Since ordinary women rarely had the opportunity to partake in the same social experiences as their menfolk, they had created their own sub-culture to satisfy their needs. To a large extent, the personal and self-contained nature of their social networks was a reflection of their comparatively low status in their communities. However, by comparing the nature and quality of the social experiences of the two sexes there has been a tendency to devalue and denigrate the informal associations forged among women.[108] Indeed, the authors of a report on coalfield society drafted in 1921 for the Ministry of Health went so far as to suggest that women in the area did not participate in any form of communal social life:

> A characteristic feature of working-class life in this Region is that males and females, both children and adults, to a large extent take their recreations separately, or perhaps it would be truer to say that adult females do not as a rule indulge in games at all. The men after their day's work resort to their clubs or public houses or other places of entertainment, and it is comparatively rare for girls to accompany their male friends or wives their husbands to the various resorts.[109]

This oversimplified interpretation of events did not take into account the significance of women's informal social patterns within the wider social and cultural context. Since working-class women had very little time or money to spend on formal social activities, their lively oral networks were not only an important means of entertainment and amusement but also provided close contact with family and friends which, in turn, fostered a deep sense of communal unity and friendship.

The physical nature of the mining valleys of south Wales, with their long rows of narrow terraces, lends particular strength to this notion, and it is known that tightly-knit communities were fostered by the close physical proximity of both family and neighbours. Moreover, as Barrie Naylor has noted, this social stability provided an important source of material and spiritual comfort in times of need:

---

[107] See, for example, Gerda Lerner, *The Majority Finds its Past: Placing Women in History* (Oxford, 1981); 'Culture and Gender: The Separate Worlds of Men and Women', editorial *History Workshop Journal*, 15 (1983), 1–3; Ellen Ross, 'Survival Networks: Neighbourhood Sharing in London Before World War I', ibid., 4–27; Elizabeth Roberts, *A Woman's Place: An Oral History of Working-Class Women 1890–1940* (Oxford, 1984).

[108] Rhys Davies, *Print of a Hare's Foot* (London, 1969), p. 88; Walter Haydn Davies, *Blithe Ones* (Port Talbot, 1979), p. 20; Stuart Macintyre, *Little Moscows: Communism and Working-Class Militancy in Inter-War Britain* (London, 1980), p. 139.

[109] *Report of the South Wales Regional Survey Committee for the Ministry of Health* (London, 1921), p. 58.

In the 'old' days in the Rhondda the street was the natural unit where good-neighbour-
liness was whole-hearted and spontaneous. A strong community spirit was forged by
two things . . . the closeness forged by sharing dangerous working conditions and the
necessity of a neighbour's support in the hard daily toil which was the woman's lot.[110]

In view of the fact that women spent considerable time engaged in chores in and
around their homes, it was natural that many friendships would be formed with
other women on doorsteps, in streets and in shops. While their husbands were at
work, the street culture formed a vital part in the daily lives of women and
children. For example, when performing household chores, such as washing
clothes or stoning the doorstep, women conversed with neighbours who were
usually engaged on similar routine tasks.[111] To some extent, therefore, there was a
very formal aspect to this feature of communal life, for it was through such
associations that local news and information were received and passed on. Indeed,
the custom of 'sitting out' on the doorstep to keep one eye on the children and an
ear open for the latest gossip was a favourite pastime of many women.[112]

Aspects of this vibrant oral culture were often denigrated, however,[113] and
conversations between women were regarded as nothing more than 'idle talk'. A
'wagging tongue' was believed by critics to characterize a lazy wife; for example, a
commentator from the Rhondda noted in 1929 that for many local women
'doorstep gossiping and pavement chatting' occupied 'a deal of the time that ought
to be devoted to housework'.[114] In 1936 a particularly intolerant correspondent
from the Rhondda expressed his dismay on discovering unwashed and dishevelled
female residents of a row of houses chatting in the middle of the morning: he
advised them to follow the advice of the late Robert Owen Hughes (Elfyn):

> Er ei ch'wilydd, rhoi ei chalon – mae hi
> Ar bob math o straeon;
> Aed i'w thŷ, a doeth i hon
> F'ai seibiant hefo sebon.[115]

---

[110] Barrie Naylor, *Quakers in the Rhondda, 1926–1986* (Brockweir, Chepstow, 1986), p. 15.

[111] Rosemary Crook, ' "Tidy Women": Women in the Rhondda between the Wars', *Oral History*,
10, no. 12 (1982), 40–6; S. Minwel Tibbott and Beth Thomas, *O'r Gwaith i'r Gwely: Cadw Tŷ
1890–1960 / A Woman's Work: Housework 1890–1960* (Cardiff, 1994).

[112] Gwyn Evans, 'Onllwyn: A Sociological Study of a South Wales Mining Community' (unpubl.
University of Wales MA thesis, 1961), p. 31; evidence of Olwen Eddy in Treanor et al. (eds.),
Green, Black and Back, p. 44; Mary Davies Parnell, *Block Salt and Candles: A Rhondda Childhood*
(Bridgend, 1991), pp. 127–8.

[113] See Rosemary Jones, ' "Separate Spheres"? Women, Language and Respectability in Victorian
Wales' in Geraint H. Jenkins (ed.), *The Welsh Language and its Social Domains 1801–1911* (Cardiff,
2000), pp. 177–213.

[114] *Rhondda Fach Gazette*, 13 July 1929. See, for example, 'Y Glepwraig' (the Gossiping Wife), a
poem by Murmurydd, *Y Darian*, 14 December 1922.

[115] *Free Press and Rhondda Leader*, 14 March 1936.

(Shame on her for setting her heart / On all manner of tales / Let her keep to her house, it would be wise for her / To spend some time with soap.)

Even when women assembled on formal occasions, similar prejudices were aired in order to belittle their discussions. In the novels of Lewis Jones and T. Rowland Hughes, derogatory references were made by male characters regarding the political and social meetings held by women in mining communities. In their opinion, the Women's Club and the Co-operative Guild were nothing more than a 'Talking Shop' or a 'Gossip Club'.[116]

Despite such derogatory remarks, women's oral networks were in reality a valuable source of power. Through their use of words, women had access to a form of authority which enabled them to correct aberrant or unacceptable social behaviour. Through the power of 'gossip', efforts were made to sustain certain moral and social values which provided society with some measure of stability and communal unity.[117] Individuals who acted in a deviant or socially unacceptable manner could expect to be shamed in public. An even worse punishment, however, was to banish 'transgressors' from the oral networks of the community by refusing to speak to them. Such verbal tactics were employed regularly during industrial disputes when strike-breakers and blacklegs came under fire.[118] A common tactic during a strike was for women to use their tongues – their 'chief weapon of offence' – to harass and abuse scabs.[119] Indeed, it was believed that the role of women in such campaigns brought even greater shame on male offenders.

Clearly, therefore, we should be wary of depicting industrial communities as harmonious, unified entities where all residents benefited from the close-knit nature of the society. As Joanna Bourke has pointed out in her study of working-class cultures, physical closeness and conformity of experience did not guarantee social unity and harmony.[120] In industrial communities, where people of different

---

[116] Lewis Jones, *We Live* (London, 1939), p. 15; T. Rowland Hughes, *William Jones* (Aberystwyth, 1944), p. 245.

[117] For further discussion on this subject, see Melanie Tebbutt, 'Women's Talk? Gossip and "Women's Words" in Working-Class Communities, 1880–1939' in Andrew Davies and Steven Fielding (eds.), *Workers' Worlds: Cultures and Communities in Manchester and Salford, 1880–1939* (Manchester, 1992), pp. 49–73; eadem, *Women's Talk? A Social History of 'Gossip' in Working-Class Neighbourhoods, 1880–1960* (Aldershot, 1995).

[118] Angela V. John, 'A Miner Struggle? Women's Protests in Welsh Mining History', *Llafur*, 4, no. 1 (1984), 72–90; Rosemary A. N. Jones, 'Women, Community and Collective Action: The "Ceffyl Pren" Tradition' in Angela V. John (ed.), *Our Mothers' Land: Chapters in Welsh Women's History, 1830–1939* (Cardiff, 1991), pp. 17–41. Similar tactics were used in the South Wales Coalfield during the miners' strike of 1984–5; see Hywel Francis and Gareth Rees, ' "No Surrender in the Valleys": The 1984–85 Miners' Strike in South Wales', *Llafur*, 5, no. 2 (1989), 41–71; Vicky Seddon (ed.), *The Cutting Edge: Women and the Pit Strike* (London, 1986), p. 271.

[119] *Rhondda Leader*, 20 April 1918; *Western Mail*, 18 January 1930.

[120] Joanna Bourke, *Working-Class Cultures in Britain, 1890–1960: Gender, Class and Ethnicity* (London, 1994), p. 142.

linguistic and cultural backgrounds lived alongside one another, it was inevitable that such proximity would prove 'stifling and alienating' for some.[121] Individuals who might have felt that they did not share the social experience of the majority, or who considered themselves different in some way, did not find it easy to fit in and gain acceptance within the wider community. More often than not, such individuals attracted the unwanted attention of the 'gossiping wife', a figure characterized in a poem published in 1933:

> Mrs Hughes she has a wonderful power of speech
> Yes indeed she is a wilderness of speaking
> The stream runs quick by her door but she speaks quicker
> The soot comes down her chimney and blackens her pots
> It blacks all, even spiders behind the pictures
> But her tongue makes her friends and foes oh! *much* blacker.[122]

As D. Lleufer Thomas, stipendary magistrate for Pontypridd and the Rhondda, noted in 1919, females were generally 'a great deal harder on women than others were, particularly when one woman had been in trouble', and they frequently took collective action against ill-favoured individuals.[123] In Blaen-cwm in 1930 around a dozen women gathered outside the home of a woman accused of being a prostitute, and in two separate incidents in Clydach Vale in the early 1930s petitions were drawn up and physical attacks were made against 'unpopular' women.[124]

There was an extremely intolerant element to this sub-culture, therefore, and people who were deemed slightly 'different' were judged fair game. In some areas where the Welsh language was not so common, knowledge of Welsh, or the inability to speak fluent English, could attract the scornful attention of neighbours. In a court case in Bargoed in 1921 a woman from Ystradmynach was fined for threatening her monoglot Welsh neighbour, who had by all accounts suffered at the hands of her neighbours for some time because of her ignorance of the English language.[125] For Katie Olwen Pritchard, who migrated with her family from Tal-y-sarn in Caernarfonshire to Gilfach-goch in 1916, the experience of settling in was difficult and at times traumatic. Her mother found it especially hard to come to terms with life in an Anglicized village and the effort of communicating with others was sometimes unbearable.[126]

The stifling presence of the powerful Nonconformist culture placed additional pressures upon many Welsh women to conform and behave appropriately. Failure

---

[121] Ibid.

[122] Eleanor Boniface, 'Gossip', *The Welsh Outlook*, XX, no. 11 (1933), 309.

[123] *Glamorgan Free Press*, 30 January 1919.

[124] *Glamorgan Free Press and Rhondda Leader*, 8 November 1930, 28 May 1932, 23 September 1935.

[125] *Glamorgan Free Press*, 16 September 1921.

[126] Katie Olwen Pritchard, *Y Glas a'r Coch (Darlith Flynyddol Llyfrgell Penygroes, 1980/81)* (Cyngor Sir Gwynedd, 1981), pp. 20–2.

to maintain the exalted values of that culture invariably precipitated squabbles between women in industrial communities; consequently, great importance was placed upon protecting one's 'good name' and avoiding becoming a target for gossip. Press reports reveal, however, that many men and women suffered public humiliation, often through the medium of Welsh, because of their unacceptable moral behaviour.[127] The Nonconformist establishment was highly critical of this disrespectful and wanton practice and sharply condemned all such activity. Remarks made by several magistrates suggest that only the lower orders of society engaged in such behaviour and that the language heard in frequent slanging matches was not appropriate for women's ears, let alone their tongues! On hearing a mother from Cwm-parc using indecent language, a magistrate from Tonpentre declared her actions utterly 'abominable', while at Pontypridd in 1919 the conduct of a 49-year-old married woman who had verbally abused her neighbour was deemed to be 'unbecoming to a woman of her age and apparent respectability'.[128] Such squabbles often developed into fierce physical fights and colourful descriptions may be found of women fighting like 'Kilkenny cats' and 'wild tigers' in the streets.[129] Margaret Wilde from Caerphilly, mother of the champion boxer, Jimmy Wilde, broke her leg while trying to emulate her son's feats in a brawl with another woman outside one of the town's hostelries in 1920![130] In 1922, following violent scenes in the streets of Abercwmboi, a magistrate from Aberdare suggested that missionaries should be dispatched immediately to the village to civilize its wild women.[131] The women of Ferndale, too, according to the poet 'Cynllwyndu', were doughty fighters, but the standard of their spoken Welsh left much to be desired:

> Mi glywais ddwy fenyw – a dwy hyll eu grân,
> Mewn ymdrech tafodi a'u llygaid ar dân,
> 'A nawr te stand allan', meddai Martha o'r wlad
> 'I will to be sure dy sathru dan drad';
> Y llall oedd Gardïes a gwaeddai heb freg
> 'Mi ripia dy liver, 'rol scriwio dy geg'.[132]

(I heard two women – and two ugly ones at that / Engrossed in a slanging match, their eyes on fire / 'A nawr te stand allan', said Martha from the country / 'I will to be sure dy sathru dan drad' / The other, of Cardiganshire stock, shouted loudly / 'Mi ripia dy liver, 'rol scriwio dy geg'.)

---

[127] See the following for examples of cases brought before local magistrates' courts where the Welsh language was used to slander and verbally abuse: *Aberdare Leader*, 7 June 1919, 21 September 1935; *Rhondda Leader*, 28 July 1921.

[128] *Rhondda Leader*, 26 February 1916; *Glamorgan Free Press*, 30 January 1919.

[129] *Rhondda Leader*, 15 September 1917; *Aberdare Leader*, 25 October 1930.

[130] *Glamorgan Free Press*, 21 January 1921.

[131] *Aberdare Leader*, 29 July 1922.

[132] *Y Darian*, 8 June 1922.

Cynllwyndu suggested that the type of women who fought in streets were not likely to be troubled by the standard or medium of their speech, and some commentators went so far as to claim that the Welsh language was not even a suitable medium to express the less respectable elements of this oral culture. In 1919, during a court case in which a married woman from Pen-y-graig was accused of threatening and verbally abusing her neighbour, her solicitor claimed that she could not be guilty of such a crime for she always addressed her neighbour in Welsh! Similarly, in a case involving a man from Aber-fan who had been accused of slandering an Italian woman, the chairman of the bench suggested that the woman had slighted the Welsh language by claiming that the accused had used his mother tongue: 'There is no dirty language in Welsh, you can take that from me.'[133] Yet, the mere fact that so many Welsh women were associated with such wanton behaviour undermined the idealized image of the 'true Welshwoman'.[134] Even so, the emphasis placed by Nonconformist culture on public respectability and oral decency remained a powerful influence and even determined which subjects were deemed appropriate for discussion among women through the medium of both Welsh and English. In Aberdare in 1914 women were denied entry to a public meeting organized by the Welsh Section of the Free Church Council of the town as part of its 'Purity and Moral Crusade'. It was feared that the sensitive nature of the discussion might prove unsuitable for women and that their absence would enable men to 'take a little more liberty than they otherwise could, in discussing some very important aspects of social evils'.[135]

In spite of what the chapels and other commentators chose to believe, Welsh-speaking women were an intrinsic part of a vibrant and sharp-tongued culture. Nor were women who were members of chapels unblemished; it was claimed that two women accused of taking a prominent part in an attack on a strike-breaker in Pen-coed in 1926 were 'very respectable women, not accustomed to using bad language', and that one of them was a 'life-long member' of Pen-coed Baptist chapel.[136] Several unpleasant and personal arguments were even discussed in chapel and *seiat* meetings, and a violent incident between several women was reported outside the Welsh Baptist chapel at Senghennydd following a

[133] *Rhondda Leader*, 1 November 1919; *Aberdare Leader*, 1 August 1931.
[134] See Sian Rhiannon Williams, 'Y Frythones: Portread Cyfnodolion Merched y Bedwaredd Ganrif ar Bymtheg o Gymraes yr Oes', *Llafur*, 4, no. 1 (1984), 43–56; eadem, 'The True "Cymraes": Images of Women in Women's Nineteenth-Century Welsh Periodicals' in John (ed.), *Our Mothers' Land*, pp. 69–91.
[135] *Aberdare Leader*, 21 March 1914.
[136] *South Wales News*, 23 August 1926.

disagreement relating directly to the Welsh language.[137] However, attempts were made to deny that Welsh women were in any way capable of shameful behaviour. Llewelyn Morgan, a Wesleyan minister from Ferndale, declared in 1922 that in-migrants were responsible for every destructive act in the Rhondda valleys, and his words were echoed by a correspondent to the local newspaper who was firmly of the opinion that the 'foreign element' was responsible for the immorality and wantonness of the industrial valleys: 'From my observations, I find that the "filthy mouthed and immoral companions, unfaithful and intemperate wives and mothers" are generally of the Saxon breed, hailing from places outside the Welsh borders. It is the lower class of the foreign element that contaminates Wales.' Such women were blamed for bringing local women into disrepute, and it was claimed that only the 'Welsh element' kept the 'Rhonddas morally sound'.[138] Racist views of this kind, however, do not bear close scrutiny. There is abundant evidence in local court reports that Welsh-speaking women were guilty of a variety of offences, including abortions, gambling, drunkenness and verbal indecency. Many of them attended the courts in order to summon local men to take responsibility for their illegitimate children.[139] Although D. Lleufer Thomas, stipendiary magistrate for Pontypridd and the Rhondda, was familiar enough with this kind of evidence, in 1930 he, too, chose to air the same prejudices when giving testimony before the Royal Commission on Licensing: 'Welsh women, I mean, particularly those of Welsh up-bringing, very rarely acquire the drinking habit. It is only women who come into Wales from other parts that as a rule have or acquire this habit.'[140]

This view was shared by Elisabeth Williams, wife of Griffith John Williams, lecturer in Welsh at the University College of Wales, Cardiff. Addressing a meeting of Mudiad Mamau a Merched Cymru (the Society for the Mothers and Daughters of Wales) in Cardiff in 1932, she claimed that in comparison with non-Welsh speakers, and English and Irish in-migrants, the native Welsh-speaking population showed far greater respect for cleanliness and good appearance ('y bobl a barcha lanweithdra ac ymddangosiad graenus fwyaf yw'r Cymry Cymreig ac nid y bobl a gollodd eu hiaith a'r Saeson a'r Gwyddelod sy'n byw yn ein mysg').[141]

---

[137] Michael Lieven, *Senghennydd: The Universal Pit Village, 1890–1930* (Llandysul, 1994), p. 98. In the minutes of one Welsh Nonconformist cause in the Rhondda, it is noted that the minister and officials were forced to intervene to bring to an end a dispute between members of the church: one of the female members had accused two of her fellow-members of conducting an adulterous relationship. NLW, CM Archives E118/2. Minute Book of Libanus, Blaenclydach, 25 January 1914, 2 May 1914.

[138] Llewelyn Morgan, *Cwm Rhondda a Fu ac a Sydd* (Aberdâr, 1922); *Glamorgan Free Press and Rhondda Leader*, 3 November 1922, 7 June 1930.

[139] *Aberdare Leader*, 30 October 1915; *Rhondda Leader*, 5 July 1919; *Glamorgan Free Press and Rhondda Leader*, 25 May 1923. See Glamorgan Record Office, Q/S M38–40, Minutes of Glamorgan Quarter Sessions, 1926–44.

[140] Royal Commission on Licensing (England and Wales), *Minutes of Evidence, 16th Public Session, Tuesday, 21 January 1930* (London, 1930), question 6994/22.

[141] *Y Darian*, 3 March 1932.

Similar claims were made in 1936 in an inquiry conducted into juvenile un-employment in the industrial areas. The author noted that the homes of indigen-ous Welsh women in the Rhondda were invariably clean and tidy, in direct contrast with the homes of the females of non-Welsh origin at Merthyr, where he had not dared accept an invitation to a meal![142] In the opinion of Kate Roberts, the different cultural upbringing of Welsh women in the Rhondda had helped them cope with the harsh circumstances of the depression years, for they, unlike their Monmouthshire neighbours, had been endowed with a culture which respected craftsmanship and cleanliness:

> Yn y boreau, yn y stryd hon, fe glywch gorws o sŵn rhwbio rhywbeth tebyg i rud hyd gerrig y drws i'w gwneud yn wynion; er, mae'n rhaid imi addef, mai gwastraff ar amser yw ceisio gwneuthur cerrig drws yn wyn yn yr ardaloedd hyn. Eto i gyd, fe ddengys fod gan y gwragedd awydd i'w codi eu hunain uwchlaw'r amgylchedd. Yng Nghwm Rhondda y gwelais i'r dillad glanaf a welais erioed ar y leiniau dillad ar ddydd Llun. Ni welir ond gydag eithriad ddillad pyg ar y leiniau yma, ac fe ddywedir wrthyf, er yr holl dlodi, fod y plant yn dwt ac yn lân yn yr ysgolion . . . Nid yw ysbryd crefft wedi marw'n hollol yma. Dyma'r gwahaniaeth mawr a welais i rhwng y cymoedd yma a chymoedd Sir Fynwy. Nid yw'n dlotach yno nag yma, ond mae tai Sir Fynwy yn ofnadwy i'r llygad . . . ni welais erioed ddim byd truenusach. Pob tŷ bron yn ddibaent a'u ffenestri'n flêr. Y plant a'r merched ar bennau'r drysau ac yn fudr. Ni wn sut i gyfrif am y gwahaniaeth; onid hyn, bod rhywfaint o falchter ar ôl yng Nghwm Rhondda oherwydd bod rhywfaint o'r ysbryd Cymreig ar ôl yma.[143]

(In the mornings, in this street, you will hear a chorus of noise as something similar to grit is rubbed on the front doorsteps to make them white; although, I must admit, it is a waste of time to try and whiten the doorsteps in these districts. In spite of that, this effort shows that the women are keen to rise above their situation. It is in the Rhondda Valley that I saw the cleanest clothes ever on washing-lines on a Monday. It is extremely rare to see dirty clothes on these lines and I have been told, despite all the poverty, that the children are neat and clean in the schools . . . The spirit of craftsmanship is not completely dead here. This is the big difference between these valleys and those of Monmouthshire. People are no poorer there than here, but the houses in Monmouthshire are a sorry sight . . . I never saw anything more pitiful. Nearly every house is unpainted with untidy windows. The children and the women on the doorsteps look dirty. I know not how to account for this difference; only that some pride remains in the Rhondda Valley because some of the Welsh spirit remains there.)

The main proponents of this view were women who assembled to establish the Society for the Mothers and Daughters of Wales in September 1920. During the

---

[142] Gwynne Meara, *Juvenile Unemployment in South Wales* (Cardiff, 1936), p. 97.
[143] Kate Roberts, 'Cwm Rhondda', *Y Ddraig Goch*, 6, no. 12 (1932), 4.

centenary celebrations marking the birth of Evan Jones (Ieuan Gwynedd) (1820–52), a group of women honoured his name by pledging to keep the Welsh language in their homes and to protect, foster and promote the Christian virtues of chastity and morality among the female sex.[144] This was a reactionary movement with clearly-defined aims and objectives, but its main activities were confined to organizing occasional visits to the burial places of notable poets and hymn-writers in the Vale of Glamorgan, as well as an annual pilgrimage to the grave of Ieuan Gwynedd at Groes-wen.[145]

Despite the restricted appeal of this movement, it should be recognized that such societies gave many Welsh women their first opportunity to speak in public. Under the auspices of Mudiad y Mamau and numerous other local Welsh cultural societies, individuals such as Megfam and Moelona became experienced orators who drew upon their experiences as teachers in the industrial valleys in emphasizing in their public lectures the contribution women could make to the language cause.[146] The National Union of Welsh Societies was criticized in 1918 for insisting upon inviting male speakers to address its meetings on this important issue and for ignoring women who knew far more about the subject.[147] Since mothers knew best about the key role they could play in the language struggle, it was argued that there was a special need for women to become involved. The protagonists of such views thus continued to stress the traditional role of the Welsh woman in the home. Megfam herself believed that no woman should undertake public duties if her domestic responsibilities were likely to suffer in any way.[148] Although it was firmly believed that the mother's place was in the home, it cannot be denied that the 'society women' experienced and benefited from unprecedented opportunities to speak and debate publicly through the medium of the Welsh language. Indeed, special evenings organized by women, during which papers were delivered on a variety of historical and literary topics, were regular features in the annual programme of Welsh cultural societies in the valley communities of south Wales.[149]

[144] *Y Darian*, 30 September 1920; *Western Mail*, 13 September 1920. Evan Jones (Ieuan Gwynedd) (1820–52), Congregational minister and editor of the first Welsh-language periodical for women, *Y Gymraes*, championed the cause of the women of Wales following the 1847 Education Report's damning remarks on their character and morality. See Williams, 'The True "Cymraes"', pp. 69–91.

[145] *Y Darian*, 5 June 1930.

[146] For biographical details on Megfam, see Lieven, *Senghennydd*, pp. 88–9; and on Moelona, see *Y Genhinen*, V, no. 11 (1955), 101–7.

[147] *Y Darian*, 28 March 1918.

[148] Ibid., 20 September 1917. Megfam echoed the views of Ellen Hughes of Llanengan, who declared in 1910 that 'polishing one's shoes is just as elevating as serving on a committee!' ('Byddaf fy hun yn teimlo fod gloewi fy esgidiau yn llawn mor ddyrchafol a bod mewn Pwyllgor!'). Ellen Hughes, 'Merched a Chyhoeddusrwydd', *Y Gymraes*, XIV, no. 169 (1910), 167.

[149] The following examples are taken from the programme of the Aberdare Cymrodorion Society: November 1915, papers by Rosina Williams, 'Eu Hiaith a Gadwant', M. R. Owen, 'D. Emlyn Evans, the Musician', H. J. Watkin, 'The University of Wales'; November 1922,

At a time when the number of Welsh speakers was declining sharply, it is likely that such formal affiliations acquired even greater significance in the lives of Welsh-speaking women in the valleys. During the early 1920s Welsh cultural societies flourished in the industrial valleys of Glamorgan and their immense popularity reflected the great hunger for opportunities to socialize through the medium of Welsh. Public meetings, dramatic performances, concerts and lectures were all organized under the auspices of these societies.[150] Over the years, Welsh chapels had provided a central meeting-place for the Welsh-speaking population in the industrial districts and a full programme of weekly events kept their members busy. However, parental pressure was probably an important factor in ensuring the regular attendance of young girls at chapel meetings, since they were considered the only social centres suitable for 'tidy' Welsh girls.[151] Even so, it is clear that the chapel was a central institution in the social lives of the young female population and the 'monkey parades' which followed church services and singing festivals gave girls the opportunity to mix with male friends and meet future partners.[152]

For women of the older generation, chapels fulfilled a vital social and spiritual need. For many years, chapels had provided women with a unique opportunity to work actively on behalf of their communities, and through the temperance movement many of them had become accomplished public speakers and committee members.[153] In the years following the Great War, such women were provided with even wider opportunities to contribute to their causes through their work in the 'Zenana' or missionary committees, the Sunday schools, the Band of Hope, and, most importantly, the finance and fund-raising committees.[154] Although very few women were elected chapel deacons in the years before the Second World War, one of the main characteristics of chapel life in the period was the substantial growth in the influence and work of the sisterhoods. By

papers by Dilys Griffiths, 'Cranogwen', Sarah Evans, 'Tanymarian', Mariel Morgan, 'John Gibson – the Sculptor'; February 1925, papers by L. M. Williams, 'Owain Glyndŵr', Ann Morgan, 'The Humour of Daniel Owen'. *Aberdare Leader*, 13 November 1915, 11 November 1922, 14 February 1925.

[150] See Menna Davies, 'Traddodiad Llenyddol y Rhondda' (unpubl. University of Wales PhD thesis, 1981), p. 263; Selwyn Jones, 'Y Seiat Rydd', *Yr Efrydydd*, IV, no. 7 (1928), 190–2.

[151] MWL, tape 1375, evidence of a female from Treorci (b. 1875), and tape 7019; Beth Thomas, 'Accounting for Language Shift in a South Wales Mining Community', *Papurau Gwaith Ieithyddol Cymraeg Caerdydd / Cardiff Working Papers in Welsh Linguistics*, no. 5 (Welsh Folk Museum, 1987), pp. 55–100.

[152] Thomas, 'Accounting for Language Shift in a South Wales Mining Community'; George Ewart Evans, *The Strength of the Hills: An Autobiography* (London, 1983), p. 44; evidence of Violet Lorraine Norman (b. 1917, Llanelli) in Jeffrey Grenfell-Hill (ed.), *Growing Up in Wales: Collected Memories of Childhood in Wales 1895–1939* (Llandysul, 1996), p. 151.

[153] NLW, Undeb Dirwestol Merched De Cymru (South Wales Women's Temperance Union), Papers 190, 289; Ceridwen Lloyd-Morgan, 'From Temperance to Suffrage' in John (ed.), *Our Mothers' Land*, pp. 135–58.

[154] D. Ben Rees, *Chapels in the Valley: A Study in the Sociology of Welsh Nonconformity* (Upton, 1975), pp. 211–12.

choosing to attend Welsh chapel meetings and societies, women publicly exhibited their allegiance to the Welsh language and culture. The language fulfilled an important function in their social lives and they devoted themselves to selfless activity on behalf of Urdd Gobaith Cymru (the Welsh League of Youth) and various Welsh dramatic and literary societies. According to Gareth Alban Davies, who wrote a narrative essay on the labours of such women in the Rhondda in the 1930s, they were 'the mainstay of Welsh cultural life in the two Valleys'.[155]

However, owing to the general decline in the numbers of Welsh speakers, the task of maintaining such activities through the medium of Welsh became increasingly difficult. By the late 1920s virtually every public meeting in the industrial valleys, except those organized by chapels, was held through the medium of English.[156] Even the commitment of chapel and Welsh society members towards the language was severely tested, and no one could be sure how much Welsh would be spoken even in their meetings. In her address at the annual conference of the National Union of Welsh Societies in Cardiff in 1928, Megfam criticized women whom she had heard 'jabbering' in English on their way to and from the Welsh chapels, and appealed to them to make a concerted effort to conduct every meeting connected with the chapel through the medium of Welsh.[157] The linguistic hypocrisy of many 'cultured' Welsh people greatly concerned D. Arthen Evans, too, and in 1921 he appealed to members of Welsh societies to mend their ways. Although conscious of people's affiliation to Welsh societies and chapels, he knew only too well that English was the principal language of the vast majority of Welsh speakers in south Wales.[158] It was claimed that some of the 'Zenana' meetings in the Welsh chapels of Glamorgan were also held in English, and the annual report of the South Wales Women's Temperance Union for 1913 reveals that many of their meetings followed the same pattern.[159] The Anglicizing presence of women from the industrialized regions meant that a considerable amount of English – deeply deplored by Moelona – was spoken during the annual meeting of the movement in Newcastle Emlyn in 1921.[160]

In reality, this 'unconscious' mixing of the two languages of the valleys reflected their close daily relationship. The social and cultural life of the industrial communities did not divide neatly into two linguistic and cultural compartments and Welsh speakers switched with comparative ease from one language to another when socializing.[161] The pace of assimilation between the two languages and two

---

[155] Gareth Alban Davies, 'The Fur Coat' in Meic Stephens (ed.), *A Rhondda Anthology* (Bridgend, 1993), p. 155.

[156] *Y Darian*, 25 November 1926.

[157] Ibid., 19 July 1928.

[158] Ibid., 27 October 1921.

[159] Ibid.; *Adroddiad o Weithrediadau a Chyfrifon Arianol Undeb Dirwestol Merched De Cymru, 1913*.

[160] *Y Darian*, 3 November 1921.

[161] See Hywel Francis, 'Language, Culture and Learning: The Experience of a Valley Community', *Llafur*, 6, no. 3 (1994), 85–96.

cultures, however, had grave consequences both for the status and standard of Welsh. The Welsh press devoted considerable attention to the declining standard of colloquial Welsh in the valleys and it was feared that the habit of 'mixing English' was creating both a garbled form of Welsh and a distinctive 'Rhondda English'.[162] Welsh speakers in the industrial areas were said to possess a vulgar, grating tongue which was 'a wretched mixture of both languages, most objectionable to a Welshman and to an Englishman'.[163] One local reporter, who was appalled by the pitiful standard of the 'Welsh' regularly heard in the valleys, wondered what could be done to stamp out 'atrocities' such as: 'Our Bill ni said to me last night: Mam, cofia I must have my dillad gwaith ready bore fori and put them by the tân to dry. My scitsha newi wants new lassis; remember bara caws for the box bwyd.'[164] A correspondent from Aberdare reckoned that a typical conversation in the town was conducted in '40 per cent Welsh, 40 per cent English and 20 per cent in "unknowname" language'.[165] The Ferndale poet Cynllwyndu was so incensed by the standard of Welsh spoken by the inhabitants of the Rhondda Fach in 1922 that he expressed his 'grief' in verse form in *Y Darian*:

> Mor flin ydyw clywed rhyw estron o aeg
> A Chymry unieithog yn mwrdro'r Gymraeg.
> Wrth gerddo un bore trwy Heol y Llyn,
> Mi glywais rhyw fenyw yn dwedyd fel hyn,
> 'Wna'r plant ma ddim washo, mor black yw eu crwyn,
> Jack, dyma dy boot lace a weipa dy drwyn',
> A mam yn Brynhyfryd a waeddai yn groch,
> 'Run to school, Johnny, mae just ten o'r gloch'.[166]

(How tiresome to hear a foreign tongue / And monoglot Welsh speakers murdering their language / As I walked along Lake Street one morning / I heard one lady say like this / 'Wna'r plant ma ddim washo, mor black yw eu crwyn / Jack, dyma dy boot lace a weipa dy drwyn' / And a mother from Brynhyfryd shouted out loud / 'Run to school, Johnny, mae just ten o'r gloch'.)

Hand in hand with the decline in the standard of spoken Welsh came an appreciable decline in the support for Welsh-language reading material. Members of the Welsh societies often complained about the dearth of Welsh-language

---

[162] W. W. Harris (Arthan), 'Gall Pobun Wella ar ei Gymraeg', *Y Ford Gron*, V, no. 8 (1935), 185, 189. One newspaper columnist defined 'Rhondda English' as a bastardization of Welsh and the dialects of 'Somerset, Wilts. and Devon'. *Glamorgan Free Press and Rhondda Leader*, 28 January 1923.

[163] *Glamorgan Free Press*, 21 October 1921; Jones, *Eneideg Cenedl a Phwnc yr Iaith Gymraeg*, p. 9.

[164] *Glamorgan Free Press*, 13 January 1922.

[165] *Aberdare Leader*, 18 December 1915.

[166] *Y Darian*, 8 June 1922.

literature in local libraries and reading rooms.[167] In fact, little use was made of what little literature was available. The layers of dust which had allegedly settled on the covers of the large collection of Welsh books housed at Treharris Workmen's Library in 1914 betrayed a worrying lack of interest among the local Welsh-speaking population.[168] During 1922–3 only 357 Welsh books were borrowed from the public library at Aberdare, a pitifully low figure when compared with the 51,344 English books for children borrowed during the same period. Despite the general increase in the use made of libraries during the years of the depression, the gulf between the number of Welsh- and English-language books borrowed by readers remained immense. During 1934, 165,280 books were borrowed from Aberdare library, but only 581 of them were Welsh-language volumes.[169] Very little support was given to the Welsh-language press and it was a sign of the times when the weekly newspaper, *Llais Llafur*, changed its title to *Labour Voice* in 1915.[170] The Aberdare-based *Y Darian* struggled heroically to maintain a Welsh-language weekly for south Wales, but after many years of financial uncertainty it was wound up in October 1934 under the editorship of M. Henry Lloyd (Ap Hefin). Convinced that the apathy of the Welsh speakers of south Wales had killed the newspaper, he reiterated the comments of a reporter who had claimed that stories from 'Tit-bits' or 'Comic Cuts' were more appealing to the new generation of Welsh speakers.[171]

As inhabitants of the valleys increasingly distanced themselves from the Welsh language, it became clear to some critics that immediate action was an urgent necessity. Convinced that it was no longer sufficient to rely merely on goodwill to maintain the language, W. J. Gruffydd and W. Ambrose Bebb called for a progressive policy to raise the status of Welsh by making it a compulsory subject within the education system. They argued that unless the language could secure a place in all aspects of Welsh public life and be regarded as a language of dignity and value, its future well-being was at risk. A stirring public debate was conducted in the Welsh press at the beginning of the 1920s between Gruffydd, Bebb and their followers and the 'prophets of the hearth'.[172] Gruffydd declared that the policy of the 'nationalists of the hearth' had been an abject failure and argued that the number of Welsh speakers would continue to fall if the language was merely regarded as the language of the kitchen ('Yn enw ein hunan-barch ac yn enw

---

[167] Ibid., 25 January 1917.
[168] *Tarian y Gweithiwr*, 26 February 1914.
[169] *Y Darian*, 10 March 1923; *Aberdare Leader*, 23 June 1934.
[170] See *Labour Voice*, 9 and 16 January 1915.
[171] *Y Darian*, 11 and 25 October 1934.
[172] W. J. Gruffydd, 'Yr Iaith Gymraeg a'i Gelynion', *Y Llenor*, II, no. 1 (1923), 11–19; W. Ambrose Bebb, 'Achub y Gymraeg: Achub Cymru', *Y Geninen*, XLII, no. 4 (1924), 169–80. Cartoons appeared in the press depicting the difference of opinion between Bebb and Gruffydd and Professor W. Morgan Watkin, who argued against the proposals for a compulsory language policy. See *Western Mail*, 15 and 16 August 1924.

rheswm, ai trwy gadw ein hiaith yn rhyw law forwyn mewn ffedog fras yn y gegin yr ydym yn debig o gael pobl i siarad Cymraeg?').[173] Gruffydd drummed his message home in the Board of Education Report in 1927 in which he advocated an ambitious programme for Welsh-medium education as the only long-term solution to the language problem:

> It is clear that the policy of 'Welsh on the hearth', excellent as it is up to a point, is inadequate to preserve the language. No language can live without prestige, and prestige is to-day impossible apart from education.[174]

With the official backing of this report, many schools in the valleys were able to expand facilities for Welsh-language teaching and it was believed that a long period of campaigning by Welsh chapels and societies had finally reaped dividends. The provision for Welsh-language teaching in different areas, however, remained largely dependent on the goodwill of local education authorities and although schools such as those in the Rhondda and Cilfynydd achieved considerable success in the field, this was largely attributable to the foresight and vision of individual teachers and education officials.[175] The need for a similar campaign in the homes remained a preoccupation of many campaigners, including the Revd Fred Jones, Treorci, who believed that expanding provision for Welsh-language education was a fruitless exercise unless matched by action within the homes.[176] In an article in *The Welsh Outlook* in February 1926 D. Rees Williams also feared that 'unless the people themselves wish to foster Welsh and unless and until it becomes the language of the hearth all efforts to make it compulsory in the schools will be misplaced energy and even damaging to the cause of national progress'.[177] Some months earlier, in May 1925, Kate Roberts, who was at that time a Welsh teacher at the Girls' School, Aberdare, had suggested that there was indeed a need for such a campaign for, despite the introduction of the Welsh language as a teaching medium in the local school, the children of Aberdare spoke English on the streets and in the home.[178]

It soon became apparent that this was a pattern which would characterize the linguistic habits of the industrial community. Since so many people had distanced themselves from the Welsh language, the cultural gulf which had opened between

---

[173] Gruffydd, 'Yr Iaith Gymraeg a'i Gelynion', 17.

[174] Departmental Committee on Welsh in the Educational System of Wales, *Welsh in Education and Life*, p. 188.

[175] Rhondda Urban District Council, Education Committee, *Report by R. R. Williams (Deputy Director of Education) on the Teaching of Welsh in the Bi-lingual Schools of the Authority* (Treherbert, 1925); NLW MS 22147D, Minute Book of Undeb Athrawon Cymreig (the Union of Welsh Teachers), 1926–38; NLW ex. 1128.

[176] *Y Darian*, 12 February 1925.

[177] D. Rees Williams, 'Wales and the Future', *The Welsh Outlook*, XIII, no. 2 (1926), 39.

[178] *Y Darian*, 21 May 1925.

two generations had widened considerably. This divide was evident even within the close community of the Welsh chapels. In her short drama, *Beth Wnawn Ni?* (1937), Megfam revealed how the cultural clash had created a rift between members of the sisterhood seeking to raise funds for their chapel. The younger generation argued that lectures were as old-fashioned as the magic lantern, while the older women doggedly rejected their pleas for a dance or a whist drive.[179] The dance halls, sports-fields and cinemas were all rapidly replacing chapels as meeting-places for young women and it was difficult to resist their appeal.[180] Welsh societies were keenly aware of the competition and of their limited appeal to the younger generation. Delegates at a meeting of the West Glamorgan branch of the National Union of Welsh Societies in 1933 expressed the view that the majority of societies were wrapped up in the traditions of the past and had no vision for the future.[181]

The Welsh language was unable to adapt to the social and economic needs and aspirations of the younger generation and eventually it paid a high price for its failure. The scale of language shift among the younger age groups boded ill for the language and the institutions associated with it. These concerns deepened as commentators noticed that young girls in particular were much more likely to turn their back on the language than their male counterparts, thereby undermining their traditional role as the supporters and saviours of the language. W. J. Gruffydd believed that since Welsh girls were on the whole extremely ignorant of their native country and tongue their cultural apathy threatened the future of the language.[182] In the Welsh-language press, in the pulpit and on the public stage, Welsh girls were frequently criticized for their cultural indifference.[183] In an address delivered at the National Eisteddfod at Caernarfon in 1921, the Revd D. Tecwyn Evans claimed that the women of Wales were 'the greatest sinners' in this matter ('Merched Cymru yw'r pechaduriaid pennaf yn y cyfeiriad hwn').[184] His accusation received official support in 1927 in the report of the Board of Education which declared that 'girls in Wales are much more inclined than boys to "drift into English"'.[185] Perturbed by the linguistic preferences of his female contemporaries, one young Welshman expressed the view that it would be advisable for young girls to cling to their mother tongue, for the mongrel

---

[179] NLW, National Eisteddfod MSS. Machynlleth National Eisteddfod, 1937, no. 31.

[180] Roberts, *Oriau Hamdden ac Adloniant*, p. 2; Royal Commission on Licensing, *Minutes of Evidence*, question 6994/14.

[181] *Y Darian*, 30 November 1933.

[182] Gruffydd, 'Yr Iaith Gymraeg a'i Gelynion', 16.

[183] Ibid. See the report of a damning speech delivered by the Revd W. R. Jones (Gwenith Gwyn) before the Conference of the National Union of Welsh Societies at Hebron, Tonpentre, 12 May 1928. NLW, Gwenith Gwyn Papers A/4; *Glamorgan Free Press*, 19 May 1928.

[184] NLW MS 15797D. Scrap Book of T. E. Richards, Treherbert.

[185] Departmental Committee on Welsh in the Educational System of Wales, *Welsh in Education and Life*, p. 188.

language ('rhyw erthyl o beth') which they spoke was most certainly not English.[186] According to Caerwyn, it was a sign of the times that young girls should believe that speaking Welsh was unrefined and that those who spoke English were more cultured and superior, despite the fact that the standard of their spoken English left much to be desired.[187] The behaviour of the 'flappers' of Aberdare provided further evidence of this cultural change. According to one correspondent, local girls made fools of themselves in their attempt to speak English, a language which they associated with fashion and modernity.[188] Another local columnist went so far as to suggest that hatred of Welsh existed among the young girls of Aberdare: 'Undoubtedly, it is a type of snobbery that has taken root in the town with the advent of wireless (and Oxford accents), college education, baby cars, dancing, coffee drinking in cafés, and berets and leather coats.'[189]

Several sociolinguists have detected a general tendency among women to modify their language under social and cultural pressure,[190] and the commentators of the period under study were also of the opinion that women's 'inherent' interest in fashion and ostentation led them to favour English. The authors of the 1927 Departmental Committee Report claimed that 'social conventions and the refinements of life' made a 'stronger appeal to women than to men' and, to that end, it was only natural that 'in the years of adolescence, and during the time of courtship' young women should believe they showed 'a greater delicacy in speaking English'.[191] Iorwerth C. Peate voiced his anger in 1931 on hearing a group of women speaking what he considered to be lamentable English to one another outside a Welsh chapel in south Wales simply because they believed it was the 'genteel' tongue.[192] At a time when so much emphasis was placed on knowledge of the English language – the language of 'fashion and good form' – the Welsh language was unable to set a similar standard of cultural refinement to Welsh girls.[193] Women turned to embrace the English language because the Welsh language failed to give adequate expression to their social experiences.

---

[186] 'Cylch y Merched: Barn Llanc am ein Merched Ifainc', *Y Ddraig Goch*, 3, no. 7 (1928), 6. It appears that the author of this letter was Morris T. Williams, who married Kate Roberts in 1928. See Ifans (ed.), *Annwyl Kate, Annwyl Saunders*, p. 51.

[187] *Y Darian*, 13 September 1923.

[188] *Aberdare Leader*, 1 June 1929.

[189] Ibid., 8 August 1931. For further evidence of the linguistic 'snobbery' of the residents of Aberdare, see ibid., 18 March 1933.

[190] See, for example, Peter Trudgill, *On Dialect: Social and Geographical Perspectives* (Oxford, 1983), pp. 161–8; Ralph Fasold, *The Sociolinguistics of Language* (Oxford, 1990), pp. 89–118; Jennifer Coates, *Women, Men and Language: A Sociolinguistic Account of Gender Differences in Language* (London, 1993); Suzanne Romaine, *Language and Society: An Introduction to Sociolinguistics* (Oxford, 1994), pp. 116–25.

[191] Departmental Committee on Welsh in the Educational System of Wales, *Welsh in Education and Life*, p. 188.

[192] Iorwerth C. Peate, 'Y Capeli a'r Gymraeg', *Y Tyst*, 31 December 1931.

[193] Gruffydd, 'Yr Iaith Gymraeg a'i Gelynion', 16; *Aberdare Leader*, 26 May 1923, 8 August 1931.

However, as the sociolinguistic work undertaken by Beth Thomas in the Welsh-speaking industrial community of Pont-rhyd-y-fen has shown, further local research is required in order to understand fully the linguistic tendencies of both men and women.[194] Despite allegations that women and girls favoured the English language, there is no hard evidence to confirm that charge. Indeed, census figures reveal that a greater percentage of females than males under the age of 24 spoke Welsh in the Rhondda in 1931 (32.4 per cent compared with 30.4 per cent), while 21 per cent of females of the same age in the Ogmore and Garw valleys spoke Welsh compared with 18.1 per cent of males.[195] Nevertheless, it proved impossible to appease those Welsh language supporters who worried about the long-term implications of the decline in the number of Welsh-speaking females. It was feared that their leanings towards the English language would have a detrimental effect upon the language of homes and children in the future. After all, if the mothers of the future insisted upon speaking English while courting, English would certainly become the language of the home and there would be no likelihood of transmitting Welsh to the children.[196] Gwenith Gwyn feared that since the future of Welsh lay with girls up to fifteen years of age, many of whom were tending to reject it, the fate of the native language hung in the balance.[197]

In the light of such fears, it is not surprising that the social and political developments which affected women after the Great War received a lukewarm reception among members of the Welsh 'establishment'. Despite declaring their wholehearted support for efforts to enfranchise women and to raise their awareness of their political and social responsibilities, many saw some aspects of the new political ideology as a potential threat to the Welsh language. To supporters of the 'authentic Welsh woman', the behaviour of the new woman or 'flapper' was offensive, since her emphasis on equal rights and thirst for leisure and recreation challenged the future of the traditional Welsh home, the bedrock of the Welsh language and culture.[198] The old miner, Murmurydd, was saddened to see young girls being lured by cheap entertainment and he urged them to think more about improving their minds than their appearance.[199] Indeed, judging by the harsh words of arch-moralists such as the Revds J. Vyrnwy Morgan and T. D. Gwernogle Evans, young women of the time could scarcely be compared favourably with their virtuous mothers:

[194] Thomas, 'Differences of Sex and Sects', pp. 51–60.
[195] Census of England and Wales, 1931, *County of Glamorgan (Part I)*, pp. 36–7.
[196] NLW, CM Archives C2/23. Evidence of W. J. Nicholas, Secretary of Horeb, Treherbert, 17 September 1925.
[197] *Barry and District News*, 28 October 1927.
[198] *Y Darian*, 11 October 1934; E. Aman Jones, 'Y Foesoldeb Newydd a'r Teulu', *Y Traethodydd*, II (1933), 170–80.
[199] *Y Darian*, 11 November 1920.

The Welsh girl of this generation is very ignorant in spite of her schooling; indolent, undomesticated and wasteful. She is anxious to appear in the latest fashion and to be attractive; fond of chapel or church, and equally fond of the cinema, or places of amusement, because they all alike serve the same purpose, that is, to keep her in evidence; with the result that she gets married very easily, though, generally speaking, she proves worthless as a wife.[200]

Fears that mothers of the future could fall victim to the frivolous and superficial attractions of the inter-war years caused general concern throughout Wales,[201] but the linguistic loss inherent in these developments caused especial concern in industrial south Wales. Satirical portraits appeared in the Welsh press emphasizing the difference in character between the flighty modern girl who spoke stilted Welsh and her virtuous sister, the 'authentic Welsh woman'.[202] For instance, Eleri, the niece of William Jones, the principal character in T. Rowland Hughes's novel *William Jones* (1944), which was set in industrial south Wales in the 1930s, personified this cultural shift. Once she began frequenting dance halls and cinemas, she became disobedient and unruly and refused to help her mother with household chores.[203]

The political developments which followed the First World War were of considerable significance for women in the south Wales valleys, especially when the campaign to win the vote and political representation on local and national authorities was won. In common with miners' movements in the eastern valleys, women's political movements also utilized the English language in order to spread the socialist message. As women took up seats on local councils and committees, their affiliations with more formal, English-language social networks strengthened, and, as the unprecedented social and economic experiences of the depression years placed even greater pressure on the daily lives of ordinary women, many cultural considerations were cast aside. Women endured great hardship in their struggle to feed and clothe their families and the reports of medical officers of health during the period reveal that they paid a high price for their sacrifices.[204]

---

[200] Morgan, *The Welsh Mind in Evolution*, p. 112. See also T. D. Gwernogle Evans, *Smoking, a Message of Love to the Daughters of Wales* (Neath, 1934), p. 3.

[201] Aled Gwyn Job, 'Agweddau ar Syniadau Cymdeithasol a'r Farn Gyhoeddus ym Môn rhwng y Ddau Ryfel Byd' (unpubl. University of Wales MPhil thesis, 1990), p. 18.

[202] See, for example, 'Drama i Tair o Ferched', *Y Darian*, 15 October 1919; O. H. G., 'Dadl: Yr Iaith Gymraeg – Gwen a Lil', *Y Gymraes*, XXII, no. 261 (1918), 89–90; H. Griffith, 'Ymgom rhwng Dwy Ferch', ibid., XXX, no. 352 (1926), 12–13; A. E. Hughes, 'Cartrefi Cysegredig', ibid., XXI, no. 362 (1926), 170–1.

[203] Hughes, *William Jones*, p. 185.

[204] See, for example, Rhondda Urban District Council, *Annual Reports of Medical Officer of Health and School Medical Officer, 1920–38*; Aberdare Urban District Council, *Annual Reports of Medical Officer of Health and School Medical Officer, 1920–39*; Ogmore and Garw Urban District Council, *Annual Reports of Medical Officer of Health, 1916–45*. See also Carol White and Sian Rhiannon Williams (eds.), *Struggle or Starve: Women's Lives in the South Wales Valleys between the Two World Wars* (Dinas Powys, 1998).

The main priority of women was to unite their communities against poverty and economic oppression, and there was no room for linguistic debates in the collective campaigns against social injustice. Despite the enthusiasm and perseverance of some language campaigners, the Welsh language hardly merited a mention among people who were struggling to cope with material crisis. Cassie Davies, who was a vigorous champion of the language cause during this period, believed that the struggle for work and decent living conditions outweighed all other considerations and thrust linguistic and cultural values into the background ('Rhaid bod y frwydr gyson am waith ac amodau byw wedi gorbwyso pob ystyriaeth arall ac wedi gwthio gwerthoedd iaith a diwylliant a chenedl i'r cysgod').[205]

As the economic depression tightened its grip on mining communities, it became evident that many people would have to migrate to seek work. It was not easy, however, to abandon their native culture and society, and an industrial survey noted in 1932 that Welsh speakers were deeply reluctant to join the government's transference schemes and leave their localities.[206] Young women, however, rarely had any choice and were forced to forsake their homes for distant towns and cities. During the year of the General Strike in 1926, the minister of a chapel in the Rhondda pointed out that it was mainly young females who left their homes in order to relieve the financial burden on their families.[207] Having secured work as shop assistants or domestic servants in hotels and private houses, they sent valuable contributions back to their impoverished families. It was noted that one of the most sobering and unexpected consequences of the depression years was the appreciable number of young girls who sought work in London; by 1931 it was estimated that over 10,000 girls from south Wales were working as domestic servants in the city.[208] It was apparent by the early 1930s that greater numbers of young women than men were leaving their homes in south Wales and the Ministry of Labour confirmed that twice as many girls aged between 14 and 18 as males had left for England during the period 1930–4.[209] Moreover, female migrants tended to be much younger than males. Of those who were transferred by the government from south Wales to the Oxford area between 1921 and 1931, 77.3 per cent of the women were under 30, compared with 59.4 per cent of men.[210] Not everyone joined the state's compulsory transference schemes, however, and it is difficult to estimate exactly how many girls made their own arrangements to leave south Wales or moved to stay with friends and relatives

---

[205] Cassie Davies, *Hwb i'r Galon* (Abertawe, 1973), p. 126.

[206] Board of Trade, *Industrial Survey of South Wales* (London, 1932), p. 153.

[207] *Adroddiad Eglwys y Bedyddwyr, Libanus, Treherbert am y flwyddyn 1926* (copy).

[208] *Aberdare Leader*, 17 July 1926; *Second Industrial Survey of South Wales* (3 vols., Cardiff, 1937), II, p. 81.

[209] A. J. Chandler, 'The Re-making of a Working Class: Migration from the South Wales Coalfield to the New Industry Areas of the Midlands *c.*1920–1940' (unpubl. University of Wales PhD thesis, 1988), pp. 176–7; *Parliamentary Debates* (Hansard), 5th series, vol. 320, 2213 (25 February 1937).

[210] Goronwy H. Daniel, 'Labour Migration and Age-Composition', *Sociological Review*, XXXI, no. 3 (1939), 281–308.

who had already left Wales. It is known, however, that around 47,000 people left the Rhondda area alone between 1921 and 1935 on a journey memorably described by the writer Gwyn Thomas as 'a Black Death on wheels'.[211]

Although the likes of the Revd W. Glynfab Williams chastized migrants for turning their back on their country and language, not everyone was so blindly insensitive.[212] The Revd W. D. Lewis, Trecynon, president of the Aberdare Cymrodorion Society, had every sympathy with those who, having been forced to leave their native land, saw no benefit in maintaining the Welsh language and culture.[213] For the many thousands of young girls who left to seek work in English towns and cities, the ability to speak correct English was a vital qualification, whereas the Welsh language appeared to be of little value or status. One girl from Aberdare who worked as a servant in London believed that girls in south Wales should aim to improve their English rather than fret about the fate of the Welsh language: 'Welsh is no use outside Wales . . . Welsh may be useful at home in Wales but in other places it is useless.'[214] In his survey of Welsh life in 1938, the author Rhys Davies noted that this was the prevailing attitude among many young people. The majority were apathetic about the language and dubious of its value:

> Young men and women particularly are not eager to bother with the language. I have asked many of them their opinion, and the average reply is a vague: 'It's all right as a language', followed by a more definite: 'But it's no *use*.' They mean it's of no value to them in that climb through the world's activities with which the mind of the young is occupied – even if only with activities of amusement.[215]

As Harold Carter has noted, people were reluctant to use and maintain a language which was so restricted in its appeal and value.[216] Furthermore, as the historian John Davies has suggested, it was extremely unlikely that mothers in the valleys would make efforts to transmit the language to their children: 'what was the point of passing the language on to children who would have no future except in places like Luton or Dagenham?'[217] It was not surprising, therefore, that growing numbers of their children were raised through the medium of English. By 1938

---

[211] A. D. K. Owen, 'The Social Consequences of Industrial Transference', ibid., XXXIX, no. 4 (1937), 333; Thomas, *The Subsidence Factor*, p. 15.

[212] *Glamorgan Free Press and Rhondda Leader*, 14 November 1936.

[213] *Aberdare Leader*, 17 October 1936.

[214] Ibid., 19 October 1929.

[215] Rhys Davies, *My Wales* (London, 1938), p. 236.

[216] Harold Carter, 'Dirywiad yr Iaith Gymraeg yn yr Ugeinfed Ganrif' in Geraint H. Jenkins, *Cof Cenedl V: Ysgrifau ar Hanes Cymru* (Llandysul, 1990), pp. 151–2.

[217] Davies, *A History of Wales*, p. 582.

only 5 per cent of the children in the elementary schools of the Rhondda were recorded as Welsh speakers.[218]

The migration process clearly had a detrimental impact on the language. Yet many Welsh exiles succeeded in maintaining their cultural links because of their tendency to intermarry and to recreate their own Welsh communities in their new homes.[219] It was difficult, however, to maintain the native culture and language in such an alien environment. A married couple from Neath, who moved to Oxford in 1934 with their daughter and four sons, found it extremely difficult to come to terms with their new life in exile:

> they were all very dissatisfied with their lives. They missed the social life of their village in Wales. They wished they could speak Welsh to every one and resented such things as having to cook in a gas-oven instead of an ordinary one. The parents grieved that their children were growing up outside the chapel and beginning to lose their mother tongue. Every member of the family would prefer to live in Wales, even if the wages were much less.[220]

Young girls who left their homes to serve in private houses and who found themselves bereft of the companionship of family and friends were obliged to make a considerable effort to maintain contact with other Welsh people and institutions. The 'monoglot Welsh girl', portrayed in a poem by Ben Davies, was reckoned to deserve particular credit for making the effort to attend a Welsh-language chapel every Sunday.[221] Another commentator who lived in London maintained that many Welsh girls were overcome by their new surroundings in the capital city, and several admitted that they felt lonelier among London's millions than they could ever be on a mountain-top in Wales or in the African desert ('Y mae llawer yn tystio eu bod wedi teimlo'n fwy unig yng nghanol miliynau Llundain nag ar ben mynydd yng Nghymru neu anialdir Affrica').[222]

For those who stayed in their native districts, the burden of supporting traditional cultural and social institutions became heavier. Welsh chapels suffered greatly owing to the lack of financial and spiritual support, and secularism bred apathy among members.[223] An extremely bleak picture was presented in the annual reports of the chapels, not only regarding the devastating effects of the

---

[218] *Free Press and Rhondda Leader*, 15 October 1938.

[219] Goronwy H. Daniel, 'Labour Migration and Fertility', *Sociological Review*, XXXI, no. 4 (1939), 381; Peter D. John, 'The Oxford Welsh in the 1930s: A Study in Class, Community and Political Influence', *Llafur*, 5, no. 4 (1991), 102.

[220] Goronwy H. Daniel, 'Some Factors Affecting the Movement of Labour', *Oxford Economic Papers no. 3* (Oxford, 1940), p. 176.

[221] Ben Davies, 'Y Gymraes', *Free Press and Rhondda Leader*, 30 July 1938.

[222] *Y Cymro*, 18 January 1936.

[223] See John Roberts, 'Cyflwr Crefydd yn yr Ardaloedd Diwydiannol', *Y Drysorfa*, CI, no. 1202 (1931), 74–6.

migration of the younger population but also the spiritual and material poverty among the remaining members.[224] These losses caused grave concern to the Revd T. Alban Davies, minister of Bethesda chapel, Tonpentre, who believed that the depression had weakened every aspect of society and deprived it in particular of the young people who might have secured its future.[225] Yet, it appears that many female members remained faithful to their churches and the reports of the various denominations confirm that they worked assiduously on behalf of the churches and their co-members during the years of adversity.[226] The fund-raising work carried out by the sisterhoods not only helped to clear the debts of individual chapels but also ensured that social evenings and classes gave women a valuable opportunity to assemble and share their worries in such troubled times.

There was evidently a cultural significance to the losses of these years. As A. D. K. Owen warned in 1937: 'social *capital* is not all that there is to be lost to the nation. Whilst their importance cannot be measured in economic terms, the devitalization of provincial life and of the vigorous and distinctive national culture of Wales must surely be deplored'.[227] The work of the Welsh societies was greatly hampered by lack of interest and support, and was made all the more difficult by growing ignorance of the Welsh language. Drama festivals, which had previously staged notable Welsh-language productions, were now failing to attract any Welsh-language companies.[228] Yet it would be wrong to suggest that the social life of the industrial valleys had died; in fact, it remained vigorous and strong, though Welsh-language aspects of that social life were severely curtailed. As the English language tightened its grip on daily life, the use made of the Welsh language outside the confines of home and chapel diminished. Cassie Davies, a schoolteacher who campaigned vigorously on behalf of Plaid Genedlaethol Cymru (the Welsh Nationalist Party) in the valleys of Glamorgan, was disheartened in 1937 to find Welshness withering as the chapel and home lost their hold on the younger generation.[229] At the end of the 1930s another

---

[224] See, for example, *Adroddiadau Blynyddol Eglwys Nazareth MC, Aberdâr, 1929, 1930*; *Adroddiad Blynyddol Bethesda, Ton-Pentre, 1935, 1936*; NLW MS 12524D. Quarterly Reports of the Calvinistic Methodists in South Wales, 1936–8; *Rhondda Gazette*, 22 June 1935, 25 September 1937.

[225] T. Alban Davies, 'Rhai Sylwadau ar Adroddiad Ymchwil yr Athro H. A. Marquand yn Ne Cymru', *Yr Efrydydd*, III, no. 1 (1937), 23.

[226] See NLW MS 12524D; *Adroddiad Blynyddol Eglwys y MC yn Jerusalem, Ton, Ystrad, 1937* (Pentre, 1937); *Bethesda, Ton-Pentre, Jiwbili y Ddyled, Braslun o Hanes yr Eglwys 1876–1938* (Pentre, 1938), p. 21; S. L. George, *Bethania, Llwynypia, Braslun o Hanes yr Eglwys ar Achlysur Dathlu Jiwbili Clirio'r Ddyled* (1945), p. 18. See also B. B. Thomas, 'Yesterday and To-Day in a Mining Valley', *The Welsh Outlook*, XX, no. 12 (1933), 327–30.

[227] Owen, 'The Social Consequences of Industrial Transference', 351.

[228] *Aberdare Leader*, 19 November 1927, 31 October 1936; *Glamorgan Free Press and Rhondda Leader*, 26 January 1929, 30 January 1932.

[229] Cassie Davies, 'Yr Urdd a'r Iaith', *Heddiw*, 3, no. 1 (1937), 28.

commentator maintained that the whole atmosphere of the industrial community had been transformed:

Aflan ac amhur yw dŵr Afon Rhondda, a phob budreddi yn cael ymarllwys iddo o bob cyfeiriad. Ac y mae'r un peth yn wir am gyflwr ysbrydol a diwylliannol y cwm . . . Y mae'r ymfudo helaeth yn gyfrifol i raddau, ond ar wahân i hynny aeth bywyd yr ardal yn anghymreig ac yn wrth-Gymreig, a dylanwadau basaf Lloegr ac America yn ben arno.[230]

(The water of the river Rhondda is unclean and polluted, and every type of filth is allowed to pour in from all directions. And the same is true of the spiritual and cultural condition of the valley . . . In-migration is responsible to some extent, but apart from that the life of the area has become un-Welsh and anti-Welsh and the basest influences of England and America now rule.)

Following the outbreak of the Second World War in 1939, it soon became apparent that the military effort would have far-reaching implications for Welsh cultural life. The war undoubtedly had a devastating effect on social practices and conventions, for both work and leisure patterns were transformed by the wartime needs of the state. British aspirations permeated deeply into the Welsh consciousness and exercised considerable influence on the linguistic and cultural attitudes of the majority of the population. The stability of domestic life and social networks was destroyed as people were moved across the country and to distant parts of the world in order to meet military demands. From the industrial valleys, thousands of women, both young and old, took up munitions work at war factories in south Wales (Bridgend, Glasgoed, Cardiff and Treforest) and in industrial centres in England, where contact was made with people from all parts of Britain.[231] Thousands of evacuees flooded into the valleys from English towns and cities and it was inevitable that the 33,000 women and children who found shelter in the Rhondda would leave their mark on the language of both schools and homes.[232] In one of the Welsh chapels of the valley, it was reported that a very 'mixed' congregation now assembled for services and one commentator reckoned that 'one hears more Cockney accent in the Rhondda to-day than the Welsh language'.[233]

As tighter restrictions on public meetings were enforced, established social networks were destroyed and very few Welsh-language activities were maintained during the war years. According to one Welsh-language journal, the language was

---

[230] J. Gwyn Griffiths, 'Cwm Rhondda', ibid., 5, no. 6 (1939), 296.

[231] See Mari A. Williams, *'Where IS Mrs Jones Going?' Women and the Second World War in South Wales* (Aberystwyth, 1995); eadem, '"A Forgotten Army": The Female Munitions Workers of South Wales, 1939–45' (unpubl. University of Wales PhD thesis, 1999).

[232] E. D. Lewis, *The Rhondda Valleys* (London, 1959), p. 261.

[233] *Adroddiad Blynyddol Eglwys y MC yn Jerusalem, Ton, Ystrad, 1940* (Pentre, 1941), p. 4; *Rhondda Gazette*, 25 December 1943.

fighting for its life and was visibly wasting away.[234] It was difficult at the time to predict to what extent it might be resurrected after the war, but the minister of Jerusalem chapel, Tonpentre, was firmly of the opinion in 1940 that the future was bleak since the war was seriously weakening traditional cultural affiliations.[235] As the influence of the chapel gradually waned, linguistic decline was certain to follow and it was reported in 1943 that very few young people succeeded in maintaining their knowledge of the language once they had abandoned the chapels.[236] These fears were confirmed in evidence presented in a survey conducted by Undeb Cymru Fydd (the New Wales Union) in December 1943. It was reported that the Anglicizing tendencies in the valley towns of south Wales had been strengthened as new experiences at home and work expanded horizons and strengthened links with people from different cultural backgrounds. It was claimed that English had completely displaced Welsh as the language of institutions and societies in Aberdare, while in Maesteg and Nantgarw the war was recorded as having had a devastating effect on moral and social conventions. Among the younger generation, a general increase in the popularity of the cinema, the dance hall and public house was noted, while the 'Yanks' were said to be the most popular attraction of all among young women in Hengoed and Ystradmynach![237]

In recalling the impact of the Second World War on the social and cultural life of Gilfach-goch, Katie Olwen Pritchard felt that the whole experience had completely transformed the daily life of the mining community:

Ar ddiwedd y rhyfel sylweddolwyd fod cymeriad y cwm wedi ei llwyr drawsnewid. Daeth chwyldroad arall i'w hanes. Bu dylanwad y ffoaduriaid ar y Gymdeithas yn anferth. Profodd yr heddwch mor anodd â'r brwydro. Pan ddychwelodd y merched a'r bechgyn o'r lluoedd arfog 'roeddynt yn ymwybodol o'r cyfnewidiadau. Diflannodd bywyd egnïol crefyddol yr Eglwysi a gwelwyd safonau newydd israddol yn meddiannu'r gymdeithas.[238]

(At the end of the war it became apparent that the character of the valley had been totally transformed. Another revolution had occurred in its history. The influence of the evacuees on Society was immense. Peace proved as difficult as the battle itself. When the women and men from the armed forces returned they were conscious of the changes. The vibrant religious life of the Churches disappeared and was overtaken by new, inferior social standards.)

---

[234] Editorial, 'Y Dyfodol', *Heddiw*, 7, no. 1 (1941–2), 5.
[235] *Adroddiad Blynyddol Eglwys y MC yn Jerusalem, Ton, Ystrad, 1940*, p. 4.
[236] *Western Mail*, 21 April 1943.
[237] NLW, Undeb Cymru Fydd Papers (November 1960 collection), 165. Responses to Undeb Cymru Fydd's research questionnaire into the condition of the social life of Wales, December 1943.
[238] Pritchard, *Y Glas a'r Coch*, p. 30.

The reference to the experience of war as a 'revolution' was no exaggeration, for fundamental changes had occurred in the daily lives of the inhabitants of the industrial communities. The social experience of the majority had been widened by new work and leisure patterns, while the influence of the English-language media penetrated the most isolated valley settlements. As a result of these changes, it was not unusual for people to travel considerable distances to their workplace or to meet friends. And as women forged new social links, it was virtually inevitable that the Welsh language would lose its place in their informal conversation. Their social experiences were no longer restricted to the confines of the home and immediate neighbourhood, for the English language soon became a medium to be used daily in work and play. Gradually, the close-knit social networks which had played such an important part in maintaining the Welsh language and culture over the years were eroded. In the eastern valleys of Glamorgan it became increasingly difficult to maintain any form of social association through the medium of the Welsh language outside the walls of the chapels or home. Indeed, one correspondent complained in 1945 that the Welsh-speaking population of south Wales was being frozen out of existence.[239]

In effect, the Second World War merely confirmed and consolidated cultural trends which had been afoot for many decades. By the eve of the First World War, the Welsh language had already been isolated by economic, political and social forces. That process was accelerated by the difficult experiences of the inter-war years during which time the Welsh language was consigned to even more restricted social domains. During the same period women in the industrial valleys experienced a gradual change in their social role as political and economic developments transformed the nature of their daily experiences. It was inevitable that the majority of young women raised during this period would embrace very different linguistic and cultural values from those of their mothers. The defensive attitude adopted by supporters of the Welsh language towards the role of 'future mothers' was therefore unlikely to attract great support among women who were acquiring very different political and social ideals. Nevertheless, the Welsh language continued to satisfy the social and cultural needs of many people, notably members of the older generation. It cannot be said, therefore, that the language, together with its associated cultural values, was rejected consciously and deliberately by all members of industrial society. Ultimately, social and economic considerations were the principal factors which shaped linguistic preferences and patterns among the inhabitants of the south Wales valleys during the period under consideration, and the notion, advocated by Gwenith Gwyn and his ilk, that women could save the native tongue by championing the Welsh language in their homes was nothing but a pipedream.

---

[239] *Baner ac Amserau Cymru*, 29 August 1945.

4

The Welsh Language Movement in the First Half of the Twentieth Century: An Exercise in Quiet Revolutions

MARION LÖFFLER

THE EMERGING Welsh language movement of the first half of the twentieth century has hitherto escaped the attention of historians primarily concerned with understanding the traumatic social upheavals of the period. However, from the turn of the century a network of enthusiastic people, for whom Welsh identity was inextricably linked to the Welsh language, sought to rally a mostly unwilling nation to their cause. They trod a narrow centrist path, vulnerable to attacks both from the radical intellectuals of Plaid Genedlaethol Cymru (the Welsh Nationalist Party) and from conservative Anglo-Welsh and English forces. Following the Second World War and in the light of the more spectacular actions of a new generation of activists, their quiet revolution was largely forgotten. The following review of some of the major initiatives of the time will reveal how the sense of urgency felt by sections of the Welsh-speaking middle class in the face of the growing influence of English was transformed into organized and consistent action on behalf of the Welsh language. They planted ideas and laid foundations without which the achievements of the post-war period would not have been possible.[1]

According to the periodical *Celtia* in February 1901, the new century promised to be the 'Century of the Small Nations'.[2] Current trends seemed to confirm this opinion. Consciously emulating the example of their eastern European neighbours, cultural organizations set out in earnest to save their native tongue and support their home rule movement. In 1891 *An Comunn Gàidhealach* (the Highland Association) had been founded in Scotland. *Yn Çheshaght Ghailckagh* (the Manx Society) had been active since 1899, and in Cornwall the Celtic-Cornish Society was formed in 1901. The Irish *Conradh na Gaeilge* (the Gaelic League) was to achieve major educational goals before 1910. In 1900 a new Celtic Association was founded; it did not plan to concern itself 'with abstruse and recondite questions of Celtic ethnology' because 'we have in each of the five countries mentioned a burning problem – that of the preservation of the national

---

[1] The National Eisteddfod of Wales and the drama movement in Wales are not discussed in this chapter.

[2] *Celtia*, I, no. 2 (1901), 17; the periodical was published between 1901 and 1908.

language'.[3] The main occupation of the Dublin-based enterprise was organizing Celtic Congresses at Dublin (1901), Caernarfon (1904) and Edinburgh (1907) and issuing the magazine *Celtia* – 'the organ of militant Celticism directed mainly against the deadening and demoralising influences of modern Anglo-Saxondom'.[4] The publication was not interested in antiquarianism; rather, it presented creative work through the medium of modern Irish, Manx and Welsh, as well as English and Esperanto. The movement culminated in the Celtic Congress held at Caernarfon. Attended by over four hundred people, it brought together the learned and the quirky, the romantic and the radical, the British islands and eastern Europe, and thus provided an important link between those working in the field of minority languages in the first decade of the new century.

In Wales the arrival of the twentieth century was greeted with mixed feelings. On the one hand, visitors observed a national awakening and the emergence of a new national spirit. National institutions were founded and aspects of Welsh history were proudly displayed in colourful pageants, while the movement for the disestablishment of the Church of England in Wales gathered strength. The number of Welsh speakers was still rising and the language itself was refined by a new generation of scholars. The self-consciously titled *Wales To-day and To-morrow*, published in 1907, was optimistic: 'Herein is reflected the fair, fresh countenance of her rising Nationalism, and the expanding life of her people. The book is not reminiscent: its eyes are fixed on the present, with a brief glance at the future.'[5] However, other voices, wary of the 'English flood' which threatened to submerge the counties of Glamorgan and Monmouth, complained about the growing Anglicization of the National Eisteddfod and chapel life, and feared for the fate of the Welsh language in the next generation.[6] Both optimism and fear lay behind the foundation and re-emergence of a growing number of societies concerned with the maintenance of the Welsh language.

The first non-denominational organization to further the use of Welsh among children, Urdd y Delyn (the League of the Harp), had been founded by Mallt Williams in 1896. Mediated through the pages of O. M. Edwards's new magazine, *Cymru'r Plant*, it survived until 1906.[7] By that time, Mallt Williams had persuaded Gwyneth Vaughan to assist in the foundation of Undeb y Ddraig Goch (the Union of the Red Dragon), in order '1. To safeguard and promote the mother-tongue, 2. To revive the triple Harp . . . 3. To support Home Industries,

---

[3] Ibid., I, no. 1 (1901), 15.

[4] Ibid.

[5] Thomas Stephens (ed.), *Wales To-day and To-morrow* (Cardiff, 1907), p. xiii. A Welsh version of the book was published the following year.

[6] See D. Arthen Evans, 'Y Gymraeg a'r Llanw Seisnig', *Cymru*, XXXVII, no. 216 (1909), 34; J. Tywi Jones, 'Y Gymraeg yn y Teulu a'r Eglwys', *Tarian y Gweithiwr*, 10 and 17 April 1913.

[7] O. M. Edwards himself stressed several times that 'Miss Mallt L. Williams, Aberclydach yn nyffryn y Wysg' was the original founder of Urdd y Delyn. See O. M. Edwards, 'At Ohebwyr', *Cymru*, XIV, no. 79 (1898), 87, 100; *Celtia*, III, no. 1 (1903), 9.

4. To encourage a native Drama.'[8] Although the Union survived for less than a decade, from 1901 to about 1910, its attempts to make Welsh more attractive to children and young people by offering eisteddfod prizes for *penillion* singing, harp-playing and a knowledge of Welsh literature were warmly welcomed.[9] By 1899 the Society for Utilizing the Welsh Language for the Purpose of Serving a Better and More Intelligent Knowledge of English (1885) had changed its name to the more fitting Cymdeithas yr Iaith Gymraeg (the Welsh Language Society) and began to hold Welsh-language summer schools in 1904. In 1911 a second, more militant organization for Welsh children, Byddin Cymru (the Army of Wales), was founded and again popularized through the pages of *Cymru'r Plant*. Inspired by Irish youth organizations, it held rallies in which its members appeared in a uniform of green trousers and red scarves. Both uniform and rallies re-emerged when one of its first members, Ifan ab Owen Edwards, founded his own organization four years after the 'Army' folded in 1918.[10] A host of other organizations sprang up and disappeared again. Undeb Darllen Cymraeg (the Welsh Reading Union), established by the Welsh Language Society in 1907, Cymdeithas Siarad Cymraeg (the Society for Speaking Welsh), advertised by R. Gwylfa Roberts (Gwylfa) in 1916, and R. W. Melangell Evans's Byddin yr Iaith (the Language Army) (1923), whose members wore badges and pledged to speak Welsh only, are now little more than historical footnotes.[11] Other organizations founded during and shortly after that high tide of Welsh romantic nationalism survived and prospered. The Welsh Language Society itself (1899) and Undeb Cenedlaethol y Cymdeithasau Cymraeg (the National Union of Welsh Societies) (1913), which later assisted in the foundation of Urdd Gobaith Cymru (the Welsh League of Youth) (1922) and Undeb Athrawon Cymreig (the Union of Welsh Teachers) (1926), as well as local Cymrodorion, Cymreigyddion and other literary societies, were active throughout the period leading up to the Second World War. This chapter will concentrate on the main aspects of their work.

In 1959 Brinley Thomas argued, contrary to received wisdom, that industrialization saved the Welsh language. Since then, scholars have been unable to agree on the matter, but it is clear that Welsh speakers moving into industrial areas brought their language with them and developed their own Welsh-language

---

[8] Undeb y Ddraig Goch (the Union of the Red Dragon), *English Report for 1904* (Carmarthen, 1905), p. 3.

[9] *Celtia*, III, no. 9 (1903), 146; *Cymru*, XXVIII, no. 166 (1905), 260; ibid., XXXI, no. 183 (1906), 190; *Y Gymraes*, VIII, nos. 88–94 (1904).

[10] 'Byddin Cymru. Ysbiwyr y Frenhines. Y Rhestr Gyntaf: rhifau 35 a 36. Ifan ab Owen, Hâf, merch Owen, Neuadd Wen, Llanuwchllyn', *Cymru'r Plant*, XX (1911), 156; 'Gwisg Ysbiwyr', ibid., XXII (1913), 136; *Tarian y Gweithiwr*, 12 June 1913; Urdd Gobaith Cymru, *Gwisg yr Urdd* (Corwen, n.d.).

[11] *Adroddiad Cymdeithas yr Iaith Gymraeg am 1907* (Casnewydd-ar-Wysg, 1908), p. 26; R. Gwylfa Roberts, 'Cymdeithas Siarad Cymraeg', *Y Tyst*, 13 September 1916; R. W. Melangell Evans, 'Byddin yr Iaith', *Cymru*, LXIV, no. 381 (1923), 159.

culture in their new homes.[12] Even when the Welsh language and its culture began to retreat under pressure from English-speaking incomers, there remained islands of urban Welsh speakers, many of them middle class and therefore well equipped to defend their mother tongue and their traditions. Unlike Ireland and the Highlands of Scotland, Wales could boast that 'some Welsh is spoken in every part of Wales, and in all our large towns right up to Offa's Dyke. Here are to be found . . . vigorous and influential groups and societies of Welsh-speaking Welshmen ready at all times to press the needs of Wales and of the language'.[13] Members of such societies not only strove to safeguard the Welsh language in their own areas, but also reached out into Welsh-speaking Wales, where a command of English remained the desired goal of education, and also into the Anglicized border counties, where English had reigned supreme for generations. Fears about the endangered situation of the Welsh language in urban areas were thus transferred into rural areas. Industrialization may well have led to the in-migration of large numbers of English speakers, but it also facilitated the emergence of a Welsh language movement with the ability and the desire to work on behalf of the language. The wave of founding and reviving Welsh cultural societies emanated from the urban centres and partly Anglicized regions of the south and the north-east of Wales. The reasons were clear, as the report of the Llangollen Literary Society about its foundation in 1901 reveals:

Yr oedd y pryd hwnnw yn y dref gymdeithas Saesneg gref, er mai Cymry oedd y rhan fwyaf o'i haelodau. Tuedd honno ar brydiau oedd bychanu y Cymry, eu hanes a'u traddodiadau . . . Yr oedd gennym felly ddigon o resymau dros sefydlu'r gymdeithas uchod i lanw bwlch na wnai'r gymdeithas Saesneg mohono.[14]

(There was at the time a strong English society in the town, although most of the members were Welsh people. It tended, at times, to belittle the Welsh people, their history and their traditions . . . Therefore, we had good reason to set up the above society to fill the gap which was not filled by the English society.)

Especially in south Wales, Welsh speakers realized that they were swiftly becoming a minority, that Welsh was disappearing as the language of public life, and that it was no longer safe even in the traditionally strong domains of religion and the home:

---

[12] See Brinley Thomas, 'Wales and the Atlantic Economy', *Scottish Journal of Political Economy*, VI, no. 3 (1959), 169–92; idem, 'The Industrial Revolution and the Welsh Language' in Colin Baber and L. J. Williams (eds.), *Modern South Wales: Essays in Welsh Economic History* (Cardiff, 1986), pp. 6–21; idem, 'A Cauldron of Rebirth: Population and the Welsh Language in the Nineteenth Century' in Geraint H. Jenkins (ed.), *The Welsh Language and its Social Domains 1801–1911* (Cardiff, 2000), pp. 81–99; E. G. Millward, 'Industrialisation did not save the Welsh Language', *Welsh Nation*, no. 69 (1960), 4.

[13] D. Parry-Jones, *Welsh Country Upbringing* (London, 1948), p. 104.

[14] T. Carno Jones, 'Cymdeithas Lenyddol Llangollen', *Cymru*, XLI, no. 240 (1911), 13–14.

Un o beryglon mawrion Gwent a Morgannwg heddyw yw colli'r Gymraeg fel iaith y teulu a'r gwasanaeth crefyddol. Collwyd hi eisoes fel iaith yr heol. Tyrr y llanw Seisnig megis tonn anferth dros yr holl fro, ac ofnwn mai gorchuddio'r Gymraeg wna fel y gorchuddiwyd Cantref y Gwaelod gynt.[15]

(One of the main dangers facing Gwent and Glamorgan today is that Welsh will be lost as the language of the family and the religious service. It is lost already as the language of the street. The English tide rises like a giant wave over the whole area, and we fear it will submerge the language in the same way as Cantref y Gwaelod was submerged long ago.)

In the light of this threat, 'preachers, priests and teachers',[16] the leaders of the local Cymrodorion societies, felt it necessary to change their methods and aims, and to unite in order to be stronger. Following a series of conferences, the Revd J. Tywi Jones, owner and editor of Y Darian, and D. Arthen Evans, schoolmaster and secretary of the Barry Cymrodorion, formed the National Union of Welsh Societies in Neath in November 1913. The Union had embraced seventy-two societies in south Wales by 1914, but was not content with restricting itself to the region.[17] From 1919, its general secretary D. Arthen Evans attempted to co-operate with societies in north Wales, but was forced to admit in 1923 that 'Powys and Gwynedd have as yet presented insurmountable difficulties to complete Federation. Their Literary Societies are not so aggressive as they are in the industrial districts'.[18] A campaign of public meetings 'on behalf of Welsh Nationalism' organized in these districts in 1925 proved more successful.[19] New literary societies emerged and joined the Union, mainly along the north coast and in the larger towns, where Anglicizing influences had begun to make themselves felt and where a middle-class population similar to that which led the Union in the south was to be found. As late as 1938, however, the people of Anglesey remained convinced that there was no need for branches of any patriotic Welsh movement in a county as Welsh as theirs.[20] The main centres of activity in the north developed along the eastern borders, around Crewe and in the suburbs of Wrexham.[21] Expansion in the north-east went hand in hand with a decline in south Wales caused by the economic depression as well as by the dwindling

[15] Evans, 'Y Gymraeg a'r Llanw Seisnig', 34.
[16] Y Darian, 22 April 1920.
[17] Tarian y Gweithiwr, 9 January 1913, 6 and 27 March 1913, 31 July 1913, 20 and 27 November 1913; Undeb Cenedlaethol y Cymdeithasau Cymraeg (UCCC), Llawlyfr 1914 (1914), pp. 6–9.
[18] NLW, E. T. John Papers 5552, D. Arthen Evans, 'The Tenth Anniversary of the Formation of the National Union of Welsh Societies', pp. 3–4.
[19] NLW, Box XHS 1816, pamphlets of the National Union of Welsh Societies; Y Darian, December 1924–May 1925; Y Brython, January–March 1925. Meetings took place in Blaenau Ffestiniog, Caernarfon, Colwyn Bay, Dolgellau, Lampeter, Machynlleth, Rhyl and Wrexham.
[20] Y Brython, 19 May 1938.
[21] T. I. Ellis, 'Undeb Cymru Fydd', Pamffledi Cymru, no. 1 (1943), p. 2.

numbers and growing desperation of Welsh speakers who lived in the area. The disappearance of *Y Darian – Papur y Cymdeithasau Cymraeg a'r Eisteddfod* (The Shield – Newspaper of the Welsh Societies and the Eisteddfod) in 1934, a newspaper which had served the literary societies well, made communication all the more difficult. On the other hand, *Y Brython*, published in north Wales, continued to inform its readers of the activities of the Union and of the other main patriotic movements, namely the Welsh Nationalist Party and Urdd Gobaith Cymru.[22] Despite the difficulties, the Union maintained a membership of around sixty to seventy local societies, serving about ten thousand people. In addition, an estimated further sixty local literary societies were active throughout the period before the Second World War, some of which co-operated with the Union.[23]

The geographical distribution of other organizations displayed similar characteristics. The Union of Welsh Teachers was based in south Wales, where its bimonthly publication, *Yr Athro* (est. 1928), sold most of its 2,000 copies and where the majority of its 500–600 members were organized into twenty or so branches.[24] The Union also attempted to include north Wales in its activities, but encountered similar problems to the National Union of Welsh Societies.[25] On the other hand, during its early years Urdd Gobaith Cymru appealed mainly to children and teachers in the counties of Caernarfon, Denbigh and Merioneth, probably because its founder lived in Merioneth and *Cymru'r Plant* seemed to be targeting an audience in those areas. Nevertheless, expansion into south Wales was soon facilitated by the National Union of Welsh Societies, Welsh chapels and literary societies, as well as by the Union of Welsh Teachers. The National Union of Welsh Societies organized lectures on behalf of Ifan ab Owen Edwards and called for support in its meetings, while individual Cymrodorion societies, chapels and Welsh teachers founded or supported Urdd branches.[26] When Ifan ab Owen Edwards and R. E. Griffith, the first full-time organizer of the Urdd, decided to concentrate on independent branches and rely less on schools, it became clear that the most active areas were industrial south and north-east Wales, and along the north coast, while large parts of Cardiganshire and Anglesey remained apathetic.[27] Reporting that 'there is much greater Urdd activity in the anglicised areas of Wales than in the purely Welsh areas . . . there is much more enthusiasm . . . in those parts where the Welsh language and culture are in danger', R. E. Griffith

---

[22] *Y Brython*, 7 January 1937, 24 March 1938.
[23] Membership figures are based on the list of member societies and their subscription rates, which were published annually in the report and the accounts of the National Union of Welsh Societies.
[24] *Yr Athro*, IV, no. 1 (1931), 3; ibid., IV, no. 5 (1931), 196–7; ibid., IX, nos. 8 and 9 (1936), 229.
[25] 'Nodiadau Golygyddol', ibid., VII, no. 2 (1934), 53–5; ibid., VII, no. 5 (1934), 139.
[26] UCCC, *Rhaglen Cyfarfodydd y . . . Gynhadledd Flynyddol* (1924), p. 10; *Cymru'r Plant*, XXXIV (1925), 398 (Abercynon); ibid., XXXV (1926), 397 (Abercynon, Cilfynydd, Ynys-y-bŵl, Pontypridd); 'At y Plant', ibid., XXXVII (1928), 255, 286; *Cronicl yr Urdd*, II, no. 2 (1930), 29–30 (Denbigh), 40–1 (Llanelli).
[27] *Cronicl yr Urdd*, II, no. 3 (1930), 40; ibid., II, no. 10 (1930), 154.

drew the conclusion that 'there is something wrong, either with the Urdd or with the Welsh rural areas'.[28] The probable explanation is that a language which is an integral part of the community does not need overt efforts to sustain it. Cultural movements pursuing such aims gain influence only when and where a language is in danger of being superseded by another.

Unlike the other organizations mentioned, the influence of Urdd Gobaith Cymru grew swiftly. In February 1923, when it was just a year old, its 784 members took only three weeks to organize a petition of 7,000 signatures in protest against the drowning of Glyn Ceiriog.[29] The circulation of *Cymru'r Plant* rose from 6,250 copies a month in 1920 to over 15,000 copies in 1928–9, the highest circulation since its foundation.[30] By December 1930 the membership figures of the Urdd stood at 26,454, surpassing those of the Boy Scouts, the largest youth organization operating in Wales, which had 16,091 members. By 1940 the membership of the Urdd (57,548), organized into 670 branches all over the country, some of them attached to schools or chapels, and some independent, exceeded the total membership of all other youth organizations in Wales.[31]

The working methods of the various organizations were very similar. After all, they shared a common *raison d'être*: the salvation of the Welsh language. Differences arose from the domains in which they worked and the type of people they reached. The Welsh Language Society remained a small group of educationalists whose object was 'to promote (a) the use of Welsh as a means of education, and (b) the better teaching of Welsh in the Welsh-speaking, English-speaking and bilingual districts of Wales'.[32] The Union of Welsh Teachers, founded later in the century and certainly influenced by the more radical spirit of the 1920s, took these aims a step further:

> Credwn fod Cymru yn wlad ag iddi hunaniaeth genedlaethol, a . . . daliwn mai Cymraeg a phynciau diwylliannol Cymreig a ddylai gael y flaenoriaeth yn nhrefniant addysg ein gwlad. Dyna'n hawl, ac ni ofynnwn am ddim llai. Rhwymyn ein cyfamod yw, 'Cymraeg i Gymru', a'r neb nid oes ganddo Gymraeg, nid ydyw Gymro ychwaith.[33]

---

[28] 'Urdd Notes', *Western Mail*, 15 December 1937.

[29] *Cymru'r Plant*, XXXII (1923), 59, 133.

[30] D. Tecwyn Lloyd, 'Hanes Masnachol Rhai o Gyhoeddiadau Syr O. M. Edwards', *NLWJ*, XV, no. 1 (1967–8), 55–71.

[31] *Cronicl yr Urdd*, II, no. 12 (1930), 177; *Fourth Annual Report of the Welsh Scout Council for the year ending 30 September 1930* (1930), p. 3; NLW, Urdd Gobaith Cymru Archives (A1989/30), A56. It must be remembered that the membership of the National Union of Welsh Societies and the Union of Welsh Teachers was renewed every year, whereas, before the Second World War, members of Urdd Gobaith Cymru were registered once, on entering the organization. Between 2,000 and 4,000 children joined the Urdd annually.

[32] The Welsh Language Society, *Scheme and Rules of the Society* (Bangor, 1901), p. 16.

[33] Tom Jones, 'Rhagair: Ein Safbwynt a'n Hamcanion', *Yr Athro*, I, no. 1 (1928), 3.

(We believe that Wales is a country with its own national identity, and . . . we believe
the Welsh language and Welsh cultural subjects should have priority in the educational
system of our country. That is our right and we ask for nothing less. 'Welsh for Wales'
is the bond of our covenant and he who speaks no Welsh is not a Welshman.)

The Union's main objectives were to secure priority for the Welsh language and
for the literature, music and history of Wales in schools. It would provide a
platform for Welsh teachers, further co-operation between them, prepare statistics
on the state of the education system, and provide Welsh-language teaching
materials.[34]

Both the National Union of Welsh Societies and Urdd Gobaith Cymru
pursued wider aims and appealed to a much wider circle of people. They
endeavoured to form mass organizations that would further the use of Welsh in all
spheres of life. 'Iaith Nas Arferir, Iaith i Farw Yw' (A language that is not used is
a dead language), was the theme of one of the Union's nascent meetings at the
Abergavenny National Eisteddfod in 1913:

Ni waeth pa mor gyfoethog ei llenyddiaeth, na pha mor ddyfal y'i hefrydir gan
ysgolheigion byd, na pha faint o arian a werir i'w dysgu yn yr ysgolion dyddiol, na pha
mor ddiffuant y'i molir gan Wasg a Llwyfan, bydd yr Iaith Gymraeg farw oni SIAREDIR
hi. Felly, heddyw, yn nydd du ei hesgeulusdod ar aelwyd, mewn capel, a masnach, a
chymdeithas, os am achub rhag difancoll yr Iaith Gymraeg a phopeth a olyga hi i
Gymru . . . rhaid Siarad Cymraeg, Gohebu'n Gymraeg, Darllen Cymraeg.[35]

(No matter how rich its literature, or how avidly it is studied by international scholars,
or how much money is spent to teach it in day schools, or how sincerely it is praised by
the Press and from public Platforms, the Welsh Language will die if it is not SPOKEN.
Therefore, today, in the darkest day of neglect on the hearth, in chapel, in the market
place and in the community, if Welsh and everything it means to Wales is to be saved
from perdition . . . we must Speak Welsh, Correspond in Welsh, Read Welsh.)

The Union's objectives, laid down in its first handbook, included assisting the
foundation of new societies throughout Wales and acting as a link between them.
It proposed to support the Welsh language and its literature and to secure its use
in every circle of Welsh life. It would raise the national spirit and oppose every
movement which did not do so, thereby 'serving Wales along national lines'.[36]
The aims of Urdd Gobaith Cymru, displayed on every membership certificate,
were broadly similar. Among other things, the young members vowed to speak
Welsh with other children, to read and to buy Welsh literature, to sing Welsh

---

[34] Ibid.
[35] UCCC, *Y Cymdeithasau Cymreig: Gweithrediadau Cyfarfod Y Fenni, Awst 7, 1913* (1913), p. 6.
[36] Idem, *Llawlyfr 1914* (1914), p. 5.

songs, to play in Welsh all the time and never to deny that they were Welsh or to betray their country.[37] A threefold promise, to be faithful 'to Wales, to Fellow Man, and to Christ' ('i Gymru, i Gyd-ddyn ac i Grist'), was added in 1932.[38]

All the societies were committed to strictly constitutional methods through which they sought to influence public opinion and change the attitude of institutions. Apart from holding public meetings and organizing social events held through the medium of Welsh, this mainly took the form of petitioning and respectable protest. However, there were different ways of influencing public opinion. Whereas the Welsh participants of the Celtic Congress at Bangor in 1927 simply removed 'God Save the King' from the programme,[39] the Urdd sought to gain respect for the Welsh national anthem by direct action:

Fe'r ydym wedi sylwi mai ychydig iawn o barch a gaiff ein hanthem genedlaethol gennym ni yn ein cyrddau yng Nghymru. A wna bechgyn yr Urdd, gan hynny, sefyll ger drysau pob cyfarfod y digwyddant fod ynddo tua'i ddiwedd, a rhwystro pobl allan tra chenir 'Hen Wlad fy Nhadau'. Trwy hyn, dysgwn y Cymry i barchu eu hanthem genedlaethol eu hunain.[40]

(We have noticed that our national anthem is but little respected in our meetings in Wales. Will the boys of the Urdd, therefore, stand by the doors towards the end of every meeting at which they happen to be present and prevent people from leaving while 'Hen Wlad fy Nhadau' (Land of my Fathers) is being sung. This way, we will teach the Welsh people to respect their own national anthem.)

One cannot fail to be impressed by the achievements of the voluntary organizations active in Wales at a time when the country was riven by economic crises and received only minimal financial support from a state which at best pursued a 'policy of benign neglect'.[41] All the societies mentioned survived almost exclusively on members' subscriptions and on substantial donations from individuals. For instance, Mallt Williams and J. M. Howell donated the £200 which enabled Ifan ab Owen Edwards to hold the first Welsh summer camp for members of the Urdd. They sponsored eisteddfod prizes for reciting in Welsh and writing Welsh plays, and paid the entrance fees for Urdd members attending the National Eisteddfod. In addition to subsidizing Cymru'r Plant in the 1920s, J. M. Howell's gift of £1,000 laid the financial foundation for establishing the Urdd as

---

[37] Cymru'r Plant, XXI (1922), 6. For an example of a membership certificate, see Marion Löffler, 'Iaith Nas Arferir, Iaith i Farw Yw': Ymgyrchu dros yr Iaith Gymraeg rhwng y Ddau Ryfel Byd (Aberystwyth, 1995), p. 12.

[38] R. E. Griffith, Urdd Gobaith Cymru: Cyfrol I. 1922–1945 (Aberystwyth, 1971), p. 132.

[39] The anthem was cut out overnight, see Morning Post, 22 July 1927.

[40] Cronicl yr Urdd, IV, no. 37 (1932), 20.

[41] Phillip M. Rawkins, 'The Politics of Benign Neglect: Education, Public Policy, and the Mediation of Linguistic Conflict in Wales', International Journal of the Sociology of Language, 66 (1987), 27–48.

a limited company and facilitated its phenomenal expansion in the 1930s. A later donation of £500 paid for the production of the first film with a Welsh soundtrack.[42] From its inception, Mallt Williams annually donated the fees for up to three teachers to attend the Welsh summer school. She also paid substantial subscriptions to the Welsh Language Society, the National Union of Welsh Societies and later the Welsh Nationalist Party.[43] Government support was rare. The Welsh Language Society and the National Union of Welsh Societies received financial support only in the form of education authority grants for teachers attending their summer courses, and grants towards Welsh language, literature and history classes held in conjunction with the Workers' Educational Association (WEA) or the extramural departments of the University of Wales. When grants for teachers failed to materialize in the 1930s, the summer school of the National Union of Welsh Societies ceased. In contrast, English youth organizations were given financial support by charities such as the Carnegie Trust, as well as by the government. The South Wales Federation of Boys' Clubs was subsidized with about £12,000 in 1931–2 and the National Association of Boys' Clubs received £40,000 in 1937–8. The sum of £10,000 was given to the National Association of Girls' Clubs to maintain their libraries, while Young Farmers' Clubs were supported by the Ministry of Agriculture and Fisheries. The Urdd, however, did not receive its first government grant for work in the distressed areas until 1935. Only after the National Fitness Council was established in 1938, with the aim of preparing British youth for the physical strains of the anticipated war, did independent Urdd branches receive about £12,350, mainly for the acquisition or extension of buildings. The first Urdd grant from the Board of Education did not arrive until 1939.[44] Government subsidies for Welsh-language publications were also not forthcoming. Y Darian succumbed to financial difficulties in 1934, while Cymru'r Plant, despite relatively high circulation figures, proved a heavy financial burden for Ifan ab Owen Edwards throughout the inter-war years, and survived through private donations.[45] Y Capten, an ambitious magazine for older children

---

[42] Griffith, Urdd Gobaith Cymru: Cyfrol I, pp. 78, 94–5; 'Cronfa yr Urdd', Y Capten, I, no. 10 (1931), 222.

[43] D. James, 'Yr Ysgol Haf Gymraeg, 1904', Cymru, XXVII, no. 160 (1904), 229–35; idem, 'Yr Ysgol Haf Gymraeg', ibid., XXXII, no. 186 (1907), 65–72; Gerald Morgan, 'Dannedd y Ddraig' in John Davies (ed.), Cymru'n Deffro: Hanes y Blaid Genedlaethol 1925–75 (Talybont, 1981), p. 23; annual reports of the Welsh Language Society, the National Union of Welsh Societies and Urdd Gobaith Cymru. For an insight into the life and interests of Mallt Williams, see Marion Löffler, 'A Romantic Novelist', Planet, 121 (1997), 58–66.

[44] J. Glynn-Jones, 'Boys' Clubs and Camps', The Welsh Outlook, XX, no. 8 (1933), 214–17; A. E. Morgan, The Needs of Youth: A Report Made to King George's Jubilee Trust (London, 1939), pp. 280, 322, 343; National Fitness Council for England and Wales, Report of the Grants Committee to the President of the Board of Education for the period ended 31st March 1939 (London, 1939), pp. 14–55.

[45] NLW, W. J. Gruffydd Papers II, 252, letter from Ifan ab Owen Edwards to W. J. Gruffydd, 14 March 1936.

and teenagers, folded in 1933 after only three years. *Yr Athro* survived, largely because of the revenue from advertisements and because none of the contributors received payment.[46]

Financial difficulties were not the only problems facing Welsh cultural organizations. Especially after the foundation of the Welsh Nationalist Party and in the tense atmosphere of the late 1930s, it became important for cultural societies to distance themselves from politics, while at the same time continuing to work for the Welsh language and, as many people saw it, for the Welsh nation. This was an especially acute problem for Urdd Gobaith Cymru and for the National Union of Welsh Societies, which had professed nationalist political aspirations before 1925. Following a vote taken in the annual general meeting of 1919, members of the Union had been obliged to use every legal means to stress the right of Wales to self-government ('defnyddio pob moddion cyfreithlawn i bwysleisio hawl Cymru i Ymreolaeth').[47] However, when the matter was raised again in 1922, a decision was postponed because of the opposition of leading council members.[48] Although the progress of the Welsh Nationalist Party was furthered on several levels,[49] the Union nevertheless eventually decided to abandon politics and concentrate on the preservation of the Welsh language. D. Arthen Evans, general secretary of the Union, informed H. R. Jones, organizer of the Welsh Nationalist Party, that the Union would henceforth confine itself to issues relating to the Welsh language while the Party could concentrate on the political aspects of Welsh nationalism ('gall ein Hundeb ni i weithio ym myd yr iaith neu yn narn yr iaith o faes mawr cenedlaetholdeb ac y gall y *Blaid* weithio yn y darn politicaidd o'r maes hwnnw').[50] Thus resources could be concentrated on language preservation and, perhaps more importantly, the organization would remain more acceptable to the Welsh middle classes than the 'Welsh Sinn Feiners', as the Welsh Nationalist Party was dubbed by some.

It is clear from letters and articles written by Ifan ab Owen Edwards that he

---

[46] *Yr Athro*, IV, no. 6 (1931), 211; ibid., XII, no. 12 (1939), 341.

[47] UCCC, *Rhaglen Cyfarfodydd y . . . Gynhadledd Flynyddol* (1919), p. 5.

[48] NLW, E. T. John Papers 3138–4133, correspondence between D. Arthen Evans and E. T. John 1922–3; UCCC, *Rhaglen Cyfarfodydd y . . . Gynhadledd Flynyddol* (1922), p. 3; idem, *Rhaglen Cyfarfodydd y . . . Gynhadledd Flynyddol* (1923), p. 5.

[49] The report of the Dyfed region for 1924 mentions that its annual meeting heard lectures by 'Mr Ambrose Bebb, MA, o Brifysgol Paris' and by 'Mr D. J. Williams, BA, Yr Ysgol Sir, Abergwaun'. UCCC, *Rhaglen Cyfarfodydd y . . . Gynhadledd Flynyddol* (1924), p. 6. One wonders if the annual meeting was part of the Union's 'campaign on behalf of Welsh Nationalism'. Apart from the above founder members of the Welsh Nationalist Party, H. R. Jones, its first secretary, R. E. Jones, its second secretary, and Saunders Lewis lectured widely in Union meetings in 1924 and 1925. The former two also served as Union secretaries, H. R. for Eifionydd and Arfon and R. E. for Blaenau Ffestiniog. UCCC, *Rhaglen Cyfarfodydd y . . . Gynhadledd Flynyddol* (1925), p. 19. Evidence of the ways in which organizations such as the Union were used by the founders of the Welsh Nationalist Party is found in T. Robin Chapman, '"Ein Ffydd Genedlaethol Ni": Tri Llenor a Chychwyn y Blaid Genedlaethol', *Taliesin*, 94 (1996), 101–17.

[50] NLW, Plaid Cymru Archives B2, letter from D. Arthen Evans to H. R. Jones, 30 July 1926.

viewed Urdd Gobaith Cymru as an instrument not only for the preservation of the Welsh language but also for building a sense of Welsh national identity that the older generation did not possess.[51] Although, following an early campaign devoted to 'Self-Government for Wales', politics was officially excluded from its agenda, the Urdd often found itself caught in a crossfire.[52] It was attacked by some for its alleged connections with the Welsh Nationalist Party and by others for its anti-nationalist tendencies. Time and again Ifan ab Owen Edwards and R. E. Griffith stressed that the Urdd was a wholly non-political and non-sectarian organization. In 1930, for instance, the following declaration was made: 'Once and for all, there is no connection at all between the Urdd and the Welsh Nationalist Party' ('Unwaith ac am byth, nid oes dim cysylltiad o gwbl rhwng yr Urdd a'r Blaid Genedlaethol').[53] R. E. Griffith, himself a member of the Welsh Nationalist Party, complained in 1942:

> Fe synnech cymaint yr ydym ni wedi gorfod ei ddioddef yn dawel oherwydd y pethau y mae'r Blaid yn sgrifennu amdanom, ac yn eu dweud amdanom. Mae'r Llywodraeth yn disgyn arnom am bob dim a glywir neu a welir, a swyddogion y Ministry of Information ar eu heithaf yn casglu pob tystiolaeth fel yna.[54]

> (You would be surprised how much we have had to suffer in silence because of the things the Party says and writes about us. The Government descends on us because of everything it hears or sees, and officials from the Ministry of Information do their utmost to assemble all such evidence.)

Such publicity certainly had adverse affects. The Welsh Language Petition of 1938, for instance, ran into early difficulties on Merseyside because the opening meeting there had been conducted by Saunders Lewis and not, as in many other places, by the respective regional secretary of the National Union of Welsh Societies. People were anxious not to be connected with a campaign organized by the Welsh Nationalist Party, but were willing to lend their support to one conducted on 'non-political national' lines.[55]

Some attacks were motivated by concerns other than party politics. The English and Anglo-Welsh press were always ready to pour scorn on campaigns relating to the Welsh language and to voice the complaints of English speakers. The grievances of several 'English-speaking Welshmen' were published in the newspapers of south Wales and in 1927 a protest about the incorrect

---

[51] Ifan ab Owen Edwards, 'A yw y Cymry'n Genedl?', *Cymru*, LXIII, no. 372 (1922), 1–3.

[52] 'Hunan Lywodraeth i Gymru', *Cymru'r Plant*, XXXII (1923), 286.

[53] *Cronicl yr Urdd*, II, no. 10 (1930), 154.

[54] NLW, Urdd Gobaith Cymru Archives A58, letter from R. E. Griffith to J. O. Williams, 7 May 1942.

[55] *Liverpool Daily Post*, 25 March 1939, 2 June 1939; *Wrexham Leader*, 28 April 1939.

pronunciation of Welsh names on the radio evoked a spate of satiric verse under headings such as 'Wales Wails' in newspapers across Britain.[56] In 1929 *Punch* made light of a campaign to secure bilingual cheques, reporting that 'we should hate to hear our bank manager saying what he thought of our overdraft in Welsh'.[57] At times the difficulties must have seemed overwhelming. Poems like 'Cwynfan Gwent' (Lamentation of Gwent) and 'Angladd y Gymraeg' (Funeral of the Welsh Language), both composed in connection with Cymrodorion meetings in south Wales, captured the acute sense of hopelessness:

> Mae'r Iaith Gymraeg yn marw, a'r Beibl yn ei llaw,
> A'i phlant yn llawn mursendod ffol, a'u Saesneg brâs, di-daw;
> Nid gormes Llan na Chapel yw'r achos, medde nhw,
> Ond pawb o'r Cymry yn 'u tai'n baldorddi, – 'How d'ye do?'

> . . . Mae Cymrodorion Ebbw, bob gaea'n noddi'r Iaith,
> Ond Saesneg drwy y flwyddyn hir, ar Sul, a Gwyl, a Gwaith;
> Diflanna swyn y Ddrama, a'r Ddarlith bob yn ail,
> Tra'r hên Estrones yn y tŷ yn cloddio dan eu sail.[58]

(The Welsh language is dying, with the Bible in her hand / Her children are full of affectation, with their coarse and endless English / The reason is not, they say, the oppression of Church or Chapel / But all the Welsh themselves babbling – 'How d'ye do?' – in their houses.

The Ebbw Cymrodorion support the Language every winter / But it is English throughout the long year, on Sundays, holidays and at work / The charm of the Drama and of the Lecture disappear one after the other / While the old Foreigner in the house undermines the foundations.)

The language policy of the BBC, the development of 'talkies' in the cinema and the increasing quantity and availability of cheap English-language literature all posed new threats to the Welsh language. Older issues, including the neglect of the language in education and by public institutions, and its exclusion from the legal system, remained unresolved. On the other hand, the founding of the Welsh Nationalist Party in 1925 extended the framework of radical opinion within which cultural organizations operated.[59] As a consequence, language preservation activities on both a regional and a national level in the domains of education,

---

[56] *South Wales Daily News*, 8 June 1923. For examples of the poems, see *Yorkshire Observer*, 14 June 1927; *Daily News*, 16 June 1927.

[57] *Western Mail*, 27 May 1929; *Punch*, 5 June 1929.

[58] Evan Price (Ieuan Gorwydd), 'Cwynfan Gwent', *Cymru*, LXII, no. 371 (1922), 212–13; H. Lloyd, 'Angladd y Gymraeg', ibid., LXVIII, no. 404 (1925), 86–7.

[59] D. Hywel Davies, *The Welsh Nationalist Party 1925–1945: A Call to Nationhood* (Cardiff, 1983), pp. 3–58.

broadcasting, publishing and official life intensified, coming to a peak in the years immediately before the Second World War. Each of these will be examined in turn.

The first campaigns for reintroducing the Welsh language into the domain of secular education had been fought by the Welsh Language Society in the last quarter of the nineteenth century. It was through its efforts that the Intermediate Education Act 1889 recognized the Welsh language as a special subject, a position which was further developed in the 1907 Educational Code. Education authorities which administered what was known as a bilingual system and allowed the teaching of Welsh as a subject in their schools did so on the basis of the scheme laid down by the Society in the first decade of the new century.[60] In 1910 a more detailed scheme was developed and published by David James (Defynnog), the Society's secretary.[61] An active and prominent member of the language movement, James published more than a dozen educational pamphlets and books on the teaching of the Welsh language and the history of Wales in the years that followed. The efforts of the Welsh Language Society were given wider scope when the National Union of Welsh Societies was founded in 1913. From its inception it organized public conferences and lobbied government institutions in order to draw attention to the place of Welsh in the educational domain. A first report, *Adroddiad ar Safle Addysgu Llên Cymru yn ein Hysgolion Canolraddol* (Report on the Place of Teaching the Literature of Wales in our Intermediate Schools) was published by the Union in 1915.[62] Conferences on the teaching of Welsh were held under its auspices from 1916.[63] In 1921, following the passing of the Fisher Education Act, it published *Schemes of Welsh Studies*, which demanded from the Departmental Committee on the Organisation of Secondary Education in Wales that Welsh should be made a compulsory subject in every type of educational institution in Wales.[64] The annual conference of 1923 urged the Board of Education to conduct research into the place of Welsh in the education system. It was argued that the Welsh language in Wales should be treated in the same way as English in the schools of England.[65] Similar sentiments were conveyed to the press following the annual conference of the Union in Barry in 1925, the year in which

---

[60] The Welsh Language Society, *Scheme and Rules of the Society*, pp. 5–6; idem, *Adroddiad Cymdeithas yr Iaith Gymraeg am 1906* (Casnewydd-ar-Wysg, 1907), pp. 5–12; idem, *Adroddiad Cymdeithas yr Iaith Gymraeg am 1910, 1911, a 1912* (Caerdydd, 1913), pp. 5–10.

[61] *Rhondda Scheme for Teaching Welsh, Compilers: D. James, Treherbert; H. Howells, Treorchy (at the request of the Rhondda Head Teachers' Association)* (Cardiff and London, 1910).

[62] Undeb y Cymdeithasau Cymraeg, *Adroddiad ar Safle Addysgu Llên Cymru yn ein Hysgolion Canolraddol, gan T. Matthews* (Dundalk, 1915).

[63] See 'Addysg Mewn Cymraeg' (Cardiff), *Y Darian*, 30 March 1916; 'Y Gymraeg ar yr Aelwyd ac yn yr Eglwysi' (Cardiff), UCCC, *Rhaglen Cyfarfodydd y . . . Gynhadledd Flynyddol* (1916); 'Addysg Genedlaethol' (Swansea), *Y Darian*, 8 January 1920.

[64] UCCC, *Schemes of Welsh Studies, or, Proposals for Securing for the Welsh Language its Proper Place in a System of Education in Wales and Monmouthshire, under the Education Act, 1918* (Barry, 1921), p. 2.

[65] Idem, *Rhaglen Cyfarfodydd y . . . Gynhadledd Flynyddol* (1923), p. 8.

a commission was appointed to inquire into the place of the Welsh language in the educational system of Wales.[66] Among the committee members who compiled the influential final report were Philip Thomas, chairman of the Union, D. Lleufer Thomas, one of its former presidents, and Ellen Evans, the influential head of Barry Training College and one of the Union's most faithful suppporters. Ellen Evans was the only female member.[67] After the publication of the report in 1927, William George, by now president of the Union, and Ellen Evans organized public meetings to discuss its recommendations and to develop schemes for its application.[68] The report fuelled public discussion in Wales for months, if not years, and thus put the status of Welsh in education on the national agenda. Even though many of its recommendations were not implemented until after the Second World War, it gave local groups and individuals a basis on which to demand new rights and to conduct experiments. Ellen Evans, for instance, saw the opportunity to develop her ideal of Welsh-language playgroups for the Anglicized industrial areas of Wales. Since mothers whose priorities lay with the feeding and clothing of their children could not be expected to concern themselves with the language of the hearth, she argued:

byddai sefydlu 'Ysgolion Meithrin' i blant Cymraeg o ddwy flwydd i bum oed, yn arbennig yn yr ardaloedd poblog . . . yn help sylweddol i gadw iaith plant Cymry Cymreig yn bur a dilediaith hyd at oedran dechrau yn yr ysgol.[69]

(the establishment of 'Nursery Schools' for Welsh children between the ages of two and five, especially in the populous areas . . . would be a great help in keeping the language of the children of Welsh speakers pure and undefiled until they reach school age.)

With extraordinary energy and commitment, Evans set about turning her dream into reality.[70] Having visited existing nursery schools, she called a conference in Barry to prepare for the establishment of such schools in south Wales. The first 'ysgol feithrin' (nursery school) was set up in Dowlais on 10 October 1930.[71] Other success stories followed the publication of the 1927 report and were championed as exemplars in Yr Athro. In 1930 an elementary school was established in Llandudno, in which about sixty children between the

---

[66] See copy of the list of motions on education in Wales prepared by E. T. John for discussion at the Barry conference, NLW, Plaid Cymru Archives B2, letter from L. May Roberts to H. R. Jones, 20 March 1925.

[67] Departmental Committee on Welsh in the Educational System of Wales, *Welsh in Education and Life* (London, 1927), p. xvii. A number of Union members gave evidence. For the proposals of the Union, see pp. 155–7 of the report.

[68] *Wrexham Advertiser*, 10 September 1927 (Harlech); *Western Mail*, 22 February 1928 (Tonypandy).

[69] Ellen Evans, 'Y Plant Bach a Phwyllgor Ymchwil y Gymraeg', *Yr Athro*, I, no. 2 (1928), 42.

[70] For a portrait of Ellen Evans, see Cassie Davies, *Hwb i'r Galon* (Abertawe, 1973), pp. 71–4.

[71] *Y Ddraig Goch*, 7, no. 11 (1933), 3.

ages of five and seven were taught in Welsh. At Cilfynydd Boys' School, half the lessons were given through the medium of Welsh from 1930 onwards. The pupils emerged fluent in both English and Welsh and the headmaster John Phillips was thus able to demonstrate 'that it was possible for a school, even in Glamorgan, to be bilingual'.[72] Just as national developments were manifested locally, local campaigns often radiated into the rest of the country and initiated nationwide developments. From the early 1920s Cymrodorion societies, chapels and later the Union of Welsh Teachers petitioned the education authority in the Rhondda until an experiment in bilingual education was carried out at schools in Blaenrhondda, Treherbert, Treorci, Ton, Clydach Vale, Alaw and Maerdy between 1920 and 1925.[73] The success of the experiment was reported by R. R. Williams in 1925 and, following more petitioning, progressive guidelines for the teaching of Welsh in schools and the training of future teachers were adopted by the local authority.[74] The Education Committee of the Rhondda Urban District Council divided the schools falling under its responsibility into 'Grade A. – to include those schools which are situated in districts favourable to the development of the work and which have previously been recognised as Bilingual Schools', and 'Grade B. – to include all other Schools.'[75] The minimum requirement, even for 'Grade B' schools, was that 'all instruction in Infants' Schools shall be through the medium of Welsh at the end of three years, and all the Upper Schools . . . shall be bilingual in ten years'.[76] From 1928 onwards teachers who did not have the requisite qualification to teach Welsh were to be dismissed. These guidelines ensured that all elementary school pupils received about three hours Welsh-language instruction per week, and that Welsh was a compulsory part of the entrance examination to secondary schools in the area. Following a proposal in 1937 that Welsh should no longer be a requirement for entrance to secondary schools, a second campaign was conducted by the Rhondda societies and churches.[77] Public meetings were held, questionnaires were sent out to local election candidates, and a deputation met members of the Board of Education.

---

[72] Katie Griffith, 'Babanod Llandudno a Barddoniaeth', *Yr Athro*, VI, no. 4 (1933), 137; 'Nodiadau Golygyddol: Llwyddiant Eithriadol y Gymraeg mewn Ysgol', ibid., VI, no. 3 (1933), 97–8; 'Nodiadau Golygyddol: Ysgol Bechgyn Cilfynydd ar y Blaen', ibid., VIII, nos. 8 and 9 (1935), 236; Pontypridd Education Committee, 'A Scheme of Welsh in a Bilingual System of Education as Practised at the Cilfynydd Boys' Council School, Pontypridd', ibid., IX, nos. 8 and 9 (1936), 249–55.

[73] *Y Darian*, 25 November 1920, 18 June 1925, 10 September 1925; *Western Mail*, 28 July 1921, 4 January 1923; O. J .O., 'Llwybr Addysg Cymru'r Dyfodol', *Cymru*, LXII, no. 370 (1922), 163.

[74] Rhondda Urban District Council, Education Committee, *Report by R. R. Williams (Deputy Director of Education) on the Teaching of Welsh in the Bi-lingual Schools of the Authority* (Treherbert, 1925). R. R. Williams was one of the founder members of the Union of Welsh Teachers.

[75] Idem, *Scheme for the Teaching of Welsh in the Schools of the Authority* (Treherbert, 1926), p. 6.

[76] Ibid., p. 7.

[77] *Y Brython*, 25 March 1937, 1 April 1937, 6 May 1937, 13 January 1938; *Western Mail*, 11 and 31 March 1937, 3 June 1937.

On this occasion the efforts of the societies were not crowned by success, mainly because of the counteraction of the Head Teachers' Association, which had never completely agreed with the new regulations.[78]

However, the Rhondda example had resolute followers. In 1924 a 'Memorial on the Teaching of Welsh', presented by the Swansea Cymrodorion Society to the local education authority, asked, after it had 'carefully examined the experiments . . . tried by various Authorities', for a bilingual education scheme. The Society demanded that a Welsh-language organizer be appointed, that competence to give instruction in Welsh should be a *sine qua non* for employing teachers, and that the Welsh language should be recognized in secondary school entrance scholarship examinations. A proposed bilingual scheme was appended.[79] In a 1925 circular the National Union of Welsh Societies urged all education authorities to follow the 'resolutions duly adopted by the Glamorgan Education Committee and the Carmarthenshire Education Committee, respectively'.[80] By 1928 knowledge of Welsh was compulsory for entrance to secondary schools in the counties of Caernarfon, Carmarthen and Glamorgan.[81]

Efforts to improve the position of Welsh in the education system were reinforced by practical help, both for teachers who wanted to use it as a medium of instruction or teach it as a subject, and also for those who simply wanted to learn the language. The Welsh summer schools, organized by the Welsh Language Society since 1903, provided two weeks of instruction for teachers. Although attendance figures never regained the early peak of 179 in 1904, every year until 1939 an average of ninety teachers received training in the teaching of the Welsh language and its literature, as well as the history of Wales.[82] Another 'holiday' school was established by the National Union of Welsh Societies in 1918 and it survived until 1933, providing two weeks of lessons in the language, literature, history and religion of Wales for around sixty people from all professions. The official language of both schools was, of course, Welsh. The proceedings of the Union's summer schools were published as introductions to the Welsh language, its literature and folk songs.[83] Local Welsh societies and branches of Urdd Gobaith Cymru offered an increasing number of Welsh classes, often in co-operation with institutions such as the extramural departments of the

---

[78] 'Welsh Federation of Head Teachers: Annual Conference', *The Head Teachers' Review*, XXI, no. 2 (1930), 58–61; *Western Mail*, 8 April 1937, 6 May 1937.

[79] Swansea Cymrodorion Society, *Memorial on the Teaching of Welsh, presented by the Swansea Cymrodorion Society to the Swansea Education Authority / Deiseb ar Ddysgu'r Gymraeg, a gyflwynir gan Gymdeithas Cymrodorion Abertawe i Bwyllgor Addysg Abertawe* (Wrecsam, 1924), pp. 1–4.

[80] NLW, E. T. John Papers 5550.

[81] *Yr Athro*, I, no. 5 (1928), 147.

[82] James, 'Yr Ysgol Haf Gymraeg, 1904', 229–31. No summer school was held between 1916 and 1919.

[83] The reports about the 'holiday' school are to be found in the annual reports of the National Union of Welsh Societies from 1919 to 1934. The volumes published were *Doethineb Llafar* (Abertawe, 1925), *Camre'r Gymraeg* (Abertawe, 1926) and *Alawon Cymru* (Abertawe, 1927).

University of Wales and the WEA, to which the National Union of Welsh Societies subscribed from 1920.[84] Classes were held in Carmarthen, Cefncoedycymer, Merthyr Tydfil, Pontypridd, Deiniolen, Penfforddelen, Newtown and Fishguard.[85] According to a report from Pen-y-parc class in 1922, they were perceived as 'one of the best weapons to keep the Welsh language alive among the people' ('un o'r arfau goreu i gadw'r Gymraeg yn fyw ymhlith y werin').[86] Many of them were short-lived, but others, such as the Welsh classes held at Morriston and Ammanford, survived for many years and taught over thirty students annually.[87] The record figure for attendance was reached by members of the Treorci Cymrodorion, who started a Welsh class in 1920. By 1922, thirty-two students had committed themselves to a three-year advanced course conducted by the Revd Fred Jones, while more than a hundred were attending three preparatory classes.[88] As in the case of the literary societies, membership was not restricted to middle-class and middle-aged people. Encouraging news came from the class at Rhydlewis in Cardiganshire: 'The majority of the class are young girls and boys, who walk long distances to be present' ('Merched a bechgyn ifanc yw'r rhan fwyaf, yn cerdded pellter ffordd i fod yn bresennol').[89] R. Williams Parry's Welsh literature class at Llanrug was attended by students whose ages ranged from sixteen to over sixty, and included quarrymen, farmers, businessmen, teachers, public officials, university graduates and some of the older pupils of the local county school.[90] By the late 1930s classes and courses were also organized under the auspices of Urdd Gobaith Cymru. The 233 young people who were members of Aelwyd Aberystwyth in 1936–7, for instance, were able to choose between a course in Welsh history, organized in conjunction with the University's Extramural Department, and several Welsh classes conducted under the auspices of the local education authority.[91] Especially in south Wales, *adrannau dysgwyr* (learner branches) sprang up, whose sole aim was to familiarize their members with the language and literature of their country. The strength of the movement is underlined by the number of books borrowed from the National Library of Wales for use in adult classes. In 1927–8, of the 4,603 books sent out, 2,056 were for classes in economics and political science and 656 for those in Welsh language and literature. By 1930–1 the total number of books borrowed was 7,846, of

[84] *Y Darian*, 25 March 1920; UCCC, *Rhaglen Cyfarfodydd y . . . Gynhadledd Flynyddol* (1920), p. 4.
[85] *Y Darian*, 15 January 1920, 8 April 1920, 18 November 1920, 5 March 1925, 22 October 1925; UCCC, *Cylchlythyr Gorphennaf* (1915); idem, *Rhaglen Cyfarfodydd y . . . Gynhadledd Flynyddol* (1930), pp. 14–15; idem, *Rhaglen Cyfarfodydd y . . . Gynhadledd Flynyddol* (1933), p. 13; idem, *Rhaglen Cyfarfodydd y . . . Gynhadledd Flynyddol* (1939), p. 7.
[86] 'Atodiad i Cymru', *Cymru*, LXIII, no. 377 (1922), 1.
[87] Ibid., 2–3.
[88] Ibid., 4–5.
[89] 'Atodiad i Cymru', ibid., LXIV, no. 378 (1923), 4.
[90] 'Atodiad i Cymru', ibid., LXIV, no. 381 (1923), 2.
[91] *Y Brython*, 27 May 1937.

which 1,537 dealt with economics and 1,984 with Welsh language and literature.[92]

Another form of practical assistance came from the Union of Welsh Teachers. Their magazine, *Yr Athro*, consisted almost entirely of Welsh-language teaching materials, from nursery rhymes and model lessons for five year-olds to scientific vocabulary and detailed descriptions of chemistry experiments for county school pupils. In addition, Union members gave 'demonstration lessons on modern methods of teaching Welsh' and showed 'the play way of teaching Welsh to infants' in the summer schools.[93]

The crowning achievement of the period before the Second World War was the foundation of the first 'ysgol Gymraeg' (Welsh-medium school) in Aberystwyth. It came not as a result of a long campaign, but from the personal intervention of a man whose dreams had already transformed several aspects of life in Welsh-speaking Wales. Ifan ab Owen Edwards realized the necessity of establishing his own private school when, in 1939, Aberystwyth was inundated with evacuee children who were swiftly changing the linguistic character of the small primary school attended by his elder son. Reluctant to await a change of policy by the local education authority, he launched his own private school of seven pupils. By 1944 fifty-six pupils were in attendance and four years later it was included in the Ministry of Education's 'list of efficient schools'. By then, similar institutions had also been established in Cardiff, Holywell, Llandudno, Llanelli, Rhyl and Mold.[94]

The 'ready-made culture' of radio and cinema, especially popular among the young, insinuated the English language into predominantly Welsh-speaking areas and threatened to supplant traditional forms of entertainment. Shortly after the BBC had begun transmitting radio programmes, the council of the National Union of Welsh Societies reported that it would carefully monitor their linguistic influence, and radio stations were visited to ensure that programme-makers paid due attention to the Welsh language and culture.[95] The problem was brought before the House of Commons in 1926 when Ellis Davies, Liberal MP for Denbighshire, demanded a relay station at Colwyn Bay to enable 'Welsh addresses, lectures and religious services' to be broadcast. According to John Davies: 'Thereafter, such appeals and protests loom so large that there may be a

---

[92] 'Editorial Notes', *Cambria*, no. 5 (1931), 3.

[93] G. H. Livens, 'Addysgu Mesuroniaeth yn yr Ysgolion', *Yr Athro*, I, no. 3 (1928), 78–80 and ibid., II, no. 1 (1929), 18–21; C. Harris Leonard, 'Gwersi Syml ar Wyddoniaeth', ibid., VI, no. 1 (1933), 32–4; ibid., VI, no. 2 (1933), 80–2; ibid., VII (1934) [series of articles]; Thomas D. Jenkins, 'Ymarferion gyda'r Geiriadur ar gyfer Dosbarthiadau sy'n Dysgu'r Gymraeg fel Ail Iaith', ibid., XII, nos. 8 and 9 (1939), 237; *Liverpool Post and Mercury*, 19 August 1931; *Manchester Guardian*, 17 August 1931.

[94] Griffith, *Urdd Gobaith Cymru: Cyfrol I*, p. 347; idem, *Urdd Gobaith Cymru: Cyfrol II. 1946–1960* (Aberystwyth, 1972), pp. 74–7.

[95] NLW, E. T. John Papers 5548, 'Adroddiad Cyngor yr Undeb 1924–25', p. 3.

tendency, in discussing the history of broadcasting in Wales, to give them disproportionate attention.'[96] It is clear, however, that without such protests there
would not have been a separate Welsh Region of the BBC by 1937 and that
broadcasting in Wales would have taken an entirely different course. The
condemnation of the policies of the BBC in the 1927 report, *Welsh in Education
and Life*, gave the protests hitherto voiced by individuals and voluntary
organizations the stamp of authority:

> the wireless telephone is surely achieving the complete anglicisation of the intellectual
> life of the nation, and the language itself is as surely going the way of the intellectual life.
> We regard the present policy of the British Broadcasting Corporation as one of the most
> serious menaces to the life of the Welsh language, and think that our general
> recommendations will lose much of their value unless the matter is put right . . .
> Nothing short of the full utilisation of the Welsh language in broadcasting, by whatever
> means this may be effected, will meet the case.[97]

The flood of protests from all sides was not to abate for years to come. The
National Union of Welsh Societies regularly sent the BBC and the Welsh
Parliamentary Party memoranda urging the establishment of a separate Welsh
radio station. At every given opportunity they voiced publicly their grievances
concerning the policies of the corporation and urged their members to send
Welsh letters of protest to the headquarters of the BBC.[98] Similarly, Urdd
Gobaith Cymru and the Union of Welsh Teachers made frequent appeals in their
publications for a radio station for Wales.[99] Public bodies such as the Court of
Governors of the University of Wales, local authorities and county councils also
protested and drafted petitions, while the Welsh Nationalist Party considered a
campaign of withholding licence fees. Listeners' letters, loud with complaints,
flowed into the headquarters of the BBC. In 1928 a first 'Advisory Committee',
consisting of the representatives of several cultural societies, succeeded in lifting
the ban imposed on spoken Welsh on the radio. In 1932 the broadcasting committee of the Welsh Parliamentary Party (formed in 1931) secured a fortnightly
programme and religious service in the Welsh language. Several more deputations
and commissions were to venture out before, in 1933, a ten-man committee was

---

[96] John Davies, *Broadcasting and the BBC in Wales* (Cardiff, 1994), p. 35. For a detailed outline of the
years before the establishment of the Welsh Broadcasting Region, see ibid., chapter 2, pp. 39–100.

[97] Departmental Committee on Welsh in the Educational System of Wales, *Welsh in Education and
Life*, pp. 174–5.

[98] UCCC, *Rhaglen Cyfarfodydd y . . . Gynhadledd Flynyddol* (1927), p. 20; *Manchester Guardian*,
5 October 1926; *Western Mail*, 13 June 1927, 26 May 1931.

[99] 'At y Plant', *Cymru'r Plant*, XXXVII (1928), 121; *Cronicl yr Urdd*, III, no. 34 (1931), 238–9, 283;
ibid., III, no. 36 (1931), 283; *Y Capten*, II, no. 5 (1932), 101; 'Nodiadau Golygyddol', *Yr Athro*, I,
no. 4 (1928), 109; ibid., II, no. 5 (1929), 150–1; ibid, IX, no. 4 (1936), 100.

appointed by the Council of the University of Wales. It included men of differing political views and personalities, such as Emrys Evans, David Lloyd George, William George, W. J. Gruffydd and Saunders Lewis, who were united only in their demand for an adequate Welsh-language radio service. Their arguments gradually wore down the resistance of the BBC and by 1937 seven hours of Welsh-language programmes per week had been secured, broadcast by the newly-established Welsh Region.[100]

Concerns about the Anglicizing influence of the cinema, which drove others to condemn the medium,[101] prompted Ifan ab Owen Edwards to initiate the first film in Welsh, written and directed by John Ellis Williams, and acted by members of his Urdd branch in Blaenau Ffestiniog. Between 1935 and 1940 the 'Sinema Gymraeg', featuring the first Welsh 'talkie', *Y Chwarelwr* (The Quarryman), as well as films of the mass gymnastic displays of Urdd Gobaith Cymru, travelled all over Wales. The films were shown in over 120 locations every winter.[102]

The Welsh publishing industry had been in decline since the last quarter of the nineteenth century, mainly as a result of the fall in the number of monoglot Welsh speakers. Publishers had failed to adapt to a changing readership and to modernize the production and distribution of Welsh literature.[103] As a result, organizations like Byddin Cymru, the Welsh Language Society, the Union of the Red Dragon, Urdd y Delyn, the National Union of Welsh Societies and Urdd Gobaith Cymru endeavoured to change the reading habits of young Welsh speakers by holding competitions based on Welsh literature and distributing Welsh books as prizes. In addition, several attempts were made to establish book clubs and home reading unions. Like his father Owen M. Edwards, Ifan ab Owen Edwards was deeply concerned about the situation and expressed his anxieties in a letter to T. Gwynn Jones in 1920: 'As you know, it is not easy to get booksellers to stock Welsh books and, therefore, because they do not see them, people do not buy the books which have been prepared for them. Before long, the situation will be such that publishing Welsh books will no longer be possible' ('Fel y gwyddoch anhawdd iawn yw cael llyfrwerthwyr i stocio llyfrau Cymraeg, ac felly, am na welant hwy, tuedd y werin yw peidio prynu'r llyfrau ddarperid ar eu cyfer. Cyn bo hir fe ddaw pethau i'r fath sefyllfa na fydd yn bosibl cyhoeddi llyfr Cymraeg').[104] Edwards planned to remedy the situation by reviving the tradition of selling Welsh books at country fairs. In 1921, supported by the Books Council

---

[100] Davies, *Broadcasting and the BBC in Wales*, pp. 46–72; William George, *Atgof a Myfyr* (Wrecsam, 1948), pp. 197–9.

[101] *Y Brython*, 6 January 1938; William George, 'Brwydr yr Iaith yng Nghymru', *Seren Gomer*, XXIV, no. 4 (1932), 173.

[102] Cwmni Urdd Gobaith Cymru, *Pumed Adroddiad Blynyddol ynghyd â'r Cyfrifon am y Flwyddyn Ebrill 1af 1935–Mawrth 31ain 1936* (Aberystwyth, 1936), p. 9; NLW, Urdd Gobaith Cymru Archives (A1989/30), A55, A56.

[103] I owe this point to Philip Henry Jones.

[104] NLW, T. Gwynn Jones Papers G1154, letter from Ifan ab Owen Edwards to T. Gwynn Jones, 27 November 1920.

of the National Union of Welsh Societies, he announced the foundation of Urdd y Cyni (League of Distress), whose members promised to buy at least one book a month during the following year.[105] However, like many campaigns in this field, it proved short-lived. Nevertheless, it had assembled a membership of some 480 people by November 1921. Had all members kept their promise and bought a book every month, at least 2,000 Welsh volumes would have been sold.[106] The book club founded by E. Prosser Rhys in Aberystwyth was more successful: between 1937 and the death of its founder in 1945 forty-four volumes were published.[107] Local Cymrodorion societies were particularly concerned about the lack of Welsh books in the new public libraries which clearly failed to reflect or satisfy the interests of Welsh readers.[108] One of the first activities of the Barry Cymrodorion, founded in 1906, was to collect £10 in order to buy Welsh books for the town's public library.[109]

The National Union of Welsh Societies concentrated its efforts on organizing exhibitions of Welsh books, which were inaugurated in connection with a conference, held in Cardiff in 1915, on the position of the Welsh language in family and chapel life. The first Welsh Book Festival was held in 1930 to mark the celebration of St David's day. 'The late Sir Owen Edwards', wrote the *Western Mail*, 'who will be best remembered for his efforts in the expansion of modern Welsh literature, a reaction from the almost tyrannous supremacy of the English tongue in education in Wales, would have been gladdened in heart could he have been present at the exhibition.'[110] He would have been particularly gratified by the re-emergence of an idea which he had favoured before the turn of the century and which his son, Ifan ab Owen Edwards, would realize after the Second World War, namely 'the creation of a central depot where all current Welsh books may be obtained'.[111] Between 1930 and 1939 nine national exhibitions of Welsh books on different themes were organized, including 'The Economic and Social Development of Wales' (1932), 'Religion in Wales' (1933), 'The Contribution of Wales to Science' (1937) and 'The Eisteddfod Past and Present' (1938).[112] Since a

---

[105] 'Apêl ar ddydd Gwyl Dewi, 1921', *Cymru*, LX, no. 355 (1921), 97; NLW, E. T. John Papers 5548, 'Y Pwyllgor Cyhoeddi Llyfrau, Cyfarfod, 8 Hydref 1921'; UCCC, *Rhaglen Cyfarfodydd y . . . Gynhadledd Flynyddol* (1921), p. 7.

[106] *Cymru*, LX, no. 357 (1921), 145; ibid., LX, no. 358 (1921), 177; ibid., LX, no. 359 (1921), 214; ibid., LXI, no. 360 (1921), 36; ibid., LXI, no. 361 (1921), 49; ibid., LXI, no. 363 (1921), 121; ibid., LXI, no. 364 (1921), 167.

[107] J. Tysul Jones, 'John David Lewis a Hanes Gwasg Gomer', *Ceredigion*, VIII, no. 1 (1976), 42.

[108] See T. Elwyn Griffiths, 'Caernarvonshire and its Libraries: Development of the First County Library in Wales', *TCHS*, 33 (1972), 170–89.

[109] NLW, O. M. Edwards Papers, Box 7, Class A: General Correspondence 1900–6, Bundle 1906 12(d), letter from D. Arthen Evans to O. M. Edwards, 17 November 1906.

[110] *Western Mail*, 24 February 1930.

[111] Ibid. I am indebted to Philip Henry Jones for the reference to Sir O. M. Edwards.

[112] *Western Mail*, 26 November 1929, 26 February 1930, 23 February 1931, 22 February 1933, 26 February 1934, 21 February 1938; *Radio Times*, 12 February 1932; *Manchester Guardian*, 25 February 1935; *Sunday Times*, 19 February 1939.

visit to the exhibition was part of the schools' St David's day celebrations, up to 4,000 children, mainly from south Wales, attended annually.[113] On the radio programme 'Welsh Interlude', the success of the festivals was celebrated, thus popularizing and furthering the sale of Welsh books. Wales was in the vanguard in adopting European marketing ideas. The Cardiff series was the first of the great book festivals held in Britain, and in the wake of these events, exhibitions were organized locally to coincide with conferences and day schools held at Coleg Harlech, the University College of North Wales, Bangor, and in the towns of Bala, Machynlleth, Swansea and Llanelli.[114] *Y Brython* acknowledged these efforts more than once:

> Y mae'n ddyled arnom i gydnabod gwasanaeth ymarferol y mudiadau a'r cymdeithasau Cymreig a roddodd hwb amserol i lenyddiaeth Gymraeg yn ddiweddar . . . Cyfeiriwn yn arbennig at ymdrech fawr Urdd Gobaith Cymru, at gymwynas werthfawr Undeb y Cymdeithasau Cymraeg, ac at feddylgarwch y rhai a drefnodd arddangosfeydd o lyfrau Cymraeg mewn amryw leoedd . . . Yr oedd yn ddrwg gennym ddeall na lwyddodd yr Undeb i gael gwerthwr llyfrau i deithio o fan i fan. Credwn y gellid llwyddo gydag antur felly gyda dyfalwch a chynllunio doeth.[115]

> (It is our duty to acknowledge the practical help of the Welsh movements and societies which have, of late, given Welsh literature a timely lift . . . We refer especially to the great efforts of Urdd Gobaith Cymru, the valuable service of the Union of Welsh Societies, and the thoughtfulness of those who organized exhibitions of Welsh books in various places . . . We were sorry to learn that the Union's attempts to revive the travelling booksellers have failed. We believe that a venture like this could still succeed if planned wisely and pursued diligently.)

Although attempts to revive the profession of the travelling bookseller failed, the National Union of Welsh Societies was successful in instigating the foundation of Undeb y Cyhoeddwyr a'r Llyfrwerthwyr Cymreig (the Union of Welsh Publishers and Booksellers) at a meeting convened by Ernest Hughes and Gwilym Brynallt Williams (Brynallt) in February 1938.[116] Hindered in its activities by the outbreak of the Second World War, the Union was reconstituted in 1945 in the wake of the Welsh Books Campaign organized by Urdd Gobaith Cymru. The aim of a competition, devised by R. E. Griffith in 1938, was to sell as many books

---

[113] Figures quoted for 1931 state the attendance of 4,872 schoolchildren and 1,347 adults. UCCC, *Rhaglen Cyfarfodydd y . . . Gynhadledd Flynyddol* (1933), p. 18. According to the *Western Mail*, 21 June 1938, the 1938 festival was attended by about 3,500 children and 2,000 adults.

[114] *Y Darian*, 30 January 1930; *Y Brython*, 25 March 1937 (Harlech), 11 November 1937 (Bala), 10 November 1938 (Wrexham).

[115] *Y Brython*, 1 April 1937.

[116] Ibid., 17 February 1938. For an account of a book-pedlar's experiences in the 1930s, see F. G. Payne, 'Pacmon yng Ngheredigion', *Y Llenor*, XI, no. 2 (1932), 90–8; ibid., XI, no. 3 (1932), 140–57.

as possible in the weeks leading up to St David's day. Beginning modestly, with fourteen of the best Urdd branches selling 1,025 books in the first year, it reached its peak in 1944 when 219 branches sold 54,043 Welsh books.[117] Both the new Union of Welsh Publishers and Booksellers and the Books Campaign were still prospering long after the Second World War. A memorandum from the Union, drafted in June 1951, led to the appointment of a Committee for Welsh Language Publishing, whose report on the 'Crisis in Welsh Publishing' resulted in government subsidy from 1956, and ultimately the establishment of the Welsh Books Council.[118] By the time of the final Books Campaign sponsored by the Urdd in 1965, its members had sold 415,329 Welsh books.[119]

The use of Welsh in public circles had been a bone of contention throughout the nineteenth century.[120] Initiatives associated with the early establishment of home rule or a Welsh free state during the first two decades of the twentieth century ushered in discussion about the legal status the Welsh language might enjoy in the future. Indeed, the quest for official recognition of Welsh remained on the agenda long after hopes for political independence had been abandoned by all but a few. The National Union of Welsh Societies, Urdd Gobaith Cymru, the Union of Welsh Teachers, as well as the Welsh Nationalist Party, all used Welsh as their official language. They published material, held conferences, meetings and summer schools, and kept their accounts in Welsh. Concessions were made only in press releases to English newspapers and in petitions and memoranda to authorities, which were usually sent out bilingually. An explicit policy with regard to achieving equal legal status for Welsh and English in Wales was pursued by the National Union of Welsh Societies and the Welsh Nationalist Party. Although the protection of the Welsh language had been one of the original aims of the National Union of Welsh Societies, it was not until the 1920s, following a series of lectures given by W. Morgan Watkin, Professor of French at the University College of Wales, Cardiff, that a clear policy of official bilingualism for Wales was adopted.[121] From 1923 onwards, the 'special aim' of the Union was to secure complete equality for Welsh and English in every sphere of Welsh life. In order to achieve this, every opportunity was to be taken to use Welsh – in church and courtroom, at public meetings, conferences, offices, etc., and every Welshman

---

[117] Griffith, *Urdd Gobaith Cymru: Cyfrol I*, pp. 204, 290, 338.

[118] Home Office, *Report of the Committee on Welsh Language Publishing / Adroddiad y Pwyllgor Cyhoeddi Llyfrau Cymraeg* (London, 1952) (PP 1951–52 (Cmd. 8661) XVIII).

[119] R. E. Griffith, *Urdd Gobaith Cymru: Cyfrol III. 1960–1972* (Aberystwyth, 1973), p. 397.

[120] Hywel Moseley, 'Gweinyddiad y Gyfraith yng Nghymru', *THSC* (1974), 16–36; Watkin Powell, 'Y Llysoedd, yr Awdurdodau a'r Gymraeg: Y Ddeddf Uno a Deddf yr Iaith Gymraeg' in T. M. Charles-Edwards, Morfydd E. Owen and D. B. Walters (eds.), *Lawyers and Laymen* (Cardiff, 1986), pp. 287–315; Hywel Teifi Edwards, 'Helynt Homersham Cox' in idem, *Codi'r Hen Wlad yn ei Hôl 1850–1914* (Llandysul, 1989), pp. 173–86. For these and other references to the nineteenth century, I am indebted to Dr Mark Ellis Jones.

[121] Morgan Watkin, 'Polisi Ieithyddol i Gymru', *Y Geninen*, XLI, no. 1 (1923), 16–29.

was urged to take advantage of his right to use his mother tongue in all his activities.[122] The Welsh Nationalist Party adopted a language policy whose aim was to make Welsh the only official language in Wales, despite Watkin's warning that such a strategy might 'divide the country as Ireland was divided over another matter' ('r[h]annu'r wlad fel y rhannwyd Iwerddon ar bwnc arall').[123] However, since the Party's viewpoint on this matter changed several times before the Second World War, no consistent campaign was pursued to realize this objective.[124]

During the general elections of 1922, 1923 and 1924 the National Union of Welsh Societies sent out questionnaires asking all candidates standing in Wales and Monmouthshire whether they were in favour of home rule for Wales, and whether they were 'in favour of making both English AND WELSH official languages in Wales under the new regime – both languages to be treated on a footing of equality, and to possess and enjoy equal freedom, rights and privileges'.[125] Somewhat surprisingly, in 1922 positive or partly positive replies were received from over forty-five candidates, half of whom were sitting MPs.[126] These were the only Welsh questions asked in these elections. The first attempt by the National Union of Welsh Societies to influence the attitude of a public body occurred in 1924, when the Postmaster General was urged to place a list of Welsh place-names in every post office in Wales, so that no letter addressed in Welsh would be lost or delayed.[127] The attempt was repeated in 1927 and, when no list was forthcoming, it was agreed that the Union should prepare one itself. It was dispatched to the Postmaster General in 1929, together with the further demand that a knowledge of Welsh place-names should be a condition for employment in post offices in Wales.[128] After the matter had been raised by Welsh MPs, the list was officially acknowledged in 1929. Although this did not necessarily ensure that it was widely applied, it sanctioned the use of Welsh place-names on letters and telegrams.

Following the election of William George as president in 1926, the Union and its branches sought to force the authorities to acknowledge the language by urging members to correspond with official bodies, address their letters, and write bank cheques in Welsh. This policy went hand in hand with lobbying public bodies to accept Welsh as an official language and protesting against the appointment of

---

[122] UCCC, *Rhaglen Cyfarfodydd y . . . Gynhadledd Flynyddol* (1923), p. 3.

[123] Watkin, 'Polisi Ieithyddol i Gymru', 20.

[124] See Davies, *The Welsh Nationalist Party*, pp. 73–9.

[125] National Union of Welsh Societies, *The General Election, November 15, 1922: Questions to Candidates* (Y Barri, 1922).

[126] UCCC, *Cymru ac Ymreolaeth* (Y Barri, 1922).

[127] Idem, *Rhaglen Cyfarfodydd y . . . Gynhadledd Flynyddol* (1927), p. 22.

[128] Idem, *Rhaglen Cyfarfodydd y . . . Gynhadledd Flynyddol* (1928), p. 8.

monoglot English speakers to important public posts.[129] Many of the attempts
were significant only in so far as they challenged existing practices and attitudes
and highlighted the problems of Welsh speakers in particular spheres. Plans to
arrange for the use of Welsh bank cheques, for instance, ran into early difficulties.
A Welsh cheque printed by Barclays Bank in Aberystwyth was rejected by the
Counting House.[130] Other campaigns proved more successful. In 1931, by
approaching the Registrar General, the Union succeeded in securing a supply of
Welsh-language census schedules as of right for all bilingual and monoglot Welsh
speakers.[131] St David's day pamphlets were sent to every local society advising
their members to use Welsh-language forms, and an article to that effect appeared
in *Y Ford Gron*.[132] The success of the operation is indicated by the following
passage in the official census report:

> Census schedules printed in Welsh were provided, as at previous Censuses, for the use of
> those householders who were unable to speak English and care was taken to appoint
> enumerators able to write and speak Welsh for duty in those parts of Wales in which
> such persons were likely to be enumerated. It was not contemplated, at this or any
> previous Census, that schedules printed in Welsh would be demanded for use by persons
> able to speak both English and Welsh, yet such was the case at the 1931 Census.[133]

Thus began a decade of campaigning, lobbying and arguing on behalf of Welsh
speakers. Demands ranged from the right to keep local council minutes and to
hold public inquiries in Welsh to the establishment of a Welsh telephone service
and the appointment of Welsh-speaking officials.[134] In 1938 the Coed-poeth
Welsh society, 'Y Felin' (The Mill), launched a successful campaign to promote
the use of Welsh in local homes and official circles and it was reported that 'scores
of families had pledged themselves to support the language, and the parish council
had capitulated, following the threats by individuals and local bodies to ignore
communications in English from the council'.[135] The leading campaign of the

---

[129] *Y Darian*, 14 May 1925, 23 October 1930; *Y Brython*, 25 November 1937; UCCC, *Cylchlythyr
Dechrau'r Flwyddyn* (1923); idem, *Rhaglen Cyfarfodydd y . . . Gynhadledd Flynyddol* (1924), p. 13;
idem, *Rhaglen Cyfarfodydd y . . . Gynhadledd Flynyddol* (1927), pp. 8, 22; idem, *Rhaglen Cyfarfodydd
y . . . Gynhadledd Flynyddol* (1932), p. 11; idem, *Rhaglen Cyfarfodydd y . . . Gynhadledd Flynyddol*
(1935), p. 13.

[130] *Western Mail*, 27 May 1929, 13 June 1931.

[131] UCCC, *Rhaglen Cyfarfodydd y . . . Gynhadledd Flynyddol* (1930), p. 10; idem, *Rhaglen Cyfarfodydd
y . . . Gynhadledd Flynyddol* (1931), p. 1.

[132] Idem, *Cylchlythyr Gwyl Dewi* (1931); 'Ein Barn Ni: Cyfri'r Bobl', *Y Ford Gron*, I, no. 6 (1931), 3.

[133] Census of England and Wales, 1931, *General Report* (London, 1950), 'Part VII – Welsh Language',
p. 182. I am indebted to Dr W. T. R. Pryce for this reference.

[134] J. Graham Jones, 'The National Petition on the Legal Status of the Welsh Language, 1938–1942',
WHR, 18, no. 1 (1996), 111. This article provides the full history of the Welsh Language Petition.

[135] *Manchester Guardian*, 13 June 1938.

1930s, however, was that to ensure equal status for the Welsh language in courts of law in Wales. The public argument was launched by Judge Ivor Bowen in his lecture on 'Quarter Sessions and Grand Juries in Wales'. Bowen revealed that the notorious 'language clause' of the Act of Union 1536 had never been repealed and that it was still illegal to use the language in a legal context.[136] A report commissioned by the National Union of Welsh Societies and published in 1935 demanded that Welsh should have equal status with English and that non-Welsh speakers should not be appointed to the bench.[137] This was followed by a campaign to reinforce pleas on behalf of the Welsh language in the courts made by Sir Thomas Artemus Jones and Judge H. W. Samuel to the Royal Commission on the Despatch of Business in the King's Bench Division.[138] In their report, issued in January 1936, the commissioners admitted that they had 'heard the evidence of a representative deputation which presented a Welsh national petition demanding the appointment of a High Court Judge who could not only understand but speak Welsh and who would be capable of conducting a case throughout in the Welsh language', but had come to the conclusion that 'it is impossible to recommend that such a request should be acceded to'. However, they conceded that 'it is vital that there should be attached to every court a competent interpreter and a shorthand writer capable of recording evidence in shorthand in Welsh as well as in English'.[139] The failure of the Royal Commission to concur with the deputation disappointed many who had believed in the impartiality of the British legal system. In the wake of the trial of Saunders Lewis, Lewis Valentine and D. J. Williams, following the burning of the RAF bombing school at Penyberth in Llŷn in 1936, the argument about the status of the Welsh language in the legal system became increasingly acrimonious. Yet, cultural nationalists still nursed hopes of positive action by Parliament until a Private Bill on the Administration of Justice in Wales, brought before the House by Ernest Evans, MP for the University of Wales, was talked out on its Second Reading on 26 February 1937.[140] Other courses of action seemed more promising. In November 1937 the *Manchester Guardian* reported that an important meeting had taken place at Caernarfon:

> The launching of a national movement to have the Welsh language established as the official language of the courts of Wales was suggested in a discussion on 'Welsh in the courts' at the Cymmrodorion Society here to-night. The society adopted a resolution asking Mr E. V. Stanley Jones . . . Mr W. R. P. George . . . and Mr Hugh Griffith . . . to collaborate in furthering the idea and to consider means of arousing national feeling

[136] *Western Mail*, 14 February 1934.
[137] Ithel Davies, *Adroddiad ar Weinyddu'r Gyfraith yng Nghymru a Lle'r Gymraeg yn ein Llysoedd Barn* (Abertawe, 1935).
[138] *Manchester Guardian*, 15 April 1935.
[139] Ibid., 31 January 1936.
[140] *Western Mail*, 9 November 1936, 27 February 1937.

in favour of it, with a view to the Government being asked at the opportune time to promote the necessary legislation.[141]

In the months which followed William George delivered lectures to several other Cymrodorion societies demanding that the 'oppressive' act of Henry VIII be abolished.[142] In June 1938 the Revd John Pierce, secretary of the National Union of Welsh Societies in Anglesey and a member of the Welsh Nationalist Party, sent an open letter to the Welsh press suggesting that a national petition be organized to improve the legal status of the Welsh language.[143] At the annual conference of the Union on 11 June, William George announced that the time was ripe to launch an aggressive movement in support of the language ('Mudiad Ymosodol o Blaid yr Iaith'). He urged members of the Union, the Welsh Nationalist Party, and Urdd Gobaith Cymru to unite to form a kind of 'Welsh Party' with the aim of organizing a national petition demanding equal status for Welsh with English in the law courts and the abolition of the 'language clause' of 1536.[144] In July 1938 the Welsh Nationalist Party declared its intention of concentrating all its resources into a united movement to press for a Welsh Language Act.[145] At a meeting of fifteen societies, convened by the Union at the Cardiff National Eisteddfod in 1938, it was decided to form a working committee.[146]

Established in September 1938, the Welsh Language Petition Committee, with its full-time secretary Dafydd Jenkins, found a home in the headquarters of Urdd Gobaith Cymru in Aberystwyth. Within a month it had published a petition with the following demands: '(1) to put the Welsh language on the same footing as the English language in all proceedings for the administration of justice and public services in the Principality, and (2) to repeal the existing statutory provisions which make English the only official language in Wales.'[147] Between November 1938 and February 1939 public meetings, mainly under the auspices of the National Union of Welsh Societies, were held in most areas of Wales.[148] Members of the Union, the Urdd and the Welsh Nationalist Party began to collect signatures in a house-to-house campaign. In March, when the lists were returned to the central office in Aberystwyth, it became clear that in many areas more than 90 per cent of the adult population had signed the petition. In some places,

---

[141] *Manchester Guardian*, 20 November 1937.
[142] William George, ' "Beth a Wnawn Ni?" Polisi Ymarferol i Gymdeithasau Cymraeg', *Yr Eurgrawn*, CXXIX, no. 12 (1937), 454.
[143] *Y Brython*, 9 June 1938.
[144] William George, *Mudiad Ymosodol o Blaid yr Iaith* (Pontarddulais, 1938); *Y Brython*, 16 and 23 June 1938.
[145] *Y Ddraig Goch*, 12, no. 7 (1938), 8.
[146] *Y Brython*, 11 August 1938.
[147] *The Welsh Language Petition* (Aberystwyth, 1939), p. 1.
[148] *Carmarthen Journal*, 18 November 1938; *Y Brython*, 24 November 1938; *Wrexham Advertiser*, 2 December 1938; *Manchester Guardian*, 5 December 1938; *Llandudno and North Wales Weekly News*, 19 January 1939.

including Betws Leucu, Llangernyw and Lledrod, the figure was 100 per cent.[149] Over 360,000 signatures were collected in less than a year and in October 1939 the petition was presented to Parliament. In 1942 the Welsh Courts Act was passed and, although it fell far short of what had been demanded, it finally abolished the 'language clause' of the Act of Union.[150]

The inter-war years, remembered chiefly for their strikes and hunger marches, were also paradoxically the years during which the idea of leisure came to the fore. Commercial enterprises, voluntary organizations and the state itself all interested themselves in the use of leisure time.[151] The working week, established at around forty-eight hours a week by 1920, was considerably shorter than it had been at the end of the nineteenth century.[152] In many rural Welsh-speaking areas, the chapels still provided the basis for social activities in the form of Sunday schools, prayer meetings, eisteddfodau, singing festivals, bazaars and tea parties.[153] However, new pastimes and societies, introduced into every part of Wales, often ushered in the English language. Especially in urban areas, commercial forms of mass entertainment, such as the cinema, racing and dancing, were almost exclusively in English, but in the voluntary sector education and entertainment were also offered through the medium of Welsh, mainly by local literary societies and Urdd Gobaith Cymru. In addition to the evening classes discussed earlier, literary societies and clubs founded by the Urdd from the early 1930s onwards offered members a variety of Welsh-language activities, including knitting, dancing, and staging plays, thereby creating opportunities to socialize through the medium of Welsh. While literary societies confined themselves to weekly or fortnightly meetings and traditional entertainment, members of Urdd Gobaith Cymru sometimes met as frequently as five times a week and developed new spheres of activities.

Much time was devoted to preparing for local eisteddfodau, with the ultimate aim of participating in the National Eisteddfod. Eisteddfodau for children had been held locally since the mid-nineteenth century. In 1918 a children's day was introduced in the National Eisteddfod at the request of Rhys J. Huws and with the help of the teachers and Cymrodorion societies in south Wales.[154] Under the auspices of the Urdd, it soon became one of the great attractions of the National Eisteddfod before the organization founded its own national event in 1929. The Urdd National Eisteddfod, preceded each year by about thirty regional

[149] *Manchester Guardian*, 13 and 22 April 1939; *Welsh Gazette*, 25 May 1939.

[150] Jones, 'The National Petition', 123.

[151] See Dorothy E. Roberts, *Oriau Hamdden ac Adloniant* (Wrecsam, 1924); H. Durrant, *The Problem of Leisure* (London, 1938).

[152] Stephen G. Jones, *Workers at Play: A Social and Economic History of Leisure 1918–39* (London, 1986), pp. 34–86.

[153] Alwyn D. Rees, *Life in a Welsh Countryside: A Social Study of Llanfihangel yng Ngwynfa* (Cardiff, 1961), pp. 131–41.

[154] O. M. Edwards, 'Y Plant a'r Eisteddfod', *Cymru*, LV, no. 328 (1918), 129–30.

eisteddfodau, took its place alongside the National Eisteddfod. Its fiercely Welsh character, based on the all-Welsh rule in its constitution, compared favourably with the adults' national festival and left many correspondents as 'forcibly impressed' as the one who reported from Aberystwyth in 1938:

> While I was at the Eisteddfod several aspects of the festival greatly impressed me. One of these was the future of the Welsh Nation. We have often been told that the native tongue of our forefathers is in imminent danger of becoming extinct, but I have no further trepidation. The sight of five thousand children reciting and singing in the Welsh language dispelled from my mind any fears which I might have had . . . But perhaps one of the most inspiring scenes of the entire eisteddfod was the procession on Saturday morning. Never will I forget the thrill which I received when I saw six thousand of the youth of Wales attired in the colourful dress of the Urdd, marching through the streets of the town headed by three brass bands and their beloved leader.[155]

The young generation criticized its elders for printing eisteddfod tickets in English, permitting the use of the English language in the proceedings, and placing too much emphasis on monetary prizes.[156] This certainly fuelled the protests which preceded the 1937 National Eisteddfod in Machynlleth, when, following W. J. Gruffydd's lead, eight adjudicators resigned because of the proposed appointment of Caradoc Evans as adjudicator of the novel and of Lord Londonderry as the festival's president. The result was the 'completely new' phenomenon of a National Eisteddfod held in 'Welsh from the beginning to the end' in Old Colwyn in 1941, and ultimately the adoption of the all-Welsh rule.[157]

Both local Cymrodorion societies and Urdd Gobaith Cymru played an important role in arranging summer activities through the medium of Welsh. Annual summer outings to the homes of famous Welsh people and other places of historical interest enabled members of local societies to learn more about their heritage, while the Urdd gave the current fashion for hiking a Welsh complexion by organizing similar pilgrimages. Likewise, the competition from the growing number of camps run by the Boys' and Girls' Clubs in south Wales and by the Welsh Schoolboys' Camp Movement[158] was taken seriously: 'At the moment, there is much uncertainty, but one thing is essential, we must have summer camps for the older members . . . we must learn from the English movements that the

---

[155] *Wrexham Advertiser*, 24 June 1938; *Western Mail*, 3 June 1929; 'Nodiadau'r Golygydd', *Y Llenor*, XII, no. 2 (1933), 68–9.

[156] *Western Mail*, 1 June 1929; *Wrexham Advertiser*, 22 August 1931; *Y Capten*, I, no. 8 (1931), 169.

[157] *Western Mail*, 22 February 1937. A synopsis of the 1937 argument can be found in 'Nodiadau'r Golygydd', *Y Llenor*, XVI, no. 2 (1937), 65–8; 'Eisteddfod Hen Golwyn', *Y Ddraig Goch*, 15, no. 9 (1941), 3.

[158] T. I. Ellis, 'The Welsh Schoolboys' Camp Movement', *Cambria*, no. 2 (1930), 36; Glynn-Jones, 'Boys' Clubs and Camps', 214–17; Margaret E. George, 'Girls at Camp', *The Welsh Outlook*, XX, no. 10 (1933), 269–72.

character of children must be developed through playing and living with one another' ('Ar hyn o bryd nid oes dim yn sicr iawn, ond y mae un peth yn hanfodol, rhaid cael gwersylloedd haf i'r aelodau hynaf . . . Rhaid dysgu gwers y symudiadau Saesneg, – mai trwy gyd-fyw a chyd-chwarae y rhaid datblygu cymeriadau plant') was the battle cry of Ifan ab Owen Edwards in 1927.[159] Summer camps for members of Urdd Gobaith Cymru were held from 1928 onwards. The only conditions for admission were membership of the Urdd and the ability to speak Welsh. According to camp rules, the use of English could lead to expulsion.[160] In 1930 the Welsh-language camps offered places for 600 children, but by 1938 the number of children attending had risen to 1,443.[161] In the same year, seventy-two young people of both sexes attended the first 'Welsh-speaking adult holiday camp'.[162] This was a revolutionary development and resulted in a flood of applications. From 1934 until 1939, those who had the money and leisure to take an annual holiday abroad were provided with an opportunity to cruise in an entirely Welsh atmosphere. During these years, the Orduña, a ship chartered by Ifan ab Owen Edwards, took about 500 Welsh speakers to various parts of Europe, from Scandinavia to the Mediterranean.[163]

Arguably the most important contribution of Urdd Gobaith Cymru to the preservation of the Welsh language in the inter-war years was its willingness and ability to utilize contemporary international trends in a Welsh context. Unlike other cultural organizations, the Urdd was not defensive. Its leaders believed that the only way of saving the Welsh language was to develop and expand its use. It therefore set about matching all the activities that organizations like the Scouts and the Guides, the Boys' Brigades and the St John's Ambulance Association had to offer. In the Urdd magazine, Cymru'r Plant, the rules of rugby and association football were explained, perhaps for the first time, in the Welsh language. A Welsh football association, set up in 1931, organized an annual cup competition for Urdd members.[164] The pinnacle of Ifan ab Owen Edwards's attempts to introduce sports in the Welsh language for young people were his 'mabolgampau' (sports games), held from 1932 onwards. Such games, especially fashionable in Denmark, Sweden and Germany, were already reflected in the Jamborees of the

---

[159] Ifan ab Owen Edwards, 'Ar Ddiwedd Un Mlynedd ar Bymtheg ar Hugain', Cymru, LXXII, no. 431 (1927), 163.

[160] 'Cronicl yr Urdd', Cymru'r Plant, XXXVI (1927), 455; 'Torri Rheolau'r Gwersyll', Gwersylloedd yr Urdd 1932 (1932), p. 3.

[161] Cronicl yr Urdd, II, no. 1 (1930), 3; Cwmni Urdd Gobaith Cymru, Wythfed Adroddiad Blynyddol ynghyd â'r Cyfrifon am y Flwyddyn Ebrill 1af 1938–Mawrth 31ain 1939 (Aberystwyth, 1939), p. 8.

[162] Western Mail, 24 August 1938.

[163] NLW, Urdd Gobaith Cymru Archives (A1989/30), C3; Yr Ail Fordaith Gymraeg: Trefniadau Miri Orduña (Liverpool, 1934); Gareth Alban Davies, 'The Fur Coat' in Meic Stephens (ed.), A Rhondda Anthology (Bridgend, 1993), p. 153.

[164] 'At y Plant', Cymru'r Plant, XXXVI (1927), 33; 'Cymdeithas Pêl Droed yr Urdd' in Urdd Gobaith Cymru (ed.), Llawlyfr yr Urdd (Aberystwyth, 1932), p. 63; idem (ed.), Llawlyfr Cymdeithas Genedlaethol Pêl Droed Urdd Gobaith Cymru: Rheolau (Conwy, n.d., [c.1931]).

Scouts.[165] Thoroughly Cymricized by Ifan ab Owen Edwards and Tom Davies, the Urdd's sports organizer in south Wales, they encouraged branches to practise gymnastics throughout the year and provided the movement with another mass event of high propaganda value. The games attracted thousands of young people annually and were the only sports event broadcast by the BBC in Welsh during that period. Criticisms that young Welsh people were being militarized were countered by R. E. Griffith on the grounds that:

> trwy wrthwynebu a llwyr ymwrthod y bydd i'r datblygiad hwn beryglu bywyd y genedl fwyaf. Yr unig ffordd i rwystro hynny yw trwy ni ei Gymry [sic] ymroddi i'r gwaith o sicrhau'r datblygiad corfforol newydd hwn yn unol â'n traddodiadau ni fel cenedl.[166]

> (opposing and refusing this development would endanger the life of the nation most. The only way to prevent this is to apply ourselves to the work of ensuring that this new physical training is in harmony with our national traditions.)

Through the pages of *Cymru'r Plant* and, between 1931 and 1933, *Y Capten*, members of the Urdd were also introduced to science and technology. *Y Capten* was geared towards older children and teenagers and included articles such as 'Teithio yn y Dyfodol' (Travelling in the Future), in which modern developments, including the construction of helicopters and cars, were explained. A special issue on electricity and the radio was published and members of the newly-formed Council for the Preservation of Rural Wales contributed a series of articles on the preservation of the rural environment.[167]

Other youth organizations active in Wales at this time were presented with a choice between co-operating with or competing against the Urdd. The St John's Ambulance Brigade chose to co-operate. Welsh speakers received their training through the medium of Welsh within the Urdd, but were awarded a Welsh certificate from the Brigade. Moreover, the Urdd translated the Brigade's literature into the Welsh language.[168] The relationship with the Scouts and Guides, on the other hand, remained somewhat tense, since their ideology, based on the contribution of imperial heroes such as Wellington and Nelson, was essentially alien to the pacifist traditions of Henry Richard and others expounded in *Cymru'r Plant* and Urdd handbooks.[169] Although members of the Urdd were informed

---

[165] Walter Z. Laqueur, *Young Germany: A History of the German Youth Movement* (London, 1962), pp. 87–203.

[166] *Y Brython*, 6 January 1938.

[167] 'Car bach Cyflym – Awyren Enfawr', *Y Capten*, II, no. 3 (1932), 60–1; 'Teithio yn y Dyfodol', ibid., II, no. 4 (1932), 84–5; ibid., II, no. 5 (1932) [special issue on electricity and radio]; 'Y Prydferth yng Nghymru', ibid., III (1933) [series of articles].

[168] *Cronicl yr Urdd*, III, no. 27 (1931), 69; ibid., IV, no. 44 (1932), 190; R. Davies, *Amgeledd i'r Anafus* (Wrecsam, 1931); idem, *Nyrsio Gartref* (Wrecsam, 1931).

[169] See 'Henry Richard', *Cymru'r Plant*, XXXII (1923), 152–3; Urdd Gobaith Cymru, *Llawlyfr yr Urdd*, pp. 15–16; idem, *Llawlyfr yr Urdd* (2nd ed., Aberystwyth, 1933), p. 4 (portrait).

through the pages of *Cymru'r Plant* and *Y Capten* that scouting was a pastime to be respected, they were also advised to consider carefully whether its aims were appropriate for Welsh children.[170] Private correspondence shows that there was no love lost behind the scenes; this was a battle for souls and territory.[171] The 1930s saw the Urdd triumphant. In 1933 its membership was still rising, whereas that of the Scouts and Guides had begun a steady decline.

There can be no doubt about the important influence of the Urdd on the use of the Welsh language by children and young people. From the turn of the century, however, attempts to establish a Welsh-language movement of comparable stature for women floundered.[172] In this context it is indeed ironic that the first Women's Institute, progenitor of a movement that would come to be particularly associated with Englishness, was established at Llanfair Pwll-gwyngyll in Anglesey in 1915. The Institutes restricted their activities to rural areas and became phenomenally popular in north and mid-Wales. The speed of their development is comparable only to that of the Urdd. Praised by some for their democratic spirit and their service to the supposedly ingenuous womenfolk of the countryside, they were condemned by others for their alleged Anglicizing influence.[173] More research is required to assess their linguistic influence in detail and with confidence. Nevertheless, it is clear that the programmes of Women's Institutes were generally in English, with the Welsh language reserved for special Welsh occasions such as St David's day and the annual eisteddfod. It would appear that most of their lectures were also delivered in English. The following account of a nightly visit to a farmhouse in Cardiganshire, presented at the second meeting of the north Cardiganshire branch of Pwyllgor Diogelu Diwylliant Cymru (the Committee for the Defence of the Culture of Wales), might well have applied to the situation in many other Welsh-speaking rural districts:

> Pan gyrhaeddais y gegin y noson honno yr oedd y fam hithau yno, a'r llanc un ar bymtheg, sydd yn yr Ysgol Sir . . . Cymraeg yw'r iaith rhyngddi hi a'i gŵr a'r bechgyn, ond yn Saesneg bron yn ddieithriad y sieryd â'i merch, sydd erbyn hyn oddi cartref, yn nyrs, yn Llundain . . . O ie, ni ddylid anghofio'i ffyddlondeb i'r *Women's Institute*. Teimla hi'n fraint aruthrol i gael eistedd yn yr un ystafell â gwraig y Plas – llywyddes flynyddol y gymdeithas, a chael siarad Saesneg trefol a swyddogol, ac ymfalchïo'n dawel bach bod ei Saesneg yn debycach i eiddo'r llywyddes na nemor un o'r aelodau eraill . . . Nid oes angen sôn rhyw lawer i'n pwrpas yma am John. Achubodd Cwrs Cymraeg yr Ysgol Sir ef i Gymru. Ymfalchïa'n fwy llafar na'i dad mai Cymro yw. Gŵyr hanes

---

[170] 'Yr Urdd a'r Boy Scouts. Cronicl yr Urdd', *Cymru'r Plant* (1929), 114; *Cronicl yr Urdd*, III, no. 25 (1931), 20.

[171] NLW, Urdd Gobaith Cymru Archives (A1989/30), A55, letter from R. E. Griffith to Tom Davies, 29 November 1939; ibid., A56, letter from Tom Davies to Ifan ab Owen Edwards, 1 January 1940; ibid., A57, letter from G. P. Hopkin Morris to R. E. Griffith, 14 July 1941.

[172] See Löffler, '*Iaith Nas Arferir, Iaith i Farw Yw*', pp. 10–11.

[173] Gwenllian Morris-Jones, 'Women's Institutes', *The Welsh Outlook*, XX, no. 9 (1933), 239–41; *Yr Herald Cymraeg*, 16 February 1926.

ei wlad, a chryn dipyn am ei llenyddiaeth . . . Y mae'n aelod selog o'r Urdd hefyd
. . . Synnwn i ddim na bydd yn Aelod o'r Blaid Genedlaethol hefyd . . .[174]

(When I reached the kitchen that night the mother, and the sixteen year-old son, who
is in the County School, were there . . . Welsh is the language used between her, the
husband and the boys, but almost without exception she speaks English with her
daughter, who by now has left home and is a nurse in London . . . Oh yes, one should
not forget her loyalty to the Women's Institute. She considers it a great honour to sit in
the same room as the Lady of the Manor – the annual president of the society, and to
speak 'town' and official English, and quietly pride herself that her English is more akin
to that of the president than that of any other member . . . For our purposes, it is not
necessary to say much about John. The Welsh Course at the County School saved him
for Wales. He prides himself on being a more outspoken Welshman than his father. He
knows his country's history and a good deal about its literature . . . He is also a zealous
member of the Urdd . . . I would not be surprised if he also joined the Welsh
Nationalist Party . . .)

The outbreak of the Second World War was an important watershed in the
history of the Welsh language movement in the twentieth century. It deepened
the crisis in Welsh publishing, reduced the hours of broadcasting in the Welsh
language, and brought large numbers of evacuees and refugees to Welsh communities at a time when thousands of young Welsh speakers were leaving Wales.
Nevertheless, it also provided an incentive and an opportunity to develop new
alliances and movements. Following the publication of a letter by Saunders Lewis
and J. E. Daniel in the *Manchester Guardian* on 8 September 1939, the Council of
the National Eisteddfod convened a 'Conference for the Protection of Welsh
Culture'. Twenty-five Welsh organizations were represented. As a result, the
Committee for the Defence of the Culture of Wales was founded, to which the
likes of W. Ambrose Bebb, Ifan ab Owen Edwards, Ellen Evans, William George,
W. J. Gruffydd and Saunders Lewis contributed in an attempt to counter the
negative effects of the war. Among the subjects addressed were the influx of
evacuees into Wales, the effects of mandatory youth service, the military
occupation of Epynt Mountain, the predicament of Welsh speakers in the armed
forces, and the use of the Welsh language on wartime radio.[175] At the Old
Colwyn National Eisteddfod in 1941, the National Union of Welsh Societies and
the Committee for the Defence of the Culture of Wales merged to form Undeb
Cymru Fydd (the New Wales Union).[176] The issue of Government Circular
1577, which required every teenager aged between sixteen and eighteen to

---

[174] T. Eirug Davies, 'Diogelu'n Diwylliant', *Yr Efrydydd*, VII, no. 1 (1941), 10–11.
[175] NLW, Urdd Gobaith Cymru Archives (A1989/30), A56, Memorandum *Y Gynhadledd
Genedlaethol er Diogelu Diwylliant Cymru* (Dinbych, 1940).
[176] R. Gerallt Jones, *A Bid for Unity: The Story of Undeb Cymru Fydd 1941–1966* (Aberystwyth, 1971),
pp. 18–21.

register with a youth organization, resulted in the founding of a wave of new Welsh youth clubs by the Urdd.[177]

The Second World War ended an era in which nineteenth-century efforts and ideas had been seized and developed to form a firm basis for the Welsh language movement which would emerge in the second half of the twentieth century. Attempts to establish mass cultural organizations and resuscitate local Cymrodorion and Cymreigyddion societies at the turn of the nineteenth century had been modestly successful. By 1925 they had spawned a range of voluntary organizations which catered for different strands of nationalism and different parts of the Welsh-speaking population. In terms of membership and ideology, Urdd Gobaith Cymru was by far the most dynamic. Towards the end of the 1930s it reached a greater percentage of Welsh-speaking children and teenagers than any other youth organization in Wales before or since. Its nominally non-political ideology profoundly affected Welsh life and imbued a whole generation with new confidence. More overtly political campaigns were organized by groups like the National Union of Welsh Societies and its member branches, by local literary societies, by branches of the Union of Welsh Teachers and by the Welsh Nationalist Party. Nevertheless, on questions considered to be of grave importance to the survival of the Welsh language, all strands of opinion united, and these common campaigns held the key to success in fields such as broadcasting. They convinced English officials that not only so-called extremists but also moderates supported their demands and that they should be heeded. In the case of the Welsh Language Petition of 1938, virtually the whole nation, regardless of party politics, stood behind the campaigners. The foundation of the Welsh Region of the BBC in 1937 and the campaign for the Welsh Language Petition in 1938 are highly significant milestones in the history of the Welsh language movement in the twentieth century. Alongside these national campaigns, countless local battles were also fought over the language. These did not always achieve tangible results but they had the effect of heightening public consciousness of the position of the Welsh language and the difficulties its speakers experienced daily. Local campaigns and practical work, in particular in the field of Welsh-language classes or the publishing of teaching material in Welsh, might not have been as spectacular or as well-publicized as the Welsh Language Petition, but they sowed ideas, created precedents and established institutions which would be developed after the Second World War. Finally, in a sea of chrysanthemum societies, Women's Institutes and Working Men's clubs, in an age of new media and of English mass entertainment, Welsh cultural societies modestly, but importantly, provided opportunities for leisure activities through the medium of the Welsh language.

---

[177] Board of Education, *Circular 1577: Registration of Youth* (London, 1941).

5

The Legal Status of the Welsh Language in the Twentieth Century

GWILYM PRYS DAVIES

AT THE TURN of the nineteenth century the status of the Welsh language in the courts and in public administration in Wales was still governed by section 17 (the 'language clause') of the first Act of Union 1536.[1] The section directed that the language of the courts in Wales would be English, that oaths, affidavits and verdicts be given in English, that court records be kept in English, and that no person should hold public office unless he spoke English. In short, the legal status of the Welsh language in Wales had been relegated to that of a foreign language.

Yet, notwithstanding section 17, at the beginning of the twentieth century, as in the centuries since the Act of Union, the courts exercised a discretion to allow Welsh to be spoken by a party who pleaded 'Cymraeg, os gwelwch yn dda' (Welsh, if you please), provided the plea did not arise out of 'obstructiveness'. However, the basis and scope of the discretion were not defined by statute, case-law or Rules of Court and considerable uncertainty prevailed. Since each court determined for itself the terms upon which a party could testify, or not, in Welsh, much depended on the predilection of the chairman or judge of the individual court.

An editorial in a north Wales newspaper in 1872 welcomed the enlightened approach of the Lord Chief Justice, Lord Cockburn, and Baron Channell towards Welsh speakers who had appeared in recent assizes and whom they had encouraged to testify in the language of their choice.[2] In 1890 the Lord Chief Justice, Lord Coleridge, in an address (probably to the Grand Jury) during the Dolgellau Summer Assize, gave judicial benediction to the principle that 'a Welsh-speaker who knows English moderately well but who habitually spoke Welsh should be

---

[1] It was believed in some quarters that the Statute Law Revision Act 1887 had repealed the 'language clause' of the Act of Union, but owing to a muddle over the numbering of the 1887 Act this result had not been achieved. Even if the clause had been repealed by the Act of 1887, it can be argued that two Acts of George II would have ensured that the proceedings of the courts in Wales were conducted in the English language.

[2] *Carnarvon and Denbigh Herald*, 12 October 1872, editorial.

permitted to give his evidence in his mother tongue. It was "but natural"'.[3] Moreover, after 1872, in response to petitions and parliamentary pressure, it became the general policy to appoint Welsh-speaking county court judges and registrars throughout Wales, except for the Cardiff–Newport circuit.[4] A letter from Judge Moss, a North Wales County Court judge, bears out the picture in his district in 1907: 'there is hardly a County Court where I do not try one, & sometimes 3 or 4 cases *entirely* in Welsh. (I believe this is not strictly legal, by the way, but all my notes are in English . . .)'.[5] These developments commanded the respect of Sir John Rhŷs and David Brynmor-Jones, who concluded in *The Welsh People* (1900):

> The establishment of the modern county courts, and the gentler and more tactful treatment of Welsh witnesses by the judges of the High Court during recent years, have done much to remove any grievances special to the people of Wales in regard to the administration of justice.[6]

Yet, we may be allowed to question whether the conclusion was too optimistic. Although the persuasive influence of High Court judges of the calibre of Cockburn and Coleridge upon the attitudes of the lower courts cannot be underestimated, the fact remains that, at the beginning of the twentieth century, a Welsh speaker with little or no understanding of English who came before a court in his own country faced serious problems and obstacles. He could be debarred from giving evidence in his mother tongue. He could feel a sense of inequity and humiliation. The oath could not be taken in Welsh, except through an interpreter, and he had no right to be tried by a jury who understood his language. The translation of his evidence into English for the court's benefit could be undertaken by the clerk, court officials or the police, and could be of extra-

---

[3] University of Wales Bangor Library [UWBL] MSS 27634–28204, Papers of Judge Sir Thomas Artemus Jones KC, extract among the papers. Surprisingly, the statement was unreported. The Assizes Minute Book (Crown Court) ASS 61/24 1883–95, contains no reference to a case where the language was in issue which suggests that the statement was made in the course of his charge to the Grand Jury.

[4] Speaking in 1846, when the County Court system was established, the Lord Chancellor expressed the view that it was desirable that judges in Welsh-speaking areas should be Welsh speakers. This was more or less a dead letter until 1872 when George Osborne Morgan presented eighty-nine petitions to Parliament. *Parliamentary Debates* (Hansard), 3rd series, vol. 209, 1648 (8 March 1872). In 1928 Hopkin Morris urged that 'the custom' be extended to the appointment of judges of the High Court. *Parliamentary Debates* (Hansard), 5th series, vol. 213, 830–1 (14 February 1928).

[5] Nevertheless, Moss also believed that complaints about the interpretation facilities in the assizes were well-founded, PRO LCO 2/4420 (3201/3). For the experiences of a solicitor in Anglesey Magistrates' Courts in the period 1905–14, see Cyril O. Jones, 'Cydraddoldeb yr Iaith Gymraeg a'r Iaith Saesneg' in Aled Rhys Wiliam (ed.), *Arolwg 1967* (Abercynon, 1968), pp. 28–30.

[6] John Rhys and David Brynmor-Jones, *The Welsh People: Chapters on their Origin, History and Laws, Language, Literature and Characteristics* (5th edn., London, 1909), p. 392.

ordinary low quality,[7] while the evidence given against him in English would not be interpreted in Welsh for his benefit. In civil cases in the assizes and in all cases in the magistrates' courts, he could be compelled to pay the interpreter's fee.[8] There is evidence to suggest that at the turn of the century much mischief lay in the operation of the magistrates' courts.[9] In this respect it is important to remember that of the total number of 91,421 cases heard in Wales in 1900, only 578 were heard in the High Court, 300 in the Quarter Sessions, and 36,031 in the county courts (of which only 2,938 were before a judge), while a staggering 54,512 (59.6 per cent) were heard in the magistrates' courts.[10] Calls for a legislative remedy became clamant and from time to time cases were brought directly to the attention of central government and Parliament.[11] Although two of the grievances were pursued in adjournment debates in the Commons in 1911,[12] officials and ministers concluded 'that nothing was to be done or needed to be done at this time' and that the complaint 'should stand over'.[13]

The place of Welsh in public administration in Wales fared equally poorly at the beginning of the twentieth century. Indeed, the Welsh language remained

[7] UWBL MS 28108, memorandum, pp. 1–2, 4; *Parliamentary Debates* (Hansard), 3rd series, vol. 209, 1648 (8 March 1872), speech by George Osborne Morgan.

[8] Under Statutory Order made in 1858, the Court had power to pay a reasonable allowance in criminal cases in the assizes. In 1892 the Home Secretary advised that the magistrates' courts had no discretion in the matter of costs if the amount was reasonable, PRO HO 45/16838/A46949/9, letter from Herbert Asquith to Abraham H. Thomas, 25 November 1892. See the decision of Is-dulas Magistrates' Court, Denbighshire, disallowing the prosecution's application for costs, *Parliamentary Debates* (Hansard), 3rd series, vol. 347, 339–40 (18 July 1890).

[9] See 'Yr Iaith Gymraeg mewn Llysoedd Barn', *Baner ac Amserau Cymru*, 16 February 1881, and Ithel Davies, *Adroddiad ar Weinyddu'r Gyfraith yng Nghymru a Lle'r Gymraeg yn ein Llysoedd Barn* (Abertawe, 1935), p. 7. This would also be consistent with the widespread criticism of the Welsh magistracy in the nineteenth century.

[10] *Judicial Statistics, England and Wales, 1900* (PP 1902 (Cd. 953), CXVII); *County Courts (Plaints and Sittings)* (PP 1901 (329) LXI).

[11] In 1902–3 the Lord Chancellor refused an application from Caernarfonshire to appoint an interpreter for civil cases, but on 13 December 1911, as a result of a Commons debate and the efforts of David Lloyd George and W. Llewelyn Williams, the Treasury issued a letter (no. 21103 II) authorizing payment of interpreters' fees in civil cases in assizes in Wales out of public funds, but it appears to have been disregarded on the South Wales Circuit until 1942. In April 1942, in Llangadog Petty Sessions, defendants were ordered to pay the interpreter's fee.

[12] *Parliamentary Debates* (Hansard), 5th series, vol. 27, 4–5 (19 June 1911), question by W. Llewelyn Williams; ibid., vol. 30, 414–19 (26 October 1911), Adjournment Debate on motion of Ellis Davies.

[13] PRO HO 45/16838; ibid., A46949/9, correspondence between Abraham H. Thomas and Herbert Asquith, 1892; PRO LCO 2/4420 (3201/3), letter from J. Herbert Lewis to the Lord Chancellor, 20 December 1906; *Parliamentary Debates* (Hansard), 5th series, vol. 30, 414–19 (26 October 1911), Adjournment Debate on motion of Ellis Davies, but see also, PRO HO 45/16838, letter from Home Secretary to Lord Chief Justice Alverstone and reply 17 November 1911, and PRO LCO 2/4420 (3201/Part 3), correspondence between W. Llewelyn Williams and the Treasury, August–December 1911; UWBL MS 27856, letter from W. J. Gruffydd to T. Artemus Jones re. *Rex v. Sweeney*, Caernarfon Assize *c.*1892–4; *Parliamentary Debates* (Hansard), 5th series, vol. 213, 830–1 (14 February 1928); *Justice of the Peace*, XCII, no. 8, 25 February 1928, 137.

excluded, except for limited purposes in a few areas of social and welfare policies.[14] Although three statutes[15] and some thirty abstracts of industrial regulations had been issued in Welsh during the latter part of the nineteenth century,[16] this development was discontinued. In 1889 a golden opportunity to secure an official role for the use of Welsh in public administration was lost when the newly-created Merioneth County Council decided, on the advice of the Attorney-General, Sir Richard Webster, that it could not keep its minutes in Welsh. Although the matter was raised in the House of Commons,[17] the legality of his ruling was not challenged and was treated as binding by all Welsh county councils.[18] Twenty-six years later, having contemplated issuing National Health Insurance contribution cards in Welsh, the newly-created Welsh Board of Health concluded that Webster's opinion was still authoritative and prevented it from doing so.[19]

By 1913 leaders of Welsh cultural societies, especially in south Wales where considerable English in-migration had occurred, saw the need for an effective pressure group to 'foster and preserve the language'. To this end they founded the umbrella movement Undeb Cenedlaethol y Cymdeithasau Cymraeg (the National Union of Welsh Societies). By 1920 it claimed about 100 affiliated societies, representing a total membership of 10,000.[20] It campaigned vigorously for reform of the status of the language not only within Glamorgan but also in the courts and schools of Wales. By 1925 it was perceived by the Welsh Department of the Board of Education 'as an influential body, especially in south Wales'.[21]

Grievances about the position of Welsh in the courts of Wales appear to have slumbered between 1912 and 1921. But anyone tempted to believe that there were no special problems in the courts received an awakening on 21 February 1923 following a ruling by Daniel Lleufer Thomas, stipendiary magistrate for Pontypridd

---

14 The Births and Deaths Registration Act 1837 allowed for marriages to be registered in Welsh in those districts where the Welsh language was commonly used or professed; the Pluralities Act 1838 empowered the bishops of the Welsh dioceses to make knowledge of Welsh a condition of the licensing of clergy; the Coal Mines Regulations Act 1887, Quarries Act 1894 and Factories Act 1901 provided for the appointment of Welsh-speaking works' safety inspectors in Wales.

15 Local Government Act 1888, Local Government Act 1894 and Intermediate Education (Wales) Act 1889.

16 For the list, see Royal Commission on Land in Wales and Monmouthshire, *Report* (London, 1896), pp. 93–4, and Appendix A in *Bibliographical, Statistical, and Other Miscellaneous Memoranda, being Appendices to the Report* (London, 1896), pp. 1–78.

17 *Parliamentary Debates* (Hansard), 3rd series, vol. 333, 1155 (7 March 1889).

18 The advice, however, was not followed by many district and parish councils in predominantly Welsh-speaking districts.

19 NLW, D. Lleufer Thomas Papers, evidence presented by the Welsh Board of Health before the inquiry of the Departmental Committee of the Board of Education into the position of the Welsh language in the educational system of Wales, 1927 (copy).

20 Undeb Cenedlaethol y Cymdeithasau Cymraeg, *Rhaglen y Seithfed Gynhadledd Flynyddol a gynhelir yng Nghaerfyrddin* (Barry, 1920).

21 PRO ED 91/57 W/490, minute Welsh Department of Education, G. Prys Williams to Sir Alfred T. Davies.

and the Rhondda.[22] Unpalatable though it may have been,[23] D. Lleufer Thomas forced the Welsh people to confront the inferior legal status of their native language and to demand reform by ruling that the oath could be taken in Welsh only through an interpreter. Expressing sympathy with a Welsh-speaking witness who appeared before him at Pontypridd, Thomas encouraged him to pursue with his MP 'whether the Home Secretary could not be induced to bring in a short Bill to put the Welsh language on a footing of equality with English in this matter of taking the oath'. The matter was raised by William Cope, MP for Llandaff and Barry. On 28 February the Home Secretary confirmed that the ruling was correct, but 'did not see his way clear to introduce legislation'. But D. Lleufer Thomas persisted and took the unusual step of expanding on his ruling in lengthy letters published both in the *Western Mail* and the *South Wales News*.[24] The second letter – supported by the *Western Mail*'s editorial – listed reforms which were required and which Lleufer Thomas believed could be secured by amending the Criminal Justice Bill currently before Parliament: Welsh versions of documents ranging from oaths to cautions should be issued; they 'should have equal validity with the English originals'; and the courts should pay the cost of interpretation.

Three years later, Sir Alfred T. Davies, Permanent Secretary at the Welsh Department of the Board of Education, provided D. Lleufer Thomas with a forum within which he could advance the case for reform. In March 1925 the Board set up a Departmental Committee of Inquiry into the teaching of Welsh in the schools of Wales. It was hoped that the committee would do for Welsh what the 1919 Departmental Committee had done for the English language in the schools of England.[25] Among its members were D. Lleufer Thomas[26] and W. J. Gruffydd, who were to ensure that the committee extended its remit to enable it to consider the place of the Welsh language in the courts. The committee published its report, *Welsh in Education and Life*, in August 1927.[27]

---

[22] D. Lleufer Thomas was a founder member of Cymdeithas Dafydd ap Gwilym, secretary to the Royal Commission on Land in Wales and Monmouthshire (1893–6), president of the National Union of Welsh Societies (1914–16), and chairman of the Welsh panel of the Commission of Enquiry into Industrial Unrest (1917–18). For an insight into his views on the status of the Welsh language in the courts, see D. Lleufer Thomas, 'Y Sessiwn yng Nghymru', *Y Geninen*, X, no. 2 (1892), 19–22.

[23] *Y Tyst*, 28 February 1923.

[24] *Western Mail*, 12 March 1923, 7 April 1923; *South Wales News*, 12 March 1923, 7 April 1923.

[25] Departmental Committee on the Position of English in the Educational System of England, *The Teaching of English in England* (London, 1921).

[26] In the 'revised final list' of possible members, D. Lleufer Thomas was designated the chairman of the Committee. PRO ED 91/57 W/40, list at 12 February 1925.

[27] Departmental Committee on Welsh in the Educational System of Wales, *Welsh in Education and Life* (London, 1927). Although the report was given a generally favourable reception in Welsh educational and cultural circles, others were not so enamoured with its recommendations: see Herbert M. Vaughan, 'The Welsh Language in Life and Education', *Edinburgh Review*, 247, no. 504 (April 1928), 262–73. A 'slashing criticism' of the report was also said to be circulating in the Home Office, PRO HO 45/16838/A46949/39.

The report, while acknowledging the benefits of the 'gentler and tactful treatment' received by Welsh witnesses in the law courts during recent years, went on to recommend the following reforms: that the offending section of the Act of Union be repealed (recommendation 70); that the oaths, affirmations, cautions and explanation of charges be provided in Welsh (recommendation 71); and that there be one general code of instructions relating to interpreters who should be provided and remunerated by the state (recommendation 72).[28] The first was a new point. The other two were a re-draft of the proposals contained in the letters sent by D. Lleufer Thomas to the press in 1923. Inter-departmental exchange of minutes reveals that urgent consideration was given to suppressing these recommendations, but the idea was quickly abandoned.[29]

On 23 February 1928 the Home Secretary was asked in the Commons whether his attention had been drawn to the committee's recommendations and whether he would repeal section 17 of the Act of Union. He replied that repeal raised important issues and promised to look into the matter. By April the Home Office had completed its review of the recommendations and compiled its conclusions in a long, detailed and defensive minute.[30] Of the general case for reform, it claimed that in recent years 'agitation' had never been more than fitful. Section 17 contained very little that could be objected to, and its repeal would be a 'very strong step'. As for taking the oath in Welsh, no provision was required. On the questions of payment of interpreters' fees and translation of documents, it was reported that since only a handful of questions had arisen during the previous forty years, the translation of English documents into Welsh would be costly and troublesome, opening up 'never-ending vistas', while the translation of Welsh documents into English was considered 'preposterous'. Government officials suspected that the Departmental Committee was intent not only on providing for the needs of Welsh people who were handicapped if they had to use English in the courts, but also for the needs of bilingual Welsh people who preferred to use Welsh in the courts even though they were not placed at a disadvantage by having to give evidence in English. The courts were already dealing with the first issue, and it was deemed that no provision needed to be made for the second. The author of the minute concluded that the grievances were 'mainly sentimental' and that no action was necessary:

Having begun with a good deal of sympathy for Welsh feeling, I find no case for action. The Committee went outside the terms of reference . . . only, I think, under the

---

[28] Departmental Committee on Welsh in the Educational System of Wales, *Welsh in Education and Life*, pp. 314–15.

[29] PRO LCO 2/4418 (3201/3 Part 1 and 3201/2 Part 7). This explains the significance of the note on p. xx of the report which makes it clear that the report should not be expected to lead to reform in fields for which the Board of Education had no responsibility.

[30] PRO LCO 2/4418 (3201/3 Part 1), minute *Welsh in the Courts* (copy).

personal influence of Mr D. Lleufer Thomas; and, in doing so, the Committee had no real hardship or grievance in mind.

He added:

one cannot help feeling that the Committee is fighting a losing battle against the natural tendencies of their own people, and that Welsh is now doomed to gradual extinction as the tongue of every day life.

The minute was sent to the Lord Chancellor's Office. Within a week Sir Claud Schuster, its Permanent Secretary, responded that the Lord Chancellor saw 'no reason to suppose that the circumstances are such as to call for any action at any time'.[31] Despite having been revived by the 1927 Departmental Committee, D. Lleufer Thomas's 1923 initiative (which is known to have earned the staunch support of Sir Alfred Davies)[32] had been blocked.

During the 1930s, however, the need for reform was to be clearly demonstrated by four significant court events which led to an outcry at the treatment of the Welsh language in the courts.

In 1933 a case came before the Caernarfonshire Quarter Sessions in which the defendant, the witnesses, the advocates, the jurors and the chairman (David Lloyd George) were Welsh speakers. The chairman suggested that the trial should proceed in Welsh, but since the court's shorthand writer knew no Welsh the case had to be conducted in English.[33] This incident led Caernarfonshire County Council to seek the appointment of a Welsh-speaking shorthand writer to serve the needs of the Sessions, subject to the approval of the Lord Chancellor and the Lord Chief Justice. In March 1936, following a delay of two years and four months, they refused to grant approval. Lloyd George consulted Judge Sir Thomas Artemus Jones, the Deputy Chairman of the Sessions, who regarded the incident as 'part and parcel of the bigger question' of the administration of justice in a bilingual society and immediately wrote a memorandum outlining the

---

[31] Ibid., letter (copy).

[32] PRO ED 91/57 W/145, letter from Sir Alfred T. Davies to the President of the Board of Education, 12 April 1923 (copy), where a 'strong plea' for support of the proposals put forward by D. Lleufer Thomas – 'a Welshman of high repute who knows what he is talking about' – was made. See also PRO HO 45/16838/A46949/27, minute from President of the Board of Education to the Home Secretary (copy) and a negative reply, 24 April 1923. For a very different view of the policy of 'equality of the two languages' on the part of the younger reformers, see W. Ambrose Bebb, 'Achub y Gymraeg: Achub Cymru', Y Geninen, XLI, no. 3 (1923), 113–26.

[33] UWBL MS 28108, pp. 2–5; Judge Sir Thomas Artemus Jones, Without my Wig (Liverpool, 1944), pp. 166–82.

reforms which he considered necessary.[34] A copy of the memorandum was sent to Lloyd George, Sir Claud Schuster, W. J. Gruffydd and David Hughes Parry.

Complaints about injustice in the courts became more pronounced in 1933 following two controversial judgements. The first was that of the Court of Criminal Appeal in the case of *Rex v. Robert Llewelyn Thomas* (1933 IKB 48), an appeal from Merioneth Quarter Sessions. The appellant had been convicted of sheep-stealing and sentenced to twelve months' imprisonment with hard labour. He sought leave to appeal against his conviction on the grounds, among others, that two of the jurors who were Welsh-speaking had insufficient knowledge of English to enable them to follow the proceedings which had been conducted partly in English and partly in Welsh. His appeal was dismissed. The decision was perceived as the worst wrong committed against Wales for many years.[35]

On the very date upon which this judgement was given, the same point lay before the Judicial Committee of the Privy Council in the case of *Ras Behari Lal v. The King Emperor* (50 TLR). This case involved an appeal from India against a conviction of murder on the grounds that one of the jurors did not understand English, the language in which some of the evidence had been given, the addresses of counsel had been made and the charge to the jury had been delivered. The Privy Council quashed the decision. Lord Atkin of Aberdovey, the immensely influential law lord who delivered the judgement, explicitly disagreed with the decision in the *Thomas* case. He held that the effect of the incompetence of a juror to follow the proceedings was 'to deny to the accused an essential part of the protection afforded to him by law, and that the result of the trial in the present case was a clear miscarriage of justice'.

Manifestly, these two decisions contradicted one another. In Wales (and beyond) it came to be seen that the principle enunciated by Lord Atkin should have equal force throughout the Empire. The net result of the two cases was that a prospective Welsh juror who had no understanding of English would be asked to stand down and be discharged from serving in a trial. Yet, the new practice demonstrated that there was something fundamentally unfair with a legal system which deprived a monoglot Welsh speaker of his constitutional privilege of serving on a jury in his own country solely on the grounds that he spoke no English, while a monoglot English speaker could sit in judgement on him in a court in Wales.

At this time, Judge Artemus Jones became aware that 'court officials are accused in the press of an anti-Welsh attitude'. He claimed that the fault lay 'not with the officers of the court but with a juridical practice, which is neither wholly bilingual

---

[34] UWBL MS 28108; PRO LCO 2/4418 (3201/3 Part 1). The memorandum is reproduced almost in its entirety in his Lenten Reading, 'Bilingual Justice', delivered on 29 April 1937 to the Honourable Members of the Middle Temple and briefly reported in *The Times*, 30 April 1937; see T. Artemus Jones, 'Deddf Harri VIII yng Ngolau'r Gwreiddiol', *Y Llenor*, XV, no. 4 (1936), 232–7.

[35] UWBL MS 28108, p. 10.

nor wholly monoglot'.[36] At its council meeting on 3 February 1934 the National Union of Welsh Societies responded to the growing dissatisfaction with the position of the Welsh language in the courts, and called for Welsh to be made 'an official language alongside the English language throughout all the courts of Wales'.[37] The resolution was sent to the Prime Minister, Ramsay MacDonald. It was acknowledged, dispatched to the Home Office and the Lord Chancellor's Department with the enquiry 'Is this a matter for you?', then filed away.[38]

The inferior legal status of the Welsh language could not have been demonstrated more starkly than in *Rex v. Saunders Lewis, Lewis Edward Valentine and David John Williams*. This case arose out of the burning by three Welsh nationalists of the RAF bombing station at Penyberth in the Llŷn peninsula in 1936.[39] The contemptuous treatment of the Welsh language by the trial judge was to be exacerbated by the Attorney-General's subsequent ill-judged decision to remove the second trial (after the jury had failed to agree on their verdict) from Caernarfon to the Old Bailey.[40] This was viewed as an insult to Welsh juries and to Wales. It had its repercussions in Parliament, but not before T. A. Levi, Professor of Law at the University College of Wales, Aberystwyth, had written to the *News Chronicle* in October 1936 urging Welsh-speaking witnesses to stand 'mute' and decline to give evidence, except in their mother tongue, a tactic advocated in the nineteenth century.[41]

In February 1937, no sooner than the three nationalists were in Wormwood Scrubs prison, Ernest Evans, MP for the University of Wales, having consulted with Artemus Jones, introduced a Private Member's Bill, The Administration of Justice (Wales) Bill, to secure the right of Welsh speakers to use Welsh in the courts in Wales (clause 1), and to provide that a trial could only be removed from one Welsh county to another county in Wales (clause 2). The Bill received a brief and disappointing Second Reading Debate on 26 February 1937 and did not proceed further. It was opposed by the Attorney-General on the grounds that the first clause was undesirable and the second unnecessary. Lloyd George then made a telling intervention:

> Supposing a Welshman understands English and can speak it, but he prefers to give his evidence in his own language. Would the judge be entitled in that case to say: 'You understand English and speak it well; therefore I cannot allow you to speak in Welsh?'[42]

---

[36] UWBL MS 2804, letter from J. E. Daniel to T. Artemus Jones.
[37] UWBL MS 28101, p. 10.
[38] NLW MS 17203C, Minute Book of the National Union of Welsh Societies, 3 February 1934.
[39] See Dafydd Jenkins, *A Nation on Trial: Penyberth 1936* (Cardiff, 1998).
[40] The Attorney-General subsequently informed Schuster that the removal of the trial had been a mistake and that he had been willing to alter his application to move it to Cardiff, but the defendants did not respond; PRO LCO 2/4419, minute 25 February 1937.
[41] *News Chronicle*, 27 October 1936.
[42] *Parliamentary Debates* (Hansard), 5th series, vol. 320, 2428 (26 February 1937).

When the Attorney-General replied that the answer was in the discretion of the judge, the flaw had been exposed.

The Bill had drawn a great measure of support from organizations in Wales, notably the vigilant National Union of Welsh Societies. It also represented the beginnings of a sea change in Welsh public opinion, which the observant E. Morgan Humphreys, writing in the *Liverpool Daily Post* in January 1937, believed he had identified:

> There are indications, I think, of a complete reorientation of Welsh thought upon political questions. In the past we have been inclined to think of Welsh success in terms of the personal success of individual Welshmen. We have rejoiced in the triumphs of our fellow-countrymen outside Wales. We have gloried in the political promotion – very small promotion sometimes – of Welshmen and in their success in commerce, in science, and in other walks of life. In future, I think, we shall think more of service to Wales than of individual success.[43]

In the following year, yet another unsuccessful attempt was made in the Commons to improve the status of the language in the courts during the Committee stage of the Administration of Justice (Miscellaneous Provisions) Bill 1938.

Wales had been shaken by these events and possibly also by the worsening position of the language in the magistrates' courts, as was pointed out by Ithel Davies in his 1935 report to the National Union of Welsh Societies.[44] Against this background, the Union embarked on another initiative. At its council meeting in October 1937, it called on the MPs of Wales to take immediate steps to secure the removal of the offending Act of Henry VIII from the statute book. Disappointed when only six MPs bothered to reply, it resolved at its annual conference in June 1938 to appeal to Welsh public opinion to demand the repeal of section 17 and to this end to organize a National Petition to present to the Commons.[45] The petition was launched at a national conference chaired by Alderman William George and held in Cardiff City Hall during the 1938 National Eisteddfod. Some MPs and Saunders Lewis were present. The petition called for:

> an Act of Parliament placing the Welsh language on a footing of equality with the English language in all proceedings connected with the Administration of Justice and of Public Services in Wales.

[43] *Liverpool Daily Post*, 21 January 1937.
[44] Davies, *Adroddiad ar Weinyddu'r Gyfraith yng Nghymru*, p. 7.
[45] NLW MS 17203C, 29–30 October 1937, 18–19 March 1938 and 10–11 June 1938.

Public meetings, conferences and meticulous doorstep canvasses were organized throughout Wales and the petition drew support from members of political parties and non-party members alike.[46]

Unbeknown to the Welsh public, in the early part of 1939 three memoranda calling for reform of the legal status of the language were received in the Lord Chancellor's Department. The first to arrive was written by David Hughes Parry, Professor of Civil Law at the London School of Economics (and a member of the National Petition Committee), in consultation with Judge Artemus Jones. In November 1938 they had decided to seek an early meeting with Sir Claud Schuster in order to persuade him that there was a strong case for setting up a departmental committee to consider the position of the Welsh language in the courts with a view to the removal of the disabilities. At about the same time Robert Richards, the well-informed Labour MP for Wrexham, was expressing to Hughes Parry his scepticism that anything would come of the petition. Could not Hughes Parry and Artemus Jones make a direct appeal to the Lord Chancellor's Department? Richards was well-acquainted with Schuster and it was agreed that he should make an approach. A meeting was duly arranged for 30 January. In preparation for this meeting, Hughes Parry sent Schuster a copy of the National Petition and the six-page memorandum which he had agreed with Artemus Jones.[47]

The memorandum was written in a lucid and analytical style and displays Hughes Parry's patriotism. It argued for the repeal of the offending 'language clause' of the Act of Union and of 'the grant of a measure of official recognition to the Welsh language'. He based the case on two separate grounds. The first was the 'national reason', namely the unfair discrimination against Welsh speakers who found themselves in a court of law debarred 'from expressing themselves in their mother tongue on their own soil' and the resultant sense of indignity and humiliation. Secondly, there was the 'legal reason', in that a Welsh speaker could find himself handicapped in the exercise of three fundamental legal rights: to know what he is accused of; to cross-examine witnesses; and to put his defence before the court in his own language. Hughes Parry advised:

> So far the movement in Wales is non-political. I have some fear – and this feeling is shared by His Honour Judge Sir Thomas Artemus Jones K.C. – that political capital may be made out of it. If some steps could be taken to deal with these questions fairly soon, there would be a good deal of satisfaction felt throughout the Principality and our fears lest the question should become more complicated by its growth into a political one would be removed.

This moderate memorandum appealed to Schuster.

[46] NLW, Undeb Cymru Fydd Papers (November 1960 collection), 154a, Minute Book of the National Welsh Language Petition.

[47] UWBL MS 28121, letter from David Hughes Parry to T. Artemus Jones, 28 November 1938 and reply 3 December 1938; PRO LCO 2/4419, letters from David Hughes Parry to Sir Claud Schuster, 17 December 1938 and 26 January 1939.

None the less, the document was silent on the status of the language in public administration. The probable explanation for this omission is that the use of Welsh in public administration was beyond the remit of the Lord Chancellor's Department. However, the meeting with Schuster touched four issues: the position of the monoglot or semi-monoglot juror, the appointment of inter-preters, the need for an official translation of the oath into Welsh, and the repeal of the language section.[48] Schuster reflected on all this.

A week earlier, on 23 January, J. Pentir Williams, who was Coroner for Caernarfonshire and on the point of retiring as town clerk of Bangor, wrote a particularly interesting letter to the Attorney-General.[49] He noted that there was 'a great deal of agitation at this time in Wales about the injustice Welshmen are supposed to be suffering' as a result of 'the language provisions' and that meetings were being held in all parts of Wales inviting people to sign the National Petition. He suggested that a short Bill should be introduced to remove the injustice. It is believed that Pentir Williams's parents were monoglot Welsh and that he had a keen appreciation, therefore, of the potential difficulties which could face either of them if they found themselves in a court of law as a party, a witness, or a juror. Since he was a member of the University of Wales Advisory Board of Law (which had in 1935 made a submission to the Royal Commission on the Despatch of Business at Common Law that a witness should be entitled as of right to testify in Welsh),[50] he had a broad understanding of the history of the legal status of the Welsh language. His letter was considered by the Attorney-General to be sufficiently important to obtain the opinion of Parliamentary Counsel's Office. Within a week the Second Counsel, John Stainton, had produced a powerful memorandum reviewing the merits and demerits of repeal of section 17.[51] One of the strongest arguments in favour of repeal was that it was 'scandalous that legal proceedings should be conducted in English in a Welsh-speaking country'. In his view, the decision in *Rex v. Thomas* was deplorable. On the other hand, his fundamental argument against repeal was that 'the recognition of Welsh as an official language of the Court would necessarily give impetus to the Welsh national movement with political consequence which may be undesirable'. He concluded that repeal was undesirable.

[48] PRO LCO 2/4419 (3201/3 Part 2), note of meeting. The two lawyers agreed to a suggestion by Schuster that they should submit a memorandum to Lord Roche's Committee on Conditions of Service of (Justices') Clerks which was then sitting and which they did on 4 April 1939, but it is not acknowledged in the *Report of the Departmental Committee on Justices' Clerks* (London, 1944) (PP 1943–4 (Cmd. 6507) IV). A copy of the memorandum exists in UWBL MS 28109.

[49] PRO LCO 2/4419 (3201/3 Part 2), letter (copy). See *Yr Herald Cymraeg*, 23 January 1939, for a report of an address by Pentir Williams to the monthly meeting of the Calvinistic Methodist churches of Arfon.

[50] University of Wales, *Minutes of the Proceedings at the Annual Collegiate Meeting of the University Court, held at Bangor, 21 and 22 July 1936* (Cardiff, 1936).

[51] PRO LCO 2/4419 (3201/3 Part 2), memorandum (copy).

However, the Attorney-General was not so sure. On 31 January he sent a copy of Stainton's memorandum to Schuster claiming that a contrary view was possible. He believed that 'Section 17 is worded in terms which may well be regarded as objectionable by the Welsh' and might be the basis of a grievance which 'is not altogether easy to answer'. Fortunately, Schuster had read the Hughes Parry memorandum and had had the benefit of the discussion with him and Artemus Jones on the previous day. He profoundly disagreed with the tenor of Stainton's paper and confided to the Attorney-General his strong criticism of his approach:

> Stainton writes of the Welsh language . . . as if it were on a par with any other foreign language . . . It is far too late to attempt to persist in this point of view.[52]

He added that Stainton 'appears to me not to realise what really takes place on the political and national situation in Wales'. Within a month, Stainton in turn was confiding to the Permanent Secretary at the Ministry of Health that the Attorney-General 'has gone all Welsh lately'.[53]

Schuster's impression of the political position in Wales was soon to be strengthened by an unexpected document, namely the Iwi memorandum.[54] Edward F. Iwi was a London solicitor who dabbled in intricate constitutional issues.[55] He had lived in Llandudno from 1913 to 1925 and had been educated at John Bright Grammar School. On 30 March 1939 he presented the Lord Chancellor, Lord Maugham, with a remarkable memorandum entitled, 'The Problem of North Wales', in which he warned that, with the threat of a European war looming, this was a potential danger to the unity and strength of Britain. He claimed that the root cause of the language demands in Wales was the policy of Anglicization which had culminated in the Act of Union. This ancient wrong had to be redressed. He also proposed that the distinguishing title of 'a Welsh Duchy of Cymru' should be created to pass to the sovereign's eldest daughter in order to strengthen the link between the Crown and the Principality. The second suggestion was not within the scope of the Lord Chancellor's functions, but the first concerned him.

This document made an impact on the Lord Chancellor, so much so that he had a copy sent in confidence to Major Gwilym Lloyd George, National Liberal MP for Pembrokeshire, and invited him to discuss it with him.[56] The invitation was accepted, but the files do not contain details of the meeting, if it ever took

---

[52] Ibid., correspondence.
[53] Ibid.
[54] PRO LCO 2/4419, memorandum (copy). In September Iwi sent a memorandum on the same subject to the Home Office, but this has not been traced.
[55] *Who was Who 1961–1970. Volume VI* (London, 1972), p. 585.
[56] PRO LCO 2/4419 (3201/3), letter from Schuster to Gwilym Lloyd George (copy).

place. Maugham's letter also contains evidence which indicates that reform of the legal status of the language was being contemplated by the Department, but, as the country became engulfed in war, the question of reform was either dropped or postponed by the government. In Wales, however, the campaign shifted into top gear. It was taken over by Undeb Cymru Fydd (the New Wales Union), which felt deep anxiety about the risks and dangers which the war posed for the language. It intensified the drive to collect signatures so that the petition could be presented to Parliament at an early date.[57]

On 15 October 1941 the National Petition, signed by 365,000 people and supported by thirty of the thirty-six Welsh MPs, was presented to the House of Commons by the secretary of the Welsh Parliamentary Party (WPP). On 4 February 1942, at the request of the WPP, the Home Secretary, Herbert Morrison, accompanied by his Permanent Secretary and Sir Claud Schuster, met for the first time a deputation from the WPP led by its Chairman, Sir Henry Morris-Jones, National Liberal MP for Denbighshire, to discuss the petition.[58] It was an amicable session. It contained an allusion to the war aims. The Home Secretary indicated 'off the record' that he personally 'was very sympathetic to the case', and he suggested that the WPP should concentrate on the practical measures which could be taken.

Within weeks the WPP had formulated the following proposals: that the Welsh language be placed on a basis of equality with English in the courts; that section 17 be repealed; that all formal court documents should be provided in Welsh and English; that all persons should be entitled to have their case conducted in any court in Wales in the Welsh language; that the costs of interpreting be borne by the state; that all new enactments should be translated into Welsh; and that in any court 'where Welsh is used or which may be called upon to administer justice in the Welsh language, the Tribunal should be qualified to conduct proceedings in Wales'.[59]

Months of inter-departmental argument followed. Viscount Simon, the Lord Chancellor, took the lead, claiming a 'personal and special interest' in the reform and that he was 'half a Welshman'. Although Simon believed that the demand for the repeal of section 17 was 'largely sentimental', he was adamant that it should be removed from the statute book. But his reasoning did not address the basic question of principle: whether a Welsh speaker should be entitled as of right to testify in Welsh in a court in Wales. To his mind, the right to testify in Welsh should be limited to those cases where a Welsh speaker would be at a disadvantage in testifying in English by reason of his natural language being Welsh. In May

---

[57] See R. Gerallt Jones, *A Bid for Unity: The Story of Undeb Cymru Fydd 1941–1966* (Aberystwyth, 1971).

[58] PRO LCO 2/4419 (3201/3), minute of meeting.

[59] Ibid., minute on House of Commons notepaper.

1942 Simon took the highly unusual step of drawing up a first draft of the Bill.[60] (It was unusual because since 1869, when the Parliamentary Counsel's Office was set up, it has been exceptionally rare for a Department to draw up a Bill which it promoted; but this was wartime.) His draft contained three main proposals: it made provisions regarding the use of interpreters where a party 'uses Welsh as his natural language of communication'; it repealed section 17; and it provided for the oath to be taken in Welsh. However, Parliamentary Counsel propounded a very different approach. He advocated that two separate bills be introduced simultaneously: a Welsh Language Bill would be introduced in the Lords which would circumvent the need for repeal, while concurrently a Payment of Interpreters Bill would be introduced in the Commons to apply new provisions for interpreters in all courts in Britain generally, whenever a person gave evidence in a foreign language.[61]

While Simon was skirmishing with the Parliamentary Counsel's Office, the WPP was perturbed at the delay. In June it pressed for accelerated legislation which would repeal section 17 and confer an absolute right to testify in Welsh. On 10 July Simon issued a warning:

> Legislation in war time on a matter not arising out of war is, as you know, difficult and I should fear that unless there is agreement as to the proposal legislation, the chance of introducing and passing it would be by no means improved, so I hope you and your friends will do your utmost to co-operate; you know where my sympathies on the matter lie.[62]

At a WPP meeting on 22 July, David Lloyd George brought the wrangling to a head. He persuaded his fellow Welsh MPs to demand a joint meeting with the Lord Chancellor and the Home Secretary and to bring the matter to the floor of the House. He insisted on seeing the Chief Whip and the Speaker himself in order to secure an Adjournment Debate on 6 August. It seems this was Lloyd George's first involvement with the Bill and it prompted Morris-Jones to wonder why he had decided to become involved. Was it his love of Wales or his hatred of Simon? But he avoided an answer.[63] Could the answer lie with the involvement of his brother William?

A week later a strong WPP deputation had a final meeting with Morrison and Simon. That evening Morris-Jones wrote in his diary: 'Morrison is direct and straight. Simon was wriggly and uncertain.'[64] Even so, he believed that progress had been made: the Adjournment Debate was called off and the Welsh MPs left

---

[60] Ibid., minute by Viscount Simon.
[61] Ibid., minute by Parliamentary Counsel.
[62] Ibid., letter from Viscount Simon to James Griffiths, 10 July 1942 (copy).
[63] Clwyd Record Office [CRO], Sir Henry Morris-Jones Papers, diary of Morris-Jones.
[64] Ibid.

London. Although the form of the Bill had been settled by ministers by 21 September, there remained a flaw in the crucial opening clause which defined the right to testify in Welsh. When, three days later, the Lord Chancellor happened to meet Clement Davies, Liberal MP for Montgomeryshire, he told him that he had kept his word, but would not promote the Bill unless the WPP would treat it as non-controversial. Davies replied:

> it would make all the difference if LG was spoken to about it before-hand in which case he might give the Bill his blessing, and all would be well. On the other hand, if he made some disgruntled comments this would have more effect than any harm anyone else could do.[65]

Acting on this hint which had been relayed to him by Simon, and also believing that this would flatter Lloyd George, Morrison called on him the following afternoon. This was a calculated risk, but Morrison secured his support. On 29 September the Legislation Committee authorized the introduction of the Bill, provided that it was acceptable to the Welsh MPs. The following day Lloyd George arrived at the WPP meeting and produced the Bill. The only known account of the meeting comes from Morris-Jones's diary:

> LG brought in a Bill in draft of 'Welsh Language in Court'. Says Morrison Home Secretary had sent it to him saying the PM has said 'Show it to LG and if he approves it, it is alright for us (War Cabinet)'.[66]

Lloyd George approved it. Given his great authority and in view of Simon's earlier veiled threat that the Bill could be lost altogether, it is not surprising that those members who may have had grave reservations about the wording of clause 1 which contained the Bill's inherent weakness were silenced.

On 7 October 1942 the Welsh Courts Bill was introduced in the Commons. It was a slender four-claused Bill. Clause 1 repealed section 17 and enacted that 'the Welsh language may be used in any court in Wales by any party or witness who considers that he would otherwise be at any disadvantage by reason of his natural language of communication being Welsh'. Clause 2 laid upon the Lord Chancellor the duty to make rules prescribing a Welsh form of any oath or affirmation, and clause 3 (i) empowered him to make rules for the employment and remuneration of interpreters. But clause 3 (ii) ensured that English stood as the language of record.

The Committee of the Associated Law Society of Wales had 'protested most strongly' both to the Lord Chancellor and to the Home Office against the repeal

---

[65] PRO LCO 2/4419 (3201/3), letter from Viscount Simon to Herbert Morrison (copy).
[66] CRO, diary of Morris-Jones.

of section 17 being introduced in the middle of a war.[67] From the other side, the Bill was fiercely criticized by Plaid Genedlaethol Cymru (the Welsh Nationalist Party) as being totally inadequate.[68] Yet it received an unopposed Second Reading and a Committee stage proved to be unnecessary. On the night of the Second Reading and following the debate, Morris-Jones wrote in his diary: 'Great triumph for Wales: for the Parliamentary Party and for me. It terminates my year of office in great style.' But the entry shows that the mood was not one of triumph everywhere: 'Just as I sat down after my speech a telegram [was] handed to me from the Welsh Nationalists saying we would be traitors if we did not oppose the measure.'[69]

Within a year, the Llandudno Magistrates' Court refused to allow a Welsh defendant to testify in Welsh. Its refusal went to the heart of the ambiguity in section 1 of the Act. Did the court have discretion in deciding whether or not a party could use Welsh? On 24 September 1943 the Home Secretary announced in the Commons that the court had no such discretion. The following week his Department issued guidance to that effect. But the guidance proved worthless when, twenty-five years later, the High Court came to a very different conclusion in *Reg. v. Justices of Merthyr Tydfil ex. parte Jenkins* (1967 1AER 636), when the Lord Chief Justice ruled that it was not enough for a party to claim that he was under a disadvantage if he had to testify in English; the court had to be satisfied either that he was under a disadvantage or that he at least genuinely thought himself to be under a disadvantage.

The 1942 Act did not achieve the objects of the National Petition by a long way. It is a fact scarcely noted that the Financial Memorandum (endorsed on the Bill) shows that the Department correctly predicted that the additional expenditure in implementing the Act would be minimal.[70] In some quarters, there was an acute sense of betrayal of the petition and there were recriminations.[71] Morris-Jones contented himself with the reflection that the status of the Welsh language 'will probably never be adequately settled outside a Welsh Parliament'.[72]

---

[67] PRO LCO 2/4419 (3201/3 Part 2), letters from the Committee of the Associated Law Society of Wales to Schuster and the Home Office claiming to speak for some 800 members of the local Law Societies, March and April 1942.

[68] Ibid., letter from the president and secretary of the Welsh Nationalist Party to the Lord Chancellor, 21 October 1942.

[69] CRO, diary of Morris-Jones.

[70] The Financial Memorandum states that £8.8.0 had been incurred on the employment of interpreters in 1939–40, £6.16.6 in 1940–1 and £1.10.0 in 1941–2. For a cynical assessment, see PRO BD 23/170, minutes between G. P. Coldstream and E. C. Martin, 9 and 24 November 1942: 'It is quite obvious that nothing whatever needs to be done, and that everything will go on as before.'

[71] R. E. Jones, *The Petition was Betrayed* (Caernarfon, 1943).

[72] Sir Henry Morris-Jones, *Doctor in the Whips' Room* (London, 1955), p. 125.

The criticism persists. In 1992 the Act was condemned by Judge Watkin Powell as 'a mockery'.[73]

Despite all the criticisms that can be properly levelled at the Act, it was clearly a landmark. It may be seen as the first legislative step since the Act of Union towards the restoration of the legitimacy of the Welsh language in the courts of Wales. It led directly to the issue of the Welsh Courts (Oaths and Interpreters) Rules 1943 (Statutory Instrument 1943 683/L14), prescribing the Welsh translation of twenty-two oaths and affirmations which were then in common use. The translation had been approved by the Welsh language scholar, Professor Ifor Williams. Schuster sent the Order in draft to John Morgan, the Welsh-speaking Clerk of Assize on the Chester and North Wales Circuit, for his comments, which provide an insight into the thinking of a senior bureaucrat about Welsh-speaking witnesses.[74] He envisaged that post-1942 there would probably be two classes of such persons. There would be the 'pre-Act type, the monoglot Welshman' and there would be 'the Welshman of higher education who may claim his right although he understands and speaks English as perfectly as anyone in Court':

> For the pre-Act type of witness the interpreter we already have in the Criminal Court is suited. He is of the working type and is to them 'one of us'. There is nothing professorial or 'high brow' about him. But I doubt whether his Welsh will be sufficiently classical for the second class. The witness who gives his evidence in Welsh merely as a matter of principle might prove something of a problem. 'Pidgin' Welsh would not do for him, although even he might occasionally find himself in some difficulty. For although for agricultural purposes Welsh is a complete every day language, it is not so for industrial purposes. The advent of industry seems to have caught the Welsh language napping. English words, pronounced in a Welsh way are constantly used in industry.

Schuster then cleared the draft Order with the Lord Chief Justice, Lord Justice Caldecote. But a terse reply reveals that the Lord Chief Justice was out of sympathy with the Order: 'It [Welsh] is of course a foreign language to me and, to

---

[73] Dewi Watkin Powell, *Language, Nation and Legislation: Towards New Attitudes / Iaith Cenedl a Deddfwriaeth: tuag at Agweddau Newydd* (Llys yr Eisteddfod Genedlaethol, 1990), p. 19. For a different view, see CRO, Morris-Jones Papers, letter from Dr William George to Morris-Jones, 19 October 1942: 'It is not by any means the full answer to the Petition, but in my opinion it is a substantial step in the right direction' ('Nid yw, o lawer, yn ateb llawn i gais y Ddeiseb, ond yn fy meddwl i y mae'n gam sylweddol i'r iawn gyfeiriad'); PRO LCO 2/4419 (3201/3 Part 2), note from T. Artemus Jones to Schuster; the editorial of *The Times*, 13 October 1942, expressed the view that the Act provided the Welsh language with 'a recognition long overdue'; Kenneth O. Morgan has argued that: '[it] gave legal validity to the use of Welsh in court proceedings', Kenneth O. Morgan, *Rebirth of a Nation: Wales 1880–1980* (Oxford, 1981), p. 270.

[74] PRO LCO 2/4422 (3201/3 Part 6), letter 9 November 1942.

tell you the truth, I do not know that I feel very sympathetic to this plan for keeping alive what, like Erse and Gaelic is really a dying language.'[75]

The political momentum behind the Welsh Courts Act 1942 swiftly subsided after its passage. In the post-war years, when Wales was immersed in the enormous challenge of rehabilitating its economy and building its welfare structure, the status of the Welsh language was no longer seen as a central concern. Although there was a spectacular row in May 1953, when the judge at the Dolgellau Assize (John Morgan was the clerk) – in breach of the provisions of the 1942 Act – discharged two Welsh-speaking prospective jurors who had asked that they should be allowed to take the oath in Welsh,[76] it was not until the early 1960s that a new phase of reform began. The question of the legal status of the language, indeed of its survival, was then ushered onto centre stage by the combination of a judgement in the High Court, a radio lecture, and a report produced by a government standing advisory committee.

The High Court case, *Evans v. Thomas* (1962 2QB), involved an election petition. At a council election at Ammanford in 1961, a nomination form made out in Welsh was rejected by the returning officer on the grounds that it was not in English. A petition was brought before the High Court and in May 1962 the court held that since the nomination form in Welsh was a 'form to the like effect' as the English prescribed form which could be adapted 'so far as circumstances require', its rejection was invalid.

This judgement was viewed by language reformers as an important victory. Indeed, Saunders Lewis described it as the 'most important High Court judgement in London for Wales for two centuries if not more' ('Dyna'r dyfarniad pwysicaf yn yr Uchel Lys yn Llundain i Gymru ers dwy ganrif os nad rhagor').[77] But equally it became a cause for concern that the court had rejected the contention by Watkin Powell, counsel for the petitioner, that since the Welsh Courts Act 1942 the Welsh language had acquired a legal status equivalent to that of English. It became clear that this judgement turned on the particular facts which the court was addressing: that 79 per cent of the electorate were Welsh speakers and that the returning officer had on his staff Welsh-speaking officials. It was not a precedent for the proposition that a nomination form in the Welsh language would always be valid in every part of Wales. Instead, everything would depend on the facts. From the reformers' standpoint, a nomination form for any election in any part of Wales should be valid if it were in Welsh and not invalid on other grounds. This led to the call that Welsh should be given the status of an 'official language'. It was articulated in particular by Undeb Cenedlaethol

---

[75] Ibid., letter 12 April 1943.

[76] *Parliamentary Debates* (Hansard), 5th series, vol. 515, 177–8, Written Answers (21 May 1953). See also PRO LCO 2/5273 (3485/6), exchange of minutes between the Attorney-General and Schuster, and John Morgan, Clerk of Assize, and Schuster.

[77] Saunders Lewis, 'Tynged Darlith', *Barn*, 5 (1963), 143.

Athrawon Cymru (UCAC) (the National Union of Teachers in Wales) in letters sent in September 1961 to the Minister for Welsh Affairs and the WPP. It will be seen that these letters were to bring about significant changes. But they were not the only factors at work.

Saunders Lewis, the veteran nationalist leader, had also returned to the arena. On 13 February 1962 he delivered his celebrated radio lecture, *Tynged yr Iaith* (The Fate of the Language).[78] In his lecture, Lewis predicted that 'Welsh will end as a living language, should the present trend continue, about the beginning of the twenty-first century'.[79] He urged the Welsh people to build a powerful language movement, using 'revolutionary methods' to fight in those areas where Welsh was in daily use to ensure that Welsh became an official language in the local and civil administration.[80] No other Welsh-language broadcast has equalled its impact. Within six months an impatient younger generation had rallied to his call and founded the defiant language movement, Cymdeithas yr Iaith Gymraeg (the Welsh Language Society). Its members demanded not only the right to use Welsh with public authorities, but that the authorities should also use Welsh in their dealings with them.[81] This fresh development did not go unnoticed in Whitehall.[82] Court cases against Society members for breaking the law in protest against government policies, which they saw as a violation of their fundamental rights as Welsh speakers, became increasingly frequent. A few years later Whitehall would be startled by the open sympathy of many magistrates in predominantly Welsh-speaking areas, and not exclusively in such areas, towards language activists summoned before their courts for politically motivated offences.[83]

Meanwhile, the Council for Wales and Monmouthshire, the government's standing advisory body on Welsh affairs (composed of twenty-six distinguished Welsh people), set up a panel, chaired by Professor Richard I. Aaron, the Council Chairman, 'to study and report upon the situation of the Welsh language at present'. The panel collected extensive evidence of the extent to which Welsh was being used. Some of it was immensely worrying. Thus, a 'personal' letter to

---

[78] Idem, *Tynged yr Iaith* (London, [1962]). For the English translation, see Gruffydd Aled Williams, 'The Fate of the Language (1962)' in Alun R. Jones and Gwyn Thomas (eds.), *Presenting Saunders Lewis* (Cardiff, 1973), pp. 127–41.

[79] Williams, 'The Fate of the Language', p. 127.

[80] Ibid., p. 141.

[81] Magistrates' Court Aberystwyth, 2 January 1963. The case of Geraint Jones and Emyr Llewelyn, who demanded that the summons be issued in Welsh.

[82] PRO MO/1295/62, minute from Blaise Gillie, 12 February 1963.

[83] In 1970 a Swansea magistrate was not prepared to impose a fine for such an offence and was removed from the bench in 1972. In April 1972 the Cardiff stipendiary magistrate granted an absolute discharge to two defendants who had pleaded guilty to using television sets without licences in order to draw attention to the inadequacy of Welsh-language television facilities. When the Lord Chancellor made it known to him that he had acted wrongly, the stipendiary acknowledged his error.

the panel secretary from a Home Office official revealed that both his Department and that of the Lord Chancellor had studiously avoided monitoring the implementation of the 1942 Act:

> I should be glad if you would not put the contents of this letter before the Council. As you know, the use of Welsh is a surprisingly explosive issue . . . and we are particularly uneasy about the effect of any inquiry about the proportion of Welsh-speaking clerks and assistants. We fear that this, coming from us, would be regarded as the first in a move to make knowledge of Welsh a requirement for employment, and would thus stir up a hornets' nest. We could not in any case make the inquiry about justices; this would be for the Lord Chancellor's Office, and they have shown no enthusiasm for the making of any enquiry at all.[84]

It appears that this letter was withheld from members of the panel. The oral evidence of the clerks of the Welsh local authorities was equally depressing: 'They all consented to the opinion that it [the use of the Welsh language in local government] had no future at all, especially in view of the trend towards the establishment of larger local government units' ('Tybient i gyd nad oedd iddi ddyfodol, yn arbennig yn wyneb y duedd i sefydlu unedau llywodraeth leol mwy').[85]

The panel's wide-ranging survey, *Report on the Welsh Language Today*, was completed by the end of 1962 and was presented to the Minister for Welsh Affairs in April 1963.[86] The Council took the 'fundamental standpoint' that it wanted the language to survive. The report, which was well received in Wales, contained thirty-four recommendations, but in this chapter we are interested in the two which Aaron had identified in the *Western Mail* on 21 November 1963 as 'the most important', namely that Welsh be an official language in relation to certain functions and that a permanent body be set up to care for its interests. The concept of an official language for specified purposes was novel. Aaron had studied the situation of the Irish language closely during the early 1950s. Moreover, he had had private discussions with senior officials at the Department of Education in Dublin on 17–18 October 1961 about the state of the Irish language, and it is possible that this recommendation may have emanated from his interpretation of article 8 (3) of the Irish Constitution 1937.[87] The permanent body proposals were also new. Their genesis is to be found in a submission to the panel by Alun R. Edwards, the innovative Cardiganshire County Librarian, and

---

[84] PRO BD 23/177, letter from R. L. Jones to B. H. Evans, 6 March 1962.

[85] PRO BD 23/170, minute 22 September 1961.

[86] The Council for Wales and Monmouthshire, *The Welsh Language Today* (London, 1963) (PP 1963–4 (Cmnd. 2198) XX).

[87] PRO BD 23/170, letter from Richard I. Aaron to B. H. Evans, 16 July 1961.

they had strong attractions for Aaron.[88] The details of these two key proposals had not been closely worked out in the report, but if their underlying principle had been acceptable to ministers, expertise in drafting and constitutional law would have been available to the government to work them through. But both were unpalatable to ministers. The rebuff probably came as no great surprise to Aaron,[89] but it must have been a blow since he had chosen to work constructively with ministers. Nevertheless, through the instrument of this report, Aaron had presented Wales with powerful ideas which would provide debate for another day.

While the panel was studying the general well-being of the language, the WPP had been approached by UCAC as a result of the *Ammanford Case (Evans v. Thomas)* to secure official recognition for the Welsh language. In response, the WPP, at its meeting in October 1961, invited two of its lawyer members to prepare a memorandum on the issues. These were considered in a document prepared by John Morris, Labour MP for Aberafan.[90] After reviewing the Acts of 1536 and 1942, Morris advised that with the repeal of section 17 'there was nothing to prohibit the use of Welsh in any form'. Nevertheless, in order to remove doubt, he advised that the WPP should request the government:

> to introduce a Bill, in the nature of an Interpretation Act, which would merely state that any form, minute or document, written in the Welsh language would have equal validity as if it were written in the English language.

His colleagues accepted his opinion and sought a meeting with ministers. After much procrastination, a meeting took place on 6 November 1962 between R. A. Butler, the Home Secretary, Sir Keith Joseph, the Minister for Housing and Local Government and Welsh Affairs, and a WPP deputation led by Lady Megan Lloyd George.[91] Blaise Gillie, the able if eccentric senior civil servant at the Cardiff office of the Ministry of Housing and Local Government, compiled a defensive briefing note.[92] He told ministers that there were some ten MPs who 'seriously favoured' making Welsh an official language, but that very few of the others 'would incur the odium of opposing it'. But the issue was not raised. Lady Megan Lloyd George explained that the concern arose out of the *Ammanford Case*. When John Morris and Goronwy Roberts suggested that a departmental committee should be appointed to examine the issues, Joseph was sympathetic,

---

[88] NLW, Richard I. Aaron Papers. Edwards had in mind the Royal Commission on Ancient and Historical Monuments or the Andrew Carnegie (UK) Trust.

[89] PRO BD 25/120, letter from Richard I. Aaron to Blaise Gillie, 5 July 1962 and reply 13 July 1962.

[90] PRO BD 24/186, memorandum (copy).

[91] PRO MO/1295/62, briefing 29 October 1962. The Lord Chancellor's Department chose not to be involved, since it felt there was no uncertainty about the law.

[92] Ibid., minute 9 November 1962.

but claimed that ministers would have to consider its implications and arrange to meet the WPP again.

Gillie, who had listened to the discussion, reported to his Permanent Secretary, Dame Evelyn Sharpe, that it had been a half-hearted presentation.[93] He supported an inquiry since it was often 'the simplest way of satisfying everybody that there is really not much in it', but she was not convinced.[94] Even when ministers had agreed in principle to set up a small committee of inquiry, Dame Evelyn Sharpe was still wary:

> This could be a dangerous exercise as it could be difficult to assemble a committee of persons who understand the Welsh language, who could be regarded as sympathetic, and who yet wouldn't go hay-wire over having Welsh much more widely used despite the relatively few people who can understand it.[95]

Since ministers had willed the inquiry, she did everything in her power to ensure that it would deliver results which would be acceptable to her Department. Civil servants took soundings on the candidates for the chair. A lowly official on Gillie's staff described Aaron as an effective chairman, but that 'his objectivity was sometimes clouded'.[96] After the Lord Chancellor had ruled that the inquiry did not justify the appointment of a High Court judge, David Hughes Parry became the leading candidate. The Home Office initially feared that he was too closely identified with the Welsh-speaking lobby, although there is no evidence that they were aware of his behind-the-scenes work in 1939. Finally they came round:

> Not only is he highly regarded in Wales, but his reputation in legal matters generally is for conservatism and caution. These qualities may not be unimportant in the Chairman of an enquiry of the kind in contemplation.[97]

Dame Evelyn Sharpe gave her conditional support: 'If we can feel satisfied that Sir David Hughes Parry would be safe enough, we should go for him as chairman.'[98] She advised that the committee would also 'need a very hard-headed secretary as we don't want to get landed with suggestions for a considerable enlargement of people's legal rights to use the Welsh language'.[99] The legal adviser at the Cardiff office of the Ministry of Health, who was about to retire, was appointed to the post.

[93] Ibid., minute 15 July 1963.
[94] Ibid., minute 12 February 1963.
[95] PRO BD 23/170, minute 22 September 1961.
[96] Ibid.
[97] Ibid.
[98] Ibid.
[99] Ibid.

On 30 July 1963, in reply to an arranged question, Sir Keith Joseph announced in the Commons that he was appointing a small committee with the tight remit 'to clarify the legal status of the Welsh language and to consider whether any changes in the law are required'. Its chairman was Sir David Hughes Parry, by then seventy years of age. This meant that the Aaron recommendations had been set aside, although this was not clear at the time. The committee took two years to prepare its report, *The Legal Status of the Welsh Language*.[100] Having taken evidence, it deliberated whether the status of the language should be based in future on any one of three principles: *necessity* (i.e. that of the Act of 1942, that Welsh could be used only where an individual believed that he/she would be under a disadvantage in English because his/her natural language of communication was Welsh); *bilingualism* (i.e. all legal and administrative business be conducted in English and Welsh side by side); and *equal validity* (i.e. 'that any act, writing or thing done in Welsh in Wales should have the like legal force as if it had been done in English'). It did not examine the principle of *official status for prescribed purposes* (the recommendation of the Council for Wales which had been supported in a detailed submission to the committee by UCAC). The report unhesitatingly rejected the first two options and unanimously recommended that Welsh should be accorded *status of equal validity* with English for legal purposes and in public administration in Wales, that the new status should be applied without exception throughout the whole of Wales, and that it should be embodied in statute. The committee made thirty other recommendations which were regarded by many as a blueprint for action to give effect to the new principle.

There is a striking similarity between the report's main recommendation of 'equal validity' and the 'equal validity' proposal in the Morris report to the WPP. John Morris states that these conclusions were arrived at independently.[101] But since the Morris proposal – which had been warmly received by the WPP – was highly relevant to the committee's inquiry, it is very likely that his memorandum would have been discussed with, if not shown to, the committee by representatives of the WPP. When the committee produced its report, it was promptly presented to Parliament by James Griffiths, the first Secretary of State for Wales. The Official Opposition secured a debate on it in the Welsh Grand Committee on 14 December 1964. It was opened by Peter Thomas (Shadow Welsh Secretary), who made a supportive and well-researched speech. There was no doubt about the commitment of both Griffiths and Goronwy Roberts, his Minister of State, who respectively opened and closed the debate on behalf of the government. Both had consulted Hughes Parry. Like Peter Thomas, both were

---

[100] The Welsh Office, *Legal Status of the Welsh Language: Report of the Committee under the Chairmanship of Sir David Hughes Parry, 1963–1965* (London, 1965) (PP 1964–5 (Cmd. 2785) XXIII).

[101] Interview with John Morris, December 1994.

firmly opposed to affirmative discrimination in favour of the language. On the other hand, their backbenchers, Iorwerth Thomas, MP for Rhondda West, and Leo Abse, MP for Pontypool, who represented a significant section of the Welsh Labour Party which a Labour government could not alienate, were predictably hostile and some of their criticism was echoed by Peter Thorneycroft, MP for Monmouth, who wound up for the Opposition. Nevertheless, that evening Welsh Office ministers could draw encouragement from the broad thrust of the debate, although they also knew that opposition could be stirring.

Following the general election in April 1966 there was a Cabinet reshuffle. A new ministerial team arrived at the Welsh Office. Cledwyn Hughes was appointed Secretary of State and George Thomas became his Minister of State. The minds of the two ministers ran in very different ways in terms of their aspirations for the Welsh language. Undoubtedly the Minister of State ensured that the criticisms voiced by Iorwerth Thomas and Leo Abse in the Welsh Grand Committee again surfaced within the Welsh Office.[102] On the other hand, the language had been a vital part of the upbringing of the new Secretary of State. He saw it as a defining feature of Welsh nationhood and sought to achieve a settlement which would confer on it a status worthy of a national language.

Cledwyn Hughes was a leader of Welsh-speaking Wales. He was a pragmatic politician and a consensus-builder. But events conspired against him. The threat represented by Plaid Cymru's unexpected by-election victory at Carmarthen in July 1966, followed by its striking success in a by-election in Labour's heartland, Rhondda West, alarmed Labour MPs in south Wales. Cledwyn Hughes had been working for some years on a proposal to establish an all-Wales elected council with executive powers as part of the reform of Welsh local government. Many of his backbenchers now sharpened their opposition both to the elected Welsh Council proposal and the principle of 'equal validity', perceiving them to be part and parcel of the nationalist agenda which had to be confronted. At the same time, the Secretary of State also came under attack from members of the Welsh Language Society, who charged him with lack of direction and energy. His position became all the more difficult against a volatile background involving the emergence in 1966 of the Patriotic Front set up by the Free Wales Army, the activities of the Anti-Investiture Campaign Committee and a bombing campaign waged by the underground group, Mudiad Amddiffyn Cymru (the Movement for the Defence of Wales). In this tense atmosphere, the Secretary of State was in some difficulty. A quarter of a century later, he commented: 'The practical course was to introduce a short enabling Bill, because a longer and detailed Bill, which I would have preferred, would have attracted even more bitter opposition.'[103]

---

[102] George Thomas, *Mr Speaker: The Memoirs of the Viscount Tonypandy* (London, 1985), p. 96.
[103] Interview with Cledwyn Hughes, July 1994.

Cledwyn Hughes was very well served by his Permanent Secretary, Goronwy Daniel. He was an exceptional higher civil servant who genuinely understood the significance of the Welsh language for the people of Wales. He also knew the ways and wiles of Whitehall and appreciated better than anyone else that the brand-new Welsh Office was a very junior institution. It became one of his urgent duties after April 1966 to explore the way forward with senior officials of the main departments concerned. He was to find that the Lord Chancellor's Department was unsympathetic, as was to be confirmed by the Lord Chancellor's surprising intervention in the course of the Second Reading Debate on the Bill.[104]

There is evidence that stiff resistance to the proposed legislation would have continued within Whitehall had it not been for key decisions taken in relation to the Investiture of the Prince of Wales in 1969, upon which Daniel had advised. By the spring of 1967 it was agreed between the government and the Palace that Prince Charles would prepare himself for the Investiture by spending the spring term of 1969 studying 'the history and problems of Wales and its language and literature' at the University College of Wales, Aberystwyth. It was also agreed that, unlike the precedent of 1911, the Welsh language would be given an honourable place in the Investiture ceremony itself at Caernarfon Castle. It is believed that this royal benediction lessened the obstructionism in unsympathetic quarters of Whitehall.[105]

The Bill team proceeded to prepare instructions to Parliamentary Counsel. These were sent in draft form to Hughes Parry for his comments. After consulting his two committee members, he suggested a few amendments, but they seemed to be minor drafting points which did not cause problems.[106] Eventually, in May 1967, the draft Bill was cleared with the Lord Chancellor's Office. In his supporting memorandum to the Legislation Committee, the Secretary of State explained that the principle of bilingualism had 'been completely rejected', there would be no 'absolute right to have business conducted in Welsh excepting a right to speak Welsh in legal proceedings', and that ministers would retain the right to decide when Welsh would be used by their departments.[107] He believed that the Bill would enhance the status of the language and 'as such it should be acceptable to all shades of opinion in Wales'. The wording of the memorandum reflects the tacking and trimming within the Welsh Group of the Labour Parliamentary Party and the compromises within Whitehall departments.

The 1967 Act contained five sections. It began with a preamble acknowledging that 'it is proper that the Welsh language should be freely used by those who so desire in the hearing of legal proceedings in Wales and Monmouthshire'. It then went on to state that 'further provision should be made' for the use of Welsh

---

[104] *Parliamentary Debates* (Hansard) (House of Lords), 5th series, vol. 284, 89–91 (27 June 1967).
[105] Private information.
[106] NLW, Sir David Hughes Parry Papers.
[107] Emyr Price, *Lord Cledwyn of Penrhos* (Bangor, 1990), p. 55.

'with the like effect as English, in the conduct of other official or public business', but no light was thrown on the precise meaning of the 'further provision'. Section 1 corrected the inherent defect in section 1 of the 1942 Act and entitled any person to use Welsh in any legal proceedings if he so wished. Sections 2 and 3 empowered a minister to prescribe Welsh versions of statutory documents or forms of words, and to provide that in the event of a discrepancy between the two texts, the English should prevail. The Act retained the provision that English was the language of record.

As had been the case in 1942, the Bill was passed unopposed and without amendments being tabled. It was nodded through the committee stage. This may seem strange in the circumstances of 1967, for many of the MPs were aware of the painful and long-running dispute between Eileen and Trefor Beasley and the Llanelli Rural District Council over the issue of Welsh-language rate demands, a dispute which had involved sixteen court appearances between 1952 and 1961. Moreover, what had become of the ten MPs who, according to Gillie, wanted to confer 'official status' on the language? The explanation may well lie in an unwillingness to jeopardize the compromise which had been negotiated.

A mixed response greeted the Act in Welsh political, cultural and legal circles. Alwyn D. Rees roundly condemned the new legislation in the magazine *Barn*,[108] and it received a hostile reception from the Welsh Language Society. But Hughes Parry seems not to have been disappointed with the fruits of his labour and would not be drawn into criticism of the government. Immediately after its enactment, he was reported in *Y Cymro* as describing the Act as an important step forward, although he believed that further legislation would be required to implement the new principle.[109] Although the Act undoubtedly enhanced the status of the language, its weakness was soon to emerge. It lacked teeth. The decision whether to adopt equal validity, and if so, to what extent, was discretionary. While local authorities in Gwynedd and some local authorities in Dyfed were to adopt a maximalist approach to the new principle, most of the others took a minimalist approach. Two factors in particular were to contribute to the expectations of the Act being frustrated. Firstly, it was difficult to overcome the assumptions, values and practices to which people had been accustomed for generations. Secondly, the more unsympathetic officials and local politicians were often to prove deliberately obstructive. To believe that public bodies throughout Wales would leap to implement a language policy based on equal validity was an idealistic view. As a result, in many parts of Wales equal validity remained a reform that had yet to prevail and a symbol of what the status of the language ought to be.

By the late 1960s, as the gap between the theory of equal validity and its practice became increasingly apparent, reformers called for the setting up of a

---

[108] *Barn*, 57 (1967), editorial.
[109] *Y Cymro*, 10 and 17 August 1967.

Welsh language standing commission along the lines recommended by Aaron and the Council for Wales. The demand was supported by Urdd Gobaith Cymru, the Honourable Society of Cymmrodorion and by influential Welshmen such as Sir Ben Bowen Thomas and Sir Goronwy Daniel. In September 1973, in response to pressure, Peter Thomas, the Secretary of State for Wales, appointed a non-statutory advisory committee which he called the Council for the Welsh Language. It was chaired by Ben G. Jones, an eminent London solicitor and a leading figure in Cymmrodorion circles. The Council made little immediate impact, but it produced some worthwhile papers, including a major report, *A Future for the Welsh Language* (1978).[110] The report advocated government action to save the language and the adoption of a 'positive policy of effective bilingualism'. In addition, it proposed that the Council should itself be replaced 'as soon as possible' by 'a permanent body'. The report was submitted to John Morris, who had become Secretary of State. Although Morris had a solid commitment to the language, he was at that time concentrating on the proposal for setting up an elected Welsh Assembly by 1979. He concluded that it would not be wise at that juncture to adopt the main recommendations of the report. In his judgement, to do otherwise might weaken the government's main policy of establishing an elected Assembly. That may have been right or wrong, but it was the opinion of those who were closely promoting the devolution policy that his decision, in the circumstances of 1978, was fully justified. Whether the government should have appointed a Royal Commission to examine the language issue with a view to producing a basis of policy for future action – a contribution equivalent to that of the Kilbrandon Commission on the constitution – is a matter which has not been publicly discussed. In the event, the Council's report did not achieve any significant changes.

The collapse in 1979 of the Welsh Assembly policy and the election of a Conservative government with its concerns for competition and market forces made it necessary for the reformers to rethink their priorities. There was disquiet that so little action had been taken on the reports of the Council for the Welsh Language, and also considerable anxiety as to what would be the policy of the new government towards the language. These concerns were raised at an overflowing public meeting convened by the Cymmrodorion at the National Eisteddfod at Caernarfon in 1979. The meeting resolved that a deputation be sent to the new Secretary of State, Nicholas Edwards. For reasons which are unclear, however, the Cymmrodorion failed to press the case for a meeting with Edwards.

However, the Secretary of State moved quickly. In April 1980, in an important speech to representatives of Gwynedd County Council at Llanrwst, he set out the new government's policy on the Welsh language. Satisfied that the legal status of the language had been resolved by the Hughes Parry Report, the Secretary of

---

[110] The Council for the Welsh Language, *A Future for the Welsh Language* (Cardiff, 1978).

State was anxious to encourage the use of Welsh as a living language, but he would not be a party to 'universal bilingualism'. He was opposed to 'a new and expensive quango'. There would be no question of compulsion. To add weight to his argument, he announced that the order of precedence for the two languages on bilingual road signs would be determined henceforth by each individual council; this announcement represented the first departure from the principle of universality established by Hughes Parry, but its implications were barely appreciated at the time.[111]

By early 1982 the Welsh Language Society was calling for a campaign for a new Welsh Language Act. In July of the following year, at a very poorly-attended meeting in Newtown, chaired by Professor Dafydd Jenkins, a Working Party for a New Welsh Language Act was established to examine the import of the 1967 Act and to make recommendations. For the next seven years or so, the Working Party and the Welsh Language Society – with Dr Meredydd Evans providing the vital link – made common cause in demanding a replacement Act. The public campaign began in earnest with a pamphlet published to coincide with a national conference on 3 November 1984 in Cardiff City Hall.[112] The conference was presided over by the former Archbishop of Wales, the Right Revd G. O. Williams. Thereafter the campaign was strengthened by the involvement of the language rights' movement Cefn and Y Fforwm Iaith (the Language Forum).

By July 1986 a Private Member's Bill and a draft Bill had been drawn up and sent to the Welsh Office.[113] Within three months the Secretary of State invited comments on their content from all the Welsh public bodies – a total of about two hundred.[114] The responses were never published, but there were indications that – apart from those of the nominated bodies – they were favourable to the principle of new legislation. In launching the consultation exercise, it is possible that Edwards had no greater objective than to make a sympathetic gesture before the 1987 general election, while giving himself a pretence for avoiding a decision on the merits. But his decision to consult was immensely important to the Working Party. At one blow it seemed to have destroyed the argument that there was no case for fresh legislation. At the same time, it helped to prepare public opinion to be receptive to the case for change.

Following the general election of 1987 Peter Walker was appointed Secretary of State for Wales. Although he knew very little about the Welsh language, he was optimistic about its future. In July 1988, in response to the growing pressures for a new Welsh Language Act, Walker resorted to the device of setting up

---

[111] The Welsh Office, *The Welsh Language. A Commitment and Challenge: The Government's Policy for the Welsh Language* (Cardiff, 1980), p. 4.

[112] The Working Party for a New Welsh Language Act, *A New Welsh Language Act: Recommendations* (Aberystwyth, [1984]).

[113] The Private Member's Bill was introduced by Dafydd Wigley MP and supported by eleven other MPs; the Draft Bill was produced by the Working Party for a New Welsh Language Act.

[114] Consultative letter, 1 October 1986.

another language advisory committee, which he styled Bwrdd yr Iaith Gymraeg (the Welsh Language Board), consisting of a chairman and eight members who were known to be supportive of the language, but who had little direct experience of Welsh political life.[115] As required by Walker, the Board drew up voluntary guidelines for the public and private sectors, but it is believed that they were not heeded in any significant way.[116] The Board then drew up a draft Bill which it sent to the Secretary of State in November 1989. It was followed in February 1991 by a revised version which had three main aims: to confer upon the language the status of an 'official language'; to provide criteria governing the meaning and the practical implementation of equal validity; and to establish a statutory board with a 'duty to promote the language and facilitate its greater use'.[117] Although it was widely felt among reformers that the Board's Bill had failed in many respects to learn from the experience of the 1967 Act, it was still a significant contribution and it may have surprised the Welsh Office.

Throughout the 1980s the government had been resolutely opposed to new Welsh language legislation. But, by 1992, for reasons which are unknown, it had changed its position. On 27 February 1992, on the eve of another general election, David Hunt, the Secretary of State, announced in the Commons that the government would be bringing forward new legislation which would give practical effect to the 'principle of equal validity'. Apart from discussions with the non-statutory Board – whose chairman would later criticize some of the provisions of the government's Bill – there were, as far as is known, no consultations between the Welsh Office and any other party over the proposed Bill.

The eagerly awaited Bill was unveiled on 17 December 1992. It established a Welsh Language Statutory Board with advisory and promotional functions and an independent secretariat. Its chairman and members were to be appointed by the Secretary of State and made subject to his directions. But the existence of a statutory Board was an acknowledgement by the government that the state itself was under an obligation to promote and facilitate the use of the Welsh language in Welsh public life. The Act replaced the 1967 principle of equal validity with that of 'a basis of equality' (section 3(2)(b)). However, the term approximates to the 'footing of equality', a term probably first used in 1923 by D. Lleufer Thomas and also used in the 1938 National Petition. It is not clear whether this change of terminology has any significance in law or in practice. The distinction is a very fine one, but it could be argued that 'equality' has a more positive meaning than 'validity'. What seems likely is that the new principle may only be fully workable

---

[115] Statement by Peter Walker, 20 July 1988.

[116] The Welsh Language Board, *A Bilingual Policy: Guidelines for the Public Sector* (Caerdydd, 1989); idem, *Practical Options for the Use of Welsh in Business* (Caerdydd, 1989).

[117] The Welsh Language Board, *Recommendations for a New Welsh Language Act: A Report by the Welsh Language Board to the Secretary of State for Wales, the Right Honourable David Hunt MBE MP* (February 1991).

in conjunction with a 'language scheme', but this has yet to be tested. A 'language scheme' was another new concept introduced by the Act. It was intended to be the means of translating the principle of 'basis of equality' into a detailed and workable policy in a local or service-specific scheme.

The Board was required by the Act to produce statutory guidelines identifying the matters to be reflected in a language scheme 'so far as is both appropriate in the circumstances and reasonably practicable' (sections 5 and 12). It was perceived that, as a result of these limitations, the language scheme would largely reflect the status quo and would not bring about substantial or swift improvements in the language policy of a public body. Others were encouraged by the fact that the scheme-making procedure provided an opportunity for the Board to enjoin a public body to develop, however reluctantly, a more favourable linguistic policy to guide its future actions. The failure of a public body to discharge its obligations under its language scheme does not of itself render it liable to penalty, but it may be the subject matter of a complaint by or to the Board (section 18), which may hold a formal inquiry (section 17) and can lead to a recommendation by the Board that the public body takes action to remedy its failure. If it fails to implement such recommendations, the Board may refer the issue to the Secretary of State (section 20), who may give directions to the public body, and in the event of non-compliance he may at his sole discretion apply to the court for a compliance order. It is the Secretary of State alone who can have resort to the court. To what extent the exhaustive procedure of complaint / formal investigation / recommendation / directions will ultimately provide an effective mechanism remains to be seen.

The Act re-enacted the absolute right to use Welsh in the courts. In addition, it empowered the Lord Chancellor to make rules for the use of Welsh-language documents in legal proceedings. It repealed the 1942 and 1967 provisions requiring the record of the court to be kept in English and repealed the 1967 presumption that, in the event of discrepancy between a Welsh and an English text, the latter would prevail. Although strenuous efforts were made in Parliament to strengthen and broaden the scope of the new legislation, the impact of the opposition parties was minimal. The government firmly opposed any amendments which would revise the Bill in any material way. In the event, the Act failed to address a number of key issues, each involving an important point of principle: although the boundary between the public and private sectors had become blurred since 1979, the Act was confined to the public bodies as defined in section 6(1) and therefore excluded the privatized utilities; it did not resolve the potential conflict between an employment condition which requires language proficiency and the anti-discrimination provisions of the Race Relations Act 1976; it did not entitle a party, where the trial of his or her case is heard in Welsh, or substantially in Welsh, to have the case heard before a Welsh-speaking jury; it failed to confer a right on an individual who had been adversely affected by a breach of the provisions of a language scheme to sue or recover damages.

But the single greatest cause of concern was the rejection by the government of a 'purpose clause' declaring the Welsh language to be an official language in Wales.[118] Adopting such a clause would have been an expression of the high constitutional status of the language. It would have given a firm purpose to the Act and provided guidance to the executive and to the courts, when in doubt, about the application of any of its provisions. The government was vigorously lobbied by public authorities, churches and voluntary organizations to incorporate an 'official language' amendment in the Bill. Appropriate amendments were tabled in both Houses, but the government ensured they were defeated. The government response was surprising. The Prime Minister and ministers maintained that such amendments were superfluous since Welsh was already an official language in Wales. 'We believe', declared John Major in the Commons on 13 July 1993, that 'Welsh already enjoys official status in Wales.' This contention was unconvincing for it did not correspond to reality. But if the Prime Minister's claim was right, then what objection could there be to the principle being written into the Bill? The Welsh Language Act 1993 came into force in December 1993. Although it is too early to commit ourselves to a firm judgement about its impact, it may prove to be the most important of the three Welsh Language Acts of the twentieth century.

Notwithstanding deep-rooted obstructionism and lack of understanding in Whitehall, and inertia, or even resistance, on the part of many officials and members of Welsh public authorities, there has been substantial movement during the twentieth century to reinstate the Welsh language to its proper place as the national language of Wales. At the beginning of the century, the status was dependent upon discretion. By the end of the century, it had achieved a status on the basis of equality with English. The movement can be viewed as a shift from a position of humiliation and reliance on a non-statutory discretion towards a position of pride underpinned by an accretion of statutory rights. That movement may fit into some wider scene, but it would be a mistake to suggest that it was a smooth and inevitable transition. It had to be fought for. The impetus for change came from a tiny group of intellectuals and the innovative persistence of generations of reformers, sometimes at considerable cost to themselves.

---

[118] For the meaning of 'purpose clause' see *The Preparation of Legislation: Report of a Committee appointed by the Lord President of the Council* (London, 1975) (PP 1974–5 (Cmnd. 6053) XII), pp. 62–3.

6

The Attitude of Political Parties towards the Welsh Language

J. GRAHAM JONES

In 1866 John Thaddeus Delane commented in the columns of *The Times* that the Welsh language was 'the curse of Wales', a persistent hindrance to progress and prosperity in the relatively opulent mid-Victorian age.[1] In fact, although moderate successes were achieved by the end of the nineteenth century in anchoring the Welsh language in the education system, these were not paralleled by similar progress in the fields of administration, law and commerce. Late nineteenth-century Welsh people were indeed notably 'pusillanimous when it came to their linguistic rights'.[2] Although Welsh speakers far outnumbered Nonconformist communicants, the legitimate claims and rights of Welsh speakers were almost totally ignored, while the campaign to disestablish an 'alien Church' consistently occupied a central position in Welsh political life. Only rarely did Welsh-language columns appear in the *South Wales Daily News*, the Cardiff Liberal daily newspaper which, until its demise in 1928, was a somewhat pedestrian rival to the more lively Tory *Western Mail*. While the Liberal Party had firmly established itself as 'the party of Wales and the vehicle for its growing national consciousness',[3] it had in no sense embraced the cause of the Welsh language.

The sharp decline in the monoglot Welsh population between 1891 and 1911 and the growth of a largely bilingual populace, especially in the southern coastal areas and the north-east, did not lack relevance for the political life of Wales. New attitudes rapidly sprang up as a result of the transformation in the linguistic composition of Wales. There appeared strong justification for giving priority to English in local activities, while no longer did there seem to be any need to provide an extensive range of literature in Welsh on every subject. Material published in English was within the reach of almost the entire population of Wales. In the industrial valleys of Glamorgan and Monmouthshire, it appeared that the well-being of the Welsh language was being almost daily undermined by

---

[1] *The Times*, 8 September 1866.
[2] Janet Davies, *The Welsh Language* (Cardiff, 1993), p. 52.
[3] Kenneth O. Morgan, 'The New Liberalism and the Challenge of Labour: The Welsh Experience, 1885–1929', *WHR*, 6, no. 3 (1973), 290.

Anglicizing influences, the chief of which were the partly immigrant working population and the centralizing pressures of the new industrial technology.

The period of rapid population growth in the South Wales Coalfield witnessed the emergence of the dominant forces of socialism, trade unionism and labour politics. Following the lengthy and bitter coal strike of 1898, the South Wales Miners' Federation (SWMF) was set up and, in 1900, J. Keir Hardie was elected the Labour Representation Committee MP for Merthyr Tydfil, the storm centre of industrial conflict and soon to be dubbed 'a hotbed of anti-capitalist and syndicalist propaganda'.[4] Members of the Welsh working classes found themselves drawn into British trade unions which entertained no sympathy for specifically Welsh issues, including the Welsh language, which some came to view as socially divisive and likely to undermine highly cherished notions of class solidarity and fraternity. As the novelist Gwyn Thomas put it: 'The Welsh language stood in the way of our fuller union and we made ruthless haste to destroy it. We nearly did.'[5] Wil Jon Edwards, a native of Aberdare, recorded in his autobiography that the new socialist philosophy was considered, first and foremost, as 'English ideas'.[6] So strong had been the bonds between political Liberalism, religious Nonconformity and the Welsh language that the rejection of one seemed inevitably to lead to a repudiation of all three. Whereas the Welsh language had served as the matrix of the entangled association of Liberalism and Nonconformity, the young Labour Party increasingly emerged as the natural political home of Welsh radicals. It was a movement which proudly stressed its international and cosmopolitan credentials, and it was increasingly viewed as a secular, English-based movement.

Although Keir Hardie presented himself to the electors of Merthyr Tydfil as 'a Welsh nationalist'[7] and although the Labour Party conference in 1918 advocated 'separate statutory legislative assemblies for Scotland, Wales, and even England, with autonomous administration in matters of local concern',[8] the young Labour Party generally gave short shrift to the Welsh language. The influence and ethos of the socialist gospel which swept through south Wales on the eve of the First World War were overwhelmingly English. This was reflected in the bulging bookshelves of the miners' libraries: their rows of books on philosophy, economics, politics and social history were almost totally English. The content of the highly influential and widely read *Llais Llafur*, published at Ystalyfera in the heart of the Welsh-speaking Swansea valley, was around 85 per cent Welsh when it made its first appearance in 1898. A quarter of a century later, it had become 'the

---

[4] NLW, Thomas Jones Papers, letter from Thomas Jones to Neville Chamberlain, 13 August 1920 (copy).

[5] Gwyn Thomas, *A Welsh Eye* (London, 1964), p. 103.

[6] Wil Jon Edwards, *From the Valley I Came* (London, 1956), p. 36.

[7] Kenneth O. Morgan, 'The Merthyr of Keir Hardie' in Glanmor Williams (ed.), *Merthyr Politics: The Making of a Working-Class Tradition* (Cardiff, 1966), p. 70.

[8] Resolution XIII on 'Constitutional Devolution', *Report of the Eighteenth Annual Conference of the Labour Party* (London, 1918), p. 70.

premier Labour paper in Wales',[9] but it was now called *Labour Voice* and its Welsh-language content was confined to the occasional isolated column. The widely popular *Rhondda Socialist*, first published in 1912, was overwhelmingly English, and its editors were ever ready to jettison Welsh-language items in the event of a surplus of material. Labour and trade union meetings conducted in Welsh became increasingly rare events.

Nor did Welsh Liberals give pride of place to the well-being of the Welsh-language; their main concerns were religious, educational and temperance reform and, perhaps above all, personal advancement. Any Welsh patriotism they espoused was closely linked to respect for Royalty and the glories of the British Empire, an emphasis wholly abhorrent to members of the Welsh Independent Labour Party (ILP), who rejoiced in the emergence and strengthening of a Welsh working class and the development of new, democratic organizations. The Annual Conference of the ILP, convened in 1911, resolved that all its branches should be grouped together as a single administrative unit – significantly to be known not as the Welsh ILP, but as 'Division 8'. Younger miners' agents like Charles Stanton in Aberdare, David Watts Morgan in the Rhondda and Vernon Hartshorn in Maesteg were totally committed to a British Labour Party, and this new emphasis marked the breakdown of the old 'Lib-Lab' consensus politics.

Yet, among the sponsors of E. T. John's Government of Wales Bill, a unique measure introduced in the House of Commons in March 1914, were two stalwarts of the SWMF – its president, William Brace, and general secretary, Thomas Richards.[10] John's abortive home rule campaign, however, was very much in the Cymru Fydd tradition, directing its attention to the Westminster Parliament and seeking the support and co-operation of the Scots. John depicted a Welsh Parliament as the key to the solution of the social and economic ills of the nation, but no linguistic or cultural dimension figured in his campaign, and scant attention was paid to the evidence of the 1911 census. John's Bill was attacked on this score by the young W. Ambrose Bebb, former editor of *Y Wawr*, who argued that Welsh should at least enjoy parity with English by being granted official status.[11] John's earnest efforts were also derided by the 'syndicalists' of the valleys of south Wales, who depicted a Welsh Parliament as an élitist, bourgeois institution. 'Llafurwr', who wrote in the *Rhondda Socialist*, observed in 1912:

Gair mawr rhyw bobl heddyw ydyw Cenedlaetholdeb Cymreig . . . Beth ydyw? Beth a olyga i weithwyr Cymru? Pa fodd y mae yn cyfarfod ag anesmwythyd y werin a'i chri am well amodau bywoliaeth? Yn mha le y saif Plaid Llafur yn ei pherthynas a'r peth? etc. Cydnabyddwn nad ydym yn glir ar y pwnc hwn.[12]

[9] Robert Griffiths, *Turning to London: Labour's Attitude to Wales, 1898–1956* (n.p., [1980]), p. 5.
[10] J. Graham Jones, 'E. T. John and Welsh Home Rule, 1910–14', *WHR*, 13, no. 4 (1987), 453–67.
[11] W. Ambrose Bebb, 'The Welsh Home Rule Bill', *The Welsh Outlook*, VI, no. 5 (1919), 136–7.
[12] *Rhondda Socialist*, 14 September 1912.

(Welsh Nationalism is much talked about by some people these days . . . What is it? What does it mean for the workers of Wales? How will it soothe the unrest of the working class and meet their cry for a better way of life? Where does the Labour Party stand in relation to this? etc. We acknowledge that we are not clear on this issue.)

Nor was the attitude of pre-war Liberal MPs any more convincing. The professional and commercial classes which formed the backbone of the Liberal Party in Wales displayed little determination to wrest home rule for Wales or to secure official status for the Welsh language. Even Lloyd George, 'the personification of Welshness at the highest pinnacles of politics',[13] came increasingly under fire for his apparent lack of interest in Welsh issues. Yet his progress to the zenith of political power in December 1916 was greeted in much of Wales with an euphoria seemingly divorced from the horrors and pressures of 'total war'. A whole generation of native Welsh speakers, perhaps as many as 20,000 people, was lost to Wales during the Great War, the best known of whom was Ellis Humphrey Evans (Hedd Wyn), the shepherd poet of Trawsfynydd, who was tragically killed while on active service in 1917. Moreover, the advent of war on such a scale brought the incursion of the state – an overwhelmingly Anglicizing influence – into the lives of ordinary Welshmen to an extent previously unimaginable. In the words of A. J. P. Taylor: 'Until August 1914 a sensible, law-abiding Englishman could pass through life and hardly notice the existence of the state, beyond the post office and the policeman.'[14] In a wholesale broadening of Welsh horizons during the war years, thousands of young Welshmen set foot outside their native Wales for the first time in their lives and shed their parochial outlook in the trenches of Flanders and France.

Post-war Wales was characterized by the shattering of the Liberal consensus, the severe undermining of Nonconformist optimism, and the first manifestation of industrial and economic imbalance, a precursor to severe depression. The sale of portions of most of the great estates – centres of Anglicization from the sixteenth century onwards – did little to stimulate rural communities which seemed destined to suffer the ravages of depression and severe depopulation. Aware of the impending cultural crisis, Undeb Cenedlaethol y Cymdeithasau Cymraeg (the National Union of Welsh Societies) declared formally in favour of home rule in 1919 and adopted more forceful tactics in pressing for recognition for the Welsh language. In the general election of November 1922 it circulated candidates in Wales with a questionnaire enquiring whether they supported home rule for Wales and the extended use of Welsh in schools, the civil service and Parliament. Twenty-four candidates responded in the affirmative, and one negatively, but a large number did not reply.[15] The Union, it seemed, was

---

[13] Kenneth O. Morgan, *Rebirth of a Nation: Wales 1880–1980* (Oxford, 1981), p. 139.

[14] A. J. P. Taylor, *English History, 1914–1945* (Harmondsworth, 1970), p. 25.

[15] Gerald Morgan, *The Dragon's Tongue: The Fortunes of the Welsh Language* (Cardiff, 1966), pp. 58–9.

labouring largely in a political wilderness. Half-hearted efforts to achieve a measure of home rule – a Welsh Parliament or the appointment of a Secretary of State for Wales – during the immediate post-war years did not include any concession to the Welsh language.[16] In a celebrated article in the patriotic journal *The Welsh Outlook* in 1919, Watkin Leyshon dismissed Welsh MPs as 'an undisciplined mob of time-servers and office-seekers'.[17]

Supporters of the Welsh language were plunged into gloom when the evidence of the population census of 1921 revealed that the percentage of Welsh speakers had slumped to 37.1 per cent. The figures revealed for the first time an absolute decline of 55,271 Welsh speakers since the previous census in 1911; the fall in the number of Welsh monoglots was particularly striking. Although doubts were cast on the accuracy of the census,[18] the overall results were melancholy in the extreme. To nationalists like W. Ambrose Bebb, the outlook for the Welsh language was increasingly gloomy: 'One fact faces [the Welshman], and stares him in the eyes. And that is that the number of those able to speak Welsh is decreasing. Slowly perhaps; but surely for all that.'[19] His concern was shared by W. Morgan Watkin, Professor of French at the University College of Wales, Cardiff, who, in a fascinating proposal, urged that any future Welsh Self-Government Act should ensure equality of status for the Welsh and English languages similar to the linguistic legislation governing the English and Afrikaan languages in South Africa:

Dylai fod y ddwy iaith a leferir yng Nghymru yn meddu cyfartal hawl i'w harfer yn yr ysgolion, yn adrannau gweinyddol gwlad, ym mharatoad, yn nadleuad ac yng nghyhoeddiad pob cyfraith a phob rheol a gosodiad y byddis yn eu llunio er budd Cymru. Dylid trefnu sefydliadau addysgol Cymru yn y fath fodd fel y gallo pob disgybl dderbyn rhan sylweddol o elfennau ei addysg yn ei iaith naturiol ef ei hun.[20]

(The two languages spoken in Wales should have an equal right to be used in schools, in the administrative departments of the country, in the preparation, debate and publication of every law and every rule and order formulated for the benefit of Wales. The educational institutions of Wales should be so organized that every pupil can receive a substantial proportion of the elements of education in his own natural language.)

He urged against encouraging the over-ambitious ideals of linguistic nationalists:

---

[16] J. Graham Jones, 'E. T. John, Devolution and Democracy, 1917–24', *WHR*, 14, no. 3 (1989), 439–69.

[17] Watkin Leyshon, 'Honour and Honours', *The Welsh Outlook*, XI, no. 2 (1919), 31.

[18] *Baner ac Amserau Cymru*, 1 May 1924.

[19] Quoted in D. Hywel Davies, *The Welsh Nationalist Party 1925–1945: A Call to Nationhood* (Cardiff, 1983), p. 73.

[20] Morgan Watkin, 'Polisi Ieithyddol i Gymru', *Y Geninen*, XLI, no. 1 (1923), 19.

Goreu po gyntaf, yn fy ngolwg i, yr ymwrthodo pob diwygiwr â'r gredo fod yn ddichon ar yr unfed awr ar ddeg yr ydym yn byw ynddi wneuthur y Gymraeg yn unig iaith swyddogol Cymru o dan Ymlywodraeth . . . Byddai ymgais benderfynol i wneuthur Cymraeg yn unig iaith swyddogol Cymru yn ddigon i rannu'r wlad fel y rhannwyd Iwerddon ar bwnc arall.[21]

(The sooner the better, in my opinion, every reformer rejects the belief that it is possible in the eleventh hour in which we live to make the Welsh language the only official language of a self-governing Wales . . . A determined attempt to make Welsh the only official language of Wales would be enough to divide the country as Ireland was divided over another matter.)

Although his ambitious strategy won the avid support of the National Union of Welsh Societies, Bebb disagreed with this view on the grounds that Watkin's strategy lacked the vital element of compulsion (already in force in other countries) which, in his opinion, was essential to success.[22] Saunders Lewis, too, placed the language at the heart of his emphasis on the value of tradition in Welsh life, arguing that the well-being of the native language was central to the task of sustaining Welsh civilization:

Ffrwyth cymdeithas yw iaith, peth hanfodol i wareiddiad, a thrysorfa holl brofiadau ac atgofion cenedl. Hi sy'n cadw dychmygion a dyheadau a breuddwydion y genedl, ac yn eu trysori mewn llenyddiaeth. Hyhi sy'n cadw atgof y genedl, ei gwybodaeth am ei dechreu, ei hieuenctid, ei blinderau a'i helbulon a'i buddugoliaethau, – y cwbl sy'n cyfansoddi hanes cenedl.[23]

(Language is the fruit of society, is essential to civilization, and is the treasury of all the experiences and memories of a nation. It keeps the visions and desires and dreams of the nation and treasures them in literature. It holds the memory of the nation, its knowledge of its beginnings, its youth, its suffering, its troubles and its victories, – all that constitutes the history of a nation).

These emphases, advocated by Bebb and Lewis, dictated the theme of the programme adopted by the newly-formed Mudiad Cymreig (the Welsh Movement) in 1924.[24]

Diehard nationalists like Saunders Lewis and W. Ambrose Bebb despaired of achieving any gains for the Welsh language through the agency of either the Liberal or Labour Parties. Following the failure of the Liberal conference at Shrewsbury in March 1922, a meeting which was described as 'a fiasco . . .

---

[21] Ibid., 19–20.
[22] W. Ambrose Bebb, 'Achub y Gymraeg: Achub Cymru', *Y Geninen*, XLI, no. 3 (1923), 122.
[23] *Baner ac Amserau Cymru*, 6 September 1923.
[24] Davies, *The Welsh Nationalist Party*, pp. 35–8.

uninstructed and degenerate beyond words',[25] the ailing Liberals had no credible platform on Welsh issues. When Lloyd George fell permanently from office a few months later, it was an easy task for the Labour Party to attempt to don the discredited emperor's clothes. Shortly afterwards, in a bold editorial entitled 'Labour and Nationalism', the *Labour Voice* asserted: 'There is no national cause of which the Labour Party is not the natural champion. The Welsh language, Welsh education, the Eisteddfod, Welsh literature, are in safer keeping with Labour than with Liberalism or Toryism.'[26] At an eisteddfod organized by the National Union of Welsh Societies at Mountain Ash in May 1923, Morgan Jones, Labour MP for Caerphilly and an ILP stalwart,[27] was prominent in ensuring the proscription of English from the festival's activities. The new all-Welsh rule immediately provoked a furious controversy and prompted the *Western Mail* to launch a virulent attack on the 'Welsh Sinn Feiners'.[28] Although prominent Welsh Labour politicians like T. I. Mardy Jones, MP for Pontypridd, and Robert Richards, MP for Wrexham, readily leapt to the defence of the Welsh language, their cultural and linguistic interests remained firmly isolated from their views on politics and the economy. No doubt at least half the membership of the SWMF spoke Welsh habitually during the 1920s, but its journal, *The Colliery Workers' Magazine*, rarely referred to the existence of the language. 'Under a Labour Government every facility would be afforded for fostering the Welsh language', proclaimed W. W. Henderson, secretary of the Joint Publicity Department of the Trades Union Congress and Labour Party, in the *Labour Voice* on the eve of the general election of December 1923.[29] But when a minority Labour government came into being a few weeks later, its sole action in this direction was to appoint a committee of inquiry into devolution, whose purpose, according to the Prime Minister Ramsay MacDonald, MP for Aberavon, might be 'to clear the air'.[30]

The general elections of 1922, 1923 and 1924 were fought almost totally on British issues. Of the eighty-one candidates who stood in the Welsh divisions in December 1923, only nineteen chose to respond to a questionnaire circulated by the National Union of Welsh Societies. Its secretary, D. Arthen Evans, complained: 'Comparatively small consideration is given to Welsh questions and Welsh Nationalism at a general election . . . Wales and Welsh questions do not loom large in the political world at the present moment.'[31] 'Welsh politics', agreed the *South Wales News*, 'have been dormant, if not dead, for a quarter of a

---

[25] *The Welsh Outlook*, IX, no. 5 (1922), 103–4.
[26] *Labour Voice*, 20 January 1923.
[27] See Dylan Rees, 'Morgan Jones, Educationalist and Labour Politician', *Morgannwg*, XXXI (1987), 66–83; Keith Robbins, 'Morgan Jones in 1916', *Llafur*, 1, no. 4 (1975), 38–43.
[28] *Western Mail*, 24 May 1923.
[29] *Labour Voice*, 1 December 1923.
[30] *Parliamentary Debates* (Hansard), 5th series, vol. 173, 2189–90 (21 May 1924).
[31] *South Wales News*, 7 December 1923.

century.'[32] Although the election literature of Liberal candidates in Wales was printed in Welsh, its content made no reference to the Welsh language.[33] When the Labour government fell from office within a year, heralding yet another general election, *The Welsh Outlook* could justifiably claim that 'at no election that we remember has so little attention been paid in Welsh constituencies to purely Welsh questions'.[34] It had already lamented, with justification, that 'politically and nationally' the Welsh people were 'at the ebb of our fortune'.[35]

Supporters of the Welsh language clearly had good reason to feel alarmed, and their concern was manifested in the formation of an array of nationalist groups dedicated to sustaining the language, among them Byddin yr Iaith[36] (the Language Army) and Cymdeithas Cymru Well (the Better Wales Society), whose leading light was William George, brother of Lloyd George.[37] Foremost among them was Y Gymdeithas Genedlaethol Gymreig (the Welsh National Society) – generally known as 'Y Tair G' ('The Three Gs') – formed at the University College of North Wales, Bangor, as early as 1921.[38] Soon to be charged in the south Wales press with 'aping the tactics of de Valera',[39] the new society earned the profound respect and admiration of Saunders Lewis.[40] It was in this atmosphere of alarm regarding the distressing and growing plight of the language, and despair at the patent apathy and inactivity of the Liberal and Labour Parties, that Plaid Genedlaethol Cymru (the Welsh Nationalist Party, later to become Plaid Cymru) was founded at the Pwllheli National Eisteddfod in August 1925. The new party was the result of the merger of the Penarth-based Mudiad Cymreig, which was formed in January 1924, and Byddin Ymreolwyr Cymru (the Self-Government

---

[32] Ibid. During the 1923 general election campaign, D. Arthen Evans wrote to E. T. John: 'Wales is one with England politically. She is scarcely mentioned in this election and very little Welsh is used in meetings' ('Y mae Cymru yn un a Lloegr yn wleidyddol. Nid oes fawr os dim son am dani yn yr etholiad hwn ac ni ddefnyddir fawr o Gymraeg ychwaith mewn cyfarfodydd'). NLW, E. T. John Papers 4052, letter from D. Arthen Evans to E. T. John, 1 December 1923. John responded that, while that may have been true of the south, the situation was very different in north Wales: 'Although Welsh may not be used very much in your parts, things are very different here in the North. I understand Welsh is used in the North, in Cardiganshire and, I believe, in Carmarthenshire. I also held Welsh meetings in many parts of Brecon and Radnorshire' ('Er feallai na ddefnyddir y Gymraeg rhyw lawer yn eich cyffiniau chwi, y mae y pethau yn wahanol iawn yma yn y Gogledd, ac yr wyf yn deall y defnyddir y Gymraeg yn y Gogledd, yn Sir Aberteifi, ac mi gredaf yn Sir Gaerfyrddin. Yr oeddwn hefyd yn cynhal cyfarfodydd yn Gymraeg mewn cryn nifer o ardaloedd yn Mrycheiniog a Maesyfed'). Ibid., 4053, letter from E. T. John to D. Arthen Evans, 3 December 1923 (copy).

[33] Chris Rees, 'The Welsh Language in Politics' in Meic Stephens (ed.), *The Welsh Language Today* (Llandysul, 1973), p. 235.

[34] *The Welsh Outlook*, XI, no. 11 (1924), 288.

[35] Ibid., X, no. 3 (1923), 60.

[36] *Baner ac Amserau Cymru*, 6 September 1923.

[37] Ibid., 16 August 1923.

[38] J. E. Jones, *Tros Gymru: J. E. a'r Blaid* (Abertawe, 1970), p. 25.

[39] *South Wales News*, 11 August 1923.

[40] NLW, Moses Gruffydd Papers, letter from Saunders Lewis to Moses Gruffydd, 14 August 1923.

Army of Wales), a north Wales group established in the following September by H. R. Jones, a young salesman from Caernarfonshire, who was fascinated by the national struggle in Ireland.[41] From the outset Saunders Lewis, the movement's foremost theorist whose views were to form the backbone of the new party's philosophy, insisted that the primary aim of the Welsh Nationalist Party should be to establish a Welsh-speaking Wales by enforcing the language as the medium of education and local authority business. He was also determined that the new movement should be autonomous of existing political parties and that candidates successful in parliamentary elections should 'boycott' the Westminster Parliament.[42] In June 1926 the first issue of the Party's Welsh-language journal, *Y Ddraig Goch*, was published. Not until 1932, following a wide-ranging review of Party policy, did the English-language paper, *The Welsh Nationalist*, make its first appearance. At the Party's first annual summer school, convened at Machynlleth in August 1926, the most significant lecture was 'Egwyddorion Cenedlaetholdeb' (The Principles of Nationalism), delivered by Saunders Lewis, who argued that the Welsh language should be accorded a position of primacy, not simply equality, in Welsh education, government and life, and be acknowledged as the sole official language of the country. To Lewis, the language was the very essence of Welshness, the fundamental manifestation of the Welsh national identity.[43] On this specific issue he had made his uncompromising position crystal clear in *Canlyn Arthur* (1938): 'It is bad, and wholly bad, that English is spoken in Wales. It must be deleted from the land called Wales: *delenda est Carthago*' ('Drwg, a drwg yn unig, yw bod Saesneg yn iaith lafar yng Nghymru. Rhaid ei dileu hi o'r tir a elwir Cymru: *delenda est Carthago*').[44] This emphasis meant that the young Party's primary concerns were intellectual, cultural and moral rather than political. Curiously, self-government did not become part of the manifesto of the Welsh Nationalist Party until 1932.

Many of the sentiments which culminated in the formation of the Welsh Nationalist Party in 1925 had three years earlier led to the foundation of a new organization to minister to the Welsh-speaking young – Urdd Gobaith Cymru (the Welsh League of Youth), a movement, strongly steeped in Christian moral-ity, which sought to infuse among young people a love of their native language and culture.[45] From the outset the Urdd was highly patriotic in inspiration, but it

---

[41] J. Graham Jones, 'Forming Plaid Cymru: Laying the Foundations, 1923–26', *NLWJ*, XXII, no. 4 (1982), 427–61.

[42] NLW, Plaid Cymru Archives, letter from Saunders Lewis to H. R. Jones, 1 March 1925.

[43] On the political philosophy of Saunders Lewis, see Dafydd Glyn Jones, 'His Politics' in Alun R. Jones and Gwyn Thomas (eds.), *Presenting Saunders Lewis* (Cardiff, 1973), pp. 23–78; Richard Wyn Jones, 'Saunders Lewis a'r Blaid Genedlaethol' in Geraint H. Jenkins (ed.), *Cof Cenedl XIV: Ysgrifau ar Hanes Cymru* (Llandysul, 1999), pp. 163–92.

[44] Saunders Lewis, *Canlyn Arthur: Ysgrifau Gwleidyddol* (Aberystwyth, 1938), p. 59.

[45] Gwennant Davies, *The Story of the Urdd 1922–72* (Aberystwyth, 1973); R. E. Griffith, *Urdd Gobaith Cymru* (3 vols., Aberystwyth, 1971–3).

always remained stubbornly aloof from political life. At its foundation, the Welsh Nationalist Party was equally firmly detached from mainstream Welsh politics. In the political foreground remained a burgeoning Labour Party which had captured the industrial divisions of south Wales and was well capable of making successful forays into semi-rural constituencies further afield, and a somewhat ailing Liberal Party which had already retreated to its rural fiefdoms in the north and west of the country. Both these parties displayed little concern for the national rights of Wales, still less the well-being of the Welsh language.

The Labour Party in particular displayed a curious ambivalence towards such matters during the 1920s. On the one hand, its MPs (apart from a handful of ILP representatives like Morgan Jones, Ramsay MacDonald and R. C. Wallhead), still more its local councillors and aldermen, were firmly grounded in the old 'Lib–Lab' tradition. Steeped in Nonconformity (many served as deacons and lay preachers), most of them had earned their spurs in the coal-mining industry and trade union hierarchy and secured election as miners' agents and checkweighmen in the SWMF. Labour MPs like Vernon Hartshorn, Will John and William Jenkins, and a little later, more influential figures such as James Griffiths and S. O. Davies, belonged firmly to this tradition, spoke and read Welsh freely, and wrote in Welsh regularly. Some styled themselves 'Welsh Nationalists' in their generally bilingual election addresses and leaflets. On the other hand, a distinctive 'new socialism', which emerged decisively in the aftermath of the abject failure of the general strike of May 1926 and the subsequent nine-month lock-out in the coal industry, preached the virtues of moderation, respectability and constitutionalism, coupled with an emphasis on social and economic issues, which it was hoped would prove Labour a party worthy of government and a movement capable of winning the trust of the electorate. Many Welsh Labour MPs – among them James Griffiths, S. O. Davies, Aneurin Bevan, Ness Edwards and W. H. Mainwaring – had studied at the Marxist Central Labour College in London, an institution financed jointly by the National Union of Railwaymen and the SWMF for the avowed purpose of 'equipping the organised workers with the knowledge adequate for the accomplishment of their industrial and political tasks'.[46] Its rigid syllabus gave no place for the study of the language, literature, history and culture of Wales and its working classes, and within its walls talk of regionalism and national sentiment was positively unwelcome. Had the South Wales Plebs' League, with which Noah Ablett and James Winstone were closely associated, succeeded in establishing a South Wales Labour College in 1909, the course of Welsh Labour politics might well have followed a dramatically different route, possibly similar to that pursued by students who attended the Scottish Labour College. Welsh Labour politicians might then, in the words of Robert

---

[46] NLW, James Griffiths Papers A1/15, bound volume with 'The Labour College, 1922' on spine, p. 3.

Griffiths, 'have turned a blind eye to the socialist mirage fabricated by the obsessions with nationalisation and winning a majority in the English Parliament. The long line of sub-marxist British Parliamentarians, from Bevan through Michael Foot to Neil Kinnock, might never have begun'.[47] As things turned out, although Welsh speakers gained positions of power and influence after 1945, they gave priority to British interests above all else.[48]

Nor did the small group of Liberal MPs from Wales who survived into the second half of the 1920s display more than lip-service to the cause of the Welsh language. Not a single Liberal MP represented a Glamorgan or Monmouthshire division after the 1924–9 Parliament. The momentous general election of 30 May 1929 was characterized above all by Lloyd George's plans to tackle the scourge of unemployment and its concomitant social and economic ills. It was summarized in the famous 'Orange Book', *We Can Conquer Unemployment*, published on the eve of the election. This policy document was published in a Welsh translation as *Gallwn Goncro Diffyg Gwaith*, printed by the Cambrian News, Aberystwyth.[49] This manifesto supported a number of Liberal leaflets in the Welsh language, ranging from *Dylai Merched Votio i'r Rhyddfrydwyr* (Women Should Vote for the Liberals) to *Rhowch y Ffermwyr yn Rhydd* (Set the Farmers Free), but their style was generally stilted and artificial, and they sometimes contained glaring errors of grammar and syntax.[50] Generally by this time there was hardly a specifically Welsh dimension to Liberal politics. Although Lloyd George had succeeded Asquith as Party leader in 1926, his closest advisers and confidants were by then all Englishmen, and many Liberal MPs from Wales consciously distanced themselves from his policies and pledges.

There was no significant change in the attitude of the political parties towards the Welsh language during the 1930s, when the language suffered considerably in the eastern communities of the South Wales Coalfield – the heartland of political Labour – as a result of large-scale migration to places like Luton and Dagenham. The severity of the ravages of the depression intensified the feeling that the Welsh language was an irrelevant anachronism. By the mid-1930s English had certainly eclipsed Welsh as the linguistic medium of most Labour and trade union activities, even in north and west Wales, and the trend was intensified by the disintegration of the Welsh-language pro-Labour press. In Gwynedd the once influential *Y Dinesydd Cymreig* ceased publication in 1929 and so did *Y Werin* in 1937. *Llais Llafur*, once the Welsh-language pace-setter of the Labour movement in south Wales, shrivelled into an undersubscribed English-language broadsheet, its circulation confined to the valleys of west Glamorgan. Renamed *Labour Voice*, and

---

[47] Griffiths, *Turning to London*, p. 21.
[48] Morgan, *The Dragon's Tongue*, p. 60.
[49] *Yr Herald Cymraeg*, 30 April 1929.
[50] J. Graham Jones, 'The General Election of 1929 in Wales' (unpubl. University of Wales MA thesis, 1980), II, pp. 474–6.

later *The South Wales Voice*, its radical political content was jettisoned almost completely. *Tarian y Gweithiwr*, published in the coalfield's heartland in Aberdare, contained only local, cultural and religious news by the 1930s, and its new title, *Y Darian*, fittingly reflected the contraction in its circulation and influence. By the early 1930s every Welsh-language Labour paper in Wales had ceased to exist, a demise which bore witness to ever increasing Anglicization in speech and outlook.[51] This trend was intensified still further by the penetration of London newspapers into much of Wales, in the wake of which sales of Welsh-language periodicals and papers plummeted. The growing popularity of the cinema from 1927 onwards and the beginnings of English-medium broadcasting, from Cardiff in 1923 and Swansea in 1924, further threatened the well-being of the Welsh language. The severe shrinkage in the number of monoglot Welsh speakers was also a significant trend. In such a climate, Saunders Lewis's insistence that the Welsh Nationalist Party should adhere strictly to its original 'Welsh only' policy was wildly anachronistic and impractical. Lewis's obsessive emphasis on Welsh monoglottism was sharply criticized by R. T. Jenkins:

> There are those among us who regret in particular the rapid shrinkage in the number of Welsh monoglots, whom they regard as essential to the preservation of the language – a view which, whether tenable or not in theory, is in practice rapidly becoming irrelevant. Isolation has undoubtedly preserved Welsh in the past. But nowadays, universal teaching of English in the schools, English daily papers on every breakfast-table, a steady bombardment of Welsh ears, in the remotest recesses of the country, by English broadcast transmissions, have radically altered the conditions. Most Welshmen would agree that if Wales cannot be bilingual, it cannot be Welsh-speaking at all.[52]

However, Lewis remained obstinately immune to such overtures. He insisted that the primary aim of his Party was to 'take away from the Welsh their sense of inferiority . . . to remove from our beloved country the mark and the shame of conquest'.[53] His views were not always accepted by his colleagues within the Party, some of whom adopted more challenging attitudes. The House of Commons' 'boycott' policy had been overturned in 1930. Thereafter, D. J. Davies, a colourful product of the anthracite coalfield, argued consistently that the Party should campaign vigorously among the English-language communities of Wales, a viewpoint which won many influential converts to the movement. Yet, throughout the 1930s the Welsh Nationalist Party remained an overwhelmingly Welsh-language movement. In the first half of 1938 *Y Ddraig Goch* sold an average of 7,000 copies each month; its English counterpart *The Welsh Nationalist* sold

[51] Griffiths, *Turning to London*, p. 22.

[52] R. T. Jenkins, 'The Development of Nationalism in Wales', *The Sociological Review*, XXVII, no. 2 (1935), 180–1.

[53] Quoted in John Davies, *A History of Wales* (London, 1993), p. 591.

rather less than 2,000.[54] The high-point of Party activities in the 1930s came with the burning by Saunders Lewis, Lewis Valentine and D. J. Williams of the RAF bombing school at Penyberth, near Penrhos aerodrome, in the Llŷn peninsula. Their subsequent trials, initially at the Caernarfon Assizes and later at the Old Bailey, where, it was claimed, the three defendants would be tried by an 'alien law, an alien language and an alien morality',[55] evoked immense and generally sympathetic public interest far beyond the ranks of the Welsh Nationalist Party. The rapid return of a 'guilty' verdict, the imprisonment of the three men in Wormwood Scrubs, and their subsequent triumphal return to Wales, gave spectacular prominence to the question of the inferior status of the Welsh language in the legal system. The symbolic abandonment at Penyberth of the deeply-entrenched Welsh tradition of non-resistance led to a notable predisposition among the rank and file of the Welsh Nationalist Party for non-violent law-breaking, exemplified by the adoption at the 1937 Party conference at Bala of a proposal that a 'non-co-operative movement' should be established to campaign for an enhanced status for the Welsh language. The principal speaker at the conference was a young, eloquent student at Oxford named Gwynfor Evans.[56] Party activists soon adopted a more aggressive stance, insisting upon using the Welsh language on all possible occasions, and directing the Party executive to refuse to fill in English official forms or to insist upon completing them in Welsh.[57] The executive soon agreed to support a campaign involving the non-payment of income tax and appealed for further ideas regarding 'non-co-operation'.[58]

The Penyberth incident and the resultant attention given to the deplorable status of the Welsh language in the legal system were in part responsible for the organization of a mass petition to be presented to parliament to press for a remedy. This movement was launched in 1938 at the National Eisteddfod at Cardiff by the National Union of Welsh Societies.[59] County committees were formed throughout Wales, a concerted effort was made to raise financial resources, and an array of bilingual literature was published and circulated. Ultimately, in July 1941, a monster petition bearing some 365,000 signatures (including those of thirty of the thirty-six Welsh MPs), was presented to Parliament calling for an Act which would give Welsh equal status with English ('yn unfraint â'r Iaith Saesneg') in all aspects of the administration of justice and the public services in Wales.

The eventual outcome of the intensive, if intermittent, campaign was the highly disappointing Welsh Courts Act of 1942, which permitted witnesses to give evidence in Welsh in a court of law provided they swore on oath that using

---

[54] NLW, Plaid Cymru Archives, Annual Report for 1938.
[55] *The Welsh Nationalist*, VI, no. 1 (1937), 1.
[56] *Y Ddraig Goch*, XI, no. 9 (1937), 1.
[57] Ibid.
[58] NLW, Plaid Cymru Archives, Executive Committee minutes, January 1938.
[59] *Baner ac Amserau Cymru*, 9 August 1938. The chairman of the movement was William George.

English would place them under a disadvantage. Henceforth the costs of inter-preters were to be borne out of public funds rather than by the prisoner or witness.[60] This was very much a pyrrhic victory and immediately gave rise to considerable disappointment and bitterness. By the time the agitation had reached its climax, however, the matter had to some extent been overshadowed by intense concern over the dangers of conscription, the potential Anglicizing effect of the presence of English evacuees within Wales, and the extent of the government's wartime powers to direct labour out of Wales.[61] The convention of a Welsh national conference in December 1939 led to the establishment of the Committee for the Defence of the Culture of Wales (Pwyllgor Diogelu Diwylliant Cymru), which embarked on an impressive range of activities and which soon merged with the National Union of Welsh Societies to form Undeb Cymru Fydd (the New Wales Union) in August 1941.[62] Most of the new supporters of the body were active members of the Welsh Nationalist Party, who were convinced of the need to operate through non-party organizations during wartime. Generally the decline of the Welsh language, the victim of the ever-growing impact of English newspapers, film newsreels and radio, continued apace throughout the war years. Indeed, some individuals harboured heartfelt fears that the distinctiveness of Wales might well be obliterated by a further experience of total war. W. J. Gruffydd, one of the staunchest supporters of Britain's wartime policy, believed that the Second World War would have a far more detrimental impact on the Welsh language and culture than the Great War: 'the influence of this one [the war] on the future of Wales and the Welsh language will be much worse . . . we in Wales must realize that England can win the war and Wales can lose' ('bydd dylanwad hwn [y rhyfel] ar ddyfodol Cymru a'r iaith Gymraeg yn anhraethol fwy . . . rhaid i ni yng Nghymru sylweddoli y gall Lloegr ennill y rhyfel a Chymru ei cholli').[63] Such alarm, however, was substantially unfounded: casualties proved to be only about a third of those sustained in the First World War. The majority of the adult evacuees (some 200,000 people moved into Wales) stayed only briefly, and the English children billeted on Welsh-speaking households were relatively quickly assimilated. Most of the land commandeered by the War Office was promptly returned to civilian use after 1945, with the sole and startling exception of Mynydd Epynt in Breconshire, an area of 40,000 acres, which became a permanent military training ground, thereby dispersing a closely-knit Welsh-speaking community of some 200 individuals.

Party political divisions were largely ignored during the years of the Second World War in the wake of a party truce. No general election took place for ten

---

[60] J. A. Andrews and L. G. Henshaw, *The Welsh Language in the Courts* (Aberystwyth, 1984), p. 12.

[61] See the letter from Saunders Lewis and J. E. Daniel in the *Manchester Guardian*, 8 September 1939.

[62] Undeb Cymru Fydd, *Undeb Cymru Fydd, 1941–1947* (Aberystwyth, 1947), p. 2; R. Gerallt Jones, *A Bid For Unity: The Story of Undeb Cymru Fydd 1941–1966* (Aberystwyth, 1971), p. 19.

[63] 'Nodiadau'r Golygydd', *Y Llenor*, XVIII, no. 3 (1939), 132–3. See also Davies, *The Welsh Nationalist Party*, p. 232.

years after 1935. No census was taken in 1941. But the appointment of Ernest Evans to a judgeship led to a venomously acrimonious by-election in the University of Wales division in January 1943, on which occasion Saunders Lewis, supported by an impressive list of nominators, was selected as the Nationalist candidate, while, contrary to all expectations, Professor W. J. Gruffydd (a vice-president of the Welsh Nationalist Party in the 1930s), became the Liberal aspirant. The ensuing contest created a deep-rooted rift in nationalist ranks in Wales which persisted for a generation. Gruffydd easily headed the poll and was re-elected comfortably in the general election of July 1945.

Generally, however, there was a notable leftward drift in Welsh politics during the war years, a movement fostered by a dogged determination that there should be no return to the poverty and deprivation of the 1930s. Socialist thinking tended to extol the virtues of centralist planning with no specifically Welsh dimension. Demands for the appointment of a Secretary of State for Wales were hastily brushed aside in 1943 as in 1938, although the wartime Coalition government did establish a 'Welsh Day' in the House of Commons. When the first such debate took place on 17 October 1944, the status of the Welsh language did not feature in the proceedings; pride of place was given to the difficulties associated with post-war reconstruction, notably employment and the location of industry and communications. On the eve of the election, a policy statement entitled 'Labour and Wales' appeared which projected a somewhat clouded vision:

> The true freedom of Wales depends not only on political control of her own life, but on economic control as well . . . True freedom for Wales would be the result and product of a Socialist Britain, and only under such conditions could self-government in Wales be an effective and secure guardian of the life of the nation.[64]

Interestingly, even among more patriotic Welsh socialists, the language was not raised as an issue meriting attention. Patriotic Labour candidates in north-west Wales, such as Cledwyn Hughes and Goronwy Roberts, produced an unofficial policy document entitled 'Llais Llafur', which advocated establishing a Secretary of State, a Welsh economic planning authority, a Welsh radio corporation, an end to emigration, and establishing a north–south road link, but which made no reference to the language. In July 1946 when the Prime Minister, Clement Attlee, again refused to consider the appointment of a Welsh Secretary of State, he provoked an angry reaction, encapsulated in the response of W. H. Mainwaring, MP for Rhondda East: 'There is a growing conviction that, in present govern-ment circles, Wales does not count as a nation, that at best it is a province of

---

[64] National Museum of Labour History, Manchester, Labour Party Archives, Morgan Phillips Papers, draft of *Labour and Wales*, June 1945.

England, with little or no claim to its special development.'[65] Two months previously, the government's half-hearted attitude towards Wales had been confirmed by Sir Stafford Cripps, President of the Board of Trade, during the annual 'Welsh Day' debate: 'With an area and population so small as that of Wales', he declared, 'it would be quite impossible to maintain the standard of administration in purely Welsh services, as high as that which is possible when these services cover the entire country' [i.e. Britain].[66] In fact, government concessions to Welsh national sentiment were extremely meagre, culminating in autumn 1948 with the reluctant granting of an Advisory Council for Wales and Monmouthshire, a body which contained nominated members.[67]

Although Wales benefited immensely from the imaginative and radical economic, industrial and health policies of the post-war Labour governments, their attitude towards Welsh national sentiment and the language was generally unsympathetic. In the early 1950s, when some Labour politicians called into question the 'Welsh only' rule at the National Eisteddfod, Hywel D. Lewis responded vigorously in his address to the north Wales quarrymen: 'Nobody who speaks like that can know the time of day in Welsh Wales, but I fear that is the case with many of our Labour leaders in Wales' ('Nid yw neb sy'n siarad fel yna yn gwybod faint yw hi o'r gloch yng Nghymru Gymreig, ond ofnaf fod hynny'n wir am amryw o'n harweinwyr Llafur yng Nghymru').[68] Yet the Labour Party organization within Wales was not totally immune to the importance of the language. In the general election of October 1951 the Party ensured that a Welsh-speaking canvasser was always sent to areas with a high proportion of Welsh-speaking electors.[69] In the following general election in May 1955 some candidates of all parties printed at least part of their election addresses in Welsh, with 'the Liberal candidates giving more prominence to the language than Labour, and Labour more than the Conservatives, though none, of course, using it so much as the Welsh Nationalists'.[70] In fact, the format and linguistic content of election addresses in much of Wales in the 1950s bore a close resemblance to those of the 1880s.[71]

Shortly before the Attlee government fell from office, the 1951 census – the first for twenty years – revealed further disturbing trends concerning the vitality of the Welsh language. The number of Welsh speakers had fallen to 714,686 (28.9 per cent), with the most alarming fall – 33 per cent – occurring in Glamorgan. The use of the Welsh language as the daily medium of conversation was, by the

---

[65] *The Observer*, 17 December 1946.
[66] *Parliamentary Debates* (Hansard), 5th series, vol. 428, 314–15 (28 October 1946).
[67] PRO, CAB 129/29 CP (48) 228 (11 October 1948).
[68] Hywel D. Lewis, 'Sosialaeth Bur', *Y Crynhoad* (1952), 7.
[69] D. E. Butler, *The British General Election of 1951* (London, 1952), p. 205.
[70] Idem, *The British General Election of 1955* (London, 1955), p. 30.
[71] Rees, 'The Welsh Language in Politics', pp. 234–5.

second half of the twentieth century, confined largely to the rural areas. Less than 10 per cent of the population of Cardiff spoke Welsh. The monoglot element had almost ceased to exist.[72] The fateful twin impact of depression and war was thus starkly revealed in the 1951 census returns when it became apparent that the language was faltering in vibrant valley communities like Treorci and Aberdare. The situation was remedied to some extent by the establishment of Welsh-medium primary schools; the first official Welsh-medium school had opened its doors in Llanelli in 1947,[73] to be followed by another dozen within four years. Forty-one had come into existence by 1970. The Labour Party tended to favour the setting up of Welsh units within existing schools, a practice which generally evoked the scorn and derision of educationalists and parents alike. Welsh-medium secondary schools were also beginning to spring up – Ysgol Glan Clwyd in 1956, Ysgol Maes Garmon in 1961 (both in Flintshire) and Ysgol Rhydfelen in Glamorgan in 1962 – to be paralleled by increasing provision for Welsh-language teaching in the constituent colleges of the University of Wales.

But while the language was accorded a distinctly enhanced status in the education system, it lacked any kind of official status. A few bilingual signs began to be erected on county boundaries, but official forms and public notices were almost always in English. Generally, road signs were in English, and there was no place for the Welsh language in the activities of the Post Office and the telephone service. In 1952 Eileen and Trefor Beasley of Llangennech began a long campaign in order to receive a bilingual rate demand from the Llanelli Rural District Council; this eventually led to the seizure of their property and prolonged agitation until the council finally yielded in 1960.

By this time a more distinctive Plaid Cymru presence was manifesting itself in both national and local political life. Whereas in the general election of 1955 eleven candidates contested seats and secured a total of 45,119 votes, in 1959 twenty candidates polled a total of more than 77,000 votes. The progress of the Party was hastened by increasingly vocal demands for a Welsh Office and by the dramatic resignation of Huw T. Edwards in October 1958, both as chairman of the Council for Wales and as a member of the Labour Party, in order to join the ranks of Plaid Cymru. There emerged a general consensus regarding specific Welsh political issues and a tendency for both Labour and Conservative parties to publish literature dealing with Wales, publications which included at least a passing reference to the Welsh language. Both the main parties now at least paid lip-service to the language and expressed some concern for its future, although no specific programme of action was ever outlined. In both *Labour's Policy for Wales* (1954) and *Forward with Labour* (1959), the Labour Party simply expressed support for the movement to establish Welsh-language schools,

[72] Davies, *The Welsh Language*, pp. 65–6.
[73] A private Welsh-medium primary school had been established by Urdd Gobaith Cymru at Aberystwyth as early as 1939.

reflecting its general tendency to endorse action already taken rather than to initiate change itself.

Nor did the succession of Conservative governments from 1951 to 1964 prove totally unsympathetic to the plight of the Welsh language, although the Conservative Party was generally considered to be incorrigibly unionist and irretrievably Anglicized. Anthony Eden's administration initiated government support for Welsh publishing by providing an annual grant of £1,000 in 1956, a sum which was subsequently increased. This trend eventually culminated in the setting up of the Welsh Books Council (Cyngor Llyfrau Cymraeg) in 1961. The Welsh Theatre Company and Cwmni Theatr Cymru came into being with government assistance in 1962, while a Private Member's Bill proposed by Peter Thomas, MP for Conwy, a future Conservative Secretary of State for Wales in 1970, permitted local authorities to make use of the rates to lend support to the National Eisteddfod. The Conservatives never received the credit they deserved for these positive actions on behalf of the language. Much more publicity was given to the Tryweryn episode and to the decision in 1960 to appoint Rachel Jones, a non-Welsh speaker, as chairman of the Broadcasting Council for Wales.[74] While there was genuine substance in Tom Hooson's claim that the Tories were anything but 'alien to Welsh cultural values',[75] the popular imagination was captured to a far greater extent by the decision to give the Forth Bridge priority over the Severn Bridge,[76] and by the government's patent lack of success in evolving effective policies to revive economically-depressed areas in Wales.

Yet it was under a Conservative government that the Central Advisory Council for Education (Wales) had completed in 1953 its report on *The Place of Welsh and English in the Schools of Wales*. The authors took a firm stand on the relationship between the Welsh language and Welsh ethnic identity, arguing that: 'The culture of Wales is so bound up with its linguistic expression that separated from the latter it has very little meaning or worth.'[77] A firm recommendation followed:

> Having due regard, therefore, to the varied abilities and aptitudes of pupils, and of the varied linguistic patterns in which, at present, they live, the children of the whole of Wales and Monmouthshire should be taught Welsh and English according to their ability to profit from such instruction.[78]

Indeed, in some respects Conservative attitudes towards the Welsh language and culture were healthier than those of the Labour Party, whose eagerly awaited

---

[74] *The Times*, 3 June 1960.
[75] Tom Ellis Hooson, 'St. David's Day Speech', *Wales*, VII, no. 38 (1959), 33.
[76] *The Times*, 12 September 1957, 11 October 1957.
[77] Ministry of Education, Central Advisory Council for Education (Wales), *The Place of Welsh and English in the Schools of Wales* (London, 1953), p. 52.
[78] Ibid., p. 55.

Labour's Policy for Wales (1954) gave pride of place to an attack on the tenacious Parliament for Wales campaign and to a defence of the record of the Labour government of 1945–51 in relation to Wales. It recommended a revision of the constitution of the Council for Wales and Monmouthshire and the retention of the post of Minister for Welsh Affairs (a Conservative creation in 1951), with a Cabinet seat and without departmental responsibilities.[79] In this comprehensive policy document, only three short paragraphs were devoted to the Welsh language; they contained not a single idea for the promotion or defence of the language. Labour politicians generally were at best uninterested, at worst overtly hostile to the Welsh language. Many Labour-controlled local authorities were slow to respond to clearly-expressed parental demands for Welsh-medium education. Others accused BBC Wales of harbouring 'a nest of Nationalist plotters', allegations which led in 1956 to an official inquiry by the Postmaster General. The eventual report refuted the 'conspiracy theory', but pointed to judgemental errors in the corporation's coverage of political affairs. This hornets' nest was gleefully whipped up again by Leo Abse, MP for Pontypool, in the early 1960s. The outcome, according to Robert Griffiths, was an increase in 'working-class distrust of an emergent petty bourgeoisie in Welsh public life – whose obvious badge of identity was the possession and advocacy of the Welsh language'.[80]

Yet the language had its advocates within the ranks of Labour, notably among local councillors in Glamorgan and Llanelli who pioneered Welsh-language education, and among MPs like James Griffiths and S. O. Davies. Aneurin Bevan's attitude, however, was ambivalent. Described as 'a strong critic of Welsh separateness',[81] he was capable on occasion of rushing to the defence of the Welsh language. In an article entitled 'The Claim of Wales' which appeared in the journal *Wales* in 1947, he wrote:

> People from other parts of the country are surprised when they visit Wales to find how many Welsh people still speak Welsh, and how strong and even passionate, is the love of the Welsh for their country, their culture and their unique institutions.[82]

During the 'Welsh Day' debate (the holding of which he had originally criticized) of 8 December 1953, he asserted:

> Although those of us who have been brought up in Monmouthshire and in Glamorganshire are not Welsh-speaking, Welsh-writing, Welshmen, nevertheless we are all aware of the fact that there exists in Wales, and especially in the rural areas and in

---

[79] *Labour's Policy for Wales* (Cardiff, 1954), pp. 11–12.
[80] Griffiths, *Turning to London*, p. 22.
[81] Kenneth O. Morgan, *The Red Dragon and the Red Flag: The Cases of James Griffiths and Aneurin Bevan* (Aberystwyth, 1989), p. 11.
[82] Aneurin Bevan, 'The Claim of Wales', *Wales*, VII, no. 25 (1947), 152.

North Wales, a culture which is unique in the world. It is a special quality of mind, a special attitude towards mental things which one does not find anywhere else. We are not prepared to see it die.[83]

Yet he remained a consistent critic of the 'Welsh only' rule at the National Eisteddfod and so great was his empathy with the Anglo-Welsh culture of his native Monmouthshire valleys that he could sometimes be paranoid about the Welsh language. In October 1946 he warned his fellow Welsh MPs:

> that the culture and cultural institutions of Wales do not belong entirely to North Wales or Mid-Wales. There exists in the English-speaking populations of Monmouthshire, Glamorganshire, and some parts of Carmarthenshire, a culture as rich and profound as that which comes from the Welsh speaking people of North Wales. There is too great a tendency to identify Welsh culture with Welsh-speaking . . . What some of us are afraid of is that, if this psychosis is developed too far, we shall see in some of the English speaking parts of Wales a vast majority tyrannised over by a few Welsh speaking people in Cardiganshire . . . the whole of the Civil Service of Wales would be eventually provided from those small pockets of Welsh-speaking, Welsh-writing zealots, and the vast majority of Welshmen would be denied participation in the government of their country.[84]

Certainly Bevan was no supporter of the resilient Parliament for Wales campaign of the early 1950s,[85] and in March 1955 he conspicuously failed to support S. O. Davies's Government of Wales Bill in the House of Commons. The movement, which won the active support of five independent-minded Labour MPs, was largely conducted in the Welsh language at the executive level and, in spite of pleas that it was 'entirely a non-party movement working outside party politics', it was closely associated with Plaid Cymru. Indeed, when Elwyn Roberts became the campaign's national organizer in September 1953, he was seconded from his post as a Plaid Cymru official. It was an easy task for opponents to claim that the Welsh language would become compulsory in a Welsh Parliament, thereby exacerbating divisions and tensions within Welsh society.

The years of the Parliament for Wales campaign between 1950 and 1956 have been described by Peter Stead as 'strange and angry years . . . a period with an anguish and a temper all of its own'.[86] In the 1960s, however, a more general consensus of support for the Welsh language emerged in Welsh society. The 1961 census revealed that the language was spoken by about 650,000 people, including

---

[83] *Parliamentary Debates* (Hansard), 5th series, vol. 521, 1920 (8 December 1953).

[84] Ibid., vol. 428, 400–1 (28 October 1946).

[85] J. Graham Jones, 'The Parliament for Wales Campaign, 1950–56', *WHR*, 16, no. 2 (1992), 207–36.

[86] Peter Stead, 'The Labour Party and the Claims of Wales' in John Osmond (ed.), *The National Question Again: Welsh Political Identity in the 1980s* (Llandysul, 1985), p. 104.

a clear majority in the counties of Anglesey, Caernarfon, Merioneth, Cardigan and Carmarthen, and by 198,960 people (17 per cent of the population) even in Glamorgan. In 1966 the Labour Party's policy document, 'Signposts to the New Wales', urged the establishment of a television service of 'Welsh content in both languages', a notable breakthrough following the report of the Pilkington Committee in 1964. A similar resolution had already been passed by the Welsh Regional Council of Labour as early as 1961, heralding a marked softening of its attitudes towards the language. This gradual change of emphasis coincided with a more dramatic upturn in the fortunes of Plaid Cymru, which sprang in part from the Tryweryn affair of the late 1950s and more especially from a new concern for the future of the Welsh language intensified by the alarming findings of the 1961 census. This anxiety was reflected in the promotion of Welsh-medium schools in generally English-speaking regions, in the protests against the closure of small village schools in rural communities, and in the campaign for enhanced Welsh-language provision on radio and television. Some began to press for a separate Welsh-language television service. Renewed pressure built up (following the defiant stand made by Eileen and Trefor Beasley) to accord a much improved legal and official status to the language.[87]

The whole question of the role and status of the Welsh language was brought into sharp relief in the summer of 1962 by the formation of Cymdeithas yr Iaith Gymraeg (the Welsh Language Society), a movement set up in response to a radio lecture, delivered the previous February by Saunders Lewis, entitled *Tynged yr Iaith* (The Fate of the Language). As the Society began its radical activities, attention was focused even more on the status of the language by the publication of the *Report on the Welsh Language Today* (1963) by the Council for Wales and Monmouthshire, which took as its brief a review of the role of the Welsh language in most aspects of national life. Invaluable statistics and information came to light, especially relating to the status of the language in local government and county councils. The recommendations of the report were far-reaching: the right to use Welsh in law courts, public inquiries and tribunals, the bilingual publication of documents relating to Wales, and the increased use of the language in local government, in elections, and in documents such as tax demands.

The establishment of the Welsh Office and the appointment of a Secretary of State for Wales with a seat in the British Cabinet in 1964 – the climax of some eighty years of intermittent agitation – were achievements of seminal importance, for they created a new context for the discussion of the role of the language in the public life of Wales. The initial range of powers and responsibilities of the Welsh Office, however, were disappointingly modest. Its role in 1964 was little more than that of a co-ordinating agency within Wales for policies conceived at Whitehall, and, as such, its foundation served only to fan the flames of Welsh

---

[87] Morgan, *The Dragon's Tongue*, pp. 68–72.

nationalist discontent. Even so, a symbolic victory, capable of future enhancement, had been scored.

The public's perception of the generally subservient role of the Welsh language was sharpened still further by the publication in October 1965 of the Hughes Parry *Report on the Legal Status of the Welsh Language*.[88] The report's authors did not mince their words. They asserted that, education excepted, the Welsh language had been 'in effect ignored by the British state machinery'.[89] Legal and public administration throughout Wales had traditionally remained the preserve of English: 'there is no sphere of activity where tradition can hold such a tight grip on practice as in these two fields'.[90] Within central government departments there was 'little evidence to suggest that Welsh is used to any great extent', while in the nationalized industries and the health service the situation was even less satisfactory.[91] While Welsh was used to some extent in local government meetings, this provision generally did not extend to council minutes, reports or forms, an unhappy situation mitigated only by a much more extensive use of the language at parish council level. The report recommended the setting up of a translation panel attached to the Welsh Office and the appointment of additional Welsh-speaking officials. It anticipated that the removal of most of the legal obstacles to the use of the language would result in 'reasonable demand' for greater provision and that local authorities would 'respond sympathetically'.[92]

While the Welsh language was thus emerging as a political issue of some consequence, Welsh political life was enlivened on 14 July 1966 by the dramatic victory of Gwynfor Evans of Plaid Cymru in the Carmarthenshire by-election. His party's standing and morale were at once transformed by the outcome of the poll; widespread indifference and disillusion gave way to a new-found confidence and vigour. Although it is probable that Plaid Cymru's victory could be attributed more to the glaring economic failures of the Wilson government and to profound local resentment regarding widespread pit closures in the Gwendraeth and Aman valleys than to concern about the plight of the Welsh language, Gwynfor Evans struck a symbolic blow for the language in Parliament by declaring his intention of taking the oath of loyalty in Welsh.[93] Another theme prominent at the time was the seemingly callous attitude of the Labour-controlled Carmarthenshire County Council towards the well-being of local rural schools. Evans's victory was soon to have repercussions in by-elections at Rhondda West (1967) and Caerphilly (1968) in what had traditionally been much less promising territory for Plaid Cymru in the industrial south.

[88] The Welsh Office, *Legal Status of the Welsh Language: Report of the Committee under the Chairmanship of Sir David Hughes Parry, 1963–1965* (London, 1965) (PP 1964–5 (Cmd. 2785) XXIII).
[89] Ibid., p. 35.
[90] Ibid.
[91] Ibid., pp. 30–3.
[92] Ibid., p. 58.
[93] Morgan, *The Dragon's Tongue*, pp. 92–3.

This striking nationalist upsurge coincided with the passage in 1967 of the Welsh Language Act which gave Welsh 'equal validity' with English and the unrestrained right to use Welsh in the courts. The Gittins Report of 1967 was a further stimulus to a discussion of the role of the Welsh language in the education system and it quickly influenced informed opinion. A decade later, members of the Council for the Welsh Language – a body established in 1973 – was responsible for the preparation of yet another report, *A Future for the Welsh Language* (1978), in which the authors stated categorically:

> We find the concept of 'equal validity' totally inadequate to the needs of the Welsh language today. Nor do we share the Hughes-Parry concept of bilingualism. To us, bilingualism means that throughout Wales every individual should be enabled and encouraged to achieve sufficient facility in both Welsh and English to *choose* which of the two languages to use on all occasions and for all purposes in Wales.[94]

This sequence of significant events in the fortunes of the Welsh language occurred during the term of office of Labour governments in the 1960s and 1970s. During that period a distinct change took place in the social composition of the Parliamentary Labour Party; large numbers of Labour MPs came from the professions, especially journalism, university and secondary school teaching, and the law. By 1970 only S. O. Davies, MP for Merthyr Tydfil, and Gwilym Davies, MP for Rhondda East, were direct nominees of the National Union of Mineworkers, although as late as 1959 ten miners' MPs still represented Welsh constituencies. Many of the new breed of MPs had not even a nodding acquaintance with the Welsh language. By the early 1970s, only fourteen of the thirty-six Welsh MPs spoke Welsh. Yet the Welsh language had certainly acquired the status of a political issue. It was debated within the three 'British' political parties, though the opinions expressed were 'often so disparate as to make a consensus virtually impossible'.[95]

Within the ranks of the Labour Party, both positive and negative attitudes towards the Welsh language were vocally expressed. While on a whistle-stop tour of the constituencies of north Wales during the 1970 general election, George Brown, the deputy leader, urged his listeners to forget about the 'bloody language'. The viewpoint of George Thomas, MP for Cardiff West, who served as the third Secretary of State in Wales from 1968 to 1970, was not very different. In his desire to protect the rights of non-Welsh speakers in Wales, he referred to the need to form a defence organization among the threatened majority, an attitude which he shared with Leo Abse. Some Labour-controlled local authorities zealously exerted pressure on the National Eisteddfod Council to

---

[94] The Council for the Welsh Language, *A Future for the Welsh Language* (Cardiff, 1978), p. 49.
[95] Rees, 'The Welsh Language in Politics', p. 244.

modify its commitment to the exclusive use of Welsh in all competitions. On the other hand, Tom Ellis, MP for Wrexham, firmly supported a Welsh-language television service and fully bilingual road signs, while Elystan Morgan, MP for Cardiganshire, on more than one occasion made the more radical suggestion that a Government Commission should be set up to safeguard and promote the language. Arthur Probert, MP for Aberdare, a non-Welsh speaker, criticized the lack of recognition for Welsh within the European Economic Community (EEC).[96]

Yet the attitude of each of the 'British' political parties towards the Welsh language was ambivalent, smacking of a lack of commitment and perhaps even sincerity. In the early 1970s the Conservative Party asserted its desire 'to advance Welsh culture', while the chairman of the Welsh Liberals appealed for an all-party assembly to debate the issue of the language. Yet no party ever set up an official study group to consider the topic or appointed an official spokesman to pronounce on language matters.[97] This apparent indifference became all the more conspicuous when the 1971 census revealed a disquieting decrease in the number of Welsh speakers, most of whom were now concentrated in clearly delineated pockets in north, mid- and west Wales, areas of generally high unemployment with notably meagre job prospects for young people.

At the same time as the crisis facing the Welsh language seemed most acute, the Labour Party reached the zenith of its strength and influence in Wales, dramatically capturing thirty-two of the thirty-six Welsh seats in the general election of May 1966, and enjoying a similar impregnable ascendancy over local government in the industrial areas. The sole credible challenger to its hegemony was a reinvigorated Plaid Cymru, which enjoyed a striking renaissance in both parliamentary by-elections and in elections for some urban district councils. The Liberal Party had long since retreated to the rural north and west of Wales, which had remained one of the Party's few strongholds during the years after 1945.[98] Of the twelve Liberal MPs who sat in the 1945–50 parliament, no fewer than seven represented Welsh constituencies, all of them native Welsh speakers. The two most prominent in their ranks – Clement Davies, MP for Montgomeryshire who served as Party leader from 1945 to 1956, and Lady Megan Lloyd George, who represented Anglesey between 1929 and 1951 – consistently advocated devolutionary solutions. But no Welsh Liberal MP made a spirited stand on behalf of the Welsh language. During the 1970s, however, the remaining Liberal MPs – Emlyn Hooson, MP for Montgomeryshire, and Geraint Howells, MP for Cardiganshire – were native Welsh speakers who took great pride in the language.

[96] Ibid., pp. 244–5.
[97] Ibid.
[98] J. Graham Jones, 'The Liberal Party and Wales, 1945–79', WHR, 16, no. 3 (1993), 326–55; Lord Hooson, Rebirth or Death? Liberalism in Wales in the Second Half of the Twentieth Century (Aberystwyth, 1994).

By this time the omens for the future of the Welsh language were more favourable. These included an encouraging increase in bilingualism among schoolchildren (in part a reflection of a more enlightened attitude on the part of English-speaking parents), more goodwill among local authorities, greater sensitivity within government departments, and a steady increase in the number of hours of Welsh-language broadcasting by both the BBC and HTV. In July 1978 James Callaghan's Labour government gave its blessing to a fourth television channel to be devoted entirely to Welsh-language broadcasting.

Yet the language issue did not feature prominently in the devolution debate which dominated Welsh politics from the publication of the Kilbrandon Report in 1973 to the referendum of 1 March 1979. During the lengthy prelude to the crucial vote, the question of the language as a divisive factor was raised by the opponents of devolution, notably Neil Kinnock, MP for Bedwellty, and Leo Abse, MP for Pontypool, both of whom consistently pressed the view that the proposed Welsh Assembly might endanger the interests of the non-Welsh-speaking majority. Some nationalists argued that Welsh speakers might equally become the victims of a Cardiff-based Assembly inevitably controlled by the great mass of representatives from the populous counties of Glamorgan and Gwent. This argument was redolent of attitudes prevalent at the time of the Newport meeting of January 1896, which had heralded the ignominious downfall of Cymru Fydd.

Within a few weeks of the referendum, the election of a right-wing Conservative government at Westminster meant that the omens for Wales and the Welsh language were distinctly unfavourable. Whereas the attitude of Edward Heath towards Welsh affairs had been curiously ambivalent, that of his successor, Margaret Thatcher, was overtly contemptuous. The honeymoon period of the Thatcher administration was marked in Wales by a spate of arson attacks on holiday homes and resultant arrests and prosecutions. But it was the issue of Welsh-language broadcasting which dominated the scene in Wales in the early 1980s. The alleged 'betrayal' by the government on the question of a Welsh-language fourth channel led to an intensive campaign of civil disobedience by Plaid Cymru members, 2,000 of whom withheld payment of television licences. Gwynfor Evans declared his intention to fast until death from 6 October 1980 unless the government announced a change of heart. A government volte-face took place on 17 September when it was announced that Welsh-language pro-grammes would be broadcast on a fourth channel under the control of a Welsh Broadcasting Authority. Sianel Pedwar Cymru (S4C) first went on the air on 1 November 1982. By the time of the death of Saunders Lewis, the father of Welsh nationalism, in September 1985, it was widely felt that his unremitting emphasis on the well-being of the language as the foremost priority of Welsh nationalism had borne fruit in the flourishing structure of Welsh-language broadcasting and the well-established system of bilingual schools.

During the second half of the decade, attention focused increasingly on provision for the teaching of the Welsh language in the new Education Bill. The government's initial indications that Welsh was to be excluded from the list of priority subjects elicited clamorous protests which resulted in a compromise solution that Welsh would become a 'core' subject in Welsh-medium schools and a 'foundation' subject in other schools in Wales. Linked to the role of the Welsh language in the education system were the passionate protests of the Welsh Language Society, and the sinister activities of Meibion Glyndŵr, against the purchase of second or holiday homes in much of rural Wales. In many areas, traditionally Welsh-speaking schools found it increasingly difficult to assimilate non-Welsh-speaking children. The response of Peter Walker, the Secretary of State for Wales, was to reject calls for a new Welsh Language Act and to set up, as an alternative, a non-statutory Welsh Language Board (Bwrdd yr Iaith Gymraeg) which produced its first report in June 1989. The campaign for a Language Act, however, continued undeterred, and in November of the same year the Board revealed its own draft Language Bill.

The same themes persisted into the 1990s, especially concern over the ever-increasing influx of English in-migrants into the Welsh heartland of Dyfed, Gwynedd and Powys. The teaching of Welsh in schools was a particular bone of contention in Dyfed where Dr Alan Williams, Labour MP for Carmarthen, became heavily involved in bitter controversies. More rewarding was the outcome of the 1991 census which revealed some encouraging trends, notably a significant advance in the number of Welsh speakers among younger age groups, notably in the more Anglicized districts.[99] In December 1992 the eagerly anticipated Welsh Language Bill was published and immediately attracted criticism for its failure to prescribe equal rights for Welsh speakers. Its enactment in July 1993 was accompanied by a statement in the House of Commons by the Prime Minister, John Major, to the effect that Welsh already enjoyed official status in Wales. Shortly afterwards the new Welsh Language Board was set up, with Lord Elis-Thomas, former Plaid Cymru MP for Meirionnydd Nant Conwy, as its chairman.

The changing role of the Welsh language in the governance and political affairs of Wales was given further impetus in February 1995 following John Major's announcement in the House of Commons that the government proposed to grant Northern Ireland its own Assembly, a major departure from the Conservative Party's traditional opposition to the establishment of regional assemblies on the grounds that such institutions might presage the break-up of the United Kingdom. The appearance of the Labour Party's proposals for a Welsh Assembly in May led to apprehension that the party under Tony Blair was less committed to devolution. In June 1996 Blair announced (apparently on his own initiative)

---

[99] Davies, *The Welsh Language*, pp. 67–8.

Labour Party proposals that referenda would precede the setting up of national assemblies in Wales and Scotland. His cavalier attitude suggested a deep-rooted schism in the ranks of the Labour Party in Wales over devolution, similar to that which had persistently dogged the 1979 referendum campaign. However, it seemed that popular support within Wales for a measure of devolution and for the well-being of the Welsh language was increasing, partly as a result of the apparent weakness of the twenty-two new unitary authorities set up as a result of the local government reorganization of 1 April 1996.

In May 1997 the Labour Party swept to power with a remarkable landslide majority, capturing no fewer than 418 of the 659 seats in the House of Commons, including 34 of the 40 Welsh constituencies, while not a single Conservative candidate was returned in Wales. Ron Davies, MP for Caerphilly, became Secretary of State for Wales, and immediately championed a new 'inclusive' politicial ethos as an intrinsic part of his advocacy of devolution. The fateful referendum was held on 18 September 1997. The outcome remained uncertain until the final result from Carmarthenshire gave approval to the government's devolution proposals by the narrowest of margins – 559,419 votes (50.3 per cent) to 552,698 (49.7 per cent). Predictably, support for the establishment of an assembly was strongest in the Welsh-speaking areas of north and west Wales, but the more Anglicized industrial valleys of the south also came out solidly in favour.

In December 1997 an Advisory Group was set up by the Secretary of State in order to produce recommendations regarding the working arrangements of the National Assembly. In its consultation document and final recommendations published in 1998, the Group strongly recommended that Assembly members should be able to use Welsh and English in debates and committee meetings; that members of the public should be able to use Welsh and English when communicating with the Assembly; that publications, documents and papers produced by and submitted to the Assembly should be made available in Welsh and English, and that simultaneous translation be used in plenary sessions and committee meetings.[100] Although language campaigners were quick to draw attention to the many practical barriers which prevented the implementation of a comprehensive and effective bilingual policy,[101] no one could doubt that the Welsh language was firmly rooted in the Welsh political agenda.

To conclude. Even though around a million people spoke Welsh in 1911, fears were expressed that the native tongue would not survive the century. Indeed, at the height of the First World War, *The Welsh Outlook* predicted that the language would be extinct by the mid-twentieth century. Yet within a few years there had emerged a vigorous campaign, driven by the foundation of the Welsh Nationalist Party in August 1925 and to some extent by Urdd Gobaith Cymru in 1922,

---

[100] National Assembly Advisory Group Consultation Paper (1998), pp. 26–7.
[101] Elin Haf Gruffydd Jones, 'Bilingualism in the Assembly', *Planet*, 131 (1998), 77–81; Cymdeithas yr Iaith Gymraeg, *Dwyieithrwydd Gweithredol / A Working Bilingualism* (Aberystwyth, 1998).

specifically to protect and foster the Welsh language. Subsequent evidence that the language was consistently losing ground, particularly in the industrial valleys of the south and the border areas, led to increasingly intensive efforts to perpetuate it. There was basically no doctrinal obstruction which might have prevented the full participation of all political parties in such a worthy campaign. The Communist Party had a well-deserved reputation for linguistic conservation in many parts of the globe. The well-being of minority interests was an intrinsic element in the traditional Liberal philosophy, while the native language of the common people of Wales could well have emerged as a natural priority for Welsh socialists. Even the Conservatives cherished as a central strand of their political outlook a respect, even veneration, for tradition, which might well have extended to a concern for the vitality of the Welsh language. Yet few significant attempts were made to launch initiatives which would strengthen the position of the Welsh language and regenerate confidence in its future. Only from the 1960s, as a result of the far-reaching resolution and successes of the language movement, and the institutional growth which came in the wake of the establishment of the Welsh Office, did the language issue acquire a more central role in the political life of Wales.

7

Journalism and the Welsh Language

ROBERT SMITH

One may deplore that a wider constituency has not been sought by the writers, and yet it is impossible not to feel proud of this spectacle – nowhere else visible in the whole wide world – of a national press, the literary contents of which are produced by the people for the people. It is a democracy of letters where all enjoy the widest freedom as to form and substance, and where the only reward hoped for and expected is the good opinion of a little world.[1]

THESE OBSERVATIONS were written by David Davies, editor of the *South Wales Daily Post* in 1897, during the golden age of the Welsh-language newspaper press. The late nineteenth century witnessed the emergence of a multitude of titles which sought not only to report that which occurred in the localities they served but also to guide public opinion. As Davies emphasized, newspapers were democratic and accessible; they were committed to the promotion of religious, social or political ideals and provided a platform for rigorous analysis and debate at a time when Wales was able to project a progressive and self-confident image. This tradition continued in the Edwardian period when issues with a specifically Welsh dimension such as disestablishment and education were addressed and when theological, political and social questions were debated in the light of new ideas. The exuberance which characterized the press coincided with a period of economic and industrial prosperity. It was assumed that the new era presented unrivalled opportunities for Welsh people to exhibit their talents and develop the full potential of the nation. The First World War, however, highlighted the fact that this was in many ways a delusory image. Previously concealed fault lines within Welsh society were exposed and more critical judgements were made of Welsh society. In this climate Edwardian aplomb began to be seen as premature and complacent and the press was obliged to consider critically the new crises which faced Welsh society.

---

[1] David Davies, 'The Journalism of Wales during the Victorian Era', *Young Wales*, III, nos. 31–2 (1897), 184–8.

Four critically important decades – the 1920s, the 1940s, the 1960s and the 1980s – have been selected for particular attention in this chapter, although brief consideration will also be given to the intervening decades. In the 1920s the census figures of 1921 galvanized an influential section of Welsh leaders into a more determined effort to support the language. A new sense of urgency was apparent from the declarations of local Welsh societies and their national body, Undeb Cenedlaethol y Cymdeithasau Cymraeg (the National Union of Welsh Societies), which made strenuous attempts to secure a greater priority for the language in key areas of Welsh life. In the 1940s, although Wales began to overcome the economic difficulties which had bedevilled life in the inter-war years, the decline of the Welsh language remained unarrested. The 1960s witnessed a growing appreciation that a much more determined effort was required if Welsh was to remain a language of daily use in Wales and this campaign led to the enhancement of the legal status of the language. The 1980s, a decade of considerable success for some aspects of the campaign to preserve and promote Welsh, nevertheless witnessed economic and demographic changes which threatened to undermine the language. This study will, therefore, trace the development of debates regarding the Welsh language as reflected in the Welsh press, and will also seek to demonstrate the variety of opinions held and the means by which newspapers set the agenda and also reacted to fluctuating trends in public opinion.

The Welsh newspaper press had enjoyed considerable influence in the second half of the nineteenth century. Local titles proliferated, as did political and especially denominational papers.[2] Local newspapers, however, rarely confined themselves to strictly local issues, and several of them reported and commented upon matters relating to British and international affairs. Nevertheless, at no time did Wales succeed in producing a national, Welsh-language daily newspaper. Of the English-language daily papers in Wales, only the *Western Mail*, founded in 1868, made a determined effort to project itself as the national newspaper of Wales. It achieved the goal of broadly making itself available throughout the country by the late 1940s, but, in spite of its own claims, it never achieved the status of *The Scotsman* in Scotland or the *Irish Times* in Ireland. This was mainly because it was aimed at a more popular market and also because its political editorial policy rarely reflected the views of the majority in Wales.[3]

The geographical distribution of the Welsh newspapers did not reflect demographic patterns in Wales. A vibrant vernacular press, centred mainly in north Wales, had a considerably higher ratio of titles per head than the more populous south. As a result, the evidence gained from those papers inevitably

---

[2] For a history of the development of the press in Wales, see Aled Gruffydd Jones, *Press, Politics and Society: A History of Journalism in Wales* (Cardiff, 1993).

[3] *The Scotsman*, founded in 1860, and the *Irish Times*, founded in 1859, achieved far greater recognition as national newspapers in their respective countries, not least because distance meant that London-based titles were unable to reach them as easily as they reached Wales.

favoured the preoccupations and outlook of Welsh-speaking communities. Welsh-language papers in south Wales, however, were unable to withstand the process of Anglicization. The demise in the early 1930s of *Y Darian*, a Welsh-language newspaper serving central Glamorgan, reflected the area's inability to sustain a vernacular paper. Equally significant was the decision in 1915 to turn *Llais Llafur* into an English publication, entitled *Labour Voice*, thereby demonstrating that a Welsh-language paper was no longer viable even in the strongly Welsh-speaking areas of west Glamorgan.

The late nineteenth century was undoubtedly the heyday of both English- and Welsh-language titles in Wales. By the period under consideration in this chapter, several titles had already been amalgamated or had ceased publication. This was in many respects linked to the demise of the editor-proprietor form of ownership, which had characterized much of the Welsh press in the nineteenth century. Titles were purchased by large conglomerates and many were closed down as companies sought to create a monopoly for a single paper in areas which had previously been served by several newspapers.[4] The 1920s witnessed an intensification of this trend, caused mainly by the development of other forms of communication and higher production costs. Local newspapers increasingly contained syndicated news, together with a few columns of purely local interest and a growing section devoted to advertisements. Indeed, by the last quarter of the twentieth century ownership had become concentrated in the hands of a tiny number of companies. A survey conducted in 1981 discovered that the Celtic Press owned by the Thomson Group (which included the *Western Mail*) controlled eleven titles, with a circulation of 115,000 in south Wales, while the independently-owned North Wales Newspapers controlled eight titles, with a circulation of 120,000.[5] Conglomerates such as these placed local newspaper publishing on a firmer financial footing, notably in terms of generating advertising revenue. Yet this was often achieved at the cost of editorial independence and continuity.

Three newspapers have been selected for particular attention in this study; each had its own standpoint and sought to reflect different strands of opinion relating to the Welsh language. *Yr Herald Cymraeg* was part of the Herald conglomerate in Caernarfon, a Welsh-language sister paper to the older *Carnarvon and Denbigh Herald*. Both Welsh and English titles had been strongly Liberal in politics, although the English paper favoured a more moderate version of Liberalism. The papers catered for different audiences in north Wales, and this explains to some degree the more radical political outlook of the Welsh paper. The views of R. J. Rowlands (Meuryn), editor of *Yr Herald Cymraeg* from 1922 to 1954, also had a major effect in determining the more radical outlook of the Welsh paper.

---

[4] Wynford Vaughan Thomas, *Trust to Talk* (London, 1980), pp. 93–5.
[5] *Arcade*, 4 September 1981.

Y Cymro was a much more recent title: conceived in 1920 by William Evans of Dolgellau, it was an independent paper with a religious bias.[6] The founder's aim was to provide a bold, modern newspaper which promoted the general moral, religious and cultural well-being of Wales. In July 1921 the paper launched an English-medium supplement, partly in response to the growth of English-medium religious worship. Although this proved a short-lived venture, it indicated the extent to which all-Welsh titles were declining in popularity by the 1920s. The *Western Mail* was a daily paper which claimed to be the national newspaper of Wales, an increasingly justifiable claim in the years after the Second World War when it extended its circulation. Yet in terms of its preoccupations and journalistic coverage, the *Western Mail* remained the paper of south Wales. In common with all other daily newspapers in Wales, such as the *South Wales Daily Post* and the *Cambrian Daily Leader*, it was an English-medium newspaper with few Welsh-language articles. Traditionally regarded as the paper of the coal-owners of south Wales and a paper of the political right, its editorial policy did not reflect the radical political outlook of Wales in the late nineteenth and early twentieth centuries.

The 1920s was a decade of central importance to the fortunes of the Welsh language since this was a period during which the complacent attitudes towards the language issue held by leaders of public opinion in Wales during the nineteenth century were supplanted. *Yr Herald Cymraeg* developed a strongly nationalist, if politically Liberal, outlook between 1920 and 1929. *Y Cymro*, too, strengthened its opinion on the preservation of the Welsh language during this period, despite occasional signs of complacency on the issue. The outlook of the *Western Mail* also became increasingly sympathetic towards the preservation of the language, although its commitment varied according to particular circumstances. The changes which occurred in the viewpoint of these papers cannot be attributed to changes in editorship, for R. J. Rowlands at *Yr Herald Cymraeg*, William Evans at *Y Cymro* and William Davies at the *Western Mail* remained at the helm throughout the 1920s. All three were Welsh speakers. Rowlands, better known by his bardic title 'Meuryn', was a chaired bard and a pioneer of Welsh children's fiction; his name would become synonymous with popular bardic contests. William Evans was a leading Calvinistic Methodist who believed that *Y Cymro* could inherit the traditions of *Y Goleuad*, the long-standing Methodist paper which had traditionally commented on a wide range of religious, political and moral issues. William Davies, editor of the *Western Mail*, and a Welsh-speaking native of Talyllychau, had spent most of his life working in the Anglicized industrial communities and only gradually overcame his initial indifference towards the well-being of the Welsh language.

---

[6] The last issue of *Y Cymro* appeared in September 1931. It was subsequently purchased by Rowland Thomas, who relaunched the paper in a very different style in December 1932.

The evidence assembled for this study reveals clearly that each paper realized that the future of the Welsh language was in jeopardy as a result of the Anglicizing influences which were rapidly permeating areas previously regarded as strongholds of the language. Both *Yr Herald Cymraeg* and *Y Cymro* swiftly noted the detrimental impact of the arrival of radio and gramophone on the fortunes of the language, particularly since they brought the English language directly into the home, often for the first time.[7] Yet *Y Cymro* did not advocate any determined measures to counteract this development. Although a special article in 1926 lamented that programmes broadcast from Manchester and intended for audiences in north Wales were dominated by the English language, no consistent attempt was made to press the issue.[8] The paper's editorial column rarely raised the issue of Welsh-language broadcasting and only occasional references were made in the comments section. New forms of cultural activities, often associated with the village halls which were mushrooming throughout Wales, also threatened more traditional forms of Welsh culture. *Yr Herald Cymraeg* was particularly critical of the Women's Institutes as well as certain sporting activities which used the English language in Welsh-speaking areas.[9] Yet the paper believed that the greatest threat to the language came from within the Welsh-speaking community itself. It deplored the tendency of Welsh people to converse in English for fear of embarrassing English speakers in their presence,[10] and it also denounced the notion that Welsh was an ungenteel tongue.[11]

Concern for the future of the language had long been apparent in the columns of *Yr Herald Cymraeg* and the publication of the linguistic evidence of the 1921 census merely strengthened the determination of the paper to press the issue. The census evidence, however, failed to make as great an impression on the editor of *Y Cymro*. Although the paper admitted that the figures were disappointing, it noted that the greatest decline in the number of Welsh speakers had occurred in the period from 1911 to 1921 – 'fruitless years' for the nation in general – and it forecast that the future was likely to be brighter.[12] Adopting a more cautious outlook, the *Western Mail* warned against the very real danger of ignoring the evidence of decline. It noted that although the 1921 census had revealed a decline in the number of Welsh speakers, robust Welsh-speaking communities still remained in most parts of Wales, with the exception of Monmouthshire. At the same time, the *Western Mail* was acutely aware that growing numbers of Welsh

---

[7] *Y Cymro*, 21 January 1925. For a detailed consideration of the conflicting arguments presented to the BBC on the issue of Welsh-medium broadcasting, see John Davies, *Broadcasting and the BBC in Wales* (Cardiff, 1994), pp. 46–66.

[8] *Y Cymro*, 18 August 1926.

[9] *Yr Herald Cymraeg*, 16 February 1926.

[10] Ibid., 7 March 1922.

[11] Ibid., 20 April 1920.

[12] *Y Cymro*, 27 April 1927.

speakers were turning their back on their native tongue[13] and it accused leading figures in public and education circles of failing to practise in their homes the Welshness they publicly but fleetingly espoused on St David's day.[14]

Anglicizing influences were felt particularly strongly within Nonconformist denominations. From the mid-nineteenth century onwards English-medium Nonconformist chapels had grown in Wales, partly as a result of the Anglicization of communities in the south. By the 1920s this trend had accelerated, reflecting the widely-held view that Nonconformity needed to adapt to modern society (in organization and language if not in theology). The argument in favour of catering for the needs of English speakers in Nonconformist chapels elicited enthusiastic support from *Y Cymro*,[15] but *Yr Herald Cymraeg* was implacably opposed to such initiatives, and vented its spleen on ministers who deliberately encouraged Anglicization:

> Ofnwn fod yr eglwysi yn ddyfnach na neb yn y camwedd o adael i'r ieuenctid lithro gyda'r lli Seisnig. Mae lliaws o'r gweinidogion, yn wir, yn gwneuthur eu goreu i helpu'r llanw estronol. Gwyddom am ambell un sydd yn malu Saesneg yn fingul ddigon mewn capel lle mae pob un o'r aelodau yn deall Cymraeg yn llawer gwell na Saesneg . . . Gweinidogion fel y rhain sydd yn gwneuthur mwyaf i ladd ein hiaith.[16]

> (We fear that the churches are as much to blame as anyone for the error of allowing the young to follow the English flood. Many of the ministers evidently do their utmost to encourage the alien tide. We know of several who labour to preach in affected English in chapels where every one of the members speaks Welsh much better than English . . . It is ministers such as these who do most to destroy our language.)

The position of the Welsh language was traditionally weaker in the Anglican Church and, with some exceptions, the attitude of many of the higher clergy continued to be antipathetic to the Welsh language, a factor which tended to colour the outlook of the church as a whole. Nevertheless, the disestablishment of the Church in 1920 (and the subsequent democratization of its constitution) was regarded in many circles as an opportunity to redress the balance between Welsh and English. Even so, the *Western Mail* was wary regarding the place of the Welsh language in the Church in Wales, arguing that divisions had been exaggerated and that the language of worship was a minor consideration in the debate.[17]

Since the late nineteenth century the education system had been considered one of the principal factors which had contributed to the decline of Welsh. By the 1920s, however, it was also perceived as a vehicle which might help to save the language. Arguing that the ethos of Welsh schools needed to change in order to

---

[13] *Western Mail*, 19 April 1927.
[14] Ibid., 26 March 1928.
[15] *Y Cymro*, 6 July 1927.
[16] *Yr Herald Cymraeg*, 7 August 1923.
[17] *Western Mail*, 17 June 1926.

arrest the decline in the fortunes of the language,[18] *Yr Herald Cymraeg* launched a scathing attack on the Caernarfonshire Education Authority for failing to promote a greater sense of Welshness[19] and for failing to insist on the ability to speak Welsh as a condition of employment in its schools.[20] *Y Cymro* was equally forthright in its comments on the Welshness of schools and argued strongly in favour of the proposal that education authorities should permit teachers leave of absence to attend classes in order to improve the standard of teaching of Welsh,[21] and that Welsh should become a compulsory subject in elementary school examinations.[22] The *Western Mail* also expressed sympathy for the argument that the acquisition of Welsh sharpened the intellect at an early age.[23] In 1923 an editorial rejected the argument that bilingualism merely led to an inadequate understanding of both English and Welsh by pointing to examples of successful bilingualism in Europe.[24] The paper also displayed scant sympathy for those teachers who perpetually bemoaned the difficulty of teaching Welsh and who deplored the notion that Welsh was a qualification of little practical benefit.[25]

Nevertheless, the inconsistency which was to characterize the attitude of the *Western Mail* throughout the period under consideration was already in evidence. Two years after the paper declared its support for bilingualism, an editorial warned that if Welsh were introduced too early children would acquire an inadequate grasp of both Welsh and English, and Wales would find itself an inarticulate and educationally-backward nation.[26] Moreover, the paper remained implacably hostile to compulsory teaching of the Welsh language.[27] In 1925 it noted that strong resistance had emanated from English-speaking Radnorshire to any attempt to compel education authorities to develop policies aimed at the preservation and promotion of the Welsh language. Pointing to what it believed to be the failure of compulsion in Ireland, the *Western Mail* argued:

> It is not everybody who is sufficiently racially-conscious or politically-minded to view with sympathy the compulsory (or even voluntary) restoration of a national language, especially where it is suspected that the revival would injure one's own children in respect of convenience and adequacy of study and language-utilisation in after-years.[28]

---

[18] *Yr Herald Cymraeg*, 23 March 1920.
[19] Ibid., 15 April 1924.
[20] Ibid., 17 June 1924.
[21] *Y Cymro*, 6 April 1921.
[22] Ibid., 28 August 1929.
[23] *Western Mail*, 21 July 1921.
[24] Ibid., 17 October 1923.
[25] Ibid., 7 July 1921.
[26] Ibid., 6 November 1925.
[27] Ibid., 28 January 1926. The paper reiterated this point in response to the report of the Departmental Committee on Welsh in the Educational System of Wales, *Welsh in Education and Life* (London, 1927).
[28] *Western Mail*, 7 November 1925.

In response to the 1927 Departmental Committee Report on the position of the Welsh language in education,[29] the paper called for the adoption of a distinctive 'Welsh flavour' rather than a specific commitment to the Welsh language.[30] Paradoxically, however, it also advocated increased spending on new resources for the teaching of Welsh and the development of Welsh-medium textbooks.[31] In its general approach, the paper emphasized the need for patience on the language issue, the adoption of tolerant attitudes on both sides of the linguistic divide, and the avoidance of any rash solutions.[32]

The role of institutions of higher education in promoting the language also commanded the attention of the Welsh-medium newspapers. In August 1922 *Yr Herald Cymraeg* denounced the University College of Wales, Aberystwyth:

> Lle i fagu snobyddion Sais-addolgar yw Coleg Aberystwyth, a barnu oddiwrth ei holl weithrediadau. Dywedir bod hyd yn oed rhai athrawon mewn Cymraeg yno yn gwrthod siarad yr iaith pan gyferchir hwy yn Gymraeg, a bod eu plant yn bricsiwn hyd y dref, fel enghreifftiau o Ddic Sion Dafyddion.[33]

> (Aberystwyth College is a place to nurture snobs who worship the English, judging by all its actions. It is said that even some teachers of Welsh there refuse to respond to greetings in Welsh, and that their children are ridiculed in the town as Dic Sion Dafyddion.)

Aberystwyth was not alone among the paper's targets. The University College at Bangor was said to be so heavily Anglicized that the town itself had become an island of Englishness in a sea of Welsh-speaking villages. Attacks by Beriah Gwynfe Evans on the manner in which candidates for the Welsh-speaking ministry were trained through the medium of English received strong support from *Yr Herald Cymraeg*,[34] while *Y Cymro* argued that the only means of countering such developments was to ensure that knowledge of Welsh was considered when appointing to academic posts in Wales. The paper particularly emphasized the importance of the University's links with the wider community

---

[29] Departmental Committee on Welsh in the Educational System of Wales, *Welsh in Education and Life*, pp. 307–15.

[30] *Western Mail*, 13 February 1928. The call for a 'Welsh flavour' to be given to the school curriculum in Wales would prove a recurring theme and it reached its climax in the late 1980s.

[31] Ibid., 29 August 1927, 10 February 1928.

[32] Ibid., 29 August 1927.

[33] *Yr Herald Cymraeg*, 1 August 1922. Dic Siôn Dafydd, a fictional character created by John Jones (Jac Glan-y-gors) (1766–1821), was an illiterate Welshman who prospered as a tailor in London. For pretentious reasons he pretended not to speak Welsh. He was eventually to return to Wales in humiliating circumstances and was shunned by the local community. His name became a familiar term of abuse for those who denied their Welshness in the twentieth century. Meic Stephens (ed.), *The New Companion to the Literature of Wales* (Cardiff, 1998), p. 180.

[34] *Yr Herald Cymraeg*, 23 March 1926.

and its role in Welsh life in general.[35] This responsibility, it insisted, was not fulfilled by the appointment of monoglot English speakers, a trend which was all too apparent in the newly-opened college at Swansea.[36] Although the *Western Mail* took an active interest in the development of Welsh scholarship and the part played by the University in demanding a report on the status and use of the language, it remained lukewarm on the question of Welsh-medium teaching and opposed any suggestion that priority should be given to Welsh speakers in making appointments within the University.

A major feature of the debate regarding the Welsh language in the 1920s was the growing campaign to extend its use to domains such as commercial activity, legal affairs and public life. The introduction of Welsh into the law courts found favour with the *Western Mail*. Apart from regarding the failure of the courts in the past to permit the use of Welsh as a stigma and a mark of inferiority, it argued that Welsh-speaking individuals, notably monoglot Welsh speakers, had failed to articulate themselves in court since they were obliged to speak in a foreign tongue, a handicap which had inevitably led to miscarriages of justice.[37] The *Western Mail*, however, did not share the view of both *Y Cymro*[38] and *Yr Herald Cymraeg*[39] that Welsh was an appropriate language for commercial transactions. Moreover, suggestions that a language qualification should be imposed in the civil service and in other public offices were also rejected on the grounds that, although a knowledge of the Welsh language was desirable, it was not essential because the vast majority of the people of Wales were conversant with English and because English was the language of the majority.[40]

The argument in favour of the extension of Welsh into public affairs was also advanced in relation to local government. Local councils were free to determine the language in which their business was conducted and in Welsh-speaking areas the right to hold meetings through the medium of Welsh was frequently demanded.[41] *Yr Herald Cymraeg* gave the issue considerable prominence, remind-ing local authorities of their responsibility to conduct business through the medium of Welsh, and arguing that, in strongly Welsh-speaking areas like the north-west, such a practice should be considered entirely natural. Its columnist, 'Twr yr Eryr', argued:

y mae'n sicr na roddir hanner digon o le i'r iaith Gymraeg yng nghynghorau cyhoeddus Cymru. Yr iaith Gymraeg a ddylai fod yr iaith swyddogol ym mhob un ohonynt, gyda

---

[35] *Y Cymro*, 6 May 1925.
[36] Ibid., 3 June 1925.
[37] *Western Mail*, 24 February 1928.
[38] *Y Cymro*, 4 August 1926.
[39] *Yr Herald Cymraeg*, 13 July 1927.
[40] *Western Mail*, 11 March 1926.
[41] Gwilym Prys Davies, *Llafur y Blynyddoedd* (Llandysul, 1991), pp. 129–66.

chaniatad i'r Sais o fewn ein pyrth i siarad Saesneg, os dymuna gael ei ystyried yn ddyn anwybodus.[42]

(certainly Welsh is not given nearly enough attention in the public councils of Wales. Welsh should be the official language of each one, with permission for the Englishman among us to speak English if he wishes to be considered ignorant.)

Despite occasional victories, such as the decision of councillors in Blaenau Ffestiniog[43] and Pwllheli[44] to keep bilingual minutes, the evidence of the news columns indicates that the majority of councillors were not prepared to meet the expenses of bilingualism,[45] an attitude reinforced by the hostility of local government officers to such propositions.[46] The 'Llen Lliain' column in Yr Herald Cymraeg in February 1929 complained:

Lle i gwyno sy gennym ni yng Nghymru na roddir i'n hiaith ei lle priodol yn mywyd cyhoeddus y wlad. Clywir beunydd am swyddogion na feddant yr wybodaeth leiaf o'n hiaith, na'r gronyn lleiaf o gydymdeimlad a'n cenedligrwydd, yn cael eu penodi i swyddi cyhoeddus pwysig, hyd yn oed yn y rhanbarthau mwyaf Cymreig o Gymru. Yr ym ninnau, greaduriaid diysbryd, yn goddef y cyfan, ac yn fynych yn llyfu'r llaw sy'n tynhau'r gadwyn am ein gyddfau.[47]

(We in Wales have reason to complain that our language is not given its appropriate place in the public life of the country. We hear daily of officials without the slightest knowledge of our language and without a whit of sympathy with our nationality, who are appointed to important public positions, even in the most Welsh parts of Wales. We spiritless ones suffer all of this and often lick the hand which tightens the chain around our necks.)

As was the case with so many other issues, Yr Herald Cymraeg was the most forthright and militant campaigner on this issue. Y Cymro adopted a more moderate position, limiting its comment to a call for greater use of Welsh and the inclusion of a compulsory section in basic Welsh in the civil service examination in Wales.[48] The Western Mail chose to ignore the issue, partly because the concept of Welsh as a medium of official public business was to a large extent reckoned to be irrelevant in south Wales, given the extent of the Anglicization of commerce and government. That a paper which purported to appeal to all communities in

---

[42] Yr Herald Cymraeg, 28 February 1922.
[43] Ibid., 30 January 1923.
[44] Ibid., 1 May 1923.
[45] Ibid.
[46] Ibid., 7 February 1928.
[47] Ibid., 26 February 1929.
[48] Y Cymro, 14 December 1921.

Wales and which styled itself the national newspaper of Wales should have failed to comment on this important topic is of no small significance.

The severity of the economic depression of the 1930s and its effect on Welsh society, particularly the large-scale migration of population from Wales, is well-documented. The effects of the depression were felt in both rural and industrial areas and the impact on the Welsh language was undeniable. Welsh-speaking communities were deprived of a substantial number of young Welsh speakers, a factor which clearly had long-term repercussions. The extent of these changes was highlighted by the Welsh press, which deplored the government's failure to adopt a more positive remedy than devising schemes to transfer labour from Wales. It was inevitable that public debate in Wales would be dominated by issues such as economic and industrial regeneration, public assistance, especially the Means Test, and with associated problems such as poor housing and the lack of educational opportunities. The Welsh language was deemed to be of secondary importance in these circumstances. Welsh chapels in south Wales found it increasingly difficult to sustain any form of activity other than the weekly service because of financial difficulties. Of equal significance was the fact that initiatives organized by social and political organizations such as readers' groups and radio-listening clubs were conducted through the medium of English, thereby accentuating the dwindling role of Welsh. Although Welsh continued to be the language of daily life in many rural communities, it was inevitable that cultural activities would suffer from the general malaise of the period.

Despite the fact that economic priorities increasingly dominated discussion, the Welsh language remained a priority for a vociferous minority in Wales. Plaid Genedlaethol Cymru (the Welsh Nationalist Party), founded in 1925, pursued vigorous campaigns to highlight the insufficient provision made for Welsh in public circles in Wales. Both the Welsh Nationalist Party and the National Union of Welsh Societies were particularly active in a campaign to urge the BBC to produce more Welsh programmes, an effort which was partially rewarded when Wales gained regional broadcasting status in 1937. Two other developments were of especial significance in this period. The government's decision to site a bombing school at Penyberth in the Llŷn peninsula as part of a rearmament programme was opposed by Welsh cultural leaders who feared that it would threaten the well-being of the language in one of its principal strongholds. The Penyberth issue hardened opinion in many circles and attitudes became further entrenched following the burning of the bombing school by three leading nationalists in September 1936.[49] At the same time initiatives of a more constitutional nature to promote the language were maintained. The campaign for a Welsh Language Act, led mainly by the National Union of Welsh Societies, gained momentum in the closing years of the decade and pressure was exerted on

---

[49] These issues are discussed in Dafydd Jenkins, *A Nation on Trial: Penyberth 1936* (Cardiff, 1998).

the government to clarify the legal status of Welsh. Yet, in spite of the importance of the language issue to its zealous champions, linguistic issues did not fire the popular imagination in Wales in the 1930s. Those who were active in language campaigns were a minority, mainly drawn from the professional classes in Wales and largely free of the daily struggle to survive which characterized so many Welsh households throughout the decade.

By 1940, however, the sense of urgency regarding the language issue, perceived in the columns of *Yr Herald Cymraeg* as early as the 1920s, was gaining widespread recognition. Although no census was conducted in 1941 and the need to concentrate on the war effort meant that the debate over Welsh lost much of its impetus, several private reports exposed the plight of the language.[50] Although the government was involved in considerable information-gathering activity during the war years, statistics for the Welsh language were not accorded much importance. Although no official attempt was made to record the number of Welsh speakers living in England and English speakers in Wales, reports commissioned by individuals provided evidence of such significant decline[51] that some predicted that the 1951 census would mark an irreversible fall in the number of Welsh speakers.[52]

The war years themselves witnessed further Anglicization. The drift of Welsh speakers from Wales was accelerated by the introduction of military conscription, and large areas of Wales were taken over for military purposes. The policy of evacuating children from English cities into Welsh communities also caused alarm within Welsh cultural circles. The extent of in-migration was considerable, with incomers accounting for up to 20 per cent of the population in certain areas. *Yr Herald Cymraeg* reacted strongly against the evacuation policy on linguistic grounds, and *Y Cymro* adopted a similar, though more conciliatory, approach. In the opinion of the *Western Mail*, however, Wales was likely to gain rather than lose from in-migration. The depression of the 1930s, it argued, had resulted in substantial demographic losses from rural Wales which threatened the viability of communities as economic and social units.[53] An influx of people, it predicted,

---

[50] In a report on Aberystwyth in 1942, T. I. Ellis expressed the opinion that the position of the Welsh language in the town was under threat. The strong English ethos of the local county school had a powerful influence and the homes of many professional people, a number of whom were active in Welsh life, were becoming increasingly Anglicized. In a town located in the heart of Welsh-speaking Wales, the only secular Welsh-medium cultural activity was provided by Urdd Gobaith Cymru (the Welsh League of Youth). *Y Cymro*, 24 January 1942.

[51] A survey by Denbighshire County Council showed that only 30 per cent of the county's children were Welsh speakers, a figure which fell as low as 2 per cent in certain parts of Wrexham.

[52] *Y Cymro*, 14 March 1947.

[53] The problem of rural out-migration was highlighted by the Council for Wales and Monmouthshire, *A Memorandum by the Council on its Activities: Report of the Panel on Depopulation of Rural Areas* (London, 1950) (PP 1950 (Cmd. 8060) XIX), pp. 20–64. Rural depopulation inevitably led to a reduction in economic activity, particularly in the decline of service industries. The *Western Mail* would also have been influenced by the considerable attention given to this

would inject fresh energy and new life into rural communities which were in danger of stagnating.[54] Opposition to evacuation, it was argued:

> can be traced to a small group of disgruntled Nationalists who are so obsessed by morbid and imaginary grievances, and so hostile to the Government, as to be quite incapable of viewing the problems created by the war impartially, while their general conception of 'culture' is positively abhorrent to the common-sense of the Welsh people.
>
> Their real concern is not culture but their forlorn political prospects. They have manufactured a bogey which they fondly believe will persuade the Welsh people that they and they alone are the only faithful custodians of our national traditions.[55]

Despite many pessimistic predictions, the arrival of large numbers of evacuees did not have the adverse effects which many had feared. Although some compositions written by evacuees in schools appeared to draw inspiration from the ideas of Caradoc Evans, relations remained harmonious in the vast majority of cases.[56] Indeed, Saunders Lewis claimed that evacuated families showed a greater commitment towards, and pride in, the Welsh language than did native Welsh speakers,[57] a view with which Y Cymro concurred following its own investigations in the Llanbryn-mair area.[58]

During the war years, those who called for action to preserve the language secured some concessions from central government. Agitation in support of an Act to give legal status to Welsh, led mainly by the National Union of Welsh Societies in the late 1930s, came to fruition in 1942. The Welsh Courts Act permitted court proceedings to be conducted in Welsh wherever it might serve the interests of justice. This legislation was warmly welcomed by the *Western Mail*, which, while admitting that the Act simply clarified that which had become a *fait accompli* in a number of Welsh courts, argued that it was a step in the right direction and bore witness to the 'intelligent and sympathetic' attitude of all parties in Parliament towards the claims of Wales.[59] The Welsh Courts Act, however, failed to meet the expectations of language campaigners, and Undeb Cymru Fydd (the New Wales Union) regarded it as no more than a prelude to a much stronger Act, a sentiment echoed by Y Cymro.[60] In its view, the lack of clarification in the legislation and the retention of considerable local discretion

---

problem during the 1930s by organizations such as the Council for the Protection of Rural Wales, the Welsh Housing and Development Association, the Council for Social Service in South Wales and Monmouthshire and the National Town Planning Association.

[54] *Western Mail*, 12 February 1941.
[55] Ibid., 17 April 1940.
[56] *Y Cymro*, 17 May 1941.
[57] Ibid., 26 July 1941.
[58] Ibid., 14 September 1940.
[59] *Western Mail*, 15 October 1942.
[60] *Y Cymro*, 26 December 1942.

meant that there was little hope of establishing concrete legal rights on the language issue, for the matter would be decided according to custom and practice rather than legal definition. The refusal of certain magistrates to permit the use of Welsh[61] served only to confirm the view of those who espoused linguistic equality that the Act of 1942 was woefully inadequate. The 'Llen Lliain' column in *Yr Herald Cymraeg* angrily complained:

Cynyddu a chryfhau y mae'r argyhoeddiad mai mesur diwerth hollol oedd Mesur yr Iaith. Rhoddwyd pwyslais ar hynny yn ynadlys Caernarfon ddydd Llun pan ganfuwyd na ellid gorfodi'r bargyfreithiwr a erlynai i siarad Cymraeg, er ei fod yn Gymro, ac er mai yn Gymraeg yr oedd y gweithrediadau . . . Ni bydd neb yng Nghymru yn fuan heb gredu mai bradychu achos Cymru a wnaeth yr aelodau a dderbyniodd yr erthyl hwnnw o fesur.[62]

(There is a growing and strengthening conviction that the Language Act was a totally useless measure. This was demonstrated at Caernarfon magistrates' court on Monday when it was discovered that the prosecuting counsel could not be compelled to speak Welsh, although he was Welsh, and despite the fact that Welsh was the language of the proceedings . . . Soon there will be no one in Wales who will not believe that Wales's cause was betrayed by those members who accepted that still-born piece of legislation.)

A much warmer welcome was given to proposals made by R. A. Butler to reform the education system. In the view of the *Western Mail*, his approach indicated that the anti-Welsh spirit encapsulated in the notorious Education Report of 1847 was a thing of the past, and that no longer would the continued decline of the Welsh language be attributed to the hostility of central government towards the language. Rather, the paper maintained, the determination of successive ministers of education to press for greater recognition of Welsh in the schools of Wales was in sharp contrast to the opinions of local education authorities and school governors.[63] *Yr Herald Cymraeg* and *Y Cymro* also welcomed the provisions of the 1944 Education Act[64] and neither perceived any serious deficiency in its proposals regarding the teaching of Welsh and Welsh-medium education in general.

Nevertheless, despite the positive attitude demonstrated by the Board of Education and by certain education authorities regarding the teaching of Welsh and the development of Welsh-medium education, opposition to the implementation of the policy continued. The *Western Mail* became the vehicle for a

---

[61] The Llangadog bench levied translation costs on two defendants in January 1942. *Western Mail*, 30 January 1942. The Llandudno bench refused to allow two witnesses to testify in Welsh in October 1943. *Y Cymro*, 2 October 1943.

[62] *Yr Herald Cymraeg*, 15 February 1943.

[63] *Western Mail*, 18 June 1942.

[64] *Yr Herald Cymraeg*, 19 October 1942; *Y Cymro*, 31 July 1943.

prolonged debate among its readers on the issue during the summer of 1949. Percy Rees, the proprietor of a private school in Llanelli, roundly condemned both the provisions for Welsh embodied in the 1944 Education Act and attempts by certain local authorities to develop Welsh-medium education. In his opinion, the promotion of Welsh in the schools of Wales was attributable to the influence of Welsh nationalists in the civil service, and any attempt to discover greatness in Welsh literature was akin to 'looking for a black cat in a dark room'. 'Pathetic' Welsh literature could never compete with the 'majesty' of English literature, which he believed included Aeschylus and Dante as well as Milton and Shakespeare.[65] The reaction to these strictures was swift: 90 per cent of the correspondence on the issue was hostile to Rees and of especial significance were tirades against him from English speakers living in the Anglicized areas of south Wales.[66] The *Western Mail* itself made no comment, but the general tone of its editorials indicate that the paper had little sympathy with the views of its provocative correspondent. *Yr Herald Cymraeg* angrily denounced attitudes espoused by the likes of Percy Rees. Despite increased resources given to Welsh-medium education and the launching of detailed research work by the Central Welsh Board, the paper remained dissatisfied with the ethos of Welsh schools:

Y drwg andwyol heddiw ydyw mai awyrgylch Seisnig hollol sydd i'r rhan fwyaf o lawer o ysgolion Cymru, hyd yn oed a chyfrif yr ardaloedd Cymraeg. Mae dylanwad y prifathro yn falltod mewn ambell ysgol yn yr ystyr yma. Sut y gall awyrgylch ysgol yng Nghymru fod yn iach a'r prifathro'n gwrthod siarad yr un gair byth o Gymraeg â'i ddisgyblion, er ei fod yn Gymro trwyadl?[67]

(The greatest ill of our times is that the majority of schools in Wales have a completely English atmosphere, even those in the Welsh-speaking areas. The influence of the headmaster is a blight in some schools in this respect. How can the atmosphere in a Welsh school be healthy when the headmaster refuses to speak Welsh with his pupils, even though he himself is thoroughly Welsh?)

The end of the war ushered in new factors which threatened the well-being of the language. The migration of non-Welsh speakers into Wales as permanent settlers became a major cause for concern. As early as October 1945 *Y Cymro* warned that Wales was in danger of becoming a land of second homes,[68] a problem which was compounded by the number of Welsh farms bought by English and Polish incomers.[69] The Forestry Commission, too, was accused in

[65] *Western Mail*, 19 July 1949.
[66] Among those most critical were Idris Davies, Rhymney, and others who could not be described as 'nationalist' in any real political sense. All were involved mainly in Anglo-Welsh literary circles in south Wales.
[67] *Yr Herald Cymraeg*, 12 November 1945.
[68] *Y Cymro*, 19 October 1945.
[69] Ibid., 26 March 1948.

Y Cymro of destroying Welshness by its policy of afforestation.[70] No area, however remote, was immune from powerful Anglicizing influences. Yet, all attempts to counter these influences proved largely unsuccessful. A vociferous campaign waged in favour of new bilingual road signs in the late 1940s, strongly supported by *Y Cymro*, achieved little success and attracted only limited popular support.[71]

As the long-term effects of the war left their mark, the process of Anglicization continued in the 1950s. A generation of Welsh men and women had been removed temporarily from Wales, both as active service personnel and as factory workers in other parts of Britain, and it was inevitable that, following their prolonged absence from Wales at an impressionable age, their taste in culture would change appreciably. The pages of the local Welsh press testify to the fact that dancing had become an increasingly important feature of popular culture during the 1950s and that English was the language of popular songs. The British cinema, characterized by the productions of the Ealing studios, enjoyed a revival during this period and gained large numbers of devotees in Welsh-speaking areas. Influenced by America, this culture had a global appeal, offering Welsh people an experience which differed little from that of any other town or village in Britain. Public leaders in Wales were alarmed by the pervasive new culture, which they regarded as decadent and out of keeping with Welsh traditions. The decline of the culture of the chapel vestry, the local eisteddfod or the local literary class also alarmed them. The small numbers of mainly elderly people who attended discussions on Welsh poetry contrasted sharply with the multitudes who now flocked to cinemas and concert halls throughout Wales. At the same time, the failure of economic planning measures to arrest rural depopulation meant that the drift of young people from rural communities continued, thereby further undermining the vitality of the native language and culture.

Such changes were also reflected in the appearance and content of newspapers. The new era was marked by the bold, racy tones of newspapers such as the *Daily Mirror*, which contrasted sharply with the staid traditions of the Welsh press. *Yr Herald Cymraeg*, however, resolutely refused to change its style. It retained its traditional layout and content and its columns, therefore, appeared dated in comparison with other papers of the same period. The *Western Mail* proved more adaptable to new trends, placing news stories on its front page and making better use of headlines as a means of attracting readers. Yet it was *Y Cymro* which did most to change its style to suit the new demands of the age. Its editor, John Roberts Williams, who had long nursed a cherished ambition to produce a modern, up-to-date Welsh weekly paper, succeeded in fulfilling his dream. By the mid-1950s *Y Cymro* had achieved a circulation of over 20,000 and had become

---

[70] Ibid., 19 September 1947.

[71] The pre-war road signs had been taken down as a precaution in the event of invasion; the Ministry of Transport was compelled to produce new signs since the majority of those of the pre-war period had been used as scrap.

noted for its excellent use of headlines and photographs and for its variety of columns designed to appeal to a wide audience. The writing was clear and concise, demonstrating that Welsh could be used to discuss topics relevant to the modern age. The success of Y Cymro was also marked by the fact that the new style did not compromise the level of debate or the quality of argument. Indeed, it was one of the few papers, either Welsh or English, which succeeded in becoming a popular paper without indulging in the carnal preoccupations displayed by the popular titles of Fleet Street.

Although Welsh leaders feared that the dynamic new culture of the 1950s boded ill for Welsh, there were significant developments which foreshadowed healthier attitudes towards the language. Undeb Cymru Fydd emerged as an articulate successor to the National Union of Welsh Societies and, like its predecessor, it succeeded in overcoming party political divisions. Its role as a pressure group on Welsh issues, especially the Welsh language, was crucial in promoting the language in the 1950s. Pressure was exerted on the BBC to produce television as well as radio programmes in Welsh and the University of Wales was persuaded to develop its provision for Welsh-medium teaching. A prolonged campaign to obtain state subsidies for Welsh books proved successful and the scheme was expanded gradually during the decade. Subsidies encouraged new writing in Welsh, particularly fiction and books for young people, thereby making good a serious deficiency in Welsh literature.[72] The 1950s also witnessed the expansion of Welsh-medium primary education, especially in Anglicized communities.

Although the effective campaigning of Undeb Cymru Fydd and the more positive attitude demonstrated by public authorities in the 1950s ensured that Welsh issues remained prominent on the public agenda, the 1961 census revealed that the number of Welsh speakers had declined within a decade from 28.9 per cent to 26 per cent.[73] Almost immediately, a sense of urgency informed the editorials of Y Cymro. As early as 1960, prior to the publication of the census returns, the paper had warned that unless current trends were reversed Welsh would cease to be a living language within the lifetime of the present generation.[74] In May 1962 the paper published the alarming results of a survey which showed that the language would perish in strongholds such as Anglesey unless

---

[72] Welsh literature had been dominated by biographies, historical works and books of a religious nature. Such material was out-dated and clearly could not compete with the more popular English-language works published in the period after the First World War.

[73] John Aitchison and Harold Carter, A Geography of the Welsh Language 1961–1991 (Cardiff, 1994), pp. 41–4. The census was not the only statistical evidence available. In a survey commissioned by Y Cymro, D. Jacob Davies noted that whereas 80 per cent of the children of Carmarthenshire had been Welsh speakers in 1936, the percentage had fallen to 45 per cent by 1960, the greatest decline occurring after 1950. Y Cymro, 3 August 1961.

[74] Y Cymro, 24 March 1960.

immediate action was taken to reverse the decline.[75] Not surprisingly, therefore, *Y Cymro* strongly supported the call to arms made by Saunders Lewis in his celebrated radio lecture, *Tynged yr Iaith* (The Fate of the Language) in 1962:

> Y perygl – ac nid yw heb ei ragweld – yw y bydd y bobl yn cael y feddyginiaeth yn waeth na'r dolur. Canys mae'n galw am safiad unol a gwrol. Heddiw ychydig o bobl sy'n barod i sefyll, ychydig sy'n wrol dros egwyddorion; aeth egwyddor yn beth prin.[76]

> (The danger – already foreseen – is that the people will find the medicine worse than the ailment. For it calls for a united and valorous stand. Today few show valour on matters of principle; principle has become a rarity.)

The paper returned to the theme in its St David's day editorial:

> Trwy'r blynyddoedd yr ydym wedi ceisio mynd o leiaf hanner y ffordd i gyfarfod pob math o bobl a sefydliadau ac awdurdodau ar fater y Gymraeg. Efallai i ni gael ein trwytho'n ormodol a'r gyfran honno o grefydd y Sais sy'n dweud mai'r peth i'w wneud a phob egwyddor yw ei bargeinio ymaith hyd oni ddaw'n rhywbeth sy'n dod a chytundeb tawel a digyffro rhwng anghredinwyr. Ond yn awr yr ydym yn dechrau gweld na fedrir bargeinio ag egwyddorion, a rhaid troi at bobl fel Mr Saunders Lewis a Dr Peate, gan gydnabod i ddechrau nad oes Gymru heb y Gymraeg. Os medrwn argyhoeddi ein hunain o hynny – mae gobaith i ni.[77]

> (Over the years we have sought to go at least half way to meet all sorts of people and institutions and authorities on the Welsh issue. We have perhaps immersed ourselves excessively in that part of the English belief which decrees that every principle is to be bargained away until it becomes a matter of silent and tranquil agreement between unbelievers. But now we are beginning to see that it is impossible to bargain with principles, and we must turn to the likes of Mr Saunders Lewis and Dr Peate, whilst acknowledging first that there would not be a Wales without Welsh. If we can convince ourselves of that – there is hope for us.)

The reaction of the *Western Mail* to Saunders Lewis's plea was unusually sympathetic. The paper declared that his lecture, particularly the prediction of the imminent demise of the language, contained many home truths:

> Not only have we absorbed waves of immigrants, but legislation since the Act of Union has mitigated against the continuance of Welsh. Universal free education in English, the vast availability of English newspapers and books, better transport and then radio and television have accelerated the process.

[75] Ibid., 24 May 1962.
[76] Ibid., 15 February 1962.
[77] Ibid., 1 March 1962.

In recent years efforts have been made to stem the tide. Over most of the country children are given regular Welsh lessons. The recent surveys in Carmarthenshire and Flintshire show that even this is not saving the language. Significantly, even in homes where both parents speak Welsh the trend is obvious . . . If Wales is to save her own language she must spontaneously show more signs of wanting to preserve and expand its present use.[78]

When the gloomy evidence of the 1961 census was published in the following year, the *Western Mail* was adamant that a determined effort was required to preserve the language and reverse its decline.[79]

By 1960, however, a significant change had occurred in the editorial policy of *Yr Herald Cymraeg*, both politically and in relation to the Welsh language. Following the appointment in 1954 of J. T. Jones (John Eilian) as editor, the paper adopted a Conservative standpoint as well as an increasingly antipathetic attitude towards the Welsh language at a time when public opinion on the issue was moving in the opposite direction. Saunders Lewis's radio broadcast in 1962 (in many ways reminiscent of editorials in the *Herald* during the 1920s and 1940s) was rejected by the paper as a lament for a dying language:

rhyw siarad niwlog o'r gell ydyw siarad fel hyn. Y gwir am yr iaith Gymraeg ydyw ei bod hi eisoes wedi hen farw o Forgannwg, Sir Frycheiniog, Sir Faesyfed, ac o ran helaeth o Sir Benfro, Sir Drefaldwyn, Sir Ddinbych a Sir Fflint . . . mewn geiriau eraill yn y Gogledd-Orllewin a'r Gorllewin yn unig y siaredir hi'n helaeth.

Lle mae'r iaith wedi colli 'does dim gobaith ei chael yn ôl . . . Rhyw duedd i geisio 'gosod' yr iaith sydd wedi bod – ei gosod a hyd yn oed, i raddau, ei gorfodi. Ond 'thâl hyn ddim ac y mae arnom ofn y bydd ffigyrau siroedd eraill y Gogledd (a'r Sensws) yn dangos yr un duedd ag a ddengys ffigyrau methiannus Sir Fflint.[80]

(this is but hazy talk from the secluded study. The truth is that the Welsh language has long since died in Glamorgan, Breconshire, Radnorshire and the greater part of Pembrokeshire, Montgomeryshire, Denbighshire and Flintshire . . . in other words it is spoken widely only in the North-West and the West.

Where the language has died, there is no hope of a revival . . . There has been a tendency to 'impose' the language – to impose and even to a certain extent to compel it. But this will be to no avail and we fear that the figures for other counties in the North (and the Census) will show the same trends as the failing figures for Flintshire.)

There can be no doubt, however, that pressure applied on the government and local authorities on the language issue was now greater than at any other

---

[78] *Western Mail*, 15 February 1962.
[79] Ibid., 12 September 1962.
[80] *Yr Herald Cymraeg*, 19 February 1962.

preceding period covered in this study. Cymdeithas yr Iaith Gymraeg (the Welsh Language Society), born in response to Saunders Lewis's radio broadcast, became involved in increasingly robust demonstrations. Its campaign of civil disobedience elicited a mixed response even among those who were sympathetic to the language.[81] *Y Cymro* warned that the Society was in danger of alienating the great majority of Welsh speakers,[82] and it expressed particular alarm at the assertion made by Dafydd Iwan that the Society's campaigns had hitherto been 'too docile' ('rhy ddof').[83] These views did not necessarily reflect those of the paper's readership. 'Piniwn' declared its support for direct action,[84] and there were repeated accusations that opponents of the Society, rather than its members, were responsible for the greater part of the violence associated with its activities.[85] On individual issues, however, the editorial line was more sympathetic. In 1966 it declared that the practice of processing Welsh applications for tax disc forms through the Inland Revenue (when English forms were freely available in post offices) was intolerable,[86] and it also demanded that Wales should become a single postal region in order to circumvent the anti-Welsh animus of the Post Office management in England,[87] a policy which might also apply to the telephone system.

On the other hand, *Yr Herald Cymraeg* reflected the hostile views of John Eilian towards bilingualism. In 1963 it launched a scathing attack on the Welsh Language Society, arguing that in a bilingual country the question of the medium of transacting official business was irrelevant. It insisted that the majority of people, even in the most Welsh-speaking districts, preferred to conduct official business through the medium of English:[88]

'Does neb tebyg i'r rhai selog dros y Gymraeg am wrthod wynebu ffeithiau ac felly am wneud drwg i'w hachos eu hunain . . . Saesneg ydyw'r bwysicaf o'n dwy iaith, ond nid ydyw hynny yn ddim rheswm dros inni beidio â choleddu a gloywi'n Cymraeg.[89]

[81] In his column in *Y Cymro*, I. B. Griffith criticized the Welsh Language Society for refusing to accept that non-members could be totally committed to the preservation of the language, and warned that the Society was losing the sympathy of a significant proportion of Welsh speakers. *Y Cymro*, 2 March 1967.

[82] Ibid., 22 October 1969.

[83] Ibid., 28 December 1968.

[84] Ibid., 13 October 1966.

[85] Ibid. See also ibid., 22 October 1969. In February 1963 the Cardiganshire Constabulary was accused of neglecting its duty by failing to prevent elements opposed to the Society from attacking its members during a demonstration at Aberystwyth. Ibid., 7 February 1963. In October 1966 violence at a demonstration at Cardiff was again attributed to opponents rather than Society members. Ibid., 13 October 1966.

[86] Ibid., 6 October 1966.

[87] Ibid., 9 December 1965.

[88] *Yr Herald Cymraeg*, 15 July 1963.

[89] Ibid., 28 May 1962.

(None are more prone to refuse to face facts and thus harm their own cause than those who are ardently Welsh . . . English is the more important of our two languages, although that is no reason for us not to cherish and improve our Welsh.)

The *Western Mail*, on the other hand, changed its attitude to demands for Welsh documents. Whereas the paper had ridiculed those who had demanded Welsh official documents in 1963 on the grounds that no language had ever been preserved by forms,[90] three years later the paper regarded the provision of such items as a basic right of the individual and a crucial feature of the battle to preserve the Welsh language:

> Unless it is ensured by statutory action there can be little hope that Welsh, with all that it has meant and still means for our cultural traditions, will survive as a living tongue.[91]

Education also acquired a prominent profile in the 1960s. As early as 1961 *Y Cymro* called for an inquiry into the status of Welsh in technical colleges and demanded that additional resources be made available for Welsh-medium teaching.[92] The real campaign for Welsh in education came, however, as a result of the increasingly vociferous demand for Welsh-medium schools. Throughout both Welsh-speaking and Anglicized areas it had become apparent that policies pursued by local education authorities, many of which boasted of their commitment to the Welsh language, were inadequate in the light of deep concerns about the future of the language. Progress in Welsh-medium education had been slow, even though the ability of Welsh-medium schools to attract pupils and achieve impressive levels of academic success was evident. The publication of the Gittins Report in 1967, which included a recommendation that a bilingual education should be an option for every child in Wales, was warmly welcomed,[93] although *Y Cymro* added that additional financial resources would be required by local authorities in order to fund such developments. The expansion of Welsh-medium education was accompanied by efforts by other authorities, notably Glamorgan and Flintshire, to develop schemes to teach Welsh as a second language. While *Yr Herald Cymraeg*, under John Eilian, adopted a sceptical attitude, the *Western Mail* was sympathetic to such developments and showed little regard for campaigns in opposition to the policy.[94] The paper supported proposals by Undeb Cymru Fydd to send children from Anglicized areas to the Welsh-speaking heartland during their summer holidays as a means of immersing them in

---

90 *Western Mail*, 1 March 1963.
91 Ibid., 10 October 1966.
92 *Y Cymro*, 9 March 1961.
93 Ibid., 25 January 1968.
94 *Western Mail*, 6 December 1966, 17 January 1969.

a Welsh atmosphere.[95] Yet it was far from wholehearted in its support for Welsh-medium education and chose to raise the 'linguistic apartheid' argument in its comments on attempts to establish separate Welsh-medium halls of residence for university students. It claimed that there was so much more to be gained from maintaining a cosmopolitan atmosphere at university and that the establishment of 'tribal reservations' would prove inimical to the spirit of academia:[96]

> both Welsh hostels and a Welsh college are entirely opposed to the true purposes of university education. These are, among other things, to broaden the mind, to teach tolerance and to experience it by living alongside a wide range of fellow students. None of these purposes would be served by isolating Welsh-speaking students in a monolinguistic cultural camp. If there have been frictions between Welsh and English students they could have been resolved by discussion and by commonsense compromises . . . Fortunately, the all-Welsh hostels may yet defeat themselves by lack of support.[97]

Within Welsh-speaking areas, however, the consensus of opinion was moving firmly in the direction of stronger measures to preserve and enhance the status of the language. As a result, Yr Herald Cymraeg found itself increasingly isolated. Partly in response to the change in public attitudes and partly as a result of a temporary decline in John Eilian's influence,[98] the paper tempered its anti-Welsh pronouncements. In 1965, for instance, it lent its support to the staff of Brewer Spinks Company factory at Blaenau Ffestiniog when a group of workers were dismissed for refusing to abide by a rule that no Welsh was to be spoken in the factory.[99]

The attitude of the three papers towards the Welsh language was clearly reflected in their responses to the David Hughes Parry Report on the legal status of Welsh, published in 1965, and the legislation which followed. The report was an attempt to analyse the position of Welsh and to establish a basis for legislation relating mainly to the legal status of the language. Y Cymro welcomed the recommendations as 'bold but practical', while Yr Herald Cymraeg called for a longer period of reflection. A similarly cautious attitude was adopted by the Western Mail. In 1963 the paper had argued that there was little antipathy towards

---

[95] Ibid., 2 March 1968.
[96] Ibid., 27 November 1967. In a survey carried out at Bangor in 1963, Euryn Ogwen Williams noted that of the 445 first-year students enrolled, 122 were from Wales and only 42 were Welsh speakers. He attributed this situation both to the college's recruitment policy and the tendency of an increasing number of Welsh students to attend English universities. Y Cymro, 10 October 1963.
[97] Western Mail, 7 May 1968.
[98] John Eilian was selected as Conservative candidate for Anglesey in March 1964 and contested the seat at the 1966 and 1970 elections. Fearing a conflict of interest, the Herald Group reduced his day-to-day editorial responsibilities during this period.
[99] Yr Herald Cymraeg, 21 June 1965.

the language, but it subsequently insisted that attempts to impose an artificial status of equality could prove costly and impractical. In 1965 its editorial reiterated the argument that the measure of goodwill towards Welsh which prevailed in the Anglicized areas could be jeopardized if the Welsh language were imposed on the English-speaking majority and a policy of appointing Welsh speakers to public offices adopted:[100]

> The danger of the Hughes-Parry recommendations is that under the guise of righting an ancient wrong, a minority in Wales would be imposing on the majority an irrelevant and hampering burden. The Welsh language, as the tongue of the hearth and the living literature of our nation, must be helped in every way possible – but short of sacrificing sense and logic in the conduct of our public affairs.[101]

Yet, within a month of its original statement on the Hughes Parry Report, the *Western Mail* had modified its views. Noting that the debate on the report had been remarkably muted, it renewed its support for initatives to strengthen the language, pointing to the success of the policy of encouraging the Hebrew language in Israel.

Although the Welsh Language Act of 1967 clarified and significantly strengthened the 1942 Act, the response it engendered was mixed. *Y Cymro* declared that the Act was a step in the right direction, but argued also that there was a need to strengthen its provisions gradually in order to progress towards equal validity for both languages,[102] a view it continued to hold for the remainder of the decade. *Yr Herald Cymraeg* was broadly sympathetic to the Language Act by the late 1960s, but the news articles clearly demonstrate that a large section of the paper's readership believed that the measures implemented by the Act were unacceptably modest, and this view was increasingly shared by the *Herald* itself by the early 1970s. The *Western Mail* declared that the Welsh Language Act had avoided the demands of 'extremists' and had preserved the pre-eminence of English as the language of the Anglicized areas of Wales, but that it had also demonstrated the government's intention to deal equitably with the Welsh language. But whatever sympathy the paper might have shown towards equal validity for the Welsh language was not reflected in its attitude towards the renewed (and more militant) campaigns of the Welsh Language Society. The sign-daubing campaign was denounced as 'senseless', and the paper demanded that the Society should expel any member convicted of violent behaviour.

As nationalist and pro-Welsh language sentiments gained wider support, the 1970s witnessed an intensification of the campaigns of the Welsh Language

---

[100] *Western Mail*, 21 November 1963.
[101] Ibid., 26 October 1965.
[102] *Y Cymro*, 15 June 1967.

Society. Particular attention was given to the demand for a Welsh television channel as well as to the bilingual road signs campaign. In addition, pressure of a more constitutional nature was exerted on both central and local government. Welsh-medium secondary schools continued to be established, although the focus of the activity now tended to be in the Welsh-speaking districts, whereas in Anglicized areas Welsh-medium education was less favoured by local authorities. A promising development occurred with the *papur bro* movement, a non-profit-making venture which provided local newspapers in Welsh. Forty-eight titles were launched between 1971 and 1979.[103] Although highly localized and often devoid of editorial comment, the papers nevertheless provided a valuable medium for the dissemination of information and reports on Welsh activities and were a source of ideas for the maintenance of a Welsh culture both in Welsh-speaking and Anglicized communities in Wales. The growth of the movement to teach Welsh to adults continued with some striking successes, although the total numbers were not sufficient to make a substantial impact on census figures. Despite these achievements, the decline in the number of Welsh speakers continued. Of equal significance was the worsening economic outlook of the period (together with the fear that Wales might witness the kind of exodus of population which had occurred in the inter-war years) and the right-wing ideology which threatened the Keynesian consensus which had recognized that economic policy should be concerned as much with the preservation of communities as with profit and loss. Many feared for the future of villages which had traditionally been regarded as Welsh-speaking strongholds but which were now economically isolated.

By the early 1980s statistical data provided further evidence of the failure to arrest the decline in the number of Welsh speakers. Whereas 20.9 per cent of the population had been Welsh-speaking in 1971, the proportion had fallen to 18.9 per cent by 1981.[104] The census revealed that although the rate of decline in the number of Welsh speakers had decreased, and indeed that positive signs of recovery for the language were evident in certain areas, mainly in south-east Wales, the process of decline had continued, particularly in west Wales.[105] Indeed, the position in traditional strongholds such as Carmarthen, Dinefwr, Llanelli and the Lliw Valley was particularly alarming, as was the evidence that the language was associated increasingly with the elderly in those communities.[106] Bedwyr Lewis Jones, Professor of Welsh at the University College of North Wales, Bangor, expressed fears in the *Western Mail* in February 1982 that the Welsh

---

[103] 1971 (1 title), 1973 (2 titles), 1974 (4 titles), 1975–7 (8 titles per annum), 1978 (7 titles) and 1979 (10 titles). Some of these newspapers were short-lived, but the majority have become permanent features of Welsh life in the Welsh-speaking parts of Wales.

[104] Aitchison and Carter, *A Geography of the Welsh Language*, p. 50.

[105] *Western Mail*, 28 April 1982.

[106] Aitchison and Carter, *A Geography of the Welsh Language*, pp. 50–8.

language was in danger of becoming an élitist phenomenon increasingly associated with the intellectual community, and that this trend was never likely to counteract the decline of the language in its traditional strongholds.[107] While perceiving genuine causes for optimism in south-east Wales, the *Western Mail* concurred with his sentiments:

> That [the] decline has actually been reversed in some areas, and the increase in its use is not at all confined to the 'new middle class' efforts in the South-East to revive the language as a cultural accomplishment. At the same time there is cause for real concern in the growing disuse of the language in its traditional community strongholds like Carmarthen, Dinefwr and Llanelli – sometimes apparently through misplaced fear among parents that to pass it on to their children would put them at a disadvantage in making careers.[108]

Surprisingly, in view of the attitude demonstrated towards the campaigns of the Welsh Language Society in the 1970s, the paper congratulated the Society on the way in which it had influenced opinion and ensured that the language had remained on the agenda of public debate.[109]

The publication of these figures coincided with unfavourable economic prospects both for the rural and industrial areas of Wales.[110] *Y Cymro* made the need for economic regeneration the cornerstone of its policy on the language, declaring that the battle against the deindustrialization of Wales should take precedence over the campaign for a Welsh television channel.[111] Yet the focus of the language campaigns remained similar to that of twenty years earlier; it concentrated mainly on four areas: the status of Welsh in public life, education, in-migration and broadcasting. Welsh language campaigners succeeded in the domains of education and broadcasting, but issues regarding in-migration and appointments in public life continued to create difficulties. The issue of imposing a language qualification for certain public posts arose regularly throughout the 1980s, particularly in north and west Wales. In Gwynedd, the Health Authority, the University College of North Wales, Bangor, and, to a lesser extent, the County Council were accused of being reluctant to appoint Welsh speakers to senior positions.[112] On the other hand, the appointment of Welsh speakers was

---

[107] *Western Mail*, 3 February 1982.
[108] Ibid., 28 April 1982.
[109] Ibid., 11 July 1983.
[110] In a very depressing report on the effect of economic recession on the Welsh language, West Glamorgan County Council highlighted the linguistic decline in areas such as the Afan valley, the Dulais valley and the Swansea valley, where young families were forced out by lack of job opportunities. Ibid., 13 August 1982.
[111] *Y Cymro*, 29 January 1980.
[112] Ibid., 17 March 1981. For instance, in 1981 Gwynedd Area Health Authority failed to appoint a Welsh speaker as its chief officer. Similar criticisms were voiced, at various times, against Dyfed County Council, the University of Wales and the Welsh Office.

challenged in the courts. The Commission for Racial Equality became involved in a series of disputes with Gwynedd County Council, during which it was alleged that the appointments policy of the authority was racist in so far as it excluded non-Welsh-speaking applicants.[113] The *Western Mail*, which had hitherto aired its considerable reservations about insisting on the ability to speak Welsh in the appointment of personnel, nevertheless lent its support to the County Council by declaring:

> Many inmates of the residential homes concerned use Welsh as their first language. Life for the elderly and the handicapped, in even the happiest of such homes, is sufficiently unsettling in itself, without the added strangeness of being dealt with by helpers who do not understand or speak what is to them the language of normal life. It should have been seen that Gwynedd County Council . . . was carrying out a humane duty.[114]

The attitude of the *Western Mail* was based on the pragmatic need for Welsh speakers to fulfil specific caring roles rather than on the conviction that knowledge of the Welsh language should be made an essential qualification for certain occupations.

Both *Y Cymro* and *Yr Herald Cymraeg* were also greatly exercised by the detrimental linguistic effects of large-scale migration into rural areas during the late 1970s and early 1980s. Very few individuals, and certainly none of the papers studied in this survey, supported the holiday-home arson campaign. The question of holiday homes, however, became acute in the early 1980s, especially as growing numbers of outsiders settled in rural communities as permanent dwellers. This influx renewed the pressure on the Welsh language in many of its strongest areas. Education authorities such as those of Dyfed and Gwynedd, which had recently introduced Welsh-medium policies in education, faced a situation in which more than 50 per cent of pupils came from non-Welsh-speaking homes, thereby compounding the difficulties of implementing the policy.[115] The *Western Mail* chose not to advocate any form of amendment of housing or planning legislation in the light of linguistic considerations. Rather, it placed its faith in the development of peripatetic second-language teachers ('athrawon bro') and the introduction of intensive residential courses for pupils to learn Welsh.[116] The highlighting of the in-migration issue as one of paramount concern in Welsh-speaking communities coincided with the development of a more resolutely-

---

[113] In 1985 the Commission for Racial Equality supported two non-Welsh-speaking care assistants who alleged that the Council had discriminated against them. *Western Mail*, 15 August 1985.

[114] Ibid., 16 August 1985.

[115] The problem became acute in Gwynedd, ibid., 6 January 1982 and later in Dyfed, *Y Cymro*, 18 June 1985. Cynog Dafis referred to the fact that 30 per cent of the primary school pupils in the Teifi valley came from English-speaking homes. The failure of such children to learn Welsh adequately resulted in serious integration problems. *Western Mail*, 19 January 1980.

[116] *Western Mail*, 7 May 1982.

Welsh attitude on the part of *Yr Herald Cymraeg*, whose editorship passed to a succession of young editors actively committed to the preservation of Welsh. By 1989 its stance was unequivocal:

> Am ormod o amser, rydan ni wedi bwriadol anwybyddu'r mewnfudiad cyson sy'n boddi'n pentrefi. A'r pris rydan ni'n ei dalu am hyn ydi prysur fynd yn estroniaid yn ein gwlad ein hunain. Mewn geiriau eraill, mae'r sefyllfa'n dechrau mynd yn anobeithiol. A ddylen ni byth anghofio peth mor ddifrifol ydi anobaith. Mewn anobaith y mae trais yn ffynnu . . . Heb inni fedru gwneud rhywbeth ynglŷn â'r llifeiriant estron, bydd yr holl gonsesiynau a enillwyd i'r Gymraeg dros y blynyddoedd dwytha'n ddiwerth, a'r holl ymgyrchu drosti wedi bod yn gwbl ofer.[117]

> (For too long we have deliberately ignored the constant in-migration which is drowning our villages. The price we are paying for this is that we are fast becoming strangers in our own land. In other words, the situation is becoming hopeless. And we should not forget that to be without hope is a serious condition. Hopelessness breeds violence . . . Unless we do something about the foreign influx, all the concessions that have been won for the Welsh language during recent years will be worthless, and all the campaigns in its favour will have been totally in vain.)

Y Cymro advocated the introduction of linguistic considerations into the planning policies of local authorities. It believed that Welsh authorities would benefit from the experiences of their counterparts in the Lake District, where deliberate attempts were being made to prevent large-scale in-migration.[118] Despite mounting pressure, the Welsh Office remained hostile to any proposal to place legal restrictions on the housing market, but the transformation of the linguistic profile of large parts of Welsh-speaking Wales did not augur well for the future of the language. The drift of young Welsh speakers from rural communities meant that those who continued to speak the language in those areas were elderly people.[119] As a result, the social life of villages became Anglicized and the leading role in local sociocultural activity was often taken by newcomers.

Despite the serious threat posed to the pre-eminence of Welsh in its natural heartland, the 1980s witnessed other gains apart from those associated with the development of Welsh-medium education in south Wales. Despite grave financial problems, attractive language-learning centres, such as that at Nant Gwrtheyrn (an area which had long endured the effects of rural depopulation), were established.[120] At the same time, the Welsh Office, in spite of its reluctance to legislate on housing and planning, increased expenditure on the Welsh language. This was partly in order to fulfil the promise made in 1980 by Nicholas Edwards, Secretary

[117] *Yr Herald Cymraeg*, 11 March 1989.
[118] *Y Cymro*, 24 November 1981.
[119] *Yr Herald Cymraeg*, 14 October 1989.
[120] Ibid., 20 April 1982.

of State for Wales, that the alleged anti-Welsh image of the Conservative Party would change radically.[121] Expenditure on the language brought spectacular results in the field of broadcasting. The failure of the BBC and HTV to make adequate provision for Welsh-language programmes had been a major complaint among language activists throughout the period discussed in this chapter, and when the Conservative government decided in the winter of 1979 to renege on its commitment to establish a separate Welsh television channel there were furious protests throughout Wales. Both the *Western Mail* and *Y Cymro* regarded the decision to undermine a cross-party consensus on the need for a Welsh fourth channel as a wholly unacceptable breach of faith. But *Yr Herald Cymraeg*, still strongly influenced by the views of John Eilian, gave the announcement a cautious welcome. Alone among the papers examined in this chapter, it declared that the future of Welsh broadcasting lay in acquiring a greater number of hours on existing channels rather than inaugurating a separate channel which would not be watched by the vast majority of the people of Wales.[122] When the government eventually honoured its pledge to establish a fourth channel for the Welsh language, its decision received a lukewarm response from *Yr Herald Cymraeg*:

Pan wnaeth Mr Gwynfor Evans ei apêl at Angau, fe ganwyd yn iach i bwyll a gwybodaeth a barn, ac fe guddiwyd yr holl fusnes gan ddryswch a thristhad. Problem y ddwy A fawr sy'n ein hwynebu yn y diwedd, sef Arian ac Adnoddau. Mae mwy o oriau'n golygu mwy o staff, a phentyrru costau, i'r BBC a'r teledu masnachol, a bydd y cwmni masnachol . . . mewn gwaeth twll am ei fod yn dibynnu ar hysbysebion gwerthu nwyddau a'r rheiny'n gyndyn (fel ar hyn o bryd) i ganlyn rhaglenni Cymraeg.[123]

(When Mr Gwynfor Evans made his appeal unto Death, we bade farewell to caution and knowledge and judgement, and the whole business was cloaked in confusion and sadness. Two problems face us at the end of the day, namely Finance and Resources. More hours means more staff and mounting costs for the BBC and commercial television, and the commercial company . . . will be worse off since it depends on advertisements to sell goods and advertisers may be reluctant (as they are at present) to follow Welsh programmes.)

As has been indicated earlier, education featured prominently on the agenda of the debate in the 1980s, both as a means of preserving the language against external pressures in its traditional heartland and as a means of promoting the

---

[121] *Western Mail*, 16 April 1980.

[122] *Yr Herald Cymraeg*, 23 September 1980. Somewhat surprisingly, Professor Jac L. Williams of Aberystwyth, a staunch supporter of Welsh-language broadcasting, agreed with this view and consistently advocated that more Welsh programmes should be broadcast at peak times on the existing channels. *Yr Herald Cymraeg* supported such arguments on financial grounds.

[123] Ibid.

language in south Wales. The Welsh Language Society launched a campaign in support of a Welsh-Language Education Development Body that would be charged with the co-ordination and development of Welsh-medium education. The Society's demands were partly influenced by discouraging evidence from Her Majesty's Inspectors concerning the standard of the teaching of Welsh, particularly as a second language. The *Western Mail* highlighted reports which painted a bleak picture of the failure of schools to deliver Welsh as part of the curriculum, and of the failure of pupils to use Welsh upon leaving school.[124] *Y Cymro* declared that the campaign for a Welsh-Language Education Development Body was the most important initiative in the Society's history:

Drwy hap a damwain a brwdfrydedd unigolion y cadwyd pethau gystal ag y maent. Corff parhaol i gytgordio'r ymdrechion a darparu adnoddau a chyngor proffesiynol drwy'r wlad yw'r unig ffordd i sicrhau nad yn ofer fu holl ymdrechion y gorffennol.[125]

(Things are as well as they are through good luck and the enthusiasm of individuals. The only way to ensure that all past efforts will not be in vain is to establish a permanent body to co-ordinate efforts and provide resources and professional advice throughout the land.)

Even so, the paper warned that the campaign would fail to fire popular imagination as previous campaigns had done because the benefits of securing such a body were less apparent. By the time the campaign reached its peak *Yr Herald Cymraeg* had declared its support for the creation of an entirely new body, independent of the Welsh Joint Education Committee and local education authorities:

er y gall y Cyd-Bwyllgor Addysg fod yn rhan o beirianwaith gweithredu'r bwriad, mae'n rhaid i'r ysgogiad a'r arweiniad ddod o gorff cwbl newydd na fydd ar drugaredd maffia gwrth-Gymraeg nifer o'n siroedd. Mewn gair, mae'n rhaid rhoi'r gwin newydd mewn costrelau newydd.[126]

(although the [Welsh] Joint Education Committee can be part of the machinery for implementing what is intended, the initiative and leadership must come from a completely new body which will not be at the mercy of the anti-Welsh maffia in many of our counties. In short, new wine must be poured into new bottles.)

The Society's demands were met, albeit partially, in 1987 with the establishment of a working group on Welsh in education. The committee was established at a significant juncture during the more general discussion concerning the desirability of introducing Welsh into the curriculum in Wales. In the view of the working

[124] *Western Mail*, 23 June 1981, 30 January 1987.
[125] *Y Cymro*, 26 February 1985.
[126] *Yr Herald Cymraeg*, 6 May 1985.

party, the compulsory teaching of Welsh from the age of 5 to 16 was desirable.[127] This was granted in 1988,[128] although certain schools were exempted. Fulsome in its praise, the *Western Mail* claimed that the policy was likely to prove the greatest boon for the Welsh language since the translation of the Bible:

> The vast majority of people in Wales, whether they speak Welsh or not, recognise the language as a priceless heritage which they would like, if possible, to pass on to their children – even if they themselves never had the opportunity to learn. Their active support is also required if the vision is to become a reality.[129]

Efforts to enhance the position of the Welsh language in education coincided with demands for a new and stronger Welsh Language Act. This tide was already growing by the mid-1980s,[130] although, as *Y Cymro* pointed out, those who believed that a single piece of legislation would preserve the language were mistakenly naive.[131] But those who advocated legislation as a means of strengthening the position of the language were arguing from a much stronger position in 1987 than their predecessors had been able to do twenty years previously. The vast majority of those who had been consulted recognized the need to safeguard the Welsh language by some legislative means, and the differences between them arose only over the extent of that legislation.[132] The publication by Bwrdd yr Iaith Gymraeg (the Welsh Language Board) of a consultative document *The Welsh Language: A Strategy for the Future* in 1989 received a mixed response, especially since it failed to accept the need for wholesale legislative changes. Rather, the Board called for legislation which would grant Welsh equal validity with English. While acknowledging the need for some legislation to strengthen the position of the language in terms of economic and housing development, the Board insisted that, as far as private business was concerned, codes of conduct should remain voluntary. Indeed, the thrust of the Board's argument concerned not the status of Welsh but the need for propaganda to promote and popularize the language and to give positive encouragement for individuals to learn Welsh. The *Western Mail* welcomed the proposals, although it admitted that a strong commitment from government agencies would be required in order to enable them to work:

---

[127] *Western Mail*, 2 October 1987.

[128] Ibid., 10 February 1988.

[129] Ibid., 7 July 1989.

[130] In 1985, for instance, Dafydd Wigley and Gwilym Prys Davies both produced separate proposals which were circulated among public bodies in Wales. Dafydd Wigley's proposals were deemed unacceptable, but the measures suggested by Gwilym Prys Davies, which were considerably more radical than those included in the 1967 Act, were welcomed.

[131] *Y Cymro*, 6 November 1984.

[132] *Western Mail*, 2 January 1987.

the board is out to win the hearts and minds of the majority to the view that Welsh is a priceless asset and that it can be conserved and developed for the benefit of all in Wales. It is a strategy to be applauded. It now needs a sympathetic Government and Secretary of State, and a statutory board with the resources for the job.[133]

According to *Y Cymro*, however, the document was an insult. In its view, the principle of equal validity was inadequate and since the proposals did not apply to private companies they would not relate to an increasingly influential sector in Welsh life. The Welsh Language Board, it alleged, was so preoccupied with producing recommendations acceptable to the Secretary of State that it had failed to view the problem with sufficient vision:

> Gellid maddau i rywun am ddyfalu mai dull y Bwrdd o weithredu oedd rhagdybio yn gyntaf beth a fyddai'n dderbyniol i Peter Walker a'r Senedd a mynd am hynny yn hytrach na chymryd safiad a dweud beth sydd ei wir angen er gwaethaf amhoblogrwydd hynny yn y Swyddfa Gymreig. Adroddiad y pragmatydd yw hwn yn hytrach nag un o weledigaeth . . . Saunders Lewis a ddywedodd mai trwy ddulliau chwyldro yn unig y mae adfer yr iaith Gymraeg. Dydi hwn ddim yn ymddangos yn adroddiad sy'n mynd i esgor ar chwyldro – boed hwnnw yn chwyldro tawel yr ydym oll yn ei ddeisyfu. Trwy nacau'r un peth pwysig [Deddfwriaeth] y mae'n debycach o esgor ar ragor o ymgecru a ffraeo y gallem yn hawdd wneud hebddo.[134]

(One could be forgiven for imagining that the method adopted by the Board was to anticipate that which might be acceptable to Peter Walker and Parliament and opting for that, rather than making a stand and declaring what is truly needed, however unpopular that might be in the Welsh Office. This is the report of a pragmatist rather than a visionary . . . Saunders Lewis stated that only by revolutionary means could the Welsh language be restored. This does not appear to be a report which will lead to revolution – the quiet revolution which we all desire. By rejecting the one important thing [Legislation] it is likely to lead to further argument and disunity that we could well do without.)

The publication of the new Welsh Language Bill in December 1992 was greeted with derision by both *Y Cymro* and *Yr Herald Cymraeg*, although the *Western Mail* adopted a more sympathetic attitude. In many ways, the Bill constituted a more restrained version of the radical proposals published by the Welsh Language Board in 1989. *Y Cymro* made no attempt to conceal its disappointment:

> Wedi deng mlynedd o feichiogrwydd ymddengys mai esgoriad braidd yn hunllefus a gafodd babi Nadolig y Mesur Iaith. A'r argraff gyntaf yw nad yw'n plesio, gyda'r

---

[133] Ibid., 23 June 1989.
[134] *Y Cymro*, 28 June 1989.

Llywodraeth ei hun yn son am fân driniaethau llawfeddygol iddo hyd yn oed cyn inni i gyd ei weld yn iawn a chael cyfle i graffu arno.[135]

(After ten years of gestation it seems that the Christmas baby, the Language Bill, has had rather a nightmarish birth. And the first impression is that it has not won approval, with even the Government itself talking in terms of minor surgical treatment even before we have seen it properly and had an opportunity to examine it.)

The paper exposed inconsistencies in the Bill which meant that, in certain respects, the new proposals were weaker than the measures included in the 1967 Act. It also expressed particular concern at the failure to address the issue of the newly-privatized utilities. The reluctance of the government to accept any real amendments to the Bill during its passage to the statute book resulted in a hardening of attitude on the part both of language activists in Wales and sympathetic newspapers such as *Y Cymro* and *Yr Herald Cymraeg*. *Y Cymro* lamented the failure of the government to produce an Act sufficiently strong to defuse the language issue:

Y tristwch yw y bydd yn rhaid gwastraffu eto fyth ynni y goreuon o'n pobl ifainc yn ymgyrchu dros rywbeth a ddylid fod wedi cael ei ennill yn barod.[136]

(The sadness is that we must again dissipate the energies of the best of our young people in a campaign for something which should have been won already.)

The response of each of the three papers to the 1993 Act reflected convictions which they had held throughout the greater part of the 1980s. By 1984 both *Yr Herald Cymraeg* and *Y Cymro* were demanding comprehensive measures to protect the Welsh language against outside pressures, notably the influx of migrants from England, and to promote the language through an extension of its legal status. The *Western Mail* took a more pragmatic approach, insisting that although the measures advocated by *Y Cymro* and *Yr Herald Cymraeg* were desirable, any legislation relating to the language needed to be based on consensus and to be capable of operating within reasonable limits.

★　★　★

Throughout this chapter inconsistencies in the views expressed by the three newspapers on matters relating to the Welsh language have been emphasized. Clearly the influence of the editor was a powerful factor in the declarations of

[135] Ibid., 23 December 1992.
[136] Ibid., 21 July 1993.

each newspaper. The outlook of the *Western Mail* invariably reflected the opinions of its editor. William Davies (1901–31) was sympathetic but inconsistent, D. R. Prosser (1942–56) did not regard the issue of the language as being of great importance in the years during and immediately after the Second World War, while in the 1960s, under D. G. H. Rowlands (1959–64), J. G. Davies (1964–5) and J. C. Giddings (1965–73), the paper was prepared to address the need to preserve the language while opposing the tactics of language campaigners. The development of a strongly pro-Welsh attitude continued under J. S. Rees (1981–7) and especially John Humphries in the late 1980s. The influence of the editor was also evident in relation to the Welsh-language papers. The appointment in 1946 of John Roberts Williams as editor of *Y Cymro* was a significant contribution to the strengthening of the paper's commitment to the language and his outlook, in general, has remained the basis of its editorial policy.[137] Likewise the right-wing standpoint of John Eilian was a major influence on *Yr Herald Cymraeg* until 1983. Yet the change thereafter in its outlook and its resolutely pro-Welsh attitude was not simply a reflection of editorial views. *Yr Herald Cymraeg* increasingly sought to reflect the views of its readers in the Welsh-speaking community in Gwynedd and west Clwyd, where perceptions of the language and voting patterns had changed. Where once the paper had sought to preach a Conservative message to its audience, it now began to develop a new role in articulating the views of the society it served, thereby revealing how a community could influence the views of its newspaper.

The newspapers studied in this chapter were selected on the grounds that they constituted a representative sample of the various attitudes towards the Welsh language expressed in the press during the period after 1918. Their pages testify both to the variety of opinions and the changing nature of the debate during the period under discussion. Newspapers reflected the fact that public opinion was becoming increasingly concerned with the need to preserve and promote the Welsh language. Most discussion arose regarding the extent to which this should be done and the method by which it could be achieved rather than whether it should be done at all. The debate was passionate and, at times, acrimonious, yet it avoided the extremes of racial hatred. Above all, the prominence given to the issue meant that apathy and indifference towards the native tongue, which had been rife during the early decades of the twentieth century, no longer prevailed.

---

[137] Robert Smith, *'Y Papur a Afaelodd yn Serchiadau'r Bobl': John Roberts Williams a'r Cymro 1945–62* (Aberystwyth, 1996).

8

Broadcasting and the Welsh Language

ROBERT SMITH

Wales is finding itself these days, and in this cultural renaissance we want the radio to play its part. The BBC should not have to be conscripted for this crusade; it should be in the joyous forefront of the battle, of its own free will.[1]

SO WROTE J. C. Griffith-Jones, the wireless correspondent of the *Western Mail*, in 1931. In common with several of his contemporaries, Griffith-Jones considered the intellectual and literary activity of the day as indicative of broader cultural development in Wales. Yet his words also reveal the extent of the disappointment with the early endeavours of the BBC in Wales. Indeed, broadcasting was a medium initially regarded as a threat to the language, as is testified by the fears of commentators such as R. J. Rowlands of *Yr Herald Cymraeg*. Writing in the same period, Rowlands was intensely aware of the capacity of broadcasting to reach the most isolated homes and thus undermine the traditional strongholds of Welsh culture by fostering a liking for English-language programmes.[2] Those fears were founded on the realization of the extent of the growth of Anglicized social activities, reflected in the culture of the village hall and Women's Institutes, where activities were mostly conducted through the medium of English.[3]

The views expressed by Griffith-Jones and Rowlands were early contributions to a continuing debate about the role of broadcasting in the life of the nation. In that debate the issue of the Welsh language inevitably became a major consideration. This chapter includes a review of how broadcasting policy in Wales was determined and how policy-makers were responsive to a public debate in which the language was an issue of cardinal importance, together with a broad survey of the development of radio and television provision, based on critical comments provided by the Welsh press.

The concerns of Griffith-Jones and Rowlands contributed to a debate which

---

[1] *Western Mail*, 1 December 1931.

[2] *Yr Herald Cymraeg*, 10 May 1927. See also *Y Tyst*, 28 May 1931. I am grateful to Mari A. Williams for this and numerous other references.

[3] *Y Ddraig Goch*, 8, no. 4 (1934).

had already broached the issue of the structures by which broadcasting could meet the needs of a bilingual nation. In December 1926 *Y Cymro* advocated the establishment of a separate Welsh corporation and *Yr Herald Cymraeg* was equally forthright, urging that the Welsh studio should be removed from Cardiff to the strongly Welsh-speaking areas of the north-west, not least in order to imbue the corporation's staff with a stronger sense of Welsh identity.[4] These pronouncements formed part of a much wider campaign as cultural organizations, represented by Undeb Cenedlaethol y Cymdeithasau Cymraeg (the National Union of Welsh Societies), adopted an increasingly robust approach.[5] The prominence given to the issue prompted the Court of the University of Wales to establish a committee to inquire into the development of broadcasting in Wales, partly as a result of agitation by members led by William George.[6] The Court initiated its own investigations and concluded that the BBC had failed to nurture Welsh culture, most notably its music and drama. Moreover, it demanded the appointment of a representative for Wales, conversant with the Welsh language and culture, to the governing body of the BBC,[7] and that greater efforts should be made to provide a service for the substantial numbers of Welsh speakers who desired a service in their own language.[8] The Welsh Parliamentary Party, a cross-party body established to exert pressure on the government on Welsh issues, joined the agitation and proved particularly vocal in demanding parity of esteem for Wales and Scotland.[9]

The failure of representatives of moderate opinion in Wales to secure concessions from the BBC resulted in a far more vigorous effort on the part of Plaid Genedlaethol Cymru (the Welsh Nationalist Party).[10] The Party's journal, *Y Ddraig Goch*, regularly denounced the BBC for neglecting Wales and the Welsh language in particular.[11] Significantly, the Party sought to counter the technical arguments deployed by the BBC, most notably by publishing the findings of E. G. Bowen, a physicist and a prominent figure in the nationalist movement, who accused the BBC of wasting wavelengths which could be used to provide a separate service for Wales.[12] It is clear that public opinion was infuriated by the impression that the BBC had little interest in overcoming the difficulties caused

---

4   *Y Cymro*, 15 December 1926; *Yr Herald Cymraeg*, 10 May 1927.

5   *Western Mail*, 14 October 1930. For details of the National Union of Welsh Societies, see Marion Löffler, '*Iaith Nas Arferir, Iaith i Farw Yw*': *Ymgyrchu dros yr Iaith Gymraeg rhwng y Ddau Ryfel Byd* (Aberystwyth, 1995).

6   *Western Mail*, 16 December 1933; University of Wales, Minutes of the Annual Collegiate Meeting of the University Court, December 1933.

7   *Western Mail*, 22 July 1931; University of Wales, Minutes of the Annual Collegiate Meeting of the University Court, July 1933.

8   *Western Mail*, 1 December 1928; University of Wales, Minutes of the Annual Collegiate Meeting of the University Court, December 1928.

9   *Western Mail*, 10 November 1932.

10   So determined was the Party in its demand for a separate Welsh channel that serious consideration was given to launching a campaign of non-payment of licence fees. *Western Mail*, 26 May 1932.

11   Ibid., 17 November 1933.

12   Ibid., 14 February 1933.

by a mountainous terrain and by what was perceived as the corporation's disregard for the aspirations of Welsh speakers. Moreover, this discontent was not confined to nationalist circles. Gwilym Davies, a leading figure in the internationalist movement and an active social reformer, argued the case for wireless autonomy in a prolonged campaign in the columns of the *Western Mail*.[13] Davies was one of the first to realize the relevance of the new medium to Wales and the Welsh language. In his estimation, the concept of 'Wales and the West' was unacceptable because the region lacked any real sense of community and because the arrangement did not present an opportunity for national self-expression.[14]

Yet the BBC was keenly aware of differing motives among those committed to change, and it clearly sought to divide those who advocated a Welsh-language service from those who desired greater autonomy for Welsh broadcasting as a whole.[15] As one of the corporation's pamphlets claimed in 1932:

> There are some who would even say that nothing but Welsh should be broadcast over Wales, but whilst the BBC broadcasts a great deal of Welsh material from its studios each week, it believes that it can best serve Wales by giving also the best of British and international art. In following this policy it believes that it has the support of the vast majority of Welsh people.[16]

The BBC further alleged that there was insufficient interest in either Welsh-language programmes or programmes relating to Wales to merit the creation of a separate service. Indeed, so resolutely were Welsh demands resisted by the BBC that the *Western Mail* questioned whether the corporation actually believed in the existence of Wales as a national entity or even a unified region.[17] What may have incensed opinion was the complacent satisfaction which the BBC took in its concessions to the Welsh language. When, in 1931, the corporation included a Welsh page in its annual report, J. C. Griffith-Jones was singularly unimpressed:

> Consciously or otherwise, the BBC has conveyed the impression that we are rather a troublesome little people, that for such a handful we are rather impertinent in our demands. When the Corporation has given, it is in a somewhat patronising way, and it does not hesitate to use its gifts in evidence against us.[18]

[13] Alun Oldfield Davies, 'Gwilym Davies and Broadcasting' in Ieuan Gwynedd Jones (ed.), *Gwilym Davies, 1879–1955: A Tribute* (Llandysul, 1972), pp. 38–59.
[14] *Western Mail*, 19 April 1934, 13 February 1935.
[15] Ibid., 30 August 1927.
[16] Ibid., 9 December 1932.
[17] Ibid., 16 November 1929.
[18] Ibid., 1 December 1931.

Despite the initial opposition of BBC managers in London, the agitation secured the establishment of Wales as a separate broadcasting region.[19] Its announcement in 1934 led to confident predictions that Wales was on the verge of a revolution in wireless broadcasting. Yet the magnitude of the task facing Wales remained. As the *Western Mail* warned:

> It is not enough to have a Welsh region and a Welsh director. What is now required is that there shall be organised national co-operation to provide the best possible programmes, and this cannot be wholly achieved by the staff, however competent. There is no dearth of talent in Wales, but much of it is waiting to be discovered by the BBC, and to maintain and extend the distinctively Welsh character of the programmes will necessitate the introduction of many newcomers to the microphone.[20]

It is also noticeable that significant issues remained unresolved, among them the extent to which the new regional service should concentrate on the provision of programmes in Welsh. That the sensibilities of Welsh speakers were prominent in the minds of the corporation's managers were reflected in the strenuous efforts made to appoint a Welsh speaker as regional director.[21] The eventual choice, Rhys Hopkin Morris, was regarded as acceptable largely because of his Nonconformist background and his role as a critic of the BBC in the 1920s.[22] Yet, despite his reservations concerning its early activities, Morris was wholeheartedly committed to the BBC and to the principle of retaining a single broadcasting corporation for the whole of Britain. Although he undertook a punishing routine of public engagements throughout Wales in an attempt to keep abreast of the changes in public opinion, his attempts at consultation were increasingly regarded as opportunities to convince leaders of opinion in Wales of the virtues of the corporation rather than occasions for them to voice their grievances. Morris was equally determined that the BBC in Wales should, as a matter of policy, reflect the aspirations of English speakers in Wales and ensure that Welsh would not become the new region's sole medium of broadcasting. In his opinion, an effort should be made to create a broadcasting service which reflected the diversity of Wales and the needs of both linguistic communities.[23] His efforts reaped some rewards, not least in the creation of a small body of producers whose creative capabilities were reflected in the quality of the transmissions from the Cardiff and Swansea studios. They created a confidence in the ability of broadcasters in Wales to provide valuable service and to improve the standing of the BBC among an influential body of Welsh speakers.

---

[19] Ibid., 12 June 1935.
[20] Ibid., 5 July 1937.
[21] Ibid., 25 February 1936.
[22] John Emanuel and D. Ben Rees, *Bywyd a Gwaith Syr Rhys Hopkin Morris* (Llandysul, 1980), pp. 48–58.
[23] *Western Mail*, 16 January 1937.

Following the declaration of war in 1939 the BBC adopted an emergency plan which included the curtailment of Welsh-language broadcasting, partly in order to ensure that one message was relayed throughout the United Kingdom and partly in order to release airwaves by which Allied broadcasts could be conveyed to the Continent. Although the restrictions on Welsh broadcasting were gradually reduced as the war progressed, the Welsh-language service was not fully restored until hostilities ceased. The reaction of Welsh newspapers was unusually muted on the issue. *Yr Herald Cymraeg* did not include wartime broadcasting among its priorities for the defence of Welsh culture in October 1939,[24] while *Y Cymro* conceded the need for emergency measures during the war.[25] The fact that broadcasting activities within the Welsh Region had been drastically curtailed and that a reorganization of broadcasting would occur in peacetime, either to restore the pre-war service or to develop a new provision, meant that broadcasting gained increased prominence as a topic for public debate in Wales as the war drew to a close. Despite the seriousness with which the promoters of Welsh viewed the coming of the radio in the inter-war years, their concern related mainly to its potential effect. The severe economic depression which affected both industrial and rural Wales meant that radio did not penetrate a large number of Welsh homes. By the end of the war, however, radio was no longer the preserve of a minority since the natural desire to gain access to regular news bulletins had led to a dramatic increase in the ownership of private sets. As a result, the debate regarding Welsh broadcasting now had relevance for a far greater number of people.

This debate was given further impetus by the expected reorganization of the service after the war. During this period it was anticipated that the service would be expanded in Wales, but at the same time there were also demands that the service established before the war should be strengthened.[26] Two developments proved crucial to this discussion. Firstly, the establishment of the Welsh Advisory Council of the BBC in 1946 created a focus for many of the arguments concerning the future of broadcasting in Wales and, secondly, the appointment of a committee chaired by Sir William Beveridge in 1949 to examine broadcasting in Britain provided an opportunity for Welsh organizations to consider and articulate their views in relation to the changed circumstances of post-war Britain.

The deliberations of the Advisory Council indicate that although there had been a consensus in Wales in favour of greater autonomy for Welsh broadcasters in the 1930s, there were also deep divisions, relating mainly to the determination of an appropriate balance between the English and Welsh service. The novelist Kate Roberts, a member of the Council, regularly accused its members of being preoccupied with the plight of English speakers in Wales. The task of the BBC in

---

[24] *Yr Herald Cymraeg*, 2 October 1939.
[25] *Y Cymro*, 7 October 1939.
[26] Ibid., 26 January 1942.

seeking to maintain a balance between two conflicting viewpoints was un-enviable.[27] Certainly many leading members of staff believed that, were it not for the language, there would be no fundamental need for a separate Welsh service, an argument which generated animosity among the rising generation of Anglo-Welsh writers who complained, with some justification, that their counterparts who wrote in Welsh were much more likely to have their work broadcast.[28]

These standpoints were vociferously articulated when, in 1945, the leadership of the BBC in Wales passed to Alun Oldfield-Davies, a Welsh speaker with strong Nonconformist allegiances. Oldfield-Davies dominated the corporation's activities for a generation. He developed a pragmatic approach, seeking to secure greater autonomy for Wales by circumventing the influence of London rather than inviting open confrontation. He was certainly aware of the demands of the Welsh speakers, yet he was equally concerned that English speakers might be tempted to tune into the service emanating from the west of England and thus deprive the Welsh service of a potential audience and also deprive those listeners of English-language programmes with a Welsh dimension.[29]

The differing perceptions of the role of broadcasting in Wales were also reflected in submissions made to the Beveridge Committee, the first of four government-appointed committees which considered the role of broadcasting in Britain.[30] The thrust of the deliberations in the Welsh-speaking areas focused on the demand that Wales be granted its own broadcasting corporation. For newspapers such as *Yr Herald Cymraeg*, the issue was of cardinal importance. It devoted considerable editorial comment to the issue, thereby reflecting the renewed concern for the future of the Welsh language and the emphasis placed on the role of broadcasting in its preservation.[31] Undeb Cymru Fydd (the New Wales Union), formed in 1941 and incorporating the National Union of Welsh Societies, also launched a vigorous campaign for greater autonomy for Wales, and eventually advocated the establishment of a separate broadcasting corporation. The demands of Undeb Cymru Fydd reflected Scottish claims for greater freedom in broadcasting, though few Scottish organizations went so far as to demand a separate corporation.[32] In Wales the demand for separation was fuelled by the need to develop a distinctive approach in order to serve a bilingual community.[33]

The view that a Welsh corporation was required in order to promote a stronger sense of Welsh nationality, as well as to strengthen the Welsh language and

---

[27] BBC Wales Archive, 3605.

[28] Ibid.

[29] The Monmouthshire Ratepayers' Association, for instance, urged its members to turn their aerials in the direction of Bristol if they were unhappy with the service from Wales.

[30] The Beveridge Committee (1949), Pilkington Committee (1963), Crawford Committee (1974) and Annan Committee (1977).

[31] *Yr Herald Cymraeg*, 5 August 1946.

[32] *Western Mail*, 19 July 1944.

[33] PRO, HO 254/10.

culture, was actively promoted by a broad coalition in Wales, including Plaid Cymru, the Welsh Parliamentary Party, and a significant number of Welsh local authorities.[34] Support for a separate corporation, however, was by no means unanimous, even within the Welsh-speaking community. *Y Cymro*, a newspaper whose commitment to the language was indisputable, warned against undue haste, declaring that a service devoid of resources and which failed to deliver high-quality programmes would do little for Welsh self-esteem.[35] As a result of this lack of unanimity (and the fact that the BBC made a determined effort to maintain its monopoly over broadcasting), the proposal to grant Wales its own corporation was rejected. Instead, the Welsh Region was granted enhanced status in advance of that given to English regions and equal to that granted to Scotland and Northern Ireland under the new legislation.[36]

The greater part of this debate on broadcasting in Wales was concentrated on the influence and potential of radio. Yet it was already clear that television would eventually become the more powerful broadcasting medium.[37] The provision of Welsh-language programmes after 1953 had an inauspicious beginning,[38] since the BBC was initially reluctant to allow stations outside London to develop television programme-making facilities.[39] This attitude was noted by Aneirin Talfan Davies:

> There is a metropolitan belief, seldom stated in plain honest words, that these [Welsh television programmes] are deviationist exercises by a few romantic Celts on the Cardiff staff. Welsh language programmes either are or are not the obligation of the BBC; according to its charter and crown ministers in parliament they are. Their demands on staff and equipment should therefore be recognised categorically.[40]

A further impetus to the debate concerning television and the language was provided by the development of commercial television after 1955.[41] The ethos of commercial broadcasting was suspect, not least because it was feared that an emphasis on profits and the division of programmes into 'lucrative' and 'loss-making' productions would inevitably mean that few Welsh-language programmes would

---

[34] Ibid.
[35] *Y Cymro*, 18 August 1944, 14 April 1950.
[36] PRO, HO 256/55, HO 256/57.
[37] NLW, Aneirin Talfan Davies Papers, Box 17.
[38] The first programme was broadcast on St David's day 1953 but only a sporadic service was provided until *c*.1956.
[39] *Western Mail*, 12 September 1955.
[40] BBC Wales Archive, 3606/4.
[41] *Y Cymro*, 12 November 1954. The Welsh Labour Group was particularly critical of the introduction of commercial television. Ness Edwards, who was responsible for broadcasting during his period as Postmaster General 1950–1, described commercial television as 'a racket'. *Western Mail*, 30 November 1953.

be provided on the commercial channel.[42] Despite the initial distrust of commercial television, Welsh-language programmes produced by these companies
won admiration and were regarded as imaginative experiments. *Y Cymro*, for
instance, declared that Granada's provision of Welsh programmes was an example
that the BBC would do well to follow,[43] and the service that Television Wales
and West (TWW) provided for Welsh speakers was by no means derisory. Yet by
1960 there was an awareness that neither the BBC nor the existing commercial
companies were providing an adequate service to Welsh viewers.[44] This inspired
an attempt to develop a comprehensive service for Wales: in 1961 a distinctly
Welsh commercial company, Wales West and North (WWN), was established.
WWN (which assumed the name 'Teledu Cymru') was motivated to a large
extent by a desire to limit profits in order to subsidize peak-time Welsh-language
programmes.[45] Its directors included several individuals who had made a notable
contribution to the literary and cultural life of Wales: B. Haydn Williams was a
pioneer of Welsh-medium education in Flintshire, T. I. Ellis was secretary of
Undeb Cymru Fydd, and T. H. Parry-Williams and Thomas Parry were
prominent academics. WWN aimed to produce programmes which were as good
if not better than those of the BBC and its ethos was not characterized by the
avarice which was associated with other commercial companies in this period.
However, the company was hampered by financial and technical difficulties and
by the fact that it had been allocated a broadcasting region which was exceedingly
difficult to serve.[46] In the event, WWN proved a commercial failure and, following its collapse, its region was amalgamated with that of TWW. The experience
created an awareness of the difficulties of broadcasting in Welsh on a commercial
station. The economic reality was that advertising revenue was highest during the
transmission of English programmes and commercial companies were extremely
reluctant to provide Welsh programmes at peak viewing hours.

Partly as a result of the failure of WWN and the fact that a company catering
primarily for a Welsh-speaking audience was not commercially viable, attempts
were made to encourage co-operation between the BBC and commercial
companies in the production of Welsh programmes. The concept of co-operation
was not new, although previous suggestions had been rejected, notably by Lord

---

[42] 'Lucrative' programmes were those which attracted a large audience and hence the ones that
advertisers coveted. 'Loss-making' programmes had fewer viewers and generated less advertising
revenue. Given that Welsh-language programmes had a limited potential audience, they
invariably fell into the latter category.

[43] *Y Cymro*, 19 September 1957.

[44] This view prevailed, especially among supporters of Undeb Cymru Fydd, who held a conference
to discuss the issue in Cardiff in October 1959. This conference was the focus for discussions
which eventually led to the establishment of WWN. PRO, BD 23/50.

[45] *Western Mail*, 26 June 1962.

[46] *Y Cymro*, 14 December 1961, 2 May 1963.

Macdonald[47] and other representatives of the BBC.[48] Alun Oldfield-Davies was initially sympathetic, but he, too, became opposed to the idea and pointed to the inevitable tensions which would arise between the public-service ethos of the BBC and the profit motive of commercial television.[49] As a result, the concept of co-operation in serving the Welsh-speaking community would not be realized for another generation.

It was in this climate that the report of the government-appointed Pilkington Committee on broadcasting in Britain was compiled. Submissions received from Wales were indicative of continuing discontent. In many ways the coalition of organizations seeking to influence opinion in the early 1960s – Urdd Gobaith Cymru (the Welsh League of Youth), Undeb Cymru Fydd and the Court of the National Eisteddfod – were of the same ethos as those which had agitated successfully for changes in the 1930s.[50] The growing frustration within Welsh circles was reflected in the submission made by the television committee of the Court of the University of Wales:

> The few years that have elapsed since the introduction of television have made it abundantly clear that the grievously inadequate space and time given to programmes of a Welsh character, whether in Welsh or in English, under the existing unsatisfactory arrangements must have disastrous consequences for the future survival of the national culture and for the distinctive contributions that Wales can make to the common stock ... The undue absence of things Welsh from the programmes of the television services in Wales must unconsciously affect the attitude of the Welsh people, and especially the young, towards their traditional culture and the language which is its principal organ.[51]

Significantly, the Pilkington Report took full account of those submissions and advocated the establishment of BBC Wales as a television as well as a sound broadcasting unit.[52] Thus, although the commercial companies were to retain the connection between Wales and the west of England, there was at least one service for the whole of Wales.

Despite the important advances secured in the wake of the Pilkington Report, they proved insufficient to meet the demands of an increasingly assertive body of opinion in Wales, most notably that of Cymdeithas yr Iaith Gymraeg (the Welsh Language Society).[53] The Society's campaign concentrated mainly on two aspects of policy. On the one hand, they considered the existing service to be inadequate

---

[47] *Western Mail*, 22 December 1958.
[48] Ibid., 27 September 1961.
[49] Ibid., 30 June 1958.
[50] PRO, BD 23/151.
[51] Ibid.
[52] *Western Mail*, 28 June 1962.
[53] *Y Cymro*, 11 January 1968, 1 February 1968.

because of the limited number of hours reserved for Welsh programmes and the fact that such programmes were broadcast at inconvenient times. On the other hand, they questioned the ethos in which Welsh broadcasters worked, alleging that many became affected by the English culture which derived from metropolitan influences.[54] The BBC adopted a cautious attitude in response to such manifestations of discontent, but both the Broadcasting Council for Wales (BCW), established to replace the Welsh Advisory Council in 1953,[55] and John Rowley, Controller of the BBC in Wales, had acknowledged the desirability of establishing a separate Welsh-language channel by the end of 1971.[56] Within two years the BCW had also committed itself to the concept of working with commercial companies in order to produce programmes for the Welsh service, a decision of great significance for a corporation wedded to the concept of public service broadcasting.[57] Further impetus for the development of a Welsh-language channel was provided by the report of the Crawford Committee, published in November 1974, which supported the immediate establishment of a separate channel. Its recommendations were accepted in principle by the government although it delayed their implementation because of technical difficulties. The government's decision to inquire into these difficulties, however, was believed to be evidence of procrastination and as a result the Welsh Language Society renewed its vigorous campaign for a Welsh channel in August 1975.

Fears that the government was deliberately dragging its feet was one of the major themes of Welsh submissions to the Annan Committee, established in 1974. Attitudes had already been hardened by the fact that the implementation of the policy had been delayed for a second time owing to financial constraints. The sense of frustration felt by many in Wales was expressed by Urdd Gobaith Cymru in its submission:

> As a movement we do not participate in sit-ins or law-breaking activities, but we can, however, understand the sincere feelings of the many Welshmen who are driven to act in this way by the very serious state of affairs prevailing at the present time . . . One prominent Welshman has said that no dictator wishing to make a captive nation forget its identity could have devised a more effective way than the one in which the television and broadcasting services have been developed in Britain. It has also been said that television must be seen to any intelligent Welsh speaker as a machine for brainwashing his children out of their language and culture . . . The people of Wales will tell you that when such a sane and moderate movement as the Urdd talks in such strong language, there must be something radically wrong and that the sooner it is righted the better. We speak on behalf of 50,000 children and young people, their parents, teachers and leaders; we have their interests at heart. We cannot remain silent

[54] BBC Wales Archive, 3453.
[55] *Y Cymro*, 14 April 1971.
[56] Ibid., 11 August 1971.
[57] Ibid., 20 September 1973.

when we witness the erosion and the decline of our national language; it is the time for all of us to make our voices heard and to act in a direct and practical way, strictly within the law of course, before it is too late.[58]

Despite the strength of opinion in support of the concept of a separate Welsh-language channel, the proposal did not gain unanimous support. The Annan Committee received representations which argued that the establishment of the channel constituted an unnecessary expense. A second argument against separation was also waged by a small but significant group whose commitment to the Welsh language was undisputed. In a radio broadcast in 1972, Aneirin Talfan Davies warned of the dangers of establishing a 'Patagonian wilderness' on a separate channel whose inadequate service might fail to attract viewers. At the same time, however, he was deeply suspicious of the motives of some of the leading advocates of the proposal:

When I see Mr George Thomas and Mr Leo Abse, and others of their kind, rushing to embrace Mr Dafydd Iwan, I would suggest that only the most naïve of God's children would be prepared to believe their motives were the same.[59]

In his opinion, the best option was a channel for Wales based on the principles of public service rather than commercial broadcasting, in which Welsh programmes were mixed with programmes in English relating to Wales. Davies was later to modify his position but he did not take a leading part in this aspect of the debate. The doubts he expressed were also robustly advocated by Jac L. Williams, Professor of Education at the University College of Wales, Aberystwyth, and a fervent champion of the Welsh language. His argument focused on the danger of isolating the language on one channel, thereby robbing English speakers in Wales of the opportunity to hear Welsh.[60] In his opinion, separation was a convenient rather than a suitable answer:

A separate channel system would annoy very few people. It may give great satisfaction to a tiny minority of Welsh speakers, but knowing that minority well, I can assure you that it will immediately start complaining of the low quality of the all-Welsh channel. Broadcasting, in my view, should have a more noble aim than soothing the lips and ears of a cultural minority on its deathbed. It should help to extend their culture and promote the revival of the Welsh language by spreading awareness of it among the population in general.[61]

---

[58] PRO, HO 245/714; similar sentiments, usually conveyed in forthright terms, were expressed in submissions by the Gorsedd of the Bards, religious denominations and cultural organizations. PRO, HO 245/745; HO 245/296; HO 245/704.

[59] NLW, Aneirin Talfan Davies Papers, Box 3.

[60] *Y Cymro*, 26 July 1973.

[61] PRO, HO 245/732.

But these arguments failed to secure any significant support. The demand for a separate Welsh channel was an easily understood concept which attracted considerable support from Welsh public leaders and the public at large. The principle was accepted by the government, but when the newly-elected Conservative government reneged on its commitment to the channel, which had been included in its manifesto in 1979, the issue was vigorously debated. The prospect of losing the Welsh channel was greeted with acute disappointment, if not outrage, in many circles in Wales. The National Broadcasting Committee, a body representing fifty Welsh organizations, issued one of its strongest declarations in condemning the policy.[62] A campaign for the non-payment of television licences was launched and the Welsh Language Society entered one of its most active phases, organizing some spectacular demonstrations and winning support from a broad alliance of political groups.[63] The veteran nationalist leader, Gwynfor Evans, threatened a fast unto death unless the government reconsidered and by the summer of 1980 the combination of economic difficulties and the stratagems of language activists meant that Conservative leaders were reluctant to visit Wales.

As a result of these vigorous protests and the pressure exerted by representatives of moderate opinion in Wales, especially the delegation consisting of Lord Cledwyn of Penrhos, Archbishop G. O. Williams and Sir Goronwy Daniel who met the Home Secretary in July 1980, the government was forced to concede a separate Welsh fourth channel. The service was to provide twenty-four hours of programmes a week, ten provided by the BBC, nine by HTV, and five by free-lance independent producers. On 1 November 1982 the new service began its transmissions. For the first time, the BBC engaged in co-operation with commercial companies, an approach which inevitably involved complex agreements involving issues such as advertising and revenue. A different ethos existed within the two sectors and it was clearly necessary to avoid duplication. Despite initial difficulties, for instance in determining the precise demarcation between news gathering (a BBC responsibility) and current affairs (awarded to HTV), a general consensus developed which recognized that the maintenance of a separate service for Welsh speakers in both sound and television broadcasting was the most suitable means by which Welsh speakers could be provided with a comprehensive peak-time service. By the time of the review of the operations of Sianel Pedwar Cymru (S4C) in 1985, the channel had established itself to such a degree that its abandonment was no longer a serious proposition, a view later reaffirmed in the Broadcasting White Paper of December 1988. An important feature of the White Paper was its recognition of the success achieved in providing a high-quality service for a comparatively small audience and the potential for further developments.

---

[62]   *Y Cymro*, 16 October 1979.
[63]   Ibid., 2 October 1979.

There is no doubt that the establishment of S4C invigorated the Welsh language. The media industry provided opportunities for Welsh speakers to conduct their daily work largely through the medium of Welsh. The service also enabled a generation of broadcasters and producers to develop a professional expertise and led to considerable investment in Welsh broadcasting which itself betokened a new confidence in the future of the language. The expansion of the independent sector and the decision to locate the majority of its operations in Welsh-speaking areas, notably in Gwynedd, was responsible for the regeneration of economic activity, and although the media industry did not provide a solution for problems such as rural depopulation and lack of employment opportunities it nevertheless brought some hope to communities which had suffered as a result of their inaccessibility to the manufacturing industry.[64]

The ability of Welsh speakers to maintain a full broadcasting service proved to be a major achievement and, together with the strengthening of the legal status of the language, ranks among the greatest achievements of the Welsh language movement in the twentieth century. The complacent and pusillanimous attitudes of the 1920s were abandoned in the face of constant pressure and vocal agitation. The pressure exerted by nationalist opinion in the 1930s and the Welsh Language Society from the 1960s onwards undoubtedly contributed to these changes. Yet it is also the case that the strenuous efforts of representatives of more moderate opinion in Wales, both inside and outside the broadcasting authorities, were essential to the development of broadcasting in Welsh. It remains to be seen whether broadcasting will contribute to an increase in the number of Welsh speakers or whether its impact will merely arrest the rate of decline of Welsh speakers.

★ ★ ★

In the course of fifty years they have created the audience and the people who demanded and got S4C. It was conceived, not in the protest and mayhem which preceded its birth, but in the years and years of broadcasting from Bryn Meirion.[65]

These words were written by Ifor Bowen Griffith in a tribute to Sam Jones, representative of the BBC in north Wales and doyen of a generation of Welsh broadcasters. The comments could also be applied more broadly to encompass the Welsh-language output of the BBC and the commercial companies in its entirety. Fundamentally, the demand to develop a separate Welsh service was fuelled by the desire for programmes which satisfied differing needs and tastes. This section

[64] *Wales Monthly Monitor*, no. 16 (1988).
[65] Ifor B. Griffith, 'A Personal Note' in Dyfnallt Morgan (ed.), *Babi Sam yn Dathlu Hanner Can Mlynedd o Ddarlledu o Fangor 1935–1985* (Caernarfon and Bangor, 1985), p. 130.

will consider the extent to which this was achieved and will also examine in detail public reaction to a sample of Welsh programmes. It will consider whether such programmes merely mirrored that which was provided by the British network in English or whether they possessed their own distinctive content and style. Moreover, it will examine the reaction of critics and the wider public. Finally, the influence of broadcasting on spoken and written Welsh will also be discussed, especially in relation to the debate between those who advocated broadcasting a standard form of Welsh and those who favoured more colloquial forms.

Throughout the early 1930s those who commented on the BBC in Wales made few references to the actual programmes, although some were irritated by the constraints imposed by the strict regulations of the corporation on the style of programmes. The majority of broadcasts produced in Welsh consisted of talks or lectures, usually of fifteen minutes' duration. Their style was influenced by the literary essay pioneered by T. H. Parry-Williams, who also contributed many broadcast talks. The publication of such talks, in collections such as *Dal Llygoden* and *Trwm ac Ysgafn* by T. J. Morgan or *Meddwn I* and *I Ddifyrru'r Amser* by Ifor Williams, testify to the way in which broadcasting had become a stimulus to Welsh letters.[66] This tradition was maintained in prose and verse for many years after the war, both in radio broadcasts and in anthologies published by the BBC. The launching of the journal *Llafar* under the editorship of Aneirin Talfan Davies in 1951 was a significant landmark which gave such literary creations an important and durable form. The radio talk evolved quickly from the staid and amiable style of *Cymru Ddoe ac Echdoe*, a series presented by the popular preacher and poet, the Revd H. Elvet Lewis (Elfed), to the more outspoken works of scholars such as Thomas Parry and Saunders Lewis,[67] whose contributions did not always conform to the BBC ruling that broadcasters should not be judgemental in their comments or in the material they selected.[68] An equally important tradition was forged with the establishment in 1938 of the BBC's annual lecture, delivered alternately in Welsh and English. These occasions were often milestones in the development of the ideas which shaped contemporary Wales, and people as diverse as W. J. Gruffydd (1938), J. D. Vernon Lewis (1954), T. H. Parry-Williams (1958), Ifor Williams (1960) and Saunders Lewis (1962) seized their opportunity to broadcast penetrating reflections on Wales and the Welsh language.[69]

Despite the more liberated style of radio talk which emerged in the 1930s, the BBC remained vulnerable to accusations that its programmes were bland. This

---

[66] T. J. Morgan, *Dal Llygoden ac Ysgrifau Eraill* (Dinbych, 1937); idem, *Trwm ac Ysgafn: Cyfrol o Ysgrifau* (Caerdydd, 1945); Ifor Williams, *Meddwn I* (Llandybïe, 1944); idem, *I Ddifyrru'r Amser* (Caernarfon, 1959).

[67] *Y Cymro*, 11 September 1937.

[68] *Western Mail*, 2 November 1936.

[69] W. J. Gruffydd's lecture 'Ceiriog', transmitted in 1938, was the first Welsh annual lecture. No annual lectures were delivered between 1939 and 1950.

point was made forcefully by radical commentators, such as 'Dwyryd' of the *Daily Herald*, who complained that the influence of the BBC in London was stultifying Welsh-language programmes, not least by preventing the production of broadcasts which had a distinctively Welsh flavour.[70] In Wales, as in Scotland, the BBC was reluctant to recognize the claims of a specific national identity and, as Paddy Scannell and David Cardiff have argued, there was a failure to appreciate that a distinctive identity generated a need for different types of programmes.[71] These complaints did not disappear when Wales became a broadcasting region in 1937. The BBC's 'Leisure and Listening' conferences regularly witnessed demands for more Welsh programmes.[72] Yet it was more often the case that such meetings heard calls for a change in the nature of what was provided. At a conference in Swansea, Ithel Davies demanded more programmes relating to history, literature and poetry.[73] Gwenan Jones called for a greater number of educational and literary programmes and lamented the decline in programmes relating to social and political subjects.[74] In demanding greater recognition for the traditional Welsh Sabbath, Evan D. Jones argued that religious talks were appropriate programmes for Sunday evenings in Wales.[75] Such representations reflected widely-held views among Welsh cultural leaders. However, John Ellis Williams, a leading figure in the Welsh drama movement, was particularly critical of the extent to which Welsh broadcasting tended to confine itself to religious themes and to neglect light entertainment. His comments concurred with those made by 'Theomemphus', broadcasting critic for *Heddiw*, who made constant references to the disparity between the professional defects of the service and the gifts of amateur performers.[76]

The BBC took active steps to address these cultural needs, notably in the field of Welsh drama. The evolution of Welsh drama had been curtailed in the nineteenth century, partly because Nonconformist opinion had been so hostile to its development. Although a number of local drama groups had emerged in the years immediately after the First World War, production techniques were often rudimentary. There was a dearth of Welsh plays and the issues discussed were often confined to matters such as temperance, immorality and resisting temptation.[77] Most productions were performed to small, if appreciative, audiences, and evoked little critical comment.[78] In the inter-war years, however, striking

[70] *Daily Herald*, 19 December 1936.
[71] Paddy Scannell and David Cardiff, *A Social History of British Broadcasting, Vol. 1, 1922–39: Serving the Nation* (Oxford, 1991), p. 333.
[72] *Western Mail*, 13 February 1935, 4 March 1935.
[73] Ibid., 25 October 1937.
[74] Gwenan Jones, 'Radio Cymru', *Yr Efrydydd*, II, no. 3 (1937), 60–2.
[75] Evan D. Jones, 'Radio Cymru', ibid., III, no. 3 (1938), 46–9.
[76] Theomemphus, 'Drama a Radio', *Heddiw*, II, no. 6 (1937), 221–3.
[77] Idwal Jones, 'Y Ddrama yng Nghymru', *Cambria*, I, no. 1 (1930), 31–2 and D. Haydn Davies, 'Y Ddrama yng Nghymru', ibid., I, no. 7 (1932), 32–5.
[78] Dafydd Gruffydd, 'Radio a Theledu' in Meredydd Evans (ed.), *Gŵr wrth Grefft* (Llandysul, 1974), pp. 48–9.

advances were made. The influence of dramatists such as R. G. Berry and D. T. Davies led to both an improvement in the quality of written works and the consideration of a broader range of topics. In an attempt to encourage further developments, the BBC sponsored a prize at the National Eisteddfod and a series of workshop sessions was organized for the benefit of untutored broadcasters.[79] As a result, the BBC in Wales opened its doors to a wider variety of outside contributors than was the case in England, a factor of crucial importance in the development of Welsh programmes in later years. Moreover, the BBC in Wales commissioned original work. During the course of the legal proceedings arising from the burning of the bombing school at Penyberth, Saunders Lewis was invited to write a play set in the age of the saints. He complied by composing in his cell in Wormwood Scrubs *Buchedd Garmon*, a verse play broadcast on 2 March 1937. Produced by T. Rowland Hughes, with accompanying music by Arwel Hughes, the broadcast provided clear evidence of the high calibre of a small group of producers employed by the BBC in Wales.

The desire to encourage talent which existed outside the corporation's own staff also extended to performers. The valleys of south Wales were combed for suitable Welsh-speaking talent, especially for schools broadcasting,[80] and such initiatives won widespread approval. Collie Knox, the radio correspondent of the *Daily Mail*, was particularly impressed:

> South Wales has taught the BBC a whale of a lesson. If the BBC wishes to keep or to regain any sort of reputation in this country it will clasp this lesson to heart.[81]

These initiatives accorded with the desire of the BBC to integrate broadcasting into the life of the community and were also reflected in the pioneering work of Owen Parry, the corporation's education officer between 1934 and 1937.[82] His efforts were an important influence on the policy of the BBC in the years after the war, especially in the fostering of amateur talent. Yet the most outstanding success was achieved by Sam Jones, the corporation's representative in Bangor. His ability to discover and nurture local talent resulted in some spectacular successes, as will be noted below.[83] Inevitably, however, jealousies between regions and localities arose from the adoption of this policy. Evan D. Jones complained that there were few opportunities to draw on the talent of mid-Wales since the studio at

[79] Huw Ethall, *R. G. Berry: Dramodydd, Llenor, Gweinidog* (Abertawe, 1985), pp. 37–61; *Y Cymro*, 14 August 1937; *Western Mail*, 15 September 1938.

[80] John Davies, *Broadcasting and the BBC in Wales* (Cardiff, 1994), p. 116.

[81] *Daily Mail*, 22 February 1937.

[82] *Western Mail*, 31 October 1934. Owen Parry developed close links with organizations such as the Council for Social Service in south Wales and was particularly active in encouraging unemployed groups as listeners and potential contributors.

[83] *North Wales Pioneer*, 3 December 1936; Robin Williams, 'Y Noson Lawen' in Morgan (ed.), *Babi Sam*, pp. 83–92; R. Alun Evans, *Stand By! Bywyd a Gwaith Sam Jones* (Llandysul, 1998).

Aberystwyth was utterly inadequate.[84] Likewise, drama groups in north Wales, led by Albert Evans-Jones (Cynan), complained that, despite the best efforts of Sam Jones, the north was seriously under-represented and the airwaves dominated by southern accents.[85] Such petty jealousies apart, and despite the adverse comments of élitists who believed that utilizing 'amateur' actors was likely to lead to reduced standards, the inclusion of local talent became one of the strengths of Welsh broadcasting in the Welsh language and, to a lesser extent, in English.[86]

Following the outbreak of war in 1939, two developments occurred within Welsh-language broadcasting which would prove to be of considerable importance in later years. Firstly, a new impetus was given to the process of establishing a standard form of Welsh which was understood by people in all localities. The curse of mongrel Welsh had been a source of considerable vexation to commentators from the beginnings of Welsh broadcasting.[87] Welsh lacked equivalents for many technical and modern terms and there was a pressing need to develop a form of standard Welsh which balanced dialect and 'pulpit Welsh'. This issue was of particular relevance during the war since words which had no Welsh equivalent, like air raid, aeroplane and ration, became common currency. Remarkable progress was made in this respect, largely through the efforts of Alun Llywelyn-Williams, who regarded the modernization of the Welsh vocabulary and the identification of an appropriate spoken idiom as essential to the success of Welsh broadcasting.[88]

A second development which proved crucial to the success of Welsh-language broadcasting occurred in response to the government's directive to produce popular programmes which would keep public morale buoyant in the face of wartime adversity. The new emphasis was evident in *Sut Hwyl* (BBC, launched in 1942), a miscellany produced in Swansea by John Griffiths, which sought to provide a Welsh counterpart to the popular ITMA programme.[89] *Sut Hwyl* demonstrated that Welsh programmes were not necessarily concerned with dry-as-dust matters and it helped to secure a younger audience.[90] Part of the success of *Sut Hwyl* also lay in the fact that it was largely written and presented by leaders of amateur dramatic societies in the Swansea area, a factor which gave the programmes a distinctive humour and idiom.

[84] Jones, 'Radio Cymru', 46–9.
[85] *Manchester Guardian*, 11 May 1936.
[86] *Carnarvon and Denbigh Herald*, 6 February 1937.
[87] BBC Wales Archive, 3605.
[88] Ibid., 3463; *Daily Express*, 23 September 1938; Alun Llywelyn-Williams, 'Y Gymraeg ar y Radio', *Y Llenor*, XIX, no. 3 (1940), 143–54 and idem, *Gwanwyn yn y Ddinas* (Dinbych, 1975), pp. 111–57.
[89] The degree to which the more élitist elements in Wales recoiled from the popularity of Tommy Handley and the ITMA team among Welsh speakers is illustrated by John Roberts Williams in *Y Cymro*, 14 and 21 January 1949.
[90] *South Wales Evening Post*, 20 October 1952.

This experiment continued to enrich Welsh broadcasting during the immediate post-war years and provided an alternative to the restrained, almost patrician, style which had been encouraged by the BBC in London. In this respect, Welsh broadcasting owed a particular debt to Sam Jones. His liberal outlook emphasized the benefits that would accrue by making the airwaves accessible to local talent. But he also insisted on rigorous standards of writing and presentation.[91] His aim was to ensure that Welsh programmes were a source of enjoyment and enlightenment to audiences and that no longer would people be obliged to listen to an inferior programme out of a sense of duty. Moreover, he ensured that the Welsh service had sufficient material in order to justify the demand for more hours.[92] Under his guidance Bangor emerged as a school for new talent which initially expressed itself through the popular *Noson Lawen* (BBC). Broadcast on Saturday nights from various local halls, *Noson Lawen* attracted a wide audience throughout Wales, mainly as a result of its freshness and the variety of talents displayed by gifted contributors like 'Triawd y Coleg' (Meredydd Evans, Robin Williams and Cledwyn Jones), who specialized in light music, presenters such as Huw Jones, and the impressionist, Richard Hughes (Y Co' Bach), who specialized in monologues in the dialect of Caernarfon.[93] Significantly, the highly localized nature of the programme did not affect its popularity in other areas of Wales. The imaginative approach developed in Wales was also evident in outside broadcasts such as *Brethyn Cartref* (BBC, 1950),[94] a series which reflected the wealth of talent and enthusiasm which existed within Welsh-speaking communities and which also provided an impetus for many local cultural groups on which they depended.[95]

Significant progress was also made in two other areas of activity. Firstly, the service for children was consolidated by building on the foundations of *Awr y Plant* (BBC, launched in 1939), produced initially by Nest Jenkins and later by Nan Davies. *Awr y Plant* was revitalized in the years immediately after the war and made an immeasurable contribution to nurturing the young in the Welsh language. *Jim Cro Crwstyn* (BBC, 1955), a request programme for children and *Wil Cwac Cwac* (BBC, 1953), won widespread critical approval and maintained the homely ways which had characterized the production of *Awr y Plant*.[96] *Galw Gari Tryfan* (BBC, 1952) was a pioneering attempt to provide a detective serial for

---

[91] *Cambrian News*, 21 June 1946; *Y Cymro*, 26 July 1946.

[92] Gruffydd, 'Radio a Theledu' in Evans (ed.), *Gŵr wrth Grefft*, p. 50.

[93] British Broadcasting Corporation, *Annual Report and Accounts for the Year 1950–51* (London, 1951) (PP 1950–1 (Cmd. 8347) VIII), pp. 34–5; Williams, 'Y Noson Lawen' in Morgan (ed.), *Babi Sam*, pp. 83–92.

[94] British Broadcasting Corporation, *Annual Report and Accounts for the Year 1953–54* (London, 1954) (PP 1953–4 (Cmd. 9269) X), pp. 40–2; other programmes of a similar nature included *Ein Pentre Ni* (BBC, 1950), *Curwch Hon* (BBC, 1950) and *Raligamps* (BBC, 1951).

[95] British Broadcasting Corporation, *Annual Report and Accounts for the Year 1950–51*, pp. 34–5.

[96] Idem, *Annual Report and Accounts for the Year 1953–54*, pp. 40–2; idem, *Annual Report and Accounts for the Year 1955–56* (London, 1956) (PP 1955–6 (Cmd. 9803) XI), pp. 124–6.

children in Welsh. Despite some trite use of language, it succeeded in securing a loyal audience among a generation of older children who were particularly vulnerable at that time to the powerful Anglicizing influences of the cinema and English-medium popular culture. The determination of Welsh broadcasters to encourage the use of Welsh among young people was also reflected in numerous programmes which offered the opportunity to express views on air. *Llwyfan yr Ifanc* (BBC, 1952),[97] *Ymryson Areithio* (BBC, 1955),[98] and *Clorian yr Ifanc* (BBC, 1956)[99] provided opportunities for expression which had not been enjoyed by any previous generation of Welsh speakers and also familiarized them with the techniques of broadcasting.[100]

Sports coverage was the second domain captured by Welsh broadcasting in this period. The service was pioneered in a Saturday-evening programme broadcast from the Swansea studio, in which Eic Davies and Jack Elwyn Watkins reviewed the day's events on the rugby field and offered shrewd and sometimes improbable advice to Welsh selectors. The sports service rapidly established itself as an integral part of Welsh radio and made an immense contribution by providing Welsh equivalents for words such as lock ('clo'), outside-half ('maswr') and second row ('ail reng') which became common currency in a very short period of time. Gradually the Welsh sports service was expanded, initially to cover association football and later to a range of sports in highly specialized coverage. Indeed, following the establishment of S4C, sport became one of the strongest areas of Welsh-medium provision and, as the channel secured the sole direct transmission rights to certain events, it succeeded in attracting viewers who might not otherwise have tuned in.

Advances in entertainment, children's programmes and sports coverage in the period immediately after the Second World War coincided with a determined effort to expand Welsh drama in four ways. The BBC commissioned original material written specifically for broadcasting; it commissioned translations of the great dramatic works of Europe; it produced drama series based on adaptations of existing literary works and new material; and it broadcast celebrated Welsh stage plays.[101] Some of the best works of Welsh literature were presented in successful adaptations of *William Jones* (BBC, 1946) and *Chwalfa* (BBC, 1948), both novels by T. Rowland Hughes, a former producer with the BBC in Wales who was fully conversant with the techniques of writing for radio.[102] The BBC also broadcast

---

[97] Idem, *Annual Report and Accounts for the Year 1952–53* (London, 1953) (PP 1952–3 (Cmd. 8928) VII), pp. 92–3.

[98] Idem, *Annual Report and Accounts for the Year 1955–56*, pp. 124–6.

[99] Ibid.

[100] Idem, *Annual Report and Accounts for the Year 1958–59* (London, 1959) (PP 1958–9 (Cmd. 834) IX), pp. 130–2.

[101] Gruffydd, 'Radio a Theledu' in Evans (ed.), *Gŵr wrth Grefft*, p. 52.

[102] British Broadcasting Corporation, *Annual Report and Accounts for the Year 1948–49* (London, 1949) (PP 1948–9 (Cmd. 7779) XII), pp. 16–17; Edward Rees, *T. Rowland Hughes: Cofiant* (Llandysul, 1968), pp. 141–2.

adaptations of other Welsh literary classics such as *Gŵr Pen y Bryn* (1952) by
E. Tegla Davies and *Tywyll Heno* (1960) by Kate Roberts.[103] Lighter drama was
also expanded through the popular *Teulu Tŷ Coch* (BBC, 1951), a serial based on
everyday life and presented in colloquial Welsh.[104] The cast was largely drawn
from the same amateur circles which had become prominent in *Sut Hwyl* during
the war, and the success of the programme lay in its ability to attract a loyal
audience in industrial areas which were swiftly Anglicizing.[105] The series continued until 1952[106] when it gave way to *Teulu'r Siop* (BBC, 1955), an equally
successful venture which followed a similar format to *Teulu Tŷ Coch*, though
based on village life in north Wales.[107] The emphasis on indigenous literature did
not prevent the BBC from providing a broader cultural experience through the
medium of Welsh. Several translations into Welsh of some of the classics of
European literature were commissioned, notably a translation of *Antigone* (BBC,
1950) by W. J. Gruffydd and Saunders Lewis's translation of *Le Médecin Malgré Lui*
by Molière (BBC, 1950).[108] An outstanding contribution to Welsh literature was
also secured with the commissioning of verse plays broadcast in the *Pryddestau
Radio* series (BBC, 1951). Works such as *Angau* (1951) by Rhydwen Williams and
Sŵn y Gwynt sy'n Chwythu (1952) by J. Kitchener Davies figure among the classic
literature of modern Wales and certainly contributed to the consolidation of the
role of the BBC as the patron of creative Welsh writing in the immediate post-
war years.

Such productions required performers conversant with the techniques of
broadcasting. As a result, a small group of people was retained, usually on a part-
time basis, to take part in drama productions and other broadcasts. The majority
were not professional broadcasters and consequently the amateur element played a
far more important role in Welsh broadcasting than was the case in England.[109]
Although academics and ministers of religion formed an appreciable proportion of
the amateur element, an effort was clearly made to develop the talent of the
community as a whole and to include the cultured *gwerin* in the programmes. This
was entirely consistent with the outlook of Aneirin Talfan Davies and Alun
Oldfield-Davies and was best exemplified in the efforts of Sam Jones in Bangor

---

[103] British Broadcasting Corporation, *Annual Report and Accounts for the Year 1969–70* (London, 1970)
(PP 1970–1 (Cmnd. 4520) VI), pp. 191–4; D. Tecwyn Lloyd, 'Y Nofelydd' in Islwyn Ffowc Elis
(ed.), *Edward Tegla Davies: Llenor a Phroffwyd* (Lerpwl, 1956), pp. 84–105; Huw Ethall, *Tegla*
(Abertawe, 1980), pp. 45–214.

[104] British Broadcasting Corporation, *Annual Report and Accounts for the Year 1951–52* (London, 1952)
(PP 1951–2 (Cmd. 8660) VIII), pp. 37–9.

[105] *Western Mail*, 3 November 1952.

[106] *South Wales Evening Post*, 1 July 1952.

[107] British Broadcasting Corporation, *Annual Report and Accounts for the Year 1955–56*, pp. 40–2.

[108] Idem, *Annual Report and Accounts for the Year 1950–51*, pp. 34–5.

[109] Geoff Mulgan, 'Culture' in David Marquand and Anthony Seldon (eds.), *The Ideas that Shaped
Post-war Britain* (London, 1996), p. 205.

and John Griffiths in Swansea.[110] There was general agreement among Welsh commentators that the airwaves should be more genuinely reflective of the community which they served and that listeners should not become passive recipients of programmes conceived by a small, insular, professional group of broadcasters. These were worthy ideals, but it would be wrong to regard the Welsh Region of the BBC as a pioneer of a new form of broadcasting. The emphasis on amateur contributions owed much to the dearth of professional performers and writers and the extent of popular participation should not be exaggerated since it was mainly confined to the realm of light entertainment. More serious talks and, with few exceptions, discussion programmes were monopolized by the intellectual élite in Wales, as was the case in England. As more resources became available, Welsh broadcasting became increasingly professional and the reliance on community participation was slowly abandoned.[111] The fact that the Welsh broadcasting authorities opted for professionalism rather than amateurism – the approach favoured by Sam Jones – meant that one avenue along which a distinctive Welsh broadcasting style might have been developed was closed.

Television became a substantial factor in the expansion of salaried broadcasting in Wales and led to radical changes in the techniques of broadcasting and the nature and content of programmes. In August 1954 the BBC was deprived of its monopoly in relation to television broadcasting and now faced competition from the powerful, populist service provided by commercial companies. Their programmes were characterized by a bold, racy style which contrasted sharply with the rather earnest and staid productions of the BBC. Initially, Welsh broadcasters were denied the opportunity to contribute to the development of the new medium. Welsh programmes were largely confined to the occasional sermon on St David's day[112] and experimental adaptations of Welsh short stories.[113] In contrast, the Welsh service provided by the commercial sector in the late 1950s was more satisfying. From the outset, commercial television was intended to develop a provincial style and the contracts of commercial companies stipulated their obligation to provide programmes which reflected the distinctive characteristics of the regions they served. Neither TWW nor Granada was primarily concerned with the development of a service for Wales, but their service to Welsh speakers was not derisory and in many ways was more extensive than that provided by the BBC. Granada (a company noted for its commitment to the

---

[110] *Western Mail*, 14 November 1949.

[111] This occurred at a time when commentators such as Raymond Williams began to advocate the principle of accessible, democratic broadcasting as a matter of policy rather than as a financial expedient. Raymond Williams, *Communications* (London, 1962), pp. 111–29.

[112] British Broadcasting Corporation, *Annual Report and Accounts for the Year 1953–54*, pp. 40–2.

[113] For instance, *Cap Wil Tomos* by Islwyn Williams was broadcast in 1955. Williams was an experienced short story writer who had written considerable material for radio; British Broadcasting Corporation, *Annual Report and Accounts for the Year 1955–56*, pp. 124–6.

production of programmes with a distinctive regional flavour)[114] and TWW began pioneering work for Welsh television by transmitting magazine programmes such as *Amser Te* (TWW, 1958)[115] and *Dewch i Mewn* (Granada, 1958).[116] Both programmes demonstrated considerable initiative and a willingness to experiment with a variety of techniques and subjects and, despite the rather contrived format, *Dewch i Mewn*, in particular, proved to be a worthy effort, largely because of the personal appeal of presenters such as Rhydwen Williams, D. Jacob Davies and John Ellis Williams.[117]

These efforts provided a fresh impetus to the development of the BBC's Welsh television service which progressed apace following the Pilkington Report. One notable feature of this expansion was the increase in the number of permanently employed personnel in Welsh broadcasting. Actors such as Rachel Thomas, Dilys Davies and Charles Williams were now able to concentrate on work in the Welsh language, while other actors who had participated in pioneering work in Welsh sound drama were also recruited to television. Although many of these recruits had received little formal initial training, they took part in several acclaimed productions, demonstrating great versatility and a sound command of both colloquial and standard Welsh. The expansion of Welsh drama personnel coincided with the expansion of the Welsh news and current affairs service. This process was assisted by the recruitment of some of the finest print journalists in Wales such as John Roberts Williams, T. Glynne Davies and Harri Gwynn.[118] Although broadcast journalism was undoubtedly enriched by their arrival, it was also the case that the strict rules of impartiality imposed upon broadcasters deprived Wales of the benefit of the opinions of seasoned and perceptive commentators in a period when mature analysis and reflection were often lacking.

The expansion which occurred in this period resulted in a remarkable increase both in the quantity and the quality of Welsh programmes. Indeed, several successful productions indicate the extent to which the Welsh-language television service had matured in a relatively short period of time. The topical programme *Heddiw* (BBC, launched in 1963) was a notable success, partly because of the way in which it combined news with more general items and also because it identified salient social trends. The fresh approach seen in *Heddiw* was also apparent in a number of acclaimed documentaries, most notably *O Tyn y Gorchudd* (BBC, 1964), a programme which examined the lives of three blind brothers from Dinas

[114] Caroline Moorhead, *Sidney Bernstein* (London, 1984), pp. 244–6.

[115] British Broadcasting Corporation, *Annual Report and Accounts for the Year 1966–67* (London, 1967) (PP 1966–7 (Cmnd. 3425) XXIII), pp. 162–5.

[116] *Y Cymro*, 8 June 1961. Both programmes contained a miscellany of Welsh songs, items on food or travel, and conversations with prominent individuals.

[117] John Ellis Williams, *Inc yn fy Ngwaed* (Llandybïe, 1963), pp. 134–7; Donald Evans, *Rhydwen Williams* (Cardiff, 1991), pp. 20–9.

[118] The background to these appointments is given in John Roberts Williams, *Yr Eiddoch yn Gywir* (Pen-y-groes, 1990), p. 144.

Mawddwy,[119] *Ymhell o Bwyl* (BBC, 1964), a study of the Polish community in the Llŷn peninsula which had ostracized itself from the rest of the community,[120] and *Y Llygad Coch* (BBC, 1965), a particularly moving portrayal of life in the Nantlle valley.[121] Another success in this period was *Nant Dialedd*, a documentary notable for the quality of the camera work of Wil Aaron. Aaron was influenced by the work of the Italian producer Zavattini, who was committed to the development of a television equivalent to the kind of accessible, representative broadcasting culture which had been advocated in relation to sound broadcasting in the late 1940s and 1950s. Such work was restricted by the regulations of the BBC and by the resistance of professional broadcasters to the inclusion of amateur performers. As a result, the notion of democratic broadcasting had limited impact on the philosophy of Welsh broadcasters.[122] The gradual improvement in the quality of Welsh-language television was not confined to the BBC. Commercial companies developed a different but no less successful news and current affairs service in Welsh. *Y Dydd* (TWW, launched in 1963) was admired for its imaginative presentation of news, especially its use of captions and film. Likewise, *Yr Wythnos* (TWW, launched in 1963), a current affairs auxiliary to *Y Dydd*, became noted for the quality of presentation and also for its mature and candid examination of events.[123]

Another notable feature of this period was the emergence of the BBC as a patron of creative writing in Welsh. Considerable sums of money were paid each year to writers for poems, drama, essays, talks, feature programmes and other broadcast material during a period when full-time Welsh writers were otherwise largely unsupported. As Aneirin Talfan Davies proudly proclaimed, the BBC in Wales was:

> a loyal patron and supporter of the community in all its multifarious activities. It has done this not only because it has recognised Wales as an entity. It has always been conscious that it is serving a nation with a language of its own, traditions of its own, and all this symbolised in national institutions . . . The advent of the BBC gave to the writer in the Welsh language a market for his products; and more than a market, it gave him adequate payment for his labours. If you have been a constant reader of journals and books in the Welsh language during the last quarter of a century, you cannot have helped noticing how much they have owed to the existence of the BBC as a patron of the arts. This has been, perhaps, one of the more worthwhile functions of the BBC in a country where the language is in decline. I believe it to be worthwhile because I believe the maintenance of the Welsh language in Wales is of the utmost importance not only for the sake of Welsh speaking Wales, but for the whole of the nation, whether they use it or not.[124]

[119] *Y Cymro*, 15 October 1964.
[120] Ibid., 9 April 1964.
[121] Ibid., 14 October 1965.
[122] Wil Aaron, 'Byd y Ffilmio' in Evans (ed.), *Gŵr wrth Grefft*, p. 64.
[123] *Y Cymro*, 26 May 1971.
[124] NLW, Aneirin Talfan Davies Papers, Box 3.

Writers such as John Gwilym Jones,[125] John Ellis Williams, Idwal Jones and Islwyn Ffowc Elis[126] rapidly established themselves as writers for sound broadcasting in the 1950s and the flowering of Welsh sound drama undoubtedly contributed to the later success of its televised equivalents. Apart from commissioning new works, the BBC also continued its practice of producing successful television adaptations of Welsh literary works. A television adaptation of *Chwalfa* (BBC, 1966) met with considerable critical acclaim[127] and there was also a favourable reception for *Lleifior* (BBC, 1969), a series based on *Cysgod y Cryman* and *Yn Ôl i Leifior*, two novels by Islwyn Ffowc Elis.[128] Other works, notably those written by John Gwilym Jones and Islwyn Ffowc Elis, indicated the willingness of Welsh broadcasters to produce material which challenged traditional notions of Wales and which examined more controversial aspects of life.[129] These had much in common with the social realism of English film productions of the late 1950s and early 1960s and, although the urban and industrial experiences of Wales were initially neglected, they represented a desire to offer a candid portrait of life in the most Welsh-speaking areas and did not flinch from considering the less savoury aspects of life in those communities. The 1960s witnessed the emergence of honest and realistic characterizations which challenged the deferential tradition of British broadcasting.[130] This development was consolidated in *Broc Môr* (BBC, 1968), which posed important questions about the relationship between the emerging class of Welsh professionals and the community values they endorsed but no longer sustained.[131] The work of a new generation of writers included plays by Gwenlyn Parry, especially *Tŷ ar y Tywod* (BBC, 1969) and a later production, *Y Tŵr* (BBC, 1980), works noted for their simple format (each included only three characters) and their effective consideration of the significance of religious faith in a modern context.[132] The erosion of the traditional concept of Welshness (especially the decline of Nonconformity) was strongly reflected in these works and was also evident in sound drama, notably in *Yr Oedfa* (BBC, 1971) by John Gwilym Jones.

These challenging works were the precursors of other plays, broadcast in the late 1970s and early 1980s, which reflected a more general sense of social

---

[125] British Broadcasting Corporation, *Annual Report and Accounts for the Year 1967–68* (London, 1968) (PP 1967–8 (Cmnd. 3779) XVII), pp. 170–4; John Rowlands, 'Agweddau ar Waith John Gwilym Jones' in J. E. Caerwyn Williams (ed.), *Ysgrifau Beirniadol III* (Dinbych, 1967), p. 223.

[126] Gerwyn Wiliams, 'Holi Doethor Lleifior', *Taliesin*, 82 (1993), 14–20.

[127] British Broadcasting Corporation, *Annual Report and Accounts for the Year 1966–67*, pp. 170–4.

[128] Idem, *Annual Report and Accounts for the Year 1969–70*, pp. 191–4.

[129] Idem, *Annual Report and Accounts for the Year 1964–65* (London, 1966) (PP 1965–6 (Cmnd. 2823) IV), pp. 174–5; among the most notable were *Pry Ffenast* (BBC, 1964) and *Gŵr Llonydd* (BBC, 1966) by John Gwilym Jones, *Gwanwyn Diweddar* (BBC, 1964) by Islwyn Ffowc Elis and *Cariad Creulon* (BBC, 1966) by R. Bryn Williams.

[130] David Cardiff and Paddy Scannell, 'Broadcasting and National Unity' in James Curran, Anthony Smith and Pauline Wingate (eds.), *Impacts and Influences: Essays on Media Power in the Twentieth Century* (London, 1987), p. 170.

[131] *Y Cymro*, 8 August 1968.

[132] Dewi Z. Phillips, *Dramâu Gwenlyn Parry: Astudiaeth* (Caernarfon, 1982), pp. 13–65, 92–131; *Y Cymro*, 2 January 1969.

disillusionment.[133] By their very nature, such works were bound to generate a variety of responses. Most of the drama productions of the late 1970s and early 1980s were written by a new generation of Welsh writers and many rejected the traditional perceptions of Wales. More secular and worldly, the plays were regularly placed in an urban context and often examined the darker side of the human character. The outstanding feature of such works was their maturity and lack of inhibition. Adaptations of Welsh novels also created several successful series. One of the most successful developments occurred in the field of historical drama, with notable adaptations of *Y Stafell Ddirgel* (BBC, 1971)[134] and *Y Rhandir Mwyn* (BBC, 1973) by Marion Eames, and *Enoc Huws* (BBC, 1975), based on the novel by the nineteenth-century author Daniel Owen.[135] The success of these series was based on the strength of the writing and the willingness of the BBC to devote considerable resources to period drama. Considerable advances were also made in the field of light entertainment, an aspect of broadcasting which had received much adverse criticism in the late 1950s and early 1960s. The shortcomings of Welsh entertainment contrasted sharply with popular programmes available in English, especially those produced by the commercial sector. In response, the commercial company, TWW, developed a format which included a significant amount of comedy, games and light-hearted interviews,[136] a modern approach which guaranteed a substantial audience for commercial television in Wales. However, such programmes lacked any distinctive Welsh characteristics or any creative originality,[137] and it is also noticeable that the content of programmes changed little over the years. For instance, programmes such as *Hamdden, Dan Sylw* and *Ble yn y Byd*, broadcast by HTV in 1976, were in essence no different from *Cymru fy Ngwlad, Dringo'r Ysgol* and *Amser Swper* broadcast by TWW ten years earlier.[138]

Within the BBC major changes were initiated during these years. Welsh light entertainment was reinvigorated following the appointment of Dr Meredydd Evans as its head. Evans, who joined the corporation in 1963, was remembered as one of the most popular entertainers in the *Noson Lawen* broadcasts from Bangor in the late 1940s, and he appreciated the value of the amateur talent which had been the cornerstone of the programmes produced by Sam Jones. At the same time, he recognized the need to combine that tradition with a modern approach

[133] *Y Faner*, 24 March 1978, 12 and 26 December 1980. Among these works were *Mater o Egwyddor* (BBC, 1978) by R. Gerallt Jones, *Nos Sadwrn Bach* (BBC, 1980) by Michael Povey, and *Marwolaeth yr Asyn o'r Fflint* (BBC, 1980) and *Y Graith* (BBC, 1980) by Siôn Eirian.

[134] *Y Cymro*, 17 February 1971.

[135] Ibid., 13 May 1975.

[136] Ibid., 5 July 1962.

[137] For instance, *Siôn a Siân* was one of the most popular programmes to be broadcast on TWW (and later on HTV). Its format mirrored that of *Mr and Mrs*, also produced by HTV and broadcast on the network.

[138] Davies, *Broadcasting and the BBC in Wales*, p. 270.

to light entertainment. Having first-hand experience of the dangers of the commercially-orientated entertainment dominant in the United States, he rejected the notion that Welsh light entertainment should consist of pale imitations of English programmes. He was determined to ensure that Wales developed its own style and several groundbreaking programmes were launched which revitalized this aspect of Welsh broadcasting. *Stiwdio B* (BBC, 1966), which bore a passing resemblance to the English satirical miscellany *That Was The Week That Was*, became renowned as a bold, satirical programme not averse to upsetting fastidious commentators.[139] *Stiwdio B* introduced a number of new personalities, notably Ryan Davies,[140] Ronnie Williams, Hywel Gwynfryn and Derek Boote, who were to play a major role in the development of light programmes such as *Hob y Deri Dando* (BBC, 1965), *Disc a Dawn* (BBC, 1969), and *Alaw ac Olwen* (BBC, 1969).[141] Although such programmes included traditional elements like Welsh folk music, they were presented in the modern idiom.[142] Considerable progress was also made in the field of comedy. Ryan Davies and Ronnie Williams proved to be immensely successful, partly because their routine combined the popular format of English comedy pairs with a Welsh-based humour. The success of *Ryan a Ronnie* coincided with several popular situation comedies: *Y Dyn Swllt* (BBC, 1964), the tribulations of a clothes club collector,[143] and *Ifas y Tryc* (BBC, launched in 1966), the exploits of a rural lorry owner,[144] both of which were written by W. S. Jones (Wil Sam)[145] and starred two excellent character actors, Charles Williams and Stewart Jones.[146] The most successful comedy of this period, however, was *Fo a Fe* (BBC, 1970), written by Gwenlyn Parry and Rhydderch Jones. The success of the comedy derived from its clever use of three points of friction – the relationship between the generations, the conflicting lifestyles of the club and the chapel, and the contrasting perceptions of the people of north and south Wales. Each element could have provided the basis for a comedy series but, skilfully combined, they ensured that the programme enjoyed unprecedented success. Most of all, its success was based on situations which were distinctive to the Welsh experience.

Welsh broadcasters fulfilled another long-standing ambition by producing a successful serial chronicling daily life, a genre which invariably required a sizeable

---

[139] *Y Cymro*, 5 August 1965.

[140] Rhydderch Jones, *Cofiant Ryan* (Abertawe, 1979), pp. 52–72.

[141] British Broadcasting Corporation, *Annual Report and Accounts for the Year 1969–70*, pp. 191–4; the success of *Disc a Dawn* was even more remarkable considering the low fees paid to artists. In 1972, for instance, it was reported that a professional artist received only £10 for twelve hours' work. Given such a budget, the standards achieved were remarkable.

[142] British Broadcasting Corporation, *Annual Report and Accounts for the Year 1964–65*, pp. 174–5.

[143] *Y Cymro*, 1 October 1964.

[144] Ibid., 7 April 1966.

[145] Gwenno Hywyn (ed.), *Wil Sam* (Caernarfon, 1985).

[146] *Y Cymro*, 16 January 1969. Individual productions, like *Y Drwmwr* (BBC, 1969), based on the work of Islwyn Williams, were also praised for their humour and perceptiveness.

cast and the commitment of considerable resources to a single series. The BBC had attempted a project of this nature with *Byd a Betws* (BBC, 1967),[147] a series which drew some criticism because of its dated portrayal of Welsh life. This was eventually abandoned, as was another effort, *Tresarn* (BBC, 1971).[148] The third initiative, *Pobol y Cwm* (BBC, launched in 1974), proved more durable mainly because its cast included experienced actors and because of its simple format and credible characters. Although the standard of the dialogue often drew adverse comment, the programme was able to provide an authentic representation of a Welsh community without overtly adopting a moralistic or crusading stance.[149] Initially launched as a weekly series broadcast during the autumn and winter months, *Pobol y Cwm* rapidly established itself among the most popular programmes in Welsh and eventually the series was able to sustain a daily presentation throughout the year. By the 1990s the total number of viewers of *Pobol y Cwm* was much greater than that of any other television programme in Welsh. Despite this success, the standard of Welsh television programmes in the late 1970s and early 1980s fluctuated and the variety of responses was undoubtedly fuelled by the fact that the Welsh service sought to cater for all tastes and all age groups. The truth is, however, that Welsh television broadcasters lacked the resources to provide a comprehensive service which would satisfy all tastes, a defect which strengthened the campaign for a separate Welsh service.

The inadequate television service provided in this period contrasted sharply with the commendable sound service provided in Welsh. Following its launch in 1977 Radio Cymru demonstrated that Welsh broadcasting possessed the talent to sustain an extensive service. It was responsible for launching highly successful initiatives such as the morning programme, *Helô Bobol* (BBC, launched in 1977), presented in a light-hearted manner by Hywel Gwynfryn, and in light entertainment with programmes such as *Pupur a Halen* (BBC, 1981) a witty satire which proved successful at a time when television entertainment was at its weakest. *Talwrn y Beirdd* (BBC, 1977) used a format reminiscent of the 1950s, but was eminently successful, largely because of the instinctive humour and the natural talent evident in the contributions of the poets. Despite the undoubted quality of the radio service, the audience was still limited by the fact that the new service was largely confined to daytime and early evening. Broadcasting authorities might have stressed the continued importance of sound in their planning, but television possessed the more powerful influence.

The launch of S4C in 1982 posed new challenges to Welsh television broadcasters who were required to demonstrate that a twenty-four hour service could be sustained by Welsh speakers and that the quality of the programmes

---

[147] *Y Cymro*, 4 May 1967.
[148] Ibid., 17 November 1971.
[149] *Y Faner*, 4 May 1979.

would compare favourably with those provided by other channels. The prospects offered by the new channel fired the imagination of a significant body of Welsh speakers because of the opportunities they offered for experimentation and expansion. The viewing figures for the first months of S4C and the reaction of the television critics indicated that the public in general approved of the programmes and the resources which had been allocated to the enterprise.[150] The news and current affairs provision on the new channel was widely acclaimed, most notably the detailed investigations of *Y Byd ar Bedwar* (HTV, launched in 1982) and the humorous way in which serious topics were discussed by *Y Byd yn ei Le* (HTV, 1982). A popular but well-researched historical series, *Almanac* (Ffilmiau'r Nant, launched in 1982), attracted a wide audience both on account of the peerless style of its presenter, Hywel Teifi Edwards, and the variety of topics discussed.[151] Its producers were later responsible for *Hel Straeon* (Ffilmiau'r Nant, launched in 1982), a miscellany of interviews and items of general interest which resembled the early versions of *Heddiw* in the 1960s. Presentations for children also built on the success of programmes such as *Miri Mawr* (HTV, launched in 1971) and *Teliffant* (BBC, launched in 1975). Indeed, programmes for younger children gained the most consistently positive reviews of all programmes broadcast on the new channel. The provision for young people was less successful, and programmes were regularly criticized for their lack of initiative and preoccupation with media personalities.[152]

The provision of light entertainment became a matter of regular debate both within the Welsh press and further afield. Competitions and game shows, many openly based on English programmes, accounted for a large proportion of these productions, much to the dismay of the critics. Yet such programmes held attractions for broadcasting administrators, partly because their costs were minimal. Comedy programmes generated a similarly vigorous debate. Traditional comedy adaptations of literary works such as *Storïau'r Henllys Fawr* and *Hufen a Moch Bach* were well received, although their humour did not appeal to many younger viewers. Indeed, few comedy series managed to attract the level of support enjoyed by *Fo a Fe* and *Glas y Dorlan* in the 1970s.

Despite the impetus given to Welsh drama by the new channel, financial difficulties continued to limit the number of works that could be produced. Those which were broadcast, most notably the works of Siôn Eirian[153] and Michael Povey,[154] maintained the tradition of intense social portraits established in the late 1960s. Yet the drama series produced for S4C can be said to have broken the

---

[150] For example, an estimated 200,000 watched *Pobol y Cwm* on a regular basis during the first months. The new channel also succeeded in attracting a sizeable audience over the Christmas period. *Y Faner*, 15 July 1983.

[151] Ibid., 11 February 1983.

[152] *Barn*, 322 (1989), 34–5.

[153] *Y Faner*, 6 March 1987.

[154] Ibid., 12 December 1980.

mould of Welsh broadcasting. The channel sought to appeal to a broad audience, to entice viewers who had not previously watched Welsh programmes, and to produce works which were diverse and pioneering and which reflected changing popular tastes. Inevitably many initiatives failed to gain critical approval, including some which proved immensely popular. The long neglect of the Welsh industrial and urban experience was largely overcome and the channel strove to eschew an inward-looking, parochial attitude. Welsh programmes increasingly became a focus for popular discussion, a development which in itself served to raise the profile of the language. Moreover, even though many were unhappy with the content of the programmes, very few questioned the desirability of the concept of a Welsh-language television channel.

★   ★   ★

Throughout the period considered in this chapter, Welsh broadcasting generated a lively and vigorous debate concerning several recurring themes. The concept of a separate Welsh service became firmly established and only a very small minority were hostile to S4C and Radio Cymru. The nature of the service provided, however, continued to be a matter of debate. For instance, issues such as the impact of broadcasting on the quality of spoken Welsh remain unresolved. Broadcasters were often regarded as the purveyors of standard Welsh and there can be no doubt that properly prepared news bulletins and scripted contributions made a large number of listeners conversant with a mode of expression in which traditional standards were respected and also familiarized the audience with the new vocabulary consonant with the needs of modern life. At the same time, the greatly increased use of readily available recording facilities brought to radio and television unscripted interviews in which the spoken language was woefully corrupted. This was especially the case when interviews were conducted with subject specialists whose command of the language was defective, though at the same time listeners were made aware of the extent to which persons from various professions were making a creditable effort to convey matters of technical complexity in Welsh and saw merit in doing so. Other language issues also placed programme-makers in a difficult predicament, especially when broadcasters sought to portray Welsh-speaking communities in Anglicized areas in which it would have been unrealistic to fail to acknowledge the presence of a large English-speaking community.[155] Many Welsh drama productions chose purity rather than authenticity, especially for those programmes subtitled for the benefit of learners. Yet it was also the case that the broadcasting authorities sought to dilute the Welsh language in certain programmes in an effort to attract a wider audience, notably in *Heno* (Agenda, launched in 1992), broadcast from Swansea

---

[155] *Golwg*, 7 and 14 February 1991.

with the aim of attracting viewers in industrial south-west Wales. From 1994 onwards a mixture of English interviews and English songs was introduced into Welsh-language programmes on Radio Cymru, again in a deliberate effort to appeal to a wider and younger audience. The decision generated heated debate, during which the broadcasting authorities were criticized for failing to correct grammatical mistakes and careless presentation.

The need to address the requirements of Welsh learners was another constant topic. Welsh broadcasters acknowledged their responsibility towards this significant and vociferous group. The popularity of Welsh classes coincided with the development of the Open University and the methods which had been refined by educational programmes provided an important model for programmes such as *Croeso Christine* and radio broadcasts. In addition, reading materials were produced in association with those programmes, many of which were noted for their high standards of presentation and relevance. The implications of the need to cater for Welsh learners were also relevant to 'mainstream' programmes. By the late 1980s subtitling was a technical possibility which was fully utilized as a means of assisting both Welsh learners and those whose command of the language was limited. The needs of learners were also considered in relation to the standard of the Welsh that was to be broadcast, although the extent to which programme content should be diluted (and the use of English permitted) continues to be a matter of some controversy.

The amount of time devoted to individual localities was another recurring issue. During the 1930s the BBC had been criticized for its bias towards Cardiff and especially for failing to give due attention to the large Welsh-speaking community in north-west Wales. During the early years of S4C it was claimed that Cardiff and Gwynedd were receiving too much attention at the expense of other areas although, according to research undertaken by S4C itself, such concerns did not prevent the channel from attracting a significant audience in all areas.[156]

Broadcasting has undoubtedly played a historic role in strengthening the unity of the nation which it serves.[157] During the 1930s the BBC deliberately sought to strengthen the unity of the United Kingdom by developing a communal identity and ensuring that a common service was made available to all areas. Within Wales this was achieved only partially. A greater awareness of Wales was fostered by Welsh broadcasters and the deliberate effort to draw on the wealth of talent which existed in all areas was a notable achievement. The barriers between the Welsh speakers of north and south Wales were removed and a greater sense of common heritage and an appreciation of the strength which could be derived from the

---

[156] *Wales Monthly Monitor*, no. 28 (1991); *Golwg*, 17 June 1993.
[157] Cardiff and Scannell, 'Broadcasting and National Unity' in Curran, Smith and Wingate (eds.), *Impacts and Influences*, p. 157.

diversity which existed within Wales was fostered. Yet broadcasting alone was not sufficient to promote Welsh cultural identity, partly because of the linguistic divisions which separated English and Welsh broadcasting in Wales.[158] Significantly, Welsh-language broadcasting was less distinctive in the 1990s than it had been in earlier periods. As has been noted, Welsh characteristics were in evidence in the field of light entertainment in the 1940s and in the 1960s. Certainly many of the works of this period, particularly drama, concentrated on a view of Wales which emphasized characteristics such as adherence to religion, a love of learning, and the image of an enlightened people. 'Buchedd A', as classified by David Jenkins, was strongly represented on the airwaves and there were aspects of the Welsh character which were ignored by the Welsh-language service. Yet this was also the case in relation to English broadcasting. With some notable exceptions, the view of England presented by broadcasters was very limited. In essence, it reflected the values of the home counties and professional classes in tone, outlook and accent.[159] The presentations of Wales and the Welsh people may also have been narrow in terms of the modes of living portrayed, but it succeeded in depicting a much broader range of social groups.

During the twenty-five years after the Second World War, Welsh broadcasting produced its own material and was able to resist the influence of the powerful American culture which was gradually affecting English broadcasting. The early manifestations of the 'Welsh style' rejected the emphasis on élites which characterized a substantial amount of the output of the BBC in London. Ironically, however, as the autonomy of Welsh broadcasting increased from the 1980s onwards, a decline in this distinctiveness became apparent. In part this was the result of the need to provide a comprehensive sound and television service in Welsh despite finite resources. Yet it was also the case that Welsh broadcasting deliberately emulated English and American programmes in an attempt to broaden the appeal of the Welsh channel. This coincided with the realization that the traditional Welsh society, rooted in the rural areas and in the values represented by Alun Oldfield-Davies and Aneirin Talfan Davies, was in decline. An element of what Raymond Williams described as 'residual culture' (this was associated in Wales with the industrial heritage, Nonconformity and political radicalism) continued to influence Welsh programme-makers, but they had a much less clear view of Wales by the late 1990s than that held by their predecessors.[160] The representation of Wales on the airwaves was complicated by issues such as in-migration from England to Welsh-speaking areas and the increase

[158] The role of the media in the forging of a Welsh national identity is emphasized by Emyr Humphreys, *Diwylliant Cymru a'r Cyfryngau Torfol* (Aberystwyth, 1977), pp. 21–4.

[159] These points are examined by, among others, Arthur Marwick, *British Society since 1945* (London, 1982), p. 138 and Mulgan, 'Culture' in Marquand and Seldon (eds.), *The Ideas that Shaped Post-war Britain*, pp. 195–213.

[160] See Cardiff and Scannell, 'Broadcasting and National Unity' in Curran, Smith and Wingate (eds.), *Impacts and Influences*, p. 157.

in the number of Welsh speakers in the south-east, as well as other trends such as the decline of the influence of Nonconformity and a more diverse pattern of employment. As new groups within the Welsh-speaking community demanded representation on the air, broadcasters were required to balance different tastes and demands while retaining distinctive characteristics. The difficulties of achieving this in the context of an increasingly powerful, global broadcasting culture were immense and presented Welsh broadcasting with what, arguably, remains its greatest challenge.

9

The British State and Welsh-Language Education
1914–1991

W. GARETH EVANS

ONE OF the most challenging questions facing the Welsh language on the eve of the Great War was the extent to which it would figure in future years in the educational domain. By 1914 the Welsh Department of the Board of Education was committed to promoting a bilingual policy in the schools and colleges of Wales. The publication in January 1914 of a bilingual pamphlet, *Dydd Gŵyl Dewi (St David's Day)*, offering suggestions to teachers concerning appropriate programmes of work to mark St David's day epitomized official support for the advancement of the nation and for enabling the youth of Wales to appreciate 'higher ideals of patriotism'.[1] Among the summer schools supported by the Welsh Department during the same year was one organized by Cymdeithas yr Iaith Gymraeg (the former Society for Utilizing the Welsh Language) at Brecon, which aimed to provide elementary and secondary school teachers with opportunities for acquiring knowledge of the methods of teaching Welsh language and literature.[2] Alfred T. Davies, Permanent Secretary to the Welsh Department of the Board of Education, claimed with much justification in 1916 that 'the Welsh Department cannot be charged with having been slow in showing the realisation of the great value of utilising and fostering the Welsh language to the utmost extent possible'.[3] Davies contrasted the constant support for the native language through annual reports and exhortation by school inspectors with the considerable apathy evident in many parts of Wales. He strongly believed that the time was ripe for local authorities and people throughout Wales 'to rouse themselves and do their part on behalf of the mother tongue'.[4] If full advantage was to be taken of the policies promoted by the Welsh Department 'the necessary driving force . . . must . . . be supplied by people on the spot who are in a position to influence public opinion'.[5]

---

[1] Board of Education (Welsh Department), *Dydd Gŵyl Dewi (St David's Day)* (London, 1914), p. 4.
[2] Idem, *Table of Summer Schools in Wales* (London, 1914), p. 7.
[3] PRO ED 91/57, letter 1 July 1916.
[4] Ibid., letter 6 July 1916.
[5] Ibid.

Led by the Permanent Secretary, Alfred T. Davies, and the Chief Inspector, O. M. Edwards, the Welsh Department continued unflinchingly in its support for the Welsh language in education. The enthusiasm evident in Whitehall, however, was often in sharp contrast to the attitudes prevailing in many parts of Wales, particularly in conjunction with the intermediate schools. In the *Regulations for Secondary Schools in Wales* (1917), which superseded those in force since 1909, it was reiterated that 'in districts where Welsh is spoken, the language, or one of the languages, other than English should be Welsh' and that 'any of the subjects of the curriculum may (where the local circumstances make it desirable) be taught, partly or wholly in Welsh'.[6] In reality, however, Welsh was often given insufficient attention in the curriculum 'of schools, particularly in comparison to the time allocated to French. Even when Welsh was taught, English was often used as the language of instruction, and too much time was allocated to grammar. It had also become evident that many pupils were seeking to avoid Welsh because of the exacting standards of the Central Welsh Board (CWB) examinations, which were regarded as difficult even for native Welsh speakers. In these circumstances some headteachers not unnaturally were advising their pupils to take an easier language.[7] However, the examination system was only partly responsible for the unsatisfactory position of the Welsh language in the intermediate schools. The annual report of the Board of Education for 1920 referred to the possible 'indifference on the part of the parents' and also to the possible 'indifference and even hostility on the part of the heads of schools or their staffs'.[8] Outmoded methods of teaching were also unhelpful. In 1915 O. M. Edwards clashed with the Rhondda Education Committee following his objection to a proposal by the headmaster of Tonypandy Higher Elementary School to introduce French and Latin into the school curriculum. French and Latin, rather than Welsh and technical education as advocated by the Chief Inspector, were regarded as essential for occupational and social mobility among the children of working people.[9]

The year 1920 was a significant landmark in the history of Welsh education. The *Report of the Departmental Committee on the Organisation of Secondary Education in Wales*, under the chairmanship of W. N. Bruce, recommended that a National Council of Education for Wales be set up. Although the report gave no significant attention to the native language, it recognized that 'Wales is bent on preserving its

---

[6] Board of Education (Welsh Department), *Regulations for Secondary Schools in Wales* (London, 1917) (PP 1917–18 (Cd. 8571) XXV), p. 13.

[7] Idem, *Report of the Board of Education under the Welsh Intermediate Education Act, 1889, for the year 1914* (London, 1915) (PP 1914–16 (239) XVIII), p. 7; idem, *Report . . . for the year 1917* (London, 1918) (PP 1918 (39) IX), pp. 6–7; idem, *Report . . . for the year 1919* (London, 1920) (PP 1920 (Cmd. 689) XV), pp. 3–4.

[8] Idem, *Report . . . for the year 1920* (London, 1921) (PP 1921 (Cmd. 1282) XI), p. 9.

[9] W. Gareth Evans, 'Secondary and Higher Education for Girls and Women in Wales 1847–1920' (unpubl. University of Wales PhD thesis, 1987), p. 630.

language'.[10] On 15 May 1920 O. M. Edwards died, aged sixty-two, at Llanuwchllyn. Tributes at the time of his untimely death and the considered judgement of historians have highlighted his titanic contribution to the cause of education in Wales. His unfailing advocacy of the teaching of the Welsh language was central to his educational philosophy and efforts to create a new order in Welsh education. 'O. M.' was justifiably a synonym for 'the Patriot, the Crusader, the Pioneer',[11] and his influence on the policies of the Welsh Department continued after his death. Alfred T. Davies, his colleague for fourteen years, praised Edwards's 'incomparable services to Wales, to her language, her education and her culture generally'.[12] Wynne Lloyd, Chief Inspector at the Welsh Department in 1962, accurately judged that his famous predecessor's primary contribution had been 'that of a catalyst who, unchanging himself, caused changes to come about . . . who gave to the education of his countrymen a new direction and a coherent ideal, which remains with us who work in Welsh education'.[13]

However, not all teachers, headteachers, administrators and parents were similarly enthused by the educational policies championed by O. M. Edwards. Although the judgement of history has been generally highly complimentary, Gareth Elwyn Jones has highlighted the chasm which existed between the demands of the Welsh people and the vision of the Chief Inspector: 'It was his personal achievement, not his educational principles, which exerted most influence.'[14] The Welsh people desired an academic, examination-orientated education which would be the agent of social mobility to white-collar occupations beyond their immediate localities. Influenced by the ideas of Ruskin and moulded by his upbringing in rural Merioneth, O. M. Edwards espoused a philosophy of education which gave particular attention to the Welsh language, literature, history and craftwork. He wanted the schools of Wales to serve the needs and interests of Welsh communities and not be mere imitations of English grammar schools. Yet the academic, curricular straitjacket allegedly imposed by the CWB was vigorously condemned, and tensions ensued as attempts were made to implement the policy. Comparatively little had been achieved by the time of Edwards's death nor indeed by 1944. In the turbulent inter-war years of Labour-controlled south Wales, only a small minority were attracted to these seemingly anachronistic ideas. In 1989 it was claimed that O. M. Edwards had been both

[10] Board of Education, *Report of the Departmental Committee on the Organisation of Secondary Education in Wales* (Bruce Report) (London, 1920), p. 92.

[11] Alfred T. Davies (ed.), *'O. M.' (Sir Owen M. Edwards): A Memoir* (Cardiff and Wrexham, 1946), p. 10.

[12] Ibid., p. 64.

[13] Wynne Ll. Lloyd, 'Owen M. Edwards (1858–1920)' in Charles Gittins (ed.), *Pioneers of Welsh Education: Four Lectures* (Swansea, 1962), pp. 98–9.

[14] Gareth Elwyn Jones, *Controls and Conflicts in Welsh Secondary Education 1889–1944* (Cardiff, 1982), p. 18.

'reactionary' and 'colonial'.[15] The people of industrial south Wales had rejected the philosophy of the Chief Inspector as 'a reactionary irrelevancy', which locked 'working class children into the "environment" of an idealised "Gwerin"'.[16] Somewhat anachronistically, Professor J. E. Caerwyn Williams argued that O. M. Edwards failed to appreciate the dangers of bilingualism. He claimed that the Chief Inspector might have endeavoured to promote the Welsh language as the language of the whole nation rather than only part of it.[17]

It is undeniable that during the period 1907–20 the Welsh Department was often in advance of public opinion in Wales regarding the importance of the Welsh language in education. The annual reports of the CWB revealed its firm commitment to the Welsh language, even though there was no advocacy of the compulsory teaching of the native language to all pupils. In 1917 the Chief Inspector, William Edwards, emphasized that it was the duty of the intermediate schools to do everything possible 'to conserve and strengthen the position of the Welsh Language in the intellectual life of the nation'.[18] For many in Wales, schooling was synonymous with mastering the English language. The Chief Inspector was deeply critical of parents who argued that 'no time at all need be given in school to the home language as it can, in their view, take care of itself'.[19] Others believed that learning French was more useful than learning Welsh. Often the attitudes of headteachers of secondary schools and the examination regulations of the CWB placed pupils in the invidious position of having to choose between their native language and French. In 1918 Dr G. Perrie Williams condemned the examination regulations of the CWB which, by grouping subjects, 'discourages the study of Welsh'.[20] Pupils could not study Welsh with French and Latin – 'Welsh being regarded entirely as a foreign language and treated as such'.[21]

Thus, despite receiving the support of the Board of Education (Welsh Department) and the Chief Inspector of the CWB, the position of the Welsh language in the secondary schools remained precarious. One problem which greatly hindered the progress of Welsh-language teaching was the lack of qualified teachers. Although 141 students were studying Welsh in the training colleges by 1920, G. Prys Williams HMI was concerned that their numbers were insufficient. In 1920 only 3,853 pupils from 82 schools were examined in Welsh, while 5,924

---

[15] T. I. Williams, 'Patriots and Citizens. Language, Identity and Education in a Liberal State: The Anglicisation of Pontypridd 1818–1920' (unpubl. University of Wales PhD thesis, 1989), p. 174.

[16] Ibid., p. 204.

[17] J. E. Caerwyn Williams, 'Gweledigaeth Owen Morgan Edwards', *Taliesin*, no. 4 [1962], 26.

[18] Central Welsh Board, *General Report: Inspection and Examination of County Schools, 1917* (Cardiff, 1917), Appendix A, Chief Inspector's General Report, p. 25.

[19] Ibid., *General Report . . . 1918* (Cardiff, 1918), Appendix A, Chief Inspector's General Report, p. 31. See also idem, *General Report . . . 1919* (Cardiff, 1919), Appendix A, Chief Inspector's General Report, p. 21.

[20] G. Perrie Williams, *Welsh Education in Sunlight and Shadow* (London, 1918), p. 27.

[21] Ibid., p. 26.

pupils from 101 schools were examined in French and 4,988 pupils from 102 schools in Latin. In 1917 Frank Smith, who was engaged in important research into bilingualism at Aberystwyth, maintained that 'it would be charitable to describe the Welsh teaching of many schools as half-hearted; in very truth it is grotesquely inadequate and mischievously amateur'.[22]

Despite the difficult years of the First World War and much indifference concerning the teaching of Welsh, considerable voluntary effort was carried out by societies and individuals in support of the Welsh language. The Society for Utilizing the Welsh Language had been reconstituted in 1901 and, inspired by its hard-working secretary, David James (Defynnog), it continued its pre-war activities in support of the native language by organizing summer schools and evening classes to promote the teaching of Welsh.[23] Inspired by much optimism in 1913, several Welsh societies formed a Union committed to promoting the Welsh language, namely Undeb Cenedlaethol y Cymdeithasau Cymraeg (the National Union of Welsh Societies). The Union held conferences and summer schools, organized Welsh classes in conjunction with the Workers' Educational Association (WEA) and extramural departments, petitioned the CWB and the Welsh Department, and pressurized local education authorities to promote the teaching of Welsh. It also worked in conjunction with Urdd Gobaith Cymru (the Welsh League of Youth), founded in 1922, in emphasizing the value of Welsh, and influenced the growth of Plaid Genedlaethol Cymru (the Welsh Nationalist Party), established in 1925.[24] During this period a number of individuals also published schemes designed to encourage more effective teaching of Welsh. They included *Dysgu'r Gymraeg* (1916) by D. Arthen Evans, *The Value of the Welsh Language for English Youth in Wales* (1917) by O. Jones Owen, and *Y Gymraeg yn yr Ysgolion* (1916) by Huw J. Huws, written to assist the teachers of Newport. In 1921 William Phillips published *The Theory and Practice of Teaching Welsh to English-speaking children, without the aid of English.*

Some education authorities were also beginning to reveal a more positive attitude towards the Welsh language. Under the provisions of the Education Act of 1918, local education authorities were able to include provision for the teaching of Welsh in their schemes to be submitted to the Board of Education.

---

[22] Frank Smith, 'Welsh Schools and the Language Problem', *The Welsh Outlook*, IV, no. 1 (1917), 27.

[23] Gwilym Arthur Jones, 'David James (Defynnog) 1865–1928, in the Context of Welsh Education', *THSC* (1978), 267–84.

[24] Undeb y Cymdeithasau Cymraeg, *Adroddiad ar Safle Addysgu Llên Cymru yn ein Hysgolion Canolraddol, gan T. Matthews* (Dundalk, 1915); Undeb Cenedlaethol y Cymdeithasau Cymraeg, *Schemes of Welsh Studies, or, Proposals for Securing for the Welsh Language its Proper Place in a System of Education in Wales and Monmouthshire, under the Education Act, 1918* (Barry, 1921). See also Marion Löffler, '"Eu Hiaith a Gadwant": The Work of the National Union of Welsh Societies, 1913–1941', *THSC*, new series, 4 (1998), 124–52.

But the financial stringencies following the 'Geddes Axe' of 1921 made any significant expansion of the provision for the teaching of Welsh unlikely. At Newport the education authority rejected, by a small majority, a recommendation by its own elementary committee in 1913 to discontinue the teaching of Welsh. O. M. Edwards encouraged the local inspector R. E. Hughes HMI to pressurize Newport Local Education Authority to continue to teach Welsh.[25] In spite of significant opposition, Welsh was made optional in Standards 1–4 in 1914 and extended on a similar basis into senior departments. At Swansea, in January 1914 the authority's Superintendent of Education, T. J. Rees, submitted a report, *The Teaching of Welsh in Elementary Schools*, which advocated the teaching of Welsh rather than French. However, the differing attitudes of headteachers to Welsh led to a lack of linguistic uniformity in the schools of the authority. In contrast to the neglect of the language at schools in Neath, much more support for Welsh was evident at Barry, where a conference of teachers in 1913 led to the formulation of the 'Barry Syllabus' for teaching Welsh. In the Rhondda, where Welsh was taught in elementary schools by 1911, petitioning by members of the National Union of Welsh Societies and inspiring leadership by R. R. Williams, Deputy Director of Education, led to the classification of elementary schools at Blaenrhondda, Treherbert, Treorci, Ton, Clydach Vale, Alaw and Maerdy in 1920 and in 1925 as bilingual schools where experimental work could be carried out.[26] In 1926 the Rhondda Education Committee resolved to make Welsh the medium of teaching in infants' schools. Welsh was also to be taught in all secondary schools and its use as the medium of instruction in other subjects was also advocated. In Carmarthenshire, however, there was no such enthusiasm. Likewise in Cardiganshire, no high priority was given to the native language by the education authority which had fashioned its linguistic policy in 1907 on the following dubious philosophy: 'During the 1st and 2nd years of the school life of the normal Welsh child, his reading should be Welsh; there should be composition in Welsh throughout the school; but the time devoted to Welsh should be diminished as the time devoted to English increased up the school.'[27]

There was also academic interest in the study of bilingualism in the 1920s. At the Department of Education, University College of Wales, Aberystwyth, the first serious empirical work into bilingualism by D. J. Saer, Frank Smith and John Hughes led to significant publications and conferences.[28] In March and June 1922, Saer published two papers on the bilingual question in *The Journal of Experimental*

[25] PRO ED 91/57 W/490.

[26] Marion Löffler, *'Iaith Nas Arferir, Iaith i Farw Yw': Ymgyrchu dros yr Iaith Gymraeg rhwng y Ddau Ryfel Byd* (Aberystwyth, 1995), pp. 5–6.

[27] Ministry of Education, Central Advisory Council for Education (Wales), *The Place of Welsh and English in the Schools of Wales* (London, 1953), p. 18.

[28] W. Gareth Evans (ed.), *Fit to Educate? A Century of Teacher Education and Training 1892–1992 / Canrif o Addysgu a Hyfforddi Athrawon* (Aberystwyth, 1992), pp. 119–22.

Pedagogy. In July 1923, his article on 'The Effect of Bilingualism on Intelligence' appeared in *The British Journal of Psychology*.[29] Earlier in January 1923 the same journal included an article by Frank Smith on 'Bilingualism and Mental Development'.[30] These publications led to much debate and discussion in the English and Welsh press. In 1924 *The Bilingual Problem: A Study based upon Experiments and Observations in Wales* was published.[31] On the basis of empirical research into the school performance of bilingual and monoglot children, it was claimed that the monoglot child derived greater intellectual advantages from schooling than the bilingual child. It was also argued that the results of intelligence tests taken by 939 students at the University College of Wales, Aberystwyth, over a three-year period confirmed the superior intelligence of monoglot over bilingual students, 'thus suggesting that this difference in mental ability as revealed by intelligence tests is of a permanent nature'.[32]

This research attracted considerable attention. Some regarded it as an attack on bilingualism, for the work suggested that bilingualism *per se* was an obstacle to the intellectual development of children. Others, however, remained unconvinced. Ellen Evans, Principal of Barry Training College, who was awarded an MA degree in 1924 for a thesis on bilingualism, attributed the differences recorded by Saer and Smith to the neglect of the mother tongue as a medium of instruction. She argued that the research underlined the need for children to be taught initially through the mother tongue.[33] In the 1930s further research by Ethel M. Barke and D. E. Parry Williams at Cardiff and W. R. Jones at Bangor questioned the validity of the research undertaken at Aberystwyth.[34] It was shown that, when using non-verbal IQ tests, there was little difference in the scores of monoglot English-speaking children and bilingual children. It was suggested that the different scores in verbal IQ tests reflected the nature of the tests themselves rather than confirming the lower innate intelligence of bilingual children.

At the CWB, too, the validity of the research was questioned. In 1923 it was doubted 'whether the research, ingenious and painstaking as it was, justifies the conclusion, for everything depends on the previous treatment of the bilingual'.[35]

---

[29] D. J. Saer, 'The Effect of Bilingualism on Intelligence', *British Journal of Psychology*, XIV, part 1 (1923), 25–38.

[30] Frank Smith, 'Bilingualism and Mental Development', ibid., XIII, part 3 (1923), 271–82.

[31] D. J. Saer, Frank Smith and John Hughes, *The Bilingual Problem: A Study based upon Experiments and Observations in Wales* (Wrexham, 1924).

[32] Ibid., p. 53.

[33] Ellen Evans, *The Teaching of Welsh: An Investigation into the Problem of Bilingualism together with a Discussion of Schemes for the Teaching of Welsh* (Cardiff and London, 1924), p. 49.

[34] Ethel M. Barke and D. E. Parry Williams, 'A Further Study of the Comparative Intelligence of Children in Certain Bilingual and Monoglot Schools in South Wales', *British Journal of Educational Psychology*, VIII, part 1 (1938), 63–77; W. R. Jones, 'Tests for the Examination of the Effect of Bilingualism on Intelligence' (unpubl. University of Wales MA thesis, 1933).

[35] Central Welsh Board, *General Report: Inspection and Examination of County Schools, 1923* (Cardiff, 1923), Appendix A, Chief Inspector's General Report, p. 31.

At the Welsh Department, Alfred T. Davies, who had chaired the committee on 'Bilingual Teaching' at the Imperial Conference on Education, realized that the research work of Saer at Aberystwyth could embarrass or even threaten the policies of the Board of Education in support of the Welsh language.[36] This was a period when there was increasing awareness in Wales of the Anglicized nature of the intermediate schools and dissatisfaction with the peripheral attention given to Welsh. E. T. John, MP for East Denbighshire, had published *Cymru a'r Gymraeg*, and called regularly for proper attention to Welsh in schools up to matriculation level.[37] D. J. Williams called for 'a certain standard knowledge of Welsh' to be made 'obligatory for the school-leaving certificate',[38] while W. Ambrose Bebb advocated the adoption of extreme measures to promote the native language compulsorily ('dulliau eithafol i ddysgu'r iaith a'i gorfodi').[39] W. Morgan Watkin, Professor of French at the University College of Wales, Cardiff, presented a petition to the Lord Mayor on behalf of the Cymrodorion, calling for equal treatment for both English and Welsh.

The publication of the Newbolt Report on the teaching of English in England in 1921 led to demands for a similar inquiry into the teaching of Welsh.[40] G. Perrie Williams wrote to Alfred T. Davies calling for a 'Welsh Newbolt'.[41] Ellen Evans claimed that 'England is now realising the importance of special training in the mother tongue'.[42] It was thus essential that Welsh should occupy a much more central role in the schools of Wales. In 1922 the Welsh Department launched a series of national courses for teachers to encourage the teaching of Welsh and the study of Welsh literature and history. These were held each summer until 1938. The Board's annual reports noted the adverse effects of the CWB examination requirements, which made it necessary for pupils to choose between French and Welsh. But public apathy was also diagnosed. By 1924 both the University of Wales and the CWB were pressing the government for the appointment of a committee to report on the position of the Welsh language in the educational institutions of Wales and to offer suggestions for the better teaching of the language. Initially Alfred T. Davies was reluctant to agree to an official inquiry, fearing that the revelation of divisions of opinion concerning the language in education might be a retrograde step.[43] However, in the face of increasing demands, particularly from the University of Wales, the CWB and the National Union of Welsh Societies, the Welsh Department was obliged to act.

[36] PRO ED 91/57.

[37] E. T. John and J. Dyfnallt Owen, *Cymru a'r Gymraeg* (Y Barri, 1916), pp. 21–8.

[38] D. J. Williams, 'Compulsory Welsh for Matriculation', *The Welsh Outlook*, XII, no. 5 (1925), 129.

[39] W. Ambrose Bebb, 'Achub y Gymraeg: Achub Cymru', *Y Geninen*, XLI, no. 3 (1923), 125.

[40] Departmental Committee on the Position of English in the Educational System of England, *The Teaching of English in England* (London, 1921).

[41] PRO ED 91/57, letter 11 November 1921.

[42] Evans, *The Teaching of Welsh*, p. 4.

[43] Williams, 'Patriots and Citizens', p. 241.

A deputation representing the University of Wales and the CWB visited the Board of Education on 19 February 1925. Recognizing the sensitivity of the bilingual issue, the Permanent Secretary succeeded in restricting the terms of reference of the committee appointed in 1925 'to inquire into the position occupied by the Welsh Language and Literature in the educational system of Wales', and to advise how its study might best be promoted. A recent study has argued that Alfred T. Davies manipulated the committee's terms of reference by ensuring it did not question the desirability of teaching Welsh nor the provision of a pivotal role for the native language.[44] Unsurprisingly, the membership of the Departmental Committee, which included Ellen Evans, W. J. Gruffydd and D. Lleufer Thomas, was also carefully selected. In January 1923 Alfred T. Davies had stated that 'it is fairly certain that no Government Department within the British Empire or indeed any Central Government has ever given such warm encouragement to the use of the Mother Tongue over the last 16 years as has the Welsh Department'.[45] He regarded the designation of the terms of reference and membership of the Departmental Committee as his final and most important decision.

The terms of reference of 23 March 1925 stipulated that the Departmental Committee was to inquire into the position of the Welsh language in the educational system of Wales and to offer advice to the President of the Board of Education on its promotion in all types of educational institutions. It was clearly stated, however, that the committee had no executive or legislative powers. Public meetings were held in Cardiff, Swansea, Carmarthen, Aberystwyth and Bangor, where large audiences showed 'remarkable interest' in the issues being investigated. As many as 170 witnesses gave oral evidence and numerous other individuals and bodies submitted written statements. The final report, *Welsh in Education and Life*, which comprised over 300 pages, was published in 1927.[46] It provided a wide-ranging survey and analysis of the linguistic situation at the time. It concluded that 'the traditional defences' of the Welsh language had been greatly weakened over the previous half century, and that the salvation of the Welsh language in the future would depend on the impact of the schools. The relationship between language, culture and identity was particularly emphasized: 'The language of a people is the outward expression of its individuality. With the loss of its language some essential part of its character is at least obscured.'[47] It was therefore essential to safeguard the national birthright. The language should be learnt for its own sake. However, the indifferent attitude of many Welsh-speaking parents and teachers towards the native language was also noted. In spite of the

---

[44] Ibid., p. 242.
[45] PRO ED 91/57, memorandum to President, 4 January 1923.
[46] Departmental Committee on Welsh in the Educational System of Wales, *Welsh in Education and Life* (London, 1927).
[47] Ibid., p. 180.

supportive policies of the Welsh Department of the Board of Education towards the teaching of Welsh since 1907, nowhere had Welsh 'been established as *the* medium, the pervasive everyday language' of the secondary schools.[48] Indeed, it was often used merely as an adjunct to English. Inevitably, the extent to which Welsh was used as a medium of instruction might vary considerably from district to district, but it was claimed that as well as being the language of the people, Welsh was also 'the language of that society called Wales, it is the instrument of the national life'.[49] It was thus essential that Welsh be given prestige in schools in order to become an integral part of the national culture. In Anglicized districts many teachers were misguided in opposing the teaching of Welsh and in advocating the introduction of French, but the teaching of Welsh as the second language was likely to be more effective than a foreign language like French.[50] The seventy-two principal recommendations were directed at the Board of Education, the University Colleges, training colleges and theological colleges, local education authorities, the CWB, teachers and Welsh societies. More vigorous policies of bilingual teaching were necessary in the schools if the decline of the language was to be arrested and its preservation ensured. Local education authorities were urged to ensure that their schemes for the teaching of Welsh were carried out more effectively.[51] They were also urged to provide training and refresher courses in the best methods of teaching Welsh. The need for an adequate supply of trained teachers was essential for the effective teaching of Welsh. The CWB was urged to assist the secondary schools in order to ensure that curricular and examination arrangements for French did not adversely affect the teaching of Welsh. The provision of appropriate books – the tools of language – in Welsh was also emphasized, as well as the full utilization of the Welsh language in broadcasting. On the basis of differing linguistic profiles, a threefold classification of schools and accompanying linguistic policies was advocated.[52] The report was non-prescriptive regarding the districts where English was preponderant or was the sole language. It recognized that local authorities might not be convinced that it would be advantageous to teach Welsh, but it was hoped that eventually the advantages of a knowledge of Welsh – in industrial, business and social life – would become self-evident throughout Wales.

The report generally received a good press. It was seen as 'moderate and reasoned in its scope', and embodying valuable recommendations.[53] However, there was also criticism of its failure to recommend a policy of full bilingualism which would necessitate the compulsory teaching of Welsh.[54] More recently the

[48] Ibid., p. 228.
[49] Ibid., p. 183.
[50] Ibid., p. 222.
[51] Ibid., pp. 99–100.
[52] Ibid., pp. 194–215.
[53] *South Wales News*, 29 August 1927, editorial.
[54] *Baner ac Amserau Cymru*, 6 September 1927.

report has been accurately judged as 'a landmark' whose recommendations 'entailed no radically new departure'.[55] It was also undoubtedly 'very pro-Welsh language', yet 'incredibly . . . managed to say very little about the minefield of bilingualism'.[56] The Departmental Committee had been steered away from a thorough study of the prevailing controversial issues concerning bilingualism. The emphasis on the cultural and educational importance of the Welsh language epitomized arguments deployed by O. M. Edwards and the Welsh Department since 1907, while the classification of elementary schools according to their different linguistic and cultural surroundings was already evident in the reports of the Welsh Department. The report also fell short of prescribing the compulsory teaching of Welsh to all pupils. Unsurprisingly, the teaching of Welsh as a subject was given more attention than its comprehensive use as a medium of instruction.

The report clearly inspired many Welsh educationalists and ensured that the status of the Welsh language in education and many other issues received national attention. On 3 September 1927, following the opening of Coleg Harlech, the report was discussed by the recently formed Welsh Nationalist Party, which issued a special appeal to local education authorities and other organizations to implement the recommendations.[57] In the harsh financial and economic climate of the late 1920s and 1930s, however, inadequately equipped schools, high levels of unemployment, financial constraints, as well as migration from rural and urban areas and the accompanying decline in Welsh speakers, meant that the recommendations were unlikely to be implemented. For the majority of Welsh parents and councillors, particularly in Anglicized south-east Wales, campaigning for the abolition of fees and the hated Means Test in order to ensure the provision of free secondary schooling was more important than working to secure a higher profile for the Welsh language in the education system. In 1931 the Board of Education's pamphlet no. 88, *Educational Problems of the South Wales Coalfield*, highlighted mass unemployment (especially among youth), poverty and migration as factors which would have a devastating effect on the Welsh language.[58]

But the 1920s also saw the formation of three national organizations – Urdd Gobaith Cymru in 1922, the Welsh Nationalist Party in 1925, and Undeb Athrawon Cymreig (the Union of Welsh Teachers, later to become Undeb Cenedlaethol Athrawon Cymru [UCAC]) in 1926 – which, over the following half century, were to be in the vanguard of campaigns to seek higher priority for Welsh and Welsh-medium education in schools and colleges.[59] Ifan ab Owen

---

[55] Kenneth O. Morgan, *Rebirth of a Nation: Wales 1880–1980* (Oxford, 1981), p. 250.
[56] Jones, *Controls and Conflicts in Welsh Secondary Education*, pp. 125–8.
[57] *Western Mail*, 5 September 1927.
[58] Board of Education, Educational Pamphlet no. 88, *Educational Problems of the South Wales Coalfield* (London, 1931).
[59] R. E. Griffith, *Urdd Gobaith Cymru* (3 vols., Aberystwyth, 1971–3); D. Hywel Davies, *The Welsh Nationalist Party 1925–1945: A Call to Nationhood* (Cardiff, 1983); Mel Williams (ed.), *Hanes UCAC: Cyfrol y Dathlu* (Adran Lenyddiaeth UCAC, 1991).

Edwards, founder of the Urdd, was motivated by a determination to infuse the youth of Wales with pride in their Welshness and especially in the Welsh language at a time when the language was facing 'a crisis of survival and the Welsh people were conditioned into an apathy of inferiority'.[60] The National Union of Welsh Societies was also active. It gained the support of Will John, MP for Rhondda West, who made repeated representations in the 1920s to the Board of Education concerning the failure of Llandovery College to fulfil its statutory obligation to teach Welsh. Parliamentary questions on 21 March and 25 July 1929 to Lord Eustace Percy, President of the Board of Education, caused the Board to pursue the problem of the Welsh language at Llandovery with even greater vigour. The Board stressed that the school ought to take positive steps 'to establish in the minds of parents its special responsibility towards the Welsh language'. In 1931 W. Beynon Davies, a first-class honours graduate in Welsh, was appointed to teach the language, and a Welsh society was formed in 1932. W. J. Gruffydd, a prominent member of the Departmental Committee and editor of the influential Welsh quarterly *Y Llenor*, had also been actively involved in criticizing the neglect of the Welsh language at Llandovery College. Archbishop A. G. Edwards, formerly warden at Llandovery from 1875 to 1885 and Archbishop of Wales from 1920, became the target of Gruffydd's vitriolic pen. Justifiably, he was blamed for remodelling Llandovery College as an English public school and for banishing the Welsh language.[61]

In the 1927 report it was recommended that the Board of Education should include a chapter on the teaching of Welsh in its *Suggestions for the Consideration of Teachers* as soon as practicable and that inspectors should make special reference to the position of Welsh in individual schools. In 1929 the Welsh Department published memorandum no. 1, *Education in Wales: Suggestions for the Consideration of Education Authorities and Teachers*, which was designed to offer guidance in accordance with that report. While recognizing that differing linguistic circumstances would lead to different types of primary schools, it advocated a positive approach to Welsh in all parts of Wales. Indeed, local authorities were urged to realize that all children seeking careers in Wales could be affected by the degree of attention given to Welsh in the schools. Yet, it was deemed politic to assure parents that the Welsh child's 'mastery over English' would not be adversely affected, nor his 'prospects as a future citizen of the British Empire'.[62] Reason and modest encouragement rather than compulsion underpinned the policy of the Welsh Department regarding the Welsh language in the late 1920s and 1930s.

---

[60] Gwennant Davies, *The Story of the Urdd 1922–72* (Aberystwyth, 1973), p. 8.

[61] W. Gareth Evans, *A History of Llandovery College: The Welsh Collegiate Institution* (Llandovery, 1981), pp. 92–7.

[62] Board of Education (Welsh Department), Memorandum no. 1, *Education in Wales: Suggestions for the Consideration of Education Authorities and Teachers* (London, 1929), pp. 27–8.

In 1930 memorandum no. 2, *Entrance Tests for Admission to Secondary Schools*, emphasized that every candidate, irrespective of 'the linguistic conditions of the neighbourhood' in which he lived, was entitled to take the language paper of the entrance examination in either language or 'in both English and Welsh in varying proportions'.[63] In several areas, the Welsh Department organized courses for teachers and inspected the teaching of Welsh. Principles relating to language teaching highlighted in the 1927 report and 1929 memorandum were reasserted. Cardiganshire Education Authority and elementary schoolteachers were complimented in 1931 for their 'intelligent and sincere response' to the publications issued by the Board of Education,[64] but it was also recognized that fulfilling the elementary schools' aim of producing 'equi-lingual children' was virtually impossible.

However, official reports in the 1930s still viewed the Welsh language in terms of a linguistic problem. In 1930 the report of the Departmental Committee, *Education in Rural Wales*, identified the 'bilingual difficulty' at a time when financial stringency and the reorganization of all-age elementary schools according to principles enunciated in 1926 in the Hadow Report, *The Education of the Adolescent*, was causing problems.[65] However, no specific attempt was made to evaluate the language 'problem' or advocate greater usage of the native language as a medium of education in rural areas. The importance of acquiring English was deemed essential, and the 1927 report, *Welsh in Education and Life*, together with the 1929 memorandum, were deemed to provide sufficient guidance on the issues concerning the Welsh language in education.[66]

Although the 1926 Hadow Report, *The Education of the Adolescent*, had failed to appreciate the complexities of the linguistic situation in Wales, the 1931 Hadow Report, *The Primary School*, included a brief section on 'The Problem of the Two Languages in Primary Schools in Wales'.[67] It claimed that its conception of the curriculum in terms of 'activity and experience rather than of knowledge and of facts to be stored' would significantly alleviate 'the language difficulties in the Welsh schools'.[68] It would enable the second language – English or Welsh – to be 'taught as a living language, so that gradually it may become to some extent a medium of expression and instruction'.[69] While recognizing that the home

---

[63] Idem, Memorandum no. 2, *Entrance Tests for Admission to Secondary Schools* (London, 1930), pp. 1–2.

[64] Cardiganshire Education Committee, *A Statement based on an Investigation into the Teaching of Welsh in the Elementary Schools of the County of Cardigan, by Her Majesty's Inspectors of Schools* (Aberystwyth, 1932), pp. 18–19.

[65] Departmental Committee on the Public System of Education in Wales and Monmouthshire in Relation to the Needs of Rural Areas, *Education in Rural Wales* (London, 1930), pp. 78–9.

[66] Ibid.

[67] Board of Education, *Report of the Consultative Committee on the Primary School* (London, 1931), pp. 165–7.

[68] Ibid., p. 165.

[69] Ibid., p. 166.

language – English or Welsh – should be the only language of the infant school, the formal teaching of the second language, whether English or Welsh, ought to begin at the age of seven. However, the usage of Welsh should not 'imperil the ultimate proficiency of the children in English',[70] for the needs of the Welsh-speaking child in English were likely to be greater in later life than those of the English-speaking child in Welsh. The Spens Report of 1938, which advocated a tripartite system of secondary education for England and Wales, included a chapter entitled 'Welsh Problems'.[71] It asserted that it had been the policy of the Board of Education and the local education authorities for many years 'to give to the Welsh language a prominent place in the curriculum'. There was no advocacy of greater usage of Welsh in the new secondary schools other than a recommendation for a generous provision of English and Welsh books. As in previous reports, Welsh was equated with 'the difficulties of bilingualism'. However, the native language was to be tolerated since the consultative committee was confident that 'the eventual standard in English to be expected of the boy or girl in a Welsh Grammar School need not be lower than that in the Grammar Schools of England'.[72] In the inter-war years, the CWB was aware that its examination system was criticized for the marginalization of the Welsh language in the secondary schools. It was often simply an alternative to French. But the CWB regularly insisted that its powers to influence schools were limited. It maintained that its own *ex cathedra* pronouncements and the reports of its inspectors fully encouraged the teaching and use of Welsh.[73] Yet, many headteachers and governing bodies remained hostile to the Welsh language. In 1938 the National Union of Welsh Societies protested to the CWB because Welsh lagged behind English, French and Latin in popularity in the secondary schools. On the eve of the Second World War there were far fewer candidates in the examinations for both the School Certificate and Higher School Certificate examinations in Welsh than in French, Latin and English.

In spite of the policies of the Welsh Department and the publication in 1927 of *Welsh in Education and Life*, secondary education in Wales remained firmly located in its English mould. W. J. Gruffydd contrasted the enlightened attitude of the Welsh Department – 'Whitehall "Seisnig"' (Anglicized Whitehall) – with the languor, hostility and betrayal of the Welsh cause by headteachers, councillors and local authorities. Their failure to implement the recommendations of the 1927 report was heartily condemned.[74] However, at a time of increasing tension and

---

[70] Ibid., p. 167.

[71] Board of Education, *Report of the Consultative Committee on Secondary Education with Special Reference to Grammar Schools and Technical High Schools* (London, 1938), pp. 342–8.

[72] Ibid., p. 346.

[73] Central Welsh Board, *General Report: Inspection and Examination of County Schools* (Cardiff, 1925), Appendix A, pp. 30–1; idem, *General Report* (Cardiff, 1933), Appendix A, p. 26.

[74] 'Nodiadau'r Golygydd', *Y Llenor*, XXI, no. 4 (1942), 106–7.

gathering gloom over Europe, there was a glimmer of hope for the Welsh language. Deeply aware of the increasingly perilous position of Welsh following the arrival of English-speaking evacuees, Ifan ab Owen Edwards established a small, independent Welsh-medium primary school at the Urdd headquarters in Aberystwyth on 25 September 1939. Ysgol Gymraeg Aberystwyth proved to be a success and exerted a profound impact on the growth of Welsh-medium education in the post-war years.

While the arrival at Aberystwyth of evacuees from Liverpool raised fears about Anglicization and accelerated the provision of Welsh-medium schooling, Welsh remained the main medium of communication in many rural communities and many young evacuees soon became fluent Welsh speakers. In general, however, the location of war industries and military camps as well as the presence of evacuees – 10,000 children in Caernarfonshire and Carmarthenshire, 4,000 in Cardiganshire, 3,000 in Merioneth and Montgomeryshire, 2,000 in Anglesey and 33,000 in Glamorgan – exercised a significant Anglicizing influence in many Welsh-speaking communities.[75]

Despite having a disruptive and destructive impact on British society, the Second World War also unleashed powerful constructive forces. It highlighted social deficiencies and motivated the forces of reconstruction and reform. Planning for post-war education reconstruction began within the Board of Education in November 1940. The White Paper, *Educational Reconstruction* (1943), formed the basis of the subsequent Education Act (1944).[76] In 1942 R. A. Butler, President of the Board of Education, showed a positive approach towards the Welsh language when he disassociated himself from the 'obscurantist' attitude of the Commissioners of Inquiry of 1847. He expressed his wish 'to make amends for that attitude' and invited local education authorities to develop robust language policies and participate in courses to be promoted by the Board of Education.[77] The White Paper in 1943 confirmed these sentiments and acknowledged that 'the place of the language in the schools is not that of one additional subject in the curriculum, but, if it is to be handled hopefully and successfully, it must . . . become a live part of the social as well as the intellectual life of each pupil'.[78] However, there was still no clear, unambiguous advocacy of Welsh-medium primary and secondary schooling. Significantly, national aspirations in Wales at the time were equated with notions of 'free secondary education' and 'secondary education for all'. In October 1942 the Welsh Department issued Circular (Wales) no. 182, *The Teaching of Welsh*, to all local education authorities, schools and colleges in Wales, calling for a general reappraisal of the

---

[75] Ministry of Education, Central Advisory Council for Education (Wales), *The Place of Welsh and English in the Schools of Wales*, p. 20.

[76] Board of Education, *Educational Reconstruction* (London, 1943) (PP 1942–3 (Cmd. 6458) XI).

[77] *Parliamentary Debates* (Hansard), 5th series, vol. 380, 1411 (16 June 1942).

[78] Board of Education, *Educational Reconstruction*, p. 31.

situation regarding the teaching of Welsh.[79] The following year saw the publication of the Norwood Report, *Curriculum and Examinations in Secondary Schools*,
which included a chapter on 'Wales and the Teaching of Welsh'. It recognized
that 'the question of the maintenance of the language' had to be 'in the foreground' of the provision of education in Wales.[80] All pupils in Welsh secondary
schools should become familiar with the language, history and traditions of Wales.
While recognizing the essential relationship between education and the society of
which the child was a member, the report did not advance the cause of the native
language by advocating Welsh-medium secondary schools because, as well as
being a citizen of Wales, the Welsh child was also a member of the British
Empire.[81] It was thus essential that educational standards should be recognized as
comparable to those prevailing elsewhere. Such sentiments had often been
recorded in earlier pronouncements. Thus, in spite of its seemingly enlightened
attitude, the Norwood Report was 'replete with the paradoxes of decades'.[82]

In May 1944 the McNair Report, *Teachers and Youth Leaders*, recognized that
Welsh was the mother tongue of half the population. In recommending that 'the
University of Wales and its constituent colleges should assume the future
responsibility for the education and professional training of teachers in Wales', the
duality of being Welsh and British was again highlighted.[83] As well as training
teachers to teach Welsh and through the medium of Welsh, it was essential that
they and their pupils be 'conscious members of the British community, fully
qualified and free to serve on equal terms within it'.[84]

The 1944 Education Act, the coping stone of wartime educational reconstruction, made no specific reference to the Welsh language. However, clauses in the
new legislation were to prove important in its promotion in the post-war years.[85]
The Minister of Education, empowered to ensure 'the progressive development
of institutions' associated with the advancement of the education of the people of
England and Wales, would, arguably, have to give due recognition to the Welsh
language. There was also an obligation to ensure that adequate and suitable
provision of teachers existed for the schools. Furthermore, under section 76,
children were to be educated in accordance with the wishes of their parents,
provided such desires were 'compatible with the provision of efficient instruction

---

[79] Board of Education (Welsh Department), Circular (Wales) 182, *The Teaching of Welsh* (London, 1942).

[80] Board of Education, *Curriculum and Examinations in Secondary Schools: Report of the Committee of the Secondary School Examinations Council appointed by the President of the Board of Education in 1941* (London, 1943), p. 134.

[81] Ibid., p. 135.

[82] Jones, *Controls and Conflicts in Welsh Secondary Education*, p. 192.

[83] Board of Education, *Report of the Committee appointed by the President of the Board of Education to Consider the Supply, Recruitment and Training of Teachers and Youth Leaders* (London, 1944), p. 127.

[84] Ibid., p. 126.

[85] 'Sir Ben Bowen Thomas in Dublin', *Y Ddinas: The London Welsh Magazine*, 12, no. 1 (1957), 17.

and training and the avoidance of unreasonable public expenditure'. The significance of this clause was soon to be tested by parents demanding Welsh-medium primary and secondary schooling.

The immediate post-war years witnessed yet another flurry of official publications, courses for teachers, conferences and reports in which the educational importance of the Welsh language was highlighted. Ben Bowen Thomas, the urbane Permanent Secretary at the Welsh Department, was steeped in Welsh culture and a staunch advocate of the teaching of Welsh. In 1945 the Welsh Department's pamphlet no. 1, *Language Teaching in Primary Schools*, endeavoured to review the position of language-teaching in schools in the light of experience and developments since the publication of memorandum no. 1 in 1929. It acknowledged that considerable diversity existed, reflecting geographical, economic and cultural differences. In classifying areas according to language – Welsh-speaking, linguistically-mixed and non-Welsh-speaking – the approach adopted in *Welsh in Education and Life* (1927) was emulated. But there was little new in the pamphlet and it was reluctant to highlight the virtues of bilingualism. It rather lamely stated that the limited amount of research prevented a categorical statement on the effect of bilingualism in Wales.[86] Language policy in the primary school would thus need to be 'related to the present linguistic situation and to the needs of the future'.[87] The pivot of a sound language policy was 'a thorough grounding' in the child's home language, whether English or Welsh, and thereafter the teaching of a second language. At a time of increasing Anglicization, there was no reference to the possible emulation of the new venture at Ysgol Gymraeg Aberystwyth. It remained the responsibility of each local education authority to formulate and implement a language policy appropriate to the schools of an area in general, and to individual schools within that area.

In 1947, on the occasion of the centenary of the Report of the Commission of Inquiry into the State of Education in Wales, the Welsh Department published pamphlet no. 2, *Education in Wales 1847–1947*. The preface by the Minister of Education, George Tomlinson, condemned the 1847 Education Commissioners' strictures concerning the adverse influence of the Welsh language. Two further pamphlets appeared in 1949: pamphlet no. 3, *Education in Rural Wales*, and pamphlet no. 4, *Bilingualism in the Secondary School in Wales*. These emphasized the need for continuity of language policy between the primary and secondary schools. The Welsh Department was clearly becoming more critical of the linguistic position in the secondary schools. Several schools in Welsh-speaking rural districts were condemned for their Anglicized ethos and were urged in unambiguous terms to reconsider their relationship with the local community.

---

[86] Ministry of Education (Welsh Department), Pamphlet no. 1, *Language Teaching in Primary Schools/Dysgu Iaith yn Ysgolion Cynradd* (London, 1945), p. 19.

[87] Ibid., p. 11.

Ben Bowen Thomas was critical of the failure of the secondary schools to give 'due consideration to the Welsh language as a means of instruction' and 'a satisfactory place in the curriculum'.[88] There was much evidence to justify such strictures. Of a total of 52,412 pupils in the grammar schools, only 21,515 (41 per cent) studied Welsh in 1946, and English, French, German and Latin all took precedence over the native language. Only 8,198 pupils (34 per cent) were examined in Welsh in the School Certificate Examination and in only 10 out of 151 secondary schools did all pupils study Welsh to School Certificate level. Unsurprisingly, the usage of Welsh as a medium of instruction was 'even less satisfactory'. Indeed, not only the secondary schools but also the training colleges and the University of Wales had 'never seriously attempted to use Welsh as a medium of instruction'.[89] The secondary schools of Wales were unequivocally condemned for being 'imitative', for having 'modelled themselves far too much in curriculum and in method, on the lines of the English grammar school', and for failing to address their own language problems.[90]

In the same year, the first report of the Central Advisory Council for Education (Wales), *The Future of Secondary Education in Wales*, reiterated the same standpoint: 'It is regrettable that French is more extensively studied than Welsh in the secondary schools of Wales . . . We doubt whether the present stress on French at the cost of neglecting Welsh is educationally sound.' It was stressed that Welsh had 'special relevance to the life of any child in Wales'. In the Welsh-speaking areas, the commercial value of the language was also recognized.[91] Here, it was recommended that the native language should not only be a subject of study but also a medium of instruction. In linguistically-mixed areas, Welsh and English-medium streaming should be adopted.[92] The neglect of Welsh was exemplified at Ardwyn School, Aberystwyth, where 306 of the 543 pupils were Welsh speakers in 1948, but where Welsh was used only as a medium of instruction in the Welsh language and literature lessons: 'For the rest, the atmosphere of the school and the medium of instruction are English.'[93]

By contrast, the nearby Ysgol Gymraeg located since 1946 at Lluest, Aberystwyth, received a highly complimentary report of inspection in 1948. The standard of work, the richness of the curriculum and the 'lively Welsh

---

[88] Idem, Pamphlet no. 4, *Bilingualism in the Secondary School in Wales / Y Broblem Ddwyieithog yn yr Ysgol Uwchradd yng Nghymru* (London, 1949), p. 2.

[89] Ibid., p. 9.

[90] Ibid., p. 22.

[91] Ministry of Education, *Report of the Central Advisory Council for Education (Wales): The Future of Secondary Education in Wales* (London, 1949), p. 50.

[92] Ibid., p. 52.

[93] Ministry of Education (Welsh Department), *H.M.I. Report 1948: Ardwyn Secondary School Aberystwyth* (London, n.d.), p. 2.

community' were warmly praised.[94] As a result, the opportunity was taken to distribute a thousand copies of the report in order to publicize the new experiment in Welsh-medium education. The success of the school owed much not only to the inspiration of Ifan ab Owen Edwards but also to the leadership of its headteacher, Norah Isaac, and the single-mindedness of primarily professional and middle-class parents. As the school became an increasing financial burden on the Urdd, negotiations began with the Cardiganshire Education Authority which, since 1951, had been considering the feasibility of establishing a Welsh-medium primary school.[95] The principle of a specifically Welsh-medium primary school had by then been accepted by the Welsh Department. Consequently, following much deliberation and some public dissent, primary education in Aberystwyth was reorganized. A Welsh-medium local education authority school opened in September 1952, with 164 pupils. But Llanelli was to claim the honour of opening the first designated local education authority Welsh-medium primary school. Parental pressure – mainly from professional people – persuaded the Carmarthenshire Education Authority to open Ysgol Gymraeg Dewi Sant, Llanelli, with thirty-four pupils on St David's day 1947.[96] Elsewhere, including Anglicized Wales, the momentum for designated Welsh-medium schools was increasing. Dr B. Haydn Williams, Flintshire's Director of Education, believed that the Welsh language was in jeopardy since it was taught as a subject in only fifty-seven of the county's primary schools in 1948. In September 1948 proposals were made to the local education authority to establish several designated Welsh-medium schools and the following year Welsh-medium schooling became available in Anglicized Rhyl, Mold and Holywell. Although there was opposition to this development, the Director gained the support of Welsh-speaking and non-Welsh-speaking councillors. Elsewhere in Wales, Cassie Davies, HMI with responsibility for Welsh, exerted a powerful influence in favour of the establishment of Welsh-medium schools. By 1950 there were fourteen designated Welsh-medium schools with a total of 926 pupils in seven local education authorities. A new movement – Undeb Cymdeithasau Rhieni Ysgolion Cymraeg (the Union for the Parents' Societies of Welsh Schools) – was formed, highlighting the dawn of a new era for the Welsh language in the primary schools of Wales. However, the secondary schools remained incorrigibly English in their ethos and outlook.

In 1951 the report of the Central Advisory Council for Education (Wales), *The County College in Wales*, advocated that in predominantly Welsh-speaking areas the work of county colleges for 15–18 year-olds should be conducted in

---

[94] Idem, *Report by H. M. Inspectors on Ysgol Gymraeg (The Welsh School), Aberystwyth, Cardiganshire. Inspected on 13 February 1948* (London, n.d.).

[95] Davies, *The Story of the Urdd*, pp. 179–81.

[96] Ministry of Education, Central Advisory Council for Education (Wales), *The Place of Welsh and English in the Schools of Wales*, p. 34.

Welsh. While English would be the medium of instruction in the predominantly English areas, it was recognized that the problems of the linguistically-mixed areas would require enlightened resolution which might involve linguistic grouping.[97] In pamphlet no. 6, *The Curriculum and the Community in Wales* (1952), the Welsh Department recognized the difficulties of cementing the appropriate relationship between education and the community in a bilingual country: 'The coexistence of Welsh and English, especially when one is a minor tongue and the other a dominating world language, poses serious educational problems.'[98] Inevitably, the degree of mastery of Welsh would vary considerably from area to area, but significantly it was stated that irrespective of where they lived, children whose mother tongue was Welsh should be taught through its medium 'not only in the primary school but to the utmost degree possible in the secondary school also'.[99] Objections to the extended use of Welsh which had focused on the lack of a technical vocabulary and of Welsh books, examination requirements and the dearth of competent teachers, highlighted difficulties which were not believed to be insurmountable. Indeed, teachers' courses were being held to deal with the problems of second-language teaching.

The publication in January 1953 of the report of the Central Advisory Council for Education (Wales), *The Place of Welsh and English in the Schools of Wales*, showed that much had been achieved in promoting the cause of the Welsh language. But there were still considerable variations not only in the linguistic policies of the local education authorities but also in their methods and their determination to implement the policy advocated by the Welsh Department. It was also noted that the recently established Welsh-medium primary schools might indicate 'new directions in Welsh education'. The report emphasized its commitment to a bilingual policy for the schools of Wales. Pupils should be taught Welsh and English 'according to their ability to profit from such instruction'.[100] Although it was essential for all the children of Wales to become bilingual, any attempt to impose 'a uniform aim upon all children, will be useless'.[101] Local education authorities and individual teachers would be best placed to judge and implement appropriate second-language teaching. The implementation of this bilingual policy demanded an adequate supply of suitably-trained teachers. Training college courses needed reappraisal and the introduction of advanced courses in bilingual education was recommended. Welsh should also be available as a medium of instruction not only in the schools but also in the training colleges.

---

[97] Idem, *The County College in Wales / Y Coleg Sir yng Nghymru* (London, 1951), p. 15.

[98] Ministry of Education (Welsh Department), Pamphlet no. 6, *The Curriculum and the Community in Wales* (London, 1952), p. 6.

[99] Ibid., p. 55.

[100] Ministry of Education, Central Advisory Council for Education (Wales), *The Place of Welsh and English in the Schools of Wales*, p. 55.

[101] Ibid., p. 56.

A training college to train teachers exclusively through the medium of Welsh was also advocated. Such an establishment would give 'the Welsh language status and prestige'.[102] Further research on the psychological and sociological aspects of bilingualism by a Council for Research into Education was also deemed essential.[103]

Compulsory bilingualism and the rapid development of designated Welsh-medium primary and secondary schools were not part of official policy-making concerning the Welsh language in education in the post-war years. Nevertheless, the report had made firm recommendations for the extension of bilingual education and for a higher profile for the Welsh language. Its recommendations were reaffirmed in the circular issued by the Welsh Department to mark St David's day in 1953. Local education authorities were urged to visualize Wales as a bilingual country and to define their general policies in greater detail.

In some areas Welsh was now being taught as a second language in an increasing number of schools. It was also being used increasingly as a medium of instruction and language advisers were being appointed to promote its teaching. But many local education authorities and individual schools remained indifferent and apathetic in their attitude towards Welsh. In some secondary schools, even in Welsh-speaking districts, Welsh remained an alternative to French, and in the 1950s English remained the predominant medium of teaching and learning in all the secondary schools of Wales. The ethos of the grammar schools in particular was firmly English. Even in Gwynedd, Welsh was used as a medium of instruction in only twelve secondary schools and often only for the teaching of Scripture.[104] Welsh-medium courses for teachers were established at Bangor Normal College and Trinity College, Carmarthen, but the University of Wales Faculty of Education failed abjectly in 1955–6 to establish a research centre for bilingual education primarily because of disagreement between Bangor and Aberystwyth regarding its location.[105] Primarily through parental pressure and the determination of enlightened local education administrators, headteachers and teachers, the number of Welsh-medium primary schools continued to grow in the 1950s. By 1962 there were thirty-six designated Welsh primary schools with a total enrolment of 3,795 pupils. Of even greater significance at the time, however, was the opening of two bilingual secondary schools in Anglicized Flintshire – Ysgol Glan Clwyd in 1956 with ninety-three pupils initially at Rhyl and later at St Asaph, and Ysgol Maes Garmon in 1961 with 109 pupils at Mold. The determination and foresight of Dr B. Haydn Williams proved to be of vital importance in this direction. In Glamorgan, too, parental pressure played a crucial role in influencing the local

---

[102] Ibid., p. 61
[103] Ibid., p. 72.
[104] H.M.I. (Wales), Welsh-medium work in Secondary Schools: Education Survey 9 (London, 1981), p. 6.
[105] D. Gerwyn Lewis, The University and the Colleges of Education in Wales 1925–78 (Cardiff, 1980), pp. 129–31.

education authority to open Ysgol Gyfun Rhydfelen with an enrolment of eighty pupils in 1962.

Although the Welsh language remained on the periphery of studies in the University of Wales, some important individual initiatives occurred. Within the Education Department at the University College of Wales, Aberystwyth, a supplementary course in bilingual studies for teachers was instituted in 1952–3. Under the auspices of the Faculty of Education, established in 1949, important research into bilingualism was conducted from the 1950s, and courses and conferences were organized for teachers.[106] The work which had begun under the leadership of Professor Idwal Jones in the 1950s was consolidated and developed through the careful guidance of his successor Professor Jac L. Williams in the 1960s and 1970s.[107] Growth in Welsh-medium work characterized all aspects of the activities of the Department and Faculty. Elsewhere, too, a few Welsh-medium appointments were made in university departments and at colleges of education in Bangor and Carmarthen.

In the 1960s the status of the Welsh language not only in the education system but also in other social and legal spheres became the focus of much critical attention. The 1961 census showed a further decline in the number of Welsh speakers, and Saunders Lewis's radio lecture, *Tynged yr Iaith* (The Fate of the Language) (1962), exerted a profound influence on education. In particular, it inspired growing numbers of parents to seek a higher profile for Welsh throughout the educational system. The schools of Wales came to be viewed as having a vital role to play in the survival of the Welsh language. The critical nature of the linguistic situation was further highlighted in 1963 in the *Report on the Welsh Language Today*, published by the Council for Wales and Monmouth-shire. It revealed a pessimistic picture of 'substantial contraction of the Welsh-speaking school population'.[108] Since progress in Welsh among English-speaking pupils tended to be slow and limited, local education authorities and school governors were reminded of their responsibility for implementing a language policy 'in the light of the linguistic pattern in their areas'.[109] The importance of Welsh-medium nursery education, research into the methods of teaching Welsh, ensuring an adequate supply of trained teachers of Welsh, and the extension of Welsh-medium teaching in the University were also emphasized. Above all, it was becoming abundantly clear that the Welsh language required official status. In 1965 the findings of the Hughes Parry Committee, *Report on the Legal Status of the Welsh Language*, were published. Its advocacy of equal validity for the Welsh

---

[106] Idwal Jones (ed.), *A Review of Problems for Research into Bilingualism and Allied Topics* (Aberystwyth, 1953).

[107] Evans (ed.), *Fit to Educate?*, pp. 147–66.

[108] The Council for Wales and Monmouthshire, *Report on the Welsh Language Today* (London, 1963) (PP 1963–4 (Cmnd. 2198) XX), p. 123.

[109] Ibid., p. 100.

language led to the Welsh Language Act of 1967. The report claimed that, with an increase in status, 'the learning of the language at school would seem more purposeful and worthwhile'.[110]

The election of Gwynfor Evans as MP for Carmarthenshire in 1966 epitomized the growth of a national consciousness which placed considerable importance on Welsh-medium education. In 1967 the much-acclaimed Gittins Report, *Primary Education in Wales*, called for 'a positive policy of bilingualism' in the primary schools. It welcomed the 'ysgolion Cymraeg' set up in the Anglicized areas as representing 'one of the most significant developments of the last 30 years'.[111] It also called for the extension of Welsh-medium work in secondary schools. However, a parental attitude survey carried out on behalf of the Gittins Committee revealed that a third of the parents of primary school children in Wales were indifferent to the Welsh language. In the 1960s and 1970s the growth in demand for Welsh-medium education continued unabated. By 1980 there were 54 designated Welsh primary schools with an enrolment of 9,769 pupils, which increased steadily to 64 schools and 10,788 pupils in 1984, and to 69 schools with 12,475 pupils in 1989.[112] The number of designated bilingual secondary schools also increased, as shown in Table 1.

Table 1. Number of designated bilingual secondary schools in Wales and number of pupils in attendance, 1965–90

Year	Number of schools	Number of pupils
1965	5	142
1970	6	2843
1975	8	5504
1980	11	8281
1985	16	10332
1990	18	11519

As well as in the more Anglicized areas – Llanhari, Cardiff, the Rhymney valley, Llandudno, Pontypool, Gowerton and Llanelli – bilingual secondary schools were established at Ystalyfera, Aberystwyth, Bangor, the Gwendraeth valley, Carmarthen and Llandysul. Powys was the only area without a designated bilingual secondary school. Only comparatively slowly did other secondary

[110] The Welsh Office, *Legal Status of the Welsh Language: Report of the Committee under the Chairmanship of Sir David Hughes Parry, 1963–1965* (London, 1965) (PP 1964–5 (Cmnd. 2785) XXIII), p. 35.
[111] Ministry of Education, Central Advisory Council for Education (Wales), *Primary Education in Wales* (London, 1967), p. 221.
[112] The Welsh Office, *Statistics of Education in Wales: Schools, no. 3* (Government Statistical Service, 1989), p. 52.

schools, usually in the Welsh heartland, extend their provision of Welsh-medium teaching. The number of Welsh-medium candidates in Welsh Joint Education Council (WJEC) examinations also increased.[113] Equally significant was the growth of Welsh-medium nursery classes. Voluntary part-time nursery classes were established in Cardiff and Carmarthen in 1943 and in Barry in 1951. Thereafter, their numbers increased slowly and spasmodically, aided by Cronfa Glyndŵr (the Glyndŵr fund), founded by Trefor and Gwyneth Morgan. In 1971 Mudiad Ysgolion Meithrin (the Welsh-medium Nursery Schools Movement) was formed and under its auspices (aided by government grants, which increased from £5,500 in the mid-1970s to over £500,000 in 1996), the number of 'cylchoedd meithrin' (nursery groups) increased from 65 in 1971 to 553 in 1990 and to more than 650 in 1996.[114] By 1998 over 14,000 children were associated with Welsh-medium nursery schools.[115]

The growth of bilingual and Welsh-medium education owed more to the pressure of individual parents and Cymdeithasau Ysgolion Cymraeg (Welsh Schools' Societies) than to the influence of educational administrators, inspectors and teachers, although their support was also crucial. Initially, many of the protagonists were the intelligentsia – upwardly mobile, professional, Welsh-speaking parents from 'Y Fro Gymraeg' – whose employment in administration, the media and education had taken them to the more Anglicized parts of south-east and north-east Wales. More remarkable was the growing support in the 1970s and 1980s from non-Welsh-speaking parents. The academic achievements of the bilingual schools, a more acute perception of national identity, reflected in the establishment of the Welsh Office and the cultural and economic benefits of bilingualism, led to growing demand for bilingual education. There was also an awareness of the detrimental effects of inward migration on the future well-being of the native tongue. Plausible arguments, based on natural justice and equity and a growing realization that bilingual education had no adverse effects on educational achievement, also contributed to the overall growth of bilingual education. Individuals and various groups and organizations, including Urdd Gobaith Cymru, Undeb Cymdeithasau Rhieni Ysgolion Cymraeg, Cymdeithas yr Iaith Gymraeg (the Welsh Language Society), UCAC, Merched y Wawr (lit. Daughters of the Dawn) and Plaid Cymru, all exerted pressure. The Welsh Office and the Department of Education and Science continued to support the well-established policy of bilingual education, reaffirmed in numerous surveys and reports, including *Welsh-medium Work in Secondary Schools* (1981) and *Welsh in the Secondary Schools of Wales* (1984). In the 1960s and 1970s the Schools Council

---

[113] Illtyd R. Lloyd, 'A Period of Change – Working for Progress: Secondary Education in Wales, 1965–1985' in Gareth Elwyn Jones (ed.), *Education, Culture and Society: Some Perspectives on the Nineteenth and Twentieth Centuries. Essays Presented to J. R. Webster* (Cardiff, 1991), p. 104.

[114] Catrin Stevens, *Meithrin: Hanes Mudiad Ysgolion Meithrin 1971–1996* (Llandysul, 1996).

[115] Mudiad Ysgolion Meithrin, *Adroddiad Blynyddol / Annual Report 1997–98*, p. 9.

Committee for Wales financed research projects and organized conferences concerning bilingualism, and endeavoured to promote the use of Welsh as a medium of teaching.[116] A National Language Unit was established under the auspices of the WJEC to undertake research into the teaching of Welsh as a second language. Financial support was given to the WJEC to publish Welsh-language textbooks and to local education authorities to establish a system of peripatetic Welsh teachers. Under the terms of the Education Reform Act 1988, Welsh became a statutory, compulsory subject – either a core or a foundation subject – for the first time ever in all the primary and secondary schools of Wales from the beginning of the 1990–1 academic year. Unsurprisingly, Sir Wyn Roberts, the Minister of State with responsibility for education in Wales, was at pains to underline the major significance of this legislation for the future of the Welsh language.

While the spectacular growth of bilingual education and the success of bilingual schools in the 1970s and 1980s were abundantly evident, support for the new status gained by the Welsh language was not so apparent. Nor should the overall linguistic change in these decades be exaggerated. In 1976, 25.8 per cent of primary schools in Wales taught no Welsh at all. In 1984, 23.4 per cent of primary schools were exclusively English-language establishments. As many as 98.1 per cent of primary schools in Gwent, 37 per cent of primary schools in South Glamorgan, 10.7 per cent of primary schools in Powys, and 9.7 per cent of primary schools in Dyfed did not teach Welsh. In 1983–4, 121,116 pupils or 52.1 per cent of the total secondary schools' enrolment were not taught the Welsh language.[117] In 1988 only 13 per cent of primary school pupils throughout Wales spoke Welsh fluently, and 74 per cent of primary school pupils spoke no Welsh at all. Although over 80 per cent of pupils were taught Welsh in the first year of secondary school, only 28 per cent were learning Welsh in the fourth year.[118] The provision of Welsh-medium courses in colleges of education and the constituent colleges of the University of Wales was inadequate and attracted only a comparatively small number of students.

In the post-Gittins Report era, there remained significant variations among the Welsh-language policies of the local education authorities and also among individual secondary schools in the number and range of subjects available through the medium of Welsh. In some areas, each individual secondary school decided the extent of its commitment to bilingualism on the basis of its own

---

[116] 'Two Languages for Life' – A Report of a Schools Council Committee for Wales Conference (Cardiff, 1976).

[117] The Welsh Office, Statistics of Education in Wales, no. 9 (Government Statistical Service, 1984), p. 45.

[118] John Aitchison and Harold Carter, A Geography of the Welsh Language 1961–1991 (Cardiff, 1994), p. 70.

circumstances.[119] Local education authorities varied considerably in their degree of support. Following the reorganization of local government in 1974, the new Gwynedd Education Authority pursued a successful bilingual policy, but elsewhere, particularly in West Glamorgan, there was much indifference and inertia. Rarely was a designated bilingual secondary school opened even in the more Welsh-speaking areas without much acrimony and conflict. Ysgol Penweddig in Aberystwyth, Ysgol Bro Myrddin in Carmarthen, and Ysgol Tryfan in Bangor were only established after intense communal debate and much hostility. Sometimes the more vociferous opponents of Welsh-medium education included native Welsh speakers. Organizations such as the Language Freedom Movement in Aberystwyth in the 1970s and Education First in Dyfed in the 1990s seldom disguised their hostility to the Welsh language. At times, support for Welsh-medium education was equated with social élitism and the promotion of an unhealthy nationalism.

Arguably, the comparatively limited growth of bilingual and Welsh-medium education in post-war Wales reflected the nature of the educational system. The keynote of educational policy-making and administration was the partnership of central government and local education authorities. From the era of O. M. Edwards onwards, central government, through the agency of the Welsh Department (after 1964 the Welsh Office) as well as the reports of numerous committees, advocated a policy of bilingual education. But there was no statutory compulsion until 1988. The implementation of a bilingual policy and the promotion of the Welsh language in education depended on the support, to a greater or lesser degree, of local education authorities and headteachers. Until the introduction of a national curriculum under the terms of the Education Reform Act 1988, central government was unwilling to court unpopularity by imposing a mandatory national language policy or demanding more positive action by local education authorities in establishing Welsh-medium schools.[120] At a time when the Labour governments of the 1970s adopted a firm line regarding comprehensive education, there was a marked reluctance to do likewise regarding the teaching of Welsh and Welsh-medium education. John Morris, Secretary of State for Wales, maintained that 'in education, local authorities get an enormous amount of guidance. But they also have a great amount of expertise. If I were to tread on the toes of county education committees I would be in very great difficulty'.[121] Although the support of the Welsh Office since 1964 for Welsh-medium education was crucial, it is also arguable that Wales was allowed to be distinctive in its educational development because the principal educational

---

[119] *Secondary Education in Rural Wales: A Report by the Aberystwyth Policy Group.* (Aberystwyth, 1985), pp. 40–5.

[120] Jac L. Williams, 'Troi'r Cloc yn Ôl? A yw Cylchlythyr 2/69 yn Torri Traddodiad?', *Barn*, 85 (1969), 9.

[121] Quoted in Clive Betts, *Culture in Crisis: The Future of the Welsh Language* (Upton, 1976), p. 101.

concerns of central government lay elsewhere. In charting the struggle over comprehensive education, Gareth Elwyn Jones rightly claimed that 'concessions to the Welsh language have been of marginal concern to Westminster governments'.[122]

---

[122] Gareth Elwyn Jones, *Which Nation's Schools? Direction and Devolution in Welsh Education in the Twentieth Century* (Cardiff, 1990), p. 195.

10

The Welsh Language and Religion

D. DENSIL MORGAN

Y gwir yw fod rhan fawr ac anhepgor o'n crefydd ni fel Cymry yn gymhlethedig â'n hiaith. I'r mwyafrif mawr o Gymry crefyddol golygai colli'r iaith golli eu crefydd hefyd.[1]

(The truth is that a large and essential part of our religion as Welsh people is bound up with our language. To the vast majority of religious Welsh people, losing the language would mean losing their religion as well.)

THIS VIEW was expressed during the 1920s by a Congregational minister in east Glamorgan at a time when the 'English deluge' (as he called it) threatened to sweep everything before it. Not every believer would have insisted on linking the fate of the Welsh language so closely to the fate of the faith, but there is no doubt that the relationship was extremely close. According to one historian, only a detailed analysis of this association and the nature of the changes which occurred from the mid-nineteenth century onwards can provide 'the richest clues as to the role not only of religion but also of language in society'.[2] The aim of this chapter is less ambitious: it charts the history of Christianity in Wales from 1914 to the 1990s, and suggests how the Welsh language, as well as people's attitude towards it and their awareness of it, affected that history.

The Pattern of Religion and Language up to 1914

According to the 1901 census the best part of half the population of Wales were Welsh speakers, but within a decade the proportion had fallen to 43.5 per cent. This pattern can be compared with that of religious practice: in 1905 two of every five Welsh people were church members, i.e. 743,361 out of a population of 1,864,696. By denomination, 193,081 (25.9 per cent) were Anglican

---

[1] Arthur Jones, 'Yr Eglwysi a'r Gymraeg', *Y Dysgedydd* (March 1916), 135.
[2] Ieuan Gwynedd Jones, *Towards a Social History of the Welsh Language* (Aberystwyth, 1994), p. 17.

communicants, 175,147 (23.5 per cent) were Congregationalists, 170,617 (23 per cent) were Calvinistic Methodists, 143,835 (19.2 per cent) were Baptists, 40,811 (5.4 per cent) were Wesleyan Methodists and 19,870 (3 per cent) belonged to smaller denominations such as the Unitarians, the Plymouth Brethren, the Salvation Army and so on. Geographically, over half the population of the western counties, namely Anglesey, Caernarfon, Merioneth, Cardigan, Carmarthen and Pembroke, belonged to a church, but the percentage decreased the further east one went: from 45.2 per cent in Montgomeryshire to 27.7 per cent in Flintshire. There was very little difference between rural and urban patterns in these counties. However, the percentage of believers was lower in the more populous areas and the larger towns, especially in the east: 16.8 per cent in Cardiff, 27.1 per cent in Aberdare, 29.3 per cent in Merthyr Tydfil, and 34.9 per cent in the Rhondda. In the west the proportion was higher: 40.3 per cent in Neath, 47.5 per cent in Maesteg, 52.8 per cent in Llanelli and 67.9 per cent in Ammanford.[3] When these figures are compared with the distribution of the Welsh language, a broad degree of correspondence can be seen between knowledge and use of the language and membership of a church. According to R. Tudur Jones, the general rule was that if more than 60 per cent of the population spoke Welsh, over half the population were church members, but if less than 30 per cent were Welsh speakers it was rarely the case that more than a third of the population were church members.[4] It is hardly surprising, therefore, that many people believed that Christianity was synonymous in some way or other with the 'Welsh way of life'.

The use people made of the Welsh language did not in every case correspond with their attitude towards it. Since Welsh was for many the only medium of expression, religion was wholly dependent on the language, particularly in the west. But its status, almost without exception, was lower than that of English and on occasions this was a cause of deep concern. The principal denominations afforded spiritual sustenance for both linguistic communities, and all denominations had their English-language churches. Ever since 1880, when Lewis Edwards refused to ordain Robert Ambrose Jones (Emrys ap Iwan) into the pastoral ministry, the matter of English-language provision – the 'Inglis Côs' (English cause) – had been a burning issue among Calvinistic Methodists. The bone of contention was not so much the desire to present the gospel to non-Welsh speakers as the difference in status between the languages. If Welsh was the

---

[3] R. Tudur Jones, *Ffydd ac Argyfwng Cenedl: Cristionogaeth a Diwylliant yng Nghymru* (2 vols., Abertawe, 1982), I, pp. 25–7, based on statistics recorded by the Royal Commission on the Church of England and Other Religious Bodies in Wales and Monmouthshire (London, 1910) (PP 1910 (Cd. 5432) XIV). This estimate does not include the 80,000 members of the Roman Catholic Church who were in Wales at the time, the vast majority of whom lived in Newport and Cardiff and parts of Flintshire.

[4] Jones, *Ffydd ac Argyfwng Cenedl*, p. 30.

language of the common people, English was the language of commerce, progress and the Empire, and a genuine ambition to evangelize among non-Welsh speakers could often conceal a desire to be fashionable in the eyes of the world. The speed of change in the language of worship in the Nonconformist churches of Monmouthshire (with the exception of those in the upper part of the Rhymney valley) in the 1880s, together with their willingness to abandon their ancient heritage, suggested that significant social pressures were at work, and this was also doubtless true of other areas.[5]

During these years the situation was complicated by the campaign in favour of disestablishment. In spite of the emphasis placed on promoting the 'English cause', from around 1890 Nonconformist leaders believed that their denominations best expressed the Welsh identity. But the truth is that there was nothing particularly Welsh about Nonconformity. The Congregationalists, the Baptists and the Wesleyans had originated in England, and Calvinistic Methodism was the only indigenous Welsh denomination. On the whole, the Welshness of the chapels was more pragmatic than principled. Apart from individuals such as Michael D. Jones and Emrys ap Iwan, Nonconformists who were convinced of the inherent value of Welsh were rare, and there were many like J. R. Kilsby Jones who were eagerly awaiting its demise. However, as the sense of nationhood deepened, the relationship between faith and nationality became a matter of acute concern.

For Churchmen such as Henry T. Edwards, dean of Bangor, Wales and the Welsh language were important matters. During the long centuries of their history, the Church and the nation had been one. The Celtic saints, such as Dyfrig and Illtud, Dewi and Teilo, represented a Christian culture far older than the Christianity of Canterbury, and that culture had not been impaired by the political union between England and Wales in 1536. This Celtic church had been the true national church for a millennium and more, and thus it would have continued had it not been for the destructive policy of the Stuart state, intensified thereafter by the Hanoverians. 'The policy which arrayed all the forces of nationality against the Church was not adopted in Wales until the eighteenth century', claimed Edwards, 'at that point its effect was to make the Welsh people not Romanist, but Nonconformist.'[6] He maintained that the Welsh had rejected the Church not for religious reasons but because the leading prelates of the Church had turned their back upon them. With considerable passion, Dean Edwards argued that it was still possible to reform the established Church, and that in Wales it was this Church, rather than Nonconformity, which represented the true aspirations of the common people.

Although many ordinary clerics sympathized with Dean Edwards's analysis, there was a good deal of substance to the criticism that the Church was a foreign

---

[5] See Brynmor Pierce Jones, *Sowing Beside All Waters: The Baptist Heritage of Gwent* (Cwmbrân, 1985), pp. 53–61, 84–92, 101–39.

[6] Henry T. Edwards, *Wales and the Welsh Church* (London, 1889), pp. 318–19.

institution, that it was the Church of *England* in Wales. Ironically, no one did more to strengthen this belief than Dean Edwards's brother, A. G. Edwards, the chief apologist of the rights of the Church during the disestablishment campaign. Elected bishop of St Asaph in 1889, he responded to the challenge of the supporters of disestablishment by emphasizing the privileged social status of the Church and its links with the English establishment. In contrast to Henry T. Edwards, his attitude towards Welshness was extremely ambiguous: 'I am half an Englishman and half a Welshman and I have been labouring between the two all my life.'[7] Although able to speak Welsh, he considered the language barbarous and primitive: 'Welsh', he declared, 'the last refuge of the uneducated.'[8] As W. J. Gruffydd noted: 'For years he [the bishop] has been notorious for his enmity towards the language of the Welsh' ('Y mae['r esgob] ers blynyddoedd yn enwog am ei elyniaeth at iaith y Cymry').[9] The ambivalence of A. G. Edwards towards Welshness, together with his contempt for the language, became a feature of his episcopal policy as well as the basis of his energetic campaign to defend the rights of the Anglican Church in Wales during the disestablishment campaign.[10]

This left its mark on the Church as a whole. Although Welsh was the medium of services within Welsh-speaking areas and the only language of worship in many parishes, it was accorded no official status. English was the only language of administration in the four dioceses; it was also the medium of communication between senior clergy and among many of the minor clergy as well. It was fashionable for them to speak English among themselves and very often to deprive their children of the opportunity to learn Welsh. Together with the general trend towards Anglicization which was already underway, this practice further weakened the sense of Welshness within the Church. Although provision existed for Welsh-language services in most of the populous parishes in Llandaff, the general view was that the language was in terminal decline in the diocese. The impression gained from reading the comments of William Thomas, vicar of Cymer and Porth, before the Royal Commission on the Church of England and Other Religious Bodies in Wales and Monmouthshire, was that the sooner English gained ascendancy the better. He claimed that English was the language of the younger generation everywhere and that was how it would continue: 'A very large proportion of those who do worship seemingly in Welsh know very little about Welsh. I doubt if they are capable of understanding a Welsh sermon . . . the

---

[7] George Lerry, *Alfred George Edwards: Archbishop of Wales* (Oswestry, n.d.), p. 54.
[8] Quoted in Owain W. Jones, *Glyn Simon: His Life and Opinions* (Llandysul, 1981), p. 55.
[9] 'Nodiadau'r Golygydd', *Y Llenor*, VIII, no. 3 (1929), 129.
[10] See Roger L. Brown, 'Traitors and Compromisers: The Shadow Side of the Church's Fight against Disestablishment', *Journal of Welsh Religious History*, 3 (1995), 35–53.

question is becoming a very serious one – how to provide for the youth of the district, owing to the fact that they are incapable of grasping a Welsh sermon.'[11]

There were also signs that a split was emerging between the Welsh-language culture of the Church and the culture associated with popular Nonconformity. Among the most influential religious leaders in the Rhondda in this period were Canon William Lewis, vicar of Ystradyfodwg and rural dean of the Rhondda, and the Revd William Morris (Rhosynnog), Noddfa, Treorci, the doyen of Baptist ministers in the valley. Both were patriotic Welshmen, of similar theological convictions, enthusiastic in their support of all charitable work and, despite the tensions caused by the disestablishment campaign, on friendly terms with one another. Culturally, however, they inhabited different worlds. Whereas Morris stood in the mainstream of Welsh-language Nonconformist culture, with its choirs and cantatas, its literature, plays and public lectures, Lewis ruefully admitted that very little cultural provision existed in Church circles. In a parish of 22,000 people, only 90 copies of *Y Cyfaill Eglwysig* (the Anglican's Welsh-language periodical) were distributed and even fewer of the *Church Evangelist*. Nor was any effort made to promote literacy, let alone culture and learning among the parishioners. At Noddfa chapel, on the other hand, a class of young men met every week to study the intricacies of Dewi Môn's grammar and to perfect their skills in written and spoken Welsh. Periodicals such as *Y Greal, Seren Gomer, Yr Heuwr, Seren yr Ysgol Sul, Y Geninen* and the newspaper *Seren Cymru* were widely read. When the canon was asked how well acquainted he was with the literary output of such Nonconformist neighbours as David James (Defynnog), Cynon Evans, Lewis Jones, Treherbert, Lewis Probert, Ben Bowen, David Bowen (Myfyr Hefin), D. M. Davies, Tylorstown, and the Revd William Morris himself, he was forced to admit that he had never read a word of their work![12]

This cultural divide was not unique, nor was the disagreement between Churchmen and Nonconformists regarding the future prospects of the Welsh language. The Revd R. E. Peregrine, the learned minister of Seion Congregational Church, Rhymney, insisted that the position of the Welsh language in the locality was so healthy that he was not required to use any English,[13] but Daniel Fisher, vicar of the parish, held a different view: 'The tendency of the rising generation I think is really to go in for English more than Welsh.' Fisher's predecessor as vicar of Rhymney was Canon William Evans, an accomplished Welsh writer and dedicated editor of *Y Cyfaill Eglwysig*, but when his successor was asked what he knew of Evans's literary labours he confessed that he knew next to nothing. Neither did he know of John Davies (Ossian Gwent), Thomas Jones (Gwenffrwd), David Jones

[11] Royal Commission on the Church of England and Other Religious Bodies in Wales and Monmouthshire, *Minutes of Evidence. Vol. II. Book I* (London, 1910) (PP 1910 (Cd. 5433) XV), questions 6112 and 6120.

[12] Ibid., questions 5823–67; for the replies of the Revd William Morris (Rhosynnog), see questions 8971–9739.

[13] Ibid., question 11524.

(Dafydd o Went) or any of the other Nonconformist writers of his own parish.[14] The cultural divide between Churchmen and Nonconformists was paralleled by the division between patriotically-inclined Welsh Churchmen and those who were indifferent to their cultural heritage. It was as if the inheritance of Henry T. Edwards was being undermined by his brother, who was elected first archbishop of the new disestablished church in 1920. It would take decades for the Church in Wales to rid itself of its lukewarm and anti-Welsh image.

Christianity, Socialism and National Identity 1914–c.1940

Between the outbreak of the Great War in 1914 and its conclusion in 1918, as many as 280,000 Welshmen served in the armed forces, of whom around 14 per cent died. There was not a town or village in the country which did not experience loss, anguish and grief. Although the true impact of the conflict was not assessed until later, everyone already knew that the old world had perished in the desolation of the Somme. Hedd Wyn's couplet conveyed the conviction of a whole generation:

> Gwae fi fy myw mewn oes mor ddreng
> A Duw ar drai ar orwel pell.[15]
>
> (Woe that I live in this dire age,
> When God on far horizon flees.)[16]

The influence of the war on Christian witness was mixed. For some the conflict deepened their faith in God, but for others it served to confirm scepticism and unbelief. Rather than returning to a land fit for heroes, many of the soldiers and sailors who escaped with their lives found themselves in a period of unparalleled economic depression and social upheaval. In the wake of changes in naval technology and developments in the field of transport in general, the international demand for steam coal from south Wales came to an end, and from the beginning of the 1920s cheap coal was purchased from the mines of Italy, Spain, Poland and the United States. The international markets for Welsh steel disappeared. As well as the widespread redundancies which occurred in the coalfield, thousands of men became unemployed as a result of the closure of the steel works at Cyfarthfa (1921), Blaenafon (1922), Ebbw Vale (1929) and Dowlais (1930). By 1925, 16.5 per cent of the population was unemployed; this proportion rose to 19.5 per cent within two years, and reached 26 per cent by 1930. During the 1930s the

---

[14] Ibid., questions 10815–969.
[15] Hedd Wyn, *Cerddi'r Bugail* (Y Bala, 1918), p. 146.
[16] Translated by D. Tecwyn Lloyd in 'Welsh Literature and the First World War', *Planet*, 11 (1972), 21.

situation continued to deteriorate. By August 1932, 42.8 per cent of Welsh male workers were idle and, from September 1931 onwards, financial assistance from the state was cut and a Means Test imposed on all applications for assistance. The greatest suffering was endured in the industrial areas where the language was on the wane, namely the eastern part of Glamorgan and Monmouthshire, an area which experienced large-scale out-migration. It was here too, perhaps more so than in other areas, that the churches faced pressing theological and practical problems regarding the nature of their mission.

Long before the depression the churches had been forced to grapple with the labour question. Early socialists such as Keir Hardie had employed scriptural language and biblical images in a bid to win Welsh chapel-goers to their cause. In Hardie's view, socialism was an ethical creed rather than a political or economic dogma. 'It is a Socialist scheme', claimed R. Silyn Roberts, 'and in the view of the majority of its adherents Socialism is a religion. For some Socialism is an intellectual conviction; for others it is an organizational or a political creed; but to ninety-nine per cent of the members of the I.L.P. [Independent Labour Party] Socialism possesses the vital force of a great religious truth' ('Cyfundeb Sosialaidd yw hi ac yng ngolwg mwyafrif ei haelodau crefydd yw Sosialaeth. I rai argyhoeddiad deallol yw Sosialaeth; i eraill credo drefnidol neu wleidyddol ydyw; ond i naw deg a naw y cant o aelodau'r B.L.A. [y Blaid Lafur Annibynnol] medd Sosialaeth rym bywiol gwirionedd crefyddol mawr').[17] Although the Revd T. E. Nicholas (Niclas y Glais) would later profess thoroughly Marxist convictions about the class war, he was the chief Welsh-language propagandist of the Independent Labour Party in south Wales during this early period, and he represented perfectly the links being forged between the old Welsh radical Nonconformity and the new politics. Some of the ablest of the younger ministers were attracted to the socialist ranks, among them John Jenkins (Gwili), John Morgan Jones (Aberdare, and later Bala-Bangor), Herbert Morgan and R. Silyn Roberts. Welsh 'Nonconformist' socialism heavily influenced James Griffiths, who became the leader of the miners in south Wales. Griffiths appreciated the powerful influence which Silyn Roberts had exercised on the generation which came to maturity at the advent of the Great War:

Yr oedd i'w ddyfodiad ef arwyddocâd arbennig i ni ieuenctid Deheudir Cymru. Yr oedd ef yn ddolen yn cydio'r hen a'r newydd, ac yr oedd gan yr hen eto ddigon o afael arnom i beri inni deimlo fod eisiau dolen i'n cydio wrtho. Silyn oedd y ddolen. Pregethai Dduw a Datblygiad. Yr oedd yn weinidog ac yn Sosialydd . . . Efe oedd ein hysbrydoliaeth, a'n cyfiawnhad hefyd. Gallem ddweud wrth ein rhieni a ofnai'r efengyl newydd yma y soniem gymaint amdani, 'Ond mae Silyn Roberts yn credu fel ni.' Faint o dadau duwiolfrydig pryderus a gymodwyd â Sosialaeth eu meibion gan y wybodaeth hon? Yr oedd ef yn cydio De Cymru Evan Roberts wrth Dde Cymru Keir Hardie.[18]

[17] R. Silyn Roberts, *Y Blaid Lafur Anibynnol: Ei Hanes a'i Hamcan* (Blaenau Ffestiniog, 1908), p. 6.
[18] Quoted in David Thomas, *Silyn (Robert Silyn Roberts), 1871–1930* (Lerpwl, 1956), p. 77.

(His coming had special significance for us, the young people of South Wales. He was a link binding together the old and the new, and the old had enough of a hold on us to make us feel that a link was required to bind us to it. Silyn was that link. He preached God and Evolution. He was a minister and a Socialist . . . He was our inspiration, and our justification too. We could say to our parents, who feared the new gospel of which we talked so much, 'But Silyn Roberts believes as we do'. How many pious and anxious fathers came to terms with their sons' Socialism by means of this knowledge? He linked the South Wales of Evan Roberts with the South Wales of Keir Hardie.)

This new socialism was a 'gospel', and because it spoke the language of religion it appeared to be eminently compatible with chapelgoing. Throughout the 1920s, progressive Nonconformity sought to assimilate socialist politics. 'It is rather late in the day to utter this nonsense [regarding any division between religion and socialism]', claimed one commentator, 'for there are thousands of Welshmen to-day who can find no inconsistency in singing "Diolch Iddo" and "Ar Ei Ben Bo'r Goron" with the Welsh hwyl at one meeting, and then proceeding to another meeting to sing "The Red Flag" with the same intense enthusiasm.'[19] But there were considerable problems implicit in this integration. Traditional Noncon-formists feared that the link between Christian belief and socialism was being forged at the expense of the substance of the faith. Those who were most enthusiastic for socialism and the 'Social Gospel' seemed to be furthest from the central truths of historical Christianity.

Whereas R. Silyn Roberts preached God and Evolution, T. E. Nicholas believed in the perfectibility of humankind: 'true Christian religion recognises the divinity of man, made in the likeness of God, and having the spirit of God within him, who is not a fallen being, but is continually advancing to higher levels, and who is endowed with unlimited possibilities'.[20] Orthodox doctrines such as Original Sin, the Incarnation, the Trinity, the classical interpretation of the Person of Christ and the Atonement were either reinterpreted along social and naturalistic lines or rejected as worthless relics.[21] At the same time many church leaders, in reaction against the previous association between the denominations and the Liberal Party, desisted from taking up a political stance. As far as their relationship with Labour was concerned, the tendency was to dress humanistic socialism in Sunday clothes rather than to devise a balanced and healthy social theology. The outer trappings of religion – hymn-singing, respect for the Sabbath and an appreciation of a well-constructed sermon – were still important for many, but spiritual convictions were weakening daily. By interpreting Christianity in

---

[19] *Labour Voice*, 14 April 1923.
[20] David W. Howell, *Nicholas of Glais: The People's Champion* (Clydach, 1991), p. 29.
[21] See Robert Pope, 'Y Drindod: Profiad Personol a Chymdeithasol', *Diwinyddiaeth*, XLV (1994), 92–108; idem, *Seeking God's Kingdom: The Nonconformist Social Gospel in Wales, 1906–39* (Cardiff, 1999), passim.

accordance with the fashionable philosophical Idealism, the theological liberals or 'modernists' sought to create a synthesis between humanism and faith. Many ordinary believers who championed the new politics were happy to follow them. But their efforts were bound to end in failure. By rejecting classical orthodoxy, Welsh Christians were deprived of the kind of teaching which could have enabled them to interpret social needs more effectively and in accordance with the canons of the faith. More than a decade elapsed before some of Wales's religious leaders began to realize the implications of this.

Membership of the Nonconformist churches reached its peak in 1926 when a total of 530,000 adult communicants was recorded by the different denominations.[22] These figures, however, were deceptive. Although the formal membership was increasing, complaints of slackness in Sunday observance and a general lack of loyalty to other church activities were continually aired. Above all, the number of 'adherents' – those who attended services regularly but who were not full members – was diminishing. The pattern was replicated in the case of children. By the 1930s it was clear that the future of Nonconformity was in serious jeopardy and its leaders were unable to respond to the situation.[23] Some believed that deliverance would come by means of social action, but individualism had taken so firm a hold on the Nonconformist conscience that nothing came of this. The fundamental weakness of *Yr Eglwys a Chwestiynau Cymdeithasol* (The Church and Social Questions) (1921), the report of Committee V prepared by the Restructuring Commission of the Calvinistic Methodists, and *Cenadwri Gymdeithasol yr Efengyl* (The Social Message of the Gospel) (1923), the report of the Congregationalists, was their individualism. Although both reports analysed the effect which social structures exercised on living conditions, they offered no satisfactory answers to the current situation. The paramount need, they claimed, was to adapt Christian 'principles' to social problems. This could be done by the individual and through his efforts changes in the political, social and economic order would occur. Theologically speaking, this was Pelagianism, and in political terms 'Liberalism', at least from the point of view of philosophy if not specifically of party allegiance. Whereas the pure socialism of the Labour Party and the ideals of the trade unions acted for the benefit of the mass of the working class, the denominations still placed their faith in the power of the individual. Nonconformity became irrelevant to many because it ignored class issues, and the Welsh language played its part in this rejection.

It soon became apparent that the strain upon religion would become immense in future years. Secularism was spreading: the appeal of the chapels had been undermined by the popularity of new forms of entertainment such as the cinema;

[22] John Williams (ed.), *Digest of Welsh Historical Statistics* (2 vols., Cardiff, 1985), II, pp. 272, 294, 324, 342.

[23] See R. Tudur Jones, *Hanes Annibynwyr Cymru* (Abertawe, 1966), pp. 278–95; T. M. Bassett, *The Welsh Baptists* (Swansea, 1977), pp. 392–3.

the assumption of the *Aufklärung* that education was essentially neutral with regard to religious values affected the curriculum taught in schools and colleges; and by the 1920s and 1930s there was a violent reaction against the puritanism of the Nonconformist conscience and the standards associated with it. From the mid-1920s onwards the chapels would lose more members than they gained and for every worker who succeeded in combining religion and trades unionism there was another who believed that religion and socialism were the 'opium of the masses'. 'The people now that became socialists in South Wales', declared the Communist Dai Dan Evans, 'became automatically irreligious.'[24] Despite the earlier effort to bind together socialism, Nonconformity and the Welsh language, the ties now seemed to be unravelling. Socialism signified fashionableness, modernity and progress, while the Welsh language was synonymous with puritanism and the Liberalism of the past. 'The language of socialism was English', maintains Ieuan Gwynedd Jones (referring to the experience of south Wales), and thus ' . . . to abandon Welsh became not only a valuational but also a symbolic gesture of rejection and of affirmation; the rejection of the political philosophy and the sham combination of Lib-Labism and the affirmation of new solidarities and new idealisms based upon a secular and anti-religious philosophy'.[25]

By the mid- and late 1930s, the aspirations of workers in south Wales were represented by Aneurin Bevan, MP for Ebbw Vale, a non-religious, non-Welsh-speaking materialist.[26] In the secularized Wales which was developing in the industrial valleys and beyond, religion and the Welsh language were to languish together. When the Revd E. Cynolwyn Pugh became minister of the Calvinistic Methodist chapel at Tonyrefail, Glamorgan, in 1921, he was assured that Welsh was the language both of the community and of the church, but he was soon disabused. The majority of members were miners and their families, and the class of 'adherents' – men aged from fifty to seventy – was still sizeable. However, very few of the young people were able to speak Welsh and not more than half a dozen of the eighty children were fluent. Yet, some of the church elders insisted that there was no language problem or difficulty.[27] They represented the old order and ignored the social transformation which was occurring around them. The younger generation was already siding with modernity, and English was their chosen medium of communication.[28]

[24] Quoted in Robert Pope, *Building Jerusalem: Nonconformity, Labour and the Social Question in Wales, 1906–1939* (Cardiff, 1998), p. 104.

[25] Ieuan Gwynedd Jones, 'Language and Community in Nineteenth Century Wales' in Paul H. Ballard and D. Huw Jones (eds.), *This Land and People: A Symposium on Christian and Welsh National Identity* (Cardiff, 1979), p. 36.

[26] Kenneth O. Morgan, *The Red Dragon and the Red Flag: The Cases of James Griffiths and Aneurin Bevan* (Aberystwyth, 1989).

[27] E. Cynolwyn Pugh, *Ei Ffanffer ei Hun* (Aberystwyth, 1958), pp. 56–7.

[28] For a similar situation among the Congregationalists during the same period, see D. Eurof Walters, 'Yr Annibynwyr a'r Dylifiad Saesneg' in J. E. Lloyd et al., *Hanes ac Egwyddorion Annibynwyr Cymru* (Abertawe, 1939), pp. 169–80.

Christianity, the Welsh Language and National Consciousness 1920–45

Not every Christian, however, was willing to accede to this situation, and between the wars efforts were made to restore the Welsh language to a position of dignity and honour in its own country. As well as achieving dominion status for Wales under the British Crown, the aim of Plaid Genedlaethol Cymru (the Welsh Nationalist Party), which was established in August 1925, was to safeguard Welsh culture, mainly by protecting the interests of the Welsh language. Among its founders were the Revd Fred Jones and Griffith John Williams, both of whom were Congregationalists, W. Ambrose Bebb, who eventually became a Methodist elder, Lewis Valentine, a Baptist minister, and Saunders Lewis, the son, grandson and great-grandson of influential Calvinist ministers. Of these, Lewis was the outstanding figure, and also the most independent thinker. Although still formally a Calvinistic Methodist, he had already expressed his disagreement with the major religious trend of the age. 'It seems to me', he wrote in September 1923, 'that the tendency towards a vagueness of creed is the chief characteristic of theology [today], – the condition known as "modernism"' ('Fe ymddengys i mi mai'r dwedd at amhendantrwydd credo yw prif nodwedd diwinyddiaeth [heddiw], – y cyflwr a elwir yn "modernism"').[29] Writing in 1926, the year which saw the publication of the biblical dictionary, *Y Geiriadur Beiblaidd*, a work heavily influenced by liberal theology, he maintained that the majority of Nonconformist ministers in Wales who claimed to be scholars of some sort were modernists. Their tendency, he argued:

> yw ymwadu â phob cred mewn miragl, yn y cwbl a elwid ers talm yn 'oruwchnaturiol'. Nid oes mewn sacrament – neu, yn yr hen ddull, sagrafen – ystyr iddynt o gwbl. Nid yw'n ddim ond peth i helpu'r cof a thynnu sylw, peth y gallai'r Cristion cryf ei hepgor yn rhwydd. Yn wir, gwlad ddisagrafen yw Cymru ymneilltuol heddiw.[30]

> (is to renounce all beliefs in miracle, in everything that was once called 'supernatural'. The sacrament – or, in the traditional manner, *sagrafen* – holds no meaning for them at all. It is nothing more than an aid to memory and to focus the attention, something that the mature Christian could easily do without. Indeed nonconformist Wales today is a land bereft of sacraments.)

Although alien to many Welsh people, the Catholic Church which Saunders Lewis later joined already championed the separateness of Wales and the language and cultures of small nations. Since 1895 Wales had been considered a separate apostolic vicariate and before the end of the century the diocese of Menevia had been formed from it, with Francis Mostyn, son of the patrician Mostyn family of

[29] *Baner ac Amserau Cymru*, 6 September 1923.
[30] Ibid., 8 July 1926.

Talacre, Flintshire, as bishop. 'The idea of a Welsh diocese, a Welsh bishop, and a bilingual clergy would not only make a special appeal to Welsh Catholics', claimed Cardinal Vaughan of Westminster, 'but would break down prejudice and encourage a sympathy in the non-Catholic Welsh, and so open way to conversions.'[31] The bond between Catholicism and Wales went deeper still as a result of the publication in 1916 of *Cambria Celtica*, the apostolic letter of Pope Benedict XV which created the Archdiocese of Cardiff, with Menevia as a separate diocese. 'Wales', he maintained, 'a nation of Celtic origin, differs so much from the rest of England in language, traditions, and ancient customs that it would seem in the ecclesiastical order also to call for separation from the other churches and for the possession of its own hierarchy.'[32] A year later, in his letter *Maximum Illud*, Benedict spoke of the need for a priest to be at one with his people in background, culture and language, and in *Rerum Ecclesiae* (1926) Pius XI also emphasized the need to reach people by empathizing with their principal characteristics and their national customs.

The language of the Catholic Church was Latin, and people of Irish extraction, rather than the indigenous Welsh, constituted the majority of its members. But throughout the inter-war years there were zealous Catholics who enthusiastically supported the Welsh language. Although Francis Mostyn spoke little Welsh, he was at pains to include Welsh in his pastoral letters in Menevia and in Cardiff, where he moved following his election as archbishop in 1921. A similar attitude towards the language was adopted by Mostyn's successor in Menevia, Francis Vaughan, the son of another of the old Welsh recusant families, the Vaughans of Courtfield. He also established a committee in 1934 to draw up a Welsh hymn-book and made fervent and regular appeals for Welsh-speaking priests. Since 1904 Welsh had been taught to ordinands at St Mary's College, Holywell, which was relocated to Aberystwyth in 1924, and in 1926 Dafydd Crowley of the *Venerabile*, the English College in Rome (where Morys Clynnog had once been principal), referred to the enthusiasm of some of the exiled Welsh for the language and customs of their country.[33] So great was the attachment of the priests Paul Hook and T. P. Kane and the layman James O'Brien to their adopted culture that they were admitted to the Gorsedd of the Bards of the Isle of Britain. But the most loyal to the cause of Wales and the Welsh language was Michael McGrath, an Irishman who, having been invited to Menevia by Francis Mostyn in 1921, fell under the spell of all things Welsh. He swiftly mastered the language, and as parish priest at Aberystwyth he enrolled in Professor T. Gwynn Jones's classes on

---

[31] Quoted in Anselm Wilson, *The Life of Bishop Headley* (London, 1930), p. 130; For the background, see Trystan Owain Hughes, *Winds of Change: The Roman Catholic Church and Society in Wales, 1916–62* (Cardiff, 1999).

[32] Quoted in Donald Attwater, *The Catholic Church in Modern Wales: A Record of the Past Century* (London, 1935), p. 149.

[33] D. Crowley, 'The Exile's Corner: The Welshman in Rome', *The Welsh Outlook*, XIII (1926), 24.

medieval literature. He succeeded Francis Vaughan in 1935 as bishop of Menevia and eighteen months later he visited Saunders Lewis in his cell in Wormwood Scrubs following 'the Fire in Llŷn' incident when three leaders of the Welsh Nationalist Party set fire to the military aerodrome at Penyberth. 'The Bishop of Menevia . . . came here last Thursday morning', Lewis wrote to his wife, Margaret, on 13 April 1937, 'was altogether delightful; approved definitely of the Porth Neigwl action and had let his clergy know so.'[34] It appears that McGrath, rather than the main leaders of Welsh-speaking Nonconformity, was the least ambiguous in his support for the deed at Penyberth.

Catholicism valued the Welsh language for two reasons: it could use the language as a means of winning the people back to the 'old Faith', and it possessed an intrinsic value as God's creation. 'The language question is, without doubt, the distinctive problem to be faced in any attempt to re-Catholicize Wales', wrote R. O. F. Wynne in 1934, 'for the Welsh people are very deaf to all attempts made to "reach" them in English',[35] a point reiterated by Donald Attwater a year later: 'Those Catholics who maintain that the language question has nothing to do with the conversion of Wales have usually had very little intimate association with the common people; and, quite simply, they are talking nonsense.'[36] How well Attwater knew the ordinary Welsh people is a moot point. In the counties of Flint and Monmouth, the strongholds of indigenous Welsh Catholicism, Welsh was a minority language by 1931: it was spoken by 31.7 per cent of the people of Flintshire and by 6 per cent of the people of Monmouthshire. By that time Catholics were more numerous in Glamorgan, where the proportion of Welsh speakers was 30.5 per cent and their absolute numbers declining.[37] The majority of Catholics in Wales were non-Welsh-speaking in-migrants and their descendants who had little interest in the language and little desire to evangelize among the non-Catholic Welsh. 'The major portion is of Irish or English extraction', wrote T. P. Ellis in 1936, 'with little interest in Wales as Wales. They dwell and earn their livelihood in Wales; and that is about all.'[38] Even so, there were some Catholics (including Ellis himself) who were fully committed to the language and intensely eager to support it, and the gifted group of patriotic converts – including Saunders Lewis, Catherine Daniel and H. W. J. Edwards – who joined the Catholic Church during the 1930s and who established 'Y Cylch Catholig' (a society for Welsh-speaking Catholics) in 1941 felt very much at home among them.

---

[34] Mair Saunders Jones, Ned Thomas and Harri Pritchard Jones (eds.), *Saunders Lewis: Letters to Margaret Gilcriest* (Cardiff, 1993), p. 594.

[35] R. O. F. Wynne, 'The Conversion of Wales and the Need for Welsh', *The Tablet*, CLXIV, no. 4926 (1934).

[36] Attwater, *The Catholic Church in Modern Wales*, p. 214.

[37] Robert Owen Jones, *'Hir Oes i'r Iaith': Agweddau ar Hanes y Gymraeg a'r Gymdeithas* (Llandysul, 1997), p. 340.

[38] *Western Mail*, 18 May 1936.

Although the Welsh Nationalist Party in its early years had a Catholic tinge, the majority of its members were Nonconformists. Lewis Valentine stood as its first parliamentary candidate in Caernarfon in 1929, and he and Saunders Lewis, together with the extremely un-puritan Calvinistic Methodist, D. J. Williams, were imprisoned in Wormwood Scrubs after setting fire to the bombing range at Penyberth, Llŷn, in 1936. So great was the feeling in favour of defending the national identity of Wales that the Revd J. Dyfnallt Owen (Dyfnallt) could make the following pronouncement from the chair of the Union of Congregationalists: 'It is not Hitler and his sort who are the true apostles of nationalism, but Michael D. Jones of Bala, Emrys ap Iwan, Thomas Davis, Mazzini, Grundtvig and Masaryck' ('Nid Hitler a'i fath yw apostolion gwir genedlaetholdeb, ond Michael D. Jones o'r Bala, Emrys ap Iwan, Thomas Davis, Mazzini, Grundtvig a Masaryck'). In Dyfnallt's view, the essence of Wales's distinctiveness was its language: 'Hi yw ein gwaddol cyfoethocaf. Hi yw nôd angen ein bod. Hebddi ni byddem namyn bastardiaid digymeriad' (The language is our richest endowment. It is the one distinguishing feature of our existence. Without it, we would be no more than characterless bastards).[39] One highly significant Christian theologian among the nationalists was J. E. Daniel, Professor of Christian Doctrine at the Bala-Bangor Congregational College, and the leader of the Nonconformist reaction against the liberal theology associated with Karl Barth.[40] Apart from his academic work, Daniel's main interest lay in the activities of the Welsh Nationalist Party. He twice fought general elections in its name, and served as acting president while Saunders Lewis was in prison and as president between 1939 and 1943. He, more than anyone, bore the brunt of defending the movement against accusations of Fascism, not least by Nonconformists such as W. J. Gruffydd and the Revd Gwilym Davies. By the 1940s he had begun to produce conceptual work which directly linked religion and nationalism. In his essay 'Y Syniad Seciwlar am Ddyn' (The Secular Idea of Man), he illustrated the fundamental difference between nationalism based on naturalistic assumptions and that which sprang from New Testament convictions, and in his sermon 'Gwaed y Teulu' (The Blood of the Family) he argued that fostering Wales and the Welsh language was less a threat to the unity of mankind than a contribution to the richness, variety and mutual understanding of nations:

A chredwn yn y Pentecost tragwyddol y bydd Bernard yno yn canu ei *Jesu, dulcis memoria*, a Luther ei *Ein feste Burg ist unser Gott*, a Watts ei *When I survey the wondrous cross*, a Phantycelyn ei 'Iesu, Iesu, rwyt Ti'n ddigon', heb i Bernard anghofio ei Ladin,

[39] *Adroddiad Cyfarfodydd yr Undeb a gynhaliwyd ym Mangor . . . 1936*, XI, no. 3 (Abertawe, 1941), p. 129; R. Tudur Jones, *Yr Undeb: Hanes Undeb yr Annibynwyr Cymraeg, 1872–1972* (Abertawe, 1975), p. 253.

[40] See D. Densil Morgan, ' "Ysgolhaig, Gwladgarwr, Cristion": J. E. Daniel a'i gyfraniad', *Y Traethodydd*, CLII (1997), 5–22.

na Luther ei Almaeneg, na Watts ei Saesneg, na Phantycelyn ei Gymraeg, a heb i hynny rwystro mewn unrhyw fodd gynghanedd berffaith eu cyd-ddeall a'u cydganu.[41]

(And we believe that in the eternal Pentecost Bernard will be there singing his *Jesu, dulcis memoria*, and Luther his *Ein feste Burg ist unser Gott*, and Watts his 'When I survey the wondrous cross', and Pantycelyn his *Iesu, Iesu, rwyt Ti'n ddigon*, without Bernard forgetting his Latin nor Luther his German, nor Watts his English nor Pantycelyn his Welsh, and without that hindering in any way the perfect concord of their understanding and their harmony.)

Despite his limited published output, Daniel provided Welsh-speaking Nonconformity with a powerful apologia in favour of a Christian patriotism based on the Word of God, and he convinced many of its ministers that loyalty to the Welsh language should be an aspect of their religious witness.

But Welsh-speaking Anglicans also endeavoured to deal with questions of identity. They now belonged to a disestablished Church separated from the state and free from the direct influence of Canterbury. The Disestablishment Bill passed in 1914 had been postponed until after the war, and on 1 April 1920 the new Church came into being. The first archbishop of the Church in Wales was A. G. Edwards, bishop of St Asaph, the most influential prelate in Wales and, in the view of W. J. Gruffydd, 'the most disastrous man Wales had ever seen' ('y gŵr mwyaf trychinebus a welodd Cymru erioed').[42] Reference has already been made to his views on Wales and the Welsh language. The higher clergy of the new Church and many of its members were extremely reluctant to abandon the privileged position which had been theirs when the link with the state was secure. Social status counted as much as ever, and by 1935 the governing body of the Church included six barons, ten baronets, five knights, eleven titled ladies, three sons of peers, two generals, one vice-admiral, one brigadier-general, and sixteen colonels, as well as a motley array of ex-army officers and other gentry.[43] Despite this, two developments helped to restore the less patrician and Welsh-speaking tradition within the Church.

The first of these occurred at Saint David's College, Lampeter, an institution of considerable importance to the life of the Church. Since the majority of the clerics were educated here, it was capable of exerting substantial influence on parish life. The aim of the institution under Principals Llewellyn Bebb and Gilbert Cunningham Joyce[44] had been to produce 'respected gentlemen, good Tories,

---

[41] J. E. Daniel, *Torri'r Seiliau Sicr: Detholiad o Ysgrifau J. E. Daniel gyda Rhagymadrodd gan D. Densil Morgan* (Llandysul, 1993), pp. 171–5.

[42] Quoted in T. I. Ellis, *Ym Mêr fy Esgyrn* (Lerpwl, 1955), p. 41.

[43] See A. J. Edwards, *Archbishop Green: His Life and Opinions* (Llandysul, 1986), p. 87.

[44] D. T. W. Price, *A History of Saint David's University College, Lampeter. Volume Two: 1898–1971* (Cardiff, 1990), pp. 35–6.

moderate Anglicans . . . and committed supporters of the Establishment', but, following the appointment of Dr Maurice Jones in 1923, a major change occurred. The new principal was the son of a Trawsfynydd shoemaker and a cousin of the well-known Methodist minister, the Revd J. Puleston Jones. Maurice Jones was a sound scholar and a prolific author. Between 1923 and his retirement in 1938 he placed the college on a firm financial footing, increased the number of students from 90 to 200, attracted far more candidates for holy orders from the county grammar schools than from the public schools in Llandovery and Brecon, and secured a more prominent place for the Welsh language in the syllabus and activities of the institution. Although this unnerved some Churchmen, Jones took pride in his Welshness and remained a true man of the people. This had a salutary effect on his students and thereby on the whole province.

The second important event in the process of making the Church more sympathetic towards the Welsh language was the appointment in 1931 of Timothy Rees to succeed the veteran Joshua Pritchard Hughes as bishop of Llandaff. As a member of the Community of the Resurrection at Mirfield, Yorkshire, Rees, like Maurice Jones, had spent the major part of his ministry outside Wales, but, unlike Jones, he was a High Churchman. The Welsh were fully aware of this, but did not realize that his brand of High-Churchmanship was far more radical than the conservative and pietistic type embraced by the Welsh Tractarians and that he took pride in every aspect of Welsh-language culture. Despite his uncompromising catholicism, Rees was a powerful preacher, a fine hymn-writer in both languages, and a man who respected the Nonconformist piety in which he had been raised in Cardiganshire. A catholic evangelical, he embodied all the values of the late Dean Henry T. Edwards. Although the form of service for consecrating bishops had been included in the Welsh-language version of the Book of Common Prayer since 1662, it was never used until Rees was enthroned as bishop of Llandaff. This was a new departure, and many, including Nonconformists, believed that his advent to Llandaff in the midst of the depression was a sign of a new dawn in the history of the Church in Wales.[45] Unfortunately, Rees's career at Llandaff was short-lived. He worked tirelessly for reconciliation and relief in the coalfield, and, like the Congregationalist, the Revd T. Alban Davies, Tonpentre, he insisted on taking the people's case to Whitehall to press for greater economic support from the government. Alas, as the social and political situation worsened, his health deteriorated and he died in April 1939. This was a grievous blow to the testimony of the Church in Wales, as well as to the efforts of some of its clerics and members to join the mainstream of Welsh national and popular life.

---

[45] See J. Lambert Rees, *Timothy Rees of Mirfield and Llandaff: A Biography* (London, 1945), p. 101; Dafydd Jenkins, 'Timothy Rees CR, Esgob Llandaf', *Ceredigion*, XI, no. 4 (1992), 405–24.

Soon the people of Wales were at war once more. Mercifully, the trauma of the 1939–45 conflict was not as great as that of the Great War, and Wales was spared the terrible destruction and suffering experienced in so many European countries in Europe. The atmosphere in 1939 was free from the jingoism of 1914, and the general consensus about the evils of Hitlerism meant that there was less ambiguity about the aims of the war than had been the case a generation earlier. Military conscription was administered in a way which alleviated tensions between those who chose to join the armed forces and those who demurred, and the stand taken by conscientious objectors was accepted and for the most part respected. Religious life continued much as usual and the main difference between the attitude of Anglicans and Welsh Catholics to the conflict and that of the Nonconformists was that, for chapel people, pacifism was a more valid option.[46]

The Welsh Language and the Crisis of Nonconformity c. 1945–75

From the standpoint of both religion and the Welsh language, the period between 1945 and the mid-1960s was one of considerable anxiety. According to the 1951 census the proportion of Welsh speakers had fallen to 28.9 per cent and by 1961 it had fallen again to 26 per cent. The geographical pattern of the Welsh language was changing. Welsh-speaking Wales was now predominantly rural, and a substantial linguistic decline had occurred in industrial Glamorgan (apart from parts of the Swansea valley above Clydach) and in the more populous area of Denbighshire and Flintshire.[47] Moreover, monoglot Welsh speakers were dying out. The vast majority of Welsh speakers in south and north-east Wales were now elderly, and virtually all Welsh speakers in the west could also speak English. This would have serious implications for the Christian mission throughout the country.

The religious statistics were also gloomy. Between 1945 and 1955 the membership of the Calvinistic Methodists had fallen from 172,954 to 150,027, the Congregationalists from 160,519 to 142,597, the Baptists from 110,328 to 79,750, and the Wesleyan Methodists from 45,089 to 40,945. The total number of children in the Sunday schools of all the denominations (excluding the Wesleyans) had fallen from 363,190 in 1935 to 219,282 by 1955.[48] But despite the decline in chapel membership, Nonconformity was still a powerful movement. In a country with a population of two and a half million people, the main denominations could claim the loyalty of about 505,000 Welsh people – still a very substantial figure – and in the rural and industrial areas where Welsh was a living language (east Denbighshire around Rhosllannerchrugog, the quarrying areas of Merioneth and

[46] See Dewi Eirug Davies, *Protest a Thystiolaeth: Agweddau ar y Dystiolaeth Gristionogol yn yr Ail Ryfel Byd* (Llandysul, 1993).

[47] Jones, 'Hir Oes i'r Iaith', pp. 344–5.

[48] Williams (ed.), *Digest of Welsh Historical Statistics*, II, pp. 273, 295, 325, 328.

Caernarfonshire, the Gwendraeth and Aman valleys and the Llanelli area in Carmarthenshire, and parts of west Glamorgan), the appreciable contribution of the chapels to the bustle of social and cultural activity could not be ignored. During the celebrations associated with the Festival of Britain in 1951, W. J. Gruffydd could still claim, with little incongruity, that 'by the end of the first quarter of the 19th century, Wales had become what it substantially is today, a nation of Evangelical Christians'.[49]

Others were markedly less sanguine. 'What we see is Welsh-speaking Wales becoming more irreligious every year and its grasp of Christianity becoming more tenuous' ('Gweld y Gymru Gymraeg yr ydym ni yn mynd yn anghrefyddolach o flwyddyn i flwyddyn a'i gafael ar Gristnogaeth yn eiddilach'), wrote Lewis Valentine in 1954.[50] Eight years later he was still dismayed by the chill of 'these recent dismal and morose years . . . this age of uncertainty and hazy half-belief, of sporadic lukewarm worship and a frigidity in hearing the Word, of shameless spurning of responsibility' ('y blynyddoedd blwng a sarrug diwethaf hyn . . . [d]yddiau'r ffydd amhendant, a dyddiau'r hanner credu niwlog, dyddiau'r addoli llugoer ysbeidiol, a'r gwrando rhew, a'r ymwrthod digywilydd â chyfrifoldeb').[51] Valentine was not by nature a pessimist, but throughout the 1950s and early 1960s he issued grave forecasts and regular warnings about the spiritual deficiencies of the churches. In *Y Dysgedydd* in 1955 the Congregational leader Iorwerth Jones, minister of Pant-teg chapel, Ystalyfera, referred to the condition of a reputedly 'strong' church located in a town in the south-west where 44 per cent of the 324 members did not frequent the services. Their explanations for absence were as follows: ill-health (32), fatigue (25), disagreement with fellow-members (19), being weary of constant requests for money (17) and dissatisfaction with the minister (8). More serious were the specifically *religious* reasons given for non-attendance. Twenty-seven claimed that they did not derive any benefit from the services and fourteen stated that they did not attend because they were non-believers, despite the fact that they were fully baptized members. In one sense, the reasons given by the regular attenders were even more disturbing: sixty-two came out of force of habit, thirty-four 'for the sake of the children', twenty-seven 'out of respect for the minister', twelve because of the singing and twelve – all young people – because their parents forced them to attend. Among the regular attenders, only thirty-four came 'to worship God'. The minister, who had laboured among them for thirty-five years was by all accounts a fine and enlightened preacher. Iorwerth Jones noted that the sad probability was that the overwhelming majority of Congregational churches were in a similar situation ('Y tebygolrwydd trist yw bod mwyafrif llethol ein heglwysi mewn sefyllfa gyffelyb').[52]

[49] W. J. Gruffydd, 'A Portrait of South Wales' in Geoffrey Grigson (ed.), *South Wales and the Marches* (London, 1951), p. 57.
[50] 'Nodiadau Golygyddol', *Seren Gomer*, XLVI, no. 1 (1954), 5.
[51] 'Araith Llywydd yr Undeb', ibid., LIV, no. 2 (1962), 42.
[52] 'Dyddlyfr y Dysgedydd', *Y Dysgedydd* (September 1955), 239–41.

The Calvinistic Methodists, too, were troubled by the decay and apathy. 'It is difficult to get our people to realize that what the Gospel has to offer is a matter of life and death' ('Anodd cael ein pobl i sylweddoli bod yr hyn sydd gan yr Efengyl i'w gynnig yn fater bywyd'), claimed J. E. Hughes, Brynsiencyn: 'Too many of our people are too self-satisfied and self-sufficient, too much at ease in Zion. Words such as "Sin" and "Grace" convey almost nothing to them, and spiritual forces are a closed book to them' ('Mae gormod o'n pobl yn rhy hunan-fodlon a hunan-ddigonol, yn rhy esmwyth arnynt yn Seion. Nid ydyw geiriau fel "Pechod" a "Gras" yn cyfleu nemor ddim iddynt, a llyfr caeëdig iddynt ydyw y nerthoedd ysbrydol').[53] One of the most passionate responses to the crisis came from the Calvinistic Methodist writer, W. Ambrose Bebb. The words of his last testimony, Yr Argyfwng (The Crisis), published shortly after his death in 1955, were profoundly moving:

Yr Eglwys? Dduw Dad, a oes gennym ni'r dirgelwch hwnnw heddiw? Yr Eglwys? Onid hi – neu'r sefydliadau sy'n derbyn yr enw – sy'n cadw draw? Y mae Crist yn galw ac yn denu, â'i Groes yn denu ac yn tynnu sylw. Ond, am yr Eglwys, y mae hi, mor aml â pheidio, yn gyrru oddi wrthi. A ydwyf fi'n dweud celwydd, neu'n cablu, wrth fwrw drwyddi fel hyn? Ofn sydd arnaf nad ydwyf fi ddim. Mi roddwn i lawer iawn am weled gwir Eglwys, deilwng o Grist, yng Nghymru heddiw, ac yn denu'r myrdd miloedd i mewn i'w chôl. Ond nis gwelaf ar hyn o bryd.[54]

(The Church? Oh, heavenly Father, do we still possess that mystery? The Church? Is it not she – or the institutions which go by that name – which stand afar? Christ calls and draws people to him, and the Cross beckons and calls for attention. But as for the Church, she, more often than not, drives people away. Am I lying, or blaspheming, in railing like this? My fear is that I am not. I would give much to see a true Church, worthy of Christ, in Wales today, attracting many thousands to her bosom. But at present I do not see one.)

The most tangible symbol of the old puritanism was 'the Welsh Sabbath' and the fact that the desire to safeguard it was diminishing bore witness to the social changes afoot. Throughout the early 1950s the councils of Rhyl, Wrexham, Cardiff, Swansea and other towns decided in favour of opening their cinemas on Sundays, and it also became increasingly acceptable to hold sports and other leisure activities on a Sunday. Since they were private establishments, licensed Working Men's clubs and those connected with rugby and football clubs were able to open their doors on Sundays. In 1961 the government acknowledged the historical influence of Nonconformity on the life of the nation by allowing a local poll to be held, in accordance with the conditions of the new Licensing Act, in

[53] J. E. Hughes, 'Pregethu'r Efengyl i'n Hoes', Y Drysorfa, CXXI, no. 10 (1951), 255.
[54] W. Ambrose Bebb, Yr Argyfwng (Llandybïe, 1955), p. 29.

order to decide whether public houses should be open in Wales on Sundays. The 'Sunday opening question' became a focus for the Nonconformist conscience which was still linked in the minds of many with the 'Welsh way of life'. In the Welsh-speaking areas of Anglesey, Caernarfonshire, Denbighshire, Merioneth, Cardiganshire, Pembrokeshire, Montgomeryshire, and Carmarthenshire the influence of the chapels proved sufficiently strong to ensure that people voted against Sunday opening of licensed premises in the referendum held in November. But the populous and Anglicized areas of Glamorgan, Monmouthshire, Brecon and Radnor, Flintshire, Cardiff and Swansea voted in favour of opening public houses on Sundays. According to Kenneth O. Morgan, the result of the poll 'was a somewhat pathetic commentary on the waning authority of organized religion'.[55]

It became clearer than ever that the Nonconformist concern for matters such as temperance, gambling and keeping the Sabbath was becoming ever more irrelevant in the complex modern age. In a period of material progress on the one hand and fears of nuclear war on the other, the negative attitude of the chapels and their moralistic stance appeared out of step with the age. It became more difficult for Nonconformist causes to convince their own members of the value of the puritan heritage, let alone try to mould a whole society in accordance with their standards. For this reason, an undertone of melancholy characterized the celebrations held in 1962 to mark the tercentenary of the 'Great Ejection' in 1662, an event which created modern Nonconformity. Of all the literature published to mark the occasion, the contribution of the Revd R. Ifor Parry, a Congregational minister at Aberdare, offered the most penetrating analysis of the situation. He was in no doubt that Nonconformity was facing its most serious crisis ever, and among the reasons for this was its association with the Welsh language: 'On the whole, wherever people retain their Welsh, they also remain loyal to the chapel . . . the fate of Nonconformity is bound up, therefore, with the fate of the language in many areas' ('At ei gilydd, lle bynnag y ceidw pobl eu Cymraeg, cadwant hefyd at y capel . . . O ganlyniad, y mae tynged Ymneilltuaeth ynghlwm wrth dynged yr iaith mewn llawer ardal').[56]

Despite the decline in Welsh-speaking Nonconformity, the resurgence of national feeling experienced in the aftermath of Saunders Lewis's radio lecture *Tynged yr Iaith* (The Fate of the Language) in 1962 provided a fresh impetus. This was a decade of considerable intellectual energy, and the theological ferment created elsewhere in Britain by John A. T. Robinson's popular work, *Honest to God* (1963), by the secular theology of Paul Tillich, Rudolf Bultmann and their followers, and by the 'death of God' movement in the United States, left its mark on Welsh theological thought. Remarkably lively discussions were to be found in the pages of *Barn*, a periodical founded in 1962. Under the editorship of

---

[55] Kenneth O. Morgan, *Rebirth of a Nation: Wales 1880–1980* (Oxford, 1981), p. 355.
[56] R. Ifor Parry, *Ymneilltuaeth* (Llandysul, 1962), pp. 192–3.

Alwyn D. Rees *Barn* became a major medium for expressing the new vigour of Welsh nationalism. The discussion was provoked by the attempt by Professor J. R. Jones to adapt some of Tillich's categories to the situation in Wales. Although Jones coined the memorable phrase 'The Crisis of Meaninglessness' ('Yr Argyfwng Gwacter Ystyr') to describe the current cultural condition of the western world, his theology was capricious, idiosyncratic and poles apart from any classical interpretation of the faith. However, he was an exceptionally intelligent man who passionately declaimed his convictions in unusually fine prose.[57] He won enthusiastic supporters for his standpoint in Gwilym O. Roberts and Dewi Z. Phillips (who succeeded Jones as Professor of Philosophy at the University College of Wales, Swansea), as well as powerful opponents in Hywel D. Lewis, Professor of the Philosophy of Religion at King's College, London, and R. Tudur Jones. The discourse was made all the more compelling because of its (indirect) link with the language issue. Although their doctrinal position differed, both J. R. Jones and R. Tudur Jones were prominent in the nationalist movement, and their awareness of a religious crisis was inextricably bound up with their concern for the future of Wales and its mother tongue. In its time of crisis, both believed that Welsh-speaking Nonconformity had an important role in the task of defending the spiritual interests of the nation.

Although both the Welsh language and Nonconformity were under attack and their future in obvious danger, the late 1960s and early 1970s were a fruitful period from the point of view of the relationship between religion and the Welsh language. Some of the young activists of Cymdeithas yr Iaith Gymraeg (the Welsh Language Society) drew inspiration from the radical Nonconformist tradition and, among their leaders, Dafydd Iwan and Ffred Ffransis considered protest to be a form of Christian discipline. There were obvious Christian elements in the Society's non-violent image, and at one time as many as three Nonconformist ministers served on its senate. 'It is the duty of every Welshman, and especially the Christian Welshman, to seek to understand what is happening in the life of the nation at present' ('Dyletswydd pob Cymro, a Christion o Gymro'n enwedig, yw ceisio deall yr hyn sy'n digwydd ym mywyd y genedl ar hyn o bryd'), said one commentator, and the nature of the relationship between the Welsh language and Christianity once more became a matter for reflection:

Yng nghanol y deffroad cenedlaethol a'r berw cyfoes gwelir yr Iaith Gymraeg – y Gymraeg ac arwyddion-ffyrdd a'r teledu a'r llysoedd a bythynod-cefn-gwlad ac ymprydiau ac ymgyrchoedd protest. A diau yn y man fe bwysleisir y berthynas sydd rhwng y Gymraeg a Christnogaeth oblegid bu'r iaith Gymraeg ynghlwm wrth y Ffydd o'r pryd y ganed Cymru'n genedl yn oes dadfeiliad yr Ymerodraeth Rufeinig ac 'Oes y

---

[57] J. R. Jones, *Ac Onide* (Llandybïe, 1970).

Saint' – Dewi, Illtyd, Dyfrig, Teilo, Padarn, arweinwyr un o'r diwygiadau mwyaf a welodd Cymru erioed.[58]

(In the midst of the national awakening and the contemporary ferment, we find the Welsh language – Welsh and road signs and the television and the courts and rural cottages and hunger strikes and protest campaigns. And it is certain that emphasis will soon be placed on the relationship between Welsh and Christianity since the Welsh language has been bound up with the Faith from the time of Wales's birth as a nation in the age of the decline of the Roman Empire and the Age of the Saints – Dewi, Illtyd, Dyfrig, Teilo, Padarn, the leaders of one of the greatest revivals Wales ever saw.)

Not least among the contributions of theologians at this time was the serious reappraisal of the nature of the relationship between language, nationality and the Christian revelation, during which R. Tudur Jones, Pennar Davies and Bobi Jones produced a body of work which remains an original and substantial contribution to the understanding of our national identity.[59]

Anglicanism, Catholicism and the Welsh Language 1945–70

If the situation among the Nonconformists was discouraging, this was not the case among Anglicans. Vitality and optimism characterized the Church in Wales from the end of the Second World War onwards. This was reflected in the Province's Youth Council, set up in 1945, and in the youth movement known as 'Cymry'r Groes'. Although complaints were still to be heard that the English-speaking, upper-class influence lay heavily on Anglicanism in Wales, there was abundant evidence that the Church had drawn nearer to ordinary people and that it was becoming more sympathetic towards Welsh-language culture. So great was its appeal that it could boast of having attracted to its ranks patriotic laymen such as T. I. Ellis (who had been an Anglican for some time), Aneirin Talfan Davies and D. Gwenallt Jones (Gwenallt), and to its ministry able poets such as Euros Bowen and G. J. Roberts, and scholars such as Gwynfryn Richards, H. Islwyn Davies and G. O. Williams. These were all former Nonconformists, and the Church clearly benefited from attracting prominent leaders in the public and cultural life of Wales.

Two of the most influential bishops in this period were John Charles Jones at Bangor and Glyn Simon at Llandaff. A Calvinistic Methodist from Llan-saint, Carmarthenshire, Jones had become an Anglican in his college days. Before his appointment as vicar of Llanelli he had been a missionary in Uganda, and his work

---

[58] *Seren Cymru*, 16 February 1973.
[59] R. Tudur Jones, *The Desire of Nations* (Llandybïe, 1975); Bobi Jones, *Crist a Chenedlaetholdeb* (Pen-y-bont ar Ogwr, 1994) and the various essays in the following volumes: Dewi Eirug Davies (ed.), *Gwinllan a Roddwyd* (Llandybïe, 1972), and Ballard and Jones (eds.), *This Land and People*.

in the diocese of Bangor (1949–56) was characterized by evangelistic zeal. He combined missionary vigour, Anglo-Catholic theology and the spiritual values of the ordinary Welsh-speaking people, and in this he was very similar to Bishop Timothy Rees. His untimely death in 1956 was a considerable blow to the Church. In style and background, Glyn Simon, bishop of Llandaff (1957–71) was totally different. The son of a clergyman, he had been brought up in the sounds of the battles over disestablishment, and although a contemporary of J. E. Daniel at Jesus College, Oxford, he had little sympathy with Nonconformity, its values or its language. He was, in fact, a somewhat aristocratic prelate in whom A. G. Edwards would have taken pride. In view of this background, his reaction to the election of Alfred Edwin Morris as Archbishop of Wales in November 1957 surprised many. Morris was an Englishman and formerly Professor of Theology at Saint David's College, Lampeter; he had no experience of parish ministry before becoming bishop of Monmouth in 1940. Gwenallt protested loudly against his election before abandoning the Church and returning to the Calvinistic Methodism of his youth.[60] Simon's reaction, though more discreet, was no less sharp. 'The recent elections', he declared, 'have revealed an anti-Welsh and pro-English trend, and, in some cases a bigotry as narrow and ill-informed as any to be found in the tightest and most remote of Welsh communities.'[61] As in Gwenallt's case, Simon's main criticism of the appointment was that Morris was a non-Welsh speaker, and subsequently his zeal for the Welsh language increased markedly. By the time of the Investiture of the Prince of Wales at Caernarfon Castle in 1969, Glyn Simon had himself been elected Archbishop of Wales and not the least daring of his actions at that time was to visit Dafydd Iwan, chairman of the Welsh Language Society, who had been imprisoned for his part in the campaign for bi-lingual road signs. The constant refrain of the new leader of the Church in Wales was: 'There is nothing unscriptural or un-Christian in nationalism as such.'[62]

Even so, only a minority of Anglicans and Catholics were disposed to embrace things Welsh. In spite of the influence of bishops such as Simon and G. O. Williams within the Church in Wales and the enthusiasm of Archbishop McGrath and, to a lesser extent, Bishop Daniel Hannon (who learnt Welsh) and John Petit, who succeeded him in Menevia in 1948, churches continued to reflect trends within secular society and throughout these decades Welsh lost ground. For the majority of people Welshness was still synonymous with Nonconformity. Whereas 'the chapels are the outposts of traditional Wales in these areas', commented J. M. Cleary in 1956, 'the Catholic churches are sure to have statues of St Patrick and the *Cork Weekly Examiner* on sale at the door.'[63] In 1960 a Catholic as fervent as Victor Hampson-Jones could confess that he felt an 'alien

---

[60] D. Gwenallt Jones, 'Yr Eglwys yng Nghymru', *Y Genhinen*, VIII, no. 2 (1958), 86–91.

[61] Quoted in John S. Peart-Binns, *Edwin Morris: Archbishop of Wales* (Llandysul, 1990), p. 119.

[62] Jones, *Glyn Simon: His Life and Opinions*, p. 124.

[63] J. M. Cleary, 'The Irish and Modern Wales', *The Furrow*, 7, no. 4 (1956), 205.

inside the Church' because of his loyalty to the Welsh language.[64] With the publication in 1963 of *Sacrosanctum Concilium*, the Second Vatican Council's document on liturgy, which insisted that the Mass should be celebrated completely in the indigenous languages, Latin yielded to English rather than to Welsh. This was a bitter blow for several Welsh Catholics, including Saunders Lewis and his friend, the artist and Anglo-Welsh poet, David Jones. Jones referred to 'the possibilities of a most ironical situation arising in Wales whereby Yr Eglwys Lân Rufeinig [the Holy Roman Church] might attach to herself the stigma of anglophilism and anglicization which once attached to the Church of England in Wales'.[65] Saunders Lewis lapsed into even greater despair. 'Alas', he wrote to R. O. F. Wynne in November 1965, 'I have no atom of influence with the bishops. I had rather a fierce quarrel with his Grace of Cardiff over the vernacular liturgy and we are barely on speaking terms.' Lewis suggested that Cardiff and Menevia could merge for purposes of worship in order to conduct more Welsh-language services, but the bishop's response was negative: 'Not he', said Lewis, '*He* couldn't interfere in Menevia, and he was a dutiful and obedient son of the Church. I told him that that was the Nazi officials' excuse for Belsen. And so we finished.'[66]

Until the mid-twentieth century and thereafter in areas where Welsh was still the principal language, religion was the only domain in which Welsh had a strong foothold. In all other spheres – government, commerce, education (apart from the primary schools), the mass media such as radio, television, the cinema and the main newspapers, and modern Anglo-American culture – English was the medium. This divide proved detrimental to religion and the Welsh language alike. Any dichotomy between the sacred and the secular undermines religion since it sets limits on God's sovereignty and denies the lordship of Christ over his whole creation. In Welsh-speaking areas the tendency was to limit 'religion' to specific religious activities such as chapel attendance, worship, prayer, Sunday school activities and aspects of personal morality. Just as religion was prevented from proclaiming its lordship over secular matters, whether politics, economics, aesthetics or social morality, so bounds were set on the ability of the Welsh language to encompass all aspects of life since English was the language of 'the world'.

By the 1950s and early 1960s, the secularism already at work in continental Europe had reached Wales, including Welsh-speaking Wales. This created a missionary problem for the churches, namely how to safeguard the spiritual heritage and at the same time seek to extend the area of Christ's lordship in a society which was no longer familiar with the fundamental principles of Christianity. However, the problem for the Welsh language was rather different.

---

[64] *Western Mail*, 17 February 1960.
[65] NLW, David Jones Papers, Box I/3.
[66] Hazel Walford Davies, *Saunders Lewis a Theatr Garthewin* (Llandysul, 1995), p. 369.

For the language to survive it would need to establish itself in secular fields from which it had formerly been excluded. In the case of Christian believers who were also patriotic Welshmen, this could create considerable tension. H. W. J. Edwards voiced a somewhat similar dilemma in the context of Welsh-speaking Catholicism: 'As a Catholic I am glad that there are more Catholics. As a Cymro I am afraid that . . . the rise of Roman Catholicism in Wales will mean the destruction of Welsh speech and ways.'[67] By the 1960s Christians from all backgrounds were fearful that extending the domains of the Welsh language would go hand in hand with secularizing the nation. Of course, they could do no less than rejoice that the Welsh language was acquiring a new status, but they were also deeply conscious of the dangers involved.[68] By the end of the 1970s, then, Christians had to come to terms with religious and cultural pluralism.

Christianity, Pluralism and the Welsh Language c.1979–90

When, in 1983, the results of a survey of the state of the churches in Wales were published, it became obvious that organized religion was swiftly losing its authority and influence. Out of a population of c.2,850,000, the total church membership in 1982 was 523,100 (24 per cent). The number of attenders (280,000) was substantially lower and 45 per cent of these were over 50 years of age. The Church in Wales, the strongest body, had 137,000 communicants, the Catholic Church 129,600, the Calvinistic Methodists 79,900, the Congregationalists 65,200, the Baptists 50,200, the Wesleyan Methodists 25,300 and the other denominations 35,300. A comparison with the evidence of the survey carried out in 1978 reveals that every denomination except the Catholics had lost members. Although membership of the Church in Wales had generally fallen, the number of those attending its services had increased, the increase being as much as 14 per cent in Dyfed. Beyond its stronghold in the north-west, Calvinistic Methodism was swiftly declining, with a considerable decrease recorded in Clwyd and Dyfed and a critical fall in Glamorgan. According to one Presbyterian minister, the situation in south Wales was extremely serious and he feared that the Welsh-speaking churches in Glamorgan had not profited from the success of the Welsh-language schools in the area ('Difrifol yw sefyllfa'r Presbyteriaid yn Ne Cymru . . . mae'n amlwg nad yw'r eglwysi Cymraeg . . . wedi elwa ar lwyddiant Ysgolion Cymraeg y cylch').[69] Although no serious percentage decline had occurred in the membership of the Congregationalists, it was revealed that the Baptists were prospering only in the English-language churches of Gwent, while the Welsh-speaking Wesleyans were in parlous straits. English was the medium of worship among the smaller

---

[67] *Western Mail*, 18 December 1952.
[68] See Jones, *'Hir Oes i'r Iaith'*, pp. 361ff.
[69] D. Ben Rees, 'Daearyddiaeth Crefydd yng Nghymru' in Peter Brierley and Byron Evans (eds.), *Yr Argoelion yng Nghymru: Adroddiad o Gyfrifiad yr Eglwysi, 1982* (London, 1983), p. 10.

denominations, such as the 169 Pentecostal churches which had now established themselves throughout the country, the churches linked to the Baptist Union of Great Britain and Ireland, and various evangelical and charismatic fellowships. Although they were located in Wales, the atmosphere and ambience of these congregations reflected English mores and customs.[70]

By the final decade of the century, the assumptions of Welsh-language institutions were, in the main, secular, particularly in the case of the broadcasting media (despite the fact that 'sons of the manse' were strongly represented among their staff), and, although the churches still maintained their mission, they had become highly marginalized. Nevertheless, there were still solid gains in some religious fields, the most substantial of which was the New Welsh Bible, published in 1988, one of the masterpieces of twentieth-century scholarship. It sold remarkably well and swiftly took its place as an intelligible and attractive translation of God's Word in modern guise. There were also gains in the field of ecumenism and inter-church relations, especially following the foundation of Cytûn, the body which replaced the Council of Churches for Wales in September 1990. The great difference between Cytûn and the Council was the fact that the Catholic Church was now an active member. Even more important was the change of climate among Welsh Christians and the less mistrustful, less factious, and more creative spirit which flourished among them. The same was also true of believers of a more evangelical persuasion. This was chiefly attributable to the Evangelical Alliance, a movement established in Wales in 1986, which was more tolerant and broadminded in character than the Evangelical Movement of Wales which had been active since 1955. By the 1990s Welsh Christians were more willing to emphasize those aspects of the faith which they held in common than those which kept them apart, especially in the face of the secular challenge which threatened to undermine Christian truths and values.[71]

Despite many complexities and ambiguities, the relationship between religion and the Welsh language during the twentieth century was, on the whole, extremely close. The fate of the Welsh language was a matter of no small concern to religious believers, including those who adopted pragmatic and practical standpoints at the beginning of the century and those who espoused more doctrinal and principled considerations in a later period. Since religion, by definition, deals with people's core values, and Christianity, among all the faiths, is based on a revelation of the Word, this could hardly have been otherwise. Whatever the new millennium holds in store, the use made of the Welsh language for religious purposes in the twentieth century will remain a clear reflection of its value to the wider community.

[70] See D. W. Bebbington, *Evangelicalism in Modern Britain: A History from the 1730s to the 1980s* (London, 1989), pp. 229–76; Adrian Hastings, *A History of English Christianity, 1920–1990* (London, 1991), pp. 602–71.

[71] D. Densil Morgan, *The Span of the Cross: Christian Religion and Society in Wales 1914–2000* (Cardiff, 1999), pp. 260–79.

11

Welsh Literature since 1914

R. GERALLT JONES

Mae'r hen delynau genid gynt
Yng nghrog ar gangau'r helyg draw,
A gwaedd y bechgyn lond y gwynt
A'u gwaed yn gymysg efo'r glaw.[1]

(And there, the weeping willow trees,
Bear the old harps that sang amain,
The lads' wild anguish fills the breeze,
Their blood is mingled with the rain.)[2]

THUS DID the final stanza of a short lyric, little noticed at the time, announce that the world had changed for ever and that literature must change with it. Much the same happened to English literature, too, between 1914 and 1918. The English Georgian poets, by and large, entered the Great War not only with the same romantic jollity that had informed the previous generation's approach to imperial conquests and the faraway adventure in South Africa, but also with the same poetic vocabulary. The war changed that vocabulary; what had begun with Rupert Brooke's 'Grantchester' ended with Wilfred Owen's 'Anthem for Doomed Youth'. In Wales, it was simply an added irony that the author of the sharpest poetic comment on the war in the Welsh language, Ellis Humphrey Evans (Hedd Wyn), was also Wales's most celebrated victim.

It is, of course, a mistake to associate literature too closely with the social and political events which run parallel to it, for they run parallel to it rather than create it. Literature, like all art, is made up of individual writers' responses to the intensity of individual experience, and individual experience is infinitely repetitive as well as infinitely varied. Love is love and death is death, whether written about in medieval Welsh or in modern English. Nevertheless, at any one

---

[1] Hedd Wyn, *Cerddi'r Bugail* (Y Bala, 1918), p. 146.
[2] Translated by D. Tecwyn Lloyd in 'Welsh Literature and the First World War', *Planet*, 11 (1972), 21.

time and in particular parts of the globe, certain determining factors are inescapable. In the case of Welsh writers writing in Welsh during the course of the twentieth century, two such factors stand out among many subsidiary ones: the Great War and the status and condition of the language itself.

In a perceptive essay, 'Llên Cyni a Rhyfel' (The Literature of Want and War), D. Tecwyn Lloyd described the Great War as 'the wound that will never close' ('y clwy na all byth gau').[3] In the same essay, he pointed out that comparatively little 'war literature' was written in Welsh during and immediately after the Great War, and that for two reasons. Firstly, middle-aged, established writers who dominated the literary landscape between 1914 and 1918 – poets and academics like John Morris-Jones, John Jenkins (Gwili) and John Owen Williams (Pedrog) – played no part in the war and still lived and wrote as though the long Edwardian afternoon would never end. When the war itself finally ended, they condemned uncomprehendingly the changed moral attitudes and patterns of behaviour of the young men returning home from the trenches. They themselves had been responsible in their day for dragging Welsh poetry out of the morass of hectoring moralism into which it had sunk during the second half of the nineteenth century and restored to it certain criteria of aesthetic taste and linguistic purity that it had long lost; they were not inclined to accept another and seemingly contradictory revolution so soon. Secondly, the young men themselves had no wish to write about the war; they wanted to put it behind them and get on with their new lives. As D. Tecwyn Lloyd says, it was the deepening gloom of the depression in the late 1920s and through into the 1930s – when it became apparent that the hopes and dreams for which the war had ostensibly been fought, to create a 'world fit for heroes', were unattainable – that 'unlocked floodgates of anger and distress which had been kept hidden when the war ended' ('Cyni'r dirwasgiad fu'r allwedd i ddatgloi llifddorau'r digofaint ac enbydrwydd profiad a gadwesid o'r golwg ar ddiwedd y rhyfel').[4]

The war in fact had changed everything, even though poets like Eliseus Williams (Eifion Wyn), in many ways the epitome of the easy pre-war romanticism into which John Morris-Jones's *fin de siècle* aesthetic revolution had already declined, went on writing as though it had never been. It was not only that the young men who were to become major literary figures as the century wore on – Saunders Lewis, T. H. Parry-Williams, R. Williams Parry and W. J. Gruffydd – were deeply affected in different ways by their experience in and out of war; it was also the fact that a global catastrophe had impinged terminally upon a rural cultural landscape that had remained essentially unchanged for five hundred years. And Wales, for all the industrialization of the southern valleys, was

---

[3] Idem, *Llên Cyni a Rhyfel a Thrafodion Eraill* (Llandysul, 1987), p. 36.

[4] Ibid., p. 37.

a rural country in 1914, dominated by the traditionalism of small rural communities and translating the conservatism of these village communities even into the new patterns of urban living in the industrial areas. The industrialized valleys of south Wales were still essentially a collection of village communities, dominated though they were by coal-tips and steel mills; they did not acquire the urban values of Cardiff and Swansea until the rest of Wales did, following the Second World War. As far as Welsh-speaking communities were concerned, the depredations of industry and the earlier depredations of the 'press gang', ever feared in coastal areas, were as nothing to the wholesale depredations of war epitomized in the phrase 'Y rhwyg o golli'r hogiau' (the wrench of losing the boys).[5] One only has to enter any rural church or pause by any village war memorial to sense the bewilderment created in thinking minds by such depredations. One churchyard memorial in a remote village in the hill country of Ceredigion commemorates young men from farms with deeply evocative names, speaking eloquently of stability and continuity – Garth-fawr, Llaindelyn, Hafod-las Isaf, Gilfach-goed, Penglan-owen Fawr – lying dead 'ar faes y gad' (on the battlefield) and naming in turn all those places which have become synonymous with the Great War – Ypres, the Somme, Gallipoli, the Dardanelles.[6] What had the one to do with the other? Even communities long accustomed to man's inhumanity and the quirks of fortune had to ask what malign fate had taken these young men, and thousands like them, from their fields and slain them far away? It was a question which was to haunt in various ways a literature dominated from then on by the search for identity in a fractured world, a world in which Welsh literature would no longer be the product of settled, interdependent communities.

For the Welsh-language writer, the *angst* which afflicted the whole of post-war Europe was deepened by an inevitable concern about the state of the language itself, the writer's *raison d'être*. The decline of the language was not, of course, a new phenomenon. The percentage of those able to speak Welsh had been declining since the mid-nineteenth century, but not until the 1901 census were Welsh speakers shown to be a minority of the population.[7] And even these figures, as far as Welsh literature was concerned, provided a misleading statistic. For although parts of Wales were indeed becoming – or had become – Anglicized, and although a neglect amounting to hostility within the education system was a cancer that had been gnawing away at the language for a very long time, nevertheless most of the young writers who went to war, as well as the

---

[5] From the *englyn* 'Ar Gofadail' by R. Williams Parry, published in *Yr Haf a Cherddi Eraill* (Y Bala, 1924), p. 110.

[6] This particular monument stands among the gravestones in the churchyard in Llangwyryfon, Ceredigion.

[7] According to the 1901 census, 49.9 per cent of the population of Wales was able to speak Welsh.

previous generation which did not, had been brought up in rural communities in north and west Wales which were still, for all practical purposes, monoglot, especially in day-to-day oral communication. As far as they knew from their own personal experience, the state of the language was healthy enough. It was the Great War and its aftermath which triggered an accelerated and obvious decline that was to continue until the 1991 census returns at last appeared to show that the decline had been checked.[8]

But to return to 1914 and to the fact that social, political and even linguistic changes in society are only seen in literature through the filter of individual experiences. In 1914 Saunders Lewis, the greatest dramatist to write in the Welsh language and probably the century's most erudite and perceptive critic and scholar, was still studying French and English at the University of Liverpool; he would soon be serving in France, then in Italy and Greece, as an officer in the South Wales Borderers. T. H. Parry-Williams, who was to become a major poet and the virtual creator of the personal essay form in Welsh, had already achieved prominence as a result of his successes at the National Eisteddfod[9] and was beginning his academic career as a young lecturer in Aberystwyth. During the war, as a result of his pacifism, he was to suffer traumatic experiences which would remain with him into old age.[10] His cousin, R. Williams Parry, regarded by many as the most sensitive and artistic of all modern Welsh-language poets, had also already established himself, mainly by means of the seminal Eisteddfod *awdl*, 'Yr Haf' (The Summer). At the time he was a schoolteacher in rural Wales but before long he, too, would be drawn into the conflict, writing melancholy letters home as a private soldier from safe but dismal camps in the south of England, within hearing of the guns of Flanders. W. J. Gruffydd, the hugely influential and often scathing editor of the literary journal, *Y Llenor*, from 1922 to 1951, was lecturing in the Department of Welsh at the University College of Wales, Cardiff. Before long he would be in the Royal Navy, patrolling the Persian Gulf and finding, as one biographer has said, 'the tedium of the desert countries and the boredom of the Red Sea really unbearable';[11] he contracted malaria and dysentery, ailments which would continue to afflict him and make him extremely irritable and impatient as the years wore on.[12] Kate Roberts, certainly the finest prose writer of the twentieth century, was completing her studies at Bangor under John Morris-Jones; by 1918 she would have lost one brother in the war and another would suffer permanent ill-health as

---

[8] According to the 1921 census, 37.1 per cent of the population of Wales was able to speak Welsh.

[9] At the National Eisteddfod held at Wrexham in 1912, he won the Chair for an *awdl* entitled 'Y Mynydd' (The Mountain) and the Crown for his *pryddest* 'Giraldus Cambrensis'. He repeated the feat at Bangor in 1915, when the *awdl* was entitled 'Eryri' (Snowdonia) and the *pryddest* 'Y Ddinas' (The City). Of these, 'Y Ddinas' was the only one he gave any credence to in later life.

[10] There is a detailed account of these events and their effect on T. H. Parry-Williams in David Jenkins, *Thomas Gwynn Jones: Cofiant* (Dinbych, 1973), pp. 267–71.

[11] T. J. Morgan, *W. J. Gruffydd* (Cardiff, 1970), p. 42.

[12] Ibid.

a result of it. We have her own testimony that grief drove her to write as a form of personal therapy.[13] Albert Evans-Jones (Cynan), the only poet apart from Hedd Wyn significantly to incorporate his war experiences in his poetry – which he did notably in his Eisteddfod *pryddest*, 'Mab y Bwthyn' (The Cottage Son) – served throughout the war, first as a private soldier, but then as a chaplain, his views becoming more and more pacifist as the war went on. Even D. Gwenallt Jones (Gwenallt), who was later to write powerfully of his experiences of poverty in industrial south Wales, and who was only fifteen years old in 1914, was to see the inside of Wormwood Scrubs and Dartmoor as a conscientious objector before the war ended. His stance was born of an explosive mixture of Christian pacifism and international socialism, one of the root causes of which was the death of his father in a vat of molten metal.[14] The greatest writer of the previous generation, T. Gwynn Jones, already forty-three in 1914, was beginning a second career as an academic at Aberystwyth. Because of the absence of others at war, he was effectively running the department before his appointment to the Gregynog Chair of Welsh Literature at the College in 1919; he, too, was deeply influenced, if indirectly, by the war and he incorporated his feelings powerfully in fine, symbolic poems.[15]

The war did not form the majority of these writers; apart from Kate Roberts and Gwenallt, they were already established writers. It was rather that the experiences they endured in and out of it changed their world view and fundamentally influenced their mature work, thereby influencing in turn the whole direction of Welsh writing after the war.

T. H. Parry-Williams had seen the clouds gathering before 1914. Following a brilliant career as a student at Aberystwyth and Oxford, he had gone to Paris and Freiburg to study Comparative Philology. What he witnessed in both places, particularly in Freiburg, shocked him. In Germany he was brought face to face with the war-like and militaristic attitudes of many of the young men he met in the university,[16] and when he took up his post at Aberystwyth he expressed his grim foreboding in poems and essays published in the college magazine, *Y Wawr*.[17] His experiences of city life in Paris led him to write vividly of corruption and prostitution in an Eisteddfod *pryddest*, 'Y Ddinas' (The City), which won him the Crown for the second time in 1915. It was not surprising, however, that Eifion Wyn, one of the adjudicators, disliked the poem intensely.

---

[13] Kate Roberts, *Y Lôn Wen* (Dinbych, 1960).

[14] Gwenallt dealt with this event and the background to it in his long-awaited and unfinished novel, *Ffwrneisiau* (Llandysul, 1982).

[15] 'Madog' (1917), 'Broséliâwnd' (1922), 'Anatiomaros' (1925), 'Argoed' (1927). All were notable also for their experimental use of the strict metres and they were later published in T. Gwynn Jones, *Caniadau* (Wrecsam, 1934).

[16] This is strikingly evident in an essay which he contributed to the magazine of the Theological College in Aberystwyth in November 1914. See T. H. Parry-Williams, 'Criafol', *The Grail (Y Greal)*, VIII, no. 23 (1914), 24–5.

[17] Idem, 'Y Pagan', *Y Wawr*, III, no. 1 (1915), 9; idem, 'Yr Hen Ysfa', ibid., III, no. 3 (1916), 88–92.

Whether consciously or not, he no doubt sensed as he read it that his comfortable day was done.

Not that this became immediately apparent. When W. J. Gruffydd launched *Y Llenor* in 1922 he had cause enough to chastize outdated and hypocritical attitudes and was not loath to do so, although his own taste in poetry was pre-modernist enough for him to have stated in his introduction to his widely used and, for a time, highly regarded anthology, *Y Flodeugerdd Gymraeg* (1931), that the Welsh penchant was for lyric rather than epic verse, and for the contents of the anthology to reflect, faithfully enough on the whole, the aesthetic of John Morris-Jones.[18]

But times were changing, and a clear indication of this was the gradual growth of a genuine body of Welsh fiction to set beside what was still largely a poetic tradition. It is true that Daniel Owen had written fine novels at the end of the nineteenth century and that others had also turned their hands to the novel, largely as a vehicle of social and moral propaganda; but Daniel Owen had been a remarkable and individual phenomenon and if one wished to be taken seriously as a writer in pre-war Wales, it was an advantage to write verse. Although there were serious precursors of a creative prose tradition, especially in the short stories of Richard Hughes Williams (Dic Tryfan) and W. Llewelyn Williams, it was with the appearance in 1923 of E. Tegla Davies's novel, *Gŵr Pen y Bryn*, and of Kate Roberts's first volume of short stories, *O Gors y Bryniau*, in 1925, that markers were really put down for the development of a modern tradition. Both in terms of stance and of language use, it was clear that something new was taking place. In E. Tegla Davies's case, it was no more than a marker, for the story of an affluent farmer's spiritual struggles during the Tithe Wars of the 1880s, although it possessed a genuine sparseness and artistic sensitivity, was to be his only venture into the field of the serious novel. For Kate Roberts it was to be the beginning of a long and unique career as a writer of prose fiction in Welsh. Before she died in 1985, aged ninety-four, she had published ten collections of short stories, six novels and an outstanding autobiography, and it is impossible to overestimate her influence on the writers who followed her.[19]

In the first place, her stance was entirely specific and contemporary. She set out to interpret baldly and uncompromisingly the grim struggle for survival of the people among whom she had grown up. These were the families of quarry

---

[18] Incorporated in his study of Welsh prosody, *Cerdd Dafod* (Rhydychen, 1925), and in his eisteddfod adjudications.

[19] The volumes published in the interim were: *Deian a Loli* (Caerdydd, 1927); *Rhigolau Bywyd* (Caerdydd, 1929); *Laura Jones* (Aberystwyth, 1930); *Traed mewn Cyffion* (Aberystwyth, 1936); *Ffair Gaeaf* (Dinbych, 1937); *Stryd y Glep* (Dinbych, 1949); *Y Byw sy'n Cysgu* (Dinbych, 1956); *Te yn y Grug* (Dinbych, 1959); *Y Lôn Wen* (Dinbych, 1960); *Tywyll Heno* (Dinbych, 1962); *Hyn o Fyd* (Dinbych, 1964); *Tegwch y Bore* (Llandybïe, 1967); *Prynu Dol* (Dinbych, 1969); *Gobaith* (Dinbych, 1972); *Yr Wylan Deg* (Dinbych, 1976); *Haul a Drycin* (Dinbych, 1981).

workers living along the hillsides between Caernarfon and the huge complex of slate quarries around Llanberis. They were not, however, purely industrial communities, for almost all these families also farmed smallholdings in order to eke out a bare and precarious income at the rock-face. They were communities desperately concerned with making ends meet. All her early work, from *O Gors y Bryniau* onwards – *Rhigolau Bywyd* (1929), *Ffair Gaeaf* (1937) and her first novel *Traed Mewn Cyffion* (1936) – deals with the grim struggle for survival in such a society and faces its starkness with an almost contrary honesty. It is only when she depicts its children, in *Deian a Loli* (1927) and much later in the beautifully sunlit *Te yn y Grug* (1959), that she allows the brighter side of this society to shine through – its essential innocence and simplicity. On the whole, as far as adults are concerned, human beings and human qualities do survive, but only just, and Kate Roberts evolves a suitably spare, even puritanical, style to relate the tale she has to tell. Liberally sprinkled through this style are words and phrases gleaned from the rich oral tradition of a monoglot community, and the very syntax is a distillation of the language patterns she had heard as a child. It is not too much to claim that, just as the translation of the Bible in 1588 created such a fusion of dialect and classical forms that it could serve as a model for prose usage for three hundred years and more, so did Kate Roberts fuse onto the oral usage of her childhood a spare classical syntax, thereby creating a flexible and contemporary model suitable for a very different and more creative contemporary usage than that which would still be provided for many years to come for preachers and others by William Morgan's Bible.

In formulating her model, and in building a body of work that would have marked her out as a major writer in any language, Kate Roberts was aided by one substantial fact which she refers to more than once in her autobiography.[20] The society she grew up in and wrote about used the Welsh language creatively to express contemporary emotions; it was a growing, organic medium. Furthermore, it was a society whose culture was still primarily a literary culture, one which set considerable store by language use. She points out in her autobiography that the chapel, as she knew it, was not primarily a religious institution, but a cultural one.[21] And its role as a cultural institution was highly linguistic. There were, it is true, regular singing practices on the tonic sol-fa modulator, but there were even more opportunities for learning and reciting poetry, whether scriptural or not, writing essays, conducting debates, even performing suitably bland playlets. The Welsh-language writer, throughout the inter-war years, was operating within a cultural context that was literate and linguistically aware. Kate Roberts, together with D. J. Williams, who began late, but who complemented Roberts's work with his marvellous sequence of short story collections set in rural

---

[20] Roberts, *Y Lôn Wen*, p. 48.
[21] Ibid.

Carmarthenshire – *Storïau'r Tir Glas* (1936), *Storïau'r Tir Coch* (1941) and *Storïau'r Tir Du* (1949) – was able to presuppose a readership that possessed literary touchstones; without any artistic deception, both could depict a society for whom spoken and written language were important. In *Storïau'r Tir Glas* in particular, and in his first volume of autobiography, *Hen Dŷ Ffarm* (1953),[22] D. J. Williams created a south Wales equivalent to Kate Roberts's Rhosgadfan, distinct but essentially the same. It is interesting to note that, as the 1930s moved into the 1940s and another war came and went, he could see this society changing before his eyes. His third volume of stories, *Storïau'r Tir Du*, is very different from the first, both in style and content; it depicts a society that is disintegrating, both morally and linguistically. The decline from the moral stance, the harsh puritanical probity, of Kate Roberts's Rhosgadfan to what she certainly regarded as the moral and linguistic decadence portrayed in her later work, is equally clear, if painted in more forgiving colours, in a progression through D. J. Williams's work.

T. Rowland Hughes, too, wrote of the same quarrying communities as Kate Roberts in the 1940s. Although his novels are based in the main on the sizeable industrial villages of Llanberis and Bethesda, he could draw on similar experiences and assume the existence of the same literate and bookish audience. Hughes was a conscious craftsman in the field of the novel and in a succession of works, in particular in the outstanding *Chwalfa* (1946), in which he dealt with the historical topic of the quarrymen's strike and the subsequent 'lock-out' in the Penrhyn quarries at the turn of the century, he succeeded in setting within the wider context of the quarrying industry, its industrial relations and its conditions of work, the personal suffering which Kate Roberts had placed under a more precise and limiting microscope.[23]

What was true for prose writers was, of course, true for poets. Parry-Williams, Williams Parry and Gwenallt comprised the last generation of poets who could write out of a community that was not only naturally Welsh-speaking but also well versed in the Bible, so that scriptural allusion could be the bread and butter of their imagery, creating a common bond between the poet and his audience. This common bond was not necessarily used for theological purposes, and it would never again be valid for any artist.[24] In terms of content and of the writer's stance, the literature of the 1920s and 1930s displayed an increasing attempt to come to terms with the fundamental changes which had occurred in Welsh

---

[22] A second volume was published six years later. See D. J. Williams, *Yn Chwech ar Hugain Oed* (Aberystwyth, 1959).

[23] The others were: *O Law i Law* (Llandysul, 1943); *William Jones* (Llandysul, 1944); *Yr Ogof* (Llandysul, 1947).

[24] Following his adjudication in the Chair competition at the Cardiff National Eisteddfod in 1960, when the Chair, offered for an *awdl* on the subject 'Dydd Barn a Diwedd Byd' (The Day of Judgement and the End of the World) was withheld, Gwenallt pointed out in the Literary Pavilion that poets were no longer able to write convincingly on such a topic since, by and large, they did not believe in the Day of Judgement.

society since the Great War and were continuing to take place, and in particular with the fact that the world of Welsh Wales was no longer a series of self-sufficient rural enclaves. The larger world, having so rudely thrust itself into these enclaves during the Great War, was now constantly injecting into the old ways disturbing doses of new ideas and new values – urban, alien and dangerously libertarian. Henceforth, Welsh literature would be the literature of individuals who happened to be Welsh speakers, rather than the literature of integrated communities.

In poetry, Parry-Williams continued to be the pioneer who forced the reader of Welsh literature to come to terms with that new, oblique and questioning literary stance which would come to be known as 'modernism' and which impelled the poet to muse rather than declaim, to converse rather than sing. The generation motivated and informed by John Morris-Jones and his *Cerdd Dafod* (1925) had already resolved, a quarter of a century earlier, to reject wordy and prosaic Victorian moralizing in favour of a deliberately 'poetic' style, suitable for dealing with selectively 'poetic' subjects – 'romantic' love (that is, love poetry which was, by definition, non-explicit as far as sex was concerned), poems celebrating the prettier aspects of the natural world, and the like. They had also, though less explicitly, rejected the Nonconformist apologetics of the Victorians in favour of a more secular, not to say agnostic, aesthetic.

In Parry-Williams's work, a harder and more analytical intellectual approach blew the softness away, and eventually modernism in that sense undermined the romanticism of the early years of the century. R. Williams Parry's first volume of verse,[25] although including deeply agnostic elegiac poems for those killed in the Great War, was, by and large, a demonstration of his superb artistry as a maker of lyrics. His god during his early years was unquestionably Keats, whose various poetic invocations, from 'Beauty is Truth, Truth Beauty; that is all ye know on earth and all ye need to know' to 'O for a life of emotions rather than of thoughts', would have suited well his own early approach to poetry. In Williams Parry's case, although the Great War certainly had an effect, it was the symbolic deed at Penyberth in 1936 which finally marked the end of the old world and the coming of a new, more unsettled and less civilized time; a number of his poems written subsequently presage the coming of another war. From then on his themes were in general more socially conscious, the language sparer and the tone far sharper. The Williams Parry of *Cerddi'r Gaeaf* (1952) was so different from the Williams Parry who was universally known as 'Bardd yr Haf (The Poet of Summer) that the contents of this major volume deeply disappointed many who still fed on the honeydew of Eifion Wyn and who yearned to seek shelter in a self-contained literary world which bore as little relation as possible to that which was

---

[25] Williams Parry, *Yr Haf a Cherddi Eraill*. It is interesting to note that none of these poems contained any element of Christian hope of a resurrection.

going on around them. W. J. Gruffydd too – majestically romantic in his great lyric, 'Ywen Llanddeiniolen' (The Yew Tree of Llanddeiniolen), and similar early poems – seemed to be a different writer when he published 'Gwladys Rhys' and other later verse in irregular metres, which contained much of the social satire found in his editorial notes for *Y Llenor*.

T. Gwynn Jones who, in a series of fine poems written between 1917 and 1927, had expressed in traditional forms and by the indirect means of Celtic myth and legend what he saw as the tragedy of modern man, overrun by philistine materialism and in danger of losing altogether the sensitivities of a civilized society, turned to *vers libre* and to a harder, more detached stance for his ultimate condemnation of barbarism in his last volume. It is no doubt significant that he felt impelled to publish this volume under a pseudonym.[26] It was Parry-Williams, however, with his first volume of verse, *Cerddi* (1931), and his first volume of creative essays, *Ysgrifau* (1928), who marked the sea change which was taking place; in many ways these two volumes introduced the modernist interpretation of literature to Welsh Wales. He, like Kate Roberts in prose, but even more radically, created his own vocabulary for the way in which he wanted to express things, especially in his 'ysgrifau' (essays) which were a far cry from the *belles lettres* essays on topics like 'Bedknobs' which were at the same time finding favour in English periodicals, although these may well have been one of his starting points. Parry-Williams used the essay as a vehicle for an intense examination of his own experience, and, as a body, they comprise an ambivalent and elusive spiritual and intellectual autobiography. They bear a closer relation to the work of Montaigne than they do to the English Georgian essayists. His stance was that of an ordinary man sharing common thoughts in day-to-day language with anyone who might be inclined to listen. The 'ysgrifau', complex and unrelenting in their thought processes, are nevertheless full of linguistic inventions based on the remembered oral language of his native Rhyd-ddu and thus are extraordinarily vibrant and direct in their prose style. In this they were unquestionably influential, although it must also be said that many who continued to write poetry in the old ways seemed unaware of the passage of time. Moreover, many of the essay writers who imitated T. H. Parry-Williams during the inter-war period appeared to have little grasp of the special nature of his contribution and used the essay as a vehicle for self-indulgent musings in a style more suited to *fin de siècle* escapism than to the challenges of the new century.

It was not long, however, before a younger generation of poets followed in Parry-Williams's wake: Gwenallt, only twelve years his junior, but not so quickly

---

[26] [T. Gwynn Jones], *Y Dwymyn* (Llandysul, 1944). Published under the pseudonym, 'Rhufawn', it contained one of his finest poems, 'Cynddilig'. The series of poems contained in *Y Dwymyn* were first published singly during the 1930s in *Y Traethodydd*, the journal of the Calvinistic Methodists.

into his stride,[27] Caradog Prichard,[28] Gwilym R. Jones,[29] J. M. Edwards,[30] Aneirin Talfan Davies,[31] W. H. Reese, E. Prosser Rhys and J. T. Jones (John Eilian)[32] were among those poets who, in different ways, spoke with fresh voices during the 1920s and 1930s, sometimes employing irregular metres, sometimes bringing the worlds of industry and technology into their poems, and almost always challenging what they regarded as the outmoded attitudes of their elders. When E. Prosser Rhys wrote of homosexual love in an Eisteddfod *pryddest* in 1924,[33] and Gwenallt similarly challenged the convention of reticence regarding sexual matters in an *awdl* in 1928,[34] the same kind of outrage which T. H. Parry-Williams had provoked with 'Y Ddinas' was paraded and questions of propriety rehearsed.

Lurking in the wings throughout the period and representing a very different response to the tumults of change was Saunders Lewis. His presidency of the newly founded Plaid Genedlaethol Cymru (the Welsh Nationalist Party) from 1926 to 1939, his early plays based on early Welsh themes, his political essays written for *Y Ddraig Goch*, the journal of the Party, between 1926 and 1937, and later to be continued in *Baner ac Amserau Cymru*, his critical reinterpretations of major Welsh literary figures and not least his symbolic picture of what he saw as a contemporary moral decline into degradation in his novel *Monica* (1930), all argued for a retrenchment of moral and spiritual values through political action. Wales could recover its soul and counter many of the worst excesses of modern materialism if it became an independent nation responsible for its own actions, recovering at the same time an informed sense of pride in the best of her past. Saunders Lewis was a highly erudite man, well versed in Latin, French and Italian literature, and he certainly wished to think of Wales within the context of a wider

[27] *Ysgubau'r Awen*, his first volume of verse, was published in Llandysul in 1939.

[28] A journalist working in London, he won the National Eisteddfod Crown in 1927, 1928 and 1929, all with poems which were highly personal, contemporary and to some extent controversial. He later won the National Eisteddfod Chair in 1962.

[29] The editor of *Baner ac Amserau Cymru* from 1945 to 1977, he was one of the few to have won all three major literary awards at the National Eisteddfod.

[30] He also won the Crown three times and wrote much about the influence of industry and technology on modern life, notably in his long poem, 'Peiriannau' (Machines).

[31] Later an enlightened Head of Programmes for BBC Wales and a significant and wide-ranging literary critic, he first gained recognition with a volume of *vers libre*, *Y Ddau Lais*, published jointly with W. H. Reese in 1937.

[32] Later first editor of *Y Cymro*, founder of *Y Ford Gron* and for many years chief editor of the *Herald* newspapers in Caernarfon, he published an early volume of contemporary verse, *Gwaed Ifanc*, jointly with E. Prosser Rhys in 1923. He also won the National Eisteddfod Chair and Crown in 1947 and 1949 respectively.

[33] 'Atgof' (Memory). In spite of the adjudicators' unease, this *pryddest* did win the Crown.

[34] 'Y Sant' (The Saint). Both Elfed and the Revd J. J. Williams agreed with their fellow-adjudicator, John Morris-Jones, who dismissed the work as 'a pile of filth' ('pentwr o aflendid'). See E. Vincent Evans (ed.), *Cofnodion a Chyfansoddiadau Eisteddfod Genedlaethol 1928 (Treorci)* (Caerdydd, 1928), p. 4.

world. In his case, however, it was the ordered world of Catholic Christendom, a world which went back to the great strict-metre poets of the fourteenth and fifteenth centuries. He longed to see this balanced universe reflected in contemporary Welsh literature and he believed it would be possible if Wales became an independent nation separate from its English neighbour. It was the sense of permanence incorporated in integrated communities which he wished to see restored and he might well have agreed with Yeats's famous couplet: 'How but in custom and in ceremony/Are innocence and beauty born?'[35] Yeats was in fact an early influence upon him, as were Maurice Barrès and the Welsh writer, Robert Ambrose Jones (Emrys ap Iwan), although, as he developed, he turned more and more to French Catholic writers like Claudel, Mauriac and Maritain, and to Italian critics like Croce. Lewis himself was admitted into the Roman Catholic Church in 1932. His spectacularly different response to the problems of the modern world compared with that both of the early aesthetes and of the modernists gained a growing response among many Welsh writers for the remainder of the century; much Welsh writing became more overtly and more politically nationalistic and there was also, as we shall see, a return to religious affirmation, if not to Catholicism, among many of the poets who came to prominence after the Second World War.

If imaginative literature may be said to rest on the three prongs of poetry, prose and drama, while prose began to assume its proper place side by side with poetry during the inter-war years, drama remained a Cinderella. Of the three branches, drama requires a much more developed support structure than the other two. Although the role of the individual writer in the creation of literature has been stressed, it is nevertheless true that for any body of literature to develop a shape and a direction, it requires support systems in the society within which it is operating. The poet may perhaps continue to produce work of quality, irrespective of any assumed audience or any publishing mechanism. The novelist, on the other hand, presupposes an audience and some form of publication is essential to his *raison d'être*. But it is the dramatist who is really dependent on outside forces; for him to function properly, there must be a theatre, actors, audiences; a play on paper is nothing without performance. As Saunders Lewis himself was to comment acidly more than once, there was in effect no theatre in Wales. When asked disingenuously on one occasion why his work was so 'heavy' and why he did not write more comedies, he replied that the performance of comedy required acting skills that were not available in Welsh Wales; and lest anyone believed that this was a joke, he repeated it later in the preface to one of his plays.[36] Although there was a thriving amateur tradition, it was based on village halls and chapel vestries, and serious drama requires more. There were, in fact,

---

[35] From 'A Prayer for my Daughter', written in June 1919.
[36] Saunders Lewis, *Problemau Prifysgol* (Llandybïe, 1968).

during the inter-war period, some 500 amateur drama companies in Wales, performing what they liked to call 'village drama' in Welsh.[37] Most of the writers providing material for these companies satisfied themselves with superficial sketches, but there were a few writers of genuine talent, like R. G. Berry, J. O. Francis and D. T. Davies, who endeavoured to deal with matters of genuine social concern in dramatic terms, but who were largely operating in a vacuum. There were others, like T. Gwynn Jones and W. J. Gruffydd, whose main areas of activity lay elsewhere, but who also contributed both original plays and translations. Several small theatres were established as the century wore on, notably that of R. O. F. Wynne in his country house at Garthewin, in converted barns and the like, and flourished briefly until the coming of television saw support for them gradually wither. Serious playwrights like John Gwilym Jones, Huw Lloyd Edwards and Gwenlyn Parry, who emerged in the post-war period, were dependent on their posts as college and university lecturers, or, in Gwenlyn Parry's case, as a BBC drama editor, to provide them with a captive company and a select audience to enable them to write and produce serious plays which would otherwise have found neither actors to perform them nor audiences to appreciate them.

Both John Gwilym Jones and Huw Lloyd Edwards worked in Bangor colleges, the one in the University and the other in the Normal College. John Gwilym Jones, in particular, wrote his plays largely for his student company, and he himself was a gifted drama director. Until they were recreated for television in later years, however, fine plays like *Y Gŵr Llonydd* (1958), *Y Tad a'r Mab* (1963), *Hanes Rhyw Gymro* (1964) and the outstanding *Ac Eto Nid Myfi* (1976) were either effectively produced by the author himself for one tour or, in some cases, heard by listeners in sound radio versions. Some of John Gwilym Jones's later plays were written specifically for radio and he had himself been a radio drama producer before joining the Department of Welsh at the University College of North Wales, Bangor. Scarce opportunities for performance afflicted the finely crafted contemporary parables of Huw Lloyd Edwards even more and important plays like *Y Gŵr o Gath Heffer* (1961), *Y Gŵr o Wlad Us* (1961) and *Pros Kairon* (1967) were rarely performed to a professional standard. There were other able dramatists active in other colleges and elsewhere, dependent on dwindling numbers of good amateur companies and occasional National Eisteddfod performances for any kind of showing for their work. In such a situation, the call for a national professional theatre in Wales was heard more than once and several abortive attempts were made to establish such a theatre. These always foundered, although Cwmni Theatr Cymru, which gained autonomy in 1968 with the support of the Welsh Arts Council and Wilbert Lloyd Roberts as its director, achieved much for a time until it lost the necessary financial support. Professionalism entered the theatre in

---

[37] 'Drama' in Meic Stephens (ed.), *The New Companion to the Literature of Wales* (Cardiff, 1998), pp. 185–7; Hywel Teifi Edwards, *Codi'r Llen* (Llandysul, 1998).

another way later on and on a more modest scale. Groups of actors assembled to form small touring companies, sometimes with a base provided by a local education authority theatre-in-education provision, and the best of these companies, notably Theatr Bara Caws and Brith Gof as far as the Welsh language was concerned, achieved a high standard of performance by concentrating on contemporary social issues. Their work, however, emphasized mime, movement, music and the like at the expense of a set script and although they encouraged a new kind of writing for the theatre, they were not major sponsors of the written word. Gwenlyn Parry, one of the most important of Welsh playwrights, enjoyed a privileged position within the BBC and most of his plays, which were heavily influenced by the anti-naturalistic techniques of the French Theatre of the Absurd, were also comparatively easily adapted to television. Parry, however, was fundamentally a man of the theatre and the highly theatrical situations of plays like *Tŷ ar y Tywod* (1968) and *Y Tŵr* (1978) demanded theatrical production of the highest calibre and rarely, if ever, received it. It is one of the tragedies of Welsh literature that the post-war period produced a crop of able dramatists, thoroughly familiar and in sympathy with the new departures of modern European theatre and likely to have been able to supply a fully professional live theatre with a body of outstanding, forward-looking plays had such a theatre existed.

Apart from the National Eisteddfod, support structures in Welsh Wales between the 1920s and the 1950s were few and impoverished, and the Eisteddfod itself still unashamedly reserved its best attentions for poetry and often represented outdated attitudes. It was nevertheless an institution of the greatest importance as far as public encouragement for writers was concerned. It confirmed public perception of literature as an integral part of life, it provided a forum for national debate regarding literary standards, and it lent distinction, at least temporarily, to successful writers. Where poetry was concerned, however, it was no coincidence that many of the literary milestones of the period were provided by prize-winning Eisteddfod poems. Support for the publication of books was piecemeal and partial, as it always had been in Wales. There were several well-established printers like Gwasg Gee in Denbigh, Hughes a'i Fab in Wrexham and the Gomerian Press (later Gwasg Gomer) in Llandysul, who were also publishers and indeed subsidizers of important journals and periodicals[38] and who, in addition, published books as one-off projects; but none of them possessed a proper book-publishing programme and their activities were in no way co-ordinated.

There were also the literary periodicals which, because of the lack of a properly developed publishing infrastructure, had always played a disproportionately important role in the history of Welsh literature. Although dominated by

---

[38] For example, Gwasg Gee published *Baner ac Amserau Cymru*, Gwasg Gomer *Y Gen(h)inen* and Hughes a'i Fab *Y Llenor*.

Y Llenor, a variety of periodicals provided a platform for aspiring writers from the 1920s to the 1950s. The long-standing *Y Traethodydd* and *Y Gen(h)inen* played their part, while *Y Ford Gron*, which was extant between 1930 and 1935, although primarily intended as a periodical for Welsh expatriates, perhaps represented the mood of the 1930s better than any of the others. Although the denominational periodicals were much concerned with theological and philosophical matters, they, too, provided a platform for creative writing. The national newspapers, *Baner ac Amserau Cymru*, founded in 1859, acquired a new lease of life and a new interest in literature under the editorship of the poet, E. Prosser Rhys, between 1923 and 1945, and *Y Cymro*, founded in 1932 and also edited in the first instance by a poet, John Eilian, had a strong literary bias. Even regional newspapers like *Yr Herald Cymraeg*, published in Caernarfon, played their part. All this ensured that both poetry and prose appeared regularly before the public and most established writers contributed frequently to one or more of the periodicals. It made for a lively and varied literary scene, but it was all rather *ad hoc* and in no sense did it comprise an organized support structure. That was to come later.

The coming of the Second World War did not have the same obviously traumatic effect on Welsh literature as the coming of the First World War. In many ways the damage had already been done and, in any case, there was a kind of resignation abroad, a sense of inevitability linked to the growing bitterness and disillusionment that had deepened as the 1930s wore on. The war itself certainly hastened the continuing decline in the number of Welsh speakers and nipped in the bud many of the literary activities which had been set in motion in the late 1930s, notably the publication of the two periodicals *Heddiw* and *Tir Newydd*,[39] but in terms of the nature and content of the literature being produced immediately beforehand and immediately afterwards, it did not form the kind of watershed created by the Great War. The major writers who had already made their mark continued to write and the war produced few new writers, although it did have a major influence on the work of two major poets. Alun Llywelyn-Williams, a poet known mainly for his editorship of *Tir Newydd* during the late 1930s, published a first volume of lyrical and moving war poems in 1944[40] and often revisited his wartime experiences in later poems, adopting a quiet and cultured stoicism in the face of the barbarities of war and of modern post-war life. Waldo Williams, on the other hand, a remarkable visionary and mystical poet, found that the Second World War simply deepened and matured ideas and attitudes which he had grown up with as a child during the Great War. Both his parents had been pacifists and he nursed a deep regard for them and for their

---

[39] Fifty-eight issues of *Heddiw*, edited by Aneirin ap Talfan (Aneirin Talfan Davies) and Dafydd Jenkins, were published by Gwasg Heddiw between 1936 and 1942, and seventeen issues of *Tir Newydd*, edited in Cardiff by Alun Llywelyn-Williams, appeared between 1935 and 1939.

[40] Alun Llywelyn-Williams, *Cerddi 1934–1942* (Llundain, 1944). His collected poems, *Y Golau yn y Gwyll*, were published in 1979.

attitudes. During the Second World War he suffered a severe personal trauma from which he never truly recovered, namely the death of his wife barely a year after their marriage. He suffered deprivation because of his own pacifist stance and was deeply affected by the threat posed to the communities of the Preselau mountains in Pembrokeshire – communities he revered as models of simple co-operative living in tune with nature – by the appropriation of 16,000 acres of land for an artillery range. A witty, intellectually gifted man, sociable by nature and often hilarious as a storyteller, the war made him into a strongly militant pacifist and an active political nationalist who was later imprisoned for his refusal to pay taxes for warlike purposes and who took Christian solace in his membership of the Society of Friends. The transparent goodness of his utter commitment to the brotherhood of man, together with his one volume of verse *Dail Pren*,[41] not published until 1956, exerted a strong influence on younger poets and made him an extremely influential literary figure during the post-war period.

It is significant that both these major writers came from backgrounds very different from those which had produced even the generation immediately preceding them. Waldo Williams spent the first seven years of his life in an English-speaking home in Haverfordwest in south Pembrokeshire, where Welsh was not only not spoken but also regarded as alien; he became a convert to rural Welshness when the family moved to Mynachlog-ddu, where he learnt Welsh from the children there. Alun Llywelyn-Williams was born in Cardiff, the son of a doctor, and his stance and attitudes remained thoroughly urban.[42] Both writers represented the fact that the emerging literature of the post-war period was to reflect a far wider spectrum of experience and of language use than had been the case during the first half of the century, although the second of these considerations was to be the cause of much soul-searching and critical comment regarding the impoverishment of idiom and vocabulary as a result of the dilution and dispersal of the old rural community.

Writing in 1945, in an appendix to his standard *A History of Welsh Literature*, Thomas Parry took a gloomy view of what he saw.[43] It was clear that the lack of what he regarded as a committed approach among writers themselves, together with the near collapse of what had been at best a patchy system of publication and distribution, had considerably reduced literary activity. Brave attempts to plug the gap by such ventures as the Clwb Llyfrau Cymraeg (the Welsh Books Club), begun in the 1930s and spanning the war years, were clearly inadequate. The very continuation of a published literature in the Welsh language came to depend even more on existing periodicals during the financial constraints of the immediate post-war period. Another commentator, Islwyn Ffowc Elis, describes the scene as he saw it as late as 1950:

---

[41] Waldo Williams, *Dail Pren* (Aberystwyth, 1956).

[42] Alun Llywelyn-Williams, *Gwanwyn yn y Ddinas: Darn o Hunangofiant* (Dinbych, 1975).

[43] Thomas Parry, *Llenyddiaeth Gymraeg 1900–1945* (Lerpwl, 1945).

Rhyw 50 o lyfrau Cymraeg a gyhoeddid mewn blwyddyn i oedolion, a rhywbeth tebyg ar gyfer y plant. Doedd dim grant i'w chael o unman at gyhoeddi na llyfr na chylchgrawn Cymraeg, dim Cyngor Llyfrau Cymraeg, dim Cyngor Celfyddydau Cymru. Doedd y mwyafrif o awduron Cymraeg yn derbyn yr un ddimai goch am ysgrifennu llyfr; roedd y cyhoeddwyr yn cyhoeddi'n aml ar golled.[44]

(About fifty Welsh books were published annually for adults and about the same number for children. There was no grant to be obtained anywhere for publishing Welsh books or periodicals, no Welsh Books Council, no Welsh Arts Council. Most Welsh authors did not receive a single halfpenny for writing a book; publishers often published at a loss.)

The tone of those words, written in 1986, when Elis was editor of the Welsh Books Council publication *Llais Llyfrau*, is an indication of the changes which had been set in motion. There is no doubt that, notwithstanding all the new writing and the development of a more urbane approach within wider horizons, the most significant developments which occurred during the second half of the twentieth century were changes to the support structure, rather than to the nature of the literature itself. These changes, taken side by side with the establishment of Welsh-language television as a universal experience for Welsh speakers, transformed the situation for the Welsh-language writer during the post-war period.

Whereas the National Eisteddfod continued to be an important focus of writing and a provider of financial crumbs to winners of major prizes, there was growing unease among some writers because its sponsorship of literature, especially poetry, was entirely competition-based. There was even greater concern that some poets did not appear to write at all except in order to win major prizes. Others argued that the Eisteddfod was a unique folk festival whose business it was to defend traditional values associated with the *gwerin* and that professionalism in literature was inconsistent with the Welsh tradition. The dispute rumbled on for some twenty years, to no good purpose, but eventually died out as it became increasingly apparent that Welsh literature was in fact finding its place in the new world by becoming at least a semi-professional, subsidized activity. A body which drew a good deal of the fire of the *gwerin* school, Yr Academi Gymreig, was set up in 1959 specifically to defend and maintain standards of literary excellence. One of its founders, the poet Bobi Jones, was one of the main protagonists in the literary debate. Yr Academi Gymreig found an acceptable role in due course and gave birth to an English-language offspring for Anglo-Welsh writers.[45] Although neither wing of the organization quite lived up to the expectations of their

---

[44] Islwyn Ffowc Elis, 'Doedd Neb yn Ddiogel Rhagddo', *Llais Llyfrau* (October 1986), 4.

[45] The English-language section was established in 1968. Its inaugural meeting is described by Meic Stephens, 'Yr Academi Gymreig and Cymdeithas Cymru Newydd', *Poetry Wales*, 4, no. 2 (1968), 7–11.

founders, they performed valuable tasks within a growing network of support, and were responsible for a number of significant publications and, as far as the Welsh-language section was concerned, sustained an important literary journal, *Taliesin*.

There was no question, however, that the National Eisteddfod, throughout the period, remained the most important social focus and an important platform for debate; the strengthening of its 'Welsh-only' rule made it into a vital symbol of cultural nationhood at a time when the currency of the language was still declining, even if the standards of its major competitions, including those submitted for the Prose Medal, which had been added to the Chair and the Crown in 1937, were variable.[46]

An interesting and sophisticated debate was conducted during the 1960s with regard to the writer's duty as a propagandist and even as an active participator in the increasingly militant protests and demonstrations for greater official recognition of the language which occurred following the formation of Cymdeithas yr Iaith Gymraeg (the Welsh Language Society) in 1962.[47] It was felt in some quarters that the writer's comfortable ivory tower was no place for a true Welshman when the struggle for the language was raging all around. Others believed that the writer's chief concern was to write, and that the purpose of literature was to express some aspect of truth about human experience, whatever the prevailing circumstances. Others believed that the writer should use his or her gifts to attract wider audiences to literature by ensuring that whatever was written was widely accessible and would therefore contribute to the survival of the Welsh language. Alun R. Edwards, the energetic and charismatic County Librarian for Cardiganshire, was prominent among these and he coined the phrase 'sothach da' (good rubbish) to describe the kind of popular fiction which he believed was required in order to persuade library users to borrow and read Welsh-language books.[48] Some writers responded and one of them, Islwyn Ffowc Elis, a novelist of genuine ability, deliberately set out to produce novels that would attract a wider audience. In pursuit of this aim he published on average a book a year during the late 1950s and early 1960s.[49] These were extremely good, readable,

---

[46] Welsh was declared the official language of the National Eisteddfod as early as 1937, but English was still used to some extent until 1950 when the 'Welsh Rule' which has subsequently been strictly observed came into effect.

[47] For further details recording the establishment and founding of the Society, see Cynog Dafis, 'Cymdeithas yr Iaith Gymraeg' in Meic Stephens (ed.), *The Welsh Language Today* (Llandysul, 1973), pp. 248–63; Dylan Phillips, *Trwy Ddulliau Chwyldro . . .? Hanes Cymdeithas yr Iaith Gymraeg, 1962–1992* (Llandysul, 1998).

[48] The story of Alun R. Edwards's populist campaigns may be found in his memorial volume, Rheinallt Llwyd (ed.), *Gwarchod y Gwreiddiau: Cyfrol Goffa Alun R. Edwards* (Llandysul, 1996).

[49] They were: *Cysgod y Cryman* (Aberystwyth, 1953); *Yn Ôl i Leifior* (Aberystwyth, 1956); *Wythnos yng Nghymru Fydd* (Caerdydd, 1957); *Blas y Cynfyd* (Aberystwyth, 1958); *Tabyrddau'r Babongo* (Aberystwyth, 1961). *Ffenestri Tua'r Gwyll* (Aberystwyth, 1955) was of a different order and appeared to be aimed at a different readership. However, it was not well received and in his next volume Elis returned to the style and intention of *Cysgod y Cryman*.

contemporary stories which attracted new young readers by virtue of their freshness and contemporaneity and the fact that the author had succeeded in evolving a lively, modern style which combined a genuine mastery of the language with an easily accessible informality. It was a style which proved to be a model for others to follow. Whether or not some of the sterner critics were right in claiming that Islwyn Ffowc Elis had sacrificed his potential as a major novelist on the altar of populism, he unquestionably established the novel as a viable form of modern literature. It was he, far more so than Kate Roberts, who pioneered the way forward for the new generations of prose writers. In any case, populism or not, it was clearly impossible for any writer to ignore the state of the language and the fight for survival that was taking place, and this was inevitably reflected in much Welsh writing of the time, often in a different view of foreboding from that of the 1930s.

One abiding truth about writing in Welsh underlay all this: the Welsh-language writer, however serious his intention and however professional his attitude, was fated at best to have a partial and incomplete literary career, writing as opportunity allowed, but always earning his living in some other occupation. Until the establishment of the Welsh-language television channel it was not possible for a professional Welsh-language writer to exist; writing was an amateur activity, conducted in one's spare time, and many fine talents had to be satisfied with partial and incomplete careers as writers. It was certainly no coincidence that the most professional and committed of writers, Kate Roberts, published nearly twice as many books after her sixtieth birthday as she had published before; there was always a likelihood, apparently unrecognized by critics like Thomas Parry, that Welsh literature would forever be a literature of aspiring youngsters and old-age pensioners. It is certainly not coincidental that the large majority of major Welsh-language writers during this century have either been ministers of religion or academics. Such a limiting combination does not make for a truly varied and representative body of literature.

In response to an increasing sense of cultural crisis during the post-1945 years, Sir David Maxwell Fyffe, Minister for Welsh Affairs, on the instigation of the Council for Wales and Monmouthshire, under the energetic and literate chairmanship of Huw T. Edwards, set up a committee to consider the needs of Welsh publishing. The committee's report was published in October 1952 and became known as the Ready Report (its chairman was A. W. Ready, a director of the publishers, Bell and Sons). The report recognized that the needs were great and made a substantial number of recommendations. It is interesting to note that Huw T. Edwards, writing to the minister, was able to sum them up in this way: 'It appears to me that they have recommended the only successful approach to what is a very difficult problem, i.e. the setting up of a Welsh Books Foundation.'[50]

---

[50] Llwyd (ed.), *Gwarchod y Gwreiddiau*, p. 120.

What was clear to Edwards, however, was not clear enough to the minister and his civil servants, and although Alun R. Edwards and others set a number of projects in motion in order to improve the situation, it was not until 1961 that the Welsh Books Council was established, and even then not as a result of central government action but by means of co-operative effort on the part of a number of local authorities and the comparatively recently-formed Undeb Cymdeithasau Llyfrau Cymraeg (the Union of Welsh Book Societies). The Welsh Books Council was established specifically to promote the production and marketing of 'popular' books for adults, but over the years its scope widened hugely, so that by the 1990s it was concerned with the whole range of book production and had spawned in 1979, in conjunction with the Welsh Arts Council, a Welsh National Children's Literature Centre, based on the same site in Aberystwyth as the Books Council itself. The Council began at once to implement a scheme for the payment of grants to authors, to introduce book tokens for Welsh books and, not least, to set up a wholesale distribution centre. The Welsh Arts Council, which came into being as a separate entity in 1967,[51] was a major funder of the Books Council and enabled it in the early 1970s to expand significantly until it was eventually able to offer a central service to authors, publishers and booksellers through its four departments, dealing with editing, design, publicity and marketing. The Welsh Arts Council itself, through its literature department, under its energetic director, Meic Stephens, supported literature which was deemed to have particular literary merit by means of production grants, writers' bursaries, grants to periodicals and the like. By the mid-1990s the literature department of the Welsh Arts Council was disbursing over a million pounds in grants, while the Welsh Books Council, as well as disbursing some £600,000 of government money annually, was also providing substantial organizational support for all aspects of literature through its full-time staff of 42 members at the Aberystwyth headquarters. When one adds to this the fact that the Welsh Joint Education Committee[52] also became responsible for developing textbooks in Welsh, it is fair to say that there existed by the end of the century a substantial support structure for writing in Welsh.

What difference did this make? It did not alter the situation fundamentally, for it was still not possible for the Welsh writer to earn a full-time living by writing, except on a temporary basis, funded by a bursary or a specific commission. But it meant that published writing was reimbursed, if not adequately reimbursed, and that a whole army of organizers, editors, designers, translators and even publishers

---

[51] It had previously had a much more limited role as the Welsh Committee of the Arts Council of Great Britain.

[52] Established in 1948 to represent all local education authorities in Wales and since 1949 to act as the main examining board for Wales, it has played an increasingly significant role, especially since it has administered augmented grants under the 1980 Education Act, as a funder and commissioner both of Welsh-language textbooks and school reading books.

were able to earn a full-time living on the margins of literature. It also meant a substantial increase in the number and variety of Welsh books published. Fifty titles were published in 1950. By 1972 the number had risen to 199, by 1982 to 390 and by 1992 to 550, including reprints.

As far as the literature itself was concerned, a younger generation of prose writers, producing novels rather than short stories, emerged in the shadow of Islwyn Ffowc Elis during the late 1950s and early 1960s and produced a succession of novels dealing with the emerging problems of the post-war world, the rebellion of youth, rootlessness, the shadow of the bomb, as well as the continuing patterns of rural life. Writers such as John Rowlands, Eigra Lewis Roberts, Harri Pritchard Jones, Marion Eames, Jane Edwards and Rhiannon Davies Jones were serious writers of fiction, while other established writers, better known for their work in other fields, like Pennar Davies, Caradog Prichard and T. Glynne Davies, turned to the novel and made a distinctive contribution. Pennar Davies, whose novels were experimental in form and almost mystical in nature, remained highly poetic in his prose,[53] and T. Glynne Davies's long historical novel, *Marged*, while flawed, was a vibrant and ambitious work.[54] Caradog Prichard's *Un Nos Ola Leuad*, written in the oral dialect of the quarrying areas of Bethesda, was a superb but strange autobiographical novel, perhaps the finest single piece of creative prose written during the century.[55] This generation was followed by another which, although increasingly dominated by women writers like Manon Rhys, Angharad Tomos, Angharad Jones and others, included a major novelist in Aled Islwyn and powerful contributions from two young men whose work displayed a confidence and a willingness to depart from the traditional novel forms and structures, the one in a historical context and the other in a world of myth and fantasy, which marked them out as strongly individual contemporary writers. Wiliam Owen Roberts's *Y Pla*[56] and Robin Llywelyn's *Seren Wen ar Gefndir Gwyn*[57] both indicated that the Welsh novel was poised to abandon its traditional role as a naturalistic chronicler of Welsh life for more exploratory fields of activity.

The poets, as ever, went on writing. Soon after the war, the most remarkable of the younger poets, Bobi Jones, set the tone in his first volume *Y Gân Gyntaf*, published in 1957.[58] He, like Waldo Williams, was born to an English-speaking

---

[53] Notable among his fictional works are *Anadl o'r Uchelder* (Abertawe, 1958), *Meibion Darogan* (Llandybïe, 1968) and *Mabinogi Mwys* (Llandybïe, 1979).

[54] T. Glynne Davies, *Marged* (Llandysul, 1974).

[55] Caradog Prichard, *Un Nos Ola Leuad* (Dinbych, 1961).

[56] He had earlier published another idiosyncratic novel, *Bingo* (Penygroes, 1985). *Y Pla* (Caernarfon, 1987) received widespread critical praise and was later translated into English and German.

[57] *Seren Wen ar Gefndir Gwyn* (Llandysul, 1992) won the National Eisteddfod Prose Medal in 1992. The author repeated this feat in 1994 with another mythic work entitled *O'r Harbwr Gwag i'r Cefnfor Gwyn* (Llandysul, 1994).

[58] Bobi Jones, *Y Gân Gyntaf* (Llandysul, 1957). The poems were first submitted to an Arts Council competition where they were highly praised by the adjudicators, Saunders Lewis, Pennar Davies and Alun Llywelyn-Williams.

family, in his case in Cardiff, and he learnt Welsh at school, rapidly becoming a convert to the language, to nationalism and later to Christianity, all of which he espoused with passionate absolutism. His first volume of verse immediately drew attention by its daring imagery and its unusual and challenging use of language, and ever since he has continued to be a radical, challenging and controversial figure in the world of Welsh literature.[59] He was initially scathing in his criticism of the work of his elders, but more latterly he matured as an interpretive commentator on the work of his contemporaries and juniors. He consistently fought to preserve literary standards, pilloried the concept of populism, inspired young writers, and was arguably the most considerable literary figure to emerge during the post-war period. However, he was by no means the only major poetic figure. The Anglican clergyman Euros Bowen, who was born in the Rhondda in 1904, the son of a Nonconformist minister, did not start writing seriously until the post-war period. He edited the literary magazine *Y Fflam* between 1946 and 1952, with the intention of providing a platform for younger writers, and he published his first volume of verse, *Cerddi*, in 1957. Like Bobi Jones, he followed this with a constant flow of works,[60] although he confined himself in the main to verse. To the major output of these two poets must be added the work of 'Cylch Cadwgan', a group of poets who used to meet in J. Gwyn Griffiths's home in the Rhondda during and after the war. It included Griffiths himself, Pennar Davies, Gareth Alban Davies and Rhydwen Williams, later the author of several substantial novels.

By the end of the 1960s, newer and younger poets were contributing significantly. Among them were Gwyn Thomas, a poet who returned to simpler and more accessible styles and themes in his verse, Nesta Wyn Jones, Bryan Martin Davies, Gwynne Williams and others who had already published one or more volumes. There was a strong flowering of new and varied poetry during the first twenty-five years following the Second World War, mainly in irregular metres and mainly modernist, imagist and allusive in nature. More traditional and conventional poetry, often in the strict metres, had continued in parallel with this influx of new writing, often in association with the Eisteddfod, but it was not until the late 1970s that an unexpected phenomenon manifested itself. This was a very strong resurgence of strict-metre poetry among the then youngest generation

---

[59] He also publishes scholarly work and criticism under his full name, R. M. Jones. In terms of creative writing, he has published eight volumes of verse, two novels, five volumes of short stories and one long poem. He has contributed prolifically on literary topics to all major journals especially, of late, to *Barddas*. He still writes under both names with unabated energy.

[60] Like T. Gwynn Jones, he experimented widely with variations on the strict metres and, unusually, won the Crown with such a poem, entitled 'Difodiant' (Extinction), in 1950. He had also won the Crown in 1948. He published fifteen volumes of verse, together with translations of Greek plays and of Latin and French verse.

of poets. There is no doubt that the Eisteddfod achievements of Alan Llwyd,[61] the precursor of this school, matched by another representative of it, Donald Evans,[62] were to a large extent responsible for this. Alan Llwyd energetically championed strict-metre verse and encouraged young writers in yet another influential periodical, *Barddas*, and through the publishing house established under the same name, a publishing imprint which, as time went on, widened its scope to provide effective and catholic support to all forms of poetry. Alan Llwyd himself was a major poet, writing mainly but not solely in the strict metres and there is no doubt that he, by virtue of his own work, his journal and his publishing house, was the most influential poetic figure of the late twentieth century. Poetry of a more modernist type, influenced by schools and individuals outside Wales, from Seamus Heaney to Roger McGough, continued to flourish and significant new voices, much concerned with contemporary social problems, like those of Iwan Llwyd, Menna Elfyn, Gerwyn Wiliams, Gwyneth Lewis and others, insisted that Welsh poetry was directly related to events on the world scene, from Bosnia to South Africa.

A critical turning point occurred when the Welsh-language television channel, Sianel Pedwar Cymru (S4C), was established in 1982. The fourth channel opened up hitherto undreamed-of possibilities for writers in Welsh who could tailor their talents to the needs of television soap operas and situation comedies. Television had emerged as the most important influence on Welsh writing. The energies both of potential dramatists and potential novelists were diverted towards the screen and S4C produced a substantial number of dramatic series and adaptations of novels which enabled the likes of Eigra Lewis Roberts, Wiliam Owen Roberts, Manon Rhys, Gareth Miles and Ifan Wyn Williams to develop an expertise in the field while also writing more conventional work. The long-running soap opera *Pobol y Cwm* channelled the talents of a far greater number of writers for its own less exalted but well-remunerated purposes. There is no doubt that S4C brought drama in the Welsh language to far greater numbers than had ever been exposed to any literature in Welsh before.

The final comment must, however, relate to the audience for Welsh literature in published form. It is an ironic fact that at this point in history, when there is at last a satisfactory support structure for literature, when there is still a wide variety of literature of all kinds and of a good standard being produced (much of it by younger writers), the number of those who buy and read imaginative literature in Welsh is worryingly low. There is reason to believe that the influx of adult Welsh learners who have unquestionably influenced census returns for the better in 1981 and especially in 1991 are not, by and large, informed readers of Welsh literature.

---

[61] Alan Llwyd won both the National Eisteddfod Chair and Crown in 1973, and again, in controversial circumstances, at Cardigan in 1976 when Dic Jones was found to be ineligible to compete for the Chair since he was a member of one of the Eisteddfod committees.

[62] Donald Evans won both main awards in 1977 and in 1980.

Many highly literate Welsh people, brought up on Kate Roberts and T. H. Parry-Williams, have perished, and new generations of readers have not taken their place in sufficient numbers. Whether they ever will in an age dominated by visual images must be open to question. The twentieth century witnessed a resurgence of Welsh literature, unparalleled in scope and variety and finer in terms of quality and substance than anything it has seen since the fifteenth century, but whether it will prove to have been the last full century in the long history of Welsh literature remains to be seen.

12

The Riches of the Past? Recording Welsh Dialects

BETH THOMAS

Nid rhaid i mi egluro i chwi y gwaith y bwriedir ymgymryd ag ef. Cofnodi holl lên y werin ac astudio'r iaith a siaredir ym mhob cwr o'r wlad. Dylid bod wedi gwneuthur hyn hanner can mlynedd yn ôl. Heddiw, mae'r cof am a fu yn pallu, hyd yn oed yn yr ardaloedd lle y parheir i siarad Cymraeg. Ond y mae'r sefyllfa'n wir argyfyngus mewn llu o gylchoedd yn siroedd y dwyrain. Gwn am lawer plwyf a phentref lle na cheir namyn ryw un neu ddau a eill siarad Cymraeg. Bûm i fy hun yn sgwrsio â'r Cymro Cymraeg olaf mewn llawer pentref ym Morgannwg – profiad trist iawn. Wedi ei farw, wele gladdu holl olud gorffennol y pentre hwnnw.[1]

(I need not explain to you the scale of the task in hand. Recording the entire lore of the people and studying the language spoken throughout the country. This should have been done half a century ago. Today, the memory of the past is fading, even in those areas where Welsh is still spoken. But the situation is truly critical in a host of localities in the eastern counties. I know of many parishes and villages where only one or two inhabitants are able to speak Welsh. I have myself spoken to the last Welsh-speaking Welshman in numerous villages in Glamorgan – a profoundly sad experience. And with them are buried all the riches of that village's past.)

THE WELSH have always had an ambivalent attitude towards their dialects. On the one hand dialects are discouraged in the interests of standardizing the language, but on the other they are considered a mark of our identity. Among our most prominent national qualities are an attachment to locality ('brogarwch') and a longing for a supposed period in time when the Welsh language was 'pure' and free from English influence. The twentieth century has witnessed the breakdown of the concentrated, closely-knit, local networks which are crucial to the maintenance of a minority language or dialect. Despite significant advancements in the public status of Welsh, it is hard not to believe that the language is at the same time in danger of losing those local characteristics which were once so vital to its existence.

---

[1] Museum of Welsh Life [MWL], tape no. 71G/C 570–24, radio appeal by Professor Griffith John Williams on behalf of the Welsh Folk Museum, 1958.

Some assert that the proper task of the dialectologist is to safeguard the 'purity of dialects'. However, linguistic 'purity' and 'correctness' is not absolute and indisputable. The dialectologist describes the language as it is, not as he would like it to be. Nevertheless, he is also undeniably influenced by the perspectives and problems of his own age. In order to appreciate the achievements of twentieth-century Welsh dialect studies, they must be placed in their methodological and historical context.

The Welsh were extremely dilatory in applying modern linguistic methods to the recording of spoken Welsh. Until the 1930s, the period when George Wenker[2] and Jules Gilliéron[3] were undertaking the compilation of comprehensive dialect atlases in Germany and France, the main focus in Wales was collecting vocabularies.[4] Nevertheless, the influence of O. H. Fynes-Clinton's study of the Bangor dialect in 1913,[5] and the work of Alf Sommerfelt on the language of Cyfeiliog in 1925,[6] led to the inclusion of other linguistic elements. During the 1930s several University of Wales MA theses were written in the form of descriptive monographs on dialects.[7] The most innovative and scientific of these in respect of methodology was a thesis by J. J. Glanmor Davies on the spoken Welsh of the New Quay area. This study was an important landmark in the history of Welsh-language dialectology since it utilized the latest developments in linguistics and applied scientific methods already in use in other countries.

The first known attempt to make a sound recording of samples of spoken Welsh was by Rudolf Trebitsch, an Austrian linguist who was interested in the language and recorded a number of speakers on phonograph rolls in 1907–8. The original rolls are kept in the *Phonogrammarchiv* of the *Österreichische Akademie der Wissenschaften* in Vienna, although copies on tape are also available for reference in the sound archive of the Museum of Welsh Life.[8] Their quality, however, is extremely poor, and the samples recorded can scarcely be heard let alone analysed.

---

[2] George Wenker began his survey of German dialects in the 1870s, but the task of publishing the mass of material which he collected (over 52,000 completed questionnaires) fell to Werde and Mitzka, his successors at Marburg University. See F. Werde (completed by W. Mitzka), *Deutsche Sprachatlas* (Marburg, 1926–56).

[3] Jules Gilliéron and E. Edmont, *Atlas Linguistique de la France* (Paris, 1902–10).

[4] For a more detailed examination of the development of dialectology in Wales, see Robert Owen Jones, 'Datblygiad Gwyddor Tafodieitheg yng Nghymru', *BBCS*, XXXIII (1986), 18–40; D. A. Thorne, *Cyflwyniad i Astudio'r Iaith Gymraeg* (Caerdydd, 1985).

[5] O. H. Fynes-Clinton, *The Welsh Vocabulary of the Bangor District* (Oxford, 1913).

[6] Alf Sommerfelt, *Studies in Cyfeiliog Welsh: A Contribution to Welsh Dialectology* (Oslo, 1925).

[7] Daniel G. Evans, 'Tafodiaith Cwmtawe' (unpubl. University of Wales MA thesis, 1930); Cyril B. H. Lewis, 'Tafodiaith Hen Blwyf Llangatwg (Castellnedd)' (unpubl. University of Wales MA thesis, 1932); Thomas I. Phillips, 'The Spoken Dialect of the Ogwr Basin, Glamorgan' (unpubl. University of Wales MA thesis, 1933); J. J. Glanmor Davies, 'Astudiaeth o Gymraeg Llafar Ardal Ceinewydd: Ei Seineg gydag Ymchwiliadau Gwyddonol, ei Seinyddiaeth a'i Ffurfiant gyda Geirfa Lawn, a Chyfeiriad at ei Semanteg' (unpubl. University of Wales PhD thesis, 1934); Rees O. Rees, 'Gramadeg Tafodiaith Dyffryn Aman' (unpubl. University of Wales MA thesis, 1936).

[8] MWL, tape no. 6832.

In a later period, the Board of Celtic Studies of the University of Wales sought to record the south-eastern dialect using a copper disc-cutting machine. Between January 1933 and July 1938 twelve elderly Welsh speakers from Cardiff and the surrounding area and two from south-east Breconshire were recorded. These discs were also deposited in the archives of the Museum of Welsh Life, and until recently their content was inaccessible since no appropriate working equipment was available to play them.[9]

In the late 1930s a more successful and lasting attempt was made to record dialect speech by T. J. Morgan, who was at that time a lecturer in the Department of Welsh at the University College of Wales, Cardiff. In his volume *Trwm ac Ysgafn* (1945),[10] he recounts the experience of meeting the last Welsh speakers in the district of Grwyne Fechan, a valley in the old county of Brecon on the border with England. In order to secure recordings of a high standard, he succeeded in persuading the BBC to co-operate with the Board of Celtic Studies by sending a recording van from London to carry out the work. In 1939 ten people from various localities in south Wales, including Grwyne Fechan, were recorded on disc. It is difficult for us today to envisage the problems posed by field recording at that time. For practical reasons, T. J. Morgan failed to record all five of the remaining Welsh speakers in Grwyne Fechan. In response to a letter from Vincent H. Phillips in 1974, he recalled the difficulties encountered:

> Fe allaf gofio'n awr pam nad oes disg o iaith Miss Parry. Yr oedd yn byw mewn rhywbeth a oedd yn fwy distadl na thyddyn ar ochr y mynydd, y tŷ 'cynteficaf' a welais erioed . . . Llwyddais i fynd â'r car nes fy mod o fewn 80 llath i'r tŷ, er bod y ffordd yn hollol anaddas i fodur, ac erbyn bod men recordio'r BBC yn cyrraedd, nid oedd ganddynt *gable* digon hir i gyrraedd y tŷ. Ein bwriad oedd mynd yr ail dro a dod â Miss Parry i lawr i dafarn yn Llanbedr . . . ond yr oedd Miss Parry yn rhy fusgrell i gael ei symud . . . gyda llaw, yr oedd y fen a'r staff o Lundain, gan nad oedd dim o'r fath beth gan y BBC yng Nghaerdydd . . . Fel y dywedais, fe ddaeth 1939 ac ni ddaeth cyfle arall inni gael y fen recordio.[11]

(I can remember now why there is no disc of Miss Parry's language. She lived in a place more lowly than a smallholding on the side of the mountain, the 'most primitive' house I ever saw . . . I succeeded in taking the car within 80 yards of the house, although the road was totally unsuitable for a motor car, and when the BBC's recording van arrived it was discovered that the cable was not long enough to reach the house. It was our intention to return and bring Miss Parry down to a public house in Llanbedr . . . but Miss Parry was too feeble to be moved . . . by the way, the van and staff were from London because the BBC in Cardiff had no such facilities . . . As I said, 1939 came and we had no further opportunity to secure the recording van.)

[9] The discs and recording equipment have been deposited in the Museum of Welsh Life by the Board of Celtic Studies (MWL accession no. F69.329).
[10] T. J. Morgan, *Trwm ac Ysgafn: Cyfrol o Ysgrifau* (Caerdydd, 1945), pp. 14–20.
[11] See MWL accession correspondence, no. F69.329.

With the advent of the Second World War, dialectological activity in Wales ceased. Study was not resumed until the 1950s, when the work of a new school of dialectologists, including T. Arwyn Watkins, Vincent H. Phillips, Alan R. Thomas and Ceinwen H. Thomas, was published.[12] Although they maintained the monographic tradition established in the 1930s, they were also affected by new influences and responsibilities. A consideration which weighed heavily on the minds of dialectologists during this period was the fragile state of the Welsh language itself, particularly in the south-eastern areas where most of them carried out their work. One far-reaching development was the invention of magnetic tape-recording machines. The Department of Welsh at the University College of Wales, Cardiff, led by Professor Griffith John Williams, was the first to exploit the potential of the new technology to make sound recordings of Welsh-language dialects. Early in the 1950s, the Department purchased a tape recorder and dispatched Vincent H. Phillips, who was at the time a research student in the Department, to record some of the last Welsh speakers in the south-east, especially in the Vale of Glamorgan and Monmouthshire.

Thus, although a new era in Welsh-language dialectology began, it also gave rise to new dilemmas and choices. The dialectologist was now freed from the laborious task of transcribing the informant's words phonetically as he or she spoke, 'permitting the fieldworker' as W. N. Francis observed, 'to operate as a linguist as well as a recording machine'.[13] At the same time, another dimension was added to the responsibilities already assumed by dialectologists in the post-war period. They now had the choice of compiling a comparative atlas of dialects, or of carrying out detailed monographic studies of the dialects of individual areas, or of recording as much as possible of the dialects before they disappeared.

Following the establishment of the Welsh Folk Museum (now the Museum of Welsh Life) in 1948, plans were laid down for the collection of oral testimony by means of field work. The excellent recording work accomplished by the Institute for Dialect and Folklore Research in Sweden and the Irish Folk Lore Commission had already underlined the weaknesses in similar work being undertaken in Wales. With government support, Vincent H. Phillips was appointed in 1957 to carry forward the recording programme. Initially, the only technical equipment available to him was a tape recorder belonging to the Department of Welsh in

---

[12] T. Arwyn Watkins, 'Tafodiaith Plwyf Llansamlet' (unpubl. University of Wales MA thesis, 1951); Vincent H. Phillips, 'Astudiaeth o Gymraeg Llafar Dyffryn Elái a'r Cyffiniau' (unpubl. University of Wales MA thesis, 1955); Evan J. Davies, 'Astudiaeth Gymharol o Dafodieithoedd Llandygwydd a Dihewyd' (unpubl. University of Wales MA thesis, 1955); Alan R. Thomas, 'Astudiaeth Seinegol o Gymraeg Llafar Dyffryn Wysg' (unpubl. University of Wales MA thesis, 1958); E. Christopher Rees, 'Tafodiaith Rhan Isaf Dyffryn Llwchwr' (unpubl. University of Wales MA thesis, 1958); David G. Lewis, 'Astudiaeth o Iaith Lafar Gogledd-orllewin Ceredigion' (unpubl. University of Wales MA thesis, 1960); Ceinwen H. Thomas, 'A Phonological Conspectus of the Welsh Dialect of Nantgarw, Glamorgan' (unpubl. University of London MA thesis, 1960–1).

[13] W. N. Francis, *Dialectology: An Introduction* (London, 1983), p. 94.

Cardiff. In 1958, in order to raise money to purchase the required equipment, Professor Griffith John Williams broadcast the radio appeal referred to at the beginning of this chapter. With the funds raised as a result of the broadcast, together with a grant of £1,500 from the Gulbenkian Foundation, a Land Rover and tape recorder were purchased to enable the Museum to press on with the work. This heralded the formation of an archive in St Fagan's Castle, charged with the duty of surveying the oral traditions and dialects of the whole of Wales.[14]

Professor Griffith John Williams also urged his own institution, the University College of Wales, Cardiff, to promote research into Welsh-language dialects. In 1958 Ceinwen H. Thomas was appointed assistant lecturer in Dialectology in the Department of Welsh. Later, in 1967, the Welsh Language Research Unit was established to study all aspects of Welsh-language dialectology and linguistics. The Unit's researchers studied one district at a time, undertaking intensive interviewing and recording. Between 1965 and the mid-1980s, the Unit produced several monographs, mainly on the dialects of the south-east.[15] These all followed the same uniform pattern, namely structural phonemic studies of the dialect involved, together with a vocabulary. The principal aim was to produce a series of similar studies for the purpose of systematic comparison.

During the same period, the Department of Welsh at the University College of Wales, Aberystwyth, produced dialectological research theses which focused on the collection of vocabulary rather than detailed phonemic analyses, as in the Cardiff monographs.[16] Although some staff at Aberystwyth began compiling a

[14] Vincent H. Phillips, *Tape Recording and Welsh Folk Life* (Welsh Folk Museum discussion paper, Cardiff, 1983).

[15] Mary Middleton, 'Astudiaeth Seinyddol, gan gynnwys Geirfa, o Gymraeg Llafar Ardal Tafarnau Bach, Sir Fynwy' (unpubl. University of Wales MA thesis, 1965); Lynn Davies, 'Astudiaeth Seinyddol gan gynnwys Geirfa o Dafodiaith Merthyr Tudful a'r Cylch' (unpubl. University of Wales MA thesis, 1969); Gilbert E. Ruddock, 'Astudiaeth Seinyddol o Dafodiaith Hirwaun, ynghyd â Geirfa' (unpubl. University of Wales MA thesis, 1969); John T. Bevan, 'Astudiaeth Seinyddol o Gymraeg Llafar Coety Walia a Rhuthun ym Mro Morgannwg' (unpubl. University of Wales MA thesis, 1971); David A. Thorne, 'Astudiaeth Seinyddol a Morffolegol o Dafodiaith Llangennech' (unpubl. University of Wales MA thesis, 1971); Olwen M. Samuel, 'Astudiaeth o Dafodiaith Gymraeg Cylch y Rhigos' (unpubl. University of Wales MA thesis, 1971); David A. Thorne, 'Astudiaeth Gymharol o Ffonoleg a Gramadeg Iaith Lafar y Maenorau oddi mewn i Gwmwd Carnwyllion yn Sir Gaerfyrddin' (unpubl. University of Wales PhD thesis, 1977); Glyn E. Jones, 'Astudiaeth o Ffonoleg a Gramadeg Tair Tafodiaith ym Mrycheiniog' (unpubl. University of Wales PhD thesis, 1984). Theses produced at the University of Wales College, Lampeter, during the early 1980s followed in the same tradition: Philip J. Brake, 'Astudiaeth o Seinyddiaeth a Morffoleg Tafodiaith Cwm-ann a'r Cylch' (unpubl. University of Wales MA thesis, 1981); Elizabeth P. Davies, 'Astudiaeth Seinyddol a Morffolegol o Dafodiaith Trimsaran gan gynnwys Geirfa' (unpubl. University of Wales MA thesis, 1983).

[16] Gareth D. Jones, 'Astudiaeth Eirfaol o Gymraeg Llafar Rhosllannerchrugog' (unpubl. University of Wales MA thesis, 1962); Anna E. Roberts, 'Geirfa a Ffurfiau Cymraeg Llafar Cylch Pwllheli' (unpubl. University of Wales MA thesis, 1973); David W. Griffiths, 'Astudiaeth Eirfaol o Gymraeg Llafar Llanfair Caereinion' (unpubl. University of Wales MA thesis, 1975). Work carried out at the University of Wales College, Bangor, during the same period included Robert Owen Jones, 'A Structural Phonological Analysis and Comparison of Three Welsh Dialects' (unpubl. University of Wales MA thesis, 1967).

dialect atlas of Wales in the 1950s, the project was not comprehensively pursued until the 1960s when a survey was carried out by Alan R. Thomas. The findings of this survey were subsequently published in *The Linguistic Geography of Wales*,[17] a volume which remains an invaluable source to all dialectologists working on the Welsh language.

By the end of the 1960s, therefore, the prospects for the development of dialectology in Wales were bright; several dialect projects were in progress, each with a different emphasis. It seemed feasible that all dialects could be recorded, using a variety of approaches which would complement one another. However, for several reasons, these efforts were not wholly successful. The data we have today is incomplete and it is difficult to trace specific linguistic features for the whole of Wales. Some dialects disappeared without being described and others have yet to be recorded and analysed in detail.

The delay in applying modern linguistic approaches to recording oral speech meant that dialectologists in the period after the Second World War faced an enormous task. The recognition of the urgent need to record for posterity is a recurrent theme in all studies and surveys. As T. Arwyn Watkins confessed, it was difficult to know where to start:

> Superficially this geographical distribution of decline would suggest that the attention of Welsh dialectologists should be concentrated at the present time on the areas of rapid anglicisation . . . In the western and north-western parts of the country the language has held its own remarkably from the point of view of numbers. Nevertheless there is good reason not to neglect these 'safe' areas in a dialect survey . . . The growth of bilingualism has had a remarkable effect on the development of the Welsh language.[18]

Despite the paucity of human resources, ambitious plans were initiated. For instance, dialectology was only one aspect of the work of the Welsh Folk Museum. Inevitably, the focus in the early days of the archive was on collecting and recording a wider range of oral testimony, and the task of describing dialects in the form of detailed monographs across a wide area also proceeded at a slow pace. Due to the emphasis on training students in phonemic analytical methods at Cardiff and other colleges of the University of Wales, the studies tended to be repetitive and wasteful of human resources, duplicating unvarying elements rather than focusing on the fluctuating features of dialects. Because the work was so protracted, a gap of a generation existed between the informants of the earliest studies and those of more recent research projects.

---

[17] Alan R. Thomas, *The Linguistic Geography of Wales: A Contribution to Welsh Dialectology* (Cardiff, 1973).

[18] T. Arwyn Watkins, 'Background to the Welsh Dialect Survey', *Lochlann*, II (1962), 42–3.

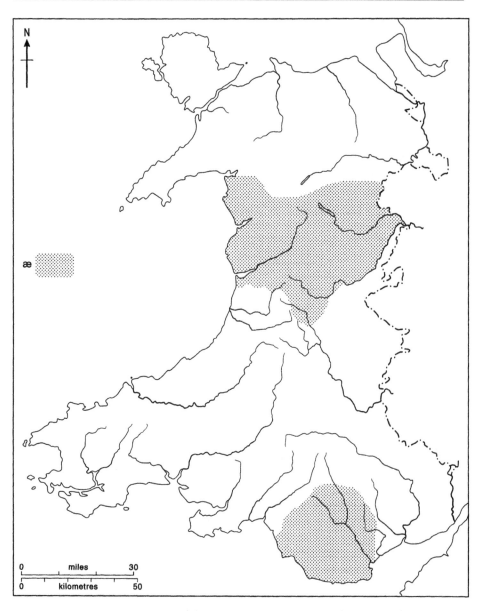

Figure 1. Territory of the *'æ fain'* (by permission of Gwasg Taf)

These considerations must be borne in mind when summing up the evidence of the various studies in order to obtain an overview of the distribution of dialectological characteristics. One of the most striking phonological features of the dialects of mid- and south-east Wales, for example, is the use of a long, half-open vowel ('æ fain' as it is commonly called) instead of the open vowel heard in most of Wales, giving **tæn** instead of **tân** and **glæs** instead of **glas**. According to the available evidence, the geographical area of this sound extends in the south-east through Glamorgan to the Afan valley and the north of the old county; in mid-Wales it is heard from the Dyfi valley to Trawsfynydd, Rhyd-y-main and Llanrhaeadr-ym-Mochnant (Figure 1).[19] It must be borne in mind, however, that the information for mid-Wales is based on work undertaken by Thomas Darlington and Alf Sommerfelt at the beginning of the twentieth century,[20] and that the distribution of the sound in the south-east reflects the fieldwork of researchers at Cardiff from the 1950s to the 1980s. Until the findings of the latest survey by the Board of Celtic Studies of the distribution of phonological and morphophonological features of dialects throughout Wales have been fully analysed,[21] the extent of change in the distribution of 'æ fain' in mid-Wales cannot be ascertained. We do have evidence, however, that this linguistic feature has been unstable for some time in the dialect of the south-east.

The first published reference to the distribution of this phonological feature occurs in an article entitled 'Tafodieithoedd Morgannwg' (The Dialects of Glamorgan) by Thomas Jones, published in *The Grail* in 1911.[22] Fascinating reference is made to the stigma attached to the sound in the early part of the twentieth century and the tendency of preachers to proscribe it from formal speech. This is supported by evidence collected by Vincent H. Phillips and Ceinwen H. Thomas which demonstrates that use of 'æ fain' varied according to generation in the Ely valley and Nantgarw. It appears that younger speakers were ashamed of it:

> Gydag ychydig iawn o eithriadau, perthyn pobl o dan y trigain i un dosbarth. Y maent yn aelodau o gapeli, ond Cymraeg bratiog, ansicr, sydd ganddynt, heb odid ddim gafael ar y dafodiaith. Y mae eu geirfa Gymraeg yn eithriadol o gyfyngedig, ac yma fe welir newid mawr yn seiniau'r dafodiaith. Nid ydynt yn caledu culseiniaid yn gywir, ac *a*: a ddefnyddiant mewn geiriau fel *tad*, *tan*, *da* yn lle (æ) y dafodiaith.[23]

---

[19] Source: Beth Thomas and Peter Wynn Thomas, *Cymraeg, Cymrâg, Cymrêg . . . Cyflwyno'r Tafodieithoedd* (Caerdydd, 1989), p. 37.

[20] Thomas Darlington, 'Some Dialectal Boundaries in Mid Wales: With Notes on the History of the Palatization of Long *A*', *THSC* (1900–1), 13–39; Sommerfelt, *Studies in Cyfeiliog Welsh*.

[21] Alan R. Thomas (ed.), *The Welsh Dialect Survey* (Cardiff, 2000).

[22] Thomas Jones, 'Tafodieithoedd Morgannwg', *The Grail (Y Greal)*, IV, no. 13 (1911), 110–13.

[23] Phillips, 'Astudiaeth o Gymraeg Llafar Dyffryn Elái', II, p. 6.

(With very few exceptions, people under sixty belong to one category. They are chapel members, but their Welsh is broken, uncertain, with very little grasp of the dialect. Their Welsh vocabulary is exceptionally limited, and a great change in dialect sounds is evident. They do not use provection correctly, and they use a: in words such as *tad, tan, da* instead of the (æ) of the dialect.)

. . . hon yw'r unig sain y mae'r siaradwyr ieuengaf yn orymwybodol ohoni pan fyddant yng ngŵydd siaradwyr tafodieithoedd eraill.[24]

(. . . this is the only sound of which the youngest speakers are self-conscious when they are in the company of other dialect speakers.)

The Afan valley is extremely peripheral in respect of the geographical distribution of 'æ fain'. The variant is not heard in areas to the west of Pont-rhyd-y-fen nor in Cwmafan, the nearest village down the valley. Inhabitants of Cwmafan use the feature to deride the villagers of Pont-rhyd-y-fen, whom they claim resemble sheep bleating ('ishta defid – mê mê ar 'yd lle i gyd'). Yet although the sound is identified locally with 'the language of Pont-rhyd-y-fen', it became evident when recording in the area that only a minority of Welsh speakers in the community made use of it, namely women born before the 1930s who attended the two chapels on the eastern side of the village.[25] Social patterning such as this can only be identified by detailed sociolinguistic sampling – work which militates against recording the language at one point in time across a wide area.

Since the majority of detailed dialect studies focus on phonology and vocabulary, it is impossible to map some grammatical features. Although it is believed, for example, that feminine forms of adjectives are used more commonly in north Wales, it was only possible to cite evidence from four areas in the volume *Cymraeg, Cymrâg, Cymrêg* to demonstrate this,[26] because of gaps in the information recorded on the subject in various monographs. Table 1 summarizes some known facts regarding the use of ten adjectival feminine forms in the districts of Bangor, New Quay, Cyfeiliog, and the Ely valley.[27]

Once more it is important to guard against drawing detailed conclusions concerning the geographical distribution of linguistic features on the basis of evidence

---

[24] Ceinwen H. Thomas, *Tafodiaith Nantgarw* (2 vols., Caerdydd, 1993), I, p. 13.

[25] Beth Thomas, 'Differences of Sex and Sects: Linguistic Variation and Social Networks in a Welsh Mining Village' in Jennifer Coates and Deborah Cameron (eds.), *Women in their Speech Communities: New Perspectives on Language and Sex* (New York, 1988), pp. 51–60; eadem, 'Amrywio Sosioieithyddol yn Nhafodiaith Pont-rhyd-y-fen' in Martin J. Ball, James Fife, Erich Poppe and Jenny Rowland (eds.), *Celtic Linguistics / Ieithyddiaeth Geltaidd: Readings in the Brythonic Languages: Festschrift for T. Arwyn Watkins* (Amsterdam/Philadelphia, 1990), pp. 41–52; eadem, 'Tyfu Mâs o'r Mæs: Pontrhyd-y-fen a'r æ fain' in Hywel Teifi Edwards (ed.), *Llynfi ac Afan, Garw ac Ogwr* (Llandysul, 1998), pp. 138–62.

[26] Thomas and Thomas, *Cymraeg, Cymrâg, Cymrêg*, pp. 52–3.

[27] Fynes-Clinton, *The Welsh Vocabulary of the Bangor District*; Davies, 'Astudiaeth o Gymraeg Llafar Ceinewydd'; Sommerfelt, *Studies in Cyfeiliog Welsh*; Phillips, 'Astudiaeth o Gymraeg Llafar Dyffryn Elái'.

Table 1. The use made of ten feminine forms in the Bangor, New Quay, Cyfeiliog and Ely valley districts

	Bangor	New Quay (elderly)	Cyfeiliog	New Quay (young)	Ely valley
gwen	+	+	+	+	+
melen	+	+	+	+	+/−
ber	+	+	+	−	−
cron	+	+	+	−	−
trom	+	+	+	−	−
bront	+	+	−	−	−
cre(f)	+	+	−	−	−
gwleb	+	+	−	−	−
sech	+	−	−	−	−
defn	+	−	−	−	−

of speakers from different generations. The speakers from Bangor whose language was recorded in *The Welsh Vocabulary of the Bangor District* were born between 1835 and 1859. There are two columns for J. J. Glanmor Davies's speakers in New Quay; the first refers to the usage of people who were already old in 1934 (they were born between 1850 and 1882) and the second to the usage of young people in the 1930s. The striking contrast between the two generations indicates the speed at which the feminine forms disappeared in that district.

In 1934 the feminine forms were commonly used by the older generation in New Quay and there appears to have been very little distinction between the linguistic patterns of these people and those in Bangor. However, in the case of those born in New Quay during the first decade of the twentieth century, most of the feminine forms had been lost, and the list is very similar to that recorded for the inhabitants of the Ely valley in east Glamorgan born between 1865 and 1899. The picture presented here therefore is a mixture of historical and geographical change.

The only study to record systematically the distribution of data across the whole country at the same point in time is *The Linguistic Geography of Wales* by Alan R. Thomas. His success lay in defining a viable task, namely, restricting the scope of his questionnaire and implementing it with the assistance of local contacts and the postal service. These methods proved effective in all parts of the country with the exception of the south-east, where the sampling methodology of the atlas was unable to tackle the complexity of the prevailing linguistic and social situation. *The Linguistic Geography of Wales* was not the only study to encounter difficulties in this complex locality.

In all countries, traditional dialectology is geographically focused; the emphasis is on recording the geographical distribution of dialect features, into which pattern is woven developments in education, transport and communications and the influence of other languages. A strong historical element pervades the work also, due to the interest in identifying old forms which have survived in dialects but have disappeared from the standard language. It is natural, therefore, for the dialectologist to focus on the most conservative elements of the population, namely comparatively uneducated and non-mobile elderly people. This is legitimate, provided that the researcher demonstrates complete integrity and consistency in selecting his sample. It was inevitable that the older generation would be selected in several studies of districts in south-east Wales, for it was they who were the last Welsh speakers in these localities. There was also a tendency to concentrate on the language of agricultural populations while this was still possible; as T. Arwyn Watkins noted in 1955: 'We agree with Professors Orton and Dieth that dialect material is best preserved in agricultural communities.'[28] However, these conservative groups of speakers were not so numerous in the coal-mining communities of south Wales. In some districts it proved difficult for Alan R. Thomas's local contacts to find suitable Welsh speakers to complete the questionnaires, for, despite having lived in the district for many years, they hailed originally from the counties of Anglesey, Caernarfon, Cardigan and Pembroke.[29]

The inability to control the sampling meant that responses obtained from the south-east produced very mixed patterns. Alan R. Thomas selected enquiry points either at the heads of valleys or on main roads in order to compare conservative retreats with the country's main paths of communication.[30] In the Afan valley, for instance, his sole enquiry point was Blaengwynfi, at the extreme end of the valley. Unlike similar communities in rural areas, this was the most recently populated community in the Afan valley, having evolved at the end of the nineteenth century as a result of the development of the coal industry in the vicinity. When the Welsh Linguistic Research Unit visited the area to record its Welsh-speaking inhabitants in the late 1970s, most of them were incomers from west Wales or the children of incomers.

More recently, Peter Wynn Thomas conducted a study based on a sample of speakers from agricultural backgrounds, using the lexical questionnaire of *The Linguistic Geography of Wales*.[31] This revealed geographical patterning in the data which was far removed from the 'typically mixed' picture which was, in Alan R. Thomas's opinion, so characteristic of the south-east. Figure 2 shows Peter Wynn

[28] Watkins, 'Tafodiaith Plwyf Llansamlet', p. 32.

[29] Quoted in Peter Wynn Thomas, 'Putting Glamorgan on the Map', *Papurau Gwaith Ieithyddol Cymraeg Caerdydd / Cardiff Working Papers in Welsh Linguistics*, no. 2 (Welsh Folk Museum, 1982), p. 95.

[30] Alan R. Thomas, 'A Contribution to Welsh Linguistic Geography', *Studia Celtica*, III (1968), 66–78.

[31] Peter Wynn Thomas, 'Dimensions of Dialect Variation: A Dialectological and Sociological Analysis of Aspects of Spoken Welsh in Glamorgan' (unpubl. University of Wales PhD thesis, 1990).

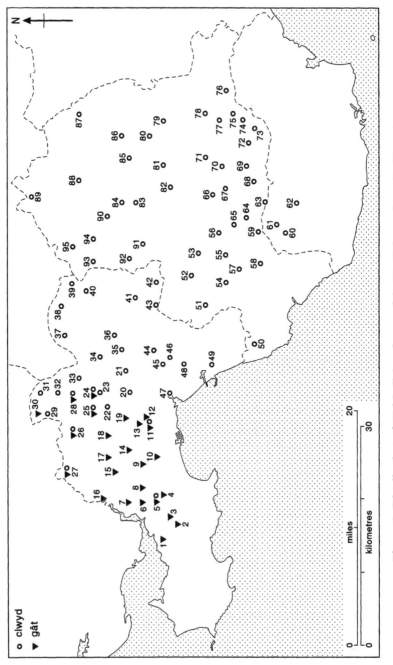

Figure 2. Distribution of Welsh dialect forms of the English word *gate* in Glamorgan

Thomas's map of the distribution of words used in Glamorgan for the English word 'gate' (item no. 105a; figure 108 in *The Linguistic Geography of Wales*).[32] 'The area to the east of the Nedd is typically mixed' was Alan R. Thomas's conclusion on the basis of responses to this item in his lexical questionnaires.[33] Although the most common response was **clwyd**, there were also isolated instances of forms which belonged to other parts of Wales, such as **llidiart** in the north, **iet** in the south-west, and **gât**, which is characteristic of west Glamorgan and east Dyfed.

This contrasts sharply with the uniform pattern discovered by Peter Wynn Thomas upon limiting the study to speakers from an agricultural background: it was discovered that **clwyd** is the native word in the east, although the doublets in the west of the county imply that the loanword **gât** is extending its territory towards the east. It is interesting to note that the south-east is the repository of the only native Welsh word we have for this particular artefact: **llidiart, iet, giât** and **gât** are all English borrowings. It is likely that the oldest of these is **llidiart** (from the English dialect word 'lidyate'), which was assimilated prior to the fourteenth century. This word has been replaced over large areas of its domain by the more recent borrowing **giât**, also borrowed many centuries previously. **Iet** in the south-east is another loanword from English dialects over the border. In England these dialect forms have only survived in place-names such as Yate (near Bristol) and Lydiate (in Worcestershire and Lancashire), while in Wales **iet** and **llidiart** are still in common usage. Clearly the borrowing of English words is not a recent phenomenon. The agricultural vocabulary recorded in *The Linguistic Geography of Wales* is permeated with borrowings which are often of crucial importance in attempting to define lexical areas.

Peter Wynn Thomas has demonstrated the importance of sampling methodology in attempting to draw conclusions on the basis of any linguistic study. The Welsh-speaking population of the south-east, even when restricted to the oldest speakers, is not a single homogeneous group but rather an overlapping network of speakers whose background and linguistic experience varied considerably. Rather than seek to study this complex pattern, monographers in particular tended to focus on the language of a limited number of selected informants, with very conservative language, and imply that they were representative of the Welsh of the whole community. In areas where there was a greater choice of elderly speakers, there was a tendency to select only those who conformed to the researcher's bias concerning the features of the indigenous dialect and to omit from the sample those who diverged from that ideal. It is not surprising, therefore, that monographers discovered in their material the uniform

---

[32] Source: Peter Wynn Thomas, 'Glamorgan Revisited: Progress Report and Some Emerging Distribution Patterns', *Papurau Gwaith Ieithyddol Cymraeg Caerdydd / Cardiff Working Papers in Welsh Linguistics*, no. 3 (Welsh Folk Museum, 1984), p. 122.

[33] Thomas, *The Linguistic Geography of Wales*, p. 183.

patterns they sought. As a result, the initial attempt to record the remnants of a dialect on the verge of extinction failed to convey the actual linguistic and social situation. This accounts for two contrasting views of the language in the south-east, that of the 'typically mixed' area recorded in *The Linguistic Geography of Wales* and that of the 'stable dialect area, in which there had been no important linguistic upheaval', described by Ceinwen H. Thomas.[34]

The opportunity to study the linguistic and dialectal cauldron which once existed in the valleys of south Wales has been lost. It is certain that the linguistic experiences of the different communities varied greatly, depending on the period, extent and direction of in-migration. Across large sections of the eastern coalfield the language was inundated by an influx of English-speaking in-migrants before a new dialect pattern could emerge and before linguists could record it. In some communities in the western valleys it appears that the native dialect held its own despite substantial in-migration from districts further west. Linguistic studies with a more sociological emphasis indicate that more recent developments are responsible for undermining these dialects.

Since the 1950s linguists in America, and more recently in Britain, have adopted sociological methods of sampling informants and sought to account for the linguistic variation within communities and within individual speech.[35] Robert Owen Jones was the first to apply these methods in his study of the Welsh language in Patagonia.[36] Since the 1980s there has been a steady increase in this type of study in Wales, mainly at the University of Wales, Swansea, and the University of Wales, Cardiff.[37] As with the traditional dialectological studies which preceded them, they tend to focus on the language of south-east Wales, especially west Glamorgan and east Dyfed. The main theme of most of these

---

[34] Ceinwen H. Thomas, 'Some Phonological Features of Dialects in South-east Wales', *Studia Celtica*, X/XI (1975–6), 347.

[35] For a more detailed introduction to the field of sociolinguistics, see K. M. Petyt, *The Study of Dialect: An Introduction to Dialectology* (London, 1980), pp. 132–70; W. Downes, *Language and Society* (London, 1984); J. Holmes, *An Introduction to Sociolinguistics* (London, 1992).

[36] Robert Owen Jones, 'Astudiaeth o Gydberthynas Nodweddion Cymdeithasol ag Amrywiadau'r Gymraeg yn y Gaiman, Dyffryn y Camwy' (unpubl. University of Wales PhD thesis, 1984).

[37] For a list of the sociolinguistic theses on the dialect of the Tawe valley, see Robert Owen Jones, 'Tafodiaith Cwm Tawe' in Hywel Teifi Edwards (ed.), *Cwm Tawe* (Llandysul, 1993), p. 239. See also A. Kevin Campbell, 'Astudiaeth Gymdeithasegol Ieithyddol o Gymraeg Cwmaman (Dyfed)' (unpubl. University of Wales MA thesis, 1984); Ann Eleri Jones, 'Erydiad Geirfaol ym Mhentrefi Clunderwen, Efailwen a Llandysilio' (unpubl. University of Wales MA thesis, 1984); Martin J. Ball, 'Sociolinguistic Aspects of the Welsh Mutation System' (unpubl. University of Wales PhD thesis, 1985); Nia Gruffydd Jones, 'Astudiaeth o Erydiad Geirfaol ym Mhontyberem' (unpubl. University of Wales MA thesis, 1986); Christine M. Jones, 'Astudiaeth o Iaith Lafar y Mot (Sir Benfro)' (unpubl. University of Wales PhD thesis, 1987); Siân Elizabeth Thomas, 'A Study of *Calediad* in the Upper Swansea Valley' in Martin J. Ball (ed.), *The Use of Welsh: A Contribution to Sociolinguistics* (Clevedon, 1988), pp. 85–96. See also the recent study by Mari C. Jones, 'Language and Dialect Death in Contemporary Wales' (unpubl. University of Cambridge PhD thesis, 1993); eadem, *Language Obsolescence and Revitalization: Linguistic Change in Two Sociolinguistically Contrasting Welsh Communities* (Oxford, 1998).

studies is how bilingual education on the one hand and the disintegration of dense community networks on the other have led to the loss of the dialect features associated with these areas.[38] One of the most notable features of south-eastern dialects is provection, that is, using the consonants **p**, **t** and **c** in words such as **sgupor** (ysgubor), **catw** (cadw) and **eclws** (eglwys), instead of the **b**, **d** and **g** used in other areas. Robert Owen Jones describes the current status of this dialect feature in the language of the Tawe valley as follows:

O'r canol oed i fyny 'roedd diffyg calediad neu ganran digwyddiad is bron yn ddieithriad ynghlwm wrth lefel addysg yn y Gymraeg ac ymwybyddiaeth o batrymau'r iaith lenyddol. Ym mysg y canol oed ifanc a'r plant, y prif erydwr yw'r gyfundrefn addysgol Gymraeg . . . Nid yw caledu bellach yn nodwedd gynhyrchiol yn llafar y cenedlaethau iau. Peidiodd y broses yn yr union gysylltiadau seinegol lle digwyddai'n ddifeth ar un adeg. Olion yn unig a erys a hynny heb fywiogrwydd a chyfoeth y gorffennol.[39]

(From middle age upwards the lack of provection or a lower percentage incidence was almost always linked to the level of Welsh education and awareness of the patterns of the literary language. Among the younger middle-aged and children, the main eroder is the Welsh-language education system . . . Provection is no longer a productive feature in the speech of the younger generations. The process has ceased in precisely those phonetic contexts where it at one time occurred without fail. Only remnants remain, and they display none of the vigour and wealth of the past.)

For generations, allegiance to the Welsh language has been linked to allegiance to local roots. The irony of the contemporary linguistic situation is that efforts to revive the language have endangered the continuation of those local variations which have formed such an intrinsic part of our identity. Rather than safeguarding our linguistic heritage, the effect has been to create a totally new linguistic and sociological situation.

Language is not a static phenomenon. One of the consequences of using a recording machine to record language was that it revealed for the first time the effect of the enquiry process on the speaker's response. It was increasingly difficult to ignore the fact that dialectology is a study of people, all with their own opinions concerning their language and how it can be adapted to suit different speech situations. It is fair to say that the interest of academic researchers, as well as the media, in dialects has left its mark on speakers. On the one hand, we have the old attitude to dialect – a sense of inferiority and humility which leads some to believe they cannot be regarded as 'real' Welsh speakers. On the other hand,

---

[38] See Beth Thomas, 'Here Today, Gone Tomorrow? Language and Dialect in a Welsh Community', *Folk Life*, 36 (1991–2), 84–95.

[39] Jones, 'Tafodiaith Cwm Tawe', p. 226.

external influences have had positive effects on certain social groups over the years. The interest of college lecturers, ministers, and the media has nurtured a sense of pride in the 'dialect', as witnessed in the following words spoken by a woman from Pont-rhyd-y-fen:

Wy'n cofio Norah (Isaac) yn dod chimod . . . i siarad a'r pwyllgor rieni, a'dd 'i'n gweud, 'Mae'n 'yfryd i gâl ysgolion Cymrâg . . . ond cofiwch, pidwch â angofio'ch tafodiath' . . . Ma tafodiath gida pob pentra chwel, a ma'n neis i gadw fe.[40]

(I remember Norah (Isaac) coming you know . . . to talk to the parents' committee, and she said, 'It's nice to have Welsh schools . . . but remember, don't forget your dialect' . . . All the villages have their own dialect you see, and it's nice to keep it.)

In a variety of ways, more direct links have been forged with Welsh speakers from other areas and some of the old linguistic myths and prejudices have been overturned. 'Dialect' – or an ideal of dialect free from English borrowing – has been elevated to a linguistic style and now wields sufficient status to be used publicly. Although these developments have often led to a feeling of greater pride in local dialects, they can also undermine them. The reinforcement of external Welsh-language networks can weaken networks within the community. In this respect, it is interesting to note the differences between women and men in their loyalty to the local dialect. In Pont-rhyd-y-fen, for instance, women are the last guardians of the 'æ fain' sound in the language of the community;[41] in his study of mutations in the Tawe valley, Martin J. Ball discovered that women use more non-standard forms than men.[42] The linguistic situation in Wales offers abundant material for those studying the spoken language, and the challenge facing Welsh-language dialectologists at the end of the twentieth century is to document and seek to understand the social processes and their effect on the language, both in areas where Welsh is strongest and where it is close to extinction.

In his thesis on the dialect of the Ely valley in 1955, Vincent H. Phillips set himself and other Welsh-language dialectologists an impossible objective:

Un o'n prif broblemau fel tafodieithegwyr yw ceisio . . . sicrhau popeth a fydd o ddefnydd inni, ac nid yn unig i ni heddiw, ond hefyd i oesoedd y dyfodol, cyn ei bod yn rhy ddiweddar. Oni wnawn hyn, geill cenedlaethau diweddarach . . . ein beio'n arw am na wnaethom y gorau o'r defnyddiau sydd ar gael yn ein cyfnod ni.[43]

---

[40] MWL, tape no. 8455.
[41] Thomas, 'Tyfu Mâs o'r Maes'.
[42] Martin J. Ball, 'Variation in the Use of Initial Consonant Mutations' in idem (ed.), *The Use of Welsh*, p. 79.
[43] Phillips, 'Astudiaeth o Gymraeg Llafar Dyffryn Elái', I, p. 86.

(One of our main problems as dialectologists is to seek . . . to preserve everything which will be useful to us, not only for us today, but also for the future, before it is too late. Unless we do this, subsequent generations . . . will be able to hold us responsible for failing to make the best of the materials which were at our disposal.)

Welsh-language dialectologists in the twentieth century have undoubtedly achieved excellent results in seeking to record the spoken language, despite a paucity of resources and incomplete data. This is clearly demonstrated in *The Linguistic Geography of Wales*, in the tens of detailed descriptions of the dialects of individual areas, and in the thousands of audio tapes deposited at the Museum of Welsh Life and the University of Wales, Lampeter.[44] It is easy to identify shortcomings with the benefit of hindsight, but the truth is that adequate human resources have never been available to document and record disappearing dialects and the process of linguistic change. As Robert Owen Jones has written:

Rhaid gochel . . . rhag synied mai casglu er mwyn gwarchod yw prif swyddogaeth y tafodieithegydd. Nid i'r archif yn unig y perthyn y tafodieithoedd. Rhan o'r gwaith yw'r casglu a'r cadw; rhaid dadansoddi a dehongli'r deunydd a gasglwyd ac a gesglir.[45]

(Care must be taken . . . not to assume that the main function of the dialectologist is to collect in order to preserve. It is not to the archive alone that dialects belong. Collecting and preserving is only part of the work; the material collected and being collected must be analysed and interpreted.)

Our instinct as Welsh people has been to strive to save the wealth of our geographical dialects from the 'archives of the grave'. Our duty now as dialectologists is to record the changes in the spoken language throughout the country, for it is only by interpreting and understanding these changes that we can best safeguard what remains of our dialectal heritage.

---

[44] See Christine Jones and David Thorne, *Dyfed: Blas ar ei Thafodieithoedd* (Llandysul, 1992), p. 88.
[45] Jones, 'Datblygiad Gwyddor Tafodieitheg yng Nghymru', 35.

13

The War of the Tongues: Early Anglo-Welsh Responses to Welsh Literary Culture

JOHN HARRIS

The very first time that I heard the late, revered, D. J. Williams was at the Plaid Cymru Conference in Cardiff in 1960. He asked one of the lecturers to explain why so many Anglo-Welsh writers were so antagonistic and contemptuous towards the Welsh language and indeed, to the nation itself . . . I wanted to get up and protest, but realised that a contrary case would be difficult to argue.[1] (Harri Webb)

IN THE ABOVE passage D. J. Williams had in mind a strain of thinking associated with the younger band of English-language writers who came to prominence in the 1930s so successfully and in such numbers as to prompt talk of a Welsh literary renaissance; they included Rhys Davies, Richard Hughes, Margiad Evans, Jack Jones, Dylan Thomas, Geraint Goodwin, Gwyn Jones, Glyn Jones, Lewis Jones, David Jones, Idris Davies and Richard Llewellyn, to mention only the more celebrated, and to stop for the moment at 1939. The outline of this 'first flowering' is familiar. What needs to be emphasized, for it was important to Anglo-Welsh identity and growing self-belief, is the range of the literary achievement, its demonstrable impact, both critically and in the market place, and the accelerating surge of publication as the decade proceeded. Anglo-Welsh literature could display its modernism (Dylan Thomas, David Jones), an authentic proletarian voice (Idris Davies, Lewis Jones), its mainstream popular winners (Jack Jones, *Off to Philadelphia in the Morning*, and Richard Llewellyn, *How Green Was My Valley*) and solid middle-brow appeal (in Rhys Davies pre-eminently). Richard Hughes, like Richard Llewellyn, had struck a universal chord, though not with Welsh subject matter; *A High Wind in Jamaica* won worldwide popularity and an international prize – the first such awarded to a Welsh writer.

But one need only glance at this list to recognize how disparate were the Anglo-Welsh, even prior to the appearance of Alun Lewis, Emyr Humphreys, Gwyn Thomas and R. S. Thomas in the 1940s. This was not a formal group with

---

[1] 'Harri Webb' [autobiographical essay] in Meic Stephens (ed.), *Artists in Wales, 3* (Llandysul, 1977), p. 91.

a common manifesto, though Keidrych Rhys tried his hand at drafting one. The very label 'Anglo-Welsh' triggered strong dissent, most writers coming to tolerate it as a literary tag of convenience.[2] How then to cast a single net over Rhys Davies and Emyr Humphreys and the Welsh worlds they represent? To Davies's way of thinking, the Welsh language was 'sunset-tinted', 'a lovely tongue' inviting quiet literary experiment, but too much used to sustain the illusion that we are different from everyone else.[3] For Emyr Humphreys, that same language lay at the heart of identity, the *sine qua non* of Edenic bliss. As he suggested to a National Eisteddfod audience: 'There lurks in the depths of every Welshman's soul an ideal – that of a country peopled entirely by monoglot Welshmen; a monolingual Garden of Eden on Earth, a Wales before the Fall – without the sound of English or the hiss of a serpent anywhere near the place' ('Am fod delfryd yn llechu yng ngwaelod enaid pob Cymro am wlad yn llawn o Gymry uniaith Gymraeg: Gardd Eden uniaith ar y ddaear hon, Cymru cyn y cwymp lle nad oes sŵn Saesneg, na sisial sarff ar gyfyl y fan').[4] The language divide was a cultural divide, with ramifications in religion and politics as much as in the field of literature; this division was fully manifest in the early 1930s and accepted almost as a precondition for the emergence of the Anglo-Welsh.

Their first popular advocate sounded a combative note: the Welsh writers whom the Cardiganshire journalist Glyn Roberts admired had emerged in the teeth of a native culture lauding 'pedagogues and pedlars of the platitude'.[5] Any English-language writer of Wales would almost certainly have to contend with parochial prejudice, if not abysmal misunderstanding and streams of childish abuse. Little wonder that those who had surmounted it should be strong personalities with something urgent to say. Roberts had in mind Caradoc Evans and, more immediately, the hysterical Welsh reception afforded *Nothing to Pay* (1930). 'It is called "realism" in the jargon of the modern school', explained the *Western Mail*, 'We prefer to call it filth.'[6] Demands for the novel's suppression accompanied pulpit reprobation – could not a Welsh MP raise the matter in Parliament? – and booksellers were urged not to stock it (Cardiff Public Library kept it under the counter).

The reception of *Nothing to Pay* dramatically focused those issues of artistic responsibility and relationship to audience which, by and large, separated English-language writers from their Welsh counterparts. Evans was the writer as social scourge: the transgressive, adversarial artist profoundly out of joint with his times.

---

[2] The label seems first to have been used by Idris Bell in *The Welsh Outlook*, IX, no. 8 (1922). In July 1931 the *Western Mail* was employing it 'for want of a better term', and it is absent from the writings of Glyn Roberts. By 1936, however, it had gained acceptance as a term of literary classification.

[3] Rhys Davies, *My Wales* (London, 1937), pp. 218–20.

[4] *Western Mail*, 8 August 1985.

[5] Glyn Roberts, 'The Welsh School of Writers', *The Bookman*, LXXXIV, no. 503 (1933), 248–9.

[6] *Western Mail*, 28 August 1930.

It was a role little exemplified in Welsh literature – the Welsh do not understand satire, said Glyn Roberts, and Evans was the greatest satirist of his people since Swift – and a role positively resented in native writers who, through their use of English, might reach an international audience. Literature was the servant of nationality, not a vehicle for parading supposed national defects before a readership all too ready to think the worst of Wales. 'Whilst he [Caradoc Evans] thus writes, English people slap their knees with delight',[7] and for pandering to such an audience he is paid his pieces of silver. English praise for Caradoc Evans incensed Welsh commentators; indeed, for one opponent, Middleton Murry's approval of *My People* (1915) had been worse than the book itself. Murry sidestepped neatly, explaining that his concern was not with west Wales but with one man's reaction to west Wales, a writer whose disciplined anger had produced an artistic triumph. It was a point Rhys Davies echoed – he, too, had been pilloried for unflattering portraits of Wales – when he spoke of a parochial attitude to literature born of feelings of inferiority. Shocking things in a well-written book should harm no one with a balanced mind and readers should learn to appreciate the value of personal truth:

> What *is* the real Wales? . . . Surely every genuine writer finds his own Wales. I don't ask people to accept my picture of Wales as the real one; it is inevitable that as people differ in temperament, in views, in beliefs, many should reject my picture of our country, should find certain elements exaggerated, others omitted. A piece of writing is mainly a sort of flowering, a fulfilment of oneself.[8]

One had to know how to read a book and not be forever poring over novels in search of 'insults to Wales'. As it was, the Welsh were too reluctant to stray beyond romantic visions of themselves ('love of land we call it').

As for the nature of the readership, recognition of Welsh writing abroad was wholly to be welcomed. This indeed was a settled Anglo-Welsh position. As Richard Hughes assured members of the Cymmrodorion Section of the National Eisteddfod in 1931, the notion of a national literature aimed solely at a national audience was anachronistic: an ambitious author naturally seeks the widest possible readership and, as for subject matter, the Welsh writer in English must, like authors anywhere, write about whatever most deeply engages him, be it the Welsh scene or not. 'If he is a true Welshman . . . and if he writes what comes from under his skin, his writing will be truly Welsh literature – as truly as "Romeo and Juliet" is English literature.'[9] If this now seems uncontentious, it was never the majority view – for which we might look to Glyn Jones's remark that

---

[7] *Carmarthen Journal*, 5 September 1930.

[8] NLW, BBC (Wales) Archives: Scripts, Radio Talk by Rhys Davies, 'How I Write', broadcast 17 January 1950.

[9] Richard Hughes, 'The Relation of Nationalism to Literature', *THSC* (1930–1), 127.

the only English thing about an Anglo-Welsh writer ought to be his language.[10] By this reckoning Hughes himself was an outsider, 'in but not of' the company, though any full-time writing Welshman remained a glamorous figure, to the young Keidrych Rhys at least. It was the professionals who excited ('They fed our imagination and provided what literary atmosphere existed'), and in exploring the Anglo-Welsh tradition Rhys portrayed a colourful, ink-stained crew:

> Ernest Rhys, providing a link with the Nineties and the Rhymer's Club, W. H. Davies, the lyricist and super-tramp, Arthur Machen who'd survived Grub Street . . . Richard Hughes with a sailor's beard, people of bohemian stamp like their fellow countryman Augustus John.[11]

The Welsh-language literary scene in contrast seemed amateurish and circumscribed, the product not just of preacher-authors but of preacher-publishers as well. The Irish and the Scots were encouraged by societies and the press, Caradoc Evans told Bangor students, whereas 'if you want a platform in Wales you must buy one in a chapel . . . If you want a thing printed you must submit it to some Liberal Nonconformist newspaper'.[12] (He excepted *Y Llenor* and the *Western Mail*.) Denied breadth and freedom of opinion, the people had succumbed to the viewpoint of their masters:

> they have dominated us for so many generations that they have fashioned our mind. They have built a wall about us. Within that wall – within that Nonconformist compound – we are born and spend our days as captives . . . He [the Welshman] may escape from Wales, he may break his tethering cord, but as long as he lives he will not escape the consequences of Nonconformity.[13]

Welsh intellectual life lay in the grip of a priest-caste, its literature the 'foolish mouthings' of sentimentalism and self-praise. It had been moulded by the petit-bourgeois Eisteddfod, that grand parade which rewarded 'the masters of the commonplace – little preachers and little lawyers, who scurry home with their money in their pockets and are heard of no more until next year'. Creative literature lives not by cash handouts but by 'bought bread and cheese'.[14]

---

[10] Glyn Jones, *The Dragon Has Two Tongues: Essays on Anglo-Welsh Writers and Writing* (London, 1968), p. 208.

[11] NLW, BBC (Wales) Archives: Scripts, Radio Talk by Keidrych Rhys, 'Welsh Writing, 1938–1948', broadcast 14 September 1948.

[12] Extracts from Evans's address to the Literary and Debating Society, University College of North Wales, Bangor, 7 November 1924, appeared in the *Western Mail* and the *Liverpool Daily Post*, 8 November 1924.

[13] Ibid.

[14] Ibid.

If others echoed Evans's strictures (though none so ferociously in public), it was not the sole Anglo-Welsh perspective. Geraint Goodwin met Evans's assertion that the Eisteddfod lacked artistic credibility – that 'cash or crown takes the winner nowhere' – by pointing out that this was not strictly true, but that even if it were, it did not matter. John Ceiriog Hughes (Ceiriog), 'the most sublime lyric poet Wales has produced', in Evans's sense 'got nowhere'. He never saw the need to; is he therefore to be judged a failure?[15] Goodwin's thinking accords more with Richard Hughes's notion of Welsh culture as essentially dispersed and communal (as opposed to centralized and metropolitan). Through his involvement with the Portmadoc Players, Hughes spoke with an insider's experience. 'The natural corollary of a country without a capital is an art independent of a few superlatively great artists', he ventured before the Cymmrodorion.[16] The Eisteddfod was not necessary for bringing to light great literature – a parcel to a publisher would suffice – 'No. The chief value of an Eisteddfod, and the peculiar values, in my eyes, of all Welsh culture, lies in the quite unparalleled public interest in literature and art and music which it exemplifies.'[17]

Meanwhile new works were emerging: fiction by Goronwy Rees, Margiad Evans, Jack Jones and Geraint Goodwin, and poetry by Glyn Jones and Dylan Thomas. Gwyn Jones, whose first novel appeared in 1935, referred to a 'kind of spontaneous combustion' that occurred around this time, regarding it as partly a response to unparalleled social conditions: 'The Anglo-Welsh writers of my generation grew up in both hard and mind-stirring times. Socialism and the class struggle . . . And mustering on the horizon the murk of Fascism and Communism.'[18] He accepted, too, that the decline of Nonconformity was a prerequisite ('the well-meaning moralist is the emasculator of art'), and that at some level this literary burgeoning reflected a sharpened sense of nationality – even if many practitioners 'found their social conscience more alert than their national'.

At first an affair of individuals, Anglo-Welsh literature developed its groupings. The earliest had Dylan Thomas as linchpin, the Swansea wunderkind whose *18 Poems* (1934) both thrilled and mystified. *The Spectator* came to pinpoint the author's genuine distinctiveness – 'He is neither English nor American, he is not in any ordinary sense a political poet, and he has avoided the universities' – and also his striking new way with language: 'His poems are written more for the voice and less for the eye . . .'[19] Thomas was 'modern' and 'difficult' and his

---

[15] Geraint Goodwin, 'Are Celtic Festivals Worthwhile?', *Evening News* [Glasgow], 4 August 1935, [Saturday Supplement], 1.

[16] Hughes, 'The Relation of Nationalism to Literature', 126.

[17] Ibid., 119.

[18] NLW, BBC (Wales) Archives: Scripts, Radio Talk by Gwyn Jones, 'Welsh Writing, 1938–1948', broadcast 7 September 1948.

[19] Desmond Hawkins, review of *Twenty-five Poems* by Dylan Thomas, *The Spectator*, no. 5659, 11 December 1936, 1058.

metropolitan impact gave the Anglo-Welsh a spectacular early boost ('leaks from Dylan Thomas's petrol can', joked Keidrych Rhys of the rest). Wales at last could claim a place in the literary vanguard. By 1934 Glyn Jones had met up with Dylan Thomas and discovered that he, too, nurtured hopes of a periodical which might serve the English-language writers of Wales, as did yet a third young poet – and one with the means to make it happen. It was the 20-year-old Keidrych Rhys who knocked on Glyn Jones's door at Rhiwbeina in the summer of 1936 and introduced himself as the founder of the next Welsh literary periodical. Rhys was as good as his word, launching *Wales* in July 1937 with encouragement from Dylan Thomas and Glyn Jones.

Keidrych Rhys warrants closer attention on the grounds of his pivotal position among the early Anglo-Welsh. The son of a tenant farmer, he spent his childhood in Carmarthenshire, a Welsh-speaking part of the country where, he was able to report, 'people are still good, sane, happy and simple-hearted'.[20] Following grammar school at Llandovery, he planned a career in journalism: he became a literary modernist and a nationalist in politics, attributes which were to irritate many in both language camps. Not that his manner helped. Literary life for Rhys invariably meant controversy, particularly in the pages of *Wales* where his machine-gun editorials strafed a range of targets. His was the archetypal 'little magazine', a vehicle for 'the younger progressive Welsh writers', as its manifesto boldly proclaimed. 'The contents should be, in the best sense, "contemporary", new and alive and original', agreed Dylan Thomas,[21] whose own contributions matched this requirement ('like no poetry that has ever come out of Swansea', judged the *Herald of Wales* uncontentiously). But Rhys also made play with the popular basis of Welsh literature – a literature enriched not by 'moneyed dilettantes, but by the small shopkeepers, the blacksmiths, the non-conformist ministers, by the miners, quarrymen, and the railwaymen'. Nor was this all Celtic blarney: Glyn Jones hoped for fresh working-class voices, while Rhys knew a countryside where poets were persons of substance. The trouble was that proletarian literature was naturally old-fashioned. Somehow Rhys had to square the circle and reconcile his populist avowals with an admiration for the élitist avant-garde. Goronwy Rees saw the dilemma:

> can we speak of ourselves as rooted in Wales when so much of the *idiom* in which *Wales* is written is that of contemporary English letters of the most fashionable and Bloomsbury kind . . . If, as you say, you really are of the People, you must write a language that the people can read.[22]

---

[20] NLW, BBC (Wales) Archives: Scripts, Radio Talk by Keidrych Rhys, 'Childhood in Carmarthenshire', broadcast 14 November 1950.

[21] NLW MS 22745D, letter from Dylan Thomas to Keidrych Rhys [n.d.].

[22] Ibid., letter from Goronwy Rees to Keidrych Rhys, August 1937.

Politics deepened the confusion, especially as Rhys's own were (in the words of the *Western Mail*) 'a very personal anarchism, although he is sympathetic to the Welsh Nationalist Party'. Nationalism was more a spiritual realm for Rhys, married to deep feelings about 'the ever-fascinating rural-intellectual repository that is the Principality'.[23] He defined himself by opponents, invariably establishment figures English and Welsh. His manifesto railed against the English ('a few individuals may be highly cultured, but the people as a whole are crass'), and claimed stewardship of the language they had so shamefully misused. Rhys judged his position as moderate – 'beyond the bigotry of unintelligent fascist nationalism'. Dylan Thomas never wanted the political dimension (nothing 'stridently Welsh in tone'), while Keidrych's public ranting embarrassed Glyn Jones. How on earth was Welsh culture going to improve south Wales? Why not simply make it clear that 'we in Wales are on the side of socialism'?[24] But, unlike the bulk of his contributors, Rhys never warmed to socialism. It marginalized more fundamental concerns. 'I wish that the Left Wing, in England and Wales, would pay more attention to Nationalism, language, the difference between the English proletariat and the Celtic Peoples, and culture generally,' he wrote a little later.[25] The challenge was to raise the national consciousness of his Anglo-Welsh contemporaries, an amorphous group but loosely tied to region which might yet be transformed into a cohesive force working to secure 'in the better English minds' sympathy for Welsh cultural ideals. These included the well-being of the language ('our separate identity ceases when the Welsh language ceases'); bedazzled by Saunders Lewis, Welsh modernist and aristo-nationalist, Rhys even came to believe that Anglo-Welsh literature might be a temporary, transitional phenomenon, a way back to the use of Welsh for all literary expression in Wales (emblematically he advertised *Wales* in Welsh in one London journal). 'The best sort of crank', said Dylan Thomas of a man who won affection in most camps of the Anglo-Welsh. The nationalists were particularly loyal, Harri Webb coming to think of him as among the great of his age, a man who almost single-handedly created a sense of community among English-language writers. Glyn Jones similarly attests how *Wales* served as a rallying point. Where previously there had been a 'vast cultural moonscape of nothing and nobody':

one could now believe in the existence of other writers, and even correspond with them and, if one was fortified sufficiently against disillusion, one could actually meet and get to know them personally. One could also read their work and compare it with one's own and come to some opinion about it.[26]

---

[23] Keidrych Rhys, 'Contemporary Welsh Literature (ii)', *The British Annual of Literature*, Vol. 3 (London, 1946), p. 19.
[24] NLW MS 22745D, letter from Glyn Jones to Keidrych Rhys [n.d.].
[25] 'Letter from Wales', *Twentieth-Century Verse*, 18 (1939), 60–1.
[26] Glyn Jones, *Setting Out: A Memoir of Literary Life in Wales* (Cardiff, 1982), p. 14.

Rhys proved a perpetual flashpoint, though others less combustible could also be made to flare: Geraint Goodwin, for instance, angered by the *Western Mail*'s dismissal of *The Heyday of the Blood* (1936) as 'sport for the Philistine',[27] in the manner of Caradoc Evans, responded with talk of the living talents of Wales 'slaughtered by neglect and embittered by abuse and jeering from the sidelines'.[28] The encounter remained with Goodwin, who deplored the ingrained Welsh prejudice against Anglo-Welsh writers ('It is not nationalism: it [is] more like trade unionism').[29] He hoped that sufficient young Welsh writers would understand that a person prepared to take 'only the approval of his countrymen (and a small proportion at that) might be a hell of a big fellow to them but a hell of a small one to a lot of others'.[30] An established author might preserve some detachment – 'Honestly', asked Richard Hughes, 'have you ever heard a Welshman have a good word for anything ever written for outside consumption about modern Wales?'[31] – but one forgets how destructive hostile critics can be at the outset of a writer's career. It was a point made regularly by Keidrych Rhys in relation to Caradoc Evans, ever the focus of strong emotion: the traducer whose savage lies set the Anglo-Welsh on a path of misrepresentation or, as Rhys insisted, the pattern of artistic survival in the face of petty parochialism.

Evans raged on, disdaining Welsh nationalism (in a talk banned on radio but published in February 1937)[32] as a 'stair-way to money-for-nothing jobs' offering Wales little beyond talk; and books forced upon inoffensive schoolchildren. Still, he had no wish to enter into squabbles with 'a Party which seems to think that words build memorials'; Penyberth and the symbolic firing of the bombing school showed the nationalists to be 'the Shadrachs, Mesachs and Abednegos of our chapellers; boys bach who scream for a fiery oven because they know there isn't one'.

These remarks came in the context of a major controversy, which began with the astonishing news of Evans's appointment as Welsh novel adjudicator for the 1937 National Eisteddfod at Machynlleth (at Port Talbot not even his portrait could be displayed, such were the nationalist threats). Evans accepted the invitation, though in little spirit of reconciliation. The Eisteddfod, he believed, was of no artistic consequence, but, rather, a parade ground for politicians 'who hunger for a bite of the Welsh electorate'. Predictably a *Western Mail* correspondence developed, touching upon the whole position of the Anglo-Welsh in relation to the Eisteddfod. Huw Menai urged their acceptance, but again in

---

[27] *Western Mail*, 31 October 1936.
[28] Ibid., 5 November 1936.
[29] NLW, Gwyn Jones Papers, *Welsh Review* correspondence, letter from Geraint Goodwin to Gwyn Jones, 25 October 1938.
[30] Ibid., letter from Geraint Goodwin to Gwyn Jones, 31 October 1938.
[31] Richard Hughes, 'Wales through the Looking-Glass', *The Listener*, XLV, no. 1160, 24 May 1951, 838.
[32] *Western Mail*, 3 February 1937.

confrontationalist terms; by canonizing Evans, was not 'drowning little Wales clutching at a straw'? (To Kate Roberts it was the Anglo-Welsh who were drowning; having failed in England, their natural arena, they now sought shelter amongst the Welsh literati.) Meanwhile, eight literary adjudicators resigned from the Machynlleth panel in protest at the growing Anglicization of the festival (Evans's appointment was not specifically raised, though Thomas Parry privately conceded that it played a part in his own thinking). Of course, Evans stoked the fire: it was idle, he told the press, to expect Eisteddfod novels to reach to any English standard so long as Welsh fiction remained the province of Nonconformist ministers – a class who imagined they had a monopoly of Welsh letters. Wales had talent enough, but no non-political platforms on which to display it. Evans hoped that examples of such talent, from 'a poor man who cannot afford to pay and can write', would come into his hands – for if the standard of work submitted was no better than in the past he would make no award.[33] He never got the chance; by March 1937 the Eisteddfod committee had dispensed with his services, explaining how resigning nationalist adjudicators should have no cause to blame them for bringing to bear anti-Welsh influences on literary competitions. To Evans it was confirmation that Eisteddfod adjudicators dare not tell the truth.

This was the cultural cauldron into which Rhys launched his *Wales*, its first issue seized upon by Iorwerth C. Peate, one of the resigning adjudicators, for a particularly hostile review.[34] The magazine made Peate feel old, very old, its modernist pretensions epitomized in Dylan Thomas, drunk this time on psycho-analysis and looking through dirty glasses on body and soul. The whole sorry business was best summed up by the opening of Glyn Jones's poem:

> This is the scene, let me unload my tongue
> Discharge perhaps some dirty water from my chest.

Keidrych Rhys, who needed his enemies, found a Peate-noire: the man and his gang were doing their best to kill off *Wales* – and apparently succeeding (by late 1937 it had run into financial difficulties). Nevertheless, one review from within the Welsh-language community was altogether more complimentary, that by (almost certainly) the astute and forceful critic, Pennar Davies.[35] With parents from either side of the Pembrokeshire *Landsker*, Davies had taught himself Welsh and begun writing poetry in both languages. He deplored the mutual suspicion which divided Welsh- and English-language writers and came to share Rhys's thinking on the cultural possibilities of the Anglo-Welsh, if only they would curb 'a raging subjectivism that persists in ignoring the audience'. An agent for public

---

[33] Ibid., 20 February 1937.
[34] *Heddiw*, 3, no. 1 (1937), 37.
[35] *The Welsh Nationalist*, VI, no. 8 (1937), 8. The review is unsigned.

action, literature must be part of a social solution. Yet, he envied the Anglo-Welsh their confidence and energy, and trusted that Rhys would dragoon his contributors into some uniform policy.

Meantime the Anglo-Welsh were everywhere, as artists and as self-promoters, teasing out on the Welsh Home Service their particular position. They must be 'a mouthpiece for that large second nation within our midst who speak and write and think in the English tongue',[36] and at the same time serious players in the business of English publishing. If the early Anglo-Welsh remained largely part-timers, their literary culture was professional. They secured themselves leading publishers (Faber, Cape, Dent, Gollancz) and entered into vital relationships with literary editors, thereby experiencing what Richard Church (with Dylan Thomas in mind) called 'the machinery of a great publishing house': the power to generate talk about a writer, with consequent sales of books – whatever the needs of authors, their books had to justify themselves commercially. Economic as well as other factors must shape the character and appeal of their art, for theirs was not a quiet coterie audience but 'the open competitive field of public taste'.[37] Rhys Davies maintained that a vigorous, full-bodied literature demanded one or two full-time writers, and that the reluctance to diversify had given Welsh publishing its 'bilious and shabby look' – witness the Welsh-language books on the second-hand stall in Swansea market, 'with that dusty dead look which testifies to the great unopened'.[38] If Welsh literature had its glories, why not have them translated? Until that happened, Wales would inevitably be represented in the world outside by its English-language authors.

By this time the Anglo-Welsh could number some thirty writers, as well as a landmark Faber anthology, the 500-page *Welsh Short Stories* (1937) displaying their talent in a genre increasingly associated with them (the collection also included four translations from Welsh). Dylan Thomas continued to flourish with his first Dent collection and a place in Michael Roberts's influential *Faber Book of Modern Verse* (1936). But first books from Glyn, David and Lewis Jones (all in 1937) proved equally significant. From the moment of its appearance, *In Parenthesis* was hailed as an Anglo-Welsh masterpiece: 'brilliant from what Dylan told me', wrote Vernon Watkins to Keidrych Rhys. Garlanded with praise, it won the Hawthornden prize, a matter of celebration for Keidrych Rhys. The Anglo-Welsh were touching new heights.

Lewis Jones's *Cwmardy* captured a very different type of audience – as its publisher intended it should. Lawrence and Wishart were the publishing arm of the British Communist Party and their Lewis Jones editions projected a worker-activist whose writings were intrinsic to the revolutionary struggle, 'written

[36] NLW, BBC (Wales) Archives: Scripts, Radio Talk by Gwyn Jones, 'Anglo-Welsh Authors', broadcast 30 September 1937.
[37] NLW, BBC (Wales) Archives: Scripts, Radio Talk by Charles Davies, 'Anglo-Welsh Authors', broadcast 15 March 1938.
[38] Davies, *My Wales*, p. 227.

during odd moments stolen from mass meetings, committees, demonstrations, marches, and other activities'. At forty-two, Jones lay dead in a Cardiff bedsit after a January day in the Rhondda appealing for food for Spain (some thirty meetings were addressed from a motor-van). As the dust-jacket of *We Live* (1939) proclaimed, 'if proletarian literature has any meaning, here is the real thing'. Jones was one of several Welsh writers seen as articulating a new class-consciousness. The *Left Review* listed them in 1937, in a 'Library of Living Books, as we would build it': Rhys Davies, Gwyn Jones, Glyn Jones, Jack Jones, Lewis Jones, Goronwy Rees, and the Faber *Welsh Short Stories*.

Around this body of writers hung the spirit of militant socialism and the desire to give expression to a unique industrial consciousness. 'The outcry of a community as well as that of an individual', ran the publicity for Idris Davies's *Gwalia Deserta* (1938); 'it expresses the hopes, betrayal, and suffering of the people of South Wales'. The longest chapter in Rhys Davies's *My Wales* (1938) considered not literature but 'The South Wales Workers'. It is an impressive account even if, as Lewis Jones maintained, it shrouded the workers in a romantic aura:

> Almost entirely within the boundaries of one Welsh county, Glamorgan, has been concentrated for the last hundred or so years a struggle which is the very breath of modern life. It is in this struggle that Wales is linked up with the rest of the world and becomes important. All other aspects of Welsh life to-day – and how charming and picturesque those aspects can be! – fade before this vital chronicle, which is not yet finished. A gloomy, bitter, tragic chronicle that is yet strangely exhilarating. Exhilarating because it contains such elements of nobility, passion, determination, and bravery.[39]

That the manifold resources of south Wales owed little to traditional culture became a commonplace in Anglo-Welsh thinking. They chose to celebrate discontinuity. The contrast was between proletarian and peasant, between a vibrant, progressive, industrial society and a backward-looking rural community, stultifying and puritanical. Inevitably, negative elements coalesced around the Welsh language: religion, or the husk of religion; declining political Liberalism; an introverted culture sealed off from contemporary influences by language and religion.

Individual writers knew both worlds, either through personal migration or from within their family. Goronwy Rees best reveals opposing bicultural perceptions when he writes of his childhood move from a manse in Aberystwyth to a suburb in Cardiff.[40] His father, a Calvinistic Methodist minister, had now to venture among the heathen, the miners emerging from their pits 'like troglodytes out of their caves'. The new paganism must be confronted, though it meant

---

[39] Ibid., pp. 44–5.
[40] Goronwy Rees, *A Chapter of Accidents* (London, 1972), pp. 22 et seq.

preaching in English – 'just as missionaries in strange lands must use the language of the heathen if he is to touch their hearts'. The child Goronwy stumbled through this new world, mingling with boys whose wits had been sharpened by living in a more complex environment. He had met them once before on a summer camp. It was like a Roman confronting the Goths. They were rougher, tougher, jeering and foul-mouthed:

> but they also seemed freer and more adult and less inhibited than the boys I had known, scornful of authority, untouched by the miasma of bigotry and hypocrisy which emanated from the twenty-five chapels of our little town.

In these lads turned socialist workers Rees invested his hopes. Makers of working-class history, they had displayed rare pride and independence and, through the South Wales Miners' Federation, a talent for self-government. 'What would be and is bombast in other Welshmen is the plain truth in the Welsh miners . . . Among them we can find our nationality.'[41] Living in England, Rees cherished beliefs about the fundamentally radical, democratic nature of Welsh society; how, 'compared with the English we are a united people, and one expression of our unity is our common wish for social change and progress'.[42] In Aberystwyth he saw things rather differently. What struck him now was the intense cultural and intellectual conservatism of the Welsh, their complacency in their national virtues. Was it an urban/rural difference? Or, as Nigel Heseltine believed, more a matter of class? ('The bourgeois Welshman is narrow, intolerant, ignorant on all subjects outside his own, and perpetually whining', he warned Keidrych Rhys of the nationalists.)[43]

Elsewhere Goronwy Rees explains his decision to become an English-language writer. 'It was as if, choosing the language of my childhood, I should have chosen to remain a child for ever . . . The trouble was, I suppose, that I wanted to grow up and felt that I could not do it in Welsh.'[44] Though the expression is provocative, his linking of such a decision with the passage of adolescence accords with Glyn Jones, whose comments on a writer's choice of language have become something of a *locus classicus*:

> It seems to me that the language which captures his heart and imagination during the emotional and intellectual upheavals of adolescence, the language of his awakening, the language in which ideas – political, religious, aesthetic – and an understanding of personal and social relationships first dawn upon his mind, is the language likely to be the one of his creative work.[45]

---

[41] Idem, 'From a Welshman Abroad', *The Bookman*, LXXXVII, no. 518 (1934), 105.
[42] NLW, BBC (Wales) Archives: Scripts, Radio Talk by Goronwy Rees, 'Beyond the Dyke', broadcast 8 June 1938.
[43] NLW MS 22744D, letter from Nigel Heseltine to Keidrych Rhys, 24 December 1937.
[44] Rees, *A Chapter of Accidents*, p. 34.
[45] Jones, *The Dragon Has Two Tongues*, p. 25.

One might adduce Idris Davies, bowled over by the English Romantics, but support for this thesis comes also from a contemporary of Goronwy Rees at Cardiff High School. Alun Llywelyn-Williams moved in the opposite direction, transferring his allegiance from English to Welsh on becoming aware of the body of Welsh creative writing: 'The discovery of this rich heritage in adolescence was a traumatic experience.'

As Anglo-Welsh literature became increasingly identified with the industrial valleys, a new south Wales literary grouping evolved as a counter to Keidrych Rhys and *Wales*. (That the 'militant journal of the Welsh literary renaissance' should have originated in Carmarthenshire was always something of a surprise.) Appropriately at the University of Wales, Cardiff, Gwyn Jones planned a broader-based cultural journal, something more substantial, more discriminating. Blackwood-born Gwyn Jones, cross-bred English and Welsh, was marked off from the firebrand Rhys in other crucial ways: he was a good eight years older to begin with, a scholarly academic with four Gollancz novels behind him, and his tone was altogether more commanding – 'shrewd and wise and nicely bitter' (in the well chosen words of one reader). By autumn 1938 Jones was sounding out likely contributors, not least among Welsh-language writers. *Wales*, it should be noted, published poems in Welsh by writers more attuned to the industrialized south (D. Gwenallt Jones (Gwenallt), Alun Llywelyn-Williams, Pennar Davies, T. E. Nicholas, Aneirin Talfan Davies and others), but Gwyn Jones had something different in mind: the publication of the very best Welsh short fiction in translations of commensurate quality. In his opening *Welsh Review* editorial (February 1939), he gave his thoughts on Anglo-Welsh literature: a manifestation of the south Wales mentality, it was interpreting Wales to the world and promising, coincidentally, to reinvigorate the exhausted body of English literature. The rift between Welsh- and English-language writers he thoroughly deplored and he hoped that he might bridge it by 'keep[ing] the English-speaking Welshmen bound to their homeland'; far from disparaging the native culture, the *Welsh Review* would do what it could to enhance it by offering a platform to its representatives, and by a policy of publishing high-quality translation.[46]

His invitation to Saunders Lewis met with an interesting reply. Lewis declined to contribute, explaining that only politics and economics would tempt him to write in English; his forthcoming lecture at Cardiff worried him because it was on a literary topic and had to be done in English: 'You see, I am willing to sacrifice for political propaganda for Welsh Nationalism, but not for anything less.'[47] The lecture, entitled 'Is there an Anglo-Welsh Literature?', was delivered before a university audience on 10 December 1938. Lewis answered his own question

---

[46] *Welsh Review*, I, no. 1 (1939), 4.
[47] NLW, Gwyn Jones Papers, *Welsh Review* correspondence, letter from Saunders Lewis to Gwyn Jones, 30 November 1938.

comprehensively in the negative, largely by comparison with the Anglo-Irish, and on the grounds that there was no such thing as an organic Anglo-Welsh society with its own separate dialect or idiom. 'A writer of literature belongs to a community. Normally, he writes for that community.'[48] Normally, the Anglo-Welsh did not; their books were 'essays in interpretation', enriching the English imagination. This lack of an assured sense of function afflicted most writers of Wales, the outcome, as Saunders Lewis saw it, of a sickness in Welsh society whose remedy was political.

Jack Jones responded immediately – he could make no sense of the argument; as a miner he was indisputably Welsh but as a miner-novelist, still 'rooted in the black depths of industrial Wales', his nationality was being denied him. Yet, apart from Jack Jones, Anglo-Welsh reaction to the lecture was muted, partly because its thrust was not new: Welsh as the essence of identity, the only language capable of expressing 'the soul of Wales'; south Wales as mongrelized and debased, a howling wilderness of philistinism ('The Anglo-Welsh . . . I never believed there were such a people', claimed Peate when dismissing *Wales*); above all, the notion of English-language writers as alienated, shaping their literature for an outside English readership.

Furthermore, Saunders Lewis as cultural commentator lacked something in credibility; a mad arsonist, as Harri Webb then saw him, whose preoccupations were irrelevant in comparison with the coming war. It was the long predicament of the 1930s, namely how to reconcile opposition to war and to a corrupt social system at home with resistance to European Fascism, but by late 1938 Lewis had retreated into political fantasy. Praising Hitler over the Sudetenland, Lewis urged total appeasement. 'All the massed forces of English propaganda are concentrated today to make Germany and Herr Hitler in particular appear the provokers of this war', he explained on the front page of *The Welsh Nationalist* in October 1938.[49] Seemingly they had succeeded. English hatred had inoculated the Welsh against reason, and it pained him that 'Welsh-speaking people of the countryside' should think Hitler a fanatical lunatic (Lewis found him 'reasonable, and above all restrained and most suggestive . . . in new ideas'). If the English failed to concede Hitler's objectives, they rather than the Germans would be morally responsible for any ensuing war. Plaid Genedlaethol Cymru (the Welsh Nationalist Party) clung to this line: Germany was to be crushed for her strength – 'It is the treatment the Philistines meted out to Samson.'[50]

To be attacked by such an analyst might be counted a positive virtue; and if the rural Welsh were beyond him, how much greater his ignorance of south Wales? Wherein lies definitive Welshness? Not, Glyn Jones would claim, in locality or

---

[48] Saunders Lewis, *Is there an Anglo-Welsh Literature?* (Caerdydd, 1939), p. 3.
[49] *The Welsh Nationalist*, VII, no. 10 (1938), 1.
[50] Ibid., VIII, no. 10 (1939), 1.

language – a Welsh life could be lived in industrial Merthyr, and through the medium of English:

> But if working-class culture, and the Radical spirit, and the feeling of belonging to a democratic, egalitarian society are elements in the concept of Welsh society, then Merthyr was much more Welsh than Carmarthenshire. I never saw a book, nor heard any song, nor any discussion of any literary, political, or religious subject, in my uncle's home – the famous countryside culture didn't exist in these parts, as far as I could see. On the other hand, I never saw anyone in Merthyr bowing or curtsying, as my aunts did in the presence of the local landowners, who were well-to-do, English-speaking Welsh people. The Welsh character means a lot more to me than the ability to speak Welsh.[51]

But Saunders Lewis had his Anglo-Welsh admirers, especially Keidrych Rhys who, though distancing himself over the war, believed that 'our greatest Welshman' had in his Cardiff lecture said 'almost all there is to be said' on the subject of Anglo-Welsh literature. The lecture was tacit recognition of the impact of the Anglo-Welsh who, so Rhys believed, must be encouraged to develop a more unified vision of Wales. He found a practical ally in Pennar Davies, himself worried by this cultural discerption ('a conglomeration of minds which, when they think of Wales, do not think of the same thing').[52] Accordingly, the two men proposed a bilingual Academy of Letters, named the New Wales Society/ Cymdeithas Cymru Newydd, which would be a fellowship of writers seeking 'to substitute energy and responsibility for the dilettantism and provincialism of Welsh life and literature'.[53] In summer 1939 some forty young writers were circularized, including, on the English-language side, Idris Davies, Emyr Humphreys, Glyn Jones (but not Gwyn), Goronwy Rees, Dylan Thomas and Vernon Watkins. Their replies make clear how serious were the rifts over politics and language: 'personally, I would wish that every member of the proposed society were a Socialist first and a Welshman afterwards', responded Idris Davies, while Emyr Humphreys, urging that the Society's Welsh name take precedence ('the native language should be always given the place of honour'), insisted that Saunders Lewis's 'short but very significant speech' at the Denbigh National Eisteddfod should provide the basis for any manifesto.[54] In that speech Lewis had declared that the problems of Welsh literature were political not literary – 'there must be a nation before there can be literature' – and that there was no hope for

---

[51] Glyn Jones, 'The Making of a Poet – Part 1', *Planet*, 112 (1995), 76. A translation by Meic Stephens of a memoir broadcast in Welsh by the BBC in 1970 and later published in Alun Oldfield-Davies (ed.), *Y Llwybrau Gynt I* (Llandysul, 1971), pp. 61–93.

[52] *Western Mail*, 10 August 1939.

[53] NLW MS 20784D.

[54] Ibid.

Wales until it became monoglot Welsh: 'any one who believes that a bilingual nation can produce real literature is talking through his hat'.[55] (Within the ranks of the Welsh Nationalist Party, it should be said, were many who believed that it was their president who was talking through his hat and that neither Welsh nor English could become a single unifying force. Better, they argued, to accept an Anglophone culture and strive to make it as Welsh as possible.)

One imagines that Goronwy Rees and Dylan Thomas were canvassed more in hope than expectation, though Rees, as assistant editor of *The Spectator*, was well placed to further Welsh interests among 'the better English minds'. Indeed, he had used *The Spectator* to advocate Welsh nationalism – fundamentally on the grounds that 'no culture is safe, or can prosper, which is divorced from political responsibility'.[56] But if he found no difficulty with nationalism, he rejected those who represented the movement in Wales; and the Welsh Nationalist Party's response to the Nazi threat elicited biting satire from a man whose stand against Fascism drove him into military service. As for Dylan Thomas, he was a well-wisher, who did more for his literary compatriots than is generally recognized (publicly reading their poems and helping them find publishing outlets); but he could summon up no enthusiasm for formal groups or societies. 'I don't think it does any harm to the artist to be lonely *as* an artist. (Let's all "get together", if we must, and go to the pictures)', he replied to Pennar Davies.[57] When the war came the New Wales Society project was abandoned, though it briefly flickered again in 1942.

One reply with a dash of arrogance disconcerted Pennar Davies. Vernon Watkins's viewpoint was that of Dylan Thomas, namely that authors wrote best when they wrote independently of groups, but he proffered some additional advice to the effect that 'those nationalists who are most bitter at this moment should try to distinguish between the imperfections of their country and the imperfections of their style'.[58] The barb struck deep and soured Davies's attitude towards the Anglo-Welsh. Whereas Saunders Lewis softened towards Dylan Thomas (and other English-language writers), Pennar Davies always maintained that Thomas in particular lacked moral substance, possessing no national, social, or for that matter, religious loyalties. His influence was pernicious, expressly on Glyn Jones who explained in a postscript to his first collection, *Poems* (1939), how, when faced with Dylan's achievement, he had questioned his previous notions, derived from socialism (and *Hen Benillion*), concerning a communal literature – one written by and for the people. Thomas seemed not to worry about readership and, under his example, Glyn Jones abandoned as hopeless and visionary his

---

[55] As reported in the *Western Mail*, 12 August 1939.

[56] Goronwy Rees, 'In Defence of Welsh Nationalism', *The Spectator*, no. 5698, 10 September 1937, 417.

[57] Paul Ferris (ed.), *The Collected Letters of Dylan Thomas* (London, 1985), p. 388.

[58] NLW MS 20784D, letter from Vernon Watkins to Pennar Davies, July 1939.

schemes for the poeticization of the masses. Pennar Davies judged *Poems* a book 'of a prodigious representative importance' since, at last, it offered the critical basis of the Anglo-Welsh.[59] He disassociated himself from it completely, recommending to all Welsh writers 'a course in Hugh MacDiarmid, militant high-brow and convinced believer in the intelligence and taste of the common people'. The future lay not with raging subjectivists but with 'strenuous individuals' like Keidrych Rhys.

Rhys busily made enemies in the cause of Wales. The self-elected spokesman of his generation, he castigated Welsh literary conservatism. The Welsh-language literary renaissance had come to falter as its leaders retreated into poetical Georgianism and *Tir na n-Óg* preoccupations. Too many Welsh writer-academics were wedded to Palgrave and Keats and once-daring intellectuals now grossly inflated the commonplace, praising any kind of 'puritan rubbish' in the belief that it kept the language alive. Avidly they hunted the modernist to protect their unhappy 'Welsh ethos'. For people like Iorwerth C. Peate, the destruction of Welshmen who wrote in English had become as important as the destruction of Hitler – 'perhaps a bit more important', Rhys reflected.[60]

With disgust Rhys noted Peate's support for 'a more dignified and monied Anglo-Welsh periodical'[61] – a periodical which nevertheless had folded, like Keidrych's own, by the end of 1939. *Wales* reappeared in 1943, the *Welsh Review* in 1944, and at either end of the intermission came two high-profile book collections, again from Gwyn Jones and Rhys. In 1940 Penguin Books published *Welsh Short Stories*, edited by Gwyn Jones, who included some translations from the Welsh (one being E. Tegla Davies's 'Samuel Jones' – which its translator, Dafydd Jenkins, believed to be perhaps the greatest short story in the language). Given Gwyn Jones's commitment to translation, it was something of a surprise that he should disappoint D. J. Williams over a version of 'Y Cwpwrdd Tridarn' (The Court Cupboard) for the revived *Welsh Review*. Williams, an admirer of Jones's editorials ('fresh, original and clinching'), took a friendly interest in the periodical, though he doubted its appeal among English speakers (his point, that those most alive to its message were readers of Welsh-language journals, was regularly made at the time). Dafydd Jenkins's translation of 'Y Cwpwrdd Tridarn' well satisfied D. J. Williams, who confidently offered it for publication. But 'The Court Cupboard' never appeared, at least not in the *Welsh Review*, for Gwyn Jones decided that the drift of the story, and in particular the revulsion of Harri, the Caeo man, at his nephew's intention to enlist, was unacceptable in time of war (the year was 1944). Williams understood Gwyn Jones's thinking, though to the best of his knowledge the story had caused no offence within his circle of

---

[59] Originally intended for *Wales*, his review appeared in *Poetry* (*London*), 5 (March–April 1941), 153–6.

[60] *Western Mail*, 23 August 1939.

[61] Ibid., 28 August 1939.

acquaintances: 'And until an Anglo-Welsh magazine can recognize the existence of such a point of view in Wales it will not be exercising its full function as an interpreter of the Welsh people to a wider public beyond Wales.'[62] What Gwyn Jones declined, Keidrych Rhys accepted, publishing the translation in *Wales* shortly after the end of the war.

A year previously Rhys had placed on Faber & Faber's distinguished list an anthology of poems by over thirty of the younger Anglo-Welsh; a bold selection (two-thirds of the poets lacked their own first collections) and boldly presented: this 'contribution of the Welsh genius' gave a better picture of the Welsh ethos than did any best-selling novel. Its title might be considered provocative, but by using 'Welsh' (not 'Anglo-Welsh') in *Modern Welsh Poetry* Rhys explained that he was seeking to denote the unity of Wales: Welsh culture was the culture of the whole nation as distinct from the purely 'Cymric' kind. A stricter nomenclature ('Cymric', 'Welsh') would help prevent the dangerous division into 'Welsh' and 'English' and stiffen the allegiance of the Anglicized regions.[63]

Keidrych Rhys and Gwyn Jones, the two great literary facilitators, shadowed each other compulsively, each coming to believe that a book publication programme was necessary for the sake of native writing and in order to bolster the chances of their periodicals (this was before the era of subsidy). In 1945 Gwyn Jones planned to launch the book arm of Penmark Press (publishers of the *Welsh Review*) not with an Anglo-Welsh title but with Kate Roberts in translation. He had already published her work in the *Welsh Review* and in his 1940 Penguin, and he shared the growing belief that in Kate Roberts Wales possessed a writer who could confidently be offered to the world. There were grounds for optimism, for eight of her short stories had already appeared in English-language periodicals (*Life and Letters Today* even produced a special issue on Kate Roberts). Immersion in another literary culture both excited and daunted the author. There were welcome financial returns – a story in Welsh, she assured Gwyn Jones, receives nothing in its original form, whereas *Life and Letters* paid two to three guineas per thousand words. But with the rewards came the brickbats; and from critics like George Orwell, whose dismissal of 'pointless little sketches about fundamentally uninteresting people' greatly disconcerted her. Could not W. J. Gruffydd open for Penmark? or maybe Gwyn Jones himself? Jones's *The Buttercup Field* would indeed lead off but (so she was persuaded) with herself to follow.

The presence of an academic editor (now Professor of English at Aberystwyth) who was also a creative writer disposed Kate Roberts to the Penmark venture; she sought Gwyn Jones's advice and took up his suggestions. By and large the translations pleased her – Dafydd Jenkins she thought brilliant, and one passage in

[62] NLW, Gwyn Jones Papers, *Welsh Review* correspondence, letter from D. J. Williams to Gwyn Jones, 10 July 1944.
[63] *Western Mail*, 14 March 1944.

Wyn Griffith's English seemed better than the original – but publishing Kate Roberts was a formidable challenge, no other publisher having yet attempted to carve out an English market for a modern Welsh-language writer. To help in the enterprise Jones recruited Storm Jameson, an accomplished author who served as London president of PEN, to provide an introductory essay. But a book is more than its text, and to his skills as commissioning editor Jones brought a taste for book design and a professional sense of the market. 'It really is a beautiful book', responded Kate Roberts appreciatively, 'I hope the reviewers will find the stories worthy of such a handsome get-up.'[64] Influential reviews were central to a marketing drive which still excites admiration. Gwyn Jones moved ambitiously, securing reviews (in the nationals and on radio) and negotiating deals with book-shop chains for a print run of 3,000. On 14 June 1946 Roberts acknowledged a cheque for royalties, the first advance she had ever received; by November a second cheque had come her way. In the event reviewers were friendly: it provided access, said Rosamond Lehmann, to a foreign culture ('our ignorance of it is only matched by our incuriosity') and an antidote to south Wales fiction, whose motifs had become over-familiar: 'No fallen angels, no blood, lust, sin, guilt, hysteria.'[65] Kate Roberts's *A Summer Day* (1946) was indeed a high watermark in collaboration across the language divide and Gwyn Jones was its ideal publisher – a man with a sound-minded appreciation of his author and of the need to achieve translation, and with a necessary practical grasp of the English publishing world. Kate Roberts wrote in thanks for all Gwyn Jones's efforts on her behalf: 'The book was published in record time and everything has been very efficiently done.'[66]

Efficiently produced indigenous books were the goal of Keidrych Rhys, whose Druid Press mirrored the Penmark enterprise (though he published one Welsh-language title). Rhys's views on the Welsh book trade were sound and far-sighted, urging a greater professionalism and some degree of public patronage:

> Authors must be paid for their work. There must be more concern for typography. Publishing must be segregated from printing. There must be more pride in the business – the *End* isn't merely having a job for your printer to do. There must be more bookshops. There should be 'Book Pages' in the Welsh newspapers. And there should be one central Wholesaler. The doyens of the Welsh book-trade still visualize an old man with a sack of books and periodicals on his back crossing the hills to remote white farmsteads on the skyline.[67]

---

[64] NLW, Gwyn Jones Papers, *Welsh Review* correspondence, letter from Kate Roberts to Gwyn Jones, 14 June 1946.

[65] *The Listener*, XXXVI, no. 915, 25 July 1946, 122.

[66] NLW, Gwyn Jones Papers, *Welsh Review* correspondence, letter from Kate Roberts to Gwyn Jones, 12 November 1946.

[67] Keidrych Rhys, 'Welsh Commentary', *Books: News Sheet of the National Book League*, no. 191 (August 1945), 58.

For his first book Rhys chose audaciously and brilliantly, as literary history (if not the finances of the Druid Press) eventually proved. *The Stones of the Field* (1946) was a first collection by R. S. Thomas, a poet known only from periodicals like the *Dublin Review* and *Wales*. On the surface this was an unlikely pairing, but the two men shared similar ideas about literary life in Wales. Thomas also deplored those authors selling 'stagey presentations of their own countries to the English capitalist publishers'[68] and, as Rhys before him, he somehow came to imagine that Anglo-Welsh literature might be but a temporary phenomenon, 'a stepping-stone back to the vernacular, as in Scotland the revival of Lallans was seen as hopefully a half-way house on the way back to Gaelic'.[69] Once more the Saunders Lewis influence was powerful (whereas Dylan pilgrimaged to Caradoc Evans at Aberystwyth, R.S. journeyed to meet Saunders Lewis) and particularly the notion of Anglo-Welsh writers as *déraciné*, having no vital relationship with a community. That English was a permanent literary language of Wales remained an article of faith among the Anglo-Welsh, but R. S. Thomas never accepted this, and turned self-consciously in the mid-1940s to the 'purer, more continuous' Welsh poetic tradition in pursuit of a distinctively Anglo-Welsh idiom. As publisher, Keidrych Rhys sought to reflect his concerns. 'These are essentially nature poems, but they are not written in the English tradition [the blurb extravagantly claimed]. Their imagery is more akin to that of those early Welsh writers, whose clarity of vision was born out of a mystical attachment to their environment.'

The Stones of the Field is often paired with Emyr Humphreys's *The Little Kingdom* as two works of 1946 which marked a turning point in Anglo-Welsh literature – a realignment graphically imaged in Pennar Davies's later reference to 'those of artistic chastity – David Jones, Glyn Jones, Emyr Humphreys, R. S. Thomas and a growing number of others – who can use English words for Babylon's overthrow'.[70] Humphreys was unambiguous in his goals, as his response to the New Wales Society attests, and a follower of Saunders Lewis even in his reading of the war: it was a clash between rival imperialisms, with English imperialism the enemy of Wales. Again, he invoked the senior literature, the epigrammatical terseness of the Welsh poetical tradition, as an influence on his own prose style which was economical and under-emphasized, in contrast to the south Wales 'bardic' school. He deliberately distanced himself from this school and its industrial proletarian preoccupations, and dismissed one of Jack Jones's novels as 'a large jelly of sentiment, made from wind, water, and words'.[71] Anglo-

---

[68] *Western Mail*, 12 March 1946.

[69] R. S. Thomas, *Cymru or Wales?* (Llandysul, 1992), p. 5.

[70] 'Pennar Davies' [autobiographical essay] in Meic Stephens (ed.), *Artists in Wales* (Llandysul, 1971), p. 127.

[71] Emyr Humphreys, review of *Off to Philadelphia in the Morning* by Jack Jones, *The New English Review*, XV, no. 4 (1947), 374.

Welsh literature did little justice to the north; indeed, it was writing it off the map of Wales.

Both Emyr Humphreys and R. S. Thomas nailed their colours to the mast of *Wales*, Thomas making plain his displeasure at the reappearance of the *Welsh Review*. 'After all *Wales* was first in the field', he wrote to Keidrych Rhys. 'If the professor wishes to pursue a similar policy, why not join forces with you? If he intends to differ, he must answer to the charge that "he who is not for us, is against us".'[72] 'The professor' felt dismay at those who, as he saw it, were setting themselves apart on account of their superior patriotism. Relations deteriorated, especially after a *Welsh Review* profile of Saunders Lewis (Winter 1946) which made it very clear why there should be more nationalists outside his Party than within it. The piece is witty and devastating, though it admitted the possibility that, as it got closer to social realities, Plaid Cymru might yet become the modern radical party of Wales. Its conclusion on Lewis is prescient: 'Rejected by his people as their political leader, he may be after all the apostle of their new awakening.'[73] A reorientated Plaid Cymru found much to applaud in the *Welsh Review*. On becoming a subscriber, Gwynfor Evans thanked Gwyn Jones for the thoughtful support of his editorials. 'Such a generous commentary is far too rare to be allowed to pass unacknowledged, and we would certainly be the stronger for finding your influential pen oftener in sympathy with us.'[74] An immediate outcome of the Saunders Lewis profile was that Jones was unable to print Lewis's 'The Essence of Welsh Literature', one of six broadcasts by eminent scholars on the Welsh literary tradition. Originally considered as a Penmark volume, the talks were rescheduled for publication in the *Welsh Review*. Five appeared in a single issue (Winter 1947), Lewis giving his own to *Wales*.

If their competitiveness was undisguised, it is only fair to stress the remarkable commitment of both Gwyn Jones and Keidrych Rhys to the idea of the Anglo-Welsh and how, with their sense of belonging to a strikingly different generation, they unstintingly promoted their contemporaries. The rivalry was of a piece with literary relations during the 1940s, when the protracted war of the tongues concealed a confusion of cultural battlefronts, sharp internecine clashes and some improbable alliances. Keidrych Rhys saw the division as more a matter of intellectual generations than one between English and Welsh, and Saunders Lewis's seeming acceptance of this, in an essay which lauded the new Anglo-Welsh assembled in *Modern Welsh Poetry*, put a spring in the editor's step. (Lewis believed the collection was of the highest significance to Wales and of a quality beyond the reach of the younger Welsh-language poets.) At last English-language

---

[72] *Wales*, no. 4 (1944) 106.
[73] 'Welsh Profile, 4: Saunders Lewis', *Welsh Review*, V, no. 4 (1946), 263. The profile is unsigned but was probably written by Gwyn Jones.
[74] NLW, Gwyn Jones Papers, *Welsh Review* correspondence, letter from Gwynfor Evans to Gwyn Jones, 7 May 1947.

writers were putting down roots in native soil, while outside Wales their stock continued to rise.

That Anglo-Welsh literature was in vogue Pennar Davies had no doubt; Welshness had become 'a quality that can, it seems, redeem talented mediocrity into impassioned genius'.[75] Acclaim for Dylan Thomas doubtless provoked his ill temper, though Davies also suggested that an acceptable kind of Welshness partly explained Alun Lewis's leap to fame: had Lewis been more emphatically, more aggressively Welsh, he would never have been accepted as an ideal English soldier-poet in the line of Rupert Brooke. In *The Welsh Nationalist*, Davies preferred to reserve his applause for those like Emyr Humphreys, R. S. Thomas and Keidrych Rhys who recognized 'the living nationhood of the Welsh people'. They stood apart from the prevailing Anglo-Welsh indifference, typified by Vernon Watkins, who existed in a social vacuum and whose poems were too often 'mere decorations upon next to nothing'.[76] Pennar Davies could not forget the remark that Welsh nationalists should cultivate their style rather than their grievances, and it additionally galled him that Rhys Davies, 'lost on the heaving ocean of English life', should pose as a national spokesman. Welshness was not to be identified with quaint theories of racial character but with a developing national life; Wales must be spoken to, not written about. Pennar Davies's criticism gained assurance from a settled view of the writer's function – he even took Emyr Humphreys to task over an unflattering portrayal of Welsh nationalism in *The Little Kingdom* – though he proved refreshingly hospitable towards the Rhondda novelist Gwyn Thomas, believing him to be curiously neglected in Wales in the late 1940s. Others, with 'not a hundredth' of Gwyn Thomas's gift and vision, were 'reverently belauded by university professors and imitated by university students'.[77]

Pennar Davies's problem with Dylan Thomas was continuous and reflects a wider Welsh ambivalence towards the nation's most celebrated poet. Gwyn Thomas recalled Thomas's iconographic significance: 'He was a sort of living revenge on all the restrictions and respectabilities that have come near to choking the life out of the Welsh mind.'[78] Less admiringly, in 1946 Keidrych Rhys agreed that it was hard to convince oneself that Dylan Thomas or Alun Lewis 'ever felt or thought as Welshmen'.[79] This was the moment of Thomas's ascendancy. In the changed climate of war, his poetry showed a new directness and accessibility, culminating in *Deaths and Entrances* (1946), which won him unstinting praise. 'And how quietly he just goes on', observed the editor of *Life and Letters* to Gwyn Jones, 'getting better and better – no careerism, no starting "movements" or

---

[75] Davies Aberpennar, 'Anti-Nationalism among the Anglo-Welsh', *The Welsh Nationalist*, XVII, no. 2 (1948), 3.
[76] Idem, 'Vernon Watkins', *Welsh Nation*, XVIII, no. 8 (1949), 6.
[77] Idem, 'A Novelist Worth Noting', ibid., XVIII, no. 10 (1949), 4.
[78] Gwyn Thomas, *A Welsh Eye* (London, 1964), p. 64.
[79] Rhys, 'Contemporary Welsh Literature', 19.

belonging to them – just quietly going on – not without its humour, really, as in private he is so far from quiet!'[80] Thomas knew much about literary movements, including those in Wales, and in a radio broadcast in 1946 he firmly disassociated himself from the poetical nationalists:

> There is a number of young Welshmen writing poems in English who, insisting passionately that they are Welshmen, should, by rights, be writing in Welsh, but who, unable to write in Welsh or reluctant to do so because of the uncommercial nature of the language, often give the impression that their writing in English is only a condescension to the influence and ubiquity of a tyrannous foreign tongue. I do not belong to that number.[81]

Welshmen, he sensibly argued, had written some good poetry in English because they were good poets rather than good Welshmen: 'It's the poetry, written in the language which is most natural to the poet, that counts, not his continent, country, island, race, class, or political persuasion.' Gwyn Jones elaborated on this viewpoint in a radio broadcast (1948), which surveyed a decade of the Anglo-Welsh:

> That literature should be the handmaiden of nationality, politics, theology, what you will, appears to me both stultifying and unnatural. It may in the nature of the special case be any one of these, but inclusive and exclusive demands upon the artist are in their nature evil. The choice is the artist's and, emphatically not the legislator's.[82]

R. S. Thomas was not convinced; three months later he emphatically legislated in the pages of *The Welsh Nationalist*, urging the would-be Anglo-Welsh writer to study Welsh history and literature, and indeed all things Welsh, then to 'write out of that full knowledge and consciousness in English, – if you can!'[83]

We need perhaps to remind ourselves that these were young writers at the outset of their careers. The attitudinizing is predictable, as is their later acceptance of the imperatives of the literary life; that it mattered more to be a writer than a Welshman, that the artist's commitment is to his art. Looking back on the turmoils of the period, on the tangle of principles and prejudices, the fierce position-taking and high-pitched cultural claims, one cannot but endorse Dylan Thomas's view that 'too many of the artists of Wales spend too much time talking about the position of the artists of Wales. There is only one position for an artist anywhere: and that is, upright.'[84]

[80] NLW, Gwyn Jones Papers, *Welsh Review* correspondence, letter from Robert Herring to Gwyn Jones, 2 May 1946.

[81] Ralph Maud (ed.), *Dylan Thomas: The Broadcasts* (London, 1991), p. 31.

[82] NLW, BBC (Wales) Archives: Scripts, Radio Talk by Gwyn Jones, 'Welsh Writing, 1938–1948', broadcast 7 September 1948.

[83] R. S. Thomas, 'Anglo-Welsh Literature', *The Welsh Nationalist*, XVII, no. 12 (1948), 3.

[84] Maud (ed.), *Dylan Thomas*, p. 220.

14

The History of the Welsh Language Society 1962–1998

DYLAN PHILLIPS

By THE beginning of the 1960s it was a matter of grave concern for supporters of the Welsh language that their mother tongue was losing on average one speaker every ninety minutes. Their conviction that the language was facing the greatest crisis in its history was strengthened following the publication of the 1961 census results which confirmed the trend of the previous sixty years of a steady decline in the number of Welsh speakers. In responding to this situation, the editor of *Baner ac Amserau Cymru* observed that the worst fears of Welsh language supporters had been realized.[1] At first sight, the census figures offered some consolation since they provided clear evidence that the rapid decrease in the number of speakers experienced between 1931 and 1951 had eased somewhat. During this period the language had lost, on average, one speaker every fifty-four minutes. Nevertheless, as Alwyn D. Rees noted in his analysis of the statistics in the periodical *Barn*: 'Dylid sylweddoli hefyd nad yw tap ar waelod casgen yn rhedeg mor gryf pan â'r lefel yn isel' (It should also be realized that a tap at the bottom of a barrel does not flow so forcefully when the level is low).[2] Since the beginning of the twentieth century the percentage of Welsh speakers had been declining at a faster rate than ever before in the history of Wales. The 1901 census recorded that 929,824 people were able to speak Welsh, approximately half the population. However, by the 1961 census the numbers had decreased to 656,002 (26 per cent of the population) – a loss of a quarter of a million speakers since the turn of the century. The language was in retreat even in its rural strongholds in the west and north: by 1961 Welsh was the main language of no more than seven of every ten inhabitants in these areas, compared with nine of every ten in 1901. An even more disturbing revelation for advocates of the language was the enormous decline in the number of monoglot Welsh speakers. There were 280,905 monoglot speakers in 1901, representing 15 per cent of the population, but only 26,223 remained by 1961, this being scarcely one per cent.[3]

---

[1] 'Gwersi'r Cyfrifiad', *Baner ac Amserau Cymru*, 20 September 1962.

[2] Alwyn D. Rees, 'Cyfri'r Cymry', *Barn*, 2 (1962), 40–1.

[3] For a statistical examination of the position of the Welsh language, see John Aitchison and Harold Carter, *A Geography of the Welsh Language 1961–1991* (Cardiff, 1994).

The stark census figures alarmed Welsh language supporters and many despaired for its future, the news being described as 'pur ddigalon' (very depressing) by *Y Cymro* and 'distressing' by the *Western Mail*. With the exception of the imperialist editor of *The Times*, who found much satisfaction in the figures and suggested benevolently that the time had come for the Welsh people to free themselves from the shackles of the past and join the modern world, the census results caused much disquiet among the editors of Welsh newspapers and magazines. It was now clear that the native tongue was in crisis and that its future as a living language was at stake. The day after the figures were published the editor of the *Liverpool Daily Post* observed: 'the period between now and the 1981 census is vital; in that period the language will be saved, or lost beyond recall'. In similar vein, *Baner ac Amserau Cymru* declared that the Welsh people should alert themselves to the danger, for the 1961 census had sounded the final warning and urgent action was required in order to preserve the Welsh language and its culture.[4]

The Need for a New Movement

Concern for the future of the language had been expressed as early as 1891 when the first census to seek to assemble data on the Welsh language had been held. As a result several campaigns were launched to protect and revive the language, and several movements and societies were established.[5] Yet, despite the notable work of movements such as Undeb Cenedlaethol y Cymdeithasau Cymraeg (the National Union of Welsh Societies), Urdd Gobaith Cymru (the Welsh League of Youth) and Undeb Cymru Fydd (the New Wales Union), by the 1950s several Welsh language supporters had become increasingly concerned at the declining prospects of the language. Economic and social problems which were particularly detrimental to the language were intensifying, such as the decline of the traditional industries in the Welsh-speaking heartland, the outward migration of Welsh speakers, and the influx of non-Welsh-speaking families seeking to escape the pressures of urban life. Furthermore, it was felt that the increasing influence of English-language and English-orientated mass media, particularly as a result of the penetration of television into almost every household, threatened the position of

---

[4] 'Rhimyn Arian', *Y Cymro*, 13 September 1962; 'Figures behind the Facts', *Western Mail*, 12 September 1962; 'The Pedigree of Nations', *The Times*, 12 September 1962; 'Decline of a Language', *Liverpool Daily Post*, 12 September 1962; 'Gwersi'r Cyfrifiad', *Baner ac Amserau Cymru*, 20 September 1962.

[5] For the background to some of these societies, see J. Elwyn Hughes, *Arloeswr Dwyieithedd: Dan Isaac Davies 1839–1887* (Caerdydd, 1984); Robin Okey, 'The First Welsh Language Society', *Planet*, 58 (1986), 90–6; Marion Löffler, *'Iaith Nas Arferir, Iaith i Farw Yw': Ymgyrchu dros yr Iaith Gymraeg rhwng y Ddau Ryfel Byd* (Aberystwyth, 1995); R. E. Griffith, *Urdd Gobaith Cymru, 1922–1972* (3 vols., Aberystwyth, 1971–3); Cassie Davies, *Undeb Cymru Fydd: 1939–1960* (Aberystwyth, 1960); Dafydd Glyn Jones, 'The Welsh Language Movement' in Meic Stephens (ed.), *The Welsh Language Today* (Llandysul, 1973), pp. 287–357.

the Welsh language in the home. Nor did it appear that the drive to establish Welsh-medium schools was having much success in stemming the decline in the number of Welsh-speaking children. However, the most obvious indicator of the subordination of the mother tongue was its lack of public status: English was the language of government departments and local authorities. No forms or official letters were available in Welsh, and English was the sole language of road signs and formal discourse.[6]

The status of the language was a cause of concern for a growing number of people. Throughout the 1950s letters and articles appeared regularly in the press claiming that the strenuous efforts of previous language movements had been unsuccessful. Frustrated supporters called for bolder measures than those put forward by the government and for positive action to make Welsh an official language equal in status with English and a mandatory subject in schools. Writing in *Y Genhinen* in 1958, E. G. Millward declared:

Rhagrith noeth (neu ddallineb anfaddeuol) ydyw clegar byth a hefyd am Gymru ddwyieithog a pholisi dwyieithog heb geisio sicrhau statws swyddogol i'r Gymraeg . . . Onis defnyddir ymhob cylch o'n bywyd, trengu a wna'r Gymraeg, a bydd yn haeddu marwolaeth.[7]

(It is pure hypocrisy (or unforgivable blindness) to harp on about a bilingual Wales and bilingual policy without trying to secure official status for the language . . . Unless it is used in all walks of life, the Welsh language will die, and deservedly so.)

By the beginning of the 1960s, therefore, on the eve of the publication of the 1961 census figures, the concern of Welsh language advocates had reached its peak. Some nationalists began to argue that it was time to abandon the tactics of the past and to adopt a radical new approach. In a letter published in the *Welsh Nation* in November 1960, John Davies suggested that a new movement should be established with the object of organizing a national campaign to persuade central and local government, public bodies and private businesses of the need for equitable treatment for the language – by unconstitutional means if necessary. The inspiration for his appeal for civil disobedience was the uncompromising stand of Eileen and Trefor Beasley in Llangennech, Carmarthenshire. Since 1952 the couple had refused to pay rates to Llanelli Rural District Council because the demands were issued in English. Although they eventually succeeded in receiving some form of Welsh rate demand, their protest cost them dearly, for the council

---

[6] See Janet Davies, *The Welsh Language* (Cardiff, 1993); Aitchison and Carter, *A Geography of the Welsh Language*; and the various articles in Stephens (ed.), *The Welsh Language Today*.

[7] E. G. Millward, 'Cymru Ddwyieithog', *Y Genhinen*, VIII, no. 4 (1958), 216–20.

employed bailiffs to seize property to the value of the debt.[8] John Davies believed
that unconstitutional action would be the only effective means of securing official
status for the Welsh language.[9]

Davies's frustration with traditional methods of conducting politics was shared
by several fellow countrymen who felt that nothing of value had been achieved by
past campaigns. Neither were the political parties active proponents of the Welsh
language: the Conservative Party was viewed by many Welsh people as a foreign
and English entity; leading members of the Labour Party such as Iorwerth Thomas,
George Thomas, Ness Edwards and Leo Abse were hostile to the Welsh language;
and it was feared that Plaid Cymru was deserting the language as it increasingly
turned its attention to campaigning in the English-speaking areas of the industrial
south. Many nationalists were also openly critical of Plaid Cymru's inertia during
this period. Indeed, John Davies's letter reflected the dissatisfaction of a substantial
proportion of the younger generation who were quickly losing patience with the
Party's lack of electoral success. Since its establishment in 1925 Plaid Cymru had
gained no electoral success in parliamentary elections and consequently pressure
was increasing from within for a change in strategy, methods and leadership. In
October 1960, at a meeting held in Aberystwyth to discuss unconstitutional means
of promoting the nationalist cause, several disaffected members and supporters of
Plaid Cymru formed a splinter group called 'Cymru Ein Gwlad' (Wales Our
Country) to promote direct forms of action.[10] Their frustration with Plaid Cymru
was further intensified by its failure to prevent the Liverpool Water Corporation
from drowning the village of Capel Celyn, with the result that some of its members
resorted to direct action at Tryweryn in 1962 and again in 1963.[11]

Some believed that the future of the language should take precedence over self-
government, since independence would be futile if Wales were to lose its native
tongue. The main advocate of this argument was Saunders Lewis, president of the
Welsh Nationalist Party from 1926 to 1939. By 1962 Lewis was convinced that the
language campaign was 'the only political matter which it is worth a Welshman's
while to trouble himself about today'.[12] He had lost patience with the strategy of

---

[8] For an account of this episode, see Eileen Beasley, 'Papur y Dreth yn Gymraeg', *Y Ddraig Goch*,
     XXXI, no. 3 (1959), 3.
[9] John Davies, 'Reforming Plaid Cymru', *Welsh Nation*, November 1960, 6.
[10] Alan Butt Philip, *The Welsh Question: Nationalism in Welsh Politics 1945–1970* (Cardiff, 1975),
     pp. 88–92; Phil Williams, 'Plaid Cymru a'r Dyfodol' in John Davies (ed.), *Cymru'n Deffro: Hanes
     y Blaid Genedlaethol 1925–75* (Talybont, 1981), pp. 121–46.
[11] For the history of the drowning of Capel Celyn and the Tryweryn valley, see Gwyn Erfyl,
     'Tryweryn: The Drowning of a Valley', *Planet*, 73 (1989), 49–53; Watcyn L. Jones, *Cofio Tryweryn*
     (Llandysul, 1988), pp. 155–283; Gwynfor Evans, *Rhagom i Ryddid* (Bangor, 1964), pp. 34–54;
     Owain Williams, *Cysgod Tryweryn* (Caernarfon, 1979). For an account of the frustration within
     Plaid Cymru following Tryweryn, see Butt Philip, *The Welsh Question*, chapter 5.
[12] Saunders Lewis, *Tynged yr Iaith* (London, [1962]), p. 29. Translated into English by Gruffydd Aled
     Williams, 'The Fate of the Language (1962)' in Alun R. Jones and Gwyn Thomas (eds.), *Presenting
     Saunders Lewis* (Cardiff, 1973), p. 141.

electoral campaigns and the failure of the language movements. On Tuesday evening, 13 February 1962, in a celebrated radio lecture, he called for a campaign of civil disobedience in support of the Welsh language. *Tynged yr Iaith* (The Fate of the Language) aimed to awaken the Welsh to the crisis facing the language and expressed Lewis's belief that 'Welsh will end as a living language, should the present trend continue, about the beginning of the twenty-first century'.[13] He called on Plaid Cymru and its leaders to abandon their electoral campaigns and to use the Welsh language as a political weapon. He, too, had been inspired by the stand of the Beasleys, and he believed that it was entirely feasible to organize an unconstitutional campaign that would make it impossible for local and central government to conduct its business without having recourse to the language:

> Let it be insisted upon that the rate demand should be in Welsh or in Welsh and English. Let the Postmaster-General be warned that annual licences will not be paid unless they are obtainable in Welsh. Let it be insisted upon that every summons to a court should be in Welsh . . . Let it be demanded that every election communication and every official form relating to local or parliamentary elections should be in Welsh. Let Welsh be raised as the chief administrative issue in district and county.[14]

The influence of Saunders Lewis's lecture on language campaigners and others was immense, and his message was widely discussed throughout Wales. It exercised its greatest influence on students at the University College of Wales, Aberystwyth, and members of the Plaid Cymru branch in the town. One member, Gareth Miles, was already involved in a legal battle concerning the language of a summons he had received following his arrest in January 1962 for illegally carrying a friend on the bar of his bicycle. He refused to obey the English-only summons and was kept overnight in the police cells after refusing to pay the fine.[15] Members of Aberystwyth branch decided to support his stand and submitted a motion to Plaid Cymru's annual conference in Pontarddulais in August calling on all branches to organize activities which would force the authorities to grant official status to the Welsh language. The implementation of Saunders Lewis's strategy had begun. In submitting the motion, which was seconded by John Davies, E. G. Millward argued that a new movement was required to co-ordinate the campaign. Both were elected secretaries of the new society and in its first meeting at the White Horse in Aberystwyth in October 1962 it was named Cymdeithas yr Iaith Gymraeg (the Welsh Language Society).[16]

[13] Williams, 'The Fate of the Language', p. 127.

[14] Ibid., pp. 140–1.

[15] See Gareth Miles, 'Incident at Aberystwyth', *Welsh Nation*, August 1962, 6.

[16] For a more detailed account of the history of the founding of the Welsh Language Society, see John Davies, 'Blynyddoedd Cynnar Cymdeithas yr Iaith Gymraeg' in Aled Eirug (ed.), *Tân a Daniwyd: Cymdeithas yr Iaith 1963–76* (Abertawe, 1976), pp. 5–39; Gwilym Tudur, *Wyt Ti'n Cofio?* (Talybont, 1989), pp. 13–26; Dylan Phillips, *Trwy Ddulliau Chwyldro . . .? Hanes Cymdeithas yr Iaith Gymraeg, 1962–1992* (Llandysul, 1998), passim.

The First Campaign

The founding of the Welsh Language Society in 1962 was a key event in the campaign to safeguard the language. It signalled a fundamental change of direction in terms of strategy and methods and the advent of a new period of confrontational campaigning and political activity. The founders were well aware of the need for an *active* and *direct* campaign to ensure the survival and revival of the Welsh language. They realized that their predecessors had been restricted by their courteous and respectful approach and their desire to avoid making the language a political issue. However, since the exclusion of Welsh from all official and legal circles following the 1536 Act of Union was a political act, political campaigning was now justified in pursuit of its revival. Society members also appreciated that they needed far more enterprising methods than those adopted by their predecessors in order to publicize their campaign. Thus commenced the 'language struggle'.

It is no surprise that the Society should choose protest as its main weapon. After all, the early 1960s was a period of worldwide turmoil and unrest. In many countries and societies minority groups and peoples were expressing their disillusion with the constitutional political process. There were protests in Paris against the French government's Algerian policy; massive peace marches in London; strikes and riots in South Africa against the injustices of apartheid; student protests from California to Warsaw in support of freedom of expression; and civil disobedience campaigns to achieve equal rights for black people in the United States of America.[17] The 1960s was an exhilarating period for many people throughout the world, and Welsh language supporters in Wales hoped that by emulating the methods of their international cousins they would be able to elevate the status of their mother tongue.

The Society began its political campaign by highlighting the various needs of the Welsh language and its inferior public status. Court summonses were its first target. The summons was a potent symbol of legal power and of the subordinate status of the Welsh language. By their refusal to accept English-only summonses, Society members challenged the language clause of the 1536 Act of Union which had made English the sole language of administration and law in Wales. At the beginning of the campaign the two secretaries followed up the incident involving Gareth Miles by requesting bilingual court summonses from Cardiganshire magistrates. However, following a long period of fruitless correspondence, the Society embarked on the path of civil disobedience. Some members flouted the law by committing minor offences involving highway regulations. Two others

---

[17] For further details on worldwide protests, see Robert Benewick and Trevor Smith (eds.), *Direct Action and Democratic Politics* (London, 1972); Norman F. Cantor, *The Age of Protest* (London, 1970); Terry H. Anderson, *The Movement and the Sixties: Protest in America from Greensboro to Wounded Knee* (Oxford, 1995).

ventured to emulate Miles's original offence by cycling unsteadily past a policeman on the streets of Aberystwyth. In protest at the language of the court, offenders refused to respond to the English summonses subsequently issued.[18] This action, however, failed to move the magistrates, and it was decided that a mass protest was required to bring matters to a head.

The protest held in Aberystwyth on 2 February 1963 targeted the Post Office, an institution which represented the public face of government in Wales and was administered totally through the medium of English. The main objective was to engineer the arrest of as many protesters as possible so that they could reject their summonses. The protest was widely publicized and seventy members and supporters, most of them students from Aberystwyth and Bangor, assembled in the town. The crowd marched to the post office and pasted posters on the windows and walls of the building proclaiming 'Defnyddiwch yr Iaith Gymraeg' (Use the Welsh Language) and 'Statws i'r Iaith Gymraeg' (Status for the Welsh Language). Since no one was arrested they proceeded to adorn the council buildings and police station. Having again failed to draw a response, some of the protesters, despite the doubts of the organizers, decided to move on to Trefechan Bridge where they sat in the middle of the road, blocking the flow of traffic into the town. Yet again no one was arrested, but the action succeeded in attracting the attention of the media throughout Wales and England, inspiring tantalizing newspaper headings such as 'They Fight for the Language of Heaven', 'A Whole Town "Welshed" On', and 'Posters, Squatters and Fights Help Give Welsh Equal Status?'[19]

This protest resulted in a swift response to the demand for Welsh-language summonses. A Welsh summons was prepared by Cardiff magistrates within a few weeks and it was also revealed that the Under-Secretary of State at the Home Office had sent a letter to Aberystwyth magistrates noting: 'The magistrate appears to be legally entitled to issue a summons in Welsh or English with a translation into Welsh.'[20] Despite the slow and uneven response within other courts, the Society had secured its first victory. It was in the wake of this campaign that it adopted its militant and uncompromising approach to political action, implementing for the first time ever direct and unconstitutional methods of promoting the cause of the Welsh language.

[18] 'Students refuse to pay 10s. fines', *Western Mail*, 25 January 1963; *Y Cymro* and *Baner ac Amserau Cymru*, 31 January 1963; Davies, 'Blynyddoedd Cynnar Cymdeithas yr Iaith Gymraeg', pp. 13–14; Tudur, *Wyt Ti'n Cofio?*, p. 21.

[19] See reports in the *Western Mail*, *Daily Express*, *Daily Herald*, *Liverpool Daily Post*, *The Times*, and *The Guardian*, 4 February 1963; *Y Cymro*, 7 February 1963; *Cambrian News*, 8 February 1963.

[20] Davies, 'Blynyddoedd Cynnar Cymdeithas yr Iaith Gymraeg', pp. 14–15.

The 1960s: The 'Struggle for the Language' Begins

Following its baptism of fire at the Aberystwyth protest and the success of its first campaign, the Welsh Language Society had demonstrated the need for a well-organized movement. As a result, efforts were made during the following months to strengthen its organization, since the two secretaries appointed at the inaugural meeting were the only officers and no administrative system or formal procedures were in place. Therefore, in May 1963, Siôn Daniel was elected to the chair and a recruitment campaign was conducted over the following months. Advertisements were placed in Welsh-language papers inviting people to join the new movement and declaring that:

Y mae aelodaeth yn y Gymdeithas yn agored i bawb a fyn statws swyddogol i'r iaith Gymraeg yng Nghymru, ac a fyddai'n barod i wneud rhywbeth amgen dros y cyfryw nod na gwisgo bathodyn brithliw.[21]

(Membership of the Society is open to all who desire official status for the Welsh language in Wales, and who would be prepared, in pursuit of such an aim, to do more than just wear a multi-coloured badge.)

At the May meeting it was also announced that the aim and function of the Society was to secure official status for Welsh on an equal footing with English in the fields of administration, government and business, and that it was prepared to engage in illegal activity in the event of its failure to achieve its aims by legal means.[22]

Following the success of its campaign for bilingual summonses, the Society concentrated its efforts on securing public status for the language. However, at its first annual general meeting held in August 1963 it was decided to postpone the direct action campaign. The government had by then appointed Sir David Hughes Parry to form a committee to examine the legal status of the Welsh language and members and supporters were urged to submit evidence to the committee. During the next two years Society officers corresponded extensively with local authorities and other bodies such as the Post Office, British Rail and the Tourist Board with regard to the status of the language in their administration and services to the public. They pressed for Welsh income tax returns, bilingual road signs, bilingual telephone and electricity bills, and they attempted to draw to a successful conclusion the long-running campaign for bilingual cheques.[23] The

---

[21] John Davies, open letter to *Y Crochan*, 1 (1963), 2.
[22] NLW, John Davies Papers 13. Welsh Language Society membership card, 1963.
[23] Davies, 'Blynyddoedd Cynnar Cymdeithas yr Iaith Gymraeg', pp. 29–31; Tudur, *Wyt Ti'n Cofio?*, pp. 21, 29.

Society's emphasis on public status for the language was wholly deliberate since the ultimate aim of its campaigns was to provide the opportunity for Welsh people to use their native tongue freely. It was argued that the subordinate status of the language had led many people over the years to believe that Welsh was of no value and was not worth transmitting to the next generation.

The truce came to an end in November 1965 when a mass protest was organized at the post office in Dolgellau. This represented the culmination of a long campaign to have the sign on the building changed from 'Dolgelley' to 'Dolgellau'. After marching around the town, the post office was occupied by over two hundred members and supporters, and once again the protest was reported extensively in the press and by the media. This time, however, it was decided to maintain the pressure, the post office at Lampeter being occupied in December and the one at Machynlleth in January.[24] By now it was clear that a growing number of Society members were determined to intensify the unconstitutional campaign. The current members of the Central Committee were more impatient than the original leaders and brought with them a new willingness to break the law. The benefits of civil disobedience were increasingly recognized. Firstly, it forced the authorities to act in favour of the language since they were anxious to avoid unfavourable publicity which highlighted the shortcomings of their language policies. Secondly, the publicity gained in the press and media provided the Society with a platform for disseminating its message. The main advantage, however, was that protest compelled the public itself to respond, to consider the message conveyed, and to decide whether they themselves should make a stand or not.

In this respect, the Society's unconstitutional strategy resembled that of several single-issue movements active throughout the world in the 1960s. Movements such as CND, the civil rights campaign in America, and student movements all used protest and civil disobedience to promote and publicize their campaigns for nuclear disarmament, equal rights and improvements in the education system. The effectiveness of this strategy persuaded the Society to escalate its civil disobedience campaign at the end of October 1965, and Central Committee members committed themselves to refusing to tax their vehicles in order to bring pressure on the Ministry of Transport to publish a bilingual application form. As a result, several members were arrested for driving a vehicle without a road fund licence, and during the following year many were fined and even imprisoned by the courts. The first to be imprisoned was Geraint Jones in April 1966 for refusing to pay fines totalling £16 imposed for driving a vehicle without a road fund licence.[25] However, the action attracted extensive press coverage which served to

[24] See *Western Mail*, 29 November 1965; *Y Cymro* and *Baner ac Amserau Cymru*, 2 December 1965; *Western Mail*, 13 December 1965; *Y Cymro* and *Baner ac Amserau Cymru*, 16 December 1965; *Western Mail*, 31 January 1966; *Y Cymro*, 3 February 1966; *Baner ac Amserau Cymru*, 10 February 1966.

[25] See *Western Mail*, 29 April 1966; *Y Cymro* and *Baner ac Amserau Cymru*, 5 May 1966.

disseminate the movement's propaganda in much the same way as the suffragettes had done in campaigning for women's suffrage and pacifists in America in calling for an end to the Vietnam War. Court cases provided an effective platform for publicizing the demand for equal status for the Welsh language, and since 1962 approximately two hundred activists have been sentenced to periods of imprisonment for their part in various campaigns.[26]

Although protest and direct action had become the main planks of Society policy, members adhered strictly to the principle of non-violence. Non-violent campaigning had been the official policy of the Society since 1966, when the general meeting rejected 'trais dwrn, trais tafod, a thrais calon' (physical violence, verbal violence, and emotional violence).[27] Its spiritual mentors were Mahatma Gandhi and Martin Luther King, the two principal advocates of non-violent protest in the twentieth century. Statements read out in court, speeches and articles all testified to their profound influence on the actions of Society members. In January 1969 Dafydd Iwan urged members to abide by Christian values, declaring that their struggle should reflect their practical Christianity and emulate the campaigns of Martin Luther King and Gandhi.[28] Other members were persuaded to accept this method of action for reasons of pragmatism and practical politics. Rather than cherishing a deeply-held conviction in the high-minded principles and spiritual value of non-violent methods, they believed, with Thoreau, that the aim of civil disobedience and unconstitutional action was to bring pressure on the authorities and compel them to yield to the demands of protesters. In 1966 Emyr Llewelyn asserted that non-violence should be adopted as a tactical necessity since the authorities had no answer to peaceful action. He argued that it was a simple matter to meet violence with violence, but a far more difficult proposition to deal with hundreds of peaceful protesters. Moreover, the use of violence would alienate the public and create hostility towards the Society's aims and objectives.[29]

The road fund licence campaign, which was not finally won until 1969, owed much to the support of a substantial number of well-respected figures in Wales. Keen to provide the older generation with an opportunity to demonstrate their admiration for the young campaigners, Alwyn D. Rees played an instrumental

---

[26] For a more detailed examination of the Society's use of civil disobedience, see Phillips, *Trwy Ddulliau Chwyldro . . .?*, chapter 4.

[27] NLW, Cymdeithas yr Iaith Gymraeg Papers 40 and 4/2. Minutes of the Central Committee, 22 October 1966, and the special general meeting 1966. See also Cynog Dafis, 'Cymdeithas yr Iaith Gymraeg' in Stephens (ed.), *The Welsh Language Today*, p. 278; Dafydd Iwan, *Dafydd Iwan* (Caernarfon, 1981), p. 54.

[28] Dafydd Iwan, 'O Gwmpas dy Draed', *Tafod y Ddraig*, 17, January 1969. See also Gareth Miles, 'Torri Cyfraith Anghyfiawn', *Baner ac Amserau Cymru*, 23 May 1968; Ffred Ffransis, 'Cymdeithas yr Iaith a'r Deyrnas', *Tafod y Ddraig*, 33, June 1970; Rhodri Williams, 'Anufudd-dod Dinesig', *Efrydiau Athronyddol*, XLII (1979), 42–56.

[29] Speech delivered by Emyr Llewelyn at the special general meeting 1966. Published as 'Trais neu Di-drais?', *Baner ac Amserau Cymru*, 1 December 1966.

role in the success of the campaign. By publishing lists of supporters in the columns of the monthly periodical *Barn*, of which he was editor, Rees organized them as an effective contingency force. The authorities were alarmed to discover that over six hundred and fifty of the readers of *Barn* had committed themselves not to display the English tax disc until the preparation of bilingual forms and discs was under way. Victory swiftly followed this intervention and all excuses and alleged practical difficulties preventing the production of bilingual documents, such as cost and computer limitations, were quickly cast aside.[30] In fact, the support of members of the older generation was critical to the success of the Society on many occasions: they became directly involved in protests, wrote letters of support to the press, defended the young protesters at public meetings, and paid their fines. Nevertheless, by the end of the 1960s it was becoming increasingly evident that the Welsh Language Society was a young people's movement and that the vast majority of its leaders were students. The younger generation were not constrained by family and employment responsibilities, and were free to concentrate on the cause and act uncompromisingly in pursuit of their beliefs.[31]

By the end of the 1960s the Society had initiated campaigns demanding a wide range of official bilingual forms and publications such as electricity bills, income tax returns, television and radio licences, salary cheques, pension payments, and certificates of marriages, births and deaths. Despite its success in compelling the Labour government to pass the Welsh Language Act of 1967, the continuing inferior status of the language spurred the Society to further action.[32] In 1967 it launched its best-known campaign, that against English-only road signs, which were reckoned to be the most visible symbols of the subordination of the Welsh language in Welsh public life. The first act of this campaign had in fact been carried out in August 1964 when the signs at 'Trevine' had been removed during the night and replaced with signs bearing the Welsh name 'Tre-fin'. The campaign was resumed in earnest in October 1967 when three students from the University College of Wales, Aberystwyth, acting without the blessing of the Society's Central Committee, damaged English-only road signs in the area. The following day the general meeting approved the new campaign and in January 1969 detailed guidelines, including what shade of green paint to use, were published in *Tafod y Ddraig*, the Society's monthly magazine.[33]

Several hundred activists joined the sign-daubing rallies held at Wybrnant and Cefn-brith, and over two hundred members attended the Post-mawr rally in

---

[30] A contemporary account of the campaign is given in *Barn*, 77–83 (1969).

[31] For a more detailed discussion on the nature of the membership, see Phillips, *Trwy Ddulliau Chwyldro . . .?*, chapter 1.

[32] See Robyn Lewis, *Second-Class Citizen* (Llandysul, 1969), pp. 59–101.

[33] See *Western Mail*, 4 August 1964 and *Y Cymro*, 6 August 1964; Tudur, *Wyt Ti'n Cofio?*, p. 49; 'Cyfarwyddiadau ynghylch Peintio Arwyddion', *Tafod y Ddraig*, 17, January 1969, 6–7.

December 1970. An even greater number were attracted to the night rallies when the actions of the Daughters of Rebecca were emulated and thousands of English road signs were pulled down or destroyed. This energetic campaign fired the imagination of many young people and resulted in the dramatic growth of the Society's membership to over two thousand at its height. In his autobiography Dafydd Iwan describes the enthusiasm and exhilaration of the period:

> Er mor ddwys a difrifol oedd y sefyllfa, ac er mor gynhyrfus y teimlem, roedd hwyl yn y gwmnïaeth bob amser. Fedra' i ddim pwysleisio gormod ar hyn oherwydd roedd yn nodwedd o holl gwmnïaeth ac ymgyrchoedd Cymdeithas yr Iaith Gymraeg yn ystod y blynyddoedd hynny. Credem i gyd yn gryf ac yn ddwfn yn yr achos yr ymladdem drosto. Ond doedd hynny byth yn trechu'r hwyl a'r asbri naturiol oedd yn rhan ohonom. Ymhob sefyllfa roedd yna achos i dynnu coes ac i chwerthin. Oni bai am hynny, mae'n debyg, byddai wedi bod yn llawer iawn anos dioddef yr amgylchiadau.[34]

> (Despite the seriousness of the situation and the nervousness we all felt, there was always an element of fun. I can't stress this enough, for it characterized the comradeship and campaigns of the Welsh Language Society during those years. We all had a firm and deep belief in the cause we were fighting for. But this never overshadowed our natural exuberance and exhilaration. There was leg-pulling and laughter in every situation. But for that it would probably have been far more difficult to carry on.)

Society members accused of causing criminal damage to road signs appeared in courts throughout Wales, the total number of cases exceeding 185, and the campaign was severely criticized by local authorities and in the press. Indeed, some protesters were assaulted by local inhabitants as they passed through Rhayader on their way to the Cefn-brith rally in 1969.[35] Judging by the number of threatening letters and phone calls he received, Dafydd Iwan, the Society's chairman, was probably the most unpopular person in Wales at that time.[36] The campaign simmered for several years, baulked by the obstinacy of successive Secretaries of State such as George Thomas, Peter Thomas and John Morris, who opposed the erection of bilingual road signs on the grounds of cost and safety. Nevertheless, the huge swell of popular support for such signs eventually forced the government to capitulate. This famous and important victory found expression in popular Welsh culture, especially in Dafydd Iwan's protest song 'Peintio'r Byd yn Wyrdd' (Painting the World Green) and the lively songs of groups such as Tebot Piws.[37] As a result, a place of honour was ensured for the road signs campaign in the recent mythology of Welsh-speaking Wales.

---

[34] Iwan, *Dafydd Iwan*, p. 82.

[35] '10 Scuffle with Sign Daubers', *Western Mail*, 17 February 1969.

[36] Iwan, *Dafydd Iwan*, p. 43.

[37] There is no doubt that the lowering in the age of the electorate from twenty-one to eighteen in 1967 had an impact on the Society's average membership age, since more young people became members.

The 1970s: Widening the Struggle

By the end of the 1960s, therefore, the campaigns on behalf of equal status for the Welsh language had firmly established the Society as a political force in Wales. This had been mainly achieved by its militant approach, together with its use of non-violent civil disobedience. Language campaigners had learnt at an early stage that protest and law-breaking were an effective means of bringing direct pressure on the authorities and also of highlighting the numerous injustices which prevented the language from flourishing in its own country. Nevertheless, this type of campaign had its drawbacks. Because of their commitment to direct action, Society members were often condemned and labelled extremists and vandals. Militant methods also incurred the wrath of the establishment, providing Secretaries of State and local government officers with an excuse to reject the Society's demands. Yet, illegal action had proved an extremely effective tool in arousing interest in the campaign to promote the status of Welsh in the 1960s.

Notwithstanding the success of their early campaigns, Society members realized by the beginning of the 1970s that securing equal status for the language was not enough, and that political solutions were required to the threats facing the Welsh language. As a result, the Society's aspirations developed far beyond those of Saunders Lewis in *Tynged yr Iaith*, which had focused solely on the status of the language as a means of communication between the government and the public. Even as early as 1965–6 the language campaign had been extended to include new domains, such as education and the mass media, and improvements in the language policy of primary schools in Cardiganshire and a Welsh-language broadcasting service had been among the priorities. During the 1960s, however, the Society's most controversial campaign was undoubtedly its opposition to the Investiture of the Prince of Wales in 1969. Despite the reservations of many supporters, an energetic programme of anti-Investiture protests and rallies was organized, thereby attracting much criticism from the authorities, the media and the general public. For example, in July 1968 the *Western Mail* condemned the 'extremists, hooligans and anarchists' for behaving in a 'shameful and disgusting' manner during the prince's visit to Cardiff.[38] Nevertheless, this diversion from the narrow path of language activism forced the Society's leaders to give serious thought to their position within the wider political arena and to develop their campaign strategy and policies.

The Society therefore developed several more politically- and socially-orientated campaigns than those of earlier years which had focused on specific issues of status. Several of its leaders were also influenced by the ideas of the philosopher, Professor J. R. Jones, whose volume *Prydeindod*, published in 1966, warned readers of the serious threat to the existence of Welsh-speaking Wales and

---

[38] 'Prince of Wales', letter by Gwynne Williams, Treherbert, *Western Mail*, 2 July 1968.

of the impending extinction of the Welsh as a separate people. If the language were to be lost, he argued, the Welsh would inevitably lose their identity and cease to exist as a distinct people.[39] This message had critical implications for members of the Welsh Language Society since it confirmed that the survival of the language was inextricably bound up with the survival of Welsh-speaking communities. The most eloquent expression of the Society's new emphasis on community is to be found in an article written by Dafydd Iwan in *Baner ac Amserau Cymru* in 1969:

> Ni ellir ysgaru iaith oddi wrth y gymdeithas y mae'n gyfrwng iddi. Nid rhywbeth i'w hystyried ar ei phen ei hun yw iaith, ond rhan annatod o wead cymdeithas gyflawn. Nid brwydro dros yr iaith Gymraeg er ei mwyn ei hun yr ydym yn y Gymdeithas hon ychwaith, eithr brwydro dros hanfod y bywyd Cymraeg. Ag eithrio ei bod ynghlwm wrth y bywyd hwnnw, does fawr o werth na phwrpas i'r Gymraeg.[40]

> (A language cannot be divorced from the society for which it is a medium. Language is not something to be considered in isolation, but as an integral part of the structure of a complete society. We in the Society are not fighting for the Welsh language for its own sake either, but for the essence of Welsh life. Unless it is an integral part of that life, Welsh has little value or purpose.)

It was in keeping with this new approach that Society members stood side by side with the inhabitants of the Senny valley in 1969 against the River Usk Authority's plan to drown the land in order to create a reservoir. The scheme not only threatened the livelihood of local farmers but also the native Welsh-speaking community. Support was also given to the parents of Bryncroes primary school on the Llŷn peninsula in their protest against Caernarfonshire County Council's decision to close the school; the building was occupied and unofficial schooling was arranged for a short period.[41] The Society was deeply aware that the number of areas where it was possible for Welsh speakers to live their lives wholly through the medium of Welsh was declining, and that it was impossible to preserve the language in a vacuum, no matter how many bilingual forms and signs were made available.

The early 1970s therefore witnessed a fundamental change in strategy as the emphasis shifted away from campaigning for specific rights. It became necessary to gather together the Society's aims and objectives in a single comprehensive document, and this resulted in the publication in 1972 of *Maniffesto Cymdeithas yr Iaith Gymraeg*. The *Maniffesto* placed the language issue in its wider historical context and carefully clarified the required minimum of 'revolutionary' conditions deemed necessary to ensure a revival in its fortunes. These included securing

---

[39] J. R. Jones, *Prydeindod* (Llandybïe, 1966), pp. 9–33.
[40] Dafydd Iwan, 'Anadl Einioes Cenedl', *Baner ac Amserau Cymru*, 4 December 1969.
[41] See *Y Cymro*, 27 May and 12 August 1970; *Western Mail*, 24 June and 6 August 1970.

equal legal and official status with English in courts of law, central and local government, and public bodies; bilingualism in commerce, business and advertising; priority for Welsh in the education system; an adequate radio and television service for Wales; and meeting local needs by protecting employment opportunities and homes in rural areas. The *Maniffesto* reflected the development and expansion of the Society's strategy, especially its new focus on safeguarding communities.[42]

In order to ensure the effective co-ordination of these new campaigns, a Senate was established in 1970, and a series of campaign groups became responsible for the various aspects of language activity, including status, education, broadcasting, planning and housing, and the economy. By this time, too, membership had increased to over two thousand, necessitating a strengthening of the Society's administrative structures. In October 1970 Ffred Ffransis was appointed its first full-time secretary, working as campaign organizer from an office above Siop y Pethe in Aberystwyth. However, by the mid-1970s the burden was such that two or three officers were required. Efforts to develop an effective administrative system were nevertheless frustrated by the inability to raise funds. Despite the assistance of many older supporters, the movement lurched from one financial crisis to another during the 1970s, and this severely restricted its potential achievements. Thus, although as many as twenty secretaries and regional organizers were employed during this period, the Society remained essentially a voluntary movement. The members themselves were responsible for strategy and direction and for constitutional and unconstitutional activities, and in the early 1970s, in an effort to facilitate campaigning in a large number of areas and to spread its message to a wider audience, the Society endeavoured to establish cells throughout Wales.[43]

The campaigns of the 1970s drew on the 1972 *Maniffesto* and increasingly focused on the socio-economic factors which were undermining the Welsh language. The Society thus transformed itself from a single-issue movement into a movement with a wider vision. For instance, it developed campaigns to secure housing and work with the aim of preserving the language. Dafydd Iwan argued that the language issue was inseparable from socio-economic issues, and that language and land were equally vital elements in the struggle for Wales.[44] In rural areas campaigns were mounted in opposition to second homes and in favour of powers which would enable the new Welsh counties to buy empty houses and let them to local people. Local authorities were urged to reject planning permission for the construction of large, unnecessary housing estates and to widen their planning policy to include culture and language statistics. They were also pressed

---

[42] Cynog Davies, *Maniffesto Cymdeithas yr Iaith Gymraeg* (Aberystwyth, 1972). For a translation of the 1972 Manifesto, see Harri Webb, 'Cymdeithas yr Iaith – the Manifesto', *Planet*, 26/27 (1974–5), 77–136.

[43] For a more detailed discussion on the organization and structure of the Society, see Phillips, *Trwy Ddulliau Chwyldro . . .?*, chapter 2.

[44] Dafydd Iwan, 'Byddwn yn Parhau'r Pysgota Anghyfreithlon', *Y Ddraig Goch*, April 1972, 3.

to create employment opportunities to stem the out-migration of young people from rural Wales, and energetic campaigns were conducted in industrial areas against the closure of plants and factories such as those at Shotton and Ebbw Vale. In 1975 the Society made its first concerted attempt to address educational issues, with the publication of *Addysg Gymraeg: Rhai Pynciau Trafod* (Welsh Education: Some Points of Discussion). At the general meeting that year it was announced that the Society's aim for the whole of Wales was the development of comprehensive Welsh-language and Welsh-orientated education from primary school to university.[45] It called for the provision of accelerated learning courses and centres for non-Welsh-speaking latecomers in order to combat the adverse impact of in-migration on the language of rural schools, and for a further education policy geared towards training young people for employment in their local communities. Courses and camps were organized for learners, a new campaign was launched to deal with the effects of tourism, and the status campaign was extended to target shops, banks and the private sector.

The success of these campaigns led to a minority backlash and the formation of anti-Welsh pressure groups which opposed equal status for the language and especially Welsh-language education. In 1973 George Thomas threatened to set up an 'English Language Society' to reverse the Society's achievements.[46] The Language Freedom Movement was formed by a circle of academics in Aberystwyth in May 1977 and Parents for Optional Welsh in 1978, the former to campaign against making Welsh a compulsory subject in schools and the latter to combat the language policy implemented in Gwynedd. In the 1990s, too, the establishment of Education First, a movement associated mainly with Dr Alan Williams, Labour MP for Carmarthen, aroused much ill feeling and resentment.[47] Although not campaigning directly against the Society, these movements were clearly founded in response to its successes and were bent on undermining the favourable attitudes towards Welsh nurtured since 1962.

Throughout the 1970s the Society was preoccupied with its broadcasting campaign and especially its campaign for a Welsh-language television channel. There was widespread concern that television was subverting the native language, with many hours of English entertainment and values assailing Welsh-speaking homes daily. The campaign was launched at the end of the 1960s when it was resolved to itensify efforts to secure bilingual radio and television licences and to

---

[45] NLW, Cymdeithas yr Iaith Gymraeg Papers 4/3. General meeting 1975.

[46] David Blundy, 'Welsh Nats out to Capture Labour Votes', *Sunday Times*, 7 January 1973. Some letters expressing support for Thomas's stand against the Welsh Language Society and interest in joining the proposed 'English Language Society' are to be found among George Thomas's personal papers. NLW, Papers of Viscount Tonypandy 48, 51, 56, 93, 115.

[47] 'Call for Language Ombudsman by Freedom Group', *Western Mail*, 3 June 1977; 'Parents Call for "Optional Welsh"', *Liverpool Daily Post*, 10 August 1978; 'Parents Group Formed as Labour Councillor Backs Review Demand', *Cardigan & Tivyside Advertiser*, 15 June 1990.

highlight the general lack of commitment towards Wales and the Welsh language on the part of the BBC. It was pointed out that the BBC radio service broadcast more hours in Arabic than in Welsh. Initially the campaign involved correspondence, petitions, public meetings and rallies, but in November 1968 the campaign intensified when BBC studios in Llandaff and Bangor were occupied in protest at the reluctance of the corporation to expand its Welsh-language service.[48] By the end of 1970 the campaign had extended beyond Offa's Dyke and in December that year traffic outside the BBC headquarters and studios in London was disrupted by activists seated in the middle of the main road and chanting 'Cymraeg ar yr Awyr' (Welsh on the Air) and 'Sianel Gymraeg yn Awr' (A Welsh Channel Now). The Society had also by this time clarified its demand for an improved broadcasting service in Welsh by insisting on the provision of two radio stations and two television channels (one in Welsh and the other in English), together with an independent broadcasting corporation, so that the whole of Wales might enjoy comprehensive coverage.[49]

For the remainder of the 1970s the campaign was characterized by mass protests, bold unconstitutional acts, and frequent unlawful deeds. Rallies and protests were held at the broadcasting centres of the BBC and HTV and at the offices of the Independent Broadcasting Authority; members scaled television transmitters and interfered with broadcasts; radio programmes were broadcast on the illegal wavelength 'Y Ceiliog' (The Cockerel); the proceedings of both the House of Commons and the House of Lords were disrupted; and television studios and broadcasting stations in Wales and England were broken into and equipment damaged. Some protesters paid a high price for their actions: more than fifty were incarcerated for periods varying from one night in a police cell to a year's imprisonment in an English prison. Several hundred people supported the campaign by refusing to pay their television licence; 250 separate cases were heard against 500 individuals for this particular offence between 1971 and 1981.[50] However, the most remarkable act of the whole campaign was the threat made by Gwynfor Evans in May 1980 to fast unto death unless the new Conservative government honoured its election pledge to establish a Welsh-language television channel. This announcement led to an escalation of the campaign throughout Wales and a determined effort by distinguished statesmen to persuade the government to set up the channel. The implications of the martyrdom of the president of Plaid Cymru were too profound for the government to bear, and accordingly it fulfilled its promise by drawing up a parliamentary Bill to establish

---

[48] See *Western Mail*, 30 November 1968; *Baner ac Amserau Cymru*, 5 December 1968.

[49] Cymdeithas yr Iaith Gymraeg, *Darlledu yng Nghymru: Cyfoethogi neu Ddinistrio Bywyd Cenedlaethol?/Broadcasting in Wales: To Enrichen or Destroy our National Life?* (Aberystwyth, 1970).

[50] For a detailed account of the campaign, see idem, *S4C – Pwy Dalodd Amdani? Hanes Ymgyrch Ddarlledu Cymdeithas yr Iaith* (Aberystwyth, 1985).

a Welsh-language television channel which would begin broadcasting in 1982.[51] A decade of unwavering and costly campaigning had secured for the Society its most famous victory.

The 1980s: Reconstruction and Consolidation

Despite its success in securing a Welsh-language television channel, the early 1980s was a period of comparative inactivity, the Society having expended much of its energy, time and resources during that relentless campaign. Some members continued to be penalized for previous actions. Wayne Williams was sentenced to nine months' imprisonment for conspiring (by virtue of his position as Society chairman between 1979 and 1981) to cause criminal damage to broadcasting stations in south-west England and was subsequently dismissed from his teaching post in Llanidloes. Membership fell to its lowest level since the mid-1960s, prompting some observers to suggest that the Society had lost direction. However, its predicament was not unique at this time. The entire national movement in Wales was afflicted by a general malaise following the bitter disappointment of the devolution referendum on St David's day 1979 and the election victory of the Conservative government of Margaret Thatcher.[52]

In recognition of the need to give its campaigning a new cutting edge, a second *Maniffesto* was published in 1982 clarifying the Society's main aim:

> In order to actively promote the revolutionary process of increasing and sharpening awareness, it was decided to write this new version of the Manifesto of Cymdeithas yr Iaith Gymraeg; the purpose of the Manifesto is to set out our policies and objectives as an organisation so as to encourage positive debate and purposeful action.

The leaders believed that the language could not survive on goodwill and symbolic status alone and that it was essential to ensure its use in all walks of Welsh life and to secure for it a healthy community basis.[53] To a large extent, the 1982 *Maniffesto* represented the culmination of the philosophical debate, conducted by the Society in the late 1970s, centred on its concept of 'Cymdeithasiaeth'. 'Cymdeithasiaeth' (a term originally used in the late

---

[51] See *Western Mail*, 18 September 1980; *Y Cymro*, 23 September 1980; *Liverpool Daily Post*, 2 October 1980; *Y Cymro*, 7 October 1980.

[52] John Davies, *A History of Wales* (London, 1993), pp. 678–81; Kenneth O. Morgan, *Rebirth of a Nation: Wales 1880–1980* (Oxford, 1981), pp. 405–7; Gwyn A. Williams, *When was Wales? A History of the Welsh* (London, 1985), pp. 296–300.

[53] Cymdeithas yr Iaith Gymraeg, *Maniffesto 1982* (English edition) (Aberystwyth, 1982), pp. 9, 100.

nineteenth century by R. J. Derfel for 'socialism') was an ambitious socio-economic ideal founded on decentralization, participative democracy, co-operation, and on social rather than commercial values. It was a reaction against capitalism and the centralizing policies of government and public authorities. But it was also a by-product of the Society's focus on the importance of community in the late 1960s.[54] The 1982 *Maniffesto* therefore assembled, in keeping with the principle of 'Cymdeithasiaeth', a series of policies and campaigns involving education, housing, tourism, linguistic and social planning, and the economy. Since the support of the material foundations of local communities was the main aim of the Society's housing, planning and economic policy, it was considered essential that local communities should exercise control over factors affecting their lives. Consequently, the Society's policies were distinguished by strong socialist overtones which bore witness to its growing political maturity since its inception in 1962. The *Maniffesto* stated:

> It was realised that the language cannot survive unless an economic and political order is established in Wales which is operated and administered in all its aspects according to Welsh socialist principles.

As the Welsh language continued to face economic and social problems involving second homes, the break-up of farms, the influx of newcomers to rural areas, the exodus of young people, the closure of schools, the effects of tourism, and the need for language planning, the Society became convinced that socialist policies were the only means by which suitable conditions for the growth of the language could be nurtured.[55]

The outcome of this new vision were several campaigns in support of the economic well-being of Welsh communities. The imposition of milk quotas and the agricultural crisis of the 1980s prompted the Society to become actively engaged in campaigns in support of farming interests, such as the opposition to the closure of dairies in Newcastle Emlyn in 1983 and Johnstown in 1986.[56] Society members were also prominent in their support of the 1984–5 miners' strike: they collected food and money for the miners and their families, provided holidays for their children, and held public meetings throughout Wales to explain the importance of protecting mining communities and thereby the language.

---

[54] For a more detailed discussion on the Society's political philosophy and strategy, see Phillips, *Trwy Ddulliau Chwyldro . . .?*, chapter 3.

[55] Cymdeithas yr Iaith Gymraeg, *Maniffesto 1982*, pp. 12–13, 101.

[56] NLW, Cymdeithas yr Iaith Gymraeg Papers 30. General meeting 1983. See also *Western Mail*, 25 June 1984, 9 August 1984, 15 and 29 January 1988, 8 and 13 February 1988.

Members also stood alongside pickets outside collieries at Aber-nant, Point of Ayr and Cynheidre.[57] Both farmers and miners appreciated the Society's support, although some observers were suspicious of its socialist motives. Its membership, after all, was predominantly middle class and it had failed to all intents and purposes, as in the past, to attract substantial working-class support. However, by becoming involved in the campaigns of the agricultural and mining communities the Society developed a deeper awareness of linguistic needs.

These forays did not mean that more familiar campaigns were abandoned. Following the publication of the 1982 *Maniffesto* the Society formulated a long-term programme, setting a series of targets to be achieved by the end of the decade. These included demands for a revised language act which would make full use of Welsh a requirement in all areas of public administration and service, the establishment of a new body of educational representatives with responsibility for developing Welsh-language education throughout the country, housing policies for local authorities based on the needs of the local community, and planning policies which gave full consideration to the needs and interests of the language.[58] Substantial administrative changes had also been made in order to enable the Society to carry out these campaigns effectively. Instead of employing two full-time secretaries based in Aberystwyth, one secretary and a national organizer were appointed from 1982 onwards to organize campaigns in the regions. The attempt to establish a network of cells in the 1970s had floundered due to their over-dependence on the enthusiasm of key individuals. The Society was therefore fortunate throughout the 1980s to benefit from the services of Jên Dafis and Helen Greenwood whose thoroughly professional approach placed the movement on a firm administrative footing. It also benefited from the contribution of intelligent and skilful chairpersons like Angharad Tomos, Toni Schiavone and Siân Howys, whose resolute leadership inspired members to campaign for the conditions essential for the preservation and development of the language, as outlined in the long-term work programme.

In the wake of the status campaigns of the 1960s and 1970s, the Society assembled all grievances concerning shortcomings in the language policies of central government, local authorities, public services and the private sector and integrated them into a single demand for a new language act. The need to press for new legislation to replace the inadequate 1967 Welsh Language Act had been identified as early as April 1975, but campaigning did not commence in earnest until after the publication of the 1982 *Maniffesto*. The Society's determination to

---

[57] NLW, Cymdeithas yr Iaith Gymraeg Papers 30. General meeting 1985. Tony Heath, 'Bridge over Troubled Water', *Radical Wales* (Winter 1984), 13; *Western Mail*, 19 August 1984; *Cambrian News*, 17 August 1984; *Liverpool Daily Post*, 27 February 1986; *Y Cymro*, 10 February 1988.

[58] NLW, Cymdeithas yr Iaith Gymraeg Papers 49.3. *Rhaglen Waith Dros Dymor Hir* (Aberystwyth, October 1982).

secure a parliamentary Bill granting equal status for both Welsh and English was strengthened by the laissez-faire attitude of the Conservative government towards the language. Nicholas Edwards, Secretary of State for Wales between 1979 and 1987, sweepingly declared at the commencement of the Conservatives' term in office that the survival of the language would be determined by the personal choice of the people of Wales rather than by parliamentary legislation.[59] The Society totally rejected this view, being convinced that it was the responsibility and duty of the government to intervene directly in language issues and embark on whatever action was required to preserve and promote it. In 1983 a booklet entitled *Llyfr Du ar Status* (Black Book on Status), which highlighted the short-comings of the 1967 Language Act and the inferior status of the Welsh language, was published and numerous campaigns were mounted throughout the 1980s to protest against the inadequate bilingual policies of Gwynedd Health Authority, British Rail, the Post Office and British Telecom. By the general meeting of 1986 the Society had published in draft its own new language act. The Conservatives, however, persevered with their policy despite growing support for a new act. Their sole concession was Peter Walker's decision in August 1988 to set up a Welsh Language Board (Bwrdd yr Iaith Gymraeg) to consult on the need for such a measure. This shrewd attempt by the government to subvert the demand for a new act was countered by an intensification of unconstitutional activity by the Society. Hundreds of members joined a popular campaign of daubing post boxes and telephone kiosks, thereby reviving the old frisson of the road signs campaign. Once more the older generation participated by painting slogans calling for a new language act on the walls of the Welsh Office in Cardiff, while younger members broke into government offices, scattering files and damaging equipment.[60] This reaction prompted the Prime Minister, Margaret Thatcher, to declare: 'Ultimately this sort of violence does nothing but harm to the image of Wales.'[61]

An equally forceful and bold campaign was waged on educational issues throughout the 1980s. The main efforts in this area from 1982 onwards centred on the demand for a Welsh-Language Education Development Body. This body (eventually established by the government as a 'Committee') would act as a national forum to co-ordinate the activities of all those working in the field of education, provide research and learning resources, and obtain and allocate funding to implement constructive policies designed to meet the needs of the language. The Society exercised its whole range of traditional campaigning techniques in pursuit of its aims: correspondence, petitions, lobbying, public

---

[59] The Welsh Office, *The Welsh Language. A Commitment and Challenge: The Government's Policy for the Welsh Language* (Cardiff, 1980).

[60] For an account of the campaign, see Cymdeithas yr Iaith Gymraeg, *Deddf Iaith Newydd: Yr Hanes 1983–1989* (Aberystwyth, 1989).

[61] 'PM's Fury at Blackmail', *Liverpool Daily Post*, 10 July 1990.

meetings and rallies, and direct action. A milestone in this campaign was the action of Meinir Ffransis, Lleucu Morgan and Dafydd Morgan Lewis, who, in 1984, broke into Conservative Party headquarters in Cardiff, causing £5,000 worth of damage to files, equipment and furniture, including a portrait of the Prime Minister.[62] Colleges of further education were also urged to increase their Welsh-medium provision; campaigns by parents in Glamorgan and Gwent for additional Welsh-language education were supported; the closure of rural schools was steadfastly opposed; and attempts were made to address the severe problems facing the education system in Welsh-language strongholds as a result of an influx of monoglot English-speaking children into local schools.

The housing and planning status campaigns were also developed. Members campaigned tirelessly against ambitious marina schemes and other tourist developments considered incompatible with local needs; resistance continued towards 'unnecessary' housing developments; and in 1987 a 'Nid yw Cymru ar Werth' (Wales is Not for Sale) working party was set up in order to highlight the problem of the purchase of houses, businesses and land in Wales by outsiders. Since house prices in Wales were much lower than in the affluent cities and counties of southeast England, the countryside experienced an unprecedented influx of newcomers during the economic boom of the mid-1980s. Local Welsh people were squeezed out of the housing market, thereby causing immense resentment. The Society called upon the government to control the housing market and to give priority to local people. To publicize their demands, they occupied second homes, daubed slogans on auction houses, and held 'For Sale' sign rallies throughout the country.[63] At the same time district councils were urged to draft detailed language plans, and a major victory was achieved in 1988 when the Welsh Office agreed to publish guidelines which granted local authorities the right to reject planning applications considered detrimental to the language.[64]

The 1990s: The End of the Struggle?

The early 1990s witnessed an increase in the tempo of unconstitutional action as three major and well-supported campaigns came to a head. By then, those who sought enhanced status for the Welsh language had become thoroughly frustrated

---

[62] For an account of the campaign, see Cymdeithas yr Iaith Gymraeg, *Yr Ergyd Gyntaf* (Aberystwyth, 1985).

[63] Idem, *For Sale. Na! Meddai CYIG – Nid yw Cymru ar Werth* (Aberystwyth, 1987).

[64] Responding to a parliamentary question by Dafydd Elis Thomas MP in October 1986, Wyn Roberts announced that it was appropriate for planning authorities to give planning status to the Welsh language. *Parliamentary Debates* (Hansard), 6th series, vol. 103, 8 Written Answers (27 October 1986). As a result, the Welsh Office issued *Circular 53/88. The Welsh Language: Development Plans and Planning Control* (Cardiff, 1988). See also Toni Schiavone, 'Cynllunio: Buddugoliaeth Llanrhaeadr', *Tafod y Ddraig*, 201 and 202, February and March 1988.

by the government's reluctance to respond to their call for a new language act. This victory was finally secured in 1993 when the Welsh Language Board was granted permanent statutory status and guidelines were announced compelling public bodies to draw up language plans giving Welsh equal validity with English in the operation of all their services. However, the Society was not satisfied and continued to call for a 'comprehensive Language Act'.[65] Having been exempted from the requirements of the 1993 Act, shops, banks and public utilities became a prime target. Pickets were organized, offices occupied, windows daubed and locks glued, especially in Cardiff where the city cell conducted a particularly effective campaign. The Education Group was forced to spend the first three years of the decade justifying the existence and continuation of the Welsh-Language Education Development Committee (WLEDC). Peter Walker decided that the Welsh Language Board should subsume the responsibilities of the WLEDC, resulting in its abolition in 1993 before it was able to achieve anything of note.[66] By the mid-1990s the education campaign was more concerned with the organization of the education system than its content, and under the slogan 'Trefn Addysg Deg' (A Fair Education System) the Society initiated a campaign of illegal action in support of its demand for an independent education system for Wales.[67] By the beginning of the decade the housing and planning campaigns had developed into a campaign for a 'Property Act for Wales'. Three fundamental principles lay at the heart of the demand for legislation in this area: housing and property should be considered a need rather than a commodity; access for local people to the current housing and property stock should be ensured; and house and property prices should reflect the local market.[68] In support of this campaign, members embarked on a series of illegal acts over the next two years, disrupting auctions, occupying second homes and picketing planning committee meetings.[69] To the government, however, a Property Act was anathema, since it challenged the Conservative Party's adherence to free market and laissez-faire principles.

This conflict between Thatcherite philosophy and the Society's emphasis on community led to the publication in 1992 of the movement's third *Maniffesto*. The Thatcherite and Conservative preoccupation with the private economy, competition and the interests of the individual were anathema to a movement which championed community politics, co-operation and democracy. It therefore developed a series of policies focused on status, education, housing and planning designed to challenge the Thatcherite 'Free Market' and advance the

---

[65] Cen Llwyd, 'Beth Nesaf? Deddf Iaith Newydd!', *Tafod y Ddraig*, 250, July–August 1993, 7.

[66] 'Diolch a Ffarwél – Bwffe ar Gael', ibid., 250, July–August 1993, 22–3.

[67] Cymdeithas yr Iaith Gymraeg, *Rhyddid i Gymru mewn Addysg* (Aberystwyth, 1994).

[68] Idem, *Llawlyfr Deddf Eiddo / Property Act Handbook* (Aberystwyth, 1992).

[69] Alun Llwyd and Branwen Niclas were imprisoned in 1991 for causing £15,000's worth of damage to government offices in Rhos-on-Sea. See *Western Mail*, 3 January 1991; *Liverpool Daily Post*, 5 January 1991; *Y Cymro*, 9 January 1991.

vision of the 'Free Community'. According to the Society, the 'existence of the most hostile British government ever to the whole concept of Welsh-speaking communities' was a major threat to the well-being of the native tongue. The Society's aim during the 1990s therefore was to offer Welsh people a simple choice between the 'Politics of the Free Market' and the 'Politics of the Free Community':

> The ability to use the language in every area of life is as much an expression of that freedom as is the right to a home or work in the community, and the right for a Welsh-medium education is part of the community's struggle for control of its own education system.[70]

However, the most important development to emerge from this clash of philosophies was the realization that the survival of the language depended on the creation of a new political order in Wales. In the past, the Society's two principal 'enemies' had been central and local government, and it was against these that it had directed all its campaigns and from these that it had elicited concessions. But by the early 1990s a new political order had been established in Wales which entrusted many of the responsibilities of central and local government to several quasi-independent bodies, or quangos, which acted on behalf of the government.[71] Since these quangos were responsible for the setting of objectives, the formulation of policy, and the allocation of funding in many spheres of public life, including the status of the language (Welsh Language Board), Welsh-language education (Curriculum and Assessment Authority for Wales), and housing and planning (Tai Cymru), they were considered to be legitimate targets for Society campaigns.

Thus, at the time of the publication of the 1992 *Maniffesto*, the campaigns in the fields of status, education, housing and planning had developed into a crusade against what was widely believed to be an undemocratic development: 'Our struggle is no less than an attempt to create democracy in Wales.'[72] The Society called for the establishment of democratic, elected bodies to replace the quangos so that the people of Wales might enjoy a more representative and accountable form of government. For the next two years intensive unconstitutional campaigns were organized to highlight the injustice of the system and members of the various quangos were urged to resign.[73] Not everyone was satisfied with this new approach and the Society was subjected to severe criticism for targeting members

---

[70] Cymdeithas yr Iaith Gymraeg, *Maniffesto 1992: A Vision of the Free Community* (Aberystwyth, 1992), pp. 1–9.

[71] See John Osmond, 'The Dynamic of Institutions' in idem (ed.), *The National Question Again: Welsh Political Identity in the 1980s* (Llandysul, 1985), pp. 225–55.

[72] Cymdeithas yr Iaith Gymraeg, *Maniffesto 1992*, p. 9.

[73] Idem, *Quangos: Dull y Toris o Reoli Cymru . . . a Sut i'w Chwalu* (Aberystwyth, 1993).

of the Welsh Language Board. Much of the Society's appeal focused on its reputation as a movement which campaigned against prominent targets embodying and perpetuating the injustices which threatened the future of the language. This explains the popularity of the mass campaigns against English-only road signs, in favour of a Welsh-language television channel, and against rural overdevelopment. Unlike road signs, however, quangos were not tangible targets, and the only means of campaigning against them was by daubing slogans on nondescript offices on the outskirts of the capital.[74]

The Society nevertheless persevered, declaring in a statement at the general meeting of 1994 that the aim of the struggle was to secure genuine democracy in Wales.[75] By 1995 members had come to the conclusion that only self-determination could guarantee that the needs of Wales and the Welsh language would be met. As a result, all campaigns were amalgamated under the slogan 'Rhyddid i Gymru' (Freedom for Wales). At the general meeting that year members were called upon to support the campaign for a Welsh Parliament.[76] In addition to continuing individual campaigns in support of 'freedom' within the education system and in the areas of language status, housing and planning, the Society held a rally in Cardiff in November 1996 where the imminent demise of the Conservative government was predicted.

Within six months the prophecy had been realized and in May 1997 a Labour government was returned to Westminster with a massive majority. The establishment of a Parliament for Wales was now an achievable aim, since devolution of central government power was a key element in Labour's election manifesto. Despite the Society's prominent role in Wales in highlighting the injustice of the quangos and deepening the unpopularity of the Conservative government, it decided not to launch a high-profile campaign in support of a Parliament for Wales. Advocates of devolution feared that the Society's association with their campaign would alienate non-Welsh speakers who regarded the Welsh language as a threat. However, many Society members canvassed tirelessly in the months before the referendum in support of the 'Yes for Wales' campaign, and in August the movement organized a national walk from Caernarfon to Cardiff under the slogan 'Mwy Nag Ie' (More Than Yes). Its aim was to call for a Welsh Parliament with greater powers than those offered by the Labour government, particularly the right to legislate and raise taxes, and with the will to act positively on behalf of the language.[77]

---

[74] The television programme, *Taro Naw*, broadcast 8 August 1994, discussed the direction of the Society's campaign against the quangos. For the response of Society leaders, see *Tafod y Ddraig*, 256, September 1994.

[75] NLW, Cymdeithas yr Iaith Gymraeg Papers 85.1. General meeting 1994.

[76] Ibid., General meeting 1995.

[77] Cymdeithas yr Iaith Gymraeg Office, Aberystwyth, Cymdeithas yr Iaith Gymraeg Papers, minutes of Senate meetings, 10 May 1997, 14 June 1997.

The Society had good cause to celebrate on 18 September 1997 when Welsh electors voted by a small majority to support the government's plans for the establishment of a National Assembly. In a special meeting of its Senate, held in January 1998, the Welsh Language Society publicly recognized that the establishment of the Assembly was one of the most significant events in its history.[78] The Society had been campaigning against the policies of a remote government in London since 1962, but it now had a new focal point for its activities in Cardiff. The advent of the Assembly was also likely to be an important development in the history of the Welsh language since it possessed the necessary powers and authority to formulate constructive policies and measures to safeguard and promote the language. When the Government of Wales Act was drawn up in 1998, it accorded full and equal status to Welsh and English in all Assembly systems and services.[79]

In the light of these astonishing developments, some maintained that the struggle for the language was over. The elevation of Welsh to an official national language within the Assembly, the establishment of a Welsh-language television channel and radio wavelength, the creation of a bilingual education system, full planning status for the language, and the existence of a statutory government body dedicated to the promotion of Welsh, all seemed to suggest that the Welsh Language Society had become redundant. It was argued that protest and unconstitutional action belonged to the past. Indeed, in August 1998, a former chairman of the Society (later appointed chairman of the Welsh Language Board) provocatively asserted that the movement no longer possessed the necessary intellectual resources to act in the interests of the language.[80]

The Society, however, viewed these momentous events as a golden opportunity to embark on a new phase in its history. It responded to its critics by streamlining its administration, employing new officers and opening a new office in Aberystwyth. The Senate held wide-ranging discussions regarding its aims and objectives and the role of the Society as a pressure group was considered. The most important development, however, was the planning of new campaigns and the publication of the *Agenda for the National Assembly: The Welsh Language in the Next Millennium?* in August 1998. In addition to outlining some of the main requirements of the language in the areas of public status, education, housing and planning, and the mass media, the *Agenda* called for guarantees that the Welsh

---

[78] Cymdeithas yr Iaith Gymraeg Office, Aberystwyth, Cymdeithas yr Iaith Gymraeg Papers, minutes of weekend Senate meeting, 9–11 January 1998. See also Angharad Tomos, 'Mae'r Cynulliad yn Cynnig Cyfle i Greu Gwell Ymdeimlad o Berthyn', *Yr Herald Gymraeg*, 17 January 1998.

[79] *Government of Wales Act 1998* (c. 38) (London, 1998), Part III, Section 47 (1–3), and *National Assembly Advisory Group Report to the Secretary of State for Wales, August 1998*, Section 4.1, recommendation 22.

[80] See *Western Mail*, 10 and 14 February 1998; ibid. (*Agenda*), 8 August 1998; *Tafod y Ddraig*, 3.1, Eisteddfod 1998.

language would lie at the heart of all activities in the Assembly. Although the document warned of the crisis still facing the language, its general tone was one of optimism and confidence. Siân Howys, the principal author of the document, declared:

> At the end of the twentieth century the state of the Welsh language is precarious, but there is nothing inevitable about its demise. With a government in Wales willing to adopt policies and act positively to further the interests of the Welsh language the language could then enjoy a prosperous future which would enrich the lives of the people and communities of Wales.[81]

This document reflected the degree to which the policies and campaigns of the movement had developed since 1962 and also the important changes which had occurred in the Welsh political scene. Throughout this period the Society had played a key role in the language politics of Wales and had succeeded in elevating the status of Welsh from one of subordination to official recognition as one of the country's two national languages. Its relentless campaigning had resulted in many significant gains, including official public bilingualism, a Welsh-language television and radio service, core status for Welsh in education, and planning status for the language. However, despite the importance of these gains in the struggle to preserve Welsh as a viable language, the success of the Society should not be measured in terms of the number of concessions wrested from the authorities. As Dafydd Iwan observed in 1974, the minor victories were less important than the impact made upon Welsh public opinion.[82] The prime objective of a pressure group such as the Welsh Language Society was to agitate and stimulate. By means of bold policies and unconstitutional action it compelled people to think about its *raison d'être*, namely, the need for aggressive and audacious action to safeguard the language. John Davies has stressed that the key aim initially was not to secure total victory in the matter of Welsh-language summonses but to draw attention to the plight of the language and thus motivate a generation of Welsh people to expect and insist upon the right to conduct their public business through the medium of their native tongue.[83] A vital element of the Society's work, therefore, was to urge the Welsh people themselves to embrace their mother tongue and to consider it their most valuable national asset.

The 'revolution' which Saunders Lewis had called for in *Tynged yr Iaith* in 1962 was a change of attitude towards the Welsh language by the Welsh people themselves. This could only be achieved by persuading them of its intrinsic value and the importance of safeguarding it. The Society never lost sight of this

[81] Cymdeithas yr Iaith Gymraeg, *Agenda for the National Assembly: The Welsh Language in the Next Millennium?* (Aberystwyth, 1998), p. 10.

[82] Dafydd Iwan, 'Pam y Safaf dros y Blaid', *Tafod y Ddraig*, 68, January 1974, 6.

[83] Davies, 'Blynyddoedd Cynnar Cymdeithas yr Iaith Gymraeg', p. 18.

objective: when the *Agenda* for the Assembly was presented to the members in 1998, they were reminded that nothing less than a revolution was required to undo the effects of centuries of oppression, deprivation of power and discrimination against the Welsh language.[84] Although the status of Welsh was far higher at the end of the twentieth century than it had been forty years previously, the Welsh Language Society resolved to continue its work and redouble its efforts. Indeed, a new slogan was adopted for the twenty-first century: 'Popeth yn Gymraeg – Y Gymraeg ym Mhopeth' (All for Welsh – Welsh for All).

---

[84] Cymdeithas yr Iaith Gymraeg, *Agenda for the National Assembly*, p. 10.

15

The Welsh Language Movement and Bilingualism: What Can Local Organizations Achieve?

MARION LÖFFLER

Anybody who learns a second language becomes to some degree bilingual, but the degree becomes significant only when he habitually uses two languages.[1]

THE END of the Second World War ushered in a period of far-reaching changes in the economic, social and political life of Wales. Rural depopulation went hand in hand with the diversification of industries in the urban areas, the decline of religion was more pronounced than in the inter-war years, and Labour replaced the Liberals as the predominant political party in the country. This brave new world offered new opportunities, but also posed new threats to the language. Through the electronic mass media, English influences penetrated deeply into areas where the Welsh language was the natural medium of communication and where English was seldom heard. As car ownership increased and more people had the time and financial means to travel, the same areas became favoured tourist destinations, and even places to set up a new home. As a result, the process of Anglicization accelerated and the number of communities with a large majority of Welsh speakers fell drastically.

In the wake of these developments, nationalist politics and the Welsh language movement were given a new lease of life: a variety of new philosophies were embraced, new objectives were pursued and new tactics employed, and the number of people involved in the movement increased. Building on foundations laid by cultural societies since the beginning of the twentieth century, the language movement grew faster in the fifty years between 1945 and 1995 than it had done in the two centuries from the foundation of the Honourable Society of Cymmrodorion in 1751 until the end of the Second World War. In the second half of the twentieth century every decade was marked by the emergence of new organizations which took campaigning for the Welsh language into every societal domain and constantly developed new ways of acting on its behalf.

---

[1] Bruce Pattison, 'Foreword' in W. R. Jones, *Bilingualism in Welsh Education* (Cardiff, 1966), p. xi.

Early attempts by Undeb Athrawon Cymreig (the Union of Welsh Teachers) (est. 1926) to further the use of Welsh in the field of education were taken up by several new societies. Individual efforts to found Welsh-speaking playgroups, begun before the Second World War, were centralized in 1971 with the emergence of Mudiad Ysgolion Meithrin (the Welsh-medium Nursery Schools Movement).[2] To further the use of Welsh in primary and secondary education, Undeb Cymdeithasau Rhieni Ysgolion Cymraeg (the Union for the Parents' Societies of Welsh Schools) was established in 1956 (since 1983 known as Rhieni dros Addysg Gymraeg, i.e. Parents for Welsh Education). It continues to act as a nationwide pressure group and supports parents who wish their children to receive Welsh-medium education.[3] In 1943 Welsh teachers founded a new national union, Undeb Cenedlaethol Athrawon Cymru (UCAC) (the National Union of Teachers in Wales).[4] In 1948 the Welsh Joint Education Committee was set up to develop teaching materials in the Welsh language and co-ordinate the activities of voluntary bodies.

Cymdeithas yr Iaith Gymraeg (the Welsh Language Society) was founded in 1962 and launched a series of non-violent campaigns of civil disobedience in defence of the Welsh language with the aim of raising its legal status to one of equality with English. Its philosophy soon widened to include questions such as the protection of indigenous Welsh-speaking communities and the creation of electronic mass media in the Welsh language.[5] Cefn was set up in 1985 to 'offer support to individuals – and to use the particular cases of wrongs to illustrate the underlying institutionalized discrimination against Welsh people and the Welsh language'.[6] It regularly espoused cases of Welsh speakers whose civil rights had been violated through discrimination against them for using the Welsh language.[7]

While designated Welsh schools brought the Welsh language within reach of children in Anglicized, mainly urban areas, it became obvious that increasing in-migration into rural Wales was threatening the Welsh language in areas which had previously counted as its strongholds. This led to the emergence of organizations searching for more fundamental answers to the problems of rural Wales, including the threat to its language. Adfer, founded in 1970, sought to re-establish a Welsh-speaking core in what was left of the heartland, but for various reasons its appeal remained limited.[8] Other ways of assisting in the revival of the rural economy and the Welsh language proved more successful. The 'designated Welsh language

---

[2] Catrin Stevens, *Meithrin: Hanes Mudiad Ysgolion Meithrin 1971–1996* (Llandysul, 1996).

[3] Rhieni dros Addysg Gymraeg, *Adroddiadau Blynyddol*, 1956–98.

[4] Mel Williams (ed.), *Hanes UCAC: Cyfrol y Dathlu* (Adran Lenyddiaeth UCAC, 1991).

[5] Dylan Phillips, *Trwy Ddulliau Chwyldro . . .? Hanes Cymdeithas yr Iaith Gymraeg, 1962–1992* (Llandysul, 1998).

[6] *Cefn – Pwy Ydym Ni / Who We Are* (n.p., n.d.).

[7] Eleri Carrog, 'Deg oed eleni . . . 1985–1995', *Asgwrn Cefn*, no. 3 (1995), 2–3.

[8] Emyr Llewelyn, *Adfer a'r Fro Gymraeg* (Pontypridd, 1976); idem, 'What is *Adfer?*' in Ian Hume and W. T. R. Pryce (eds.), *The Welsh and their Country* (Llandysul, 1986), pp. 244–52.

economic development agency', Menter a Busnes, was set up in 1989 with the brief 'to maximise the economic potential of Welsh speakers'.[9] In its wake came several regional successors, such as Menter Cwm Gwendraeth (1991) and Antur Teifi (1992). All of these conducted surveys to examine the relationship between the local economy and the Welsh language, assisted Welsh speakers in establishing businesses or developing them, and supported businesses in search of a bilingual policy.[10] Since 1990 Iaith Cyf has worked in the same field by synchronizing efforts through organizing workshops on the problems of minority regions, publishing theoretical and practical literature, and also offering practical help to businesses planning to adopt a bilingual policy.

Most of the above-mentioned organizations concentrated on improving the status of the Welsh language, while others aimed at directly furthering the use of Welsh as a community language. In 1947 Urdd Siarad Cymraeg (the League of Speaking Welsh) was founded, followed in 1965 by Undeb y Gymraeg Fyw (the Union of Living Welsh), to promote the use of Welsh among native speakers and learners. Both discovered that pre-war attitudes towards the Welsh language were changing, if slowly. Members of Urdd Siarad Cymraeg reported as follows in 1966:

> Ymunodd 168 o aelodau o'r newydd yn Eisteddfod Aberafan. Y syndod yw bod cynifer ohonynt o siroedd y gogledd. Bu cyfnod pan oedd sôn am U.S.C. yn y gogledd yn wallgofrwydd – roedd pawb yn chwerthin a gwneud sbort am ben 'Mudiad Saeson bach y De'. Hwyrach erbyn hyn fod rhai ym Môn ac Arfon wedi gweld nad ydy 'Statws' fawr o werth i iaith farw.[11]

> (168 new members joined at the Aberafan Eisteddfod. It is surprising how many of them are from the northern counties. There was a time when referring to U.S.C. in the north was madness – everyone laughed and poked fun at the 'Movement of the little English people of the South'. By now, however, several in Anglesey and Caernarfonshire have realized that 'Status' is of little value to a dead language.)

The main goal of Urdd Siarad Cymraeg was to convince Welsh speakers of the necessity of using their language in every domain of life and every social situation. To achieve this, Anglicized areas were called upon to set up *Seiadau Siaradwyr* (Speakers' Councils) in order to raise the language consciousness of Welsh speakers in those areas.[12] The Union of Living Welsh sought to support the

---

[9] 'Wales. Report by Adam Price, Project Manager, Menter a Busnes' in Llinos Dafis (ed.), *Economic Development and Lesser Used Languages: Partnerships for Action. September 24–26 1993, Proceedings* (Aberaeron, 1993), p. 89.

[10] Ibid.; Menter a Busnes / Iaith Cyf, *The Use of the Welsh Language in Businesses in Ceredigion: A Report on the Ceredigion District Council Project* (Aberystwyth, 1993).

[11] 'Urdd Siarad Cymraeg' in Aled Rhys Wiliam (ed.), *Arolwg 1966* (Abercynon, 1966), p. 73.

[12] 'Urdd Siarad Cymraeg' in R. Gerallt Jones (ed.), *Arolwg 1968* (Lerpwl, 1969), pp. 65–6.

language, especially in rural areas, by holding popular events, lobbying for its use in the public domain and in education at every level and co-operating with other organizations. It collected and published lists of Welsh words, installed a learners' column in *Y Cymro*, organized Welsh-language classes, and attempted to establish a regular magazine for learners.[13] By the early 1970s, however, its activities were largely confined to Anglesey and its annual flower show.[14]

The second half of the twentieth century also witnessed the emergence of the 'Welsh learner'. This was accompanied by an exploration of new ways of teaching Welsh, especially to adults. Local circles and groups connected with Merched y Wawr (lit. Daughters of the Dawn) and other organizations were set up to help learners use their newly-acquired skills in social situations. In 1974 those efforts were given a national framework with the foundation of Cyd-bwyllgor Dysgwyr Cymraeg (now known as Cyngor y Dysgwyr (CYD) – Welsh Learners' Council).[15] In 1997 CYD ran 85 local branches nationwide.[16] From the 1980s language centres, such as Nant Gwrtheyrn on the Llŷn peninsula, were established to offer residential courses as well as Welsh-language activities and holidays.

The two most long-standing and important societies providing Welsh-language activities within the local community were Urdd Gobaith Cymru (the Welsh League of Youth) and Merched y Wawr. The former, an organization for Welsh-speaking children, was founded by Ifan ab Owen Edwards in 1922 to counter the influence of movements such as the Boy Scouts and Girl Guides, and it reached its heyday just before the Second World War.[17] Unlike numerous other youth organizations in Britain in the inter-war years, it was able to maintain its membership at a relatively high level after the Second World War. This was partly because of its close connection with schools, but it was also the result of the readiness with which the organization reacted to and adopted contemporary cultural developments. In July 1997, 49,015 Welsh children and teenagers were registered as members of Urdd Gobaith Cymru. They were distributed as shown in Table 1.

Ironically, the first Women's Institute (WI) in Great Britain was founded at Llanfair Pwllgwyngyll in Anglesey.[18] The Institutes proved phenomenally popular, and the fact that the wives, daughters and grand-daughters of well-known personalities, such as Anita George (wife of William George), Gwenllian Morris-Jones (daughter of John Morris-Jones) and Mrs W. E. Jones (grand-daughter of John Elias, the revered preacher), were involved in the movement

---

[13] 'Cornel y Dysgwyr', *Y Cymro*, 6 January 1966; *Siarad*, nos. 1–2 (1969–70).

[14] Dafydd Glyn Jones, 'The Welsh Language Movement' in Meic Stephens (ed.), *The Welsh Language Today* (Llandysul, 1973), pp. 296–7.

[15] Bobi Jones (ed.), *Cyd yn Cydio: Deng Mlynedd yn Hanes y Mudiad i Oedolion sy'n Adfer yr Iaith ar Wefusau Pobl mewn Oed 1984–1994* (Aberystwyth, 1994).

[16] *Cadwyn CYD*, no. 27 (1997), 5.

[17] R. E. Griffith, *Urdd Gobaith Cymru: Cyfrol I. 1922–1945* (Aberystwyth, 1971).

[18] Constance Davies, *A Grain of Mustard Seed: An Account of the Founding of the First Women's Institute in Great Britain, with Extracts from its Minute Books* (Bangor, 1954).

Table 1. The distribution of Urdd Gobaith Cymru members, 1997

Area	Members
Mid Glamorgan	5630
Myrddin	5261
Gwent	4603
Swansea	4111
Eryri (Snowdonia)	3974
Ceredigion	3895
Cardiff	3326
Flint Maelor	2949
Pembroke	2914
Conwy	2902
Anglesey	2676
Denbigh	2325
Montgomery	2114
Meirionnydd	1401
South Powys	917
Outside Wales	17
Total	**49015**

Unpublished statistics of Urdd Gobaith Cymru membership. Courtesy of Deian Creunant and Tomos Davies, Urdd Gobaith Cymru, Aberystwyth.

lent it credibility.[19] However, local officials more often than not did not speak Welsh, surviving programmes and lists of lecturers are predominantly in English, and English was the official language of the movement. Although fears were voiced throughout the period that the WIs were Anglicizing Welsh women, all attempts at founding an alternative society foundered. Following the Second World War, both Plaid Cymru and Undeb Cymru Fydd (the New Wales Union) were aware of the problem and endeavoured to rectify it by publishing regular women's columns in papers such as *Y Ddraig Goch*. From 1958 onwards *Y Cymro* contained a supplement entitled *Tŷ Ni*, edited by the women's section of Undeb Cymru Fydd. In April 1956 the members organized a conference to devise ways and means of safeguarding Welsh culture in the home, in schools, and in other existing movements.[20] As a first step towards this end *Llythyr Ceridwen*, a quarterly news bulletin, was published from December 1957. In the second issue, Kate Roberts again stressed the need for a secular society for Welsh women:

[19] Gwenllian Morris-Jones, 'Women's Institutes', *The Welsh Outlook*, XX, no. 9 (1933), 239–41; Davies, *A Grain of Mustard Seed*, p. 79; Dorothy Drage, *The Growth of Women's Institutes in Wales* (Caernarfon, 1956), p. 7.
[20] 'Cynhadledd Aberystwyth, Ebrill 1956', *Llythyr Ceridwen*, no. 1 (December 1957), 1.

Mae cymdeithasau felly yn bod mewn llawer lle, megis Sefydliadau'r Merched a chymdeithasau chwiorydd mewn capeli. Eithr mae i'r cymdeithasau hyn eu hanfanteision er cystal ydynt. Yn Saesneg y cynhelir y rhan fwyaf o gyfarfodydd Sefydliadau'r Merched yng Nghymru, hyd yn oed mewn ardaloedd hollol wledig ac ardaloedd Cymreig . . . Mae gweithgarwch cymdeithasau chwiorydd y capeli wedi ei gyfyngu yn naturiol i waith y capel, a phrin y disgwyliem iddynt ymddiddori ym mhob dim sydd a wnelo â'n bywyd fel Cymry. Credaf felly y byddai'n beth da ffurfio cymdeithasau Cymraeg i ferched ymhob tref a phentref drwy Gymru.[21]

(Societies such as these exist in many places, like the Women's Institutes and the sisterhoods of the chapels. But there are disadvantages to these societies, despite their good work. Most of the meetings of the Women's Institutes are held in English, even in rural areas of Wales and communities which are thoroughly Welsh . . . The activities of the sisterhood societies of the chapels are of necessity restricted to the work of the chapel, and we can hardly expect them to be interested in everything connected with our life as Welsh people. I believe, therefore, that it would be a good thing to form Welsh societies for women in every town and village in Wales.)

A dozen or so local societies were formed, mainly to organize Welsh-language classes and circles where learners could meet native speakers, and to act as local pressure groups for the Welsh language.[22] Yet *Cylchoedd y Merched* (Women's Circles) were a far cry from a national organization for Welsh-speaking women. In March 1967 *Tŷ Ni*, already reduced from an eight-page supplement to a column, disappeared from *Y Cymro*, and by spring 1968 it was clear that both *Llythyr Ceridwen* as well as *Hon*, an ambitious but short-lived magazine for Welsh women, had failed in their attempts to gain nationwide support. Welsh-speaking women once again seemed to have retreated into the home and the Women's Institute.

At this point, however, a new movement was launched which would capture the imagination of the nation in the same way as the foundation of Urdd Gobaith Cymru had done in 1922. On 25 November 1965 a Women's Institute was set up in Parc, a small village near Bala. Like other branches in the area it was granted permission to use Welsh in its meetings. However, with the exception of the badge 'Sefydliad y Merched – Women's Institute', all administrative material, including the north Wales edition of the organization's magazine *Home and Country*, remained in English.[23] Proposals to include some Welsh reports in the magazine were rejected. The new branch therefore decided to withhold membership payments until it received Welsh forms, and informed the county

---

[21] Kate Roberts, 'Cymdeithasau Merched', ibid., no. 2 (St David's day, 1958), 1.

[22] 'Nodion o'r Canghennau', ibid., no. 27 (1967), 25–8.

[23] The WI did not publish a separate Welsh edition of its magazine *Home and Country*. Welsh women were catered for in the *North Wales Edition* and the *Hereford, Monmouth and South Wales Edition*.

Table 2. The distribution of Merched y Wawr members, 1996

Area	Members
Ceredigion	1301
Carmarthen, Llanelli, Dinefwr	1009
Meirionnydd	771
Anglesey	670
Dwyfor	574
Caernarfon	511
Glyn Maelor	473
Colwyn	457
Montgomery, Powys	445
West Glamorgan	440
Aberconwy	426
Pembroke	350
South and Mid Glamorgan, Gwent	291
Alun Dyfrdwy	202
Total	**7920**

Unpublished statistics. Courtesy of Eleri Non Griffiths, Merched y Wawr.

organization that it did not believe Welsh members should contribute towards the production of English-only leaflets. This led to the exclusion of the Parc branch from the ranks of the WI in December 1966. After a short period as an independent institute, its members decided to form a women's organization which would use the Welsh language in all its proceedings. The notion was canvassed at the annual conference of the women's section of Undeb Cymru Fydd at Llansannan in May 1967 and at the National Eisteddfod held at Bala in August 1967. By that time, the new organization had been named Merched y Wawr and a second branch had been formed at Ganllwyd, near Dolgellau.[24] By the end of 1967 the new movement had fourteen branches, by 1968 it boasted fifty-four and by the end of its second year, in 1969, there were more than ninety branches.[25] From its inception, the sole aim of Merched y Wawr was to further Welsh culture and the Welsh language by offering members of local branches activities through the medium of Welsh. Its magazine, *Y Wawr*, first published for members in 1968, had a circulation of about 7,920 in 1996, but in the 1970s and 1980s that figure exceeded 10,000. It is interesting to note that Merched y Wawr was established only a few miles from the birthplace of the founder of the Urdd. It is also striking that the distribution of the branches of both movements remains

---

[24] Zonia Bowen, *Merched y Wawr: Y Dyddiau Cynnar* (Y Bala, 1977).
[25] 'Merched y Wawr' in Jones (ed.), *Arolwg 1968*, p. 81; 'Merched y Wawr' in Ednyfed Hudson Davies (ed.), *Arolwg rhif 5* (Lerpwl, 1970), p. 65.

similar, although Merched y Wawr is largely confined to rural areas. In January 1996, 7,920 members of Merched y Wawr were distributed as shown in Table 2.

From the outset, both Urdd Gobaith Cymru and Merched y Wawr emphasized their importance as community organizations, providing leisure activities through the medium of Welsh in communities throughout Wales. In order to assess their place and that of other cultural groups *in situ*, it was decided to conduct a survey of Merched y Wawr and Urdd Gobaith Cymru in Aberaeron and Fishguard, two small towns in Cardigan Bay. These two communities were chosen for several reasons. Both are small seaside towns serving as 'local centres dominating strictly limited and immediate rural areas' and relying on a restricted range of employment, mainly administrative in Aberaeron and mainly transport-based in Fishguard.[26] The rural hinterlands which they serve have a higher percentage of Welsh speakers than the towns themselves. However, since the towns developed during different periods, their linguistic profile varied considerably.

Aberaeron hardly existed as a town until the Revd Alban Thomas Jones Gwynne decided to build a harbour and town there in 1807. Once the harbour was completed, the town grew swiftly and became a centre for shipbuilding and seafaring, especially during its heyday between 1845 and 1883.[27] However, with the development of steam-driven boats and the arrival of the railway in Cardiganshire, Aberaeron lost its importance as a centre for trade and shipbuilding and its growth was halted. Between 1921 and 1961 the population (3 years and over) decreased every decade until the first wave of in-migration into rural Wales commenced and the number of inhabitants began to increase once again, from 1,167 in 1961 to 1,460 in 1991. The fact that the hinterland of Aberaeron has traditionally been one of the most Welsh-speaking areas of Wales and that population figures for the town remained fairly constant until the second half of the twentieth century undoubtedly contributed to its robust Welsh character. We shall see, however, how recent waves of in-migration have influenced its linguistic profile. According to the 1991 census, 1,040 (71.3 per cent) of the inhabitants of Aberaeron were bilingual, and only 419 people (28.7 per cent) were returned as English monoglots.[28]

Fishguard was first mentioned as a market town in Speed's *Atlas* of 1611, but did not experience major development until the beginning of the twentieth century. Although close to the *Landsker*, it remained largely Welsh-speaking throughout the nineteenth century, as the results of the 1891 census clearly

---

[26] Harold Carter, *The Towns of Wales: A Study in Urban Geography* (Cardiff, 1965), pp. 83, 107, 110.

[27] J. M. Howell, 'The Birth and Growth of Aberayron', *Transactions of the Cardiganshire Antiquarian Society*, 4 (1926), 7–14; W. J. Lewis, *Aberaeron* (Aberaeron, 1988), pp. 8–16; Lewis Cozens, *Aberayron Transport* (London, 1957), p. 5.

[28] General Register Office, Census 1961, Wales (including Monmouthshire), *Report on Welsh Speaking Population* (London, 1962), p. 5; *The 1991 Census on CD-ROM* (Cambridge, 1994), Table 67.

demonstrate.[29] The harbour was home to a local shipbuilding and fishing industry, and little movement of population seems to have occurred. However, long-standing plans for a harbour-extension were put into practice at the beginning of the twentieth century. The steamship connection with Rosslare in Ireland was opened in 1906, followed in 1911 by the opening of the railway to London.[30] These developments rapidly changed the character of the town. Between 1901 and 1911 its population (aged 3 and over) increased by some 65 per cent, from 1,602 to 2,656. During the same period, the percentage of Welsh speakers fell from 90.3 per cent to 74.7 per cent, while the percentage of monoglot English speakers rose steeply from 9.7 per cent to 25.3 per cent.[31] From then onwards, the town of Fishguard grew with its harbour. The consistent increase in popu-lation was accompanied by a fall in the number of Welsh speakers and a con-comitant rise in the number of monoglot English speakers. By 1991 the majority of the 3,042 inhabitants of Fishguard spoke English only (1,845 or 60.7 per cent), while 1,197 people (39.3 per cent) were bilingual.[32]

In 1991 the two communities occupied opposite poles of the bilingual con-tinuum: Aberaeron with 70 per cent of its population returned as Welsh speakers and Fishguard with over 60 per cent returned as monoglot English speakers. This made it possible to measure how and to what extent language choice was influenced by membership of different organizations, and also by the different linguistic environments within the range of the bilingual continuum. In order to gain a more detailed picture of the current linguistic situation in both commu-nities, local newspapers were studied, key individuals were interviewed, and questionnaires were distributed to members of the societies under examination. As control groups for the Welsh cultural organizations Urdd Gobaith Cymru and Merched y Wawr, the following were included in the survey: the WIs in both towns; the School Club in Aberaeron, and the Young Farmers' Club in Fishguard. In all cases, questionnaires were distributed and members interviewed.

In some aspects, the fieldwork was easier than expected, in others more complex. The 'language question' was found to be a sensitive issue for many people, whatever their mother tongue. However, the fact that the researcher was neither Welsh nor English by birth was an advantage, except in the case of some monoglot English speakers for whom her fluency in the Welsh language alone gave rise to a defensive attitude. The complexity of the situation may be illustrated by some reactions during a meeting of the WI in Aberaeron. Having distributed

---

[29] Gwenfair Parry, 'Fishguard' in eadem and Mari A. Williams, *The Welsh Language and the 1891 Census* (Cardiff, 1999), pp. 237–53.

[30] Great Western Railway, *Fishguard, the Ocean Port: Its History, Situation, Development, Facilities and Advantages* (London, 1911); David John Owen, *The Origin and Development of the Ports of the United Kingdom* (London, 1939), pp. 273–4.

[31] Census of England and Wales, 1911, *Vol. XII, Language Spoken in Wales and Monmouthshire* (London, 1913), p. 46.

[32] *The 1991 Census on CD-ROM*, Table 67.

questionnaires to members, the objectives of the research were explained and the audience invited to ask questions:

A very old woman in the front row remarked that they [the members] spoke English out of politeness; even when everybody, except two or three people, were Welsh-speaking, one would speak English to be polite. At which point a younger and fashionably dressed woman in the front row replied that maybe they had been too polite for too long. A woman in the centre of the room asked whether she should fill in a questionnaire as well, because she did not speak Welsh. I said that I wanted the English speakers, too, otherwise they would not be represented. And besides, maybe her parents or her children spoke Welsh. To which she replied that there was 'zilch' Welsh in the family, and added that in her experience Welsh speakers were not always that polite and that she had been in a situation where she had introduced a speaker and then everybody spoke Welsh and she could not understand a thing. She found that very rude. She went on to say that she had taught Welsh to children in south Wales as a peripatetic teacher. I replied that she must have some knowledge of the language if she had taught it. She said yes, but she could not speak it. I asked her whether she had the impression at that time that the children she was teaching were making progress. She said yes, they were coming on great, considering most of them came from families with no Welsh.

Someone asked whether I spoke Welsh. I replied: 'Odw. Wy'n siarad Cymrâg.' A murmur went through the rows. Another woman said, 'Ugh, you are stirring up something here' . . . Then the president thanked me, wished me well . . . and asked whether I thought in Welsh . . . several members remarked it was clear that I thought in Welsh from the way I spoke English.[33]

The range of reactions indicated the ambiguous attitudes of native Welsh speakers towards their language in the company of presumed non-Welsh speakers as well as the defensive attitudes adopted by some monoglot English speakers. Similar attitudes and reactions would be encountered again and would also be underlined by the statistics.

During fieldwork, 185 bilingual questionnaires were distributed to members of the societies present in their respective meetings, i.e. 62 per cent of the total membership, of which replies were received from 99 members, representing 33 per cent of the total membership and 54 per cent of those present at the meetings. An analysis of the membership figures and the age structure of the societies gave an initial impression of vitality. According to their secretaries, the Aberaeron branch of Merched y Wawr had thirty-seven members, and the WI forty-five, while at Fishguard, Merched y Wawr boasted twenty members and the WI forty. The Aberaeron branch of Merched y Wawr was by far the youngest of the women's societies, but its membership was not as numerous as one might expect

---

[33] Field notes, 8 January 1997.

since over half the members of the local WI, which functioned through the medium of English, were Welsh speakers. Most of these women were already members of the Aberaeron WI (est. 1935) when Merched y Wawr was first established in the town in 1967. In Fishguard the membership of both societies had been declining and members were older, on average, than those at Aberaeron. This might be due to the fact that the town of Fishguard offered a wider range of leisure activities than Aberaeron. Membership of Merched y Wawr had already fallen to around twenty, and although the average age of members was below that of WI members, its days seemed numbered.

Table 3. The linguistic background of members of Merched y Wawr and the Women's Institute in Aberaeron and Fishguard

Language of parents	MyW 1		MyW 2		WI 1		WI 2	
	Number	%	Number	%	Number	%	Number	%
W1st + W1st	7	100.0	7	87.5	5	33.3	2	16.7
W2nd + W1st	–	–	1	12.5	–	–	–	–
Non-W + W1st	–	–	–	–	5	33.3	–	–
W2nd + W2nd	–	–	–	–	–	–	–	–
Non-W + W2nd	–	–	–	–	1	6.7	1	8.3
Non-W + Non-W	–	–	–	–	4	26.7	9	75.0

MyW 1: Aberaeron Merched y Wawr; MyW 2: Fishguard Merched y Wawr; WI 1: Aberaeron Women's Institute; WI 2: Fishguard Women's Institute.
W1st: native speakers of Welsh; W2nd: second-language speakers of Welsh; Non-W: non-Welsh speakers.

Membership of the youth organizations tended to fluctuate, largely because of the nature of such groups and because leaders needed to secure a steady supply of new members. The Urdd branch and the School Club, both at the comprehensive school in Aberaeron, did not keep membership statistics, but estimated that they had around forty members each in 1997.[34] The membership of the Urdd branch at Fishguard High School was less constant. In 1994, when the Urdd National Eisteddfod was held in the area, membership rose to about 120, a fact which demonstrates the importance of the festival as a Cymricizing influence. The branch usually boasted around sixty members, but membership had dropped to

---

[34] However, Urdd Gobaith Cymru central statistics give 115 members for Aberaeron Comprehensive School in 1997–8. According to two members of the Aberaeron School Club no more than sixteen pupils were members of their society, all of whom received questionnaires. See interviews with respondents 2/19 and 2/20. However, percentages have been calculated on the basis of the official figures.

Table 4. The linguistic background of members of youth organizations in Aberaeron and Fishguard

Language of parents	Urdd 1		YFC		Urdd 2		SC	
	Number	%	Number	%	Number	%	Number	%
W1st + W1st	14	93.3	5	71.4	8	34.8	2	18.2
W2nd + W1st	–	–	1	14.3	4	17.4	–	–
Non-W + W1st	–	–	1	14.3	1	4.3	–	–
W2nd + W2nd	1	6.7	–	–	3	13.0	1	9.1
Non-W + W2nd	–	–	–	–	2	8.7	2	18.2
Non-W + Non-W	–	–	–	–	5	21.7	6	54.5

Urdd 1: Urdd Gobaith Cymru Aberaeron; Urdd 2: Urdd Gobaith Cymru Fishguard;
YFC: Fishguard Young Farmers' Club; SC: Aberaeron School Club.
W1st: native speakers of Welsh; W2nd: second-language speakers of Welsh; Non-W: non-Welsh speakers.

about thirty by 1996–7.[35] The leader of the group was unable to explain this decrease. Membership of the Fishguard Young Farmers' Club had also been falling and in 1996–7 it had 48 members. As with the women's organizations, the decline in membership might be connected to the growing urbanization of the town and the wider range of leisure activities on offer.

The linguistic background of the membership sample reveals that Merched y Wawr at Aberaeron and Fishguard comprised almost exclusively native speakers whose parents also spoke Welsh (Table 3). This partly accounts for the difficulties of Fishguard Merched y Wawr in attracting new members, since the linguistic background of its Welsh speakers was increasingly mixed, as the sample of the younger speakers indicates. As Table 3 shows, very few of the women who had been brought up in families with only one Welsh-speaking parent emerged as Welsh speakers. Of those who had been brought up in homes where only one parent spoke Welsh, 75 per cent had used 'English only' at home, 12.5 per cent had used both languages and only 12.5 per cent had used 'Welsh only'. Bearing in mind that hardly any Welsh-medium education was available when those members were of school age, and that there was no tradition of teaching Welsh as a second language, it is not surprising that children of mixed marriages tended not to become Welsh speakers. Among the younger generation, a different and more complex situation emerged (Table 4).

The percentage of members from totally Welsh-speaking families was highest among members of the Urdd at Aberaeron and the Fishguard Young Farmers' Club.

---

[35] These are the figures given by the local teacher. Urdd Gobaith Cymru central statistics give 88 members for Fishguard High School in 1997–8.

Table 5. The percentage of members of different linguistic ability who chose to answer their questionnaire in Welsh

Linguistic competence in Welsh	MyW1	MyW2	WI 1	WI 2	Urdd 1	Urdd 2	YFC	SC
W1st	100.0	100.0	50.0	0.0	100.0	88.9	42.9	0.0
W2nd	–	–	0.0	–	100.0	25.0	–	0.0
fairly well	–	–	0.0	–	–	0.0	–	0.0
a little	–	–	0.0	0.0	–	0.0	–	0.0

A dash indicates that there was no member in the respective linguistic category. Otherwise, percentages are given.

MyW 1: Aberaeron Merched y Wawr; MyW 2: Fishguard Merched y Wawr; WI 1: Aberaeron Women's Institute; WI 2: Fishguard Women's Institute; Urdd 1: Urdd Gobaith Cymru Aberaeron; Urdd 2: Urdd Gobaith Cymru Fishguard; YFC: Fishguard Young Farmers' Club; SC: Aberaeron School Club.
W1st: native speakers; W2nd: fluent second-language speakers.

Both societies seemed to provide a focal point for native Welsh speakers. However, while all the activities of the Urdd branch at Aberaeron were naturally conducted in Welsh, thus providing an ideal forum for young people to socialize in the native language, English was the official language of Fishguard Young Farmers' Club. Neither observation nor interviews led to a satisfactory estimate of how much Welsh was actually used at the Club, but English certainly had pride of place. Most of the meetings attended by the researcher were conducted in English, with some Welsh conversation before and afterwards. Members' accounts were contradictory.[36] The mixed linguistic background of members of the Urdd at Fishguard underlined parents' efforts to provide their children with an opportunity to maintain or regain a Welsh cultural background. The Aberaeron School Club was the most 'English' of the youth groups, although situated in a very Welsh community. This points to a linguistic divide within the school, a fact mentioned by all of the young people interviewed.[37]

All members present in a chosen meeting of the above societies were invited to complete the bilingual questionnaires in their preferred language, to add anything they felt to be of importance and also to indicate whether they would be willing to be interviewed later. The addenda, together with field notes and interviews, were used to supplement the statistics assembled with the help of the questionnaire. The language chosen to complete the questionnaire indicated what

[36] See, for instance, interviews with respondents 2/38 and 2/51.
[37] Interviews with respondents 2/15, 2/19 and 2/20.

later analyses would underline time and again, namely that language ability cannot be equated with language use, even where Welsh is the majority language. Overall, 78 per cent of native Welsh speakers chose to fill their questionnaire in Welsh, but of the second-language speakers, only 17 per cent of those claiming to be fluent did so. All those who indicated that they spoke Welsh fairly well or a little chose to answer in English, although later interviews revealed that some of them were actually fluent in the language.

Within the ranks of native speakers, choice of language was heavily influenced by cultural affiliations as well as the linguistic character of their community. As Table 5 shows, all members of Merched y Wawr at Aberaeron and Fishguard, and of the Urdd at Aberaeron, as well as most native speakers of the Urdd at Fishguard filled their questionnaire in Welsh. On the other hand, only 43 per cent of the native speakers of the Fishguard Young Farmers' Club used Welsh. Of the whole sample, only two fluent second-language speakers, both members of the Urdd, one in Aberaeron and one in Fishguard, filled the questionnaire in Welsh. All other second-language speakers who were members of the Urdd at Fishguard, i.e. 58 per cent of the membership sample, chose English. So did all native and second-language speakers of the Aberaeron School Club, and all members of the Fishguard WI. This indicates that the relationship between linguistic ability and language use becomes especially tenuous in the case of second-language speakers.

The home and family life are generally recognized as the most important influences in ensuring language transmission from one generation to the next in minority language situations. The language used with family members of different generations will therefore be considered first, before examining how much Welsh was used with friends, in local clubs and societies, and on social occasions within the respective community. Finally, a comparison will be made of speakers' attitudes towards the Welsh language as expressed through their linguistic behaviour while initiating conversations and in the presence of people presumed to be monoglot English speakers.

In order to gain information about language use within the family, members of all societies were asked to indicate whether they used 'Welsh all or most of the time', 'Welsh and English', or 'English all or most of the time' with family members of their parents' generation, their own generation and, in the case of the women's organizations, their children. The overall picture which emerged indicated that the main factors governing the use of Welsh within the family was the presence of native Welsh speakers and, to a lesser extent, the strength of Welsh in the surrounding community. The findings will therefore be presented first for the native speakers of Welsh and then for the second-language speakers.

Of the members of women's societies, it was found that 96 per cent of the native speakers in the sample were married to people of a similar linguistic background. When addressing the older generation in their families, 88 per cent used Welsh all or most of the time, 4 per cent used Welsh and English, and 4 per cent used English all the time. Those who did not use Welsh all the time with the older generation were either married to a second-language speaker or lived in Fishguard. With relatives of their own generation 90 per cent of Merched y Wawr members at Aberaeron and Fishguard, as well as the native speakers of the Aberaeron WI, used Welsh all or most of the time, while native speakers in Fishguard WI tended to use Welsh and English. With their children, 91 per cent of the sample claimed to use Welsh all or most of the time, while 9 per cent used Welsh and English.[38] It can safely be stated that Welsh was the principal medium of communication in most of the families of native Welsh speakers in the women's sample.

Of those members of the sample who spoke Welsh as a second language, either fluently, fairly well, or a few words only, 90 per cent were married to native speakers of Welsh. This group can therefore be taken to provide a fair indication of language use in families where the male partner is a native Welsh speaker. With the older generation of their families, 10 per cent of the members of this sample used Welsh most of the time, 30 per cent used both languages, but 60 per cent used English all or most of the time. With their own generation, 30 per cent used both languages, with 70 per cent using English all or most of the time. Only 29 per cent of the sample used Welsh and English with the younger generation, while 71 per cent used English all or most of the time. Yet, significantly, 71 per cent of them stated that their children were fluent Welsh speakers, although only 14 per cent were described as native Welsh speakers.

The pattern of language use within the families of the youth organization members showed similar characteristics. All the native speakers of the Urdd at Aberaeron used Welsh all the time with their mother, father and siblings, who were all native speakers. The two native speakers of the Aberaeron School Club used Welsh all or most of the time at home. In comparison, only 77 per cent of the native speakers of the Urdd at Fishguard used Welsh only with parents and siblings, while the remaining members used Welsh and English, or mostly English. Of all the members of Fishguard Young Farmers' Club, 71 per cent used only Welsh with their fathers and 86 per cent used only Welsh with their mothers and siblings, while the others used Welsh and English with their parents and English all or most of the time with their siblings. The lower percentage of Welsh speakers in the community had led to more mixed marriages and a lower incidence of Welsh within the families of native speakers.

In the sample of youth organization members, two groups were large enough to allow comparison. Most of the fluent second-language speakers of the

---

[38] Analyses of language use with the second to fourth child did not differ significantly from the results gained from the patterns emerging with regard to the first child. Reference is therefore made to the first child only. The same applies to the siblings of the youth organization members.

Table 6. The use made of the Welsh language among friends

Society and linguistic competence of members	Number of members	Percentage of friends with whom Welsh was used					
		100	75–99	50–74	25–49	1–24	0
Urdd 1: W1st	14	10	4				
MyW 2: W1st	8	7	1				
MyW 1: W1st	7	1	3	3			
WI 1: W1st	6	2	1	3			
Urdd 1: W2nd fluent	1	1					
SC: W1st	2	1			1		
Urdd 2: W1st	9		1	4	3	1	
YFC: W1st	7		1	2	3	1	
WI 2: W1st	2		1			1	
WI 1: W2nd fluent	2			2			
WI 1: fairly well	2			2			
WI 2: a little	3			2		1	
Urdd 2: W2nd fluent	4			1	3		
SC: W2nd fluent	5		1		1	1	2
Urdd 2: fairly well	10				2	6	2
SC: a little	1						1
Urdd 2: a little	1						1
SC: fairly well	3						3
WI 1: a little	3						3

MyW 1: Aberaeron Merched y Wawr; MyW 2: Fishguard Merched y Wawr; WI 1: Aberaeron Women's Institute; WI 2: Fishguard Women's Institute; Urdd 1: Urdd Gobaith Cymru Aberaeron; Urdd 2: Urdd Gobaith Cymru Fishguard; YFC: Fishguard Young Farmers' Club; SC: Aberaeron School Club. W1st: native speakers; W2nd fluent: fluent second-language speakers.

Aberaeron School Club used English only at home. Around 80 per cent used only English with their fathers, 60 per cent used only English with their mothers, and 80 per cent used only English with their siblings. Fifty per cent of the fluent second-language Welsh speakers of the Urdd at Fishguard used only English with their fathers, 25 per cent used English and Welsh, and 25 per cent used Welsh only. However, 75 per cent of them used only English with their mothers, and the remaining 25 per cent used English most of the time. With their siblings, 50 per cent used Welsh and English, 25 per cent used English most of the time and the remaining 25 per cent used English all of the time. Despite living in a community with a higher percentage of Welsh speakers, Welsh was therefore used less frequently in the families of members of the Aberaeron School Club than in any other group.

Membership of certain societies had a greater bearing upon the language spoken among friends than the language spoken in the family domain. All members of the Urdd at Aberaeron and Merched y Wawr at Fishguard indicated that they used Welsh with three-quarters or more of their friends. So did 71 per cent of the members of Aberaeron Merched y Wawr, but only half the native speakers of the Aberaeron WI did so. At Aberaeron Merched y Wawr, 29 per cent of the members as well as the remaining 50 per cent of the native speakers in the WI used Welsh with between half and three-quarters of their friends. Table 6 indicates that native speakers in the Aberaeron School Club, along with the WI, the Urdd and the Young Farmers' Club in Fishguard, were extremely inconsistent in their use of language with friends: some members used Welsh with three-quarters or more of their circle of friends, while others never used Welsh. While all fluent speakers of the Urdd at Fishguard indicated that they used Welsh with 25–49 per cent or more of their friends, only half of the fluent speakers from the Aberaeron School Club did so; the other half did not use Welsh at all with their friends. None of those members of the Urdd at Fishguard who indicated that they spoke Welsh fairly well used Welsh with more than a quarter of their friends; indeed, most of them did not use Welsh at all. It is not surprising that those who spoke only a little Welsh rarely used the language widely within their circle of friends.

Table 7. Societies, clubs and organizations in the towns of Aberaeron and Fishguard, 1997[1]

Aberaeron	*Clwb Cinio, Cymdeithas yr Iaith Gymraeg, Cymdeithas y Tabernacl, Cymdeithas Llên a Chân Peniel, Mudiad Ysgolion Meithrin*, Ladies' Circle
Both towns	Bridge Club, Choirs, Football team, Keep-Fit Class, *Merched y Wawr*, Mothers' Union, Rugby team, Scouts/Guides/Cadets, *Urdd Gobaith Cymru*, Farmers' Union of Wales, Whist Club, Women's Institute
Fishguard	*Chwaeroliaeth y Tabernacl, Chwiorydd Hermon*, Civic Society, *Cymdeithas y Cymrodorion, Fforwm Iaith Abergwaun*, Fishguard Ladies' Luncheon Club, Floral Art Society, Gateway Club, Historical Society, Ladies' Lifeboat Guild, Soroptimists, Young Farmers' Club

[1] The list was assembled from local press reports and societies mentioned by sample members in the questionnaire.

The use made of the Welsh language by second-language speakers who were members of the WI at Aberaeron and Fishguard varied according to age. The older members tended to use Welsh with a higher percentage of their friends than the younger second-language speakers. The underlying cause for this is the different setting in which the older women learnt Welsh, i.e. within the community, as opposed to the school in the case of members of the younger generation. The older women had acquired not only the linguistic but also the social competence necessary for using any language successfully outside a classroom setting. The bilingualism of many younger non-native speakers remained artificial, i.e. their second language had been acquired in the classroom and was restricted to that particular situation.[39]

Outside one's circle of close friends, the social life of a small community revolves around voluntary associations as well as community and group events. In the two towns under study, the above societies, clubs and organizations existed at the time of observation, and were attended by members of the sample. All members of the sample were asked to note the number and kind of societies of which they were members, and which language they used in meetings. The response revealed that native Welsh speakers who were members of one or more of the Welsh societies were those most likely to use Welsh in the greatest number of other clubs and organizations (Table 7). Every member of Aberaeron Merched y Wawr used Welsh in some three other societies, while members of the Urdd at Aberaeron and of Fishguard Merched y Wawr used Welsh in some two other societies. The number of clubs in which Welsh was spoken fell to about one per member for the native speakers of the Urdd at Fishguard and the Aberaeron School Club. Only every second native speaker from the Fishguard WI and Young Farmers' Club used Welsh in any other society. Only every fourth fluent second-language speaker from the Urdd at Fishguard and only every fifth such member of the Aberaeron School Club used Welsh in any other local association. The last two examples emphasize how fluent second-language speakers in Aberaeron rarely utilized their linguistic skills outside school. Although the Welsh language was used in a wider spectrum of local organizations in Aberaeron than in Fishguard, members of the Aberaeron School Club availed themselves of such opportunities to a lesser extent than did the fluent second-language speakers of the Urdd in Fishguard.

The spectrum of voluntary associations in which Welsh was used provided additional information about members' preferences and the status of Welsh in the community outside the markedly Welsh sector. Members of Aberaeron Merched y Wawr used Welsh, or Welsh and English, in thirteen other organizations in and around Aberaeron, the majority of which were either traditionally Welsh-speaking or connected with the surrounding agricultural or rural community. Their most popular choice was the local branch of Plaid Cymru, followed by the two chapel societies, and other Welsh organizations such as CYD, Mudiad Ysgolion Meithrin, Urdd Gobaith Cymru and Theatr Felin-fach. They also used Welsh, or both languages, while playing whist and attending their crochet, bobbin-lace or luncheon clubs. The native Welsh speakers within the WI also attended the 'core organizations' of Plaid Cymru and chapel societies, but

---

[39] For an exploration of the idea of 'social competence', see Alf Isak Keskitalo, 'The Status of the Sámi Language' in Einar Haugen, J. Derrick McClure, Derick Thomson (eds.), *Minority Languages Today* (Edinburgh, 1980), pp. 158–61. For the distinction between 'natural' and 'artificial' bilingualism, see Marion Löffler, *Englisch und Kymrisch in Wales: Geschichte der Sprachsituation und Sprachpolitik* (Hamburg, 1997), p. 16.

otherwise chose a slightly different range of clubs and societies, such as the keep-fit classes, the Aeron Singers and the bridge club, where they tended to use both Welsh and English, or English only. Native Welsh speakers among the women's sample in Fishguard used the language in only six other societies in the town. All the members of Fishguard Merched y Wawr joined in the activities of the Cymrodorion Society, and the majority of them belonged either to Chwaerol-iaeth y Tabernacl or Chwiorydd Hermon, both chapel-based organizations for women. Welsh speakers among the women's sample in the town used English exclusively in nine other societies.

Almost all members of the Urdd at Aberaeron were members of a Young Farmers' Club in the rural hinterland. All claimed to use Welsh there, which is not surprising, since most of the Young Farmers' Clubs in Ceredigion conduct their activities through the medium of Welsh. Welsh drama groups were also very popular, and five members participated. Two were active members of the Welsh Language Society. All of the above-mentioned societies naturally conducted their activities through the medium of Welsh. The Welsh language was also used in the town's cricket and rugby clubs. Although the three native speakers of the Aberaeron School Club attended a Welsh core organization, namely the local Young Farmers' Club, they used English in their other regular pastimes. This was also the situation in the case of the native speakers who were members of the Aberaeron WI. None of the second-language Welsh speakers of the Aberaeron School Club used Welsh in any voluntary association in or around the town. They used English only in all their regular leisure pursuits. The young Welsh speakers from the Fishguard sample made less use of the Welsh language socially than their counterparts in Aberaeron. Half of the native speakers of the school branch of the Urdd at Fishguard also attended Aelwyd Carn Ingli, the nearest youth club conducted by the Urdd. Two native speakers also used Welsh in Young Farmers' Clubs in the area.[40] Of all members of the Urdd at Fishguard who claimed to be fluent second-language speakers or who spoke Welsh fairly well, only one used Welsh in another organization, namely a Young Farmers' Club, while another five members attended Young Farmers' Clubs where they spoke English. Members of Fishguard Young Farmers' Club used Welsh in three other organizations, a branch of Merched y Wawr, a local branch of a charitable organization and the leisure centre at Carmarthen. None of the members indicated that they used both languages together in any club or society. Native and second-language speakers alike used English in the majority of their regular leisure activities.

Communal events and festivities organized by and for all community members, or various sub-groups, constitute another, more casual and less regular facet of

---

[40] Of the fifteen Young Farmers' Clubs in Pembrokeshire, only two (Hermon and Eglwyswrw) officially used Welsh in all their proceedings. Both clubs are within travelling distance of Fishguard.

Table 8. Social events held in the towns of Aberaeron and Fishguard, 1996–7

Aberaeron	carnival, regatta, Bowls Club open day, Rugby Sevens, tug-of-war
Both towns	*cymanfaoedd canu*, discos, eisteddfodau, *nosweithiau llawen*, performances by bands, public lectures in Welsh and English, sheep-dog trials, theatre performances in Welsh and English
Fishguard	celebrations of twinning with Loctudy, ARTS-fest, Cymrodorion concert, Guides' Christmas show, *Gŵyl Gwaun*, music festival, Spirit of Youth Festival

social life in any community. For the sample members, the year preceding fieldwork had been marked by the occasions shown in Table 8. All members of the sample were asked to specify which social events they had attended and which language(s) they had used there. Space was provided on the questionnaire to add any other events they had attended. Members of Fishguard Merched y Wawr had, on average, attended the highest number (over six) of public events, and used Welsh in all of them. This is consistent with the close social network of chapel, societies and events to which they belonged.[41] Every member of Aberaeron Merched y Wawr attended nearly four events where they mostly used Welsh, and every second member attended one event in which they used English. The native Welsh speakers of the WI in Aberaeron attended around two events each, where they mostly used Welsh. However, they also attended one event each, on average, where they used both languages. Native Welsh speakers who were members of the Fishguard WI attended around two events each; Welsh was spoken in one and English in the other. Strikingly, the fluent second-language Welsh speakers in the Aberaeron WI attended around three events each where they used English mostly, but only one where they spoke Welsh.

The young generation of native speakers in Aberaeron, members of both the Urdd and the School Club, attended around six public occasions each where they used Welsh. In addition, members of the School Club attended between one and two events where they used English. The native and fluent second-language speakers of the Urdd at Fishguard and the fluent second-language speakers of the Aberaeron School Club attended between two and three events where they used Welsh, but the latter two groups attended an additional three at which they used English. Members of Fishguard Young Farmers' Club, all of whom were native Welsh speakers, made very little use of the language. They each attended around

---

[41] For an exploration into the ways close networks operate, see Beth Thomas, 'Differences of Sex and Sects: Linguistic Variation and Social Networks in a Welsh Mining Village' in Jennifer Coates and Deborah Cameron (eds.), *Women in their Speech Communities: New Perspectives on Language and Sex* (New York, 1988), pp. 51–60.

two events, at which they spoke Welsh or both languages, but also two at which they used English only.

The variety of events at which Welsh was used provides further conclusions about the status of Welsh in the social life of its speakers. A general assessment of attendance figures at community events reveals that traditionally Welsh events were among the most popular in both communities and with both age groups. In Aberaeron an eisteddfod and a Welsh drama performance attracted the highest number of attendants from all sample groups. In Fishguard the Cymrodorion concert and *cymanfa ganu* attracted the highest number of participants from the women's sample, while a *noson lawen* and an eisteddfod drew the highest number of young people. Events associated with Welsh culture therefore appear to be central to the social life of both communities and of interest to a large section of the population. The detailed analysis of the linguistic profile of these events accentuates the differences already observed regarding the language used by different age groups and by native and second-language speakers in their local clubs and societies.

In Aberaeron almost all the members of Merched y Wawr attended an eisteddfod, *noson lawen*, *cymanfa ganu* and a Welsh theatre performance. So did about half of the native Welsh speakers of the WI. In addition, the majority of Merched y Wawr members as well as some native speakers of the WI used Welsh on such occasions as the carnival and public lectures, although the percentage of Welsh-speaking members of the WI who spoke Welsh at public occasions was much lower than that of Merched y Wawr. Of all the sample groups, members of the Urdd at Aberaeron attended the widest range of communal events where they used Welsh. Not only did most of them attend an eisteddfod, *noson lawen*, *cymanfa ganu* and a Welsh drama, but the majority also spoke Welsh at the tug-of-war, carnival, rugby sevens and the school disco. Overall, members of the Urdd at Aberaeron used Welsh in a range of fourteen community events, a fact which underlines the confidence of those young speakers in situations not traditionally considered to be Welsh-speaking events. Members of the School Club, be they native speakers or fluent in the language, tended to use both Welsh and English, or English only. However, the two native Welsh speakers spoke Welsh in a range of six public events, while a small number of fluent second-language speakers used the language in the same range of occasions. English tended to be used at events such as the school disco, English theatre performances, live performances by English bands, and events associated with the school.

Overall, in Aberaeron Welsh was used at eight occasions listed by the women, English at six and both languages at another six events. Welsh was spoken at fourteen community events listed by the younger generation in Aberaeron, English at eleven and both languages at four events. The use of Welsh among the younger generation seems to have increased at the expense of bilingualism, but not at the expense of the English language.

In Fishguard members of Merched y Wawr used Welsh at a range of eleven of the twelve events listed for their age group. All attended the Cymrodorion concert and a *cymanfa ganu*, and most also attended a Welsh drama and an eisteddfod, and participated in a *noson lawen*. Members of the WI, on the other hand, spoke English almost exclusively at the same range of events, except at the *noson lawen* and the *cymanfa ganu*. Among the younger generation, traditional forms of Welsh entertainment, such as the *noson lawen*, eisteddfod, and Welsh theatre performances were the most popular events with native speakers, but the percentage of those who attended and used Welsh on such occasions was much lower than in Aberaeron. For example, the most popular event, a *noson lawen*, was attended by seven of the nine native Welsh speakers, but only five used Welsh there. On the other hand, three of the four fluent second-language speakers who were members of the Urdd branch at Fishguard frequented the eisteddfod and the *noson lawen* and practised their second language there. About half of the ten members of the Urdd at Fishguard who claimed to speak Welsh fairly well attended either the eisteddfod or the *noson lawen* and used Welsh there. It is obvious that second-language Welsh speakers who were members of the Urdd at Fishguard made an effort to attend Welsh cultural events and use the language. However, the number of other members, mainly first-language speakers, who claimed to have utilized their Welsh at a variety of other events never exceeded one or two. Thus, the range of twelve events out of nineteen at which Welsh was used is deceptive. Outside the domain of traditional Welsh entertainment, English was the language most commonly used by members of the Urdd at Fishguard. Of the seven members of the Fishguard Young Farmers' Club, only one or two attended traditional Welsh events. Overall, Welsh was used by them in a range of eight out of nineteen events, whereas English was spoken by them in five events and both languages in three. Even taking into consideration that members of the Fishguard Young Farmers' Club tended to go out less often than members of any other group, their attendance rate of Welsh events and their linguistic profile as a group was extremely low. For the younger generation at Fishguard, English was the language of live performances by bands and of discos in various venues. Only three members of the whole sample of thirty-one, for instance, had attended a live performance by a Welsh band in the year preceding the questionnaire, and only one member had used Welsh there.

Every social event consists of smaller-scale speech events. The decision as to which language is used at such occasions is influenced by the attitudes of speakers. The lower the social frequency of Welsh in relation to the use of English, the less likely the language is to be the 'normal' means of communication in the eyes of its speakers. As a consequence, they will be less sure of the acceptability of Welsh and, if in doubt, will choose English or turn to English. A positive attitude, on the other hand, created by exposure to the Welsh language in a wide range of social situations, leads to a more confident use of the Welsh language both by native and second-language speakers. In order to assess the behaviour of speakers when initiating speech events, they were asked to indicate in which language they would address a native speaker, a 'learner' – i.e. an individual who had obviously learnt Welsh as a second language – and a stranger in the community. The assertiveness of Welsh speakers in mixed linguistic situations was established by asking how likely they would be to switch to English in the presence of presumed non-Welsh speakers.

As far as initiating conversations with people known to be native Welsh speakers was concerned, the response was very positive. All members of Merched y Wawr and the Urdd at Aberaeron, all native and fluent second-language speakers of the Aberaeron WI, all but one of the members of the Aberaeron School Club, all native and fluent second-language speakers of the Urdd at Fishguard, and all members of the Fishguard Young Farmers' Club stated they would address such a person in Welsh all or most of the time. Seventy-five per cent of Fishguard Merched y Wawr, as well as half of the native speakers of the WI there and half of those members of Aberaeron WI who spoke Welsh fairly well, would also address a native Welsh speaker in Welsh all or most of the time. On the other hand, only 30 per cent of Urdd members in Fishguard claiming to speak Welsh fairly well would do so.

A smaller number stated that they would address someone known to them as a 'learner' in Welsh all or most of the time. The highest percentage was recorded among members of Aberaeron Merched y Wawr, where 86 per cent would initiate a conversation with a second-language speaker in Welsh. So would 67 per cent of the native Welsh speakers of the WI and 64 per cent of the Urdd in Aberaeron. Half the members of Fishguard Merched y Wawr, half the fluent second-language speakers of the Urdd at Fishguard and half the members of the Fishguard WI who spoke Welsh fairly well would also address a second-language speaker in Welsh all or most of the time. In a second group, a majority of members would address a second-language speaker either in Welsh or in Welsh and English: 86 per cent of the members of the Fishguard Young Farmers' Club, 80 per cent of the fluent second-language speakers of the Aberaeron School Club and 78 per cent of the native Welsh speakers of the Urdd at Fishguard would do so. All the native Welsh speakers of the Aberaeron School Club and the Fishguard WI, as well as the fluent second-language speakers of the Aberaeron WI and the one fluent second-language speaker who was a member of the Urdd at Aberaeron, would address a second-language speaker in both languages. The majority of those claiming to speak the language fairly well or a little, however, would address a 'learner' in English all or most of the time.

The data for addressing 'strangers' in their own community verified the attitude encountered in all the interviews. All speakers maintained that if they were in doubt about the linguistic or ethnic affiliation of the interlocutor, they would choose English. Of all the societies, only at Aberaeron Merched y Wawr would a majority (57 per cent) address an unknown person in Welsh all or most of the time. A further 29 per cent from their ranks would use Welsh and English. Surprisingly, one of the two native Welsh speakers in the Aberaeron School Club would do the same. In a second group, a sizeable minority of the society in question would address an unknown person in Welsh: 29 per cent of the native Welsh speakers of the Urdd at Aberaeron and of the Fishguard Young Farmers' Club would do so, as well as 25 per cent of Fishguard Merched y Wawr and the fluent second-language speakers of the Urdd in the town. A further 11 per cent of the native speakers of the Urdd at Fishguard would address a stranger in Welsh. Of the remaining sample, 33 per cent of the native Welsh speakers of the Aberaeron WI and those members of the Aberaeron School Club who spoke the language fairly well would address a stranger in Welsh and English. All the others would address a stranger in English.

The tendency to address people not known personally in English is indicative of the speakers' growing linguistic insecurity within their community. This is especially apparent among the younger generation. This factor may be of little consequence in small communities, where most inhabitants know each other and their linguistic affiliations. However, it assumes far greater significance in urban communities such as Aberaeron and Fishguard which, although relatively small, are too large for everyone to know one another personally. Consequently, the spontaneous use of Welsh is diminished, even if the majority of the population is able to speak the language.

In order to establish to what extent Welsh speakers were able to sustain Welsh conversations in mixed-language speech events, they were invited to indicate how likely they were to switch from Welsh to English in the presence of those whom they presumed to be non-Welsh speakers. The only groups with any members who stated that they never or rarely switched to English were the Urdd branches at Fishguard and Aberaeron, where this was true in the case of 33 per cent and 27 per cent of native Welsh speakers, respectively. On the other hand, 22 per cent of the native speakers who were members of the Urdd at Fishguard and 53 per cent of the Urdd members at Aberaeron stated that they occasionally switched to English in the presence of non-Welsh speakers. Only one other small group contained a majority which sometimes switched from Welsh to English in the presence of non-Welsh speakers: 57 per cent of the members of Aberaeron Merched y Wawr and one of the two native Welsh speakers of the Aberaeron School Club made this declaration. In a third group, a minority of members sometimes switched to English. In this group were 33 per cent of those members of the Aberaeron School Club who claimed to speak Welsh fairly well, 25 per cent of the native Welsh speakers of Fishguard Merched y Wawr, all the fluent second-language speakers of the Urdd at Fishguard, 17 per cent of the native Welsh speakers of the Aberaeron WI, and 14 per cent of the Fishguard Young Farmers' Club. However, over half of the sample (53 people) claimed that they switched to English in the presence of a non-Welsh speaker all or most of the time. This trend inevitably leads to the relegation of Welsh in favour of English in any bilingual situation. Most speech events which do not occur in the sector marked 'culturally Welsh', especially in communities which do not contain a majority of Welsh speakers, are likely to occur in the presence of non-Welsh speakers. The results shown above indicate that Welsh will increasingly be abandoned in such situations. Until this process is reversed, Welsh cultural organizations and events will continue to fill an important gap: in communities such as Fishguard they often provide the only opportunity for speakers to use the Welsh language.

By means of general observations, interviews, and notes and comments expressed on the questionnaires themselves, information was gleaned on an aspect of language use which the statistics collected could not provide, namely the attitude of speakers. Sometimes the urge to show feelings was stronger than the desire to complete the questionnaire correctly. For example, in reply to the question asking which language was used to address a stranger, one of the women, in addition to ticking a box, wrote: 'Os Cymro yw – Cymraeg' (If he is a Welshman – Welsh).[42] This seemingly nonsensical answer highlighted what for native (and some second-language) speakers seemed to be a strict rule: Welsh is used with people one knows to be native speakers of the language. It is not a general means of communication with people one does not know or with people one assumes to be learners. Second-language speakers, on the other hand, often feel more at home with other 'learners'. During a first visit to the comprehensive school at Aberaeron, for example, the researcher spoke to a boy of about sixteen who happened to be standing in front of the building:

'Allet ti ddweud wrtho fi ble ma' swyddfa'r athrawes Gymraeg?' – 'Ble ma' Mrs D., yr athrawes Gymraeg?' – 'Ie' – 'Sai'n siarad Cymraeg, Saesneg wy i' – 'Wel, wyt ti'n swnio'n ddigon da i fi' – 'Na, dysgu Cymraeg.'[43]

('Could you tell me where the office of the Welsh teacher is?' – 'Where is Mrs D., the Welsh teacher?' – 'Yes' – 'I don't speak Welsh, I'm English [speaking]' – 'Well, you sound good enough to me' – 'No, learning Welsh.')

The same boy figured among members of the School Club who completed a questionnaire. He added the following remarks on the last page of his copy:

You may have noticed that although I speak Welsh and am able to cope in a

---

[42] Respondent 1/23, question 30.
[43] Field notes, 20 November 1996.

conversation, I rarely do converse in the language . . . I notice there is some anti-English sentiment – it is complained about that we don't try to talk in Welsh. However, when I talk in Welsh I am often laughed at or given strange looks by the very people who want me to talk Welsh.[44]

One member of the Aberaeron School Club, who had been born in the area but was the daughter of English incomers, was fluent in Welsh and considered herself Welsh. Yet she claimed that she had been bullied for being English.[45] Another fluent second-language speaker from Fishguard, who had spent the first years of her life in Milford Haven, wrote that she used 'more Welsh with friend 1 and 2 than before. I'm not sure why but I think it's because I am now considered "Welsh"'.[46] In a later interview she said of one friend, a native Welsh speaker:

Os dwi'n gallu siarad Cymraeg, dwi yn, achos, practiso fe beth bynnag. Ond ma' hi yn gwbod bod . . . Cymraeg yw'n ail iaith i, felly ma' hi'n siarad Saesneg yn ôl, a ma' hwnna'n *really* mynd ar 'yn nerfe i o achos mi rydw i'n siarad Cymrâg ond hi'n ateb yn ôl yn Saesneg. A dwi wedi dweud *lot* o weithie, 'paid wneud hwnna', ond ma' hi'n teimlo bo' fe'n annaturiol ne' rhywbeth.[47]

(If I can speak Welsh, I do, because, to practise it anyway. But she knows that . . . Welsh is my second language, so she speaks English back, and that *really* gets on my nerves, because I do speak Welsh and she answers back in English. And I've said lots of times, 'don't do that', but she feels it is unnatural or something.)

Native Welsh speakers seem to develop this restrictive attitude at an early age. The 6-year-old daughter of a member of Aberaeron Merched y Wawr was present at the interview with her mother, during which the mother asked which language she used in the playground of the Welsh-medium primary school she attended. The girl replied that she spoke Welsh with her best friend, but English with E, to which the mother replied: 'Ond mae E yn medru siarad Cymraeg, on'd yw hi?' (But E can speak Welsh, can't she?). The girl answered: 'Ie, ond Saesneg yw hi, ni'n siarad Saesneg' (Yes, but she's English, we speak English). Having heard the other child speak English with her parents when they collected her after school, she had concluded that she must be English.[48]

Because of this unwritten cultural rule, older and younger native Welsh speakers in Aberaeron used the Welsh language widely amongst themselves, but

---

[44] Respondent 2/24, question 51.
[45] Interview with respondent 2/19.
[46] Respondent 2/37, question 51.
[47] Interview with respondent 2/37.
[48] Interview with respondent 1/2. Paradoxically, the parents of child E were both native speakers of Welsh, who had chosen to bring up their child in English.

either did not mix very much with second-language speakers or found it difficult to converse with them in Welsh. This has produced a feeling of exclusion and separateness among second-language speakers, which they sought to explain in various ways:

O ie, ma' probleme mawr gyda'r Cymry Cymraeg. Achos rhai ohonyn nhw, yn ofnus iawn gyda'r dysgwyr . . . Wel, ma' dwy rheswm yn fy marn i. Un, ma' ofan 'da nhw bod Cymraeg y dysgwyr yn well na Cymraeg nhw. Ac, y rheswm arall, fod y bobl yn meddwl mae'n gormod o straen i ddysgwyr i siarad i rywun rhugl.[49]

(Well, there are great problems with the Welsh speakers. Because some of them, are afraid of talking with learners . . . Well, there are two reasons in my opinion. One, they are afraid that the learners' Welsh is better than theirs. And, the other reason, that people think it is too much of a strain for learners to talk with someone who is fluent.)

At the secondary school, native and second-language Welsh speakers formed clearly separate groups, recognized by both sides:

Ma' rhyw fath o *segregation* i gael yn ysgol. Wel, tamed bach. Ma' rhai pobl, ma' un grŵp o Cymry Cymrâg, a dy'n nhw ddim *really* yn siarad 'da pobl sy ddim yn siarad Cymraeg, sy, fi'n meddwl bach yn wael. Fi'n meddwl bach bo' fi yn y canol, fi'n siarad â rhai Cymry Cymrâg, ffrindie fi, a rhai Saesneg. A wedyn ma' rhai Saesneg sy'n siarad â neb sy'n siarad Cymrâg. Ne', os wyt ti yn siarad 'da nhw, wyt ti'n gorfod siarad Saesneg. *So*, ma' fe bach fel 'na.[50]

(There is some kind of segregation in the school. Well, a bit. There are some people, there is a group of Welsh speakers, and they don't *really* talk to people who don't speak Welsh, which is, I think, a bit bad. I think a bit that I am in the middle, I talk to the Welsh speakers, my friends, and to the English. And then there are some English who don't speak to anyone who speaks Welsh. Or, if you do speak to them, you have to speak English. So, it's a bit like that.)

This is mirrored by the perception of second-language speakers of social life in their peer-group:

Because . . . in secondary school all my friends are English. And I'm friendly with other Welsh people, totally Welsh people, but they all seem to be English, there's four of them, and they are all English, and it's really odd. I talk to Welsh people and things like that, but, it's just turned out like that and Welsh people go round with Welsh people and they never seem to mix, and that's really strange.[51]

---

[49] Interview with respondent 1/13.
[50] Interview with respondent 2/15.
[51] Interview with respondent 2/19.

This led to a serious misjudgement about the linguistic situation in Aberaeron:

> B: There's hardly any pure Welsh speaking there. I mean, they're all, well, Welsh, speak English all the time; or else English, and, that's what the school's like. Has very few people who are Welsh and speak Welsh. That's the way I feel about the school.
> . . . A: I always assume, well, the Welsh language seems to be dying out anyway, anywhere you look.[52]

Outside the school and circle of friends in Aberaeron, the Welsh language was used widely by and among its native speakers, with the younger generation showing more confidence than their elders. Since education at the primary school is conducted through the medium of Welsh, theoretically every child should be fluent by the time he or she reaches the age of six. An informant with two small children supported this view and maintained that, by the age of six, all the children in the primary school could indeed speak Welsh.[53] There was no teenager in the sample in Aberaeron who did not speak at least some Welsh, and twenty-two out of twenty-six, i.e. 85 per cent of the sample, indicated that they were either native Welsh speakers or fluent second-language speakers. This concurs with the linguistic evidence of the 1991 census, which returned nearly 90 per cent of the inhabitants of Aberaeron aged 5–15 as bilingual, and with the opinion of two second-language speakers:

> A: But nobody in school can't speak, has the ability not to speak any Welsh at all, and everybody in school knows a bit of Welsh.
> . . . B: During assembly and stuff like that they say, 'how would you like to sing a carol?', 'I don't know any Welsh', and they *do*. Of course they do.[54]

If taken as indicative of the future of the Welsh language in Aberaeron, the growth in the number of young people able to speak Welsh gives rise to optimism. However, the rift in language use which exists between native speakers of Welsh and the majority of those for whom Welsh is their second language is often marked. Only one fluent second-language speaker in the sample participated in the activities of Urdd Gobaith Cymru. In an interview she stated that very few other learners usually enrolled in the Urdd there.[55] Thus, any social competence in the language acquired at primary school may be lost, as indicated in the interview with two members of the Aberaeron School Club, who stated that:

[52] Ibid.; interview with respondent 2/20.
[53] Interview with respondent 1/2.
[54] *The 1991 Census on CD-ROM*, Table 67; interviews with respondents 2/19 and 2/20.
[55] Interview with respondent 2/15.

in primary, we did loads of things, after school every Tuesday . . . We had different activities, I mean doing different things gives you sort of a variation of language, sometimes we did sort of a mini-sort of sports day outside, it was only sort of an hour and a half after school, I mean it was brilliant, we cooked, we made paper lamps . . . cards for Mother's Day when the occasion came around.[56]

However, the contact with the Urdd was not maintained at the comprehensive school. Instead, the two became members of the School Club which was conducted in English. Older Welsh speakers expressed disappointment regarding the lack of Welsh-speaking organizations for younger children in the town. Meetings of the Cub Scouts were conducted through the medium of English, although 'probably more Welsh speakers than English speakers' had enrolled.[57] On the other hand, the local Young Farmers' Club was singled out by interviewees as a positive influence:

Ma' . . . brawd fi'n aelod nawr hefyd. A 'na'r un lle lle ma' pawb yn siarad Cymraeg â fe. Ma' hynna'n un lle pan, es i 'na pan o'n i'n yr ail flwyddyn ysgol uwchradd, a fi'n credu gwellodd Cymraeg fi lot.[58]

(My . . . brother is also a member now. And that's the one place where everybody speaks Welsh to him. That's the one place, when I went there in my second year at secondary school, my Welsh got much better.)

Voluntary societies offering the opportunity to socialize in the Welsh language have clearly been beneficial for native speakers. However, second-language speakers rarely joined these groups and consequently felt that their linguistic skills were lying waste:

B: We don't speak enough Welsh at all, we got all this language, and we don't use it and it's such an old language.
. . . A: I'll make sure I don't, I mean I'm gonna carry on talking to people [in Welsh]. I mean I'm trying a bit more actually, because it's just the waste, I mean all those years, what is it, sort of nine years in a Welsh school?[59]

An adult learner attempted to explain why second-language speakers might shy away from contact with native Welsh speakers:

---

[56] Interviews with respondents 2/19 and 2/20.
[57] Interview with respondent 1/2 and field notes, 20 November 1996.
[58] Interview with respondent 2/15.
[59] Interviews with respondents 2/19 and 2/20.

O, fi'n iawn gyda'r dysgwyr, achos ma' pawb yn yr un sefyllfa, a 'sdim ots os ti'n gwneud camgymeriade, pawb yn gwneud camgymeriade, neb yn berffaith. Ond, y person arall bydda i'n mwy cyffyrddus byddai'r tiwtor, mae'n fel *doctor*, mae'n deall yr holl brobleme.[60]

(I'm fine with the learners, because everybody [is] in the same situation, and it doesn't matter if you make mistakes, everybody make[s] mistakes, nobody [is] perfect. But, the other person I'm most comfortable with is the tutor, he's like a doctor, he understands all the problems.)

Other features of the linguistic situation in Aberaeron point to apathy regarding the Welsh language which, in conjunction with the attitudes outlined above and the continued in-migration of English speakers, invites decline in the use of Welsh. The editor of *Llais Aeron*, the local *papur bro*, 'somehow had difficulties finding correspondents for the town, although the paper sells quite well'.[61] Although Peniel chapel was reckoned to be 'Welsh through and through', leaders of the remaining churches and chapels noted that their Welsh-speaking members were ready to accept the linguistic change from Welsh to bilingual or English in their services.[62] The Welsh language had little public presence in the town. One interviewee complained about the owners of public houses and about monoglot English advertising in Aberaeron, although most of the shops were owned and run by Welsh speakers.[63] The Welsh bookshop displayed very few titles, mainly of a religious nature.[64] For entertainment in the Welsh language, Welsh speakers relied heavily on the rural hinterland and especially on Theatr Felin-fach. This reinforced local opinion that the surrounding villages were much more Welsh than the town itself and robbed second-language speakers of opportunities of practising their Welsh in town.[65]

In Fishguard the linguistic situation experienced by Welsh speakers of different age groups was divergent. The older Welsh speakers in the sample lived in a close-knit group which provided them with sufficient opportunities to socialize in the language. Proximity to the English-speaking area of Pembrokeshire posed a threat to the Welsh language and had stirred many to take action to protect the Welsh language. It was no surprise to discover that this group had fought perceived injustices inflicted on the language in town. The Cymrodorion society numbered over 100 members in 1996–7 and, according to the minister of Hermon chapel, membership was increasing. The ministers of the three Welsh chapels took a very

---

[60] Interview with respondent 1/13.
[61] Field notes, 15 October 1996.
[62] Field notes, 16 October 1996, 14 and 19 March 1997.
[63] Interviews with respondents 1/1 and 1/2.
[64] Interview with respondent 1/2.
[65] Interviews with respondents 1/1 and 1/2.

strong stance against the use of English in their institutions and *Y Llien Gwyn*, the local *papur bro*, regularly reported on activities in Fishguard.[66] In 1986 the National Eisteddfod was held in the area, and in its wake came positive developments in the voluntary sector. A Welsh choir – Côr Ffilharmonig Abergwaun – was established for the National Eisteddfod and was still active in 1997. In May 1987 *Gŵyl Gwaun*, an annual Welsh-language festival, was held for the first time and was regarded by its organizers as a natural successor to the National Eisteddfod ('fel dilyniad naturiol o'r Eisteddfod Genedlaethol y llynedd').[67] In 1994 the Town Council threatened to withdraw financial support to the festival because the organizers had written to them in Welsh only. Consequently, the pressure group Fforwm Iaith Abergwaun (Fishguard Language Forum) was founded, which numbered around forty members in 1997.[68] In the same year, the Fforwm was finally successful in its prolonged public argument with Pembrokeshire County Council regarding the erection of bilingual signs throughout the county.[69] The Fforwm has also assisted retailers in acquiring grant-aid from Europe for bilingual signs.[70] Since 1996 a new Welsh bookshop, Siop DJ, has offered a wide range of Welsh titles, but also Anglo-Welsh and 'Welsh interest' posters and books directed at the tourist market. As a result of these developments, the Welsh language has regained a visual presence in the town which has already influenced perceptions of its linguistic profile. Several interviewees mentioned that they used more Welsh than before because shops were making more of an effort or making it more apparent that their staff were Welsh speakers.[71] A young second-language speaker stressed that she used Welsh sometimes, especially when she saw the sign 'Siaredir Cymraeg yma' (Welsh spoken here).[72] However, such improvements have been largely organized and sustained by the middle-aged or the older generation. For the young people, the Welsh language was associated with markedly Welsh events and organizations. Not one of them engaged in any activity of language promotion, although the number and percentage of children and teenagers able to speak the language was growing swiftly. In 1991, 28 per cent of the population of Fishguard aged 5–15 was counted as being bilingual, compared to 14 per cent in 1981.[73] Twenty of the

---

[66] Field notes, 6, 20 and 24 February 1997, 13 and 20 March 1997.
[67] The testimony of Shân Griffiths at a committee meeting, 3 December 1986. Private Collection, *Gŵyl Gwaun* Minute Book.
[68] *County Echo*, 11 and 18 March 1994; field notes, 24 February 1997.
[69] *County Echo*, March 1996–March 1997, passim.
[70] Ibid., 6 September 1996.
[71] Interviews with respondents 2/37 and 2/51: 'Ond mae fel *Boots*, a banciau, yn neud mwy o ymdrech . . . Ne' ma'n nhw'n neud e'n fwy amlwg fod staff yn siarad Cymraeg' (It's like *Boots*, and the banks, they make more of an effort . . . Or they make it more obvious that staff can speak Welsh).
[72] Interview with respondent 2/37.
[73] *The 1991 Census on CD-ROM*, Table 67.

thirty-one young people of the sample taken in Fishguard, i.e. 65 per cent, claimed to be first-language or fluent second-language Welsh speakers and all claimed that they spoke at least some Welsh. According to a primary-school teacher interviewed, the percentage of pupils receiving Welsh-medium education had risen steadily. In 1997, for the first time, 50 per cent of the new arrivals began their education in the Welsh-medium stream of the school. This improvement is mainly attributed to the changing attitudes of parents, who are anxious for their children to become fluent in the language. However, of the twelve new pupils in September 1997, only one came from a Welsh-speaking family. If the others are not provided with opportunities for using Welsh socially, it is likely they will encounter the same problems and develop the same attitudes as the teenagers in the sample. The small number and low percentage of native Welsh speakers at Fishguard High School and the notion that the language must not be used in the company of second-language speakers and learners militated against their use of Welsh:

> Na, ma' lot mwy o Saesneg yn yr ysgol nawr. Ma' rhai sy'n siarad Cymrâg, ti'n gwbod, *small percentage*, a wedyn pobl arall sy ddim yn deall Cymrâg, ma'n nhw'n meddwl, 'O ma'n nhw tipyn bach yn *thick* ma'n nhw'n siarad Cymrâg', o God, tamed bach o hyn yw e dwi'n meddwl.[74]

> (No, there is a lot more English in school now. There are some who speak Welsh, you know, a small percentage, and then other people who don't understand Welsh, they think, 'Oh, they're a bit thick, they're speaking Welsh', oh God, it's a bit of that I think.)

If the young people used any Welsh at all with their friends, they claimed to switch to English when joined by a third person who was not a native Welsh speaker:

> Pryd 'dyn ni 'da'n gily', dim ond y ddou ohonon ni, tymo, 'dyn ni'n siarad Cymraeg wedyn, ond os ma' ffrindie 'da ni, o achos ma'n nhw i gyd yn Saesneg ni'n siarad Saesneg wedyn . . . Shelley, Joanne a Keith yw ffrindie fi gore, i mynd ma's gyda, a'r . . . Saesneg, ti'n gwbod, yw 'u iaith gynta.[75]

> (When we are together, just the two of us, we speak Welsh then, but if we have friends with us, because they are all English, we speak English . . . Shelley, Joanne and Keith are my best friends, to go out with, and . . . English is their first language.)

One of them used to rebuke her friends for using Welsh:

---

[74] Interview with respondent 2/37.
[75] Interview with respondent 2/38.

Ma' un o ffrindie fi, Nia, ma' hi'n byw lan yn Gwdig, a ma' Nia â *habit* o hyd, siarad Cymrâg â fi. A dwi'n gweud wrthi, 'Nia, Saesneg,' a 'ma' fe'n *rude*'. Does dim rhaid ishe upseto ffrindie erill . . . Ma's, wedwch ar nos Sadwrn, ma' chwech ohonon ni, ambell waith deg. A dwi'n teimlo'n agos i *lot* o ffrindie fi. Sai'n ypseto nhw i unrhywun troi rownd i gweud '*Oh, she's Welsh, she speaks Welsh in front of us, we don't understand what they're saying.*' Achos ma' hyn yn mynd i troi nhw yn erbyn yr iaith Gymrâg, a 'na'r peth diwetha ych chi am neud.[76]

(One of my friends, Nia, she lives up in Gwdig, and Nia has a habit of always speaking Welsh to me. And I say to her 'Nia, English,' and 'it's rude'. We don't have to upset other friends . . . When we are out, say, on Saturday night, there are six of us, sometimes ten. And I feel close to a lot of my friends. And I don't want to upset them, for someone might turn round and say 'Oh, she's Welsh, she speaks Welsh in front of us, we don't understand what they're saying.' Because, that's going to turn them against the Welsh language, and that's the last thing you want to do).

This attitude, confirmed by every other teenager interviewed, prevented some native speakers from using Welsh in the Fishguard Young Farmers' Club.[77] In the Guides, young Welsh speakers were reprimanded for speaking Welsh in the presence of a non-Welsh-speaking member.[78] As a result of the low percentage of native speakers and the preventive attitude, the opportunity of using the Welsh language outside the home and the school was confined to a handful of markedly Welsh societies and situations, or to private conversations. This contributed to a loss of confidence on the part of the young people in their own linguistic ability. During interviews, they feared that their Welsh was deficient:

Os dwi'n cael, ti'n gwbod, y *choice* i neud yn Saesneg. Achos, ma' rhai geirie sai'n deall, t'weld, dim ond yn y dosbarth, ti'n gwbod, dysgu, sy ddim yn wneud geirie galed galed am arholiad, 'sdim rhaid i ni, ac wedyn sai'n deall nhw i gyd . . . Pryd dwi'n gweld mam-gu, a pethe, ma'n nhw'n siarad Cymraeg ambell waith ond dwi'n troi i'r Saesneg achos, sai'n lico fe ambell waith. [Pam?] Dwi ddim yn gwbod shwd i, ti'n gwbod, ma' rhai geirie, a dwi'n *embarrassed*.[79]

(If I'm given the choice, you know, to do it in English. Because, there are some words I don't understand, you see, [I am] only in the class, you know, the learners' [class] that doesn't do the really hard words for the examination, we don't have to, and then I don't understand them all . . . When I see grandma, and things, they speak Welsh sometimes, but I switch to English, because, I don't like it sometimes. [Why?] I don't know how to, you know, there are some words, and I'm embarrassed.)

---

[76] Interview with respondent 2/57.
[77] Ibid.; interview with respondent 2/38.
[78] Interview with respondent 2/37.
[79] Interview with respondent 2/38.

This problem is enhanced in the case of second-language speakers and learners:

Ie . . . ma'n nhw mewn dosbarth ail-iaith, ma'n nhw'n gael *spelling tests* a phethe, a ma'n nhw'n trio dysgu fi amser brêc. Wedyn edrych ar y rhestr, sai'n gwbod hanner y geirie. Felly, mewn rhai ffordd, ma' Cymrâg nhw yn fwy *grammatical correct* na un fi. Ond, falle, o achos mae'n ail iaith, 'sen ni'n meddwl ni'n *fluent*, o achos . . . os dwi'n edrych mewn i geiriadur Cymrâg, ma' 'na *billions* o'r geirie fyna sai'n gwbod. Ac wedyn fi'n meddwl sai'n rhugl, chi'n weld.[80]

(Yes, . . . they are in the second-language class, they have spelling tests and things, and they try to teach me during break. But then looking at the list and I don't know half of the words. Therefore, in some ways, their Welsh is more grammatically correct than mine. But, maybe because it is a second language, we don't think we're fluent, because . . . if I look in a Welsh dictionary, there are billions of words there that I don't know. And then I think I'm not fluent, you see.)

This situation also changed the young generation's perception of what constitutes linguistic normality in their community. Every single person interviewed in Fishguard expressed the opinion that the twinning celebrations with Loctudy in Brittany and the impending celebrations of the bicentenary of the 'French invasion' had been dominated by the English language. However, while the older generation considered this an injustice and succeeded in introducing at least a minimum of Welsh into the ceremonies, the younger generation perceived things in a different light. One member of Urdd Gobaith Cymru justified the use of English as follows:

'Na, pryd o'n nhw'n siarad, o'n nhw'n siarad Saesneg, dim byd, 'sai bobl yn siarad Cymraeg 'da'i gily', ond pryd ma'n nhw'n wneud, ti'n gwbod, *speech* a popeth, 'smo nhw'n wneud e Cymraeg a Saesneg, dim ond Saesneg, achos, ti'n gwbod, pobl o Ffrainc yn dod draw, a, ti'n gwbod, ma'n nhw'n deall tamed bach o Saesneg, ond 'sdim cliw 'da nhw ambyti'r Gymraeg.[81]

(When they were speaking, they were speaking English, nothing, people would be speaking Welsh with each other, but when they are making, you know, a speech and everything, they are not doing it in Welsh and English, only in English, because, you know, people from France come over here and, you know, they understand a bit of English, but they haven't got a clue about Welsh.)

Some pupils were even more hostile towards the Welsh language:

---

[80] Interview with respondent 2/37. See also respondent 2/57.
[81] Interview with respondent 2/38.

Mewn 'n ysgol i, 'sdim lot o pobl yn siarad Cymrâg o gwbwl, *really*. Ma'r rhan fwyaf yn siarad Saesneg, a so'n nhw'n *enthusiastic* ambyti'r iaith o gwbwl, a ma'n nhw'n gweud, 'o dwi ishe dropo fe', a ma'n nhw'n *really bitter* o achos ma' raid iddyn nhw siarad Cymrâg, i neud e fel TGAU. Felly, mewn ysgol ni, fydda i'n dweud fy hunan, falle bydd rhai pobl yn anghytuno, ond fi'n meddwl . . . dyw e ddim yn boblogaidd iawn, *really*.[82]

(In my school, not a lot of people speak Welsh, really. The majority speak English, and they're not enthusiastic about the language at all, and they say, 'oh I want to drop it', and they're really bitter, because they have to speak Welsh, and do it as GCSE. So, in our school, I would say myself, maybe some people will disagree, but I think . . . it's not very popular, really.)

The branch of Urdd Gobaith Cymru at Fishguard school seemed to be the only place where the Welsh language could be practised in a non-educational setting. However, because the branch was geared towards competitions this opportunity was only partly fulfilled. The only other two institutions where young Welsh speakers socialized naturally in the language were Aelwyd Carn Ingli and the two Welsh-speaking Young Farmers' Clubs in the county. Very few young people in the sample were members of either.[83] Opportunities for socializing in the Welsh language in culturally unmarked situations are increasingly rare, especially for young speakers. The consequences of this are a loss of confidence and a less positive attitude towards the language.

One example revealed how much can be achieved through relatively simple means even in a community like Fishguard, and why localized efforts should not be scorned and abandoned in favour of nationwide campaigns for improvements in status. All interviewees of the younger generation were familiar with the name of one Welsh pop group, although their knowledge about Welsh culture and their use of the Welsh media were otherwise extremely limited. The key to the popularity of this group among the young people of the area lay in the fact that it had performed several times at the annual festival, *Gŵyl Gwaun*.[84]

★ ★ ★

According to the *Cambrian News*, a meeting was convened in Aberystwyth in 1932 with the following aim:

to form a club to preserve the Welsh language which was in danger of being superseded by the English language . . . Welsh parents spoke English to their children with the result

---

[82] Interview with respondent 2/37.
[83] In 1997–8, membership at Aelwyd Carn Ingli stood at ten.
[84] *Gŵyl Gwaun* Minute Book; *Gŵyl Gwaun* Programme 1992; *Gŵyl Gwaun* Programme 1994.

that a large number of children in Aberystwyth could speak neither Welsh nor English properly. Another inclination in young people was to regard Welsh as a chapel language. They would listen to a sermon delivered in Welsh and sing Welsh hymns, but on leaving the chapel would converse among themselves in English . . . One danger to persons removing from rural parts into Aberystwyth was that they had no further opportunity of using their own language, and thus in time took a preference for speaking English.[85]

Over a period of some sixty years, the threats to the Welsh language have multiplied, but the symptoms of language death in urban communities, namely code-switching by an increasing number of people in an increasing number of situations, remain the same. As has been revealed in this sample from two communities, the work of voluntary bodies has gone some way to redressing the balance by providing leisure activities through the medium of Welsh and space designated for its use. However, since the publication of Joshua A. Fishman's classic *Reversing Language Shift* it is a commonplace that:

> Without intergenerational mother tongue transmission . . . no language maintenance is possible. That which is not transmitted cannot be maintained. On the other hand, without language maintenance (which is a post-transmission process) the pool from which successive intergenerational transmission efforts can draw must become continually smaller.[86]

Only functionally bilingual speakers, i.e. speakers who are familiar with applying their linguistic skills to a whole range of situations, from conversation within the family to socializing in mixed language settings and addressing strangers, will successfully transfer the language to the next generation. Therefore, more small-scale, community-based developments, offering opportunities for language use to both first- and second-language speakers, and learners alike, are required if the Welsh language is to survive.

---

[85] *Cambrian News*, 18 March 1932.
[86] Joshua A. Fishman, *Reversing Language Shift: Theoretical and Empirical Foundations of Assistance to Threatened Languages* (Clevedon, 1991), p. 113.

16

We'll Keep a Welcome? The Effects of Tourism on the Welsh Language

DYLAN PHILLIPS

THE INTERNATIONAL tourist industry witnessed an enormous expansion during the twentieth century. In 1950 it was estimated that around 25 million people spent their vacation in a foreign country, but by 1998 that number had increased to 625 million. Indeed, it has been estimated that within twenty years more than 1.6 billion people will travel to foreign climes for their annual holiday.[1] Unsurprisingly, therefore, tourism has exercised a profound impact on communities, societies and cultures worldwide. Since the end of the Second World War, tourism has been given a strategic role in the development of national economies and the augmentation of international commerce. It was quickly seen to be a lucrative source of currency and, in a bid to bolster their national balance sheets and create jobs for their citizens, governments throughout the world have endeavoured to promote and encourage the growth of the industry. According to Antonio Enríquez Savignac, Secretary-General of the World Tourism Organization, writing in 1993:

> Tourism undeniably acts as a driving force for world development. Its growth has overtaken that of international trade which in turn progresses faster than the creation of wealth . . . Tourism contributes to the transfer of wealth from North to South and from the industrialized to the developing countries . . . For them international tourism is unquestionably paramount as a creator of jobs and the most readily exploitable source of foreign earnings to finance investments or reduce foreign debt.[2]

Developed countries in the west as well as the developing countries of the Third World have therefore earmarked tourism as a vital component of their economies. During 1998 overseas tourism produced a return of 444.7 billion dollars in

---

[1] World Tourism Organization, *WTO News*, 1 (1999), 1 and 3; idem, *World Tourism 1970–1992* (Madrid, 1993). See also Paul Gallaghan, Phil Long and Mike Robinson (eds.), *Travel and Tourism* (2nd ed., Newcastle, 1994), p. 259.

[2] World Tourism Organization, *The World Tourism Organization and Technical Cooperation. I: Objectives and Procedures* (Madrid, 1993).

international revenue. The domestic tourism market is estimated to be worth ten times more than overseas tourism to most national revenues in developed countries such as Britain.[3] Consequently, tourism is widely considered to be a dynamic industry which has the potential to stimulate significant economic and social benefits.[4]

However, despite commendable efforts to enhance the economic rewards of the tourist industry, especially in developing countries, grave misgivings remain concerning its harmful effects. Considerable attention has been paid recently to the environmental impact of tourism, especially the tendency within many countries to pillage natural resources while developing holiday resorts. Indeed, tourism has been perceived as one of the greatest threats to the world's fragile eco-systems.[5] Tourism has also been indicted for introducing crime, prostitution and drug abuse into several developing countries.[6] And although the champions of tourism take great pains to ensure the advancement of an industry which is sustainable and environmentally-friendly, and which promotes understanding between different cultures, many communities have already been disfigured by unbridled development within the industry in its early days. According to Koson Srisang, former Executive Secretary to the Ecumenical Coalition on Third World Tourism:

> In short, tourism, especially Third World tourism, as it is practised today, does not benefit the majority of people. Instead it exploits them, pollutes the environment, destroys the ecosystem, bastardises the culture, robs people of their traditional values and ways of life and subjugates women and children in the abject slavery of prostitution. In other words, tourism epitomises the present unjust world economic order where the few who control wealth and power dictate the terms. As such, tourism is little different from colonialism.[7]

Developing countries are not alone in having suffered as a result of the tourist industry. Every resort has experienced problems such as traffic congestion,

---

[3] World Tourism Organization, *WTO News*, 1 (1999), 1 and 3. Receipts from international tourism would correspond to £274.5 billion, according to the currency exchange rate on 30 July 1998.

[4] Alister Mathieson and Geoffrey Wall, *Tourism: Economic, Physical and Social Impacts* (London, 1982), p. 1.

[5] See, for example, E. Goldsmith, 'Pollution by Tourism', *The Ecologist*, 48, no. 1 (1974), 47–8; A. Crittendon, 'Tourism's Terrible Toll', *International Wildlife*, 5, no. 3 (1975), 4–12; G. Mountfort, 'Tourism and Conservation', *Wildlife*, 17 (1975), 30–3; M. Tangi, 'Tourism and the Environment', *Ambio*, 6 (1977), 336–41. See also Colin Hunter and Howard Green, *Tourism and the Environment* (London, 1995).

[6] See, for example, L. R. McPheters and W. B. Stronge, 'Crime as an Environmental Externality of Tourism: Florida', *Land Economics*, 50 (1974), 288–92; Nelson H. H. Graburn, 'Tourism and Prostitution', *Annals of Tourism Research*, 10, no. 3 (1983), 437–43; A. Pizam, 'Tourism's Impacts: The Social Costs to the Destination as Perceived by its Residents', *Journal of Travel Research*, 16, no. 4 (1978), 8–12.

[7] Koson Srisang, 'Third World Tourism – The New Colonialism', *Tourism Concern in Focus*, 4 (1992), 2–3.

building developments which destroy the landscape, the inundation of peaceful communities with thousands of visitors, and competition between tourists and local residents for services and amenities. Therefore, despite the obvious economic advantages connected with tourism, many disadvantages are also prevalent. As Jost Krippendorf has observed:

> the mass phenomena of modern tourism has initiated the paradoxical process 'Tourism destroys tourism'. The landscape loses its tourist value through its use, or rather over-use, by the tourist.[8]

Although tourism enables host communities to develop economically and sustain the local population, it simultaneously destroys the very things which attracted the visitors in the first place, namely the splendid scenery and the unique culture and society of the indigenous population. Tourism, therefore, is a paradoxical industry, chequered with economic advantages and social and environmental disadvantages.[9]

Welsh Attitudes towards Tourism

This paradox is also a characteristic of the tourist industry in Wales. Although the majority of people welcome the economic and employment benefits, others berate the industry for tarnishing the environment, the landscape and the local community. In 1988 the European Centre for Traditional and Regional Cultures (ECTARC) published a study of the social, cultural and linguistic impact of tourism on Wales. Individuals, societies, groups and public bodies were invited to list the advantages and disadvantages of tourism to Wales and their response confirmed the widely-held belief that tourism was a double-edged sword. As Evan Lewis, General Secretary of the Farmers' Union of Wales, observed, many people in Wales tended to view tourism as a 'necessary evil'.[10] The study also showed that some visitors to Wales were aware of the ambivalent attitude of their hosts towards tourism. According to A. C. King, surveyor for the Camping and Caravanning Club:

> Most local authorities in Wales seem to suffer from a form of schizophrenia where tourism is concerned. From extensive experience . . . I have formed the opinion that

---

[8] Jost Krippendorf, 'Towards New Tourism Policies: The Importance of Environmental and Sociocultural Factors', *Tourism Management*, 3, no. 3 (1982), 135–48.

[9] For a full discussion on the positive and negative impacts of tourism on countries around the globe, see, for example, Mathieson and Wall, *Tourism: Economic, Physical and Social Impacts*, and Mike Robinson and Priscilla Boniface (eds.), *Tourism and Cultural Conflicts* (Wallingford, Oxon, 1999).

[10] ECTARC, *Study of the Social, Cultural and Linguistic Impact of Tourism in and upon Wales* (Cardiff, 1988). Evidence of Evan Lewis, General Secretary of the Farmers' Union of Wales, letter dated 25 March 1987.

the majority feels obliged to pay lip service to the encouragement of tourism, as a means
of economic salvation, whilst wishing that the 'foreigners' could be turned back at the
frontier, preferably leaving their money behind first.[11]

When ECTARC invited local residents at Llanberis, Newcastle Emlyn and the
Rhondda to air their views about the effects of tourism, it discovered that the
great majority were pleased to welcome tourists and that they believed that the
principal advantage of tourism was its capacity to create jobs for local people and
bring money to local shops and businesses. However, it was also feared that
tourism harmed the environment, precipitated traffic and parking problems, and
caused overcrowding in host communities.[12] In fact, the ECTARC results
corroborated several earlier studies which had come to similar conclusions. For
instance, a study carried out in north Wales in 1984 by Pauline J. Sheldon and
Turgut Var revealed that residents were keenly aware of the economic benefits of
tourism, but were also wary of its social and environmental implications.[13]

Part of the explanation for this ambivalence is the widely-held conviction that
the type of tourism developed in Wales over the years has been both unsuitable
and inappropriate to Welsh interests. Although most residents of tourist areas
appreciate the economic benefits and the additional jobs, they are critical of the
structure of the industry and its public image. A visible symbol of what is
considered to be inappropriate tourism is the static caravan park. In the mid-1960s
it was estimated that more than 40,000 caravans were located on over 1,000 sites
throughout Wales. Nearly a third of these parks were situated in north Wales.
There were sufficient beds for nearly 55,000 people in the static caravans of
Anglesey and Gwynedd alone, and along the coastline between Deeside and
Llandudno a further 70,000 caravanners were provided for.[14] The striking increase
in the number of static caravan parks caused considerable unease because of the
detrimental effect on the landscape and the natural environment, and the impact
on host communities. By the end of 1966 the Wales Tourist Board was obliged to
establish a Caravanning and Camping Committee in an attempt to regulate
further developments.[15] However, despite the attempts of local authorities to
impose more stringent controls and the campaigns against the proliferation of such
sites by bodies such as the National Parks and the Campaign for the Protection of

---

[11] Ibid., evidence of A. C. King, 'Club Surveyor' for the Camping and Caravanning Club, letter
   dated 5 December 1986.
[12] Ibid., part III, pp. 75–83.
[13] Pauline J. Sheldon and Turgut Var, 'Resident Attitudes to Tourism in North Wales', *Tourism
   Management*, 5, no. 1 (1984), 40–7. See also Wales Tourist Board, *Survey of Community Attitudes
   towards Tourism in Wales* (Cardiff, 1981).
[14] W. T. R. Pryce, 'The Location and Growth of Holiday Caravan Camps in Wales, 1956–65',
   TIBG, 42 (1967), 129–31, 140–1. See also Department of the Environment / The Welsh Office,
   Report of the Mobile Homes Review (London, 1977).
[15] Lyn Howell, *The Wales Tourist Board: The Early Years* (Cardiff, 1988), p. 5.

Rural Wales much of the damage across Wales had already occurred. At the end of the twentieth century it appeared that the static caravan was as popular as ever with visitors. According to Tourist Board figures published in 1999, the camping and caravanning sector of the industry provided nearly 45 per cent of the total available bedspaces for tourists in Wales.[16]

Another problem associated with the tourist industry in Wales is the holiday home. Following the appreciable increase in the number of visitors to the scenic rural and coastal areas from the 1930s onwards, the number of those who desired, and who could afford, to buy or rent a second home in Wales as a holiday retreat also multiplied. The rise in personal income in the decades after the Second World War enabled thousands of people, enticed by low house prices, to buy holiday homes in Wales. The greatest proliferation occurred during the 1960s and 1970s. In 1978 it was estimated that there were 26,000 holiday homes in Wales, 28.6 per cent of which were located in Gwynedd and Anglesey.[17] According to Roof, Shelter Cymru's monthly magazine, this number had risen to 30,000 by September 1983.[18] Census statistics in 1991 revealed that the highest density of holiday homes was to be found in the Llŷn peninsula. In Llanengan, for instance, 37 per cent of the total housing stock were second homes.[19] This development affected whole communities throughout Wales and there is no doubt that it was symptomatic of the general decline of rural areas. Local people could not hope to compete with affluent incomers who were able to afford higher prices for property. For example, the average house price in Anglesey in 1983 was £28,000, a price far beyond the means of most local families whose average income was 20 per cent lower than that of other families throughout Britain.[20] House prices continued to rise on the island, reaching an average of £64,535 by July 1997.[21] Holiday homes lay at the root of a host of social problems: young couples who could not afford to buy homes were forced to migrate, local schools were closed

---

[16] Wales Tourist Board, *Tourism in Wales – A Position Paper* (Cardiff, 1999), p. 9. See also Paul Ronald Fidgeon, 'Holiday Caravanning in Wales' (unpubl. University of Wales PhD thesis, 1984). In 1997, 24 per cent of all tourist nights spent in Wales by domestic holidaymakers were spent in static caravans. Wales Tourist Board, research information factsheet 1997: 'Analysis of the Domestic (UK) Visitor to Wales', p. 4.

[17] Chris Bollom, *Attitudes and Second Homes in Rural Wales* (Cardiff, 1978), p. 2; Richard de Vane, *Second Home Ownership: A Case Study* (Bangor, 1975), p. 14.

[18] Anne Grosskurth, 'North Wales: The Fire Next Time', *Roof*, 8, no. 5 (1983), 19–22.

[19] Dwyfor District Council, *Dwyfor Local Plan* (Appendix – Deposit Draft, June 1995), Table 8: 'Households and Occupancy – Community Council Areas in Dwyfor, Districts, Gwynedd and Wales – 1991 Census of Population'.

[20] Grosskurth, 'North Wales: The Fire Next Time', 19–22. See also research carried out on the social background of second-home owners in Wales and an analysis of their capital earnings in de Vane, *Second Home Ownership*, pp. 21–5.

[21] Isle of Anglesey County Council, *Housing Strategy and Operational Plan, 1998/9* (Llangefni, 1998), p. 7. See also Anglesey District Council Planning Department, *Housing Market Research* (Llangefni, 1988); Dewi Gareth Lloyd, 'Monitoring Migration and Housing Demands in Anglesey: Analysis and Policy Perspective' (Town Planning Diploma, University of Wales Cardiff, 1990).

because of the dearth of young families with children, and services such as public transport, the village shop and post office were curtailed owing to the lack of all-year-round custom. The inevitable result of this process was that not only individual houses but also whole villages lay empty for long periods of the year.[22] Little wonder, therefore, that the problem of holiday homes was prominent on the political agenda in Wales throughout the 1970s and 1980s. A civil disobedience campaign led by Cymdeithas yr Iaith Gymraeg (the Welsh Language Society) demanded legislation which would give local people priority within the property market, and in December 1979 a group calling itself Meibion Glyndŵr (Sons of Glyndŵr) resorted to firebombing holiday homes throughout Wales.[23]

Furthermore, there were grave concerns that the image of Welsh culture and society projected by the tourist industry was both contrived and inappropriate. Apart from publishing photographs of Welsh women in traditional costume in holiday guidebooks and on postcards, very little effort was made to portray Wales as a country with a distinctive culture and history. As a result, little difference could be discerned between the seaside resorts of Llandudno and Brighton or Tenby and Skegness. The Wales Tourist Board was accused of investing too great a proportion of its resources in marketing Wales to tourists from across the border rather than seeking to persuade Welsh people to sample the attractions of different areas of their own country. Ambitious plans to build marinas along the Welsh coastline at Pwllheli and Aberystwyth were bitterly criticized since, to some people at least, they reinforced the notion that Wales was simply a playground for English visitors.[24] As Robert Minhinnick, a fervent advocate of green issues, attested in 1993: 'tourism is doing its level best to destroy what many people consider the two essential characteristics of Wales – its environment and its culture'.[25] At times, marketing enterprises flagrantly discounted the native culture and history, one notable example being when the Tourist Board promoted its 'Cestyll '83 – Festival of Castles' to celebrate the seventh centenary of the building of fortifications which were instrumental in Edward I's campaign to subjugate and conquer Wales.[26] Nor could it be said that the industry had made any attempt, until recently, to offer a Welsh welcome to visitors. Tourism in Wales had a thoroughly Anglicized image, and the provision of bilingual signs and literature at

---

[22] Several studies on the effects of holiday homes have been carried out in various countries. See, for example, Michael Barke and Lesley A. France, 'Second Homes in the Balearic Islands', *Geography*, 73, no. 2 (1988), 143–5; Michael Barke, 'The Growth and Changing Pattern of Second Homes in Spain in the 1970s', *Scottish Geographical Magazine*, 107, no. 1 (1991), 12–21.

[23] See Nick Gallent, Gary Higgs and Mark Tewdwr-Jones, *Second Homes in Focus* (Cardiff, 1996).

[24] Cymdeithas yr Iaith Gymraeg, *Twristiaeth i Bwy? – Twyll y 'Marinas'* (Aberystwyth, 1984).

[25] Robert Minhinnick, *A Postcard Home: Tourism in the Mid-'nineties* (Cardiff, 1993), p. 5.

[26] Angharad Tomos, 'Dileu Symbolau', *Y Faner*, 11 March 1983.

tourist attractions was conspicuous by its absence.[27] Since the type of tourism developed in Wales over the years was felt to be inappropriate and unsuitable, many Welsh people, and especially Welsh speakers, came to regard it as an alien industry forced upon them by outsiders.

Tourism and the Welsh Language

Nowadays most visitors to Wales take a more enlightened view of the country and its culture. However, as several recent studies have demonstrated, the perception of tourism as a foreign implant has only slightly diminished over the decades. Sheldon and Var argued in 1984 that Welsh speakers tended to be more reluctant than their non-Welsh-speaking compatriots to recognize the economic advantages of tourism, and that they were also more sensitive to the social and cultural disadvantages.[28] These findings were confirmed by Richard Prentice and Jayne Hudson in a more comprehensive study undertaken in 1993.[29] Consequently Welsh speakers as a group have tended to be less inclined to take advantage of the economic opportunities afforded by the growth of the industry. Indeed, the business enterprise agency, Menter a Busnes, was so concerned by this tendency that in 1998, in an attempt to encourage Welsh speakers to venture into tourism, it initiated a project called 'Croesawiaith' (Language-welcome). In a survey of attitudes towards the industry, the 'Croesawiaith' pilot scheme, which was conducted in Anglesey, concluded that opinion leaders within the Welsh-speaking community displayed 'indifference, genuine doubts and sometimes antipathy . . . towards the industry'. Although the report claimed that young people were 'developing more unbiased and constructive perspectives about tourism, hard, persistent and sometimes unhealthy attitudes remain amongst older and influential people'.[30]

There is no doubt that the tendency among Welsh speakers to spurn tourism to some extent reflects their misgivings and suspicions about its effects on their language. For several years geographers and historians have counted tourism among the many factors which have contributed to the appreciable decline in the number and percentage of Welsh speakers during the twentieth century. In 1956 J. Gareth Thomas noted:

[27] This was one of the main findings of research carried out for the 'Croesawiaith' scheme. Menter a Busnes, *Croesawiaith Môn* (Aberystwyth, 1993), pp. 17–20, par. 4.3.1–4.3.7.

[28] Sheldon and Var, 'Resident Attitudes to Tourism in North Wales', 44.

[29] Richard Prentice and Jayne Hudson, 'Assessing the Linguistic Dimension in the Perception of Tourism Impacts by Residents of a Tourist Destination: A Case Study of Porthmadog, Gwynedd', *Tourism Management*, 14, no. 4 (1993), 298–306. However, the authors warned that it should not be taken for granted that popular opinion of tourism depends wholly on the language they speak.

[30] Menter a Busnes, *Croesawiaith Môn*, p. 3, par. 2.1–2.2.

Not only does English become the essential commercial language for Welsh people living in these regions, but their population also contains a considerable English element, not merely connected with the tourist industry, but purely as a residential class of retired people who at their time of life are not likely to learn a new language.[31]

E. G. Bowen and Harold Carter also referred to the effects of tourism on the language in 1974: 'Tourism . . . in attracting English entrepreneurs and foreign workers and bringing in its train second home ownership and retirement, must be regarded as a strong anglicising agent.'[32] And in considering the plight of the language in Anglesey, John Aitchison and Harold Carter stated in 1994:

In Anglesey the growth of tourism and the popularity of the region for retirement contributed significantly to the Anglicization of the coastal communities, with a subsequent encroachment on the strong central Welsh-speaking core area. Between 1961 and 1981 such communities as Llanbadrig, Llaniestyn Rural, Llaneilian, Llanfair Mathafarn Eithaf, Pentraeth, Llanddona, Llandegfan, Llangeinwen and Llanynghenedl, all experienced major reductions in the proportions able to speak Welsh, that is percentage differences between the dates of over 20 per cent.[33]

The language movement was also deeply apprehensive about the effects of tourism and demands for more stringent control of the industry had been voiced since the beginning of the 1970s. In the first *Maniffesto* of the Welsh Language Society in 1972, Cynog Dafis warned that the manner in which the holiday industry was being developed in Wales brought 'the least possible economic benefit and the maximum of pollution and social dislocation'. The Welsh Language Society feared that the 'Welsh countryside could easily become a social, cultural and economic wilderness, a mere playground for the English Midlands'. 'Now', warned Dafis, 'the flood of the tourist industry is destroying villages as surely and completely as the waters covered Capel Celyn. Through the traffic in holiday homes, and because of the general weakness of the rural economy, the social foundations of the most Welsh parts of Wales are being destroyed.'[34] These misgivings prompted the Society to embark on a campaign directed against all holiday homes, marinas, and other tourist developments which were reckoned to threaten the interests of local people. Similarly, the language rights movement

---

[31] J. Gareth Thomas, 'The Geographical Distribution of the Welsh Language', *The Geographical Journal*, 122, part 1 (1956), 71–9.

[32] E. G. Bowen and Harold Carter, 'Preliminary Observations on the Distribution of the Welsh Language at the 1971 Census', ibid., 140, part 3 (1974), 432–40.

[33] John Aitchison and Harold Carter, *A Geography of the Welsh Language 1961–1991* (Cardiff, 1994), p. 52.

[34] Cynog Davies, *Maniffesto Cymdeithas yr Iaith Gymraeg* (Aberystwyth, 1972), pp. 24, 39–40. Translation by Harri Webb, 'Cymdeithas yr Iaith – the Manifesto', *Planet*, 26/27 (1974–5), 77–136.

Adfer believed that since the tourist industry was a force which destabilized and despoiled communities in the Welsh-speaking heartland, it was contributing to the elimination of the Welsh nation.[35]

Studying the Effects of Tourism on Culture

Such linguistic concerns are not peculiar to Wales. Supporters of minority cultures throughout Europe have expressed similar anxieties about the destructive impact of tourism on their own indigenous languages. However, the relationship between tourism and language is a relatively new field of study, since the task of measuring its negative impacts in any capacity only began in earnest during the last two decades.[36] This was partly because of the assumption that the economic advantages of tourism outweigh any other considerations. Consequently, several studies have been undertaken with the aim of increasing and maximizing the economic and employment outputs of the industry. The disadvantages of tourism also went unheeded until recently because its associated social and environmental ill-effects were not immediately obvious. However, as the industry began to over-develop in the 1970s, concerns regarding the negative impacts on host communities also multiplied. As a result, 'sustainable' and 'green' became popular watchwords for the holiday industry, and its social and environmental impacts came under careful scrutiny. Even so, little work has been undertaken on the effects of tourism on the language and culture of host communities. This is surprising given that many popular tourist resorts, especially on the Continent, are to be found in areas with autochthonous regional or minority languages and cultures.[37]

Measuring the effects of tourism on language, however, is extremely difficult. As the ECTARC study in 1988 demonstrated, to attribute the decline of Welsh to the effects of tourism would be simplistic since so many other social and economic forces, including uniform state education, the mass media, lack of official public status, in-migration, out-migration, etc., can militate against the language.[38] However, the majority of sociolinguists acknowledge that tourism is bound to have an impact on a minority language and its culture. After all, tourism creates a situation whereby people who speak different languages and have a different culture and way of life constantly come into contact with and need to

---

[35] Mudiad Adfer, *Maniffesto Adfer* (Penrhosgarnedd, 1987), p. 9.

[36] Unfortunately, little comprehensive research has hitherto been undertaken on the effects of tourism in Wales, and virtually no work focuses on its effects on the Welsh language. However, the University of Wales Centre for Advanced Welsh and Celtic Studies plans to publish shortly the findings of its study on the relationship between tourism and the Welsh language in north-west Wales.

[37] Allan Wynne Jones, 'Indigenous Cultures Close to Home', *Tourism Concern in Focus*, 8 (1993), 14–15.

[38] ECTARC, *Study of the . . . Impact of Tourism in and upon Wales*, part IV, pp. 91–3.

communicate with one another. The few early studies which focused on the impact of tourism on language and culture certainly came to this conclusion. One such study by Davydd J. Greenwood in 1972 focused on the effects of tourism on the town of Fuenterrabia in the Basque country. Although he makes no reference to the impact on Euskara, the Basque language, the author demonstrates how the inhabitants' traditional way of life was affected by the social and economic changes caused by tourism:

> Fuenterrabia's cultural heritage has become a commodity, a neo–Basque facade packaged and promoted for tourists. As for the Basques themselves, some have identified with the new consumer way of life, whereas the rest appear to be receding into ever more private cultural worlds, leaving only the outward forms of their life for touristic consumption. In the future Fuenterrabia promises to become nearly indistinguishable from all the other tourist towns on the coast of Spain.[39]

Theron A. Nunez came to a similar conclusion: he argued that the development of tourism in the village of Cajititlán in Mexico from 1960 onwards strongly resembled a conquest by invaders. This rural village swiftly developed into a popular tourist resort for people from nearby cities who were eager to spend their weekends on the shores of the beautiful lake adjacent to the village. New houses were built as tourist accommodation and the village was transformed to make it more pleasant and appealing to visitors. However, this resulted in the erosion of local traditions and customs, such as hunting with guns, horse-racing, and outlawing the right of inhabitants to bear pistols. They were not even allowed to wear the traditional white cotton trousers (*calzones*) since they resembled undergarments and were therefore deemed to be indecent. And, of course, much good agricultural land was used for building holiday cabins and holiday homes.[40] The effect of tourism on Scottish Gaelic has also been the subject of research. When interviewed, a large minority of Sleat's inhabitants on the Isle of Skye expressed negative views of the industry, claiming that the presence of visitors inhibited the use of their native language and culture.[41]

The most important study to date on the effects of tourism on a minority language is P. E. White's study of the Romansh communities of Switzerland in 1974. In his introduction, the author states:

---

[39] Davydd J. Greenwood, 'Tourism as an Agent of Change: A Spanish Basque Case', *Ethnology*, 11, no. 1 (1972), 80–91.

[40] Theron A. Nunez Jr., 'Tourism, Tradition, and Acculturation: *Weekendismo* in a Mexican Village', ibid., 2, no. 3 (1963), 347–52.

[41] J. E. Brougham and R. W. Butler, *The Impact of Tourism on Language and Culture in Sleat, Skye* (Scottish Tourist Board, 1977).

In the last ten years a small but increasing body of studies has come to the conclusion that tourist development most often serves the interests of the tourists and does not truly act as a local economic and social stimulant, but as a superimposed irritant in the receiving areas.[42]

White revealed a direct correlation between tourism and the decline of the Romansh language in Kanton Graubünden in south-east Switzerland. By comparing the percentage of speakers with the density of tourism, the author showed that Romansh was at its weakest in areas with a high density of tourism and at its strongest in areas with a low density of tourism. For example, the lowest numbers of Romansh speakers were to be found in the popular tourist centres of Upper Engadin; in St Moritz and Pontresina, for instance, less than 25 per cent of the population spoke Romansh. On the other hand, the highest number of speakers lived in the rural areas of Lower Engadin, where very little tourism was to be found. According to the author:

> The mechanism of language change in the whole study area over the last eighty years is thus inextricably tied up with tourism. Where tourism has consistently been at a high level relative to the average position for the whole area the proportion of the population claiming Romansch as first language has declined at a much faster rate than in the communes where tourism has been at a relatively lower level.[43]

The Advantages of Tourism for the Welsh Language

Wales undoubtedly derives its greatest benefit from the economic value of tourism and its ability to create jobs. Since the Second World War considerable emphasis has been placed on tourism as a means of regenerating the Welsh economy. According to the first report of the Welsh Reconstruction Advisory Council in 1944: 'In the magnificent scenery of her mountains and coasts, Wales possesses a capital asset no less important than her resources of coal or slate, and any balanced plan of national development must provide for the full utilisation of this asset.'[44] In 1950 it was estimated that 35,000 visitors came to Wales and that they spent a total of £35 million at tourist resorts throughout the country.[45] In

---

[42] P. E. White, *The Social Impact of Tourism on Host Communities: A Study of Language Change in Switzerland* (Oxford, 1974), p. 2.

[43] Ibid., p. 23. For further discussions regarding the impact of tourism on culture in other countries see, for example, Louis Turner and John Ash, *The Golden Hordes: International Tourism and the Pleasure Periphery* (London, 1975); Mathieson and Wall, *Tourism: Economic, Physical and Social Impacts*; Robinson and Boniface (eds.), *Tourism and Cultural Conflicts*.

[44] Welsh Reconstruction Advisory Council, *First Interim Report* (London, 1944), p. 59. Quoted in William J. Jones, 'The Economics of the Welsh Tourist Industry' (unpubl. University of Wales MA thesis, 1951), p. 9.

[45] Jones, 'The Economics of the Welsh Tourist Industry', pp. 26, 35.

1961 over 4 million people spent nearly 28 million nights on holiday in Wales, and this accounted for nearly 10 per cent of the total domestic market in Britain. It was also estimated that these visitors spent £50 million during their stay. By the 1960s, therefore, tourism had established itself as the fifth largest industry in Wales, after iron, steel, coal and agriculture.[46] In 1997, according to Wales Tourist Board figures, 41.8 million tourist nights were spent in Wales by domestic visitors, and 6.4 million nights by foreign visitors. Thus domestic tourism was estimated to be worth over £1.1 billion to Wales, while overseas tourism was worth £226 million. Moreover, day-trippers added a further £550 million to the country's economy.[47] Indeed, it appears that the holiday industry, in terms of its contribution to the Gross Domestic Product (GDP), is as important to the economy of Wales as it is to the economies of Spain and Greece.[48]

Tourism also offers employment for many people. In 1926 it was estimated that 10,040 people were employed in the catering sector in Wales. This figure rose to 31,080 in 1950, when hotel employees were included for the first time in catering sector statistics.[49] By 1997 as many as 60,000 people in Wales were directly employed in the holiday industry.[50] But tourism also helps to support jobs in other sectors, such as transport, retail and public services. Indeed, it is claimed that more than 30,000 additional jobs are maintained by the holiday industry. Arguably, therefore, nearly 90,000 jobs in Wales, constituting more than 9 per cent of the whole workforce, are directly or indirectly linked to tourism.[51] At a time when their traditional industries face recession, the importance of tourism to the economy of Welsh-speaking areas is undeniable. Following the decline of agriculture and the slate industry due to pressures of modernization and international competition, tourism has helped to sustain communities which would otherwise have suffered severe hardship. It is hardly surprising, therefore, that so much emphasis is currently placed on tourism as a source of income and jobs in Wales, and that it is an integral part of the economic strategy of local authorities.[52]

---

[46] The Council for Wales and Monmouthshire, *Report on the Welsh Holiday Industry* (London, 1963) (PP 1962–3 (Cmnd. 1950) XXV), p. 11. Quoted in Pryce, 'The Location and Growth of Holiday Caravan Camps in Wales, 1956–65', 129.

[47] Wales Tourist Board, research information factsheets 1997: 'Tourism in Wales', 'Analysis of the Domestic (UK) Visitor to Wales', and 'Overseas Visitors to Wales'. See also idem, *Annual Report 1996/1997* (Cardiff, 1997).

[48] In 1987 tourism represented between 4.5 and 5.5 per cent of the Welsh GDP, and between 3 and 4 per cent of the British GDP. See Stephen F. Witt, 'Economic Impact of Tourism on Wales', *Tourism Management*, 8, no. 4 (1987), 306–16. According to the Wales Tourist Board, it represented as much as 7.5 per cent of the Welsh GDP by 1999. Wales Tourist Board, *Tourism in Wales – A Position Paper*, p. 3. See also Tim Beddoes, 'Tourism in the Welsh Economy', *Welsh Economic Review*, 6, no. 2 (1993), 40–50.

[49] Jones, 'The Economics of the Welsh Tourist Industry', p. 66.

[50] Wales Tourist Board, research information factsheet 1997: 'Tourism in Wales'. See also idem, *Annual Report 1996/1997*.

[51] Ibid.

[52] Jeremy Alden, *Review of Structure Plan Policies for Tourism in Wales* (Cardiff, 1992). See also Kenneth D. George and Lynn Mainwaring, 'The Welsh Economy in the 1980s', *CW*, 1 (1987), 7–37.

At the end of the twentieth century tourism has become a key employer in the Welsh-speaking heartland and an essential element of its economy. This was effectively demonstrated in a study conducted by the Economic Research Institute of the University College of North Wales, Bangor, in 1973. Between June and September 1973, 2.8 million tourists visited Gwynedd. Over 1.8 million (67 per cent) of these stayed overnight, while 905,000 were day-trippers. During their visit these tourists were estimated to have spent over £41 million which, through a multiplier effect, generated a total of £47.5 million to the business turnover in Gwynedd during those three months. The study also revealed that tourism was responsible for 15.3 per cent of Gwynedd's total direct income in 1973, compared with an income of 17.9 per cent from agriculture and 11 per cent from the production industries.[53] By 1999 it was estimated that tourism brought £181 million a year to the economy of Anglesey alone.[54] Moreover, tourism is a significant employer within the region. A study by Peter Sadler, Brian Archer and Christine Owen in 1973 showed how the multiplier effect of tourism also boosted Anglesey's workforce: for every nine jobs created on the island as a direct result of tourist expenditure, an additional job was created within the local economy as a result of the multiplier effect.[55] Tourism, therefore, has become a crucial aspect of the Welsh economy.

Of course, economies which are too heavily dependent on the tourist industry have many weaknesses. Tourism is, after all, a seasonal and inherently unstable industry, vulnerable to variables such as inflation, recession and fashion, not to mention the weather. The potential value of jobs associated with the holiday industry is also compromised by the fact that they are mostly part-time and poorly paid; they also instil an inferiority complex within those who are obliged to tend to visitors' needs. Moreover, even though tourism undeniably swells the ranks of the workforce during the summer months, unemployment is a heavy price to pay during the winter.[56] Research undertaken by Brian Archer and Sheila Shea in 1977 revealed that only 54 per cent of the workforce within the accommodation sector in Wales was employed throughout the year, and that the remainder were laid-off when the holiday season came to an end.[57] Furthermore, although the Welsh economy has profited considerably from tourism, the type of tourism which was developed in the past severely limited its potential economic benefits.

---

[53] Brian Archer, Sheila Shea and Richard de Vane, *Tourism in Gwynedd: An Economic Study* (Cardiff, 1973).

[54] Isle of Anglesey County Council, *Ynys Môn Visitor Survey, 1997/98* (Llangefni, 1998), 'Summary of Findings', p. 16. See also *Western Mail*, 1 February 1999.

[55] Peter Sadler, Brian Archer and Christine Owen, *Regional Income Multipliers: The Anglesey Study* (Bangor, 1973).

[56] See 'Reports Clash on Tourism's Ability to Generate Jobs', *The Times*, 21 May 1986.

[57] Brian Archer and Sheila Shea, *Manpower in Tourism: The Situation in Wales* (Cardiff, 1977), p. 16. See also R. M. Ball, 'Some Aspects of Tourism, Seasonality and Local Labour Markets', *Area*, 21, no. 1 (1989), 35–45.

According to the study carried out in Bangor in 1973, self-catering accommodation was the least profitable sector developed in Gwynedd because of its over-dependence on static caravans and holiday homes. Caravan parks generally attracted low-income tourists and caravanners and holiday-home owners contributed little to the local economy since they tended to bring their own food. The most profitable type of tourism was found to be hotel and bed and breakfast accommodation (provided the establishments were owned by local people) since the money spent by tourists was more likely to remain in the area.[58]

In recent years, however, the tourist industry has adopted a more responsible attitude and much more attention is now being paid to the economic and social needs of the inhabitants and communities of Wales. In all its policy and strategy development exercises over the past fifteen years the Wales Tourist Board has strived purposefully to increase the economic benefits and to limit the social and environmental drawbacks. As has already been pointed out, money spent by tourists permeates through many circles within society, including shops, restaurants and small local businesses. The fact that local produce, such as spring water, cheese, meat and fish, is served in many restaurants and hotels offers further employment opportunities. Tourism can also supplement rural incomes by affording people the opportunity to offer bed and breakfast accommodation to visitors, an important additional income for many farming families.[59] Indirectly, it also enables local communities to maintain services such as public transport and a wider range of activities than would otherwise be possible.[60]

Tourism, therefore, has the potential to be of considerable benefit to the Welsh language. By giving them a more secure economic base, the tourist industry can help to sustain Welsh-speaking communities, a role which the Wales Tourist Board now recognizes and lists among its policy objectives. In a report published by the Welsh Select Committee of the House of Commons in April 1987, it was suggested that the Tourist Board should include in its main policy document the following objective: 'To conserve the unique way of life, culture and environment of Wales, which gives tourism in the Principality its distinctive character.'[61] In October that year the following clause was published in *Tourism in Wales – Developing the Potential*: 'the Board believes that on balance tourism is of substantial benefit to the cause of maintaining Wales' cultural and linguistic identity, and that

---

[58] Archer, Shea and de Vane, *Tourism in Gwynedd: An Economic Study.*

[59] See W. Dyfri Jones and D. A. G. Green, *Farm Tourism in Hill and Upland Areas of Wales* (Aberystwyth, 1986) and E. T. Davies and D. C. Gilbert, 'A Case Study of the Development of Farm Tourism in Wales', *Tourism Management*, 13, no. 1 (1992), 56–63. See also Peter Midmore, Garth Hughes and David Bateman, 'Agriculture and the Rural Economy: Problems, Policies and Prospects', *CW*, 6 (1994), 7–32.

[60] Gwynedd County Council Planning Department, *Gwynedd Structure Plan: Tourism and Recreation Policy Paper* (Caernarfon, 1985), p. 7, par. 5.9.

[61] Committee on Welsh Affairs, *Tourism in Wales* (London, 1987), I, p. vi., section 3. See also 'Dylai Twristiaeth Gydfynd â Dymuniadau Lleol', *Y Cymro*, 1 April 1987.

pride and interest in this living heritage can be strengthened through tourism'.[62] In 1998 the Tourist Board and Menter a Busnes launched the 'Croesawiaith' project in an attempt to 'increase awareness and understanding of tourism within Welsh culture, and to show its relevance and potential to the local and national economy'.[63] It was also realized that tourism could actively promote wider use of the language. Research commissioned by the Wales Tourist Board revealed that a significant proportion of visitors to Wales had shown an interest in Welsh culture, and that many of them would be pleased to encounter more evidence of the language.[64] As a result, projects such as 'Sense of Place' enable the Board to award grants to private tourist enterprises in order to encourage the wider use of bilingual signage within the industry.[65] Such efforts not only help to educate overseas visitors regarding the existence of the Welsh language and a distinctive national identity, but also contribute to the important task of encouraging the normalization of Welsh as a living medium of communication and culture.

The Disadvantages of Tourism for the Welsh Language

Although tourism clearly has the potential to support, promote and revitalize the language, many people remain convinced that its effects are detrimental. The experiences of other countries and cultures indicate that tourism can have adverse sociolinguistic effects. In concluding his study of the plight of Romansh in Switzerland, P. E. White declared:

> All over Europe today – for example in southern Italy, Languedoc, and western Scotland – tourism is bringing great changes which are of benefit to the regional economic balance sheet, but which may be highly disturbing to established social patterns and maintenance of a vibrant social and cultural identity. The evidence of this paper is that tourism generally acts as a destructive force in this sphere, and one that must be weighed against the desire for general economic development.[66]

Despite recent attempts by the Tourist Board and local authorities to develop an industry which is sensitive to the needs of the language, tourism has already inflicted considerable and, perhaps, irreversible damage. Not only has it been responsible for many unsuitable and inappropriate developments within Welsh society, but it has also affected the language in a much more direct and destructive manner.

---

[62] Wales Tourist Board, *Tourism in Wales – Developing the Potential* (Cardiff, 1987), p. 20, par. 3.14–3.16.

[63] Menter a Busnes, *Croesawiaith Môn*, p. 3, par. 2.1–2.2.

[64] Ibid., pp. 13–16, par. 4.2.1–4.2.7.

[65] Wales Tourist Board and Menter a Busnes, *A Sense of Place: A Guide to Bilingual Signage* (Cardiff, 1994).

[66] White, *The Social Impact of Tourism on Host Communities*, p. 35.

Tourism directly affects language by encouraging the in-migration of outsiders to the host community. In 1985 a paper on tourism and recreation published by Gwynedd County Council warned: 'The annual influx of visitors, in many places several times larger than the local population, with their own languages and cultures, may gradually weaken the local culture, language and traditional way of life of the resident Welsh population.'[67] According to the planning officer of Meirionnydd District Council in 1975, it was estimated that the population of the district increased from 31,000 during the winter months to over 100,000 during the peak of the summer holiday season. Tourists outnumbered local residents by more than four to one in some communities along the coast. Small wonder that the percentage of Welsh speakers in places like Aberdyfi, Tywyn and Barmouth declined sharply during the second half of the twentieth century.[68] Tourism also encourages the permanent in-migration of outsiders by attracting people to settle in areas where they have previous holiday connections, thus affecting the local community on a long-term rather than on a seasonal basis. Rather than visiting for a fortnight and then returning home, these incomers settle permanently in an area, bringing their values, culture and language with them. In a letter published in the *Western Mail* in 1986, Royston Jones alleged that in-migration to rural Wales was a direct result of tourism: 'today's tourist is tomorrow's immigrant'. He referred to the north Wales coastline as 'a seaside suburb of Liverpool':

> An area that once was Welsh, has, through uncontrolled and indiscriminate tourism followed by immigration become what it is today, a hideous expanse of funfair, followed by caravan park for mile after nauseating mile, scouse in speech and sentiment. This is the future that tourism offers the rest of Wales.[69]

Despite the obvious polemic, the author's observations were not without foundation for there is reason to believe that tourism is indeed connected with three forms of in-migration, namely economic in-migration, anti-urban in-migration, and retirement in-migration.

One of the most obvious consequences of the expansion of tourism is the in-migration of people seeking employment within the industry, a process which P. E. White refers to as 'economic in-migration'. Tourism is a labour-intensive industry and wherever there is thriving trade there are also jobs and entrepreneurial opportunities. Consequently, many people migrate to the main tourist resorts in Wales each year in the hope of securing employment. A thriving holiday industry also attracts enterprising individuals who have sufficient means to procure local businesses such as the village shop or post office, a public house or

---

[67] Gwynedd County Council, *Tourism and Recreation Policy Paper*, p. 7, par. 5.9.
[68] G. F. Broom, 'Tourism in Meirionnydd', *Cambria*, 2, no. 1 (1975), 52–5.
[69] 'Costa Geriatrica', letter from Royston Jones, *Western Mail*, 11 August 1986.

restaurant, or even to convert a house bought locally into bed and breakfast accommodation. Large hotels and holiday camps import most of their managerial staff from outside the host community, leaving only the most menial jobs for local residents. Tourist ventures in Wales often rely on capital invested from outside, which also means that any profit deriving from such ventures flows out of the country.

Examples of this process are legion within popular tourist destinations throughout the world.[70] In his study of the village of Trentino Alto-Adige in the Kanton Graubünden region of Switzerland in 1974, P. E. White revealed that seven hotels employed a total of 120 people at the height of the holiday season in the summer and winter months, only three of whom hailed from the village. The remainder were all incomers, ninety of whom had moved to the area from Italy in search of work. In another village which boasted ten hotels employing between twelve and twenty people each, over 90 per cent of the staff came from South Tirol.[71] Davydd J. Greenwood came to a similar conclusion in his study of Fuenterrabia. Here, too, tourism was found to be heavily dependent upon investment and control from outside the Basque region: '[Tourism] provides economic growth, but for whom? In this case Spain has profited, but the people of Fuenterrabia are being excluded.'[72] The influx of foreign investment and management is one of the major concerns of host communities throughout the world, and is particularly acute in countries such as Hawaii, Fiji, the West Indies and Africa,[73] but it also manifests itself in many resorts in the British Isles. For example, a study of the modest tourist resort of Looe, carried out in 1988 by Gareth Shaw and Allan Williams, showed that around 90 per cent of the tourist workforce of this small Cornish town, with a resident population of 4,500 people, had been born outside Cornwall and Devon.[74]

In the wake of the thriving tourist industry, Wales has also experienced the same kind of economic in-migration. In a comprehensive study of the local labour markets of north Wales in 1989, R. M. Ball revealed that many tourist employees in resorts such as Llandudno and Colwyn Bay had migrated from outside the area. Indeed, at one important resort in Gwynedd only 15 per cent of the staff hailed from Wales while the rest came from England. Two-thirds of all the staff were natives of north-west England, and nearly 30 per cent hailed from Manchester and

---

[70] For an introduction to studies of tourist in-migration in other countries, see Mathieson and Wall, *Tourism: Economic, Physical and Social Impacts*, pp. 61–2.

[71] White, *The Social Impact of Tourism on Host Communities*, p. 17.

[72] Greenwood, 'Tourism as an Agent of Change', 90–1.

[73] For instance, see P. van der Werff, 'Polarizing Implications of the Pescaia Tourist Industry', *Annals of Tourism Research*, 7 (1980), 197–223; R. B. Potter, 'Tourism and Development: The Case of Barbados, West Indies', *Geography*, 68, no. 1 (1983), 46–50.

[74] Gareth Shaw and Allan Williams, 'Tourism and Employment: Reflections on a Pilot Study of Looe, Cornwall', *Area*, 20, no. 1 (1988), 23–34.

Liverpool.[75] As a result of economic in-migration, the tourist industry in Wales became Anglicized in both image and language. This was demonstrated in a study of employment statistics carried out by Garth Hughes and Anne-Marie Sherwood on behalf of Menter a Busnes in 1991. According to their findings, a higher percentage of non-Welsh speakers prevailed in the distribution, hotels and catering sector than in any other sector of the workforce throughout Wales. Tourism was found to be especially Anglicized in Gwynedd: only 3,450 (40.2 per cent) of the workforce in the hotels and catering sector were recorded as being able to speak Welsh in 1991, compared to the 55,220 (60.2 per cent) Welsh speakers within the entire workforce. The percentage of Welsh speakers who had managerial responsibilities within this sector (25.9 per cent) or who owned their own tourist businesses (24.3 per cent) was even lower.[76]

An abundance of anecdotal evidence also suggests that tourism and in-migration are closely associated. When questioned about the effects of tourism during the ECTARC study in 1987, several respondents reiterated the opinion that it encouraged and actively caused economic in-migration. J. R. Thomas, Liaison Officer for the Pony Trekking and Riding Society of Wales, noted that 95 per cent of their centres in Wales were in the hands of in-migrants from England. Speaking on behalf of the Welsh language movement Cefn, Eleri Carrog alleged that the vast majority of craft centres were also owned by people who had moved into Wales.[77] The editorial of the June 1986 issue of Yr Odyn, the community newspaper for the Conwy valley, claimed that 90 per cent of the tourist attractions in Gwynedd were owned by outsiders.[78] However, tourism also encouraged economic in-migration not necessarily connected with the holiday industry itself. In a study conducted in 1973, C. M. Law and A. M. Warnes revealed that 27.7 per cent of all incomers employed in Llandudno had previous holiday connections with the town.[79] Other resorts reported similar findings. The study by Shaw and Williams in Cornwall revealed that although the overwhelming majority of incomers had moved to Looe for social rather than economic reasons, they had later established businesses in the area.[80]

---

[75] R. M. Ball, 'Some Aspects of Tourism, Seasonality and Local Labour Markets', 40–3. See also idem, 'A Study of Seasonal Employment in the UK Labour Market with Particular Reference to Seasonally-sensitive Industries and Seasonal Voluntary Labour Supplies in North Wales and the North and South Midlands' (unpubl. University of Birmingham PhD thesis, 1986).

[76] Garth Hughes and Anne-Marie Sherwood, *Economic Activity and Linguistic Characteristics in Wales: Analysis of Census of Population Results, 1981–1991* (Aberystwyth, 1995), p. 10, table 3.1, and p. 13.

[77] ECTARC, *Study of the . . . Impact of Tourism in and upon Wales*, evidence of J. R. Thomas, Liaison Officer for the Pony Trekking and Riding Society of Wales, and Eleri Carrog, on behalf of Mudiad Cefn, letters dated 27 March 1987 and 11 April 1987. See also Eleri Carrog, 'Twristiaeth – Diwydiant Estron', *Barn*, 423 (1998), 19–21.

[78] 'Twristiaeth', *Yr Odyn*, June 1986.

[79] C. M. Law and A. M. Warnes, 'The Movement of Retired People to Seaside Resorts', *The Planning Review*, 44 (1973), 373–90.

[80] Shaw and Williams, 'Tourism and Employment', 23–34.

Economic motives, therefore, are not a prerequisite for the in-migration which accompanies tourism. Tourism-associated in-migration is also allied to more indirect motives and processes. Some people choose to retire to a particular area or wish to escape the pressures of urban life. These types of in-migration are less obviously associated with tourism, but there is abundant evidence to suggest that many people choose to settle in a particular place because of a previous connection as a tourist or holidaymaker. After all, the features which attract incomers are much the same as those which attract tourists, namely a beautiful landscape, a natural environment, peace and tranquillity, fresh sea air, and so on.[81] A study in Scotland published in 1986 revealed a close relationship between tourism and counter-urban in-migration to the spectacular highland region and the outlying islands.[82] Similar research has also been undertaken in Wales on the phenomenon of counter-urban in-migration and the search for the 'good-life'.[83] A study by the Institute of Welsh Affairs in 1988 revealed that 30 per cent of the incomers questioned had moved to Wales in order to escape the 'rat-race' and to settle in a healthier, more peaceful and more scenic environment. But the most revealing finding was that the majority of incomers had previously spent a holiday in the area.[84]

Another form of in-migration associated with tourism in Wales is in-migration through retirement. Tourist resorts have traditionally attracted a considerable number of retiring incomers.[85] This pattern of migration has been an established feature of coastal resorts for decades. Law and Warnes revealed in 1973 that 50 per cent of the incomers who had retired to Llandudno had visited the area as tourists.[86] More recently, the 1991 census confirmed that many of the most popular holiday centres in Wales have a higher than average percentage of retired people. In one area in Anglesey, for instance, it cannot be denied that the decline of the language is associated with tourism and in-migration. Llanbedr-goch on the eastern coastline of Anglesey has been a popular tourist resort since the early decades of the twentieth century. Tens of thousands of visitors a year are attracted by the beautiful scenery and the remarkable beach which extends from Red

---

[81] Harold Carter, *Mewnfudo a'r Iaith Gymraeg / Immigration and the Welsh Language* (Llys yr Eisteddfod Genedlaethol, 1988).

[82] Huw Jones, James Caird, William Berry and John Dewhurst, 'Peripheral Counter-urbanization: Findings from an Integration of Census and Survey Data in Northern Scotland', *Regional Studies*, 20, no. 1 (1986), 15–26.

[83] See, for instance, D. Forsythe, 'Urban Incomers and Rural Change', *Sociologia Ruralis*, XXII (1982), 23–39, and Richard H. Morgan, 'Population Trends in Mid Wales: Some Policy Implications' in Glyn Williams (ed.), *Crisis of Economy and Ideology: Essays on Welsh Society, 1840–1980* (Bangor, 1983), pp. 88–102.

[84] Institute of Welsh Affairs, *Rural Wales: Population Changes and Current Attitudes* (Cardiff, 1988), I, p. 41.

[85] H. W. Mellor, 'Retirement to the Coast', *Town Planning Review*, 33 (1962), 40–8; L. Lepape, 'Etude de la population des retraités et des personnes âgées inactives dans les villes touristes littorales', *Bull. Association de Geographes Français*, 381 (1970), 123–33.

[86] Law and Warnes, 'The Movement of Retired People to Seaside Resorts', 373–90.

Wharf Bay to Benllech. However, the substantial in-migration of retired people since the 1960s transformed the age ratio within the community. Within a period of thirty years the population of Llanbedr-goch had more than doubled, and by 1991 over 30 per cent of the inhabitants were over 65 years of age, compared to an average of 17.6 per cent for Anglesey as a whole. Moreover, according to the census, 70.7 per cent of the over 65-year-olds living in Llanbedr-goch were monoglot English speakers, while the average for Anglesey was much lower at 42.4 per cent. Small wonder, therefore, that Anglesey is sometimes disparagingly called 'Môn, the daughter of Liverpool'.

Further studies have also established a strong correlation between holiday homes and retiring incomers. Research undertaken by Richard de Vane in 1975 showed that, before buying property, 65 per cent of the second-home owners examined in his study had spent many annual holidays in the area. Indeed, 31.3 per cent of these owners bought property with the avowed intention of retiring to the area later on. A similar study compiled by the Planning Department of Caernarfonshire County Council two years previously revealed that 59 per cent of holiday-home owners intended to retire to the county.[87] In 1983 the Welsh Language Society estimated that over 7,000 second-home owners in Gwynedd would be permanent residents by 1985.[88] As Geraint Jones remarked in response to the decision by Dwyfor District Council to permit a scheme to build 700 holiday homes in Morfa Bychan: 'One swallow doesn't make a summer – but seven hundred swallows are bound to cause a destructive winter' ('Un wennol ni wna wanwyn – ond mae saith gant o wenoliaid yn bownd o greu gaeaf dinistriol').[89] Even more threatening than the direct impact of in-migration on the future of the language are the indirect effects. Several examples have been cited of incomers campaigning against the provision of Welsh-medium education since they failed to realize that the teaching of Welsh was compulsory in local schools. Similarly, examples can be cited of guest house, hotel and restaurant owners refusing to allow their locally-employed staff to speak Welsh at work.[90] During ECTARC's public consultation, Gwyneth Stephens, writing on behalf of the Ceredigion District Branch of Mudiad Ysgolion Meithrin (the Welsh-medium Nursery Schools Movement), referred to the direct relationship between tourism and the decline of the Welsh language:

---

[87] C. B. Pyne, *Second Homes* (Caernarfon County Council Planning Department, 1973). It is also worth noting that 49 per cent of holiday-home owners from England hail from the West Midlands, 25 per cent from the north-west, 9 per cent from the south-east, and 7 per cent from the East Midlands. See de Vane, *Second Home Ownership*, p. 21.

[88] 'Sefyllfa Anghyfiawn', *Y Cymro*, 20 September 1983.

[89] Geraint Jones, 'Wele dy Dduwiau, O Ddwyfor!', *Y Faner*, 30 May 1986.

[90] For example, see two cases reported in *Y Cymro*, 'Mil o Bunnau Sharon', 10 October 1990; *Yr Odyn*, 'Sacio Gŵr am Siarad Cymraeg yn ei Waith', June 1993; and *Asgwrn Cefn*, nos. 1 and 2, June and July 1993.

Efallai mai breuddwyd ffŵl yw credu y gall twristiaeth gyfoethogi'r bywyd diwylliannol. Fel canlyniad credwn yn ddi-wahân fod dylanwad twristiaeth yn elyniaethus i'n ffordd o fyw. Credwn mai twristiaeth, yn rhannol sydd wedi creu'r mewnlifiad estron . . . Yn sgil hyn gwelwn ddiwylliant ac iaith estron yn ffynnu yn y Gymru wledig, tra bo'r Gymraeg, a'i ffordd o fyw yn prysur wanychu. Dyna'n barn ar effeithiau'r diwydiant ymwelwyr ar Geredigion yn rhannol am mai dyna'r ffrwyth a welwn yn ein hysgolion Meithrin.[91]

(Perhaps it is only a pipedream to believe that tourism can enrich our cultural life. Consequently we are convinced that the influence of tourism is hostile to our way of life. We believe that tourism is partly responsible for the in-migration of outsiders . . . As a result of this we see a foreign language and culture flourishing in rural Wales, while the Welsh language, and its way of life, is swiftly withering away. This is our view of the effects of the holiday industry in Ceredigion, based partly on the fruits of our experience in nursery schools.)

Through a process known as 'acculturation', tourism can also be a destructive force by dint of its effects on the minds, traditions, culture and language patterns of the host community and its native inhabitants:

Acculturation comprehends those phenomena which result when groups of individuals having different cultures come into continuous first-hand contact, with subsequent changes in the original cultural patterns of either or both groups.[92]

The final outcome of acculturation is complete assimilation. In such cases, one culture imitates another or borrows from it to such an extent that it becomes completely undermined and loses its own unique identity. In popular tourist destinations, the language and culture of tourists inevitably conflict with the native language and culture of the tourist area. In these situations, tourists represent the 'donor' culture, while the local population represents the 'recipient' culture.[93] It is extremely difficult to measure the effect of the direct contact between the local population and tourists who speak a different language, and the way in which the local population respond or react to this situation.[94] However, research conducted by William Labov in Martha's Vineyard, Massachusetts, in 1963 revealed that residents of this popular tourist area reacted both socially and linguistically to incomers and visitors. The findings indicated that as a result of

---

[91] ECTARC, *Study of the . . . Impact of Tourism in and upon Wales*, evidence of Gwyneth Stephens, on behalf of the Ceredigion District Branch of Mudiad Ysgolion Meithrin, undated letter.

[92] Robert Redfield, Ralph Linton and Melville J. Herskovits, 'Memorandum for the Study of Acculturation', *American Anthropologist*, 38, no. 1 (1936), 149–52.

[93] Nunez Jr., 'Tourism, Tradition, and Acculturation', 347–52. See also Mathieson and Wall, *Tourism: Economic, Physical and Social Impacts*, pp. 160–2.

[94] White, *The Social Impact of Tourism on Host Communities*, pp. 8–9.

contact with outsiders natives tended either to strengthen their dialect or to repudiate it completely.[95]

In tourist destinations where a minority language is spoken the polarization which occurs during such contact has even greater implications. If contact between tourist and native results in greater use of the tourist language for the purpose of oral or written communication, this inevitably leads to a degree of acculturation which has adverse effects on the native language.[96] The greater the contact between the tourist population and the local population, the greater the strain on the minority language. Outside the home, especially in the workplace, the local shop and the post office, the domains of the native tongue can become extremely limited. The presence of considerable numbers of monoglot tourists in a bilingual society can therefore cause linguistic change in some domains as the majority language is increasingly used at the expense of the minority native language. Over the years demographic pressure on a minority language can cause members of the younger generation to adopt the majority language.[97] For instance, in 1989, in a discussion of the effects of tourism on the native population of the Algarve in Portugal, Jim Lewis and Allan M. Williams referred to 'the considerable cultural dilution in the intensely-developed coastal strips where the language, behaviour and expenditure patterns of the foreign tourists have often become dominant'.[98] Close interaction between two cultures can pose a severe threat to a minority language. Referring to the effects of tourism, it has been argued that 'the intercourse of cultures can rapidly degenerate into the destruction of the economically weaker one'.[99] In Wales, the increasing use of English in Welsh-speaking areas by tourists is likely to Anglicize the native culture and undermine Welsh as a living community language. P. E. White observed this process at work in the Engadin region of Switzerland:

It is anyway the immigration of tourist workers that appears to be at least as influential in social change as the influx of the tourists themselves. Although the individuals may in certain cases change their whole social outlook, in the study case through the adoption of a new language as their 'mother tongue', it is largely the increase in the number of roles played by non-local people – their invasion of more sociolinguistic domains – that

---

[95] William Labov, 'The Social Motivation of a Sound Change', *Word: Journal of the Linguistic Circle of New York*, 19, no. 3 (1963), republished in idem, *Sociolinguistic Patterns* (Oxford, 1972), pp. 1–42.

[96] ECTARC, *Study of the . . . Impact of Tourism in and upon Wales*, part II, p. 23.

[97] White, *The Social Impact of Tourism on Host Communities*, pp. 6–7.

[98] Jim Lewis and Allan M. Williams, 'A Secret No More: Europe Discovers the Algarve', *Geography*, 74, no. 2 (1989), 156–8.

[99] I. Cosgrove and R. Jackson, *The Geography of Recreation and Leisure* (London, 1972), p. 42. See also S. Petit-Skinner, 'Tourism and Acculturation in Tahiti' in B. Farrell, *Social and Economic Impact of Tourism on Pacific Communities* (Santa Cruz, 1977), pp. 85–7.

changes the sociocultural make-up of the whole community and the dominance of the original language.[100]

The presence of non-Welsh-speaking tourists can also undermine the confidence of the native population in their own language and culture. Several modern studies have shown that natives of host communities tend to feel inferior to tourists, especially those from more affluent societies, who profess different moral values or speak a majority language.[101] Some members of the host community seek to imitate visitors in an attempt to rise above their inferior status – a process known as the 'demonstration effect'. The results of this process are abundantly visible in Third World countries because of the considerable differences in the background, standard of living and culture of the native inhabitants and visitors to their communities. But the demonstration effect also affects developed countries and cultures. In his study on attitudes towards second homes in the rural region of Auvergne in France, Hugh D. Clout divided the local people into those with 'progressive' or 'conservative' tendencies. In an attempt to enhance their own standing within society, the most 'progressive' of the local residents would try to imitate the social values of the second-home owners. The second-home market in the Auvergne therefore induced the acculturation of the local population by encouraging them to change their social values.[102] Having to wait upon tourists can also have a scarring psychological effect on the local host population, as does their exclusion from tourist facilities and amenities such as beaches, playing fields and swimming pools. Such division of status often intensifies the feeling of inferiority, and this can lead to conflict and confrontation between tourists and local people.[103] Local inhabitants of host communities may also be resentful when plans for industrial development conflict with the interests of tourism. In discussing the situation in the Basque country, Davydd J. Greenwood declares:

> Wherever tourism occurs, this appears to present a potential source of conflict. Most Basques, though content with the economic rewards, find the tourist trade unpleasant

---

[100] White, *The Social Impact of Tourism on Host Communities*, p. 36.

[101] Mathieson and Wall, *Tourism: Economic, Physical and Social Impacts*, pp. 143–7. See also P. Rivers, 'Tourist Troubles', *New Society*, 23, no. 539 (1973), 250; J. Jafari, 'The Socio-economic Costs of Tourism to Developing Countries', *Annals of Tourism Research*, 1 (1974), 227–59; Turner and Ash, *The Golden Hordes*, p. 197.

[102] Hugh D. Clout, 'Social Aspects of Second-home Occupation in the Auvergne', *Planning Outlook*, 9 (1970), 33–49.

[103] Instances of conflict between tourists and local people have been reported in many countries. See, for example, Rivers, 'Tourist Troubles', 250, and Jafari, 'The Socio-economic Costs of Tourism to Developing Countries', 227–59. Research undertaken by Delyth Morris also shows how language and in-migration can cause friction between different groups within society. Delyth Morris, 'A Study of Language Contact and Social Networks in Ynys Môn', *CW*, 3 (1989), 99–117.

and conflictful. The summer invasion, once it is under way, is resented by all, and September is greeted by manifestations of relief that the tourists are gone.[104]

Despite all attempts in recent years to ensure that the tourist industry sustains communities and promotes the native language and culture, it is nevertheless true that in the past the development of tourism in Wales has been detrimental to many Welsh-speaking communities. Nowadays bodies such as the Wales Tourist Board and local authorities are more conscious of their obligation to formulate policies and strategies which ensure that the grievous errors of the past are not repeated. Tourism has the potential to be of considerable benefit to the language, especially in its ability to secure work and provide a living for people in Welsh-speaking areas. It can also help stem the destructive out-migration of young Welsh speakers who have been driven from their communities in search of employment. Moreover, it has the capacity to further the process of language normalization and to promote confidence in the language. Yet, having carefully considered the impact of tourism on the Welsh language during the second half of the twentieth century, it is difficult to avoid the conclusion that its principal effects have been adverse. Many areas have suffered severe linguistic decline as a result of the way in which tourism has been developed and the associated pressures of in-migration and acculturation. In Hawaii, a country well-acquainted with both the advantages and disadvantages of the lucrative 'aloha' industry, the natives describe tourism as a new kind of sugar – sweet-tasting but bad for the teeth.[105] On the basis of the available evidence, it appears that the experience of the Welsh people has been very similar.

[104] Greenwood, 'Tourism as an Agent of Change', 90.
[105] See Terry Stevens, 'Twristiaeth – Y Briwsion o'r Bwrdd', *Y Faner*, 18 February 1983.

17

The Welsh Language and Agricultural Communities in the Twentieth Century

GARTH HUGHES, PETER MIDMORE and
ANNE-MARIE SHERWOOD

THE FOCUS of this chapter is on recent economic change in agriculture and the rural economy and its impact on the Welsh language. At one time, research into agricultural economics undertaken at the University of Wales, Aberystwyth – notably through the work of A. W. Ashby who, from 1926 to 1946, held the first chair of agricultural economics in the United Kingdom[1] – covered a much wider range of issues than has been the case until comparatively recently. Ashby was not only interested in the economics of agricultural production but also the wider issues of the natural environment and rural sociology. However, since Ashby's era, the scope of agricultural economics research has narrowed, both at Aberystwyth and other centres, by concentrating on agriculture and food production to the neglect of many of the wider issues of rural society which had stimulated him. This chapter can be regarded as a contribution to the process of re-establishing the Ashby tradition by exploring some of the broader cultural issues concerning rural economic development.

Within the economics profession generally there has been a growing acknowledgement by modern economists that culture is both an important influence on economic behaviour as well as being partly its product. Thus, for example, Francis Fukuyama writes:

> We can think of neoclassical economics as being, say, eighty percent correct: it has uncovered important truths about the nature of money and markets because its fundamental model of rational, self-interested human behaviour is correct about eighty percent of the time. But there is a missing twenty percent of human behavior about which neoclassical economics can give only a poor account. As Adam Smith well understood, economic life is deeply embedded in social life, and it cannot be understood apart from the customs, morals and habits of the society in which it occurs. In short, it cannot be divorced from culture.[2]

---

[1] David Bateman, 'A. W. Ashby: An Assessment', *Journal of Agricultural Economics*, XXXI, no. 1 (1980), 1–14.

[2] Francis Fukuyama, *Trust: The Social Virtues and the Creation of Prosperity* (London, 1995), p. 13.

Linguistic theorists recognize that for minority languages to survive it is necessary that the language holds sway in at least some domains such as places of worship, the home, or the workplace.[3] This view is confirmed in some of the classic anthropological and geographical studies of Welsh rural communities, including Alwyn D. Rees's *Life in a Welsh Countryside* (1950) and *Welsh Rural Communities* (1960) edited by Elwyn Davies and Alwyn D. Rees. We shall show in this chapter that agriculture continues to be an important domain of the Welsh language, with respect to the numbers of Welsh speakers that it employs and its family farm structure. The social and economic stability of agriculture is therefore of particular significance to the survival of the language. In the past, public policy has played a critical role in this respect. Since the 1930s life in the agricultural communities of Wales has been influenced by the state's growing interventionist stance on agriculture. This has provided some stability for the agricultural sector, for example, with respect to prices. However, in the 1990s a revolution occurred in the agricultural policy-framework, led by the reform of the Common Agricultural Policy (CAP) in 1992 and the GATT agreement of 1993 (General Agreement on Trade and Tariffs). This radically changed the nature of state economic support for agriculture and will inevitably herald further changes in the twenty-first century. These changes will not only have an impact on the prosperity of agriculture and the wider rural economy, but also potentially on the sociocultural fabric of rural areas. A review of the relationship between agriculture and the Welsh language, together with the changes which are likely to take place in the economic circumstances of agriculture, therefore seems particularly appropriate at the beginning of a new millennium.

Changes in the Agricultural Communities of Wales

All developed regions have experienced long-term decline in the absolute and relative importance of agriculture as a source of employment within their economies, and this was the outstanding change affecting agricultural communities in Wales during the twentieth century. The two main records of this decline in Wales and in the rest of the United Kingdom are the annual agricultural census (the June census) undertaken by the government's Agriculture Departments[4] and the decennial population census.

---

[3] Colin H. Williams, 'New Domains of the Welsh Language: Education, Planning and the Law', *CW*, 3 (1989), 41–76.

[4] The annual June census of agricultural holdings is undertaken for England, Wales, Scotland and Northern Ireland, respectively, by the Ministry of Agriculture, Fisheries and Food, the Agriculture Department of the Welsh Office, the Department of Agriculture and Fisheries for Scotland, and the Department of Agriculture for Northern Ireland.

The June census surveys all farm holdings in the United Kingdom except the very small, which are referred to as minor or statistically insignificant.[5] Among the detailed statistics collected by this census are the number of persons engaged in agricultural work on each holding at census date and their occupational status: i.e. whether a person is a farmer or an employee, a family or a hired worker, whether the work is full-time or part-time, seasonal or casual. In total, eighteen categories of labour are distinguished by the surveys of the Agriculture Departments and these statistics are available at parish, county, regional and national levels. Unfortunately, and rather surprisingly, the agricultural census, despite having been undertaken since the mid-nineteenth century, did not include the number of farmers in its labour force statistics until 1970.

The population census provides information on the agricultural labour force as part of its overall investigation of employment in all occupations and industries in the United Kingdom, with a geographical breakdown into areas as small as enumeration districts.[6] Unlike the agricultural census, however, the population census only records a person's main occupation and thus excludes those individuals working in agriculture on a part-time basis but whose main occupation is in another industry. This could be significant. One estimate made for 1981 suggests that 28 per cent of those recorded at the agricultural census of that year may have had their principal employment outside agriculture.[7] Nevertheless, because of the predominance of farmers within the Welsh agricultural labour force and their exclusion until comparatively recently from the agricultural census, the information provided by the population census will be used to provide a long-term perspective on the absolute and relative changes in the agricultural labour force in Wales.

Population censuses reveal that during the twentieth century agriculture continued to decline in both absolute and relative terms as a source of employment for the population of Wales. However, the nature of the contraction was in marked contrast to what had been experienced during the latter half of the nineteenth century, when the overwhelmingly important factor underlying this change was the huge expansion in the industrial sector, with its voracious appetite for labour, fuelled partly by the indigenous agricultural sector but mainly by in-migration from other parts of the United Kingdom. Between 1851 and 1911 the

---

[5] Data for these holdings is obtained from occasional special surveys. A holding is minor if it meets certain threshold requirements, namely: if it is less than 6 hectares, requires less than 800 hours work a year, has no regular full-time farmer or worker, has a glasshouse area of less than 100 square metres, and the occupier makes no regular census return for any other holding. In Wales in 1993 there were about 6,800 minor holdings compared with about 30,000 holdings covered by the June census. *Welsh Agricultural Statistics* (The Welsh Office, 1995).

[6] The population census is undertaken by the Office of Population Censuses and Surveys and the economic activity tables are based on a 10 per cent sample.

[7] Garth O. Hughes, 'Agriculture and Employment in Wales', *Journal of the Agricultural Society, University College of Wales*, 68 (1987–8), 160–95.

Table 1. Changes in the agricultural labour force in Wales and Rural Wales, 1851–1991[1]

	Wales			Rural Wales[2]		
Year	Total labour force	Agricultural labour force	Percentage employed in the agricultural sector	Total labour force	Agricultural labour force	Percentage employed in the agricultural sector
1851[3]	511820	169191	33.1	265982	116618	43.8
1861	570151	149353	26.2	280492	102582	36.6
1871	621383	125356	20.2	282062	87057	30.8
1881	644393	110754	17.2	274205	77178	28.1
1891	677870	108293	16.0	278814	74952	26.9
1901	836173	104027	12.4	274792	70676	25.7
1911	1024275	116147	11.3	296798	78621	26.5
1921[4]	1093556	106094	9.7	293092	70248	23.9
1911[5]	1023275	122563	12.0	296798	81473	27.5
1921[6]	1093556	106835	9.8	293012	70641	24.1
1931	1078811	101116	9.4	279980	66199	23.6
1951	1093073	89724	8.2	271943	58467	21.5
1961	1124590	67700	6.0	265360	44230	16.7
1971	1167620	52750	4.5	264360	34490	13.0
1981[7]	1039670	37880	3.6	246980	25834	10.5
1991[7]	1110180	35560	3.2	275590	24210	8.8

[1] The occupied population which consists of those in employment and those actively seeking employment.
[2] The counties of Dyfed, Gwynedd and Powys and the old counties of Cardigan, Carmarthen, Pembroke, Anglesey, Caernarfon, Merioneth, Brecon, Radnor and Montgomery.
[3] The figures for the census returns 1851 to 1911 have been reclassified on the basis of the 1911 classification of occupations.
[4] The figures for 1921 represent an attempt to redistribute the information from the 1921 census on the same basis as that used for the period 1851 to 1911.
[5] The figures for 1911 represent an attempt to redistribute the information from the 1911 census on the same basis as that used for the period 1921 to 1971.
[6] The figures for the census returns 1921 to 1971 have been reclassified on the basis of the 1951 occupational classification.
[7] The 1981 and 1991 figures refer to those in employment.

Source: John Williams, *Digest of Welsh Historical Statistics* (2 vols., Cardiff, 1985), I.

agricultural labour force in Wales fell by around 50,000, but the total labour force almost doubled to just over one million workers; the result was that whereas one in three workers had been employed in agriculture in the mid-nineteenth century, by 1911 this had fallen to almost one in nine. Since then the number of persons in the Welsh labour force has been comparatively stable, showing only modest growth compared with the experience of the second half of the nineteenth century. However, the number employed in agriculture continued to fall from around 120,000 at the 1911 census to 35,560 at the 1991 census; in relative terms, this was a decline from about 12 to 3 per cent of the total labour force (Table 1).

This figure is relatively small when compared with the numbers employed in manufacturing and services in Wales, but it belies the importance of agriculture as an employer within the rural economy. Within what might rather loosely be described as rural Wales, namely the former counties of Dyfed, Gwynedd and Powys, which occupy about three-quarters of the geographic area of Wales, almost 9 per cent of the labour force were employed in agriculture in 1991, compared with 25 per cent at the beginning of the twentieth century.

Agriculture affects the rural non-farm economy in many different ways and when these indirect effects are taken into account agriculture's contribution to income and employment is greatly enhanced. Thus, for example, it has been estimated that one job lost in agriculture may cause a loss of about three-quarters of a job elsewhere in the economy, and that within the area of the Development Board for Rural Wales (DBRW) the contribution of agriculture, both directly and indirectly, to local employment is of the order of 15 to 20 per cent.[8]

It is also interesting to note how measurement and definition can influence the perception of the importance of an industry. At the 1991 population census a total of sixty separate industries were identified, of which agriculture was one. On this basis agriculture was ranked tenth in the number employed in Wales as a whole, rising to first position in Powys, second in Dyfed and seventh in Gwynedd. These rankings, as previously explained, do not make any allowance for the significant number of people who provide labour for agriculture in addition to their main occupation in another industry, nor do they take account of workers in ancillary industries.

There are several rather well-known reasons for the decline in the absolute and relative importance of agriculture as a source of employment; these are associated with the process of economic development and they apply in Wales just as they have done elsewhere. Firstly, the revolutionary nature of scientific and techno-logical progress has transformed the productive ability of agriculture. Correspondingly, with economic development and rising incomes, the demand for industrial goods and services accelerates while that for food slows. Thus, the changing pattern of demand for goods and services in response to economic growth and prosperity necessitates a shift in the allocation of economic resources, and especially labour, from agriculture to the rest of the economy. Reinforcing this, in the case of labour, has been the fact that it has been profitable to substitute capital for labour. Production specialization has also meant that activities once

[8] David Bateman, Nigel Chapman, Michael Haines, Garth Hughes, Tim Jenkins, Nic Lampkin and Peter Midmore, *Future Agricultural Prospects in Mid Wales: A Report to the Development Board for Rural Wales* (Aberystwyth, 1991), p. 53.

undertaken on farms have grown into large industries in their own right: for instance, the production of butter and cheese is now a factory and not a farm-based activity and the workers are part of the food manufacturing sector rather than of agriculture.

While a radical transformation has taken place in the absolute and relative importance of the agricultural labour force in Wales, significant changes in the nature of agricultural communities and the conditions under which they live and work also became apparent. Within the labour force the most striking changes were the eclipse of the agricultural worker, the decline of the tenant farmer, and the growth of owner-occupancy.[9] In addition, there occurred a diversification of income sources following the growth of pluriactivity among the farm population.[10] This initiated a change in perception of what constituted a small farmer as economic pressures caused relentless expansion in viable farm size, as well as changes in the relationship of agriculture with the rest of the economy.[11] Correspondingly, while the basic components of Welsh agricultural output remained largely unchanged – the dependence on beef, lamb and milk production has remained[12] – the methods of their production and the size of farm on which they are typically produced changed considerably in response to economic and technical change.[13]

The twentieth century, especially since the 1930s, also witnessed a significant increase in the role of the state in determining the size and structure of agriculture, its level and pattern of output, and the income derived from its production. This has been a dominant and distinctive feature of the agricultural economy of Wales in the twentieth century. Such has been the role of the state that it is worthy of further comment. In the following section, the nature of state policies and the

[9] The rise of the owner-occupier is well documented. At the beginning of the twentieth century only about 10 per cent of farm holdings and farmland in Wales were in owner-occupation, whereas by the early 1940s the proportion in each case was about one third; by 1970, 60 per cent of holdings and just over half the farmland were owner-occupied. John Williams, *Digest of Welsh Historical Statistics* (2 vols., Cardiff, 1985), I, p. 239.

[10] David Bateman, Garth Hughes, Peter Midmore, Nic Lampkin and Chris Ray, *Pluriactivity and the Rural Economy in the Less Favoured Areas of Wales* (Aberystwyth, 1993).

[11] One statistical illustration of the growing integration of agriculture and the rest of the economy is the fact that something like two-thirds of the money which farmers receive for their outputs are spent on feed, fertilizer and other intermediate inputs bought from other industries. While no comparable statistics exist for the early part of the twentieth century, the evidence that does exist would suggest a lower dependence on off-farm inputs and a less specialized farming system compared with now.

[12] Of about 30,000 farms in Wales, just over 12,000 specialize in cattle and sheep, about 5,000 in sheep alone and 4,500 in milk production. As might be expected, given the predominance of livestock farms, 28 per cent of the revenue of farmers is obtained from the production of cattle, around the same amount from sheep, and just over 30 per cent from milk production.

[13] The twentieth century has witnessed a technological revolution in agriculture, with mechanization extending to even the smallest farms. In 1930, 70 per cent of farms in Wales were 50 acres and less, whereas the current proportion is about 40 per cent.

level of protection they afford to agriculture in Wales are described. Fundamental changes in agricultural policy occurred in the final decade of the twentieth century and the implications of such changes for the agricultural communities of Wales are discussed.

The Agricultural Policy Environment of the Twentieth Century

There has been a long history of government intervention in the affairs of agriculture in the twentieth century. It began in the 1930s when some government support was provided for farmers. Prior to this the involvement of the state in agriculture was relatively small, apart from the dire and emergency circumstances of the Great War. From the repeal of the Corn Laws in 1846 to the early 1930s, agriculture was largely unprotected from foreign competition. Domestic prices were thus very much a reflection of world prices and Welsh farmers earned their living in a market largely exposed to the vagaries of international price movements. As a result of the severe downturn in economic activity and rising unemployment of the 1930s, British foreign economic policy shifted its emphasis from free trade to protecting home markets. It was this, rather than any special circumstances within agriculture, which resulted in a number of ad hoc government measures to help the farming industry in the decade leading up to the beginning of the Second World War.

Although some government support was provided in the 1930s, it was in the period following the Second World War that a comprehensive system of agricultural support was established. Emergency measures were introduced during the war to increase agricultural production and ration food but, unlike the situation following the First World War, there was to be no abandonment of agricultural support in the post-war period. Rather, the government, convinced of the desirability of peacetime agricultural support, introduced the 1947 Agriculture Act, which laid the foundations of what was to prove a continuing and growing involvement of the state in British agriculture – a policy which was largely accepted by successive governments and opposition. This provided the government with guaranteed prices for output (the so-called deficiency payments)[14] and also input subsidies. The choice of this policy, rather than, say, import taxes, enabled support to be provided for farming without breaking the British tradition, dating back to the repeal of the Corn Laws in 1846, of enabling consumers to benefit from being able to buy food on world markets wherever it was cheapest. Hence, it has often been referred to as 'a cheap food policy'. This was in marked contrast to the policy approach customary in much of the rest of Europe where support was generally provided by a tariff wall, thus pushing the

---

[14] A deficiency payment is a subsidy paid to farmers which equals the difference between a guaranteed price set by the government for a commodity and the average market price of the product. The guaranteed price is set each year at an 'Annual Review'.

cost of policy onto the consumer, through higher food prices, rather than onto the taxpayer as in the British case. This diametrically opposite approach to the traditional agricultural policy became an important issue in the Common Market debate within the United Kingdom which preceded its entry into the European Economic Community (EEC) in 1973, because it was the 'European approach' based on import taxes[15] which had been adopted for the Common Agricultural Policy (CAP).[16] Following British entry into the EEC (henceforth referred to as the European Union or EU), the Corn Laws returned to the United Kingdom after an absence of one hundred and twenty-seven years.

Although the methods of agricultural support changed as a result of joining the EU, the objectives remained broadly similar (compare the 1947 Agriculture Act with the 1957 Treaty of Rome). A review of the reasons given for policy suggest the following main objectives. Firstly, one of the most long-established was the need to provide better incomes for farmers which, in an unregulated market, would otherwise fall to unacceptable levels and show too much instability. A second objective was to maintain population in rural areas. Thirdly, there was the objective of increasing domestic food production (and its technical efficiency) for reasons of food security, although import substitution to help the balance of payments was important in the United Kingdom before EU membership. Finally, from the 1980s onwards production restraint and the promotion of a more environmentally-sensitive agriculture became important.

Considerable funds were channelled into rural areas as a result of the EU's agricultural policies, and significant financial resources were drawn directly from the national budgets of member states. Furthermore, farmers in the EU benefited both from the protection of internal markets by the CAP and from subsidized exports to world markets. The level of public expenditure on agriculture in Wales is relatively easy to measure from government statistical sources. Quantification of market-price support (for example, through trade barriers) is much more difficult because it requires estimates of what prices and output would be in the absence of the CAP. For example, identifiable public expenditure on agriculture in Wales ran at about £110 million per annum during the late 1980s, i.e. about 12 per cent of Welsh agriculture's total annual receipts. However, the addition of market-price support significantly increased this figure, since the markets for milk, beef and lamb, on which Welsh agriculture overwhelmingly depended, received substantial protection in this way.

---

[15] This was supported by EEC intervention in the domestic market to buy products to prevent their prices falling below certain predetermined levels – the so-called intervention system that gave rise to bulging food stores across the EC.

[16] Although this approach placed the burden of support on the consumer rather than on the taxpayer, it should be noted that, even with this policy, substantial costs to the taxpayer remained because of internal support for the market through EC purchases at predetermined prices, and various direct output and input related payments to farmers.

One measure that was developed to take account of all types of agricultural support, direct and indirect, market or otherwise, so that inter-country and inter-product comparisons could be made, was the producer subsidy equivalent (PSE).[17] Thus, for example, an application of the Organisation for Economic Co-operation and Development's (OECD) estimates of the EU's commodity PSEs to Wales suggests that the value of agricultural support in Wales could have been as much as 58 per cent of the average value of total farm output between 1988 and 1990, or about £500 million. The dependence of rural Wales on agricultural support is further illustrated by estimates made for the area of the DBRW. Out of a total output of £259 million in 1988, identifiable public expenditure on agriculture was estimated at £50 million and the PSE level of support at £160 million. In comparison, identifiable public expenditure within other sectors of the DBRW area was estimated at only £8 million.[18]

The influence of policy on agricultural communities is diverse and complex, but, despite the analytical difficulties, a number of general conclusions can be drawn which are relevant to this discussion of the Welsh language within agricultural communities. Firstly, there are, on a priori grounds, good reasons for believing that the number of farms is greater than would have otherwise been the case had there been no agricultural support policy.[19] Agricultural price subsidies stimulate output and hence the demand for inputs. Thus, the demand for labour, and hence employment opportunities, are greater than they would have been in the absence of policy. Farming incomes improve, at least in the short term, and this reduces the incentive to expand farm businesses, for instance, through amalgamations, or to seek alternative employment outside agriculture.[20] Land prices are also likely to be relatively higher and this makes farm expansion through amalgamations not only more difficult but also relatively expensive compared with other methods of expanding output.

While Welsh agriculture benefited from the general provision of agricultural price subsidies, it also gained because specific regional policies operated in its favour. The Less Favoured Areas policy is an important example, with its emphasis on support for farming communities in difficult farming areas. About 80 per cent of Wales is classified in this way and the livestock subsidies that the policy provides (Hill Livestock Compensatory Amounts) were important to the welfare of these farming communities. The price and marketing policies provided by the

---

[17] OECD, *Agricultural Policies, Markets and Trade: Monitoring and Outlook 1991* (Paris, 1991).

[18] Garth O. Hughes, David I. Bateman and Peter Midmore, 'Agriculture and the Rural Economy of Wales' in Jeffery I. Round (ed.), *The European Economy in Perspective: Essays in Honour of Edward Nevin* (Cardiff, 1994), p. 215.

[19] Alan Swinbank, 'A Note on Price Support Policy and Hired Farm Labour', *Journal of Agricultural Economics*, XXXVI, no. 2 (1985), 259–61.

[20] David R. Colman and W. Bruce Traill, 'Economic Pressures on the Environment' in A. Korbey (ed.), *Investing in Rural Harmony: A Critique* (Reading, 1984), p. 34.

Milk Marketing Board (MMB) from 1933 to 1996 were also instrumental in supporting many Welsh dairy farmers. Under milk marketing legislation, all producers were obliged to sell their milk to the MMB, for which they received an average market price, regardless of their location, whereas in a free market prices could be expected to fall with distance from the main population centres. In this way, dairy farms in remote areas received a higher milk price than might otherwise have been obtained. Agricultural tenancy legislation also strengthened family farming and the stability of the farming population by providing greater security of tenure and, indirectly, by promoting the growth of owner-occupancy.

The development agencies, notably the DBRW and the Welsh Development Agency (WDA), indirectly helped to retain people in agriculture by providing more opportunities for part-time working and the diversification of farm household income.[21] Finally, a more prosperous agriculture, sustained by policy, added to the general employment opportunities in rural areas through the linkage effects which exist between agriculture and the rest of the economy.[22]

It is interesting to note that although policy may have retained more small farms than would otherwise have been the case, the number of farm workers may actually be less as a result of the substitution for capital of labour, and as a result of the substitution of family labour for hired labour.[23] It is instructive that while the number of agricultural workers in Wales has declined substantially, the number of farmers has shown little change over long periods of time. It is also true that not all policy has been favourable to retention of labour in agriculture. For instance, there have been some subsidies on capital; however, the effect of these is likely to have been greatest on the demand for hired labour.

Growing dissatisfaction with these policies during the 1980s intensified the pressures for change; this culminated in 1992 with an EU agreement on the most significant change in its agricultural policy since its inception and, for the United Kingdom, since British entry into the EU in 1973. The 1992 CAP reform firmly established a new direction for policy, encompassing major changes in the method of support, from one which sustained the market prices of the various agricultural commodities at relatively high levels, by protecting the European market from foreign competition, to one in which prices were to be moved lower towards world market levels and support provided by direct payments to farmers. It also

[21] Gunther Schmitt, 'Why is the agriculture of advanced western economies still organized by family farms? Will this continue to be so in the future?', *European Review of Agricultural Economics*, 18 (1991), 443–58.

[22] The authors recognize that although the various policies enumerated in the preceding paragraphs are likely to have been helpful in sustaining family farms, it does not necessarily follow that they have been the most efficient that could have been adopted to achieve this objective. For a discussion of 'linkage effects', see Peter Midmore, 'Input–Output Forecasting of Regional Agricultural Policy Impacts', *Journal of Agricultural Economics*, 44, no. 2 (1993), 284–300.

[23] Swinbank, 'A Note on Price Support Policy and Hired Farm Labour'; Bruce Traill, 'The Effect of Price Support Policies on Agricultural Investment, Employment, Farm Incomes and Land Values in the UK', *Journal of Agricultural Economics*, XXXI, no. 3 (1982), 369–85.

confirmed and strengthened the environmental conservation dimension to agricultural policy. A full discussion of these changes and their impact on rural Wales is contained in *An Integrated Agricultural Strategy for Rural Wales*.[24] It should be emphasized, however, that despite the 1992 reform of the CAP, further 'reforms' are inevitable. In particular, changes may be necessary to facilitate the enlargement of the EU to include the six countries of eastern Europe,[25] with whom it has signed Association Agreements, and to enable it to meet its existing obligations for freer international trade under GATT, and potential future ones under its successor, the World Trade Organization. Indeed, the prospect of further international trade negotiations and an enlargement of the EU will be major catalysts pushing EU policy-makers in a more radical direction. Michael S. Davenport, for example, believes that:

> The momentum for more reform is probably unstoppable . . . Even without such special factors [for example, enlargement], the conviction that the rules that have governed the international trading system as far as industrial products are concerned should be extended to agricultural products – and incidentally, to the other main hitherto excluded textiles and clothing sector – has overwhelmingly won the day. Until the last few years the agricultural sector was, to use deliberately a French phrase, a *chasse gardée*, which could be translated as 'out of bounds' to the GATT and international rules in general. That is no longer the case.[26]

Consequently, the policy trends and pressures apparent in the 1990s suggest that there is a real possibility of a radical policy response in the longer term early in the twenty-first century.

In these circumstances, Welsh farmers will be faced with agricultural markets which are more open to foreign competition, with the inevitable prospect of lower prices, and a policy environment in which state support will increasingly be in the form of direct payments, and conditional upon environmental conserva-tion, or arguments that farmers are in some sense a special case. Moreover, food safety is an important policy issue and the crisis in the beef market that developed following the potential threat to human health of Bovine Spongiform Encephalo-pathy (BSE) poses a serious threat to the livelihoods of many farmers in Wales who depend heavily on livestock production and export markets. Indeed, the effects of BSE are likely to be deep and far-reaching and will have implications not only for other sectors of agriculture and the rural economy, but also the

[24] Peter Midmore, Garth Hughes, David Bateman, Nigel Chapman, Chris Ray, Michael Haines and Nic Lampkin, *An Integrated Agricultural Strategy for Rural Wales: A Report to the Development Board for Rural Wales* (Aberystwyth, 1993).
[25] Bulgaria, Czech Republic, Hungary, Poland, Romania and the Slovak Republic.
[26] Michael S. Davenport, 'Changes in the Pattern of World Trade in Agricultural Products' in B. J. Marshall and F. A. Miller (eds.), *Priorities for a New Century – Agriculture, Food and Rural Policies in the European Union* (Reading, 1995), p. 80.

nature of food and agricultural policy, perhaps the institutions that deliver it, and even future international relations.

In the short-term, the potential impact of the 1992 CAP reform was softened by compensation payments. Indeed, in Wales, these payments, together with the added cushion of successive devaluations of the green pound, lower interest rates and reduced inflation, provided some respite to the declining farm incomes of the late 1980s and early 1990s. In the longer term, however, the directions taken with regard to agricultural policy suggest renewed, and perhaps severe pressure on farm incomes and employment in regions such as Wales and hence on the continued survival of rural communities.[27] If there is a continued loss of agricultural employment, it is increasingly likely to focus on farmers themselves, rather than on full-time workers, and if the availability of part-time off-farm work continues to be limited it follows that the structure of traditional family farming may be weakened, with associated social as well as economic repercussions. This could have implications for Welsh-language communities and therefore in the next section we investigate the relationship between economic activity, especially agriculture, and the Welsh language. In addition, the agricultural changes now taking place are likely to have much wider implications for the long-term future of the Welsh language. Such changes will not only act directly, through their impact on the social fabric of family farming, but also, indirectly, because the existence of a Welsh-speaking agricultural community helps to sustain a wider infrastructural framework in rural Wales, a framework which reflects and supports the linguistic diversity of the area which it serves.

In this respect, it is appropriate for agricultural suppliers and other industries providing farm services in Wales to employ Welsh speakers. In rural primary schools, where the majority of local pupils are Welsh-speaking, the ability to speak Welsh is also a requirement for teachers. Similarly, banking services employ large numbers of Welsh speakers in rural Wales in order to offer a bilingual service to their clients, many of whom are engaged in the farm sector. The interaction between economic change and their cultural effects are important: if declining agricultural prosperity and employment have negative knock-on effects for the 'Welshness' of rural communities, it follows that the overall demand for services provided in Welsh may also decline. In rural areas, these processes of change might also promote a contraction in the quality and quantity of the services themselves, thereby eroding the relative stability of Welsh-speaking communities. The old maxim from the Irish Gaeltacht, cited by Colin H. Williams, is equally applicable in Wales: 'no jobs, no people; no people, no Gaeltacht'.[28] He argues that the key to the survival of the Welsh language is the degree to which its speakers are settled in economically viable communities.

[27] Garth Hughes, Anne-Marie Sherwood and Peter Midmore, *Welsh Agriculture into the New Millennium: CAP Prospects and Farming Trends in Rural Wales* (Aberystwyth, 1996).

[28] Williams, 'New Domains of the Welsh Language', 46.

Economic Activity and Linguistic Diversity in Wales

Despite the various links between culture and economic activity, little information on the economic activities of the Welsh-speaking population of Wales has been published until comparatively recently. However, data commissioned from the Office of Population Censuses and Surveys (OPCS) provided the basis for an exploratory study of the economic activities of the Welsh-speaking population of Wales.[29] This work drew on basic cross-tabulations of linguistic status and industry employment defined by the Standard Industrial Classification (SIC), for each of the county districts in Wales at the 1981 census.[30] The data was unique, in the sense that it was not part of the statistical output published by OPCS, nor had it been previously requested by any other researcher. Standing alone, however, the 1981 data was of limited value, being almost ten years out of date and representing a view of prevailing economic circumstances at a single point in time. Once the results of the 1991 census of population were made available, a fuller and more up-to-date investigation became possible, and in 1992 a further set of cross-tabulations was commissioned from the OPCS. This data was subsequently obtained in November 1994 and represents a new source of information on the Welsh-speaking population of Wales. This database provides some interesting evidence on the relationship between agriculture and the Welsh language.[31]

When examined according to SIC, there is an element of conformity as well as diversity in the patterns of economic activity shown by the Welsh- and non-Welsh-speaking populations in employment. However, in a broad comparison of the two linguistic groups (Table 2), the most immediately observable differences in industrial employment relate to manufacturing and to the agriculture, forestry and fishing sectors. These differences were evident at the 1981 census and were maintained during the intercensal period. Whereas the agricultural category accounted for 10 per cent of all Welsh speakers employed in 1991, the corresponding figure for the employed monoglot English-speaking population was considerably lower at 2 per cent. The latter group has fuller representation in the manufacturing industries, where approximately 23 per cent of the non-Welsh-

---

[29] M. Elin Jones, 'The Linguistic Implications of Agricultural Change in Wales' (unpubl. University of Wales MSc thesis, 1989); Nigel Chapman, Garth Hughes and M. Elin Jones, *Dadansoddiad o Gyfrifiad 1981 ar Weithgaredd Economaidd a'r Iaith Gymraeg / Analysis of the 1981 Census for Economic Activity and the Welsh Language* (Aberystwyth, 1990).

[30] Central Statistical Office, *Standard Industrial Classification, Revised 1980* (London, 1979); Office of Population Censuses and Surveys, Census 1981, *General Report, England and Wales* (London, 1983); Census 1991, *Definitions, Great Britain* (London, 1991); 1991 Census / Cyfrifiad 1991, *Welsh Language / Cymraeg: Wales / Cymru* (London, 1994).

[31] Garth Hughes and Anne-Marie Sherwood, *Economic Activity and Linguistic Characteristics in Wales: Analysis of Census of Population Results, 1981–1991* (Aberystwyth, 1995); Garth Hughes, Peter Midmore and Anne-Marie Sherwood, *Language, Farming and Sustainability in Rural Wales* (Aberystwyth, 1996).

Table 2. Distribution of Welsh and non-Welsh speakers in employment by industry division, Wales, 1981–1991[1]

Industrial class	Welsh speakers		Non-Welsh speakers	
	1981	1991	1981	1991
	%	%	%	%
0 Agriculture	10.3	9.6	2.5	2.2
1 Energy	5.9	2.7	5.9	2.4
2 Manufacturing	4.6	3.0	7.2	4.4
3 Manufacturing	6.5	5.1	10.5	9.8
4 Manufacturing	5.6	5.0	7.8	8.5
5 Construction	7.4	8.0	7.7	8.0
6 Distribution	16.1	16.9	19.7	20.7
7 Transport	5.5	4.4	6.3	5.2
8 Finance	4.5	6.8	5.3	7.9
9 Other services	33.7	36.9	27.1	29.5
(Not classified)	–	(1.6)	–	(1.5)
Total	100.0	100.0	100.0	100.0
All persons	182850	187590	863020	922590

[1] Usually resident persons in employment (including those on a government training scheme). Sample results have been multiplied by a factor of 10 (a 10 per cent sample): the standard error is approximated by the square root of the number of sample observations in each particular class.

Source: Office of Population Census and Surveys.

speaking workforce were employed, compared to only 13 per cent of the Welsh-speaking group.

A clearer picture of differences between the two linguistic groupings is provided by an examination of the 1991 census data at a more disaggregated level. Table 3 lists the individual industry subclasses occupying the highest twelve positions with regard to the absolute numbers of the Welsh-speaking workforce. It reveals that education employed the greatest number of Welsh speakers and, in fact, accounted for over 30 per cent of all Welsh speakers working in the combined 'other services' industry division in 1991. In terms of ranking, this category was followed by employment in the agriculture and horticulture subclass (SIC, code 01 activities), retail distribution and medical and other health services. Subclasses which contribute to the manufacturing sector are absent from the register of foremost employers.

For comparative purposes, Table 3 indicates the corresponding position of each particular industrial subclass with respect to employed non-Welsh speakers. In this

Table 3. Estimated numbers of Welsh speakers employed in the top twelve industrial classes, Wales, 1991

Ranking of industrial subclasses (SIC)[1]	Welsh speakers	Non-Welsh speakers[2]	Total persons
All employed persons	187590	922590	1110180
Industry code			
93 Education	21460	5th	77950
01 Agriculture and horticulture	17290	16th	35560
64/65 Retail distribution	16190	1st	116510
95 Medical and other health services;			
veterinary services	15700	4th	81270
91 Public administration; national defence	15190	3rd	85400
50 Construction	15100	2nd	88470
96 Other services provided to the general public	8240	8th	43810
66 Hotels and catering	8170	6th	58650
83 Business services	6470	7th	47210
61 Wholesale distribution (except dealing in scrap			
and waste)	4900	10th	30710
97 Recreational services and other cultural services	4840	14th	24860
81 Banking and finance	3790	18th	18940

[1] According to the number of Welsh speakers employed in each industry subclass: sample results have been grossed up by a factor of 10.

[2] Comparable ranking.

Source: Office of Population Census and Surveys.

case, nine of the classes listed are reordered since three-quarters of the highest twelve are common to both linguistic groups. Unsurprisingly, the retail sector emerged as the principal single employer for the non-Welsh-speaking group, with the construction trades and public administration occupying second and third places. For non-Welsh speakers, the ninth, eleventh and twelfth positions are accounted for by employment in manufacturing, reflecting the greater numbers working in these industries. Employment in agricultural and horticultural activity ranks only sixteenth.

An assessment of the relative strength of the Welsh language within each broad industry division supports the absolute positions of each linguistic group described in Table 3. Bearing in mind that nearly 17 per cent of the employed population fall into the Welsh-speaking group on an all-Wales basis, Welsh speakers figured most highly within agriculture, forestry and fishing, and account for 47 per cent (agriculture: 49 per cent; forestry: 28 per cent; fishing: 23 per cent) of all those employed in this sector in Wales in 1991. Approximately one-fifth of persons working in other services were Welsh-speaking (although this proportion rose significantly to 28 per cent in education) and 19 per cent were engaged in the energy and water supply division. However, the manufacturing industries taken as a whole exhibited a disproportionately low number of Welsh speakers. Only one in ten of the manufacturing workforce was able to speak Welsh in 1991.

The geography of the Welsh language, including proximity to the English border, has implications for the linguistic features of national employment activities and these are reflected at a regional level. Agriculture is a major employer in the predominantly rural counties of Wales where, broadly speaking, the Welsh language remains more highly represented in local communities. Conversely, employment in manufacturing and the service sectors is of greater overall significance in the relatively urban and industrialized areas of the more Anglicized districts to the south. Consequently, in 1991, agricultural activities (code 01) represented the largest numbers of Welsh speakers employed in Dyfed and Powys and ranked a close second in Clwyd. In Gwynedd the situation was not so clear cut, due to the relatively large size of the Welsh-speaking community overall: approximately 10 per cent of employed Welsh speakers were working in each of the retail distribution, education and construction subclasses, only exceeding the numbers engaged in agriculture and horticulture by a marginal 2 per cent. In the counties of Mid, South and West Glamorgan and in Gwent in south Wales, education rather than agriculture was the principal employer of the Welsh-speaking labour force in 1991.

However, two striking features emerge from a district level examination of the linguistic composition of industry of employment: the relatively lower proportions of non-Welsh speakers employed in agriculture in the most rural counties of Wales, and the comparatively higher proportions among the manufacturing workforce in the more industrialized areas of the south. Our study is mainly confined to rural counties, since this is the main focus of our interest in the census returns. In Table 4 the proportion of Welsh speakers working in the agricultural sector in individual Welsh districts is compared with that of the total workforce. With the exception of all the county districts in Gwent and South Glamorgan, the most Anglicized districts of Brecon and Radnor in Powys, Wrexham Maelor in Clwyd, and the Rhymney Valley in Mid Glamorgan, the agricultural sector across Wales employed a conspicuously higher proportion of Welsh speakers than might be expected from the linguistic structure of each district. This was a position unmatched by any other industrial grouping and applied both within and outside rural Wales although, in the latter case, the overall numbers engaged in farming were relatively small. With regard to the predominantly rural counties, the association between agriculture and the Welsh language was particularly strong in the districts of Colwyn and Glyndŵr (Clwyd) (where 75 per cent and 70 per cent respectively of those working in the sector were Welsh speaking), in Carmarthen, Ceredigion and Dinefwr (Dyfed), and in Gwynedd, where over 75 per cent of the agricultural workforce of all districts, were able to speak Welsh. Moreover, it is

Table 4. Welsh counties and local districts

County	District	Values for chi-square[1]		1991: Welsh speakers	
		1981	1991	Agriculture[2]	Total[3]
				%	%
Clwyd	Alyn and Deeside	38.53	50.42	23.6	5.7
	Colwyn	179.87	192.85	75.2	26.4
	Delyn	93.74	64.53	30.4	14.5
	Glyndŵr	79.94	142.22	69.9	39.2
	Rhuddlan	57.00	58.56	54.5	13.9
	Wrexham Maelor	94.86	90.15	4.8	10.5
Dyfed	Carmarthen	55.61	69.17	73.3	56.1
	Ceredigion	30.84	66.66	73.6	59.3
	Dinefwr	22.73	29.79	76.4	66.5
	Llanelli	66.84	40.06	64.3	42.8
	Preselau	142.38	166.62	53.4	25.2
	South Pembrokeshire	9.94	18.81	9.3	7.0
Gwent	Blaenau Gwent	9.69	17.09	0.0	1.2
	Islwyn	3.84	17.26	0.0	2.7
	Monmouth	43.94	24.86	1.0	1.9
	Newport	27.36	37.63	2.3	2.3
	Torfaen	6.68	14.69	0.0	2.2
Gwynedd	Aberconwy	120.24	91.45	76.0	35.0
	Arfon	35.01	29.58	80.6	72.8
	Dwyfor	59.28	67.18	84.0	75.1
	Meirionnydd	61.67	100.63	88.7	65.4
	Ynys Môn	44.50	86.98	90.8	62.8
Mid Glam	Cynon Valley	67.08	33.48	9.1	6.7
	Merthyr Tydfil	25.82	25.06	18.2	4.0
	Ogwr	78.52	65.82	15.9	5.6
	Rhondda	27.11	52.79	20.0	4.1
	Rhymney Valley	26.95	36.66	0.0	5.8
	Taff-Ely	75.72	75.90	12.5	7.5
Powys	Brecon	95.95	49.13	13.2	18.5
	Montgomeryshire	72.66	105.16	35.2	18.7
	Radnorshire	13.50	25.62	1.3	3.5
South Glam	Cardiff	219.45	245.95	5.9	6.1
	Vale of Glamorgan	58.03	37.63	4.7	5.7
West Glam	Lliw Valley	48.51	43.11	50.0	32.0
	Neath	24.27	51.90	22.2	10.1
	Port Talbot (Afan)	19.89	24.10	14.3	6.5
	Swansea	47.78	47.58	9.5	8.2

[1] A chi-square test was applied to all thirty-seven counties on the basis of Welsh and non-Welsh speakers employed in the ten broad industry divisions at the census. For each district this resulted in an 11 by 2 contingency table (including 'others not classified elsewhere' group). When tested at the 5 per cent and 1 per cent levels of probability, critical values for the chi-square statistic are 18.3 and 23.2 (with 10 degrees of freedom).

[2] Welsh speakers as a proportion of total employed in the agriculture, forestry and fishing division.

[3] Welsh speakers as a proportion of total employed in each district.

perhaps more significant that in those districts where the Welsh language was relatively under-represented, for example, in Preselau and Aberconwy, the ability to speak Welsh remained a characteristic of those engaged in farming.

Even in Mid and West Glamorgan in south Wales, where less than one per cent of the employed population was engaged in farming activity, the sector continued to figure significantly in the employment of Welsh speakers, despite the relatively Anglicized nature of local communities. This was particularly the case in the districts of Merthyr Tydfil, Ogwr, Rhondda and Neath. It is also notable that in the most agricultural district of the Lliw Valley in West Glamorgan, half of those engaged in farming were able to speak Welsh, compared with 32 per cent of those employed in the district as a whole.

The differences observed between the economic activities of the Welsh- and non-Welsh-speaking populations are based on the results of just one sample survey at the time of each census. This being the case, the possibility of chance results must be examined in order to determine whether or not the apparently different employment characteristics of the Welsh- and non-Welsh-speaking samples reflect true differences in the actual population. Firstly, it is assumed that there is no relationship between economic activity and linguistic status in Wales and that these two aspects of the employed population are independent. This assumption is known as the 'null hypothesis' which, if accepted, would indicate that the observed differences between the linguistic groups are the result of mere chance. Secondly, a chi-square statistic is calculated, based on observed sample results, and this value is compared with critical values for the statistic at the desired level of significance, using chi-square distribution tables. If the calculated value for chi-square is lower than the critical value, then the null hypothesis is accepted; if it is higher than the critical value, the hypothesis is rejected, indicating that real and significant differences exist between the employment patterns of Welsh and non-Welsh speakers.

The test was applied to the labour force, classified into ten industrial groups, in all thirty-seven county districts of Wales, and the results are summarized in Table 4. In most cases, the calculated chi-square values were much higher than the critical values (18.3 and 23.2, with 10 degrees of freedom) at both the 1 and 5 per cent levels of probability, suggesting a statistically significant association between the ability to speak Welsh and industry of employment (rejecting the null hypothesis), and that there is only a very small probability of error in this assertion. Furthermore, a more detailed examination of the data identified agriculture as a major contributor to the chi-square value at a district level, indicating a strong association between agricultural employment and the use of the Welsh language. Thus, a principal conclusion arising from the examination of OPCS data is that a clear relationship exists between the ability to speak Welsh and industry of employment and that agriculture is a major source of this association. In the following section we consider why this might be so.

**Table 5. Welsh speakers and non-Welsh speakers in employment
according to age, Wales, 1991**

Persons in employment[1]	All ages	16–29 years	30–44 years	45 to pension	Pension and over
	%	%	%	%	%
Non-Welsh speakers					
Total in employment	100.0	29.2	38.5	29.6	2.7
Managers/proprietors in					
agriculture and services	100.0	19.5	37.3	37.7	5.5
All other occupations	100.0	30.0	38.6	28.9	2.4
Welsh speakers					
Total in employment	100.0	26.8	36.6	32.6	4.0
Managers/proprietors in					
agriculture and services	100.0	16.2	33.6	39.3	10.9
All other occupations	100.0	28.2	37.0	31.7	3.0
All employed persons					
Total in employment	100.0	28.8	38.2	30.1	2.9
Managers/proprietors in					
agriculture and services	100.0	18.7	36.4	38.1	6.8
All other occupations	100.0	29.7	38.4	29.4	2.5
Proportion of Welsh speakers					
(a) In total employment	17	16	16	18	23
(b) In agricultural occupations	25	22	23	26	40
(c) In all other occupations	16	15	16	17	19
Ratio of (b) to (a)	1.50	1.40	1.44	1.42	1.72

[1] Excluding those on a government training scheme.

Source: Office of Population Census and Surveys.

Agriculture and the Welsh Language

The agricultural sector in Wales has remained a significant employer of Welsh speakers and, as such, represents a major source of income within Welsh-speaking communities as well as in the wider rural economy. In this section, we investigate some of the possible reasons for the existence of this important link between agriculture and the Welsh language: clearly, age structure is an influential factor. The comparison of employed Welsh and non-Welsh speakers presented in Table 5 shows that a relatively higher proportion of the Welsh-speaking workforce are to be found in the older age groups. Additionally, in comparison with the labour force overall, a higher proportion of the agriculturally-employed fall into the older age categories of both linguistic groups. It is among these that we still find a fund of 'colloquial expressions, of idioms which were current at the time when agriculture was the chief single source of employment and when most people shared the same cultural heritage'.[32]

A measure of the strength of this age effect is provided by comparing the percentage of Welsh speakers working in agriculture with that of the labour force in general for each age group: the results are given at the foot of Table 5. The ability to speak Welsh is shown to be a characteristic feature of those employed in agricultural occupations across all age groups, with a notably stronger tendency among those over pensionable age, although the absolute numbers in this category are relatively small. This would suggest that while age is a contributory factor in the association between agricultural employment and the Welsh language, it is not the only factor, and consideration must also be given to other potential causes.

The predominance of family farms in Wales and the stability and social cohesion which this has given to the rural Welsh-speaking community may be of considerable interest in this context. The significance of family farming in Welsh agriculture is illustrated by an examination of the agricultural labour force statistics compiled from the agricultural census. These reveal that only a small proportion of the labour used on Welsh farms is provided by hired workers and that labour input is dominated by farmers, their wives or husbands, and other members of the family. Furthermore, the agricultural census indicates that owner occupation, rather than farm tenancy, is the prevalent form of land tenure: of just under 30,000 farm holdings in Wales, some 21,000 are owner-occupied, and a further 3,000 or so partially farmed by their owners.

In support of the relative stability of the existing farm structure, farm sales data indicate that few holdings change hands within a locality and those that do are usually comparatively small units which become amalgamated with neighbouring farms. Only about one per cent of the million and a half hectares of agricultural land in Wales is sold annually, representing about 600 transactions or 2 per cent of holdings, and most of these sales involve farms of under 100 hectares.[33]

There are considerable obstacles to entering agriculture other than through marriage: these factors, combined with the substantial capital requirements of farm purchase (land, buildings and stock) and with competition from neighbouring local farmers wishing to expand, all help to restrict access to Welsh agriculture. Consequently, relatively few farms in Wales are sold to outsiders. These structural characteristics have promoted a high degree of stability in the farming population.

---

[32] David Jenkins, 'Land and Community around the Close of the Nineteenth Century' in Geraint H. Jenkins and Ieuan Gwynedd Jones (eds.), *Cardiganshire County History. Volume 3. Cardiganshire in Modern Times* (Cardiff, 1998), p. 96.

[33] *Welsh Agricultural Statistics* (The Welsh Office, various years).

Farms are inherited within the family and successive generations of Welsh speakers become socially and economically tied to particular localities, reinforcing the continuity of the traditional farm structure as well as the native language. Moreover, the mobility of farming families outside agriculture is often restricted by a lack of transferable skills, as well as a strong attachment to farming as a way of life. Only small numbers of farmers abandon agriculture through choice and departures from the industry are often precipitated only by financial and other external pressures. Other sectors of the economy have exhibited a far greater freedom of movement between industries, thus increasing the contact between Welsh- and non-Welsh-speaking communities.

Some additional evidence on the relationship between social factors and the survival of the Welsh language in agricultural communities is drawn from a survey, undertaken in the early 1990s, of some 300 farmers in two of the most rural and Welsh-speaking areas of Wales, namely the Cambrian mountains and the Llŷn peninsula.[34] The survey indicated that the overwhelming majority of farmers questioned felt that job satisfaction was central to their way of life, as well as their livelihood, and there was a general reluctance to give up farming, even under circumstances where financial rewards might prove to be greater. A large proportion of the farmers interviewed had been brought up on the family farm, had remained in farming all their lives, had acquired their farm through inheritance, and had lived on their existing farms for a considerable number of years within their present localities. Finally, many expressed the hope that they would be succeeded by a family member.

In summary, the geographical isolation of farms, the traditional structure of the industry and the nature of farming itself – Young Farmers' Clubs, traditional market days, the pattern of the farming year, shearing, harvesting – all help to promote a sense of identity within the agricultural community and have maintained a traditional way of life which is inextricably linked to the use of the Welsh language.

New Perspectives on Language and Cultural Diversity

Both the EU and the governments of the member states currently have policies to support and safeguard lesser-used and minority languages and cultures. While these polices are often defended in terms of the welfare and human right of individuals to be able to communicate and to conduct legal and other business in their mother tongue, it has also been recognized that there are other, new and interesting perspectives on the role of minority languages and cultures. Colin H. Williams, for example, writes:

---

[34] Garth O. Hughes and Anne-Marie Sherwood, *Socio-economic Aspects of Designating the Cambrian Mountains and the Lleyn Peninsula as Environmentally Sensitive Areas* (Aberystwyth, 1992).

> Questions about power, control, legitimacy, adequate employment, demography, development and planning are as central to the future of lesser-used language communities as are the more conventional elements of education, literature and communal values and behaviour . . . Conventionally, attention has been focused on formal education as the chief agency of language reproduction, but increasingly we are recognising the potency of regional planning, of economic development and of social policy in structuring the conditions which influence language vitality.[35]

One of the ways in which links can be made between agriculture, rural development and culture is through the debate on the meaning of sustainable development. Although a wide variety of interpretations are placed on its meaning,[36] it appears to imply greater respect for social and cultural considerations than traditional models of economic development which implicitly, if not explicitly, seem to have regarded cultural diversity almost as an obstacle to development and the loss of culture as part of the price of achieving it.

There are several ways in which culture and cultural diversity are being embraced by sustainability. Firstly, language and culture can strengthen regional identity and hence the demand for devolution in decision-making, leading to greater local autonomy and control. This can be important in promoting sustainable development and preventing what is unsustainable. One of the recommendations of *Agenda 21* – the plan of action following the United Nations' Rio Declaration 1992, on the environment and development[37] – was for greater local participation in policy-making. Secondly, by helping to maintain and strengthen regional identity and local autonomy, cultural diversity may provide a focus countering the tendency of unregulated markets towards the spatial agglomeration of economic activity, which can have external social costs, both at the centres of concentration of economic activity, for example congestion, and in declining marginal areas at the periphery, for instance, the unsustainability of local services.[38] Thus, if more dispersed autonomous control over the local economy can be exercised (following *Agenda 21*) as a result of cultural diversity, the latter has an important role to play in reducing unsustainable human activity.

The association between the use of a lesser-used language and sustainability in general may be strengthened by two further arguments, both of which are

---

[35] Colin H. Williams, 'Linguistic Minorities: West European and Canadian Perspectives' in idem (ed.), *Linguistic Minorities, Society and Territory* (Clevedon, 1991), pp. 3, 11.

[36] 'While a great deal has been written about sustainable development, it is difficult to find rigorous definitions of it.' David Pearce, Anil Markandya and Edward B. Barbier, *Blueprint for a Green Economy* (London, 1989), p. 173.

[37] United Nations, *The Declaration of Rio and its Agenda 21 Action Programme* (New York, 1993).

[38] Gunnar Myrdal, *Economic Theory and Under-developed Regions* (London, 1957); Doreen Massey and John Allen (eds.), *Uneven Re-development. Cities and Regions in Transition: A Reader* (London, 1988).

conditional until coherent supporting evidence has been assembled. The first argument relates to the changing nature of economic activity in the countryside and to the way in which this might be adapted to take advantage of the fragmentation of tourism demand. The second argument suggests that linguistic diversity is similar to biodiversity and that cultural evolution is comparable in nature to the genetic sort, shifting continuously in response to environmental changes. Some of the consequences of each argument will be considered in turn.

The long-term decline of natural resource prices (and incomes based upon their exploitation, though not necessarily the rate of their production) has reduced employment in industries such as agriculture, forestry, fishing and mining, which are proportionately over-represented in marginal, peripheral regions. This redistribution and technological transformation has also had other consequences, especially on the mobility of the urban population and on the type of activities sought for relaxation and leisure. One of the effects of the demise of conventional mass tourism is a new search for authentic experiences close to nature and a pace and lifestyle different from the everyday.[39] Linguistic diversity may thus become an asset which, since it is embedded in a different cultural tradition, can generate new income and employment. In this contemporary context, 'cultural tourism' may assist in sustaining marginal regions and their cultural integrity. The proposition is a fragile one, however, for today's tourist may become tomorrow's resident, thus weakening the essence of the initial cultural appeal.[40]

Cultural fragility is also the basis for the second set of arguments. These are that linguistic diversity, like biodiversity, is both scientifically valuable and an important part of the complex of systems which comprise and mutually support the biosphere. The first aspect has been proposed with some vigour by linguistic scientists in defence of threatened languages:

> linguistic diversity is important to human intellectual life – not only in the context of scientific linguistic inquiry, but also in relation to the class of human activities belonging to the realms of culture and art.[41]

These arguments are assembled on the basis of the need to examine diversity of grammatical structures in order to gain insight into the development of language, the fundamental building block of human societies, in much the same way that, for example, soil structure in semi-natural woodland can be used as a control to

---

[39] See John Urry, *The Tourist Gaze: Leisure and Travel in Contemporary Societies* (London, 1990).

[40] Graham Day, '"A Million on the Move?": Population Change and Rural Wales', *CW*, 3 (1989), 137–59; Bill Bramwell, 'Rural Tourism and Sustainable Rural Tourism', *Journal of Sustainable Tourism*, 2, nos. 1 and 2 (1994), 1–6; Bernard Lane, 'What is Rural Tourism?', ibid., 7–21.

[41] Ken Hale, 'Language Endangerment and the Human Value of Linguistic Diversity', *Language*, 68, no. 1 (1992), 35.

determine the extent of erosion and degradation in adjacent cultivated land.[42] The morphological and phonological structures of language are also important in cultural expression since they underpin the historical development of verse and music, crucial to the culture of Wales. Unlike genetic diversity, of course, techniques have been developed to record linguistic structures: consequently, languages without native speakers can be classified as moribund and may, to an extent, be artificially reconstructed (as with Hebrew and, possibly, Cornish). However, there may be more to the process of cultural evolution, which is not yet understood, that may have yet to be assimilated from future study of living, spoken languages. Michael Krauss compares endangered languages to the situation with regard to the most threatened biological species: perhaps 10 per cent of the 4,400 mammal species and 5 per cent of the 8,600 bird species are seriously at risk or extinct.[43] Of the 6,000 languages in the world, he predicts that 'the coming century will see either the death or doom of 90 per cent of mankind's languages', which will make the scientific task of investigating human evolution and identity considerably more difficult.

A development of arguments in this evolutionary vein draws on Richard Norgaard's ideas about the co-evolution of culture and society within the context of their natural environments.[44] He suggests that these have adapted social systems and practices which are suitable to the conditions in which they are located, and that geographical patches of linguistic and cultural diversity formerly existed between natural barriers of mountains, seas, deserts and rivers. The decline of this diversity has been due to increased mobility of information, goods, people and, latterly, services. Norgaard argues that failure to appreciate the co-evolutionary nature of social, economic and environmental changes has resulted in development failure. One of the implications of this proposition is that the co-evolutionary view is supportive of cultural pluralism, whereas conventional thinking (described as modernism by Norgaard) is antagonistic.

Conclusion

Agriculture has been a major employer of Welsh speakers and, despite its relative decline within the economy, it continues to be an important domain for the Welsh language. The future economic and social stability of agricultural communities in Wales (and their family farm structures) is therefore relevant to the future of the Welsh language. Since the economic policy environment has been a critical factor affecting the stability of these communities, future economic

---

[42] George Peterken, *Woodland Conservation and Management* (2nd ed., London, 1993), pp. 195–6.

[43] Michael Krauss, 'The World's Languages in Crisis', *Language*, 68, no. 1 (1992), 7.

[44] Richard Norgaard, 'Coevolution of Economy, Society and Environment' in Paul Ekins and Manfred Max-Neef (eds.), *Real Life Economics: Understanding Wealth Creation* (London, 1992), pp. 76–86; R. B. Norgaard, *Development Betrayed: The End of Progress and a Coevolutionary Revisioning of the Future* (London, 1994).

policies for agriculture, as well as policies for managing agricultural decline through rural development, are important issues. This is particularly significant at this point in the history of the rural economy of Wales because of the fundamental changes occurring in the policy environment.

In the past, public policy has played an influential role in determining the prosperity of Welsh agriculture: it has been largely supportive (although not necessarily ideal or without criticism), and has been relatively stable in terms of its objectives and the instruments deployed in their pursuit. The 1990s, however, represented a major turning point in the nature of agricultural policy and potentially far-reaching changes were set in motion which have not yet been fully worked out, and may, in themselves be the catalyst for further change. The directions currently being taken with regard to agricultural policy (the 1992 CAP reforms, the pressure to meet international obligations on trade and levels and methods of agricultural support, the aim of a 'competitive' agriculture, the planned move towards world market prices) suggest continued and perhaps increased pressure on farm incomes and employment in countries such as Wales and hence on the continued survival of rural communities. Any further decline in the Welsh agricultural labour force will increasingly focus on full-time farmers, rather than workers, since the decline in the number of agricultural workers appears to have reached a nadir. This, together with the limited availability of off-farm work, could lead to a weakening of the family farming structure. Given the strong link between the farming community in Wales and the use of the Welsh language, it is clear that there may be cultural implications arising from such developments.

Beyond the farm sector, too, other pressures multiply. A depopulated country-side has detrimental effects on its attractiveness for outsiders and hence on other important sources of rural income. A thriving Welsh-speaking agricultural population brings with it Welsh-speaking shopkeepers, bankers, schoolteachers – a network which will be severely weakened by further agricultural decline.

There is clearly a need for comparative study within the EU, since many of the questions relating to the fate of the Welsh language are likely to be relevant to the position of other European minority languages and cultures. A further issue is the extent to which development policies can be adapted in order to take the cultural dimension into account. Since complex and often sensitive regional considerations concerning equal opportunities and human rights necessarily become involved, it is likely that, in practice, there will be substantial obstacles to policy formulation. Increasingly, however, there is some indication that such issues are being addressed. Within the EU, with respect to agriculture and rural development, there is growing evidence of a more holistic approach.[45] While the assertion by Von Meyer that

---

[45] European Commission, *Bulletin of the European Community, 78–88* (Brussels, 1988).

'agriculture's most important contribution to rural development is no longer the production of feed and food, but the protection and promotion of rural amenity, ecological integrity and cultural identity' [46] is perhaps an overstatement, it reflects views that now appear to be widely held by policy-makers, namely that agricultural policy must be more fully integrated with policies for rural development and that development policies should give more explicit consideration to their social and cultural consequences.[47]

---

[46] Quoted in Jonathan Ockenden and Michael Franklin, *European Agriculture: Making the CAP Fit the Future* (London, 1995), p. 94.
[47] European Commission, *European Conference on Rural Development, The Cork Declaration, Rural Europe – Future Perspectives*, Cork, Ireland, 7–9 November 1996.

18

The Welsh Language and Local Authority Planning in Gwynedd 1974–1995

DELYTH MORRIS

Introduction

PRIOR TO 1974 the language used by the county councils of Anglesey, Caernarfonshire and Merioneth was at odds with the everyday language of the vast majority of the population,[1] but this situation was transformed with the establishment of the new Gwynedd County Council. By adopting a bilingual policy, supported by substantial financial and practical resources, Gwynedd County Council embarked upon a new period in the history of public admin-istration in the region, bringing the Welsh language to the heart of activities from which it had been excluded for centuries. Since being proscribed from Welsh public life following the 1536 Act of Union, the Welsh language had enjoyed neither official status nor equal validity with English until comparatively recently. In 1963 a committee was established under the chairmanship of Sir David Hughes Parry to consider the legal status of the language, but the Act which came into force in 1967 was disappointing in several respects. Indeed, it has been argued that it did more harm than good since it branded Welsh, both officially and legally, as a minority and inferior language.[2] Nevertheless, due to the changing political climate, a gradual increase occurred in the use of Welsh in public life, including local government and the media. By the end of the 1960s the activities of Cym-deithas yr Iaith Gymraeg (the Welsh Language Society) was raising awareness and stimulating change during a period of widespread political agitation.[3] It could be argued, therefore, that when Gwynedd County Council was established in 1974 the time was ripe to formulate a language policy which met the aspirations of many of the inhabitants of the county.

Gwynedd County Council was not the only body to adopt a bilingual policy. The district and borough councils – Aberconwy, Arfon, Dwyfor, Merioneth, and

---

[1] The Council for Wales and Monmouthshire, *Report on the Welsh Language Today* (London, 1963) (PP 1963–4 (Cmnd. 2198) XX), p. 38.

[2] Glyn Williams, 'Bilingualism, Class Dialect and Social Reproduction', *International Journal of the Sociology of Language*, 66 (1987), 85–9.

[3] Kenneth O. Morgan, *Rebirth of a Nation: Wales 1880–1980* (Oxford, 1981), p. 383.

Anglesey – also adopted language policies which reflected a varying degree of commitment to the Welsh language and, in the case of Dwyfor District Council, Welsh became the sole language of administration. In 1995–6 local government in Wales was again reorganized, and the new unitary authorities adopted similar language policies to the old county council. This was in fact inevitable because Gwynedd County Council had raised people's expectations and created a demand for services through the medium of Welsh. In this respect, the establishment of a formal language policy in 1974 was a pioneering advance, although this was not perhaps fully appreciated by the elected members at the time.

The number of Welsh speakers recorded in the 1991 census provided ample evidence that allusions to 'cadernid Gwynedd' (the stronghold of Gwynedd) were not mere romanticization – it was the county with the highest proportion of Welsh speakers in Wales and the highest proportion of Welsh-speaking children and young people.[4] Needless to say, it cannot be asserted that the language policy of the county council was the only factor in the development of the use of Welsh in Gwynedd, since this was the primary aim of several other organizations and movements. It must also be borne in mind that external factors, such as legal rights, as well as wider economic and political issues, often serve to restrict local authorities in the pursuit of their policies.

Gwynedd County Council remained in force between 1974 and 1996, a period of far-reaching political change in Britain which resulted in a shift of emphasis in government policy and the imposition of legal, financial and ideological restrictions on local authorities. The last few years of the county council's existence saw the passing of the 1993 Welsh Language Act and the subsequent establishment of Bwrdd yr Iaith Gymraeg (the Welsh Language Board) which influenced, at a national level, the language policies of the new unitary councils of Wales, although this occurred within the context of a neo-liberal discourse which elevates the aspirations of the individual rather than the rights of the group. The neo-liberal political trend, with its emphasis on market values, cannot promote the interests of minority language groups; to the contrary, it could be argued that it militates against them. It was necessary, therefore, for the unitary councils which came into being in April 1996 to attempt to implement their language policies within the considerable constraints which the new political ideology had imposed upon them, a situation in stark contrast to that faced by the councillors of Gwynedd in 1973–4. At that time, local government enjoyed a comparatively large degree of autonomy and could implement specific, energetic policies in particular areas, such as the education policy adopted by Gwynedd County Council in 1975. Although schools in Gwynedd, and in Wales generally, were more reluctant than English schools to opt out of local education authority control, as exhorted by the government, changes in central education policy have

---

[4] The Welsh Office, *Statistical Brief. The Welsh Language: Children and Education* (Cardiff, 1995).

inevitably affected the ability of the new councils to implement their own policies. An appropriate starting point, therefore, will be a detailed examination of the wider political framework within which the Gwynedd local authorities operate.

The Impact of the 'new Right' on Local Government Policies

The 1980s witnessed a new political shift to the right, both in Britain and in the United States of America, as Margaret Thatcher and Ronald Reagan promoted policies which stressed individualism and the free market, and which limited state interference in the lives of its citizens. The function of government was to establish order and maintain authority, in accordance with conservative moral values which promoted the family, the nation and tradition.[5] Under the new order, the concept of the rights of citizenship was abandoned with the 'freeing' of the individual within the market.

The concept of rights of citizenship has developed over a period of two centuries and, according to T. H. Marshall,[6] includes civil rights (the right to freedom of expression and the freedom to own property), political rights (the right to vote and equality under the law), and social rights (the right to an equitable measure of education, health and income). The establishment of these rights had begun early in the nineteenth century and social rights were reaffirmed and reinforced following the Second World War as the welfare state extended its activities. Rights of citizenship resulted in the diminution of economic, political and social inequality, and the establishment of a more egalitarian society in Britain and other western states.

The 'new Right', however, considered that these rights had imposed unacceptable restrictions on the working of the market and that there was no justification for seeking to redress social inequality. To the contrary, it was asserted that inequality was essential to the proper functioning of society in that it stimulated progress and development: if everyone was equal, it was argued, what incentive would there be to engage in creative and entrepreneurial activity? It was therefore important for the Right to maintain social inequality, and it did this in part by attempting to reverse the historical trend of extending rights of citizenship, the exception being property ownership, its flagship policy. Some liberals within the movement campaigned for the extension of individual rights to property ownership,[7] and at the same time for minimizing the activity of the state, so that the individual might enjoy the greatest possible level of freedom and autonomy. These liberals were not in sympathy with neo-liberal thinking which stressed

---

[5] David S. King, *The New Right: Politics, Markets and Citizenship* (London, 1987).

[6] T. H. Marshall, *Citizenship and Social Class, and Other Essays* (Cambridge, 1950).

[7] Robert Nozick, *Anarchy, State, and Utopia* (New York, 1974); Murray N. Rothbard, *For a New Liberty: The Libertarian Manifesto* (New York, 1973).

conservative religious and social values, since these undermined the freedom of the individual. Nevertheless, both liberals and neo-liberals on the new Right were united in their support of capitalism and their opposition to the state. F. A. Hayek was the most prominent and influential thinker among right-wing intellectuals;[8] he argued fervently for the curbing of state interference in the economy and society. Unlike the liberals, Hayek saw the need for the state to support certain public services and provide a legal framework; at the same time, however, he claimed that responsibility for the provision of most services should be vested in the private sector rather than a bureaucratic public sector which was, in his opinion, both ineffective and wasteful.

Margaret Thatcher's government drew heavily on the thinking of Hayek and his followers when formulating policy, although the borrowing was often eclectic, involving the marriage of new Right ideas and short-term pragmatic political considerations. The thrust of Thatcher's policies was undoubtedly radical, however, pressing forcefully for the privatization of large sections of the public sector. For local government in Wales, and Britain in general, the implications were dramatic.[9]

The year 1988 saw the passing of the Local Government Finance Act which abolished the local tax on property, and the Education Reform Act which deprived local education authorities of much of their control over schools. In Gwynedd it was estimated that the local education authority, as a consequence of these changes, lost control of a third of its total expenditure.[10] In addition, the Housing Acts of 1988 and 1989 reduced the control of district councils over the housing sector, and the 1988 Local Government Act compelled councils to privatize their services.[11] At the same time, major changes in the field of community care meant that bids now had to be submitted for many of the services normally provided by the county councils' social services departments. It was estimated at the time that English county councils would lose a third of their work as a result of these acts,[12] and it is reasonable to assume that county councils in Wales were similarly affected.

Then, in 1994, the Local Government Act (Wales) called for the establishment of three new multi-purpose councils to replace Gwynedd County Council on 1 April 1996, these being Aberconwy and Colwyn Borough Council, Caernarfon and Merioneth County Council (which later adopted the title Gwynedd Council) and the Isle of Anglesey County Council. In line with the government's policy of centralizing services, the new unitary councils had fewer statutory responsibilities

[8] F. A. [von] Hayek, *The Road to Serfdom* (London, 1944); idem, *The Constitution of Liberty* (London, 1960); idem, *Law, Legislation, and Liberty: A New Statement of the Liberal Principles of Justice and Political Economy. Vol. I: Rules and Order* (London, 1973).

[9] Ioan Bowen Rees, *Cymuned a Chenedl: Ysgrifau ar Ymreolaeth* (Llandysul, 1993).

[10] Ibid., p. 221.

[11] Ibid., p. 28.

[12] Ibid.

than the former county councils. They were, in fact, to be facilitating authorities, working in conjunction with the private sector for the benefit of the 'customer'. By buying in private-sector services, the customer would enjoy greater 'freedom and choice', 'quality service' would be provided, and 'waste' eliminated.

This forceful and persuasive political rhetoric was adopted with conviction by the numerous quangos established by the Conservatives in Wales from the beginning of the 1980s onwards. It was used extensively, for example, by the Welsh Language Board, in its guidance to the public sector, in reference to the 'cost' of implementing language schemes, the 'advantage' this might have for organizations, and the 'gain' resulting from customer satisfaction.[13] This approach was in total contrast to the language policy of the old Gwynedd County Council, which emphasized the 'right' of people to receive services in their preferred language, whether Welsh or English. There was evidently tension between the desire of the state to take an active part in the provision of services for its citizens on the one hand, and the responsibility of the individual to make the most suitable choice on the other. In the latter instance, having established the necessary framework, the state could withdraw, leaving society to function within the dictates of the market. With regard to minority language planning, however, whether at a national or local level, the problems are rather more complex. As already mentioned, the expectations of the people of Gwynedd had increased as a result of the policies of the local authority over a period of twenty years, and it was assumed that there would be an increase in demand for Welsh-medium services in the new unitary counties. According to the logic of the Right, therefore, the new local authorities would need to respond to this demand by formulating appropriate language policies.

The Language Policies of the Local Authorities of Gwynedd

Soon after their formation in 1974, Gwynedd County Council and some district and borough councils set up bilingualism panels in order to establish the principle of bilingualism within the framework of their committees, departments and services. During the following years, the use of Welsh was legitimized in several new contexts, including education (from nursery to further education), social services, libraries, planning and housing, and, in the course of time, in the workplace in general. This, in turn, led to increased pressure on other public bodies, including the health service and electricity, water and telephone utilities, to provide services through the medium of Welsh. The county council and five local district councils decided to set up the Gwynedd Bilingualism Forum, a body which would monitor bilingual provision in the county, and they were joined by sixteen major regional organizations, namely the Welsh Development Agency,

---

[13] Glyn Williams, 'Y Bwrdd a Chynllunio Iaith', *Barn*, 387 (1995), 7–9.

Gwynedd Health Authority, Gwynedd Family Health Service Authority, North Wales Police, the National Rivers Authority, the Wales Tourist Board, Nant Gwrtheyrn Language Centre, University College of Wales, Bangor, the Forestry Commission, the Countryside Council, Welsh Water, Welsh Gas, British Rail, the Chartered Institute of Bankers, TARGED and British Telecom. This forum met on a regular basis to discuss policy, but had no executive power and functioned mainly as an advisory body.[14] Nevertheless, its remit was an indication of the changing status of Welsh in Gwynedd.

The language policy of Gwynedd County Council, formulated in 1974 and reviewed in 1991, applied to all council activities, with the exception of education, since a specific policy had been adopted in this field in 1975 and reviewed in 1983. The council was to prepare all documents and signs in both languages, with Welsh given priority. In addition, individuals were entitled to deal with the council in Welsh or English. A translation service would be provided in committees to enable all members to contribute in their preferred language, and staff were encouraged to use Welsh in the internal administration of the council. Having said that, the right of staff to work in their preferred language was protected unless this was likely to 'substantially impair the effectiveness of internal communication'. In practice, of course, this meant that bilingual staff had to use English unless their colleagues could speak Welsh, and it was discovered that the majority of council workers, except in certain departments such as the Education Department, continued to use English only, or mainly, for internal administration purposes. However, over a period of years a Welsh-language culture developed among the staff, partly as a result of the forceful leadership of a large number of elected members who spoke Welsh at every possible opportunity. Non-Welsh speakers were given opportunities to attend Welsh courses and released from their duties for this purpose, although a clause in the policy permitted senior officers not to release staff if their absence was likely to affect departmental efficiency. Nonetheless, many county council workers became very proficient in the language.

The translation service undoubtedly played a crucial role in supporting the Welsh-language image of the county council and the district and borough councils. The old county councils of Anglesey and Caernarfonshire had installed translation equipment in their main chambers in the 1960s, although neither had appointed a translator; instead they employed casual translators as the need arose. It would appear, therefore, that only the main committees were served by translators, and in practice very few ventured to speak in Welsh since old habits were difficult to overcome. However, with the establishment of Gwynedd County Council in 1974, a chief translator and three translators/administrators were

---

[14] Fforwm Dwyieithrwydd Gwynedd, *Tuag at Strategaeth Iaith i Ogledd-Orllewin Cymru* (Caernarfon, 1995).

appointed, and an external simultaneous translation service was secured. Other councils followed its example, and Anglesey Borough Council, for example, appointed a full-time translator in 1979, another in 1983, and a third in 1994. In 1974–5 very few Anglesey councillors spoke Welsh in committees, but by 1995 Welsh was the most commonly-used language at all council meetings, a practice now accepted without reservation by non-Welsh-speaking members as well as the public.

In the mid-1980s the majority of elected members in the county council and in every borough and district council, except Aberconwy (47 per cent), were fluent Welsh speakers – Dwyfor (100 per cent), Merioneth (90 per cent), Arfon (90 per cent), Anglesey (86 per cent), and Gwynedd County Council (82 per cent). With the exception of Aberconwy, where 77 per cent of the staff were non-Welsh speakers, the vast majority of staff in every council were bilingual, which meant that a bilingual policy could be successfully implemented.

At the end of 1995 the new unitary councils proceeded to formulate their policies and strategies for the future, and to appoint chief officers. By and large, bilingual officers were appointed to the main posts in Anglesey and Caernarfon–Merioneth although, unsurprisingly, a majority of non-Welsh speakers were appointed by Aberconwy–Colwyn Council.[15] Furthermore, the three councils adopted bilingual policies, although with varying degrees of commitment to the Welsh language, as they had done in 1974. For example, Caernarfon–Merioneth County Council decided that Welsh would be the language of internal admin-istration, and that as a result any non-Welsh-speaking staff appointed would need to develop the 'necessary facility' in the language within a specified period of time.[16] Some criticism was levelled at this decision in the press and media; certain politicians labelled it 'racist' and the trade union Unison voiced concern over the interests of members who could not speak Welsh. A similar political debate had surfaced in 1985 when the Commission for Racial Equality took Gwynedd county council to an industrial tribunal for 'discriminating' against two women from Anglesey who had failed to secure employment at one of the old people's homes in the county due to their inability to speak Welsh. The tribunal determined that there had been discrimination, but the county council appealed against the judgement which was subsequently overturned in the Court of Appeal in London. Nevertheless, the insistence upon Welsh as a job requirement remained a contentious issue. In response to an inquiry by Caernarfon–Merioneth Council in August 1995, counsel on behalf of the Commission for Racial Equality ruled that the existing policy was a prima-facie case of discrimination against non-Welsh-speaking ethnic groups such as the English and

[15] The names of the shadow-authorities at the time of reorganization 1995–6. The names were later changed to the Isle of Anglesey County Council, Gwynedd Council and Conwy County Borough Council.

[16] Cyngor Sir Caernarfon a Meirionnydd, *Polisi Iaith / Language Policy* (Caernarfon, 1995).

Scots.[17] Elected members of the new council, on the other hand, believed that language was a skill which could be acquired and wished to respond effectively to public demand for a Welsh-medium service. The council's view was largely reinforced and justified by the Welsh Language Act and the new neo-liberal emphasis on responding to the needs and aspirations of the customer. Despite the weakness of the Act in terms of *enforcing* change, it presented opportunities for organizations and movements which sought to develop the use of Welsh. As the new unitary authorities in Wales created language schemes and policies to meet the anticipated demand from customers for Welsh-language services, they readily acknowledged the leading role played by Gwynedd councils over the previous twenty years in normalizing the use of Welsh in new areas of work and subsequently enhancing the status of the language.

Language Policy in Education

It is interesting to note that the usefulness of Welsh in the workplace was a major argument presented to non-Welsh-speaking parents in favour of the bilingual policy: 'The ability to speak Welsh is a basic qualification for many posts in education, local government, broadcasting, and commerce in Gwynedd and Wales.'[18] It could be argued that this policy, adopted in 1975, was the principal achievement of Gwynedd County Council in respect of promoting the Welsh language. Thousands of children from Welsh-speaking homes learnt to read and write Welsh with confidence, and thousands of non-Welsh-speaking children learnt to speak, read and write the language. No other county in Wales experienced such success in the field of bilingual education.

The main elements of the policy were as follows:

Primary Schools:

In the traditionally Welsh areas and the 'designated Welsh schools', Welsh will be the main medium of instruction at primary level. In these areas, non-Welsh-speaking children who enter the schools should be given an intensive course in Welsh so that they can take their place naturally in the school and in the community as soon as possible. At the same time, every effort should be made to promote the learning of English, so that a balanced progress is achieved in the children's ability in both languages.

In the less-Welsh areas, Welsh should be taught to all non-Welsh-speaking children, beginning at nursery level. Equal school-time should be allocated to both the Welsh and English languages. Care should be taken to ensure that suitable provision is made to

---

[17] Eldred Tabachnik, Q.C., *In the Matter of the Race Relations Act 1976: Advice* (London, 1995), advice to the Commission on Racial Equality.

[18] Gwynedd County Council, *Your Children in their New Schools: An Introduction to the Bilingual Policy in Gwynedd's Schools* (Caernarfon, 1981), p. 7.

safeguard and develop the mother tongue of the Welsh-speaking minorities in these areas.

Secondary Schools:

Welsh as mother tongue and second language – all pupils in secondary schools should study Welsh and English up to the end of their fifth year and all those capable should be entered for external examinations in both subjects.

Teaching through the medium of Welsh – as an extension of the bilingual education in the primary schools, teaching through the medium of Welsh should be continued in a number of subjects in the secondary schools, and pupils should be enabled to sit the external examinations in these subjects through the medium of Welsh.[19]

The adoption of this policy to some degree formalized the existing arrangements in a number of Gwynedd schools, that is, the use of Welsh as the principal teaching medium, but it was also a political response to the perceived threat to local communities in Gwynedd from the increasing influx of monoglot English speakers during the previous decade. In a report prepared by Her Majesty's Inspectors in 1977, based on a survey conducted in 1974, reference was made to a 'sudden and alarming' decrease in the number of Welsh speakers in the primary schools of Gwynedd, Dyfed and Powys over the previous twenty-five years. One predicament anticipated by the inspectors at the time was that this would eventually result in a dearth of teachers able to teach through the medium of Welsh, although the problem requiring immediate solution was the failure of schools to teach Welsh to in-migrants and newcomers. It was noted that only 5 per cent of children from non-Welsh-speaking backgrounds had learnt Welsh in Anglesey, 14 per cent in Caernarfonshire and 20 per cent in Merioneth.[20]

More incomers from England settled in Anglesey than in other parts of Gwynedd. A study conducted by Anglesey Borough Council in 1977 indicated an increase of 13.2 per cent in the population of the island, namely 12,000 people, between 1971 and 1977. Few of these spoke Welsh: over 70 per cent were from England, with a third hailing from the north-west.[21] The majority had come to Anglesey to seek employment in Wylfa Atomic Power Station, Anglesey Aluminium in Holyhead and the new industries which had been established in the area as a result of the government's regional development plans.

The process of economic restructuring in Anglesey and Gwynedd had commenced in the late 1950s, and by the 1970s it appeared that it was beginning to affect the capacity of social institutions, including educational institutions, to promote and enrich the Welsh language. The report of the inspectors for 1977 revealed that 51 per cent of pupils at Amlwch Secondary School spoke Welsh as

---

[19] Idem (Education Department), *Polisi Iaith / Language Policy* (Caernarfon, 1975), p. 7.
[20] 'Problem y Mewnfudwyr', *Y Cymro*, 27 September 1977.
[21] Anglesey Borough Council, *Anglesey Population Survey 1971–1977* (Llangefni, 1978).

Table 1. Composition of the household and the Welsh language in Gwynedd in 1981

Language of parents	No Welsh-speaking children	One or more Welsh-speaking children[1]
	%	%
Both parents Welsh-speaking	3.3	96.7
Father only Welsh-speaking	40.2	59.7
Mother only Welsh-speaking	31.9	68.1
No Welsh-speaking parent	67.1	32.9

[1]   Source: Delyth Morris, 'Ailstrwythuro Economaidd a Ffracsiynu Dosbarth yng Ngwynedd' (unpubl. University of Wales PhD thesis, 1990).

their first language, compared with 49 per cent at Menai Bridge Secondary School, 76 per cent at Llangefni Comprehensive School and 25 per cent at Holyhead Secondary School.[22] More significant, perhaps, was the fact that only 11 per cent of the non-Welsh-speaking pupils in Amlwch had succeeded in learning Welsh fluently, compared with 5 per cent in Menai Bridge, 15 per cent in Llangefni and 2 per cent in Holyhead. A similar situation prevailed in the rest of Gwynedd – in Caernarfonshire the percentage of native Welsh speakers varied from 6 per cent at Ysgol John Bright, Llandudno, to 86 per cent at Ysgol Dyffryn Nantlle, Pen-y-groes. Only 2 per cent of non-Welsh-speaking pupils at Ysgol John Bright had learnt Welsh fluently, compared with 47 per cent at Ysgol Brynrefail, Llanrug. Overall, the percentages in Merioneth were higher in respect of native Welsh speakers and good learners, a situation largely attributable to the especially high percentages of native Welsh speakers (77 per cent) and good learners (60 per cent) in the Blaenau Ffestiniog area.

The make-up of the community was clearly an important factor in the process of effective Welsh second-language learning. There is an unquestionable link between the language of the home and the language of the school, and a reduction in the number of Welsh-speaking households followed the increase in linguistically-mixed marriages.[23] As Table 1 shows, when both parents spoke Welsh the language was almost always transmitted successfully at home. In 1981 58 per cent of children in Gwynedd came from homes where both parents spoke Welsh, approximately 20 per cent from homes where neither parent spoke Welsh, and the remainder from homes where one parent spoke Welsh.[24] For those families where the language was not being transmitted successfully at home, the

[22]   *Y Cymro*, 27 September 1977.
[23]   Williams, 'Bilingualism, Class Dialect and Social Reproduction', 89.
[24]   Delyth Morris, 'Ailstrwythuro Economaidd a Ffracsiynu Dosbarth yng Ngwynedd' (unpubl. University of Wales PhD thesis, 1990), p. 357.

Table 2. Attainment of Gwynedd primary school children in Welsh

Linguistic ability	1975	1985	1987
	%	%	%
Native Welsh speakers	49.0	41.4	40.9
Fluent learners	6.0	14.1	15.0
Non-fluent learners	15.5	14.5	14.3
Little or no Welsh	20.5	26.2	26.2
Newcomers	9.2	3.8	3.6

language policy of the education authority was a crucial element in promoting the learning of Welsh. The fact that one third of children with two non-Welsh-speaking parents had learnt the language is an indication of the success of the schools. In Gwynedd County Council's review of its original language policy, *Gwynedd County Council Language Policy* (1983),[25] the education authority claimed that the language policy was a success, asserting that it had increased the use of Welsh as a teaching medium in schools and raised the attainments of children for whom Welsh was their second language, and had achieved this despite the influx of newcomers and the decrease in the indigenous population in several parts of the county.

A more detailed analysis of the statistics produced by Gwynedd Education Authority itself, however, reveals that the policy was only partially successful in its aim of teaching Welsh to all non-Welsh-speaking children in the county. In a lecture delivered at the National Eisteddfod at Newport in 1988,[26] Gwilym Humphreys, Director of Education of Gwynedd at the time, showed that the attainment of primary school children in Welsh, as assessed by their headteachers, was mixed (Table 2). Table 2 reveals that the percentage of native Welsh speakers had fallen from 49 per cent in 1975 to 40.9 per cent by 1987, mainly as a result of in-migration, but at the same time that the decline had halted by the end of this period and that the percentage of English monoglot newcomers had fallen from 9.2 per cent in 1975 to 3.6 per cent in 1987. Throughout the period, however, only a minority of children from non-Welsh-speaking backgrounds succeeded in learning the language fluently at school, despite massive investment by the education authority, which included the establishment of special centres to teach Welsh to newcomers. A schools census conducted in January 1994 showed that the situation had hardly changed seven years later (Table 3).

---

[25] Gwynedd County Council, *Gwynedd County Council Language Policy* (Caernarfon, 1983).

[26] Gwilym E. Humphreys, *Addysg Ddwyieithog yng Nghymru: Camu 'Mlaen yn Hyderus / Bilingual Education: Facing the Future with Confidence*, Orleana Jones Memorial Lecture (Casnewydd, 1988), Table 4.

Table 3. Attainment of Gwynedd primary school children in Welsh in 1994[1]
(aged 5 and over)

Unitary Authority	Fluent: language of the home	Fluent learners	Total fluent	Non-fluent	No Welsh
	%	%	%	%	%
Ynys Môn	35.2	21.2	56.4	31.3	12.3
Caernarfon–Meirionnydd	51.7	24.0	75.7	21.3	3.0
Aberconwy–Colwyn	11.7	13.5	25.1	56.2	18.7
Total	**6789**	**3955**	**10744**	**7224**	**2175**

[1] Source: The Welsh Office, *Schools Census* (Cardiff, 1994).

Although the schools had enjoyed a fair measure of success, with almost 4,000 children learning Welsh fluently as a second language, the number of failures, approximately 9,500 children, was more than twice as great. Many of those who had failed to learn the language attended schools in Llandudno, Holyhead and Bangor, where both parents and governors were possibly less committed to the language. It must also be borne in mind that the implementation of the policy was largely dependent on the goodwill of teachers and that some were more enthusiastic than others. For instance, in a document prepared by the Welsh Language Society in 1987, *Polisi Iaith Gwynedd: Chwalu'r Myth* (Gwynedd's Language Policy: Dispelling the Myth), peripatetic community teachers involved in the teaching of Welsh as a second language described the kind of problems they had encountered in some schools in Anglesey. It was noted that in certain schools children could receive their education entirely through the medium of English and that in others sub-standard Welsh was accepted. The practice was to speak Welsh with Welsh-speaking children and English with learners, with the result that after seven years of primary school many had learnt virtually no Welsh.[27] The statistics appear to confirm these claims, underlining the danger of creating a policy without at the same time establishing a framework for monitoring it closely and measures to ensure its effective and rigorous implementation.

Nevertheless, efforts were made from the outset to monitor the language policy by requiring primary and secondary language advisers to report back to the education authority annually on the pupils' linguistic progress. This could be accomplished with statistical accuracy since teams of community teachers had developed a series of tests to measure the attainment of pupils. Taking action

[27] Cymdeithas yr Iaith Gymraeg, *Polisi Iaith Gwynedd: Chwalu'r Myth* (Aberystwyth, 1987), p. 3.

against schools and teachers who failed to achieve these targets was a different matter, and perhaps this was the main weakness of the policy. By the end of the 1980s the process of measuring the linguistic attainment of pupils was becoming defunct as changes in the curriculum altered the working practices of community teachers, and the community teachers' programme itself gradually disintegrated following the introduction of a new schools' funding methodology and the fact that the governing bodies of individual schools could now determine their spending priorities. In 1991 a report published by Gwynedd Education Authority showed that only 41 per cent of the county's secondary school pupils had taken the First Language Welsh examination, 12 per cent the Extended Welsh examination, and 24 per cent the Foundation Welsh examination. In other words, nearly a quarter of the pupils had not sat any kind of Welsh language examination,[28] a disappointing percentage in the light of the money and energy expended promoting the bilingual policy over the previous fifteen years.

At the same time, some complained that the teaching of Welsh to non-Welsh speakers was being given priority over Welsh-medium education to native Welsh speakers, especially in secondary schools and colleges of further education. In the Welsh Language Society's document, *Polisi Iaith Gwynedd: Chwalu'r Myth*, several such failures of the language policy were identified. In recounting his own school days, one parent recalled that he had had to translate much of his A-level History course himself and had written to the Director of Education of Gwynedd to complain, eliciting the reply that lack of funds meant it was impossible to write or translate books.[29] Other parents were concerned that the choice of courses available through the medium of Welsh compared unfavourably with the varied and comprehensive English-language provision. Native Welsh speakers in linguistically-mixed classes were obliged to speak English during lessons: 'What's that language you're speaking? I don't understand it. Speak English', was the teacher's directive, according to one witness. In addition, claims were made that some members of staff at further education institutions were anti-Welsh, and one parent expressed surprise that it was easier to secure a Welsh-language education in Cardiff than in Gwynedd. The Welsh Language Society maintained that such flaws in the policy were legion and that Gwynedd Education Authority was more concerned with fostering the myth of an innovative and radical policy than facing the reality of the situation.

It must be recognized, however, that the policy of the education authority was a *bilingual* one and that it could be argued, therefore, that it was not practical for parents to expect a totally Welsh, or totally English, education for their children. Herein, it might be said, lay the strength of the policy, since it had succeeded in

[28] Fforwm Dwyieithrwydd Gwynedd, *Tuag at Strategaeth Iaith*.
[29] Cymdeithas yr Iaith Gymraeg, *Polisi Iaith Gwynedd*, p. 3.

creating a favourable consensus during the twenty years of its existence, notwith-standing a certain amount of dissatisfaction in some schools in the mid-1970s. It is significant that the only primary school in Gwynedd to opt out of education authority control, Caergeiliog Primary School (a school with a high proportion of pupils from families stationed at the Royal Air Force base in Valley), professed a 'bilingual policy' – an example of the normalization resulting from the language policy of Gwynedd Education Authority. Perhaps this was an indication of the shape of things to come, as the era of the county council came to a close in 1996 and governing bodies took on the responsibility of drawing up the annual plans of individual schools in line with statutory requirements. The language policy of Gwynedd Education Authority had succeeded in raising parents' awareness of the possibilities of bilingualism, and it is unlikely that the clock will be turned back.

The Welsh Language in Town and Country Planning

Another area considered crucial in securing the position of Welsh in the social life of Gwynedd was town and country planning. According to John Osmond: 'It was significant . . . that Gwynedd's chief executive, Ioan Bowen Rees . . . told his authority that official bilingualism was not the most crucial factor in the battle for the language. It was more important, he said, to enact that the Welsh language could be a deciding factor in whether or not planning permission was given.'[30] Discussions concerning the use of Welsh as a factor in planning had begun in the mid-1970s – for example, on 1 March 1978 a group called the Welsh Planning Association published a document urging local authorities to act to protect and restore the Welsh language by making use of the Town and Country Planning Act 1971 and the Town and Country Planning Regulations 1974.[31] At the same time the Association was anxious to secure official planning status for the Welsh language. The Association declared that since nobody accepted laissez-faire con-cepts in respect of the economy and, to a large degree, social life, it was therefore remarkable that this eighteenth-century philosophy should determine the govern-ment's attitude towards the Welsh language and local Welsh culture.[32] Ironically, a year later, Margaret Thatcher's Conservative Party swept to power, totally committed to this selfsame philosophy. The Welsh Planning Association could hardly have chosen a less auspicious moment to seek to restrict the housing market in such a fashion.

While recognizing that housing and work were the two most important elements in safeguarding the language,[33] the document failed to discuss employ-ment at all; rather, it focused on housing estate developments which attracted

---

[30] John Osmond, 'A Million on the Move', *Planet*, 62 (1987), 115.
[31] Cymdeithas Cynllunio Cymru, *Statws Cynllunio i'r Iaith* (Caernarfon, 1987), p. 1.
[32] Ibid., p. 2.
[33] Ibid., p. 1.

incomers, either for retirement or as second homes. Housing developments cannot, of course, be separated from the economy, and Stephen Wyn Williams has maintained that a link exists between socio-economic development and the decline in the number of Welsh speakers.[34] Subsequent research in Ynys Môn, however, has shown that it is far too simplistic to suggest that one is the direct result of the other.[35] Allowing that economic restructuring inevitably leads to changes in social structure, it does not necessarily mean that Welsh usage will be undermined, since language groups can form social networks which withstand external pressure. In addition, one of the social effects of economic restructuring in Gwynedd since the 1950s has been the fractioning of social class. Welsh-based alliances which transcend class have developed, a process which has safeguarded the use of Welsh in a number of social contexts.[36] Nevertheless, the influx of monoglot English speakers undoubtedly created difficulties in relation to the use of Welsh in the community, and it was in response to this situation that the language policies discussed above were formulated. In the same way that making Welsh a requirement for certain public posts restricted the labour market, planners sought through their policies to restrict the housing market, thus coming into conflict with government thinking after 1979.

However, until central government severely curtailed local government powers by passing a series of acts in 1988 and 1989, local authorities were free to formulate structure plans and local plans to meet the aspirations of members, officers and local inhabitants. These aspirations are reflected in several discussion documents prepared in the early 1980s, including a substantial report submitted to Arfon Planning Committee in December 1983.[37] Arfon planners used the 1981 census figures as the basis for their report, and members were presented with ideas concerning how the Welsh language could be protected in view of the legislative restrictions now imposed upon them. It was acknowledged that the language could not in itself be used as a planning factor, and that intervention in the private housing market was not possible in order to control in-migration. But despite the council's carefully-worded statement that the aim was to maintain and develop as far as possible the unique identity of the area ('cadw a meithrin hyd y mae hynny'n bosibl hunaniaeth unigryw'r ardal'),[38] the Secretary of State was unwilling to accept elements of the plan which would, in his opinion, restrict the rights of citizens to free movement within the United Kingdom. He did, however, agree that growth could be

---

[34] Stephen Wyn Williams, 'Language Erosion: A Spatial Perspective', *Cambria*, 6, no. 1 (1979), 54–69.

[35] Delyth Morris, 'A Study of Language Contact and Social Networks in Ynys Môn', *CW*, 3 (1989), 99–117.

[36] Eadem, 'Language and Class Fractioning in a Peripheral Economy', *Journal of Multilingual and Multicultural Development*, 16, no. 5 (1995), 373–87.

[37] Cyngor Dosbarth Arfon, *Sefyllfa'r Iaith Gymraeg yn Arfon a'i Hoblygiadau Cynllunio / The Situation of the Welsh Language in Arfon and its Planning Implications* (Caernarfon, 1983).

[38] Ibid., p. 2.

confined to specific areas, and following this decision Bangor, being more Anglicized, was designated such an area, while Caernarfon was restricted to natural growth only. By that time, it was evident that control of private housing and planning was impossible under the current legislation.

Nevertheless, the Welsh Language Society sought to stimulate further discussion on the subject of planning and the Welsh language at a conference held in Carmarthen in February 1985. The attention of the local district council was drawn to the decrease in Welsh speakers in the area from 87 per cent in 1931 to 62 per cent in 1981, and it was predicted that the percentage would fall further to 55.7 per cent by 1991 if in-migration continued at the same level, thereby posing a serious threat to the continuation of Welsh as the language of a living community. As a result of the significant political, economic and social changes which were transforming communities throughout Britain during the early 1980s, language campaigners and supporters in Wales were becoming increasingly concerned, a feeling encapsulated in the popular remark 'It's five minutes to midnight'. There was much interest in official figures published by the government on numbers of Welsh speakers, especially census figures, and the media, planning authorities and academics painted a gloomy picture of the future of the language. For example, according to one document prepared by Gwynedd County Council Planning Department at the beginning of the 1980s, the percentage of Welsh speakers in the county had declined from 90.8 per cent in 1891 to 61.2 per cent in 1981; the document claimed that Welsh would cease to exist as a community language when the percentage of speakers fell below a quarter of the population. It was further asserted that English was a genuine threat in those communities where only half the population spoke Welsh: 40 per cent of Gwynedd communities were in this precarious position in 1981 compared with only 6 per cent in 1891. Caution is required, however, in interpreting a static picture such as this of situations which are in fact part of a complex social network, because there is no definite evidence to support the validity of these turning points and few studies have yet been made of the *use* of Welsh in various social contexts.

Despite this, considerable use has been made of this kind of statistical analysis in seeking to promote the argument for elevating Welsh as a planning factor. Carmarthen District Council was prompted to prepare a response to the figures supplied by the Welsh Language Society, and subsequently submitted a report to the Planning Committee discussing the possibility of drawing up a planning policy which would promote and safeguard the Welsh language.[39] Legislation in respect of the preparation of structure plans and local plans allowed local authorities to consider 'social factors',[40] and the planners believed that the Welsh language came

[39] Cyngor Dosbarth Caerfyrddin, *Cynllunio a'r Iaith Gymraeg / Planning and the Welsh Language* (Caerfyrddin, 1985).

[40] The Welsh Office, *Circular 43/84. Memorandum on Structure Plans and Local Plans* (Cardiff, 1984), para 4.10.

into this category. The Welsh Office circular also noted that housing developments could be restricted in areas where environmental protection was required, limiting any development to that which was necessary to meet local needs.[41] The Secretary of State for Wales, however, did not accept that house ownership could be restricted to particular categories of people. He believed that the conditions applied under Agreement 52 in other areas which were encountering a similar increase in retirement and second homes (such as the Lake District in England) were discriminatory and unacceptable.[42] Planners recognized that the existing legislation did not permit the use of planning measures to control in-migration and recommended conducting a survey of the Welsh language in the area in order to enable planners to use the language as a planning consideration, albeit secondary, in appropriate cases. Several planning authorities in Wales followed Carmarthen's lead, conducting similar surveys in their own areas with the objective of incorporating the Welsh language as a planning issue within their structure plans and local plans. It is, however, difficult to reject planning consent on the grounds of language, and the following two cases, one in Anglesey and the other in Dwyfor, demonstrate the problems which can arise when attempting to control the housing market.

Tŷ-croes, Anglesey

In 1987 the Defence Secretary appealed to the Welsh Office following the failure of Anglesey Borough Council to respond within a designated period of time to a planning application by the Ministry of Defence to develop a holiday village on the former military base at Tŷ-croes near Aberffro. As a result, a public inquiry was held in Llangefni in July 1987. The complainants called on five planning experts (mainly surveyors) to support their case, and Anglesey Council called upon farmers and planning, conservation and economic development officers, in addition to an expert on the state of the Welsh language, Professor Harold Carter, to present their opposition to the scheme.

In its evidence, the Ministry of Defence asserted that the proposed development, in respect of the movement of people, was little different from that which had existed since 1941, and that the 3,000 soldiers in the camp had not unduly affected the local community. This, however, was a secondary consideration. The main arguments presented on behalf of the development were environmental and economic: it was claimed, firstly, that the proposed development would improve the environment by removing the old military buildings which spoilt the natural beauty of the area, and, secondly, that it would result in the creation of a substantial number of local jobs. Unsurprisingly, the promise of

---

[41] Ibid., para 4.19.
[42] Rees, *Cymuned a Chenedl*, p. 19.

jobs attracted the support of a number of local people, but there was also considerable opposition to the scheme, mainly due to the potential effect on the environment, on the quality of life in general and on the Welsh language and culture. It was feared that a major tourist development would adversely affect a community which was among the most Welsh in Anglesey. Welsh was spoken by 89 per cent of the inhabitants. In their presentation, the complainants attempted to alleviate these concerns:

> There is no reason why a tourist facility should undermine the Welsh language and culture of the area . . . the Tourist Board . . . says that 'one interesting feature of tourism in Wales has been an apparent new strength in the Welsh language due to the interest shown by visitors to Wales'.[43]

Needless to say, many of those attending the inquiry were amazed at the naivety of the Ministry of Defence, not to mention the Tourist Board.

In its response, the council focused on environmental and linguistic issues. The development, it stated, was unsuitable in an area of exceptional natural beauty and special scientific interest, and close to a site of considerable historical importance. The Inspector was also reminded that the council was committed to maintaining the social and cultural identity of Anglesey in accordance with the requirements of paragraphs 2.2.2, 2.3.4 and 2.3.7 of the structure plan, and it quoted a parliamentary reply given by the Under-Secretary of State, Wyn Roberts, on 27 October 1986:

> It is a requirement of local planning authorities in considering planning applications and of the Secretary of State and his Inspectors in considering planning appeals that they have regard to all material considerations. Policies which reflect the needs and interests of the Welsh language may properly be among those considerations.[44]

The council also summoned a Welsh-language expert to support its arguments. In his evidence, Professor Harold Carter asserted that by 1981 only five core Welsh-speaking areas remained in Wales, and that Anglesey was one of these. He stressed the fact that more than 80 per cent of the population of south-western Anglesey were Welsh speakers – a figure which, in his view, was of crucial importance to the preservation of Welsh as a community language: 'the 80 per cent level is a critical point and even the smallest degree of change could have disproportionate repercussions'.[45] He also cited other areas where similar tourist

---

[43] The Welsh Office, *Memorandum. Town and Country Planning Act 1971: Section 36, Appeal 36. Secretary of State for Defence – Proposed Holiday Complex at Tŷ Croes Camp, Aberffraw, Anglesey* (Cardiff, 1988).

[44] Ibid., p. 12.

[45] Ibid., p. 13.

developments had occurred, mainly in Clwyd and along the Merioneth coast, and the adverse effect these had had on the language. Summing up, he maintained: 'I consider that the proposed development must have an adverse impact upon the Welsh language and that in an area where its maintenance is crucial for the future.'[46]

Although arguments concerning the effect on the Welsh language were detailed and persuasive, they were rejected by the Inspector: 'I am not convinced', he said, 'that the proposed development would be likely to unduly harm the social and cultural fabric of the local community.'[47] He believed that the economic arguments in favour of job creation outweighed the linguistic considerations. Nevertheless, the appeal was rejected, mainly for planning reasons, since it was felt that the proposed development would undermine an area of outstanding natural beauty and could not be successfully integrated into the environment. The effect on the Welsh language played no part in the decision.

Llanengan, Dwyfor

In the second case, an inquiry held in Dwyfor in November 1989 overturned the decision of Dwyfor District Council to impose a 'local condition' on a strip of land at Llanengan. The condition meant that only people who had lived and/or worked in Dwyfor for a period of three years could live in the houses to be built on the land. The owner objected to the condition and appealed to the Welsh Office via his agent, a chartered surveyor from Burton-upon-Trent. In his judgement, the Secretary of State stated the council's reasons for imposing the condition:

> the Council are concerned about the increasing pressures for weekend and holiday homes and the profound effect they believe this is having on the social structure of existing communities . . . the district has a unique character and identity which is seen not only in its landscape but also in its communities, the majority of which are predominantly Welsh-speaking, and they are concerned that in a number of areas the degree and rate of change is such that it cannot be readily assimilated . . . the outward migration of young people and the inward movement of retired persons and ones occupying holiday homes has led to a decline in the Welsh language.[48]

Nonetheless, although safeguarding the Welsh-speaking community was part of Dwyfor District Council's structure plan, the Secretary of State was unsupportive.

---

[46] Ibid.
[47] Ibid., p. 20.
[48] The Welsh Office, *Memorandum. Town and Country Planning Act 1971: Section 36, Appeal by Trustees of the Estate of W. Freeman-Jones, Erection of 3 Dwellings on OS field 1395, Llanengan, Gwynedd* (Cardiff, 1989).

Despite acknowledging that it was a complex issue and that he did not wish to make a definitive statement on the principle of imposing local conditions, he allowed the appeal against the condition on economic grounds (it would lower the value of the houses built) and because Dwyfor Council had already granted unconditional planning consent in 1977 and 1980.

It appears, therefore, that the Welsh Office paid little heed to planning conditions involving the Welsh language, even when applied on the recommendation of professional officers and supported by elected members and the structure plans and local plans of Gwynedd's councils. In the light of the Welsh Office response, and what many regarded as its failure to acknowledge the severe problems faced by the county,[49] Gwynedd County Council, in conjunction with Aberconwy, Arfon and Dwyfor Councils, drew up a detailed memorandum which was forwarded to the Secretary of State in July 1988.[50] The memorandum expressed the concern of the councils and inhabitants of Gwynedd regarding the effect of in-migration on the social and cultural life of the county, especially the state of the Welsh language, and appealed to the Secretary of State to respond positively to policies incorporated in the proposed new structure plan for Gwynedd and in local plans.[51] The Secretary of State was also asked to support the 'local condition' in considering appeals against rejection of planning consent. A positive response to the memorandum was not forthcoming from the Welsh Office – indeed, it was disregarded to all intents and purposes.[52]

Since the Welsh Office, in its circular 53/88, had already reminded Welsh councils that the Welsh language could be taken into consideration in planning,[53] Gwynedd County Council proceeded to include a clause in the structure plan adopted in January 1991 which recognized that 'the Welsh language is a material consideration in assessing the implications of development in Gwynedd. This will be implemented in a manner which ensures that the aim of safeguarding and nurturing the use of the Welsh language in Gwynedd is achieved'.[54] This was a step forward in that planners would now address the objective of protecting the *use* of Welsh in the county rather than focusing on percentages of Welsh speakers by community as had been done in the past. Despite the lukewarm response of the Welsh Office, the local democratic process presented elected representatives with opportunities for formulating planning policies at their own discretion. Once the new unitary authorities had assumed responsibility for planning within their

---

[49] Rees, *Cymuned a Chenedl*, pp. 200–1.

[50] Cyngor Sir Gwynedd, *Iaith, Cynllunio a Thai yng Ngwynedd: Memorandwm at Ysgrifennydd Gwladol Cymru / Language, Planning and Housing in Gwynedd: Memorandum to the Secretary of State for Wales* (Caernarfon, 1988).

[51] Ibid., para 8.12.

[52] Rees, *Cymuned a Chenedl*, pp. 200–1.

[53] The Welsh Office, *Circular 53/88. The Welsh Language: Development Plans and Planning Control* (Cardiff, 1988).

[54] Gwynedd County Council, *Gwynedd Structure Plan: Written Statement* (Caernarfon, 1991), p. 2.

areas from 1 April 1996, the use of the Welsh language as a planning condition depended largely on the vision of the officers and elected members when drawing up their local plans. The evidence of recent years, however, suggests that the ability of any local authority to safeguard the Welsh language by means of the planning process is limited. The language has never been a major factor, or even an important factor, in rejecting planning consent anywhere, and in the future governments are unlikely to give the interests of Welsh speakers priority over their fundamental beliefs in market forces, the freedom of the individual to live and work where he wishes, and economic development. Therefore, since executive power rested in the hands of the Secretary of State for Wales, it appears that the only success of local authorities in Gwynedd in the area of planning during the period under study had been to increase public awareness of the potential of the Welsh language as a tool in the prevention of inappropriate development.

Conclusion

Ar un adeg, yr oedd modd i lywodraeth leol geisio addasu polisïau'r Llywodraeth Ganol i rannau o Gymru. Ers deng mlynedd bellach, mae holl duedd deddfwriaeth a pholisïau cyllidol y Llywodraeth wedi bod yn gwanhau'r unig gyrff etholedig y gellir gweinyddu rhannau o Gymru yn wahanol drwyddynt.[55]

(At one time, it was possible for local government to attempt to adapt the policies of Central Government in different areas of Wales. During the past decade, however, Government legislation and funding policies have served to weaken the only elected body through which parts of Wales may be administrated differently.)

As Ioan Bowen Rees argued, since 1979 political changes have undermined the power of local authorities to such an extent that they are no longer able to promote distinct, vigorous policies at the local level. The determined policy of the Conservative government to emasculate powerful local authorities in England greatly affected many levels of local government throughout Britain. In Gwynedd the result of these political changes is that the new unitary authorities are no longer able to produce as comprehensive a language policy as the old county council due to their loss of control over key areas such as education. The language strategy published by Gwynedd Bilingualism Forum in September 1995 confirms this reality. In this document, the emphasis is on 'individual choice', 'co-operation', 'monitoring performance', 'review and re-submission', and 'marketing',[56] the vocabulary and concepts of neo-liberalism which are in stark contrast to the old values of 'civil rights' or 'community rights' so highly prized in the past.

---

[55] Rees, *Cymuned a Chenedl*, t. 220.
[56] Fforwm Dwyieithrwydd Gwynedd, *Tuag at Strategaeth Iaith*, pp. 48–58.

Table 4. The use of the Welsh language in Gwynedd[1]

Social situation	Speak Welsh
	%
With doctor	69
Buying petrol	80
In the newsagents'	70
In the public house	78
With children's teacher	83
With local councillor	94
With bank manager	82

[1] Source: Delyth Morris and Glyn Williams, *Arolwg Defnydd Iaith* (unpublished research, Canolfan Ymchwil Cymru, University of Wales College, Bangor, 1995).

Table 5. Attitudes of Welsh speakers in Gwynedd[1]

Statement	Agree	Disagree
	%	%
It is a good idea that councils conduct their business in Welsh only	68	32
It is essential for all children in Wales to learn Welsh	97	3
All public sector workers should be able to speak Welsh	91	9
There is no place for Welsh in the modern world	9	91
Welsh is unsuitable for business and science	11	89

[1] Source: Delyth Morris and Glyn Williams, *Arolwg Defnydd Iaith* (unpublished research, Canolfan Ymchwil Cymru, University of Wales College, Bangor, 1995).

On the other hand, the document states that the Welsh language in Gwynedd is in a much stronger position now than it was twenty years ago – for example, according to the 1991 census figures the decline in the number of Welsh speakers has been arrested. It is further noted that the confidence of Welsh speakers has increased and that they are more likely to use Welsh in various social situations. The Forum's claims are supported by a survey of Welsh usage conducted in 1994 (Table 4). The researchers discovered that people in Gwynedd *did* speak Welsh whenever possible – i.e. when the doctor or official they wished to see could speak the language. At the same time, people's expectations of receiving services through the medium of Welsh was higher in Gwynedd than in other parts of Wales, and their attitude towards the language was generally extremely positive (Table 5).

In progressing to a new era in the history of local government administration in Gwynedd, there can be no doubt that the political changes imposed upon local councils have hampered their capacity to plan strategically for the promotion of the Welsh language. Rather, in their new role as 'enablers', the most they can expect to achieve is the establishment of the necessary framework for the people of Gwynedd to make their own language choice in respect of the services they require. This was confirmed by the Welsh Language Board in a draft document on language plans published more than a year after the passing of the 1993 Welsh Language Act. In the document, it was stated that Welsh councils and other public bodies must prepare language plans which identify how they intend to use the Welsh language and provide Welsh-language services.[57] Despite the emphasis on marketing and individual choice, the Welsh speaker is not guaranteed complete freedom of choice because local councils and other public bodies are not legally obliged to deliver services in Welsh if this is 'impracticable' or 'inappropriate'. According to the Board:

> the purpose referred to . . . is that of giving effect, so far as is both appropriate in the circumstances and reasonably practicable, to the principle that in the conduct of public business and the administration of justice in Wales the English and Welsh languages should be treated on a basis of equality.[58]

Such a situation can hardly be described as one of linguistic equality, despite the attempts of the Chief Executive of the Welsh Language Board to justify it, arguing enthusiastically that this is the best way forward for the Welsh language in contemporary Wales. There is no consensus, however, concerning language planning in Wales, and many have taken issue with the philosophy and plans of the Board. One sociologist has asserted, for example, that the Board is no more than 'an unthinking machine which operates technologically on behalf of the government' ('[p]eiriant difeddwl sy'n gweithredu'n dechnolegol ar ran y llywodraeth'),[59] and members of the Welsh Language Society have responded scornfully to the request by the Chairman of the Welsh Language Board that they forego unconstitutional methods of language campaigning. As Raymond Williams observed, the hegemonic control of the state is never complete – rather, it exists side by side with completely different and diametrically opposed methods and ways of thinking and living.[60] Although some of these anti-hegemonic ways of thinking are incorporated in the dominant social structure and are thus neutralized, others continue to operate outside the system. Such 'residual values' have a special place in challenging the existing order,[61] and the local democracy which has advanced the Welsh language in Gwynedd in recent years can probably be included among the most vigorous and radical of these.

---

[57] The Welsh Language Board, *Draft Guidelines as to the Form and Content of Schemes: Prepared in Accordance with Part II of the Welsh Language Act 1993* (Cardiff, 1994).
[58] Ibid., Part I, 1.1, p. 4.
[59] Williams, 'Y Bwrdd a Chynllunio Iaith', 9.
[60] Raymond Williams, *Marxism and Literature* (Oxford, 1977).
[61] Daniel Williams, 'Dai, Kim, and Raymond Williams', *Planet*, 114 (1996), 30–7.

19

The Other Celtic Languages in the Twentieth Century

GLANVILLE PRICE

THE SITUATION of each of the four Celtic languages other than Welsh which were alive at the beginning of the twentieth century has evolved in the course of the century in such a way as to place each of them in a radically different socio-linguistic position with strikingly different perspectives.[1] In general, there has been a marked downward trend, to the point of extinction in the case of Manx. But, with very different modalities in each case, there are also significant positive changes to be remarked upon in relation to Irish, Scottish Gaelic, and Breton. Finally, although Cornish ceased some two centuries ago to be a normal, living medium of communication, the fact that sufficient interest in the language has been generated to give rise to four different schools of thought, each seeking to revive the language as a spoken medium, is itself worthy of notice.

Firstly, consideration will be given to the Gaelic languages before moving on to the Brittonic or Brythonic languages.

Scottish Gaelic

The most striking and also the most alarming feature of the evolution of the situation of Scottish Gaelic in the course of the twentieth century was the extent to which it declined both in terms of the number of speakers and in the territorial losses it sustained.[2] Whereas, at the turn of the nineteenth century, there were extensive (though sparsely populated) areas in the far north of Scotland and,

---

[1] I am deeply indebted to Kenneth MacKinnon, Máirtín Ó Murchú, Robert L. Thomson, Humphrey Lloyd Humphreys and Philip Payton, who read and commented on early drafts of the sections on Scottish Gaelic, Irish, Manx, Breton and Cornish respectively and who saved me from numerous errors and other inadequacies. However, since considerations of space prevented me from taking full account of some of their suggestions, and since I have not asked them to read the final version, they are entirely exonerated from responsibility for any remaining blunders and omissions that must be laid solely at my charge.

[2] For an important, richly documented study, see Charles W. J. Withers, *Gaelic in Scotland 1698–1981: The Geographical History of a Language* (Edinburgh, 1984), and especially, for the more recent period, chapter 10, 'A Century of Change: Gaelic in Scotland, 1881–1981', pp. 209–51.

further south, in the highland parts of Perthshire where Gaelic was still widely spoken, the language has been all but eliminated from the eastern and central Highlands and is now virtually confined to the western coastal fringes and the Western Isles.

Before turning to consider the territorial recession of Gaelic, the global figures for numbers of speakers as provided by decennial censuses will be examined. However, given that Gaelic has never been the language of the whole of Scotland, and that much of the Lowlands and the Southern Uplands has been Scots- or English-speaking for many centuries, other statistics (and, in particular, percentages) relating to Gaelic speakers and for the whole of Scotland, though available, cannot have the same significance as those for Irish speakers and Welsh speakers in the respective countries. Indeed, they may be considered irrelevant to any assessment of the situation of Gaelic and are therefore ignored in this account.

Table 1. Gaelic speakers in Scotland, 1891 and 1901

(3 years and over)

Year	Gaelic only	Gaelic and English	Total
1891	43738	210677	254415
1901	28106	202700	230806

The first decennial census in which a linguistic question was asked in Scotland was that of 1881, but since, on that occasion, only those who claimed to speak Gaelic 'habitually' were enumerated, the data in question are of limited utility and are set aside here. The situation at the turn of the nineteenth century is reflected in Table 1, which shows the numbers of Gaelic speakers (in the whole of Scotland) in 1891 and 1901. One notices in particular the fact that, although the fall in the overall numbers was comparatively slight (4 per cent), the number of monoglots had fallen by over a third (36 per cent). Thereafter, the picture is one of accelerating decline (Table 2). It must be noted, however, that the figures for the last three censuses (1971, 1981, 1991) are not wholly comparable since there have been changes in the wording of the relevant question or questions. Moreover, although numbers fell overall, there were for the first time increases in some areas, including the Western Isles and parts of Skye.

The territorial regression of Gaelic will now be examined. Bearing in mind what has been said about the long-standing Scotticization (in the sense of the adoption of Scots rather than English as the local vernacular) or Anglicization of much of the country, only those parts of Scotland where there had been any kind of tradition of Gaelic-speaking in the previous hundred years or so are considered. The following areas will therefore be eliminated: the south-west of Scotland where some Gaelic may have lingered on for a while beyond the end of the

Table 2. Gaelic speakers in Scotland, 1911–91

(3 years and over)

Year	Gaelic only	Gaelic and English	Total
1911	18400	183998	202398
1921	9829	148950	158779
1931	6716	129419	136135
1951	2178	93269	95447
1961	974	80004	80978
1971	477	88415	88892
1981	–	–	79307
1991	–	–	65978

seventeenth century (especially in Glenapp), a few parishes south of the Moray Firth in Nairn, Moray, Banff, and the remoter parts of Aberdeenshire, where, according to the *New Statistical Account of Scotland* (1834–45), Gaelic was still spoken in the 1830s, although English was already well entrenched.

For the purposes of this study, therefore, the *Gàidhealtachd* or notionally Gaelic-speaking area can conveniently be divided into three areas. For convenience, and in line with tradition, the names of the Scottish counties (as they existed before the reorganization of local government areas in 1975) are used: (a) Outer Hebrides; (b) Inner Hebrides; (c) The Mainland.

(a) Outer Hebrides

In 1901, in Harris, Barra, North Uist, South Uist, and in the four civil parishes in the Isle of Lewis, over 86 per cent of the population was Gaelic-speaking, and in all cases except that of the town of Stornoway the proportion was at least 90 per cent and in some cases 95 per cent. Throughout the first two-thirds of the twentieth century there was a decline but no catastrophic fall. In 1961, for example, the proportion was generally well over 80 per cent, except in Stornoway

Table 3. Percentage of Gaelic speakers by age group, 1991

(3 years and over)

Age group	Gaelic speakers
	%
65+	89.5
46–64	77.0
16–44	61.0
3–15	49.0

where it had fallen to 73 per cent. According to a survey made in 1957,[3] 73 per cent of primary school children in the islands still had Gaelic as their first language. But a threat to the future of the language emerges from the report's revelation that in Stornoway only 28 pupils out of 667 (a mere 4 per cent) gave Gaelic as their first language. According to the most recent census, that of 1991, 68 per cent of the total population of the Western Islands Area (a total of 19,546) were Gaelic-speaking, but there is an ominous fall as the age groups get younger (Table 3).

(b) Inner Hebrides
In 1901 all seven parishes in Skye had over 85 per cent and in five cases over 90 per cent of Gaelic speakers and, as late as 1961, every parish except Portree (55 per cent) had proportions ranging from 66 per cent to 91 per cent. Also in 1901 the islands of Coll, Tiree, Colonsay, Jura and Islay all had 80 per cent or more, and in some parishes well over 90 per cent, of Gaelic speakers, while in 1961 in all parishes except Jura (47 per cent) the proportions ranged from 57 per cent to 74 per cent. The report referred to above gave only 51 per cent of primary school children in Skye having Gaelic as their first language in 1957, with 40 per cent in Coll and Tiree (taken together) and no more than 17 per cent in Islay. The results of the most recent census, that of 1991, reveal that in the Skye and Lochalsh district the Gaelic-speaking population accounted for 42 per cent of the total, and that even in Skye taken on its own less than half the population, namely 45.6 per cent, were Gaelic speakers.

(c) The Mainland
The Mainland zone consists, from north to south, of the former county of Sutherland, the mainland parts of Ross and Cromarty, Inverness, and Argyll, and what is known as the 'Highland District' of Perthshire (i.e. the north and west of the county). Parts of this area, which were predominantly Gaelic-speaking at least up to the First World War, are now completely Anglicized. In 1914 the Professor of Celtic at Edinburgh could state that 'West and North Perthshire is largely Gaelic-speaking',[4] but by 1971, in the Highland District, there were only 484 speakers (4 per cent) out of a total population of 11,355. Gaelic has also largely disappeared from the whole of the east coast of northern Scotland and, indeed, from much of the rest, except for a few isolated west-coast parishes. In 1971 only a little over a third of the inhabitants of the four north-western parishes in Sutherland spoke Gaelic while, further south, only Applecross had a majority of Gaelic speakers (54 per cent), a considerable drop since 1961 when the proportion was 71.5 per cent, and another seven parishes had over 30 per cent. The virtually

[3] The Scottish Council for Research in Education, *Gaelic-speaking Children in Highland Schools* (London, 1961).
[4] W. J. Watson, 'The Position of Gaelic in Scotland', *The Celtic Review*, 10 (1914–16), 69–84.

total collapse of Gaelic on the mainland is highlighted in stark relief by the report on Gaelic in schools, according to which, as long ago as 1957, of a total number of 18,901 primary school pupils in relevant mainland areas only 136 (0.7 per cent) gave Gaelic as their first language.[5]

A factor which has weighed heavily in the past against Gaelic has been the indifference or even hostility shown towards it by Gaelic speakers themselves who, seeing the restricted role it occupied in their society as compared with English, came to the inconsequential but, in the circumstances, understandable conclusion that the language was in some way inferior and unworthy of respect. A report on the teaching of Gaelic in schools published by *An Comunn Gàidhealach* (the Highland Association) in 1936 quotes the comments of teachers that 'There exists an animus against the language' and that 'Parents object to Gaelic as a waste of time',[6] and a Norwegian scholar, writing twenty years later about the Isle of Lewis, made the following observation:

> The linguistic attitude is largely one of indifference. Although many speakers take a certain pride in their Gaelic mother tongue, they are fully aware of the practical advantages of English.[7]

Such comments, which could easily be multiplied, are to some extent impressionistic, but it should be borne in mind that they emanate from sources which are themselves sympathetic to the language.

In all domains of life Gaelic has long occupied a position that, even compared with the by no means privileged position of Welsh, can be considered as underprivileged. Whereas until the middle of the twentieth century relatively little provision was made for the teaching of Gaelic in schools, improvements have occurred in the second half of the century at least to the extent that opportunities for improvement have been offered, though there has often been a regrettable failure to take full advantage of them. The Schools (Scotland) Code 1956, later reinforced by the Education (Scotland) Act of 1962, specified that:

> In Gaelic-speaking areas reasonable provision shall be made in schemes of work for the instruction of Gaelic-speaking pupils in the Gaelic language and literature, and the Gaelic language shall be used where appropriate for instructing Gaelic-speaking pupils in other subjects.

---

[5] For a detailed consideration of the decline of Gaelic, see Nancy C. Dorian, *Language Death: The Life Cycle of a Scottish Gaelic Dialect* (Philadelphia, 1981), and V. E. Durkacz, *The Decline of the Celtic Languages* (Edinburgh, 1983), in which, despite the title, the focus of interest throughout is Scottish Gaelic.

[6] An Comunn Gàidhealach, *Report of Special Committee on the Teaching of Gaelic in Schools and Colleges* (Glasgow, 1936), p. 8.

[7] M. Oftedal, *The Gaelic of Leurbost, Isle of Lewis* (Oslo, 1956), p. 14.

Unfortunately, however, the vague terms 'reasonable provision' and 'where appropriate' constituted a major flaw which would have deleterious consequences, as is revealed by a comment made when the provision in question had been in force for over twenty years:

> The terms of the code have often been narrowly interpreted at Authority and school level, and provision has in general been related much more to the teaching of Gaelic as a subject than to its use as a medium in bilingual education programmes.[8]

This is partly, but by no means entirely, to be explained on the basis of the shortage (though the situation has since improved to some extent) of suitable teaching materials in Gaelic.

A hopeful development has been the decision of *Comhairle nan Eilean*, the local government authority responsible for the Western Isles Islands Area, to take measures to broaden and strengthen the position of the Gaelic language in its schools – but only, however, for those pupils who are already Gaelic speakers. A number of Gaelic-medium nursery schools and primary school classes have also been established elsewhere in the last two or three decades, but provision for the language at all levels of education is still far below that which now exists for Welsh and there is as yet no significant provision for Gaelic-medium teaching at secondary level.[9] Another respect in which the situation of Gaelic in schools compares unfavourably with that of Welsh is that whereas Welsh now serves as the general administrative language of a number of schools this is not yet true of Gaelic.

Inevitably, given the small potential readership, publishing in Gaelic is also on a much more limited scale than in Welsh. There is one Gaelic periodical, *Gairm*, a modest number of 'house journals' published by various bodies, and a small but steady stream of books, many of them children's books or educational publications. In the broadcasting media, the position of Gaelic has improved significantly in recent years on both radio and television, but it still falls far short of the provision for Welsh in Wales.

---

[8] Murdo MacLeod, 'Scottish Gaelic (Gàidhlig)' in C. V. James (ed.), *The Older Mother Tongues of the United Kingdom* (London, 1978), p. 45.

[9] For a recent overall assessment of the position of Gaelic in education, see Kenneth MacKinnon, 'Scottish Gaelic Today: Social History and Contemporary Status' in Martin J. Ball with James Fife (eds.), *The Celtic Languages* (London, 1993), pp. 491–535. This is also highly informative on many other aspects of the current situation and contains a useful bibliography of recent work on the sociolinguistic position of Gaelic. See also idem, 'Language-maintenance and Viability in Contemporary Gaelic Communities: Skye and the Western Isles Today' in P. Sture Ureland and George Broderick (eds.), *Language Contact in the British Isles: Proceedings of the Eighth International Symposium on Language Contact in Europe* (Tübingen, 1991), pp. 495–533, and C. M. Dunn and A. G. Boyd Robertson, 'Gaelic in Education' in William Gillies (ed.), *Gaelic and Scotland: Alba agus a' Ghàidhlig* (Edinburgh, 1989), pp. 44–55.

That there have been positive developments in the last quarter of the twentieth century is undeniable. Nevertheless, the view has been expressed that Scottish Gaelic has passed the point of no return. Perhaps the two most powerful factors working against it are the very obvious fact that, like Welsh and Irish, it is confronted in all spheres of life by the all-pervasive competition of what is, if not the most widely spoken language in the world, certainly the most influential, and the less obvious but potentially more damaging fact that so many (though not all) of its speakers are either uninterested in its well-being or have given up hope.[10] However, at the threshold of the twenty-first century, at least the language still lives and perhaps one should rather adopt the view that *dum spiro, spero.*

Irish

When the question on Irish was first put at a decennial census of the United Kingdom (and in Ireland only) in 1851, it produced a figure of over one and a half million Irish speakers, nearly a quarter of the total population of Ireland. By 1901 the total number of speakers had been more than halved to 641,142 (14 per cent), of whom nearly 21,000 were monoglot Irish speakers, and by 1911, the date of the last census of an undivided Ireland, to 582,446 (13 per cent).[11]

Following the partition of Ireland in 1922, census data relating to the Irish language were no longer collected in Northern Ireland.[12] Linguistic data provided by censuses of the Republic of Ireland have to be treated with caution.[13] The increase of nearly a fifth in the number of Irish speakers enumerated in the twenty-six counties (i.e. excluding those for the six counties that were later to constitute Northern Ireland) from 453,511 in 1911 to 540,802 in 1926 can only be explained by the assumption that large numbers of those who had acquired some knowledge of Irish as a second language had been recorded (doubtless legitimately in many cases) as Irish speakers. The numbers (aged 3 and over) were later to increase steadily to 666,601 in 1936, to 716,420 in 1961, and to 1,095,830 (i.e. 32.5 per

---

[10] The following quotation provides just one indication of the lack of real support for these languages: 'The fact that today many young mothers are keen for their children to acquire Gaelic – and will now even campaign for Gaelic-medium playgroups, nursery school and primary units does not overcome the fact that one quarter of Gaelic speaking parents [in a survey undertaken in the Western Isles in 1986–8] reported that their eldest child did not speak Gaelic.' MacKinnon, 'Scottish Gaelic Today', p. 532.

[11] For a survey of data for Irish speakers produced by United Kingdom and, later, Irish censuses, see Reg Hindley, *The Death of the Irish Language* (London, 1990).

[12] A question was reintroduced at the 1991 census, by which time it can be assumed that, with the exception of a certain number of natives of the Irish Republic (e.g. students from Donegal at the University of Ulster), virtually all those enumerated as Irish speakers would be people who had acquired a knowledge of Irish as a second language.

[13] The official name of the country was the 'Irish Free State' until this term was replaced in the 1937 Constitution by that of 'Éire/Ireland'. The name 'Republic of Ireland' was first introduced in 1948 but, for convenience, the term 'Republic' is used with reference to the whole period of the existence of the independent state.

cent of the total) in 1991.[14] An attempt was made in 1926 to distinguish between native speakers and learners, but the results were found to lack plausibility and were not published, and no such attempt has been made in later censuses.[15] For estimates of the present number of native speakers (all of whom, it can be assumed, are bilingual), one must depend on the assessments of observers. These suggest that the figure is, at best, no higher than fifty to sixty thousand (i.e. lower than the figure for Scottish Gaelic which, according to the 1991 census, had some 66,000 speakers, the great majority of whom must be considered native speakers). Worse, the authoritative view of Professor Máirtín Ó Murchú, expressed in 1985, is that 'it is fairly reliably estimated that no more than 25,000 of the Gaeltacht population now use Irish consistently in day-to-day communication'.[16] (On the definition of the Gaeltacht areas, see below.) Ó Murchú has, however, commented more recently that this estimate excludes native speakers who no longer speak Irish habitually (being, for example, married to non-Irish speakers) and that the 1991 census figure of 56,469 for the Gaeltacht is probably as reliable as any census figure and that the figure for 'habitual' speakers throughout the state may be as high as 100,000.[17]

Over twenty years ago E. G. Bowen and Harold Carter drew attention to the threat posed to Welsh by the imminent danger that an 'anglicized corridor' through mid-Wales would irrevocably split the Welsh-speaking area into two.[18] They compared the decline of the language to the drying-up of a lake: 'The continuous expanse of water has disappeared and there remains a series of separate pools, patchy and uneven, slowly drying out.' This is the situation, and worse, which has been reached by Irish. In 1851 Irish was spoken by at least 25 per cent and, over much of the area, over 55 per cent of the population throughout an extensive and almost unbroken expanse of territory stretching from the north of Co. Donegal and taking in most of the west and south of the island as far as Co. Waterford.[19] By 1891 there were clear signs that this was splitting into three areas, a northern, a western, and a south-western, and within a few decades the situation was one of total fragmentation within each of these areas.

The Irish-speaking areas (the Gaeltacht) were first officially defined by a government commission which, in its report in 1926, identified seven separate areas, each of them,[20] in varying degrees, containing patches of *Fíor-Ghaeltacht*

---

[14] Apart from a fall between 1936 and 1946.

[15] The fact that, at the 1996 census, questions were added on frequency of use may provide more discriminating results.

[16] Máirtín Ó Murchú, *The Irish Language* (Dublin, 1985), p. 29.

[17] Personal communication.

[18] E. G. Bowen and Harold Carter, 'Preliminary Observations on the Distribution of the Welsh Language at the 1971 Census', *The Geographical Journal*, 140, part 3 (1974), 432–40; idem, 'The Distribution of the Welsh Language in 1971: An Analysis', *Geography*, 60, part 1 (1975), 1–15.

[19] For maps illustrating the geographical extent of Irish-speaking areas at different periods, see Ó Murchú, *The Irish Language*, pp. 26–30, and Hindley, *Death of the Irish Language*, passim.

[20] Except for the Inishowen peninsula in the extreme north-east of Donegal, which was entirely *Breac-Ghaeltacht*.

('true Gaeltacht'), where 80 per cent or more spoke Irish, and *Breac-Ghaeltacht* ('semi-Gaeltacht'), where 25 per cent to 79 per cent of the population spoke Irish.[21] The *Breac-Ghaeltacht* seems in reality to have been an area in which Irish was little used by the younger generations in particular and in which the language may well have been in a state of irreversible decline. Brian Ó Cuív, basing his comments on the number of children qualifying in 1947–8 for a grant for children from Irish-speaking homes, commented in a lecture delivered in 1950:

> In the Breac-Ghaeltacht . . . less than 3% of the homes with children of a school-going age have Irish as the home language, although according to the 1936 Census in those areas 41% of the people were Irish speakers. I could keep you here for a long time while I described my efforts to find even one local native Irish speaker in some of the so-called Breac-Ghaeltacht areas of Cork.[22]

The Gaeltacht was redefined on a narrower basis in 1956 and, although its limits have been somewhat extended since, it now covers a much more restricted area than when it was first defined in 1926. It now includes three main areas, each split into several small patches of territory separated from one another by English-speaking areas. There is one such fragmented area in each of the old provinces bordering the Atlantic:

1. in Ulster, parts of Co. Donegal
2. in Connacht, parts of Co. Mayo and Co. Galway (including the Aran Islands)
3. in Munster, three separate areas in Co. Kerry and one on the mainland of Co. Cork, together with the tiny Cape Clear Island off the south coast of Co. Cork and, further east, the small Gaeltacht of An Rinn (Ring), near Dungarvan in Co. Waterford. The Co. Cork pockets and An Rinn are all in an advanced state of decline.

In addition, in the old province of Leinster there are two areas at Baile Ghib (Gibstown) and Ráth Cairn (Rathcarran) in Co. Meath, north-west of Dublin, where Irish-speaking families from parts of the *Fíor-Ghaeltacht* were resettled in the period 1935–40.[23]

The future of Irish as a native language is gravely threatened. In the Gaeltacht areas themselves, only 56,469 (71 per cent of the population) claimed in 1991 to

---

[21] For an assessment of the extent of Irish-speaking areas from the mid-nineteenth to the mid-twentieth centuries, see Brian Ó Cuív, 'The Gaeltacht – Past and Present' in idem, *Irish Dialects and Irish-Speaking Districts* (Dublin, 1951), pp. 7–32 (esp. pp. 19–31).

[22] Ibid., pp. 30–1.

[23] The two areas in question, together with a third and even smaller one, were at first omitted when the boundaries of the Gaeltacht were redrawn in 1956 but were reinstated in 1967 (though the third was not).

be able to speak Irish and, as already noted, it is estimated that fewer than half of these – only about 25,000 – use the language consistently in their daily lives. Ó Murchú comments that, from the early 1970s onwards, 'a new decline appears to have set in',[24] which, he suggests:

> has been brought about by a modern industrialisation programme which greatly increased the number of English-speaking situations within the Gaeltacht and gave rise to an in-migration of English-speaking families; by the effects of predominantly English-speaking modern media, especially television, on small rural communities; and by new patterns of mobility which have made journeys to English-speaking areas an everyday matter.[25]

It should be recalled that no part of the Gaeltacht is more than twenty miles or so from totally Anglicized towns or villages.[26] There are also disturbing indications that parents, on whom the maintenance of a thriving community of native speakers in the next generation depends, often lack the will to ensure this continuity: 'The inability or the failure of parents to transmit Irish to their children in the home places a greater burden on the school. Indeed, some Gaeltacht communities now appear to be relying on the schools to ensure that the language is transmitted.'[27]

That, however, is not the whole picture. If census figures for Irish speakers have to be treated with considerable caution, they cannot be dismissed as of no consequence. The fact that over a million inhabitants of the Republic, or nearly a third of the population, claim to speak Irish is significant and it is misleading to give the impression that the language is virtually dead. Quoting a survey by the *Institiúid Teangeolaíochta Éireann* (the Linguistics Institute of Ireland) which revealed that, although only 5 per cent of all Irish speakers made frequent use of the language, orally or in writing, up to 25 per cent made some such use of it and 75 per cent watched Irish television programmes,[28] Ó Murchú comments that 'a high degree of passive knowledge is closely matched by the existence of a high measure of favourable attitudes towards the maintenance of Irish'.[29] He quotes figures from the same survey indicating that over 70 per cent of those questioned were in favour of the use of Irish in such public domains as television, the civil

---

[24] Ó Murchú, *The Irish Language*, p. 29.

[25] Ibid., pp. 29–30.

[26] For an assessment of the problems of the Gaeltacht, see Patrick Commins, 'Socioeconomic Development and Language Maintenance in the Gaeltacht', *International Journal of the Sociology of Language*, 70 (1988), 11–28.

[27] Bord na Gaeilge, *The Irish Language in a Changing Society: Shaping the Future* (Baile Átha Cliath, 1986), p. 11.

[28] More precisely, 18 per cent said they used it conversationally and 25 per cent that they used it 'sometimes' in the home.

[29] Ó Murchú, *The Irish Language*, p. 32.

service, and in public forms and notices. Furthermore, over two-thirds felt that it was important that children should grow up knowing Irish.

The situation of the language since the foundation of the Free State in 1922, leaving Northern Ireland within the United Kingdom, has evolved very differently in the two parts of the island. The constitution of the Republic states that 'the Irish language as the national language is the first official language'.[30] In practice, however, although 'from the 1930s until recent years, a good proportion of the internal business of the Civil Service was conducted through Irish',[31] by far the greater part of official business, in terms of the language of debates in the Dáil, the original text of legislation, documentation, correspondence, etc., is transacted through the second official language, i.e. English. The same is true to an even greater degree of semi-official, commercial, cultural and other bodies, except for the likes of *Bord na Gaeilge* (the Irish Language Board) and *Institiúid Teangeolaíochta Éireann*, which have a specific role to play in connection with the promotion of the language.

Another field where the newly independent state sought to intervene directly in fostering and strengthening the position of the language was that of education.[32] Programmes had been put in place with a view to making the teaching of Irish compulsory throughout the educational system and providing training for teachers with the ultimate aim of having all primary education (and, in due course, secondary education) taught through the medium of Irish. This policy has had at best only limited success and has been in large measure abandoned. By 1940–1 over half the primary schools in the country were teaching either partly or (in 12 per cent of the cases) entirely through the medium of Irish, but by 1980–1 only 5 per cent of such schools (161 in all, and almost all of those in the Gaeltacht areas) were using Irish only, with a further one per cent still providing some Irish-medium instruction. A *Bord na Gaeilge* report of 1986 comments that the number of Irish-medium schools outside the designated Gaeltacht areas declined from 232 in 1957–8 to only 20 by the mid-1980s (although there was a small increase later). In the same period the number of Irish-medium post-primary schools outside the Gaeltacht fell from 81 to 15 and the proportion of pupils attending Irish-medium secondary schools declined from 28 per cent in 1937–8 to a mere 1.4 per cent in 1981–2.[33]

---

[30] *Bunreacht na hÉireann* (Constitution of Ireland, 1937), article 8.1.

[31] Ó Murchú, 'Aspects of the Societal Status of Modern Irish' in Ball (ed.), *The Celtic Languages*, p. 477; this article should be consulted for its overall assessment of the position of Irish and for its bibliographical references.

[32] On this, see *inter alia* the following articles and the bibliographies thereto: Pádraig Ó Riagáin, 'Bilingualism in Ireland 1973–1983: An Overview of National Sociolinguistic Surveys', *International Journal of the Sociology of Language*, 70 (1988), 29–51; John Harris, 'Spoken Irish in the Primary School System', ibid., 69–87; Mícheál Ó Gliasáin, 'Bilingual Secondary Schools in Dublin 1960–1980', ibid., 89–108.

[33] Bord na Gaeilge, *The Irish Language in a Changing Society*, pp. 28, 42.

The position of Irish in the written and spoken media is considerably weaker than that of Welsh. Only some 2 per cent of the output of the national television channels is in Irish and there is no more than minimal provision for the language on the main radio channels, although for some years now *Raidió na Gaeltachta*, which was set up in 1972 and is available nationally on FM, has been broadcasting in Irish for some seven or eight hours daily. The average number of books in Irish published annually, many of them with the aid of subsidies from *Bord na Leabhar Gaeilge* (the Irish Books Council) established for the purpose in 1952, is about a hundred, as compared with four or five times that number in Welsh. In the field of periodical publications, too, the position of Irish is considerably less satisfactory than that of Welsh. Finally, it must be mentioned that *Bord na Gaeilge*, which was first established in 1975, has been recognized since 1978 as the official language-planning agency.

In Northern Ireland, however, Irish had no official status whatsoever until very recently. The 1991 decennial census was the first to contain a question relating to the language, and although Irish was widely taught in Roman Catholic schools there was no provision for the language in state schools until 1990. However, the Education Reform (Northern Ireland) Act of that year recognized that Irish had a role in secondary education and allowed Irish to be studied instead of a foreign language.[34] Nor was there until recently any place for Irish in the broadcasting media, though there is now some minimal regular provision for the language on BBC Radio Ulster. The signing of the Good Friday Agreement in April 1998 was an important milestone in the history of the Irish language in Northern Ireland. In addition to recognizing officially the rights of Irish speakers in the province, the agreement made a commitment to promote and encourage use of the language.

A balanced and authoritative assessment of the present situation of Irish and its prospects reads as follows:

> There is . . . in the community as a whole with regard to Irish a solid core of active competence and use and a widespread passive competence. On the other hand, its continuing low ranking on any pragmatic scale leaves Irish constantly vulnerable to extensive abandonment in any period of rapid socio-economic change. For the present, though, it still fulfils an ideological and ethnic need for a majority in the population . . . On this fact, more than any other, its survival now depends.[35]

Manx

The first attempt to obtain statistical information about the number of speakers of Manx dates from 1874, exactly a hundred years before the death of the last native speaker. This first 'census', albeit a private and unofficial one, is of considerable

---

[34] Although there was no objection in principle to the teaching of Irish at primary level, the fact is that languages other than English are not normally taught in primary schools.

[35] Ó Murchú, 'Aspects of the Societal Status of Modern Irish', p. 489.

value. It was undertaken by Henry Jenner, who addressed to the rector or vicar of each parish in the island a questionnaire designed to elicit information about the prevailing languages in each parish, the numbers, age group and social class of monoglot Manx speakers, the language or languages spoken by children, the extent to which Manx was used in church services and parish work, and the quality of the Manx spoken.[36] The results are inevitably not entirely reliable and have to be treated with caution, but so are the results provided by any linguistic census. Had the later official censuses of Manx, and indeed of the other Celtic languages, provided a similar wealth of information we should have had at our disposal a veritable treasure-house of data.

Jenner's survey showed that, of a total population of 41,084 (excluding the town of Douglas, which one can assume to have been already more or less totally Anglicized), 12,340 or 30 per cent were reckoned to speak Manx 'habitually' (which presumably means that the proportion of those who had at least a working knowledge of the language was appreciably higher). Of these, only 190, less than 0.5 per cent, spoke Manx only. The global figure conceals a considerable discrepancy between the north (the more rural part of the island) and the south, but there is no good reason not to accept it as a genuine one. In the eight northern parishes, 48.5 per cent of the population were recorded as Manx speakers compared with only 17.5 per cent in the nine southern parishes.

At first sight, these figures would seem to suggest that Manx was in a tolerably healthy state, particularly in the north of the island, but the data provided in answer to Jenner's other questions paint a much bleaker picture. In particular, Jenner's summary of the answers to the question on the languages spoken by children reveals that in only three parishes out of seventeen were they reported to be bilingual, with those in only three others having 'English and a little Manx'; children in the remaining eleven parishes were reported to speak English only. It seems, therefore, that Jenner caught the language in virtually the last stages of its more or less widespread use as a means of communication in the community. As a result, it is not surprising that, when Sir John Rhŷs visited the island on various occasions from 1886 to 1893 with the aim of studying the language, he concluded that 'with regard to the prospects of Manx as a living language, one has frankly to say that it has none'.[37] Expressing his 'grief and profound sadness to see how rapidly the men and women who can talk and read Manx are disappearing', he noted that although he had discovered fishermen in the village of Bradda, almost at the south-western extremity of the island, conversing together in Manx, they spoke English with their wives and children at home. He believed that 'perhaps Manx might be said to be more living in the village of Cregneish, on the Howe

---

[36] A detailed report on Jenner's survey is given in his article, 'The Manx Language: Its Grammar, Literature and Present State', *Transactions of the Philological Society* (1875–6), 172–97.

[37] Rhŷs's comments on the state of the language as he found it are included in the introduction to his book, *Contributions to the Study of Manx Phonology* (Edinburgh, 1894).

Table 4. Total population of the Isle of Man and total number of Manx speakers, 1931–61

(3 years and over)

Year	Total population	Number of Manx speakers
1931	47408	529
1951	52897	355
1961	46321	165

still further south', where he knew one family which still spoke more Manx than English; one member of the family, a teenage girl, was the only Manx-speaking child he recollected meeting anywhere on the island.[38]

It is regrettable that a question on the Manx language was not included in the official decennial census until 1901, half a century after such information was first elicited for Irish and twenty years after the question relating to Scottish Gaelic was included. The results of this first census confirm the collapse of the language in the last quarter of the previous century, a situation which had been forecast by Jenner and witnessed by Rhŷs. In 1901, 4,657 (9.1 per cent of the population, aged 3 and over) claimed to speak Manx, of whom 59 spoke Manx only. No breakdown by age groups is provided in the census report, but the fact that by 1921, when a similar question was next put, the number of Manx speakers had declined to a mere 1.1 per cent of the population (915 speakers, of whom 19 spoke Manx only) suggests that the great majority of those enumerated twenty years earlier were members of the oldest generation of speakers and had since died. Of the speakers enumerated in 1921, some 60 per cent were aged 65 or over and only 128 (14 per cent) were aged under forty-five.

No United Kingdom census was held in 1941 owing to the war, and by 1971 a question on the Manx language was presumably judged no longer to have any relevance. The figures for the remaining censuses taken during the lifetime of the language are shown in Table 4. No monoglot speakers of Manx were left by 1931, and the figures for bilinguals at these last censuses cannot be taken at their face value. In particular, the figure of 355 speakers for 1951 is wildly at variance with the testimony of scholars who had tried in the years immediately following the Second World War to trace and identify the last remaining speakers of the language. In an article published in 1948, A. S. B. Davies stated that in August 1946 only twenty people could be found who had been brought up to speak

---

[38] For a more extensive survey of the decline of Manx, see George Broderick, 'The Decline and Death of Manx Gaelic' in Ureland and Broderick (eds.), *Language Contact in the British Isles*, pp. 63–125.

Manx.[39] When Kenneth Jackson visited the island at the end of 1950, only ten speakers were left, most of them in their eighties or nineties, and by the time his book appeared in 1955 four of these had died.[40] In November 1957 Walter Clarke, secretary of Yn Çheshaght Ghailckagh (the Manx Society), informed the author of this chapter by letter that 'at present there are on the Island 4 native speakers still alive, one a woman'. Five years later, in June 1962, he wrote that the last woman who had been fluent in the language, a Mrs Kinvig, had died a month earlier, and that 'only one of our old native speakers remains, Mr Ned Maddrell of Glen Chiass, Port St Mary'. Maddrell, the last known native speaker, died in 1974, aged ninety-seven.

Although the Manx language is now dead, in the sense that no native speakers remain, it survived into the age of the tape recorder and so the sound of authentic spoken Manx can still be heard. In the mid-1950s Yn Çheshaght Ghailckagh, having realized that only a handful of speakers could be traced, all of them elderly, acquired an early tape recorder and, working to a programme carefully designed to bring in a wide range of vocabulary on a great diversity of subjects, made some twenty hours of recordings. The fact that these recordings exist, and that various learners of the language in the immediate post-war period acquired something of the language from the lips of Ned Maddrell and other remaining native speakers, has meant that Manx has a solid and authentic foundation for a relaunch denied to Cornish, which died out some two hundred years ago. The beginnings of the revival of Manx can plausibly be dated to the turn of the century and, in particular, to the foundation of Yn Çheshaght Ghailckagh in 1899, a society which had as one of its aims 'the preservation of Manx as the national language of the Isle of Man'.[41] In the period since the end of the Second World War, the Society has actively encouraged the learning of the language through evening classes and such measures as the organization of monthly social gatherings where learners can practise the language with those who are already fluent. Given that the latter had in many cases learned the language from the last native speakers, this means, in George Broderick's words, that 'in that respect, at any rate, the tradition of spoken Manx could be said to be unbroken' and that 'the pronunciation of Manx as spoken today . . . is essentially that of the last native speakers'.[42] The success of the movement is shown by the fact that although the question on the Manx language which had figured in previous decennial censuses was abandoned in 1971 and 1981, it was reintroduced in 1991 and produced a figure of 643 persons who claimed (doubtless with greater justification in some cases than in others) to speak the language.

[39] A. S. B. Davies, 'Cyflwr Presennol Iaith Geltaidd Ynys Manaw', BBCS, XII (1947–8), 89–91.

[40] Kenneth H. Jackson, Contributions to the Study of Manx Phonology (Edinburgh, 1955).

[41] In what follows, I draw extensively on the data provided by George Broderick in his article, 'Revived Manx' in Ball (ed.), The Celtic Languages, pp. 654–63. See also George Broderick, A Handbook of Late Spoken Manx (3 vols., Tübingen, 1984–6), and idem, 'The Decline and Death of Manx Gaelic'.

[42] Broderick, 'Revived Manx', pp. 658–9.

The Elementary Education Act of 1870 in the form adopted in the Isle of Man made no provision whatsoever for the teaching of the Manx language. However, permission was obtained to allow some teaching of the language at the discretion of individual schools, but the only school to take action in this respect, on the basis of one half-hour lesson per week, soon abandoned the idea, and another century was to pass before any official teaching of the language was introduced into the island's schools. The shortage of trained teachers competent to teach the language was inevitably a serious obstacle but, despite this, some small-scale teaching of Manx was introduced in a few primary and secondary schools in the 1970s. A GCE O-level examination in Manx, for which learners were to be prepared in evening classes, was instituted in 1982 but came to an end in 1986 when O-levels were replaced by GCSEs. However, in 1991, after a Gallup poll had revealed that 36 per cent of respondents favoured the introduction of the optional teaching of Manx in schools, the appointment of a language officer and two peripatetic teachers was authorized by the Department of Education, which also has plans to expand this kind of provision and to introduce its own certificates in the language.

There has also been some use of Manx as a written medium. In addition to the publication of folk tales and the reminiscences of elderly native speakers, such as those of Edward Faragher who died in 1908,[43] re-editions of early texts, and pedagogical materials for the growing body of learners have appeared. Robert L. Thomson informs us that 'there has been some original writing by those who learned the language from the last generation of native speakers, in *Skeealaght* (Storytelling) (1976) and John Gell's *Cooinaghtyn my Aegid as Cooinaghtyn Elley* (Memories of my Youth and Other Memories) (1977)'.[44] A significant development in the field of other media has been the production between 1983 and 1986 of five films[45] (one bilingual, four entirely in Manx), with a total running time of over three hours, designed to stimulate interest in the Manx language and the island's traditions.

Breton

Although all the surviving Celtic languages have persisted in spite of, rather than because of, the social and cultural milieu by which they have been surrounded since the late Middle Ages, if not longer, Breton can be considered to have been seriously disadvantaged even by comparison with its sister Celtic languages. Whereas Irish, Scottish Gaelic, and Welsh (and, for as long as they survived,

---

[43] See idem, 'Manx Stories and Reminiscences of Ned Beg Hom Ruy', *Zeitschrift für celtische Philologie*, 38 (1981), 113–78; ibid., 39 (1982), 117–94.

[44] Robert L. Thomson, 'Manx Language and Literature' in Glanville Price (ed.), *The Celtic Connection* (Gerrards Cross, 1992), p. 162.

[45] See Broderick, 'Revived Manx', p. 658.

Cornish and Manx) have evolved in recent centuries under the shadow of the English language, British political structures, institutions, and practices, and English or British attitudes, Breton has had to contend with the even less sympathetic and more stifling atmosphere of the French language, French political structures, institutions and practices, and French attitudes.

The hostility of the French state and its representatives towards the Breton language was publicly expressed on numerous occasions throughout the nineteenth century. To give just one example among many, one may quote the words of a government administrative official who, addressing a group of Breton primary school teachers in 1845, declared: 'Remember, gentlemen, that your sole function is to kill the Breton language' ('Surtout, rappelez-vous, messieurs, que vous n'êtes établis que pour tuer la langue bretonne'). Such attitudes continued well into the twentieth century (and, indeed, though less crudely expressed, at least in public, have still by no means disappeared from the minds of many French citizens) and were perhaps most notoriously uttered by the then Minister of Public Education, de Monzie, who, in 1925, opined that 'for the sake of the linguistic unity of France, the Breton language has to disappear' ('pour l'unité linguistique de la France, il faut que la langue bretonne disparaisse').[46]

In such circumstances, it is not surprising that the sociolinguistic situation of Breton is not only less favourable but also far less well documented than that of the other Celtic languages. Whereas questions relating to the prevalance of the relevant languages have long been asked in censuses in the United Kingdom, in France no such question has ever been put in relation to the country's many regional languages. For Breton, one is dependent for even vaguely comparable information, which in many cases cannot even be properly termed data, on a variety of unofficial estimates based on differing criteria and of widely differing reliability.[47]

What Humphrey Lloyd Humphreys describes as 'the best-informed and most meticulous estimate of the situation [of the Breton language] at the beginning of the [twentieth] century'[48] was made in 1987 by Fanch Broudic, who collated data provided by the French population census of 1905 with information derived from detailed reports on the situation (at a time when there were strong pressures to

---

[46] For these and similar expressions of opinion, see *Livre blanc et noir de la langue bretonne* (3rd ed., Brest, 1969), pp. 15–17.

[47] In what follows, in respect not only of estimates of the number of Breton speakers but of all aspects of the sociolinguistic history and present situation of Breton, I draw extensively on the work of Humphrey Lloyd Humphreys, and in particular on the following articles: 'The Geolinguistics of Breton' in Colin H. Williams (ed.), *Linguistic Minorities, Society and Territory* (Clevedon, 1991), pp. 96–120; 'The Breton Language' in Price, *The Celtic Connection*, pp. 245–75; 'The Breton Language: Its Present Position and Historical Background' in Ball (ed.), *The Celtic Languages*, pp. 606–43; 'Breton' in Glanville Price (ed.), *Encyclopedia of the Languages of Europe* (Oxford, 1998), pp. 35–40.

[48] Humphreys, 'The Geolinguistics of Breton', p. 111.

repress the language in the interests of the propagation of French) by both civil and ecclesiastical authorities. On this basis, Breton speakers would have numbered about 1,400,000, of whom some 900,000 (60 per cent) would have spoken Breton only. If, as seems likely, these estimates are even approximately correct, Breton at that time would have been by far the most widely spoken of the Celtic languages, having nearly as many speakers as the combined totals for Welsh and Irish (excluding those living outside their home countries): according to the United Kingdom census of 1901, Welsh speakers in Wales numbered 929,824 including 280,905 (30 per cent) monoglots, while Irish speakers in Ireland numbered 641,142 including only 20,953 (3 per cent) monoglots. Humphreys himself estimated the number of Breton speakers sixty years later at some 686,000, just over 50 per cent of the total population of Lower Brittany.[49]

At first sight, an estimate of well in excess of half a million Breton speakers in the late twentieth century seems encouraging rather than alarming and gives grounds for optimism about the future of the language. But when the global figures are broken down on the basis of almost any sociolinguistically relevant scale that one might choose to adopt, a far less rosy picture emerges.

Firstly, the geographical distribution of Breton speakers will be examined. If one accords to the term 'Breton-speaking area' the widest possible legitimate definition and takes it to refer to that part of Brittany in which Breton survives to any extent at all as an indigenous language, even if this is only among a small percentage of elderly people, it has included since the mid-nineteenth century, though with some retreat westwards, the area west of a line running from a little to the north-west of Saint-Brieuc to a little to the south-east of Vannes.[50] Within this 'Breton-speaking' zone, however, there are extensive areas from which the language has completely disappeared. In particular, as a result of a wide range of sociolinguistic factors which included considerable influxes of non-Bretons to Brest and Lorient, which in the seventeenth century became France's main naval base and the base for the Compagnie des Indes respectively, and the exclusive use of French for administrative purposes, the main towns have long had large concentrations of monoglot French.

Inevitably, and paralleling a situation which can be observed all over Europe where lesser-used languages have co-existed with major world languages (the other Celtic languages with English, Basque with French and Spanish, Swiss Romansh with German, Sardinian with Italian, Frisian with Dutch, Sorbian with German, to quote only a few examples from many), once Breton had been (or, rather, was in the process of being) pushed out of the towns, the influence of

---

[49] Ibid., p. 112.

[50] For a map showing more precisely the linguistic divide as calculated for various dates from the seventeenth century to 1980, with approximate estimates for the ninth and twelfth centuries, see ibid., p. 102; idem, 'The Breton Language', p. 246; idem, 'The Breton Language: Its Present Position and Historical Background', p. 622, and idem, 'Breton', p. 38.

French spread to the surrounding rural areas. The earlier stages of this process are not well documented, but Humphreys is able to conclude that 'raising children in French was already common in all but the smallest rural *bourgs* in the 1930s and extended to the scattered rural population in the course of the 1950s'.[51] It appears that it is barely possible nowadays to trace any very clear boundaries for what can properly be termed a 'Breton-speaking area', given that, in Humphreys's words, 'widespread abandonment of Breton *within* its traditional territory has made the linguistic divide far less noticeable, not only to outside observers, but also to the permanent population'.[52] In a later article, Humphreys goes further and expresses the view that, in the period since the end of the Second World War, the gradual westward shift of the linguistic border 'has paled into insignificance beside the generalized collapse of the language throughout its territory'.[53]

In referring above to the decline of Breton in the urban areas, a second sociolinguistic factor concealed by overall statistics (or, rather, estimates) for the number of Breton speakers has been touched upon. It is evident that Breton is largely confined to a relatively uneducated rural working class, while the town-dwellers, including those engaged in commerce and the generally well-educated and more sophisticated professional classes, are either ignorant of Breton or, if they happen to be of rural origin and have some (perhaps quite extensive) knowledge of the language, in many cases are at pains not to acknowledge the fact or have made a deliberate choice not to use the language.

Paradoxically, however, it is often members of an intellectual bourgeoisie who have been foremost in movements designed to foster and propagate the use of Breton in such fields as education, literature, the press, the broadcasting media, and in public life generally. Humphreys makes the valid point that 'the present Breton-speaking population falls into two contrasting categories'.[54] One is the mass of middle-aged to elderly rural speakers, most of them illiterate in Breton, who are furthermore generally reluctant to use the language even orally with strangers. The other consists of a relatively small number, perhaps ten thousand at most, of 'literate, activist speakers', many of them not native speakers of the language, mainly in intellectual or administrative occupations. Scattered as they are among communities in which the dominant language is French, they cannot themselves be considered a language community but rather a collection of individuals, sometimes constituting family groups, most of whom, in so far as they use the language outside the home, do so relatively infrequently and in a calculated way. The gulf between these two sets of speakers, the rural population for whom it is an underesteemed vernacular in respect of which they may well have what can properly be termed an inferiority complex and to which French is

[51] Idem, 'The Geolinguistics of Breton', p. 106.
[52] Ibid., p. 105.
[53] Idem, 'The Breton Language', p. 251.
[54] Idem, 'The Geolinguistics of Breton', p. 101.

to be preferred in all but the humblest contexts, and the activists (many of whom have learnt Breton) for whom it is a cause to be fought for, is one that it is likely to be difficult to bridge, though not necessarily impossible.

The third and highly important distinction which must be made among categories of Breton speakers is a generational one. This is most strikingly revealed by a sample survey made in 1982 by Humphreys in a rural parish in the east of the Breton-speaking area.[55] This revealed that, whereas 93 per cent of those aged 65 and over were fluent Breton speakers and only 7 per cent monoglot French speakers, only a small minority (less than 6 per cent) of those aged 18–25 were fluent speakers of Breton, while 44 per cent spoke French only. A broadly similar pattern emerges from a questionnaire-based survey undertaken in the same year by A.-M. Arzur in a village in north-west Brittany.[56] Humphreys also analyses the data provided by a survey undertaken in 1983 by *Radio Bretagne Ouest*, which he refers to as 'the soundest basis for an overall assessment of the present situation'.[57] This reveals a 'steep fall in proficiency and practice from the oldest to the youngest generation': not only is the proportion of those claiming to speak Breton reduced from 73 per cent among those aged 65 and over to 21 per cent in the 15–24 age group, but that of those who claim to use it 'very often' or 'quite often' falls from 52 per cent of the population to 5 per cent. Thus, the proportion of Breton speakers who make more than occasional use of the language falls from over two-thirds to only a quarter. This, of course, bodes ominously for the future of the language.

In most, and perhaps all, domains of public life, Breton has remained an underprivileged language even as compared with the other Celtic languages. In the field of education, the role of the state schools was long reckoned to be the dissemination of the knowledge and use of French. This meant not only that there was no teaching either in or of Breton, but that the use of the language was at best discouraged and at worst banned and that pupils using the language even in the playground were, at least in some schools, liable to be punished. There seems to be no evidence of any reaction against this on the part of parents, most of whom probably favoured an all-French education, since a command of the French language was seen as the key to success in life or as a means of escape from grinding poverty. Conversely, being primarily Breton-speaking was and probably still is to a large extent, envisaged (correctly, in the social circumstances of the last hundred years) as constituting an educational, economic, and social handicap. There were, nevertheless, various attempts from the late nineteenth century onwards to find a place for Breton in the state educational system.[58] But although

---

[55] Ibid., pp. 112–15.

[56] Ibid., pp. 114–15.

[57] Ibid., pp. 115–18.

[58] On these and later attempts, see idem, 'The Breton Language: Its Present Position and Historical Background', pp. 634–6.

one such initiative in 1934 was supported by half the local councils in the Breton-speaking area, like all earlier ones it met with no success. With hindsight, it is unfortunate that a limited amount of teaching of Breton was allowed in the Finistère department in 1941, i.e. during the time of the German Occupation. Coupled with the fact that a small number of extreme right-wing Breton nationalists actively collaborated with the Vichy government and the German authorities, this gave rise at the Liberation to an excessively hostile reaction, on the part of many Breton speakers as well as others, to anything to do with the fostering of Breton culture. This was a major setback to the cause of Breton not only in education but also in such fields as religion, the press, broadcasting, and public life generally.

Setting aside the abortive 1941 initiative, the first but very modest step forward came in 1951 with the passing of a law which allowed some minimal provision (voluntary for both teachers and pupils) for the teaching of four regional languages, Breton, Basque, Catalan and Occitan, in primary and secondary schools. There was to be no further improvement in the situation for another twenty years and it was not until the mid-1970s, by which time the transmission of Breton within the context of the family had virtually ceased, that such provision was significantly extended, both quantitatively and qualitatively. Since 1979 it has been possible to study Breton for four hours a week in the last four years of secondary education, and a small number of officially designated bilingual schools were established in the early 1980s. Though there is evidence that some Breton was taught as early as the beginning of the century in some private (i.e. Catholic) schools, the attitude of the ecclesiastical authorities was not in general favourable. According to Humphreys, church schools, which cater for some 40 per cent of the total school population of Brittany, are at present 'in practical terms completely integrated into the state system in so far as their syllabuses are concerned'.[59]

There have also been important developments in pre-school and post-school education. In the former case, nursery classes organized by the voluntary *Diwan* movement from 1977 onwards met with considerable success and led to the organization by the same movement of primary and, more recently, secondary classes. Even so, the numbers of pupils catered for at all levels are still tiny and are to be numbered in hundreds rather than thousands. At the other end of the educational spectrum it has been possible since 1981 to study for a degree in Breton at universities in Brest and Rennes. Degree-level courses in Breton had existed before this, but it was not then possible to take a full degree course in the subject.

During the twentieth century a catastrophic decline has occurred in the use of Breton in those activities of the Catholic Church where, even at a period when

[59] Ibid., p. 635.

the mass was said in Latin, the universal medium of communication was the vernacular, and in particular in the teaching of the catechism and in the preaching of sermons. Surveys undertaken in the late 1920s indicated that the use of Breton was widespread in rural districts, but, as one might well expect, not in the towns.[60] French, however, 'took over the catechism almost completely by 1950. Breton preaching survived a little longer but was generally abandoned in the 1960s'.[61] One might have expected that the liturgical reforms introduced by the Second Vatican Council (1962–5), one of which substituted the use of vernacular tongues for that of Latin as the language of the mass, would have led, as in the French Basque country (where, however, the language was still being transmitted to children within the family), to a widespread use of the local tongue, at least in conjunction with if not to the exclusion of French. But in Brittany this has not happened to any great extent: 'The Church as an institution', notes Humphreys, 'seems to have no place for Breton, beyond the inclusion of a Breton appendix in the three diocesan hymnals.'[62]

Not surprisingly, given the wide discrepancy in educational provision and hence of literacy between the two languages, publishing in Breton, whether of periodicals or of books, has never been even remotely on a par with that in Welsh. Nevertheless, recent decades have witnessed a significant increase. Humphreys reports that by 1983 there were about a dozen periodicals, though none had a print run of as much as a thousand, while the number of non-periodical titles published annually had risen in the course of the previous decade from 32 to 58. This is only about a sixth of what appears in Welsh and inevitably represents a very limited range, although it is important to note that children's books figure prominently.[63]

There has also been a considerable increase in the (still modest) presence of Breton in the broadcasting media, with several hours a week on radio, especially local radio, but less than two hours a week on television. But the very existence of radio and television programmes in Breton must, one imagines, have an importance incommensurate with the limited output. In the first instance, the fact that they exist at all confers on the language a badly needed measure of prestige. Secondly, the fact that listeners and viewers become accustomed to hearing a range of regional varieties of the language serves to overcome the belief that other varieties are difficult to understand, which itself tends to lead Breton speakers from any but the same or neighbouring localities to use French in conversation with one another.

---

[60] For an assessment of these and comments on the situation as it developed during the course of later decades, see idem, 'The Geolinguistics of Breton', pp. 106–9; idem, 'The Breton Language', p. 256; idem, 'The Breton Language: Its Present Position and Historical Background', pp. 633–4.

[61] Idem, 'The Breton Language', p. 256.

[62] Ibid.

[63] Ibid., p. 258; idem, 'The Breton Language: Its Present Position and Historical Background', pp. 636–7.

Some of the reasons for the decline (and perhaps collapse is not too strong a word) of Breton during the twentieth century have been outlined above. Other factors which must at least be mentioned are compulsory military service, which throws those whose first language is Breton into a (probably hostile) French-speaking environment, mixed marriages (the children of which are nowadays unlikely to be brought up to speak Breton, particularly where the monoglot French-speaking parent is the mother), the widespread boarding of children in schools, which deprives them for many weeks of contact with their families, the modernization of agriculture and concomitant rural depopulation, and, increasingly in recent decades, the development of tourism and the influx of outsiders buying up properties in Brittany as holiday cottages or second homes. In conclusion, one cannot do better than quote from Humphreys, whose sombre forecast has all too clear a ring of realism:

> Given its demographic and institutional fragility it is difficult to be optimistic about the future of Breton, whose territorial base looks as if it will have been completely eroded in fifty years' time, although isolated family groups are likely to survive. Ironically, Breton has never been so favoured by the authorities in a general climate of opinion which has been coloured by ecologism and where the moral bases of the state are widely questioned. It is tempting to wonder to what extent the present relatively liberal attitude results from the assumption that as the traditional policies have virtually done their job and Breton now seems doomed, a show of tolerance will be a cheap enough gesture.[64]

Cornish

Any consideration of attempts to 'revive' the Cornish language, which apparently died out two centuries ago, must first consider what is known or claimed about the last stages of its life and the extent to which anything of it may have persisted through the nineteenth century. In 1768 Daines Barrington made determined efforts to trace any remaining speakers of the language and eventually discovered in the village of Mousehole one old woman, Dolly Pentreath, whom he persuaded to speak 'for two or three minutes, and in a language which sounded very like Welsh'.[65] He was later informed that she could not speak English until she was over twenty (which suggests that her Cornish was good) and that she was 'positive' that no one else remained who knew any Cornish at all. In that case, Dolly, who died in 1777, would almost certainly have been the last person to have had Cornish as her first language. In a later article Barrington quoted from a letter he had received in July 1776 from a Mousehole fisherman, William Bodinar, who

[64] Ibid., p. 639.
[65] See Daines Barrington, 'On the Expiration of the Cornish Language', *Archaeologia*, 3 (1776), 279–84.

claimed that he had learnt Cornish as a boy, going to sea with his father and five others.[66] At the time he was writing, he claimed, no more than four or five people in Mousehole, all over the age of eighty, could 'talk Cornish'. Bodinar seems to have been a trustworthy witness and one can probably accept his assertion that a handful of old people still spoke the language to some extent, though presumably not fluently.

Bodinar died in 1789 and, even if one accepts the claim that he, rather than Dolly Pentreath, was the last to have had a good command of the language, Cornish still appears to have died out some two hundred years ago. John Whitaker in 1799 and Richard Warner in 1808 both sought speakers of the language, but to no avail, and one must agree with P. A. S. Pool that 'after the death of Bodinar, there is no evidence of the survival of anyone who could speak Cornish fluently, and no reliable witness claims to have met such a person'.[67]

However, tenuous links remain between the time when Cornish was a living language and the period when the first attempts were made to 'revive' or 'restore' the language. Prince Louis-Lucien Bonaparte was told by Matthias Wallis that his grandmother, Ann Wallis, who died c.1845 aged about 90, and also Jane Barnicoate, who died c.1857, had both been able to speak Cornish, although just what this implies is not clear. Later, John Davey of Boswednack (1812–91) was said to have been able to converse on simple topics, although this testimony is called into doubt by John Westlake, who collected many Cornish words from Davey but who never gained the impression that he could converse in the language.[68] The anecdotal evidence relating to Ann Wallis, John Davey and others cannot be dismissed and is sufficient to justify the assumption that a small corpus of Cornish words and phrases had passed down by word of mouth from generation to generation and that, in that limited sense, some authentic oral Cornish survived into the early twentieth century.

The beginnings of the 'revival' are associated with Henry Jenner (1848–1934), whose influential *Handbook of the Cornish Language* (1904) was 'principally intended for those persons of Cornish nationality who wish to acquire some knowledge of their ancient tongue, and to read, write, and perhaps even to speak it'.[69] Among those who began learning Cornish from Jenner's book was Robert Morton Nance (1873–1959), who later became one of the prime movers of the

---

[66] Idem, 'Some Additional Information Relative to the Continuance of the Cornish Language', ibid., 5 (1779), 81–6.

[67] P. A. S. Pool, *The Death of Cornish* (Penzance, 1975), p. 28.

[68] On the reliability of these and other reports of the late survival of elements of Cornish speech, see ibid., pp. 28–30; and R. Morton Nance, 'When Was Cornish Last Spoken Traditionally?' (a posthumously published lecture), *Journal of the Royal Institution of Cornwall*, VII, part 1 (1973), 76–82.

[69] Over a quarter of a century earlier Jenner had delivered two important lectures on the subject: 'The Cornish Language' (delivered in 1873), *Transactions of the Philological Society* (1893), 165–86; 'The History and Literature of the Ancient Cornish Language', *Journal of the British Archaeological Association*, XXXIII (1877), 137–57.

'revival'. *Inter alia*, he published a primer *Cornish for All* (1929) and a series of dictionaries. Whereas Jenner had envisaged a revival taking up the language as it had been in its last stages, Nance based his work on the language of the *Ordinalia* and other late medieval Cornish texts, but codified and standardized the orthography and grammar in a way that was not characteristic of the originals. He filled inevitable gaps in the vocabulary by creating words from authentic Cornish elements or by adaptation from Breton or Welsh. This form of the language, which came to be known as 'Unified Cornish', was adopted by most of those concerned with the 'revival' of the language for a variety of purposes, including a certain amount of original writing, and, in due course, became the official standard of the Cornish Language Board (founded in 1967).

Reservations about the authenticity of 'Unified' were expressed in many quarters and were to lead to significant developments. In 1986 K. J. George produced for the Language Board a report, *The Pronunciation and Spelling of Revived Cornish*, proposing modifications to the orthography, which he redesigned on what he claimed to be phonemic principles, and to the pronunciation, advocating a system inferred from his phonological analysis of the language of *c*.1500. Although this 'Kernewek Kemmyn' or 'Common Cornish' is in many respects based on sounder foundations than 'Unified', its orthography is even further removed from that of the authentic texts and the validity of its underlying principles has been called into question.[70] The adoption of 'Kemmyn' in place of 'Unified' by the Language Board in 1987 led to a split in the Board. One of those who espouses the claims of 'Unified' has written, with some exaggeration, that Kemmyn is 'an entirely artificial creation which does not resemble Cornish as used by Cornish people at any time in history'.[71] Yet more recently, Nicholas Williams, while believing that 'Unified' is not mistaken in principle, nevertheless identifies in it several defects which he has sought to remedy by devising a modified version which he terms 'Unified Cornish Revised' or 'UCR'. The principles underlying this and the practices to which they lead are set out in his book *Cornish Today* (1995)[72] and are applied in his manual for learners, *Clappya Kernowek: An Introduction to Unified Cornish Revised* (1997).[73]

Meanwhile, R. R. M. Gendall was working on totally different principles. Rejecting both 'Unified' and the principles on which it had been elaborated, he (following Jenner) proposed a revival based on what can be ascertained (from written sources and from Cornish relics in the contemporary English dialect of West Penwith) about the language in the last two centuries of its existence as a

---

[70] For a critical assessment of George's work, see Charles Penglase, 'Authenticity in the Revival of Cornish', *Cornish Studies*, 2nd series, 2 (1994), 96–107, and N. J. A. Williams, *Cornish Today* (Sutton Coldfield, 1995), pp. 99–122.

[71] P. A. S. Pool, *The Second Death of Cornish* (Redruth, 1995), p. 6.

[72] Williams, *Cornish Today*, pp. 169–234.

[73] Idem, *Clappya Kernowek: An Introduction to Unified Cornish Revised* (Portreath, 1997).

living tongue.[74] The orthography, grammar, and lexicon of Gendall's 'Modern Cornish', as he styles it, are all to depend on authentic written examples, while pronunciation is to be based on the speech of elderly people in West Penwith which, Gendall contends (controversially, but echoing Nance), retains many features of Cornish pronunciation.[75]

The partisans of a 'revival' of Cornish are therefore divided into four (to some extent mutually antagonistic) camps, advocating different (and, particularly in the case of 'Kemmyn' and 'Modern') radically different forms of the language in terms of its grammar, lexicon, pronunciation and orthography. Furthermore, there is an almost total lack of any 'public presence' of Cornish other than a small number of classes in the language in some schools and evening classes,[76] occasional religious services and other events on special occasions, and some small-scale publications of restricted circulation.[77] Taken together, these two factors leave little room for optimism as to the success of any kind of 'revival' of Cornish.

---

[74] See in particular R. R. M. Gendall, *A Student's Grammar of Modern Cornish* (Menheniot, 1991); idem, *A Student's Dictionary of Modern Cornish, Part 1: English–Cornish* (2nd ed., Menheniot, 1991); and idem, *A Practical Dictionary of Modern Cornish, Part 1: Cornish–English* (Menheniot, 1997).

[75] For a critical assessment of 'Modern Cornish', see Williams, *Cornish Today*, pp. 123–59.

[76] For this, and for a more general assessment of the problems faced by the 'revival' in recent decades, see Philip Payton and Bernard Deacon, 'The Ideology of Language Revival' in Philip Payton (ed.), *Cornwall since the War: The Contemporary History of a European Region* (Redruth, 1993), pp. 271–90.

[77] On this and other 'domains of usage' of Cornish at the present time, see Ken George, 'Revived Cornish' in Ball (ed.), *The Celtic Languages*, pp. 644–54.

20

Lesser-used Languages and Linguistic Minorities in Europe since 1918: An Overview

ROBIN OKEY

THE EUROPE with which this chapter is concerned emerged from the Paris Peace Conference of 1919. One of the best-known anecdotes of this conference relates Woodrow Wilson's despondent comment that when he made his celebrated affirmation of the principle of national self-determination he had not even known of the existence of many of the national groups which were now daily knocking at his door. It is important for our theme that the Welsh were not among these petitioners. The period under review here began by deepening the disjuncture between the Welsh-speaking community and several others in Europe whose circumstances hitherto, at least as far as language was concerned, had appeared not dissimilar. Varied and fluctuating as the fortunes of European small language groups were after 1918, for roughly two of the ensuing three generations they were echoed only distantly in Wales. Since the 1960s the experience and concerns of speakers of Welsh and minority languages elsewhere have shown more convergence, restoring some of the parallels that existed in the nineteenth century, if in changed forms. It is this pattern of flux and reflux which gives the post-1918 period as a whole its shape and interest for comparative purposes.

The aim here is to try to identify the various kinds of situations in which lesser-used languages were spoken in post-1918 Europe and to indicate the issues, debates and strategies to which these situations gave rise. Thus social themes are inextricably mixed with political ones for a period when language issues were heavily ideologized. Both small language groups and also members of large language groups are considered, where these constituted a minority within a given state. The hope is that a survey approach will allow readers to glimpse as many as possible of the parallels or contrasts to the Welsh experience, though inevitably at the cost of depth of coverage. Since the fate of lesser-used languages in the twentieth century has been intimately related to developments in the preceding era of 'national revivals', a preliminary review of the nineteenth-century background is indispensable, not least to establish some kind of a basis for comparison with the Welsh case.

The Nineteenth-century Legacy

Throughout the nineteenth century Welsh was one of a large and varied category of 'non-dominant' European languages, whose sway at local community level was not matched by their role in administration, education or the courts. The subordination of languages reflected the political subordination of most of the Continent's ethnic groups, and usually overlapped with lines of social and as often as not religious subordination inherited from a pre-democratic age. Even at the outset of the century, some of these languages doubtless had greater status for their speakers than did Welsh in Wales, whether they retained elements of a nobility or church hierarchy (Georgian and Armenian; Serb and Croat) or continued to be spoken by substantial bourgeois elements (Flemish, Catalan). Czech, too, by virtue of its several million speakers and presence in substantial towns, even if not beyond petit bourgeois level, should probably also be placed in this category. Of course, there were also situations where the vernacular had less salience than in Wales, among the smallest European language groups numbering from a few thousand to a few hundred thousand speakers – like Frisians, Scottish Gaels, Swiss Romansh, Sami (Lapps), Lusatian Sorbs or Balkan Vlachs – and also among the much more numerous speakers of what contemporaries still considered mere dialects of Romance, Germanic or Slav, including Belorussian and Ukrainian. Several societies remained, however, where circumstances were sufficiently close to those of Wales for us to consider them a group apart. They were small but not tiny, varying (by c.1900) from the half million speakers of Basque, a million of Welsh and Estonian, slightly more of Latvian, Lithuanian, Breton and Slovene, to almost two million Slovaks. Their social structure entering the nineteenth century was not so different from that of the Czechs but on a smaller scale, in that they included urban lower-class elements as well as peasants and sympathetic clergy, and their languages all boasted a certain number of dictionaries and grammars from the sixteenth century onwards and were quite strongly represented in religious life as a language of liturgy and/or devotional literature. In this group Welsh stood out to some extent through the age and strength of its literary heritage, but the non-dominant language most out of line with its fellows was Irish, the only one which was already a minority language among children in its ancestral area by the beginning of the nineteenth century.[1]

---

[1] For information on these languages, see José I. Hualde et al. (eds.), *Towards a History of the Basque Language* (Amsterdam, 1995); Jorj Gwegen, *La langue bretonne face à ses oppresseurs* (Quimper, 1975); R. L. Lenček, *The Structure and History of the Slovene Language* (Columbia, Ohio, 1982); D. V. Verges, *Die Standardisierung der slowakischen Literatursprache vom 18. bis 20. Jahrhundert* (Frankfurt, 1984); V. Ruke-Dravina, *The Standardisation Process in Latvian* (Stockholm, 1977); Máirtín Ó Murchú, *The Irish Language* (Dublin, 1985). For general surveys, see Meic Stephens, *Linguistic Minorities in Western Europe* (Llandysul, 1978); V. E. Durkacz, *The Decline of the Celtic Languages* (Edinburgh, 1983).

Until the 1840s the pressures of dominant state languages grew throughout the Continent, swelling the number of bilinguals in the non-dominant populations.[2] From that time the forces of 'national revival' in central and eastern Europe had begun to check, or even reverse this process, which continued to accelerate in the west. Three related features deserve attention.

Firstly, the use of different regional standards in writing came substantially to an end, the vocabulary of minority languages was modernized, and publications increased greatly in number and range of contents. By contrast, western languages previously unstandardized remained so: three of Brittany's four dialects, for example, achieved unification in 1911, but the most widely-read Breton periodical continued to appear in the Breton equivalent to Gwenhwyseg.[3] Welsh publication, which was exceeded in bulk by the Baltic languages and Slovene only towards the end of the century, by this time was stagnating and becoming increasingly narrow in range, while the latter continued to spurt forward.

Secondly, linguistic development and consciousness went hand in hand with social mobilization of non-dominant groups. The Czech historian Hroch's three-stage typology lists stage A, when interest in minority tongues was confined to a few scholars on an almost antiquarian basis, stage B, when the cause was already passionately embraced by a section of the educated minority amid a largely apathetic populace, and stage C, that of the mass movement, setting in after 1860 for the Czechs, followed a little later by Slovenes and from 1890 by the Baltic peoples.[4] Non-dominant groups acquired a fuller social profile, resting on an emancipated, increasingly literate peasantry concerned for economic improvement and populous enough to overspill into the previously semi-alien towns where a native bourgeoisie, intelligentsia and modern working class were forming. The period was characterized by the linkage of linguistic patriotism to social issues, through the proliferation of ethnic-based loan, producer and consumer co-operatives, reading rooms, and singing, gymnastic, sporting and similar societies.[5] After initial hegemony of the small nationalist middle class, similar to that wielded by Henry Richard and others in Wales, the same separating out of a distinctive working-class consciousness under socialist influence tended to occur as in Wales, but any tendency to working-class language change in multi-ethnic environments (Slovenes in Trieste, Latvians in Riga, and Czechs in German Bohemia) declined in the last decades before 1914, in contrast to Wales. This was no doubt due to the aforementioned ethnic associational network, and a press which reflected worker interests (about a quarter of the *c*.130 early

---

[2] For the growth of bilingualism en route to assimilation in eastern Europe, see J. Chlebowczyk, *On Small and Young Nations in Europe* (Wrocław, 1980), pp. 82–9.

[3] This was *Dihunamb*, published from 1905 to 1944 in the widely divergent dialect of Vannes.

[4] Miroslav Hroch, *Die Vorkämpfer der nationalen Bewegungen bei den kleinen Völkern Europas* (Praha, 1968).

[5] For an example of this process, see T. Hočevar, *The Structure of the Slovene Economy, 1848–1963* (New York, 1965), chapter 5.

twentieth-century Slovene periodicals catered for worker, artisan or socialist groupings);[6] but it was surely also due to the public salience of the mother tongue for which the nascent minority bourgeoisies were largely responsible. For stage C also saw the consolidation of the patriotic current among these groups, who could earlier be deterred by what they saw as its narrowness and lack of sophistication, to the point of deliberate de-identification, like many of their counterparts in Wales.[7]

This public salience of east European non-dominant languages, interacting with governments both tolerant and hostile, was the third feature of the revival. Formal recognition of the principle of national equality, as in the Austrian Basic Law of 1867, certainly helped Czechs to achieve and Slovenes to move to a fully-fledged mother tongue education system. But attempts to curtail minority language provision in Tsarist Russia and post-1867 Hungary had little impact on the vitality of the languages concerned because of limited state resources, earlier more generous provisions, particularly in primary education, and reluctance, even in autocratic Russia, to exercise totalitarian control over press, association and personal property rights such as the twentieth century was to know. Thus a minimum of institutional safeguards of a liberal type was available to minority communities in the period of linguistic revival. Only where mother tongue primary education was cut back and the ethnic group lacked a strong presence in an important urban centre, as among Hungarian Slovaks before 1914, did the national linguistic movement falter.[8]

An important point about this movement was that it came to assume a national society functioning, in its internal institutions, through the mother tongue only. To be sure, the ageing Czech leader František Rieger alienated younger nationalists in the 1880s when he claimed that of course educated Czechs needed a perfect knowledge of German.[9] But Rieger seems to have assumed that social life and thorough teaching of German as a subject in Czech schools would do the trick rather than bilingual education. At primary school level in particular, it was authorities hostile to the language movements which pressed for bilingual schooling. Was the concern of nineteenth-century Welsh parents that their

---

[6] Calculated from J. Šlebinger, *Slovenska bibliografija za let 1907–1912* (Ljubljana, 1913).

[7] For such a case (Dežman), see P. Vodopivec, 'Die sozialen und wirtschaftlichen Ansichten des deutschen Bürgertums in Krain vom Ende der 60-er Jahre bis zum Beginn der 80-er Jahre des 19. Jahrhunderts' in H. Rumpler and A. Suppan (eds.), *Geschichte der Deutschen im Bereich des heutigen Slowenien 1848–1941* (München, 1988), pp. 85–119.

[8] For the themes of this paragraph, see H. Hugelmann, *Das Nationalitätenrecht des alten Österreich* (Wien, 1930); P. Hanák (ed.), *Die nationale Frage in der österreichisch-ungarischen Monarchie 1900–1918* (Budapest, 1966), and for Hungary, esp. chapters by I. Dolmányos and L. Katus; E. C. Thaden, *Russification in the Baltic Provinces and Finland* (Princeton, 1981). See also R. J. W. Evans's admirable survey of Czechs, Slovenes and Slovaks, 'Language and Society in the Nineteenth Century: Some Central-European Comparisons' in Geraint H. Jenkins (ed.), *Language and Community in the Nineteenth Century* (Cardiff, 1998), pp. 397–424.

[9] O. Urban, *Česká společnost 1848–1918* (Praha, 1982), pp. 367–8.

children should learn English in the primary school a sign of a more ambitious, less sluggish common people than eastern Europe knew? Besides the arguments of educationalists, part patriotic, part practical, for mother tongue instruction, it should be borne in mind that there were more opportunities for upward mobility of east European minorities in their native tongues as the range of these expanded, and that east Europeans tended to rely on secondary schools for ambitious sons, such schools being better provided for than in Wales until 1889.

How is the strength of linguistic movements in nineteenth-century east central Europe to be accounted for? Intellectual explanations in terms of the rise of beliefs about the importance of language for ethnic identity and as the instrument of national 'missions' in a kind of world cultural ecology beg questions about the power of ideas to shape social life;[10] pleas of like emotional force have been deployed by the spokesmen of language revival in western Europe in the twentieth century without evoking a similar response. Sociological explanations point to the opportunities that 'modernization' and democratization afforded non-dominant groups for upward mobility. Ernest Gellner, in an especially influential approach, has argued that the circumstances of modern life impose the need for standardized cultural communication, so forcing late arrivals in the industrializing urban milieu (non-dominant group B) to upgrade their traditional folk culture into a 'high culture' to escape helotization at the hands of the historically dominant group A.[11] The difficulty with this approach is that Gellner conflates modernization, urbanization and industrialism and in so far as he appears to emphasize the last named he is actually wrong. The Czech language movement on which Bohemian-born Gellner's model seems based matured well before the industrial upsurge of the late nineteenth century which brought Czechs into the German Sudetenland along group A/group B lines. On the other hand, contemporaneous group A/group B situations in industrializing south Wales and Basque Vizcaya did not produce a Czech-style pattern of linguistic mobilization. It seems that ideological movements cannot be seen simply as the reflex of socio-economic processes. Attempts to explain them in this way produce the paradox that the 'modernization' of non-dominant societies in the context of a dominant culture is seen to induce linguistic revival by east European historians and assimilation in conventional Welsh assumption.

This paradox cannot be so simply resolved by arguing that the socio-economic situation of small nations in western and eastern Europe was fundamentally different. There was little to choose between them individually in sheer numbers, and Balts and Estonians were ethnically no less isolated than Celts. Balts and Slovenes were, it is true, more rural in social structure than the Welsh, though no

---

[10] See, for example, H. Kohn, *Panslavism* (New York, 1953); Elie Kedourie, *Nationalism* (rev. ed., London, 1985).
[11] Ernest Gellner, *Nations and Nationalism* (London, 1983).

more so than the Bretons. Comparative levels of monoglottism before the revivals are difficult to judge. As to economic integration in a larger whole, the Czechs inhabited the powerhouse of the Habsburg monarchy, wholly dominated at the outset of the language movement by German capital, as were the Slovenes living athwart the German-speaking world's southern outlet to the sea at Trieste. Riga was a more cosmopolitan city than Cardiff, and proportionally more Slovenes and Slovaks than Welsh made their way to America. Besides, it was in those areas of the small-nation east European economies which were most integrated into a broader capitalist world that language ambitions waxed strongest, among Czechs and the dynamic Slovene community of Trieste.[12]

The conclusion drawn in this preliminary survey is that the environment which gave rise to nineteenth-century language ideologies should be conceived more broadly than in socio-economic terms alone. Language choices varied because of differences in the total situation in which a non-dominant group felt itself to be. Here political modernization was as important as socio-economic. The rickety political structures of eastern Europe, dominated by dynastic empires in conjunction with a leading ethnic group, offered more 'windows of opportunity' for wholly new scenarios than were plausible for nineteenth-century Welsh or Bretons: the idea of a 'united Slovenia' with an official role for its language dates from 1848. Eventually, such aspirations had to be taken into account because of the high proportion of east Europeans living under alien rule. Although, one to one, the social position of small peoples in west and east can be compared, overall the numerical strength of the non-dominant in the east gave them a far greater collective saliency. We may note the not uncommon practice of mother tongue primary education already before the language revivals, and the deliberate use from Enlightenment times of secondary and seminary schooling (albeit in the dominant language) to create serviceable cohorts of educated natives. The tradition was carried over into the nineteenth-century linguistic movements, nearly all of whose leaders had a good grounding in European culture as mediated through German-medium *Gymnasien* and/or universities. Hence the international aspect of east European national movements and the openness to international fashion of their exponents. The life history of Ceiriog, as recorded in a 1906 anthology, rings ironically in comparison:

> John Ceiriog Hughes was born September 25, 1832. He was for many years clerk in the Goods Station, London Road, Manchester, and was afterwards stationmaster on the Cambrian Line at Llanidloes, Towyn and Caersws successively. He died at Caersws April 23rd, 1887.[13]

---

[12] For Slovene activity in Trieste, see Marina Cattaruzza, 'Slovenes and Italians in Trieste, 1850–1914' in Max Engman (ed.), *Ethnic Identity in Urban Europe: Comparative Studies on Governments and Non-Dominant Ethnic Groups in Europe, 1850–1940. Vol. VIII* (Dartmouth, 1992), pp. 189–219.

[13] Edmund O. Jones, *Welsh Lyrics of the Nineteenth Century* (Bangor, 1896), p. 53.

If a mutually reinforcing combination of strong language ideology and potentially favourable social and political conjunctures is to explain the east European background, how helpful is this scenario in casting light on the linguistic backdrop in the west? The most notable language movements there, in Flanders and Catalonia, can be explained in terms of the relatively favourable social background (a native bourgeoisie), the political weight of the Flemish majority in Belgium and the weakness of the Spanish state. But none of these factors was strong enough to carry the language movements to the ideological passion of their east European counterparts or wholly to overcome the regional isolation of west European non-dominant groups. The Irish movement had passion but the social basis of the language had withered away. Breton identity remained trapped in the alleged antithesis of liberal urban progress versus peasant clerical reaction into which German speakers had failed to corral Czechs and Slovenes. Welsh, for all its vastly greater literary productivity, did not altogether escape the same fate. As literacy in English grew, the tradition of 'gwybodaeth fuddiol' (edifying knowledge) in Welsh declined; the biblically-orientated contents of *Y Gwyddoniadur* were a regression, in comparative terms, on those of the translated *Addysg Chambers i'r Bobl*. While political Catholicism triumphed over liberal nationalists in late nineteenth-century Slovenia, it still largely accepted liberal hegemony in setting the cultural agenda, along modern international lines. Welsh-language culture, lacking this (ultimately politically motivated) inter-national aspiration, found a two-fold rationale, as the guardian of a unique literary heritage and as 'the language of Heaven'. This was not ideologically powerful enough to sustain language loyalty in the face of socio-economic change.

A third rationale, Welsh as the language of the *gwerin*, accessing continental romanticism and the democratizing temper of the age while not repudiating the literary and religious legacies, brought Welsh closer to the spirit of east European language movements. Its formulator, the academic O. M. Edwards, bore out what has been claimed above about the role of a sophisticated education in linguistic revival. O. M. Edwards was also innovatory in recognizing the category of English-speaking Welsh people which was beginning to create a significant difference between the Welsh and the east European situation. But in this he appears to have been rather isolated, for it does not seem that the concept was adopted by his fellow Welsh speakers. Perhaps the continuing preference among educated Welsh speakers for English in many spheres of 'high culture', in Gellner's phrase, T. E. Ellis's patriotic speeches, say, or J. E. Lloyd's *A History of Wales* (1911), reflected conscious deference to the changing situation, but it seems more likely to have been a continuance of earlier patterns of diglossia, such as had existed in east European non-dominant societies before the development of linguistic nationalism. Either way, this lopsided bilingualism of much of the Welsh-speaking élite was just as much a weakness for the language as the existence of increasing numbers of English speakers, many of whom were English in-migrants to the coalfield and great ports.

By 1914, therefore, a complex interplay between ideology and social polity, the latter setting limits to the former but also partially shaped by it, had created a pattern of differentiation between the two halves of Europe. The social position of Welsh was still, arguably, closer to that of Slovene and Estonian than that of Breton or certainly Irish. But the trajectories were diverging and the political changes of 1918 were dramatically to widen the gap which had opened up over the previous half century.

The Inter-war Experience

The First World War, Woodrow Wilson declared, was waged to make the world safe for democracy. For language activists this meant also an end to the aristocracy of language. The age-old pattern of a few dominant tongues amid a myriad varied shades of subordination was to yield to a more uniform picture, which had no place for the likes of Welsh. During the inter-war years, official recognition was given to only three kinds of language situation: that of the national language of the nation state, the basic norm; that of 'minority languages' in the nation state, with certain international guarantees; and – confined to the Soviet Union – the special status given to non-dominant languages by the socialist alternative. They merit attention in turn.

The case of the new nation states created in 1919 illustrates the capacity of politics to change the social position of languages – even if we agree with the Czech writer Chmelař that the peace settlement in central Europe was itself the inevitable result of the 'irrepressible will for life and growth' of its former non-dominant peoples.[14] While German urban islands in a Czech sea and once-Germanized Ljubljana had already been engulfed by the Slav tide before 1914, other centres like Bratislava and Košice in Slovakia, Maribor and Celje in south Styria and Novi Sad in the Vojvodina became (or became again) Slovak, Slovene and Serbian majority towns only between the wars and against the pre-war trend. In 1913, 40 per cent of the inhabitants of Riga were Latvian, a proportion which increased to 63 per cent by 1939.

The most striking symbol of the former servant peoples' determination to assert their dominance was the linguistic takeover of east-central European universities. In 1919 the Elizabeth University of Hungarian Pozsony became the Czechoslovak University of Cyrill and Methodius of renamed Bratislava; the famous German, then Russified university at Dorpat became the Estonian University of Tartu; the German university of Brünn became the Czech University of Brno and the Hungarian university of Kolozsvár became the Romanian University of Cluj. New equivalents sprouted for Slovenes in Ljubljana (1919), Latvians in Riga (1919) and Lithuanians in Kaunas (1922). This

---

[14] J. Chmelař, *National Minorities of Central Europe* (Prague, 1937), p. 10.

process had its teething troubles but that they were not crippling testified to the groundwork of the pre-1914 language movements. Terminological questions, for example, had already become a preoccupation of the Latvian Society of Riga from the turn of the century.[15] Finding qualified staff was a tougher problem. Initial appointments to the Romanian University of Cluj included several Frenchmen who taught in French and aroused resentment because of their higher salaries.[16] Only half the early lectures in Riga were given in Latvian and not until the early 1930s did the staff of Tartu University become fairly solidly Estonian.[17] The influence of Czech personnel in Bratislava University lasted longer; the medical faculty was founded by seven Czech medics who had written to the fledgling Ministry of Education about the need to train a cohort of Slovak-speaking doctors and were promptly appointed *en masse*.[18] Student numbers, however, were buoyant. Over 80 per cent of students in Tartu were Estonian; in the pre-war Russian university, 80 per cent had been Russian or Jewish.

The social elevation of native languages brought further widening of their expressive range. One and three quarter times more books and brochures – about 25,000 of them – were published in Estonian in the inter-war years than in all previous history; the first opera was performed by an all-Estonian cast in 1918–19; the first opera was written in Estonian in 1928; by 1939 there were ten permanent Estonian theatre companies, seven of them professional.[19] Slovenian periodicals trebled during the inter-war years and broached new themes; there were five on science and technology in 1939 where none had existed before 1914.[20]

The linguistic affirmation of the formerly non-dominant in higher education was the final stage in the training of a competitive native intelligentsia and its seizure of social leadership to complement the political. With twenty million members of minorities to pose a potential threat to authority (in place of the sixty million non-dominant in the pre-war period), the language battle continued. 'Besides wielding the political power, we possess the hinterland of the towns . . . With free competition, the vital forces will complete the process of purification that will pull down the fortresses of privilege . . . we, the Rumanian element, have unshaken confidence that the victory will be ours', wrote the Romanian paper of Cluj in 1924 of the battle to Romanianize Transylvania's towns.[21] 'The

---

[15] Ruke-Dravina, *The Standardisation Process in Latvian*, p. 71.

[16] Z. de Szász, *The Minorities in Roumanian Transylvania* (London, 1927), p. 288.

[17] A. Sons, 'Die Entstehung der Universitäten im Baltikum und ihre weitere Entwicklung', *Acta Baltica*, 22 (1982), 63–112.

[18] M. Tichý, 'K dejinám lekárskej fakulty v Bratislave v rokoch 1918–39', *Historický Časopis*, 37 (1989), 699–717.

[19] T. U. Raun, *Estonia and Estonians* (Stanford, 1991), chapter 8.

[20] Hočevar, *The Structure of the Slovene Economy*, p. 171.

[21] Sylvius Dragomir, *The Ethnical Minorities in Transylvania* (Geneva, 1927), pp. 53f. For a detailed modern Romanian view, see Irina Livezeanu, *Cultural Politics in Greater Romania: Regionalism, Nation Building and Ethnic Struggle, 1918–1930* (Ithaca and London, 1995).

language question is at the heart of the Minorities' problem', wrote a Hungarian of the same province, detailing successive edicts against the speaking of Magyar by officials, who for some years simply could not all be replaced by Romanians.[22] In Transylvania, northern Serbia and Polish Upper Silesia the new political masters alike legislated to ban attendance at minority schools by children who did not already speak the minority language, fearing the continued social power of old élites to lure their flock into an alien fold. Claiming that many minority language speakers were the products of previous denationalization, they often sought to extend this prohibition to children whose family names allegedly betrayed a native origin.[23] More than two hundred German-speaking teachers lost their posts in southern Styria, often being replaced by Slovene teachers who had been expelled from the Slavic borderlands of Italy that Mussolini brutally sought to Italianize.[24] The social eclipse of the old élite languages was helped by migration. Some 350,000 Hungarians, mainly the better-off, left the Hungarian minority areas for Hungary proper after 1918, as many Germans left Poland for Germany.

Thus the inter-war 'minorities problem' was born in acrimony and resentment. 'Persons belonging to racial, religious or linguistic minorities' in the so-called Succession States were to receive 'equitable' state provision for their cultural needs, according to 'minority treaties' sponsored by the League of Nations.[25] But the grounds on which some British Foreign Office officials supported minority legislation, as a means of integrating minorities into new states by judicious tolerance, showed a misreading of the situation. As G. M. Gathorne-Hardy wrote:

> It is often necessary and desirable that a specific language of the peasantry shall be recognised and used as the language of instruction in elementary or primary schools, but not in places of higher instruction; this is the situation which in fact exists in Wales and applies to those countries where the minority language is one with inferior cultural value.[26]

Were not the Welsh loyal to the Empire? This failed to recognize the upgrading in the social status of 'peasant languages' which had taken place in eastern Europe or that the new minorities were in fact mainly from the traditional dominant groups, particularly Germans and Hungarians. New states also resented the restrictions imposed by the minority treaties on their sovereignty.

---

[22] de Szász, *The Minorities in Roumanian Transylvania*, chapters 5–7. For the quotation, see p. 93.

[23] For minority school matters, see ibid., chapter 14; Dragomir, *Ethnical Minorities*, chapters 5–6; and S. Mesaroš, *Položaj Mađara u Vojvodini 1918–29* (Novi Sad, 1981), chapter 5.

[24] Hočevar, *The Structure of the Slovene Economy*, p. 214.

[25] L. P. Mair, *The Protection of Minorities* (London, 1928), p. 65.

[26] A. Sharp, 'Britain and the Protection of Minorities at the Paris Peace Conference in 1919' in A. C. Hepburn (ed.), *Minorities in History* (London, 1978), p. 58.

Thus, as far as possible, these states interpreted their obligations in the Gathorne-Hardy spirit. Yugoslav and Romanian practice allowed teaching through a non-state language on an optional basis for the first four years of schooling only, thereafter to be phased out (Romania) or immediately replaced (Yugoslavia) by the official language as the sole medium. Moreover, according to the Romanian school law of 1925 Romanian language, history and civics could be taught only in Romanian. Hungarian attempts to found private *Gymnasien* (in Yugoslavia) or a private university (in Cluj, Romania) were frustrated by the authorities.[27] By contrast, the Germans in Czechoslovakia enjoyed a fully-fledged educational system between the wars, retaining one of their two pre-war universities; they also had the right to deal with the authorities in their own language where they formed at least 20 per cent of the population, as 92 per cent of them did in 1931.[28] The most favoured minorities were those of the Baltic lands and Finland.[29] The Swedish speakers in Finland received similar rights to the Czechoslovak Germans, with only a 10 per cent (later 6 per cent) threshold. As a result of a law passed in 1925, Estonia gave minorities of more than 3,000 inhabitants the right to state-funded cultural autonomy through elective organs; minority private schools could accept children of different mother tongue and individuals were guaranteed free choice of their nationality. Latvia's provisions were similar in effect. Generosity in these cases was no doubt aided by the small size of the minorities and generally by a diminished sense of threat to the nation states.

All minorities hitherto mentioned were from formerly dominant groups. The Ukrainians and Belorussians of eastern Poland better fitted Headlam-Morley's category of 'peasant peoples'. The million Belorussians by the 1931 census (although another 700,000 from the area described themselves as speaking the 'local' language!) had had no schools in their own tongue until the wartime German occupation, but lost these in inter-war Poland; by 1937–8 there were only five bilingual schools and forty-four Polish-medium schools where Belorussian was taught as a subject. The 2,420 primary schools of the more numerous and nationally aware Ukrainians had become 420 by 1937–8, while bilingual schools increased to more than 3,000, largely as a result of the provision of the 1924 school law that wherever there were twenty Polish-speaking children in a district all education should be bilingual. Although 87 per cent of Jews had Yiddish as their mother tongue the state refused to fund any teaching through the

---

[27] See footnote 23.

[28] Chmelař, *National Minorities of Central Europe*, p. 23. For a detailed account of German minority schooling, which notes that Germans did lose many schools on the grounds of an alleged pre-war excess, see Wolfgang Mitter, 'German Schools in Czechoslovakia 1918–1938' in Janusz Tomiak (ed.), *Schooling, Educational Policy and Ethnic Identity: Comparative Studies on Governments and Non-Dominant Ethnic Groups in Europe, 1850–1940. Vol. I* (Dartmouth, 1991), pp. 211–34.

[29] See E. Maddison, *Die nationalen Minderheiten Estlands und ihre Rechte* (2nd ed., Tallinn, 1930).

medium of the language, or through Hebrew. Finally, the German community, a million strong in 1921 (only 700,000 ten years later) saw German-language schools fall from 1,039 in that year to 394, only one-third state funded, by the late 1930s. This process, which caused constant German complaints to the League of Nations until Poland withdrew from it in 1934, was cannily justified by the Polish Provincial Governor who was mainly concerned, with reference to the niggardly provision of mother tongue schools for the Polish minority in Germany – which did not have League protection.[30]

Ironically, there is no evidence that the nationalist zeal of education ministers or provincial satraps had any real impact. Minority groups retained their social cohesion, and in this they were helped by the relative tolerance shown towards their press and associational life, another echo of late nineteenth-century patterns. Thus fewer than half a million Hungarian speakers in Yugoslavia maintained four dailies and eleven weeklies.[31] What the incessant wrangles over language, particularly in education, did achieve was to keep the minorities issue a running sore, contrary to the hopes of the peacemakers. Resolutions passed at the second Congress of National Minorities (a largely German-inspired movement) in 1926 highlighted the central dilemma at the heart of minority legislation. They called for Estonian-style cultural autonomy, for the redrawing of administrative boundaries in line with linguistic ones, and for the minority language to take over the functions of the state language wherever its speakers formed a compact territorial majority.[32] For majority politicians such demands only justified the suspicion that minority rights, far from ensuring the integration of the people concerned, would be used to shore up barriers against integration, preserving a state within a state until secession to the motherland would again be possible. Suspicions of separatism were sometimes justified but not always. Under modern conditions linguistic minorities rightly feared they could no longer rely on the traditional cultural self-sufficiency of peasant folk; the pressure for cultural autonomy could be a defensive recognition of this fact rather than a prelude to secession. However, the new majorities were not to be reassured. Inter-war minority rights legislation foundered on doubts on both sides of the fence as to whether dual loyalties – to state and culture – were really possible.

This is where the Soviet Union claimed an ideological breakthrough. The dual loyalty impossible under capitalism was allegedly realized under socialism, through the principle of a system 'national in form, socialist in content'. This meant, essentially, that communism spoke to people in their own language. Soviet

---

[30] Janusz Tomiak, 'Education of the Non-Dominant Ethnic Groups in the Polish Republic, 1918–1939' in idem (ed.), *Schooling, Educational Policy and Ethnic Identity*, pp. 185–209. For Upper Silesian Provincial Governor Grażyński, see A. Chojnowski, *Koncepcje polityki narodowościowej rządów polskich w letech 1921–39* (Wrocław, 1979), pp. 106–15.

[31] Mesaroš, *Položaj Mađara*, p. 218.

[32] Mair, *The Protection of Minorities*, chapter 16.

federalism amounted to administrative units with a linguistic core, for genuine decentralization was absent; moreover, the federal units often corresponded only loosely with linguistic borders, and many smaller nationalities were actually minorities in their eponymous territories, in which Russian remained dominant. That said, the effort put into developing the Soviet state's myriad tongues, which often lacked any written tradition, reflected genuine idealism on a vast scale. Textbooks were being printed in 25 languages in 1925 and in 104 languages by 1934.[33] The number of books published in Georgian quintupled (to 650) between 1921 and 1935,[34] while Belorussian, untaught in Tsarist times, was the language of instruction in 3,794 four-grade elementary schools in the Belorussian republic by the late 1920s compared with only 27 Russian schools.[35]

Of course, the requirements of the socialist ideal set limits to the resurgence of non-dominant languages. Ukrainian faced a similar social problem to that experienced decades earlier by 'peasant languages' to the west: the towns were largely Russian-speaking. While Lenin favoured the Ukrainianization of the towns, undertaken in the 1920s by the Ukrainian party chief Skrypnyk, Stalin's suspicious centralism reversed the process and in 1933 Skrypnyk committed suicide.[36] In 1938 the Latin alphabet adopted for non-Slavic languages in the 1920s was replaced by Cyrillic and the study of Russian was made compulsory. Since the resources needed to teach it effectively were lacking, however, this measure hardly undermined the remarkable uplift Bolshevism had given to minority tongues. It fell short of its lofty propaganda not over this but in a subtler sense. The Soviet Union which claimed to be a higher form of society was in fact still less developed than the rest of Europe. The pattern of a myriad tongues kept at varying levels of development around the Russian lingua franca worked not just because of Stalin's iron hand, or the new socialist consciousness vaunted by propaganda, but because it was still accessible to the Headlam-Morley principle of integrating peasant peoples by complaisance. The Soviet Union was Europe's last empire also in the linguistic sense.

The Soviet language experience therefore did not ultimately diverge from the common pattern of the inter-war years. This was one of a working out of the pre-war legacy. In the east of the Continent the linkage of social modernization with linguistic revival and nationalism simply continued, exploding the old empires on the way, with the exception of the most backward of these which preserved itself by artfully adapting the process: Soviet policies both accelerated and imposed

[33] Michael Kirkwood, '*Glasnost*, "The National Question" and Soviet Language Policy', *Soviet Studies*, 43, no. 1 (1991), 62.

[34] B. G. Hewitt, 'Aspects of Language Planning in Georgia (Georgian and Abkhaz)' in Michael Kirkwood (ed.), *Language Planning in the Soviet Union* (London, 1989), p. 130.

[35] James Dingley, 'Ukrainian and Belorussian – a Testing Ground' in ibid., p. 183.

[36] The best account of these fluctuations is R. S. Sullivant, *Soviet Policies and the Ukraine* (Columbia, 1962), chapters 3–4.

checks upon it. In the west the lower profile of non-dominant languages did not change dramatically. The exception was Irish which was thrust by the events of 1918–22 into the position of 'national language' of the Irish Free State. Politically, its status was transformed. Ideologically, it became the symbol of the authentic Celtic nationhood whose vaunted values were to pervade the new state. The difficulty, as far as Irish as a living social medium was concerned, was that the goal of restoring the language throughout the country took precedence over the safeguarding of the actual Irish-speaking areas, with their huge economic and social problems. The 130,000 native speakers in the scattered Gaeltacht districts established in 1926 became a reservoir for teacher recruitment for the rest of the country, on 'organic intellectual' lines, but there was little otherwise to reconcile them to a system imposed from above (the Gaeltacht had no cultural or admin-istrative autonomy) which locked them into cultural isolation and poverty, through a language whose written form they often failed to master. Although twentieth-century small languages require an ideological spur, the dangers of over-ideologization in the absence of an adequate social base are shown in the time wasted in faddish disputes before Irish acquired the necessary (slightly!) simplified spelling (1948), prescriptive grammar (1958) and practical script (not finally introduced into secondary schools until 1970).[37]

Meanwhile, in Belgium universal suffrage in 1919 and a shifting demographic and economic balance between Flemings and declining Walloons revealed the power of the social base. The French speakers switched tack like the German speakers of Bohemia from the 1880s, abandoning a dominant role in Flanders with the aim of shoring up their position in a monolingual Wallonia. In 1930 the University of Ghent became Flemish (Dutch) speaking, and Flanders and Wallonia were declared monolingual regions, Brussels apart, in 1932. However, since private and, on certain terms, even publicly-funded French-medium education continued to be available in Flanders, the Flemish sense of being social underdogs continued in the inter-war years. It was nourished by the continued advance of French in Brussels, where in violation of the 1932 law Flemish parents still sent their children to French-medium schools. From 1880 to 1930 a Flemish monolingual majority in Brussels of 59 per cent became a near French monoglot majority of 43 per cent, suggesting that in two generations many originally monoglot Flemish families must have passed first to bilingualism, then to French monolingualism.[38]

---

[37] Ó Murchú, *The Irish Language*, pp. 47, 64–73. For a contemporary criticism of unimaginative approaches to Irish, see Shán Ó Cuív, *The Problem of Irish in the Schools* (Dublin, 1936).

[38] Maurits de Vroede, 'Language in Education in Belgium up to 1940' in Tomiak (ed.), *Schooling, Educational Policy and Ethnic Identity*, pp. 111–31; for Brussels percentages, pp. 119, 126. It should be noted that Flemish is officially called Dutch in Belgium, the old term being associated with the pre-standardized dialects that long obstructed language revival.

In Catalonia the language movement's sights did not go beyond bilingualism. Indeed, the 1932 Catalan autonomy statute kept control of education (except for the university) in the hands of Madrid, merely allowing a place for Catalan alongside Spanish. A flourishing Catalan press with many daily papers (though they took only a quarter of the market) and 740 books published in 1933 fills out a pattern which may have reflected the traditional social bilingualism of the powerful Catalan élite, the close similarity of the two languages and the relative lack of *de facto* centralizing pressure in a state which still left 48 per cent of Catalans illiterate in 1915.[39] The moderation of Basque linguistic demands was still more marked in relation to the dynamic political movement. The language, spoken by about 45 per cent of the inhabitants of the Spanish Basque country in 1936, had a social base in the peasantry and lower middle class in the smaller towns, with significant clerical support. But dialect divisions, and a rather puristic approach to literary standardization, incomprehensible to ordinary speakers, inhibited pioneering attempts to give it a place in education; the autonomy of 1936–7 was too brief to build on the few bilingual schools opened in the 1920s.[40]

In Brittany a stronger state than the Spanish could not greatly weaken Breton as a social force in the countryside in the inter-war years, but it had, in the eyes of a Breton observer in 1946, changed the terms of bilingualism, with the country people now requiring some French to get by in shop, office and urban market, instead of the élite needing to know some Breton as in the nineteenth century. But this observer still saw the knowledge of French as superficial enough to mean that 'educated men' in constant contact with the rural population – doctors, notaries, priests – had to use Breton.[41] There was already evidence, however, of generational decline. In 635 communes of Lower Brittany investigated in 1928 the sermon was given only in Breton in 474 and only in French in 49; but the figures for the catechism of children were 397 and 103 respectively.[42] Ironically, an upsurge of intellectual interest produced a swathe of Breton language activists, often from the French-speaking middle classes, who worked for the elevation of Breton as a language of 'high culture' – in the literary revue *Gwalarn* (1925) and the final unification of the literary language (1941) – and who challenged the negative association of things Breton in the eyes of the Left: witness the bulletin of lay teachers favouring the teaching of Breton, *Ar Falz* (1933). A petition on this

---

[39] This percentage comes from José Luís García Garrido, 'Spanish Education Policy towards Non-Dominant Linguistic Groups, 1850–1940' in Tomiak (ed.), *Schooling, Educational Policy and Ethnic Identity*, pp. 299–304; other figures are from Miguel Strubell i Trueta, 'Publishing – the Catalunyan Experience' in *Publishing in Minority Languages/Cyhoeddi mewn Ieithoedd Lleiafrifol: Proceedings of a Conference July 29–August 2, 1985* (Aberystwyth, 1986), pp. 79–99.

[40] For Basque inter-war education, see Garrido, 'Spanish Education Policy towards Non-Dominant Linguistic Groups, 1850–1914' in Tomiak (ed.), *Schooling, Educational Policy and Ethnic Identity*, pp. 304–10, and S. G. Payne's helpful book, *Basque Nationalism* (Reno, Nevada, 1975), p. 233.

[41] R. Hémon, *La langue bretonne et ses combats* (La Baule, 1947), pp. 47–51.

[42] Ibid., p. 15.

behalf, supported eventually by more than half the communes of Lower Brittany, was approved by the Educational Commission of the French Parliament in 1937 – a first ever departure from the line spelled out by the French Minister of Education in 1925 that the Breton language must be eliminated in the interest of the linguistic unity of France.

The Breton case is instructive, for its liveliness shows how placid the Welsh-speaking community was between the wars not only in relation to eastern Europe but also to its western counterparts. A comparative perspective suggests the role of ideology should be examined, as a force arising from a social background but capable of representing it selectively. The collapse of Welsh as a social medium over most of the South Wales Coalfield in this period was absorbed with surprisingly little fuss because of the strength of socialism there and the dominance in rural Wales of the O. M. Edwards synthesis of liberal Nonconformity, albeit one lacking his sense of the Anglo-Welsh dimension. Both ideologies were selective, in different directions. Overriding both, perhaps, was the fact that the state framework was little questioned even in the sense in which the French revolution had left discordant currents in France, giving Bretons access to a tradition of anti-centralism and, thereby, a greater role in the international European minority movement than Wales experienced between the wars. A single illustration may be arbitrary, but it is from a man whom Lloyd George called in 1933 the most representative Welshman of the age, the poet preacher H. Elvet Lewis (Elfed): at Niagara on the US side, Elfed felt such 'home sickness' that he determined to cross the bridge for the Canadian bank and tread on British soil ('a sangu ar dir Prydain'), but when his legs gave way on seeing the surging waters below he made his way back to the US, as he records, a 'disappointed patriot'.[43] Although the loyalty of Welsh speakers to a British imperial identity may be explained by their sense of having won a respected place within it, the ease with which most of them reconciled this sense of achievement with the continued subordination of their language still merits enquiry.

Ambiguities of 'revival': Post-war Trends in Western Europe

The events of the Second World War and their aftermath did little initially to increase Welsh awareness of language issues elsewhere, except for the work of some Welsh nationalists on behalf of persecuted Bretons. For one thing, the redrawing of frontiers and flight or expulsion of millions of people drastically reduced the number and size of minorities. The Ukrainian and Belorussian minorities of Poland largely disappeared, as did Germans and Jews throughout eastern Europe. With the change of the Italo-Yugoslav border, too, only the Hungarians of the old flashpoints were left. The whole region now formed part of

---

[43] Emlyn G. Jenkins, *Cofiant Elfed 1860–1953* (Aberystwyth, 1957), pp. 126, 137.

the communist world, largely inaccessible to western gaze, and where problems of language were declared resolved by Soviet-style federal and linguistic principles.

If in eastern Europe language problems were officially solved, in western Europe they were shuffled aside, along with the minority concept which was given part blame for the breakdown of the Versailles settlement. The omission of a reference to minority rights in the United Nations Charter and the 1948 United Nations Declaration of Human Rights was thus not accidental. Attention in the post-war world was focused on the civil rights of individuals rather than collectivities, and the unprecedented growth of living standards and new media which ensued only strengthened the trend to relegate nationality issues to the past.[44] It is interesting that the first minority to place the issue back on the agenda after the war was the one whose politics most closely related to the pre-war minority scene, rather than to the new style west European minority politics which was to emerge. This was the German-speaking minority in south Tirol, who finally in the compromise of 1969 won full rights to use German in administration and school (with state provision for university-level legal training in Innsbruck) but within a framework which made it difficult for them to avoid being bilingual.[45]

The broader change began to occur in the late 1960s. In Spain the dictatorship relaxed its grasp as the antique ideology of the Caudillo was increasingly glossed with the more pragmatic concerns of technocratic modernizers; non-Spanish publication was again tolerated as well as Basque *ikastolas* or private language schools. In Brittany the traumas of 1940–5 receded in a France moving from a society over 30 per cent peasant in the 1950s to the 90 per cent urban France of today. In retrospect the 1960s appear as a turning point in the history of industrial society in Europe, accelerating movement towards the final hegemony of an urban, secular, media-dominated society, relatively affluent compared to the past, culturally more homogeneous but also more conscious of the downside of this homogeneity. Whether it was the upswing which brought hundreds of thousands of Castilian-speaking workers to the Basque country and Catalonia, the opening up of Ireland under Lemass or the downswing of peripherality which threatened traditional employment in Brittany and Wales, all were caught up in a swiftly changing scene, characterized also by wider secondary education and awareness of international civil rights and student movements. What the Czech leader Palacký in an earlier age of change ('Railways and telegraph . . . draw all nations . . . closer together, so that the educated of the globe form almost a single great public') had called 'the law of polarity' ('the greater the nations' contacts the more they see,

---

[44] For more details, with references, see Robin Okey, 'The Minorities Concept: Definitions and Variants' in *Publishing in Minority Languages*, pp. 2–19.

[45] A. C. Alcock, 'Three Case Studies in Minority Protection: South Tyrol, Cyprus, Quebec' in Hepburn (ed.), *Minorities in History*, pp. 189–225 (189–202).

feel and become aware of their natural differences') applied in a new one.[46] Moreover, a century further on and with the antennae of democracy more sensitive, this dialectic of modernization could impact upon smaller groups than the Czechs. Securer than previous generations in their knowledge of the dominant culture, cushioned by modern welfarism and more aware of their rights, members of minority communities lacked many of the old economic and psychological incentives to disavow their ancestral tongue. The sense of new horizons opening up, of access to a new culture with the accompanying energizing excitement, could now work for rather than against the traditional language when the mother tongue of so many Breton language activists was in fact French, as English had been from the beginning for the majority in the Irish language movement. Language movements were literally rejuvenated with an influx of the young.

The emergence of a new generation of language activists in a changed social environment produced ideological shifts in language movements. Most significant no doubt was the mutual rapprochement between minority activists and sections of the European Left, as the latter's retreat from the confident centralism of traditional socialism and the embrace of theories of 'internal colonialism' encouraged the former to seek allies, in a common opposition to the socially corrosive impact of capitalism. This had much appeal in the French regions: in Brittany, where 100,000 people under the age of 30 emigrated between 1954 and 1962 and the traditional small farm was in crisis;[47] in the Midi, where Robert Lafont, the leading spokesman of French regionalism, in 1967 catalogued a history of metropolitan takeover in industry, agriculture and tourism, concentration on extractive industry and lack of an overall view of the region, leading to demographic decline.[48] The social perspective led him to criticize the non-political romanticism of the old Provençal movement of Mistral, urging language activists that the only chance for their languages was to adapt to social change.[49] On the other hand, Jean-Paul Sartre's claim apropos of the Burgos trial of Basque activists in 1970 that to speak Basque was a revolutionary act and that in fighting at the side of the Basques, the Bretons and French people were fighting for themselves against 'abstract man' was nothing if not romantic.[50] The forms that the leftist impulse could take in minority movements therefore varied widely. It could be the neo-Marxist anti-imperialism of ETA or the IRA (both of which split on the degree of socialist priorities), or a Fanonesque emphasis on the mental

---

[46] F. Palacký, *Oesterreichs Staatsidee* (Praha, 1865), p. 13.

[47] For Breton economic problems, see P. Elton Mayo, *The Roots of Identity: Three National Movements in Contemporary European Politics* (London, 1974), pp. 42–58, which also deals with Wales and the Basque country.

[48] R. Lafont, *La révolution régionaliste* (Paris, 1967), chapter 3.

[49] Lafont's foreword to P. Pasquini, *Les Pays des parlers perdus* (La presse de Languedoc, 1994), p. 7.

[50] See Jean-Paul Sartre, 'The Burgos Trials' [translation by Harri Webb], *Planet*, 9 (1971–2), 3–20.

illness induced in Bretons whose culture was ignored by the state.[51] It could be the community-orientated approach which revivified the Irish Gaeltacht in the early 1970s, pressing Dublin to set up an all-Irish radio service, *Raidió na Gaeltachta*, based in Connemara. But language movements everywhere sought to present a progressive face to a changing world and to broaden their support thereby.[52] The growing espousal of social issues by Cymdeithas yr Iaith Gymraeg (the Welsh Language Society) in the 1970s should be put in this context.

The linguistic revival movements which emerged in the late 1960s and 1970s did indeed benefit from a more favourable climate than before in majority communities. Mounting revulsion at the imperialist past, ideas of 'small is beautiful' and revived awareness of the ethnic theme through the black and anti-colonial struggle made lip service, at least, to language rights part of the mental furniture of the liberal-minded. Mitterand could declare himself a supporter of all forms of bilingualism in 1974. Allowing marks in minority languages to count towards the French *baccalauréat* in 1970 – the *Loi Deixonne* had already permitted their being taught but without credit in 1951 – more than quintupled the number of candidates sitting Breton in four years, though the state still would not give teachers of Breton full status.[53] The restoration of Spanish democracy brought autonomy statutes for Catalonia, the Basque country and Galicia (1979–81) which all introduced variations of official bilingualism. In Friesland the decision to introduce Frisian into all primary schools was taken in 1974; by 1986 an estimated two hundred people were in full-time public employ dealing with different aspects of the Frisian language.[54] In Italy twenty-nine bills dealing with minority language rights were introduced into the Italian Parliament between 1975 and 1986.[55] The Irish government, long involved in language revival, of course, but suspected by language activists of tokenism and indifference, was spurred into setting up a co-ordinating *Bord na Gaeilge* (Irish Language Board) (1978) and an economic authority for the Gaeltacht, *Údarás na Gaeltachta*, in 1980. The *Institiúid Teangeolaíochta Éireann* (the Linguistics Institute of Ireland) (1973), with a social

---

[51] P. Carrer et al., *Permanence de la langue bretonne: de la linguistique à la psychoanalyse* (Institut culturel de Bretagne, 1986). F. Morvanneau in *Le breton, la jeunesse d'une vieille langue* (Brest, 1980), p. 73, claimed there were as many psychiatric inmates in Brittany as in the whole of Britain!

[52] For interesting statements of this viewpoint, see D. Fennell, *Beyond Nationalism: The Struggle against Provinciality in the Modern World* (Dublin, 1982), esp. pp. 119–51, by an Irish intellectual active in the Connemara Gaeltacht in this period, and Morvan Lebesque, *Comment peut-on être breton?* (Paris, 1970), part of which appeared in translation as 'Becoming a Breton', *Planet*, 17 (1973), 3–20. See also Dewi Morris Jones, 'Left-Wing Nationalism in Brittany', *Planet*, 7 (1971), 21–8.

[53] Gwegen, *La langue bretonne*, pp. 51, 117.

[54] K. Boelens, *The Frisian Language* (Leeuwarden, n.d.), pp. 31, 52 (education); private information on officials in public employ from R. Walk of the Friesland Provincial Education Council, September 1986. See also K. Zondag (ed.), *Bilingual Education in Friesland* (Franeker, 1982).

[55] G. Vedovato, 'Tutela delle minoranze linguistiche: 29 projeti di legge al parlamento', *Rivista di Studi Politici Internazionali*, 53 (1986), 253–310.

linguistic emphasis, paralleled similar bodies in the Spanish regions. 'Language planning' was an in-phrase everywhere.

There was also solicitude at European level. In 1981 Gaetano Arfè, an Italian member of the European Parliament, introduced a resolution of the Committee on Youth, Culture, Education, Information and Sport in a speech noting the 'trend' in favour of minority rights and rebutting counter-arguments.[56] The resolution called for a charter of minority language rights and was instrumental in the setting up of the European Bureau for Lesser Used Languages with its head-quarters in Dublin. Its concerns interacted with growing academic interest in the issue, manifested in regular conferences, specialist periodicals and fora in which Welsh scholars now played a prominent role. On the basis of a further European Parliament resolution of 1988 endorsing the linguistic heritage of 'specific' regions as part of the European cultural identity, the Department of Welsh at the University of Wales, Cardiff, and the European Bureau for Lesser Used Languages launched an EC-funded project, entitled Citizenship 2000, which concluded: 'by promoting their own culture and traditions, and sharing in the heritage of other communities, the lesser-used language communities of Europe approach the European ideal'.[57]

But how were these enhanced ideological credentials to be translated into effective defence of minority languages at the grass roots, as social vehicles? After all, the very economic pressure and cultural uniformity which earned them intellectual sympathy heightened their actual peril. The problems were twofold. Population movements diluted the proportion of native speakers. A survey in 1983 showed that of the four million inhabitants of the Greater Barcelona area, 43.8 per cent of whom were in-migrants, Catalan was the 'usual language' of only 43.2 per cent, although it was understood 'well' by almost three-quarters.[58] The proportion of Basque speakers had at least halved from the 1930s to the 1970s, to about a fifth, according to the most convincing surveys.[59] In-migration to rural areas played a negative role in Brittany and Friesland; one village survey showed that second-home owners were two and a half times less likely to understand Frisian than permanently resident incomers.[60] Secondly, increasingly out-numbered native speakers were less likely to use the language, and the age curve spiralled downwards. This was most dramatic in Lower Brittany, where a survey in 1974 concluded that Breton was spoken by 80 per cent of those over sixty-five, by a quarter of those aged between fifteen and twenty-four, and by only 5 per

[56] For Arfè's speech, see European Communities, *Official Journal, Annex: Debates of the European Parliament 1981–82*, vol. 275, 225–6.

[57] Medwin Hughes, *Citizenship 2000 – The Lesser Used European Languages: The European Dimension in Education and Teacher Training* (Cardiff, 1993), p. 10.

[58] Strubell i Trueta, 'Publishing – the Catalunyan Experience', p. 86.

[59] For a detailed discussion, see Robert P. Clark, *The Basques: The Franco Years and Beyond* (Reno, 1979), pp. 141–6.

[60] Boelens, *The Frisian Language*, p. 27.

cent of those aged between five and fourteen – altogether 685,250 people (44.3 per cent) of whom just over three-fifths used it daily.[61] But Basque, too, according to a 1975 survey, was spoken by 30 per cent of those over fifty-five and 14 per cent of those between thirty-six and fifty-five, and only 36 per cent of all these spoke more Basque than Spanish.[62]

The response of language activists to crisis was basically education and upgrading of status. It came in two versions, according to the group's ambitions and sense of the possible. At the humbler end were Scots Gaelic proposals in the late 1970s (to apply in Gaelic majority areas) for Gaelic road signs, a Gaelic newspaper and local radio, facilities for use of Gaelic in courts, local drama festivals and schools as the centre of the community culture instead of instruments of estrangement from it.[63] Frisians, Bretons, and in Italy Friulians and Sardinians, and many others were similarly modest. On the other hand Catalans and in the longer term Basques wanted to use their new autonomous powers to create full national languages, taught at every level, with matching media in film, theatre, television and press. Other distinctions influencing policy can be made: according to whether 'national' status was claimed for a minority language or not (Sardinians quarrelled over this); whether it was spoken by a community dominant else-where; or whether or not the non-dominant language was closely akin to the relevant dominant tongue. In the last case several closely related languages had the advantage of having retained high proportions of speakers through diglossia and were much more easily learnt by incomers. But the similarity could work both ways and cause the native tongue to degenerate to the status of dialect in the eyes of its speakers, increasingly a case of younger people understanding their parents' or grandparents' patois while not speaking it themselves. The case of Occitan, understood by some 48 per cent of a large regional population of 12–13 million, of whom only 28 per cent could speak it and only 9 per cent did so habitually,[64] showed the danger Catalan and even more Frisian might face without the all-important enhancement of status. What, then, has happened?

In some ways events have gone further or faster than was anticipated. Gaelic-medium secondary education is a case in point and also the development of Gaelic television provision. Frisian, taken by only some 5 per cent of secondary school pupils in the early 1980s, became compulsory for the first three years in 1993. Galicians and Basques have television channels as well as Catalans. About 4,500 books were published in Catalan in 1991. By 1990, 90 per cent of the population

[61] Gwegen, *La langue bretonne*, p. 56.

[62] Clark, *The Basques*, p. 146.

[63] Iain Crichton Smith, 'Scottish Gaelic', *Planet*, 36 (1977), 17–21. See also, for Gaelic, Kenneth MacKinnon, *Language, Education and Social Policies in a Gaelic Community* (London, 1977).

[64] The European Bureau for Lesser Used Languages, *Mini-guide to the Lesser Used Languages of the European Community* (Baile Átha Cliath, 1993). Unless otherwise indicated, this helpful publication is also the source of figures given in the following two paragraphs.

of Catalonia understood the language.[65] Yet the danger of a language more comprehended than used was not thereby clearly overcome. The several Catalan dailies held less than 10 per cent of the newspaper market in 1986[66] and have not made a basic breakthrough since. Spanish remained the main language of commerce and intercourse between the language groups, and Catalan in many ways still retains the non-dominant position from which Flemish finally escaped in post-war Belgium. Galicians never aimed so high, with Spanish remaining the dominant medium of instruction after the first two years of primary school and only 30 per cent of secondary schools following the law on partial use of Galician as medium at secondary level. The result is a classic case of a language akin to the dominant tongue, which is very widely understood (by 91 per cent) and which with recent encouragement almost as many can speak (84 per cent) but which is habitually used by far fewer (48 per cent). This is, however, a far cry from Occitan. Frisian is not dissimilar but on a smaller scale. Already by the late 1970s it had become as much used orally as Dutch in the provincial and municipal council chambers, but it was little used in written administration; only 11 per cent could write it correctly.[67] The concern for 'correctness' reflected the perceived need for clear differentiation from Dutch norms, but ran the risk which linguistic punctiliousness has incurred in modern Wales, where people become alienated from a mother tongue with which they do not feel comfortable.

Among minority languages sharply different from those of the state, the strongest social position continued to be held by those who had compatriots over the border and were protected by international guarantees or constitutional provisions (South Tirolean Germans, Trieste Slovenes, Danes and Germans on either side of the common border). But internal state constitutional provisions could have a powerful impact, too, as the Basque case shows: £45 million was spent on a scheme to produce Basque-speaking teachers. The numbers of primary school teachers fluent in the language rose from 4.6 per cent in 1977 to 35.6 per cent in 1988.[68] In 1990, between 12 and 15 per cent of children were being taught basically in Basque, and between 18 and 20 per cent were being taught bilingually. It was an exercise in social engineering more carefully calculated than the inter-war programme of the Irish Free State, when Irish was the sole medium for all infant classes regardless of mother tongue. The language movement did not rely only on the state. The daily paper launched in 1990 (circulation 10,000) was privately funded. But it was noted that those educated in Basque did not speak it much daily; there was a high drop-out rate in adult learners' classes (79 per cent in

[65] Aureli Argemi, 'Language Laws – the European Context', *Planet*, 95 (1992), 3–6.

[66] Strubell i Trueta, 'Publishing – the Catalunyan Experience', p. 89.

[67] Boelens, *The Frisian Language*, pp. 46, 23.

[68] Elin Haf Gruffydd Jones and Patrick Carlin, 'Welsh in Gwent Schools: The Basque Example', *Planet*, 82 (1990), 107–8.

Vizcaya, 62 per cent in Guipúzcoa);[69] and there was the suspicion that patriots bought publications which remained unread.[70]

The situation in Celtic lands showed a clearer pattern of decline in traditional areas. An estimate in the 1990s gave only 300,000 Breton speakers,[71] for expanding numbers in private *Diwan* nursery schools and even the state sector were still far too few to make good the passing of the older generation. The revival of interest in Irish in the 1970s had lost much of its buoyancy by the late 1980s, with the failure to reverse the 1971 pattern in the Gaeltacht, when out of 55,000 Irish speakers only about 25,000 were reckoned to be using the language for daily communication.[72] Ironically, the relative success of *Údarás na Gaeltachta* in attracting employment meant an influx of monoglot English technical personnel. In Scotland the Outer Hebrides remained perhaps a securer fortress but, according to the 1991 census, only 68.9 per cent of the population spoke Gaelic (half that for 3–4 year olds) compared with 82.3 per cent in 1961 and the first thirty years of the century when the percentage had been stable at 90–91 per cent. A Gaelic writer summed up the trend in a reference to 'a linguistic group that is, sadly, becoming more of a network than a community'.[73] If so, the networks were substantial. Probably 100,000 people spoke Irish as a mother tongue outside the Gaeltacht; the 20,000 or so 'educated speakers' in one Breton estimate published more journals than had appeared in Breton in the 1930s, though many of the young enthusiasts could hardly communicate with elderly Breton-speaking relatives. A balanced relationship between speakers by tradition and speakers by will, such as the *Bord na Gaeilge* sought to achieve through its Action Plan, proved elusive. Some youthful language enthusiasts could dismiss the Gaeltacht as an irrelevance, Gaeltacht residents were convinced that no Dublin-based Irish organization understood their situation, and *Bord na Gaeilge* reports showed how easily public organizations shrugged aside the targets the Action Plan had assigned them – an indication, perhaps, of what awaits its Welsh equivalent.[74]

One problem with attempts to shore up languages losing their communal centrality was that the communal identities could be expressed in other ways, for

---

[69] Christopher H. Cobb, 'Basque Language Teaching: From Clandestinity to Official Policy', *Journal of Area Studies*, no. 11 (Spring 1985), 9.

[70] Suspicion reported by Ceridwen Lloyd-Morgan, 'Mamá Asunción in Donostia', *Planet*, 54 (1985–6), 24.

[71] The European Bureau for Lesser Used Languages, *Mini-guide*.

[72] Ó Murchú, *The Irish Language*, p. 29. A 1983 survey concluded that 'social norms inhibiting the use of Irish' had strengthened since a previous survey in 1973: Pádraig Ó Riagáin and Mícheál Ó Gliasáin, *The Irish Language in the Republic of Ireland 1983: Preliminary Report of a National Survey* (Dublin, 1984), p. 33.

[73] Nancy McDowell, 'An Occupation for Idealists', *Planet*, 112 (1995), 48.

[74] See Bord na Gaeilge (Irish Language Board), *Plean Gníomhaíochta don Ghaeilge 1983–1986: Tuarascáil 1985–86 / Action Plan for Irish 1983–1986: Report 1985–86* (Dublin, 1986), for example, p. 37 (University College Dublin), p. 39 (Department of Education).

example, Breton pardons, Highland pipes, and Irish music. This was a difficulty of the otherwise valid argument that languages should not be regarded simply as means of communication in a narrow, instrumental sense, but above all as bearers of values. By stressing the symbolic side of the case the way is opened for the use of other symbols, easier to apply than a declining language. Of their nature, too, symbols point away from everyday things, and a language which is made to carry too heavy a symbolic load is in danger of being put away with the Sunday best. Irish and Gaelic language activists had the further difficulty that Irish and Scottish (though not Highland!) identity obviously existed through English too.

But the problems facing minority language groups were not only internal. The famous 'goodwill' they were now so often said to enjoy from majority communities had its limits, as the caustic attacks of British Conservative MEPs on Welsh on the occasion of the Arfè report showed.[75] The pro-minorities' stance of the European Parliament and Court of European Justice was not shared by the EU Council of Ministers, particularly its British and French members. At British behest it ruled that the 'subsidiarity' principle of the Maastricht Treaty was not to apply inside individual states.[76] Some Catalans ascribed the minority status their language continued to have in public life to the imposed bilingualism of the 1978 Spanish constitution, which gave Spanish citizens the duty to know Spanish and the right to use it.[77] The Catalan sociolinguist Francese Vallverdi argued that bilingualism could not work where one language was so much stronger than the other. Influenced by him, Basque educationalists began to refer to the bilingual schools in their mixed language districts as 'zones of conflict' instead of 'zones of contact'.[78]

Was this approach, however, not in conflict with the ideology of a more co-operative, culturally pluralist world with which west European ethnic minorities had staked their modest claim for recognition? It is worth asking if frustration at the constraints on what had been achieved in Catalonia reflected valid fears for linguistic and cultural survival in a longer term or the instinct for power struggle, such as had developed from east European language movements. Certainly the Catalan rumblings sat awkwardly alongside the somewhat bland generalizations of much of modern minorities discourse. This is why a final comment on the west European experience requires an update on eastern Europe, where ethnic issues erupted so dramatically from the late 1980s. These events, too, by removing the Iron Curtain, had opened the way to a closer relationship of the two halves of the Continent.

[75] European Community, *Official Journal, Annex: Debates of the European Parliament 1981–82*, vol. 275, 273–74 (E. Forth, R. J. Cottrell).

[76] Andrew Beale, Roger Geary and Richard Owen, 'False Dawn at Maastricht', *Planet*, 98 (1993), 43–50.

[77] For these fears, see Argemi, 'Language Laws'; idem, 'Ten Years of Autonomy in Catalunya', *Planet*, 82 (1990), 29–35.

[78] Cobb, 'Basque Language Teaching', 9.

Communism and Language: The Failure of Authoritarian Pluralism

Another reason for adducing the east European experience is that many aspects of post-war language policies there resembled what west European language activists were calling for. Was there not, initially at least, tolerance of linguistic diversity, involving increased use of minority languages in schools and administration, in a framework which called for brotherhood between peoples and devised syllabuses teaching them about each other's cultures? In Yugoslavia mother-tongue education up to secondary level was provided in twelve languages and Macedonian was boldly declared to be the distinct language of a distinct Macedonian nation, and rapidly equipped with a standard alphabet, orthography, grammar and university (1945–50).[79] The Hungarian minority in Romania gained Magyar-medium teaching to university level in proportion to their numbers. For the first time a serious attempt was made by the state to provide an infrastructure to preserve the culture and language of the 60,000 Sorbs of East Germany.[80]

Of course, all this took place within a communist system, in which these generous provisions were intended to raise minority speakers from preoccupation with ethnic grievance to a loftier socialist consciousness. In the Soviet Union, the original model, this consciousness was supposed to lead non-Russians to a positive attitude to the Russian language, the natural language of inter-ethnic communication. The tendency of state policy was towards universal bilingualism with increasingly Russian weighting, expressed in the suggestive vocabulary of social scientists (pre-bilingualism, incomplete bilingualism, complete bilingualism, and post-bilingualism) and in terms first heard in the Khrushchev era – the 'drawing together' and 'merger' of nations into a Soviet nationality. Language planning prescribed that non-Russian languages should borrow new terms as far as possible from Russian; no attempt was made to de-Russify the larger towns of the non-Russian republics (there were no Belorussian-medium schools in the Belorussian capital, Minsk); higher research was largely carried on in Russian and the learning of Russian was increasingly encouraged, by such measures as abandoning the principle – dear to minorities – of compulsory mother-tongue education in 1958, introducing Russian earlier in the school, and urging greater use of it in *Komsomol* meetings and so on.[81] By 1979, 81.9 per cent of Soviet citizens could speak

---

[79] For the pre-history of literary Macedonian, see V. A. Friedman, 'The Macedonian Language and Nationalism in the 19th and Early 20th Centuries', *Macedonian Review*, 16 (1986), 280–92, and for communist attitudes, see M. Apostolski, 'Afirmacija makedonskog jezika u NOR i revoluciji', *Jugoslovenski istorijski časopis*, 21 (1986), 145–60.

[80] See P. Shoup, *Communism and the Yugoslav National Question* (Columbia, 1968); Z. M. Szaz, 'Contemporary Educational Policies in Transylvania', *East European Quarterly*, 11, 493–501 (494f.); Gerald Stone, *The Smallest Slavonic Nation: The Sorbs of Lusatia* (London, 1972), pp. 161–85.

[81] The above is mainly based on Kirkwood, '*Glasnost*, "The National Question" and Soviet Language Policy'.

Russian, which meant that well over half of non-Russians were now bilingual, with increasing numbers, indeed, not knowing their mother tongue – though often the latter were living outside their homeland, as Welsh-speaking families might lose their language in London.

We need not assume that this situation was universally unacceptable, particularly among members of small language groups and among non-Russian Slavs. The Chechens who appear on our screens do not seem to resent the Russian they use to communicate to a wider audience. But the Soviet model had two defects. Ideologically, Soviet policy made the arbitrary assumption that national consciousness was a lesser thing than socialist consciousness, and could be frozen at a certain level, beyond which only perverted 'nationalists' could wish for more. A whole *samizdat* literature of the late 1960s showed how some Ukrainian intellectuals resented the bounds imposed on the higher development and use of their language. Secondly, and relatedly, Soviet policy froze the inherited situation at the social level so that in Ukraine and Belorussia, for example, Russian predominated in the larger towns and the native tongue only in smaller ones and in the countryside. Human nature being what it is, this perpetuated negative social stereotyping of non-Russian Slavs by Russians, which helped to plant a slow fuse in the Soviet body politic.[82]

A shorter fuse existed in the Baltic republics, whose native languages had lost status under Soviet rule. In Latvia and Estonia especially, in-migration of Russian speakers threatened to swamp the native culture. Estonians fell from 88 per cent to 61.5 per cent of the population; Latvians from 75.5 per cent to 52 per cent.[83] By 1982, 41 per cent of Latvians were living in parts of their country where they were in a minority, mainly the overwhelmingly Russian-speaking larger towns. In 1989 only 17 per cent of Latvians opened a conversation with a stranger in their own language – and 96 per cent of Russians. While 65.7 per cent of Latvians spoke Russian by the 1989 census, only 21.1 per cent of Russians knew Latvian. Linguistic assimilation of other nationalities in the republic was 6 to 1 in favour of Russian, not Latvian. Russians on average were professionally better qualified than Latvians.[84] Some of these indices recall Wales.

Yet there was also a rather different side to the situation. Latvian was still the native language of 97.8 per cent of Latvians in 1979 and more Russians in Estonia habitually spoke Estonian than Estonians spoke Russian.[85] Knowledge of Russian was negligible among children aged 10 and under. Cultural self-sufficiency remained great. Although the great bulk of Estonians had some contact with

---

[82] For an impassioned dissident presentation from Ukraine, see I. Dzyuba, *Internationalism or Russification* (New York, 1974), esp. pp. 149–65.

[83] Anatol Lieven, *The Baltic Revolution: Estonia, Latvia, Lithuania and the Path to Independence* (2nd ed., New Haven, London, 1994), pp. 433–4. Figures for 1939 (Estonia 1934) and 1989.

[84] Figures from J. Dreifelds, *Latvia in Transition* (London, 1996), pp. 148, 157.

[85] Graham Smith (ed.), *The Nationalities Question in the Soviet Union* (London, 1990), p. 61; Raun, *Estonia*, p. 203.

Russians in work and study, three-quarters of them (in 1973) never read a novel in Russian and three-fifths never looked at a Russian newspaper. Seventy-one per cent of Estonians had no domestic contact whatever with Russians, but social apartheid was far from complete. Fifteen per cent of Estonian families consisted of mixed marriages and (in 1993) 32 per cent of Latvian. The remarkable characteristic of these marriages, however, was that the large majority of offspring (71 per cent) considered themselves Latvian, which in east European context very largely meant having Latvian as the first language. Hence, even in a situation of Russian language public dominance and overall figures showing a declining proportion of Latvian speakers, in the 1980s Latvian was actually gaining ground among the young. The percentage of Latvian speakers in the under 20 age group was higher than their percentage in the population as a whole.[86] This example of a community's power of assimilation on its native patch may guard against undue pessimism about inevitable gravitation to the ostensibly dominant culture. Very low figures for Welsh language maintenance in the early 1950s among the children of mixed marriages show the social Achilles heel of the Welsh language hitherto.[87]

The Soviet state ideology was strong enough to maintain its balance of linguistic pluralism and Russian language hegemony to the end. Elsewhere in the communist block the balance broke down, either in the eclipse of real language pluralism (Romania and Bulgaria) or in the loss of control by the centre, as in Yugoslavia. Massive Romanian in-migration into Transylvania had also over-turned what had remained Hungarian urban majorities between the wars (Cluj, Arad, Timişoara) and reduced the 90 per cent Hungarian level in the Hungarian heartland to around 50 per cent in its chief centre Tirgu Mureş. The result was not assimilation, however, but national and cultural stand-off between the two communities. Meanwhile, in Yugoslavia the bold decision to abandon support for cultural hegemony of local Serbs after riots in the Albanian majority province of Kosovo in 1968 had failed. Without adequate economic prospects, the scores of thousands of graduates of the programme of Albanian-language scholarization expressed their discontent through an ethnic agenda of autonomy which provoked a fateful Serbian backlash.[88] In Slovenia, too, the almost total Slovene monolingualism made all the more galling the use of Serbo-Croat in a Ljubljana

[86] Estonian figures from Francis Knowles, 'Language Planning in the Soviet Baltic Republics: An Analysis of Demographic and Sociological Trends' in Kirkman (ed.), *Language Planning in the Soviet Union*, pp. 161, 163; Latvian mixed marriage figures from Dreifelds, *Latvia*, pp. 156, 163.

[87] See Ministry of Education, Central Advisory Council for Education (Wales), *The Place of Welsh and English in the Schools of Wales* (London, 1953), p. 38. (6 per cent of children were returned as first-language Welsh speakers in families where only the father spoke Welsh; 11 per cent of children were returned as first-language Welsh speakers in families where only the mother spoke Welsh.)

[88] For problems, see P. Bodor, 'A Minority under Attack: The Hungarians of Transylvania', *The New Hungarian Quarterly* (1989), 1–35, esp. 9, 16–18, 29–31; Mark Baskin, 'Crisis in Kosovo', *Problems of Communism*, XXXII, no. 2 (1983), 61–74.

military court to try young Slovenes for criticizing the Yugoslav People's Army in 1988.

Language issues, of course, played only a small part, overall, in the upheavals of 1989 and after. Language problems following the fall of communism have been greatest concerning Hungarian minorities in Romania and Slovakia and Russian minorities in the Baltic states. The language law of newly independent Slovakia ignores the 12 per cent Hungarian minority's call for official bilingualism in Hungarian-speaking areas. Better known are the constitutional provisions of Estonia and Latvia linking citizenship to proof of proficiency in the national language. They have received international criticism but should be seen, perhaps, in the light of the bleak conclusion – for small nations – of a British expert on Soviet language questions published in the last year of the Soviet Union:

> The attempts on the part of the republics to enhance the status of their language by granting it official status are at once costly, divisive and doomed to failure so long as they remain part of the Soviet Union . . . They are doomed, because demographic patterns, and consequently patterns of linguistic behaviour, are set for many years to come. Even under the most propitious of circumstances it would take several generations to produce a radical reversal in the current trend.[89]

The discrimination against Russian speakers is not in itself a rejection of cultural pluralism but an attempt to undo the inherited weighting of that pluralism against the native majority, whereby Balts cannot look to linguistic kinship in aiding Russians to pick up their language, as can Catalans. Although nearly 100,000 non-Latvians have left Latvia since 1989, the Latvian proportion in Riga has risen only marginally, from 36.5 per cent to 37.7 per cent. But the whole controversy has shown the way in which language issues in east and west Europe stand in closer relation to each other than after 1918 and are being considered in relation to the same set of ground rules. This is not surprising in view of the aspiration of east Europeans to EU and NATO membership. Slovakia's rulers have already been told that an important factor in judging their case will be their minority policies.

Conclusion

This chapter began by pointing out the ideological dimension to the social history of European minority languages in the twentieth century. Already by its outset their fate had been politicized in the broadest sense in that it had become bound up with the shift from absolutist or oligarchic, largely rural and illiterate polities, towards more 'modern' norms characterized by democratization and social mobilization. It

---

[89] Kirkwood, 'Glasnost, "The National Question" and Soviet Language Policy', 77.

was argued that by 1918 a pattern had emerged whereby the non-dominant languages of eastern Europe had become instruments of this process, whereas those in the west had not. The reason was to be sought in the inter-relationship between social, political and ideological factors, which made ideas of linguistic revival, linked to political nationalism, come to appear relevant in eastern Europe to perspectives of change and development. The result was the collapse of the region's empires and the creation of many small nation states, each with its official national language, but with internationally monitored 'minority rights', mainly linguistic, for those of the former dominant nations who remained. The non-dominant languages of western Europe, not fitting into either category and spoken mainly by rural, bilingual populations, were all but below public perception.

The above is not quite true, of course, of inter-war Flemish, Irish, and Catalan, but they themselves were all so different that a general sense of smaller west European languages could hardly exist. After the Second World War the language question initially took a back seat. East European small nations vanished behind the Iron Curtain, where their language problems were declared solved by the Soviet system. The unenviable fate of eastern Europe before and during the Second World War, in which language disputes had played a role, put a cloud over the whole issue to a post-war generation which thought ethnic difference was being eroded by a fast-changing world.

Hence the interest that attaches to the ethno-linguistic revival of the last thirty years. To a purely socio-economic view of modernity it must remain mysterious, since the processes which had begun marginalizing small western languages in the nineteenth century only intensified. But 'modernization' has been political as well as economic, and its political driving force has been democratization, at least in the sense of the broadening of the political process to include groups previously unheard or ignored. Western language groups were able to link in to this process and to benefit from disillusionment with modern homogenizing norms and the weakening of the traditional 'nation states' to project an ideology more plausible to themselves and to an extent to others than before, giving themselves a place in a vision of the future just as east European nationalities had succeeded in doing a century before. No doubt the pluralist vision was highly generalized, as is shown by the relative sang-froid with which its original quite heavy socialist motifs were toned down as socialism waned. It faced internal and external dangers. The external danger came from the tendency of governments, while making far more concessions on matters like education and broadcasting than before, to do so from a standpoint of individual rights ultimately compatible with centralism: they still did not recognize the rights of a community to stamp its culture on a particular ancestral territory, along the lines of Professor J. R. Jones's 'interpenetration of the land of Wales and the Welsh language' ('cydymdreiddiad tir Cymru â'r iaith Gymraeg').[90] The internal danger came from

[90] J. R. Jones, *Gwaedd yng Nghymru* (Pontypridd, 1970), pp. 63ff.

the social weakness of most west European language communities, their declining hold on the traditional land, which undermined their claim to collective rights in a territory. Even where those rights were conceded, as in the autonomy statutes in Spain recognizing, for example, Catalan, as the language 'proper' to the province and co-official with Spanish, some Catalans have argued that having to co-exist in its own land with a more powerful rival risks nullifying all apparent language gains.

These doubts about official bilingualism, taken in context with the recent reaffirmation by small east European nations of unfettered language sovereignty, could be read sceptically as proof of the emptiness of recent west European thinking on minority languages in modern society. Language as the organ of a society is a jealous god which will brook no other, some might argue; it either lives to assert its sway over a sovereign nation or it dies. The verdict was clear by 1918. Bilingualism and cultural pluralism are only slogans that weak communities advocate until they are strong enough to emerge from their chrysalis and fly alone. No doubt many east European nationalists think like this and some west European ones might find it beguiling, for obvious psychological reasons. It does not seem necessary to follow them or to drive up the historic differences between the two halves of the Continent to incommunicable impasse. The experience of east Europeans shows the importance of power for an ethnic group and its language. But the absolutization of power, the zero-sum approach to ethnic relations in situations which were in fact multilingual has brought them much harm. There are degrees of power, as Spanish and Italian constitutional legislators have shown. The willingness to recognize cultural co-sovereignties in Spain is a remarkable contribution from the west European experience. It implies a different relationship between political power, ideology and language community: one in which democracy is more sensitively conceived than as a matter of individual rights alone, or as the rule of ethnic majorities who may or may not choose to offer 'minority rights' to others. In so far as the energies evident in non-dominant language societies in the last generation have had this source, they have surely not been misdirected. However, the ground covered in this chapter suggests also a further conclusion: that small language societies should remember the power of voluntary association at grass roots and not be too intimidated by global socio-economic processes on the one hand or be too hopeful of state patronage on the other.

21

Restoring the Language

COLIN H. WILLIAMS*

LANGUAGE is a powerful and mystical expression of humanity. It is far more than a communication system and a bridge for intercultural understanding. It can also be an instrument of subjugation and the marker by which subservient groups are identified and controlled. The Welsh language movement in the twentieth century became engaged in a struggle to overcome the effects of centuries of discrimination and hostility at the hands of a powerful, ethnically-differentiated state oligarchy. The movement's watchwords were survival, recognition and equality. This chapter presents key elements of this struggle in terms of a model of language survival and revitalization. Where relevant a comparative, international perspective will be introduced, for although salient features of the Welsh language movement are unique they are mediated through an international context which has profound implications for political aims and public policy.

The model of language survival may be illustrated in terms of five foci of social pressure for language change. They are:

Idealism: the construction of a vision of a fully rehabilitated 'threatened' language; this is the issue of making language and nation coterminous.

Protest: mobilizing sections of the population to agitate for a social reform/ revolution in the promotion of the lesser-used language.

Legitimacy: securing a generalized acceptance of the normalcy of exercising language rights in selected domains.

Institutionalization: ensuring that the language is represented in key strategic agencies of the state, i.e. the law, education, and public administration.

Normalization: extending the use of the language into the optimum range of social situations as a normal medium of communication in, for example, the private sector, entertainment, sport and the media.

* I am grateful to my colleagues, Mr Dylan Foster Evans, Dr E. Wyn James, Professor Glyn Jones and Ms Maite Puigdevall i Serralvo, for their constructive criticism of this chapter.

Idealism

Idealism refers to the construction of a vision of a fully rehabilitated 'threatened' language which seeks to make language and nation coterminous. It derives from the intelligentsia's attempt to impose on the popular consciousness prescriptive cultural models regarding how Wales should be interpreted and ruled. The overriding character of this discourse is its indebtedness to Welsh literature and history.[1] Idealist arguments are presented in moralistic and historical terms, with little detailed consideration given to substantive issues relating to public administration or economic policy. Deliverance rather than governance was the watchword of the nationalist intelligentsia.

The early decades of the twentieth century witnessed a plethora of social movements which were concerned that Welsh was being displaced by English as the natural medium of communication for a significant proportion of the native population. They identified intrusive capitalism, together with the burgeoning state and its attendant Anglicized culture, as the key threats to the survival of an autonomous and authentic pattern of Welsh existence. The principal agency for the transmission of the English language was the educational system. English was legislated as the official language of education in state schools under the Education Act of 1870 and subsequent acts, e.g. the Welsh Intermediate Education Act of 1889, which introduced a greater awareness of English values, culture and employment prospects and gave a powerful institutional fillip to the process of Anglicization. As a consequence of industrialization and modernization, the inhabitants of Wales, rural and urban alike, were exposed to overriding influences which sought to downgrade indigenous regional cultures and identification, and exalt the culture of the dominant state core and its value system. How the bulk of the population welcomed this 'liberation' from traditionalism and conservatism is best evidenced by the wholesale generational language shift during the period 1914–45.[2] The wider experience of state-identification made the acquisition of English a compelling necessity and the key to participation in the burgeoning British-influenced world economy.

The foundations of the language movement were laid during the period c.1890–c.1945, although two quite distinct phases were involved. In the first, 1890–1914, Cymru Fydd (Young Wales), and elements of the Liberal Party sought to secure the national recognition of Wales. In the second period, c.1921–39, dissenting intellectuals and, more particularly, Plaid Genedlaethol Cymru (the Welsh Nationalist Party) sought to anchor the fate of the language to

---

[1] For an account of the relationship between iconography and national literature, see R. M. Jones, *Ysbryd y Cwlwm: Delwedd y Genedl yn ein Llenyddiaeth* (Caerdydd, 1998).

[2] See W. T. R. Pryce and Colin H. Williams, 'Sources and Methods in the Study of Language Areas: A Case Study of Wales' in Colin H. Williams (ed.), *Language in Geographic Context* (Clevedon, 1988), pp. 167–237.

the establishment of an independent nation state. Although such ambitions always over-reached the achievement, the campaign for recognition of the separate, national character of Wales was realized in the establishment of a range of national institutions and cultural organizations. The dominant consideration, as reflected within Liberal Nonconformity, was a desire for national self-respect. Linguistic, religious and political grievances were reformulated as legitimate elements in the national struggle. The Liberal Party became a vehicle both for the promotion of cultural nationalism and for the hegemony of a Nonconformist-influenced moral and social order. At the local level, Liberalism's strident message of social reform and democratic representation was spread through the Free Church/ Nonconformist chapel system which pervaded almost every settlement. The steady growth of the Nonconformist denominations, punctuated by occasional upsurges such the religious revival of 1904–5, not only made Wales an outwardly more Christian society than hitherto but also influenced most aspects of public behaviour and private life.[3]

Culture, history and education were constant reference points for intellectual leaders: the Revd Michael D. Jones initiated a small exodus to Patagonia in 1865 to establish a Welsh migrant community known as *Y Wladfa*; Robert Ambrose Jones (Emrys ap Iwan), the first minister of religion to appear before a court of law and insist on the primacy of Welsh in legal proceedings; Dan Isaac Davies, the HMI who advocated greater use of Welsh-medium education; Thomas Gee, the publisher of the ambitious multi-volume encyclopaedia, *Y Gwyddoniadur*, and the advocate of mass circulation periodicals in Welsh; O. M. Edwards, the university teacher, writer, publisher and first Chief Inspector for Schools in Wales, who sought to establish a more tolerant approach to bilingualism by attacking the injustice associated with the Welsh Not within the school system; and his son, Sir Ifan ab Owen Edwards, who established Urdd Gobaith Cymru (the Welsh League of Youth) in 1922, which became the largest youth movement in Wales.

This collective search for identity, based on concepts of struggle, recognition and legitimacy, was also realized in national institutions, especially the development of the Welsh university and college sector, the disestablishment of the Church of England to become the Church in Wales in 1920, the formation of the Welsh Nationalist Party at Pwllheli in 1925, the 'Tân yn Llŷn' episode in September 1936 when three leading nationalists set fire to the RAF bombing school at Penyberth in the Llŷn peninsula, the presentation of a language petition to Parliament in 1941, and the Welsh Courts Act of 1942, which eradicated the 'language clause' in the original Act of Union of 1536 and gave limited statutory legitimacy to the use of Welsh in the courts of Wales.

---

[3] On religious influences, see R. Tudur Jones, *Ffydd ac Argyfwng Cenedl: Cristionogaeth a Diwylliant yng Nghymru 1890–1914* (2 vols., Abertawe, 1981–2); idem, *Yr Undeb: Hanes Undeb yr Annibynwyr Cymraeg, 1872–1972* (Abertawe, 1975).

Welsh cultural nationalism was profoundly influenced by Nonconformist principles, yet not exclusively so, for at a critical early juncture nationalism's moral philosophy was deeply imbued by the Catholicism of several of its original leaders. In comparison with Catholic Ireland between 1880 and 1921, Wales did not succumb to the power of the gun in the name of national freedom, despite several attempts to use the Irish example as an inspiration.[4] Both the constitutional and physical force traditions contributed to the ideology that in order to be reborn the Irish nation had to demand the sacrifice of martyrs for the cause. This is a common thread in the emphasis of romantic nationalism on land, language, race, a common past, and the necessity for open conflict in the struggle against oppressors. There was nothing inimical to the use of legitimate violence in Christian thought – witness the role of the Nonconformist press and leaders at the outbreak of the First World War in justifying conscription and in encouraging a disproportionate number of Welshmen to serve in Flanders. In contradistinction to most other political movements in the second phase of 1921–39, pacifism and non-violent resistance characterized Welsh nationalism.[5] It was derived in large part from the articulation of a popular belief in communal-orientated consensus politics as advocated by the two most influential presidents of the Welsh Nationalist Party, Saunders Lewis (leader from 1926 to 1939), who advocated a combination of constitutional and unconstitutional direct action, and Gwynfor Evans (leader from 1945 to 1981), a committed pacifist who moved the Party in the direction of total opposition to violence and war as a means of achieving self-government.[6]

The dominant concerns of the original nationalists were the Welsh language, national identity and Christianity. Thus the three aims of the Welsh Nationalist

---

[4] Maurice Goldring, *Pleasant the Scholar's Life: Irish Intellectuals and the Construction of the Nation State* (London, 1993); see also Terence Brown, *Ireland: A Social and Cultural History, 1922–1985* (London, 1985); and Pádraig Ó Riagáin, *Language Policy and Social Reproduction, Ireland 1893–1993* (Oxford, 1997), esp. pp. 8–15. Individual groups, notably Byddin yr Iaith (the Language Army) and Y Mudiad Cymreig (the Welsh Movement), which subsequently merged with the Welsh Nationalist Party, were more heavily influenced by the Irish direct-action methods.

[5] The exception to this pattern was the calculated symbolic use of destruction of state property in the burning of the bombing school at Penyberth. See D. Hywel Davies, *The Welsh Nationalist Party 1925–1945: A Call to Nationhood* (Cardiff, 1983), pp. 154–66.

[6] At the Welsh Nationalist Party conference held at Swansea in 1938, an overwhelming majority adopted the motion put forward by Gwynfor Evans that 'as a Party we completely reject war as a means of achieving self-government' ('fod y Blaid Genedlaethol yn ymwrthod â rhyfel fel dull i ennill hunan-lywodraeth a rhyddid i Gymru'). In contrast, Saunders Lewis had been disappointed by the performance of the Party since the bombing school incident and took consolation from the pacifist supporters' recognition of the tactical utility of adopting civil disobedience on the Gandhian pattern. In arguing that sacrifice and suffering should characterize the struggle ahead, he anticipated the actions of the language movement some thirty years hence when he asserted that: 'One path alone leads to the gateway of the Welsh parliament. That path runs directly through the prisons of England' ('Un llwybr yn unig sydd yn arwain i borth y senedd Gymreig. Y mae'r llwybr hwnnw yn rhedeg yn union drwy garcharau Lloegr'), *Y Ddraig Goch*, XII, no. 9 (1938), 5, 8. For a detailed discussion of the conference, see Davies, *The Welsh Nationalist Party*, pp. 167–8.

Party in 1925 were all related to the promotion of Welsh.[7] It was only after 1932 that Party policy adopted self-government as a means of achieving national self-respect and some semblance of autonomy.

Although preoccupied with questions of language defence, the nationalist intelligentsia were well aware of, and contributed in part to, the dominant European paradigms which focused on liberalism with its insistence on individual freedom and mutual tolerance as a means of overcoming the lack of social justice and on socialism with its materialistic explanation of inequality.[8] Control of the state apparatus in order to make it more accountable and more reformist was the principal goal. But Welsh nationalists sought a redefinition of the evolving European order in moral not materialistic terms. While the leadership, in the main, turned to the Celtic realm for moral inspiration and to post-civil war Ireland as an example of a successful national struggle, Saunders Lewis sought his authenticity in the context of a European, Catholic and Latin civilization.[9] Lewis believed medieval Europe possessed a unity of spirit and of law which protected small nations because diversity could best be accommodated within a universal European civilization. In his seminal lecture delivered in 1926, 'Egwyddorion Cenedlaetholdeb' (The Principles of Nationalism),[10] he outlined his conception of Welsh national history, which was to be influential in subsequent justification both of the language struggle and Party strategy. He argued, perhaps ironically, that it was nationalism which had destroyed the civilization of small countries. In medieval Europe individual cultures were secured because their rulers deferred to a higher authority, for 'every nation and every king recognized that there was an authority higher than state authority, that there was a law higher than the king's law, and that there was a court to which appeal could be made from the State courts. That authority was the moral authority, the authority of Christianity. The

---

[7] The original aim of the Welsh Nationalist Party was 'to keep Wales Welsh-speaking. That is, to include (a) making the Welsh language the only official language of Wales and thus a language required for all local authority transactions and mandatory for every official and servant of every local authority in Wales, (b) making the Welsh language a medium of education in Wales from the elementary school through to the univeristy'. Quoted in Alan Butt Philip, *The Welsh Question: Nationalism in Welsh Politics 1945–1970* (Cardiff, 1975), p. 14; see also Davies, *The Welsh Nationalist Party*, p. 41.

[8] Particularly significant in this respect was the work of D. J. Davies, whose admiration for Scandinavian social credit policies, economic co-operation and decentralization of power were reflected in a series of publications. See D. J. Davies, *The Economics of Welsh Self-Government* (Caernarfon, 1931); idem and Noëlle Davies, *Can Wales Afford Self-Government?* (Caernarfon, 1939). For a critique of the class versus nationalist appeals, see John Davies, *The Green and the Red: Nationalism and Ideology in 20th Century Wales* (Aberystwyth, 1980).

[9] In this respect there are many parallels to be explored between idealists such as Saunders Lewis and Sabino de Arana, Valentí Almirall, Yann Fouéré, E. MacNeill and Éamon de Valera.

[10] 'Egwyddorion Cenedlaetholdeb' (The Principles of Nationalism) was delivered at the Welsh Nationalist Party's first summer school held at Machynlleth in 1926. For the development of Saunders Lewis's ideas, see the following collections of his works: Saunders Lewis, *Canlyn Arthur: Ysgrifau Gwleidyddol* (Aberystwyth, 1938); idem, *Ati, Wŷr Ifainc* (Caerdydd, 1986).

Christian Church was sovereign in Europe, and Church law was the only final law'.[11] When state nationalism emerged in the sixteenth century it ushered in an era of state-building and tolled the death knell of smaller national-regional cultures, for state uniformity could not tolerate cultural differentiation and ethno-linguistic challenges to its hegemony. Having usurped the universal moral Christian order, state authority inaugurated a programme of state-nation con-gruence, cloaking the systematic extirpation of minorities under a veil of demo-cratic rhetoric which in time emphasized the principles of liberty and equality, if not always brotherhood, under the aegis of the state. In order that his compatriots deliver themselves from the false consciousness of British state nationalism and imperialism he advocated that they rediscover this pre-existent nationalism.

Nationalism was not an end in itself, but a necessary means by which Welsh culture would be nurtured within its own political institutions. The keystone of this culture was the promotion of the Welsh language, an issue which came to be central to the activities of the Welsh Nationalist Party (later Plaid Cymru) between 1925 and 1974. Saunders Lewis justified the selection of Welsh as the critical battleground for political action because its survival, despite centuries of state-inspired Anglicization, was proof that the Welsh had kept faith with traditional European values. At a time when Britain was acutely conscious of its role in maintaining a world empire, and of nurturing trans-Atlantic connections by virtue of its 'special relationship' with the emerging superpower of the United States of America, Lewis sought to remind the public that there was a pre-existent Europeanness to be found in the history of these isles. Wales should 'demand a seat in the League of Nations, so that she may act as Europe's interpreter in Britain, and as a link to bind England and the Empire to Christendom and to the League itself'.[12] Exaggerated though Lewis's claims were about the importance of the relationship between Wales and Europe, he did at least seek to challenge the Welsh into choosing between the Empire and the League of Nations. In this redirection of Welsh politics away from the Empire and towards contemporary Europe, Lewis set the tone for a long-standing debate within nationalism, the strains of which echoed until his death in 1985. It concerned his drawing upon Catholic Europe for inspiration and his personal advocacy of social and political policy, for he had been converted and received into the Roman Catholic Church in 1932. However, an idiosyncratic admixture of his aesthetic and ascetic strains, and his principled objection to crude materialism as revealed in his opposition to the slogan 'Bread before Beauty', did not endear itself to a Welsh audience mired in a period of acute economic depression and enamoured of socialism. Ostensibly

---

[11] Saunders Lewis, *Egwyddorion Cenedlaetholdeb / Principles of Nationalism* (Plaid Cymru, 1975), p. 3. For a variant on the same theme, see also Bobi Jones, *Crist a Chenedlaetholdeb* (Pen-y-bont ar Ogwr, 1994).

[12] Quoted in Dafydd Glyn Jones, 'His Politics' in Alun R. Jones and Gwyn Thomas (eds.), *Presenting Saunders Lewis* (Cardiff, 1973), p. 33.

radical, dissenting and Nonconformist, the Welsh populace did not approve of Lewis's political convictions and personal style. As a result, the Welsh Nationalist Party was criticized for being élitist, intellectual, and unpatriotic because leading members appeared to support quasi-Fascist movements in Europe.[13]

These opposing traditions are summarized in the exchange which took place between W. J. Gruffydd and Saunders Lewis in the pages of *Y Llenor* in 1927. In responding to criticism of the rise of a 'Neo-Catholic Movement' in Wales, Lewis distanced himself from other nationalists, such as W. Ambrose Bebb, who were charged with admiring the ideas of Barrès and Maurras and of advocating the adoption in Wales of the ideas trumpeted by *L'Action Française*. He repudiated the journal's insistence on an exclusive, racist definition of European unity, and offered instead four Catholic thinkers whose ideas were worthy of emulation: the poet and dramatist, Claudel; the novelist, Mauriac; the historian of philosophy, Etienne Gilson; and the literary critic, Jacques Rivière.[14] He also repudiated the modernist camp of Christian thought with its emphasis on 'sentimental Christianity' and the 'idea of Christ as a humanitarian visionary'. He would brook no watering down of the mystery of Godliness, nor of the conviction that faith was beyond reason. W. J. Gruffydd's reply has been described as 'an eloquent statement of that radical liberal individualism which had been Wales's main political tradition in the second half of the nineteenth century'.[15] To describe the clash as one between a conservative and a modernist, or, as Gruffydd dubbed it, between Reaction and Revolt, is to oversimplify the issues. However, at the root of the debate lay a profound difference between idealism and pragmatism, in spiritual as well as in socio-political affairs. Whereas Lewis's ideas were based on a pristine conception of what Wales could and should be, Gruffydd portrayed Wales as it was and sought to transform the country into a co-equal partner within the British state, wherein Welsh distinctiveness might be secured.

Comparisons may be drawn with idealist interpretations which inspired other ethno-linguistic movements. The closest parallel is Sabino de Arana's articulation of Basque nationalism, summarized in the six principles of his seminal work *Bizkaia por su independencia*, published in 1892. The first principle was the integrity of the Church. In comparison with the paramount role of the Catholic religion,

---

[13] For a discussion of these allegations, see Davies, *The Welsh Nationalist Party*, pp. 109–16. A re-examination of the relationship between Fascism, anti-Semitism and the views of Saunders Lewis and his colleagues is presented in Jones, *Ysbryd y Cwlwm*, pp. 324–35; Richard Wyn Jones, 'Saunders Lewis a'r Blaid Genedlaethol' in Geraint H. Jenkins (ed.), *Cof Cenedl XIV: Ysgrifau ar Hanes Cymru* (Llandysul, 1999), pp. 163–92.

[14] Jones, 'His Politics', p. 45.

[15] Ibid.

political freedom came an important (but unequivocal) second.[16] Then came the union of all Basques. Arana's case for the racial and linguistic character of nationalism was predicated on the idea that the Basque nation was coterminous with the Basque culture. This necessitated an appeal to all Basque provinces, Vizcaya, Guipúzcoa, Álava and Navarra in Spain, together with Labourd, Basse Navarre and Soule in France, summarized in the slogan *Zazpiak Bat* (Out of Seven, One). Thirdly, there was the racial justification of nationalism, which reflected nineteenth-century views on national identity. Fourthly, Arana relied heavily on the linguistic uniqueness of the Basques, since race was defined by language. Fifthly, the struggle for separation should be non-violent and adhere to parliamentary tactics if possible. In the face of a repressive regime, Basques should not engage in open rebellion, but continue the slow, steady pressure of cultural resistance, wearing away the chains of tyranny in the knowledge that moral righteousness and cultural continuity would surely win the day.[17] Sixthly, Arana insisted on the inclusive nature of Basque political organization, for he acknowledged that there was no blueprint concerning how to govern once self-government and language revival had been secured.

In similar vein the Catalan modernizer Valentí Almirall (1841–1904) sought to politicize Catalan culture through his work on linguistic normalization which involved the creation of the first Catalan newspaper, *Diari Catala* (est.1879), the organization of the First Catalanist Congress (1880), the drafting of a document in defence of Catalan law, and the foundation of the political organization, the Centre Catala (1882). In contrast to Wales, the Catalan movement was a comprehensive fusion of four social factions: cultural revivalists, progressive federalists, anti-Bourbon traditionalists and, critically, the industrial bourgeoisie. The linguistic definition of Catalan nationhood was central to the defence of Catalan interests, and when the Catalan language was subsequently attacked both by the dictatorship of General Miguel Promo de Rivera (1923–30) and by General Francisco Franco its significance increased. Cultural nationalism became the overarching ideology within which indigenous political fragmentation could be contained.

---

[16] An influential statement of Basque nationalist philosophy published in 1906, *Ami Vasco*, put it this way: 'Between seeing Euskadi in full exercise of its rights, but separated from Christ, and seeing her as in 1901 [i.e. as an integral part of Spain] but faithful to Christ, the Basque Nationalist Party would opt for the second.' Quoted in Maximiano García Venero, *Historia del Nacionalismo Vasco*, Editora Nacional (Madrid, 1969), p. 34. For elaboration, see Robert P. Clark, *The Basques: The Franco Years and Beyond* (Reno, 1979), pp. 40–9.

[17] It also required Arana to invent the name *Euskadi* to describe the Basque country. In an interpretation which had its direct parallels in Wales, Sabino argued that the true value of culture was its ability to survive the centuries and to defeat its antagonists by simply outliving them. By the 1960s, however, many had become impatient with this prescription and encouraged the direct-action methods of *Euskadi Ta Askatasuna* (ETA). See Clark, *The Basques*, pp. 153–87.

The differing impact of cultural nationalism on Catalonia and the Basque country can be explained by reference to the role of the nationalist intelligentsia.[18] In Catalonia the intelligentsia could mobilize popular support through the manipulation of language and symbols of identity, whereas in the Basque country such symbols were lacking. When political nationalism was still quiescent, the Catalan youth were drawn into the struggle for cultural regeneration. In the Basque case, the absence of a tradition of cultural nationalism resulted in political fragmentation and the alienation of Basque youth into violent forms of struggle. The Catalan leadership was able to convince its constituents that the language could be saved through their own acts of cultural regeneration, whereas in the Basque case the leadership was incapable of convincing the youth that it had the authority to determine events and that it possessed specific programmes for linguistic and political reform. In consequence, Basque radicals drifted into political violence as the only perceived answer to increasingly overt state repression. By contrast, the determining external influence on Wales was the nature of the British state and the relatively liberal political tradition of civil-state relations.

Protest

When Gwynfor Evans was elected president of Plaid Cymru in 1945 he reflected a more typical strata of Welsh nationalism, although his background was far from typical. His Christian commitment to pacifism marked him out as a principled leader of his Party who also earned grudging respect from his opponents for his consistency and strong moral demeanour. In the post-war period state-initiated, capital-intensive projects to provide water and hydro-electric power resulted in the atrophy of certain Welsh communities when several valleys were drowned in order to provide water for English cities. This occurred against the advice of most elected politicians in Wales, and despite a series of non-violent protests, in which Gwynfor Evans played a prominent role. There followed a sporadic and largely symbolic bombing campaign directed against strategic targets and state property. In comparison with many other European examples of national resistance, the interesting question is why violence was kept in check.

In 1973 Gwynfor Evans was invited to deliver the Alex Wood Memorial Lecture. He chose as his theme 'Nonviolent Nationalism', a concept which he had practised and preached all his life. In the course of the lecture he expanded on

---

[18] See Anthony D. Smith, 'Nationalism, Ethnic Separatism and the Intelligentsia' in Colin H. Williams (ed.), *National Separatism* (Cardiff, 1982), pp. 17–41. An excellent comparative analysis of Basque and Catalan nationalism may be found in Daniele Conversi, *The Basques, the Catalans and Spain: Alternative Routes to Nationalist Mobilisation* (London, 1997). For an account of the religious convictions of Valentí Almirall and the shift from a secular to a religious justification of the Catalan struggle, see also Albert Balcells, *Catalan Nationalism: Past and Present* (London, 1996), pp. 35–42.

his conviction that 'will not force' was the basis of popular social change, and that the Irish adoption of violence as a means of resisting incorporation into the British state had been tragically misguided:[19]

> Irish violence against the British led to Irish violence against the Irish . . . The Civil War of 1922 soured the nation . . . Had it relied on nonviolent methods, it would have achieved more, if a few years later . . . The exhilaration of the victorious struggle against the British was followed by the profound tragedy of Irish self-defeat.[20]

This is a telling criticism, for although Ireland has all the trappings of an independent state, such autonomy has failed to institute an indigenous national culture which was both popular and geographically widespread.[21] Evans acknowledged that 'if I thought violence could ever be justified in the pursuit of any social objective it would be to secure freedom and full nationhood for Wales, the cause in which most of my life has been spent. But even this noble cause, on which the survival of the Welsh nation depends, does not in my view justify the use of violence'.[22]

Thus was set the moral context of Welsh resistance to Anglicization and the relative neglect of Welsh interests within a British state. How the national movement, especially Plaid Cymru, developed these principles has been the subject of much debate and analysis,[23] but the best illustration of the practice of non-violent principles is the activity of Cymdeithas yr Iaith Gymraeg (the Welsh Language Society), whose primary aim was to have Welsh recognized as a co-equal official language with English in state and local authority administration.[24] A longer-term aim was to strengthen national consciousness and effect a transformation in the Welsh psychology by injecting 'a new reality into nationalism by bringing to light through the language struggle the hidden oppression in the relationship of Wales with England'.[25] The Society saw itself as the radical, anti-establishment arm of

---

[19] Gwynfor Evans, *Nonviolent Nationalism* (New Malden, 1973). For details of his life and background, see Meic Stephens, *For the Sake of Wales: The Memoirs of Gwynfor Evans* (Bridgend, 1996).

[20] Evans, *Nonviolent Nationalism*, p. 16.

[21] Desmond Fennell, 'Where it went wrong – The Irish Language Movement', *Planet*, 36 (1977), 3–13; Reg Hindley, *The Death of the Irish Language* (London, 1990).

[22] Evans, *Nonviolent Nationalism*, p. 14.

[23] See Davies, *The Green and the Red*; Davies, *The Welsh Nationalist Party*; and Williams (ed.), *National Separatism*. For an insightful treatment of the relative failure of the notion of community defence in mobilizing support for nationalism, see Laura McAllister, 'Community in Ideology: The Political Philosophy of Plaid Cymru' (unpubl. University of Wales PhD thesis, 1996).

[24] Following the Acts of Union of England and Wales (1536–43), the Welsh language was proscribed as a language of officialdom and thus did not benefit from being institutionalized in the affairs of the state. For details on relevant legislation before the Welsh Language Act of 1967, see D. B. Walters, 'The Legal Recognition and Protection of Language Pluralism. (A Comparative Study with Special Reference to Belgium, Quebec and Wales)', *Acta Juridica*, III (1978), 305–26.

[25] Cynog Dafis, 'Cymdeithas yr Iaith Gymraeg' in Meic Stephens (ed.), *The Welsh Language Today* (Llandysul, 1973), p. 249.

nationalism, willing to take risks and to mobilize young people in defence of their threatened culture. Initially there was little consensus over means and ends, but under the influence of leaders such as Ffred Ffransis the Society refused to engage in violence against persons, preferring non-violent direct action in order to highlight inequalities between Wales and the British state. In keeping with Saunders Lewis's maxim that the achievement of freedom was a prerequisite for the maintenance of a distinctive Welsh culture, the Society was always self-consciously nationalist.[26] It has been argued that it was a conservative movement by fiat, for the early campaigns appeared to have little to do with wider issues which animated the socialist, the international student, anti-apartheid and fledgling green movements.[27] However, issues such as decolonization, social justice for beleaguered peoples and a programme for international economic equalization figured in the Society's justification for direct action to redress local injustices as part of a global pattern of social reform.[28] By emphasizing the local urgency of their plight, the Society's goals were internally consistent and recognizable to a Welsh audience.

Society members felt that Plaid Cymru's insistence on socio-political change through constitutional means was insufficient to redress the declining fortunes of the Welsh language. They advocated a policy of non-violent direct action, whereby language-related grievances might be publicized through acts of civil disobedience, acts which were largely justified by reference to the inspiration offered by Gandhi, Martin Luther King and Gwynfor Evans. The leaders had quickly recognized the dependence of any government in Britain upon the mood of the electorate and had deduced that the consent of the governed had a profound effect on the formulation and discharge of the processes of political change. They hoped that sustained pressure and imaginative protest would force the government to legislate that Welsh and English be recognized as co-equal languages of the nation.

[26] However, there is a strategic qualifier to this, for recall the last impulse of Saunders Lewis's *Tynged yr Iaith* (The Fate of the Language) lecture: 'In my opinion, if any kind of self-government for Wales were obtained before the Welsh language was acknowledged and used as an official language in local authority and state administration in the Welsh-speaking parts of our country, then the language would never achieve official status at all, and its demise would be quicker than it will be under English rule.' Saunders Lewis, 'The Fate of the Language (1962)', translated by Gruffydd Aled Williams, in Jones and Thomas (eds.), *Presenting Saunders Lewis*, p. 141.

[27] In discussing contemporary causes such as student rebellions in France and the United States of America or the anti-Vietnam war campaigns, Kenneth O. Morgan argues that 'the Welsh-language movement had virtually nothing in common with any of these overseas movements; but in so far as it inspired the young and seemed to appeal to traditional folk culture in contrast to the shoddiness and false glamour of commercialized capitalism, it helped speed on militancy'. Kenneth O. Morgan, *Rebirth of a Nation: Wales 1880–1980* (Oxford, 1981), p. 385.

[28] See Colin H. Williams, 'Non-violence and the Development of the Welsh Language Society, 1962–c.1974', *WHR*, 8, no. 4 (1977), 426–55; idem, 'Separatism and the Mobilization of Welsh National Identity' in idem (ed.), *National Separatism*, pp. 145–201; idem, 'Christian Witness and Non-Violent Principles of Nationalism' in Kristian Gerner et al. (eds.), *Stat, Nation, Konflikt* (Lund, 1966), pp. 343–93.

Using the language issue as a political weapon by which support for an independent, self-governing Wales would be mobilized was in many ways the only logical choice.[29] Unlike South Africa and the southern states of the United States of America, Wales had no serious race question. It had no imprisoned dissident artists like Czechoslovakia and Hungary. It was not threatened by an imminent invasion from outside (except, of course, by a steady stream of in-migrants).[30] But it did face pernicious threats in the form of the gradual extinction of its national culture by powerful and attractive external forces. If the call to arms could not countenance the use of the Kalashnikov rifle or the Semtex bomb, it could be made in terms of a call to conscience, to self-sacrifice, and, of course, to a guaranteed amount of excitement and notoriety which involved very little risk of loss of life and an acceptable risk of forced imprisonment.

Non-violent direct action involves both non-cooperation and civil disobedience. Non-cooperation takes the form of strikes, boycotts, the closing down of businesses, refusing to hold positions, and refusal to observe, or minimum compliance with, orders that are considered morally wrong or illegal. Civil disobedience is the predetermined and publicly announced refusal to abide by laws considered illegal, together with symbolic acts of breaking unjust laws. It includes the refusal to pay taxes, to be drafted, to pay government licences, to be registered, and it can also take the form of occupation of strategic buildings. Civil disobedience is nourished by swift sanction, for punishment often gives a semblance of profundity to the act of civil disobedience and widens the publicity it receives. Both non-cooperation and disobedience were used with spectacular success in redressing the grievances of disadvantaged racial groups in South Africa, the United States of America, in the anti-Vietnam war campaign throughout the west, and in advancing the cause of many interest groups throughout Europe.[31]

---

[29] This is not to deny the structural tension inherent in the relationship between Plaid Cymru and the Welsh Language Society, as illustrated in periodic demands that the latter adopt a lower profile during election campaigns for fear of damaging Plaid's electoral performance. A second illustration is the personal cameo provided by the different trajectories taken by Gwynfor Evans and Meinir Evans, father and daughter. See Stephens, *For the Sake of Wales*, pp. 196–9.

[30] On in-migration, see Llinos Dafis (ed.), *The Lesser-Used Languages – Assimilating Newcomers: Proceedings of the Conference held at Carmarthen, 1991* (Carmarthen, 1992).

[31] For illustrations of the situation in the United States of America, see Douglas S. Massey and Nancy A. Denton, *American Apartheid: Segregation and the Making of the Underclass* (Cambridge, Mass., 1993); Harrell R. Rodgers Jr. (ed.), *Racism and Inequality: The Policy Alternatives* (San Francisco, 1975); A. M. Schlesinger Jnr., *The Disuniting of America: Reflections on a Multicultural Society* (New York, 1998 ed.); on South Africa, see Donald L. Horowitz, *A Democratic South Africa? Constitutional Engineering in a Divided Society* (Berkeley, 1991); Anthony Lemon, *Apartheid in Transition* (Gower, 1987); on central and eastern Europe, see György Litván (ed.), *The Hungarian Revolution of 1956* (London, 1996); Robert Bideleux and Ian Jeffries, *A History of Eastern Europe: Crisis and Change* (London, 1988); Misha Glenny, *The Rebirth of History: Eastern Europe in the Age of Democracy* (London, 1990); Jana Plichtová (ed.), *Minorities in Politics: Cultural and Language Rights* (Bratislava, 1992); Colin H. Williams, 'The Rights of Autochthonous Minorities in Contemporary Europe' in idem (ed.), *The Political Geography of the New World Order* (London, 1993), pp. 74–99.

Civil disobedience is often advocated by anti-establishment movements,[32] who are interested in, for example, ecology, peace, feminism, and language, as opposed to class-based issues over the allocation of material goods in society.[33]

Non-violence is normally associated with groups devoid of power who have little access to constitutional channels to effect changes, and who occupy a precarious position with regard to their legitimacy as social organizations. The Welsh Language Society suffered from its ambiguous relationship with Plaid Cymru, which projected itself as the legitimate defender of the Welsh language and culture. In contrast, members of the Society were perceived as marginal nationalists, whose reforming spirit had not yet been tempered by reality.[34] Consequently, the Society, having experienced great difficulty in impressing its claims on an unresponsive bureaucracy, adopted campaigns of direct, non-violent action. By 1971 the presence of over a hundred Welsh defendants in gaol for language-related offences was an emotionally-charged issue. Fears for cultural survival were deepened by the 1971 census figures which indicated that the number of Welsh speakers had fallen by 5.4 per cent during the preceding decade. Mapping language distributions revealed that the traditionally Welsh-speaking core areas were now subject to increased territorial fragmentation. A minority within the language movement thus began to call for the establishment of formal boundaries demarcating the Welsh-speaking heartland, a 'Fortress Wales' mentality most closely identified with Adfer and the writings of Emyr Llewelyn. The foundation of this appeal was territorial control, initially through private economic and community endeavours, and subsequently through the operation of a linguistically-differentiated public-sector service as was proposed for Canada by the Bilingual Districts Advisory Board. The rationale for this drive, from the late

---

[32] See Johan Galtung, 'The Green Movement: A Socio-Historical Exploration', *International Sociology*, 1, no. 1 (1986), 75–90; Kim Salomon, *Fred i Vår tid: En studie i 80-talets Fredsrörelse* (Malmö, 1985); idem, 'The Peace Movement: An Anti-Establishment Movement', *Journal of Peace Research*, 23, no. 2 (1986), 115–27; Sven Tägil et al. (eds.), *Studying Boundary Conflicts* (Lund, 1977); idem, 'Scale, Behaviour and Options: The Case of Sweden and General Considerations for the Future' in Otmar Höll (ed.), *Small States in Europe and Dependence* (Wien, 1983); Sven Tägil (ed.), *Regions in Upheaval: Ethnic Conflict and Political Mobilization* (Stockholm, 1984); Jürgen Habermas, 'New Social Movements', *Telos*, 49 (1986), 33–7.

[33] Salomon points to the contradictions inherent in the social structure which produces anti-establishment movements in western Europe whose 'sub-cultures are post-war phenomena which originated during a period of relative affluence'. Salomon, 'The Peace Movement', 124. Clearly the campaigns for racial equality in the United States of America or South Africa, and for workers' rights in southern California and south Asia, do not follow this pattern.

[34] 'The Fate of the Language' lecture delivered by Saunders Lewis in 1962 was aimed at Plaid Cymru not at the mobilization of a new language movement. However, there was a growing tension throughout the 1960s and 1970s between cultural nationalists, such as Adfer and the Welsh Language Society, and constitutional, parliamentary nationalists such as the Plaid Cymru leadership. For an insightful overview of the evolution and growth of the Welsh Language Society, see Dylan Phillips, *Trwy Ddulliau Chwyldro . . .? Hanes Cymdeithas yr Iaith Gymraeg, 1962–1992* (Llandysul, 1998).

1960s to the late 1970s, was the economic and social undermining of rural Wales by undifferentiated state policies, the uneven effects of regional development and capitalist penetration, tourism and the growth of second-home ownership. In contrast to Adfer, however, the Welsh Language Society refused to countenance linguistically-differentiated administrative sub-divisions, preferring a unitary Welsh state where full-scale bilingualism would be the norm, rather than language particularism.

A cultural revolution was wrought by the Welsh Language Society.[35] The most successful campaigns concerned the introduction of a bilingual road-fund licence disc, the adoption of bilingual road signs and public information signs, a commitment to the increased transmission of Welsh-medium broadcasts, and a new Welsh Language Act. The Society's attacks on production equipment and its occupation of broadcasting studios were especially important since they introduced an element of urgency into the deliberations of the broadcasting authorities.[36] The resultant establishment of Sianel Pedwar Cymru (S4C) in 1982 was one of the most critical developments in the promotion of Welsh, for it offered an opportunity for self-expression and the associated nurturing of talent, business and enterprise within the strategic and economically significant domain of the media. From the early 1980s onwards the influence of the Welsh Language Society became more diffuse as the number and range of language organizations grew. These organizations supplemented the Society by applying collective pressure on behalf of reforms in the fields of housing, tourism, planning, education, a new Language Act, a Property Act and the promotion of the bilingual character of the National Assembly. But whereas the wider language movement adopted an ecological and holistic approach to language issues, the Welsh Language Society, by retaining its independence of thought and action, has remained the most critical and galvanizing force in Welsh linguistic affairs.

Legitimacy

The success of bilingual education in Wales is one of the minor miracles of twentieth-century Europe.[37] Bilingual education advanced the aims of the language movement in several significant ways. Firstly, it legitimized the status of

---

[35] For a summary and analysis of the campaigns and incidents with which it was connected in its first decade 1963–73, see Williams, 'Non-violence and the Development of the Welsh Language Society', 439–54.

[36] Ibid.; Ned Thomas, *The Welsh Extremist* (Talybont, 1971).

[37] Were it not for the dedication of committed schoolteachers and parent associations in promoting bilingual education, the Welsh language would today be in a parlous state. For an analysis of bilingual education as a social phenomenon, see Colin Williams, *Bilingual Education in Wales or Education for a Bilingual Wales?* (Bangor, 1988); idem, 'Agencies of Language Reproduction in Celtic Societies' in Willem Fase, Koen Jaspaert and Sjaak Kroon (eds.), *Maintenance and Loss of Minority Languages* (Amsterdam, 1992), pp. 306–29.

Welsh in society and justified the place of bilingualism within the school system, the most critical agency of socialization. Secondly, it developed the value of bilingual skills in meeting the needs of the burgeoning bilingual economy and public-sector labour-market. Thirdly, it became the focus of a national project of identity reformulation. For many engaged in the language struggle, education was the principal focus and justification for their involvement. For such individuals, the advancement of Welsh-medium education was a personal and national cause requiring tremendous energy, conviction and perspicuity in arguing the case, often in the face of hostile and unsympathetic politicians, local authorities, fellow professionals and parents. Fourthly, the bilingual educational infrastructure provided a series of distinctive, interlocking sociocultural networks which validated and reinforced developments at each level in the hierarchy. This was crucial in the cultivation of a sense of national purpose for professional bodies such as Undeb Cenedlaethol Athrawon Cymru (UCAC) (the National Union of Teachers in Wales), Mudiad Ysgolion Meithrin (the Welsh-medium Nursery Schools Movement), and for pioneering local education authorities such as Flintshire, Glamorgan and, since 1974, Gwynedd Education Authority, which established the most complete bilingual system of all local authorities.[38] Fifthly, as bilingual education became both academically and socially successful, it served as an additional marker of Welsh distinctiveness within an international context.

The school's role in producing bilingual skills increased following the reforms of the 1988 Education Reform Act which insisted that Welsh be a core subject in the National Curriculum. Consequently, far greater numbers of pupils were exposed to the language and culture of their homeland, thereby reducing any latent tensions which had traditionally persisted between language communities. However, such reform also required a huge investment in teachers and resources. In the further and higher education sector a wide range of Welsh-medium vocational and non-vocational courses were made available to full- and part-time students, even if the numbers involved within any particular course were small. Even so, the trend and direction of change were significant, for they extended both the domain use and practical utility of bilingualism in society.

Undergirding education were the pillars of popular Welsh culture. Mass literacy and the development of an innovative publishing sector had contributed greatly to the promotion of Welsh since the mid-nineteenth century. By comparison with English, however, the range and overall quality of production left much to be desired, although given the constraints which face any lesser-used language the output was nonetheless remarkable. Broadcasting provided a more accurate test of the contemporary social worth and adaptability of Welsh culture. Radio paved the way with a limited range of Welsh-medium transmissions

---

[38] See Gwilym E. Humphreys, 'Polisi Iaith Awdurdod Addysg Gwynedd – Adolygu a Gweithredu ym 1986', *Education for Development*, 10, no. 3 (1987), 7–23. For an excellent overview of the system, see Colin Baker, *Aspects of Bilingualism in Wales* (Clevedon, 1985).

devoted to religious affairs, children's programmes or issues of daily life. Both Radio Wales and Radio Cymru were launched in 1977 and expanded in 1978 and 1979 respectively. One might almost describe the service on Radio Cymru as a 'friend of the family' to many Welsh speakers, for its presenters are regular household names whose aim is to provide musical and contemporary items in a manner which is simultaneously intimate and professional. Thus Radio Cymru operates as a national communication network, encouraging audience participation to a greater extent than its English-medium counterparts.

However, the greatest boost to the contemporary use of Welsh was the inauguration of S4C on 1 November 1982. It had been preceded by some thirty years of intermittent and gradually expanding Welsh-medium television output by the BBC, Teledu Cymru, TWW, and Harlech TV in particular, which had demonstrated the potential for a sustained independent channel to serve the needs of a bilingual audience. The absence of such a channel had clear implications not only for language reproduction but also for sustained dissatisfaction on behalf of the monolingual English-speaking majority in Wales. Until 1982 some 10 per cent of programmes were transmitted in Welsh, with the effect that those who preferred not to watch Welsh-medium output had tuned their television sets to English-based transmitters, thereby creating the anomaly that very many households received their daily diet of regional news and accompanying programmes from across the border.[39] This limited the appeal and impact of English-medium programmes produced in Wales and lessened the revenue from commercial advertising. Both sides of the 'linguistic divide' were thus profoundly unhappy with the situation. Identifying the problem was one thing, acting to redress it quite another, especially when there were significant political and financial implications. As the 1970s unfolded it became obvious that there was growing support in favour of a fourth channel being devoted in whole or in part to Welsh-medium programmes. In 1974 the Crawford Committee endorsed this view, as did the Conservative manifesto pledge of 1979. However, within a few months of taking office the new administration withdrew its commitment, preferring to improve the existing broadcasting arrangements. This policy change engendered the largest mass protests witnessed in post-war Wales: a plethora of social movements, political parties and non-aligned interest groups campaigned in tandem in order to force the government to honour its pledge. The focus of this campaign was the decision of Gwynfor Evans, on 5 May 1980, to fast unto death unless the government announced the creation of a separate Welsh-medium television channel.[40] To the great relief of all, on 17 September 1980 the

---

[39] Turning television aerials to receive English-based programming may also be interpreted as a partial rejection of identification with Welsh issues.

[40] For an autobiographical account of this episode, see Gwynfor Evans, *Byw neu Farw? Y Frwydr dros yr Iaith a'r Sianel Deledu Gymraeg / Life or Death? The Struggle for the Language and a Welsh T.V. Channel* ([1980]) and Stephens, *For the Sake of Wales*, pp. 220–30.

government reversed its decision and S4C was established as a major boost to the promotion of Welsh through popular and varied Welsh-medium broadcasting. S4C was a commissioning rather than a production organization, and in consequence it spawned a network of independent film and programme-makers, animators, creative designers and writers who could convert their original Welsh-language programmes into English or 'foreign' languages for sale in the international media market place. Cardiff became second only to London as a media-production centre in the United Kingdom, boasting all the technical, economic and post-production facilities and infrastructure associated with the media industry. In the latter years of the 1990s four issues dominated debates in Welsh broadcasting, namely financial self-sufficiency versus subsidy; the relaxation of certain linguistic conventions and rules regarding the appropriate mix of Welsh and English within and between programme schedules; the 'multicultural' nature of S4C, which transmitted European sport, repackaged documentaries, full-length films and co-production series in Welsh; and the impact of digital technology and multi-channel broadcasting, which gave S4C the opportunity to widen its remit within a consortia of related broadcasters.

The populist base of Welsh culture can too often be ignored in comparison with the more innovative and professional representations of material culture as transmitted by the mass media. There remained at a more voluntary level a very active network of eisteddfodau which nurtured school-based and community-based performances of musical items, poetry, Welsh plays and plays in translation, craft work, art and design and scientific projects. Unique in British life as an agency of social integration, during the twentieth century the eisteddfod system acted as a champion both for Welsh-language rights and as a vehicle for national culture, setting both the standards and prioritizing certain themes in the popular representation of Welshness. Urdd Gobaith Cymru, too, modernized its image by adding to its conventional activities go-karting, tenpin bowling, discos, and surfing 'in Welsh'. An additional voluntaristic element was provided by the myriad organizations representing different aspects of life, such as Merched y Wawr (lit. Daughters of the Dawn), Young Farmers' Clubs, many religious societies, Welsh folk dancing and musical groups.

A more linguistically self-conscious focus was provided by the 'Welsh for adults' sector which operated through Wlpan and related schemes which were geographically widespread and reasonably well subscribed. These in turn enriched the activities of Welsh clubs and social centres which might have sport, folk dancing or music as their focus but which also offered a wider entry into the indigenous culture. The cutting edge of such classes was the provision made for non-Welsh-speaking in-migrants and their children, who might attend language centres designed to hasten their integration into the local community. However, as in most unbalanced bilingual countries, there remained severe difficulties in reconciling the rights and obligations of indigenous citizens with those of incomers, some of whom were antagonistic or hostile to the legal requirement that their children attend a bilingual school.

Such was the collective force of these organizations and movements that the legitimacy and social acceptance of Welsh–English bilingualism are rarely seriously challenged today. Indeed, there occurred a profound reversal in the social perception of Welsh and in the range of favourable attitudes towards the language, in marked contrast to the climate which prevailed in the immediate post-war period.

Institutionalization

The root issue here is the power to determine the parameters of the local community and national economic development in an increasingly globalized world order. Community empowerment is an attractive notion, but one which citizens find increasingly difficult to realize because of the complexity, scale and pace of socio-economic change. Conventionally it has been argued that community ownership of the processes of social reproduction is made more difficult within bilingual or multilingual societies because of the structural tension inherent in a situation of competitive language contact. While it might be accepted that the extra frisson of inhabiting a bilingual society creates difficulties as well as joys, it is not impossible to counter these conventional arguments so long as the structural preconditions of community involvement are in place to allow the trigger of interventionist language planning to instil a fresh sense of ownership of the community's integrity and destiny. This is why language legislation and the establishment of a set of modern bilingual institutions is fundamental. Of itself, it does not guarantee success, but it does enable selected initiatives to be realized, and authorizes new patterns of language choice as a result of changes in the infrastructure.

The most recent census findings (1991) suggested that the Welsh-speaking population of 508,098 (18.6 per cent) continues to decline, albeit at a modified rate; that it was predominantly ageing; that it was concentrated in proportional terms in the north and west; that it showed encouraging signs of growth among the younger age groups, particularly in the industrial south and east; and that this growth could be largely attributed to the development of Welsh-medium education in such areas in combination with the wider scale revival of interest in the language and its institutionalization in many aspects of public life. However, many Welsh speakers found it difficult to secure adequate employment within predominantly Welsh-speaking regions, which atrophied because of the out-migration of young, fecund and well-educated people and the in-migration of non-Welsh speakers who were attracted by a variety of factors. Thus a central issue in late twentieth-century Wales was whether or not a viable Welsh culture could survive without its own heartland communities serving as a resource-base for language transmission. Could the current network of institutions sustain an alternative base and set of domains for the reproduction of a vibrant social existence?

Although Wales has a long history of initiating domain-related language policies, specific enactments of language legislation are rare. A trio of acts in the decade 1988–98 provided a new statutory infrastructure and institutional context to enable social reform in the field of language policy and planning to be realized. The domains were education, language rights and governance, as represented in turn by the Education Reform Act of 1988, the Welsh Language Act of 1993 and the Government of Wales Act of 1998, which authorized the establishment of a National Assembly for Wales following elections held in May 1999.

The first generation of professional language planners was understandably preoccupied with questions of educational curricula, the development of bilingual or multilingual public services, and the interpretation of new legal requirements to promote a previously disadvantaged language. We have already seen how the role of education, as a key agency of socialization, became central to the language struggle. In the Education Reform Act of 1988 a National Curriculum for Wales was established alongside a National Assessment Programme. The National Curriculum comprised four core subjects and eight foundation subjects. Welsh became a core subject in schools where Welsh was the main medium of instruction, and it was given a more obvious place within the school timetable of all schools in Wales. This had two implications. The granting of core status recognized the reality of bilingualism in Wales. The diffusion of Welsh as a subject in all schools made it more likely that all children would have experience (and, for some, real competence) of the language as they entered adulthood.

The Welsh Language Act 1993 provided a statutory framework for the treatment of English and Welsh on the basis of equality, thereby inaugurating a new era in language planning. Its chief policy instrument was the refashioned and strengthened Bwrdd yr Iaith Gymraeg (the Welsh Language Board), established in December 1993 as a non-departmental statutory organization. Funded by a grant from the Welsh Office, which in the year ending 31 March 1998 totalled £5,736,000,[41] its remit was as follows:

i.   Advising organizations which were preparing language schemes on the mechanism of operating the central principle of the Act, that the Welsh and English languages should be treated on a basis of equality.
ii. Advising those who provided services to the public in Wales on issues relevant to the Welsh language.
iii. Advising central government on issues relating to the Welsh language.

---

[41] Bwrdd yr Iaith Gymraeg / The Welsh Language Board, *Adroddiad Blynyddol a Chyfrifon / Annual Report and Accounts 1997–98* (Cardiff, 1998).

The Welsh Language Act 1993 detailed key steps to be taken by the Welsh Language Board and by public sector bodies in the preparation of Welsh language schemes. These schemes were designed to implement the central principle of the Act, namely to treat Welsh and English on the basis of equality. Between 1995 and 1998 a total of sixty-seven language schemes were approved, including those by each of the twenty-two local authorities. In 1998 notices were issued to a further fifty-nine bodies to prepare schemes.[42]

The primary goal of the Welsh Language Board was to enable the language to become self-sustaining and secure as a medium of communication in Wales. It set itself four priorities.[43] Firstly, in order to increase the number of Welsh speakers, it focused its efforts on normalizing the use of Welsh among young people by seeking to ensure that the provision of Welsh-language and Welsh-medium education and training was planned in conjunction with the key players. It also sought to ensure an appropriate level of provision to obtain Welsh-language education services for young people, to formulate policies and effective initiatives which ensured the appropriate provision of public and voluntary services, and to provide grants for initiatives which promoted the use of Welsh among young people. The Board's second objective was 'to agree measures which provide opportunities for the public to use the Welsh language with organisations which have contact with a significant number of Welsh speakers, provide services which are likely to be in greatest demand through the medium of Welsh or have a high public profile in Wales, or are influential by virtue of their status or responsibilities'. The third objective was to change the habits of language use and encourage people to take advantage of the opportunities provided. This was achieved through innovative marketing campaigns, including attractive bilingual public display signs, the development of a Welsh spellchecker and on-line dictionary, a direct Welsh link line for queries regarding the Welsh language and language-related services, a language in the workplace portfolio/file, a Plain Welsh campaign with excellent guidelines for writing Welsh, and other improvements to the infrastructure to enable a real language choice to be made by the general public. The Board's fourth objective was 'that Welsh-speaking communities be given the facilities, opportunities and the encouragement needed to maintain and extend the use of Welsh in those communities'. This aspect of language planning related to participation and community-level language empowerment.

A major investigation into the state of community language maintenance, *The Community Language Project* (1997), concluded that the fate of Welsh depends not only on securing an increase in the number of speakers but also on the vitality of

---

[42] During the financial year 1997–8 grants totalling £2,254,792 were distributed under the Board's main grants scheme to organizations as varied as the National Eisteddfod, the Welsh Books Council and Shelter Cymru.

[43] The Welsh Language Board, *A Consultation Document by the Welsh Language Board: An Outline Strategy for the Welsh Language* (Cardiff, 1995).

the communities which reproduce Welsh culture.[44] The essence of regenerating Welsh as a community language hinges on a shared responsibility for its condition and the promotion of its use in those daily tasks which are so psychologically important for increasing confidence and changing patterns of behaviour.

The number of domains in which Welsh was used increased significantly during the last three decades of the twentieth century, especially in education, the media, leisure and selected public services. However, there also occurred a corresponding intensification of the influence of the English language, particularly in relation to new technology. But this was not an inevitable trend, for once the infrastructure was in place the same technology could be used to facilitate the internal communication of a predominantly Welsh-medium network. A virtual community was created via e-mail and the World Wide Web with an increasing, though inadequate, range of software available. Increasingly, the home and the education system, rather than the community, took on the task of nurturing new speakers. One innovative response to the erosion of conventional social networks was the establishment of a Menter Iaith (Language Initiative) in several communities in order to stabilize linguistic fragmentation, especially in areas boasting a high proportion of Welsh speakers. In situations characterized by strong language potential but weak sociolinguistic networks, such initiatives offered a significant socio-psychological fillip for the maintenance of Welsh. As local language-promotion bodies, they functioned as a focus to create a new set of partnerships between national government, the Welsh Language Board, local government, statutory public bodies, health trusts and a variety of other voluntary agencies and private companies, thereby extending the domains within which it was possible to use Welsh.

Normalization

Catalonia provides the best European example of linguistic normalization. Four elements characterize the process. Firstly, at the political and administrative level a new language regime was ushered in by the Autonomy Statute of 1979, which established in 1980 by decree 115 the *Direccío General de Política Lingüística* (DGPL), and by decree 220 within DGPL the *Servei de Normalització de l'Ús Oficial de la Llengua Catalana* and the *Servei d'Assessorament Lingístic*. Subsequent laws included the *Llei 7/1983 de Normalització Lingüística a Catalunya*, and *Llei 20/1987*, which created *Institució de les Lletres Catalanes*. Secondly, an active marketing and promotional campaign was launched, using popular slogans denoting the role of Catalan in education, *La Premsa a l'Escola, Catala a l'Escola, Contes a cau d'orella,* and in civil society, *La Norma, catala cosa de tots, El catala depen de voste, Es nota prou*

---

[44] See Colin H. Williams and Jeremy Evas, *The Community Research Project: A Report Prepared for the Welsh Language Board* (Cardiff, 1997).

que som a Catalunya? Thirdly, wide-ranging reforms within education provided for the socialization of Catalan youth and of migrants from regions of Spain and North Africa, e.g. *Convocatoria Oposicions BUP, FP* (which involved the testing of oral and written comprehension of Catalan from 1981 onwards, and in 1986 by the decree 18 whereby all teachers contracted by public examination were obliged to demonstrate their knowledge of Catalan comprehension and expression). Fourthly, the media blossomed both in terms of Catalan editions of Spanish newspapers, e.g. *El País*, from 1982 onwards and the establishment of an autonomous third channel TV3, which began broadcasting regularly from January 1984 and which was supplemented following the Telecommunications Act of April 1988 by a wider range of broadcasts, both on television and radio.

Bilingual or multilingual decision-making assemblies are the norm in contemporary world politics, whether within European regional legislatures, such as in Catalonia and Euskadi, within the organs of the EU, or within other supranational organizations, such as the Council of Europe, NATO and the United Nations. In conforming to this international norm the National Assembly of Wales, established in 1999, signalled its intention of being a modern, representative political institution and committing itself to serving its constituents in both of the languages of Wales. The preconditions for the normalization of Welsh were already in place by this stage and an optimistic reading of the initial impact of the Assembly suggests that it could be the determining factor in realizing this potential. From the outset, the Assembly committed itself to developing a substantive bilingual policy within a multicultural context and to adopting a stronger multilingual line in keeping with the demands of a rapidly evolving European Union.

Over the next decade national language policy will focus on three important aspects. Firstly, language policy in relation to education and public administration, equal rights and the socialization of citizens within civil society. This will involve, *inter alia*, issues such as interaction with the British state and its unwritten constitution, the European Convention on human rights, European Union language policies, the development of bilingual education together with more comprehensive bilingual service provision in local government, health and social services. Secondly, economic policies and regional development initiatives which seek to stabilize predominantly Welsh-speaking communities, to create employment, and to promote bilingual working opportunities. Thirdly, consideration of the interests of Welsh language and culture as they are impacted upon by town and country/structure planning and improvements to the transport system.[45] In addition, the pressing housing, property control and rural service issues highlighted by various bodies, including Jigso and the Welsh Language Society, will receive

---

[45] Clive James and Colin H. Williams, 'Language and Planning in Scotland and Wales' in H. Thomas and R. Macdonald (eds.), *Planning in Scotland and Wales* (Cardiff, 1997), pp. 264–303.

belated attention. Strong national policies on bilingualism are likely to lead to the greater promotion of positive attitudes towards Welsh culture and heritage.

Two additional features would strengthen Welsh-language policy infrastructure. The first would be a National Language Planning Centre which would include applied research, language standardization, policy directives and the promotion of technologically innovative and proficient ways of working in a bilingual environment. The second would be the establishment of the office of a Language Ombudsman. Elements of language-related grievance and compliance could be incorporated within the remit of the current Ombudsman or there might be scope for devolving some of these functions to a strengthened Language Board.

A central issue in the normalization of Welsh is the extent to which the language can become a cross-cutting medium of governance and administration rather than be limited to its own committee for the Welsh language and culture, i.e. not become commodified and separated out as a 'problem' area. A second issue is the degree to which the operation of a bilingual Assembly influences the language-choice behaviour of the public. Critics sympathetic to the promotion of Welsh have observed that local authorities have invested heavily in statutory language schemes which in reality are of little interest to all but a handful of Welsh speakers. It would be regrettable if the Assembly's commitment were not matched by the public's adoption of Welsh as a language of interaction with national government. In turn, the Assembly will doubtless use its position as an exemplar, a testing ground, an educator and a significant actor to influence behaviour in this regard. A third issue is the constant supply of bilingual specialists to operate the Assembly who, by virtue of their daily work experience, promote the extension of bilingual capacities in hitherto unexplored domains. The Assembly will also directly influence related organizations by the manner in which it exercises its fundamental commitment to operating as a bilingual institution, including the comprehensive televising of key debates, selected committee meetings and the adoption of sophisticated telecommunication systems to disseminate information. However, although the Assembly has the potential to provide a major fillip to the future well-being of Welsh, it should not be viewed either as the 'saviour of the language' or the sole agency for language promotion.

The partial improvement in the treatment of lesser-used language communities and the resultant constructive dialogue between representatives of the various interest groups and governmental agencies at all levels in the political hierarchy of Britain and Europe obviously bodes well for the medium-term future enactment of minority rights. This improvement presupposes that the state is in some way responsive to the legitimacy of minority demands. Historically, the recognition of linguistic-minority demands is a very recent phenomenon.[46] In accordance with the resolutions proposed by European Parliamentarians, such as Arfè, Kuijpers,

---

[46] Williams, 'The Rights of Autochthonous Minorities in Contemporary Europe'.

and Killilea, from 1983 onwards the European Commission has supported action to protect and promote regional and minority languages and cultures within the European Union.[47] In 1996 some four million ECUs was expended on European sociocultural schemes (budget line B3–1006 of DGXXII). Equally significant, a raft of recent legislation and declarations upheld the rights of minorities to use their languages in several domains.[48] The British government's acceptance of the European Charter for Regional or Minority Languages as well as recent progress in the Northern Ireland Settlement hints at the creation of more formal opportunities to consider the interests of the Celtic languages in, for example, the deliberations of the Council of the Isles or pan-European agencies.[49] While there is no great expectation that the lesser-used languages will become official languages of the European Union, it is evident that the Union has committed itself to a greater recognition of lesser-used languages.

Conclusion

The twentieth century witnessed a major struggle for the normalization of the Welsh language as a medium of normal communication in the widest possible range of domains. In principle, this struggle for recognition is now over, for the bilingual National Assembly has institutionalized the existence of a Welsh bilingual society. The twenty-first century will witness the more difficult task of going beyond the provision of fragmented opportunities and a recognized right to language choice. The development of a fully comprehensive bilingual society is a project in social-engineering. It will require investment, training, encouragement and political conviction. We should not be unduly optimistic about changing patterns of behaviour over the short term, nor unduly pessimistic that most people continue to favour using English as the effective means of communication in many cases. The long gestation of the campaign for Welsh-medium education serves as a reminder of the extent to which 'reversing language shift' is an evolutionary process. Unitary authorities and central agencies like the National

---

[47] G. Arfè, 'On a Community Charter of Regional Languages and Cultures and on a Charter of Rights of Ethnic Minorities', resolution adopted by the European Parliament (Strasbourg, 1981); W. Kuijpers, 'On the Languages and Cultures of Regional and Ethnic Minorities in the European Community', resolution adopted by the European Parliament (Strasbourg, 1987); M. Killilea, 'On Linguistic and Cultural Minorities in the European Community', resolution adopted by the European Parliament (Strasbourg, 1994).

[48] Good Friday Agreement, 'Agreement Reached in the Multi-Party Negotiations, Government of the United Kingdom of Great Britain and Northern Ireland and the Government of Ireland' (Belfast, 10 April 1998). See background briefing paper for the agreement, Colin H. Williams, 'The Irish Language in Northern Ireland in Comparative Celtic and European Perspective' (Belfast, 1998); and, more generally, A. Mac Póilin (ed.), *The Irish Language in Northern Ireland* (Belfast, 1997).

[49] See Plichtová (ed.), *Minorities in Politics*. For a Welsh variant, see Cymdeithas yr Iaith Gymraeg, *Agenda for the National Assembly: The Welsh Language in the Next Millennium?* (Aberystwyth, 1998).

Assembly and the Welsh Language Board have a critical role as legitimizing agencies in the construction of new forms of partnership through statutory obligations and pump-priming initiatives. But the long-term infrastructural support will be non-governmental and grounded within local economies and communities. Hence the critical need to tackle the issue of empowering indigenous economic and cultural processes if Welsh is to realize its role as a self-sustaining language able to serve all in the increasingly complex and plural set of communities which constitute contemporary Wales.

In comparative terms the struggle for the recognition and use of Welsh has been a remarkable story of language revitalization. The Welsh case has instanced how energetic, dedicated interest groups can achieve their goal of redressing the grievances of a discriminated language group. It has also demonstrated that pragmatic adjustment to an ever-changing situation can carry the day, for so many of the reforms achieved were accomplished through unanticipated means and in diverse ways. Embedded in the national consciousness of many individuals there lies an unstinting commitment to the language and its associated culture which may be mobilized periodically. But the long-term influences have always been structural and contextual. However, for the first time in modern history the Welsh face the prospect that several of these influences will be determined from within by Welsh national institutions which possess the means of demonstrating a more responsible attitude to nurturing Welsh language and culture. The distinctly modern feature of bilingual identity in Wales is that it is based increasingly on contextualized individuality rather than on ethnic or ancestral affiliation. The challenge in this new situation is to enable the Welsh language to flourish as a co-equal anchor of multiple identities in a rapidly changing world which recognizes citizenship and civic identity, as much as linguistic birthright, as the basis of participative democracy.

Index